PHILIP'S

EASY-TO-USE FORMAT

NAVIGATOR Britain

Contents

www.philips-maps.co.uk

First published in 1994 by Philip's,
a division of Octopus Publishing Group Ltd
www.octopusbooks.co.uk
Carmelite House, 50 Victoria Embankment
London EC4Y 0DZ
An Hachette UK Company
www.hachette.co.uk

Fifth edition 2019
First impression 2019

ISBN 978 1 84907 510 7

Cartography by Philip's
Copyright © 2019 Philip's

Map data

This product includes mapping data licensed from Ordnance Survey®, with the permission of the Controller of Her Majesty's Stationery Office. © Crown copyright 2019. All rights reserved. Licence number 100011710

Data for the caravan sites provided by
The Camping and Caravanning Club.

Information for the selection of Wildlife Trust nature reserves provided by The Wildlife Trusts.

Information for National Parks, Areas of Outstanding Natural Beauty, National Trails and Country Parks in Wales supplied by the Countryside Council for Wales.

Information for National Parks, Areas of Outstanding Natural Beauty, National Trails and Country Parks in England supplied by Natural England. Data for Regional Parks, Long Distance Footpaths and Country Parks in Scotland provided by Scottish Natural Heritage.

Information for Forest Parks supplied by the Forestry Commission

Information for the RSPB reserves provided by the RSPB

Gaelic name forms used in the Western Isles provided by Comhairle nan Eilean.

Data for the National Nature Reserves in England provided by Natural England. Data for the National Nature Reserves in Wales provided by Countryside Council for Wales. Darparwyd data'n ymwneud â Gwarchodfeydd Natur Cenedlaethol Cymru gan Gyngor Cefn Gwlad Cymru.

Information on the location of National Nature Reserves in Scotland was provided by Scottish Natural Heritage.

Data for National Scenic Areas in Scotland provided by the Scottish Executive Office. Crown copyright material is reproduced with the permission of the Controller of HMSO and the Queen's Printer for Scotland. Licence number C02W0003960.

Printed in China

Road map symbols

M25	Motorway
16 — 17	Motorway junctions – full access, restricted access
	Toll motorway
Pease Pottage Services	Motorway service area
	Motorway under construction
S	Primary route – dual, single carriageway, services – under construction, narrow
Cardiff	Primary destination
25 — 26	Numbered junctions – full, restricted access
	A road – dual, single carriageway – under construction, narrow
	B road – dual, single carriageway – under construction, narrow
	Minor road – dual, single carriageway
	Drive or track
	Urban side roads
	Roundabout, multi-level junction
2	Distance in miles
	Tunnel
Toll	Toll, steep gradient – points downhill
CLEVELAND WAY	National trail - England and Wales
GREAT GLEN WAY	Long distance footpath – Scotland
YATTON / ROPLEY	Railway with station, level crossing, tunnel / Preserved railway with level crossing, station, tunnel / Tramway
	National boundary
	County or unitary authority boundary
	Car ferry, catamaran
	Passenger ferry, catamaran
CALAIS	Ferry destination
	Hovercraft
V — P	Internal ferry – car, passenger
✈ ✈	Principal airport, other airport or airfield
MENDIP HILLS	Area of outstanding natural beauty, National Forest – England and Wales, Forest park, National park, National scenic area – Scotland, Regional park
	Woodland
	Beach – sand, shingle
KENNET AND AVON CANAL	Navigable river or canal
6 — 6	Lock, flight of locks, canal bridge number
ↂ ⌂ ⌂ / ⌂ ⌂	Caravan or camping sites – CCC* Club Site, Ready Camp Site, Camping in the Forest Site – CCC Certificated Site, Listed Site *Categories defined by the Camping and Caravanning Club of Great Britain
☼ P&R ▲965	Viewpoint, park and ride, spot height – in metres / Linear antiquity
29	Adjoining page number
SY 70 / 80	Ordnance Survey National Grid reference – see inside back cover

Road map scale 1: 112 903 • 1cm = 1.13km • 1 inch = 1.78 miles

0 1 2 3 4 5 km
0 1 2 3 miles

Road map scale – Isle of Man and parts of Scotland
1: 225 806 • 1cm = 2.25km • 1 inch = 3.56 miles

0 1 2 3 4 5 6 7 8 9 10 km
0 1 2 3 4 5 6 miles

Tourist information

BYLAND ABBEY	⳨	Abbey or priory		⚓	Marina
WOODHENGE		Ancient monument	SILVERSTONE	🏁	Motor racing circuit
SEALIFE CENTRE		Aquarium or dolphinarium			Nature reserves
CITY MUSEUM AND ART GALLERY		Art collection or museum	HOLTON HEATH		– National nature reserve
TATE ST IVES		Art gallery	BOYTON MARSHES	RSPB	– RSPB reserve
1644		Battle site and date	DRAYCOTT SLEIGHTS		– Wildlife Trust reserve
ABBOTSBURY SWANNERY		Bird sanctuary or aviary		⏣	Picnic area
BAMBURGH CASTLE	🏰	Castle	WEST SOMERSET RAILWAY		Preserved railway
YORK MINSTER	✝	Cathedral	THIRSK		Racecourse
SANDHAM MEMORIAL CHAPEL		Church of interest	LEAHILL TURRET		Roman antiquity
		Country park	THRIGBY HALL		Safari park
SEVEN SISTERS		– England and Wales	FREEPORT BRAINTREE	🛒	Shopping village
LOCHORE MEADOWS		– Scotland	PRINCIPALITY STADIUM		Sports venue
ROYAL BATH & WEST SHOWGROUND		County show ground	ALTON TOWERS		Theme park
MONK PARK FARM		Farm park			Tourist information centres
HILLIER GARDENS AND ARBORETUM		Garden, arboretum		i	– open all year
ST ANDREWS		Golf course – 18-hole		i	– open seasonally
TYNTESFIELD		Historic house	NATIONAL RAILWAY MUSEUM		Transport collection
SS GREAT BRITAIN		Historic ship	LEVANT MINE		World heritage site
HATFIELD HOUSE		House and garden	HELMSLEY	△	Youth hostel
CUMBERLAND PENCIL MUSEUM	🏛	Museum	MARWELL		Zoo
MUSEUM OF DARTMOOR LIFE	🏛	– Local	SUTTON BANK VISITOR CENTRE		Other place
NAT MARITIME MUSEUM	◇	– Maritime or military	GLENFIDDICH DISTILLERY	◆	of interest

Approach map symbols

M6	Motorway
	Toll motorway
6 — 5	Motorway junction – full, restricted access
S	Service area
	Under construction
A6	Primary route – dual, single carriageway
S	Service area
⬤	Multi-level junction
⌖	roundabout
	Under construction
A195	A road – dual, single carriageway
B1288	B road – dual, single carriageway
	Minor road – dual, single carriageway
	Ring road
3	Distance in miles
COSELEY	Railway with station
LOXDALE	Tramway with station
M ⊖ ⊖ ⬤	Underground or metro station
	Congestion charge area

UK Truckstops – gourmet or gruesome?

Are Truckstops an option for the motorist?

By Stephen Mesquita, Philip's On the Road Correspondent

Can there be a better way to spend a day than eating 10 All-day Full English Breakfasts at 10 truckstops around the Midlands? We've just done it and the answer is 'yes'. Two years ago, Philip's brought you our survey of the UK's Mobile Layby Cafes (also known as Butty Vans). One of our kind readers posted a customer review on a well-known online bookshop saying that 'at least it showed that the publisher has a sense of humour'. On this latest assignment, the publisher's sense of humour wore thin.

Truckstops – not just for food

It was 6.30 on a dreary Thursday morning in early June when Philip's Sales Supremo, Stuart, and I met up just off the M1 at our first truckstop. Nine hours later, we went our separate ways having sampled ten Full English breakfasts. We could be traced by the trail of quarter-eaten breakfasts left deserted on café tables throughout the Midlands.

There were two questions we wanted to answer on this fearless exploration of roadside eateries. What is the food like in truckstops compared with other roadside eating options? And are truckstops only good for truckers – or should the rest of us give them a try?

Five things you need to know about truckstops (if you're not a trucker)

1 How do you find a truckstop?

If you're not a trucker and you're looking for something different, take a look in our *Trucker's* version of Navigator for our very useful location map of some selected UK Truckstops. All those which we sampled in our 'breakfastathon' are listed there. The list is not exhaustive. There are plenty of suggestions online (search UK truckstops or transport cafés). Or there are apps with mapping to download: we tried Iveco Hi-Stop UK Truckstops Directory (free) and Truckstop UK (£1.99)

2 Is a truckstop just another name for a café?

Truckstops are for truckers and they're not just for food. The main purpose of a truckstop is for truckers to park up and rest. Food is part of the deal but it's not the main part. Not surprisingly, you'll find lots of trucks parked up – and many truckstops offer accommodation, showers and even a shop to go with the café.

3 Are truckstops always open?

There are plenty of 24-hour Truckstops – or, at least, ones open from early in the morning till late at night. Not all the cafes are open for as long as this, although most open around 6am and close as late as 10pm. If in doubt, check in advance.

4 Will I be welcome if I'm not a trucker?

Now we get to the crunch. If you're not a trucker, will you be welcomed – and feel comfortable – eating in a truckstop? After eating at ten of them, we're pleased to report that at no stage were we made to feel unwanted.

It's true that the welcome varied from enthusiastic to peremptory. The highlight was being sent on our way with a cheerful 'Turrah, luv' in best Brummie. The lowlights were a couple of truckstops where we were served by people who gave the impression that they couldn't really be bothered. So you'll be unlucky if you're made to feel unwelcome.

But here's the crunch – could we recommend most Truckstops to non-truckers? As I sampled each one, I asked myself the question – would I be happy taking my family here? Well, I have taken my family to a truckstop – and it was fine. But, after this experience, I feel I must have been lucky to choose an exceptional truckstop. Because – with the exception of the two Truckstops that we have named and praised, I could not put my hand on my heart and say that truckstops are suitable family eating places.

Most of the Truckstops we sampled looked uninviting from the outside and, while they passed the test inside (mainly clean, reasonably comfortable if a bit basic), the overall impression of the ambiance was depressing.

Perhaps we hit a bad day – but the customers gave the impression that they were only there because they had no choice. There seemed to be none of the banter and chatty roadside welcome that was such a pleasant surprise when we tested the Butty Vans.

5 The fare

Let's start with the positives. Generally (not always) the breakfasts were cooked to order and hot. One up to truckstops over Motorway Service Areas. And the price. If cheap is the name of the game, then truckstops come out winners.

But that's where the good news ends. Because cheap isn't the same as good value. Most (not all) of the truckstop breakfasts we sampled were made from the cheapest possible ingredients. There was almost no variety in the components. Sausages were mainly artificial. Bacon was beyond salty and tough. Tomatoes were tinned. All in all it was unappetising fare (except for the fried bread – but I have to confess a cholesterol-laden soft spot for fried bread).

Many of the breakfasts came with baked beans and/or hash browns (sometimes offered as an alternative to fried bread). It's not our place to argue whether these are authentic ingredients of the Full English. All the teas were teabags (usually dangled in the cup in front of you) and all the coffee was instant (except at the Super Sausage).

Because there was so little to choose between most of the breakfasts we sampled, we've taken the unusual step of only naming those truckstops (2 out of 10) where we felt that the breakfasts were out of the ordinary. And the ordinary was very ordinary.

The proprietors would argue that they are not in the market for non-truckers and that, while non-trucking visitors are welcome, they are not the target market. And they might say that the truckers who eat there are perfectly happy with the fare.

We'd say that it's a captive market. We'd say that it's possible to offer something a little more appetising (and healthy) than this and still make a decent profit. In fact, we'd say ' Truckers – you deserve better than this'.

So well done to the two Truckstops that did offer something more appetising!

From the team's notebook

Truckstop 1 — £4.95

'*egg* overcooked'

'*bacon* very salty but it had been grilled'

'*hash browns* from the freezer – like wet paper'

'*fried bread* tasted good, as it was mainly fat'

Truckstop 2 — £3.99

'*bacon* – old leather with salt'

'*four canned tomatoes* seems a crowd'

'*sausages* – not much meat'

'*egg* was decent'

Truckstop 3 — £5.25

'*egg* overcooked and like rubber'

'*chips* (chips for breakfast??) soggy'

'*tomatoes* not just canned but chopped'

'*bacon* far too salty and quite tough'

'*fried bread* was the nicest thing'

Truckstop 4 — £5.50

'*egg* decently cooked'

'*bacon* mainly salty and very rubbery with it'

'*sausage* artificial but quite tasty'

'*fried bread* ok'

Truckstop 5 — £3.95

'*bacon* like old boots with added salt'

'*sausage* ok taste but not much meat'

'*everything else* passable'

Truckstop 7 — £5.95

'*bacon* cold and tasteless'

'*sausage* a pig hasn't bothered it with its presence'

'*egg* mainly water'

'*fried bread* was the crust taking economy to its ultimate'

Truckstop 8 — £5.45

'*sausages* not great' (signs of fatigue starting to surface among the team by now)'

'*bacon* a bit tough and salty but tasted ok-ish'

'*fried* bread tasteless'

'*eggs* ok'

'*fresh tomatoes* – at last'

Truckstop 9 — £5.49

'*edible* but unexciting'

Prices sometimes included a cup of tea or coffee.

Truckstop 6 — £4.95

Why is the picture of a half-eaten breakfast? Because your Philip's team was so amazed at stumbling upon something edible that they set upon the food and were half way through when they realised they hadn't taken a pic. Highly unprofessional – but it shows the level of desperation to which we had sunk.

So well done PJ's Transport Café, Sudbury Derbyshire! It may have a rather unpromising exterior but, for £4.95 including a cuppa, we got a very decent breakfast.

'*sausages* herby and by far the best yet'

'*bacon* salty but tasty'

'*piping hot fried bread* nice and crisp'

'*mushrooms* –YES!!!'

'*no canned tomatoes* and baked beans were optional'

'*egg* – decent'

Truckstop 10 — £5.50 (plus drinks)

Well done Super Sausage café, Towcester! But we have to add a proviso. This was on a different level because it aimed higher – as a truckstop and a family café. It was the most expensive – but it showed that if you offer quality, you can appeal to your traditional haulier's market – and to the family market.

'*bacon* tasted of bacon'

'*nice sausages* – bravo!'

'*egg* nicely cooked'

'*tea* with tea leaves'

'*real coffee*'

Restricted motorway junctions

M1 Junction 34

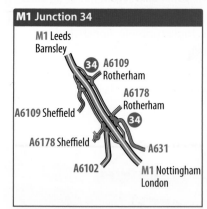

M1 Junctions 6, 6A
M25 Junctions 21, 21A

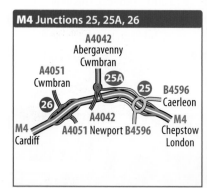

M4 Junctions 25, 25A, 26

(map)

M8 Junctions 8, 9 · M73 Junctions 1, 2 · M74 Junctions 2A, 3, 3A, 4

(map)

M5 Junction 11A

(map)

M1	Northbound	Southbound
2	No exit	No access
4	No exit	No access
6A	No exit. Access from M25 only	No access. Exit to M25 only
7	No exit. Access from A414 only	No access. Exit to A414 only
17	No access. Exit to M45 only	No exit. Access from M45 only
19	No exit to A14	No access from A14
21A	No access	No exit
23A		Exit to A42 only
24A	No exit	No access
35A	No access	No exit
43	No access. Exit to M621 only	No exit. Access from M621 only
48	No exit to A1(M) southbound	

M3	Eastbound	Westbound
8	No exit	No access
10	No access	No exit
13	No access to M27 eastbound	
14	No exit	No access

M4	Eastbound	Westbound
1	Exit to A4 eastbound only	Access from A4 westbound only
2	Access from A4 eastbound only	Access to A4 westbound only
21	No exit	No access
23	No access	No exit
25	No exit	No access
25A	No exit	No access
29	No exit	No access
38		No access
39	No exit or access	No exit
41	No access	No exit
41A	No exit	No access
42	Access from A483 only	Exit to A483 only

M5	Northbound	Southbound
10	No exit	No access
11A	No access from A417 eastbound	No exit to A417 westbound

M6	Northbound	Southbound
3A	No access.	No exit. Access from M6 eastbound only
4A	No exit. Access from M42 southbound only	No access. Exit to M42 only
5	No access	No exit
10A	No access. Exit to M54 only	No exit. Access from M54 only
11A	No exit. Access from M6 Toll only	No access. Exit to M6 Toll only
20	No exit to M56 eastbound	No access from M56 westbound
24	No access	No exit
25	No access	No exit
30	No exit. Access from M61 northbound only	No access. Exit to M61 southbound only
31A	No access	No exit
45	No access	No exit

M6 Toll	Northbound	Southbound
T1		No exit
T2	No exit, no access	No access
T5	No exit	No access
T7	No access	No exit
T8	No access	No exit

M8	Eastbound	Westbound
6	No exit	No access
6A	No access	No exit
7	No Access	No exit
7A	No exit. Access from A725 northbound only	No access. Exit to A725 southbound only
8	No exit to M73 northbound	No access from M73 southbound
9	No access	No exit
13	No exit southbound	Access from M73 southbound only
14	No access	No exit
16	No exit	No access
17	No exit	
18		No exit
19	No exit to A814 eastbound	No access from A814 westbound
20	No exit	No access
21	No access from M74	No exit
22	No exit. Access from M77 only	No access. Exit to M77 only
23	No exit	No access
25	Exit to A739 northbound only. Access from A739 southbound only	
25A	No exit	No access
28	No exit	No access
28A	No exit	No access

M9	Eastbound	Westbound
2	No access	No access
3	No exit	No access
6	No access	No exit
8	No exit	No access

M11	Northbound	Southbound
4	No exit	No access
5	No access	No exit
8A	No access	No exit
9	No access	No exit
13	No access	No exit
14	No exit to A428 westbound	No exit. Access from A14 westbound only

M20	Eastbound	Westbound
2	No access	No exit
3	No exit Access from M26 eastbound only	No access Exit to M26 westbound only
11A	No access	No exit

M23	Northbound	Southbound
7	No exit to A23 southbound	No access from A23 northbound
10A	No exit	No access

M25	Clockwise	Anticlockwise
5	No exit to M26 eastbound	No access from M26 westbound
19	No access	No exit
21	No exit to M1 southbound. Access from M1 southbound only	No exit to M1 southbound. Access from M1 southbound only
31	No exit	No access

M27	Eastbound	Westbound
10	No exit	No access
12	No access	No exit

M40	Eastbound	Westbound
3	No exit	No access
7	No exit	No access
8	No exit	No access
13	No exit	No access
14	No access	No exit
16	No access	No exit

M42	Northbound	Southbound
1	No exit	No access
7	No access Exit to M6 northbound only	No exit. Access from M6 northbound only
7A	No access. Exit to M6 southbound only	No exit
8	No exit. Access from M6 southbound only	Exit to M6 northbound only. Access from M6 southbound only

M45	Eastbound	Westbound
M1 J17	Access to M1 southbound only	No access from M1 southbound
With A45	No access	No exit

M48	Eastbound	Westbound
M4 J21	No exit to M4 westbound	No access from M4 eastbound
M4 J23	No access from M4 westbound	No exit to M4 eastbound

M49	Southbound	Northbound
18A	No exit to M5 northbound	No access from M5 southbound

M53	Northbound	Southbound
11	Exit to M56 eastbound only. Access from M56 westbound only	Exit to M56 eastbnd only. Access from M56 westbound only

M56	Eastbound	Westbound
2	No exit	No access
3	No access	No exit
4	No exit	No access
7		No access
8	No exit or access	No exit
9	No access from M6 northbound	No access to M6 southbound
15	No exit to M53	No access from M53 northbound

M57	Northbound	Southbound
3	No exit	No access
5	No exit	No access

M58	Eastbound	Westbound
1	No exit	No access

M60	Clockwise	Anticlockwise
2	No exit	No access
3	No exit to A34 northbound	No exit to A34 northbound
4	No access from M56	No exit to M56
5	No exit to A5103 southbound	No exit to A5103 northbound
14	No exit	No access
16	No exit	No access
20	No access	No exit
22		No access
25	No access	
26		No exit or access
27	No exit	No access

M61	Northbound	Southbound
2	No access from A580 eastbound	No exit to A580 westbound
3	No access from A580 eastbound. No access from A666 southbound	No exit to A580 westbound
M6 J30	No exit to M6 southbound	No access from M6 northbound

M62	Eastbound	Westbound
23	No access	No exit

M65	Eastbound	Westbound
9	No access	No exit
11	No exit	No access

M66	Northbound	Southbound
1	No access	No exit

M67	Eastbound	Westbound
1A	No access	No exit
2	No exit	No access

M69	Northbound	Southbound
2	No exit	No access

M73	Northbound	Southbound
2	No access from M8 eastbound	No exit to M8 westbound

M74	Northbound	Southbound
3	No access	No exit
3A	No exit	No access
7	No access	No exit
9	No exit or access	No access
10		No exit
11	No exit	No access
12	No access	No exit

M77	Northbound	Southbound
4	No exit	No access
6	No exit	No access
7	No exit	
8	No access	No access

M80	Northbound	Southbound
4A	No access	No exit
6A	No exit	No access
8	Exit to M876 northbound only. No access	Access from M876 southbound only. No exit

M90	Northbound	Southbound
1	Access from A90 northbound only	No access. Exit to A90 southbound only
2A	No access	No exit
7	No exit	No access
8	No access	No exit
10	No access from A912	No exit to A912

M180	Eastbound	Westbound
1	No access	No exit

M621	Eastbound	Westbound
2A	No exit	No access
4	No exit	
5	No exit	No access
6	No access	No exit

M876	Northbound	Southbound
2	No access	No exit

A1(M)	Northbound	Southbound
2	No access	No exit
3		No access
5	No exit	No exit, no access
14	No exit	No access
40	No access	No exit
43	No exit. Access from M1 only	No access. Exit to M1 only
57	No access	No exit
65	No access	No exit

A3(M)	Northbound	Southbound
1	No exit	No access
4	No access	No exit

A38(M) with Victoria Rd, (Park Circus) Birmingham	
Northbound	No exit
Southbound	No access

A48(M)	Northbound	Southbound
M4 Junc 29	Exit to M4 eastbound only	Access from M4 westbound only
29A	Access from A48 eastbound only	Exit to A48 westbound only

A57(M)	Eastbound	Westbound
With A5103	No access	No exit
With A34	No access	No exit

A58(M)		Southbound
With Park Lane and Westgate, Leeds		No access

A64(M)	Eastbound	Westbound
With A58 Clay Pit Lane, Leeds	No access from A58	No exit to A58

A74(M)	Northbound	Southbound
18	No access	No exit
22		No exit to A75

A194(M)	Northbound	Southbound
A1(M) J65 Gateshead Western Bypass	Access from A1(M) northbound only	Exit to A1(M) southbound only

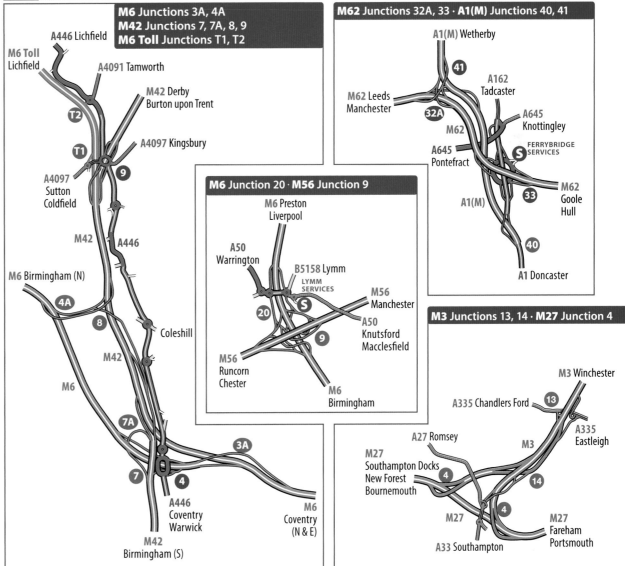

M6 Junctions 3A, 4A
M42 Junctions 7, 7A, 8, 9
M6 Toll Junctions T1, T2

A446 Lichfield
M6 Toll Lichfield
A4091 Tamworth
M42 Derby Burton upon Trent
A4097 Kingsbury
A4097 Sutton Coldfield
M42
A446
M6 Birmingham (N)
Coleshill
M42
M6
A446 Coventry Warwick
M42 Birmingham (S)
M6 Coventry (N & E)

M62 Junctions 32A, 33 · A1(M) Junctions 40, 41
A1(M) Wetherby
A162 Tadcaster
M62 Leeds Manchester
M62
A645 Knottingley
A645 Pontefract
FERRYBRIDGE SERVICES
A1(M)
M62 Goole Hull
A1 Doncaster

M6 Junction 20 · M56 Junction 9
M6 Preston Liverpool
A50 Warrington
B5158 Lymm
LYMM SERVICES
M56 Manchester
A50 Knutsford Macclesfield
M56 Runcorn Chester
M6 Birmingham

M3 Junctions 13, 14 · M27 Junction 4
M3 Winchester
A335 Chandlers Ford
A27 Romsey
M3
A335 Eastleigh
M27 Southampton Docks New Forest Bournemouth
M27
A33 Southampton
M27 Fareham Portsmouth

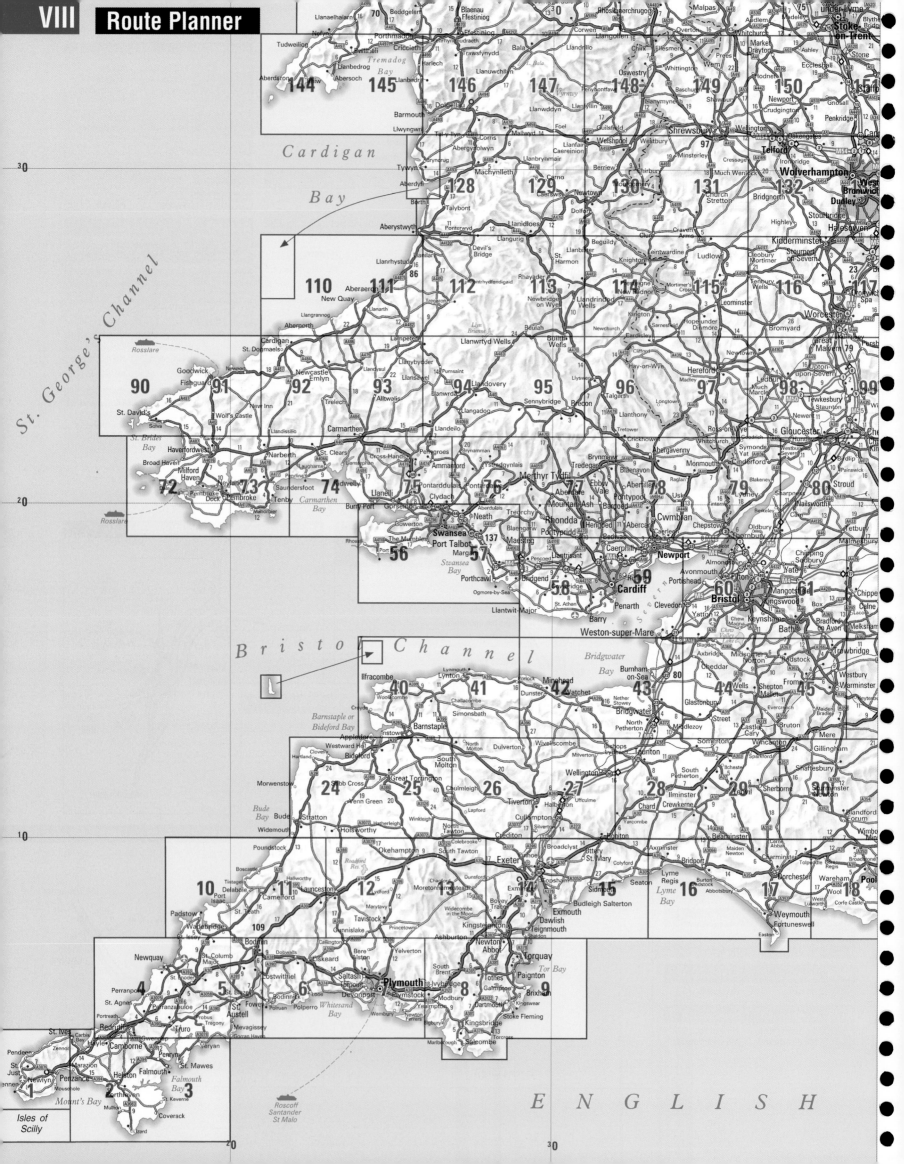

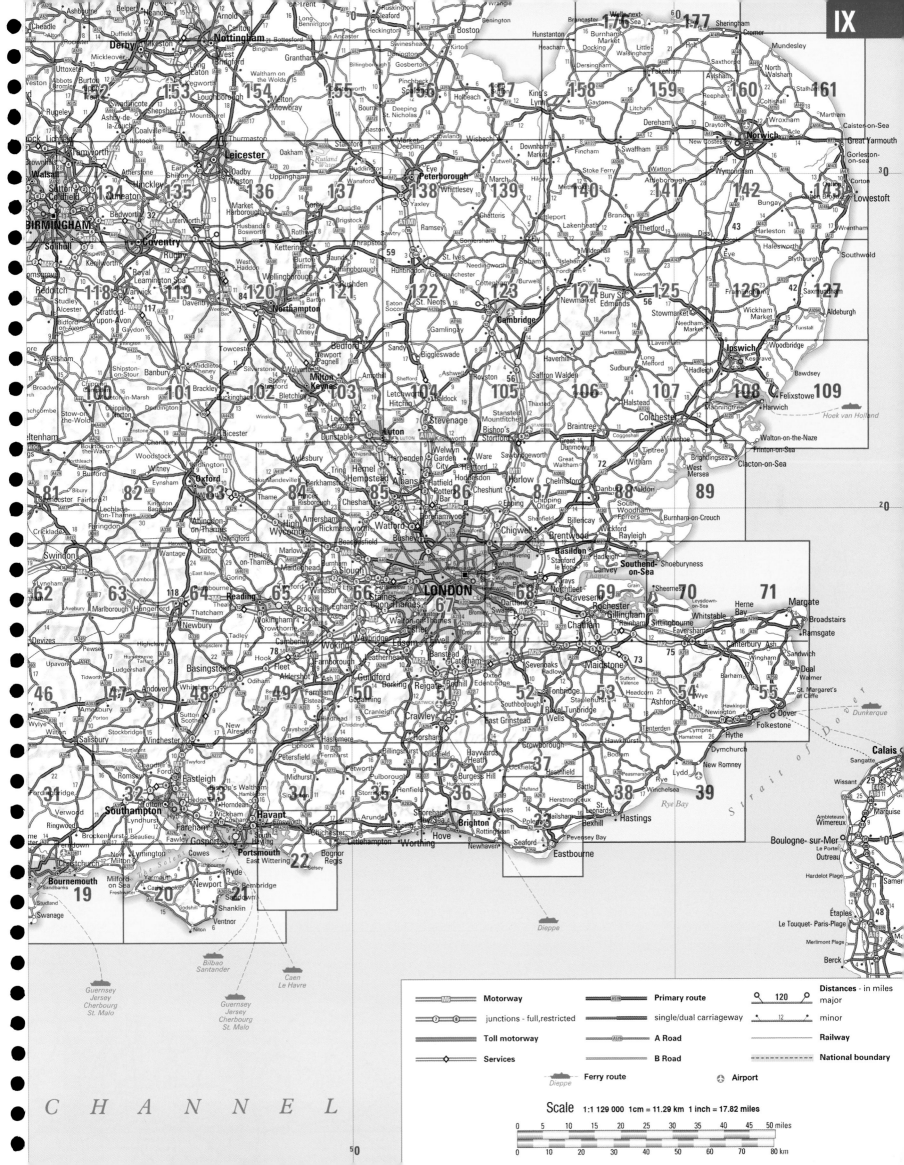

Scale

1:1 129 000 1cm = 11.29 km 1 inch = 17.82 miles

Legend	
Motorway	Primary route
junctions - full, restricted	single/dual carriageway
Toll motorway	A Road
Services	B Road
Ferry route	Airport

Distances - in miles
major / minor

Railway
National boundary

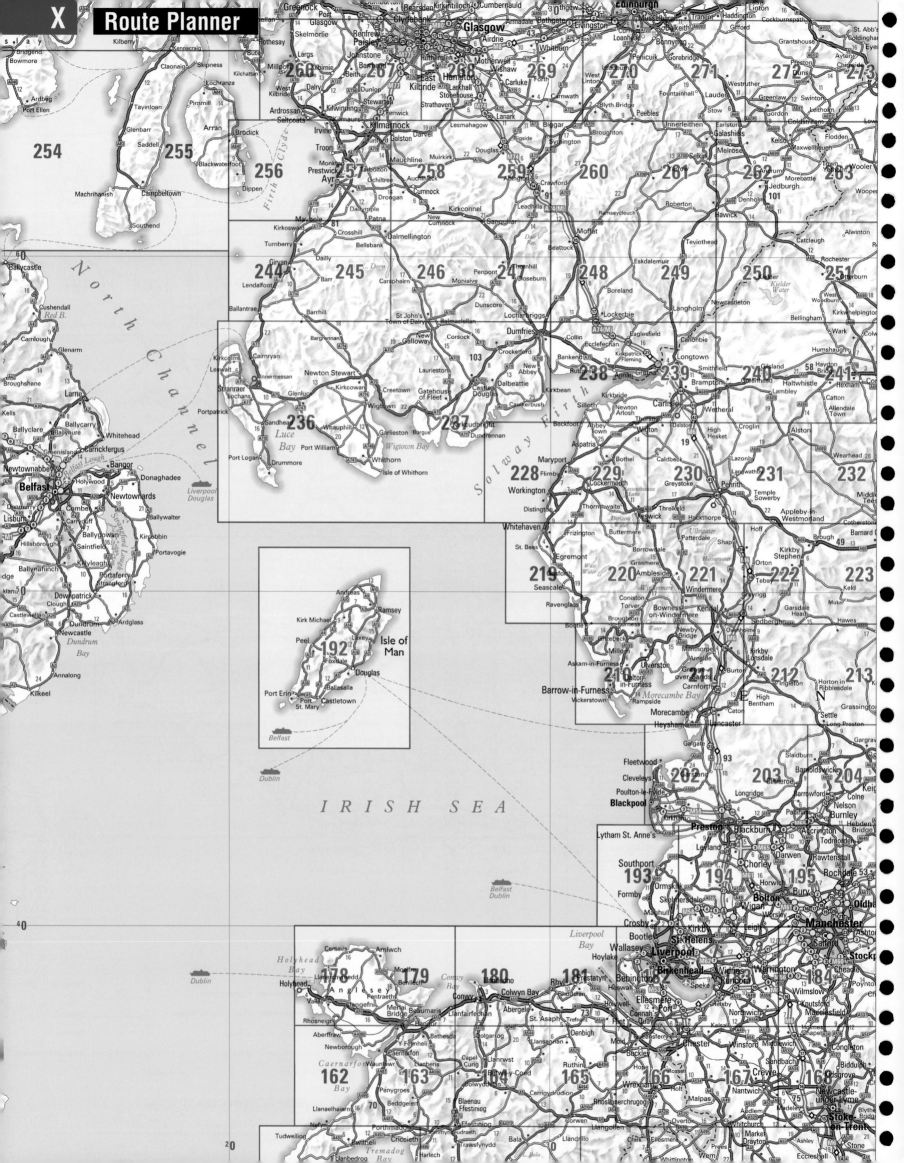

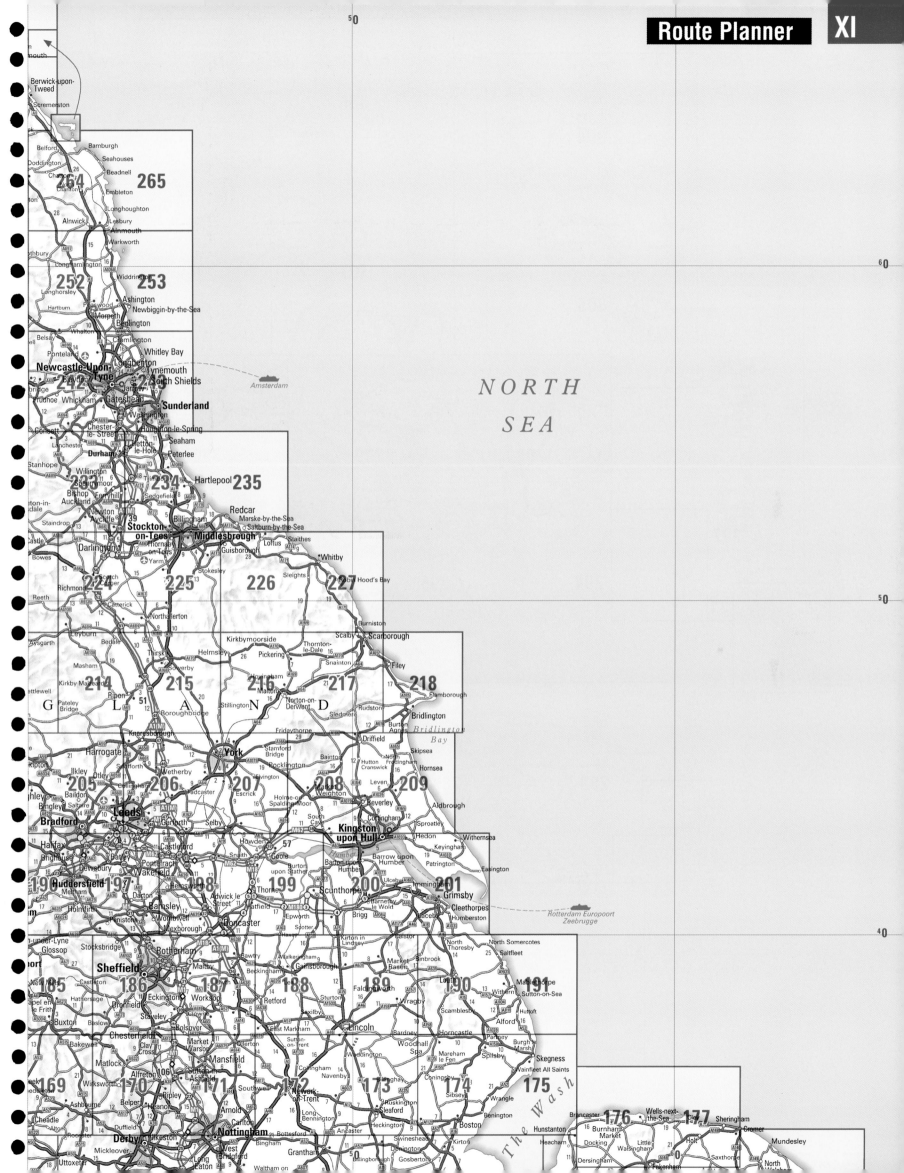

NORTH SEA

Bridlington Bay

The Wash

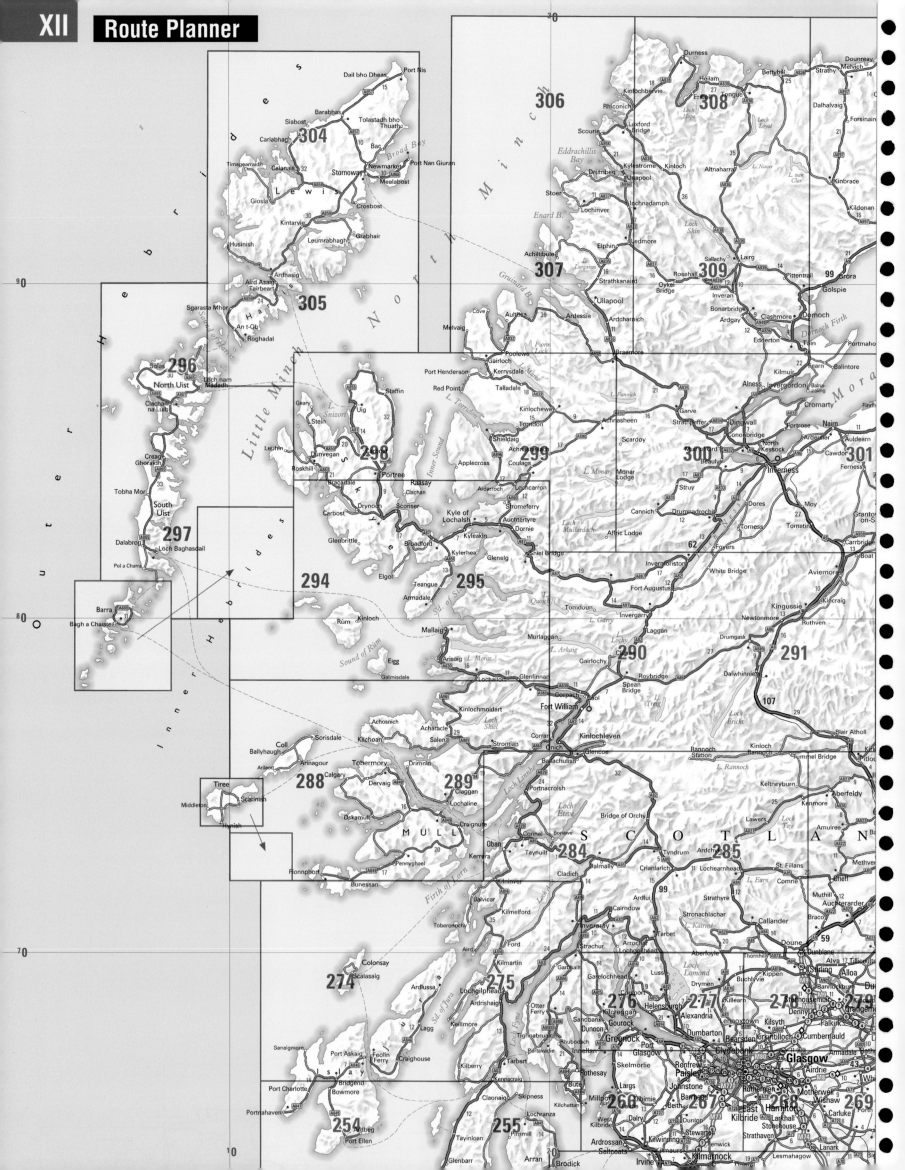

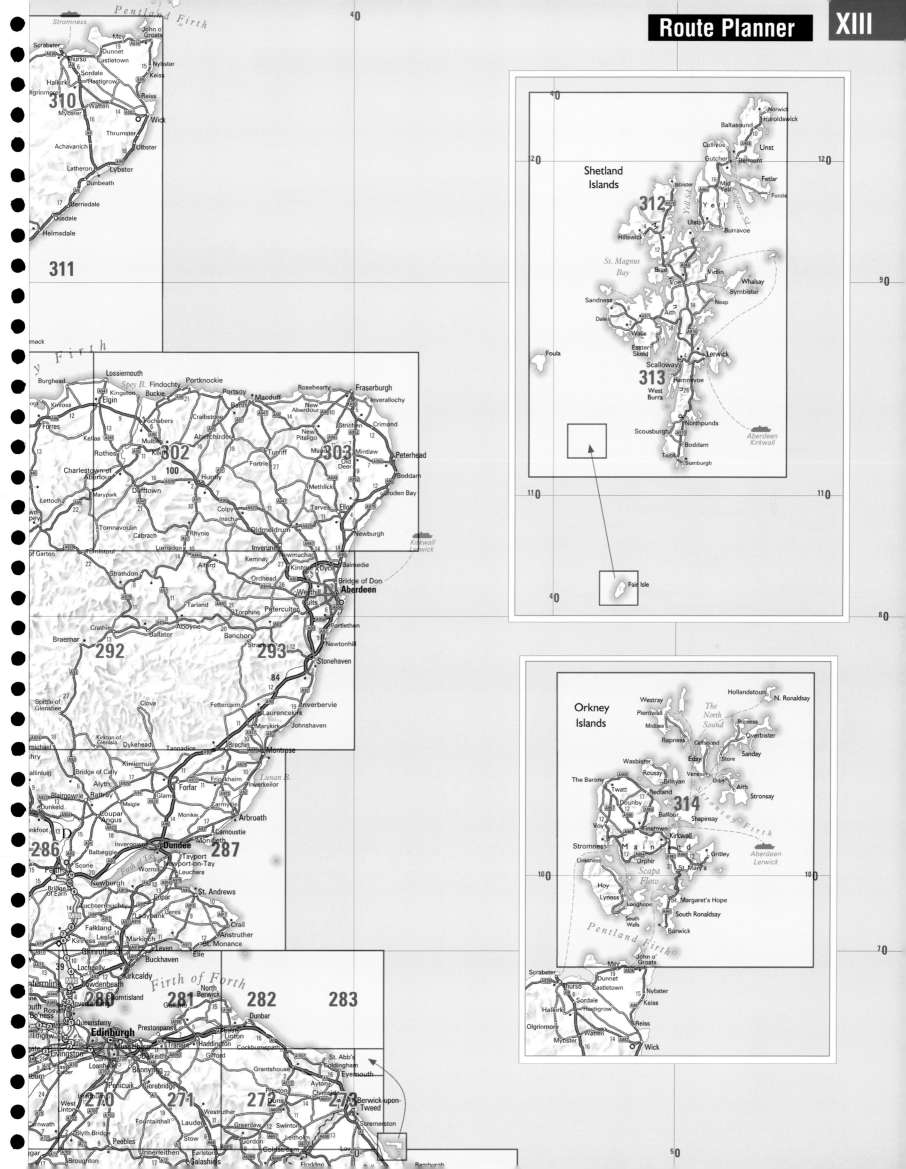

Distances and journey times

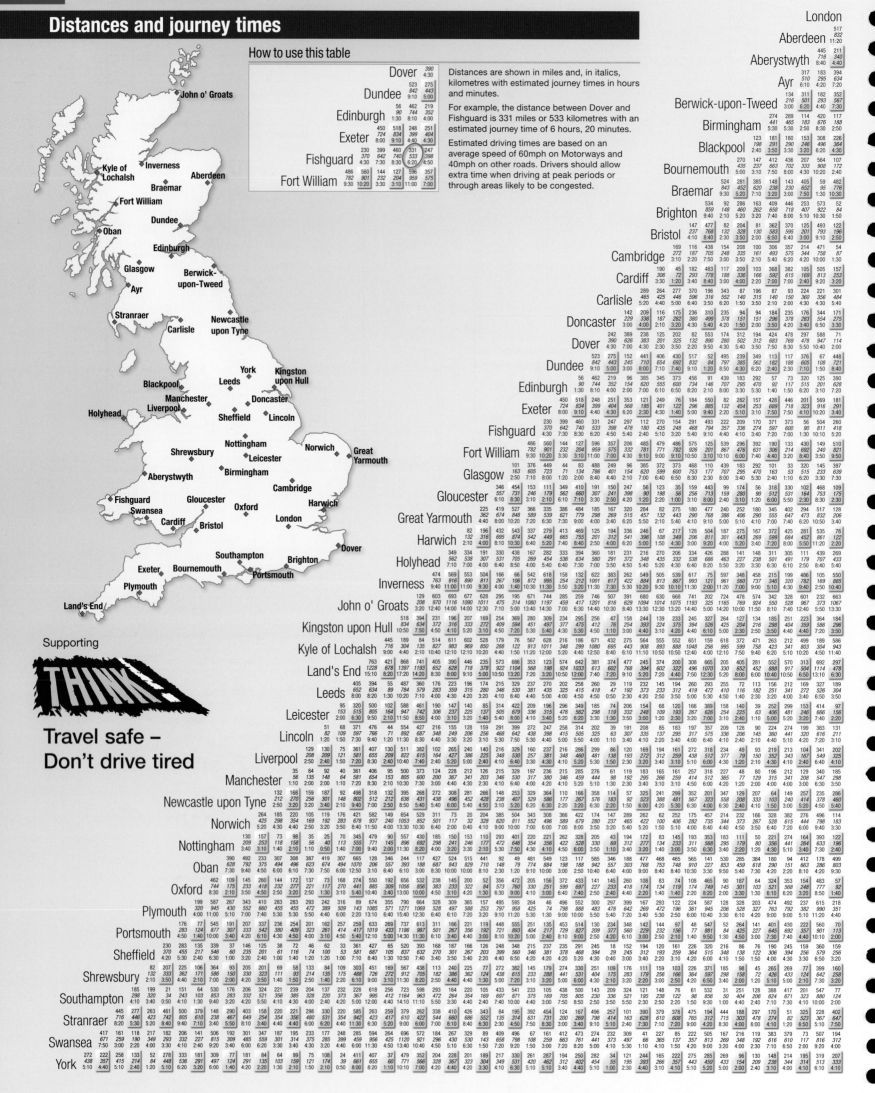

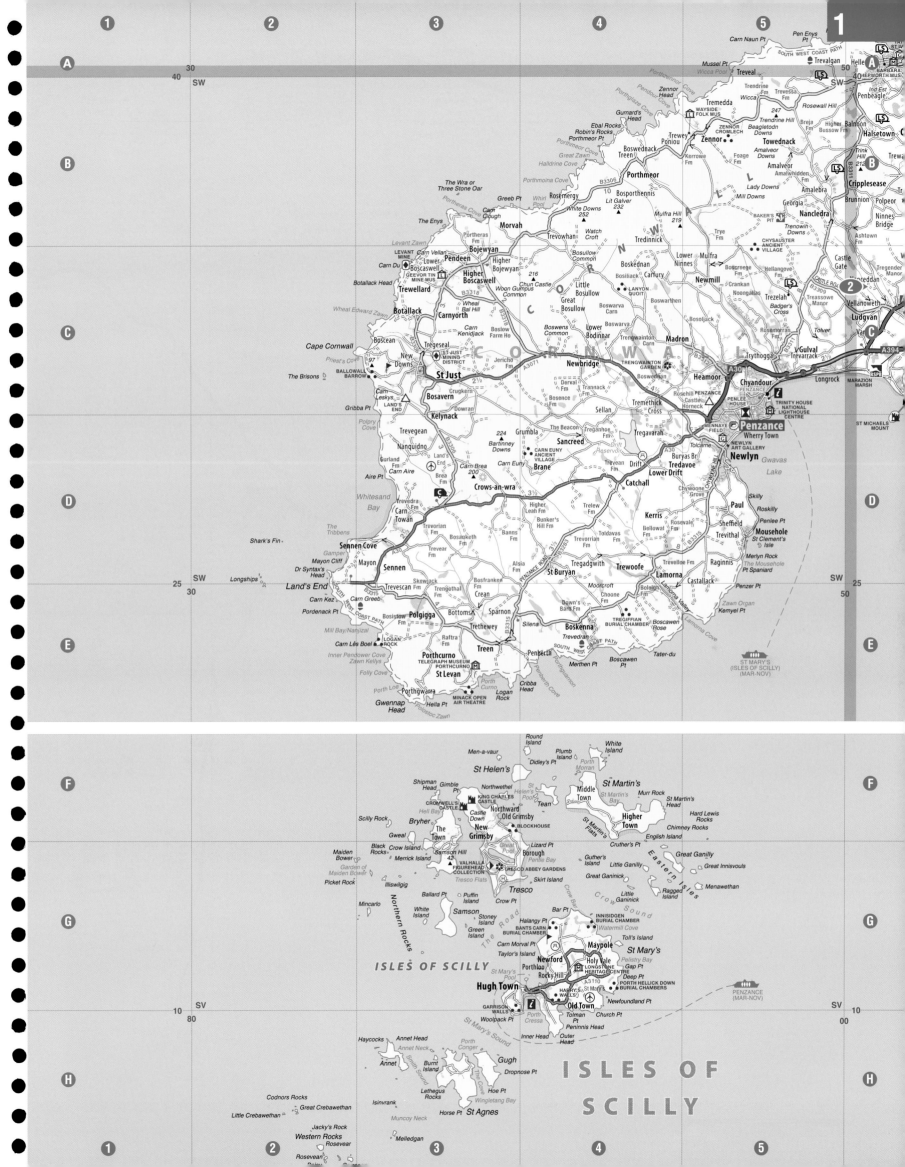

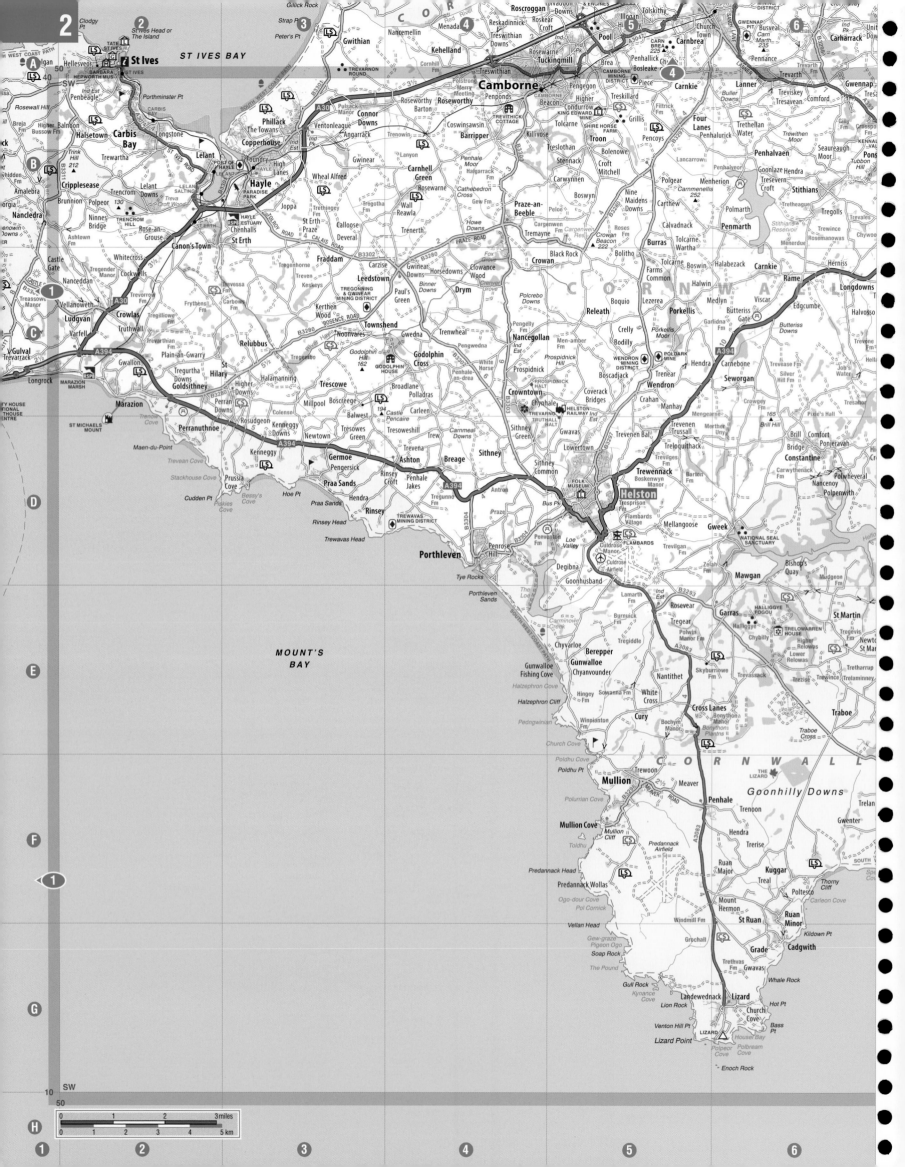

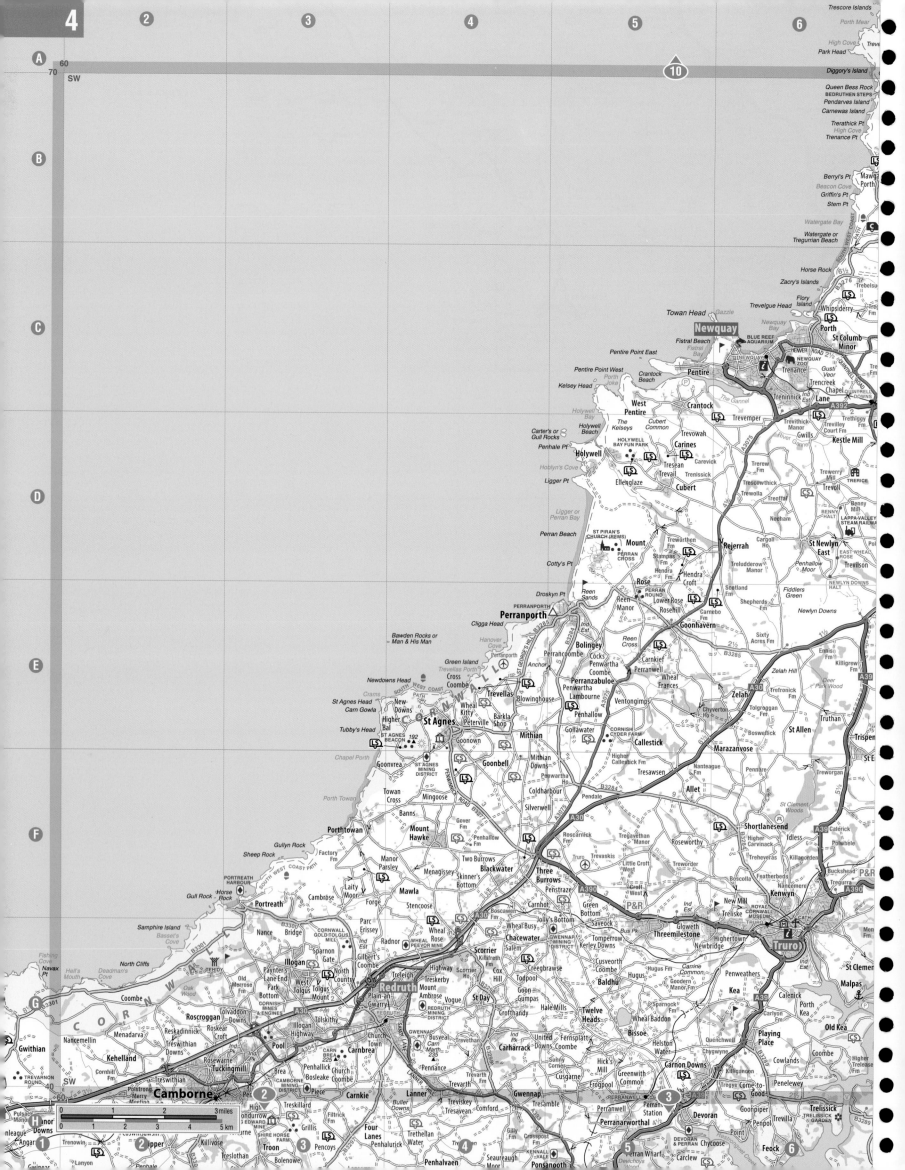

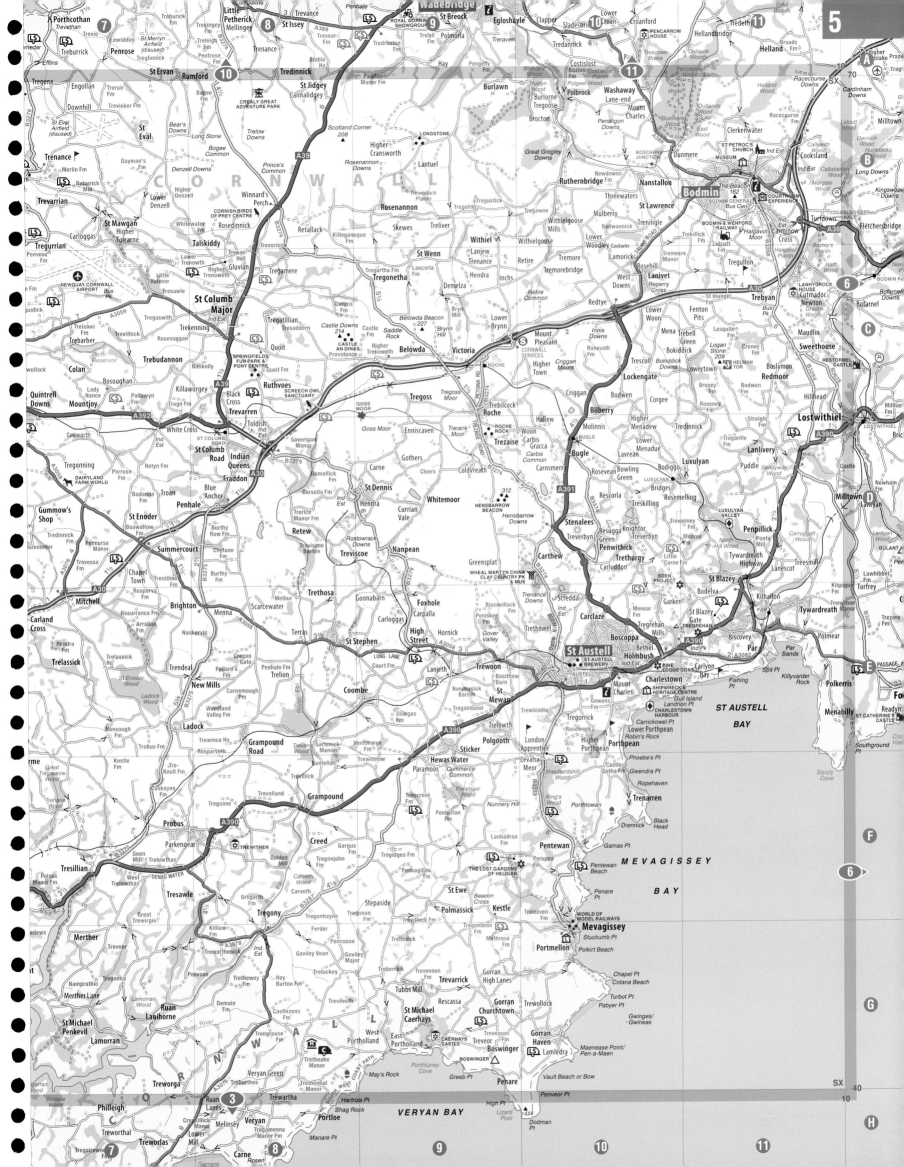

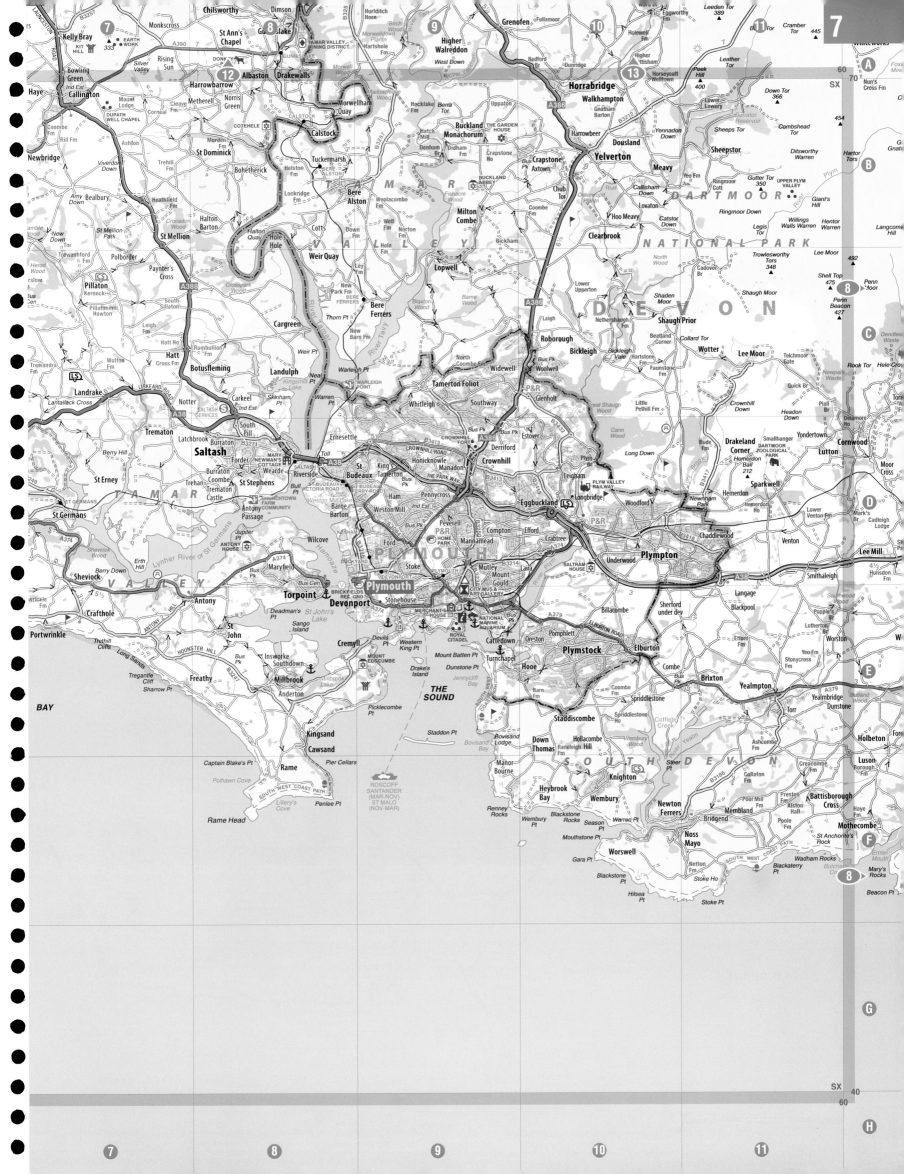

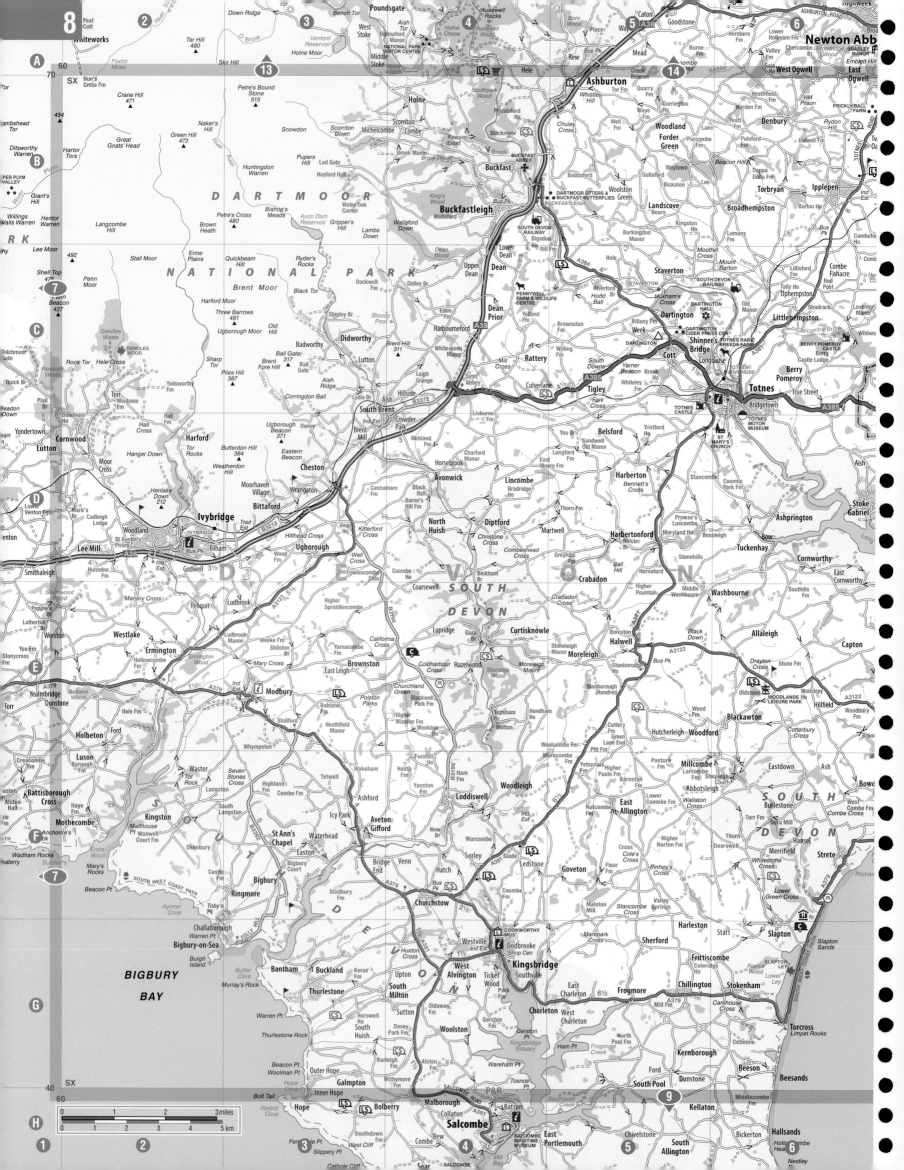

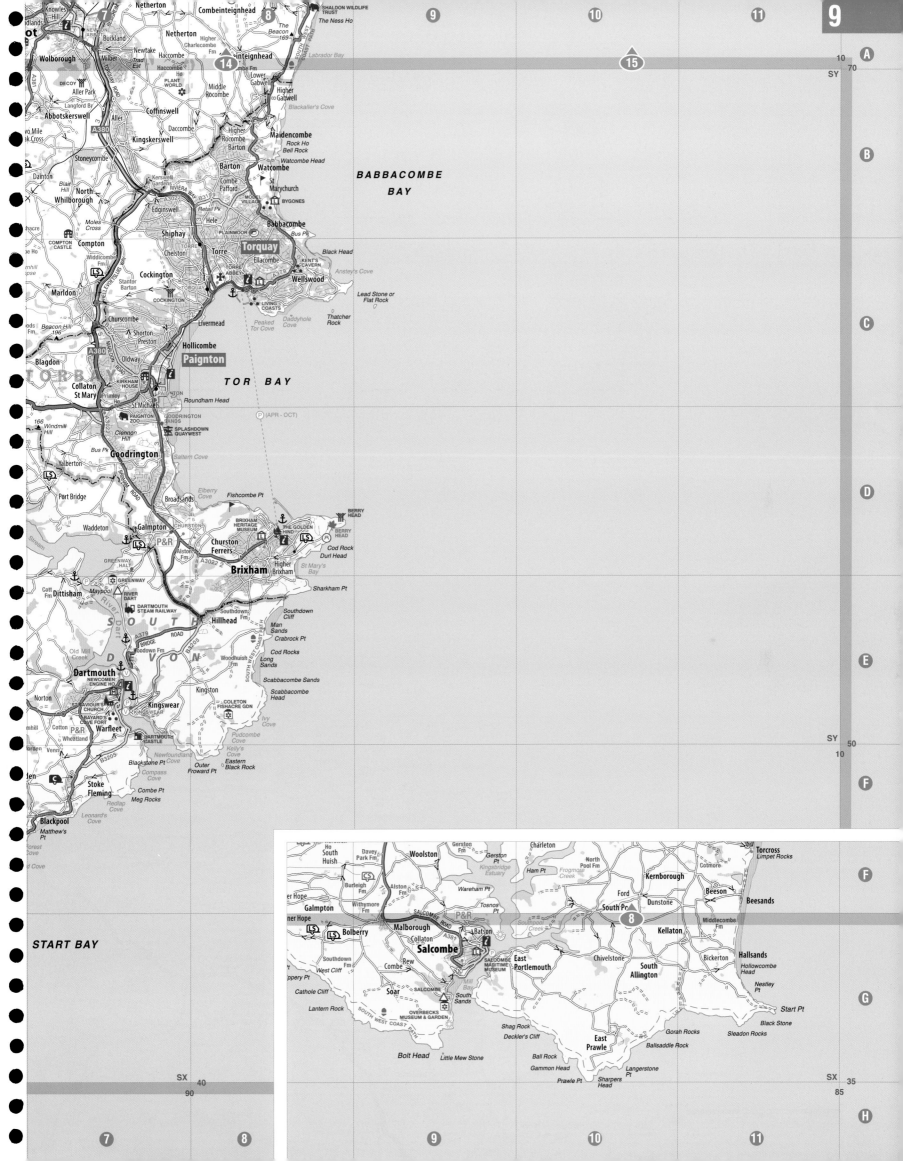

BABBACOMBE BAY

TOR BAY

SOUTH DEVON

START BAY

BABBACOMBE
BAY

Torquay
Paignton
Brixham
Dartmouth

Knowles Hill
Netherton
Combeinteignhead
SHALDON WILDLIFE TRUST
The Ness Ho
The Beacon 169
Buckland
Netherton
Higher Charlescombe
Newtake
Haccombe
Teignmouth
Labrador Bay
Wolborough
Milber
TORQUAY ROAD
Haccombe Ho
Combe Fm
Lower Gabwell
Decoy
Aller Park
PLANT WORLD
Langford Br
Middle Rocombe
Higher Gabwell
Abbotskerswell
Coffinswell
Daccombe
Higher Rocombe Barton
Blackaller's Cove
Aller
Kingskerswell
Maidencombe
Rock Ho
Bell Rock
North Whilborough
Barton
Watcombe
Watcombe Head
Blair Hill
Kerswell Gardens
RIVIERA WAY
Combe Pafford
St Marychurch
MODEL VILLAGE
BYGONES
Moles Cross
Edginswell
Hele
Retail Pk
Compton
COMPTON CASTLE
PLAINMOOR
Babbacombe
Bus Pk
Shiphay
Chelston
TORRE
Torre
Black Head
Marldon
Cockington
TORRE ABBEY
Torquay
Ellacombe
KENT'S CAVERN
Anstey's Cove
COCKINGTON
Wellswood
Churscombe
Shorton
Preston
Livermead
Lead Stone or Flat Rock
Peaked Tor Cove
Daddyhole Cove
Thatcher Rock
Hollicombe
Paignton
TOR BAY
Blagdon
Collaton St Mary
KIRKHAM HOUSE
Primley
St Michaels
Roundham Head
Goodrington
PAIGNTON ZOO
GOODRINGTON SANDS
SPLASHDOWN QUAYWEST
(P) APR - OCT
Windmill Hill
Clennon Hill
Bus Pk
Saltern Cove
Yalberton
Port Bridge
Elberry Cove
Fishcombe Pt
Broadsands
Waddeton
Galmpton
CHURSTON
BRIXHAM HERITAGE MUSEUM
BERRY HEAD
P&R
Churston Ferrers
Alston Fm
THE GOLDEN HIND
Cod Rock
Durl Head
GREENWAY HALT
Brixham
Higher Brixham
St Mary's Bay
GREENWAY
Maypool
RIVER DART
Cott Fm
Dittisham
DARTMOUTH STEAM RAILWAY
Hillhead
Southdown Fm
Southdown Cliff
Man Sands
Crabrock Pt
Old Mill Creek
Hoodown Fm
Woodhuish Fm
Cod Rocks
Long Sands
Dartmouth
NEWCOMEN ENGINE HO
Kingston
Scabbacombe Sands
Norton
ST SAVIOUR'S CHURCH
Kingswear
COLETON FISHACRE GDN
Scabbacombe Head
BAYARD'S COVE FORT
Warfleet
Ivy Cove
Wheatland
DARTMOUTH CASTLE
Pudcombe Cove
Venn
Blackstone Pt
Newfoundland Cove
Kelly's Cove
Compass Cove
Outer Froward Pt
Eastern Black Rock
Stoke Fleming
Combe Pt
Meg Rocks
Redlap Cove
Blackpool
Leonard's Cove
Matthew's Pt
Forest Cove
Cod Cove

Woolston
South Huish
Ho
Davey Park Fm
Gerston Fm
Charleton
Torcross
Limpet Rocks
Gerston Pt
Frogmore Creek
North Pool Fm
Ham Pt
Kingsbridge Estuary
Cotmore
Hope
Burleigh Fm
Alston Fm
Wareham Pt
Kernborough
Beeson
Galmpton
Withymore Fm
Tosnos Pt
Ford
SALCOMBE ROAD
P&R
Dunstone
Beesands
Hope
Bolberry
Malborough
Collaton
Batson
South Pt
Kellaton
Middlecombe Fm
Salcombe
SALCOMBE MARITIME MUSEUM
East Portlemouth
Chivelstone
Bickerton
Hallsands
Southdown Fm
Rew
Combe
East Allington
South Allington
Hollowcombe Head
West Cliff
SALCOMBE
Mill Bay
Nestley Pt
Slippery Pt
Soar
South Sands
OVERBECKS MUSEUM & GARDEN
Start Pt
Cathole Cliff
Lantern Rock
SOUTH WEST COAST PATH
Shag Rock
Gorah Rocks
Black Stone
Bolt Head
Little Mew Stone
Deckler's Cliff
East Prawle
Ball Rock
Gammon Head
Langerstone Pt
Prawle Pt
Sharpers Head
Ballsaddle Rock
Sleadon Rocks

10
70
SY
SY
50
10
SX
40
90
SX
35
85

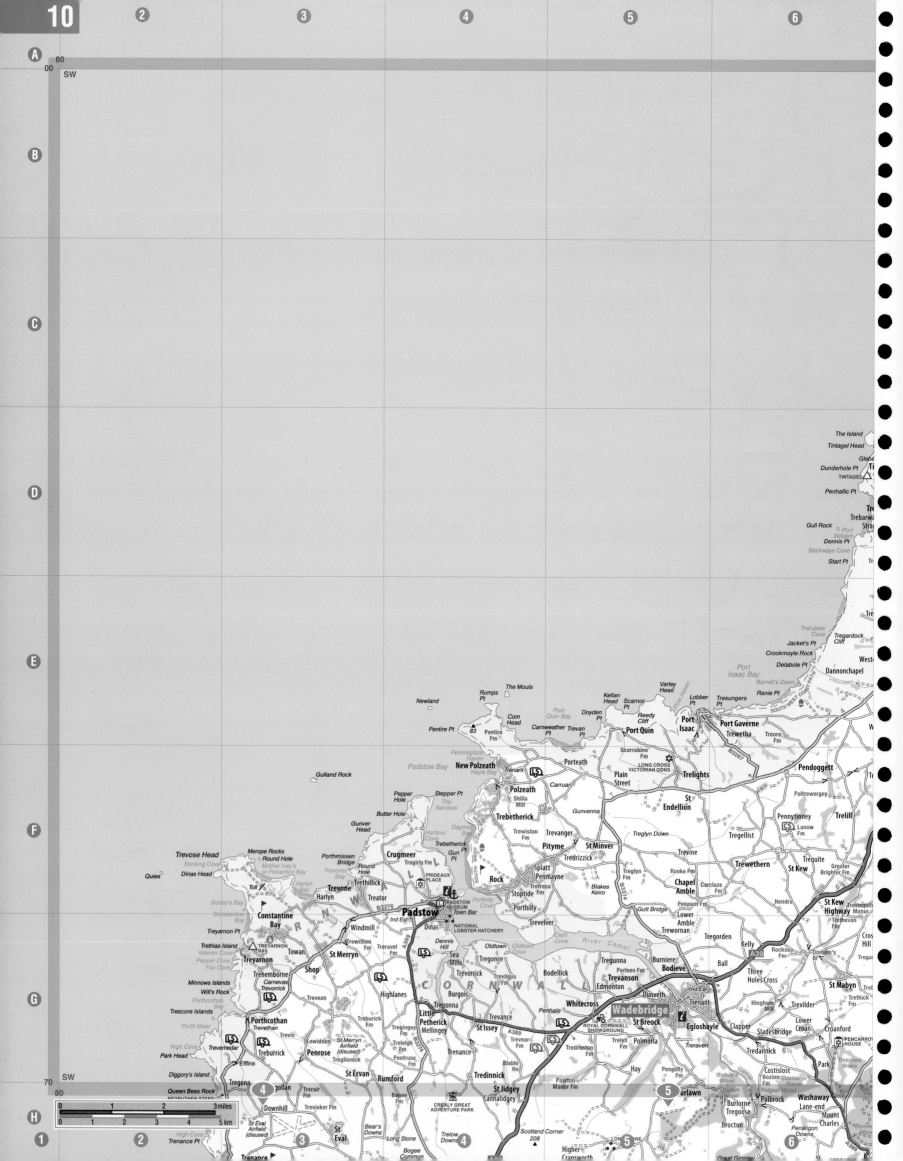

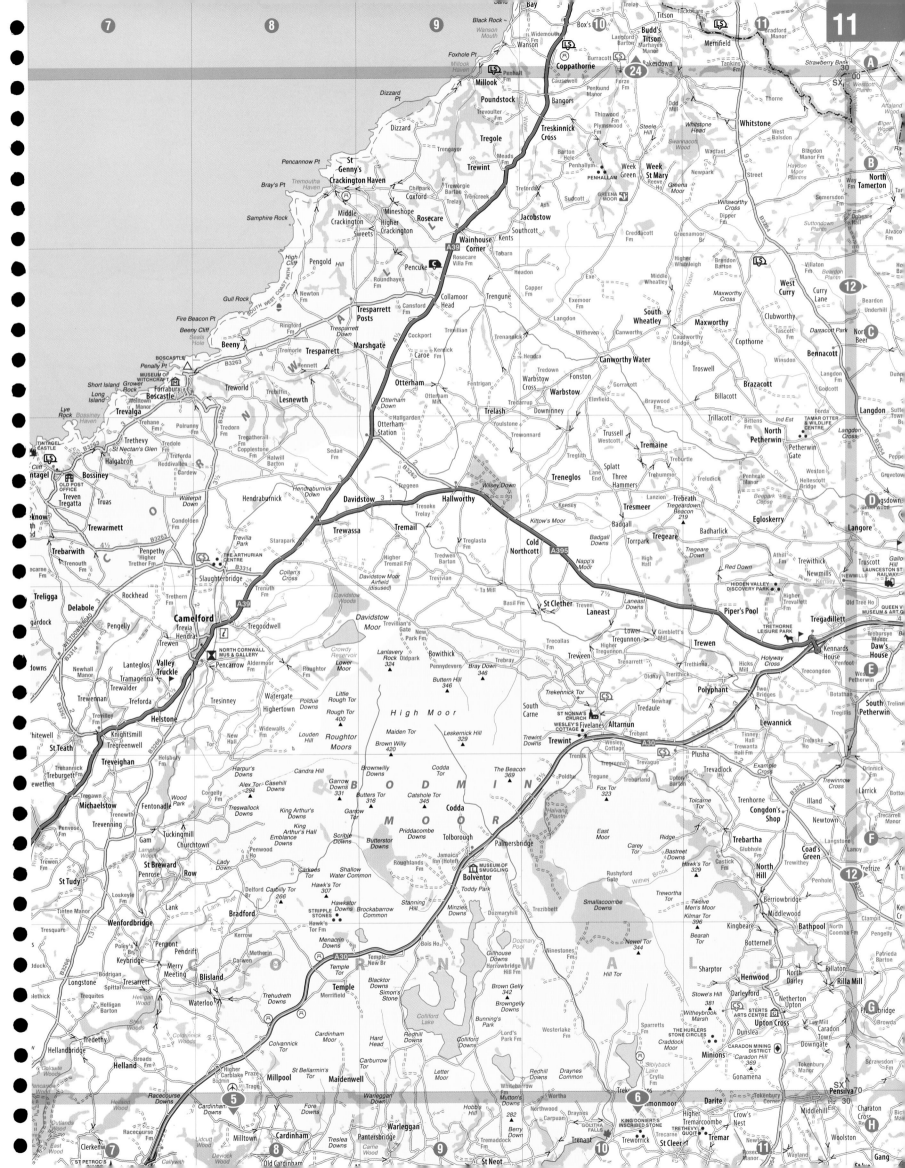

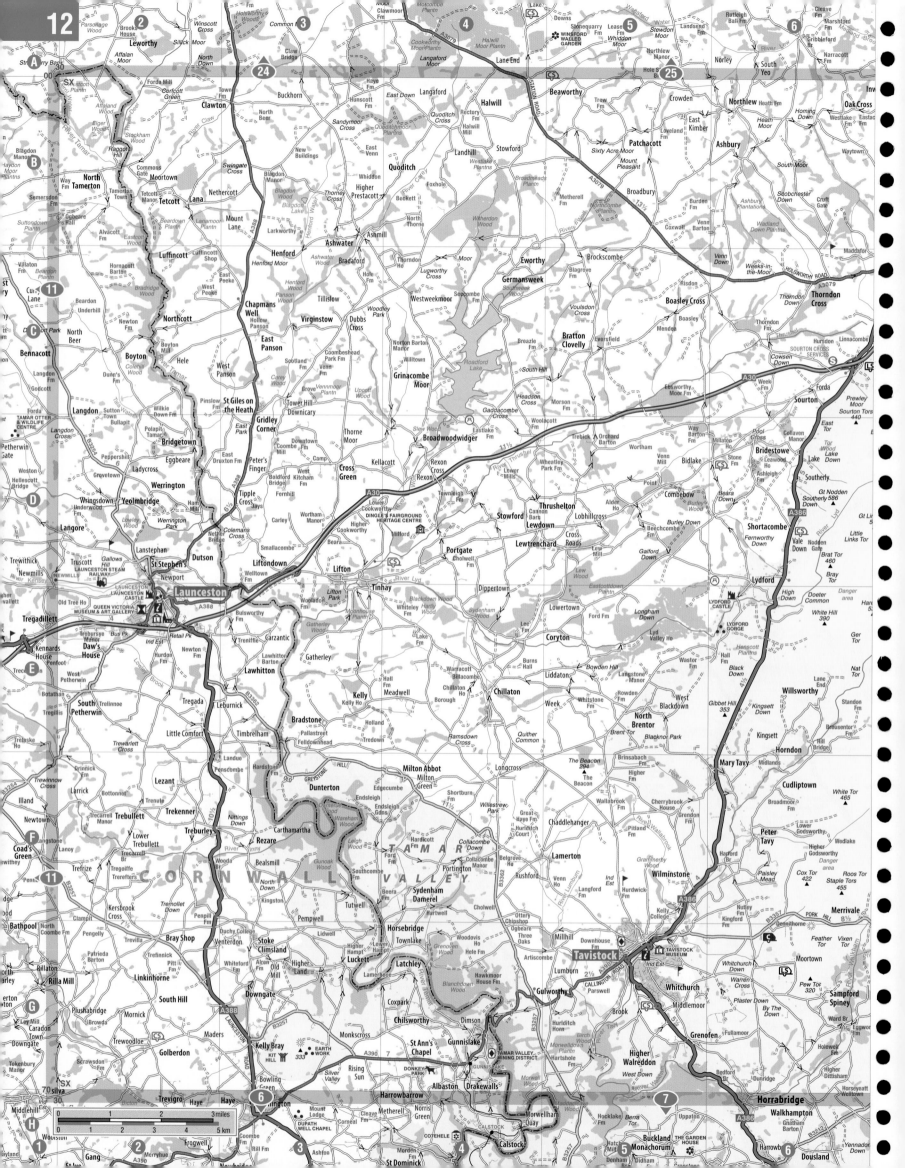

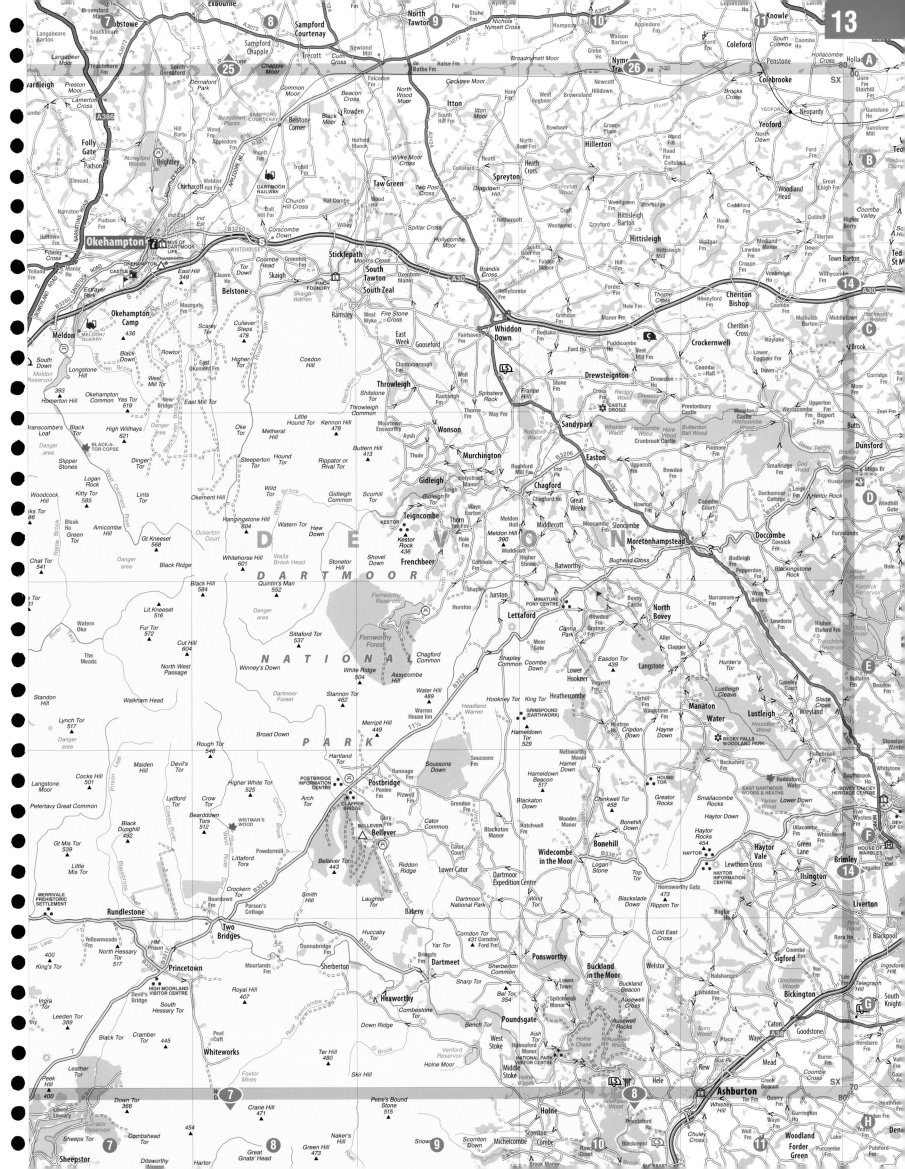

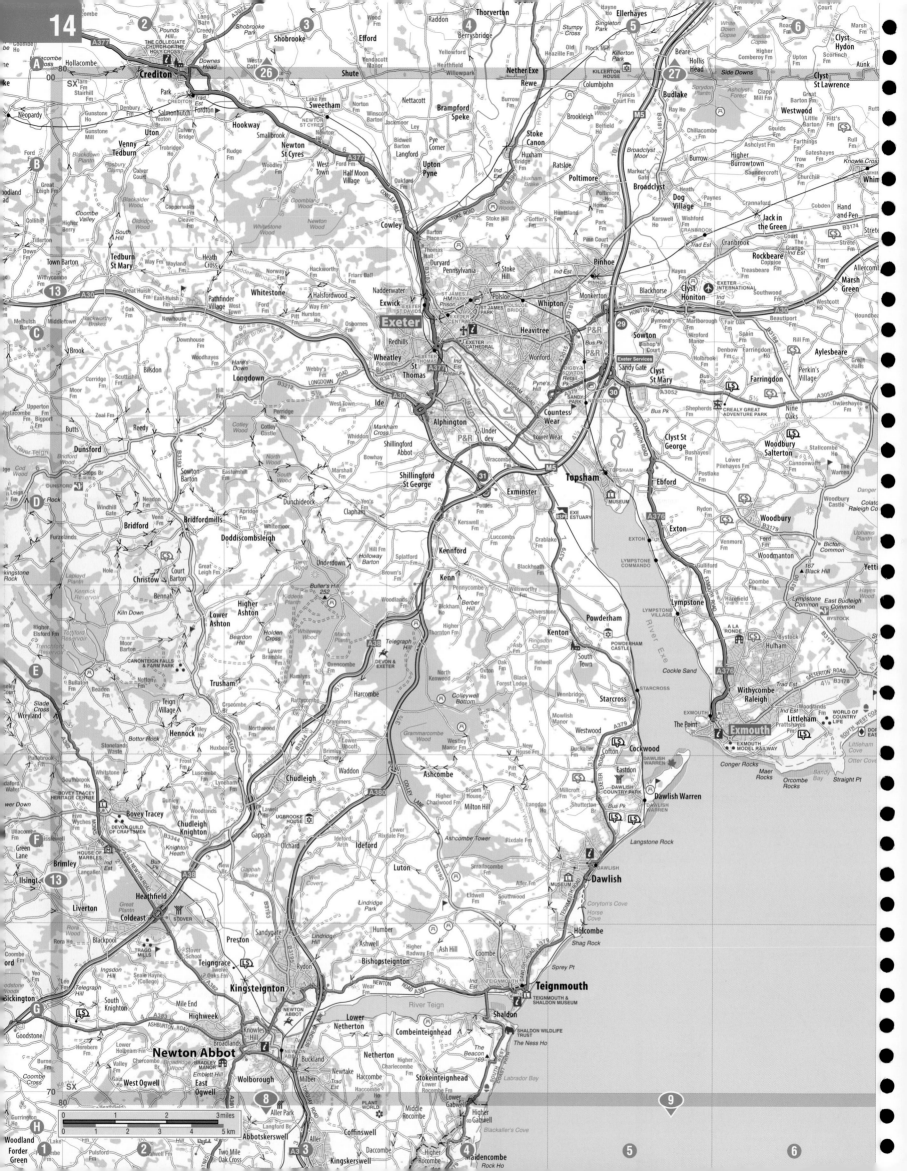

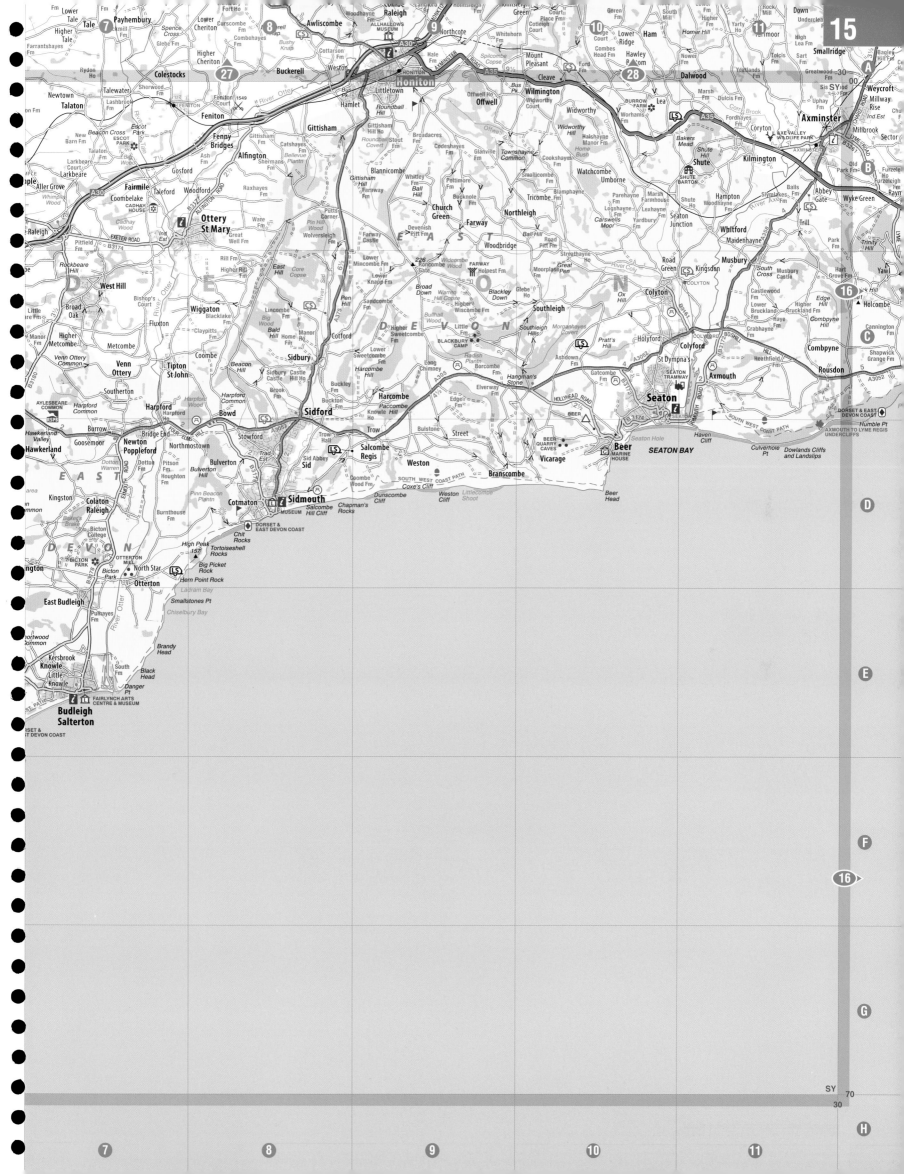

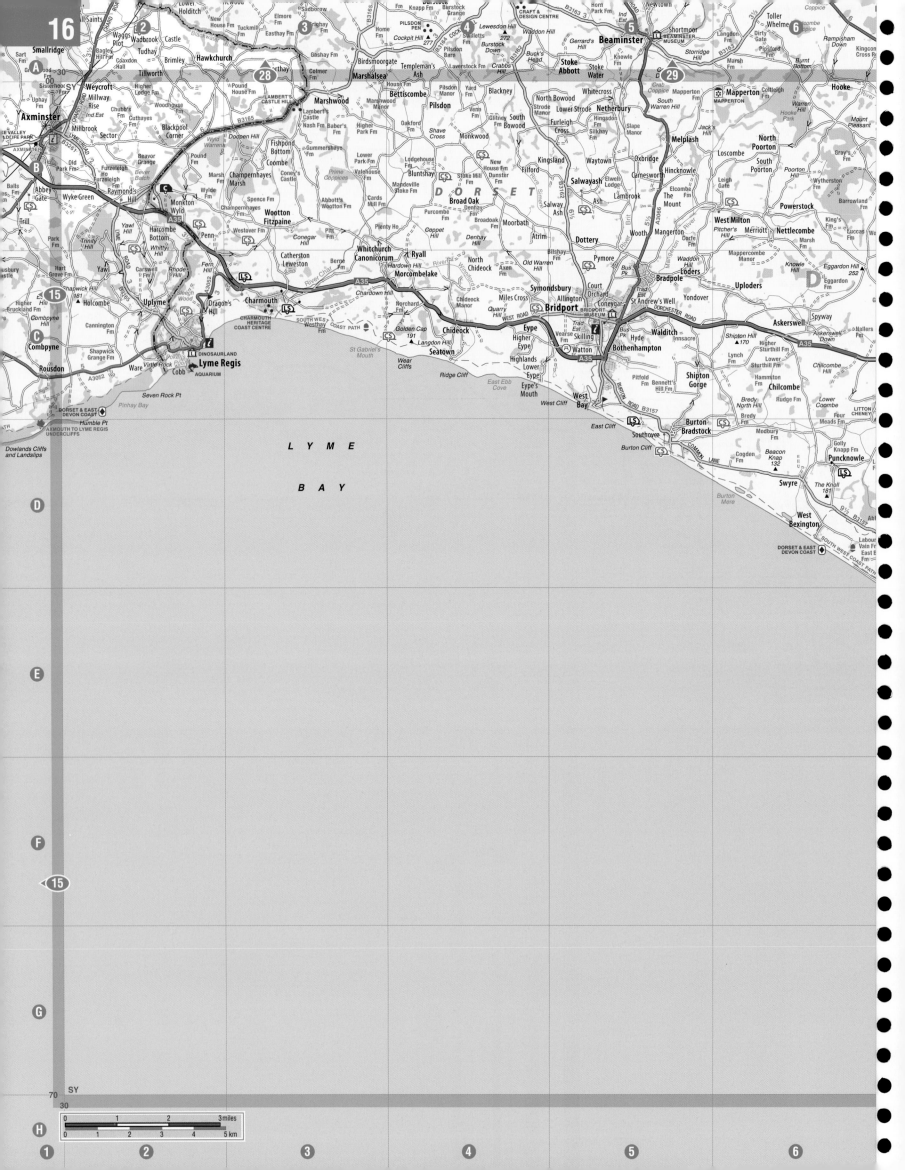

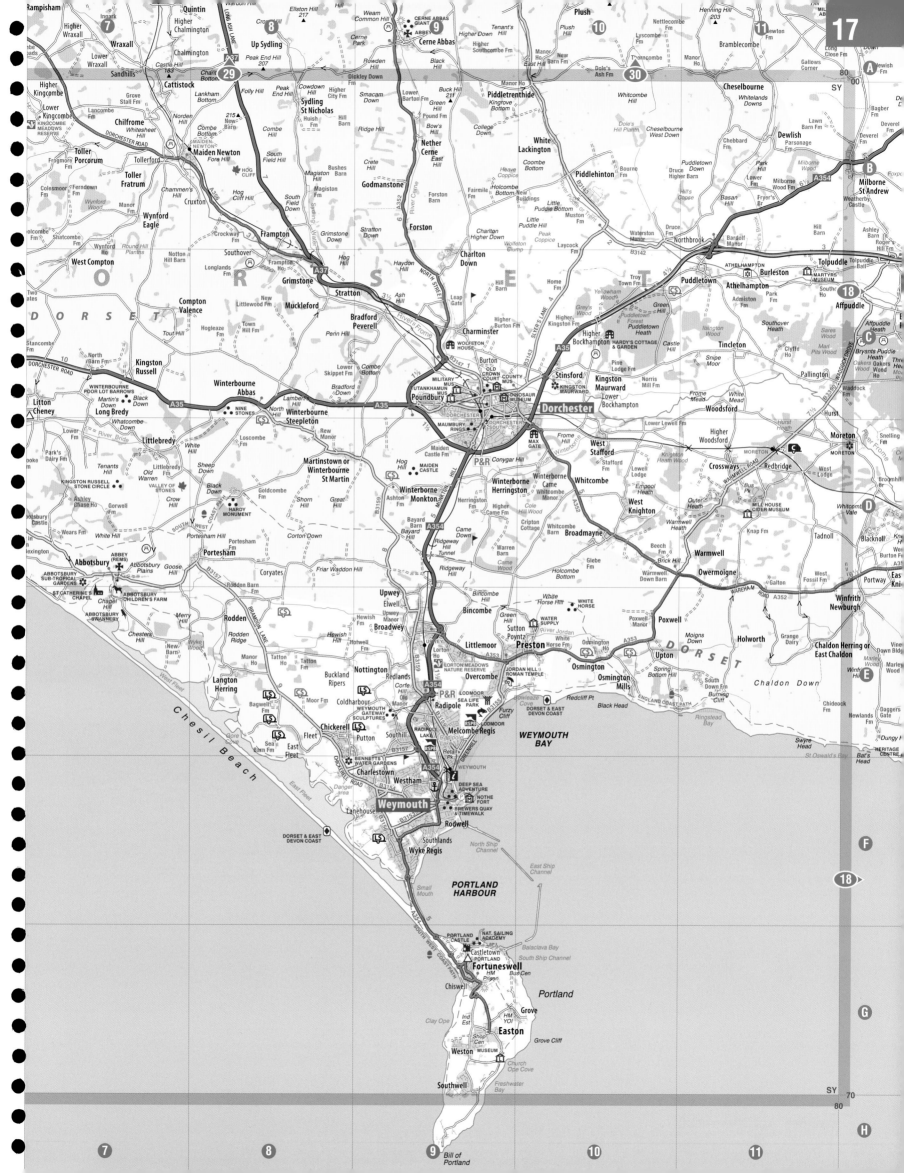

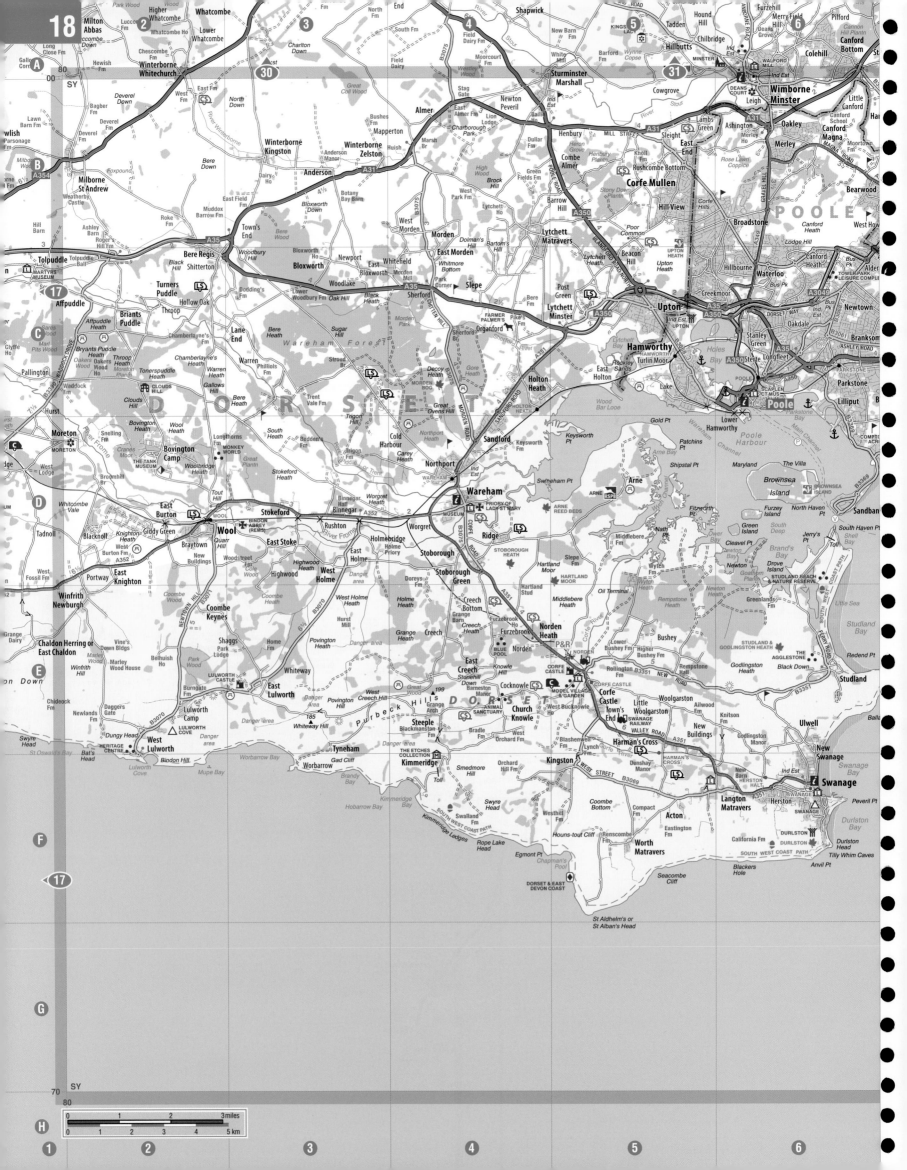

"1" /

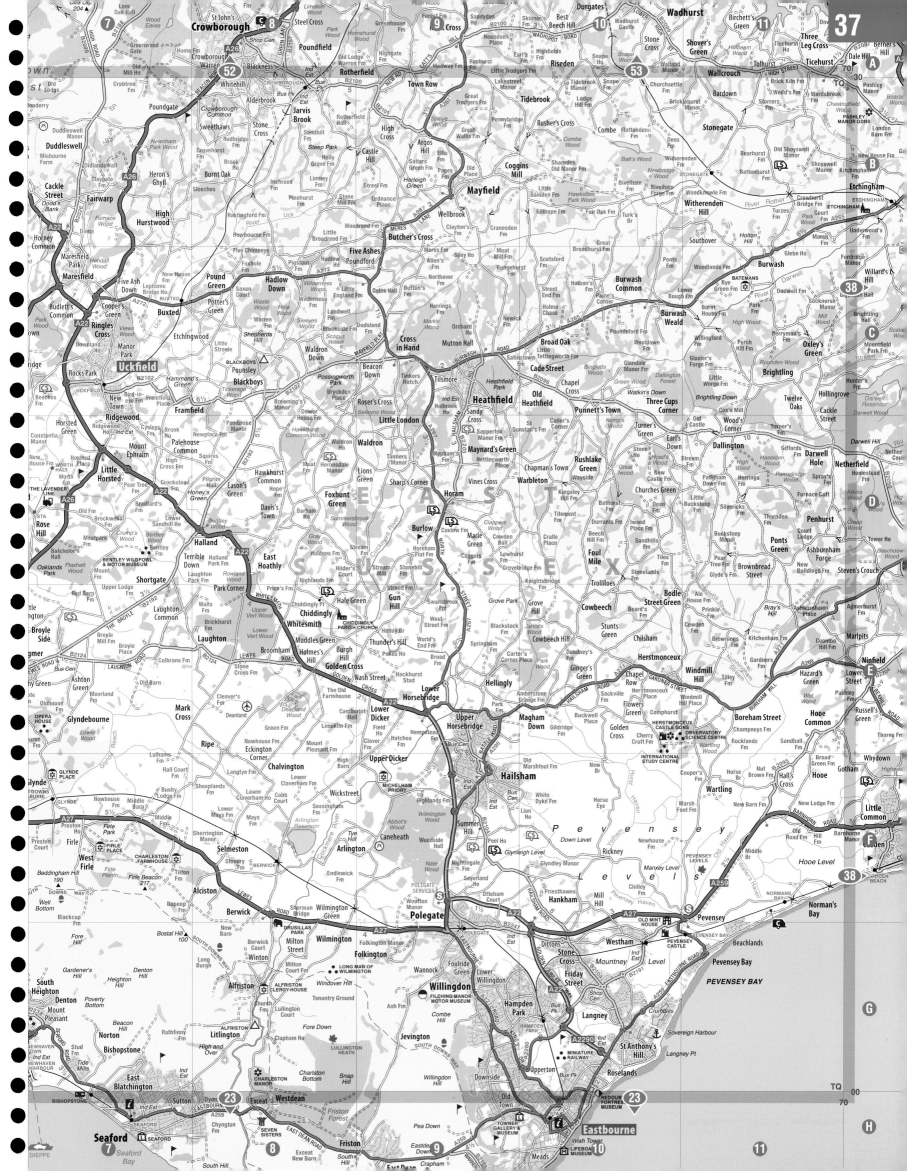

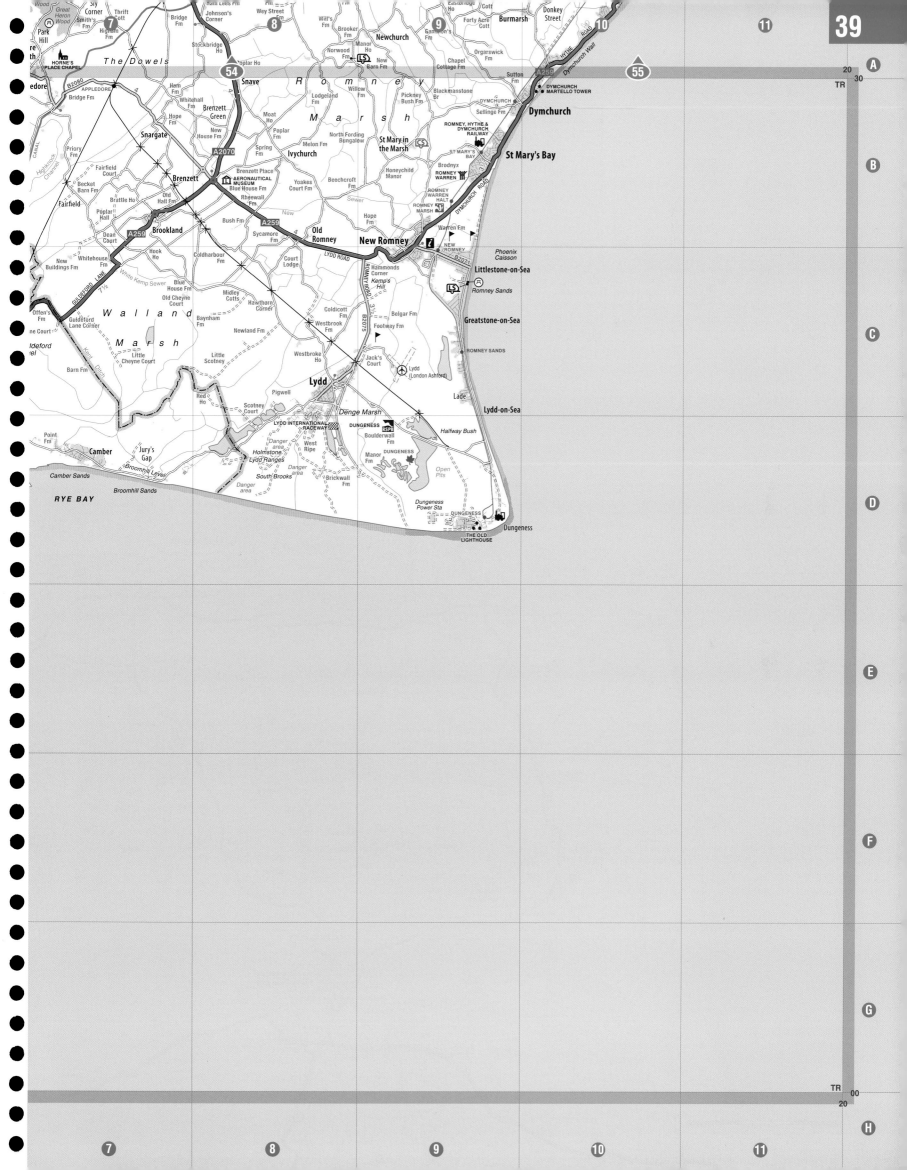

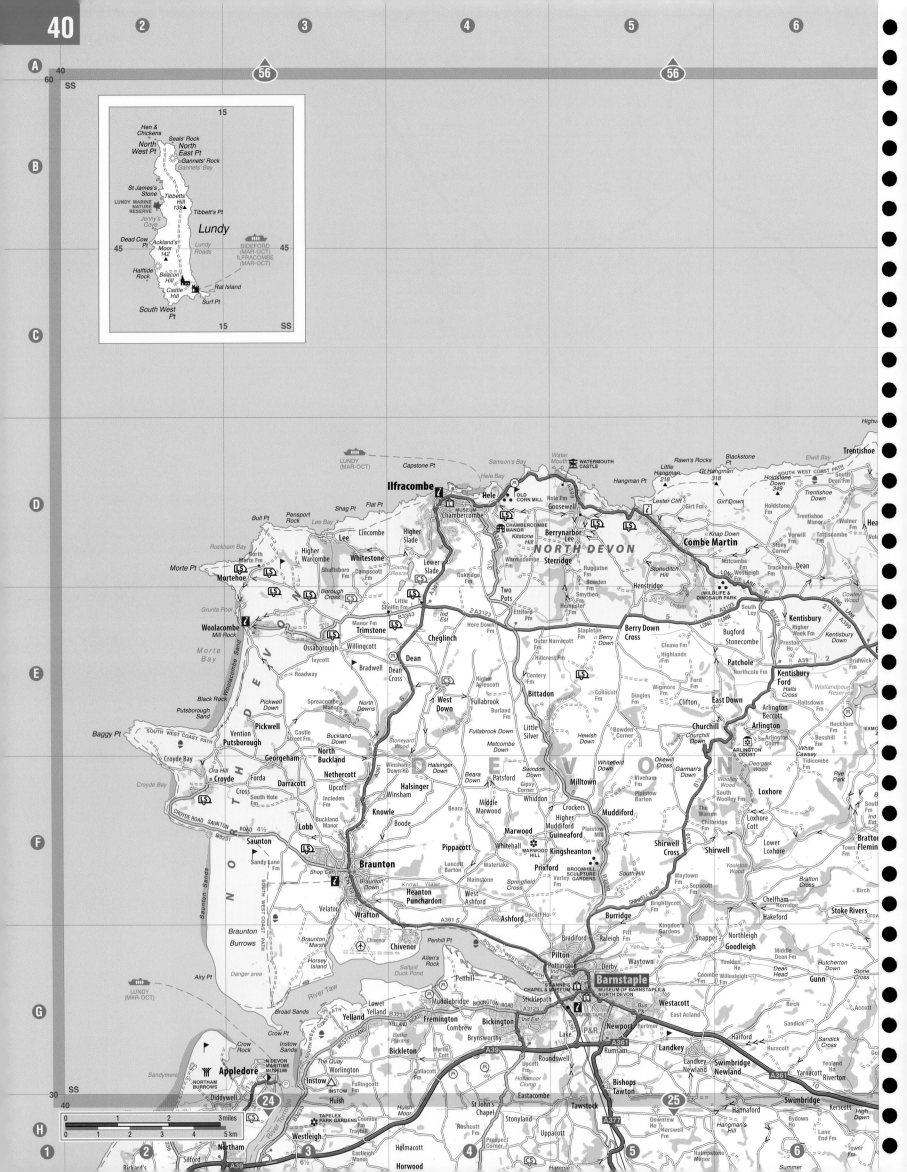

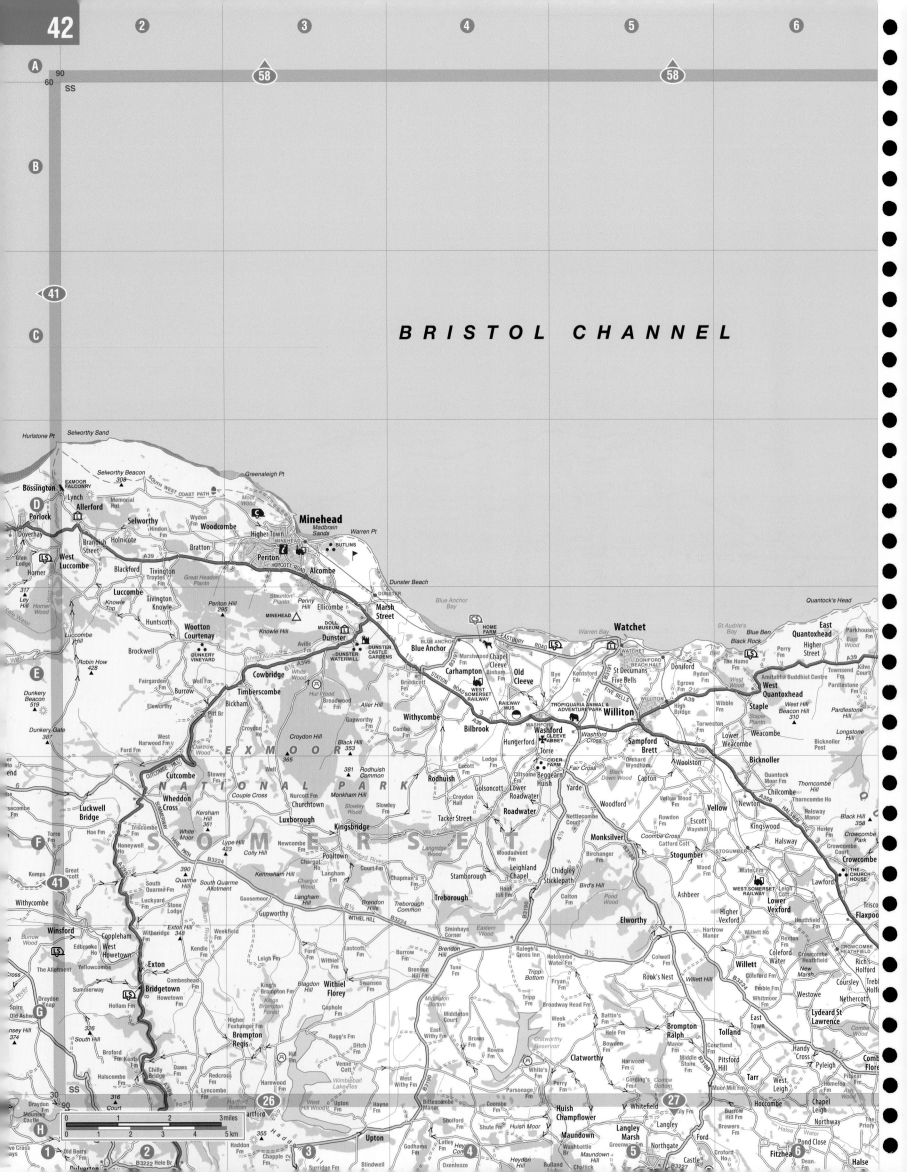

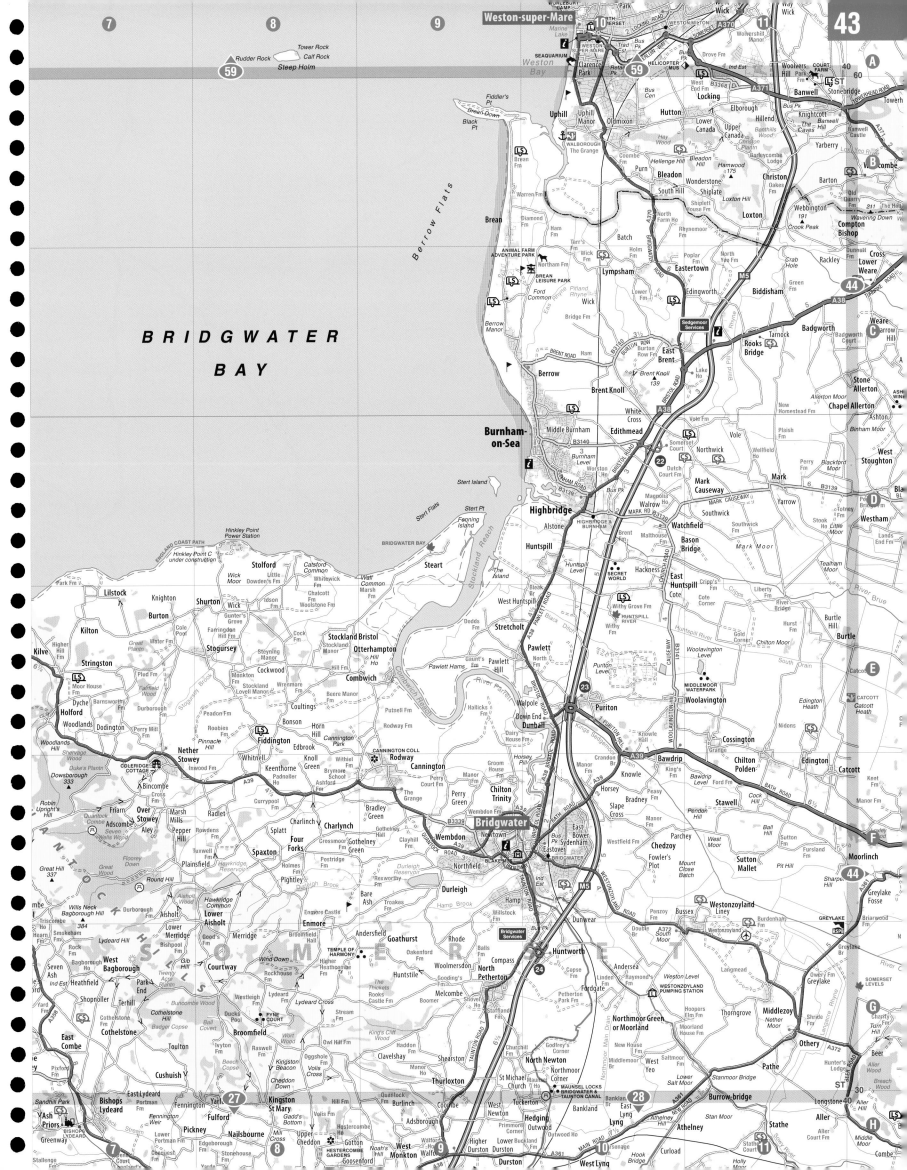

Banwell · Winscombe · Sidcot · Shipham · Star · Rowberrow · Churchill · Lower Langford · Langford · Burrington · Blagdon · Compton Martin · West Harptree · East Harptree · Litton · Farrington Gurney · Temple Cloud · Clutton · Bishop Sutton · Sutton Wick · Chew Stoke · Stanton Wick · Chelwood

Compton Bishop · Cross · Lower Weare · Axbridge · Cheddar · Charterhouse · Priddy · Chewton Mendip · Ston Easton · Chilcompton · Emborough · Ashwick · Oakhill

Weare · Stone Allerton · Chapel Allerton · Clewer · Draycott · Rodney Stoke · Westbury-sub-Mendip · Easton · Wookey Hole · West Horrington · East Horrington · Gurney Slade · Binegar

Wedmore · Blackford · Heath House · Theale · Mudgley · Panborough · Wookey · Worth · Burcott · Henton · Wells · Dulcote · Dinder · Croscombe · Downside

Westham · Westhay · Godney · Meare · Polsham · Coxley · Worminster · Shepton Mallet · Doulting

Burtle · Catcott · Edington · Shapwick · Ashcott · Glastonbury · Northover · Pilton · West Pennard · East Compton · Cannard's Grave · Prestleigh · Evercreech

Moorlinch · Pedwell · Greinton · Street · Walton · Overleigh · Butleigh · West Bradley · Parbrook · Ditcheat · Pylle · East Pennard · Wraxall

Othery · Greylake · Beer · High Ham · Henley · Dundon · Compton Dundon · Littleton · Keinton Mandeville · Lydford-on-Fosse · East Lydford · West Lydford · Alford · Castle Cary · Ansford · Sutton · Hornblotton · Alhampton

Somerton · Charlton Mackerell · Charlton Adam · Babcary · North Barrow · South Barrow

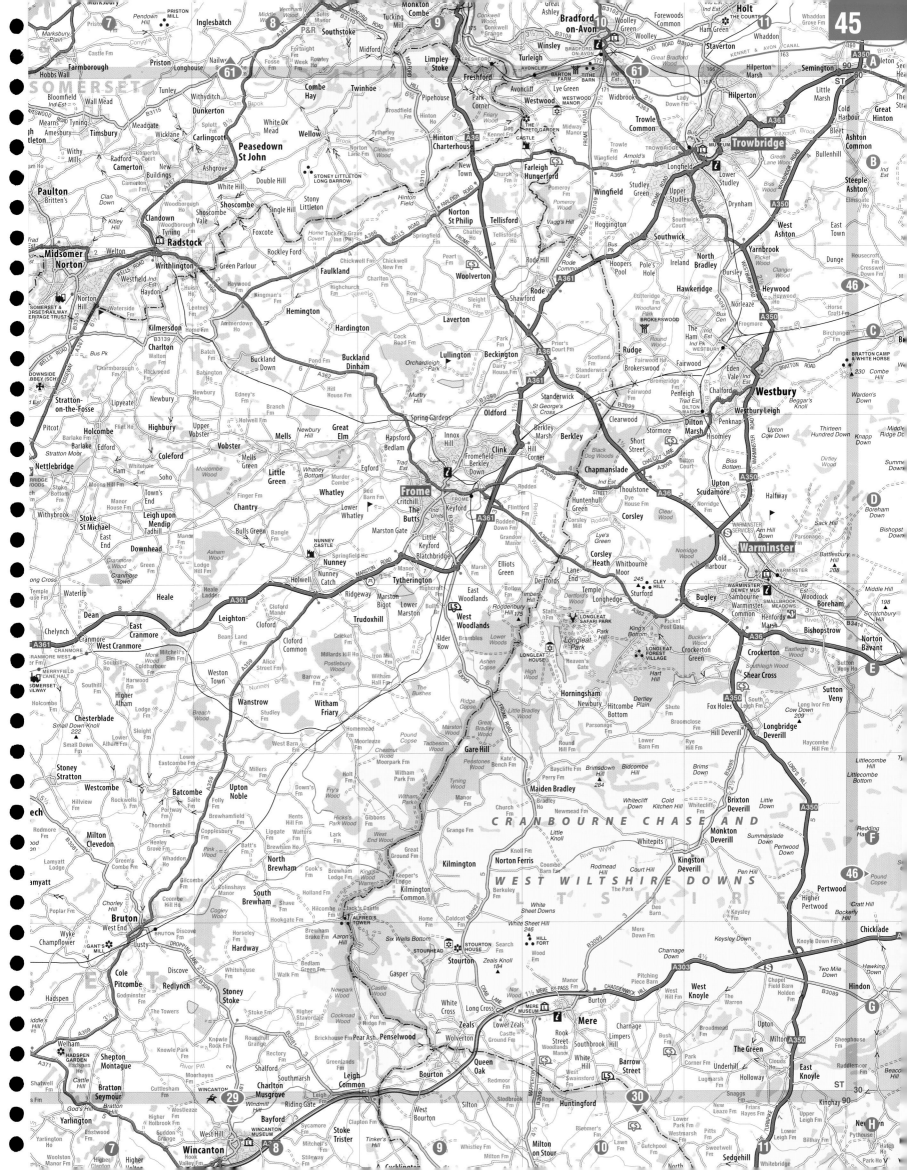

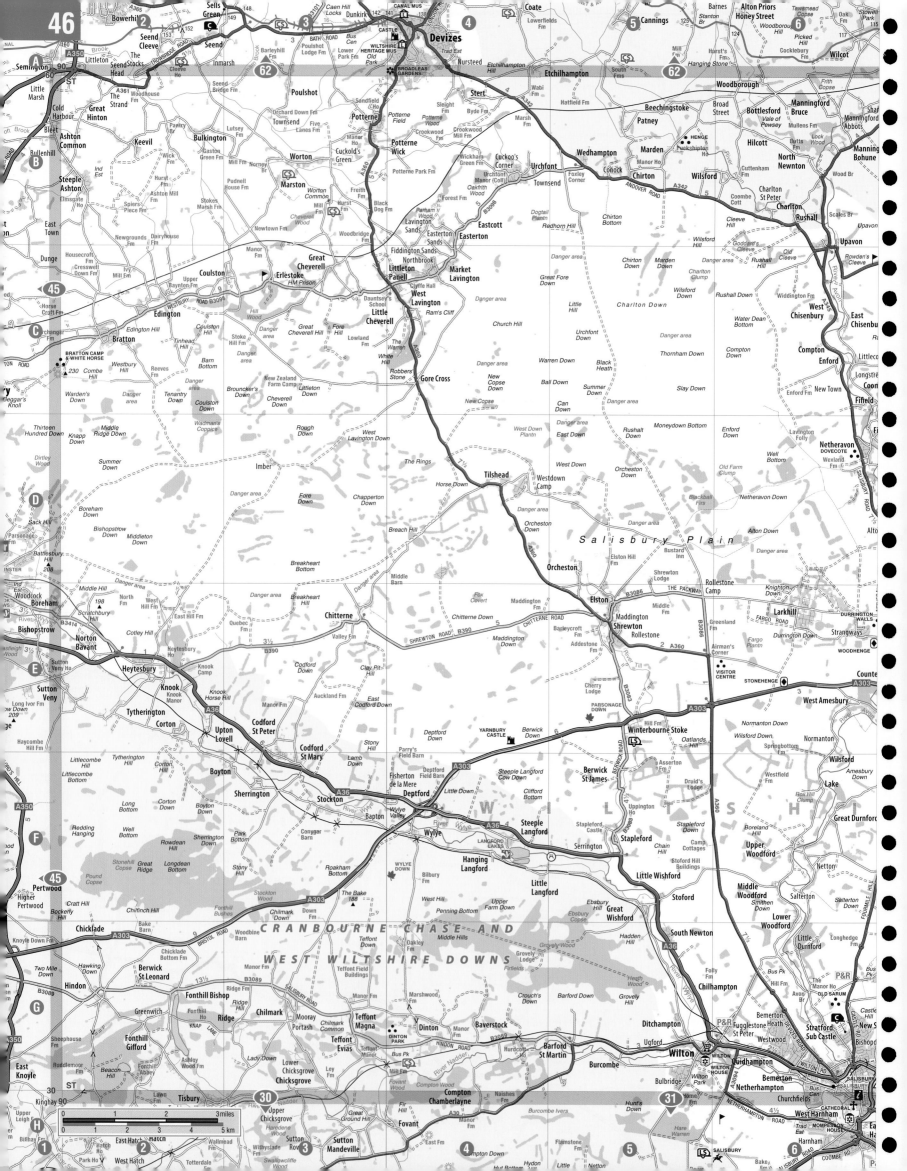

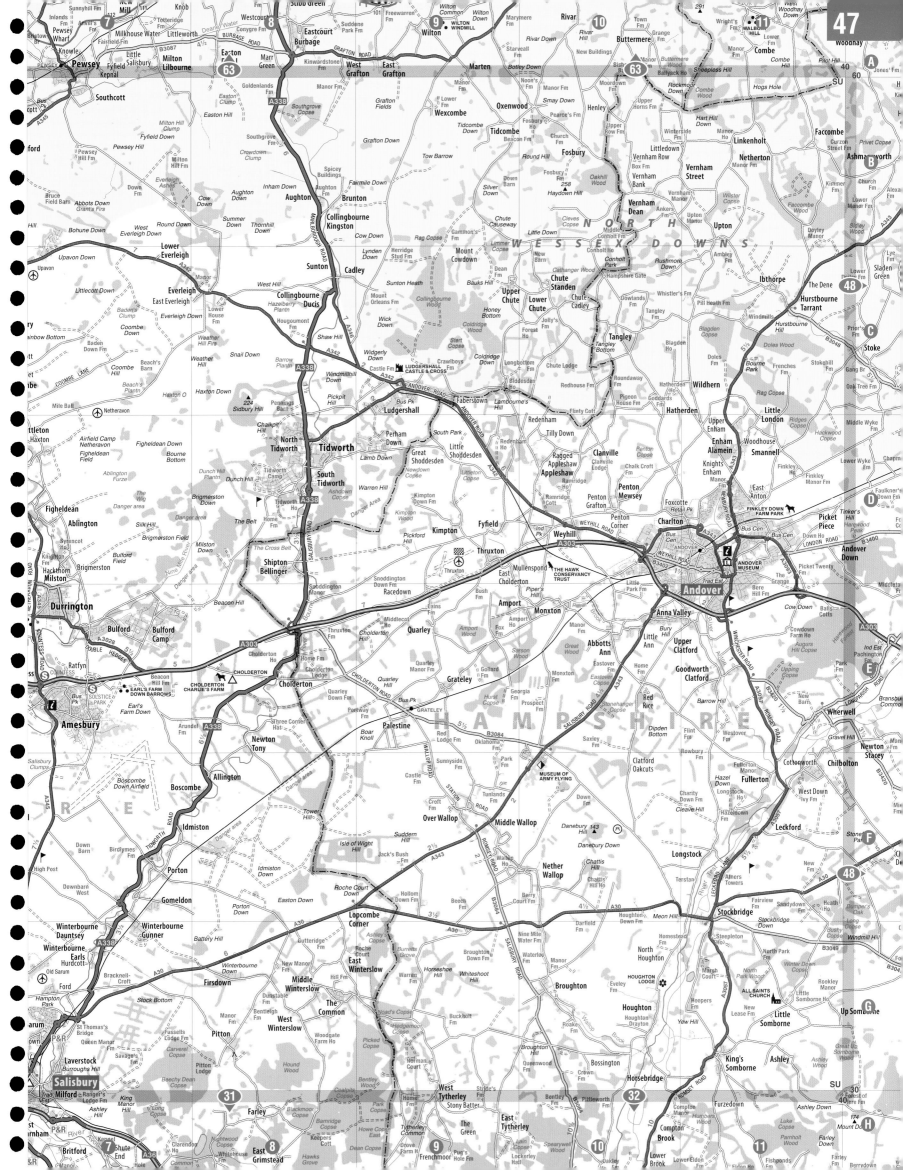

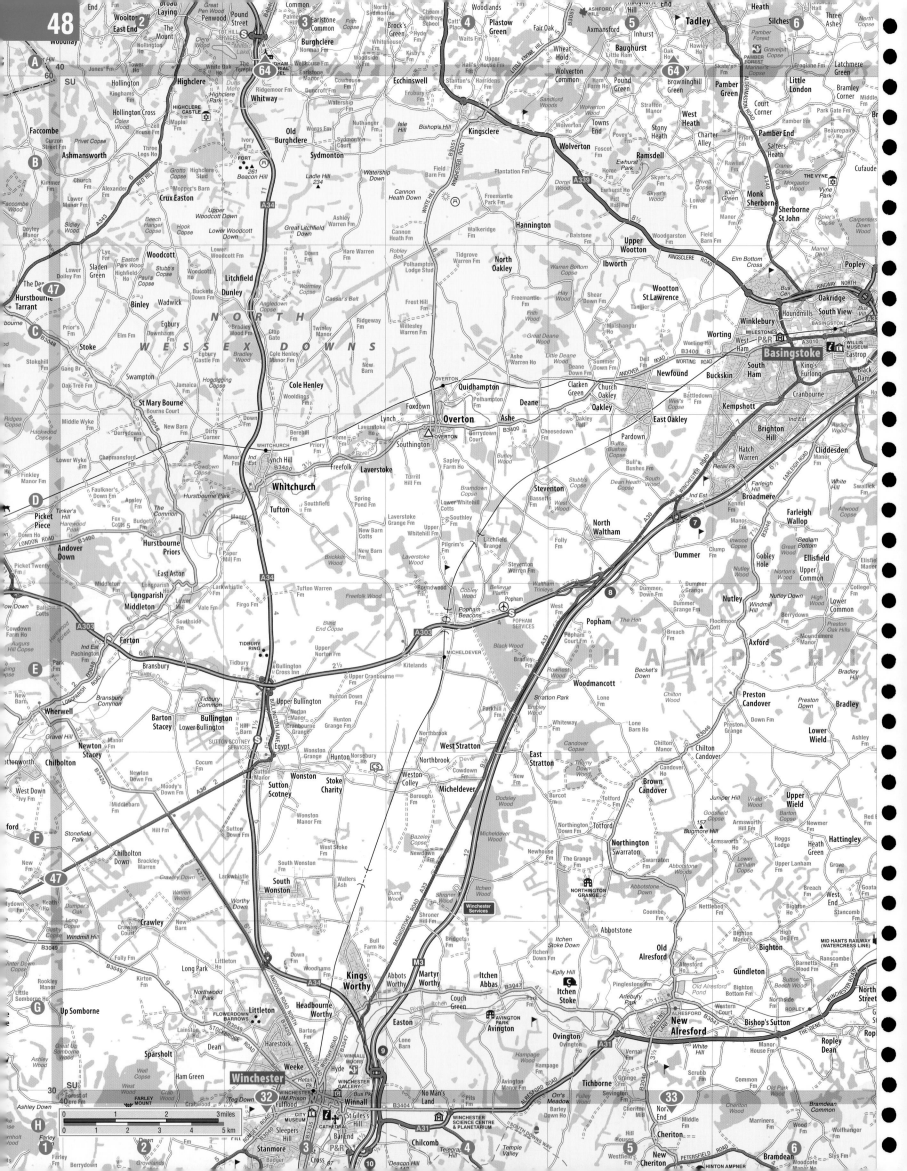

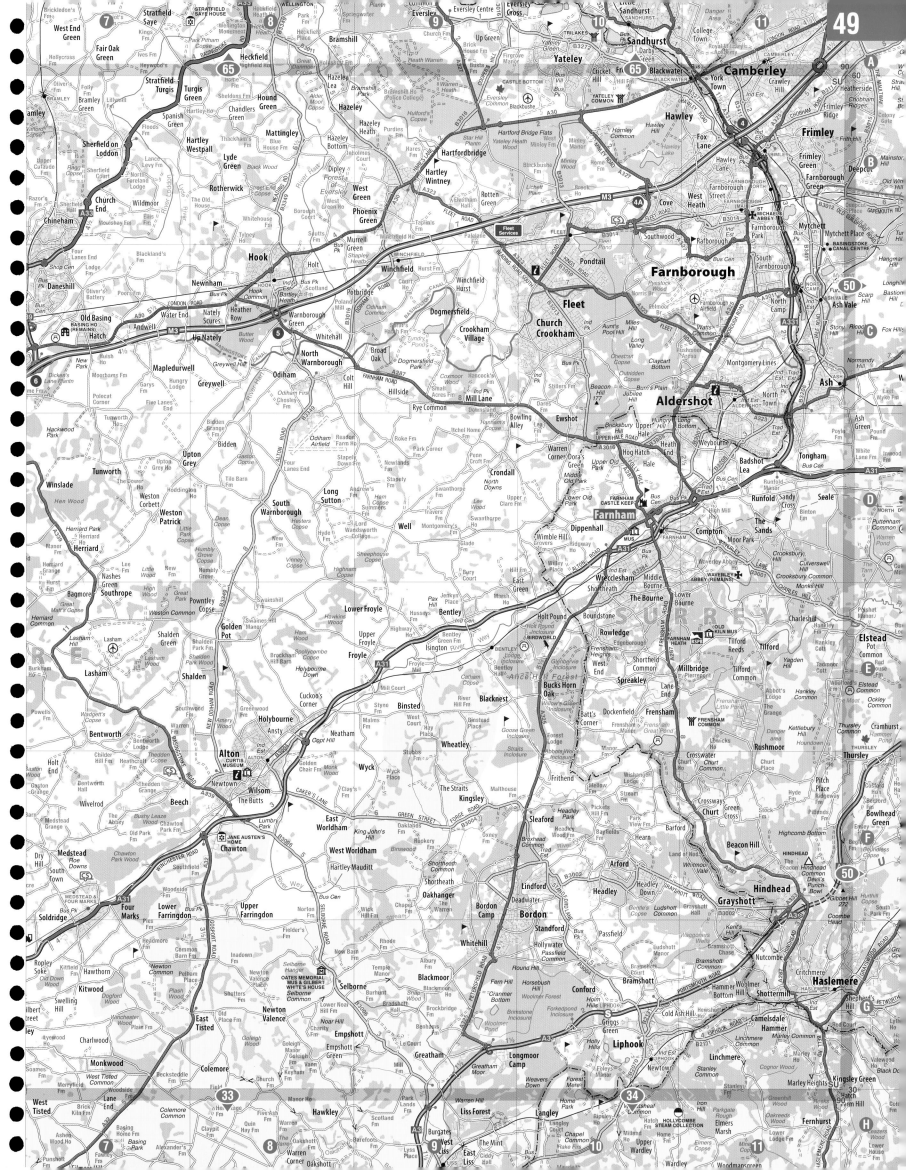

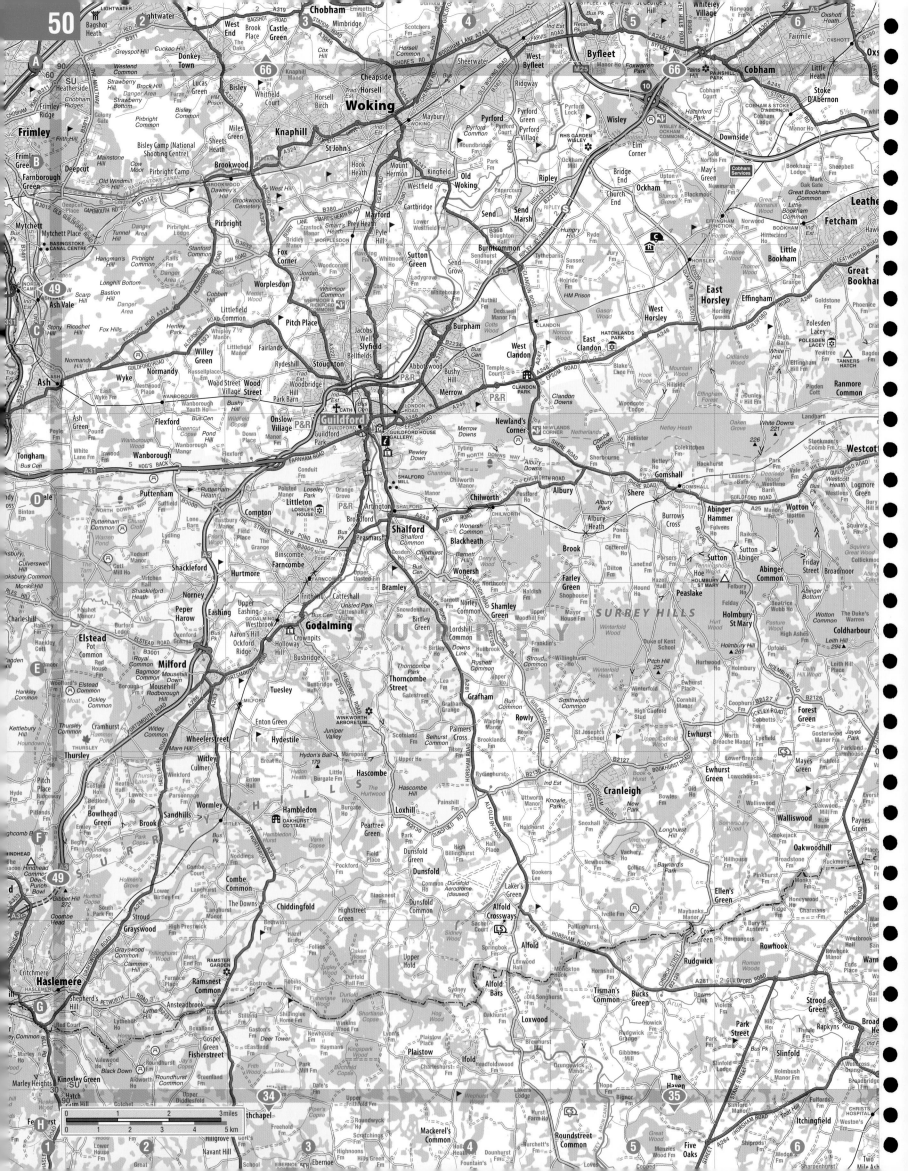

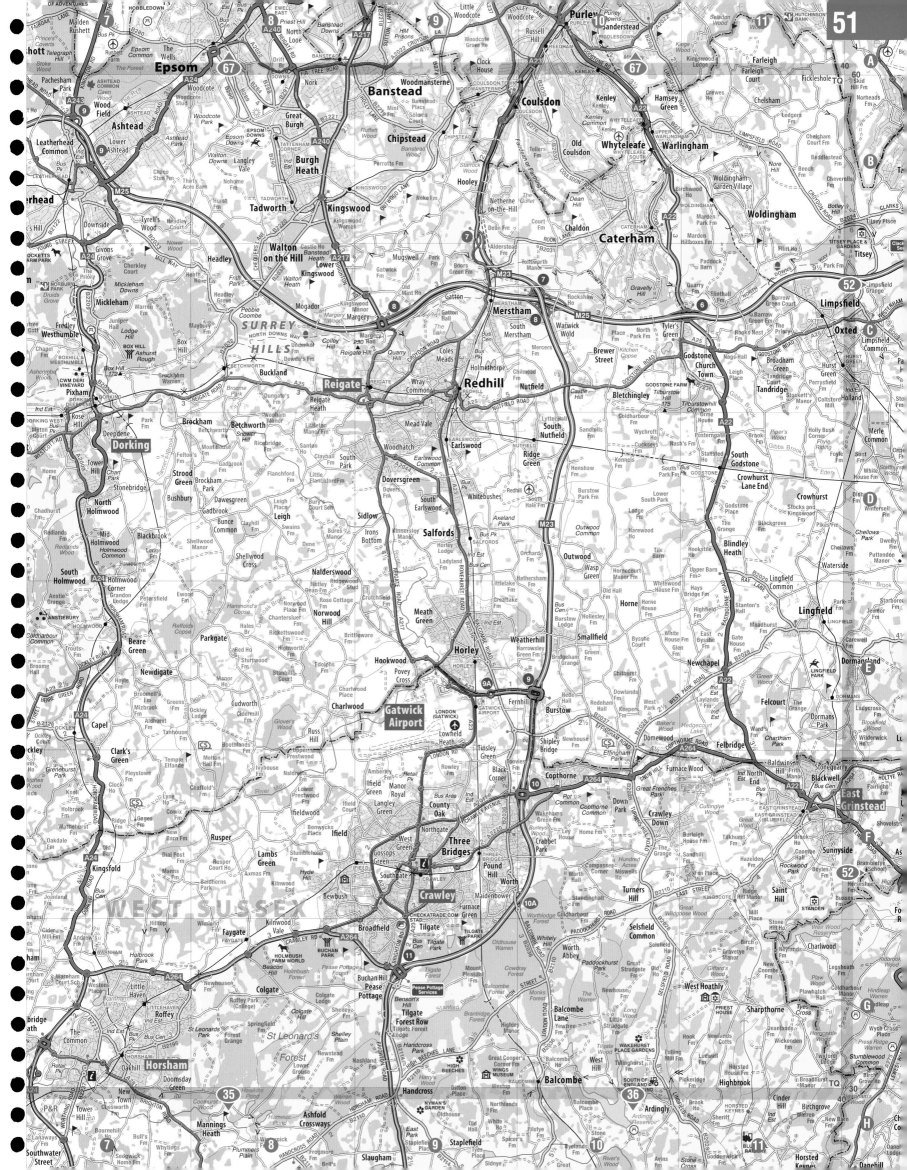

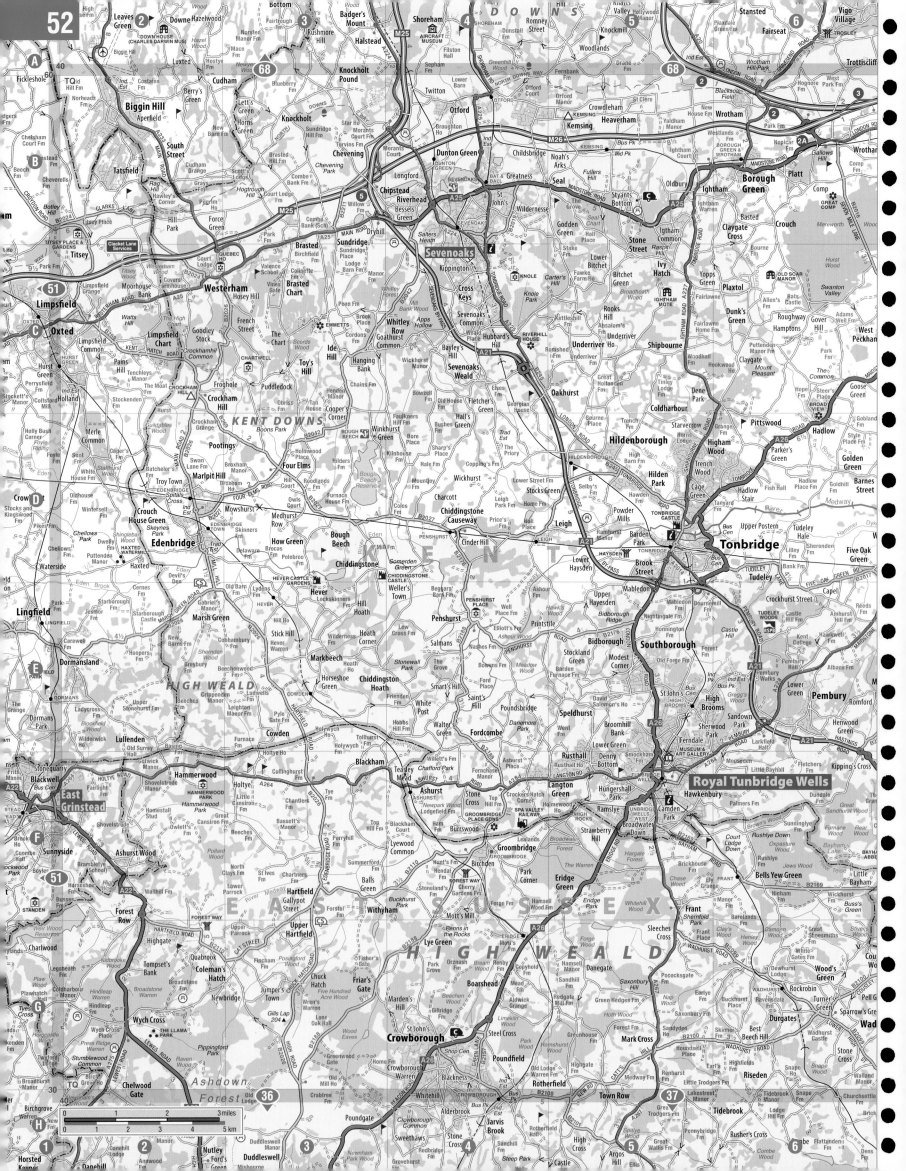

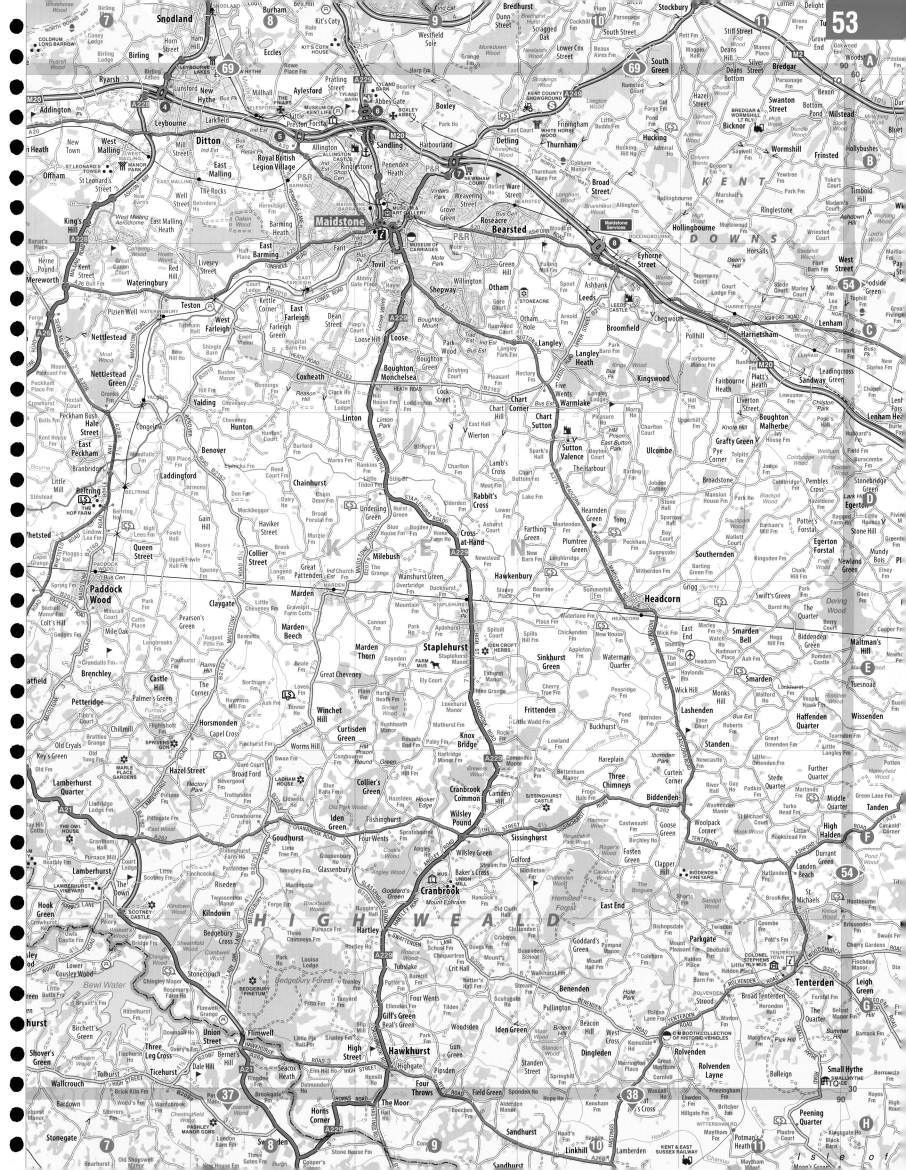

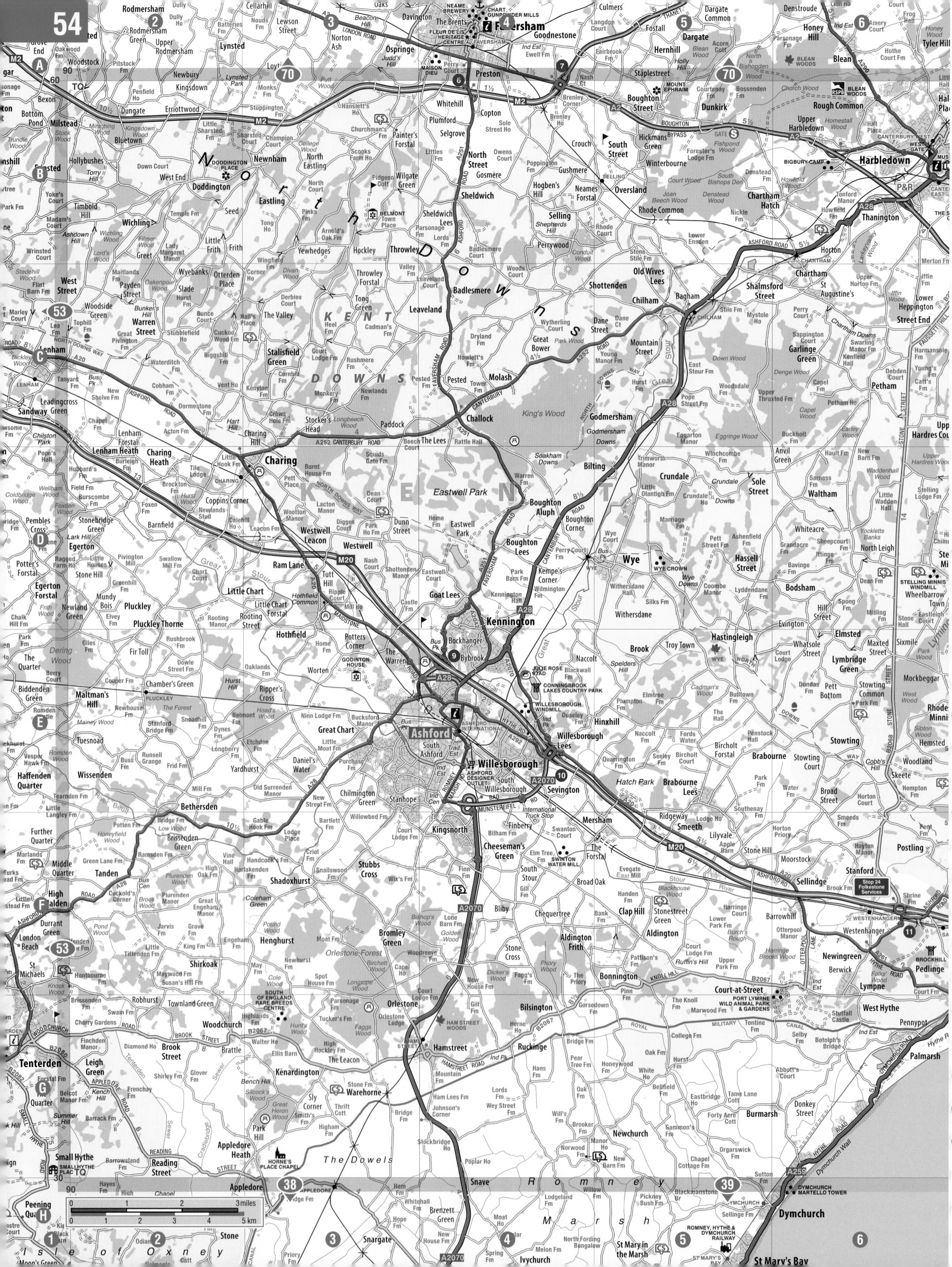

Faversham
Ospringe
Preston
Goodnestone
Dargate
Hernhill
Boughton Street
Dunkirk
Rough Common
Harbledown
Blean
Honey Hill
Tyler Hill
Rodmersham
Lynsted
Newnham
Doddington
Eastling
Sheldwich
Selling
Oversland
Chartham Hatch
Thanington
Chartham
Shalmsford Street
Chilham
Bagham
Old Wives Lees
Shottenden
Badlesmere
Leaveland
Throwley
Challock
Molash
Godmersham
Bilting
Crundale
Waltham
Petham
Garlinge Green
Lenham
Sandway
Lenham Heath
Charing
Charing Heath
Westwell
Westwell Leacon
Egerton
Pluckley
Pluckley Thorne
Little Chart
Hothfield
Ram Lane
Boughton Aluph
Boughton Lees
Wye
Kennington
Goat Lees
Brook
Hastingleigh
Elmsted
Ashford
Willesborough
Sevington
Mersham
Great Chart
Bethersden
Kingsnorth
Stanhope
Shadoxhurst
Hinxhill
Brabourne
Brabourne Lees
Smeeth
Stowting
Sellindge
Stanford
Postling
Aldington
Bonnington
Bilsington
Orlestone
Hamstreet
Ruckinge
Newchurch
Burmarsh
Dymchurch
St Mary's Bay
Lympne
West Hythe
Palmarsh
Tenterden
High Halden
Woodchurch
Appledore
Kenardington
Warehorne
Snave
Snargate
Ivychurch
Brenzett
Romney Marsh
North Downs
Kent Downs
Eastwell Park
King's Wood
Orlestone Forest
The Dowels
Isle of Oxney
M2
M20
A2
A28
A20
A251
A252
A2070
A259
70
53
38
39
0 1 2 3 miles
0 1 2 3 4 5 km

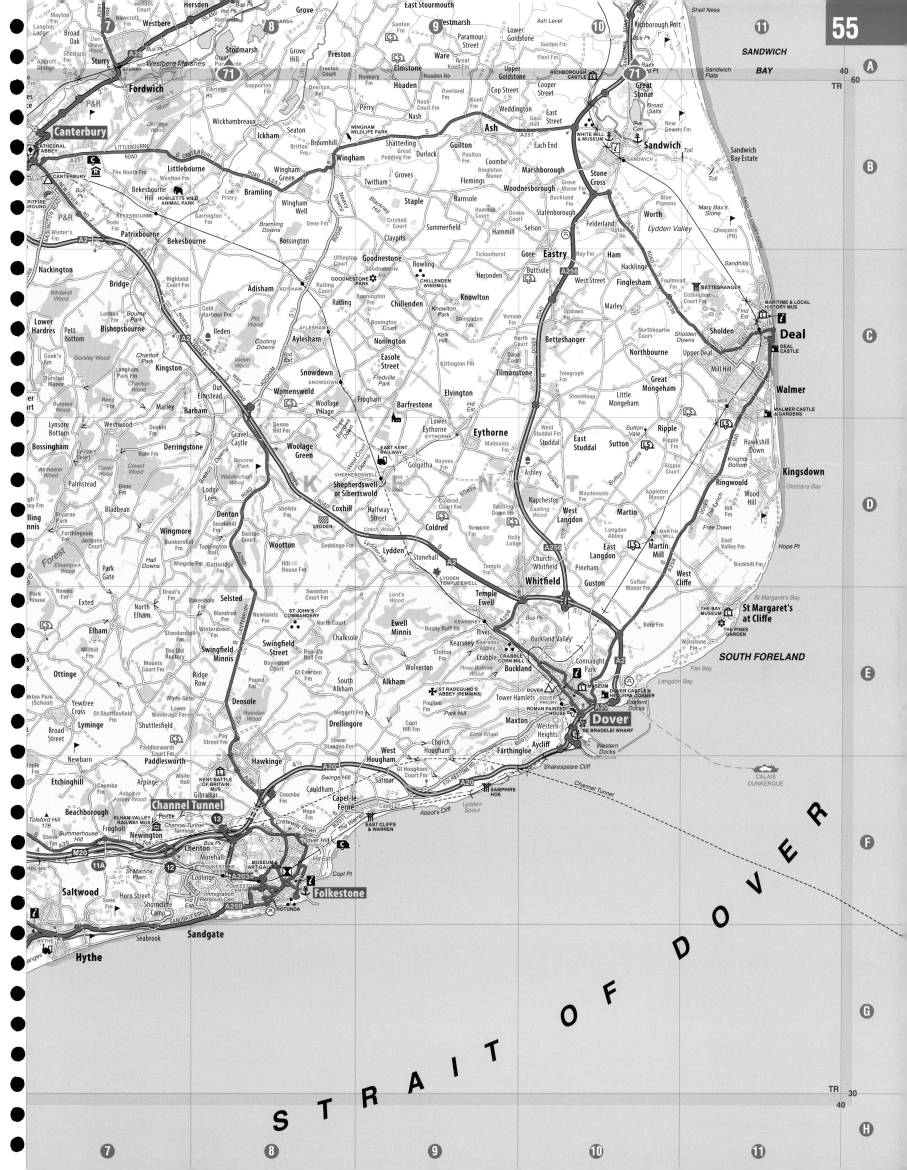

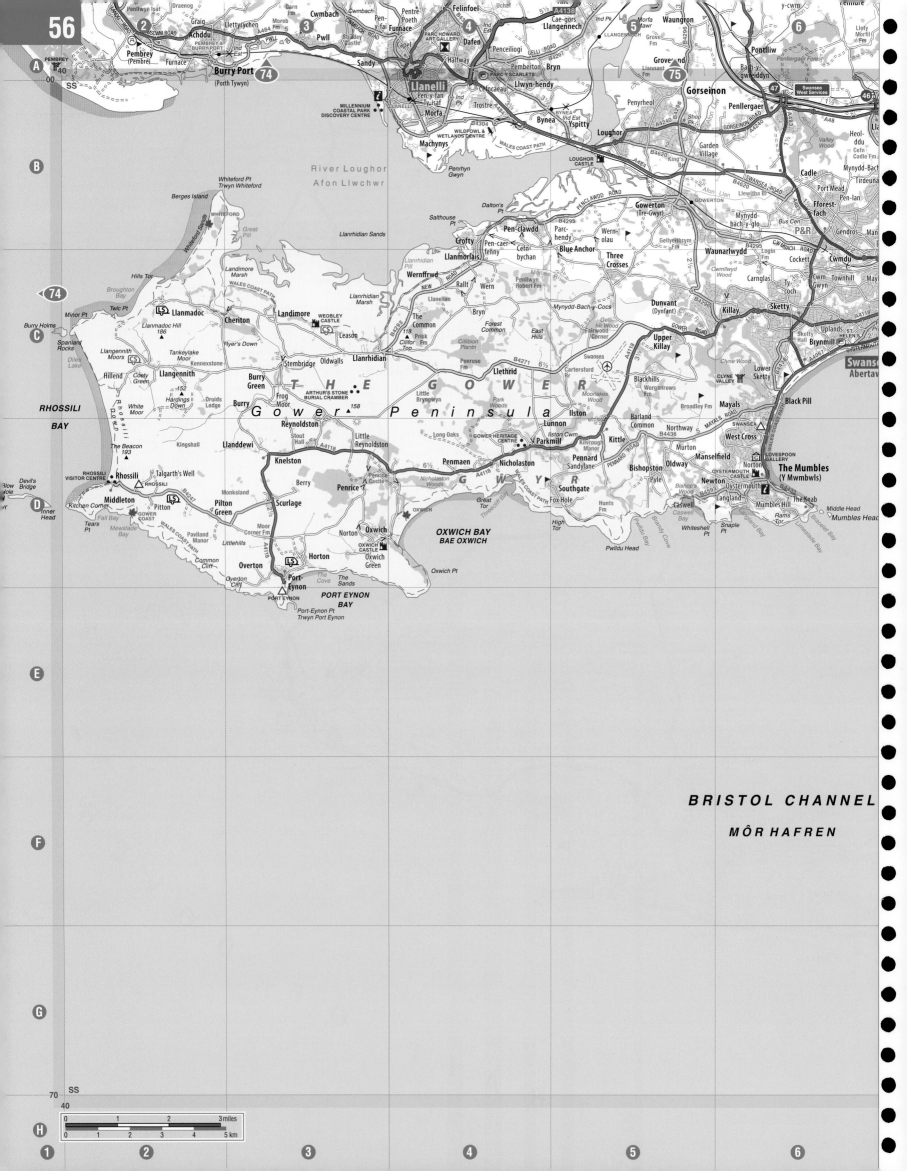

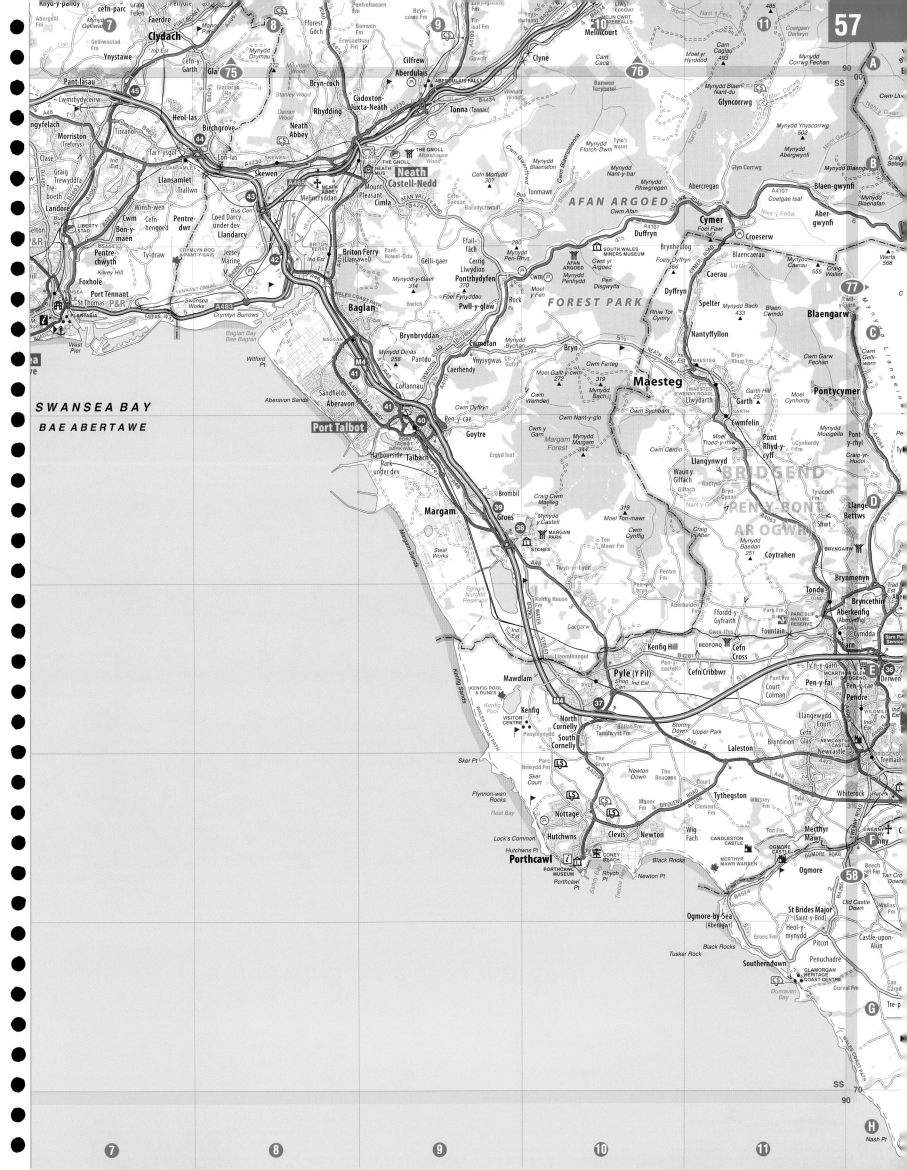

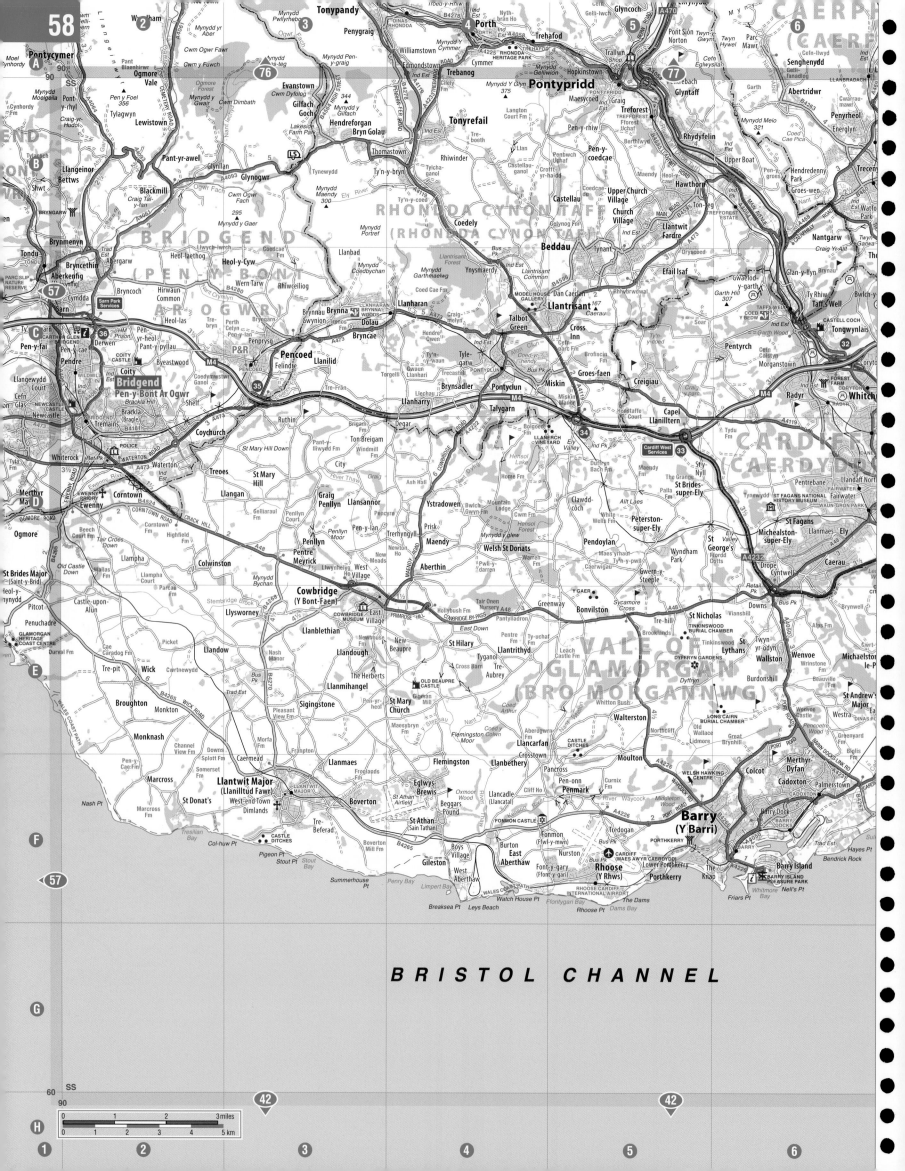

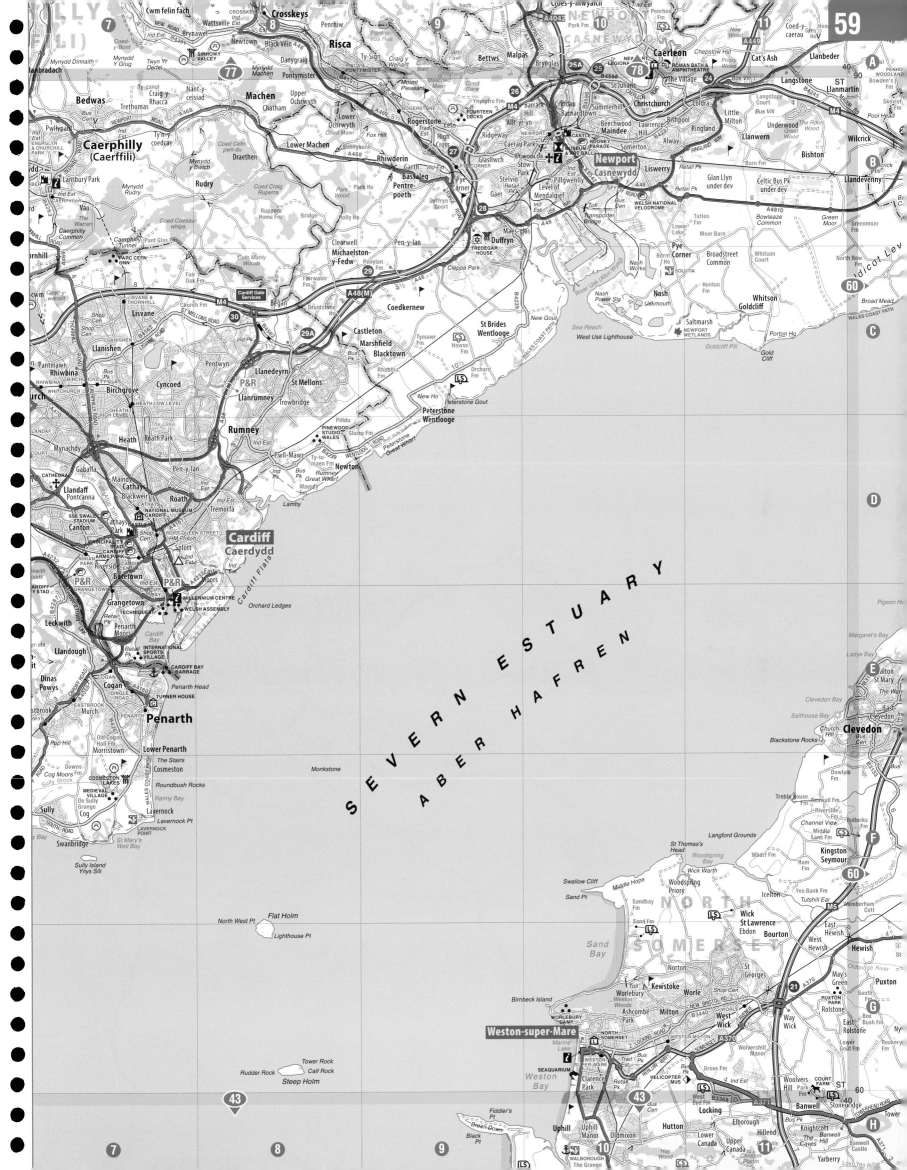

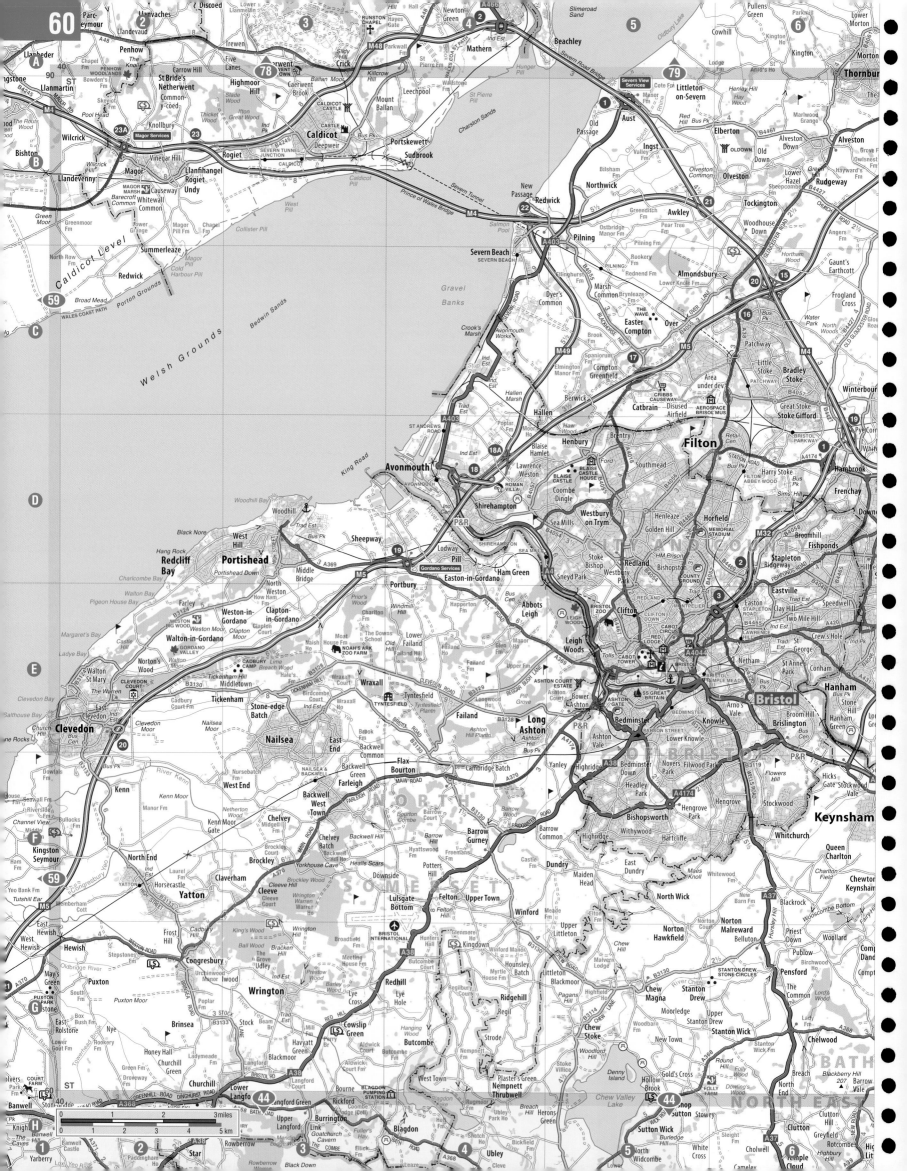

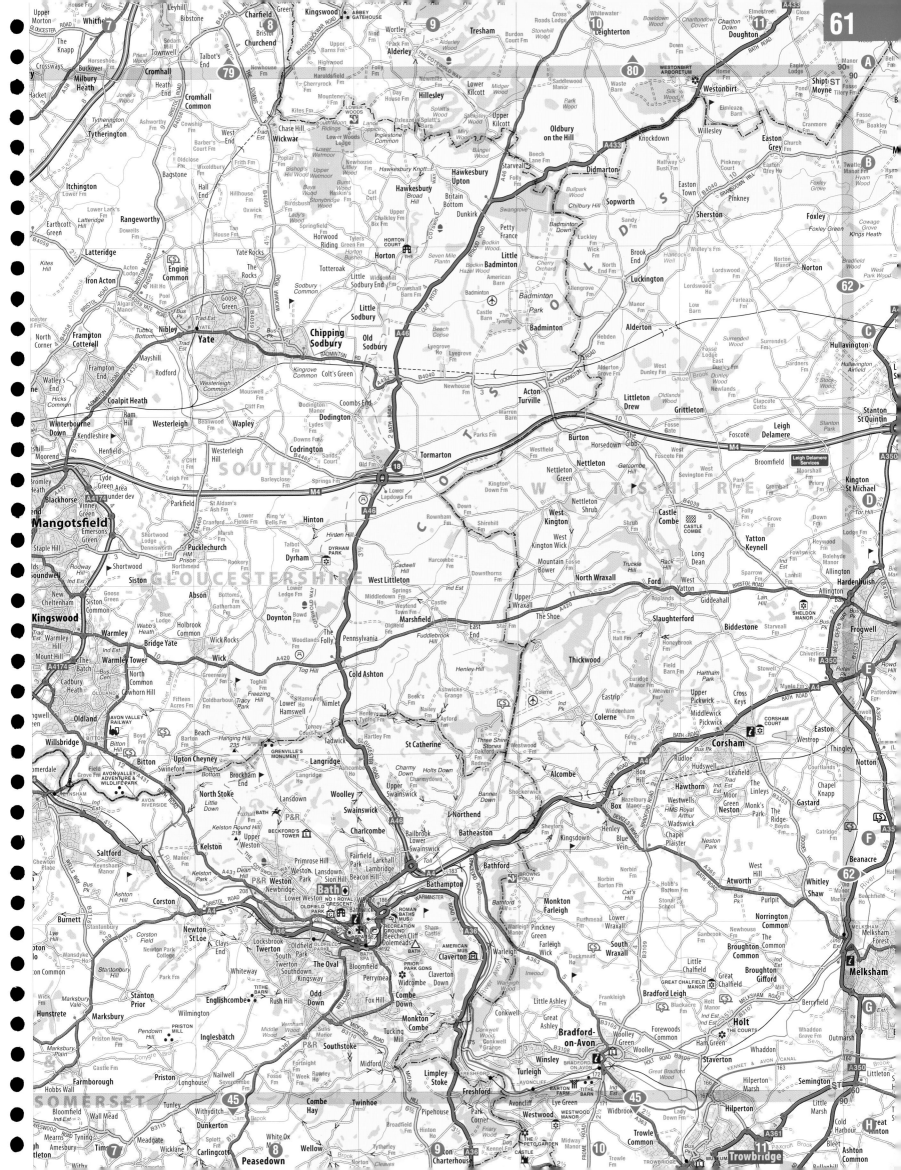

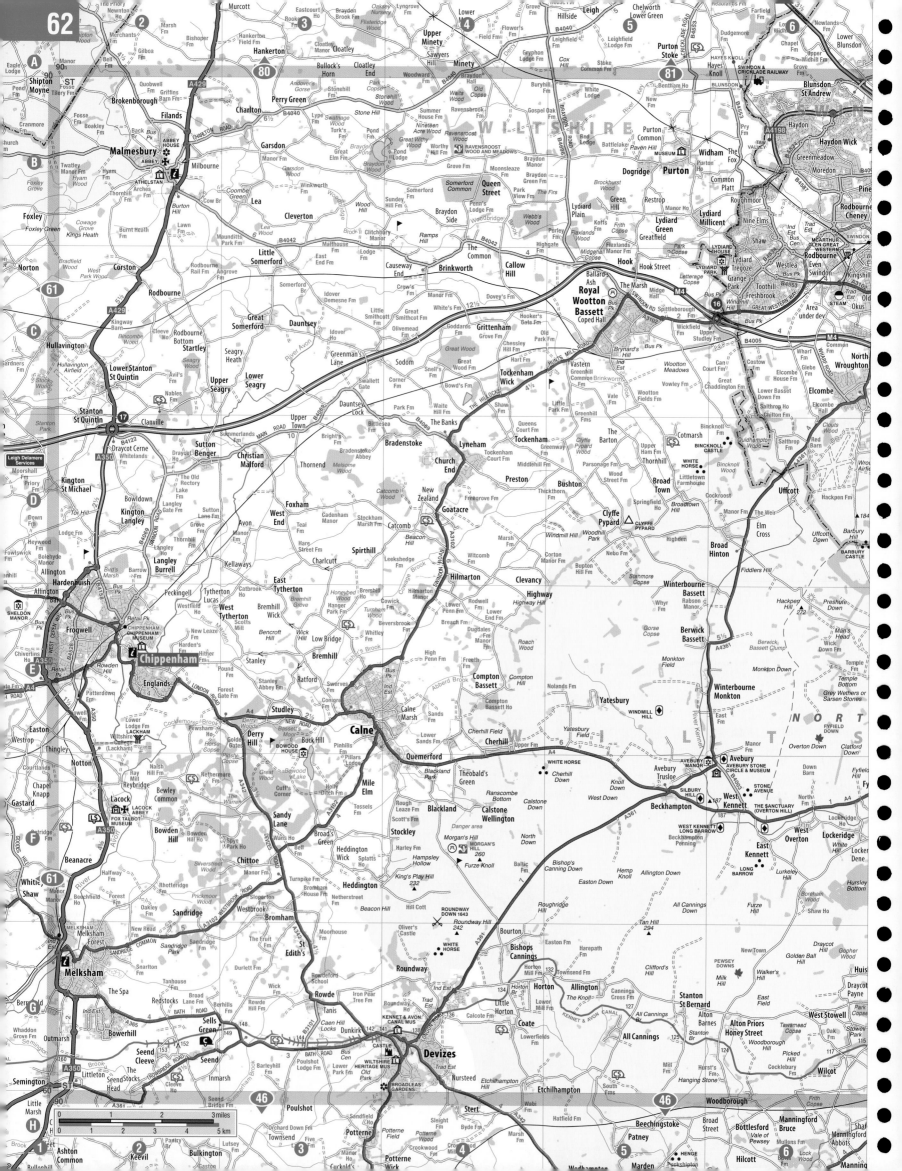

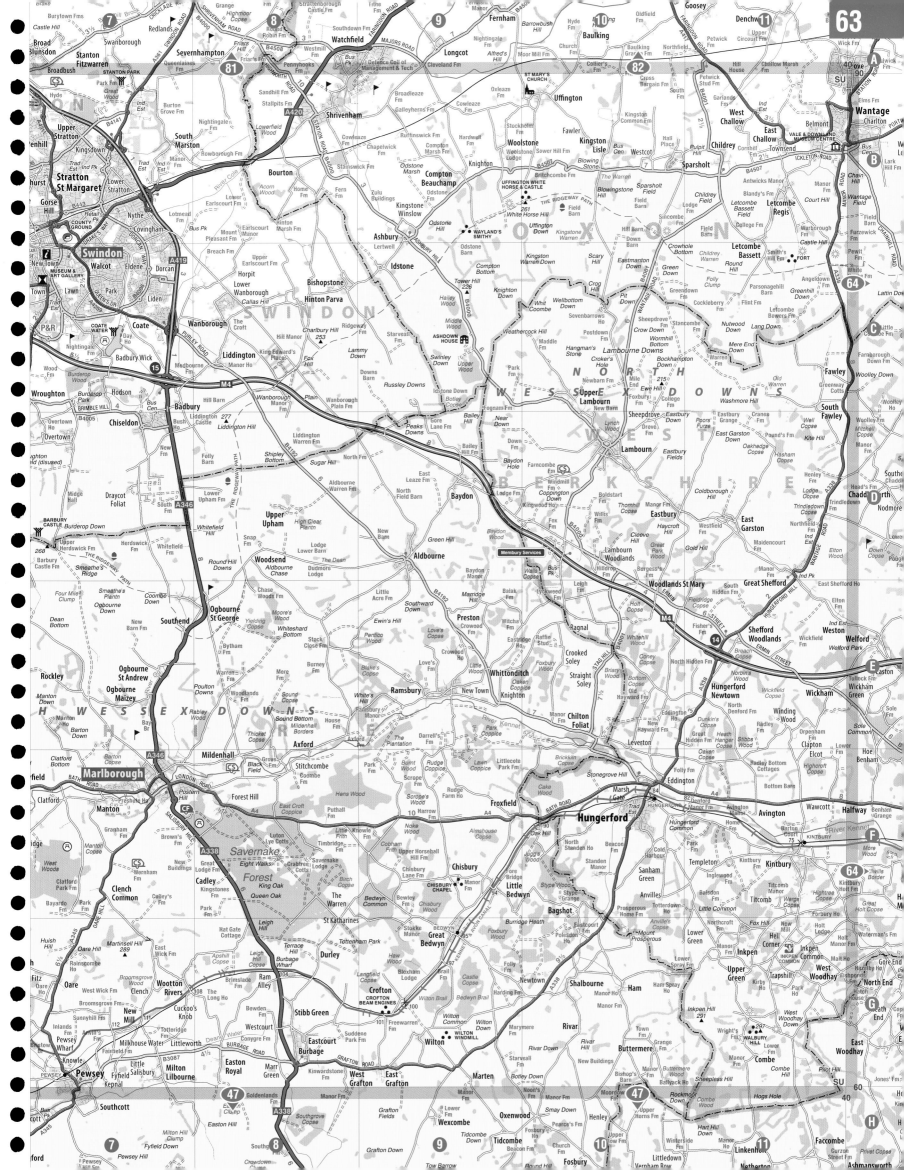

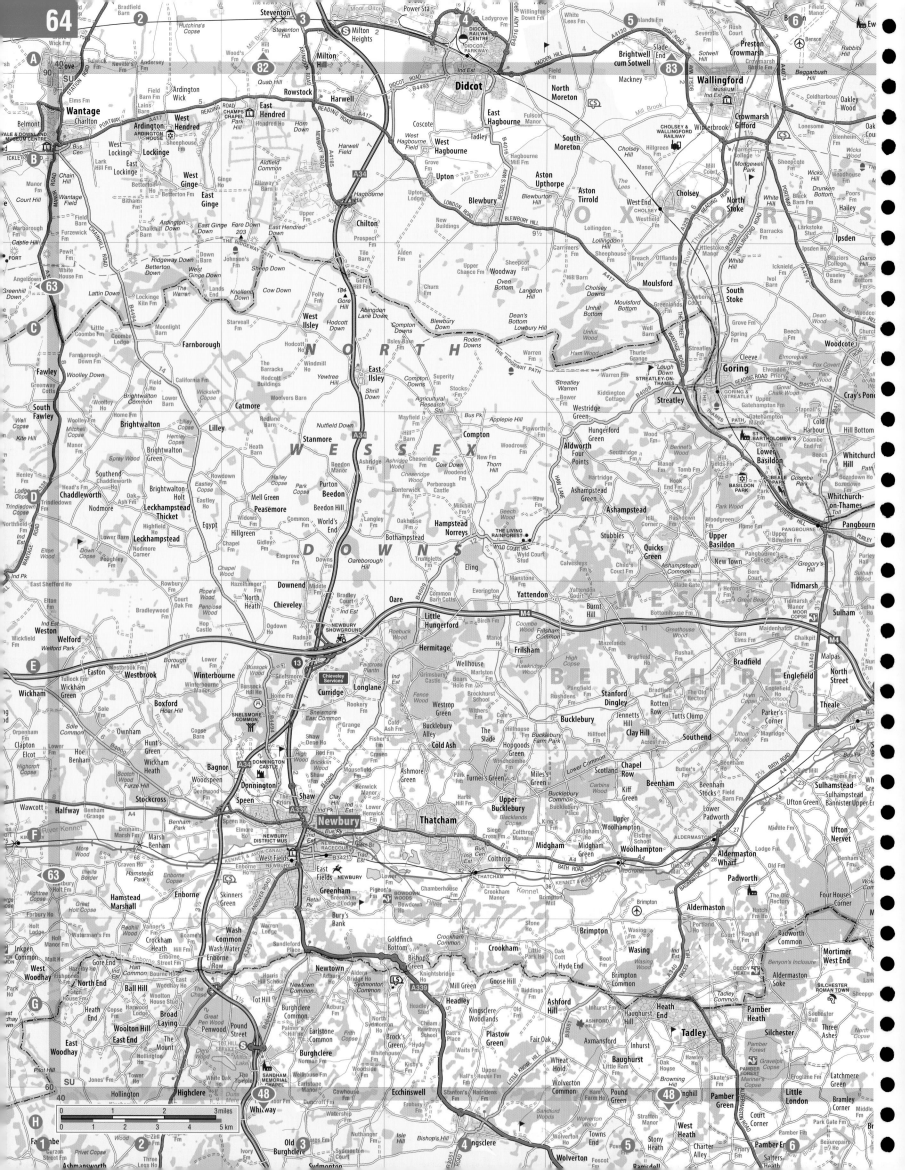

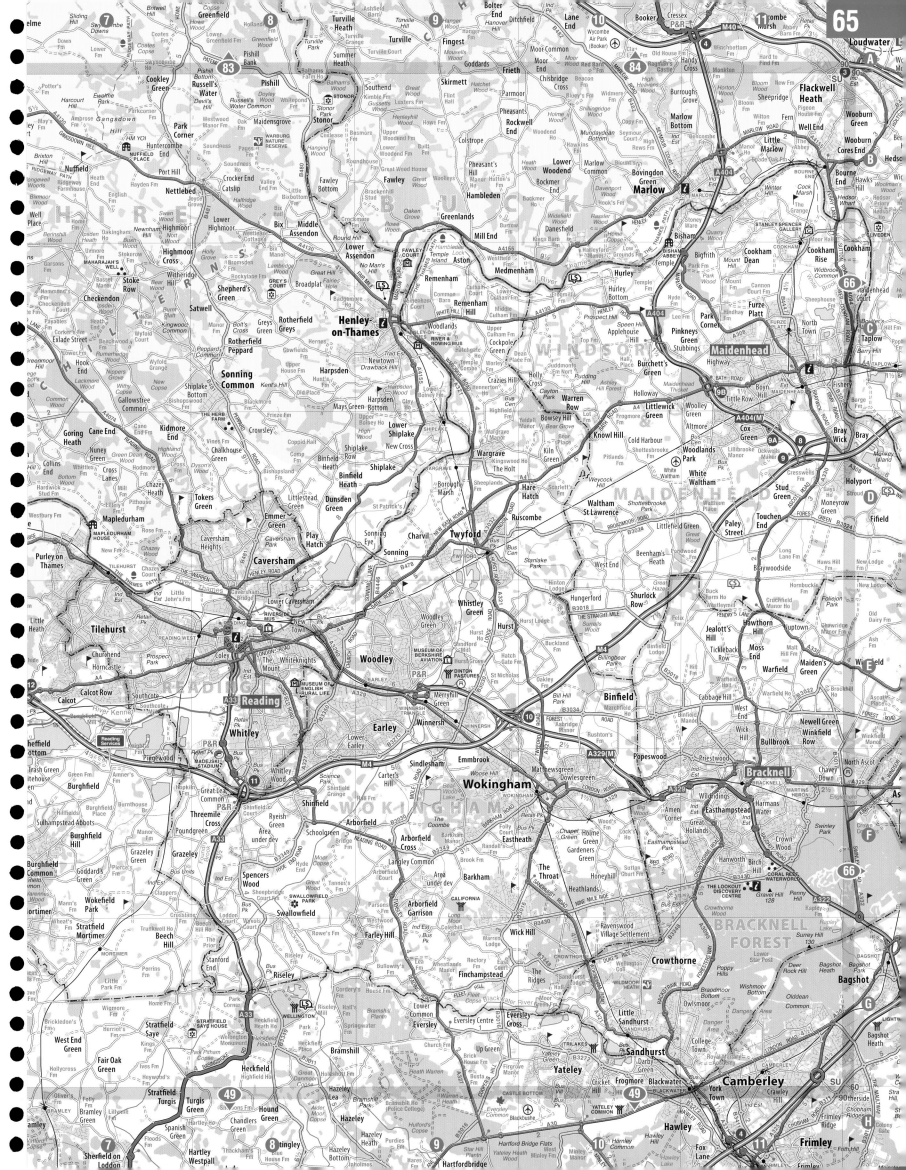

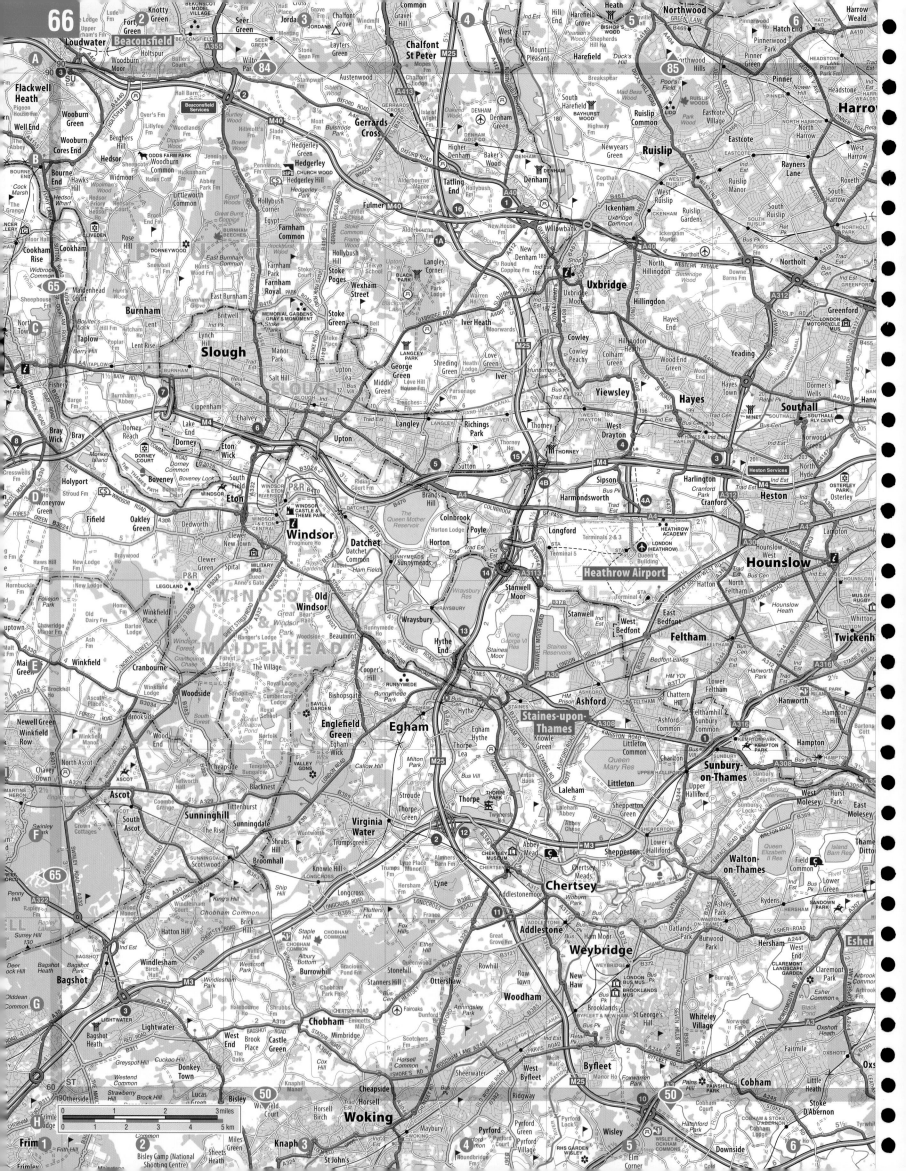

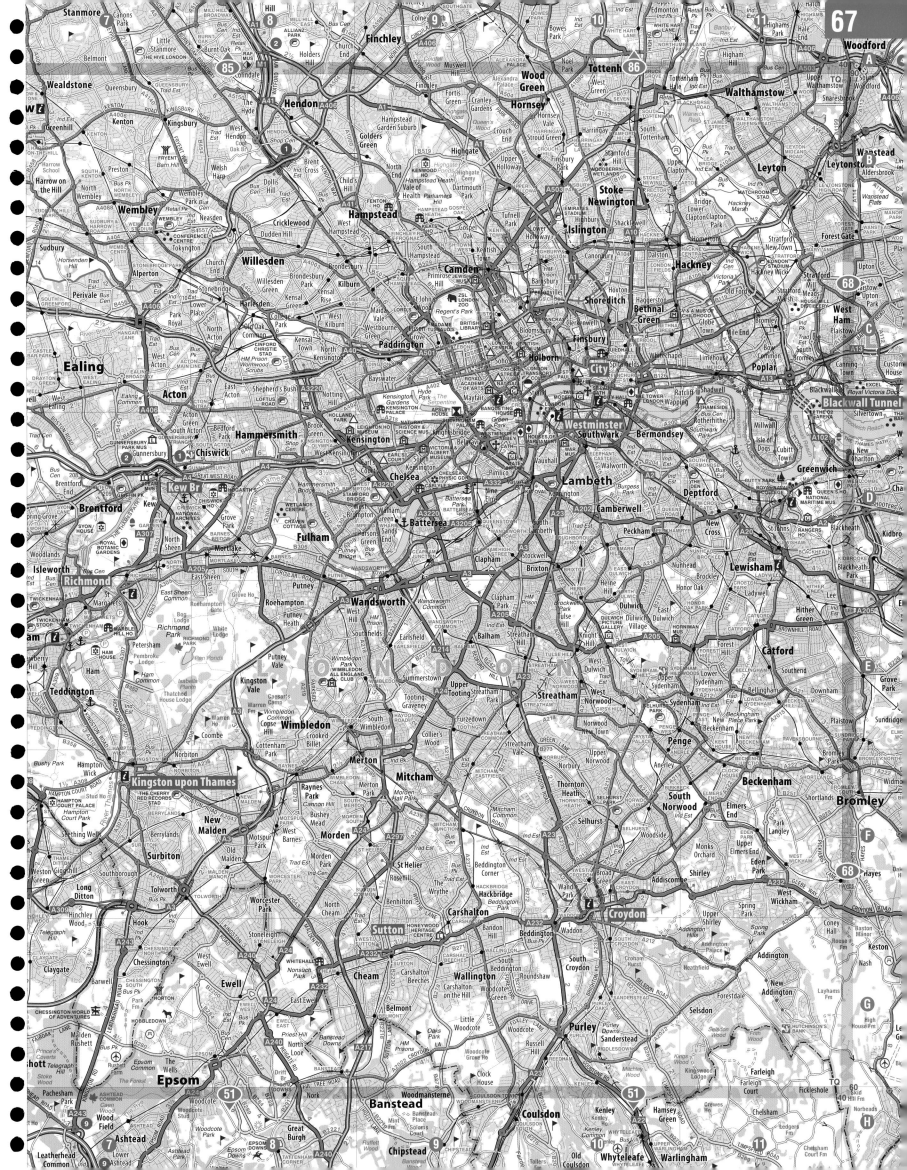

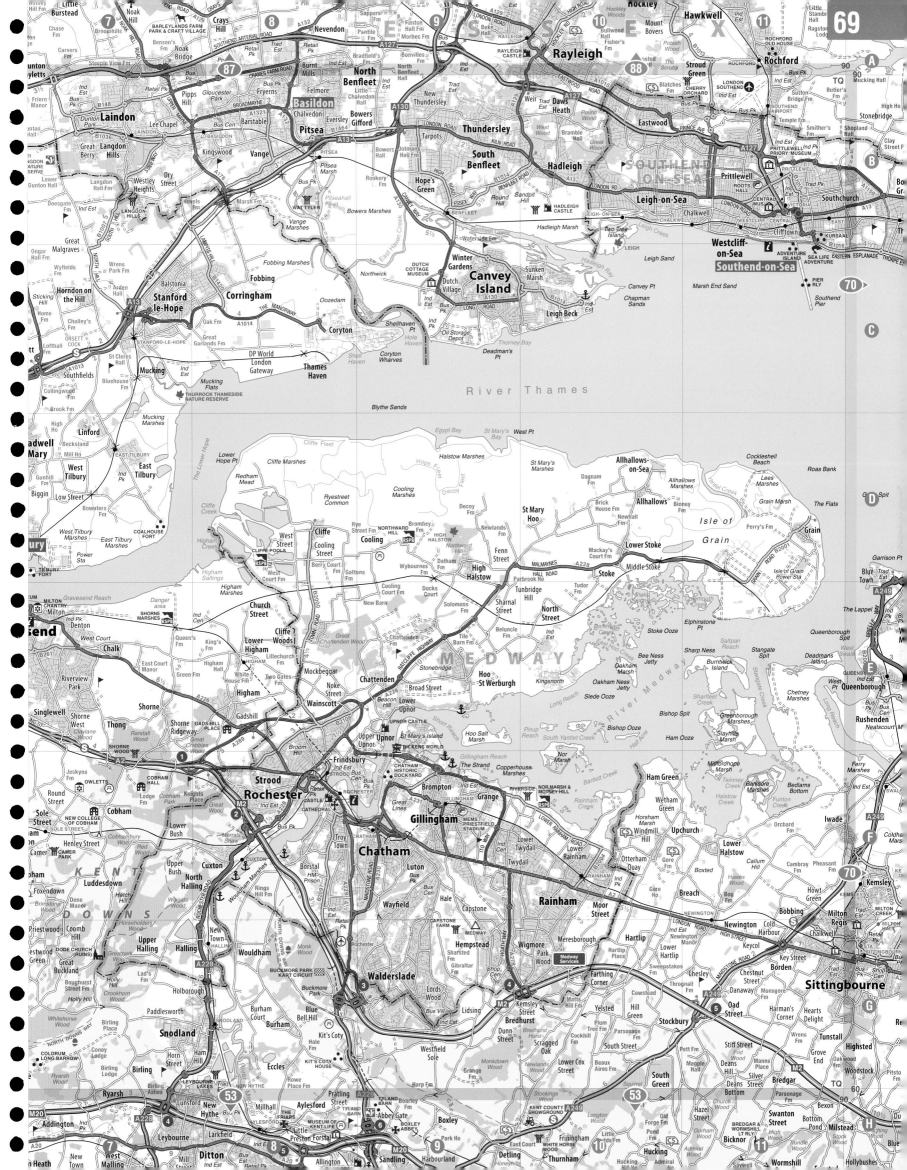

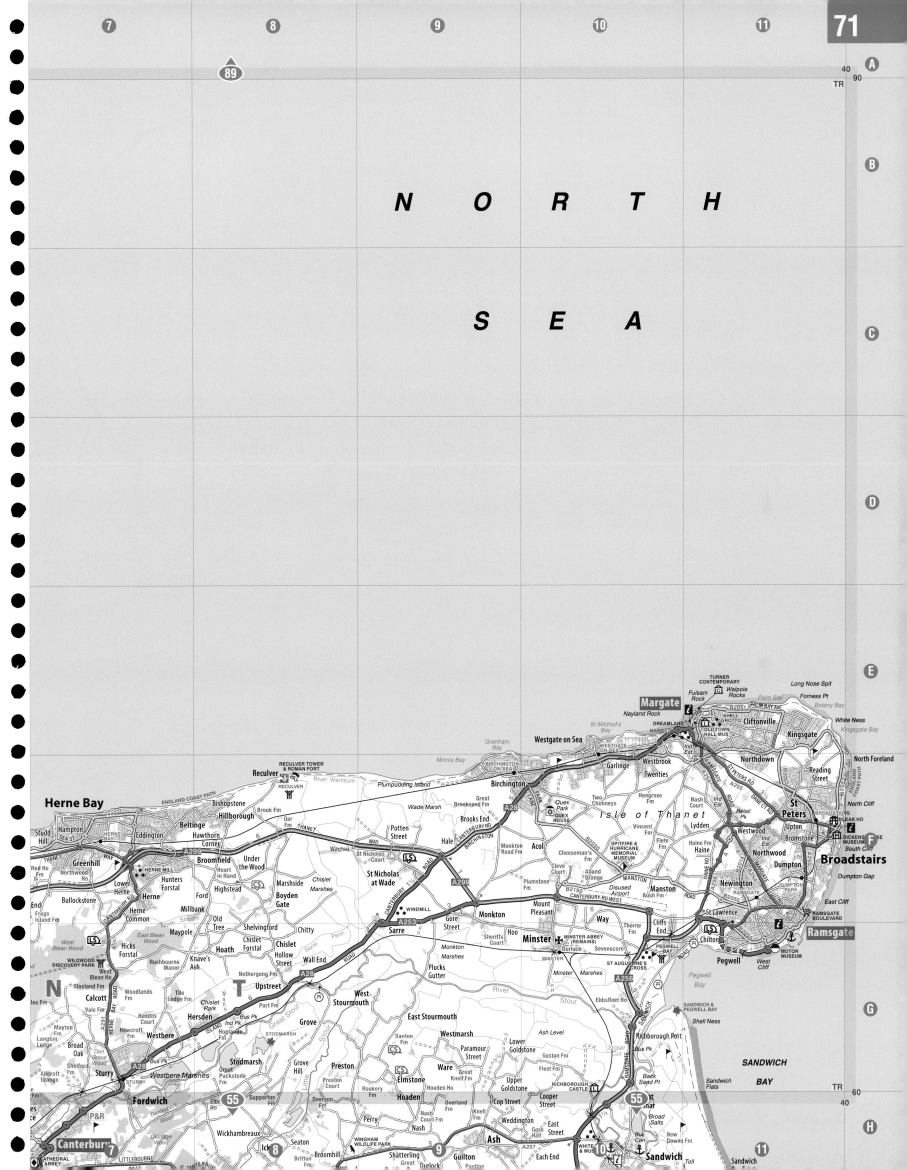

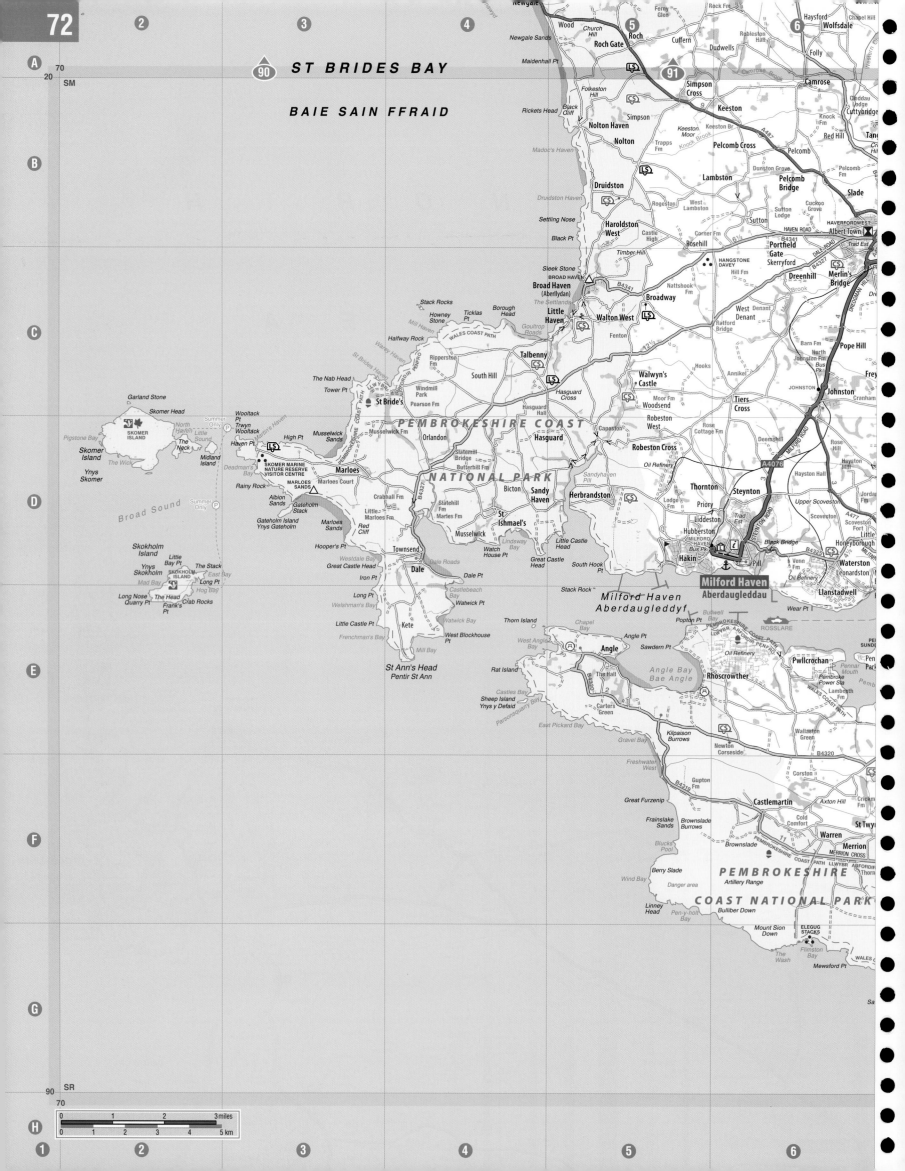

ST BRIDES BAY

BAIE SAIN FFRAID

Newgale

Wood
Church
Hill
5 Roch
Roch Gate
Cuffern
Dudwells
Ferny
Glen
Rock Fm
Haysford
Wolfsdale
Chapel Hill
Robleston
Hall
Folly
Newgale Sands
Maidenhall Pt
91
Simpson
Cross
Camrose
Camrose Brook
6 Wolfsdale
Western Cleddau
Cheddau
Lodge
Cuttybridge
Folkeston
Hill
Black
Cliff
Rickets Head
Nolton Haven
Keeston
Moor
Keeston Br
Simpson
Keeston
9
A487
Knock
Fm
Red Hill
Knock
Hill
Tang
Cri
Nolton
Trapps
Fm
Pelcomb Cross
Pelcomb
Madoc's Haven
Druidston
West
Lambston
Dunston Grove
Pelcomb
Bridge
Cuckoo
Grove
Slade
Druidston Haven
Rogeston
Sutton
Sutton
Lodge
HAVERFORDWEST
Settling Nose
Haroldston
West
Castle
High
Corner Fm
HAVEN ROAD
Albert Town
B4341
Trad Est
Black Pt
Rosehill
Trad Est
6½
Portfield
Gate
B4341
DALE ROAD
Timber Hill
HANGSTONE
DAVEY
Skerryford
B4327
Sleek Stone
BROAD HAVEN
Hill Fm
Dreenhill
Merlin's
Bridge
Dre
Broad Haven
(Aberllydan)
B4341
Nattshook
Fm
The Settlands
Broadway
Brook
Little
Haven
Walton West
Fenton
West Denant
Ratford
Bridge
Denant
Barn Fm
North
Johnston Fm
Pope Hill
Frey
Halfway Rock
Stack Rocks
Howney
Stone
Ticklas
Pt
Borough
Head
WALES COAST PATH
Goultrop
Roads
Bus
Pk
Hooks
Annikel
WALES COAST PATH
Ripperston
Fm
Talbenny
Walwyn's
Castle
JOHNSTON
Johnston
Cranham
The Nab Head
Tower Pt
South Hill
Hasguard
Cross
Moor Fm
Woodsend
Tiers
Cross
Deemshill
Rose
Hill
St Brides Haven
Windmill
Park
Pearson Fm
Hasguard
Hall
Robeston
West
Rose
Cottage Fm
Warey Haven
St Bride's
PEMBROKESHIRE COAST
Capeston
Robeston Cross
A4076
Hayston
Mill
Wooltack
Pt
Trwyn
Wooltack
High Pt
Musselwick
Sands
Musselwick Fm
Orlandon
Hasguard
Oil Refinery
Hayston Hall
Summer
Only
Merlin's Haven
Haven Pt
Statemill
Bridge
Sandyhaven
Pill
Thornton
Steynton
Upper Scoveston
Jorda
North
Haven
Little
Sound
Skomer Head
NATIONAL PARK
Bicton
Sandy
Haven
Priory
Liddeston
Scoveston
A477
Garland Stone
SKOMER
ISLAND
Midland
Island
SKOMER MARINE
NATURE RESERVE
VISITOR CENTRE
Statehill
Fm
Bittle
Marloes Fm
St
Marles Fm
Herbrandston
Lodge
Fm
Trad
Est
Scoveston
Fort
Little
Pigstone Bay
The Neck
Marloes
Crabhall Fm
St
Ishmael's
Hubberston
Black Bridge
Honeyborough
Skomer
Island
The Wick
Deadman's
Bay
MARLOES
SANDS
Marloes Court
Musselwick
Watch
House Pt
MILFORD
HAVEN
Bus Pk
Venn
Fm
B432
Waterston
Ynys
Skomer
Rainy Rock
Albion
Sands
Gateholm
Stack
Lindsway
Bay
Great Castle
Head
Hakin
Pill
Oil Refinery
Leonardston
Broad Sound
Summer
Only
Marloes
Sands
Gateholm Island
Ynys Gateholm
Red
Cliff
Little Castle
Head
South Hook
Pt
Milford Haven
Aberdaugleddau
Llanstadwell
Skokholm
Island
Hooper's Pt
Townsend
Dale Roads
Dale Pt
Stack Rock
Milford Haven
Aberdaugleddyf
Wear Pt
Ynys
Skokholm
Little
Bay Pt
The Stack
Westdale Bay
Great Castle Head
Dale
Castlebeach
Bay
Buttwell
Bay
Popton Pt
ROSSLARE
SKOKHOLM
ISLAND
Long Pt
Iron Pt
Watwick Pt
Chapel Bay
PEMBR. A HBR COAST PATH
Mad Bay
East Bay
Hog Bay
Long Pt
Welshman's
Bay
Watwick Bay
Thorn Island
West Angle
Bay
Angle Pt
Oil Refinery
Pen
Park
Long Nose
Quarry Pt
The Head
Frank's
Pt
Crab Rocks
Little Castle Pt
Frenchman's Bay
West Blockhouse
Pt
The Hall
Angle
Sawdern Pt
Rhoscrowther
Pwllcrochan
Pennar
Mouth
Pe
St Ann's Head
Pentir St Ann
Rat Island
Mill Bay
Angle Bay
Bae Angle
Pembroke
Power Sta
Pembe
WALES COAST PATH
Castles Bay
Sheep Island
Ynys y Defaid
Carters
Green
Kilpaison
Burrows
Wallaston
Green
Lambeth
Fm
Parsonsquarry Bay
East Pickard Bay
Gravel Bay
Newton
Corseside
B4320
Freshwater
West
B4319
Gupton
Fm
Corston
B4320
Great Furzenip
Castlemartin
Axton Hill
Crickm
Fm
Frainslake
Sands
Brownslade
Burrows
Cold
Comfort
St Twy
PEMBROKESHIRE COAST PATH
Warren
Merrion
Blucks
Pool
Brownslade
11
LLWYBR
ARFORDIR
Thorn
PEMBROKESHIRE
Berry Slade
Wind Bay
Danger area
Artillery Range
COAST NATIONAL PARK
Linney
Head
Pen-y-holt
Bay
Bulliber Down
Mount Sion
Down
ELEGUG
STACKS
The
Wash
Flimston
Bay
Mewsford Pt
WALES C

SM
70
20

SR
90
70

0   1   2   3 miles
0   1   2   3   4   5 km

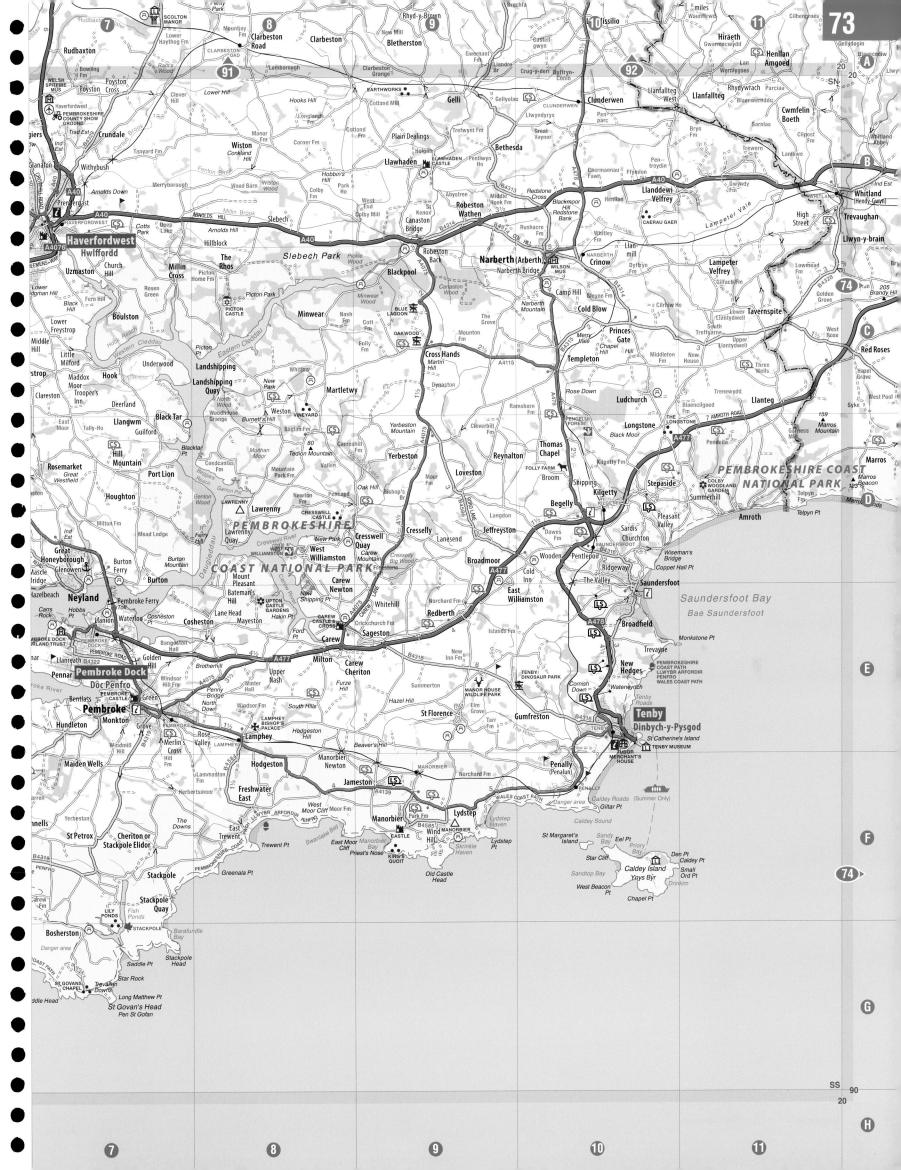

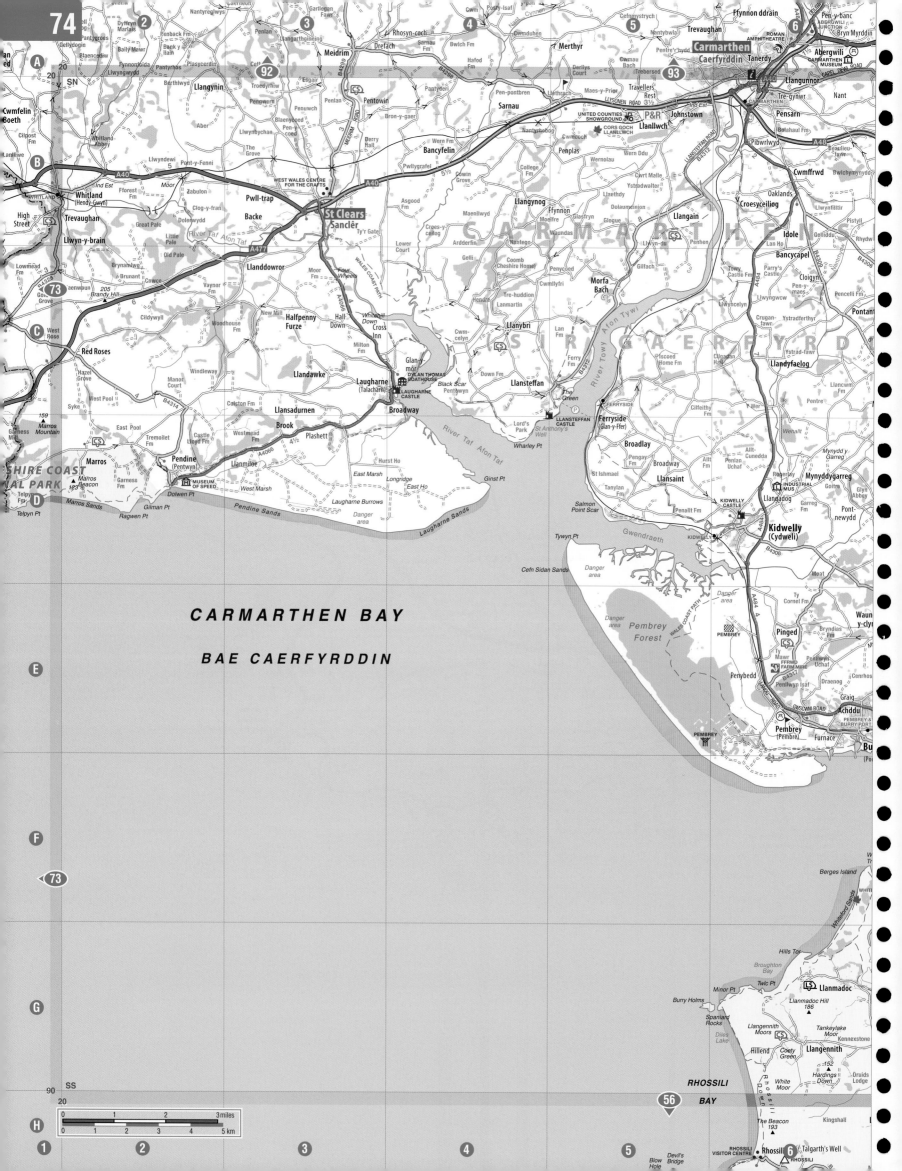

CARMARTHEN BAY

BAE CAERFYRDDIN

RHOSSILI
BAY

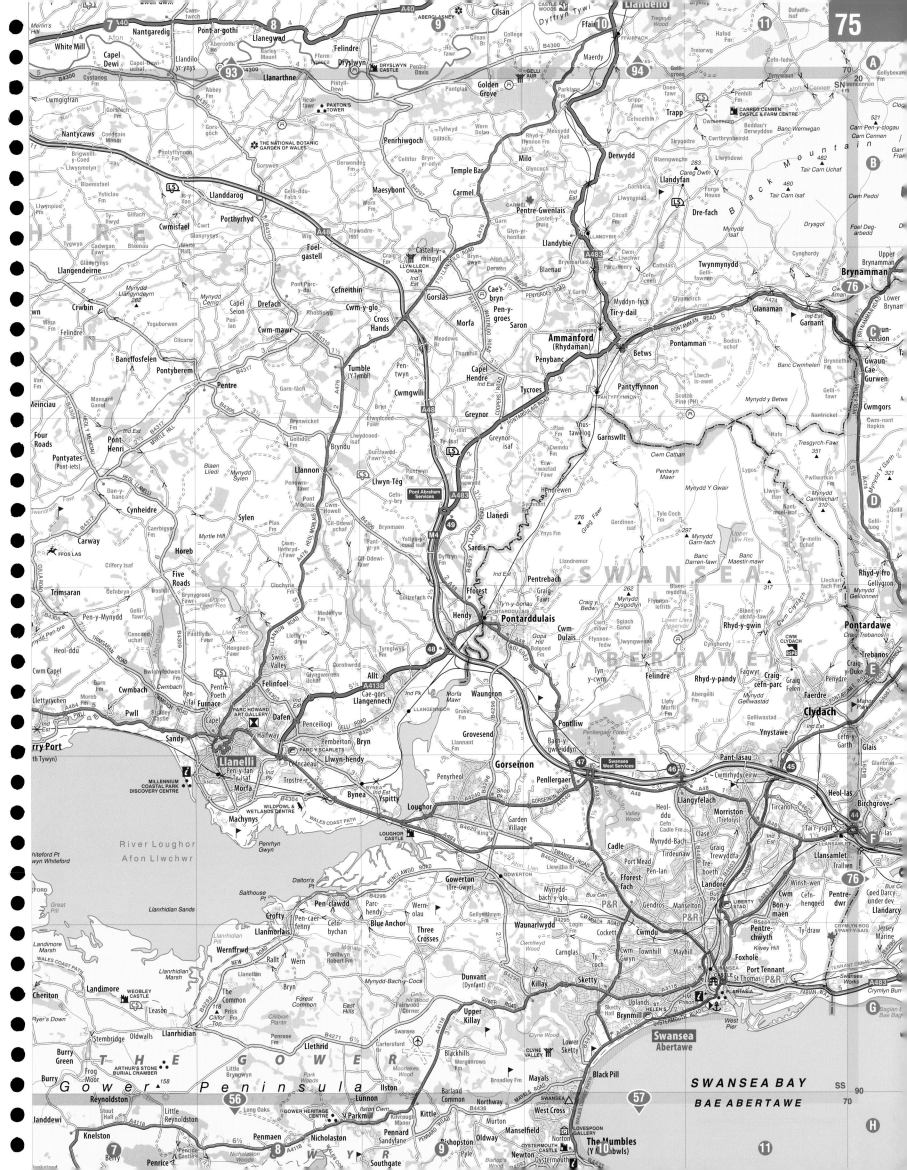

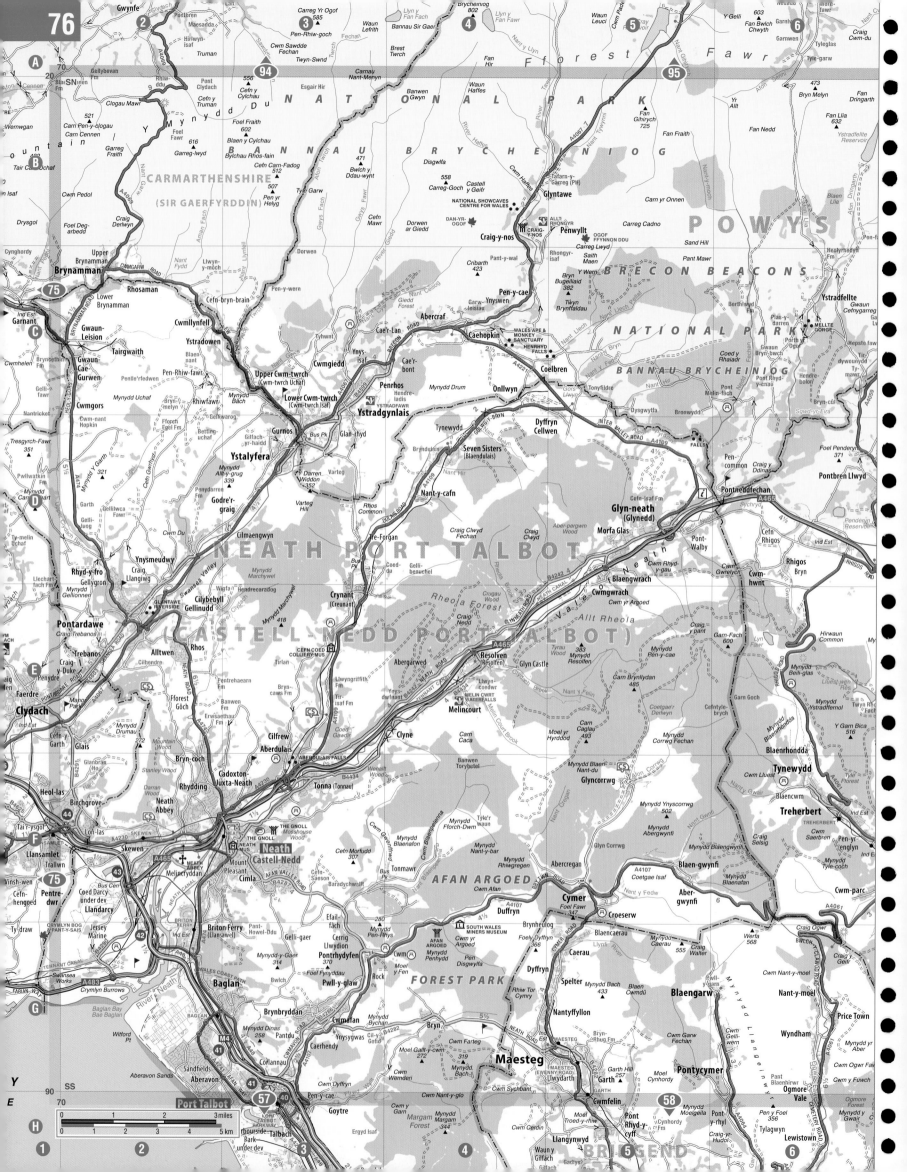

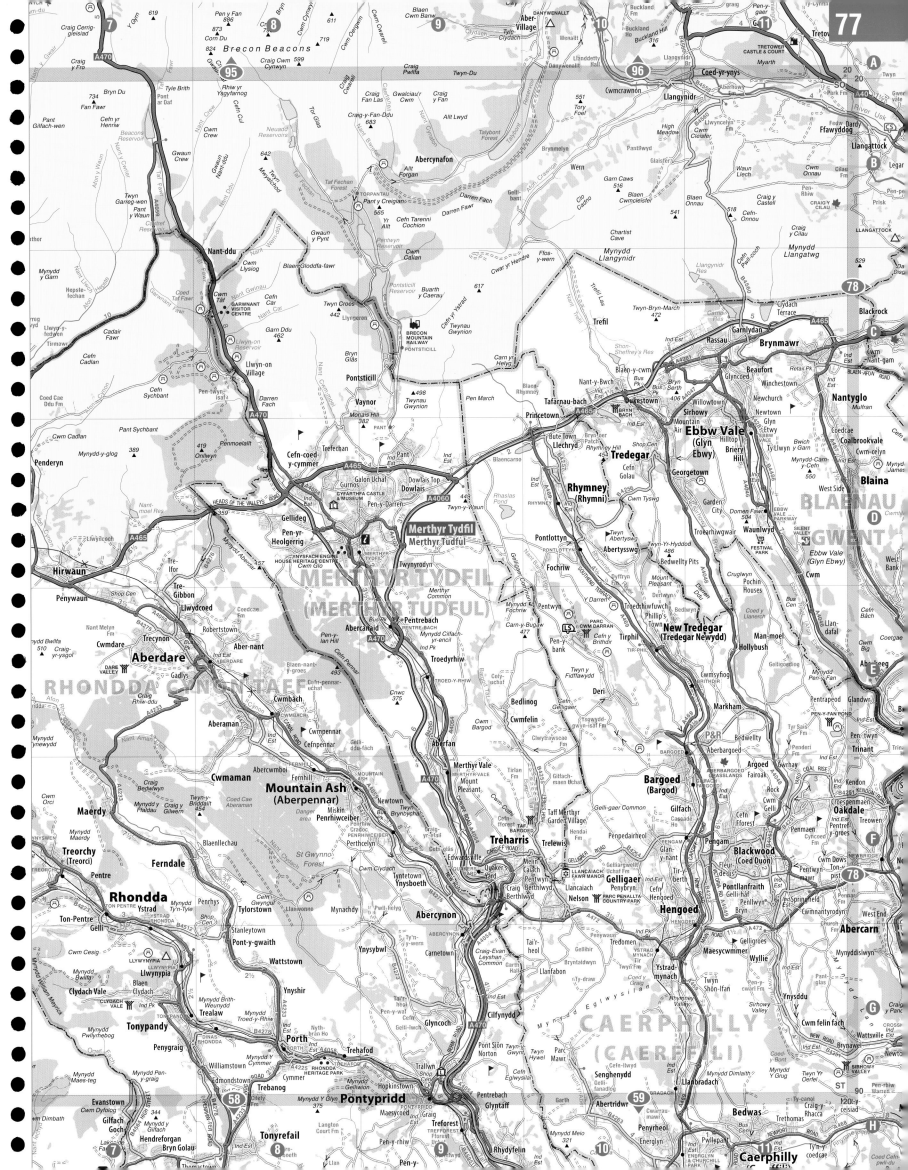

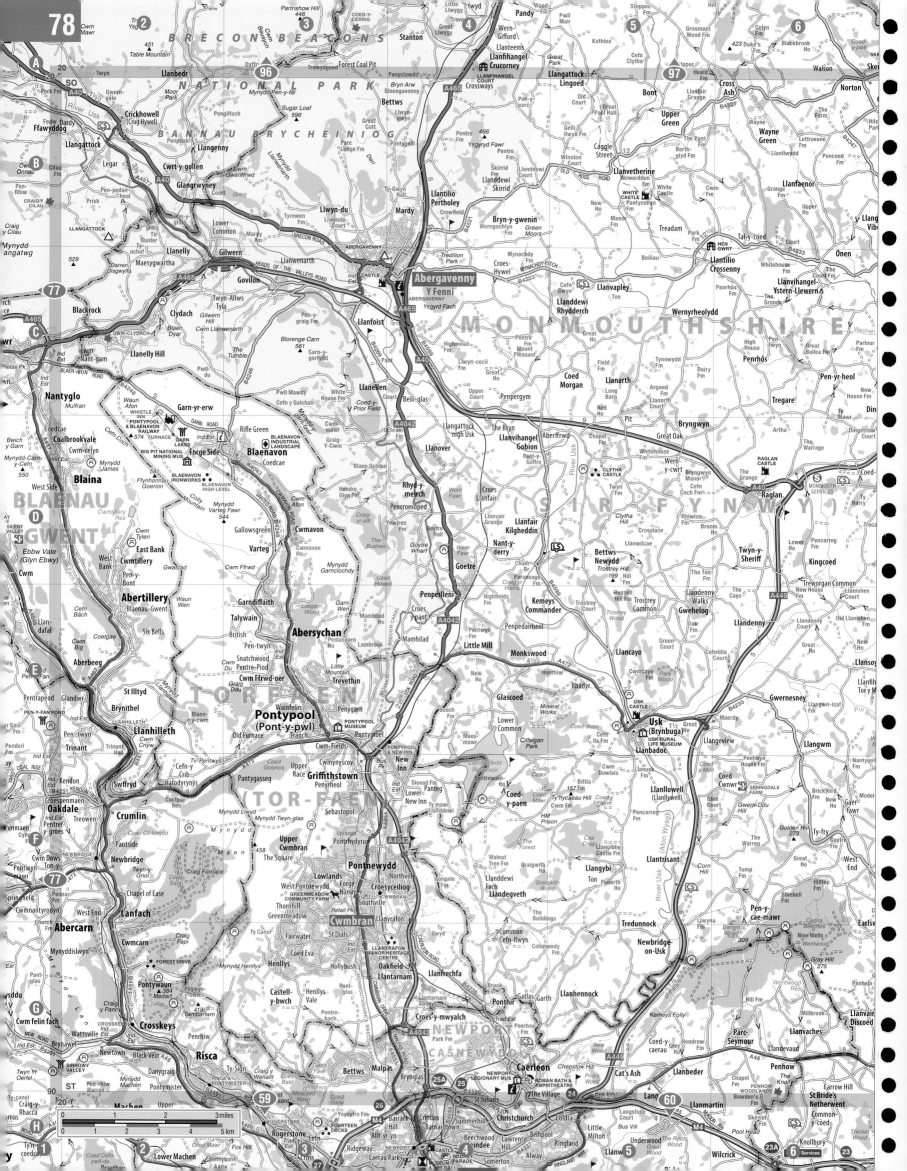

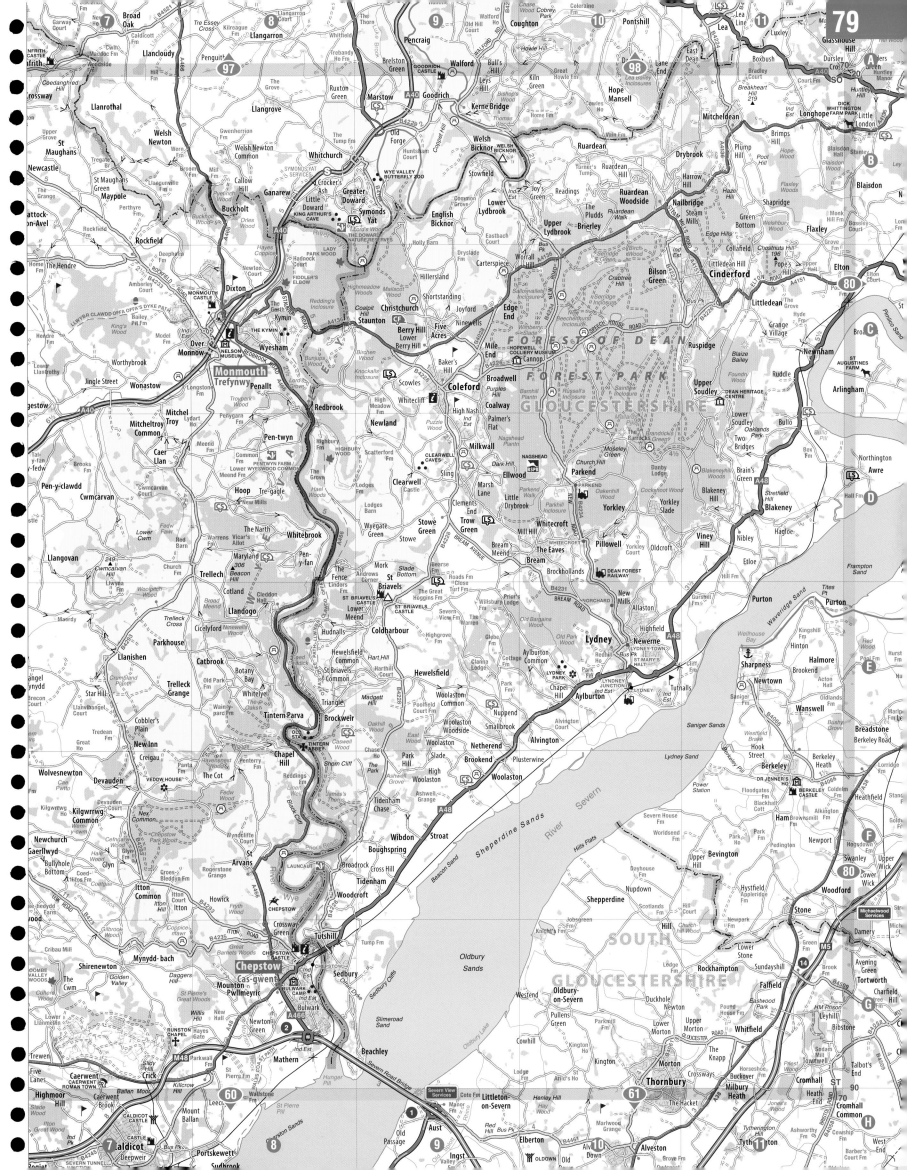

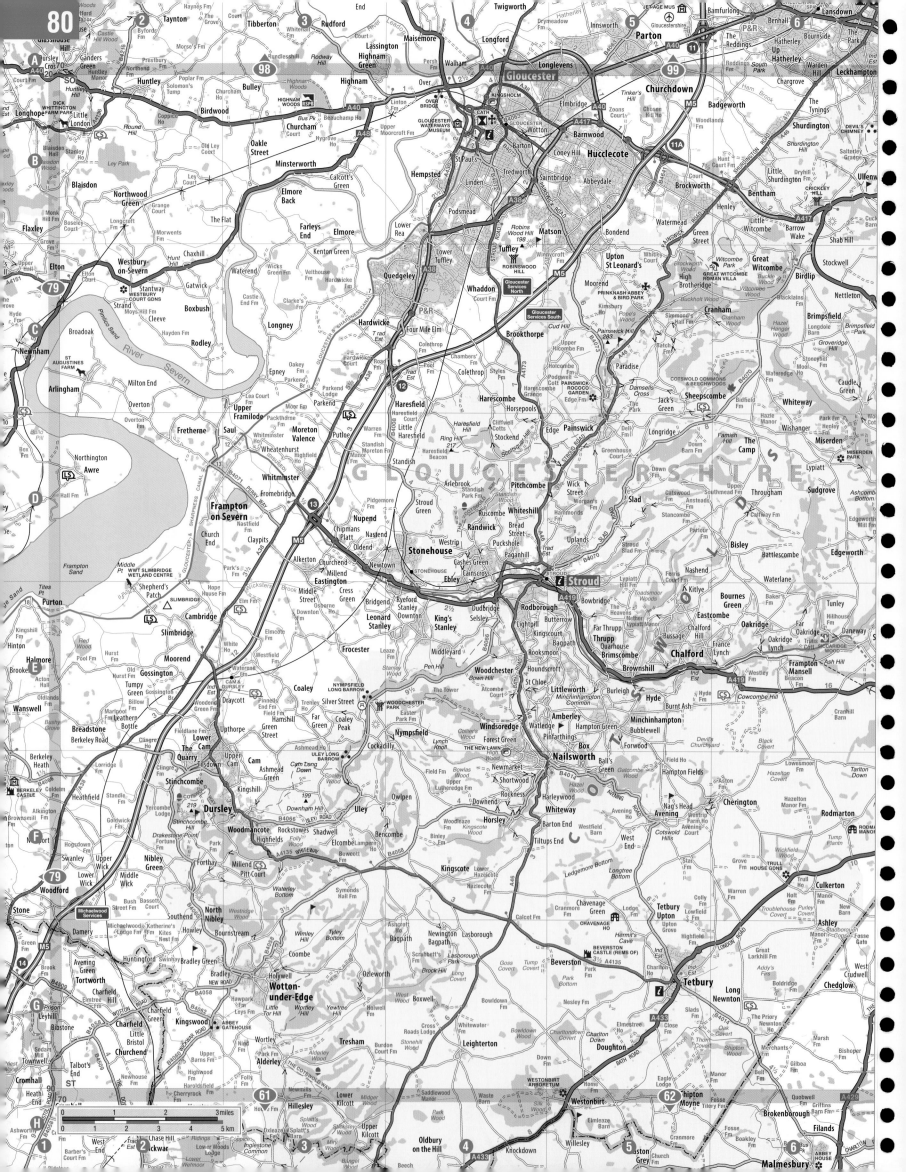

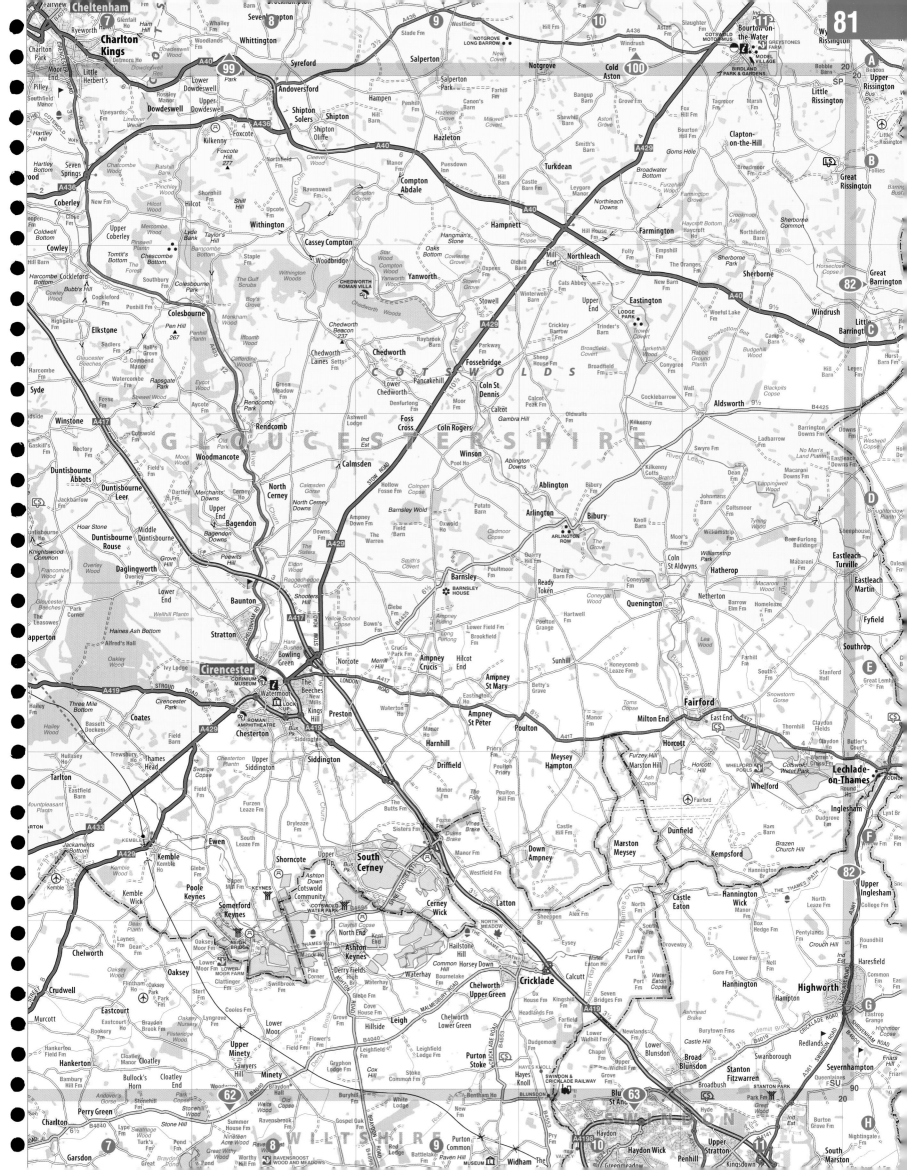

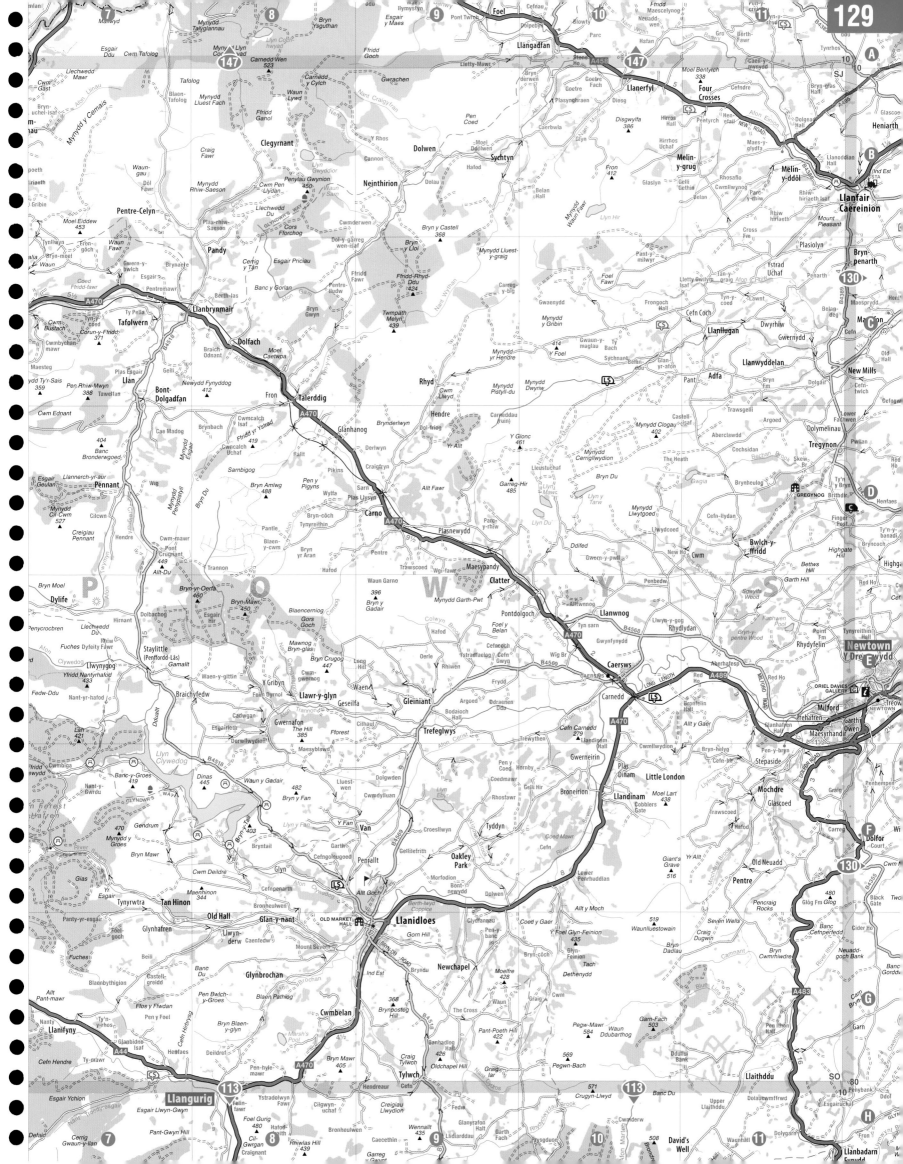

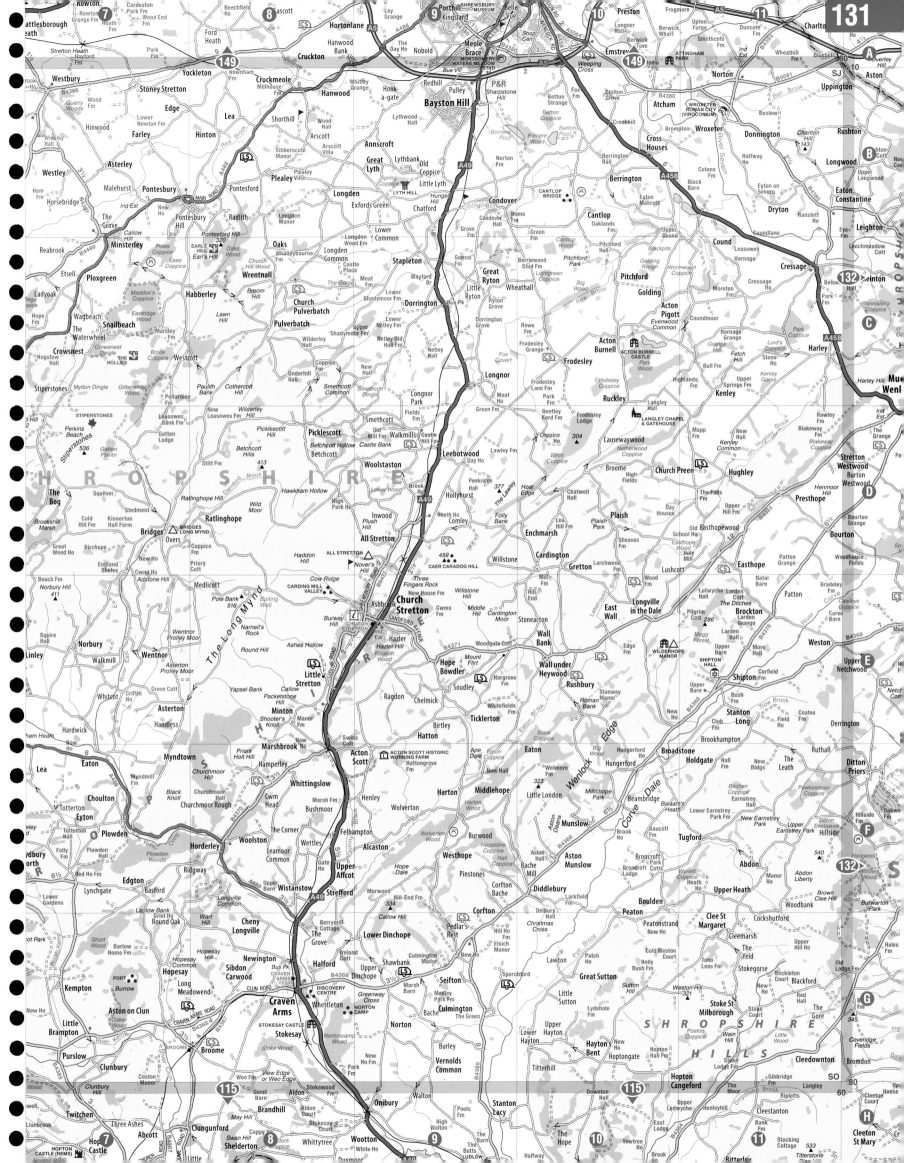

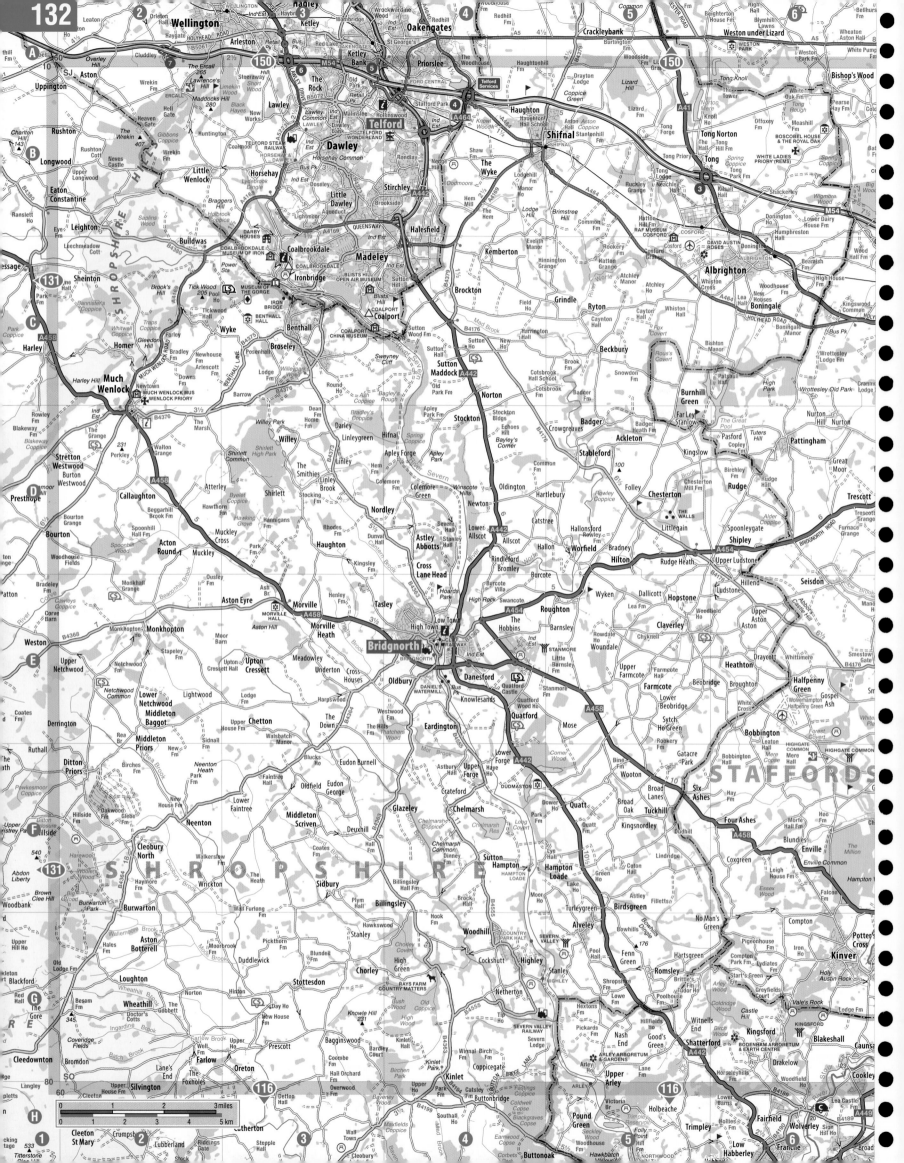

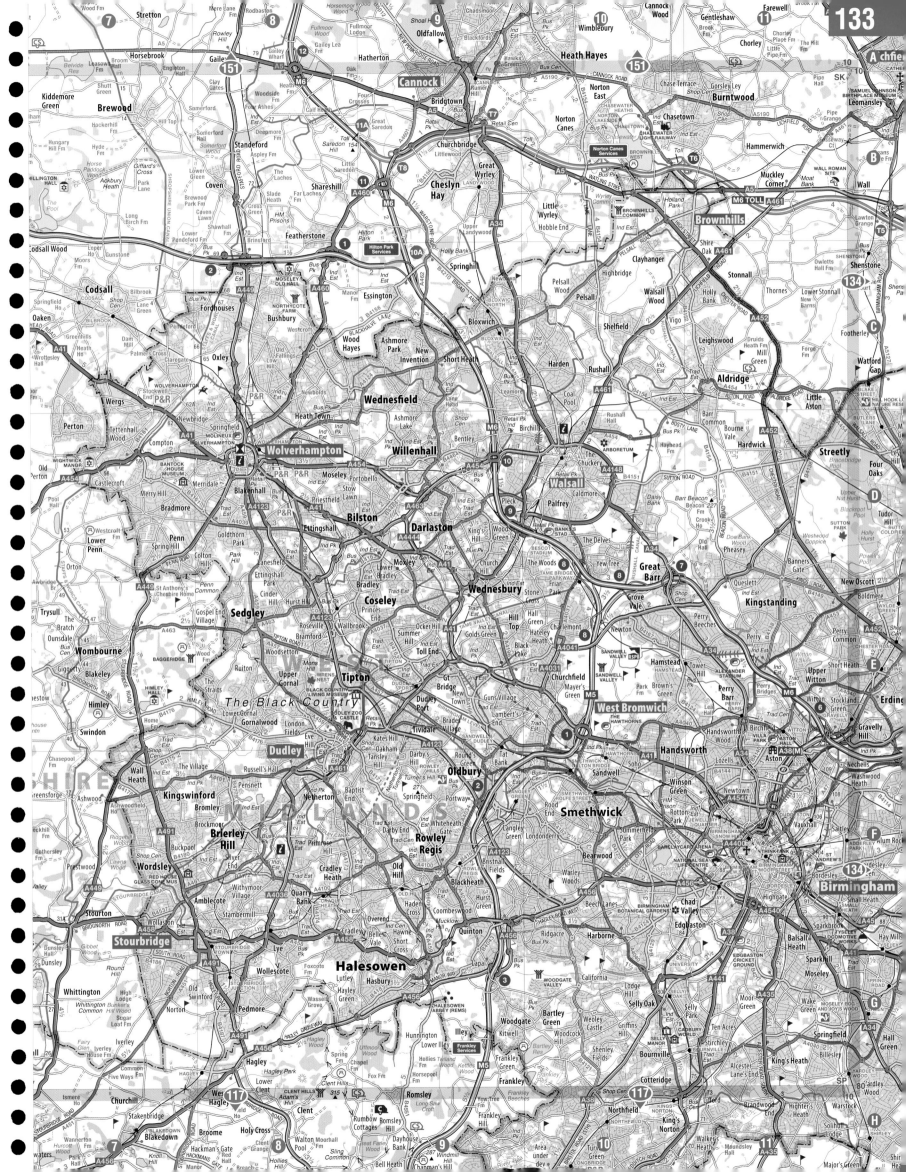

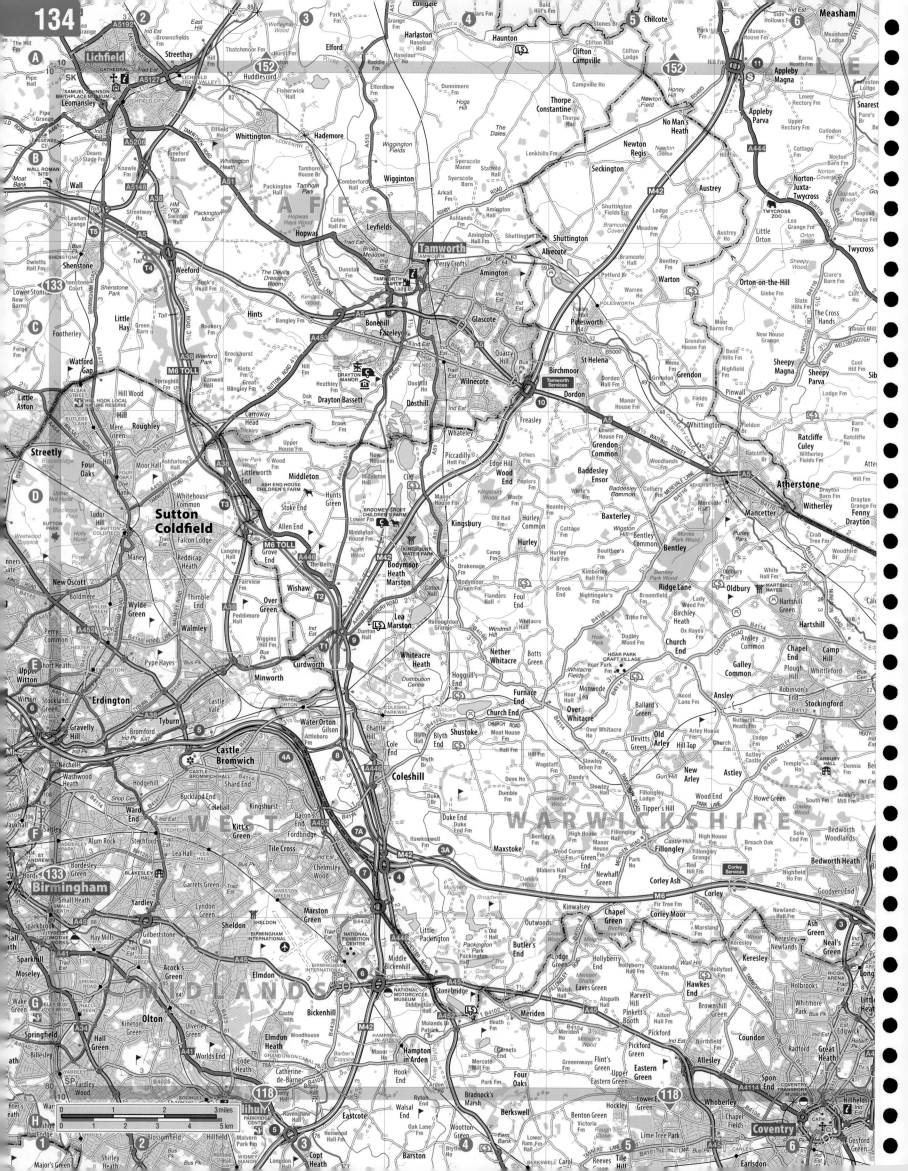

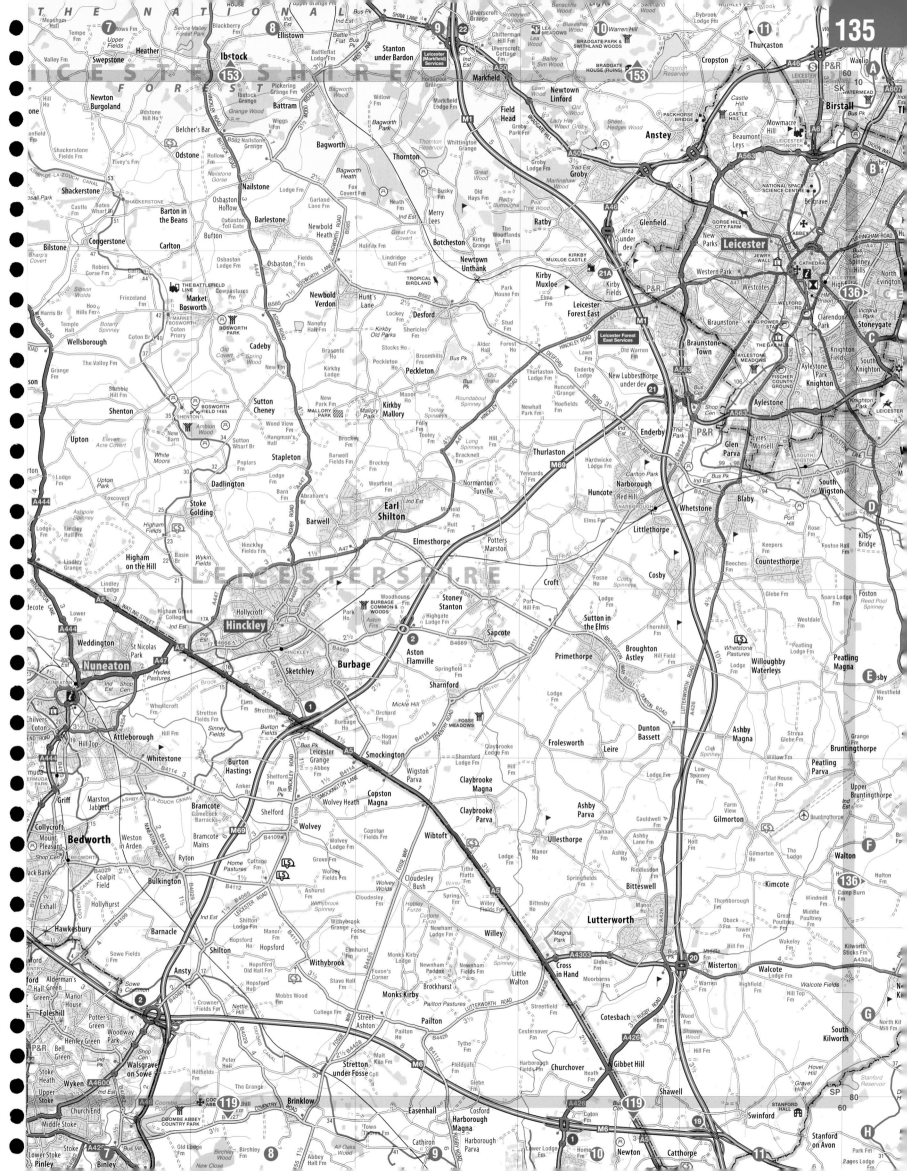

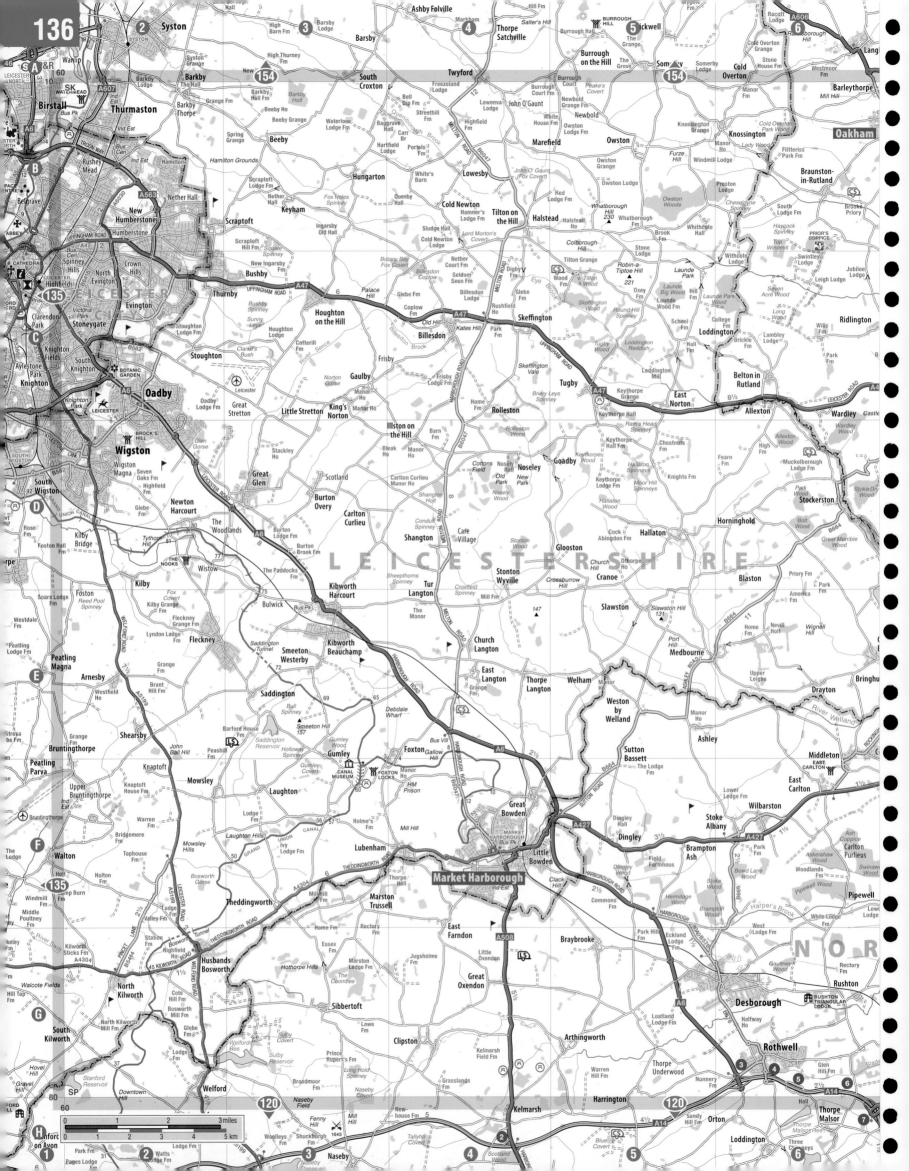

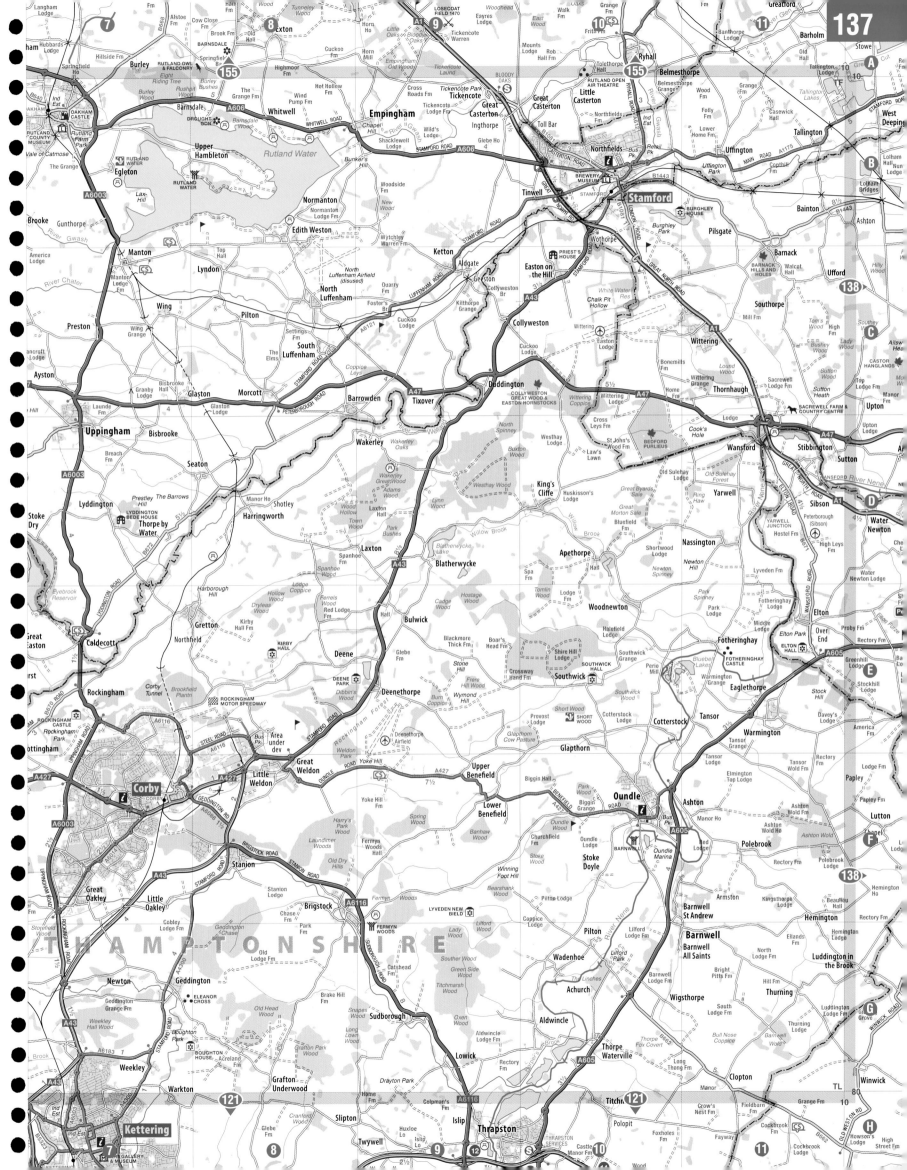

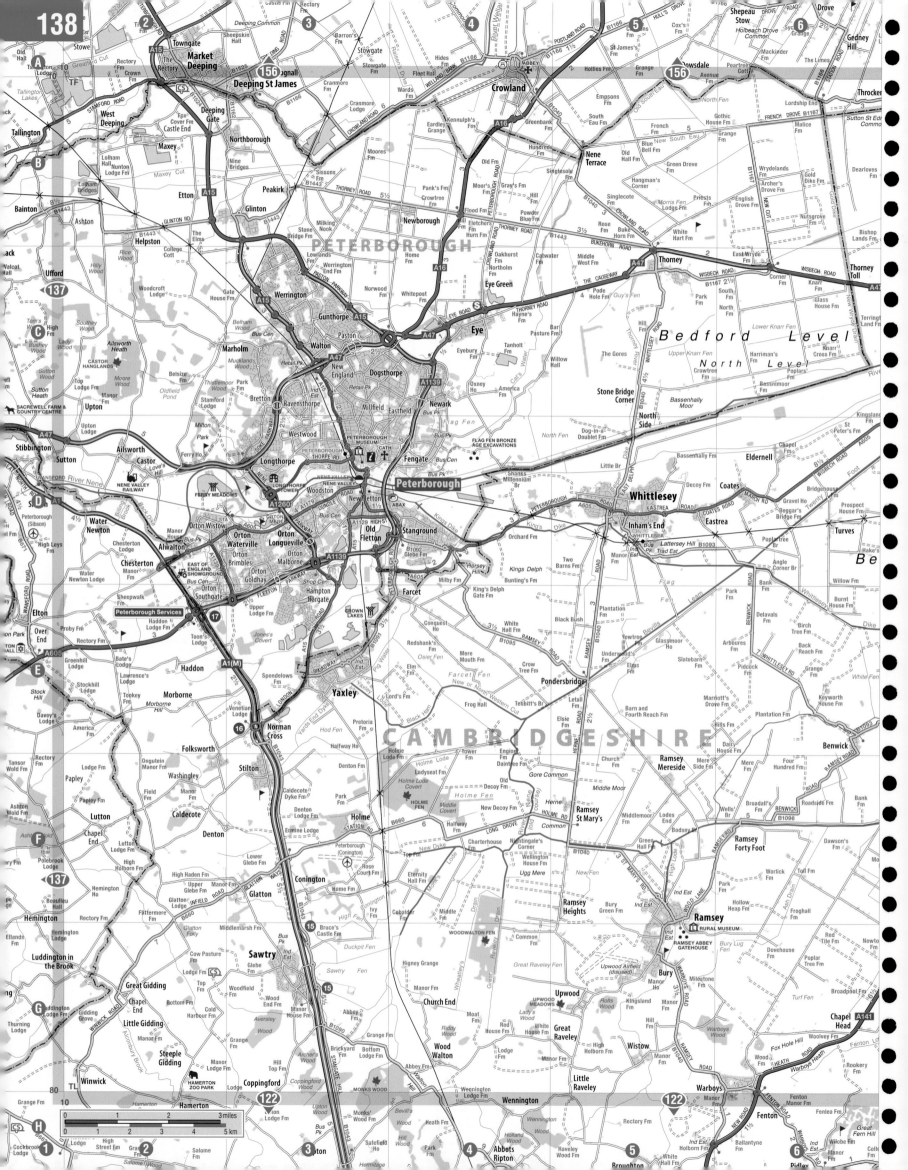

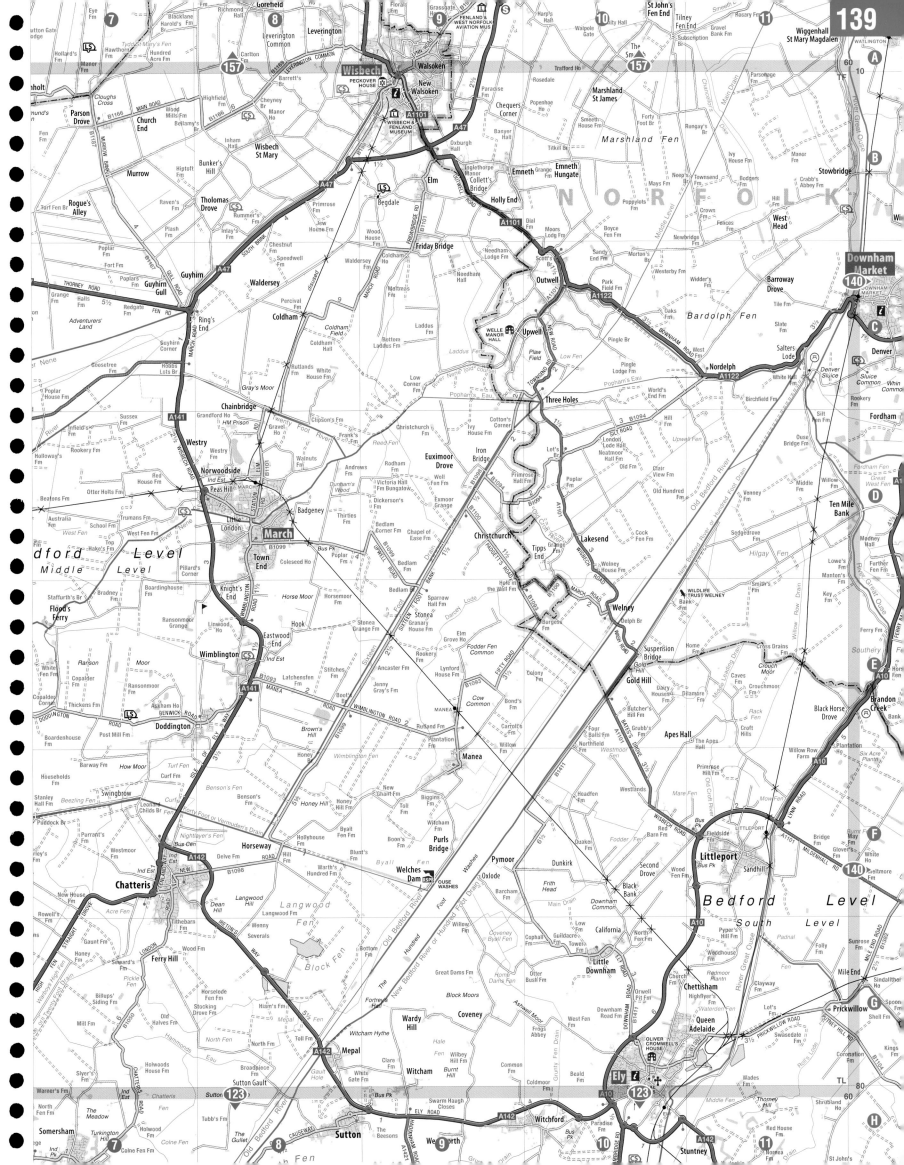

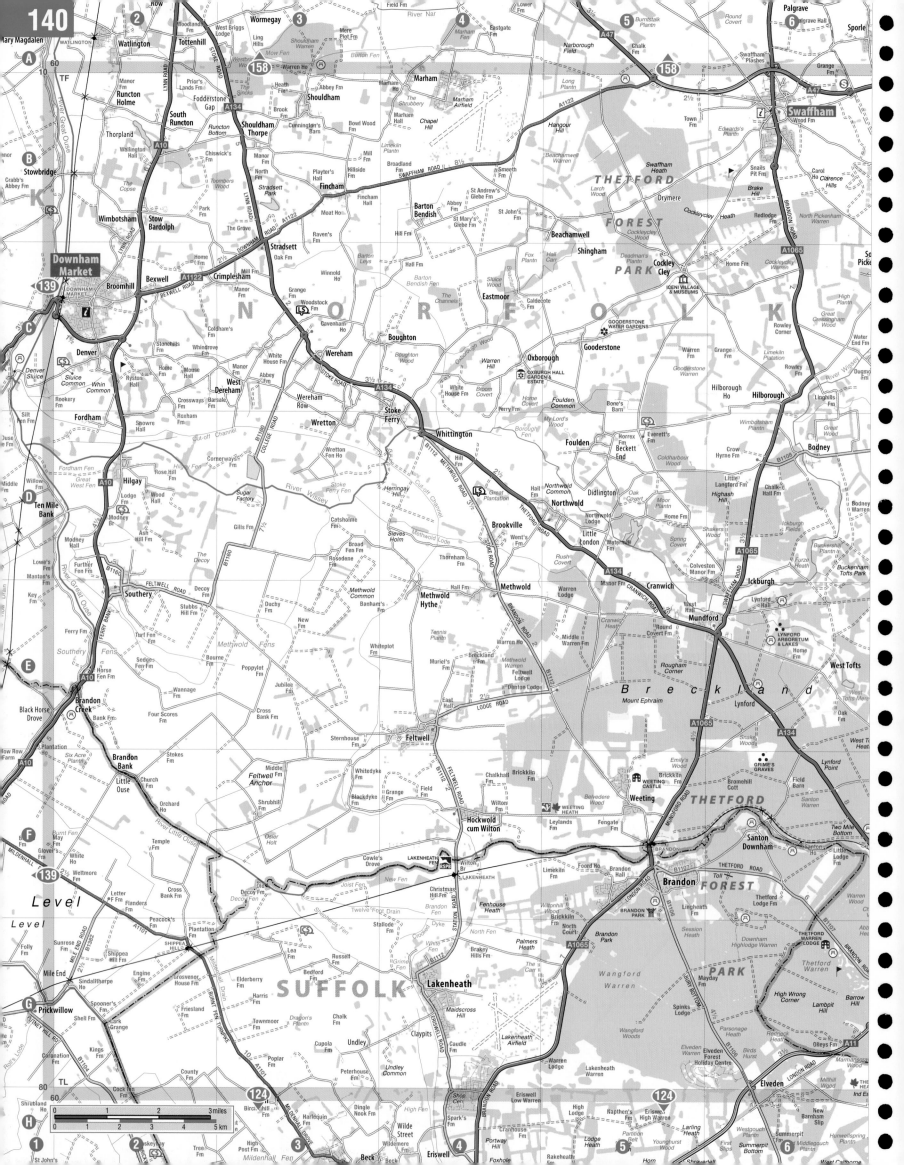

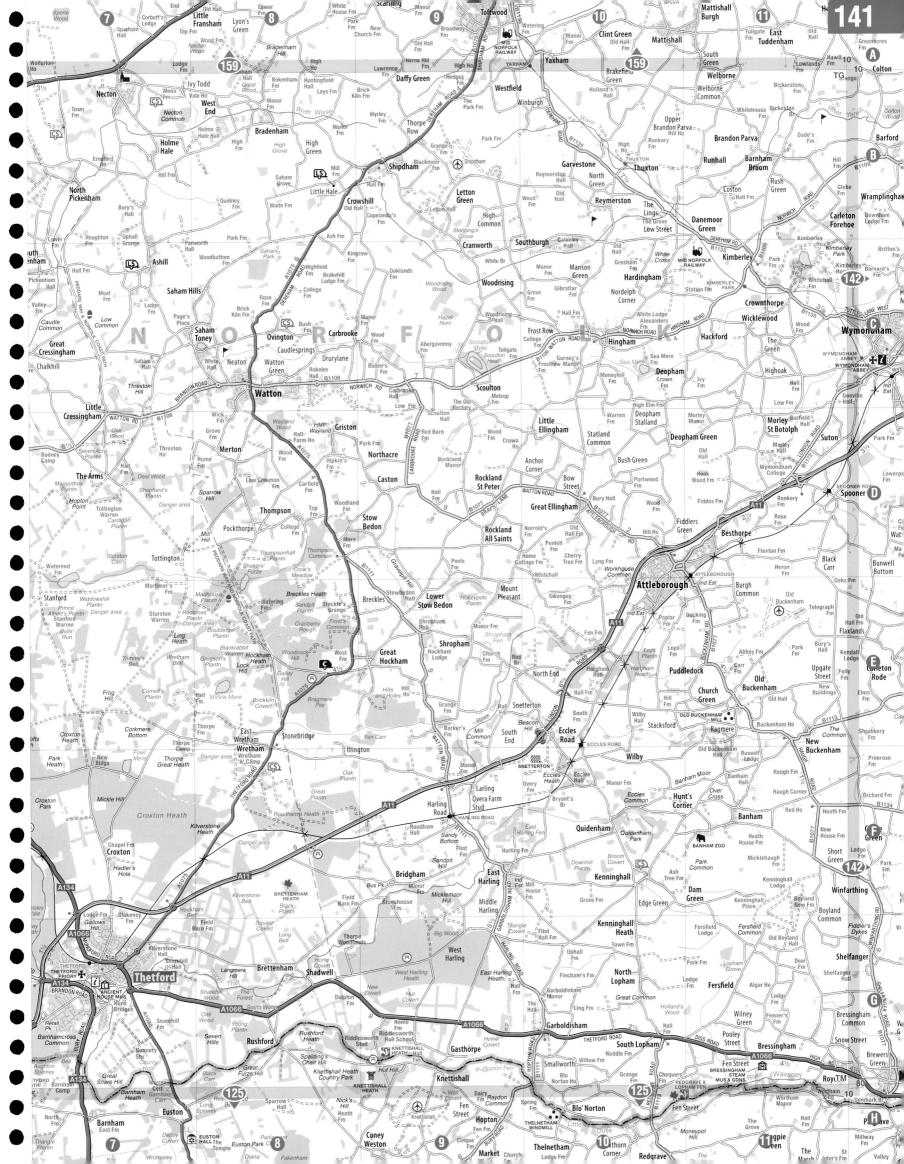

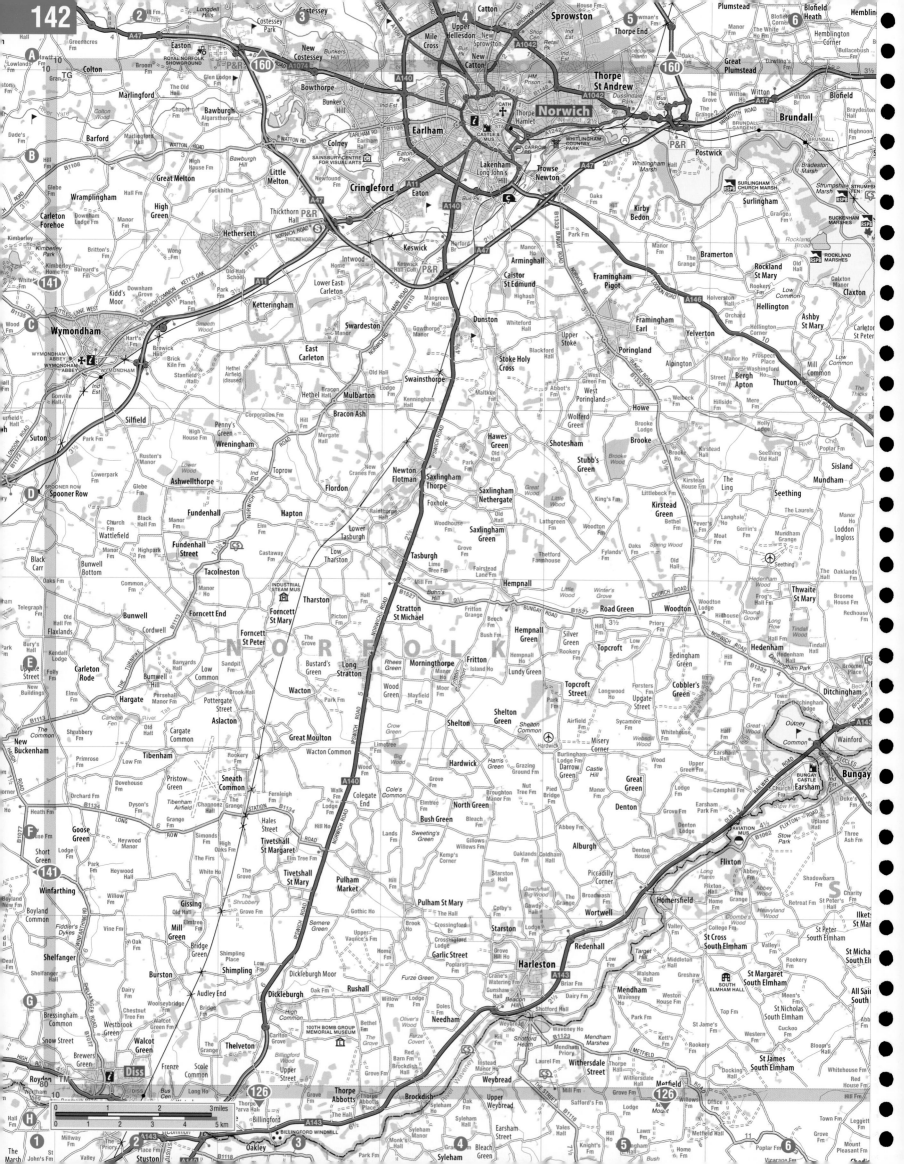

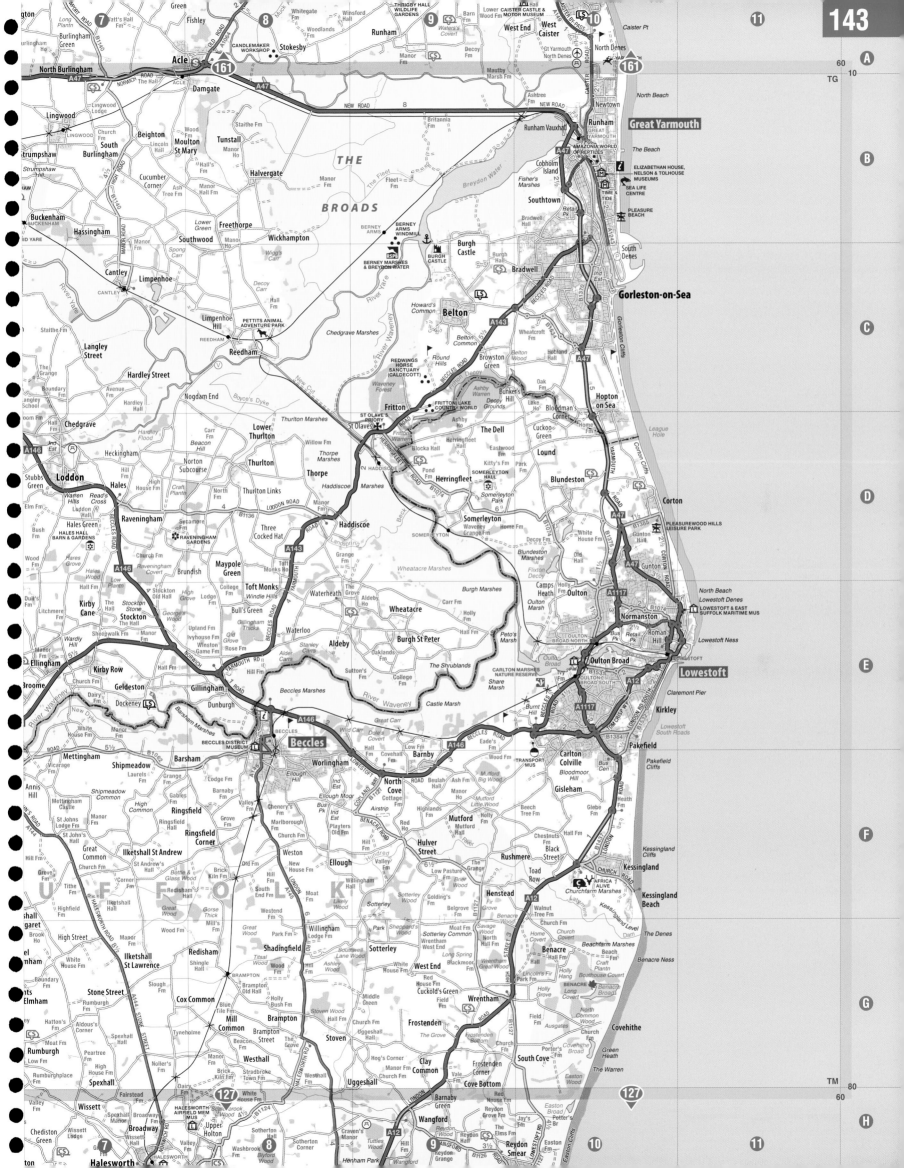

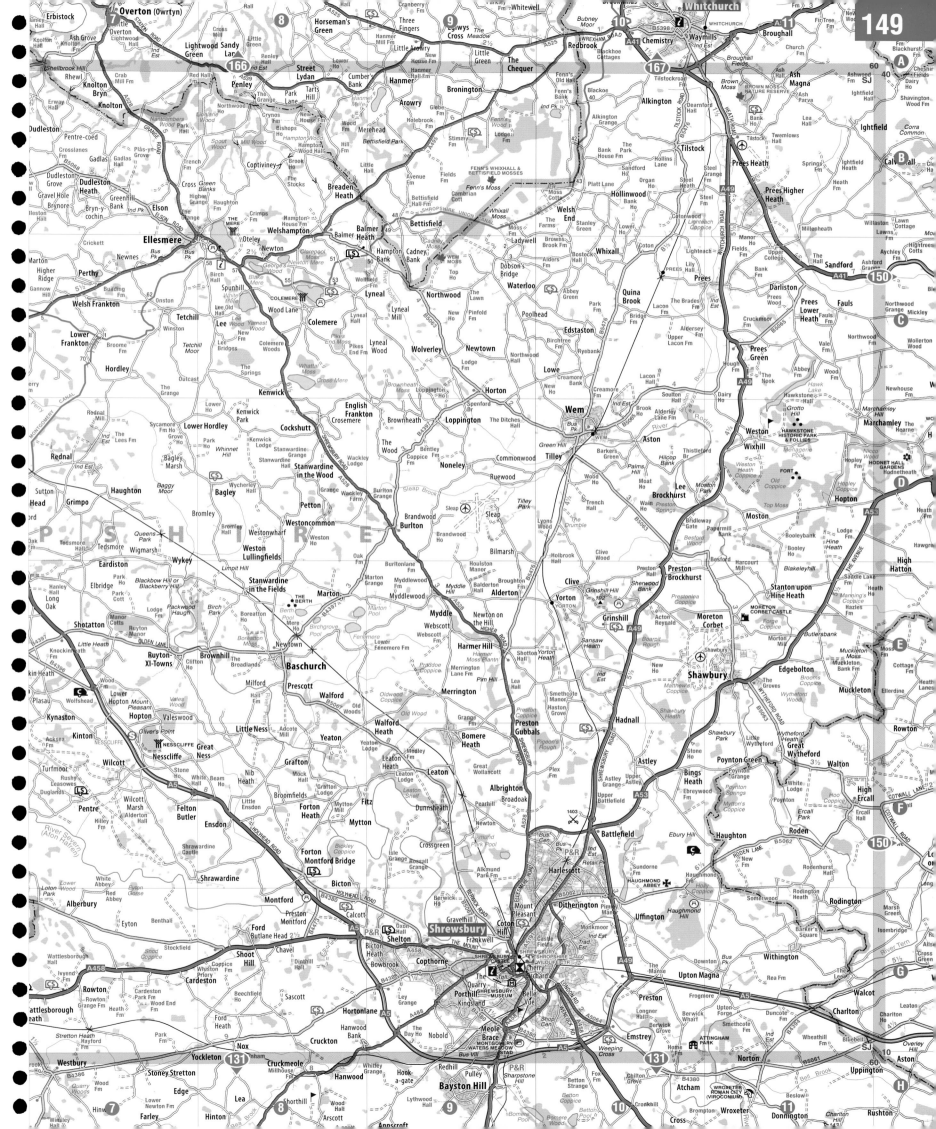

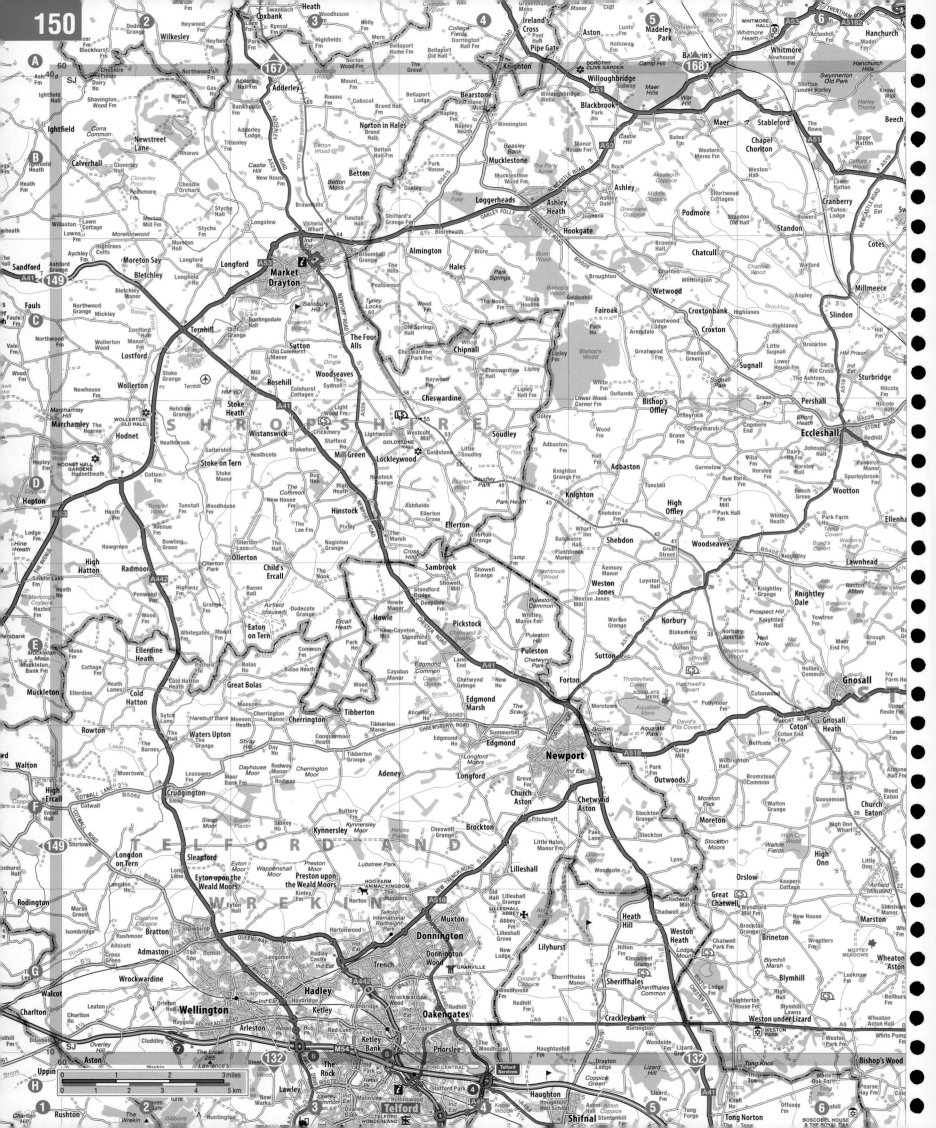

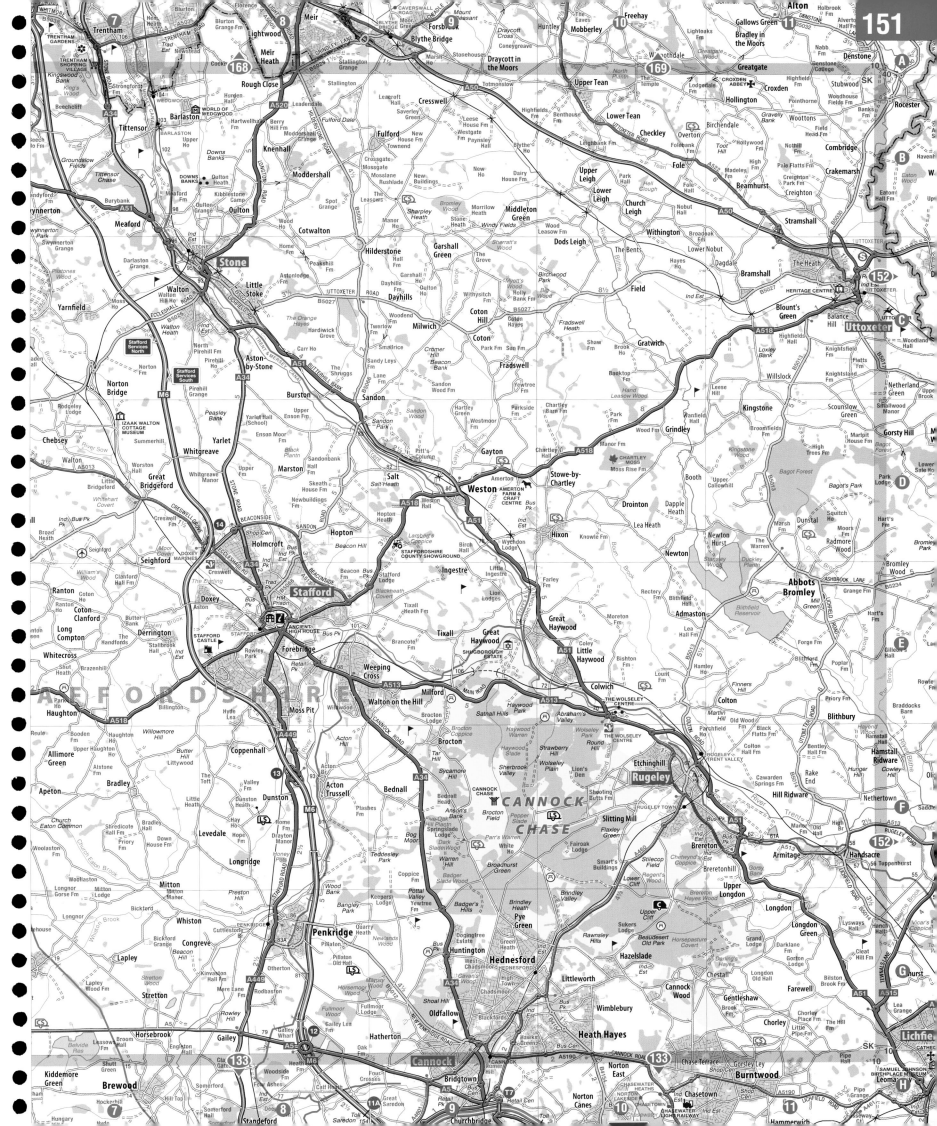

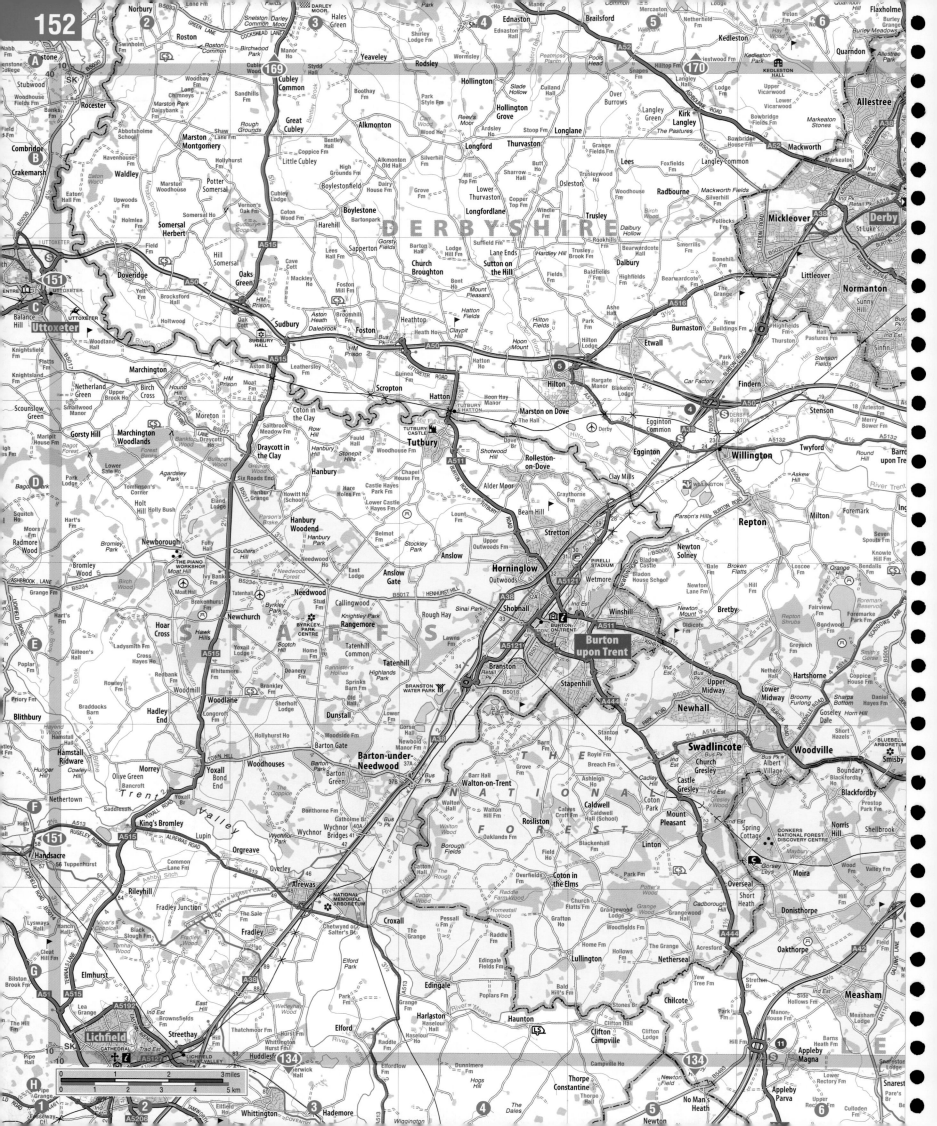

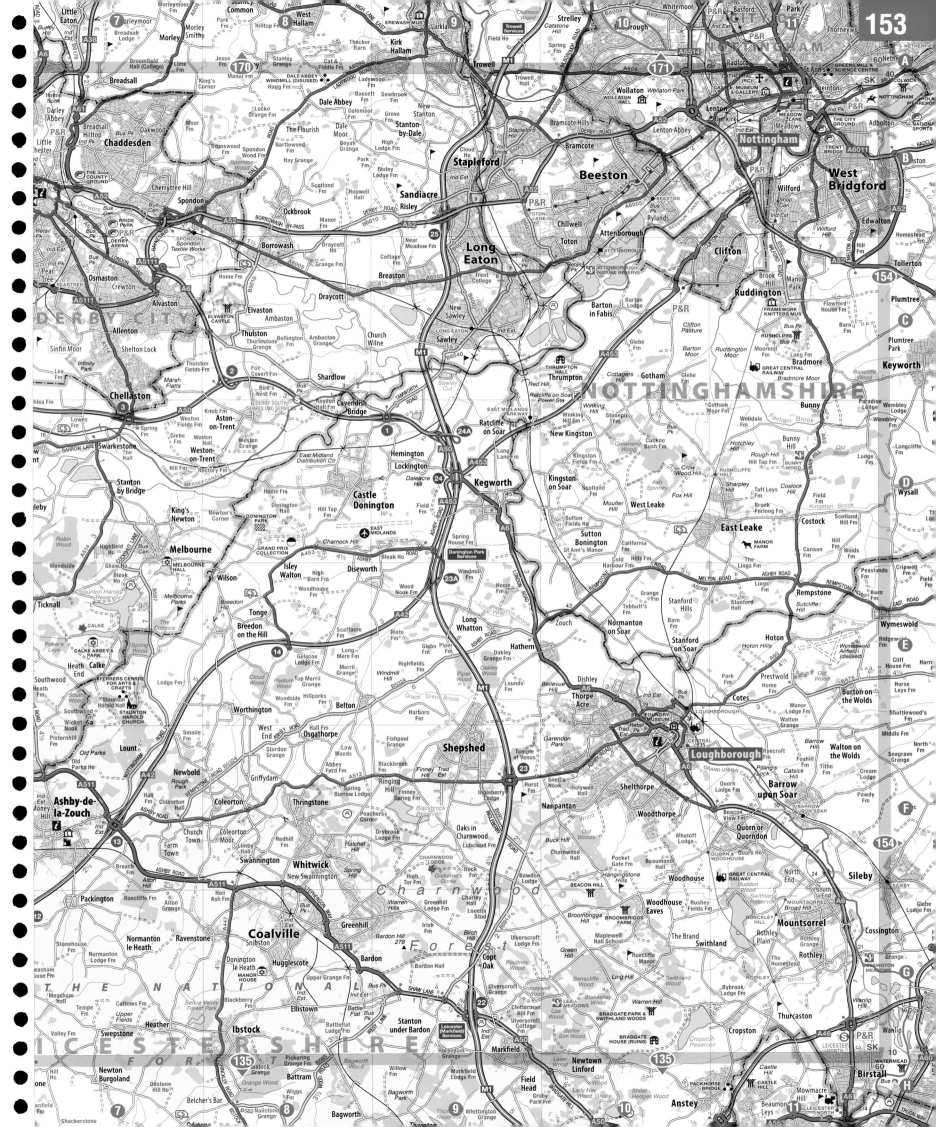

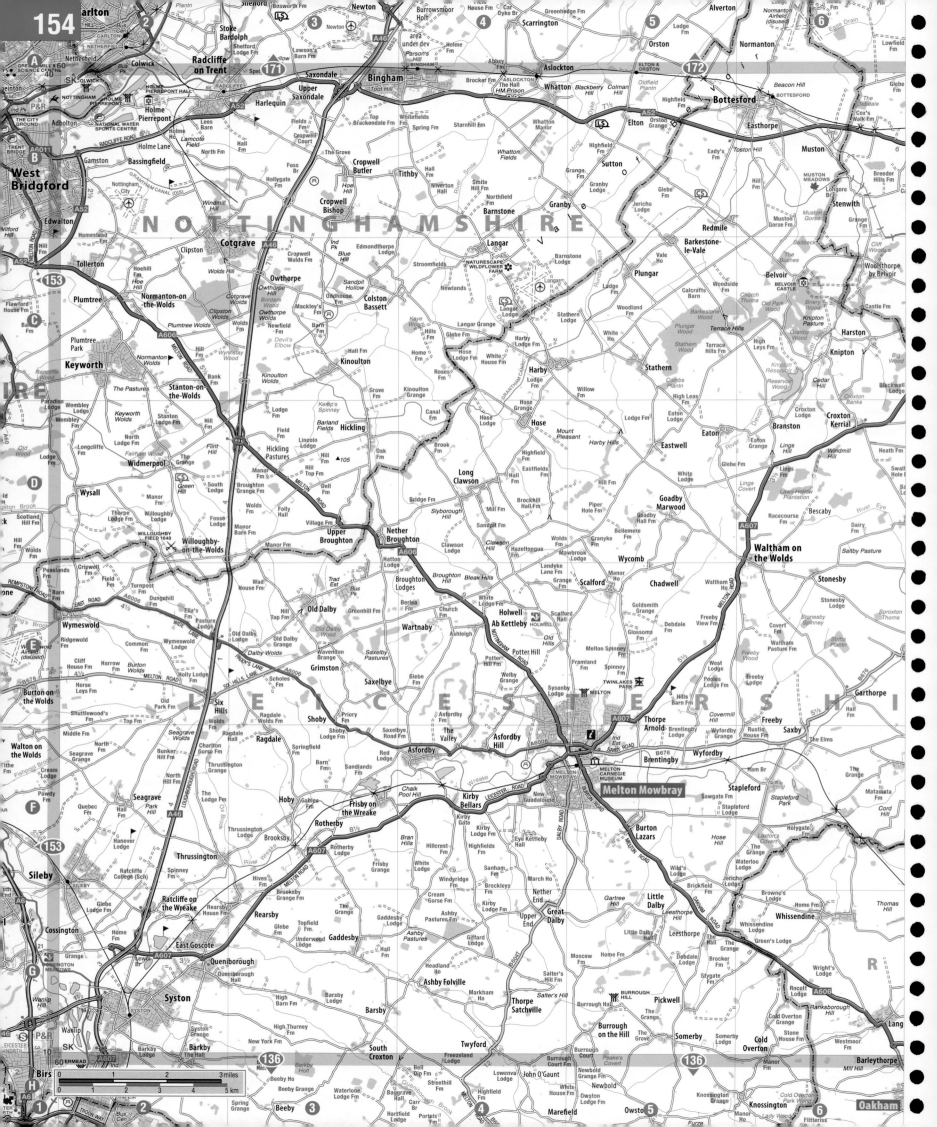

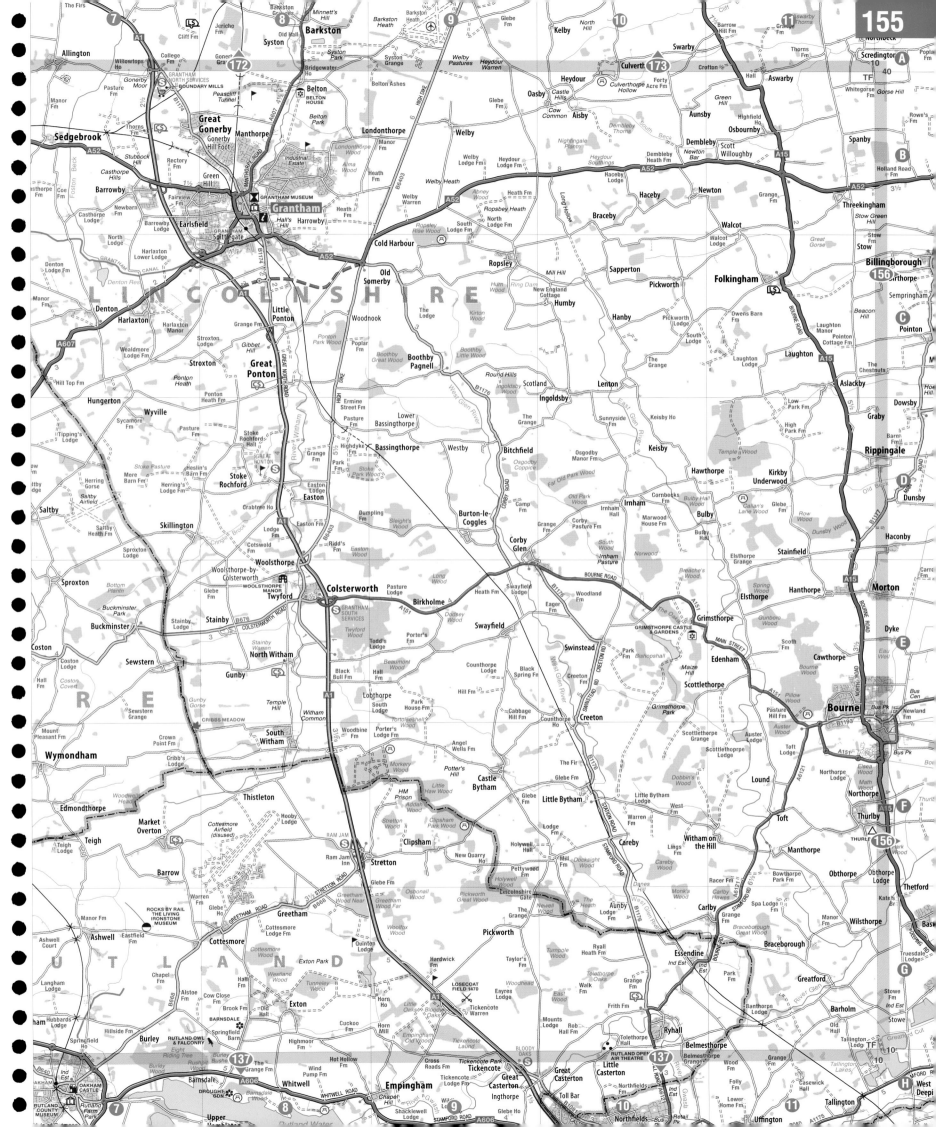

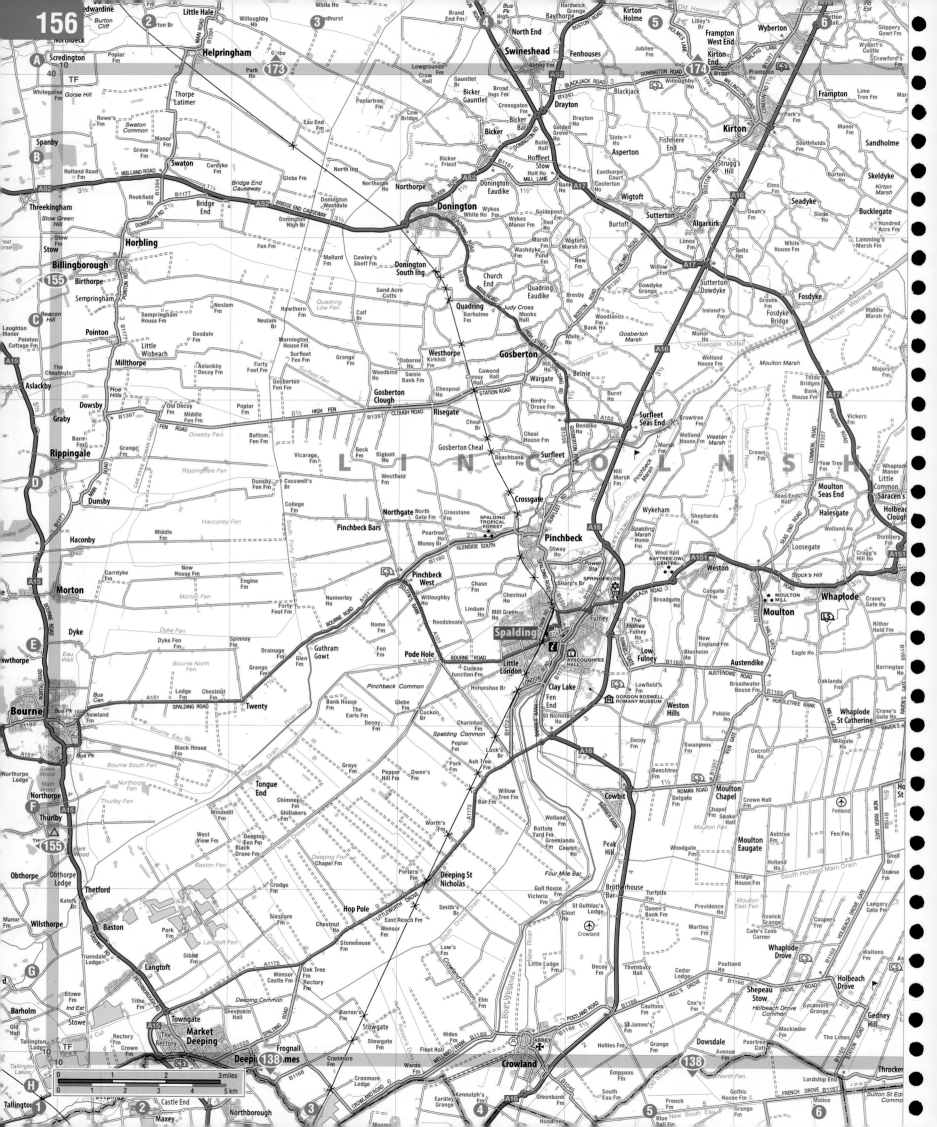

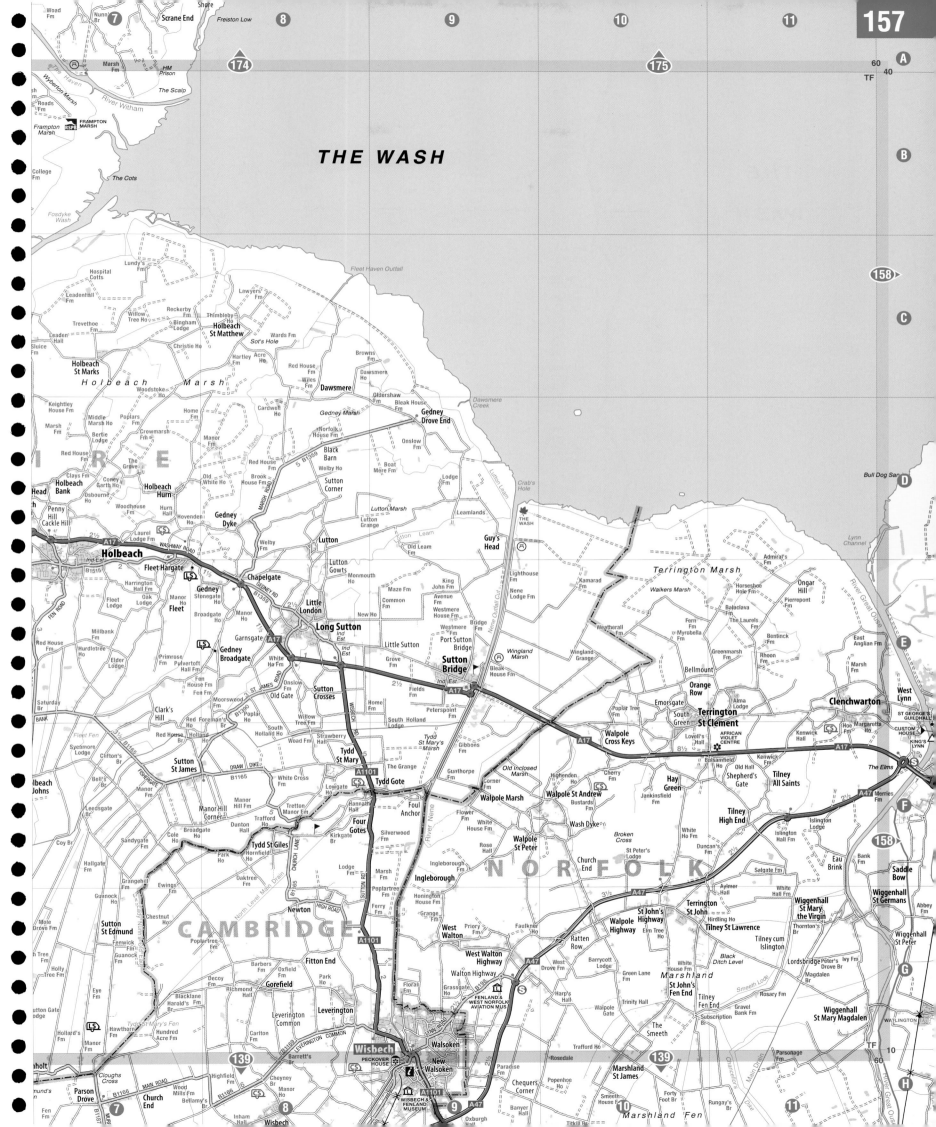

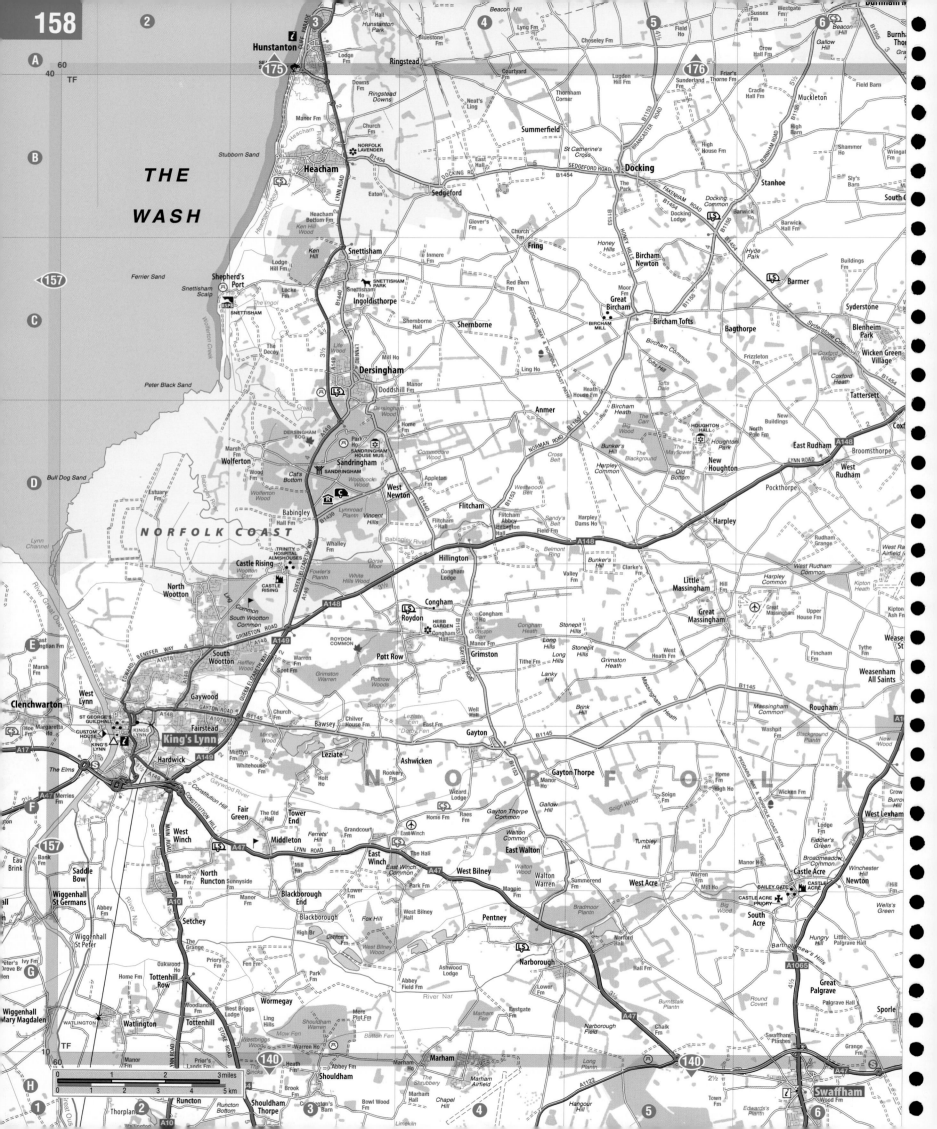

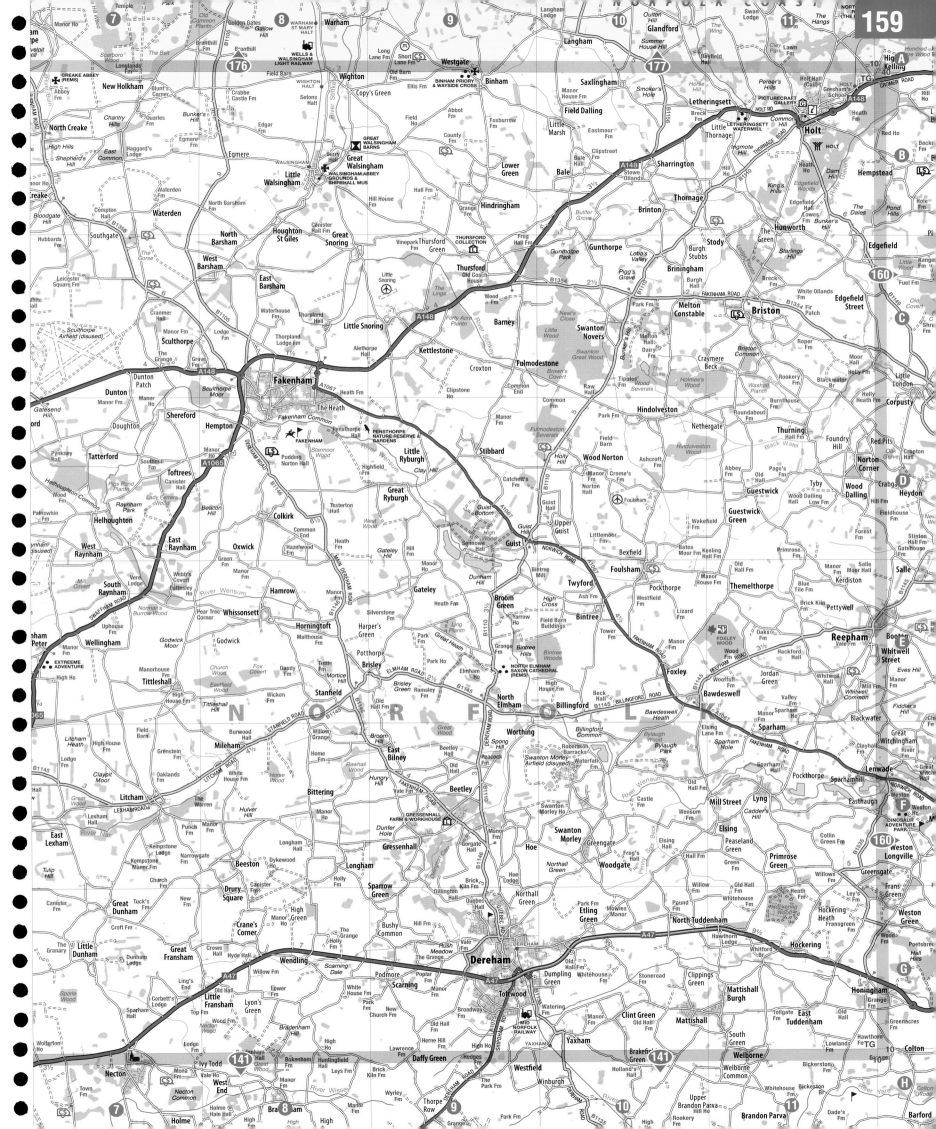

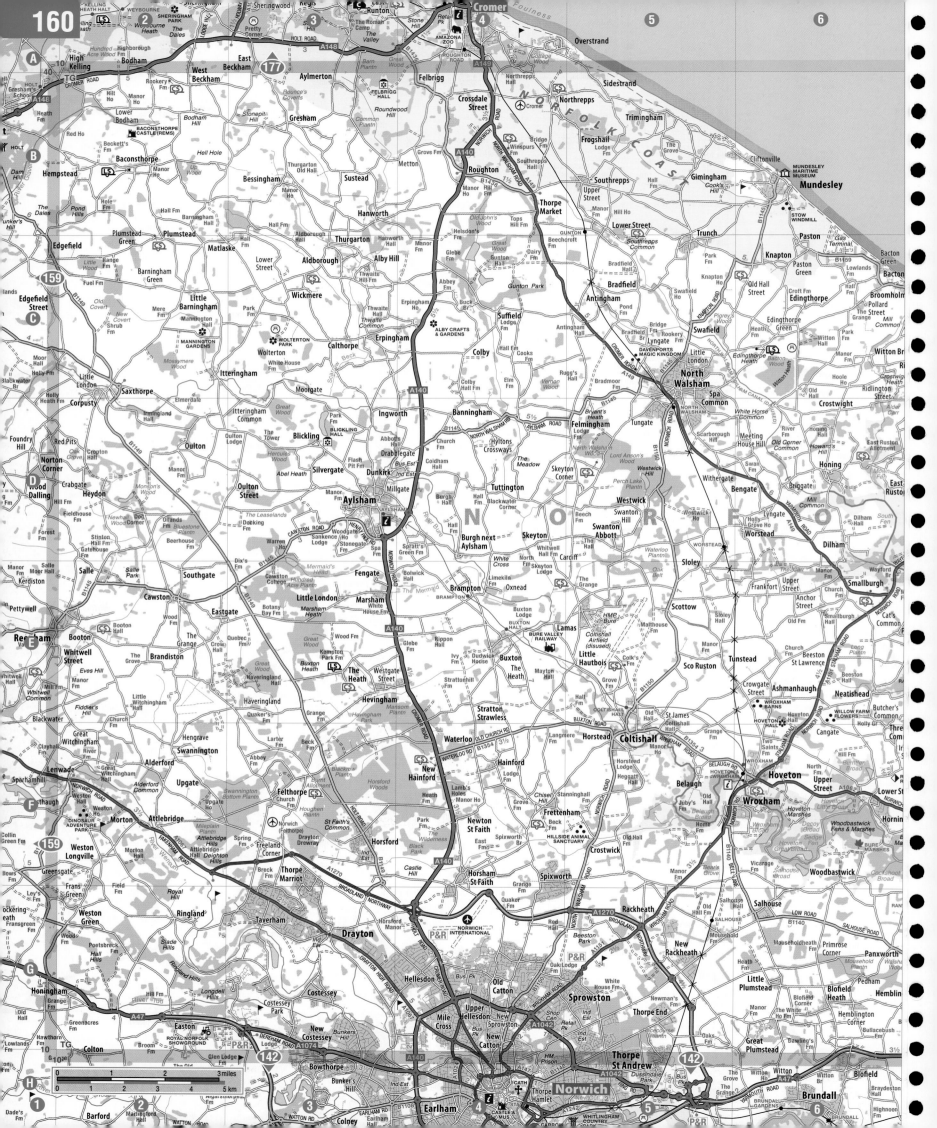

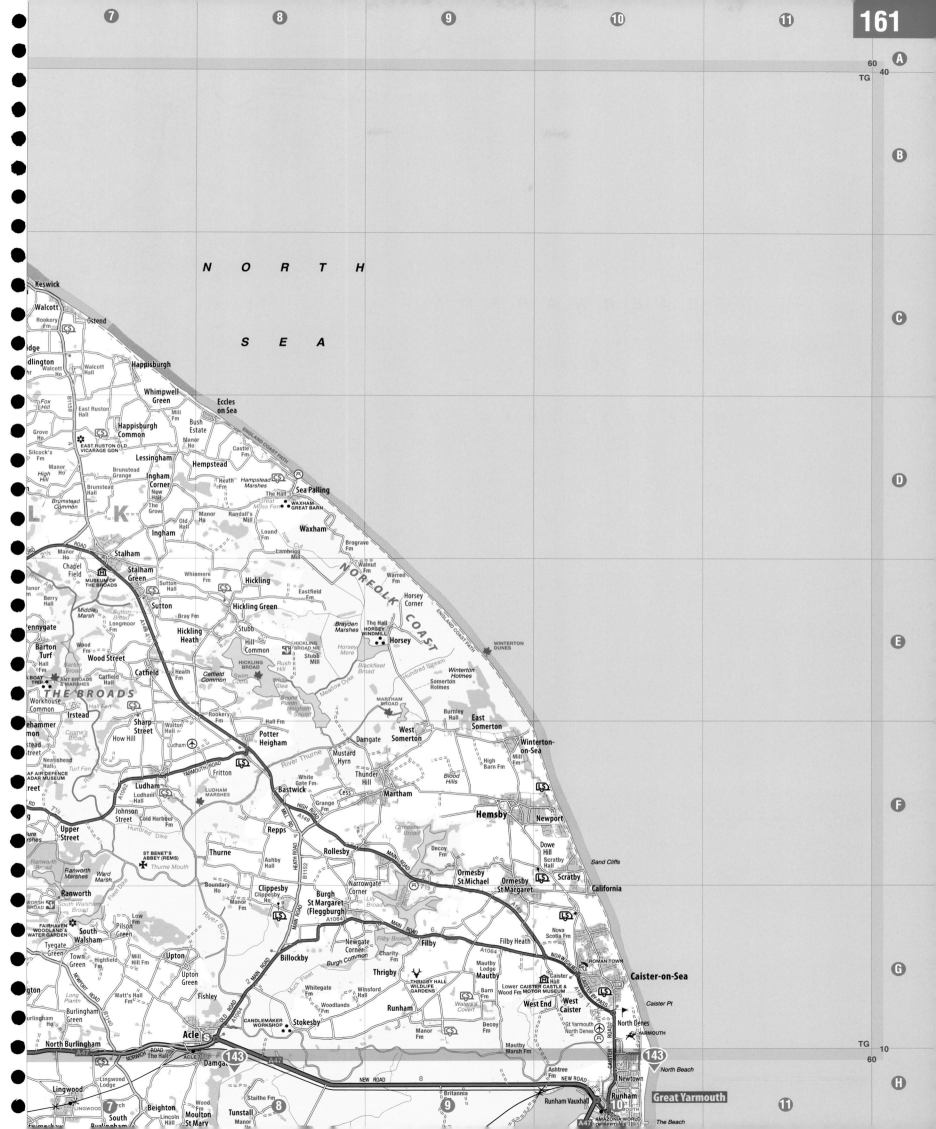

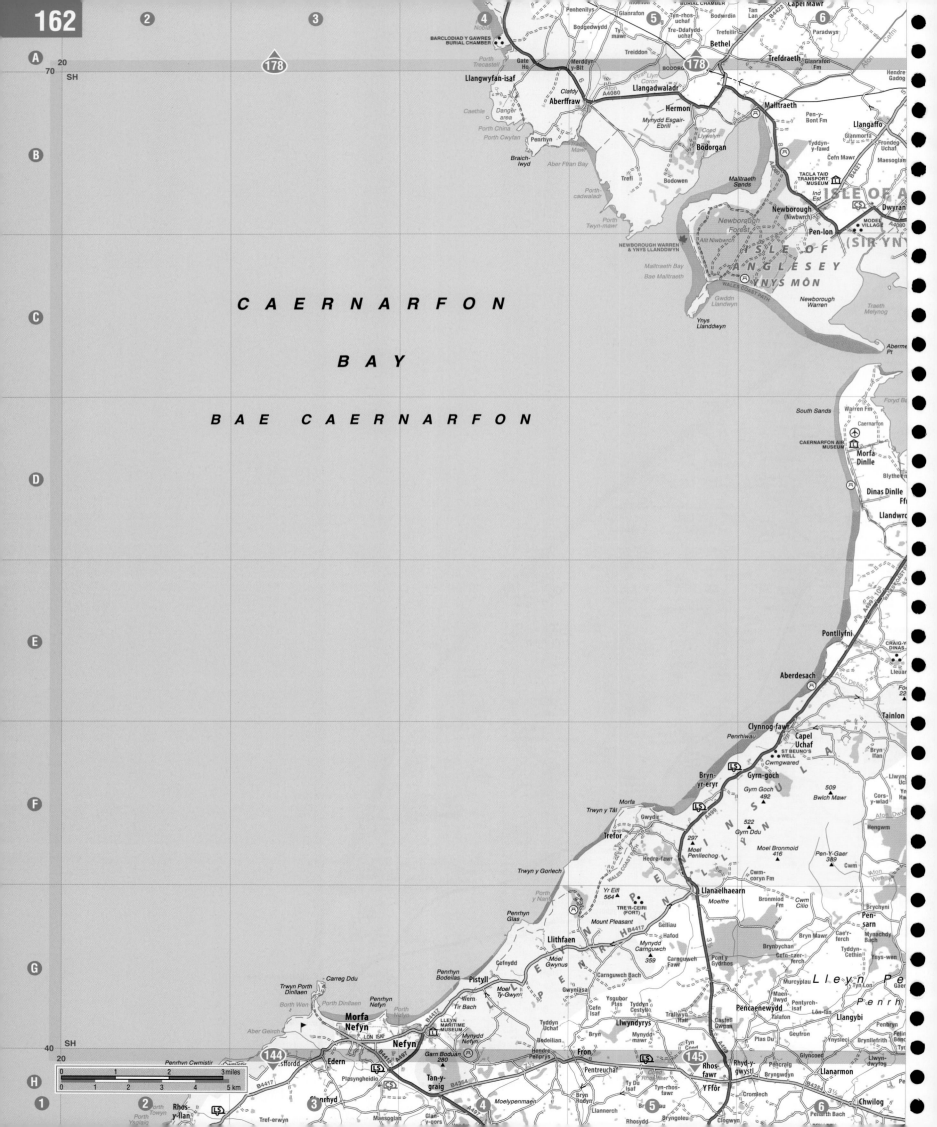

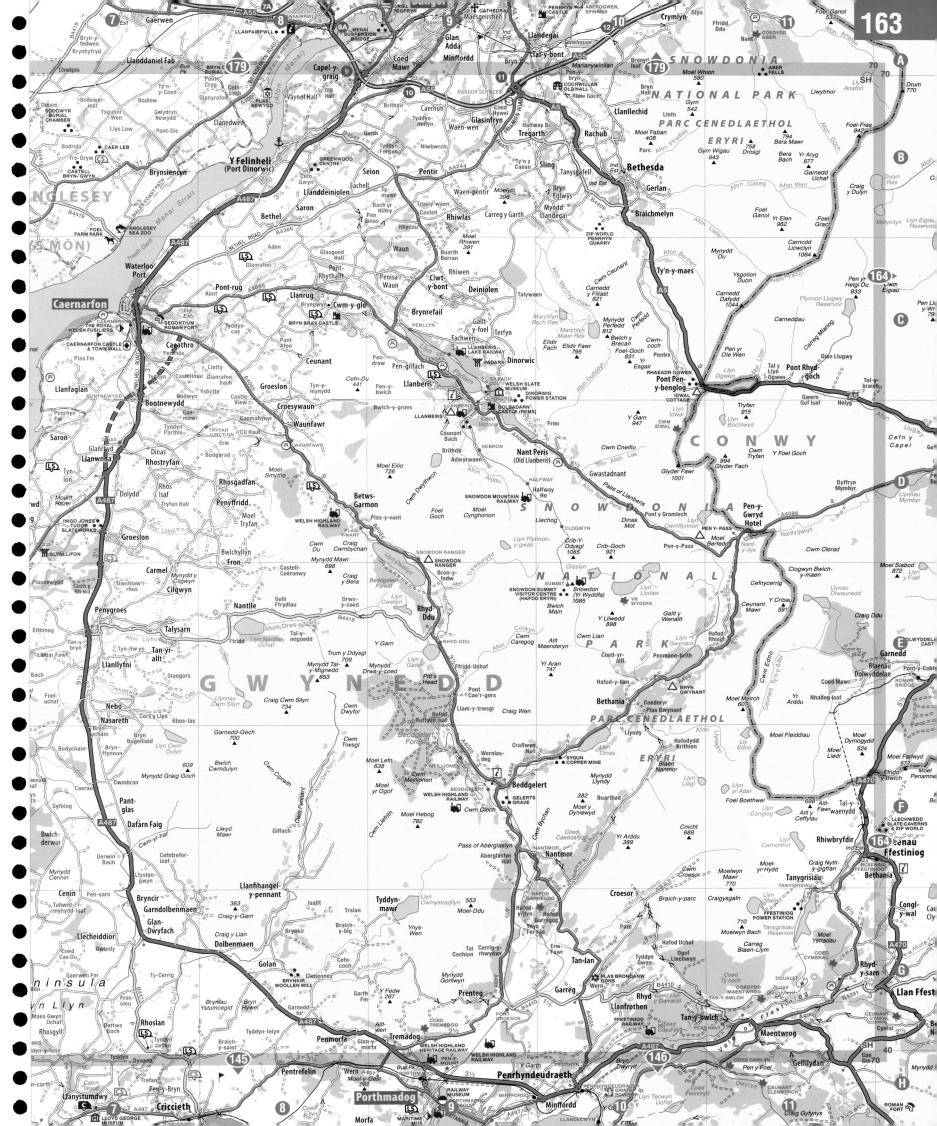

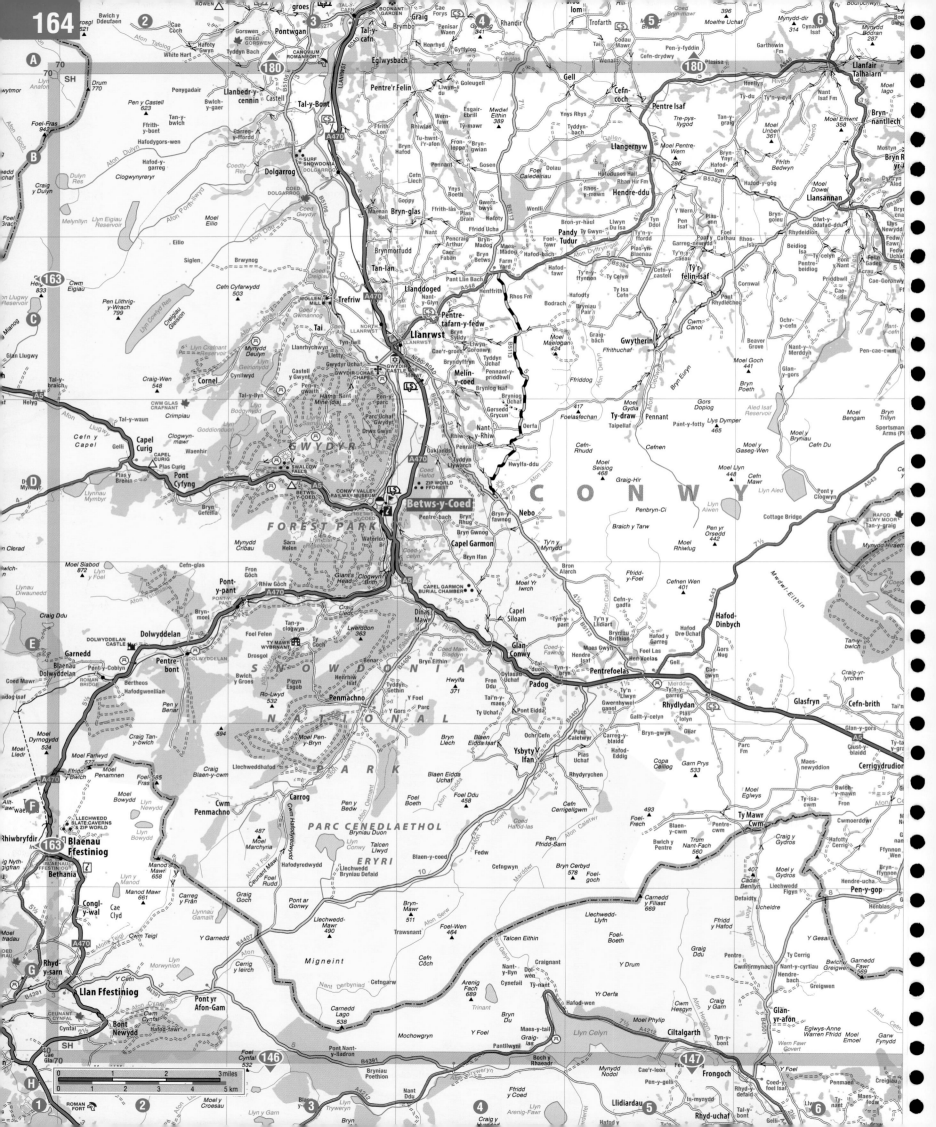

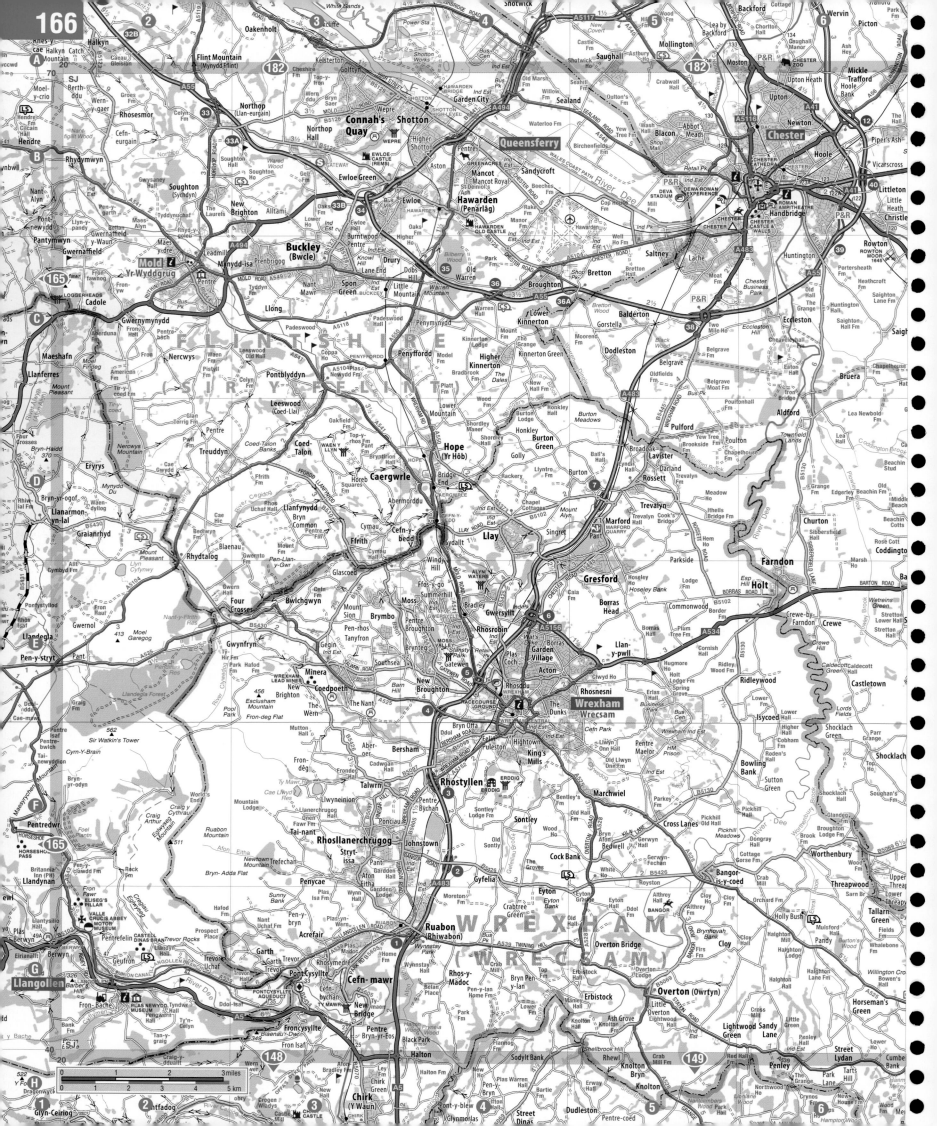

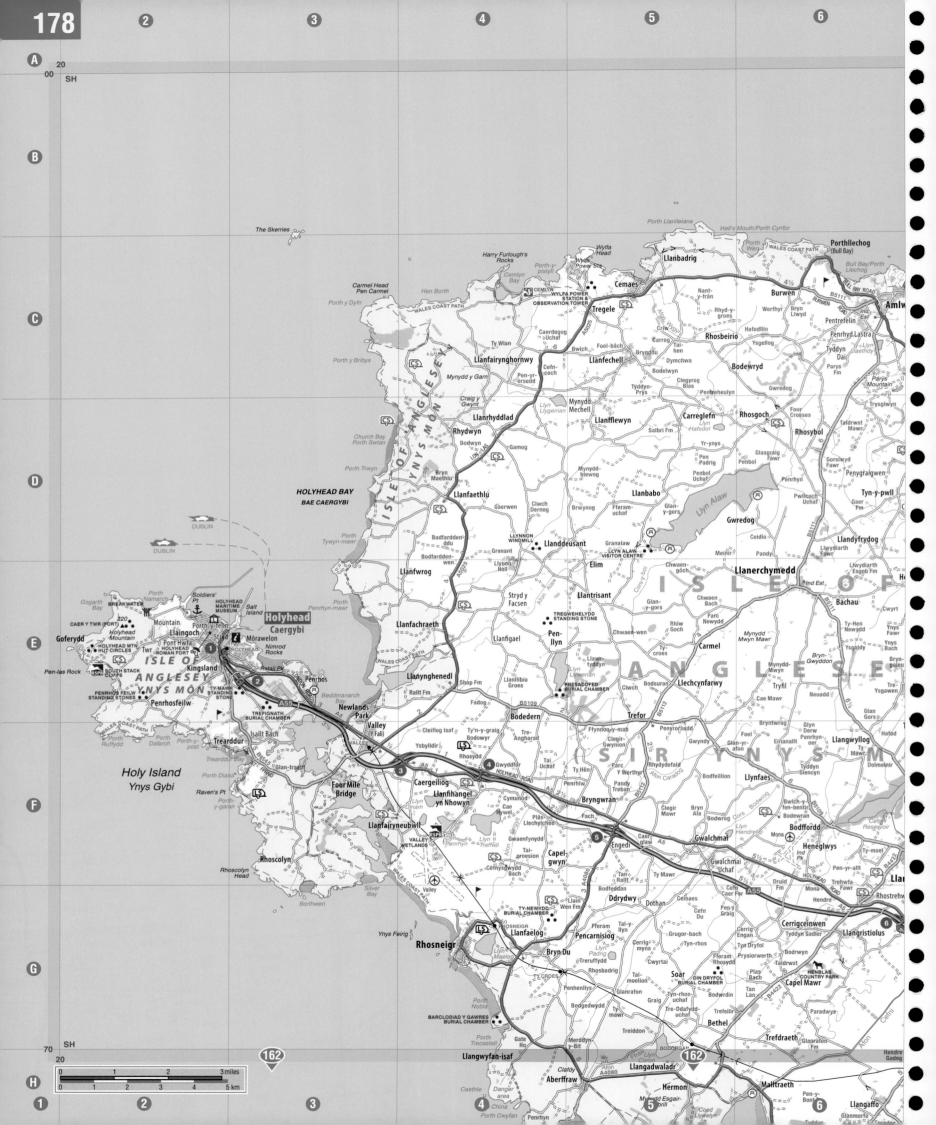

IRISH SEA

MÔR IWERDDON

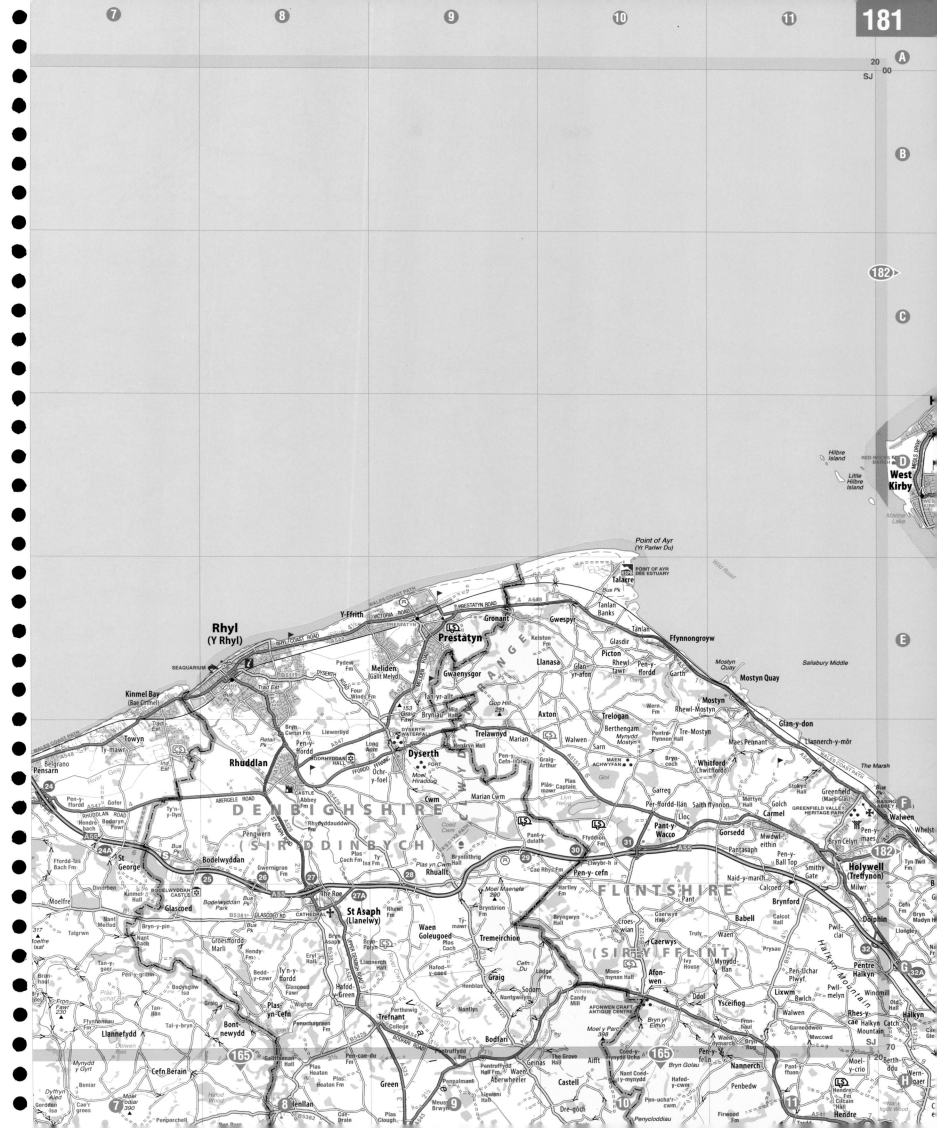

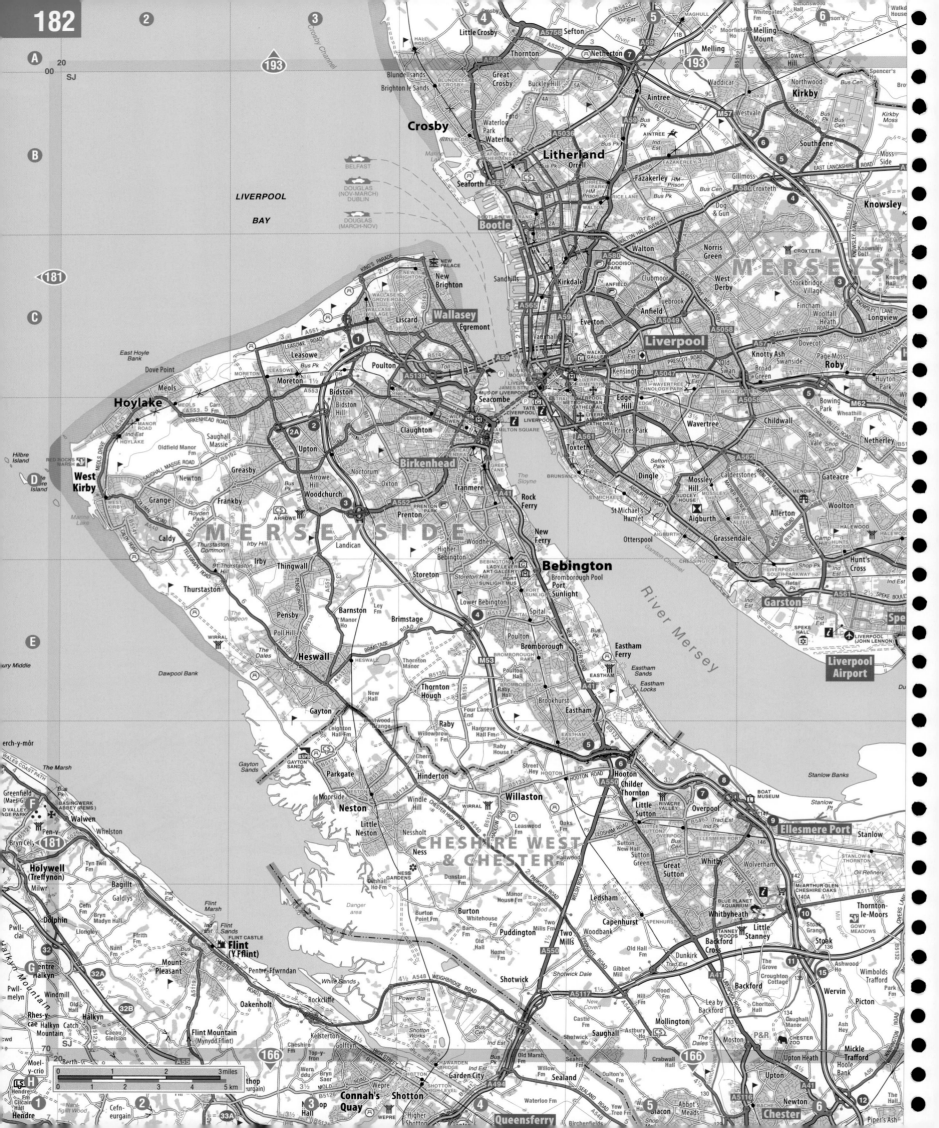

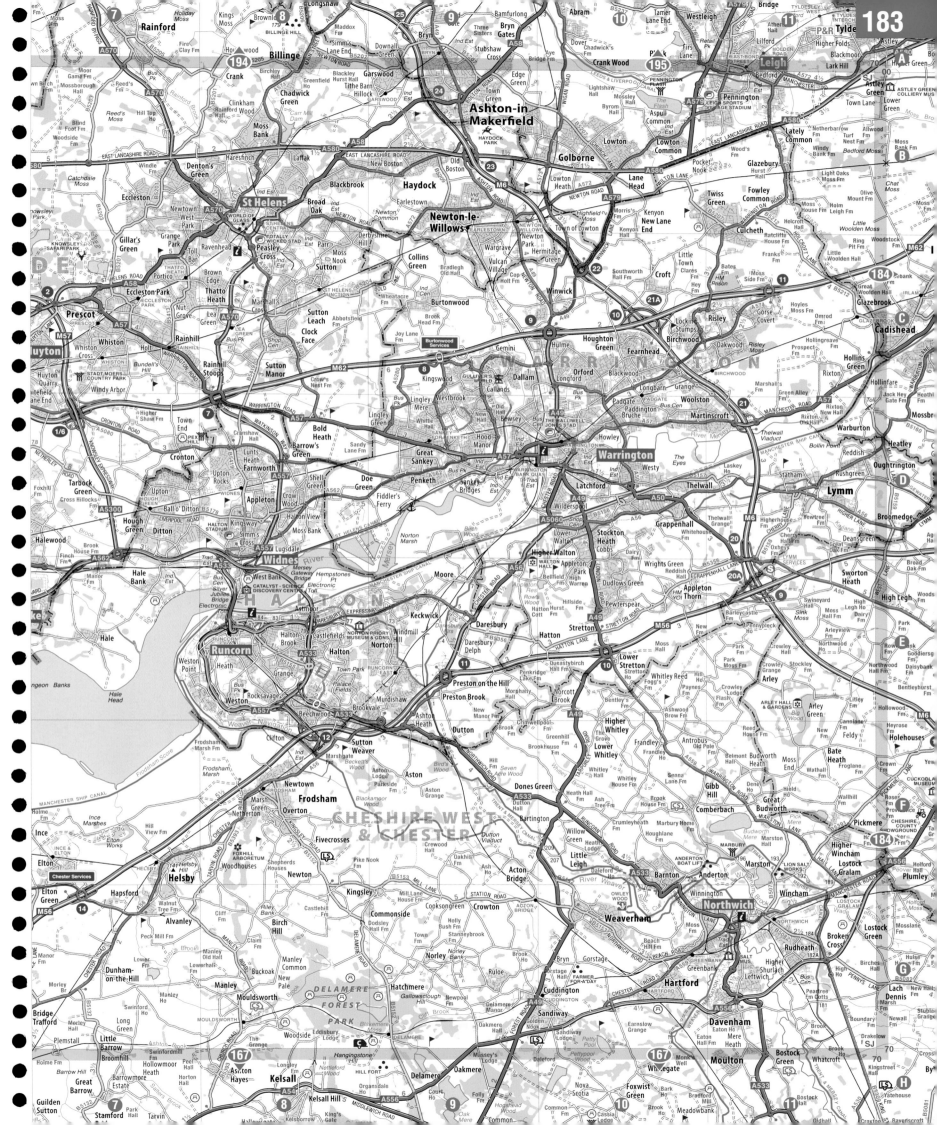

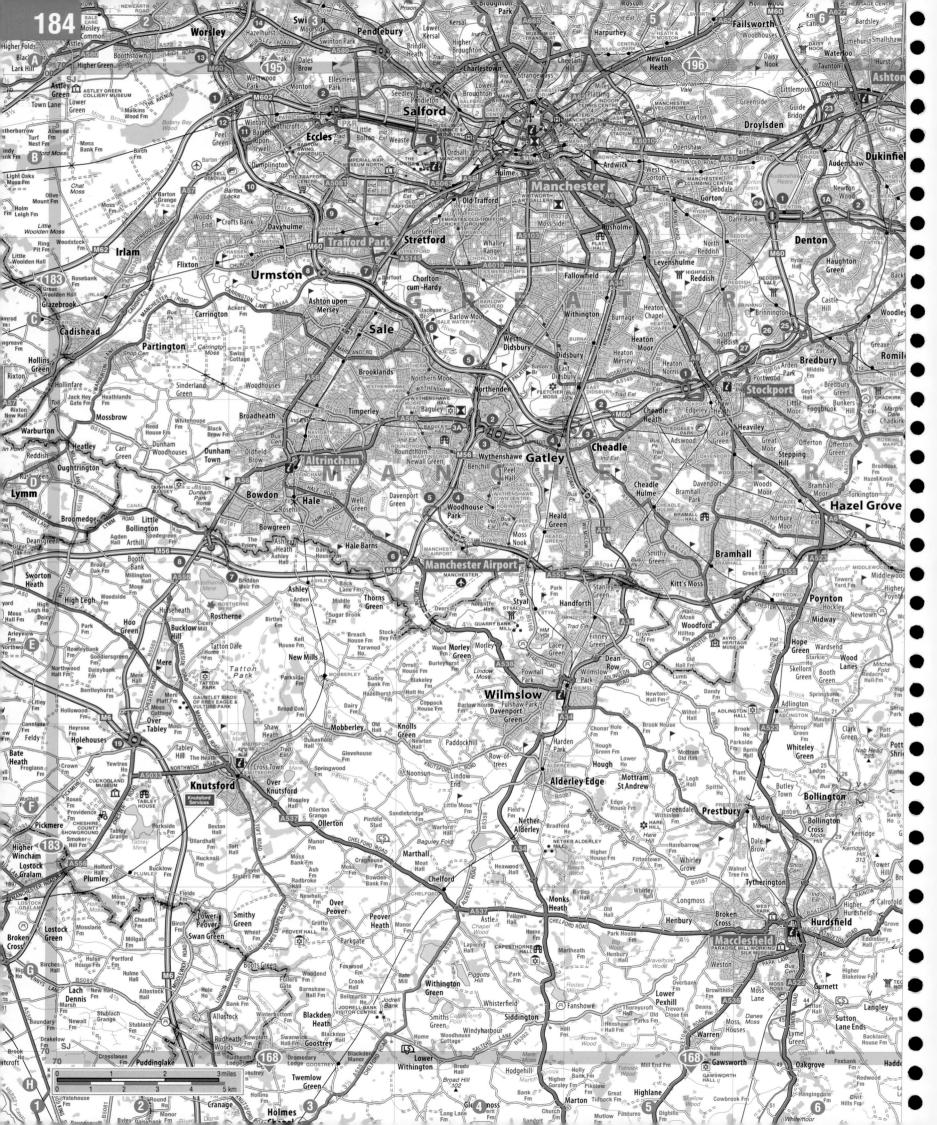

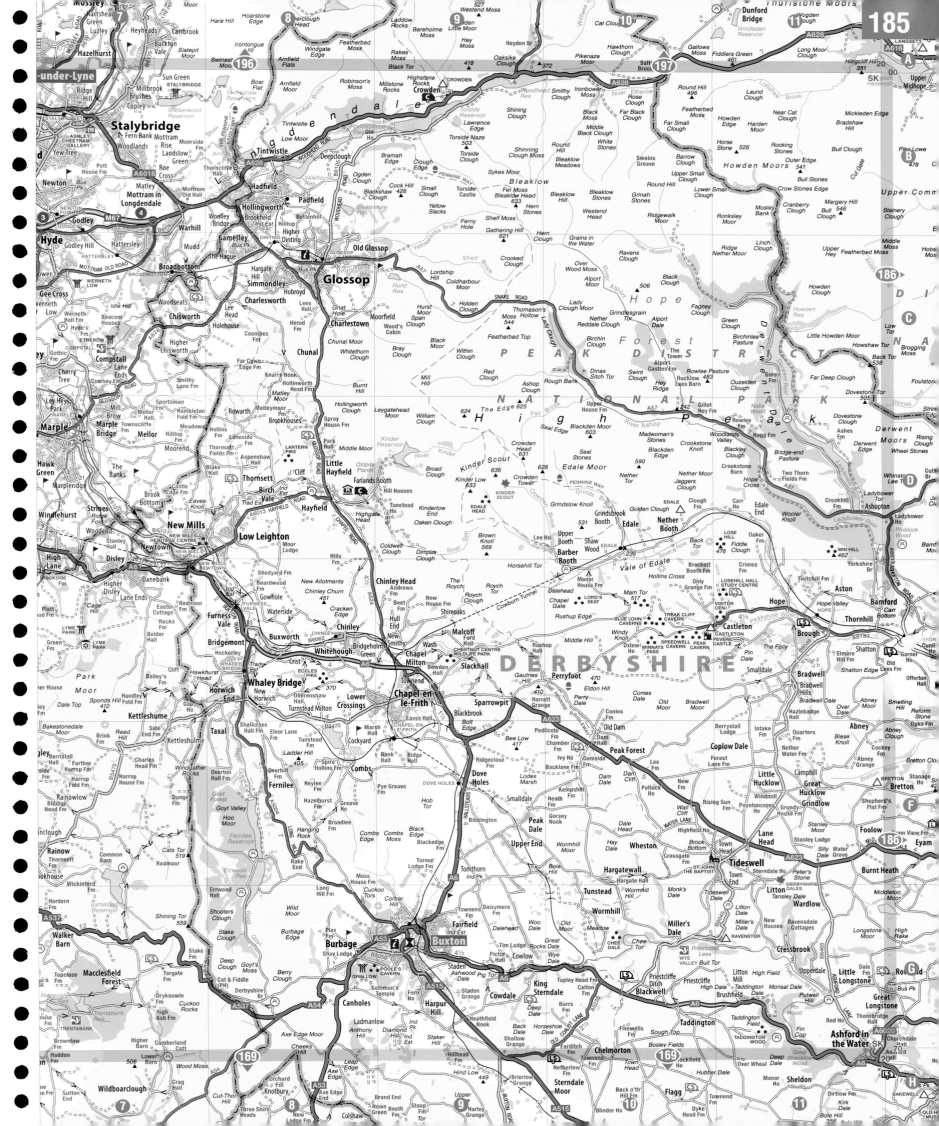

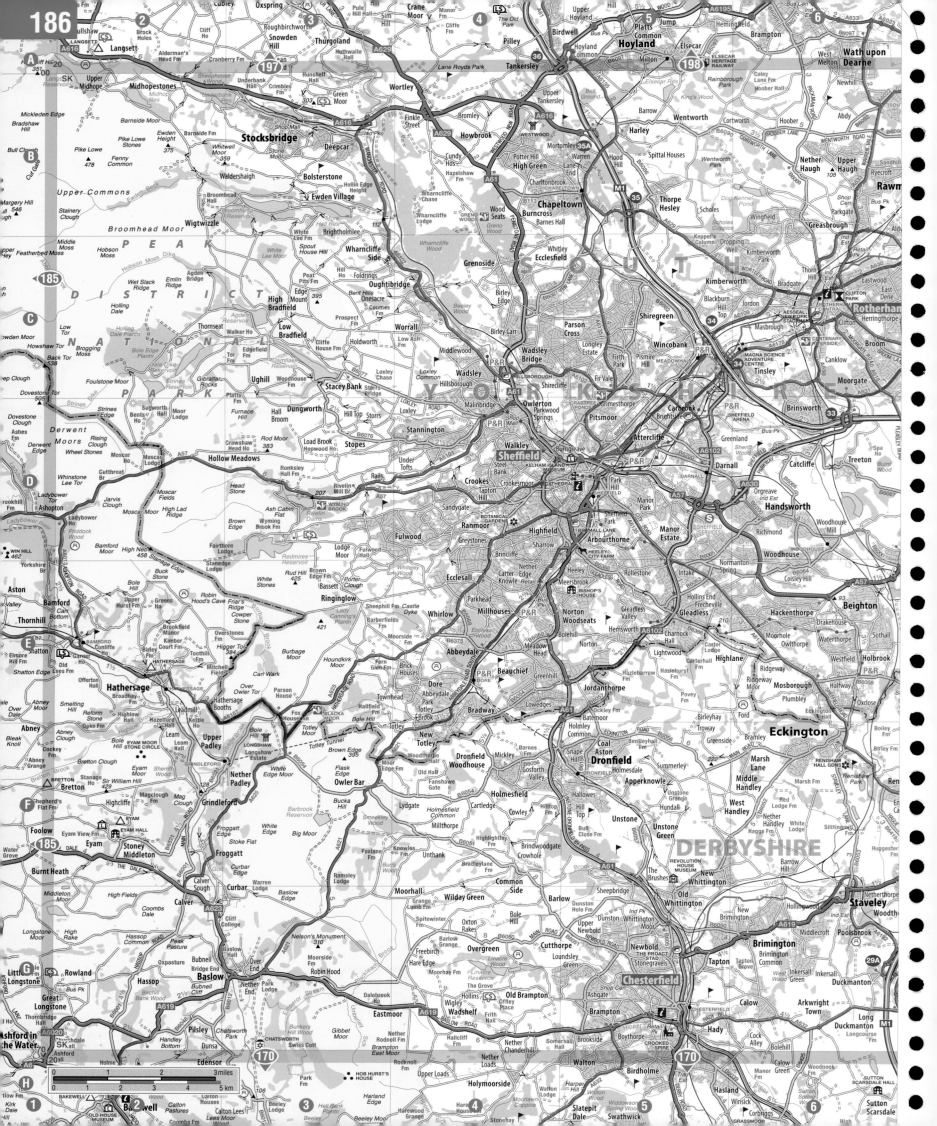

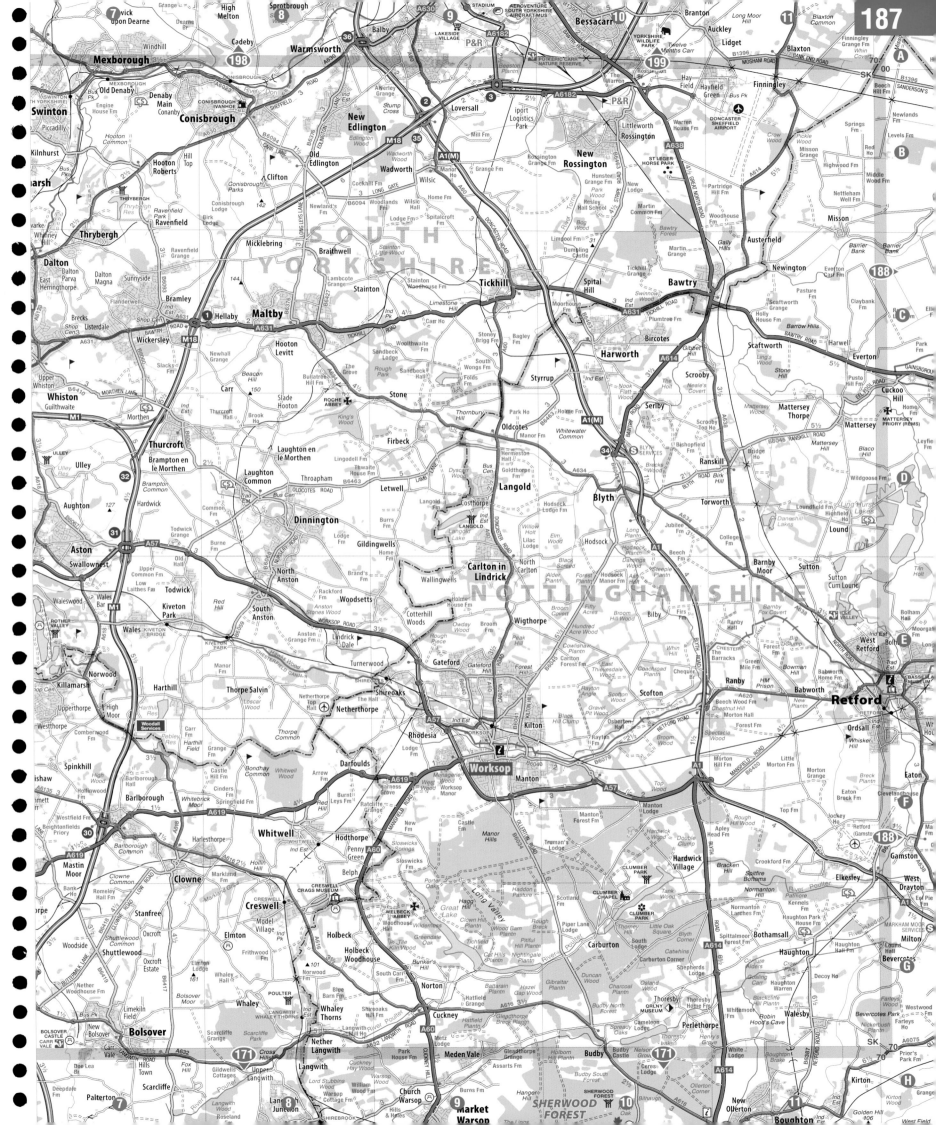

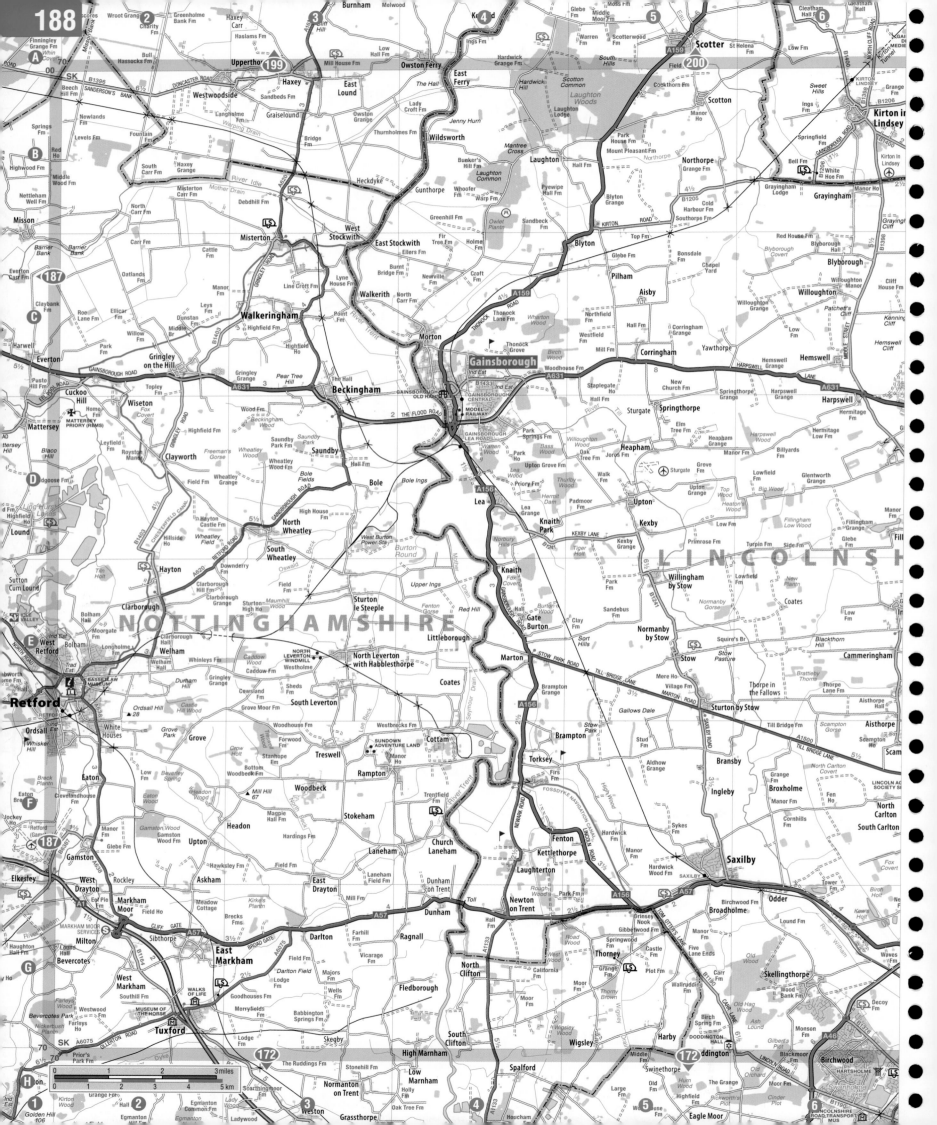

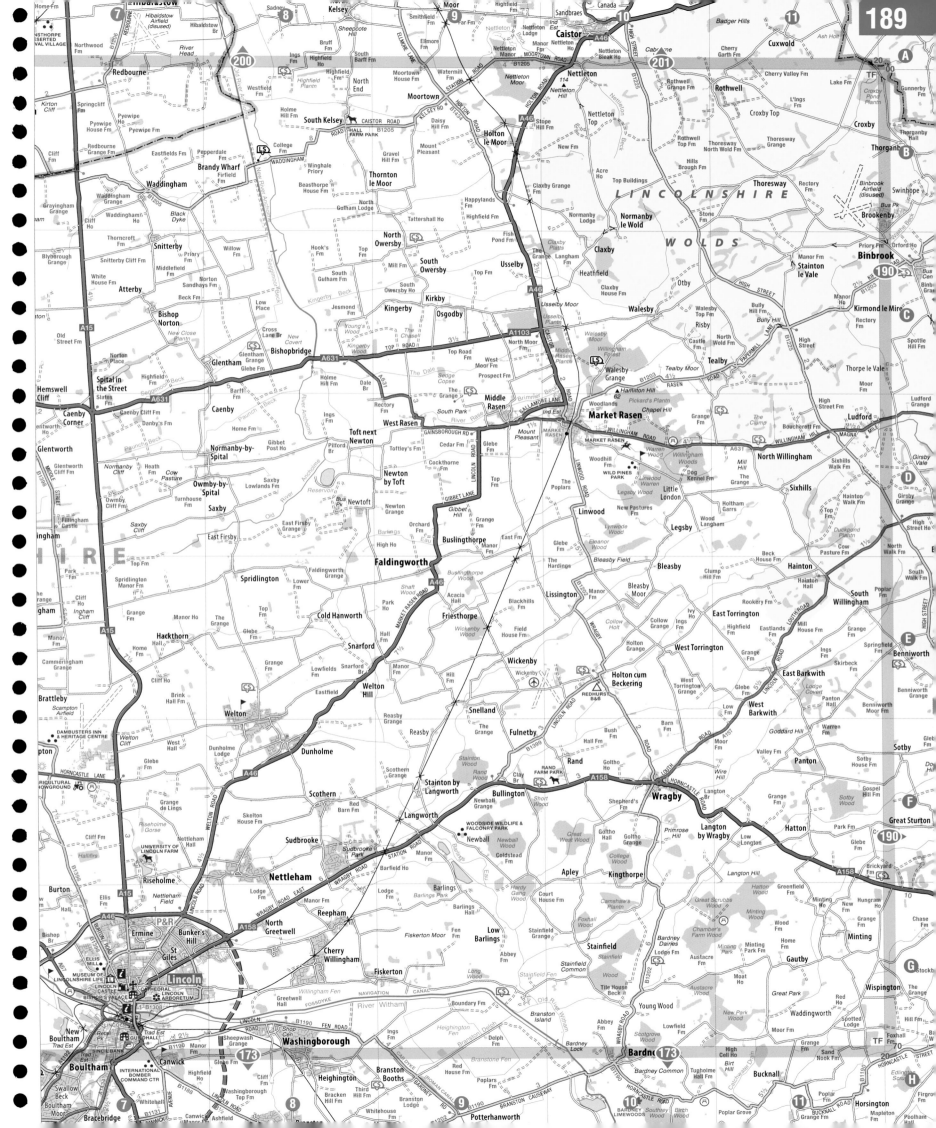

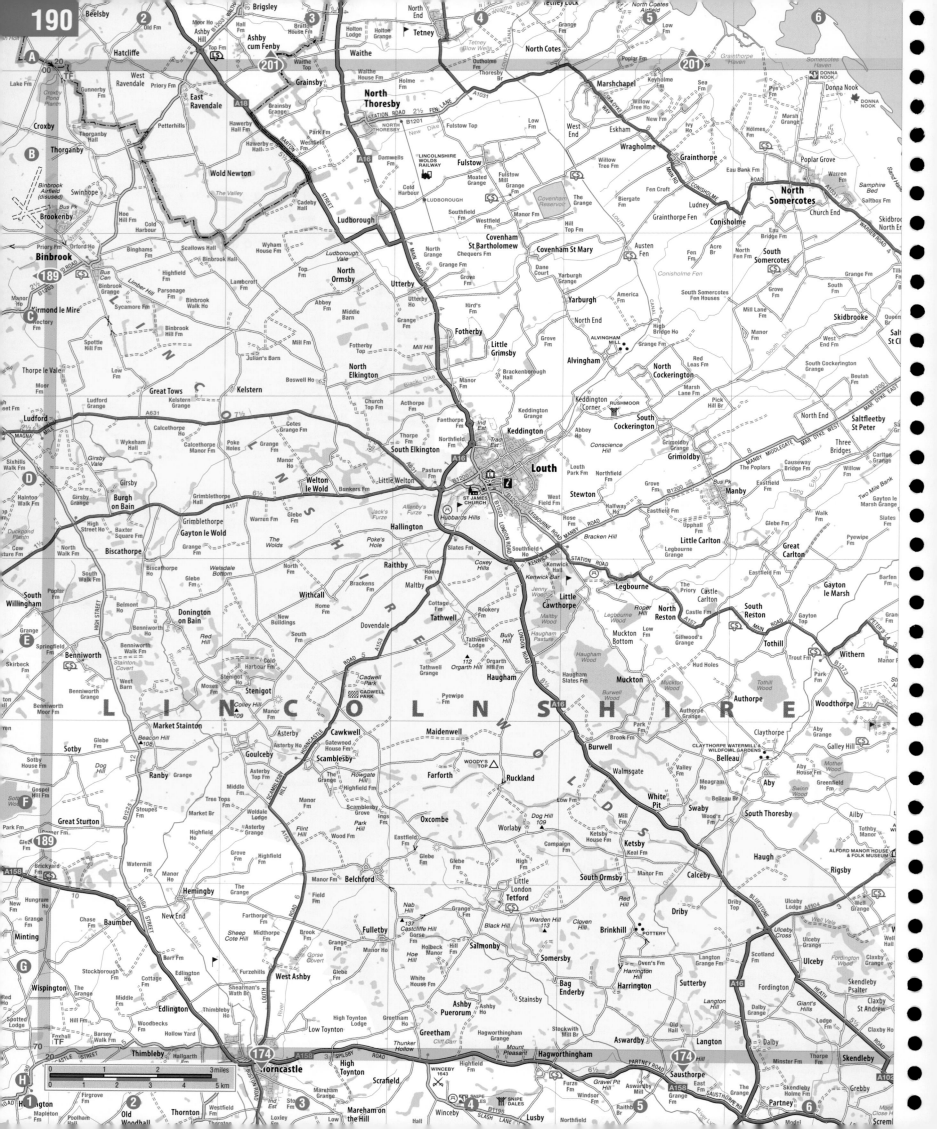

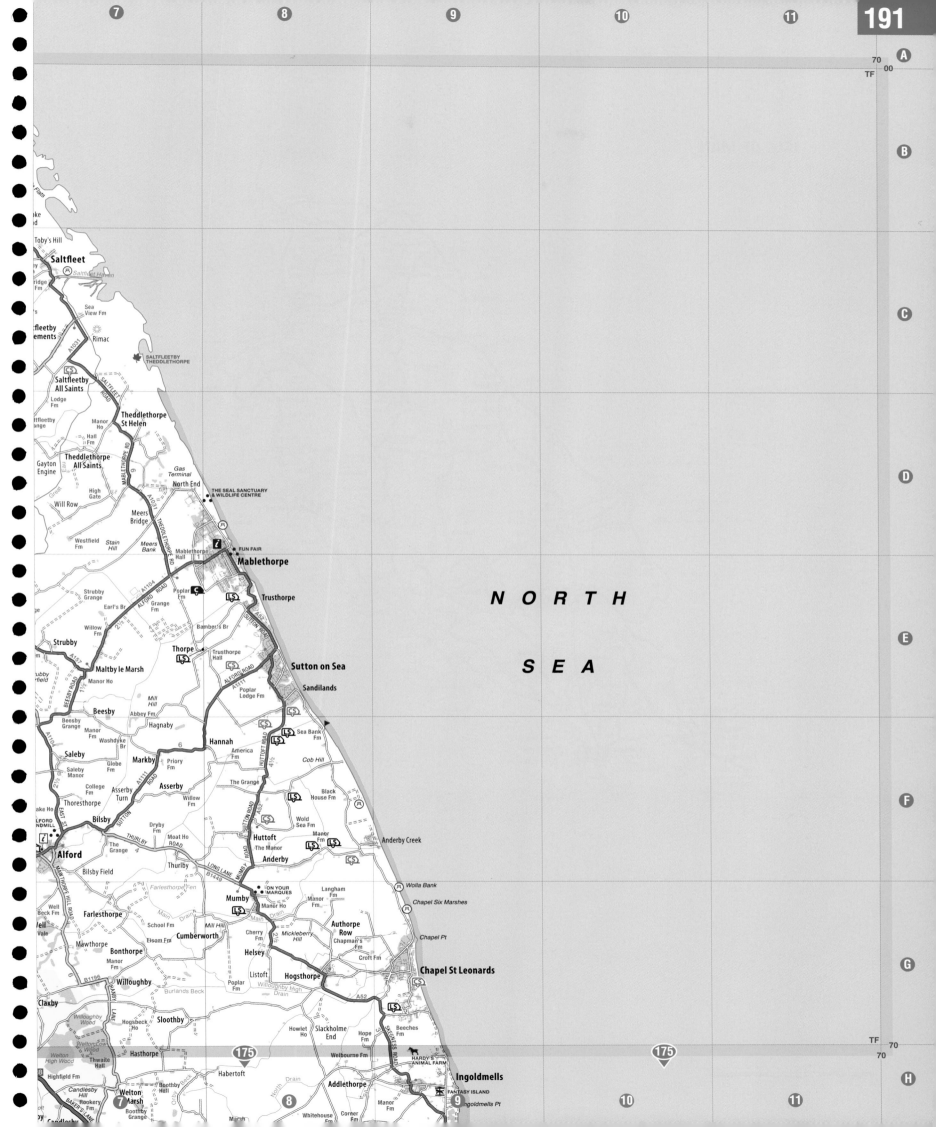

NORTH

SEA

Saltfleet

Saltfleetby
All Saints

Theddlethorpe
St Helen

Theddlethorpe
All Saints

Mablethorpe

Trusthorpe

Thorpe

Strubby

Maltby le Marsh

Beesby

Hannah

Saleby

Markby

Asserby

Thorestthorpe

Bilsby

Huttoft

Anderby

Alford

Thurlby

Mumby

Farlesthorpe

Cumberworth

Helsey

Willoughby

Hogsthorpe

Chapel St Leonards

Claxby

Sloothby

Hasthorpe

Welton
Marsh

Addlethorpe

Ingoldmells

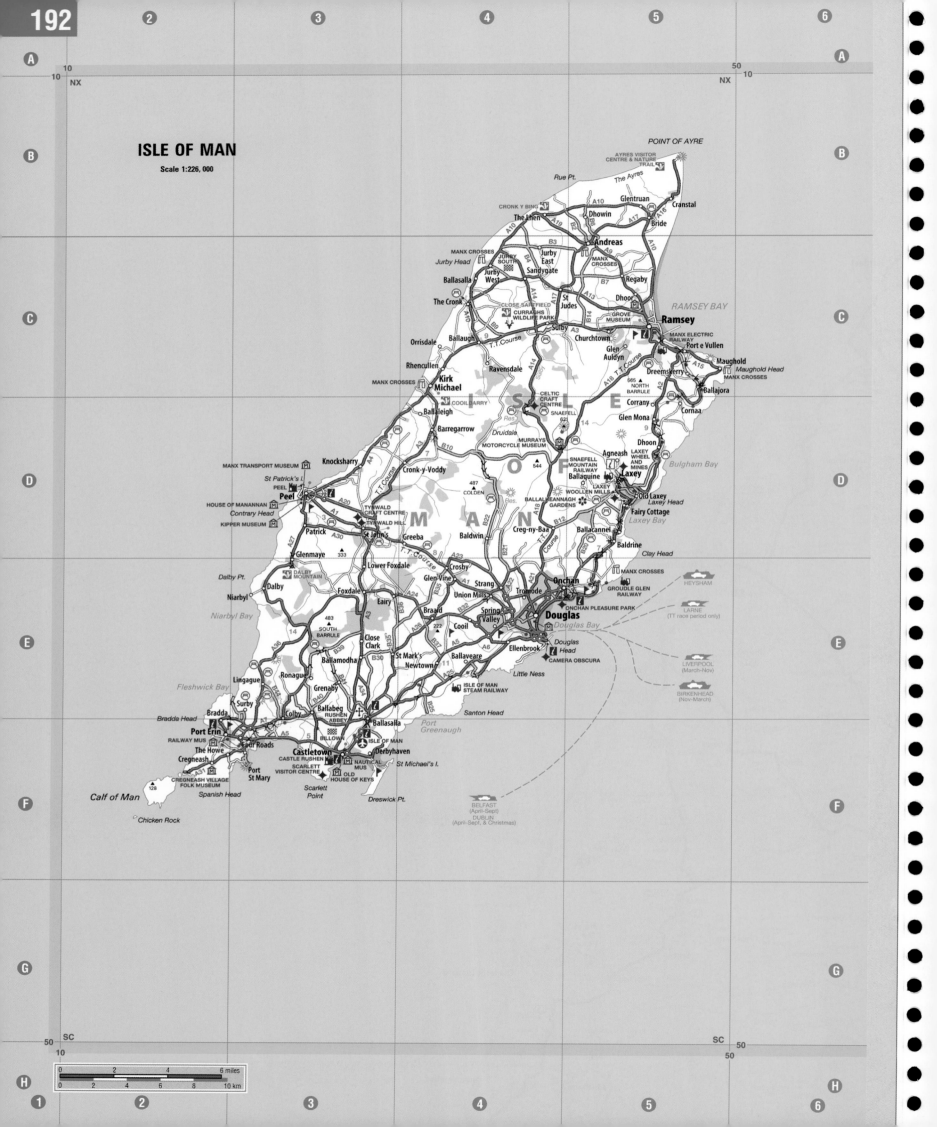

ISLE OF MAN

Scale 1:226,000

POINT OF AYRE

AYRES VISITOR
CENTRE & NATURE
TRAIL

Rue Pt.   The Ayres

CRONK Y BING   Glentruan   Cranstal

The Lhen   Dhowin   Bride

Andreas

MANX CROSSES   Jurby   Jurby
Jurby Head   East
                    JURBY SOUTH   Sandygate   Regaby
Ballasalla   Jurby
                    West
The Cronk   Dhoor   RAMSEY BAY

                    CLOSE SARTFIELD   St
                    CURRAGHS   Judes
                    WILDLIFE PARK   GROVE   Ramsey
Orrisdale   Ballaugh   MUSEUM
                            Sulby   MANX ELECTRIC
Rhencullen   Churchtown   Port e Vullen
                            T.T.Course   Glen
                                            Auldyn   Maughold
Kirk   Ravensdale   Dreemskerry   Maughold Head
Michael   MANX CROSSES
MANX CROSSES   665   Ballajora
                                        NORTH
            COOILDARRY   BARRULE
                            CELTIC   Corrany
Ballaleigh   CRAFT   621   Glen Mona   Cornaa
                            CENTRE
Barregarrow   Druidale   Snaefell   14
                    MURRAYS   Dhoon
                    MOTORCYCLE MUSEUM   Agneash   LAXEY
MANX TRANSPORT MUSEUM   Knocksharry   SNAEFELL   WHEEL
                                        MOUNTAIN   AND
St Patrick's I.   Cronk-y-Voddy   544   RAILWAY   Ballaquine   MINES   Laxey
PEEL   LAXEY   Bulgham Bay
Peel   487   WOOLLEN MILLS
HOUSE OF MANANNAN   COLDEN   BALLALHEANNAGH   Old Laxey
                    TYNWALD   GARDENS   Laxey Head
Contrary Head   CRAFT CENTRE   Fairy Cottage
KIPPER MUSEUM   TYNWALD HILL   Creg-ny-Baa   Ballacannel   Laxey Bay
Patrick   St John's   Greeba   Baldrine
                            Baldwin   Clay Head
Glenmaye   333   B21   7
                                                    MANX CROSSES
Dalby Pt.   DALBY   Lower Foxdale   Crosby   GROUDLE GLEN
        MOUNTAIN   Glen Vine   Strang   RAILWAY   HEYSHAM
Dalby   Foxdale   Union Mills   Tromode   ONCHAN PLEASURE PARK
Niarbyl   Eairy   Braaid   Onchan   LARNE
                    483   (TT race period only)
Niarbyl Bay   SOUTH   Cooil   Spring   Douglas
            14   BARRULE   222   Valley   Douglas Bay
                        Close   Douglas
            Ballamodha   Clark   Head
                            St Mark's   Ballaveare   Ellenbrook   CAMERA OBSCURA
Fleshwick Bay   Lingague   Ronague   Newtown   11   Little Ness   LIVERPOOL
                                                (March-Nov)
            Surby   Grenaby   ISLE OF MAN
Bradda Head   Bradda   Colby   Ballabeg   STEAM RAILWAY   BIRKENHEAD
        Port Erin   Four Roads   BILLOWN   Ballasalla   Santon Head   (Nov-March)
RAILWAY MUS   RUSHEN ABBEY   Port
The Howe   Castletown   ISLE OF MAN   Greenaugh
Cregneash   CASTLE RUSHEN   Derbyhaven
            Port   SCARLETT   NAUTICAL MUS
            St Mary   VISITOR CENTRE   OLD HOUSE OF KEYS
CREGNEASH VILLAGE   St Michael's I.
FOLK MUSEUM   Scarlett
128   Point   Dreswick Pt.   BELFAST
Calf of Man   Spanish Head   (April-Sept.)
                                            DUBLIN
Chicken Rock   (April-Sept. & Christmas)

0   2   4   6 miles
0   2   4   6   8   10 km

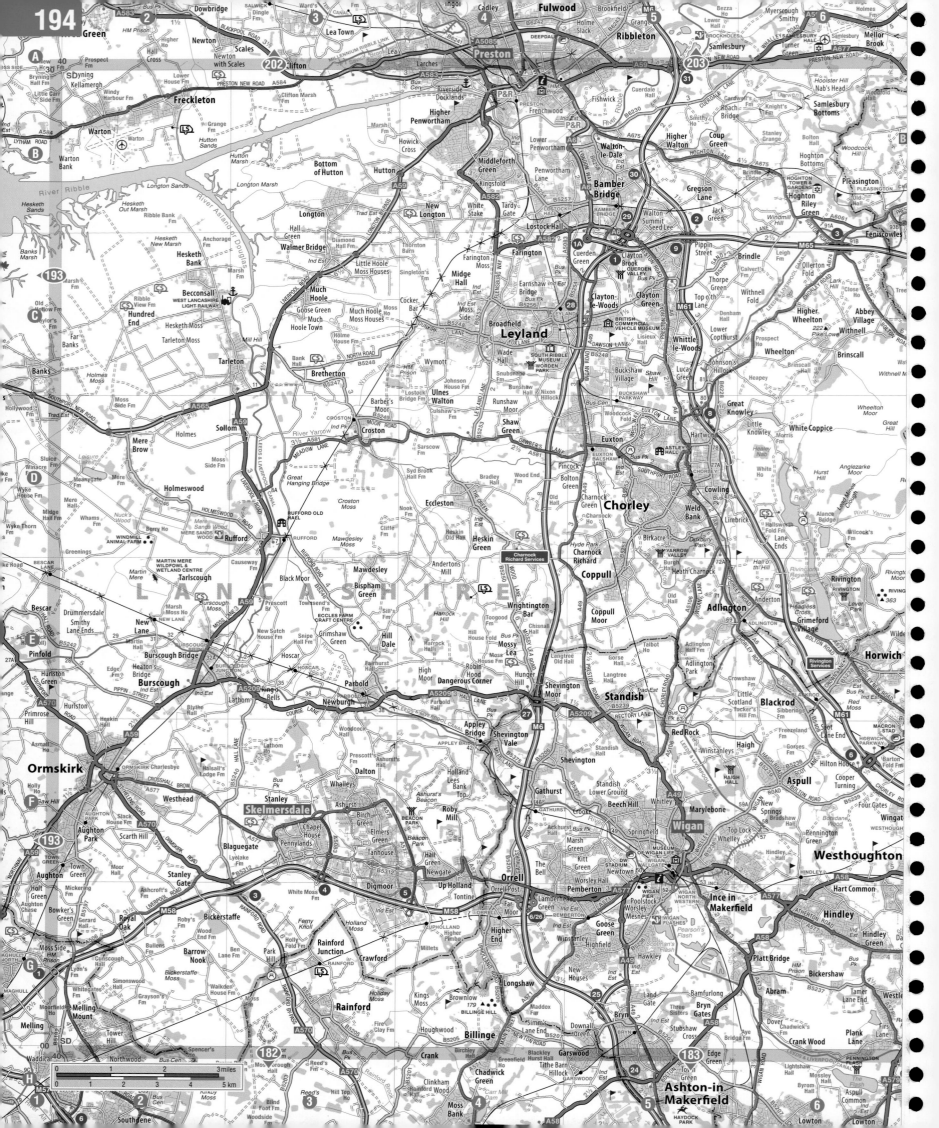

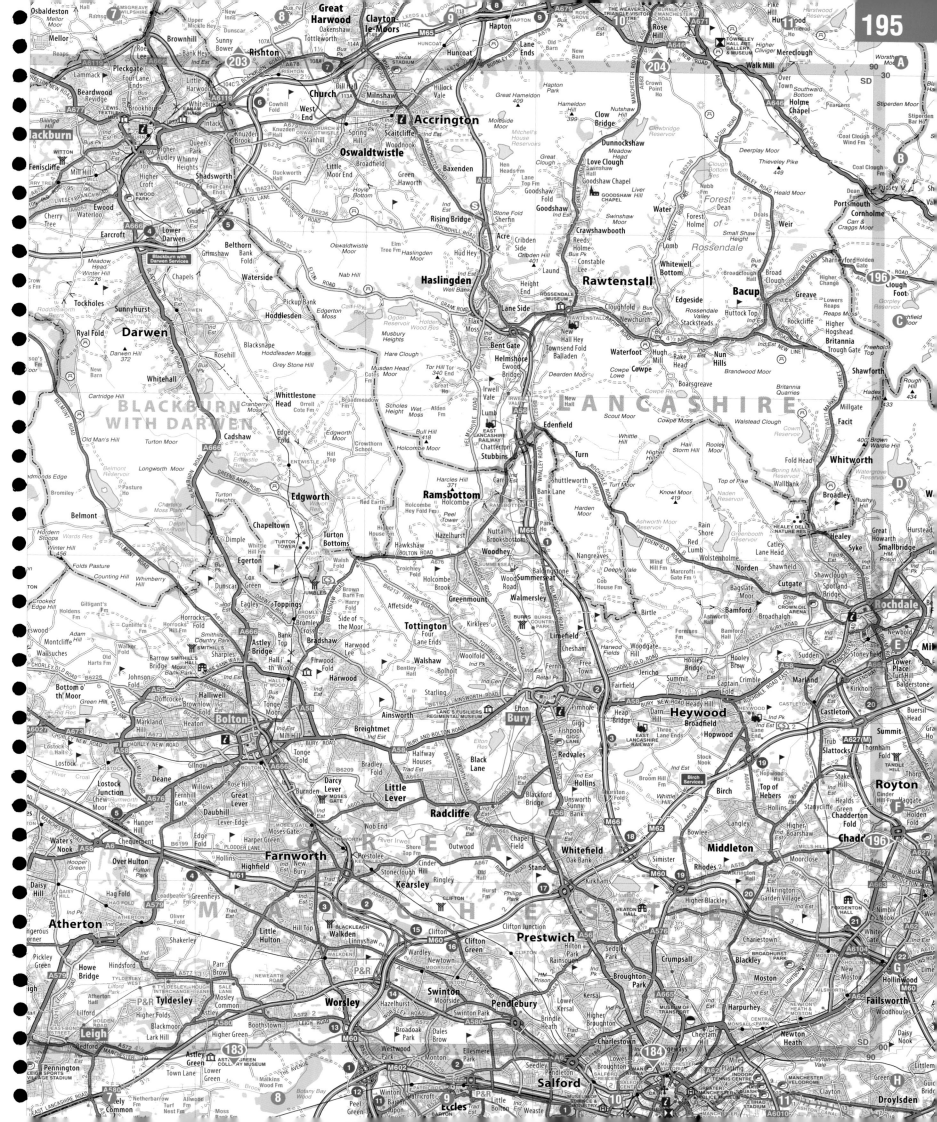

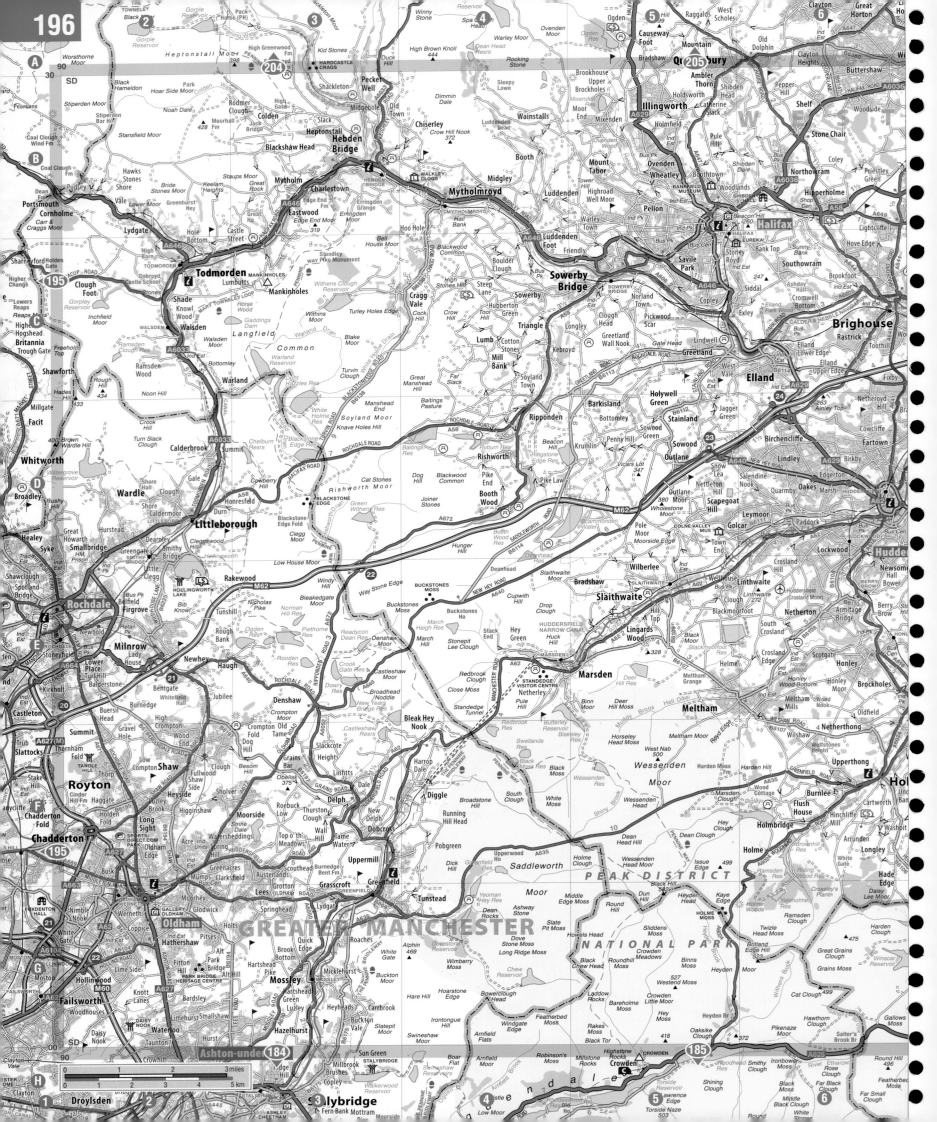

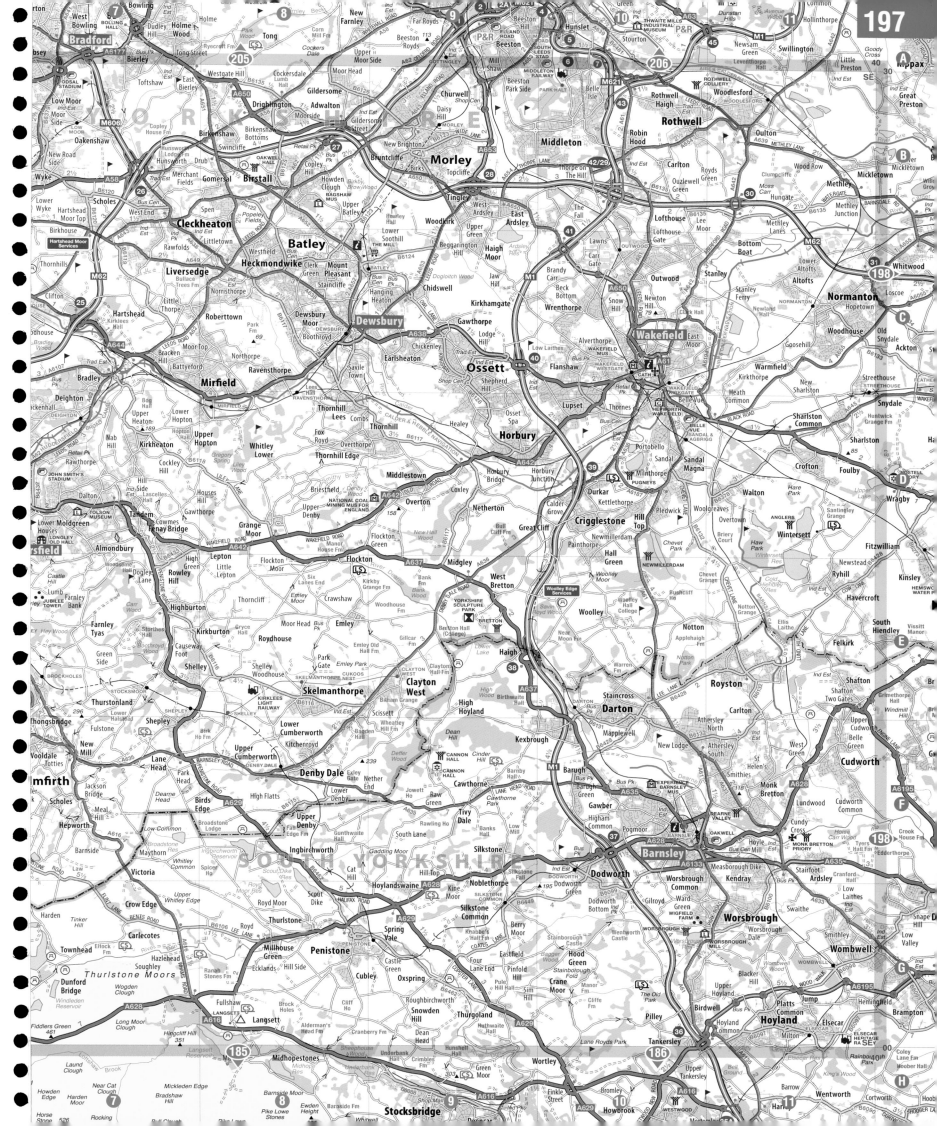

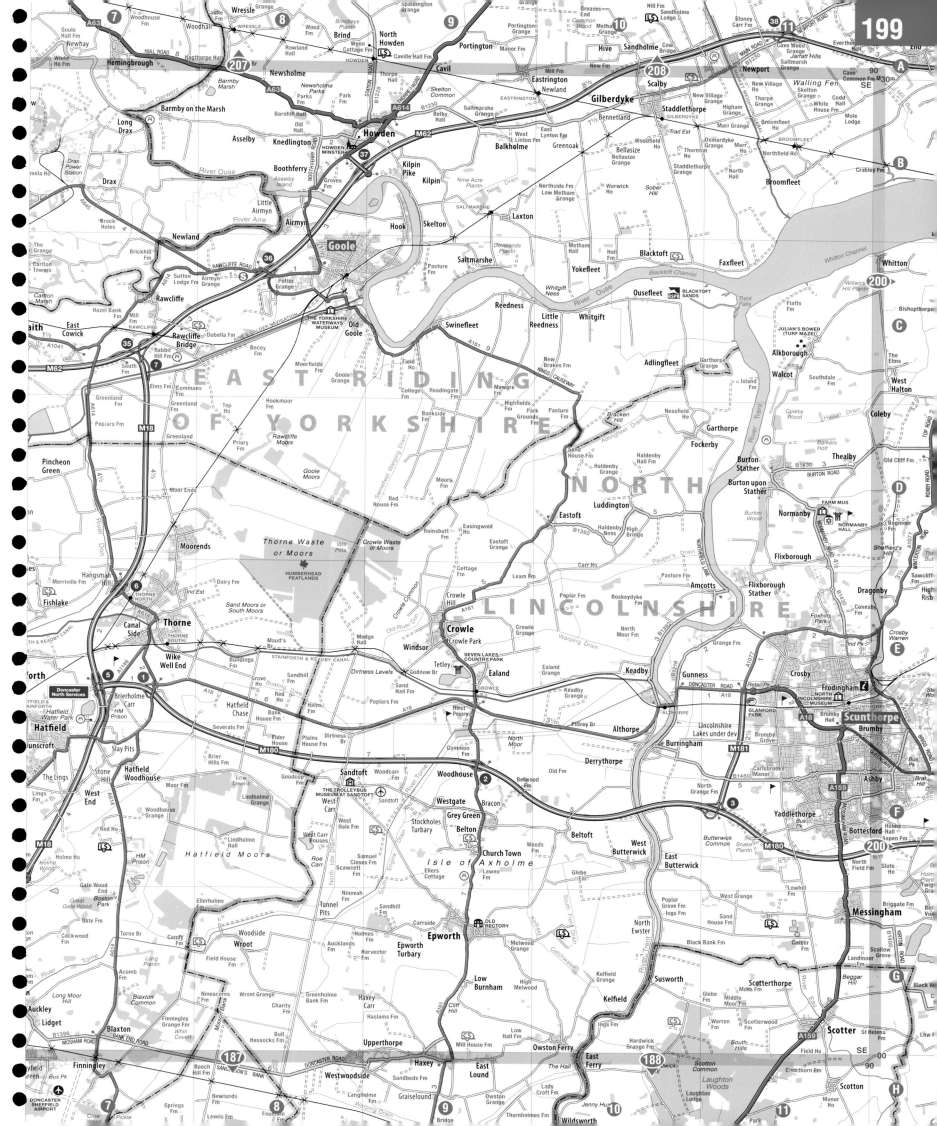

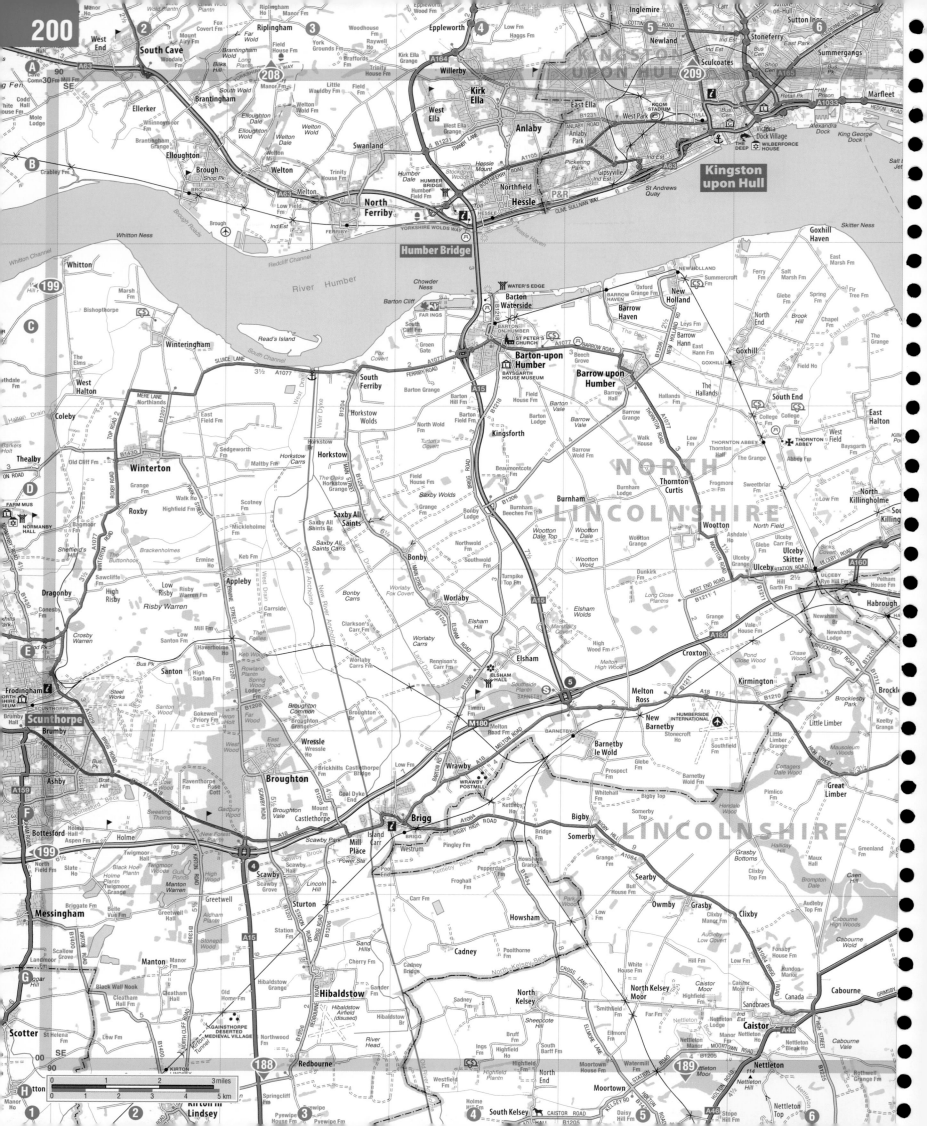

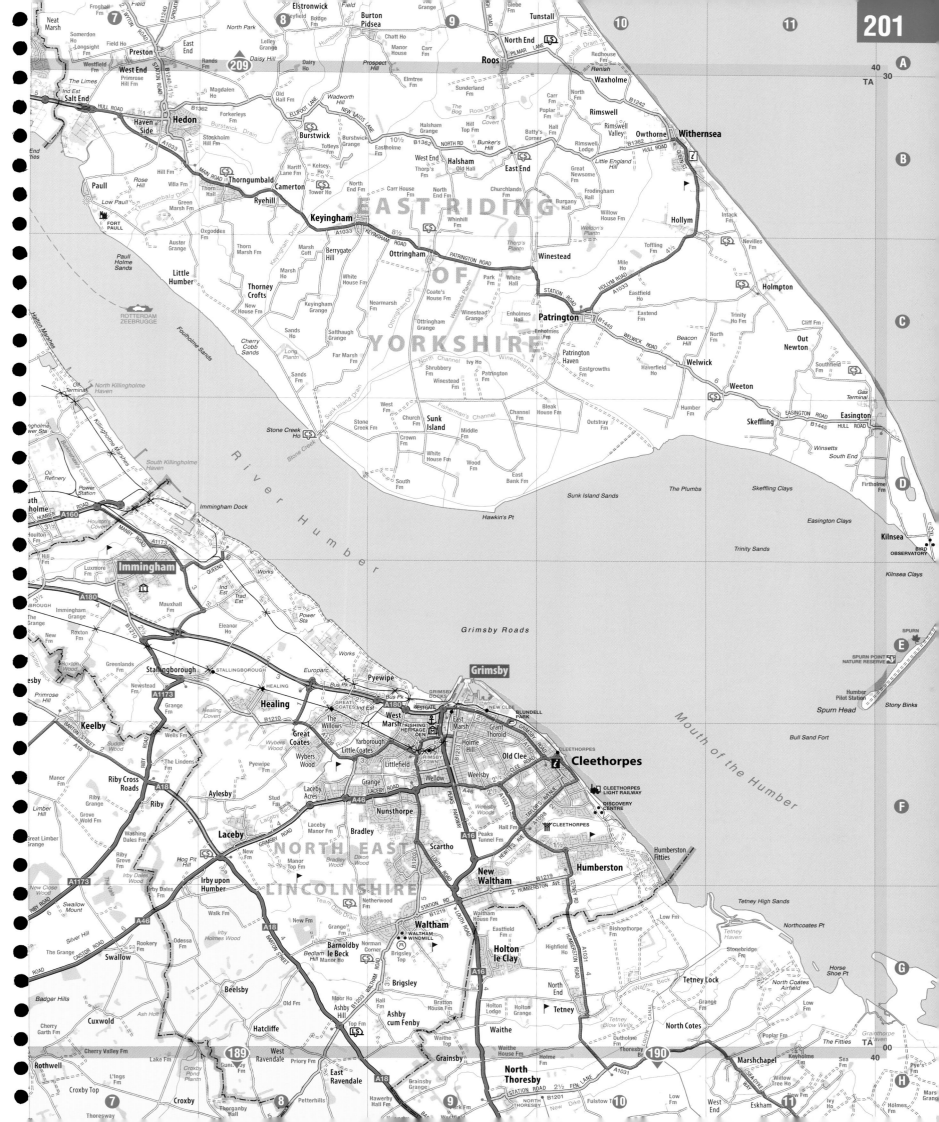

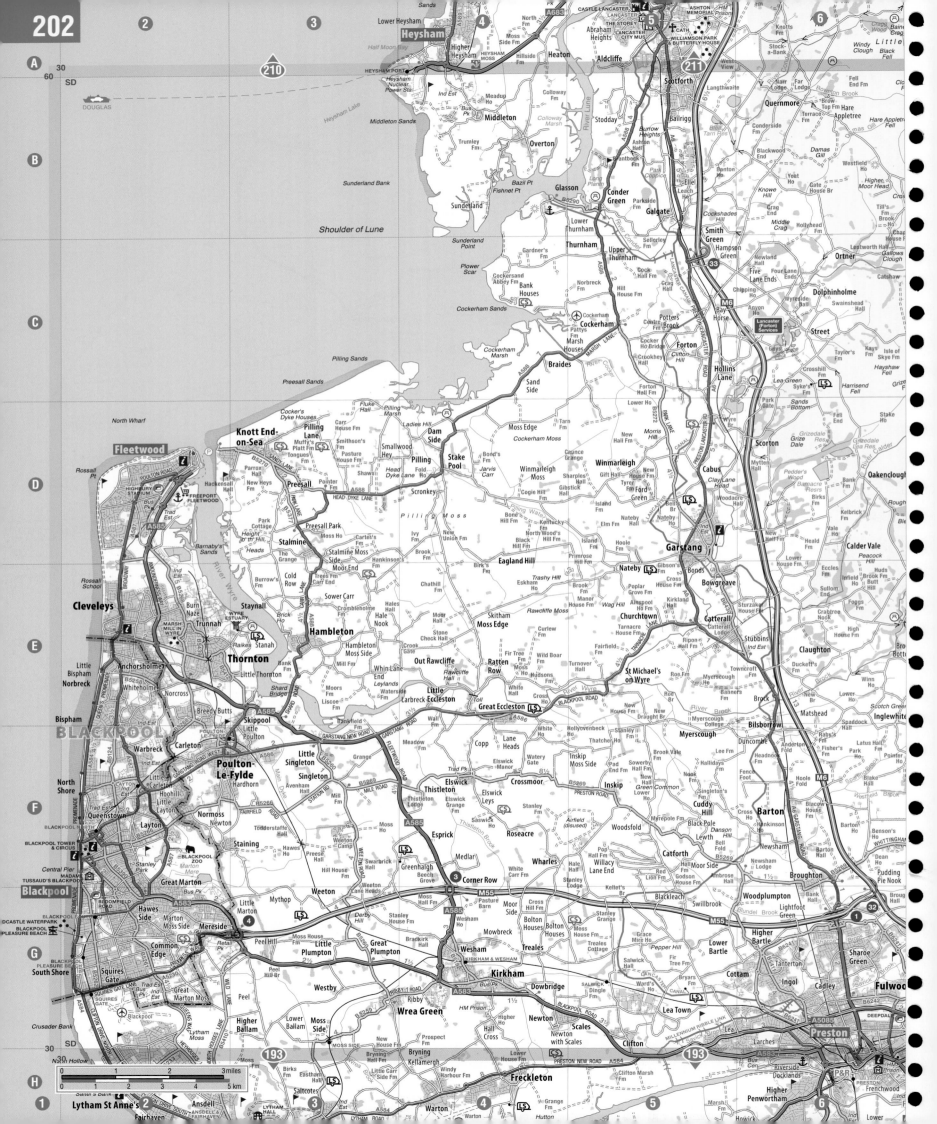

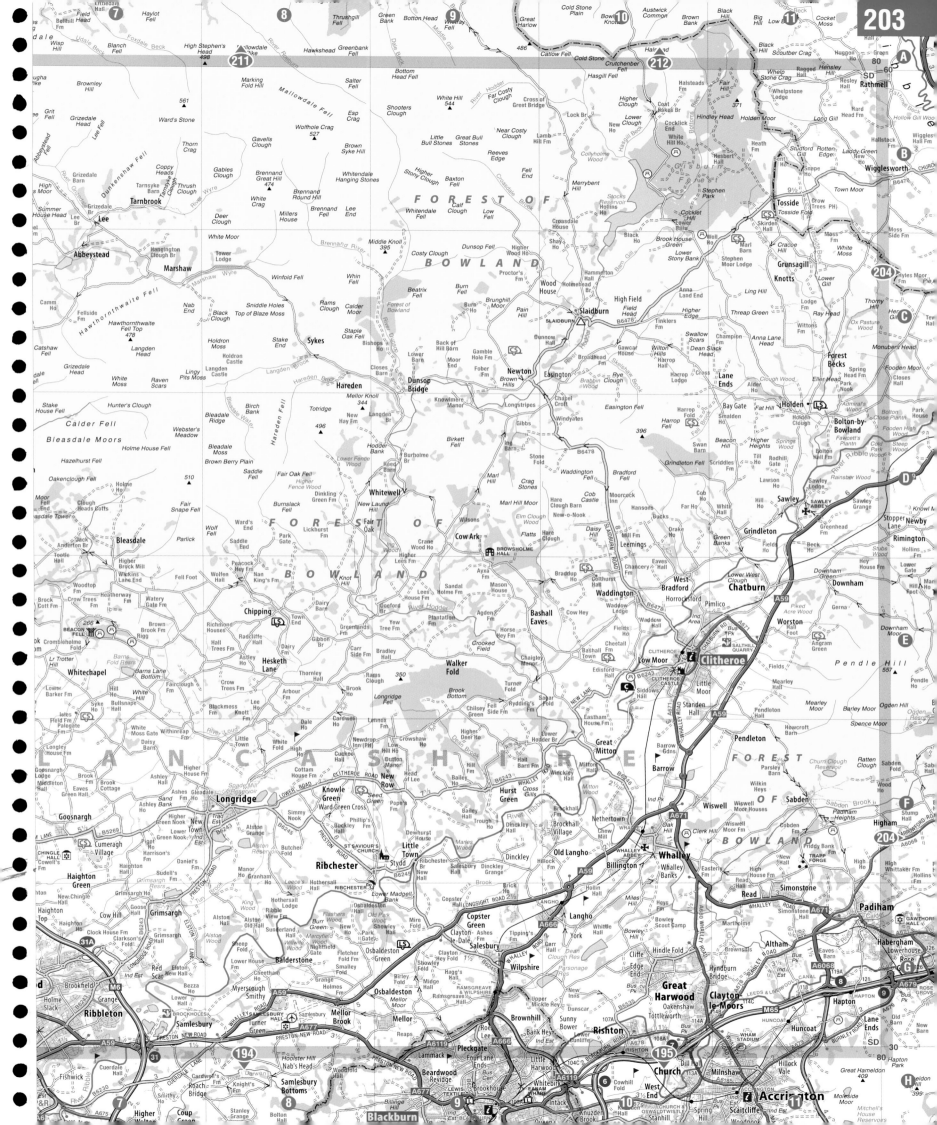

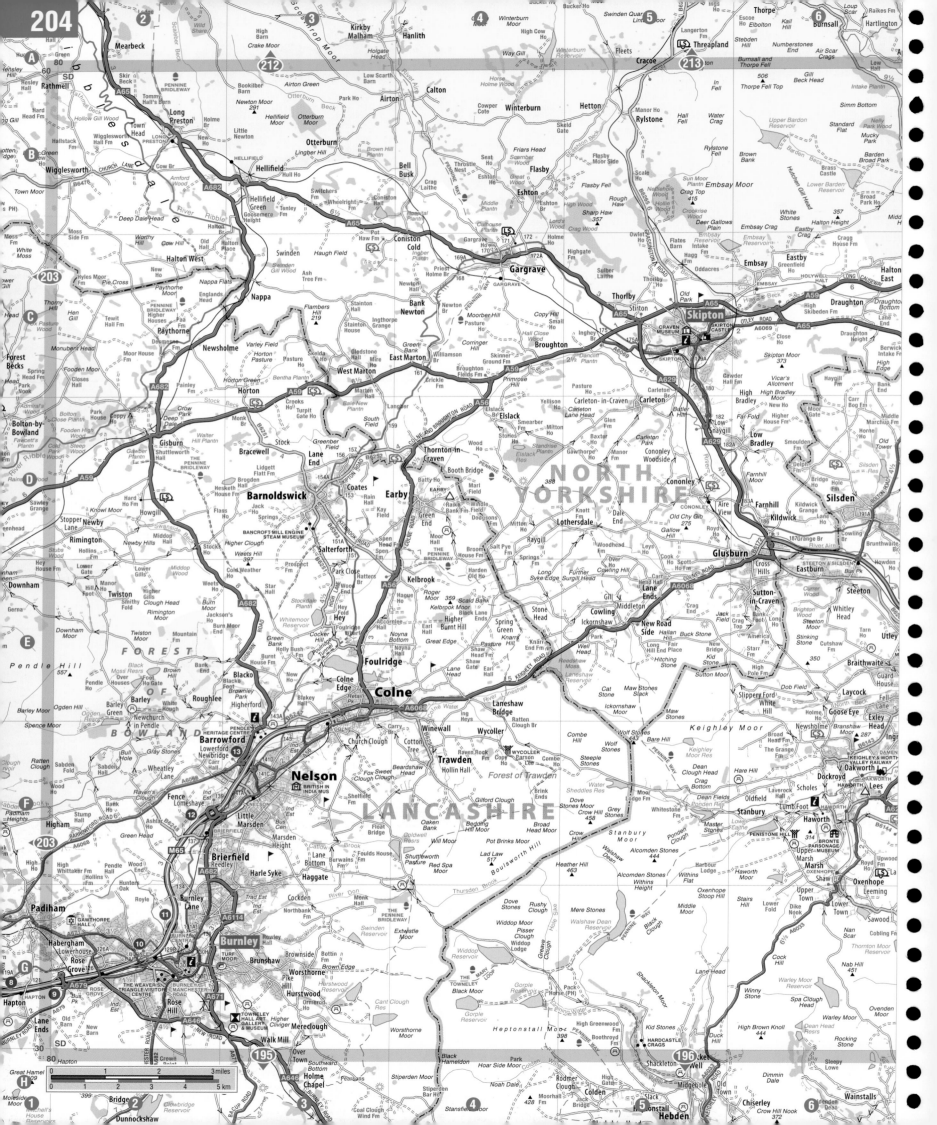

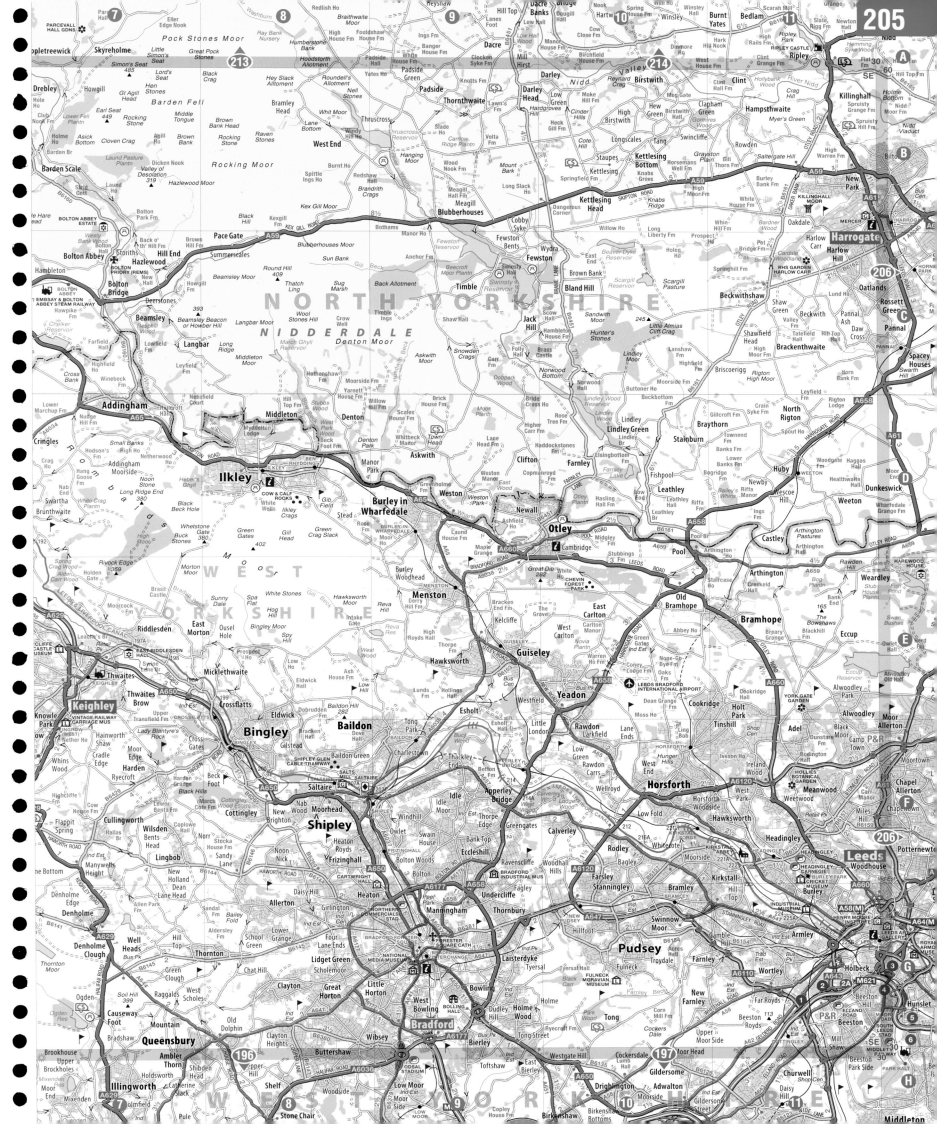

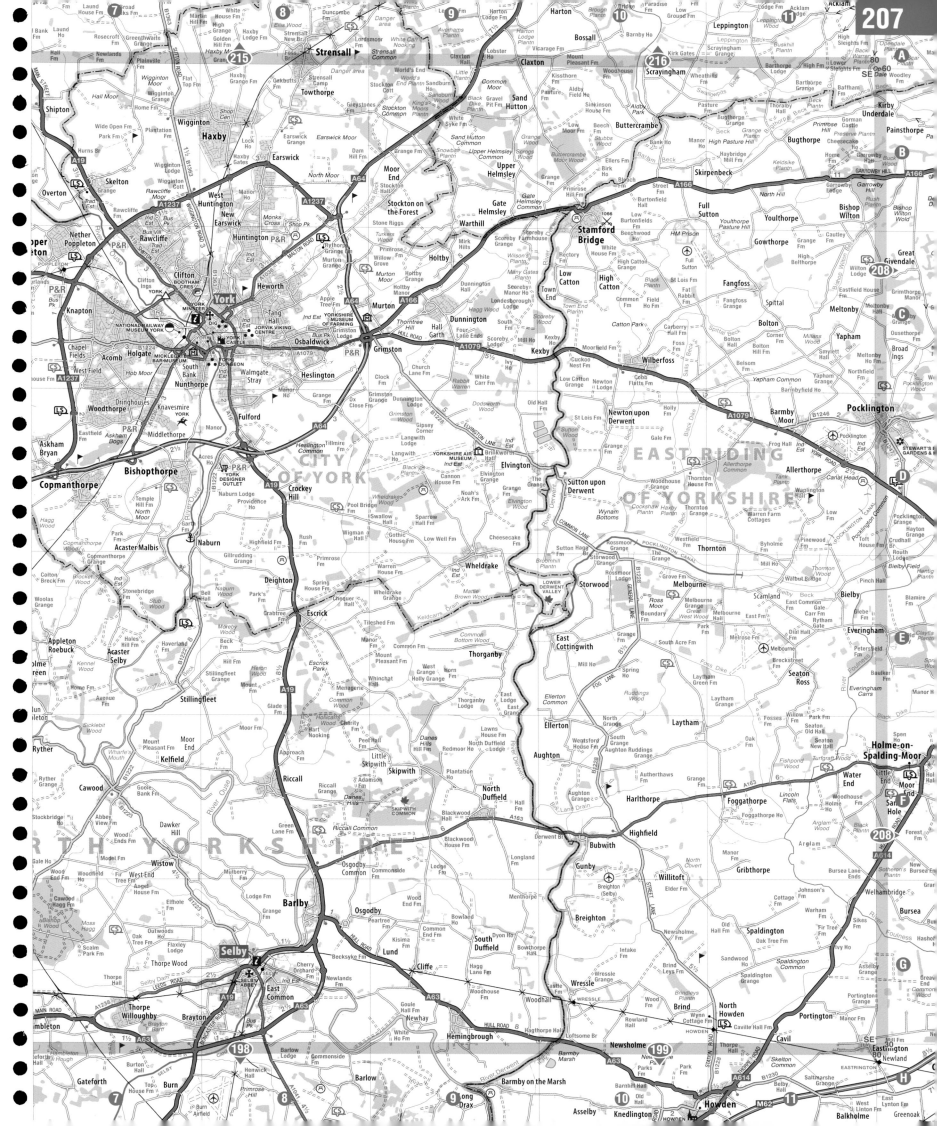

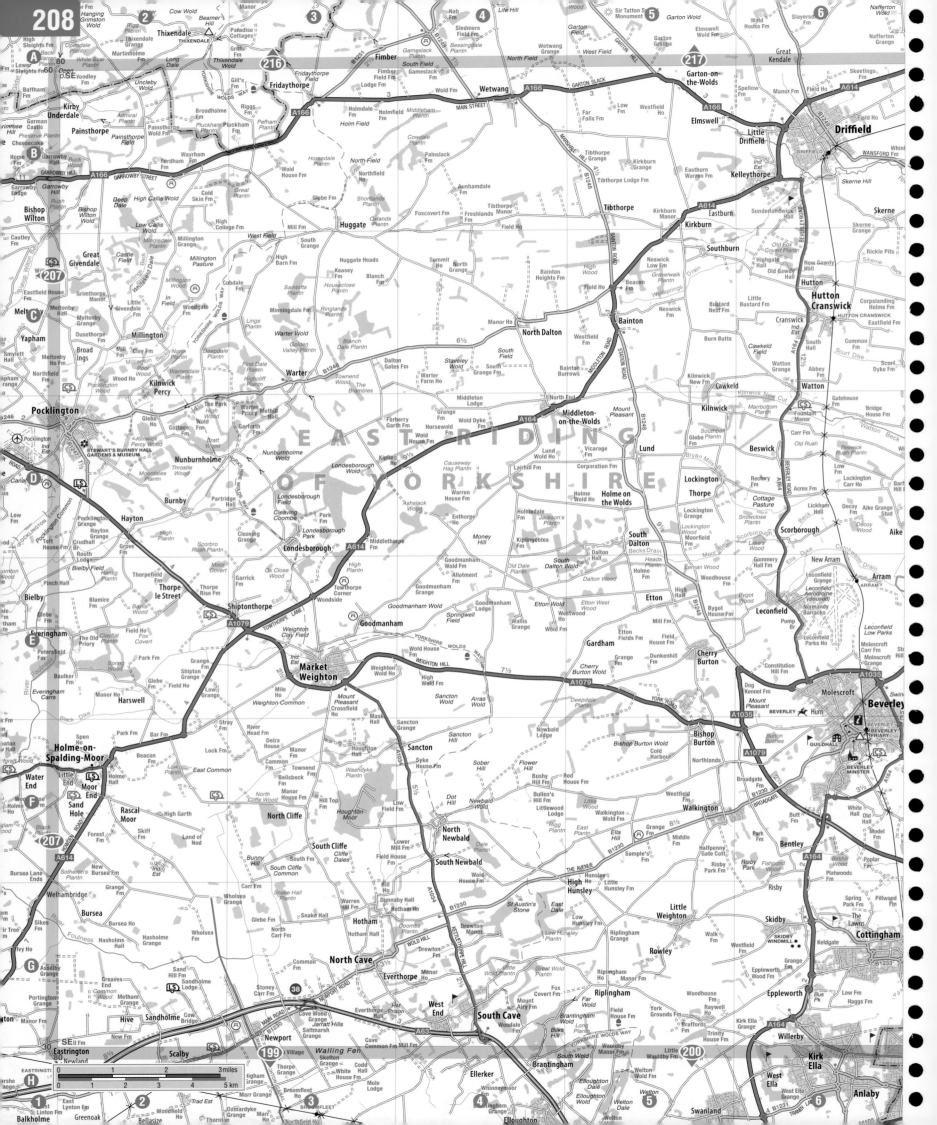

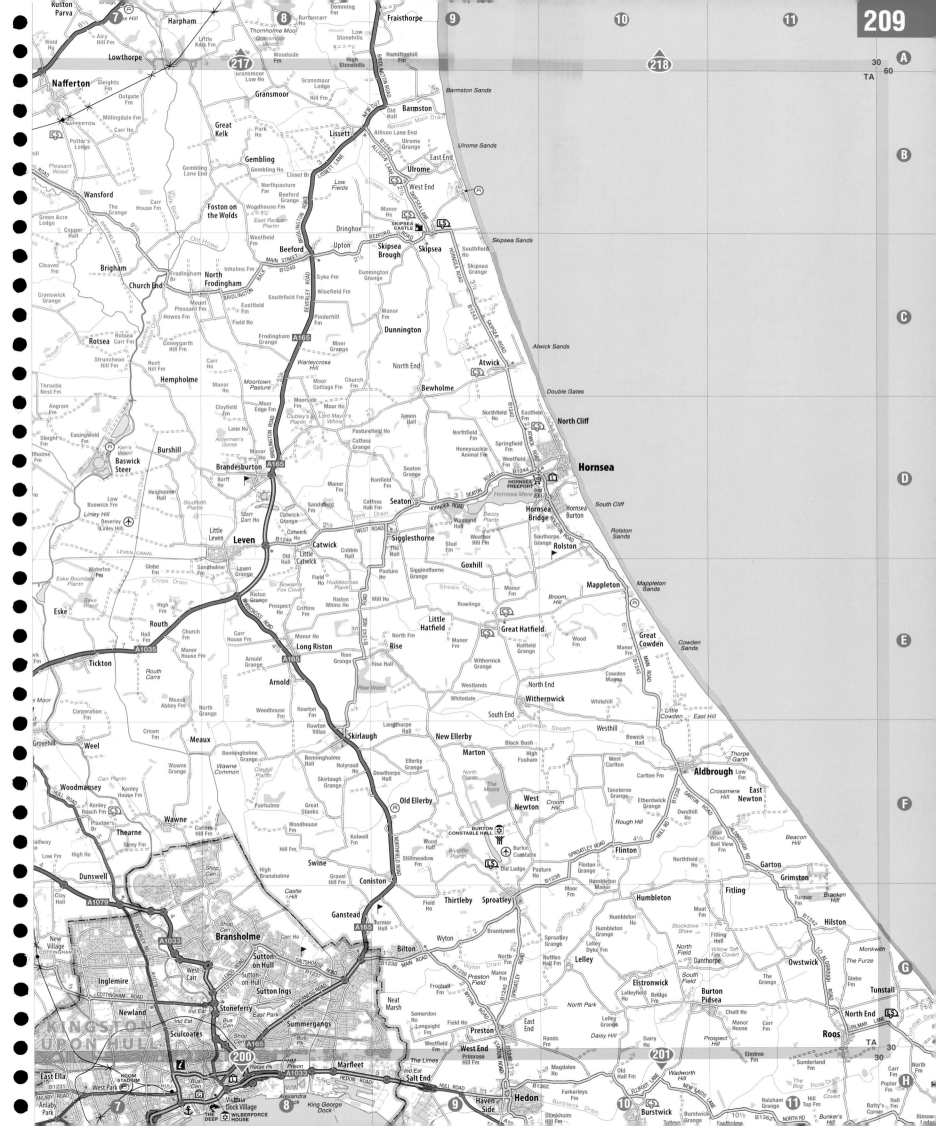

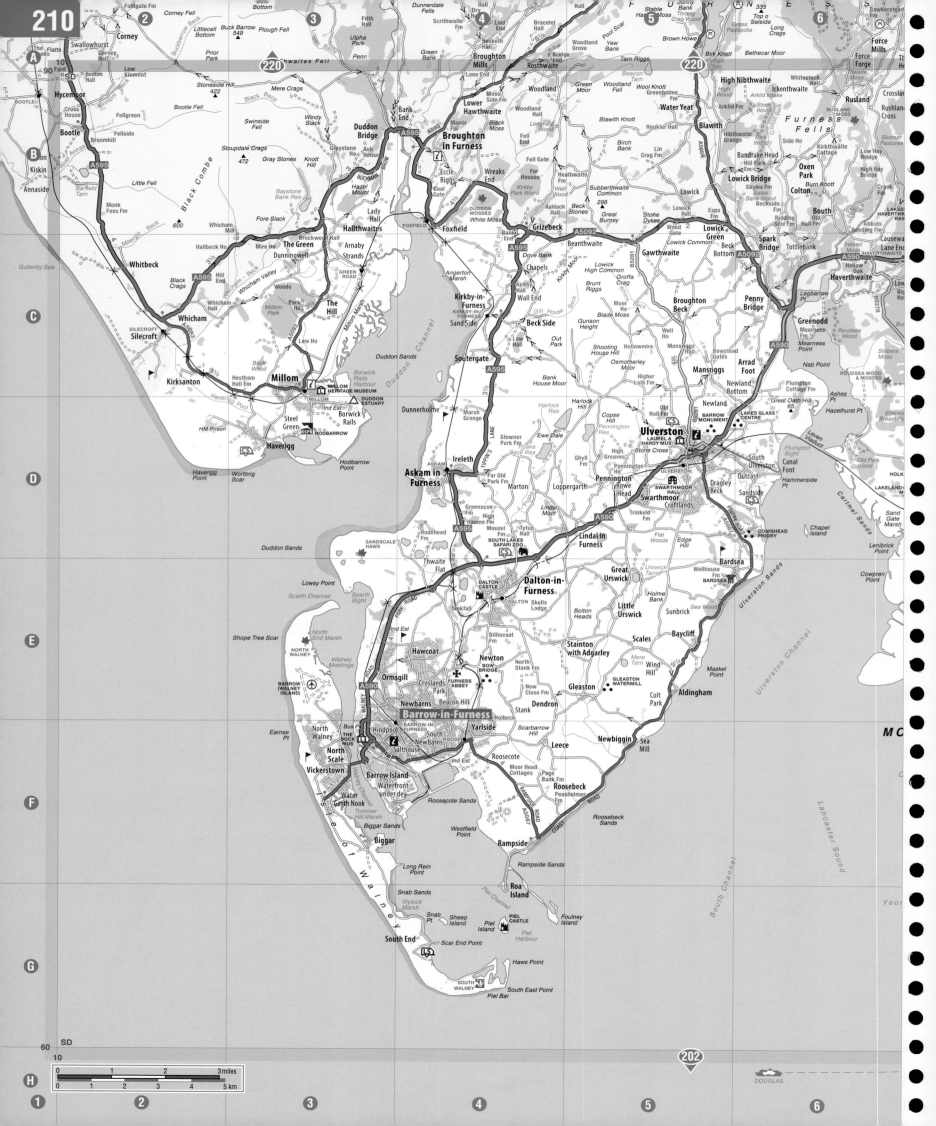

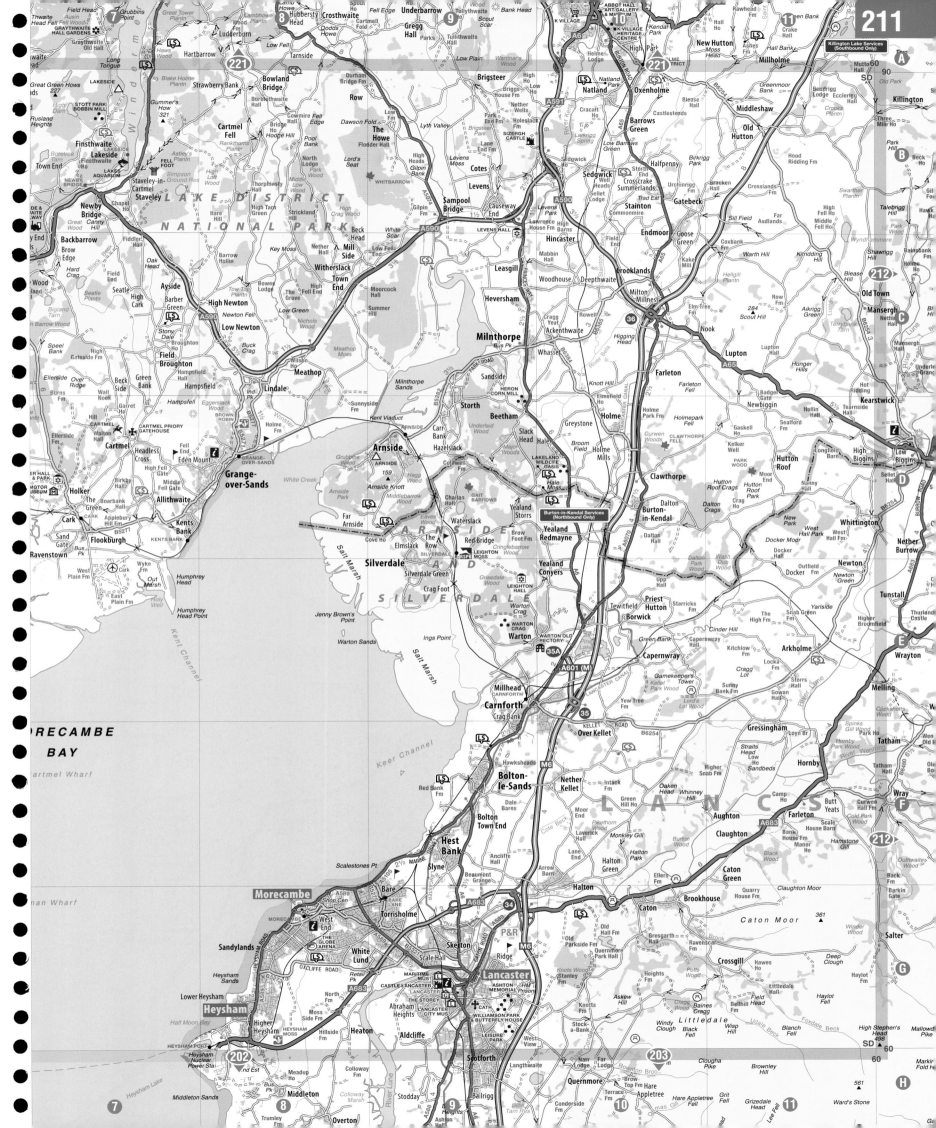

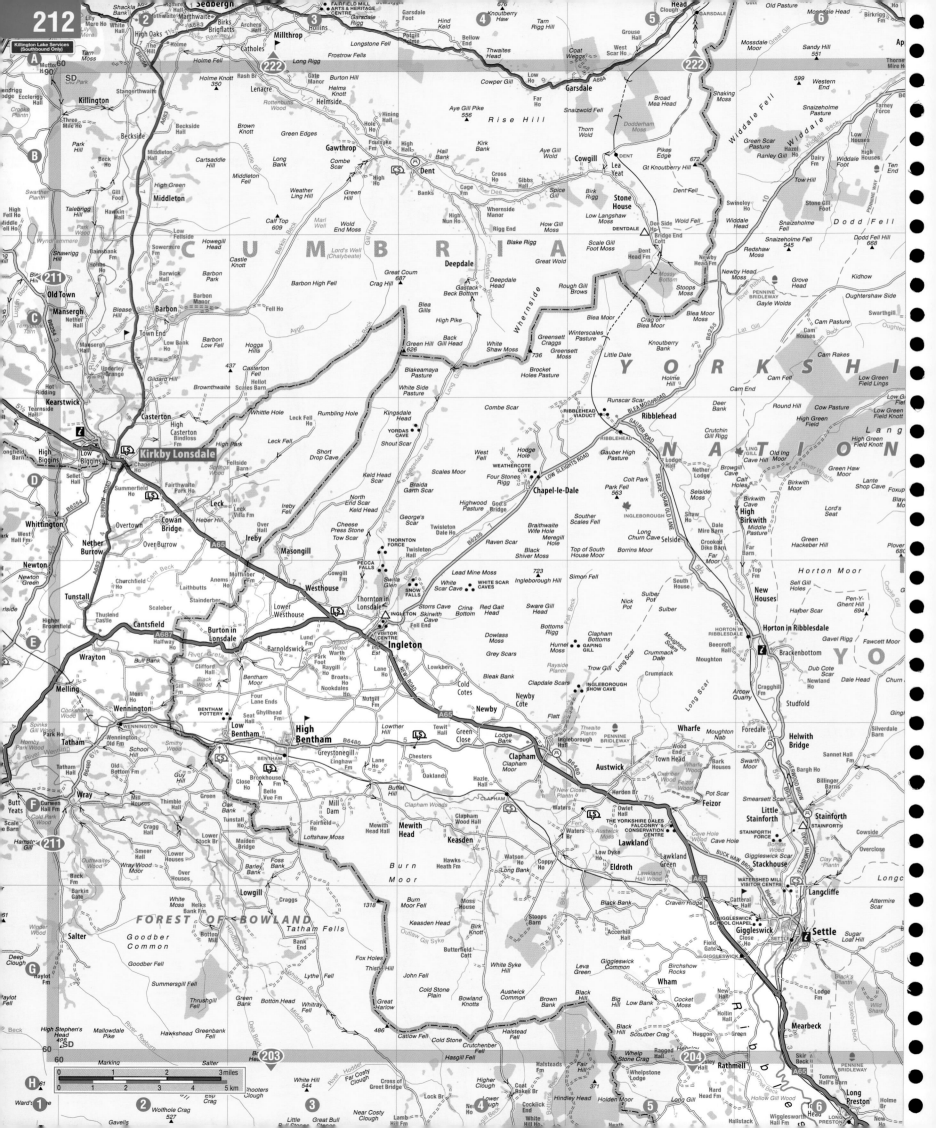

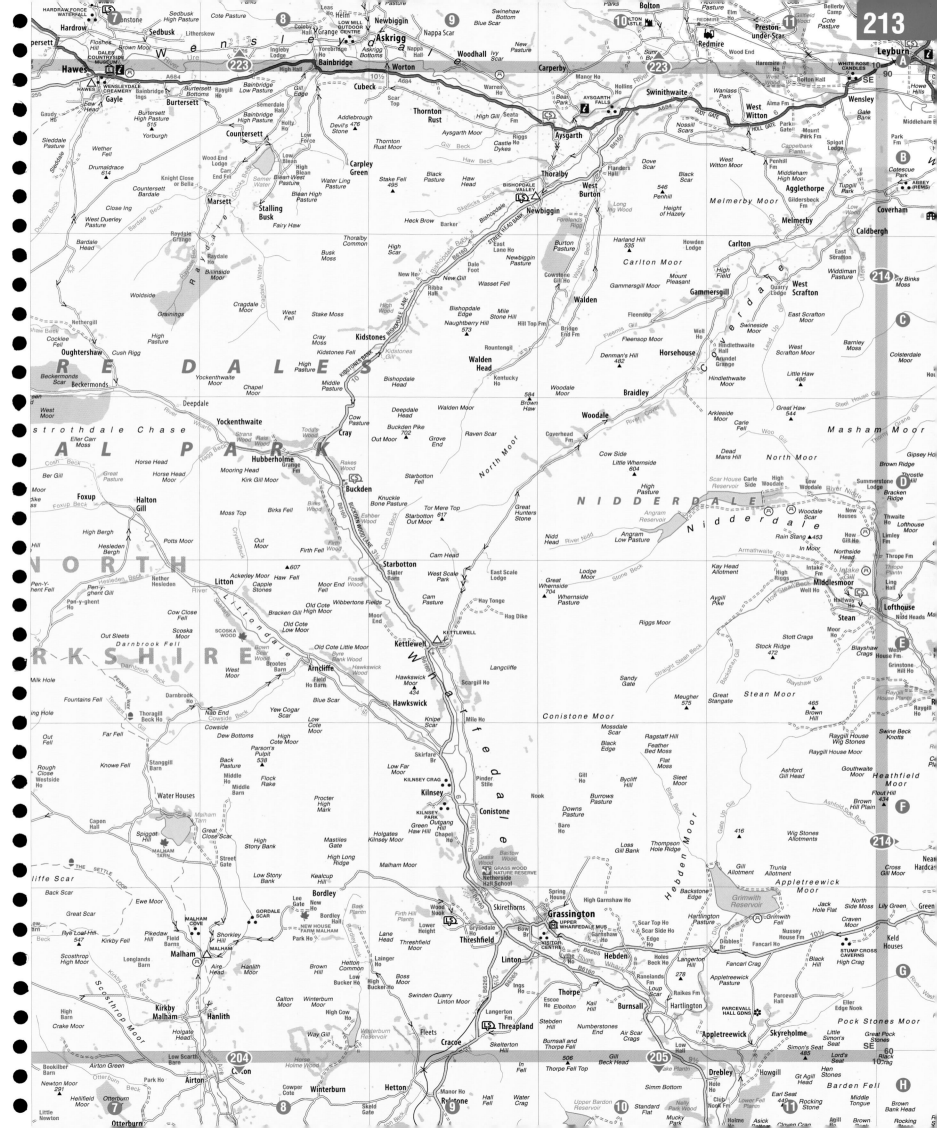

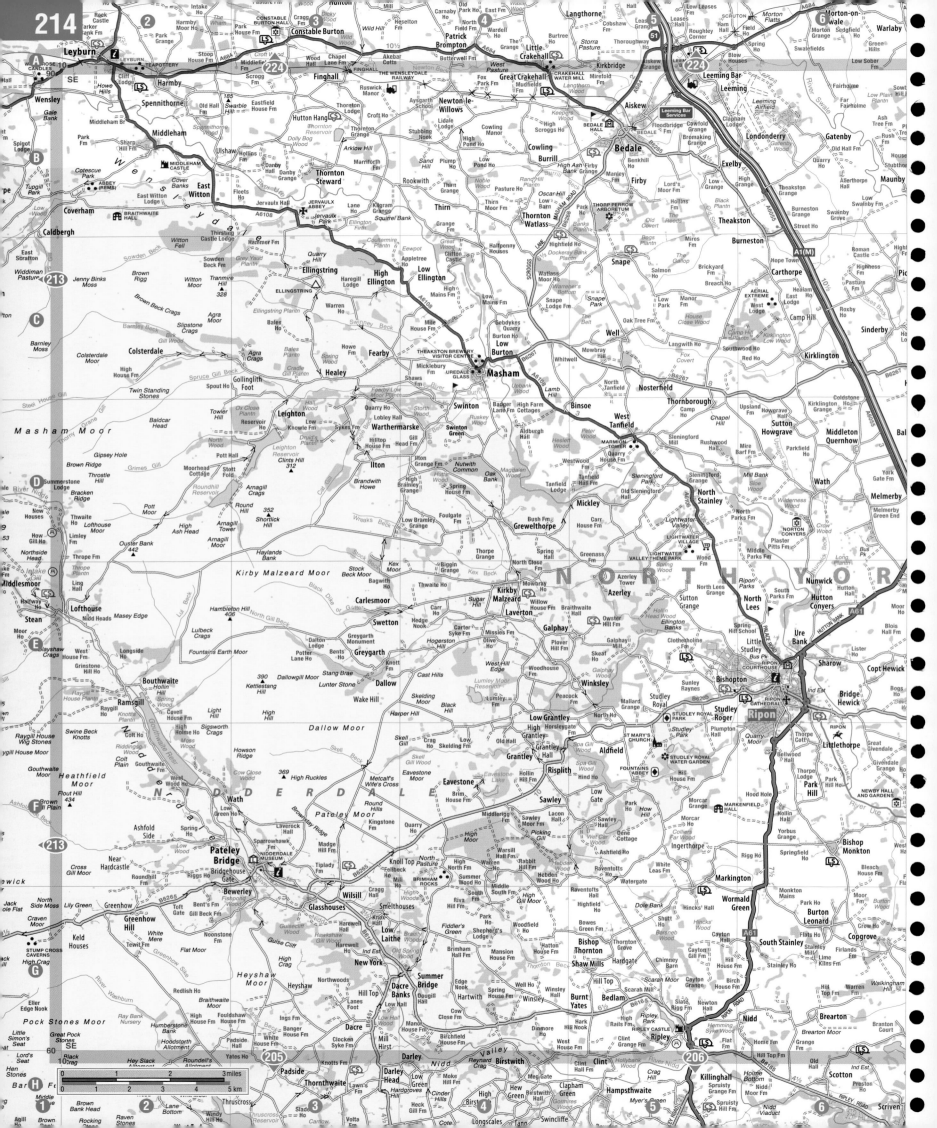

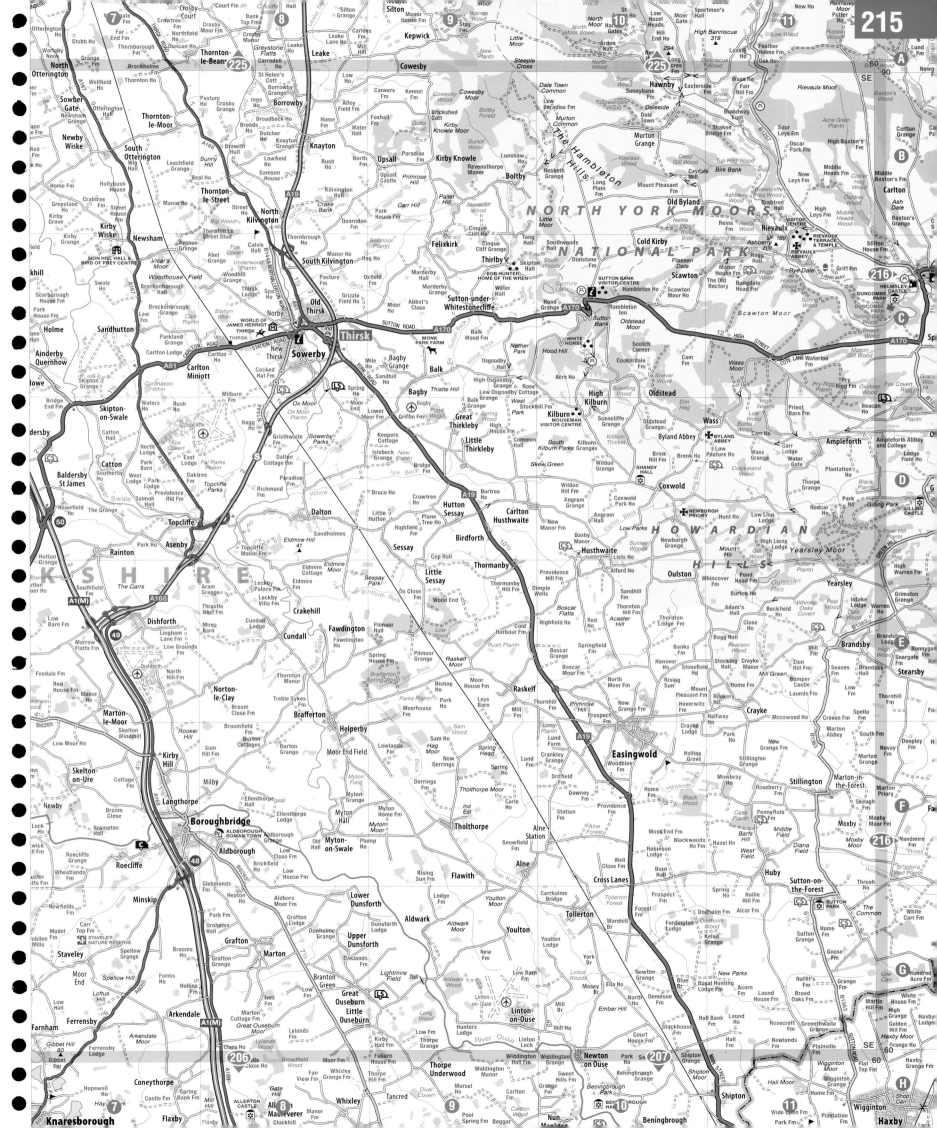

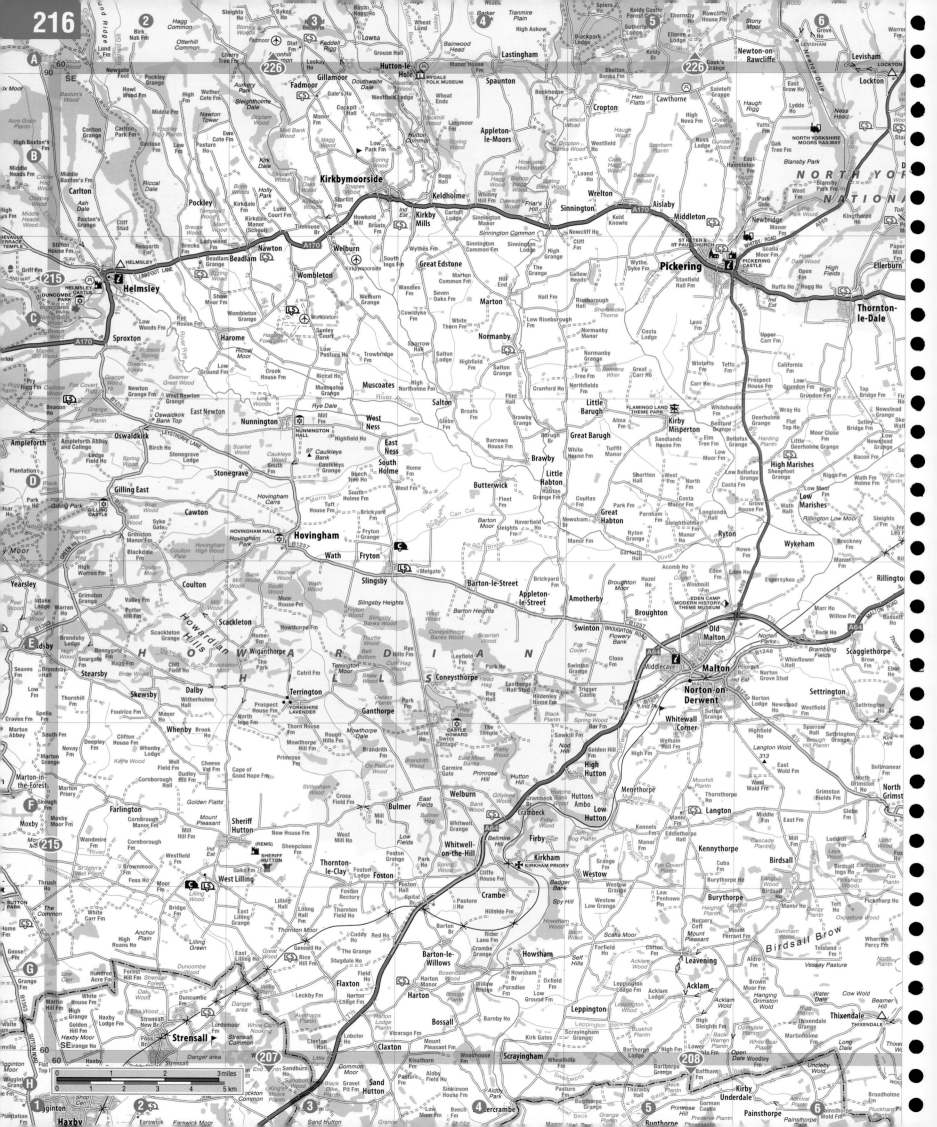

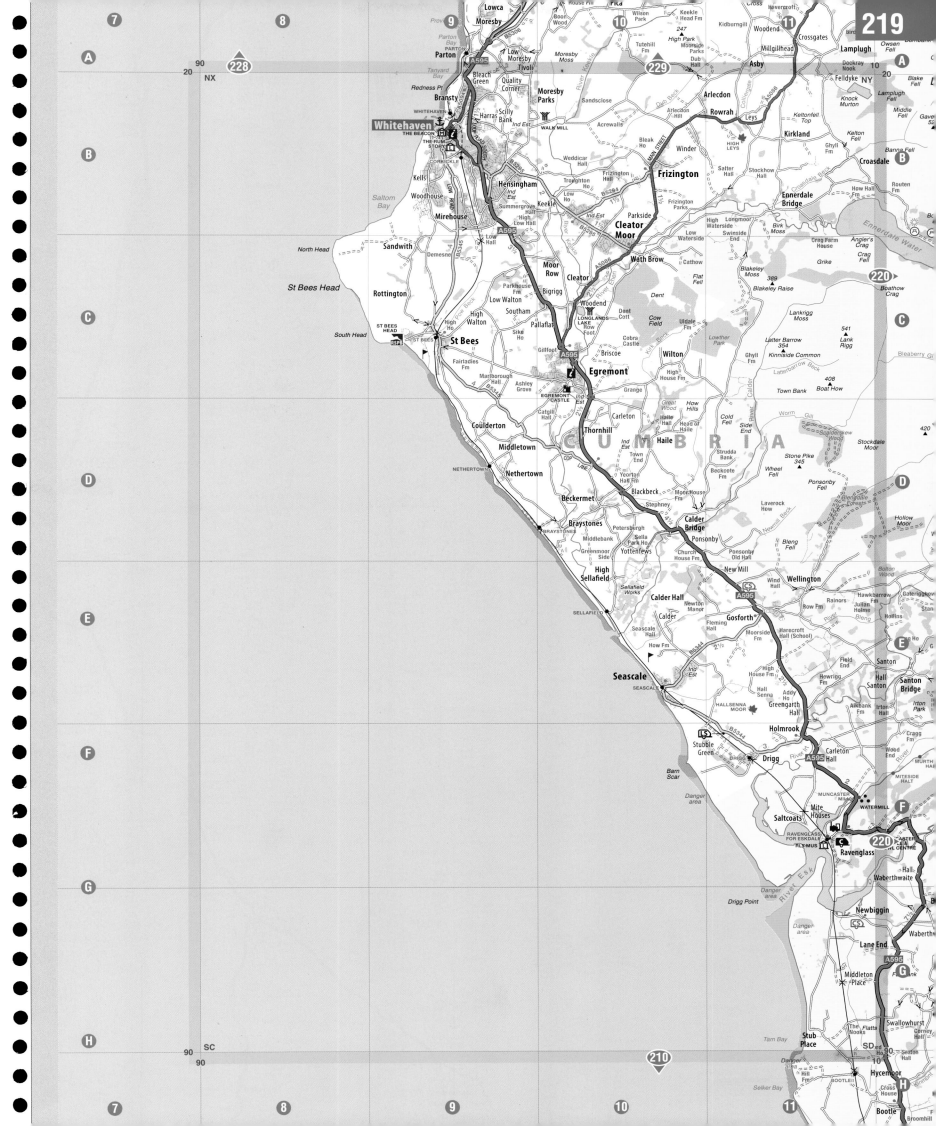

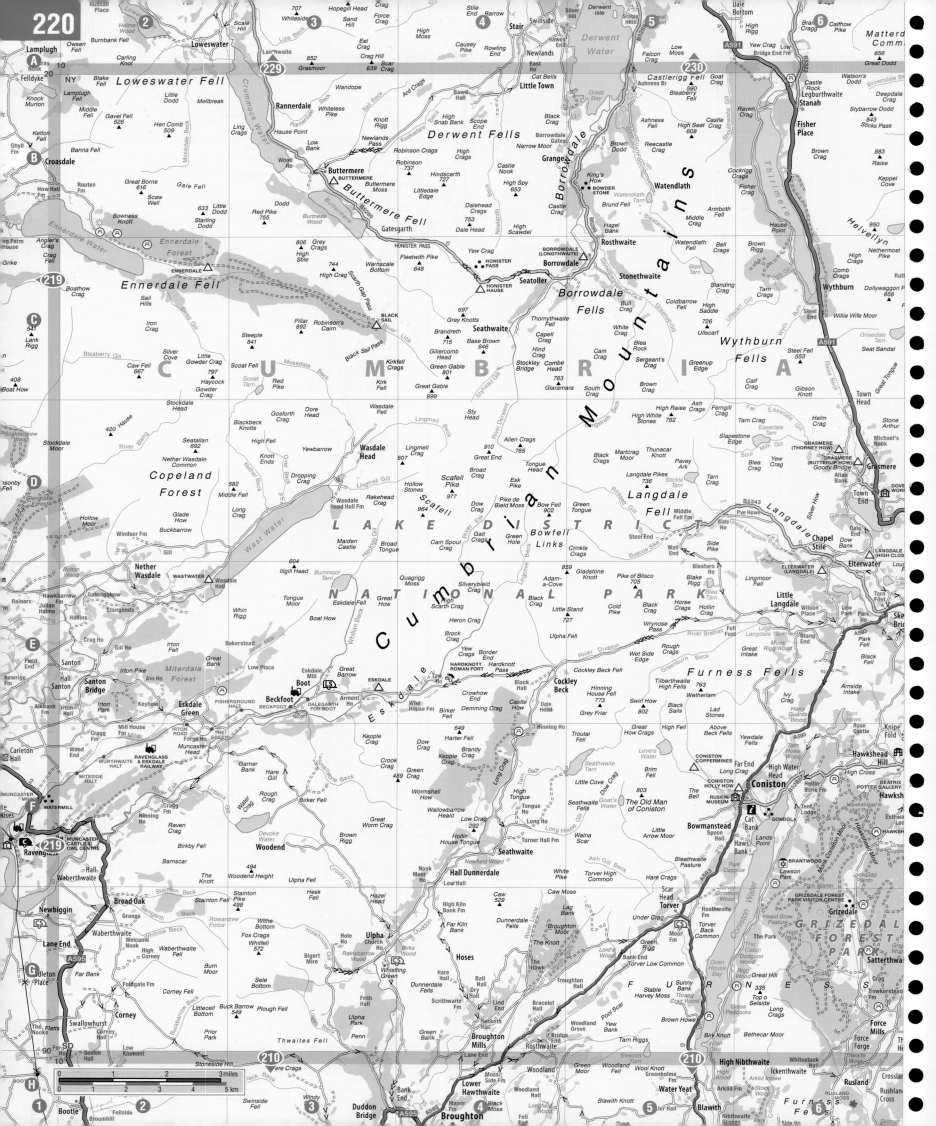

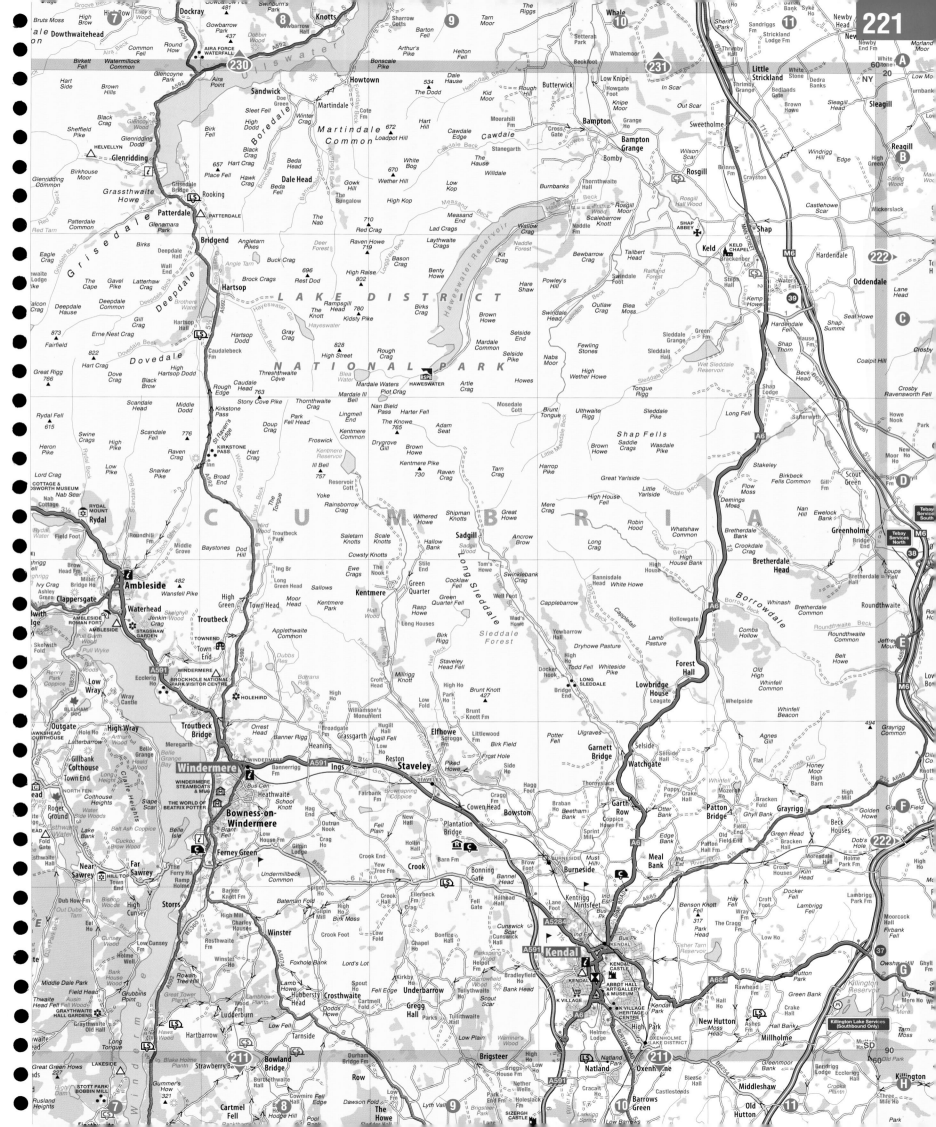

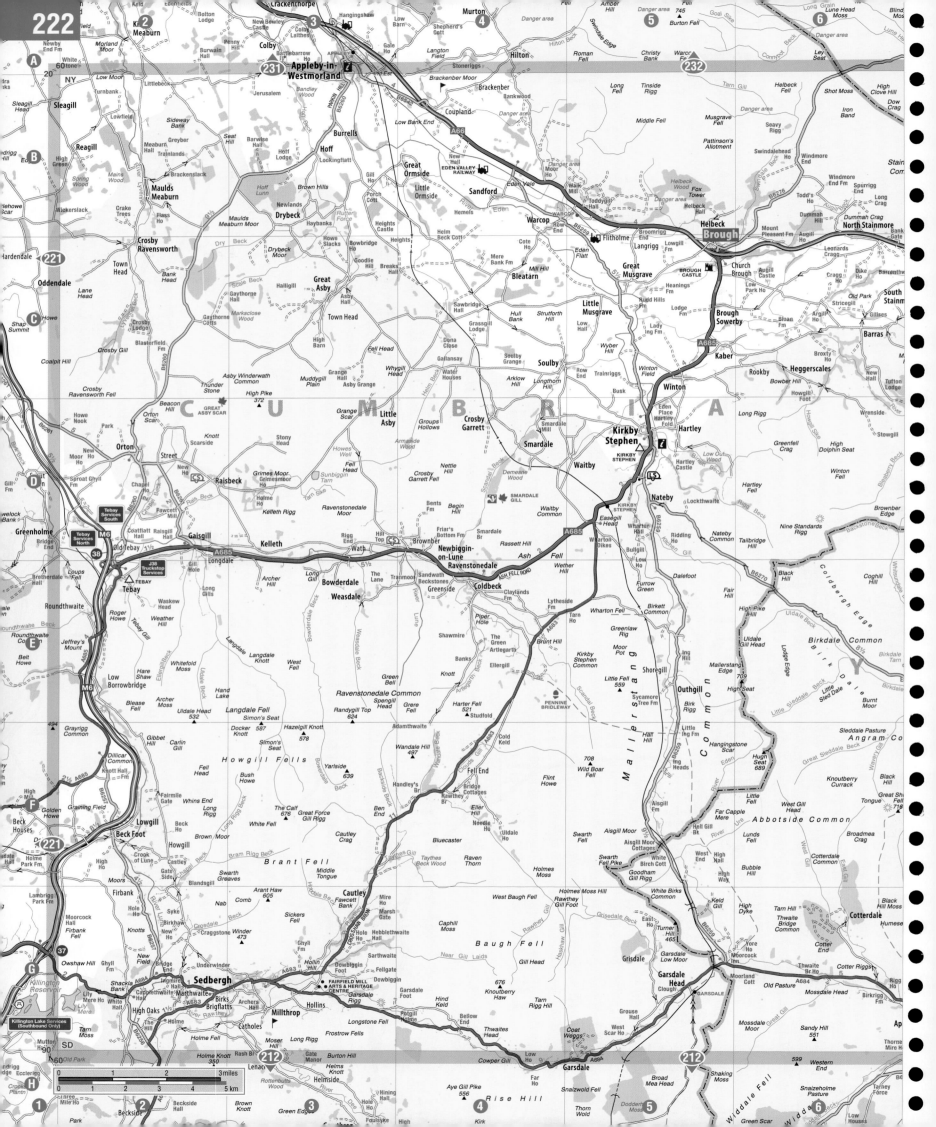

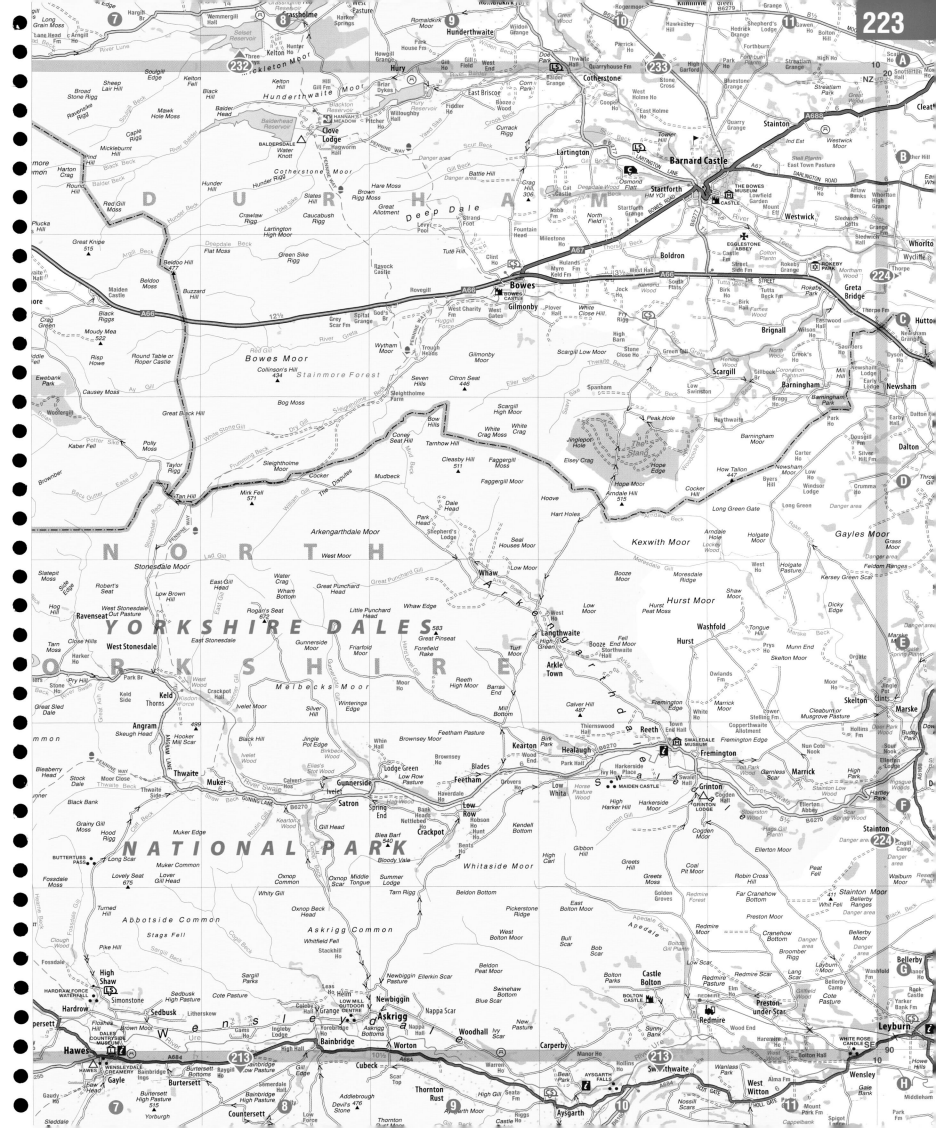

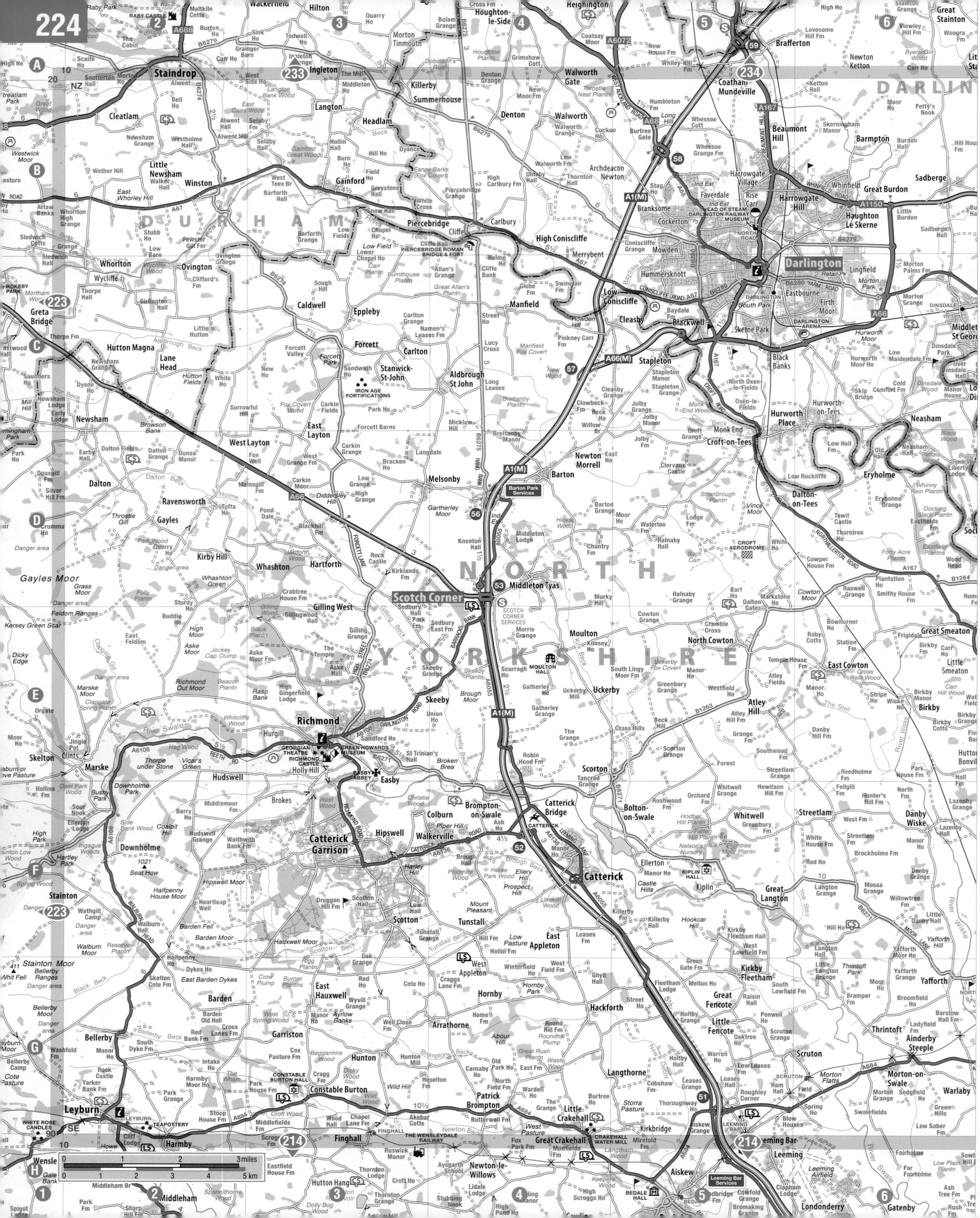
DURHAM
NORTH YORKSHIRE
DARLIN
Staindrop
Raby Castle
Ingleton
Killerby
Summerhouse
Headlam
Gainford
Cleatlam
Langton
Denton
Walworth
Walworth Gate
Heighington
Houghton-le-Side
Hilton
Winston
Little Newsham
Piercebridge
Piercebridge Roman Bridge & Fort
Cliffe
Carlbury
High Coniscliffe
Merrybent
Coatham Mundeville
Brafferton
Great Stainton
Newton Ketton
Beaumont Hill
Barmpton
Harrowgate Village
Harrowgate Hill
Whinfield
Great Burdon
Sadberge
Haughton Le Skerne
Branksome
Faverdale
Cockerton
Mowden
Hummersknott
Darlington
Head of Steam Darlington Railway Museum
Lingfield
Eastbourne
Firth Moor
Skerne Park
Low Coniscliffe
Cleasby
Blackwell
Stapleton
Manfield
Whorlton
Wycliffe
Ovington
Rokeby Park
Greta Bridge
Caldwell
Eppleby
Forcett
Carlton
Stanwick-St-John
Iron Age Fortifications
Aldbrough St John
Hutton Magna
Lane Head
Newsham
East Layton
West Layton
Melsonby
Barton
Barton Park Services
Newton Morrell
Croft-on-Tees
Hurworth Place
Hurworth-on-Tees
Neasham
Eryholme
Dalton-on-Tees
Croft Aerodrome
Dalton
Ravensworth
Gayles
Gayles Moor
Kirby Hill
Whashton
Hartforth
Middleton Tyas
Scotch Corner
Scotch Corner Services
Gilling West
Moulton
North Cowton
East Cowton
Great Smeaton
Little Smeaton
Uckerby
Atley Hill
Birkby
Skeeby
Richmond
Georgian Theatre
Richmond Castle
Green Howards Museum
Easby Abbey
Easby
Holly Hill
Hurgill
Marske
Skelton
Hudswell
Brompton-on-Swale
Catterick Bridge
Scorton
Bolton-on-Swale
Colburn
Hipswell
Walkerville
Catterick Garrison
Catterick
Kiplin Hall
Kiplin
Great Langton
Streetlam
Danby Wiske
Downholme
Stainton
Scotton
Tunstall
East Appleton
Kirkby Fleetham
Great Fencote
Little Fencote
Yafforth
Barden
East Hauxwell
Hornby
Hackforth
Garriston
Arrathorne
Bellerby
Hunton
Langthorne
Scruton
Thrintoft
Ainderby Steeple
Morton-on-Swale
Warlaby
Constable Burton Hall
Constable Burton
Patrick Brompton
Little Crakehall
Great Crakehall
Crakehall Water Mill
Kirkbridge
Leyburn
Harmby
Finghall
The Wensleydale Railway
Newton-le-Willows
Aiskew
Leeming Bar
Leeming Bar Services
Leeming
Londonderry
Gatenby
Bedale Hall
Middleham
Spennithorne
White Rose Candles
Teapottery
Wensley
A688
A67
A66
A66(M)
A1(M)
A68
A167
A6072
A1150
A6055
A6108
A6136
A684
A6136
B6274
B6279
B6275
B6280
B1263
B6271
B1264
0 1 2 3 miles
0 1 2 3 4 5 km

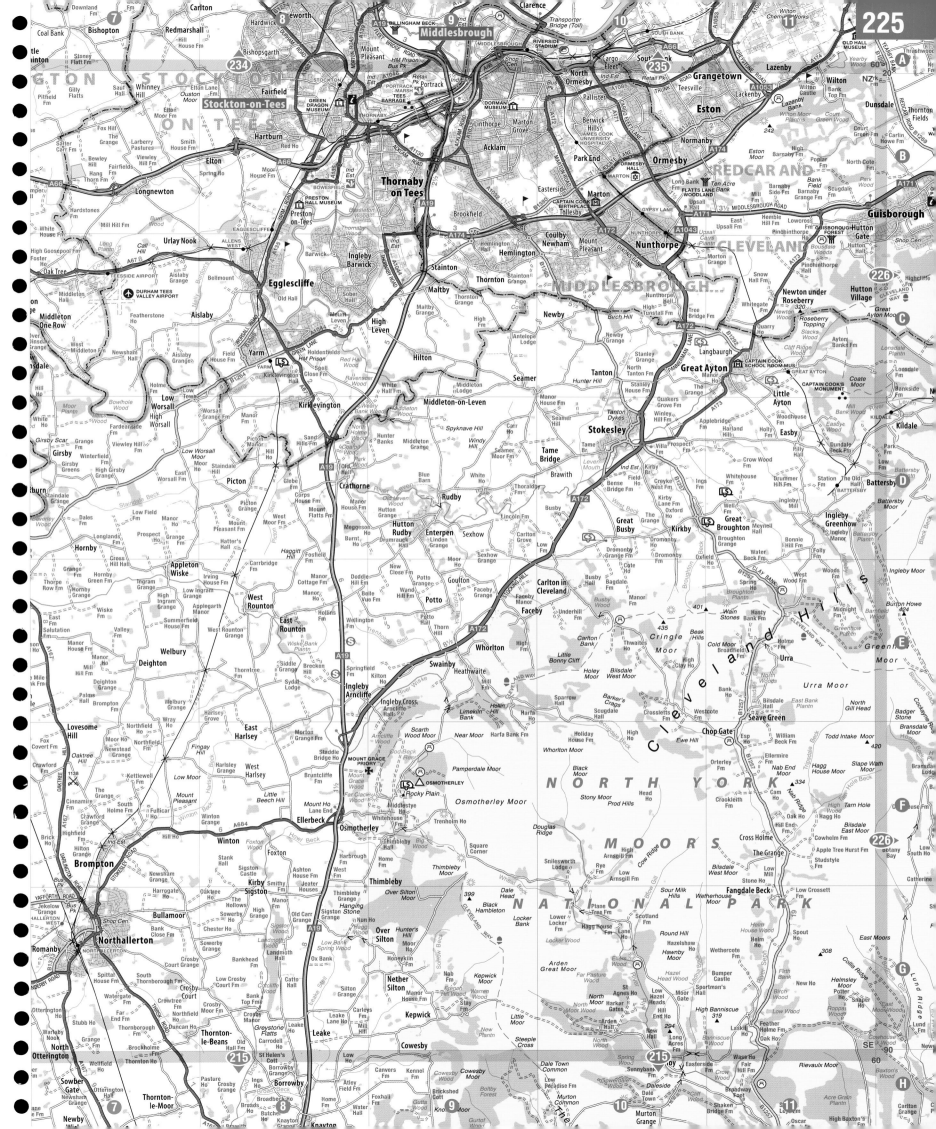

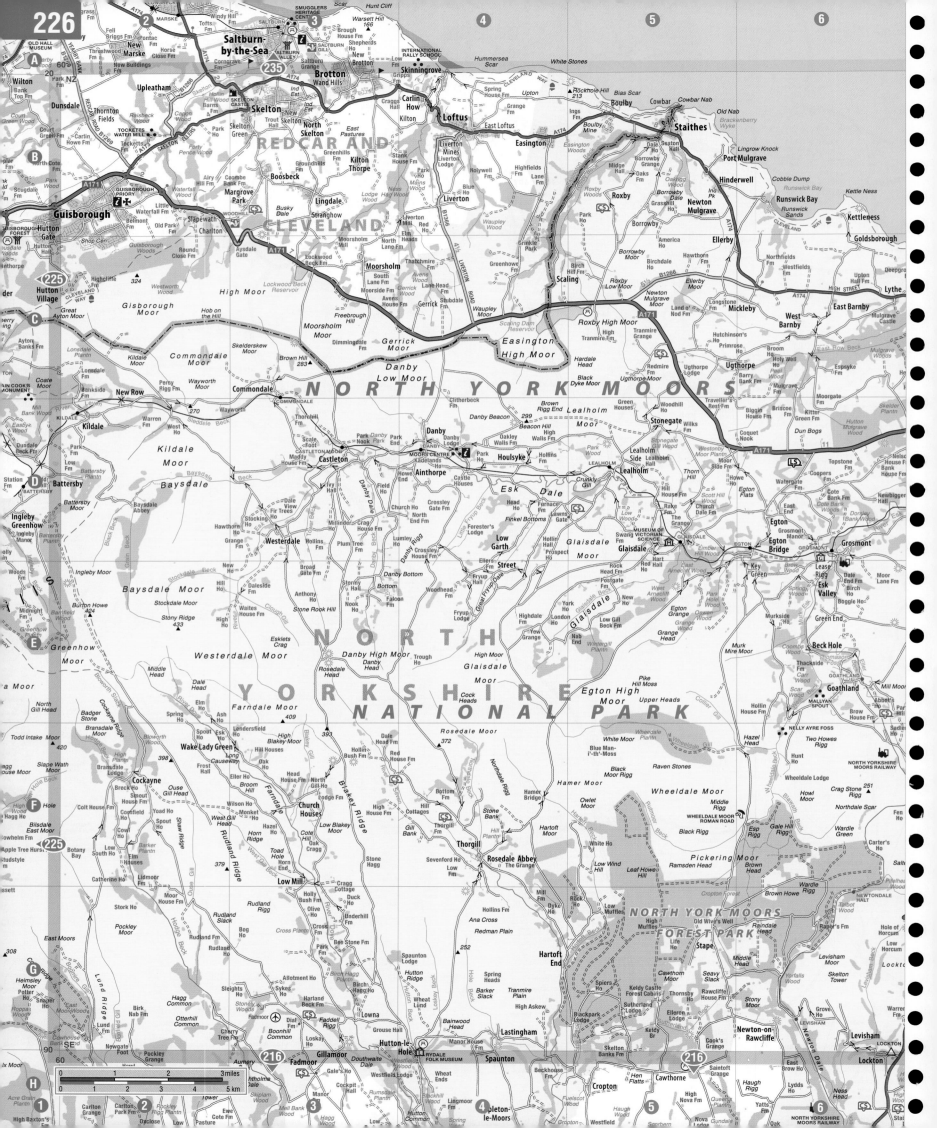

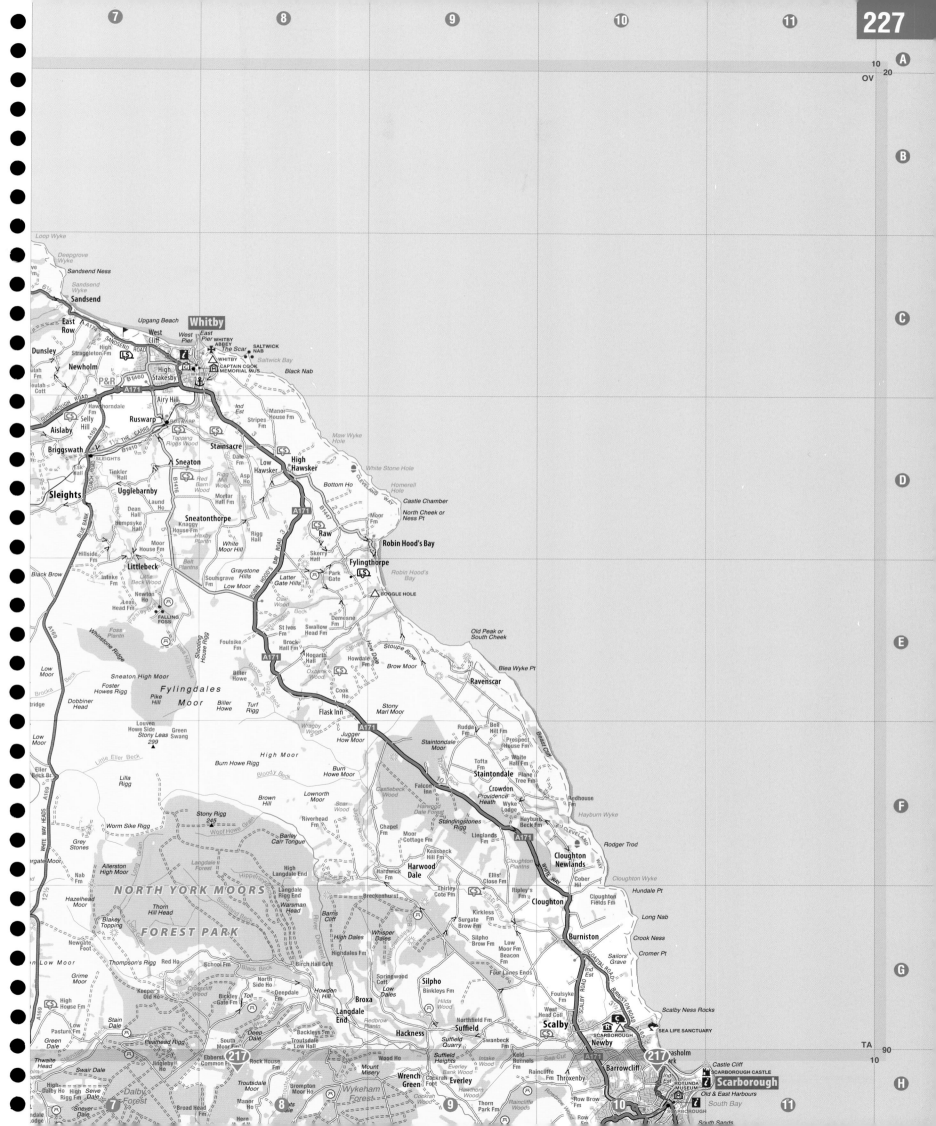

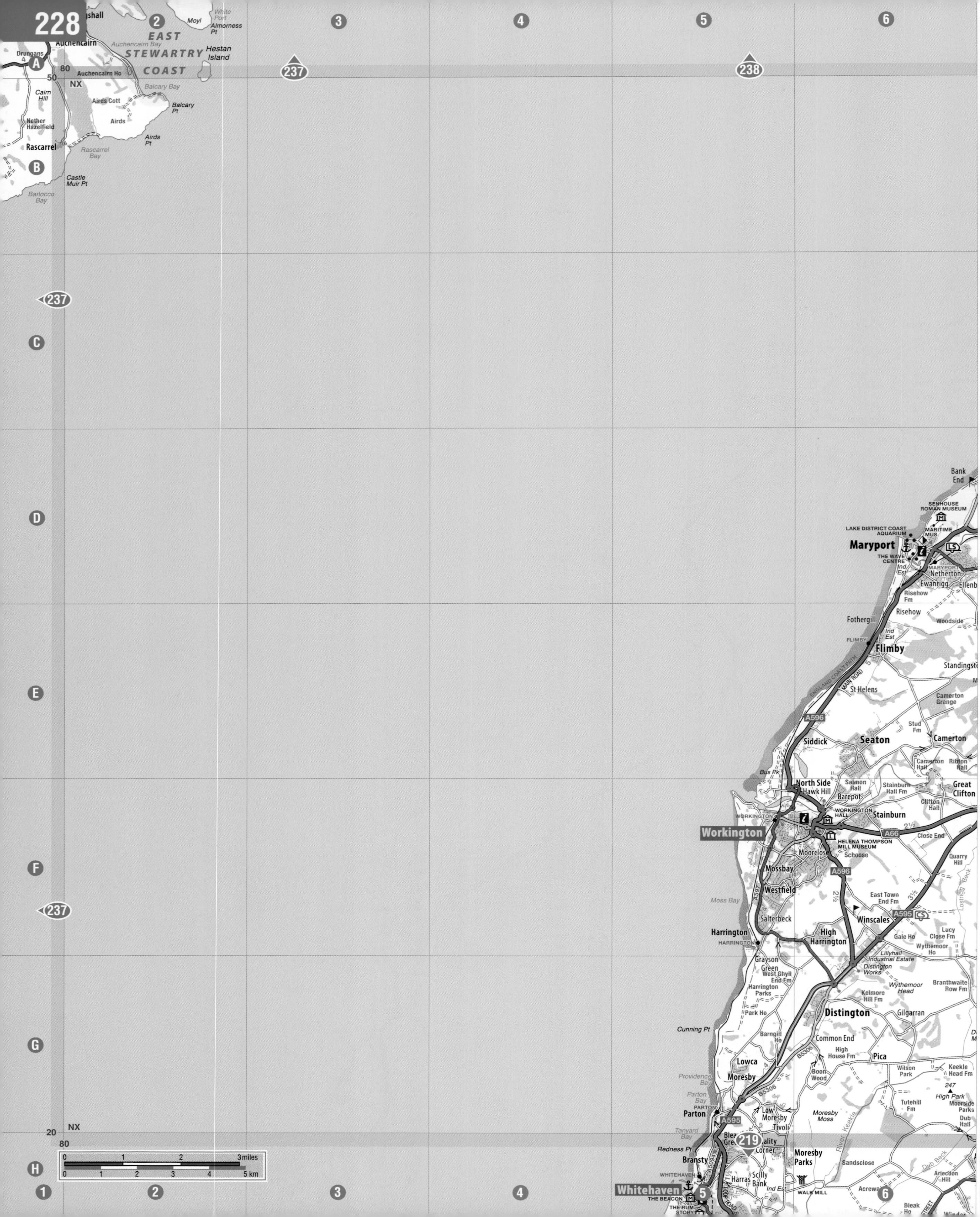

EAST
STEWARTRY
COAST

Drungans A
Auchencairn
2 Moyl
White Port
Almorness Pt
Hestan Island

A
80
50
Auchencairn Bay
Auchencairn Ho
NX
Cairn Hill
Balcary Bay
Airds Cott
Balcary Pt
Airds
Nether Hazelfield
Airds Pt
Rascarrel
Rascarrel Bay
B
Castle Muir Pt
Barlocco Bay

237

C

237

Bank End

SENHOUSE ROMAN MUSEUM

LAKE DISTRICT COAST AQUARIUM
MARITIME MUS
Maryport
THE WAVE CENTRE
Ind Est
D
Netherton
Ewanrigg
Ellenb

Risehow Fm

Fothergill
Risehow
Woodside

Ind Est
FLIMBY
Flimby
Standingsto

St Helens
CUMBRIA COAST PATH
Camerton Grange

E
A596
Siddick
Seaton
Camerton

Stud Fm
Camerton Hall
Ribton Hall

Bus Pk
Salmon Hall
Stainburn Hall Fm
Clifton Hall
Great Clifton
North Side
Hawk Hill
Barepot
WORKINGTON
WORKINGTON HALL
Stainburn
2½
A66
Close End

Workington
HELENA THOMPSON MILL MUSEUM
Schoose
Quarry Hill
Moorclose

F
Mossbay
A596

Westfield
East Town End Fm
3½
A597
Moss Bay
A595
Winscales
Lucy Close Fm
Salterbeck
Gale Ho
Wythemoor Ho
Harrington
High Harrington
HARRINGTON
Lillyhall Industrial Estate
Grayson Green
West Ghyll End Fm
Distington Works
Kelmore Hill Fm
Wythemoor Head
Branthwaite Row Fm
Harrington Parks
Park Ho
Distington
Gilgarran

Cunning Pt
Barngill Ho
Common End
G
High House Fm
Pica
Providence Bay
Lowca
Boon Wood
Wilson Park
Keekle Head Fm
Moresby
B5306
247
Parton Bay
PARTON
Moresby Moss
High Park
Tutehill Fm
Moorside Parks
Dub Hall

Parton
A595
Low Moresby
Tivoli
Moresby Moss

20
NX
80
Blea Green
Quality Corner
Moresby Parks
Redness Pt
219
Sandsclose
Tanyard Bay
WALK MILL
H
0   1   2   3miles
Bransty
Scilly Bank
Arlecdon Hill
0 1 2 3 4 5 km
Harras
Acrewa
Whitehaven
THE BEACON
Ind Est
Bleak Ho
THE RUM STORY

1   **2**   **3**   **4**   **5**   **6**

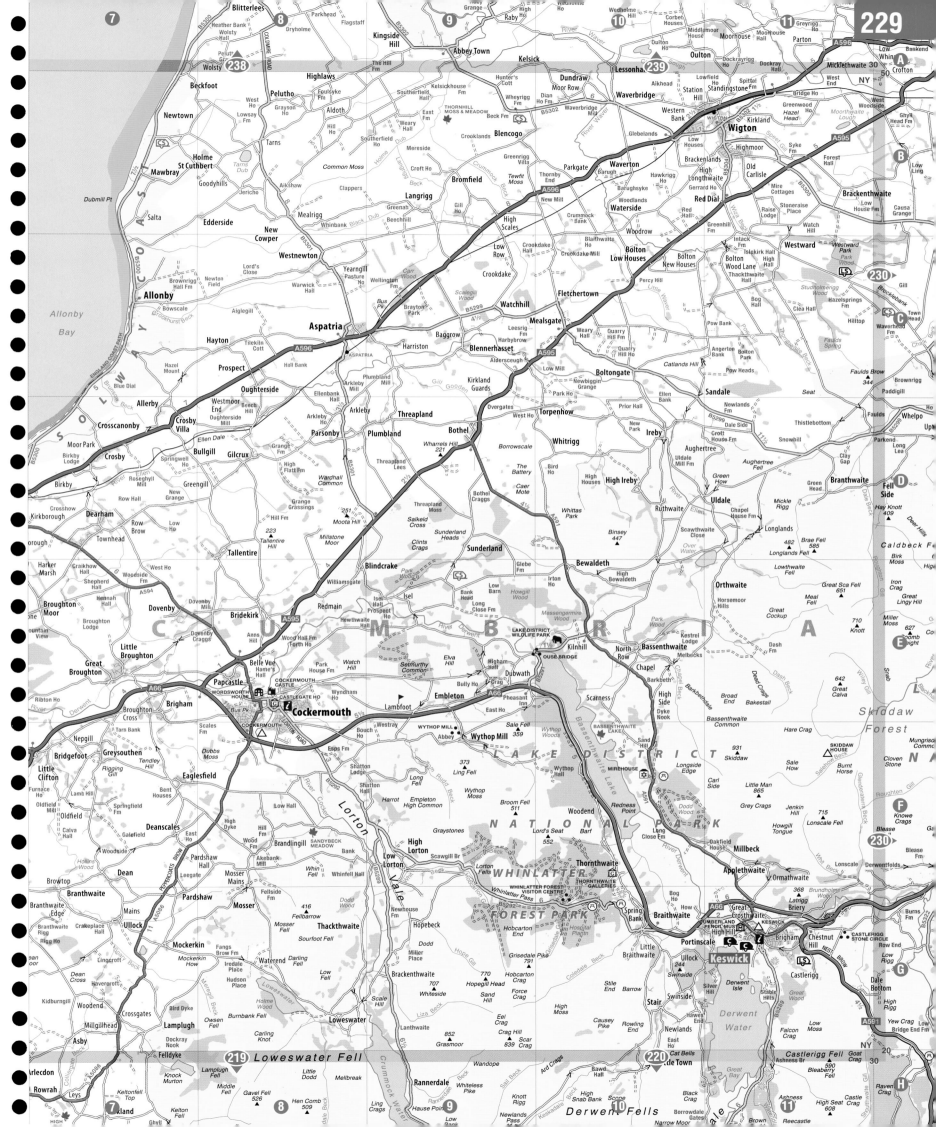

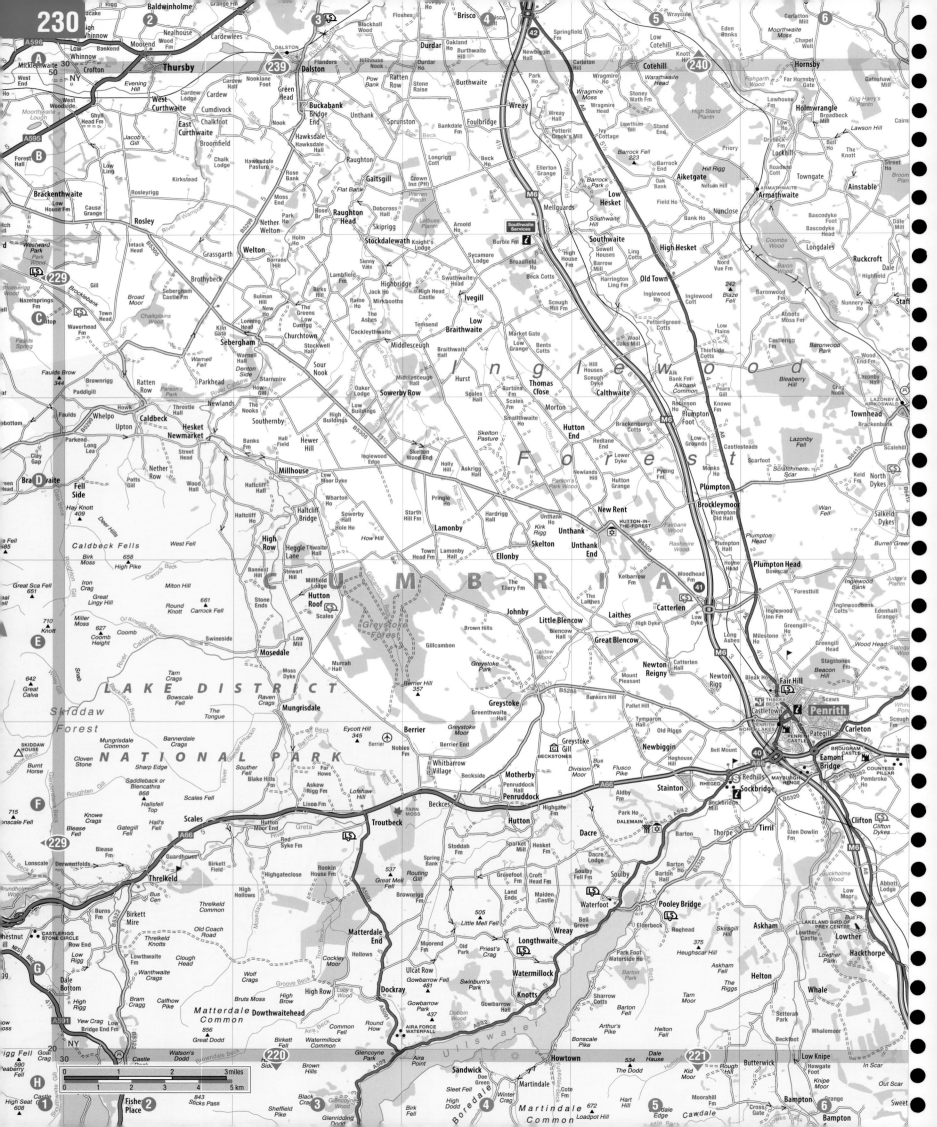

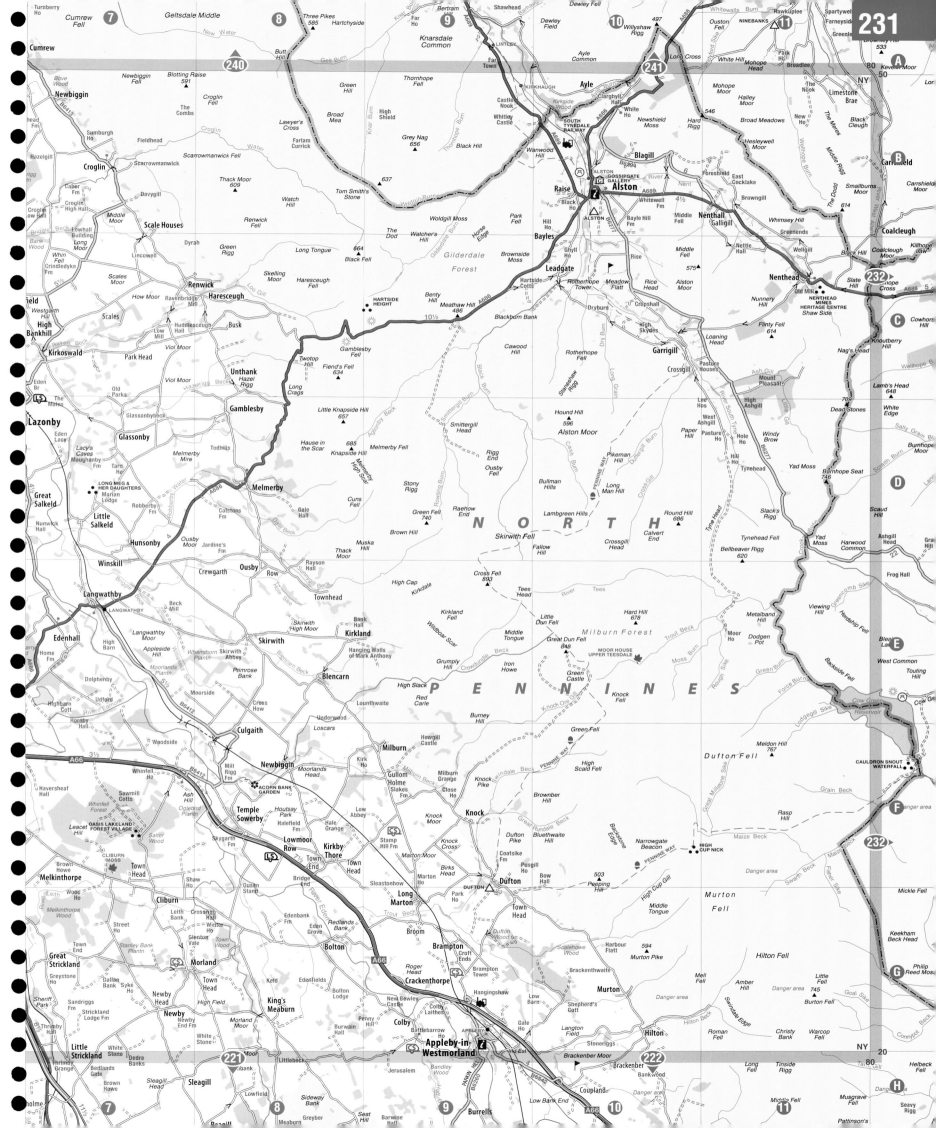

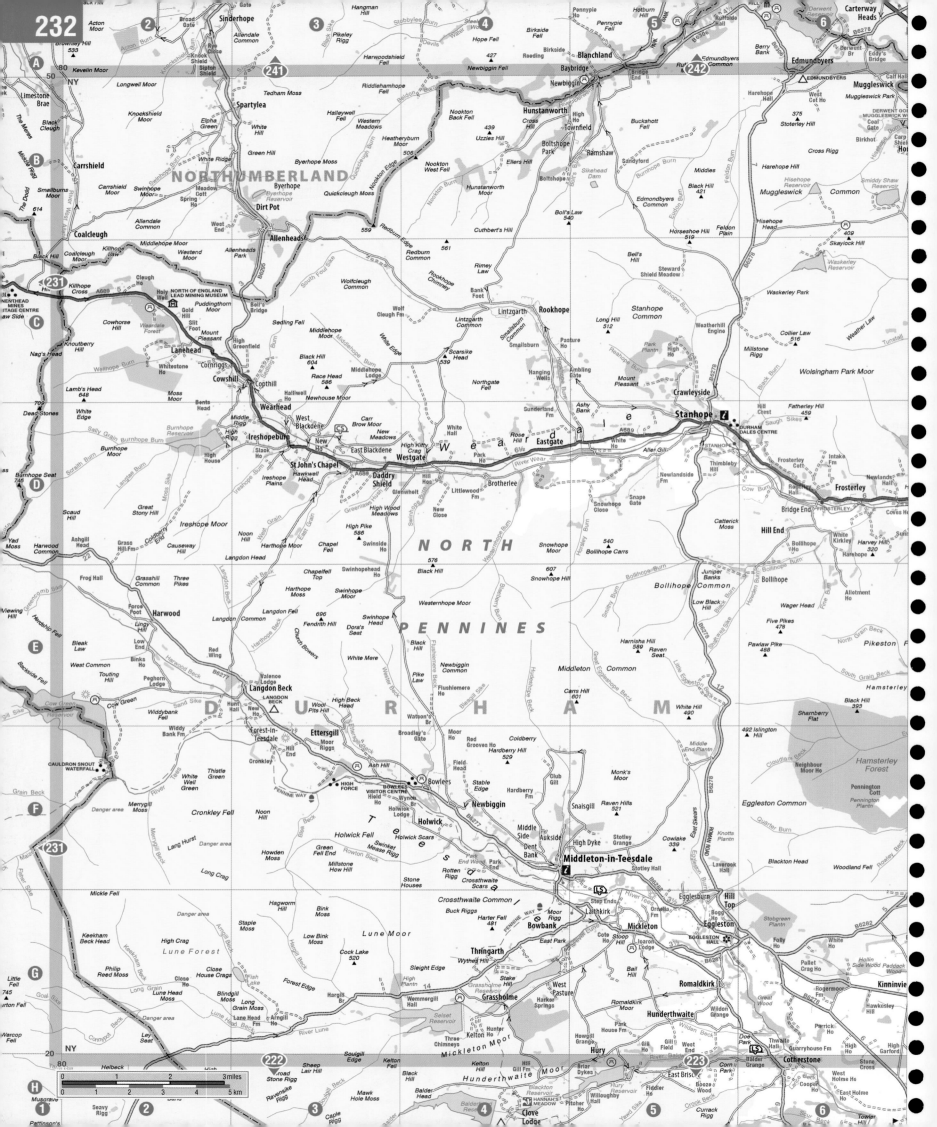

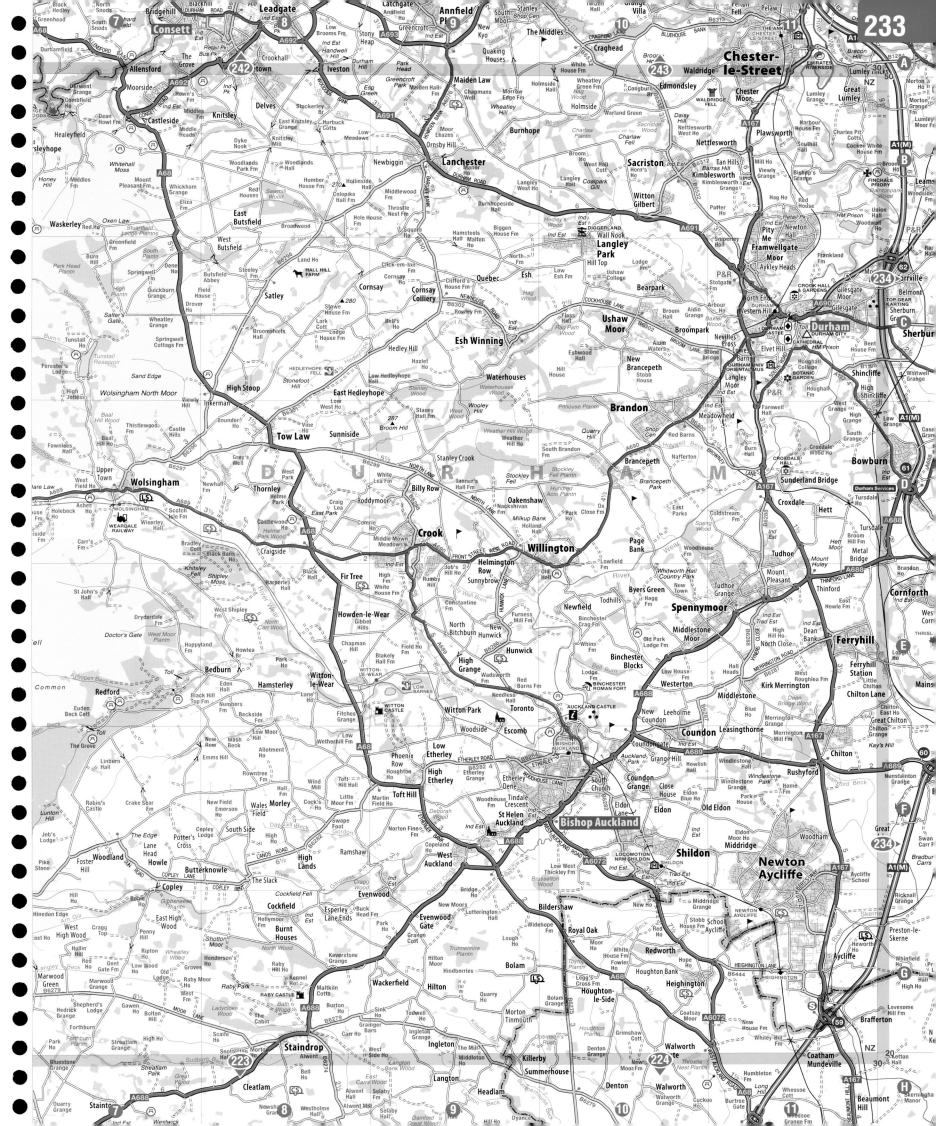

N O R T H   S E A

TEES BAY

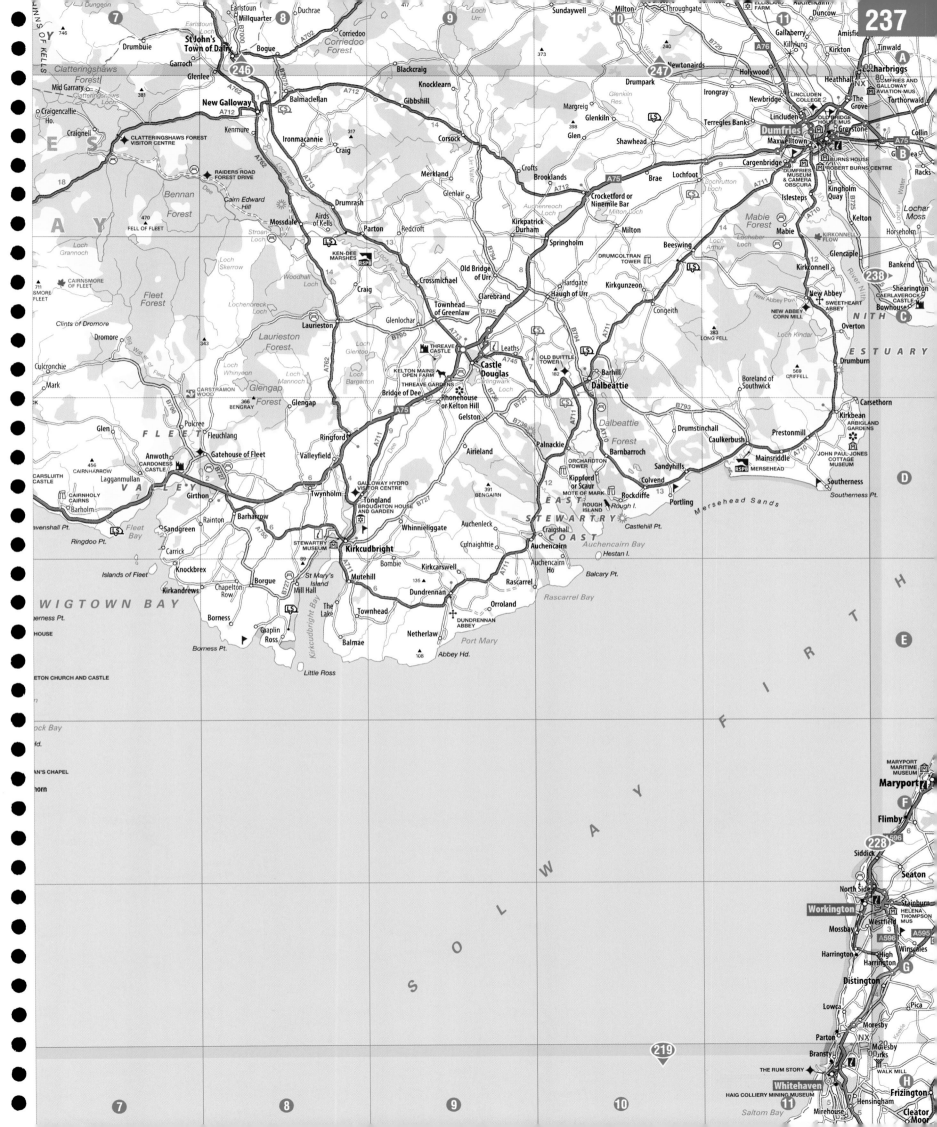

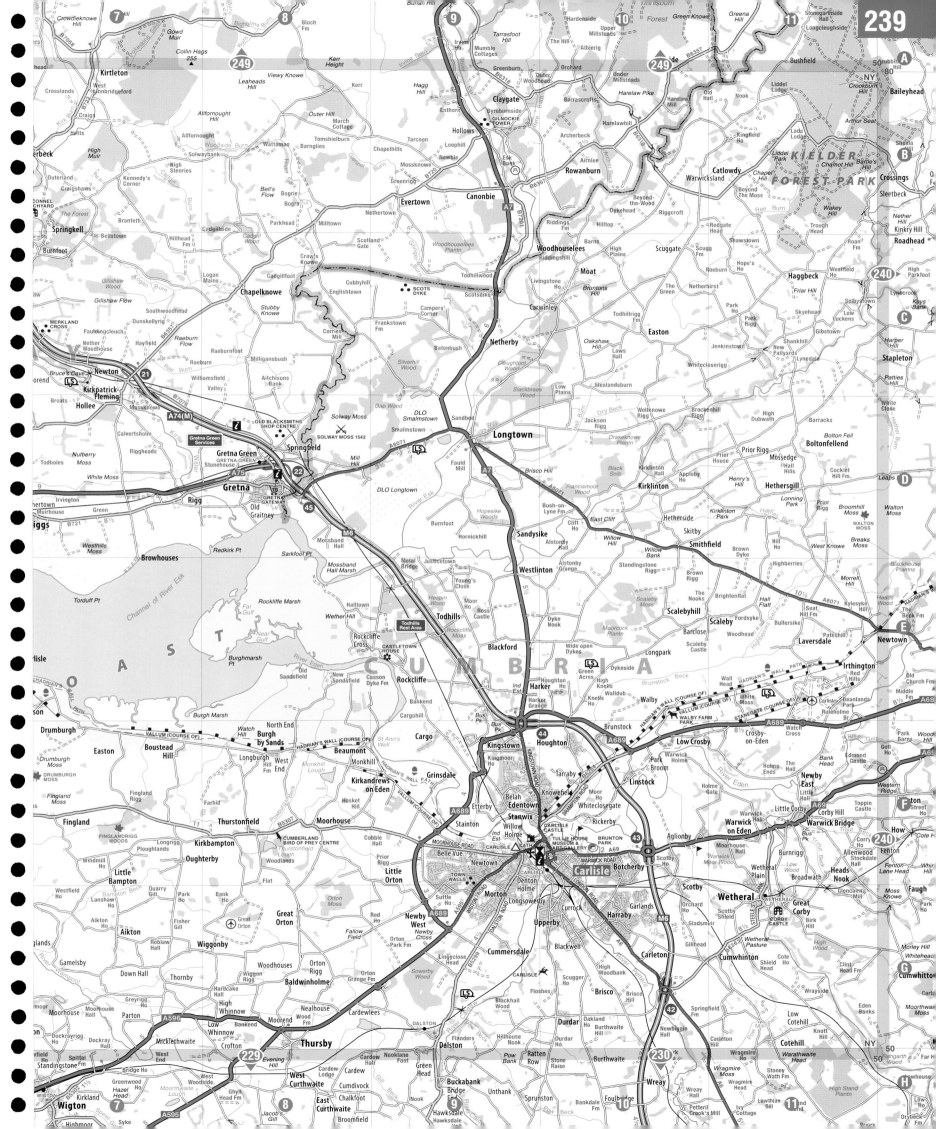

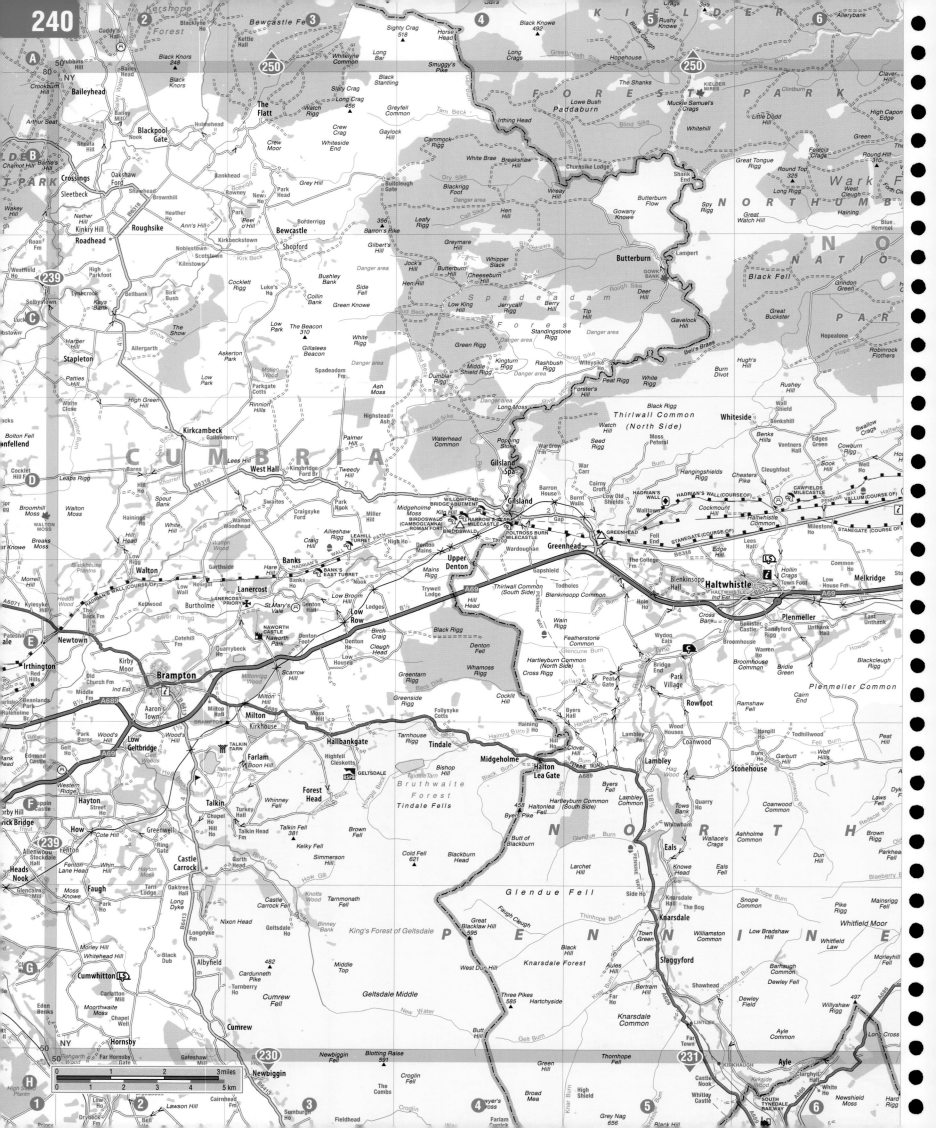

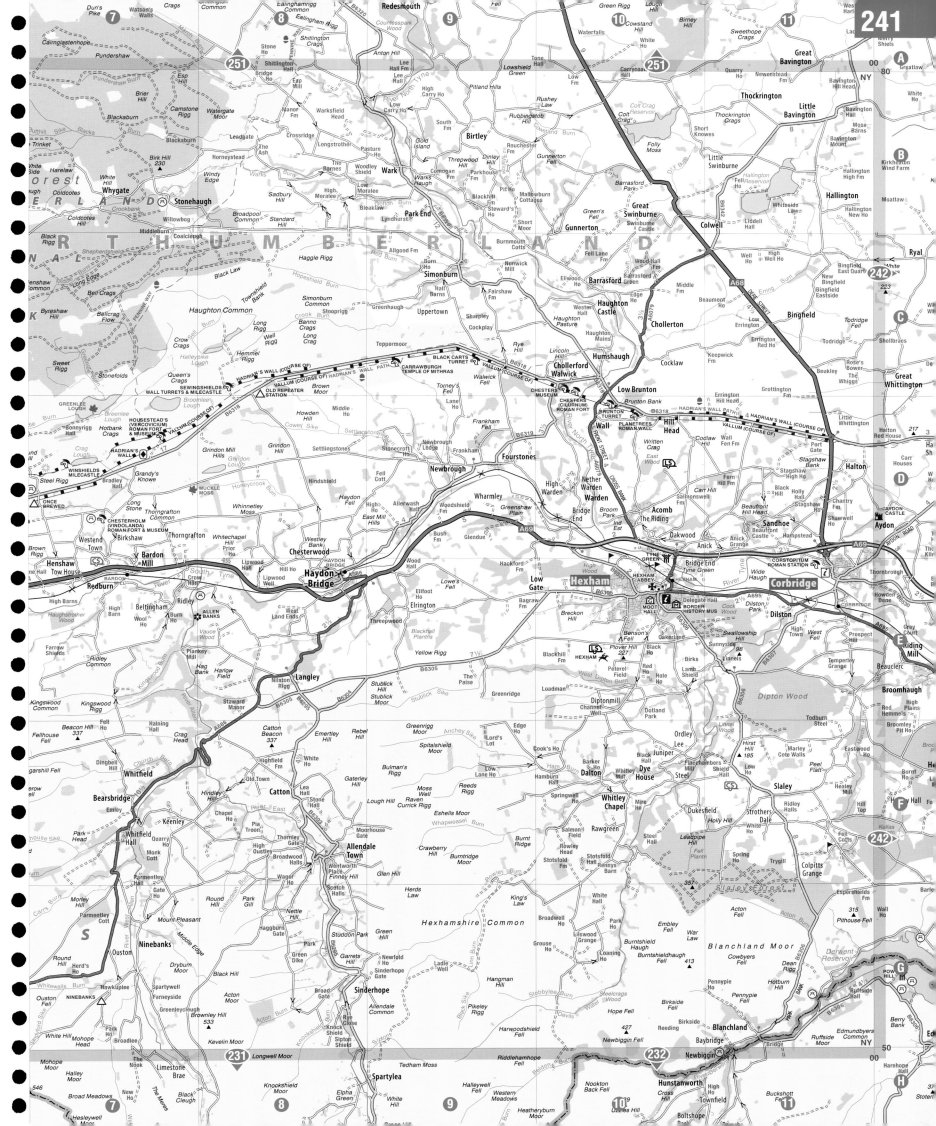

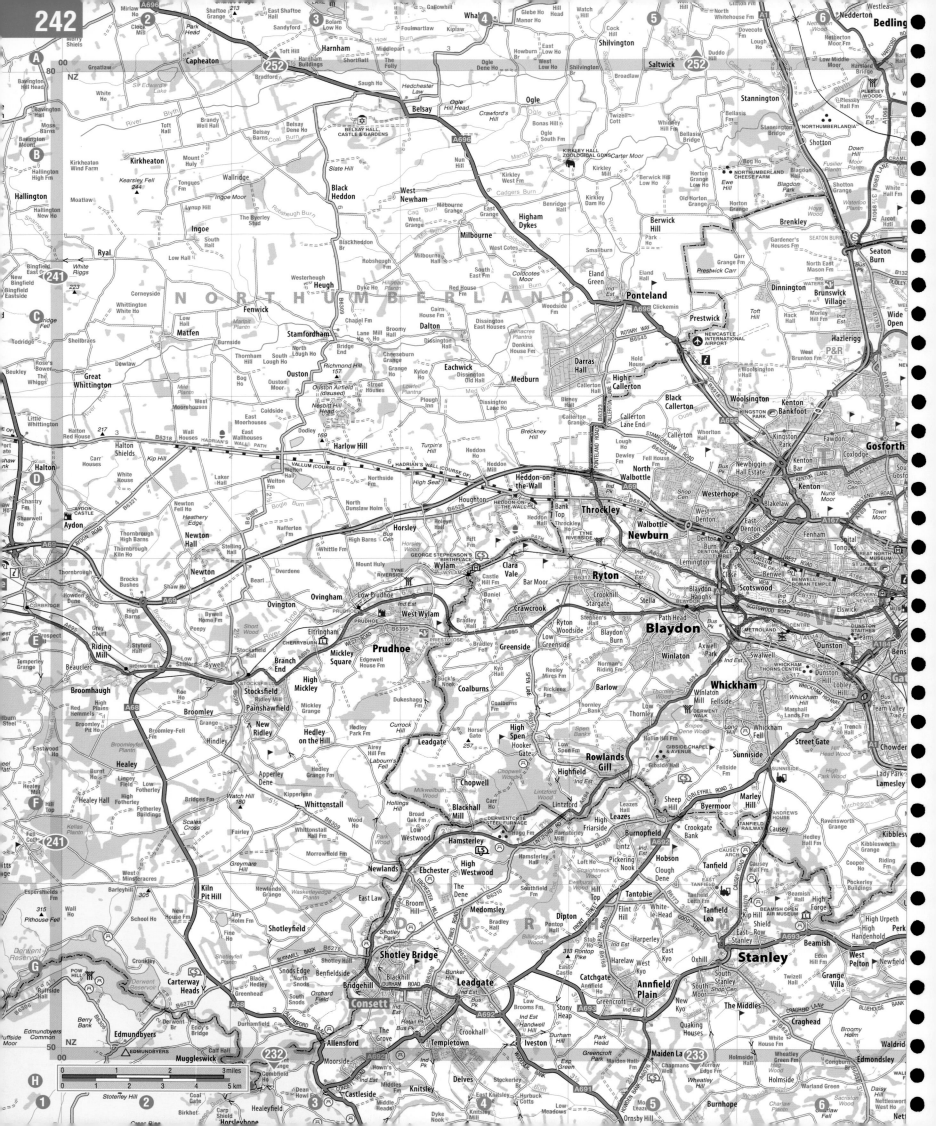

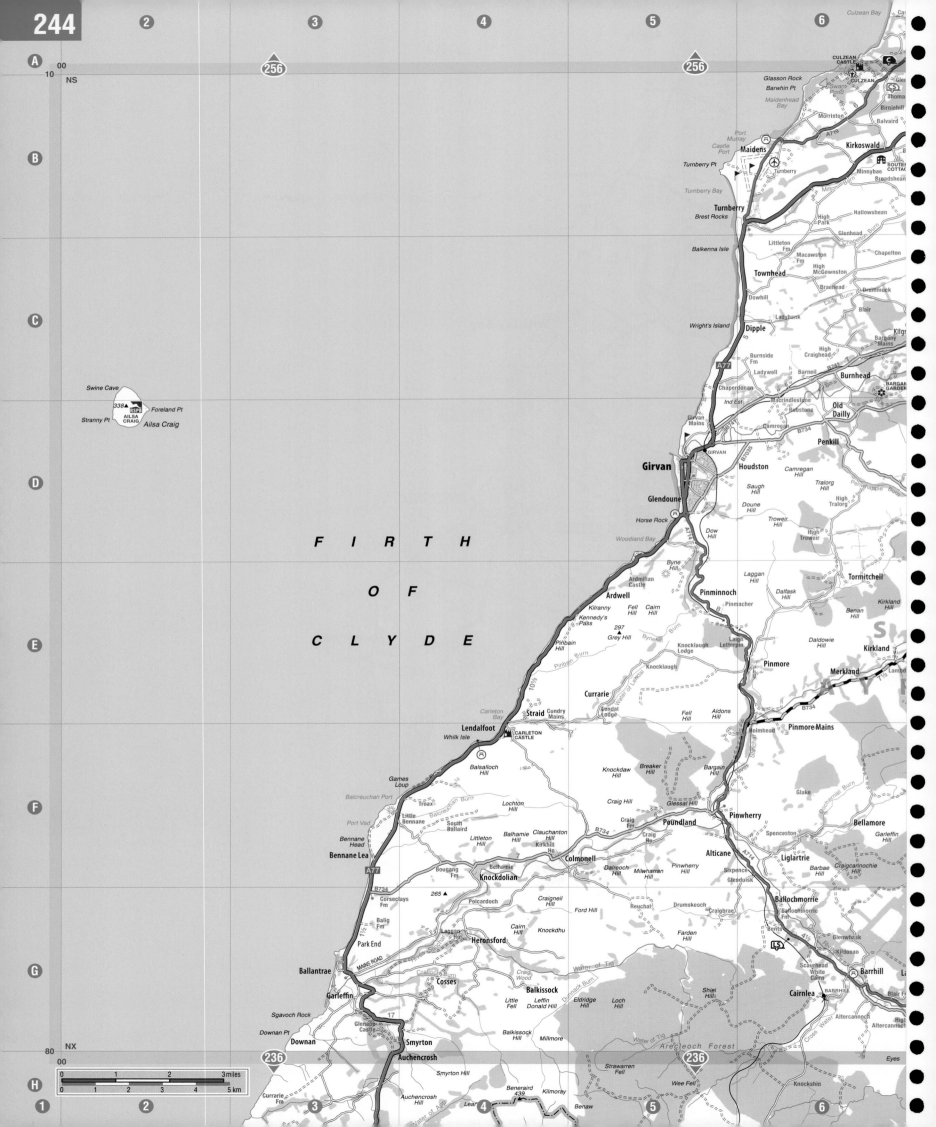

FIRTH

OF

CLYDE

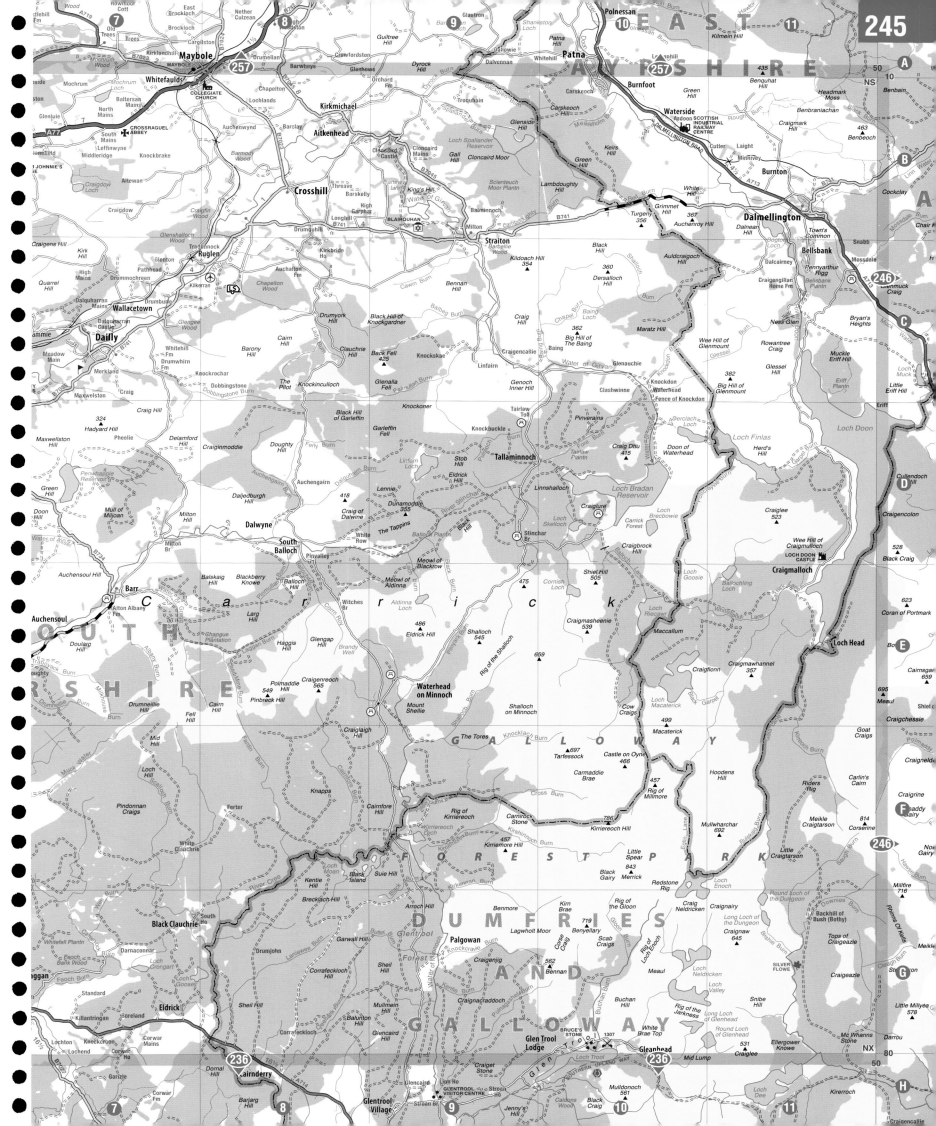

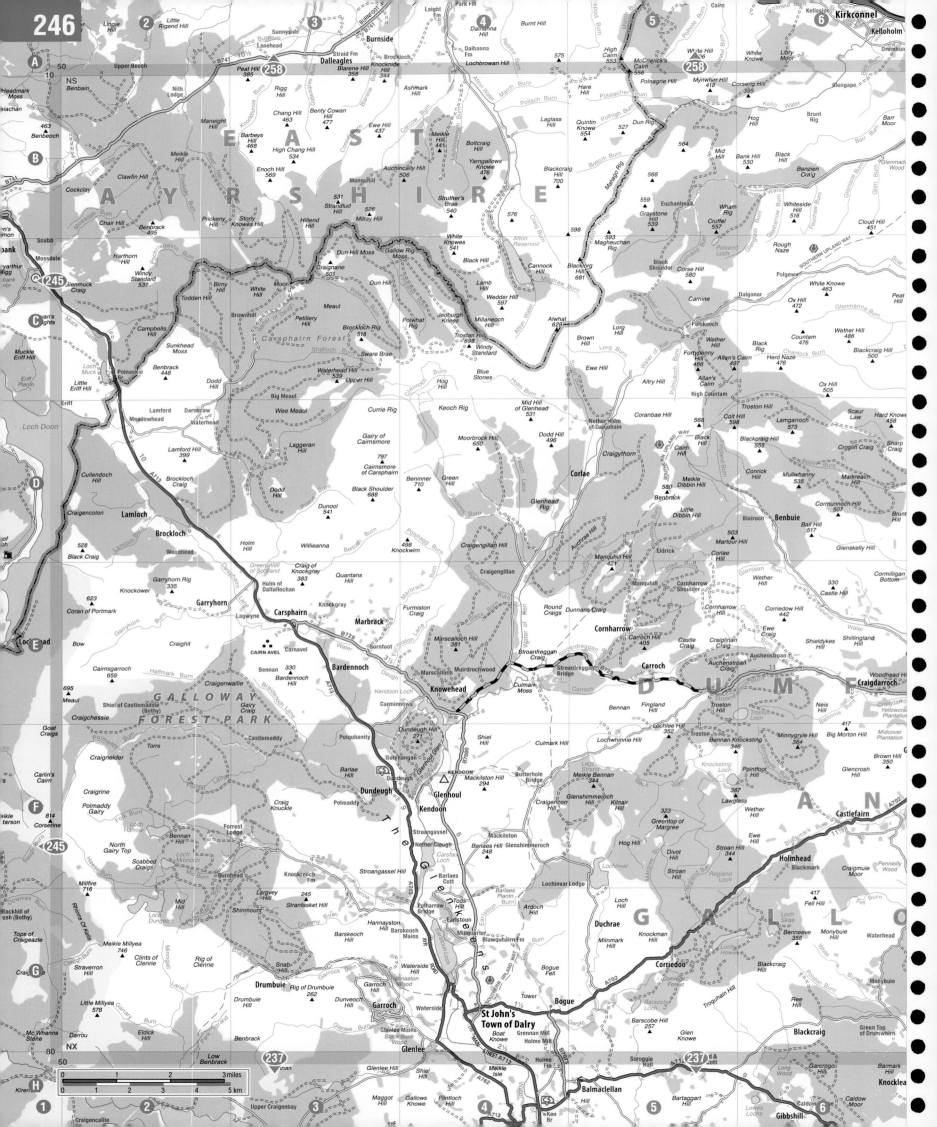

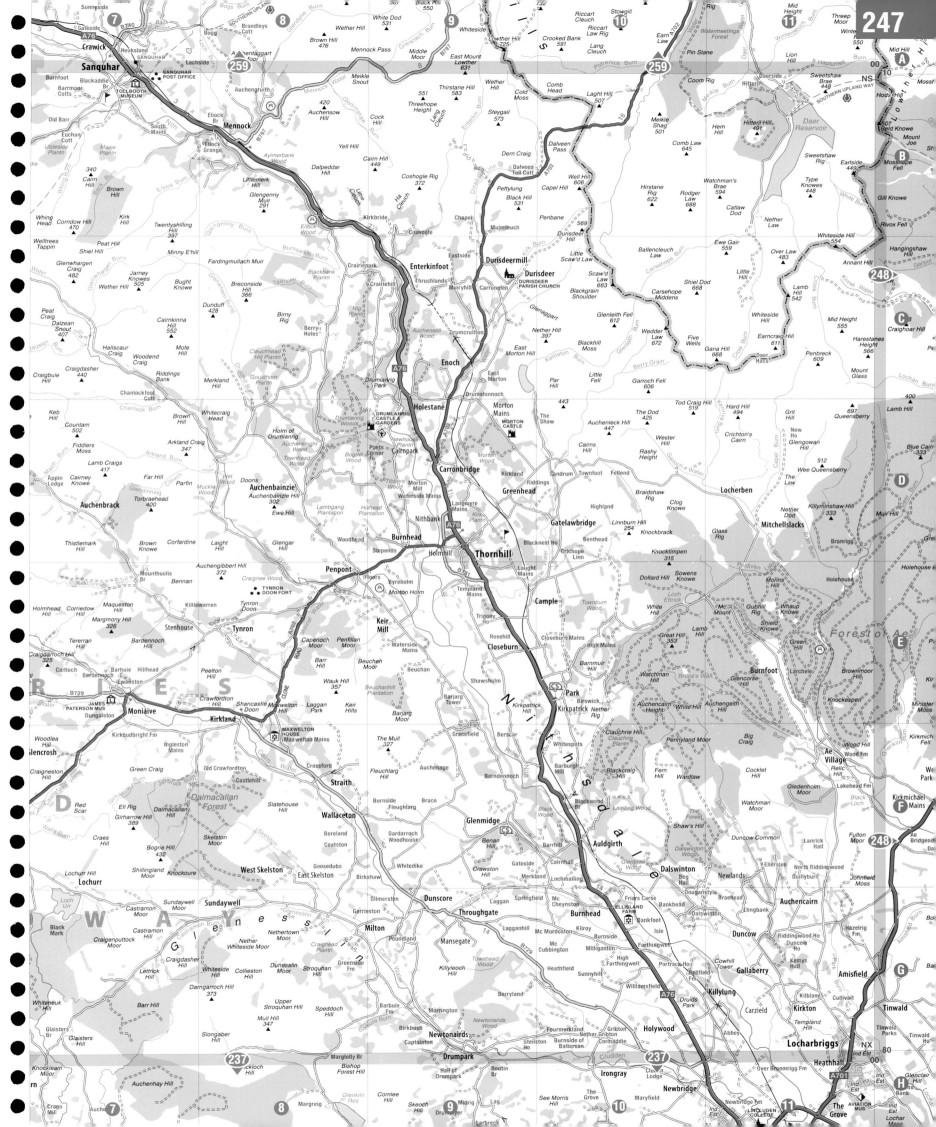

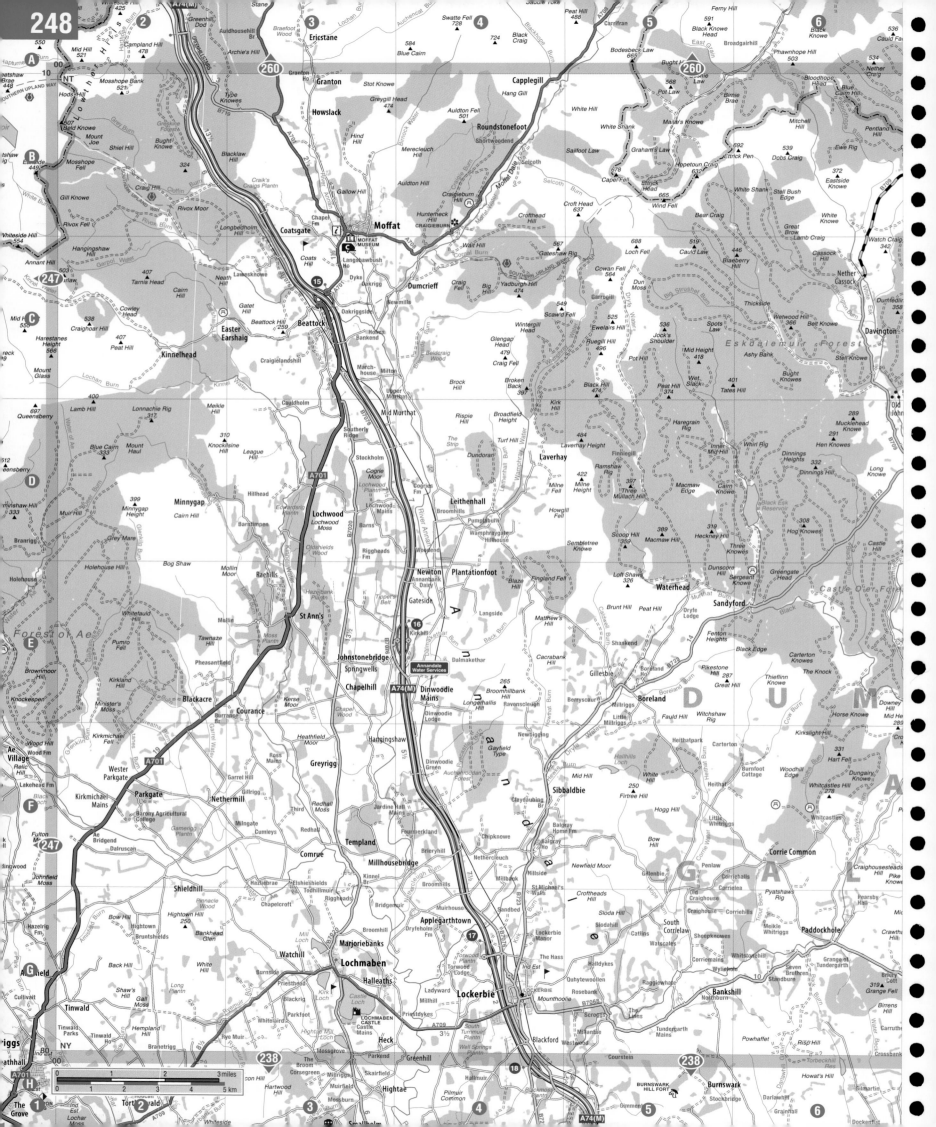

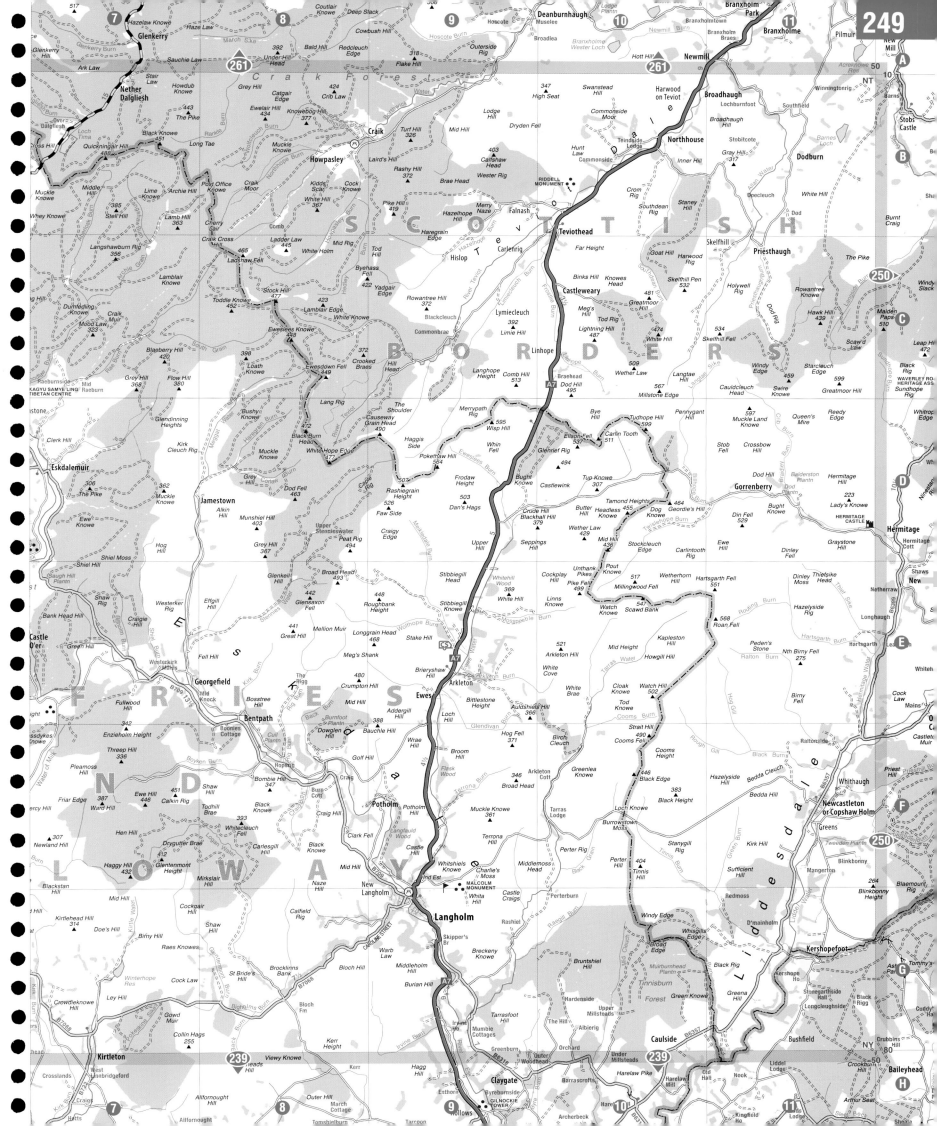

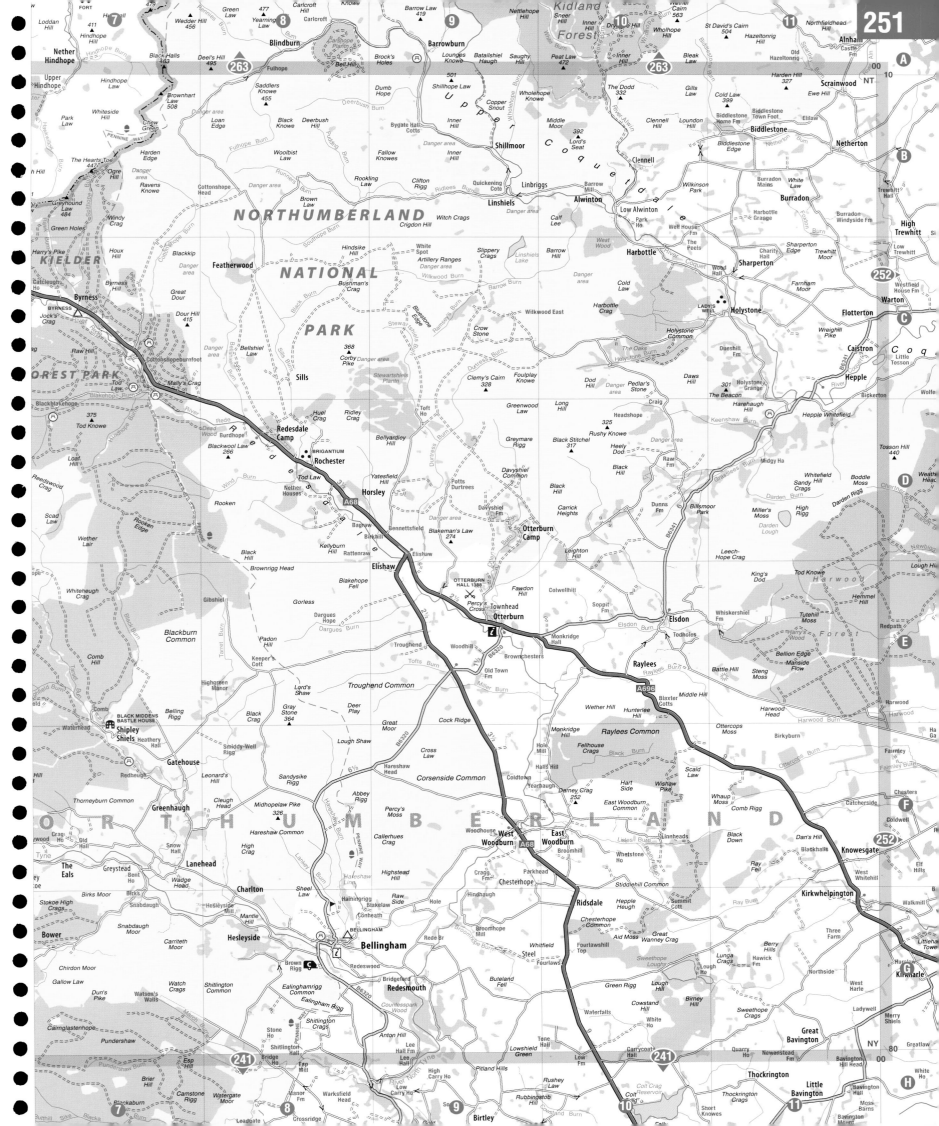

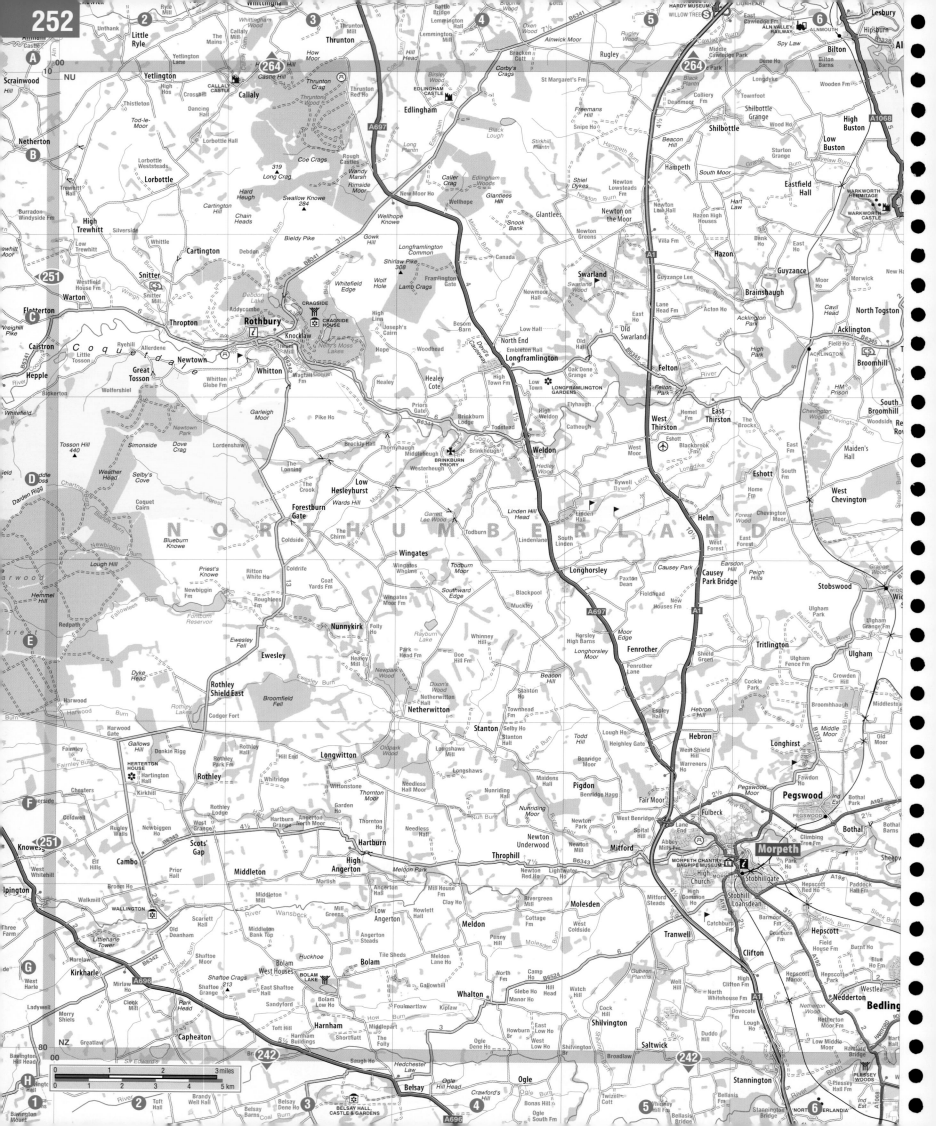

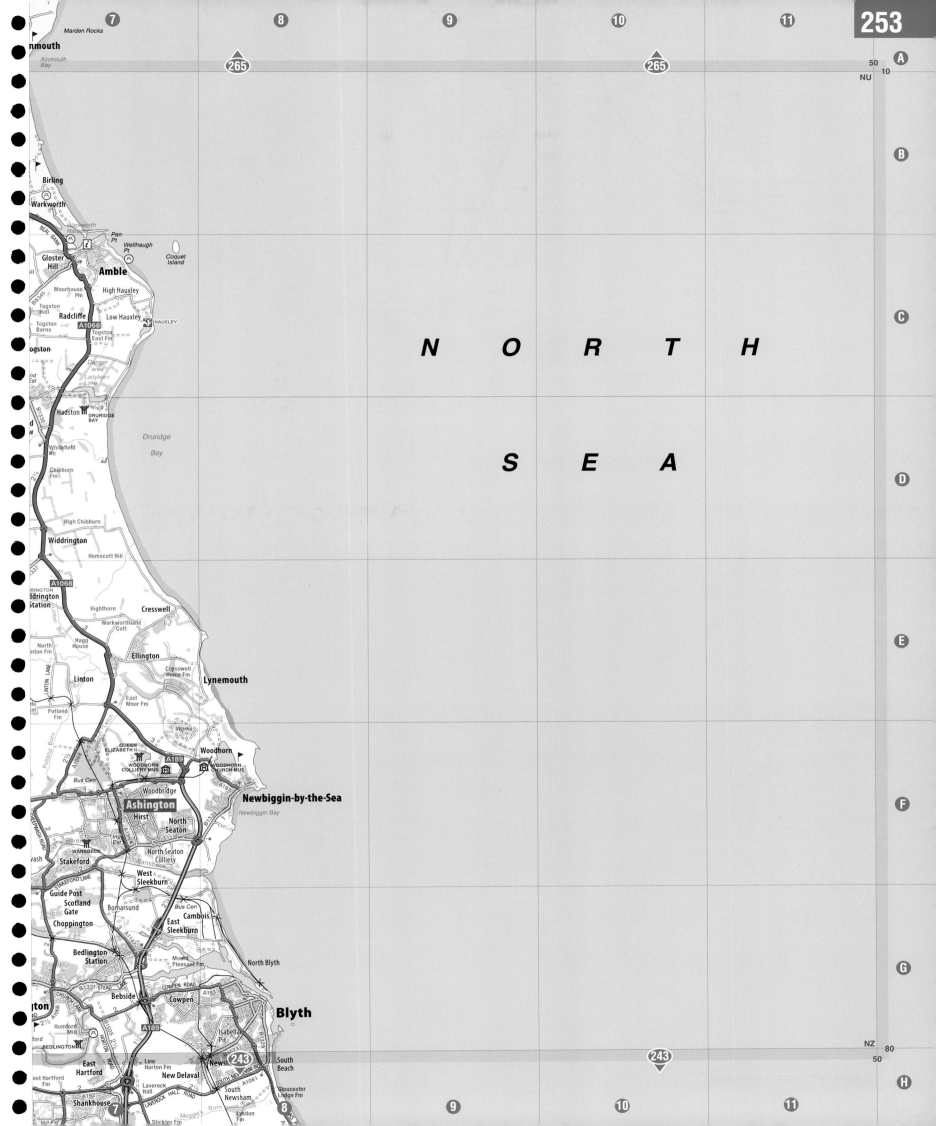

⑦ Marden Rocks

⑧

⑨

⑩

⑪

265

265

50
10
NU

A

nmouth
Ainmouth
Bay

B

Birling
Warkworth

Warkworth
Harbour
BEAL BANK
Pan
Pt
Wellhaugh
Pt
Coquet
Island

Gloster
Hill
Amble

Moorhouse
Fm
High Hauxley
B6345
Togston
Hall
Radcliffe
Low Hauxley
HAUXLEY
Togston
Barns
A1068
Togston
East Fm

Togston

C

Danger
area
Ladyburn
Lake

nd

B1330

Hadston
DRURIDGE
BAY

N   O   R   T   H

Whitefield
Ho
Druridge

Chibburn
Fm
Bay

S   E   A

D

High Chibburn

Widdrington

B1337

High Chibburn

A1068

RINGTON
ddrington
Station

Highthorn
Cresswell

Warkworthlane
'Cott

North
Linton Fm
Hagg
House

Ellington

E

LINTON LANE

Linton

Cresswell
Home Fm

Lynemouth

ds

Potland
Fm

East
Moor Fm

Pottland Burn

Works

QUEEN
ELIZABETH II
A189
Woodhorn

A1068
WOODHORN
COLLIERY MUS
WOODHORN
CHURCH MUS
Bus Cen

Woodbridge
A197
Newbiggin-by-the-Sea

F

Ashington
Hirst
North
Seaton
Newbiggin Bay

SLEEKWASH ROAD
Ind
Est
River
WANSBECK
North Seaton
Colliery

wash
Stakeford
Wansbeck
West
Sleekburn
STAKEFORD LANE

Guide Post
Scotland
Gate
Bomarsund
Bus Cen
Cambois

Choppington
East
Sleekburn

Aller

Bedlington
Station
Mount
Pleasant Fm
North Blyth

G

ton
B1331 STEAD
COWPEN ROAD
A193
Bebside
Cowpen
A193

CHURCH LANE

Humford
Mill
Blyth
BEDLINGTON
A189
NORTON ROAD
B1505
Isabella
Pit

NZ
80
50

East
Hartford
Low
Horton Fm
243
South
Beach

est Hartford
Fm
New Delaval
SOUTH NEWSHAM ROAD
A1061
South
Newsham
Gloucester
Lodge Fm
Newsha
243

H

⑦
Shankhouse
LAVEROCK HALL ROAD
Laverock
Hall
Meggie's
Burn

⑧

⑨

⑩

⑪

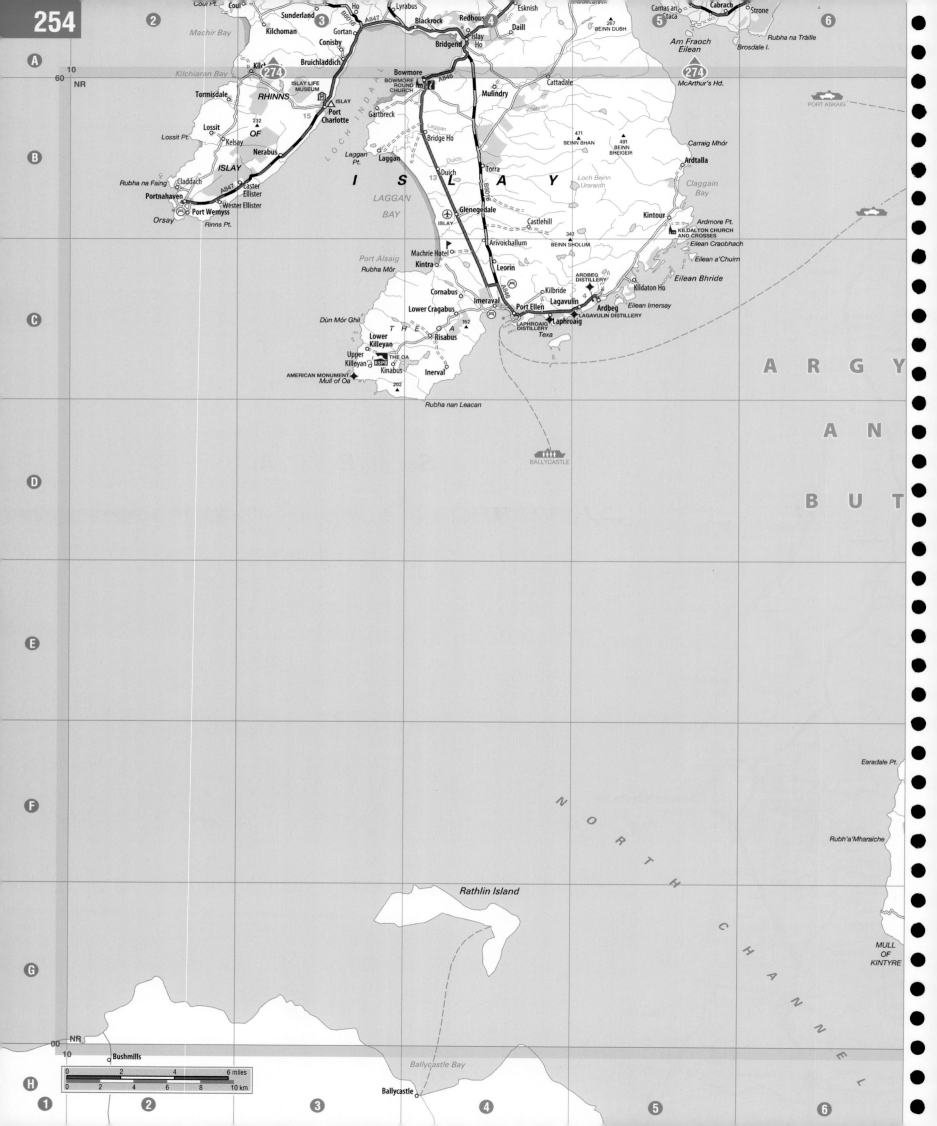

F I R T H

O F

C L Y D E

BRODICK

Saltcoats

ARDROSSAN HARBOUR
TOWN
South Bay
NORTH AYRSHIRE MUSEUM
Outer Nebbock
Inr Nebbock

CAMPBELTOWN
(May-Sept only)

255 255 266

NS
00
40

Glenshant Hill
Glen Rosa
Creag Rosa
Maol Donn 368

Merkland

Merkland Wood
Merkland Pt
Wine Port

Torr Breac
Glenrosa
BRODICK CASTLE
Cladach
Old Quay

ARDROSSAN

Glen Shurig
ISLE OF ARRAN HERITAGE MUSEUM
THE STRING
Brodick

Glen Cloy
A841

Sn Gaoithe
Strathwhillan
Corriegills Pt

Glen Ormidale
Fairy Glen
North Corriegills
Sgiath Bhán
Dun Dubh
South Corriegills

Clauchland Hills
Clauchlands Fm
Clauchlands Pt

255

Cnoc Breac
Cnoc Dubh
Meall Buidhe
Clauchlands
Margnaheglish
Kerr's Port
Hamilton Isle

Isle
Blairbeg
of
Benlister Glen
Benlister Burn
Lamlash

Mullach Beag

Holy Island

The Ross ▲ 311
Monamore Br
Arran
Cordon
White Pt
314 ▲ Mullach Mór

Monamore Glen
Gortonallister
Pillar Rock Pt

Cnoc Dubh
Urie Loch
The Knowe Fm

nvein
Auchencairn
Kingscross Pt

Glas Choirein
Knockenkelly
Kingscross

N O R T H
Borrach
North Kiscadale
Sandbraes

Cnoc Donn
Cnoc an Fheidh
Cnoc Mór
South Kiscadale
Whiting Bay

GLENASHDALE FALLS
Largymore
Auchareoch

A Y R S H I R E
Kilmory Water
Largymeanoch

Torr dubh Mór
Cnoc Craobhach
Cnoc na Garbad
Cnoc na Comhairle
Largybeg
Largybeg Pt
Port na Gaillin

Glenashdale Burn
Dippin Head

Torr a' annain
Margenaish Fm
Levencorroch Hill
Dippin

Southbank
Levencorroch
East Bennan
Auchenhew
Drumla
Porta Leacach

West Bennan
Port a'Ghillie Ghlais
Kildonan
Porta Buidhe
Port Dearg

STRUEY ROCKS
Bennan Head

Sound of Pladda
Pladda

NS
10
00

Dur

Broad Craig

Culzean Bay
Cas

CULZEAN CASTLE
CULZEAN
Glasson Rock
Barwhin Pt
Maidenhead Bay
Thoma

244 244

0   1   2   3 miles
0   1   2   3   4   5 km

Morriston
Birniehill
Port Murray
Balvaird

255

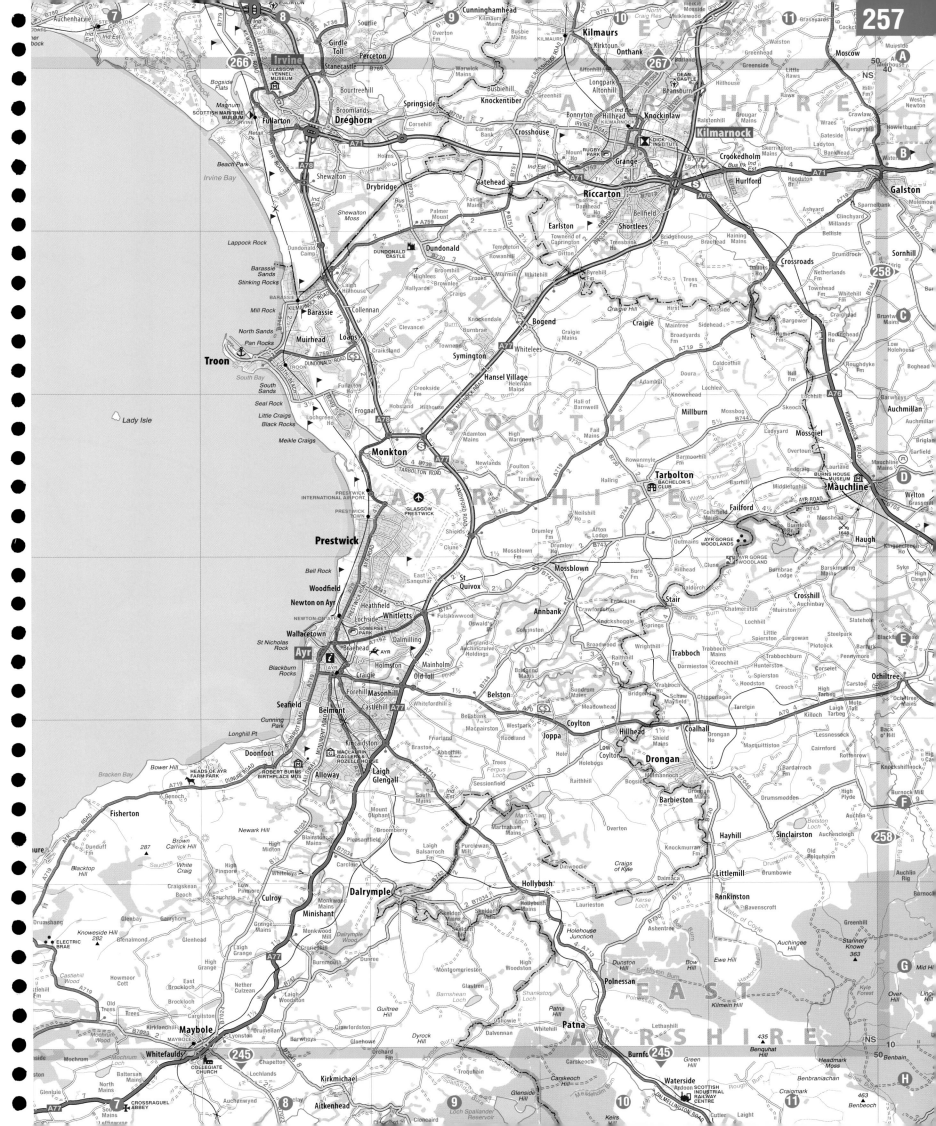

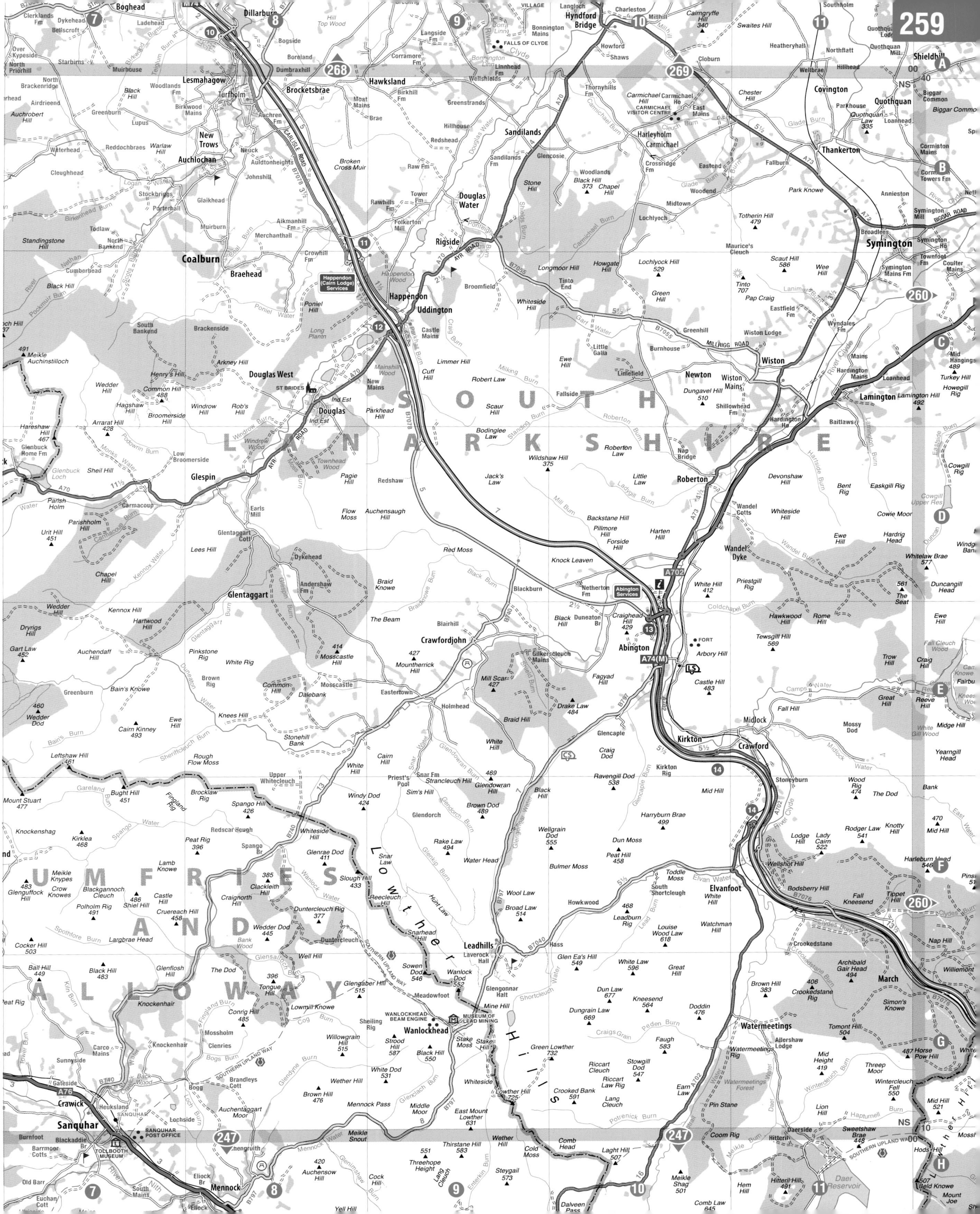
Boghead
Dillarburn
Clerklands Fm
Dykehead
Bellscroft
Ladehead
Over Kypeside
North Priorhill
Starbirns
Muirhouse
Lesmahagow
Turfholm
Boreland
Dumbraxhill
Bogside
Hill Top Wood
268
Hawksland
Brocketsbrae
Langside Fm
Corramore Fm
Corra Linn
FALLS OF CLYDE
Bonnington Mains
Bonnington Linn
Linnhead Fm
Wellshields
VILLAGE
Langloch
Hyndford Bridge
Charleston
Millhill
Cairngryffe Hill 340
Swaites Hill
Southholm
Quothquan Lodge
Quothquan Mill
Heatheryhall
Northflatt
Shieldhill
Howford
Shaws
Cloburn
Wellbrae
Hillhead
269
North Brackenridge
Airdrieend
Auchrobert Hill
Black Hill
Woodlands Fm
Birkwood Mains
Greenburn
Lupus
Auchren Fm
Birkhill Fm
Moat Mains
Brae
Greenstrands
Hillhouse
Sandilands
Thornyhills Fm
Carmichael Hill
Carmichael Ho
CARMICHAEL VISITOR CENTRE
East Mains
Chester Hill
Covington
Parkhouse
Quothquan
Quothquan Law 335
Biggar Common
Loanhead
Thankerton
Cormiston Mains
Corntown Towers Fm
Waterhead
Reddochbraes
Warlaw Hill
New Trows
Auchlochan
Neuck
Auldtonheights
Johnshill
Broken Cross Muir
Raw Fm
Redshead
Sandilands Fm
Glencosie
Harleyholm
Carmichael
Crossridge Fm
Eastend
Woodend
Fallburn
Cleughhead
Stockbriggs
Porterhall
Glaikhead
Tower Fm
Rawhills Fm
Douglas Water
Stone Hill
Woodlands
Black Hill 373
Chapel Hill
Midtown
Park Knowe
Anniestone
Symington Mill
BIGGAR ROAD
Standingstone Hill
Todlaw
North Bankend
Muirburn
Merchanthall
Aikmanhill Fm
Folkerton Mill
Rigside
Lochlyoch
Totherin Hill 479
Broadlees
Symington
Symington Ho
Townfoot Fm
Coulter Mains
Coalburn
Braehead
Crowhill Fm
Happendon (Cairn Lodge) Services
Happendon Wood
Happendon
AYR ROAD
Broomfield
Longmoor Hill
Howgate Hill
Lochlyock Hill 529
Maurice's Cleuch
Scaut Hill 586
Wee Hill
Symington Mains Fm
Cumberhead
Black Hill
Poniel Hill
Uddington
Tinto End
Whiteside Hill
Green Hill
Tinto 707
Pap Craig
Eastfield Fm
260
South Bankend
Brackenside
Long Plantn
Castle Mains
Greenhill
Wiston Lodge
Wyndales Fm
Meikle Auchinstilloch 491
Arkney Hill
Henry's Hill
Douglas West
ST BRIDES
Mainshill Wood
New Mains
Cuff Hill
Limmer Hill
Ewe Hill
Little Galla
Burnhouse
MILLRIGG ROAD
Wiston
Mains
Hardington Mains
Loanhead
Mid Hangings 489
Turkey Hill
Howgill Rig
Wedder Hill
Common Hill 488
Hagshaw Hill
Windrow Hill
Rob's Hill
Ind Est
Douglas
Parkhead Hill
Robert Law
Limefield
Fallside
Newton
Dungavel Hill 510
Wiston Mains
Shillowhead Fm
Lamington
Lamington Hill 492
Hareshaw Hill 467
Arrarat Hill 428
Broomerside Hill
Scaur Hill
Bodinglee Law
Hardington Ho
Baitlaws
SOUTH LANARKSHIRE
Glenbuck Home Fm
Glenbuck Loch
Windrow Wood
Townhead Wood
Roberton Law
Nap Bridge
Low Broomerside
Sheil Hill
Glespin
Pagie Hill
Redshaw
Wildshaw Hill 375
Jack's Law
Little Law
Roberton
Devonshaw Hill
Bent Rig
Easkgill Rig
Cowgill Rig
Cowgill Upper Res
Parish Holm
Carmacoup
Earls Mill
Flow Moss
Auchensaugh Hill
Backstane Hill
Pilimore Hill
Forside Hill
Harten Hill
Wandel Cotts
Whiteside Hill
Cowie Moor
Parishholm Hill
Urit Hill 451
Glentaggart Cott
Lees Hill
Red Moss
Knock Leaven
Wandel Dyke
Ewe Hill
Hardrig Head
Whitelaw Brae 577
Windgate Bank
Chapel Hill
Dykehead
Andershaw Fm
Braid Knowe
Blackburn
Netherton Fm
Abington Services
White Hill 412
Priestgill Rig
561 The Seat
Duncangill Head
Wedder Hill
Kennox Hill
Glentaggart
Hartwood Hill
The Beam
Blairhill
Black Hill
Duneaton Br
Craighead Hill 429
Hawkwood Hill
Rome Hill
Ewe Hill
Drygrigs Hill
Gart Law 452
Auchendaff Hill
Pinkstone Rig
White Rig
414 Mosscastle Hill
427 Mountherrick Hill
Crawfordjohn
Gilkerscleuch Mains
Abington
FORT
Arbory Hill
Tewsgill Hill 569
Fall Cleuch Wood
Trow Hill
Craig Hill
Brown Rig
Common Hill
Dalebank
Mosscastle
Eastertown
Mill Scar 427
Fagyad Hill
Castle Hill 483
Great Hill
Reeve Hill
Greenburn
Bain's Knowe
Knees Hill
Holmhead
Braid Hill
Drake Law 484
Fall Hill
Mossy Dod
Midge Hill
460 Wedder Dod
Cairn Kinney 493
Ewe Hill
Stonehill Bank
White Hill
Glencaple
Midlock
Kirkton
Crawford
White Gill Wood
Leftshaw Hill 461
Rough Flow Moss
Cairn Hill
White Hill
Craig Dod
Kirkton Rig
Stoneyburn
Yearngill Head
Upper Whitecleuch
Priest's Pool
Snar Fm
Strancleuch Hill
469 Glendowran Hill
Ravengill Dod 538
Mid Hill
Wood Rig 474
The Dod
Bank
Mount Stuart 477
Bught Hill 451
Fingland Rig
Brocklaw Rig
Spango Hill 426
Windy Dod 424
Sim's Hill
Brown Dod 489
Black Hill
Harryburn Brae 499
Knockenshag
Kirklea 468
Redscar Heugh
Glendorch
Wellgrain Dod 555
Lodge Hill
Lady Cairn 522
Rodger Law 541
Knotty Hill
470 Mid Hill
Peat Rig 396
Spango Br
Whiteside Hill
Glenrae Dod 411
Rake Law 494
Dun Moss
Peat Hill 458
Water Head
Bulmer Moss
Wellshot Hill
Harleburn Head 546
Lamb Knowe
Meikle Knypes
385 Clackleith Hill
Slough Hill 433
Lowther Hills
Toddle Moss
South Shortcleugh
Elvanfoot
Bodsberry Hill
Fall Kneesend
Tippet Hill
483 Glengufflock Hill
Crow Knowes
Blackgannoch Cleuch
486 Shiel Hill
Castle Hill
Craignorth Hill
Reecleuch Hill
Wool Law
Howkwood
White Hill
468 Leadburn Rig
DUMFRIES AND GALLOWAY
Polholm Rig 491
Cruereach Hill 458
Duntercleuch Rig 377
Broad Law 514
Watchman Hill
Louise Wood Law 618
Cocker Hill 503
Largbrae Head
Wedder Dod 445
Duntercleuch
Bank Wood
Snarhead Hill
Leadhills
Laverock Hall
Hass
Crookedstane
Nap Hill
Ball Hill 449
Black Hill 483
Glenflosh Hill
The Dod
Well Hill
Sowen Dod 546
Wanlock Dod 552
Glen Ea's Hill 549
White Law 596
Great Hill
Archibald Gair Head 494
March
Williemont
396 Tongue Hill
Glengaber Hill 515
Meadowfoot
Glengonnar Halt
Dun Law 677
Brown Hill 383
406 Crookedstane Rig
Peat Rig
Knockenhair
Conrig Hill 485
Lowmill Knowe
Mine Hill
Kneesend 564
Doddin 476
Simon's Knowe
SOUTHERN UPLAND WAY
Sheiling Rig
WANLOCKHEAD BEAM ENGINE
MUSEUM OF LEAD MINING
Wanlockhead
Dungrain Law 669
Watermeetings
Tomont Hill 504
Mossholm
Clenries
Willowgrain Hill 515
Strood Hill 587
Black Hill 550
Stake Moss
Stake Hill
Faugh 583
Allershaw Lodge
Carco Mains
Knockenhair
Green Lowther 732
Watermeetings Rig
Mid Height 419
Threeps Moor
Horse Pow Hill
Sunnyside
Riccart Cleuch
Stowgill Dod 547
Brandleys Cott
White Dod 531
Wether Hill
Whiteside
Riccart Law Rig
Watermeetings Forest
Wintercleuch Fell 550
Gateside
Bogg
Brown Hill 476
Lowther Hill 725
Crooked Bank 591
Lang Cleuch
Earn Law
Pin Stane
Mid Hill 521
Crawick
Heuksland
SANQUHAR
Auchentaggart Moor
Lochside
Mennock Pass
Middle Moor
East Mount Lowther 631
Lion Hill
Sanquhar
SANQUHAR POST OFFICE
Burnfoot
Blackaddie Br
TOLLBOOTH MUSEUM
Barrmoor Cotts
247
Meikle Snout
Thirstane Hill 583
Wether Hill
Cold Moss
Comb Head
Laght Hill 507
Coom Rig
Daerside
Hitteril
Sweetshaw Brae 448
Hods Hill
Old Barr
420 Auchensow Hill
551 Threehope Height
Cock Hill
Lang Cleuch
Steygail 573
Meikle Shag 501
Hem Hill
Hitteril Hill 491
Daer Reservoir
507 Beld Knowe
Mount Joe
Euchan Cott
South Mains
Eliock Br
Mennock
Eliock
Yell Hill
Dalveen Pass
Comb Law 645
A70
A73
A72
A74(M)
A702
A76
B7078
B7055
B740
B797
B7040
B7076
A702
NS
00
10
40

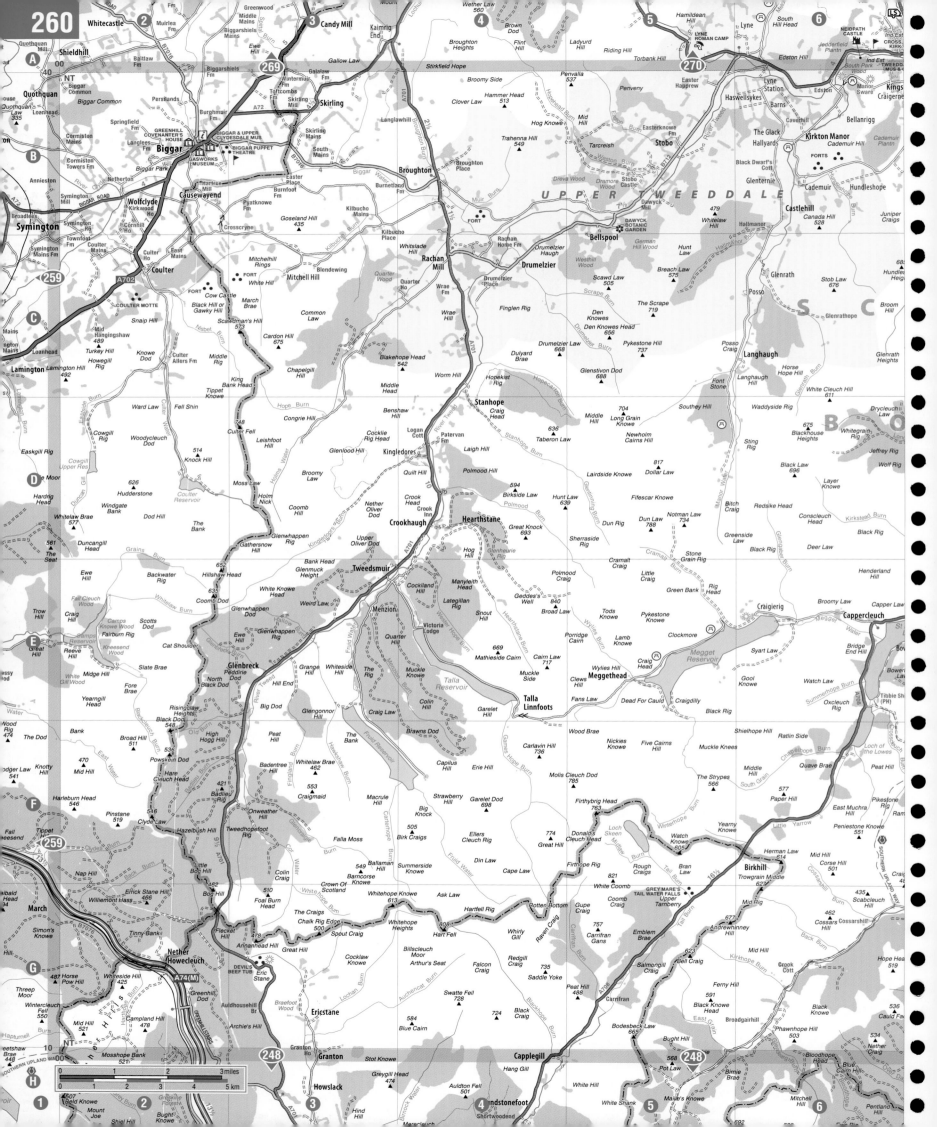

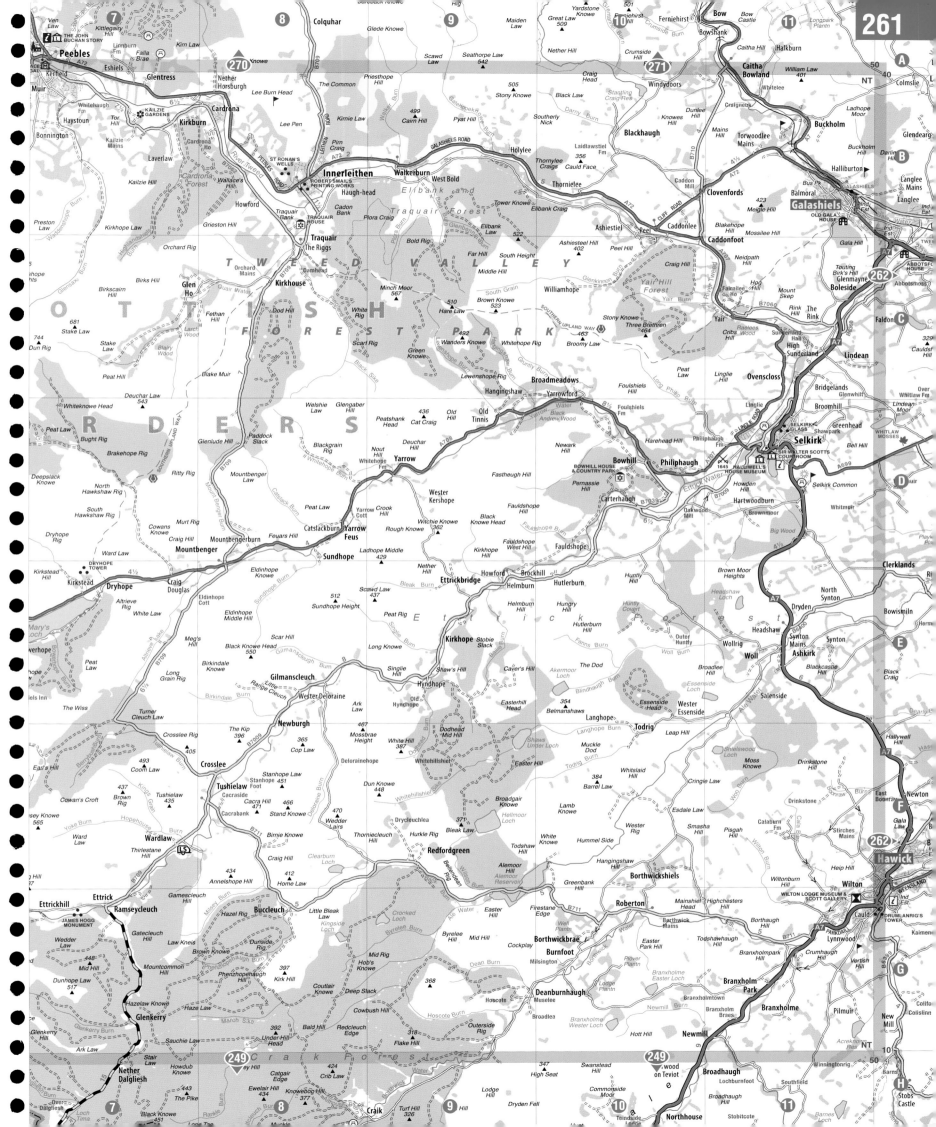

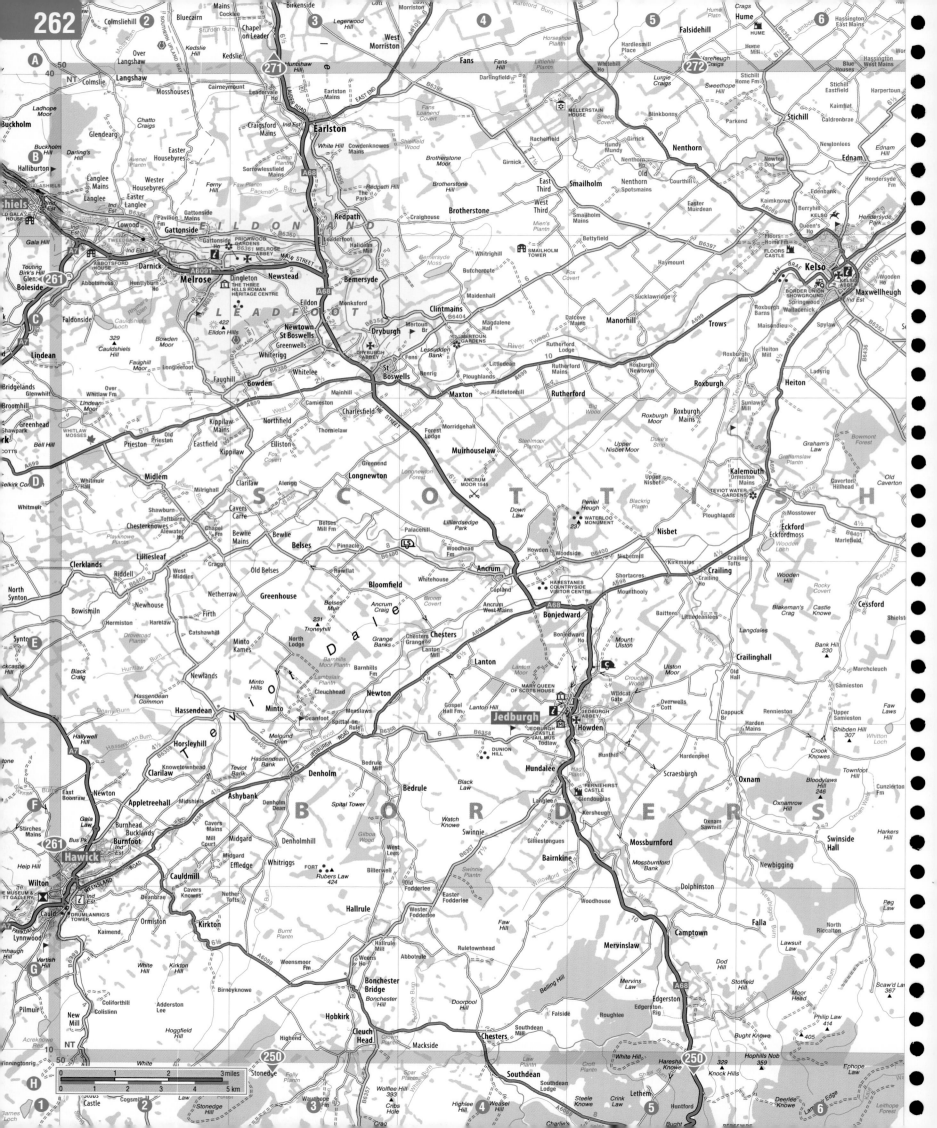

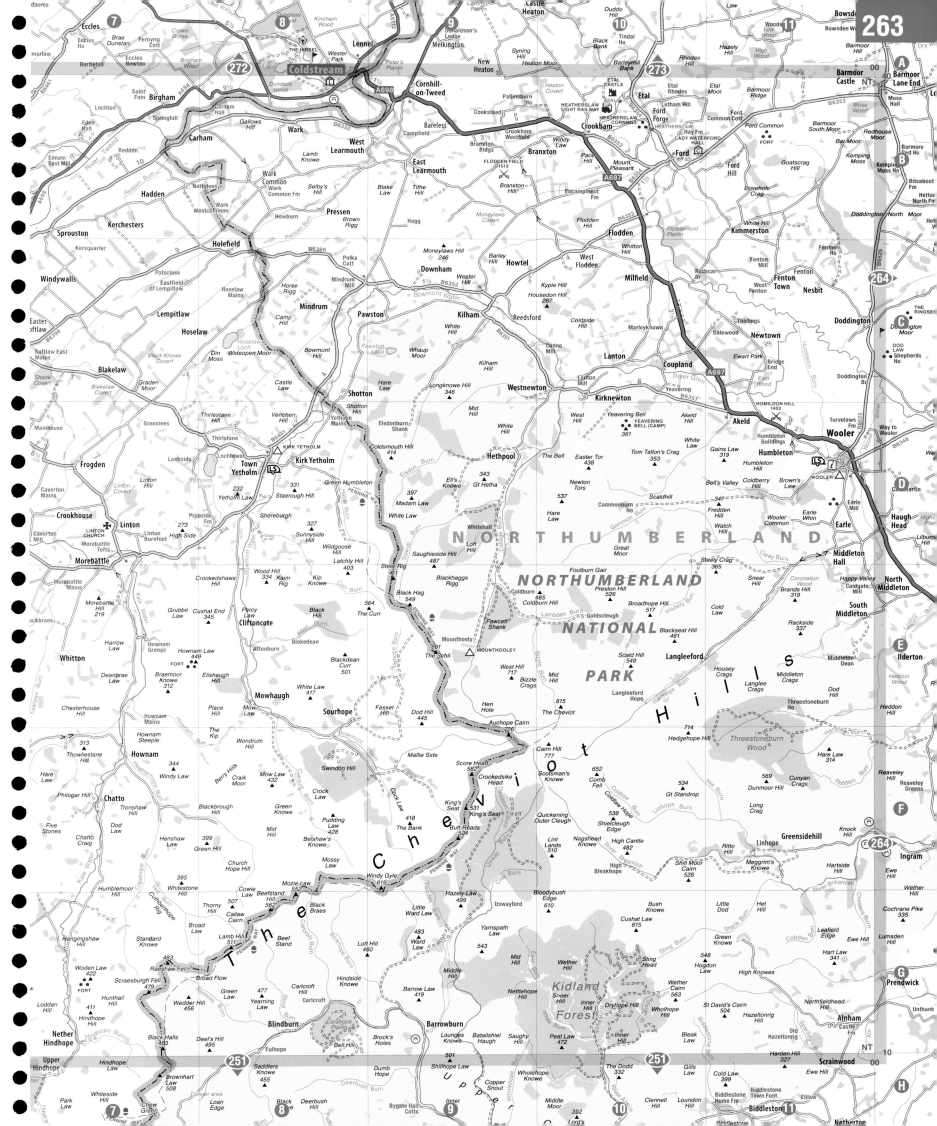

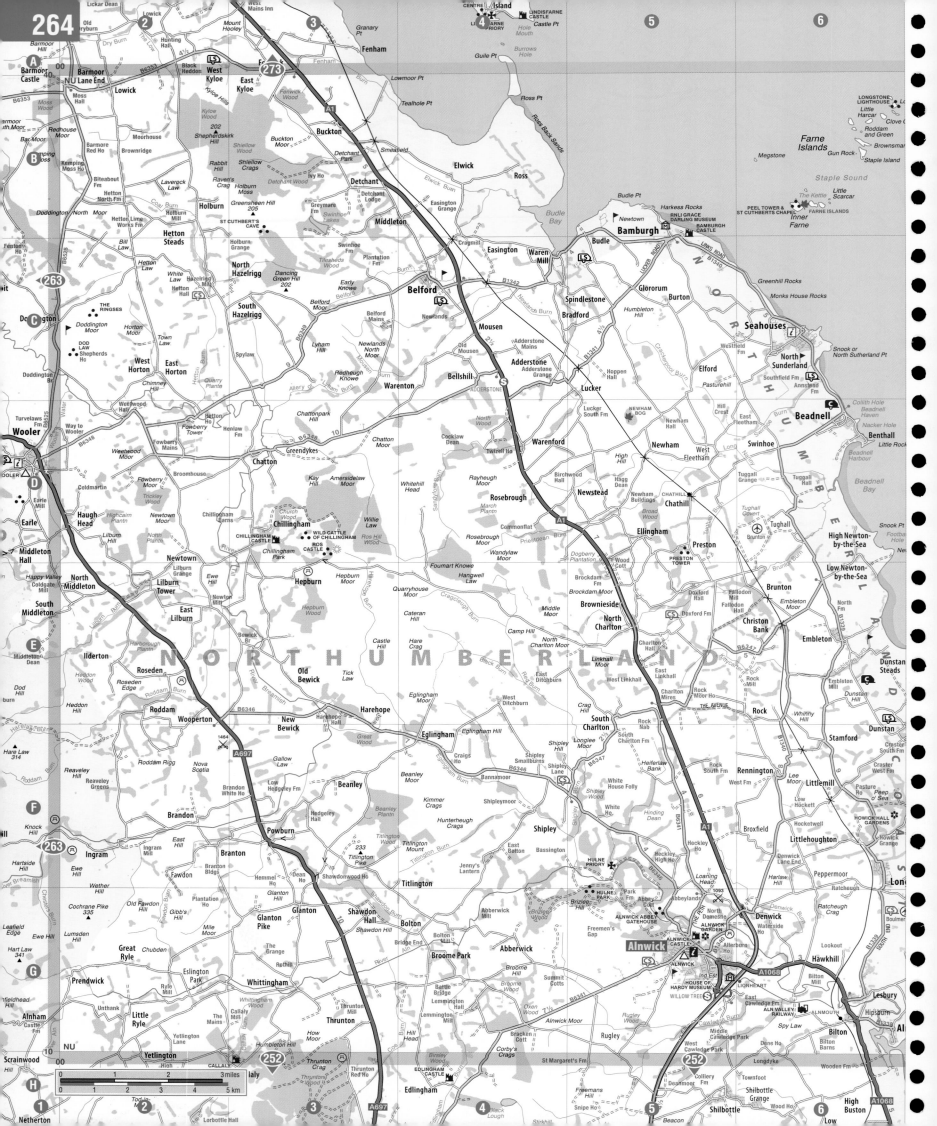

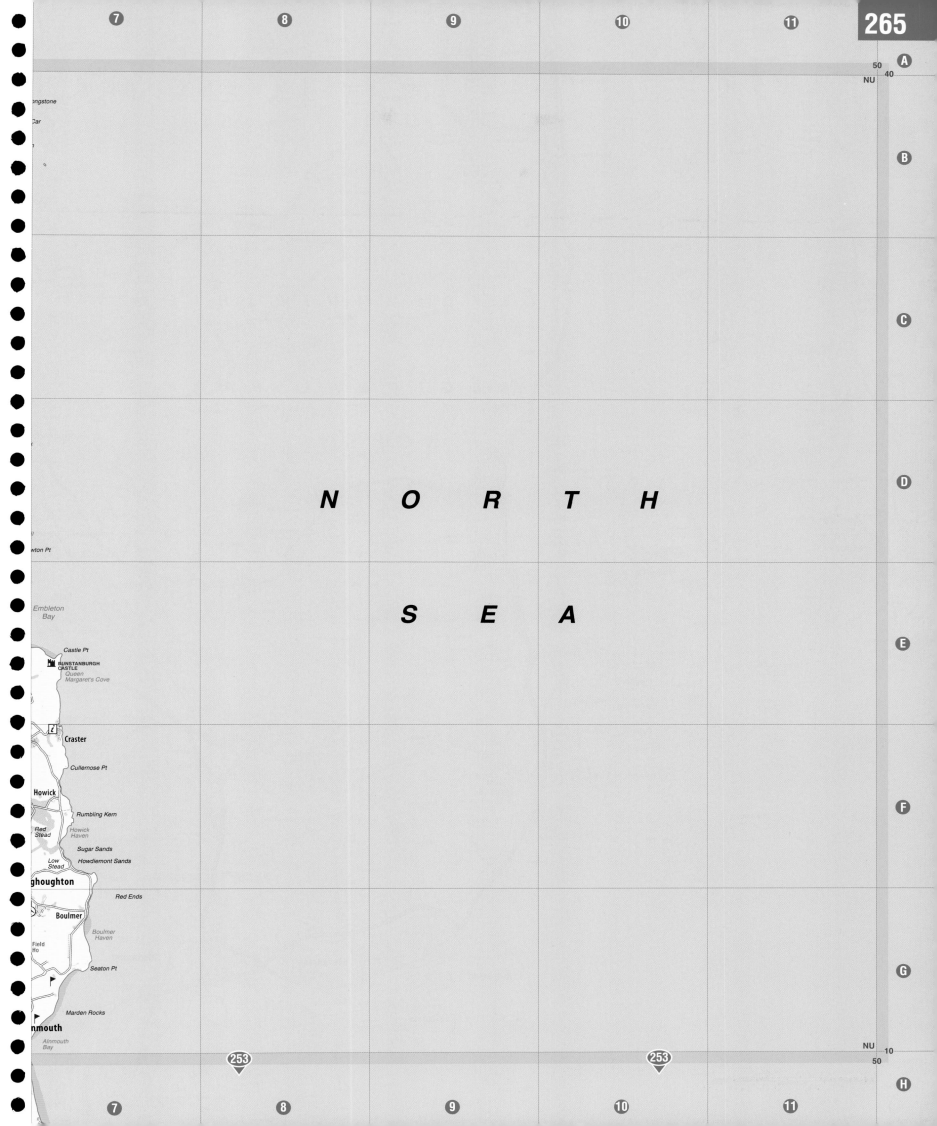

ⓐ 7 ⓑ 8 ⓒ 9 ⓓ 10 ⓔ 11

50
40
NU

A

B

ngstone

Car

C

wton Pt

D

N O R T H

S E A

Embleton
Bay

E

Castle Pt

DUNSTANBURGH
CASTLE
Queen
Margaret's Cove

ⓘ Craster

Cullernose Pt

Howick

F

Rumbling Kern

Red
Stead

Howick
Haven

Sugar Sands

Low
Stead

Howdiemont Sands

ghoughton

Red Ends

Boulmer

G

Boulmer
Haven

Field
Ho

Seaton Pt

Marden Rocks

nmouth

Alnmouth
Bay

NU
10

253

253

50

H

ⓐ 7 ⓑ 8 ⓒ 9 ⓓ 10 ⓔ 11

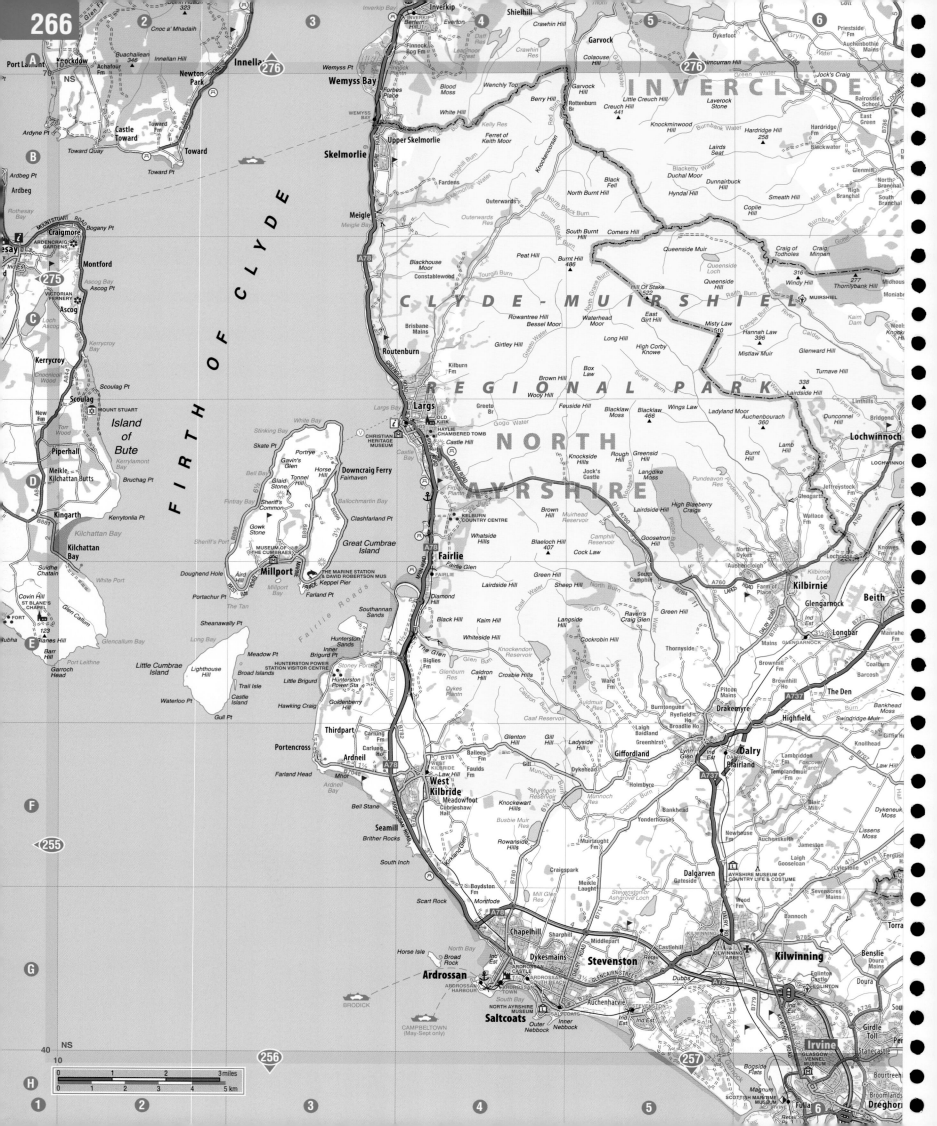

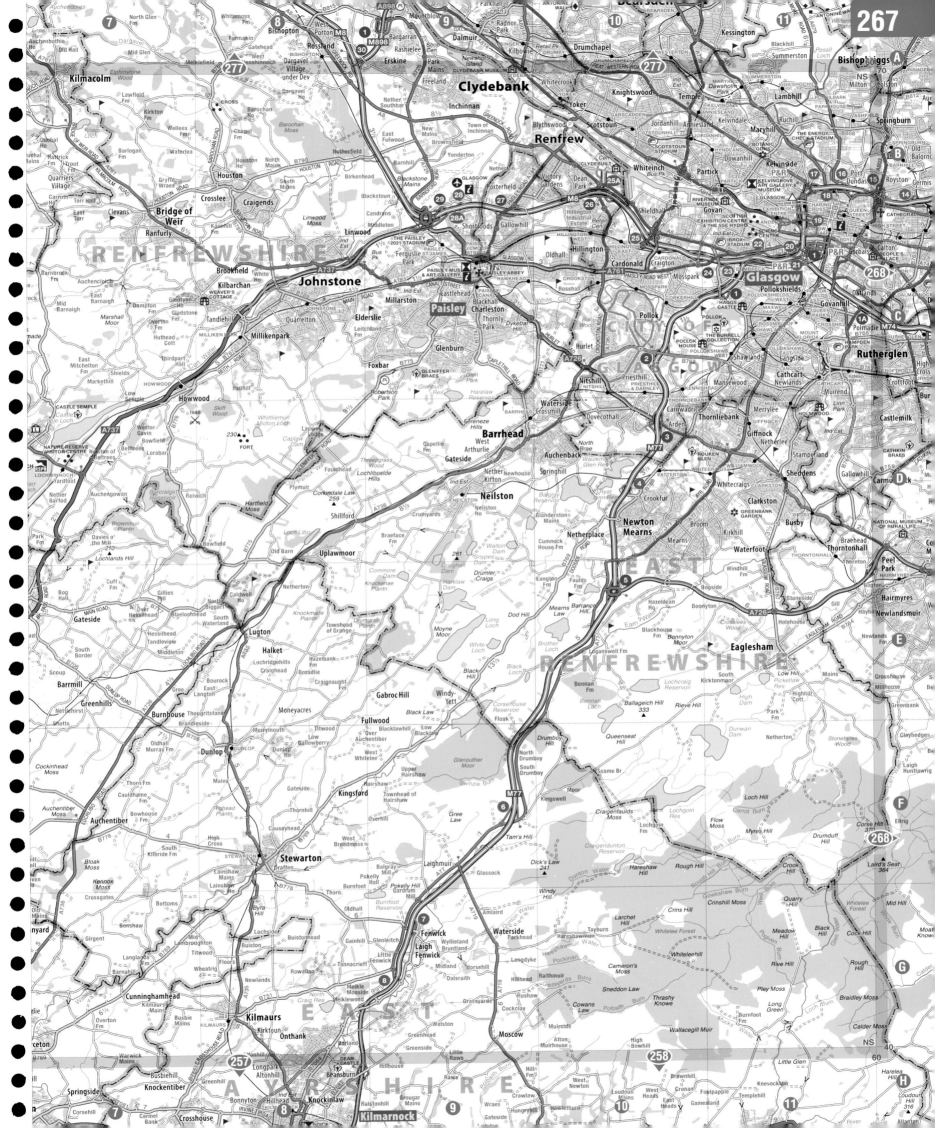

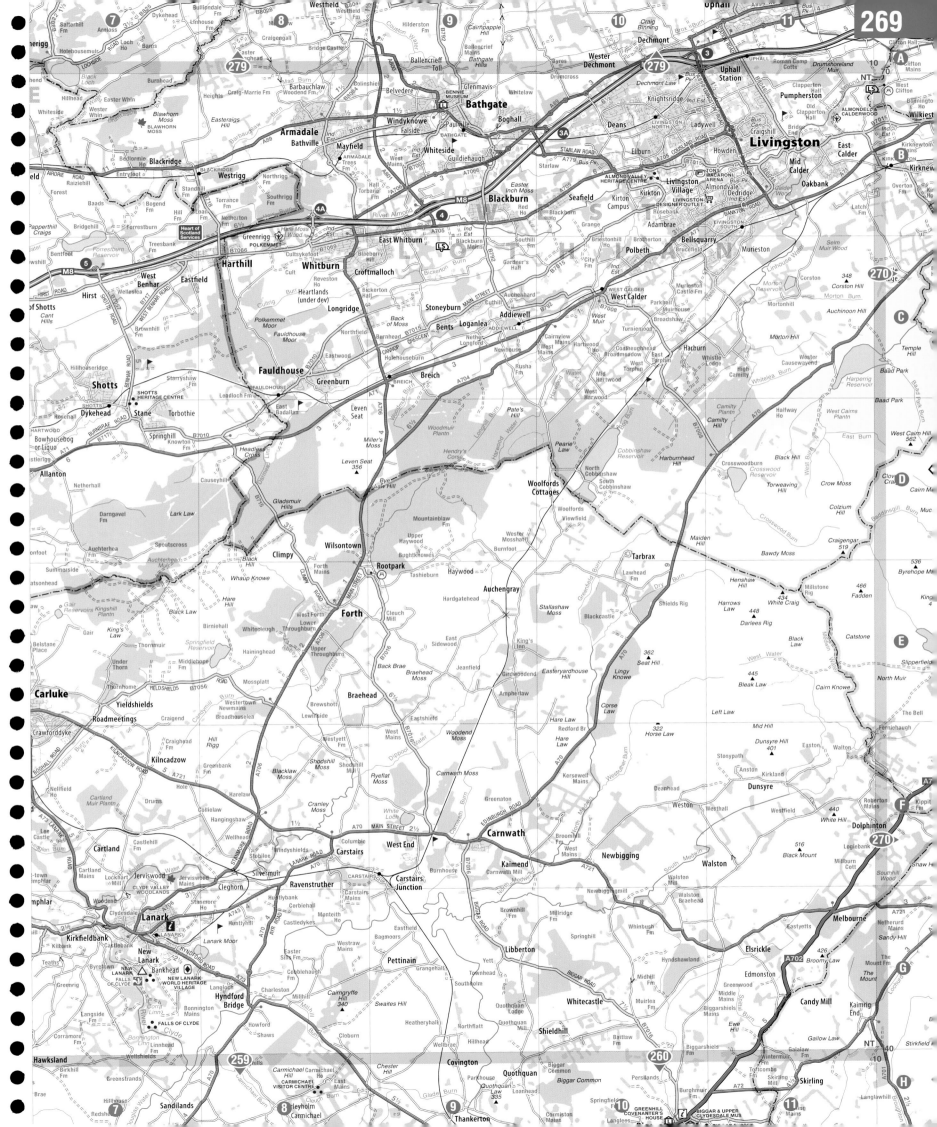

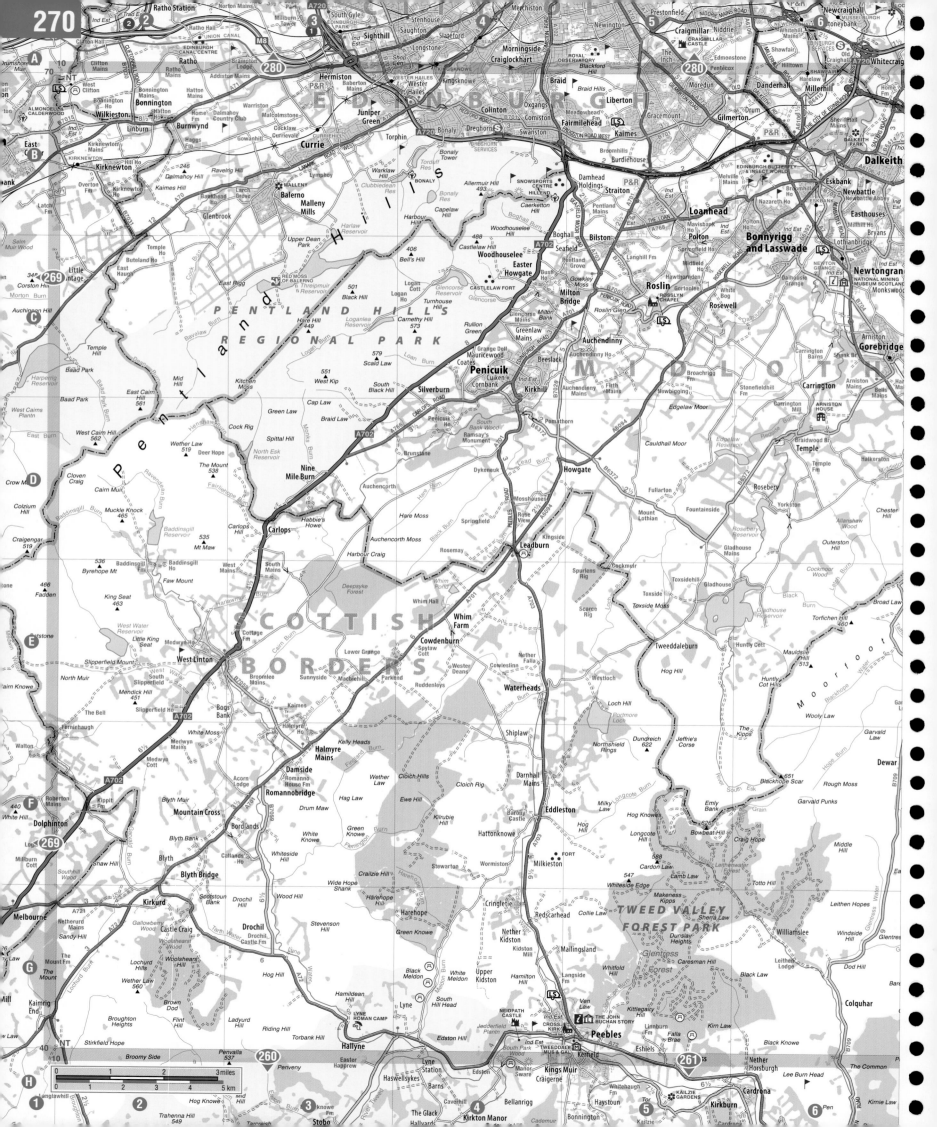

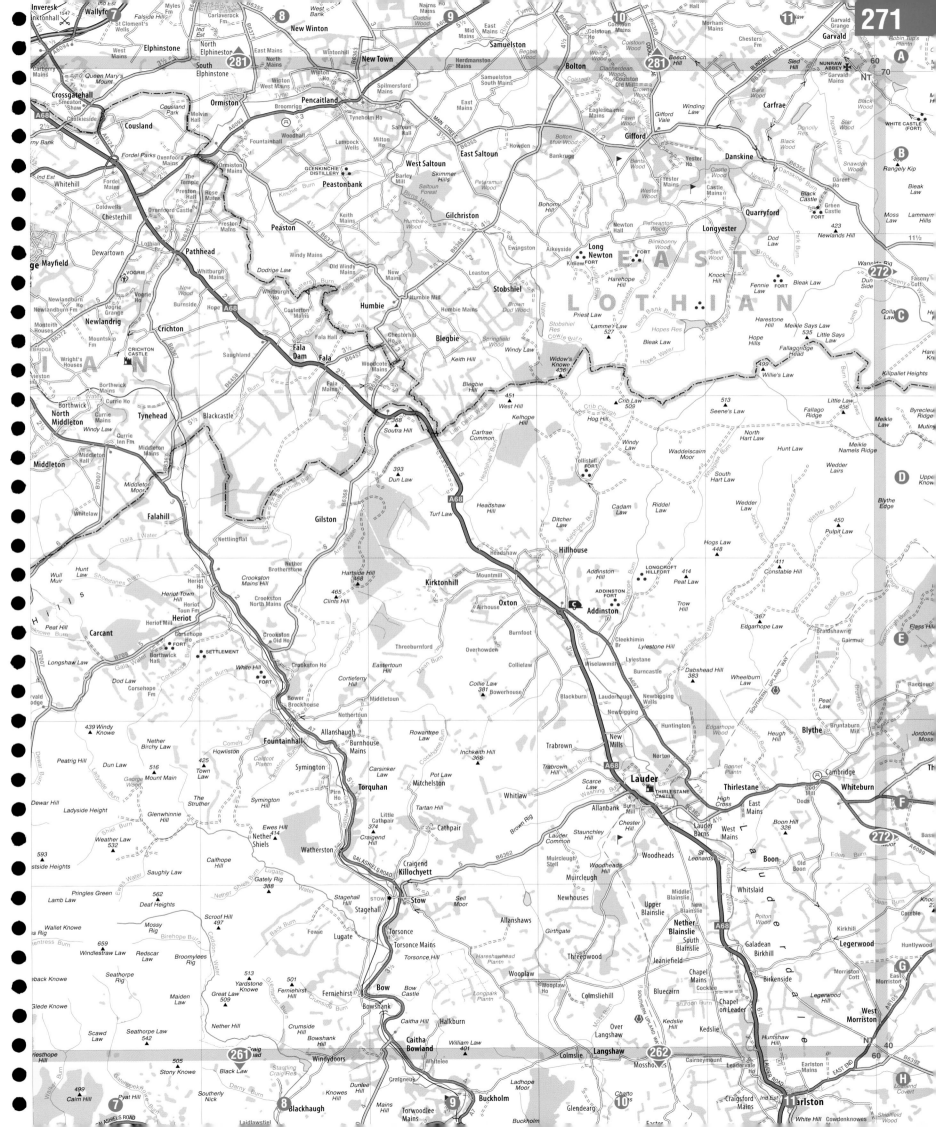

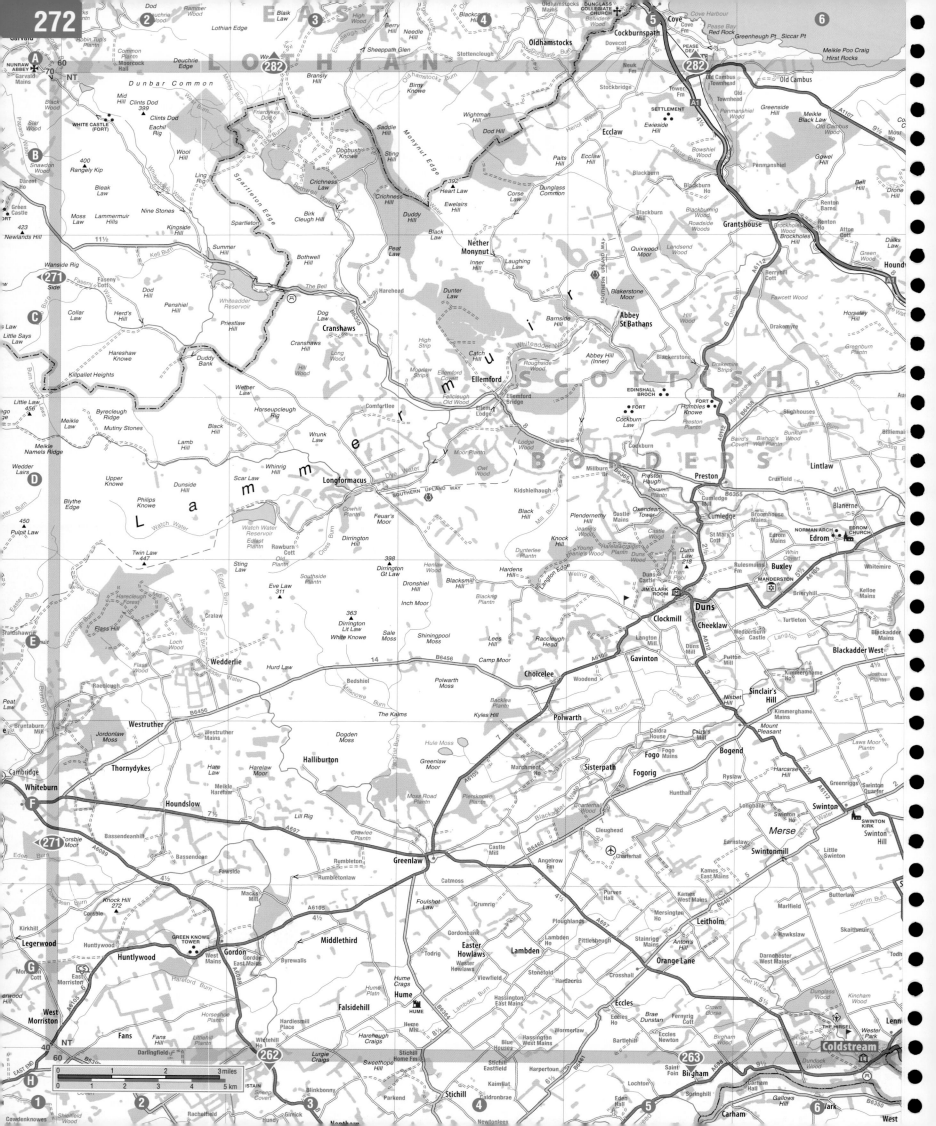

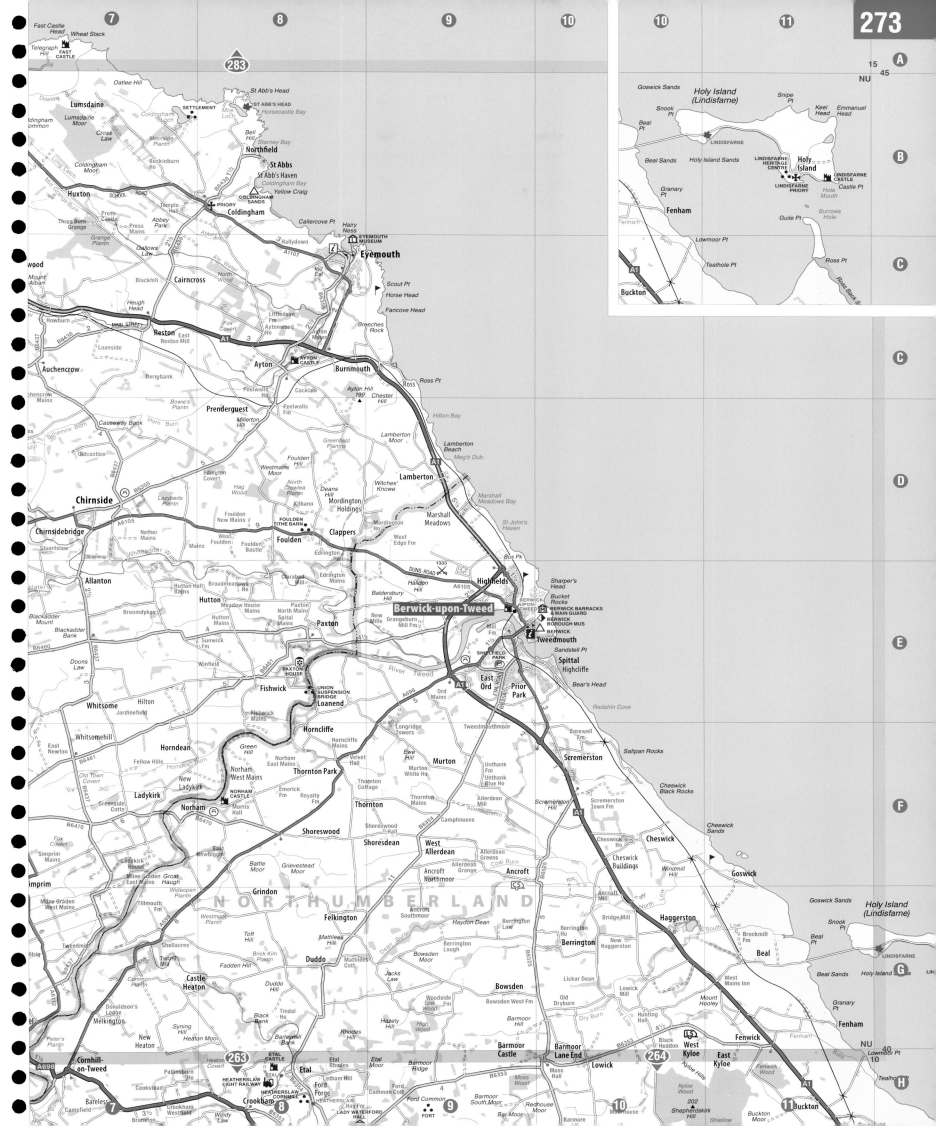

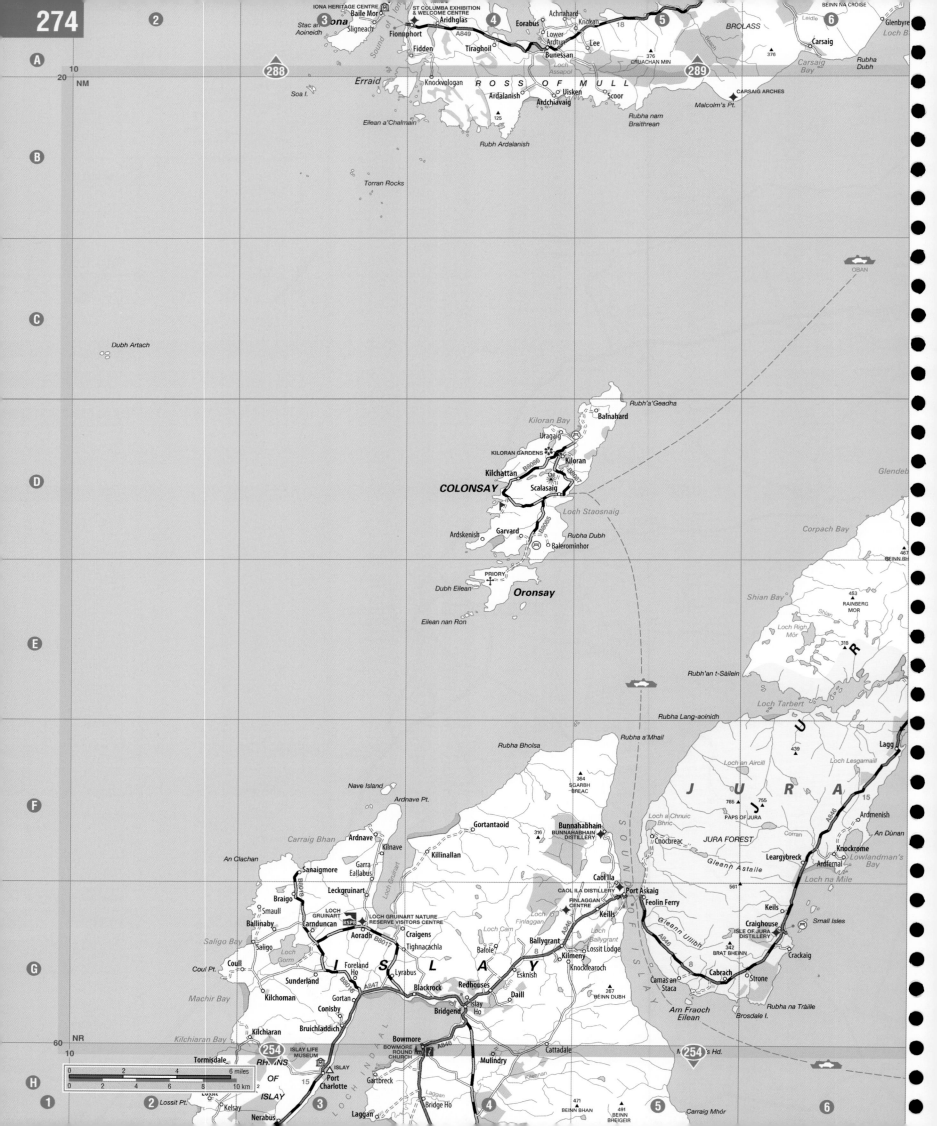

A

B

C

D

E

F

G

H

1 2 3 4 5 6

IONA HERITAGE CENTRE
ST COLUMBA EXHIBITION & WELCOME CENTRE
Baile Mor
Iona
Fionnphort
Stac an Aoineidh
Sligneach
Soa I.
Erraid
Eilean a'Chalmain
Aridhglas
Fidden
Tiraghoil
Bunessan
Knockvologan
Ardalanish
Ardchiavaig
Rubh Ardalanish
Eorabus
Lower Ardtun
Lee
Achnahard
Knokan
18
ROSS OF MULL
CRUACHAN MIN
376
Uisken
Scoor
125
Rubha nam Braithrean
Malcolm's Pt.
CARSAIG ARCHES
BROLASS
Carsaig
Carsaig Bay
Rubha Dubh
Glenbyre
BEINN NA CROISE
Loch Bk
Lèadle
376

A849
A849

288
289

10
20
NM

Torran Rocks

Dubh Artach

OBAN

Rubh'a'Geadha
Kiloran Bay
Uragaig
KILORAN GARDENS
Kilchattan
Scalasaig
COLONSAY
Balnahard
Kiloran
96
Loch Staosnaig
Ardskenish
Garvard
Rubha Dubh
Balerominor
PRIORY
Dubh Eilean
Oronsay
Eilean nan Ron
Corpach Bay
BEINN BH
467
Glendeb
Shian Bay
RAINBERG MOR
453
Shian
318
Loch Righ Mòr
Rubh'an t-Sàilein
Loch Tarbert
Rubha Lang-aoinidh
R

Rubha a'Mhail
Rubha Bholsa
Nave Island
Ardnave Pt.
Carraig Bhan
Ardnave
An Clachan
Kilnave
Killinallan
Garra Eallabus
Leckgruinart
Sanaigmore
Braigo
Smaull
Ballinaby
Carnduncan
Saligo
Saligo Bay
Loch Gorm
Coull
Coul Pt.
Sunderland
Machir Bay
Kilchoman
Gortan
Conisby
Bruichladdich
Kilchiaran
Kilchiaran Bay
Tormisdale
ISLAY LIFE MUSEUM
RHINS
OF
ISLAY
Port Charlotte
Lossit
Kelsay
Nerabus
Gortantaoid
SGARBH BREAC
364
316
Loch Gruinart
LOCH GRUINART NATURE RESERVE VISITORS CENTRE
RSPB
Aoradh
Craigens
Tighnacachla
Balole
Foreland Ho
Lyrabus
Blackrock
Redhouses
Daill
Bowmore
BOWMORE ROUND CHURCH
Mulindry
Gartbreck
Bridge Ho
Laggan
ISLAY
Esknish
Balygrant
Lossit Lodge
Kilmeny
Knockfearoch
Kilmeny
Loch Cam
Loch Finlaggan
FINLAGGAN CENTRE
CAOL ILA DISTILLERY
Caol Ila
Port Askaig
Keills
Loch Ballygrant
Loch Indaal
Bunnahabhain
BUNNAHABHAIN DISTILLERY
SOUND OF ISLAY
Feolin Ferry
JURA
JURA FOREST
PAPS OF JURA
786
755
Loch a Chnuic Bhric
Cnocbreac
Corran
439
Gleann Astaile
Leargybreck
Ardfernal
Knockrome
An Dùnan
Ardmenish
Lowlandman's Bay
Loch na Mile
561
Keils
Craighouse
ISLE OF JURA DISTILLERY
Small Isles
Crackaig
Strone
Cabrach
Gleann Ullibh
342
BRAT BHEINN
Camas an Staca
Am Fraoch Eilean
Brosdale I.
Rubha na Tràille
Carraig Mhòr
Lagg
Loch Lesgamaill
15
A846
A846
8
8
471
BEINN BHAN
491
BEINN BHEIGEIR
267
BEINN DUBH
Cattadale
Mc's Hd.
A846
A847
A846
B8018
B8017
B8016
B8086
B8085

254
254

60
10
NR

0   2   4   6 miles
0   2   4 6 8 10 km

B

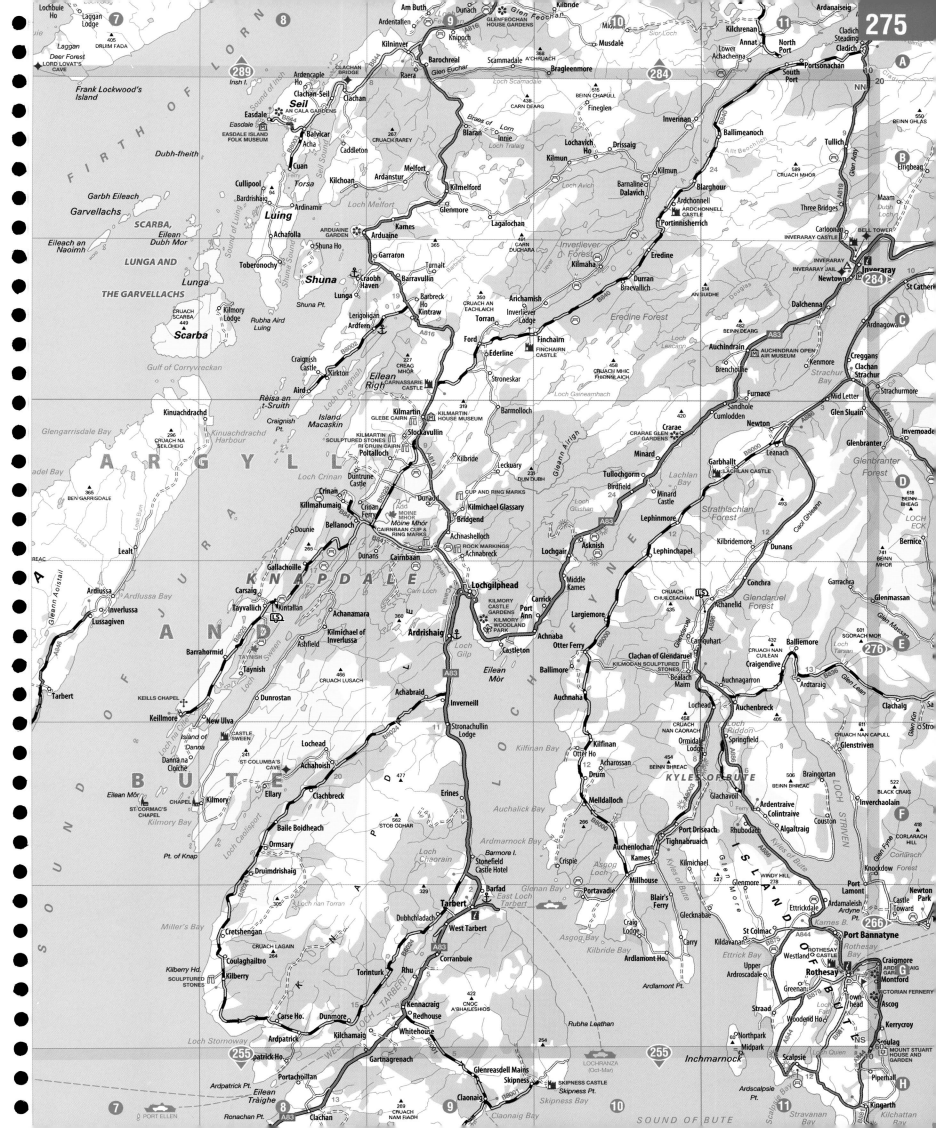

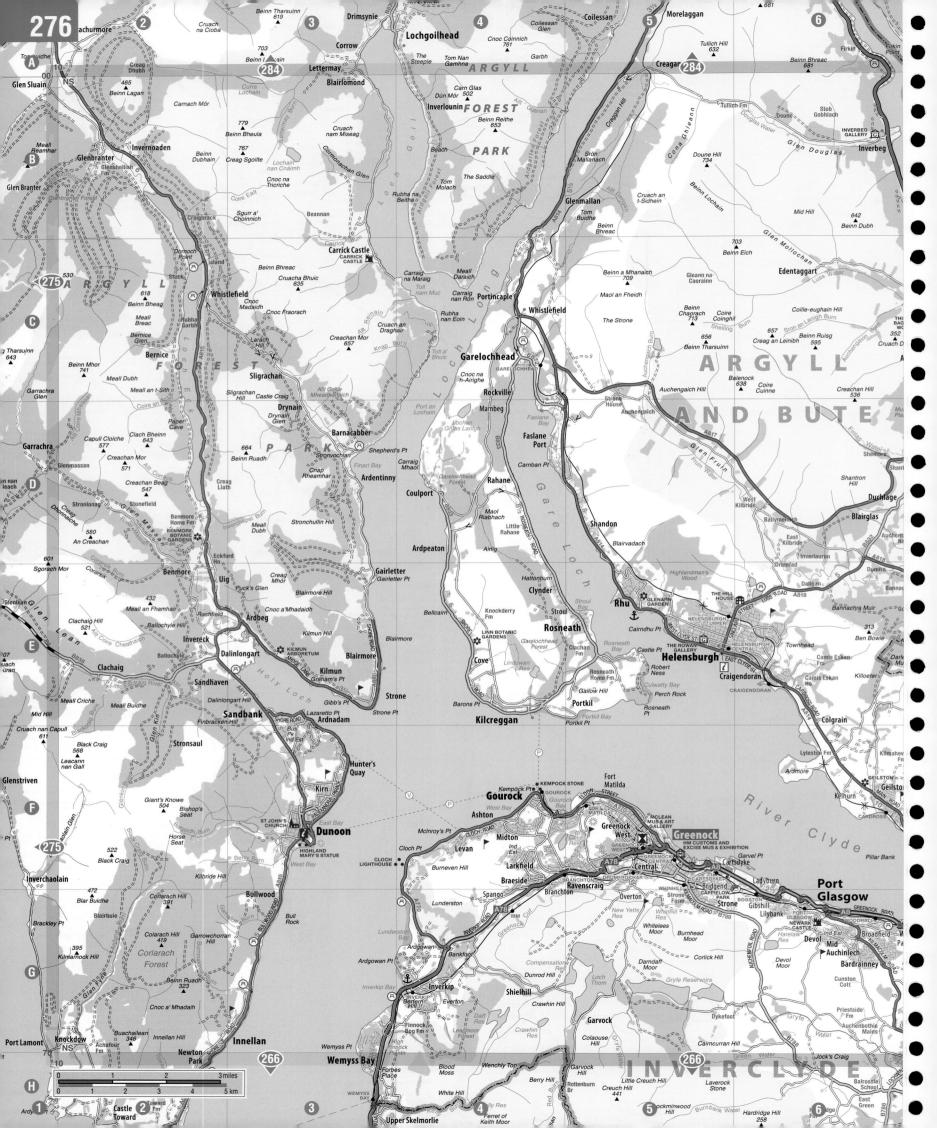

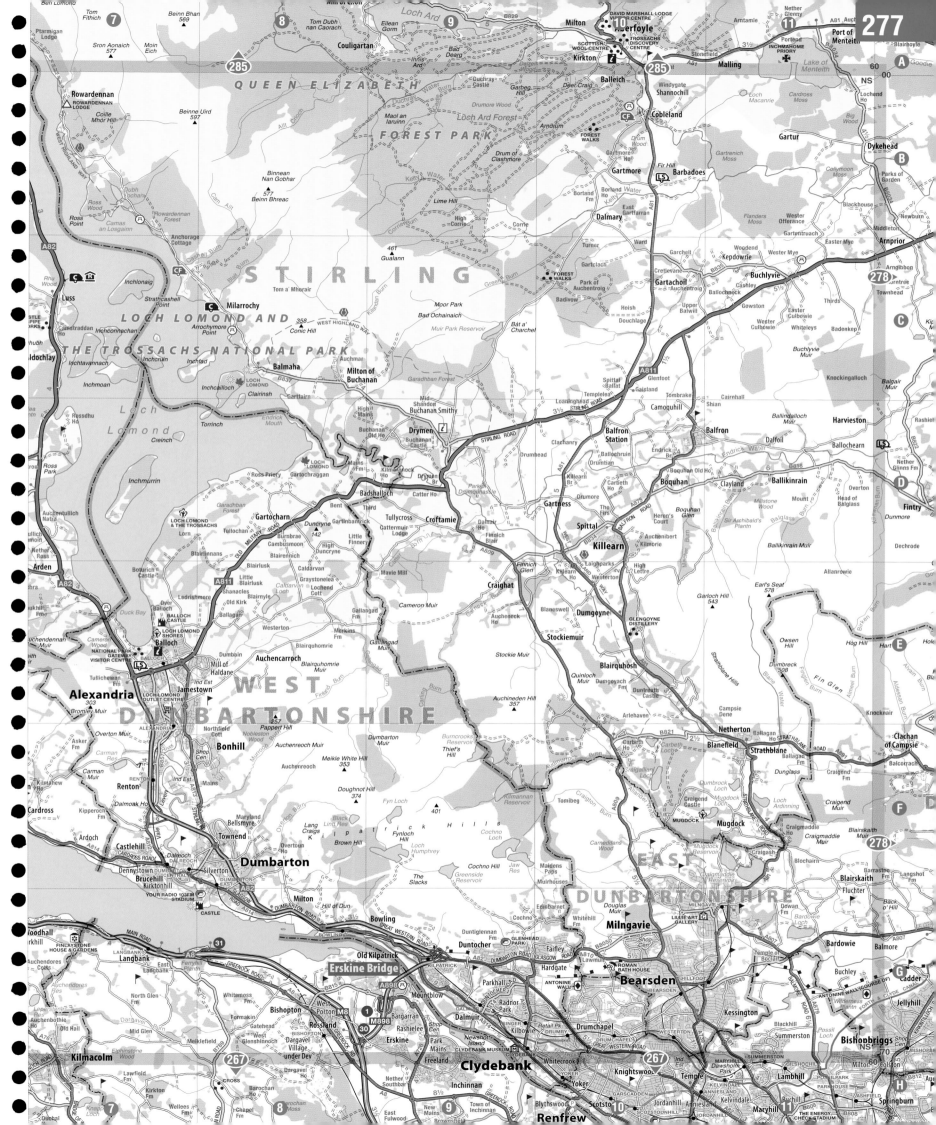

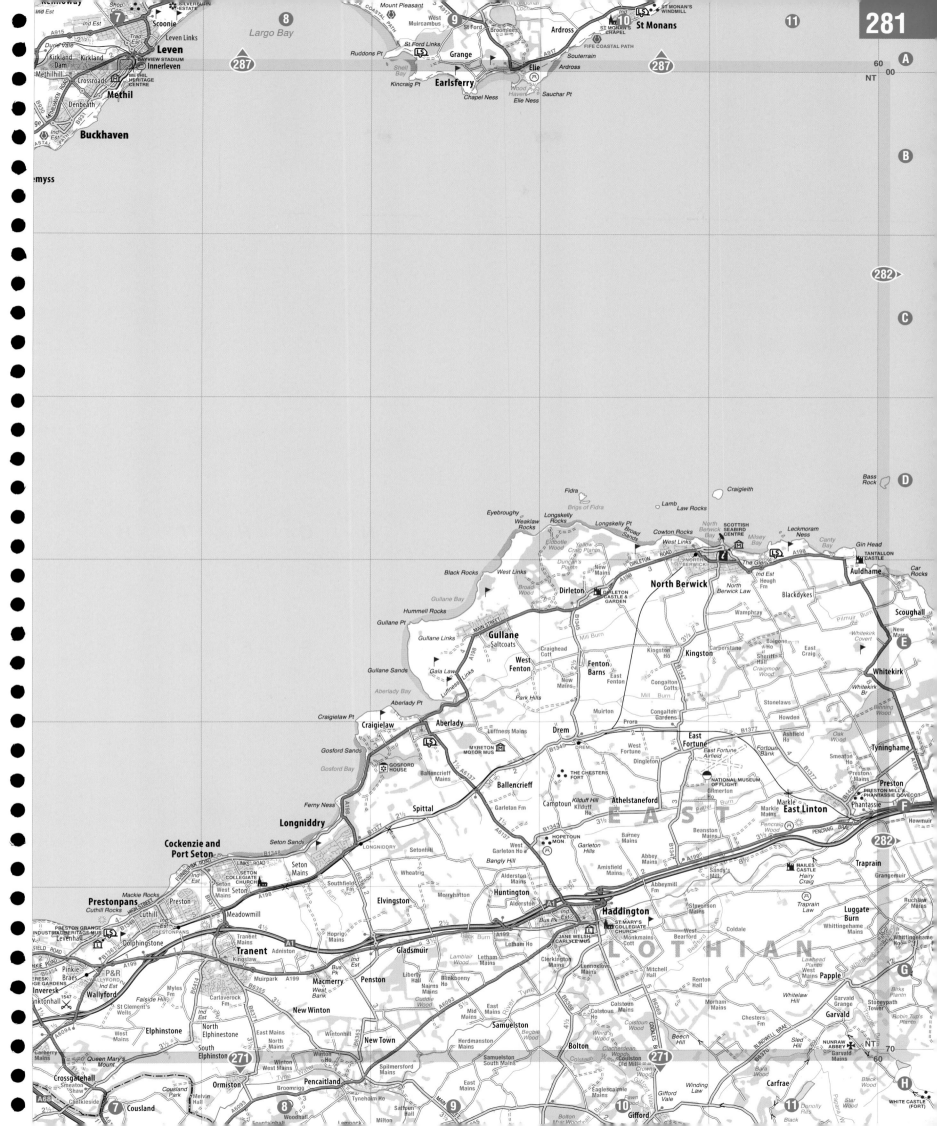

② ③ ④ ⑤ ⑥

A
60
00
NT

North Ness
ISLE OF MAY
287
Isle of May
South Ness

B

281

C

D
Bass Rock

N O R T H

S E A

Canty Bay
Gin Head
TANTALLON CASTLE
Auldhame
Car Rocks

Scoughall
Scoughall Rocks
New Mains
Peffer Sands
Whitekirk Covert

E
Pilmuir Burn
Whitekirk
Ravensheugh Sands
Frances Craig
Tyninghame Links
Whitekirk Br
Binning Wood
Tyne Sands

Oak Wood
Tyninghame
Salt Greens Plantn
Firth Plantn
Heckies Hole
John Muir
Belhaven Bay
Long Craigs
Scart Rock
Meikle Spiker
BELHAVEN ROAD
Belhaven
Dunbar
Mill Stone Neuk

Smeaton Ho
Preston
Preston Mains
Hedderwick Hill
West Barns
A1087
John Muir Birthplace
Ind Est
White Sands
Barns Ness

F
PRESTON MILL
PHANTASSIE DOVECOT
Phantassie
Knowes
A199
EDINBURGH RD
A1
Broxburn
East Barns

CRAIG BRAE
281
Howmuir
Hedderwick
South Belton
Old Belton
Spott
Dunbar Cement Works

Traprain
Grangemuir
Bielhill
Bielmill
Wester Broomhouse
Doon Hill
Little Pinkerton
Meikle Pinkerton
Chapel Pt
Skateraw Harbour
Torness Pt
Long Craig
Skateraw
Thorntonloch Power Sta.

Pitcox
Meiklerig Wood
Spott Mill
Spott West Mains
Pinkerton Hill
Thurston Manor
Crowhill
6½
Thorntonloch

Luggate Burn
Whittingehame Mains
Ruchlaw Mains
Stenton
Ruchlaw West Mains
Pressmennan Wood
THE CHESTERS (FORT)
Highside Hill
Brunt Hill
The Brunt
Thurston Mains
Innerwick
Thurston Mains Burn
A1

apple
G
Garvald
Birks Plantn
Deuchrie Dod
Rummer Wood
Halls
Blaik Law
Lothian Edge
High Wood
Berry Hill
Needle Hill
Blackcastle Hill
Old Branxton
Oldhamstocks Mains
DUNGLASS COLLEGIATE CHURCH
Belvidere Wood
Bilsdean
Reed Pt
Cove Harbour
Cockburnspath
Cove
Pease Bay
Red Rock
Greenheugh Pt
Siccar Pt

Garvald Grange
Garvald Mains
NUNRAW ABBEY
Stoneypath Tower
Robin Tup's Plantn
Common Plantn
Deuchrie Edge
Watch Law
Oldhamstocks
Dovecot Hall
PEASE DEAN
Meikle Poo Craig
Hirst Rocks

70
NT
60

E A S T   L O T H I A N

Dunbar Common
272
Bransly Hill
Birny Knowe
Stockbridge
Tower Fm
272
Old Cambus Townhead
Old Cambus

H
0   1   2   3 miles
0   1   2   3   4   5 km

WHITE CASTLE (FORT)
Cocklaw Rig
Crib Law
Fnardykes Dod
Saddle Hill
Wightman Hill
Old Hill
SETTLEMENT
Ecclaw
Penmanshiel Wood
Greenside Hill
Meikle Black Law
A1107
Cove

① ② ③ ④ ⑤ ⑥

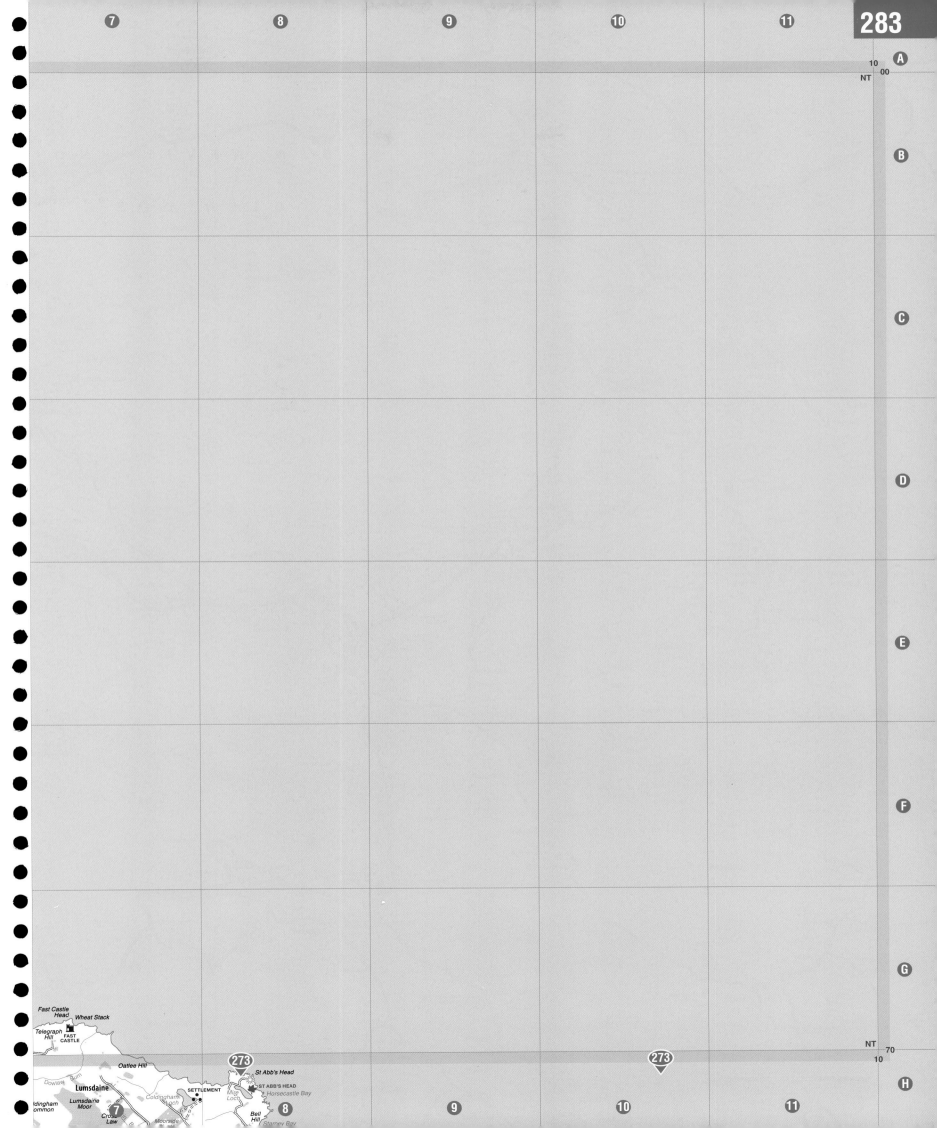

7   8   9   10   11

A

B

C

D

E

F

G

H

NT

Lumsdaine

Oatlee Hill

Moorside

Coldingham Loch

Cross Law

Telegraph Hill

FAST CASTLE

Fast Castle Head

Wheat Stack

Dowlaw Burn

Oldingham Common

Lumsdaine Moor

273

St Abb's Head

ST ABB'S HEAD

SETTLEMENT

Mire Loch

Horsecastle Bay

Bell Hill

Starney Bay

273

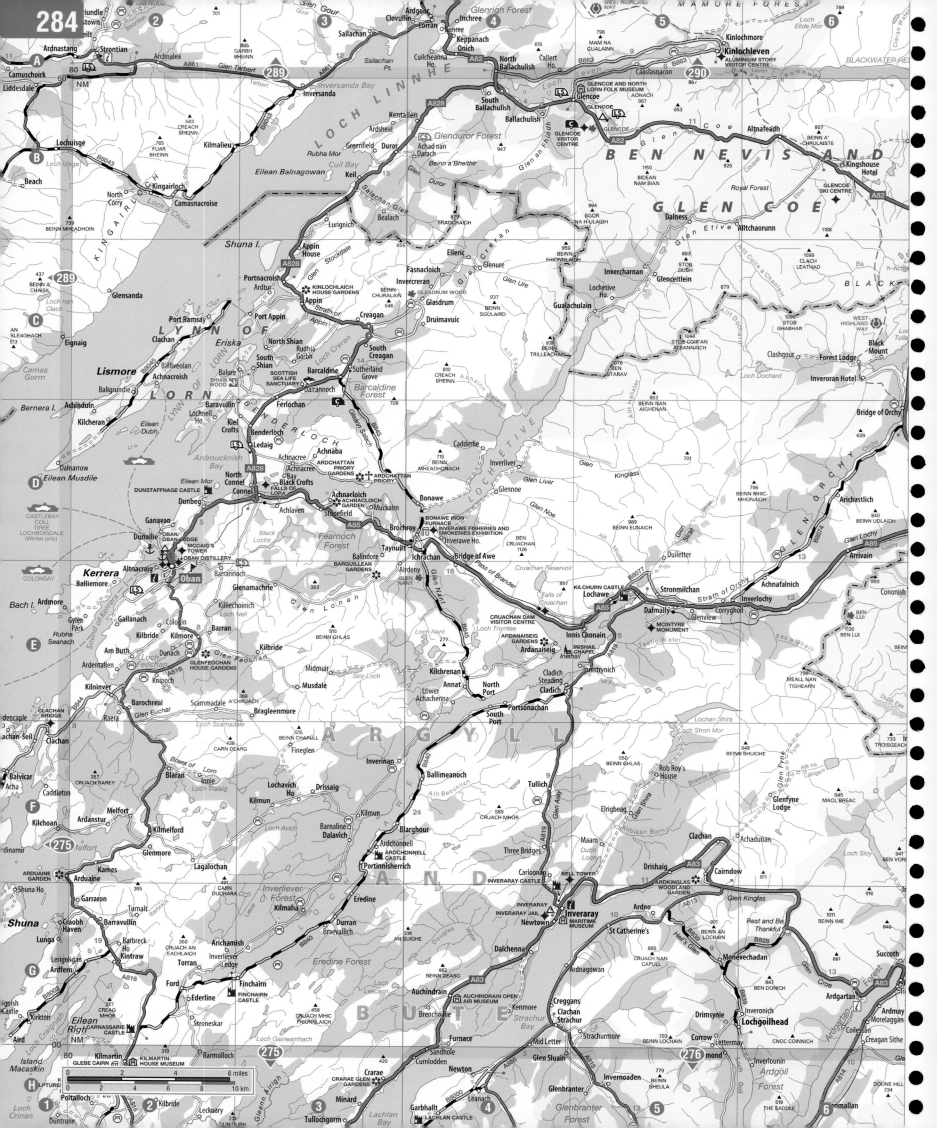

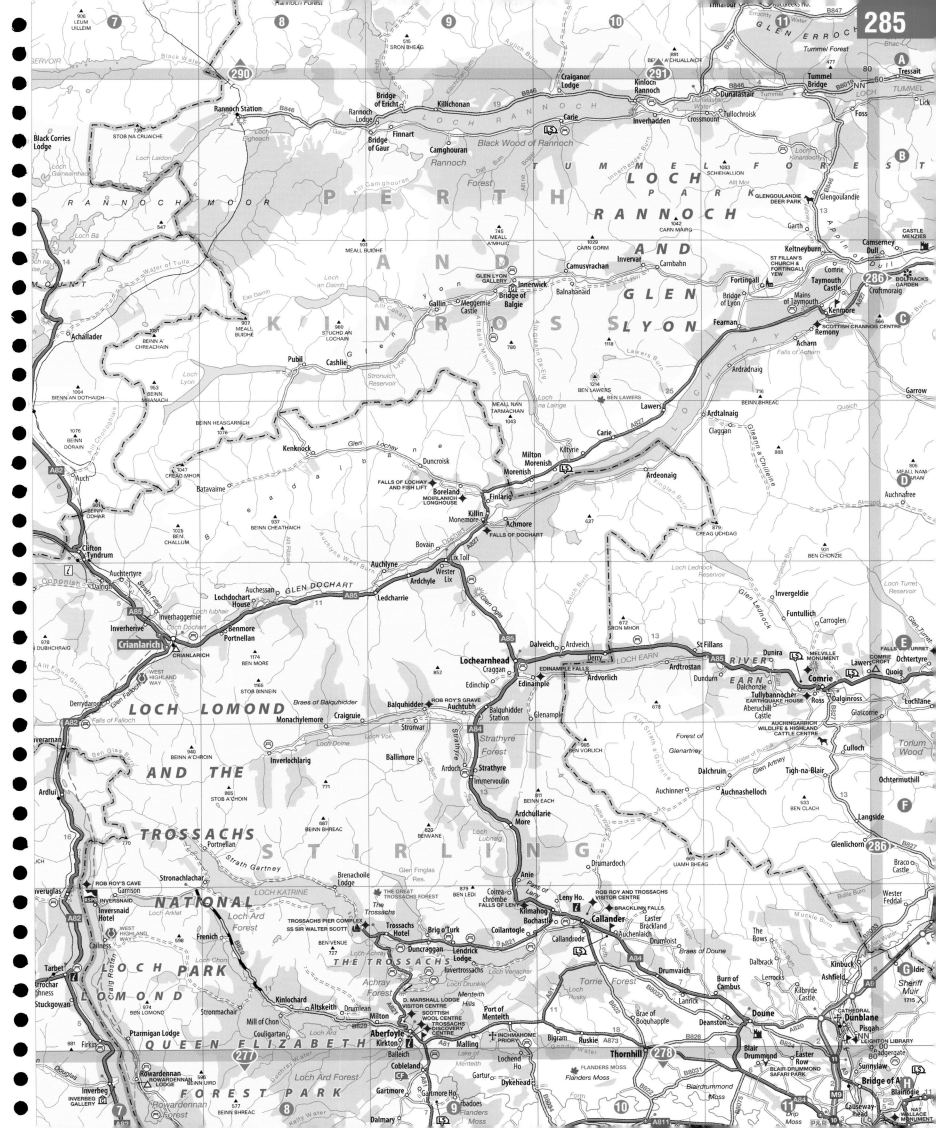

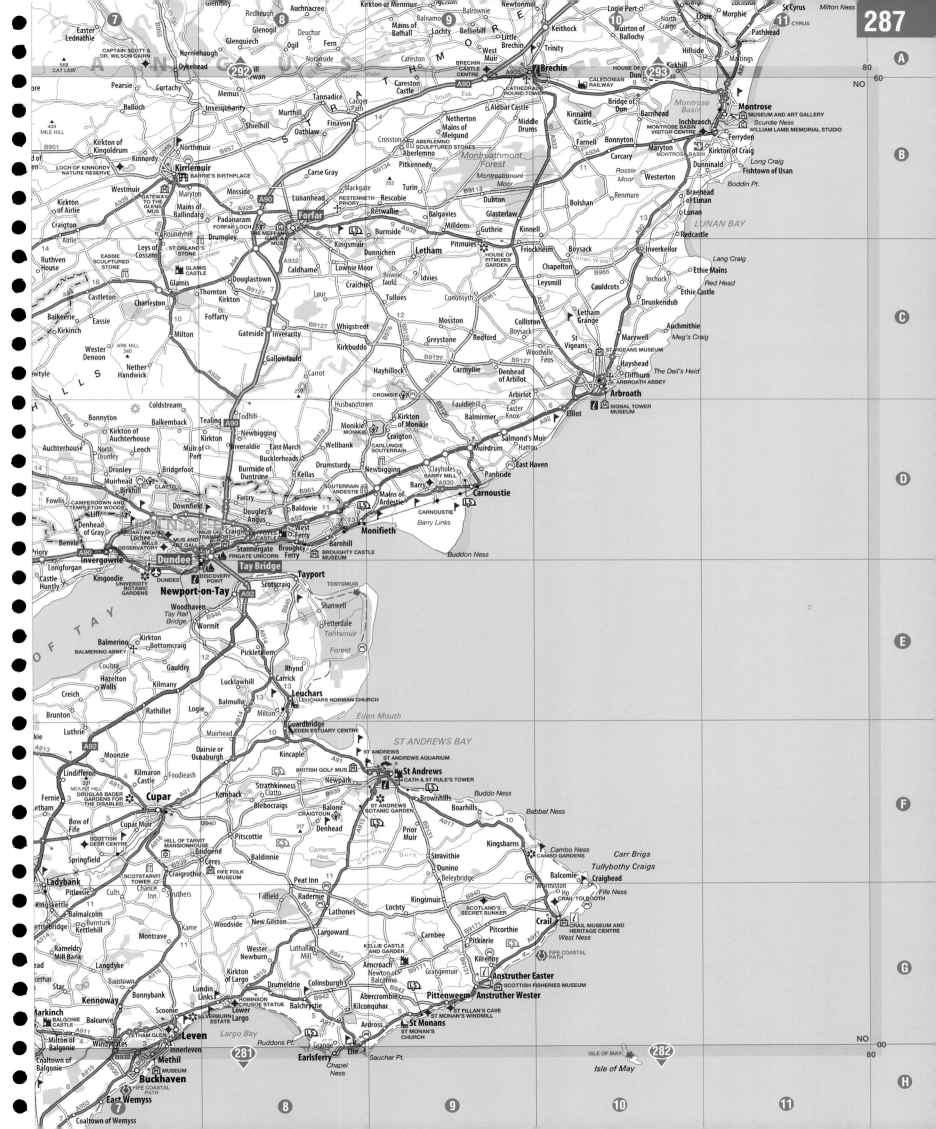

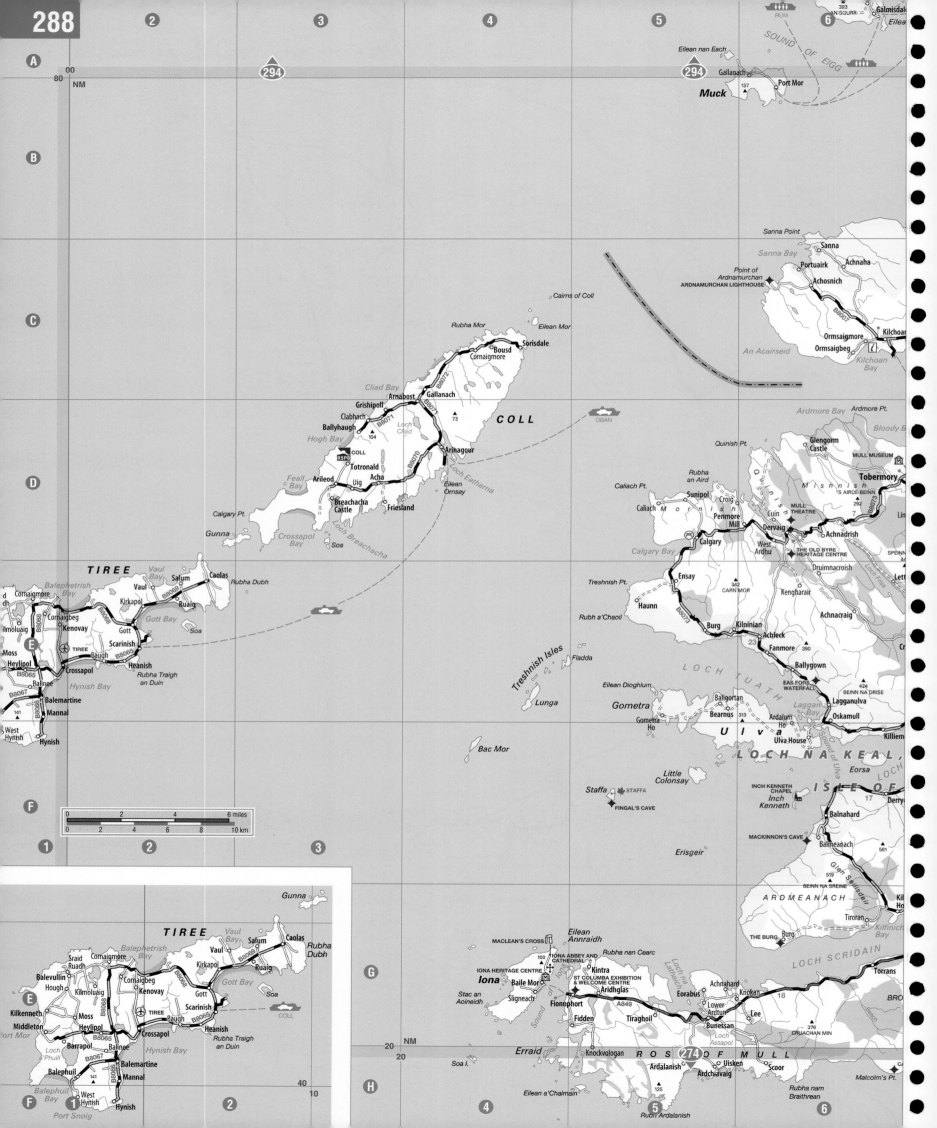

A

B

C

D

E

F

G

H

1 2 3 4 5 6

294

SOUND OF EIGG

RÙM
AN-SGURR
Galmisdale
Eilea

Eilean nan Each
Gallanach
137 Port Mor
Muck
393

294

Sanna Point
Sanna Bay
Sanna
Achnaha
Portuairk
Achosnich
Point of
Ardnamurchan
ARDNAMURCHAN LIGHTHOUSE
An Acairseid
Ormsaigmore
Ormsaigbeg
Kilchoan
Kilchoan Bay

Cairns of Coll

Rubha Mor
Eilean Mor
Bousd
Sorisdale
Cornaigmore
Cliad Bay
Arnabost
Gallanach
Grishipoll
Clabhach
Ballyhaugh
COLL
Loch
Clad
73
104
Hogh Bay
COLL
RSPB
Totronald
Arinagour
OBAN
Arileod
Uig
Acha
Loch Eatharna
Feall
Bay
Breachacha
Castle
Eilean
Ornsay
Friesland
Calgary Pt.
Gunna
Crossapol
Bay
Soa
Loch Breachacha

Ardmore Bay Ardmore Pt.
Bloody B

Quinish Pt.
Rubha
an Aird
Glengorm
Castle
MULL MUSEUM
Caliach Pt.
Sunipol
Croig
Cuin
Dervaig
Tobermory
Caliach
Mornish
Penmore
Mill
Mishnish
S AIRDE-BEINN
292
MULL
THEATRE
Achnadrish
7
Calgary Bay
Calgary
West
Ardhu
THE OLD BYRE
HERITAGE CENTRE
Druimnacroish
SPEINN
Lett
Li

TIREE
Balephetrish
Bay
Vaul
Bay
Vaul Salum
Caolas
Kirkapol
Ruaig
Rubha Dubh
Cornaigmore
Cornaigbeg
Kenovay
Gott Bay
B8069
Gott
Soa
Moss
TIREE
Scarinish
Heylipol
Baugh
Heanish
Rubha Traigh
an Duin
Balinoe
Crossapol
Hynish Bay
Balemartine
141
Mannal
West
Hynish Hynish

Treshnish Pt.
Ensay
342
CARN MOR
Kengharair
Achnacraig
Haunn
Rubh a'Chaoil
Burg
Kilninian
Achleck
Fanmore
390
Ballygown
23
EAS FORS
WATERFALL
424
BEINN NA DRISE
Lagganulva
Oskamull
Laggan
Bay
LOCH TUATH
Eilean Dioghlum
Treshnish Isles
Fladda
Baligortan
Bearnus 313
Ardalum
Lunga
Gometra
Gometra
Ho
Ulva
House
Ulva
LOCH NA KEAL
Killiem

Bac Mor

Little
Colonsay
Eorsa
LOCH
Staffa
STAFFA
INCH KENNETH
CHAPEL
ISLE OF
Inch
Kenneth
FINGAL'S CAVE
Erisgeir
Balnahard
17
Derry

MACKINNON'S CAVE
Balmeanach
561
Glen
Seilisdeir
519
ARDMEANACH
BEINN NA SREINE
Kil
Ho
Tiroran
Kilfinichen
Bay
THE BURG
Burg
LOCH SCRIDAIN

MACLEAN'S CROSS
Eilean
Annraidh
IONA ABBEY AND
CATHEDRAL
Rubha nan Cearc
100
IONA HERITAGE CENTRE
Iona
ST COLUMBA EXHIBITION
& WELCOME CENTRE
Baile Mor
Aridhglas
Torrans
Stac an
Aoineidh
Kintra
Eorabus
Achnahard
Knokan
Sligneach
Fionnphort
Lower
18
Ardtun
Lee
Fidden
Tiraghoil
A849
Bunessan
376
CRUACHAN MIN
Erraid
Knockvologan
ROS OF MULL
274
Soa I.
Ardalanish
Uisken
Scoor
Loch
Assapol
Eilean a'Chalmain
Rubh Ardalanish
Rubha nam
Braithrean
Malcolm's Pt.
125
CA

Scale:
0 2 4 6 miles
0 2 4 6 8 10 km

TIREE (inset)
Gunna
Balephetrish
Bay
Sraid
Ruadh
Cornaigmore
Vaul
Bay
Vaul Salum
Caolas
Balevullin
Hough
Kilmoluaig
Cornaigbeg
Kenovay
Kirkapol
Ruaig
Rubha
Dubh
Gott Bay
Kilkenneth
Moss
Gott
Soa
Middleton
Heylipol
TIREE
Scarinish
COLL
Port Mor
Barrapol
Baugh
Heanish
Loch
a'Phuill
Balinoe
Crossapol
Rubha Traigh
an Duin
Balephuil
Balemartine
Hynish Bay
141
Mannal
Balephuil
Bay
West
Hynish
Port Snoig
Hynish

NM
00
80

NM
20
20

40
10

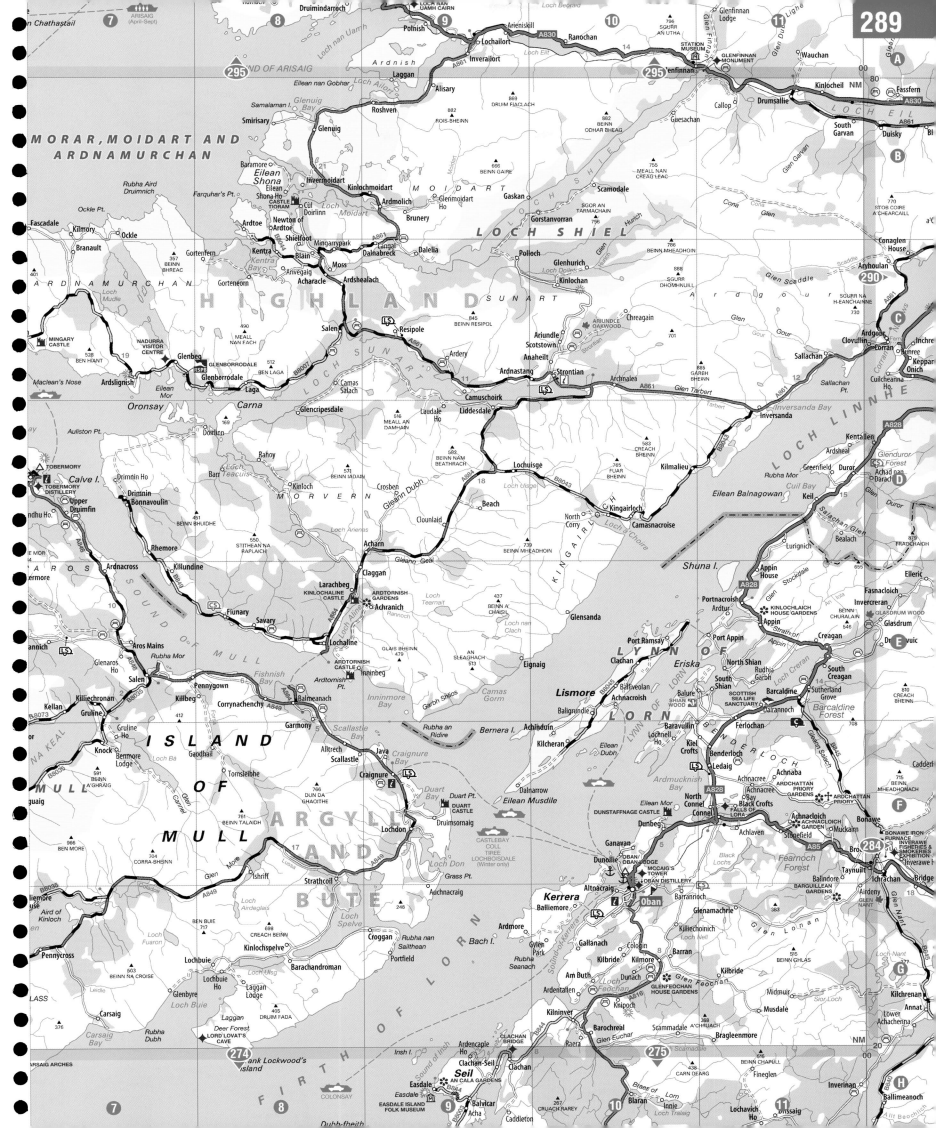

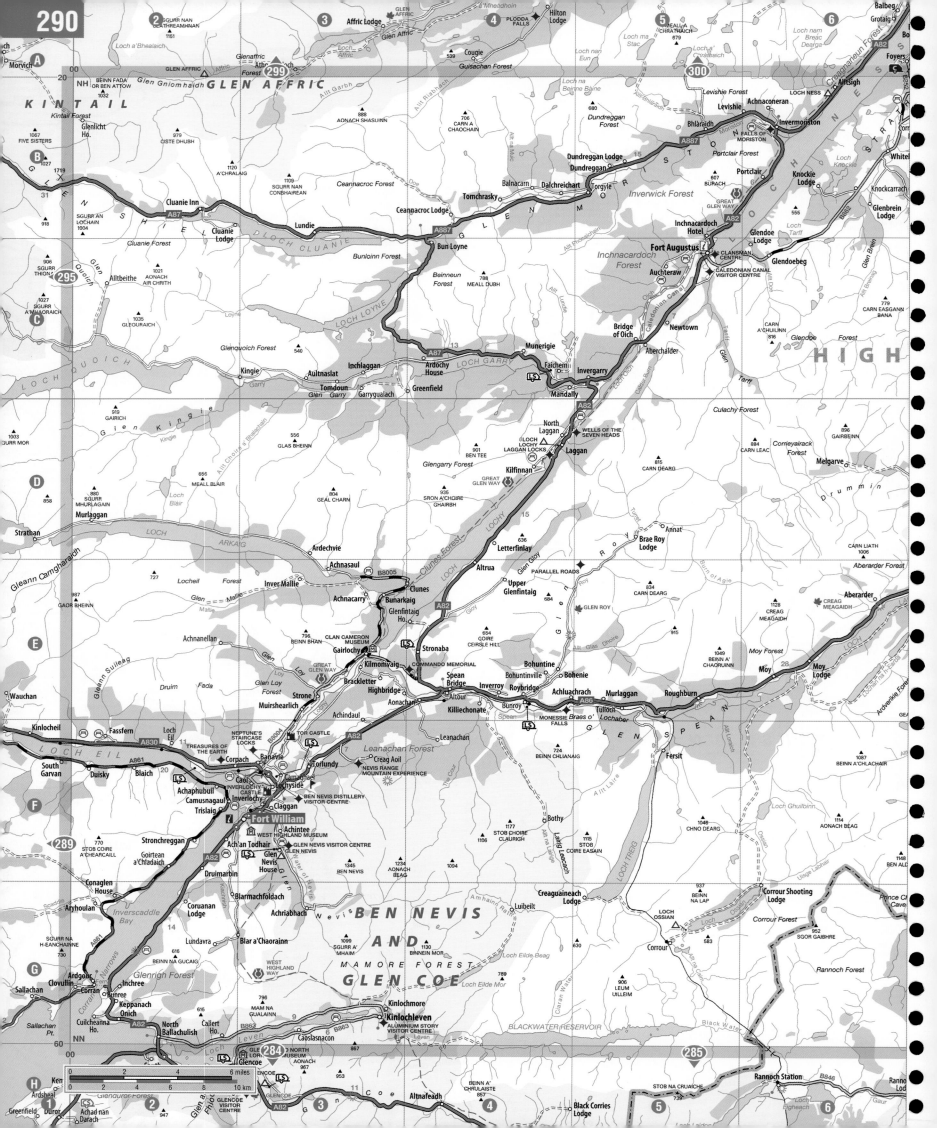

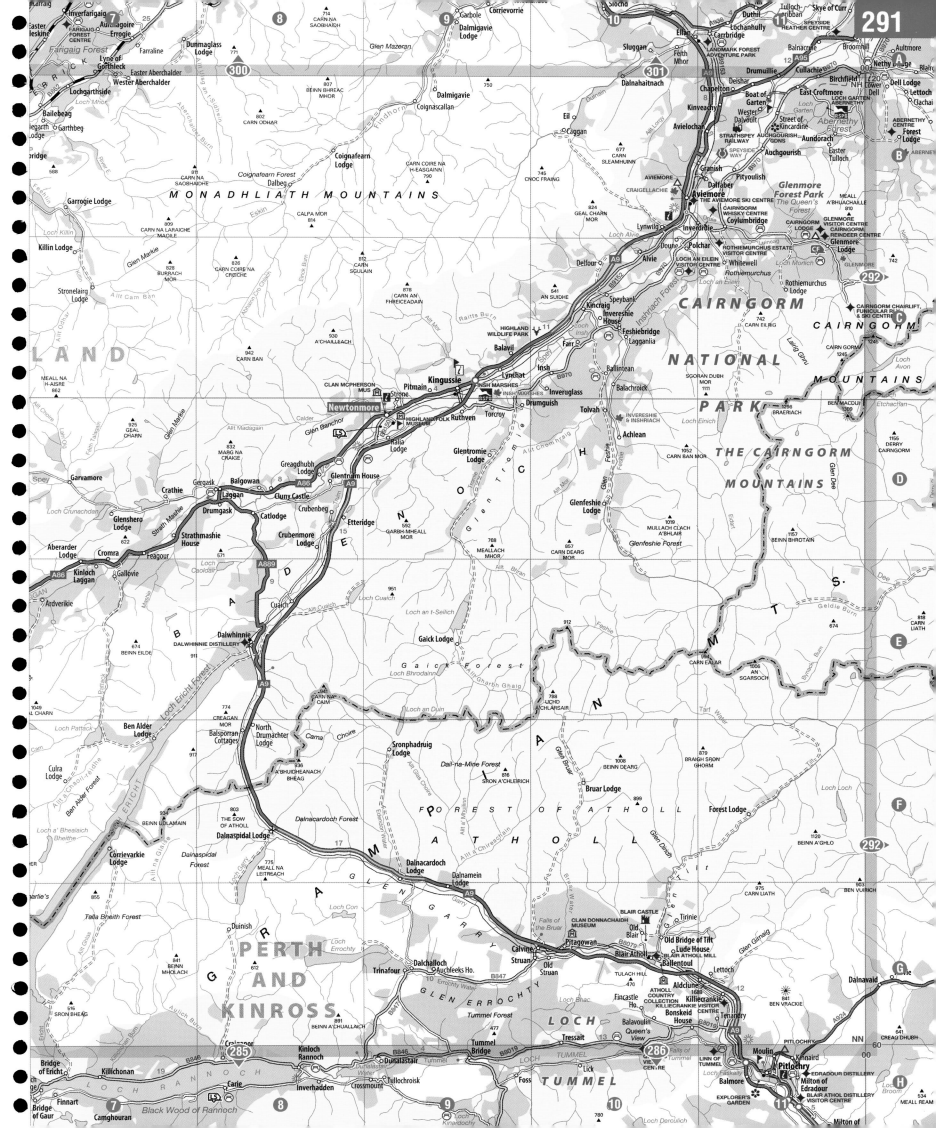

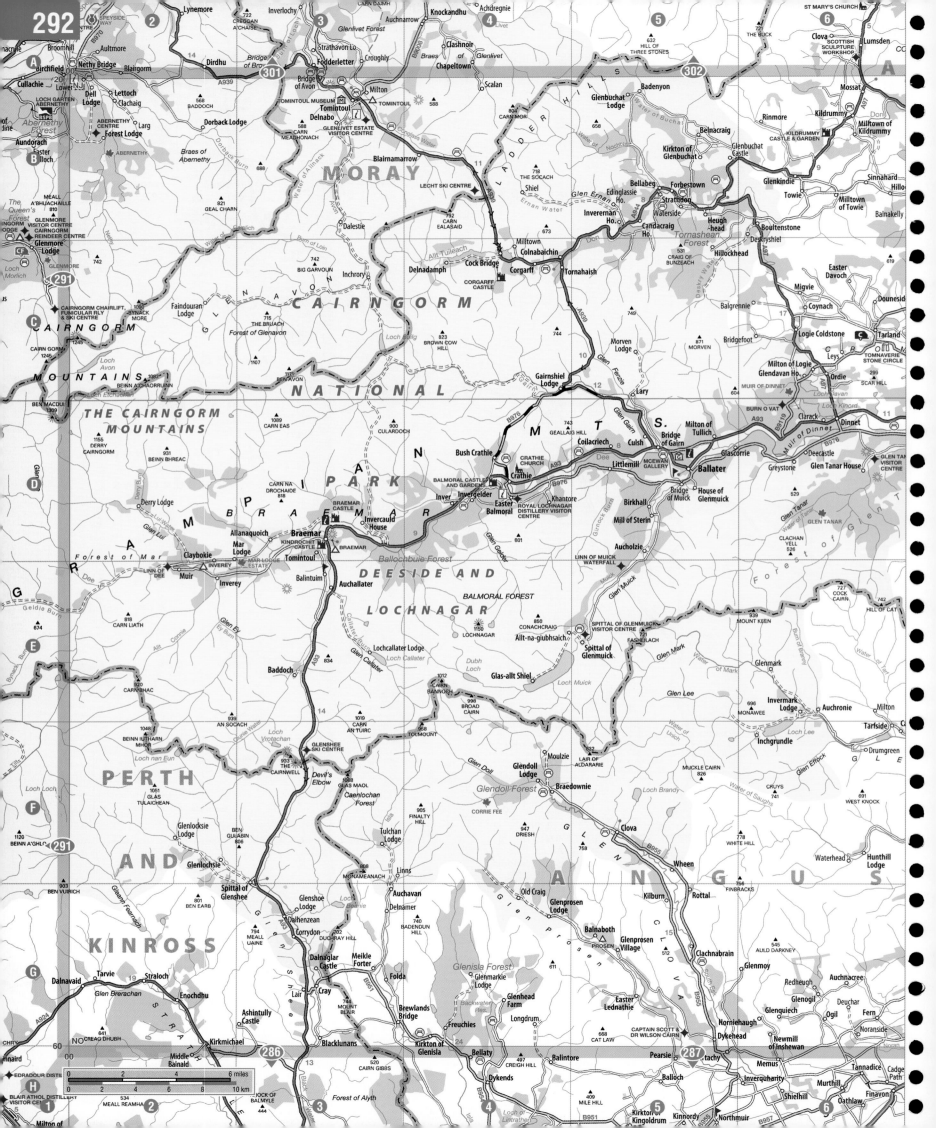

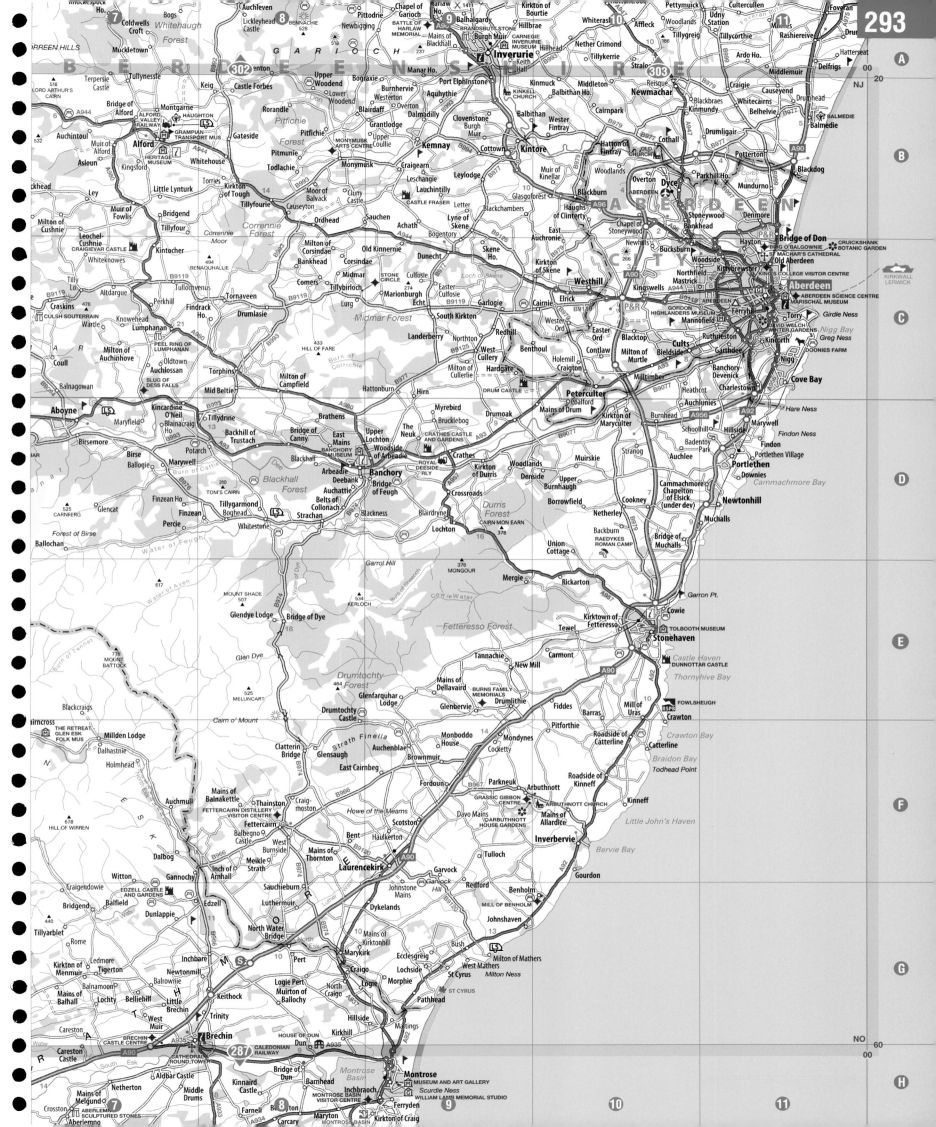

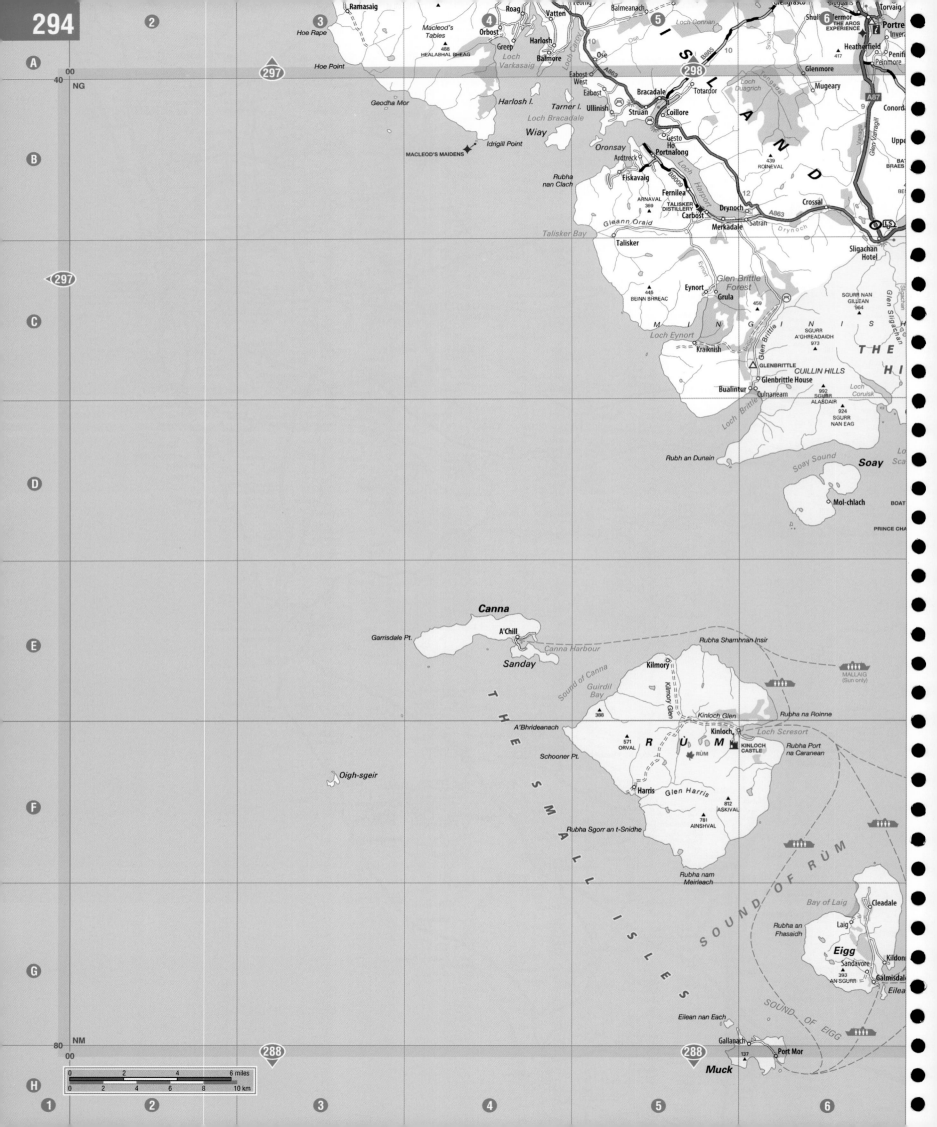

A

B

C

D

E

F

G

H

1 2 3 4 5 6

Ramasaig
Roag
Vatten
Balmeanach
Loch Connan
Shul'
The Aros Experience
Torvaig
Portre
Hoe Rape
Orbost
Greep
Harlosh
Ose
Heatherfield
Macleod's Tables
Balmore
488 HEALABHAL BHEAG
Loch Varkasaig
Eabost West
Eabost
Ose
Bracadale
Totardor
Glenmore
Mugeary
Penin
Hoe Point
Geodha Mor
Harlosh I.
Tarner I.
Ullinish
Struan
Coillore
Loch Bracadale
Wiay
Oronsay
Ardtreck
Ho
Portnalong
439 ROINEVAL
Conord
Upp
MACLEOD'S MAIDENS
Idrigill Point
Rubha nan Clach
Fiskavaig
Fernilea
Talisker Distillery
Carbost
Drynoch
Crossal
ARNAVAL 369
Gleann Oraid
Merkadale
Satran
Drynoch
LS
Talisker Bay
Talisker
Sligachan Hotel
Glen Brittle Forest
Eynort
Grula
445 BEINN BHREAC
459
SGURR NAN GILLEAN 964
Loch Eynort
Kraiknish
SGURR A'GHREADAIDH 973
THE
H
GLENBRITTLE
CUILLIN HILLS
Glenbrittle House
Bualintur
992 SGURR ALASDAIR
924 SGURR NAN EAG
Loch Coruisk
Rubh an Dunain
Soay Sound
Soay
Lo Sca
Mol-chlach
BOAT
PRINCE CHA
Canna
A'Chill
Garrisdale Pt.
Canna Harbour
Rubha Shamhnan Insir
Sanday
Sound of Canna
Kilmory
MALLAIG (Sun only)
Guirdil Bay
Kilmory Glen
388
Kinloch Glen
Rubha na Roinne
A'Bhrideanach
571 ORVAL
RÙM
Kinloch
Loch Scresort
Schooner Pt.
RÙM
KINLOCH CASTLE
Rubha Port na Caranean
Oigh-sgeir
Harris
Glen Harris
812 ASKIVAL
Rubha Sgorr an t-Snidhe
781 AINSHVAL
Bay of Laig
Cleadale
Rubha nam Meirleach
Rubha an Fhasaidh
Laig
Eigg
Sandavore
Kildon
393 AN SGURR
Galmisdal
Eilean nan Each
Eilea
Gallanach
Port Mor
137
Muck

0 2 4 6 miles
0 2 4 6 8 10 km

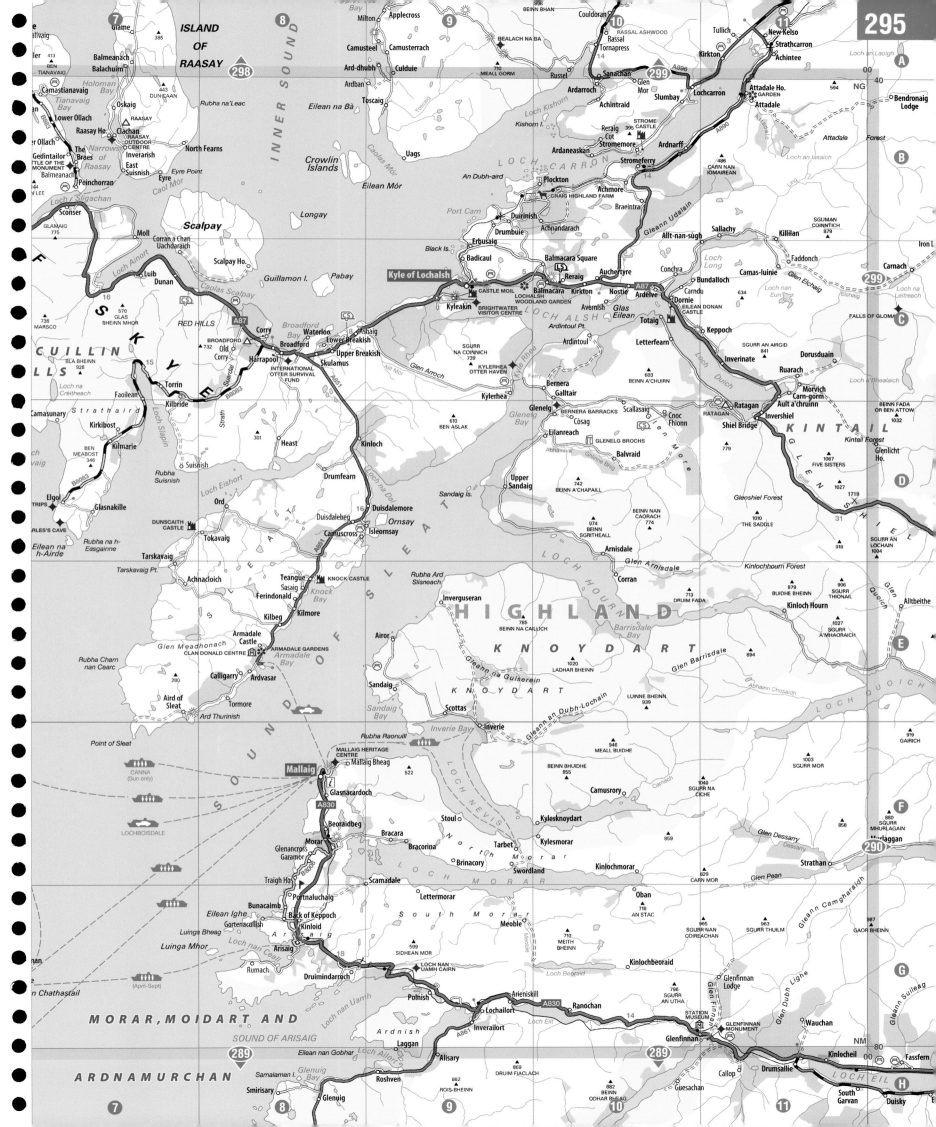

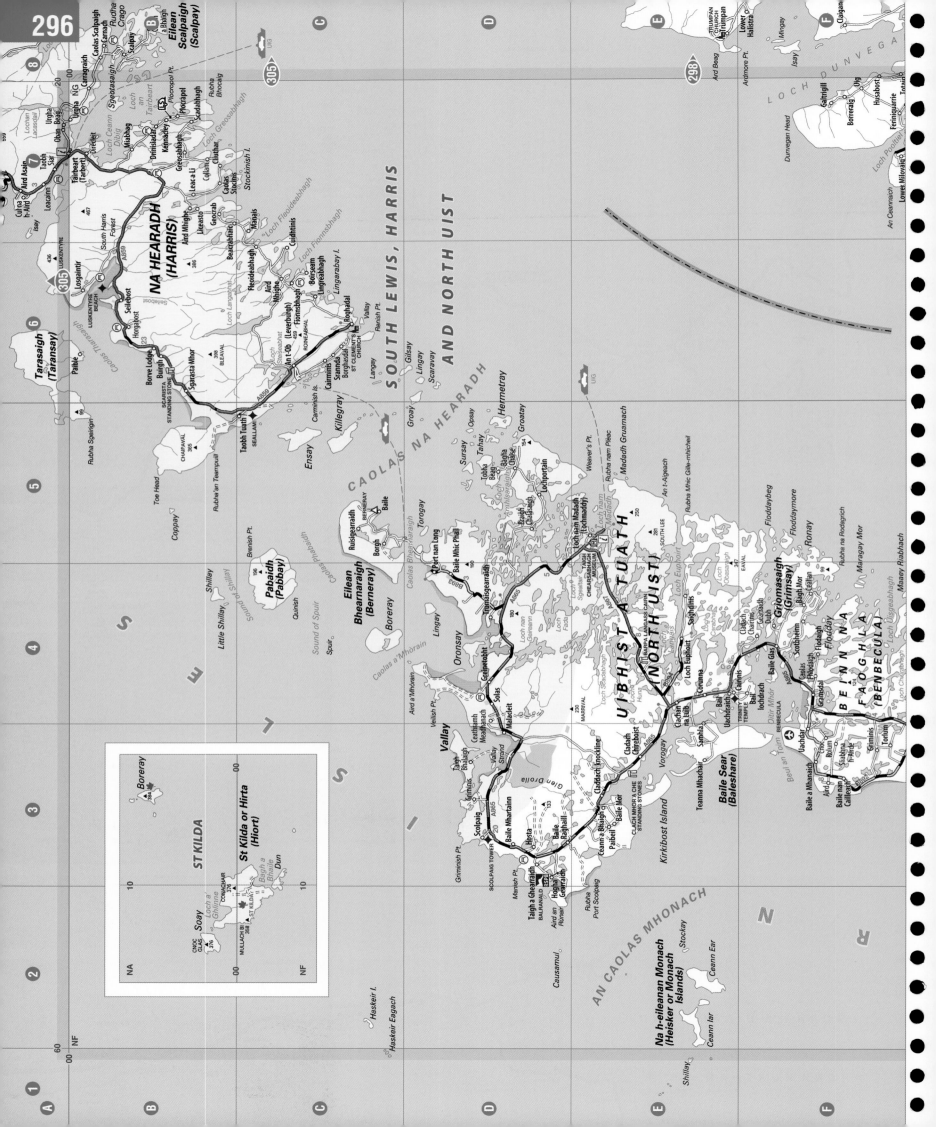

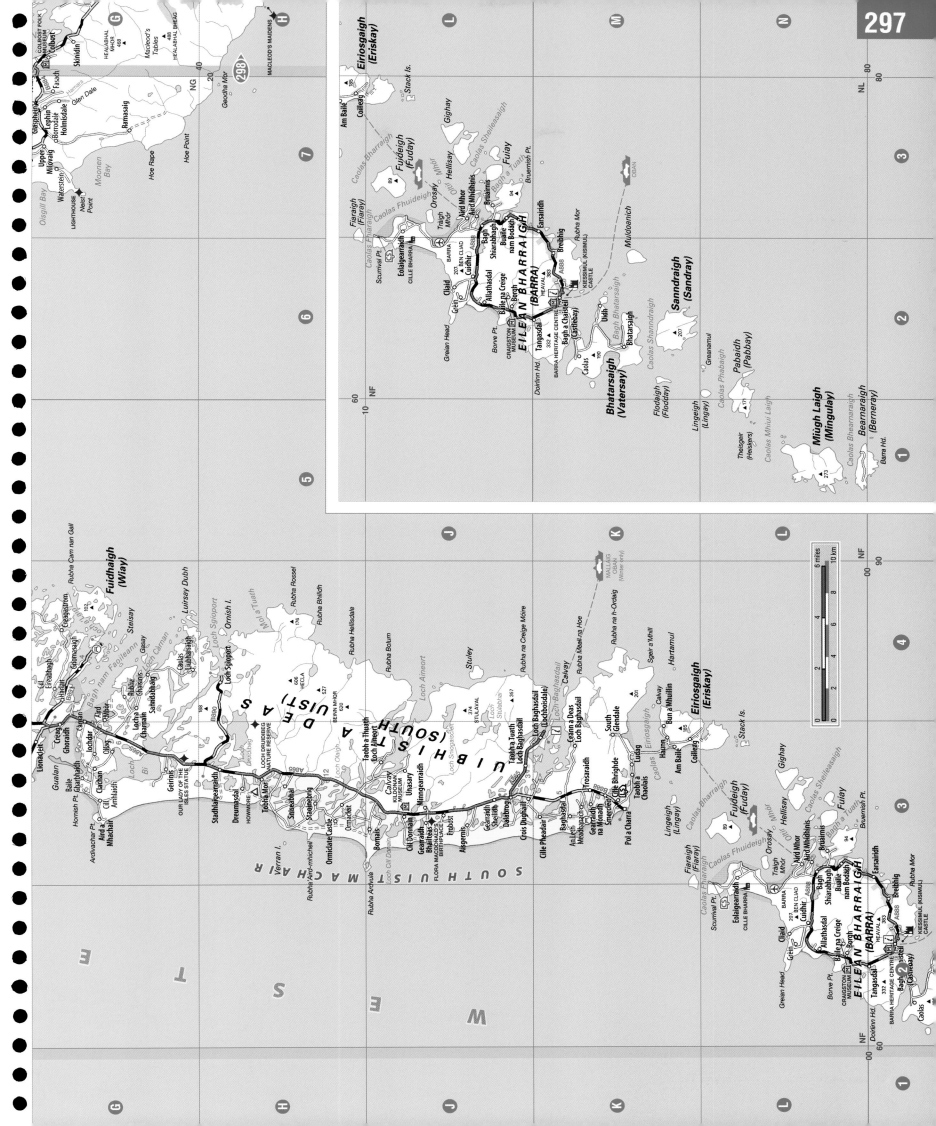

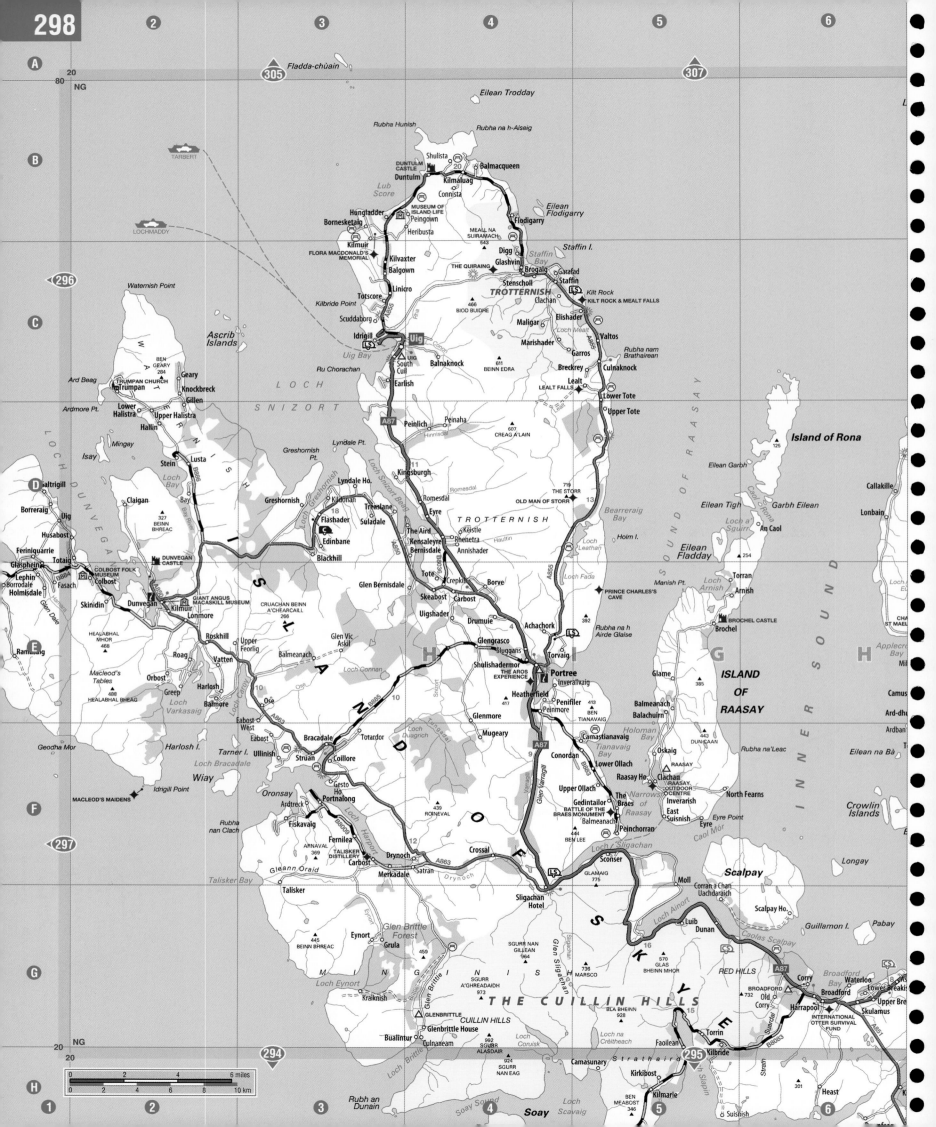

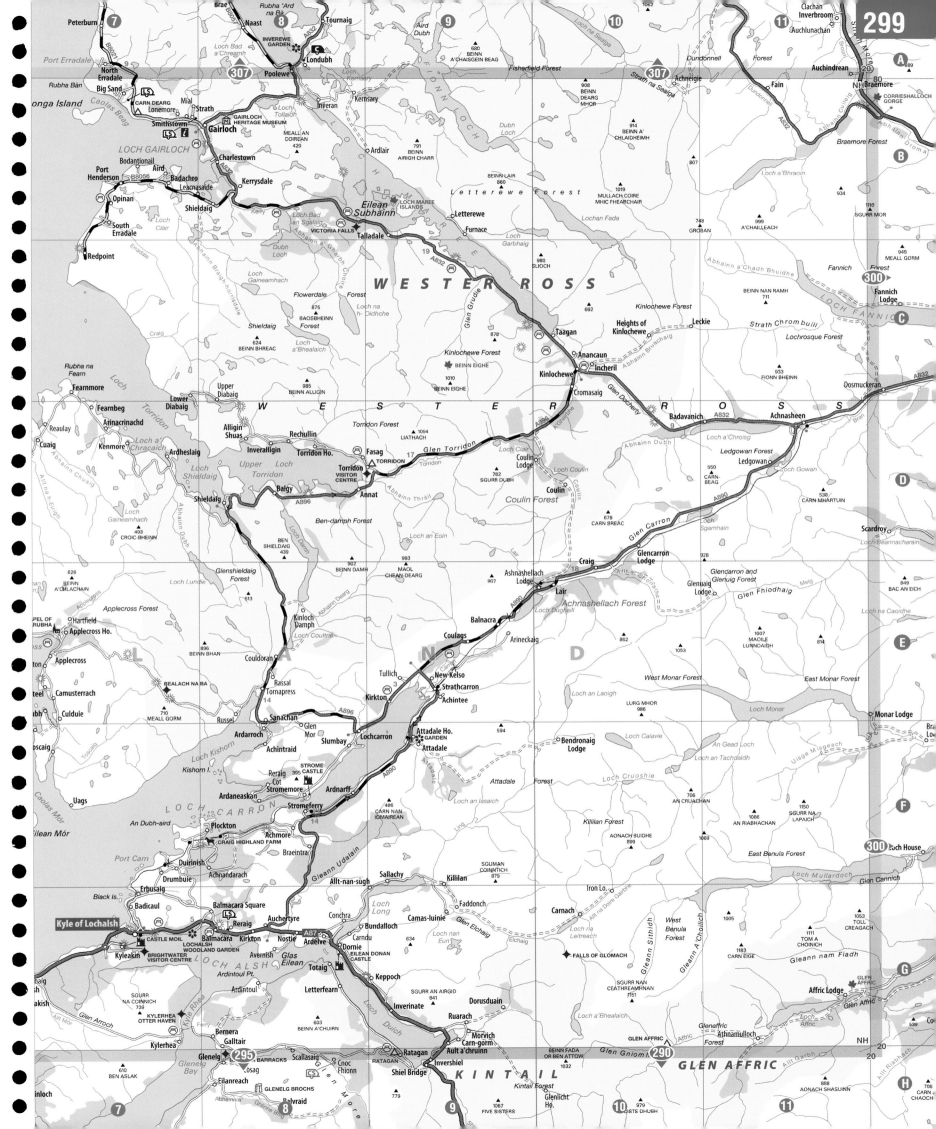

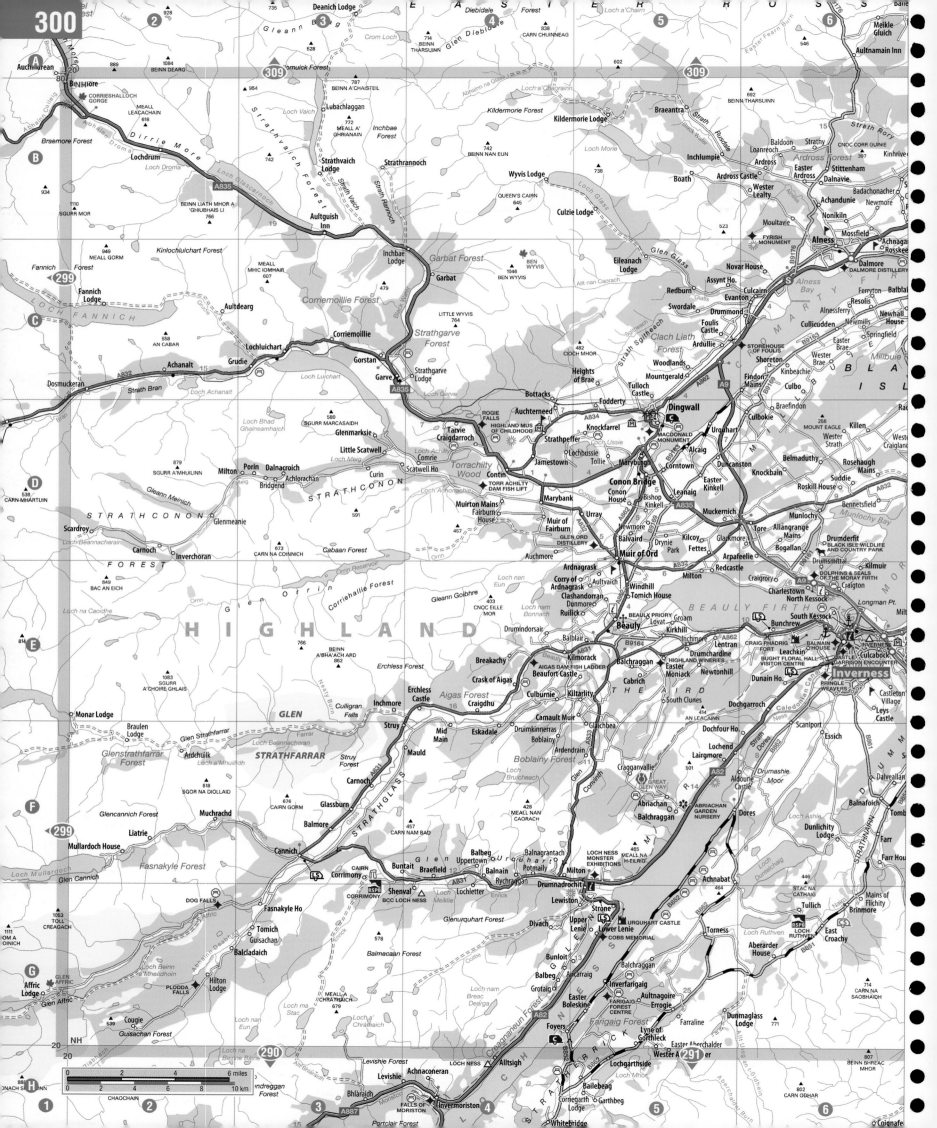

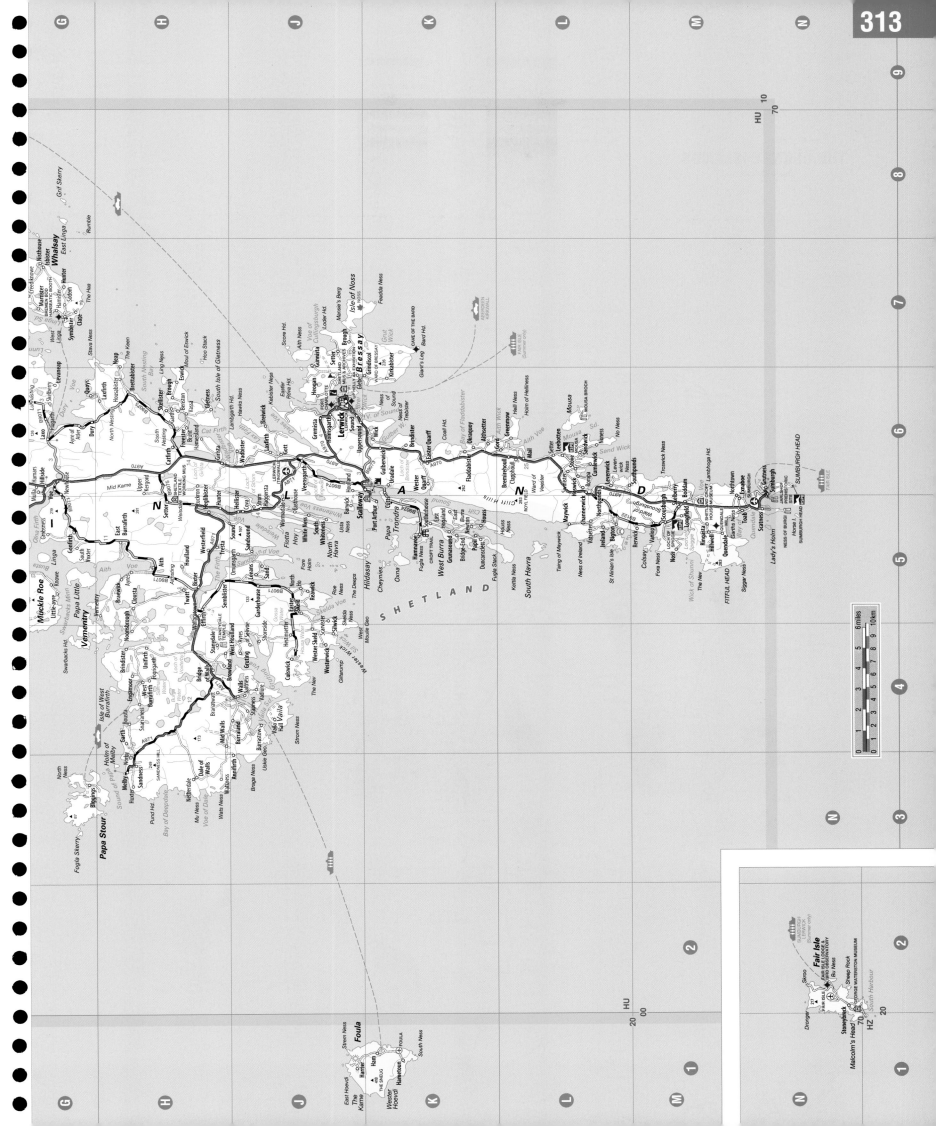

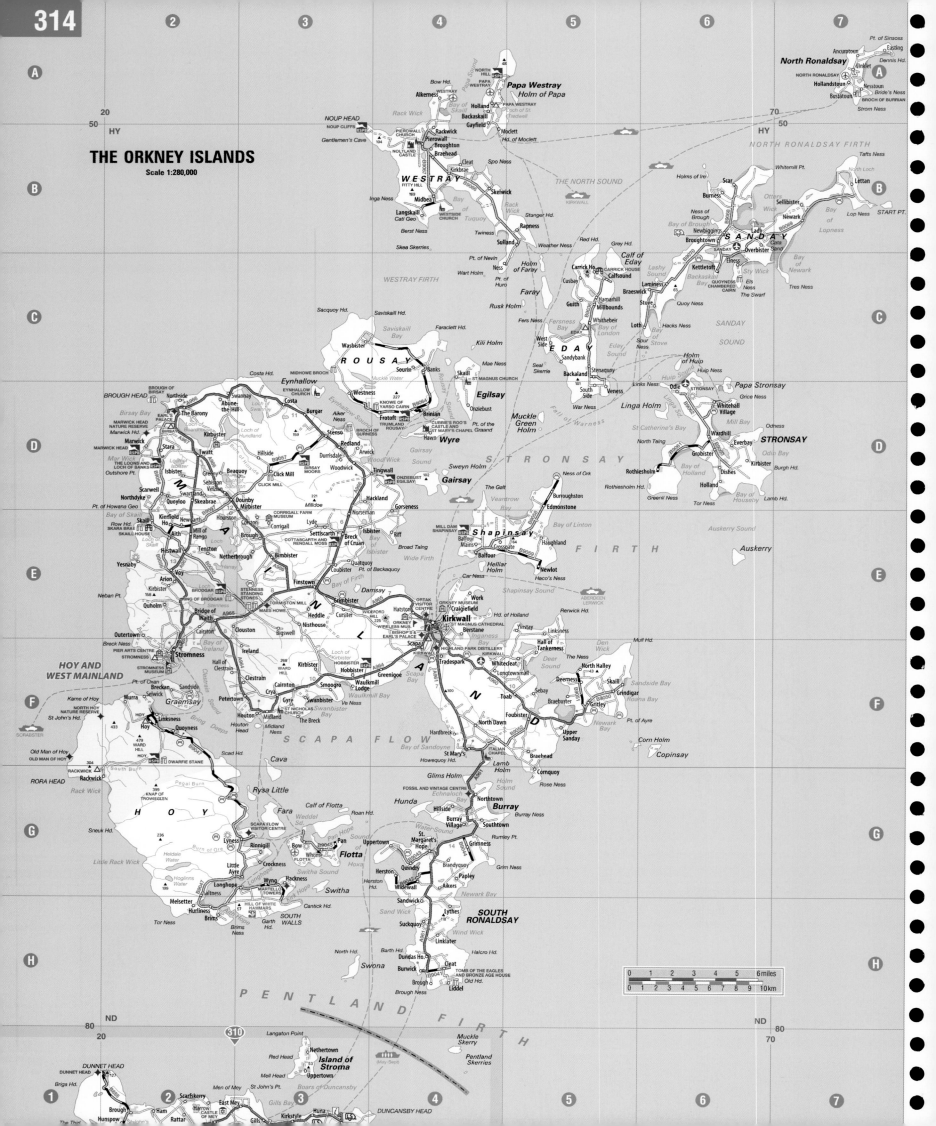

THE ORKNEY ISLANDS
Scale 1:280,000

PENTLAND FIRTH

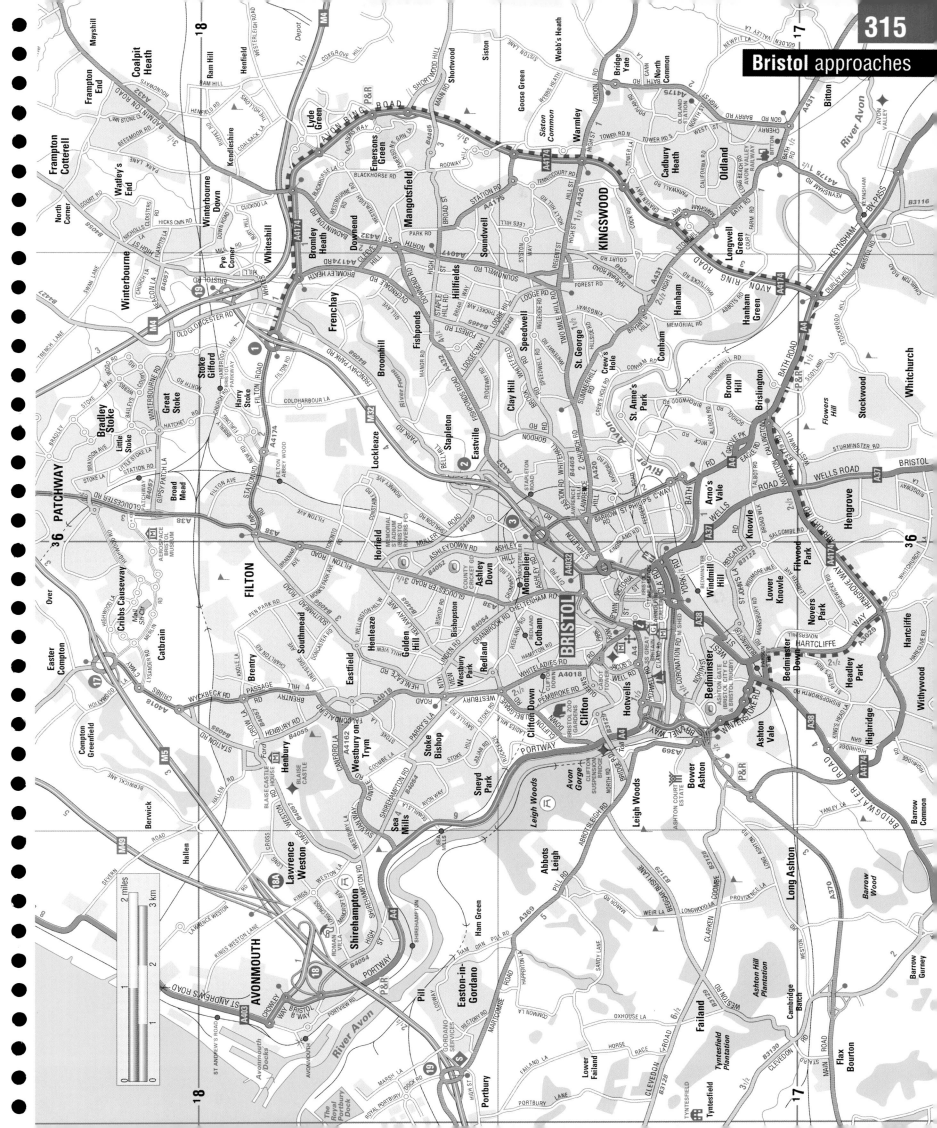

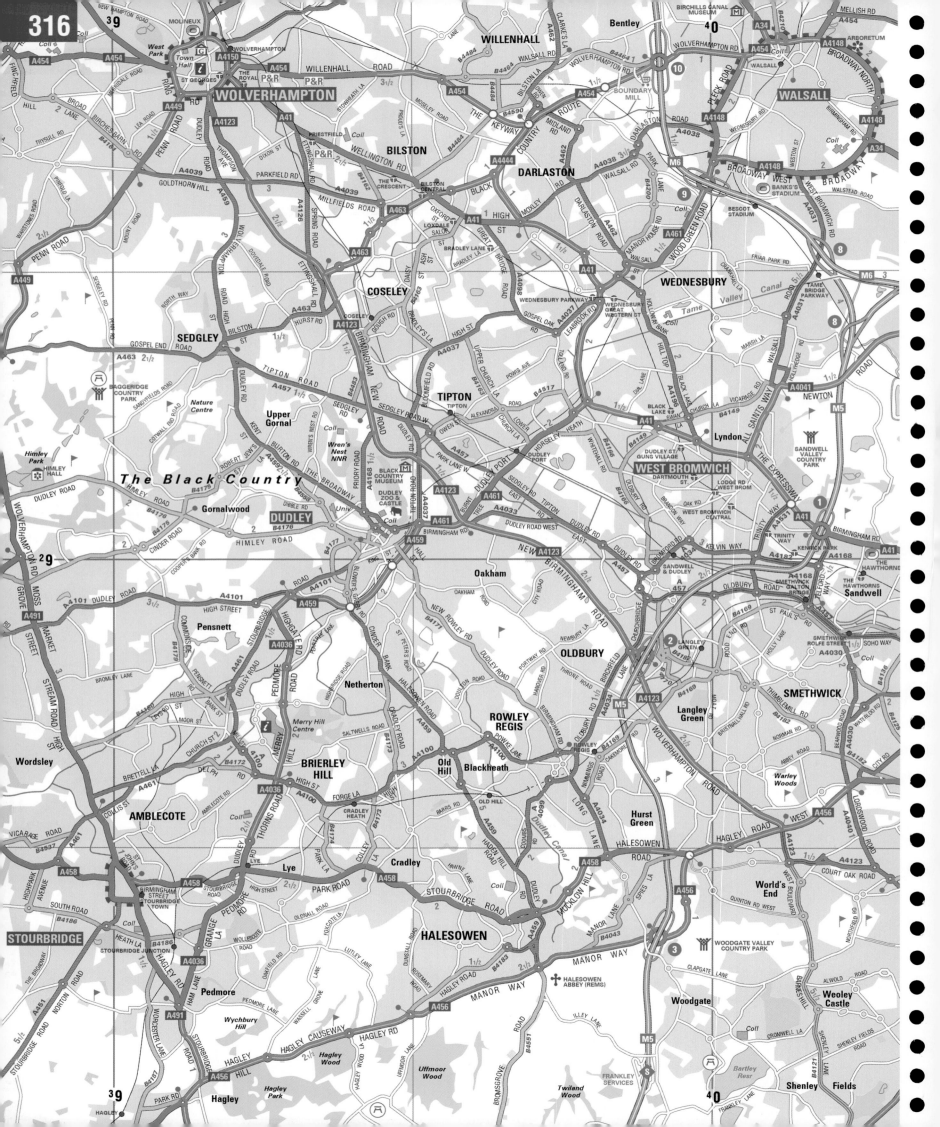

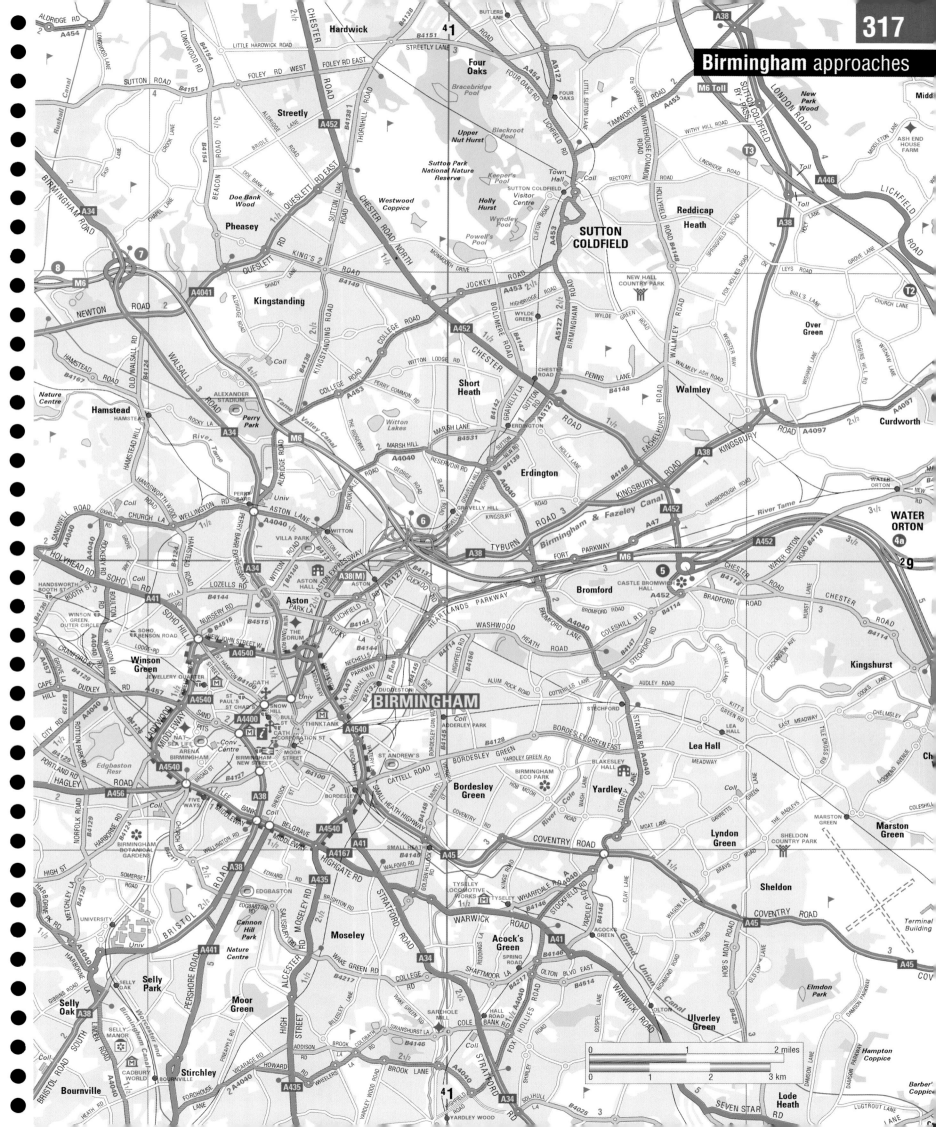

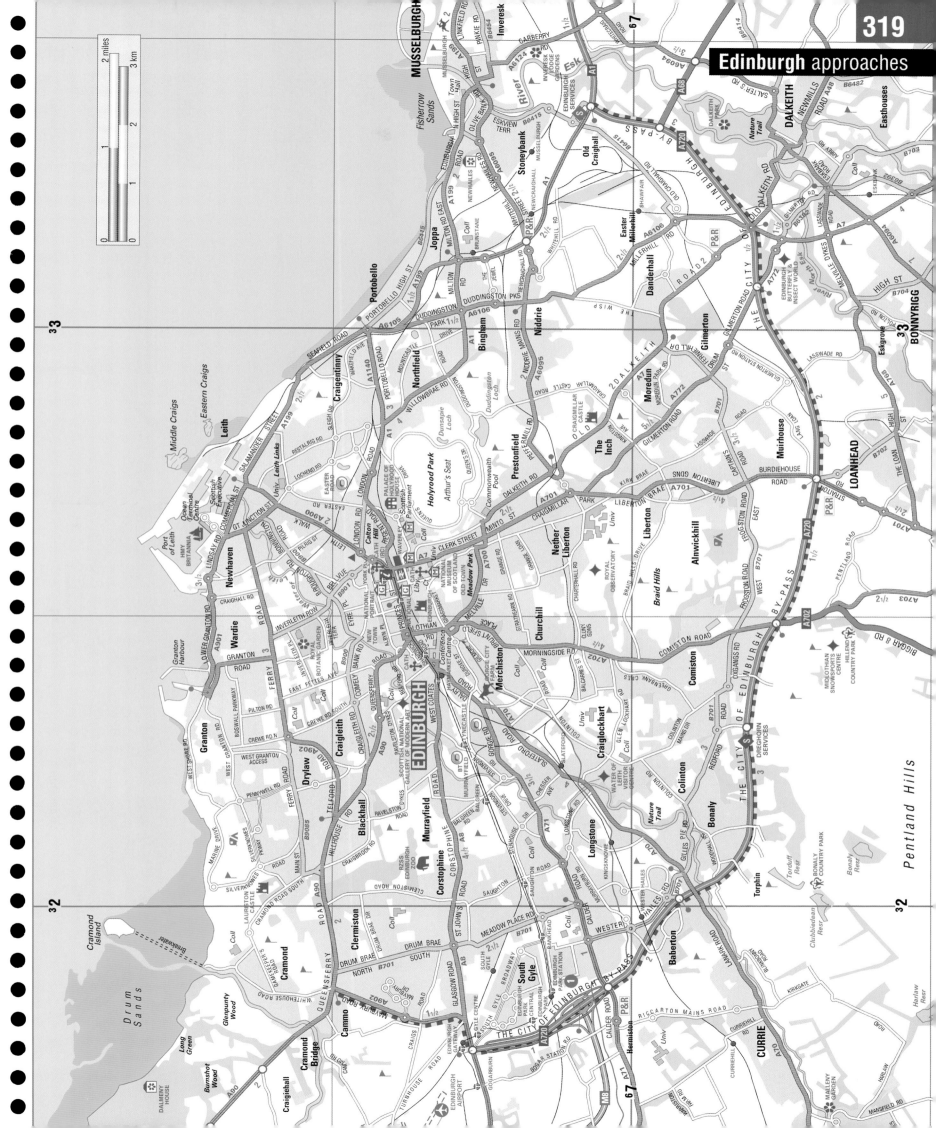

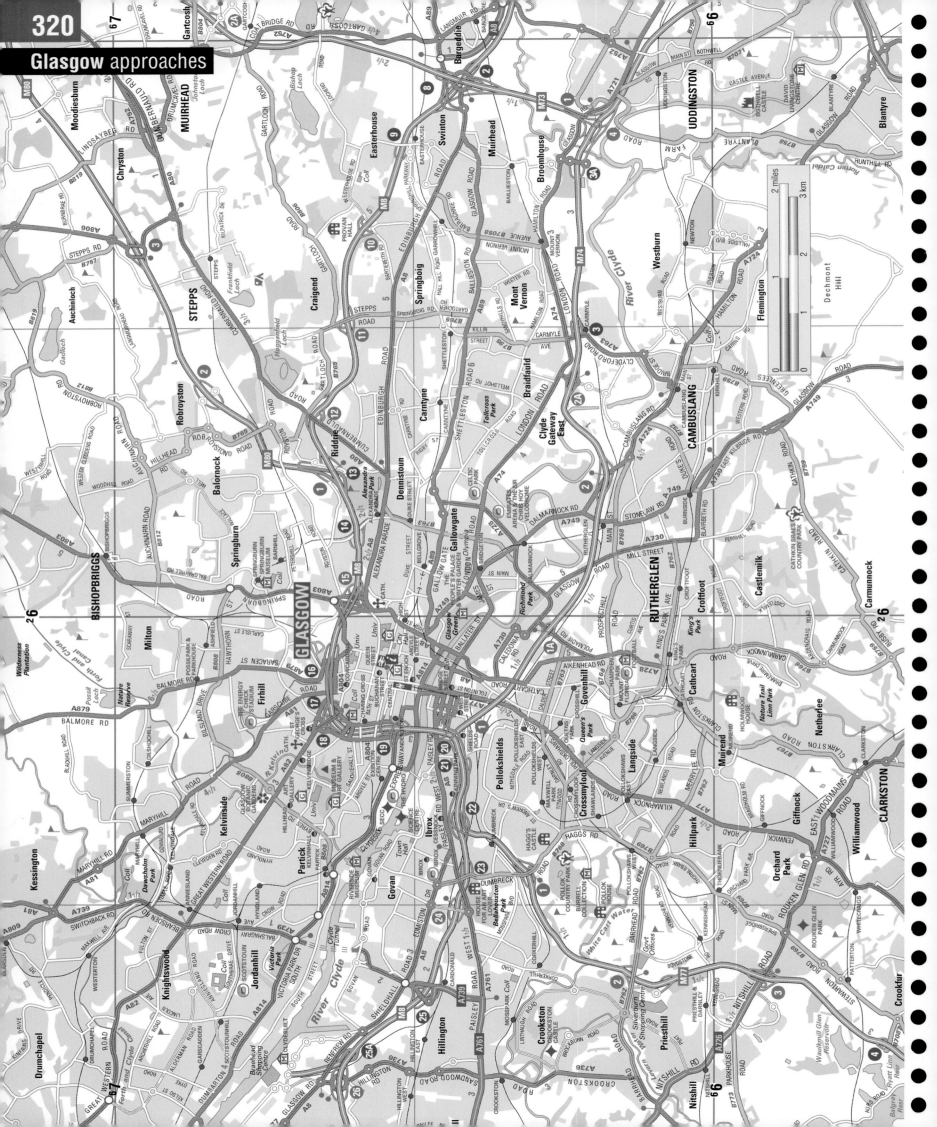

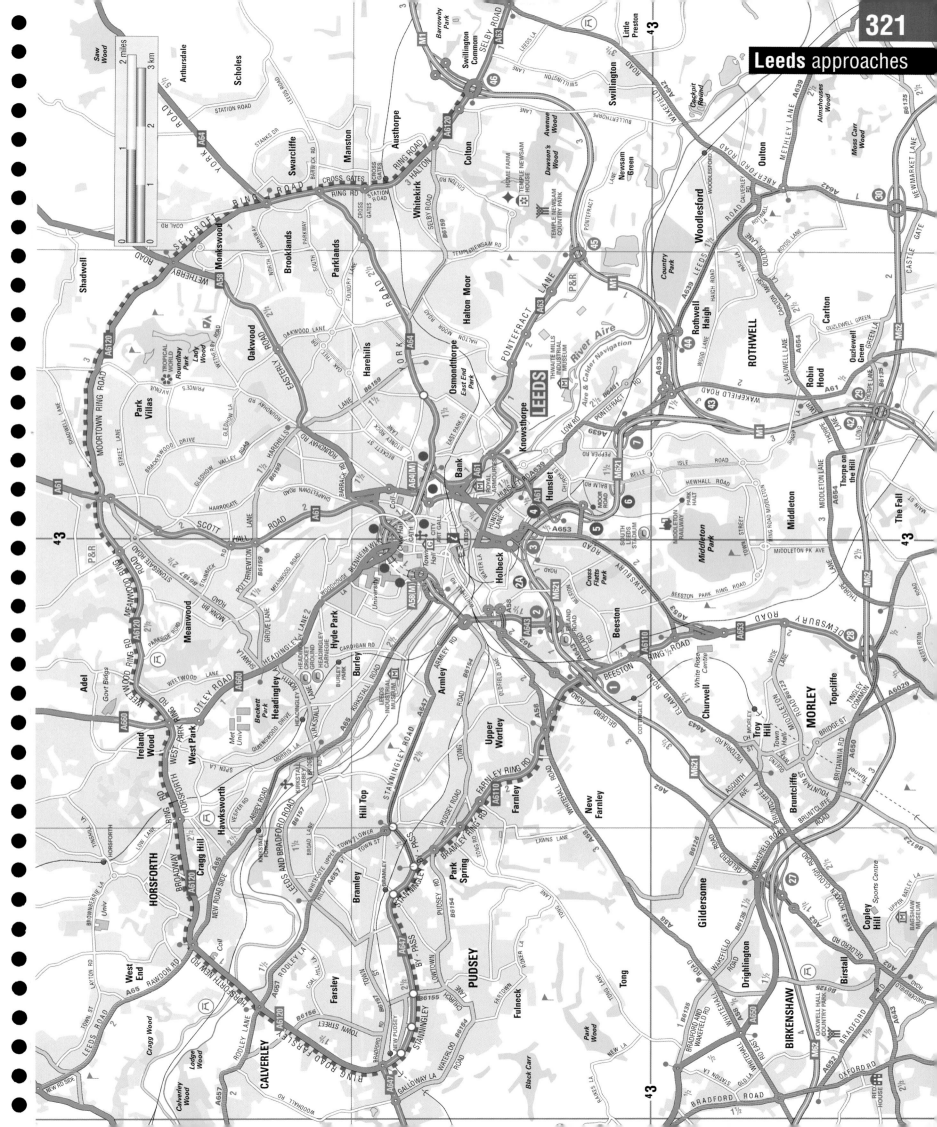

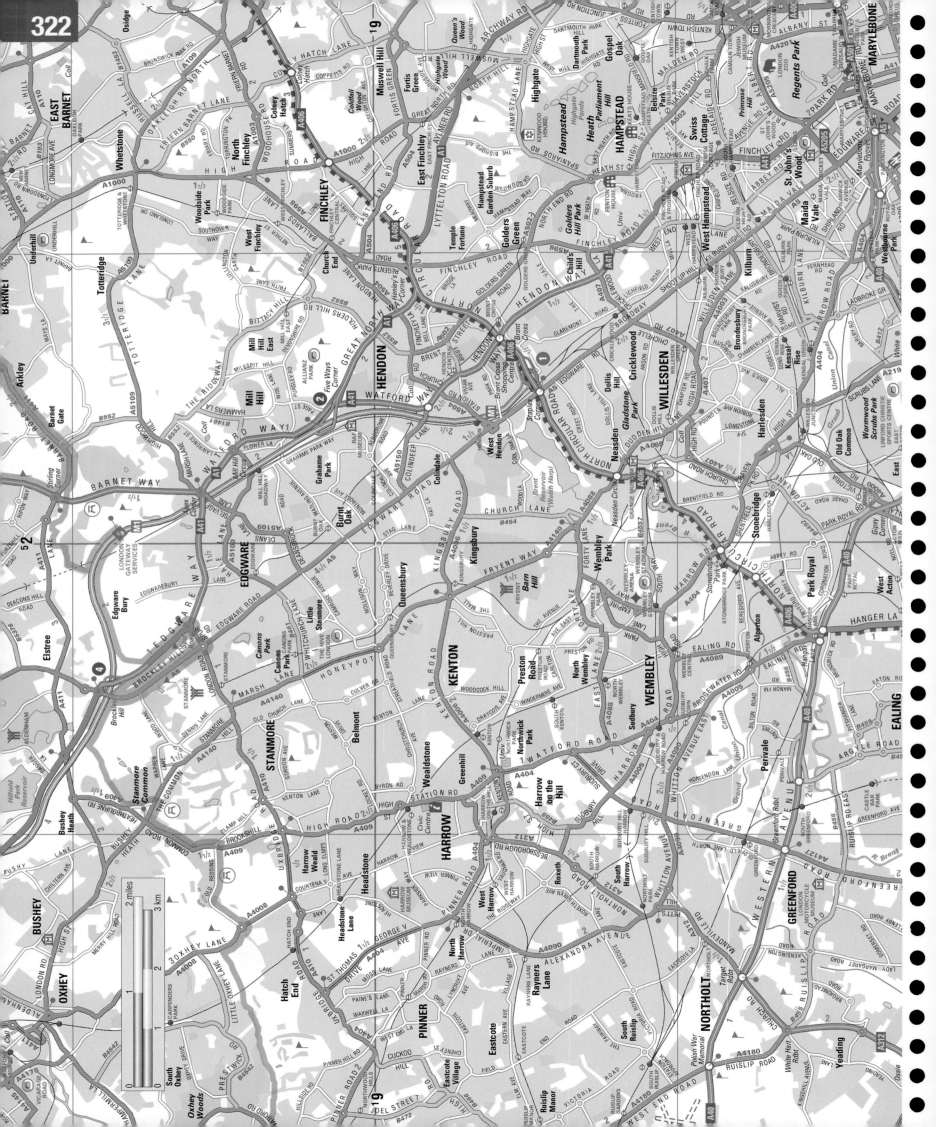

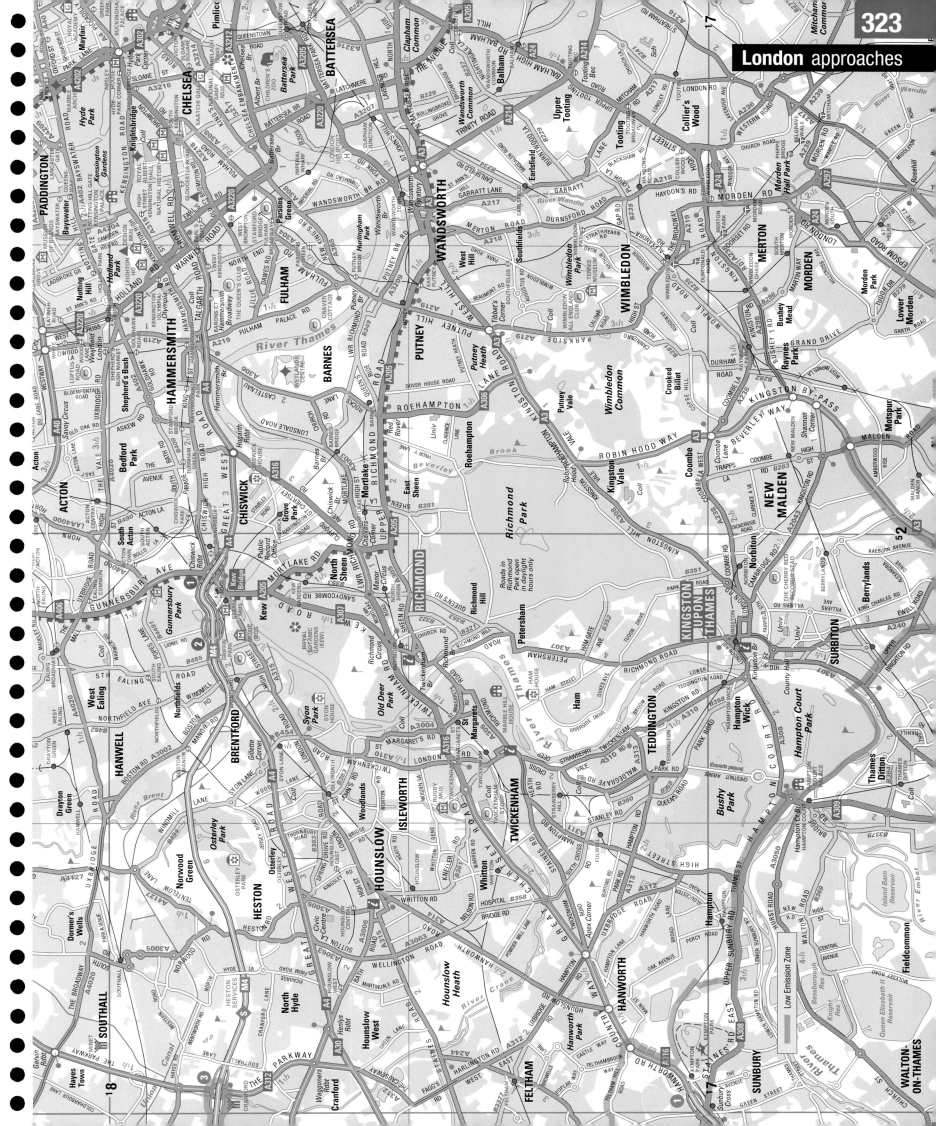

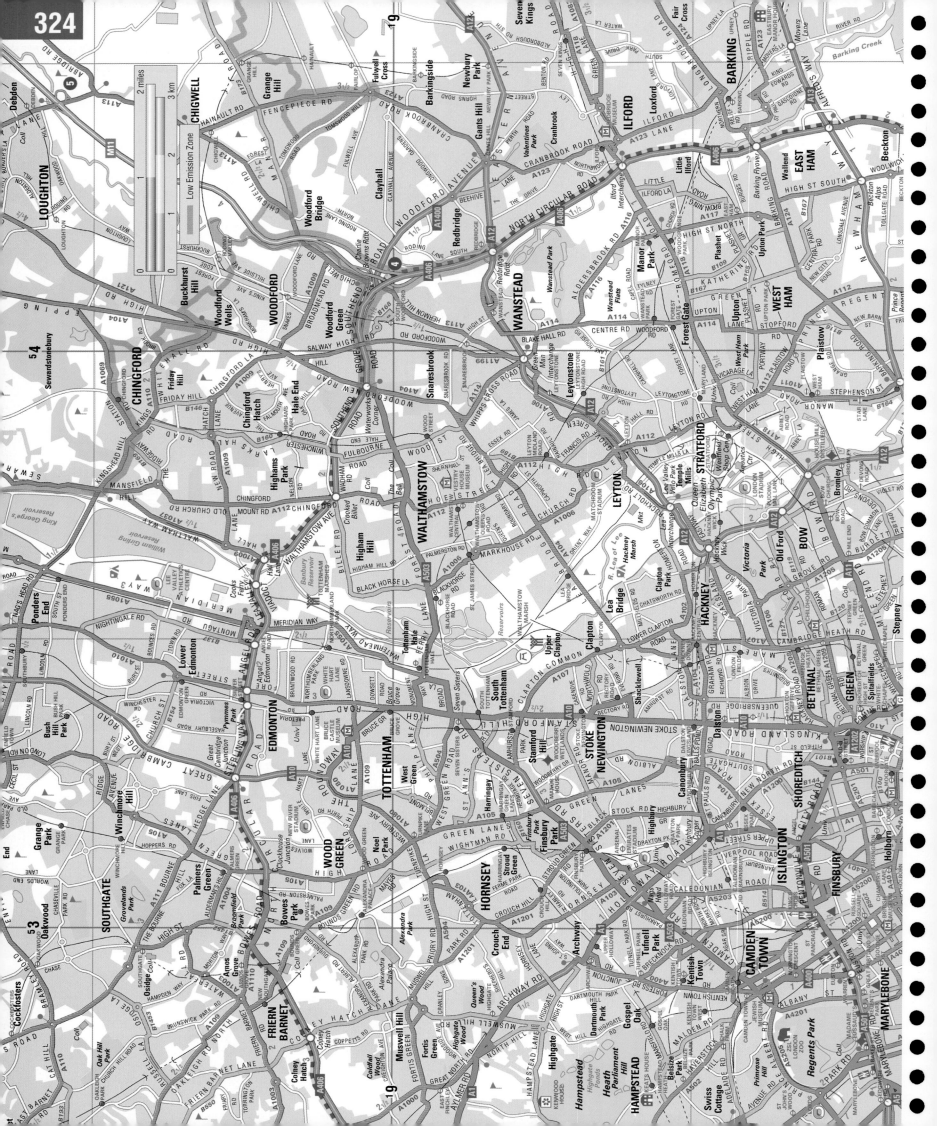

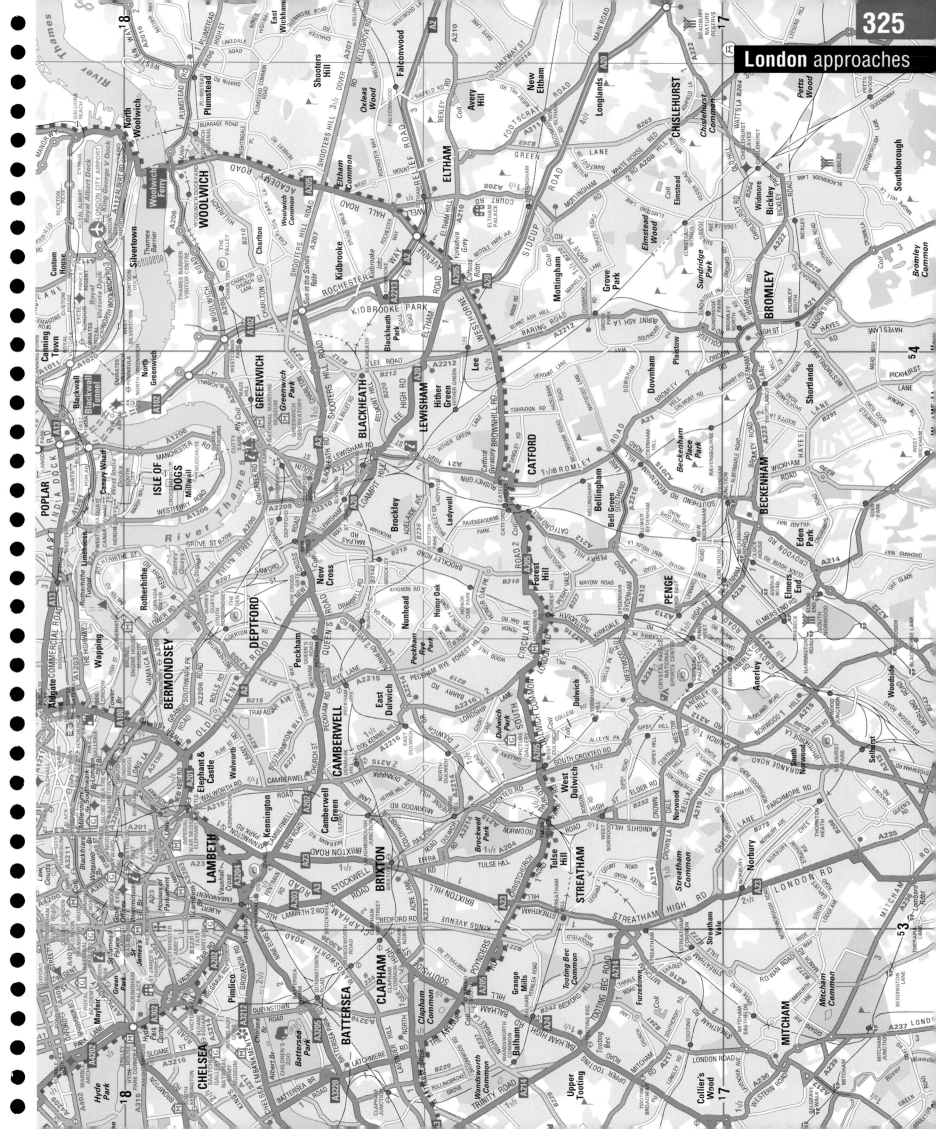

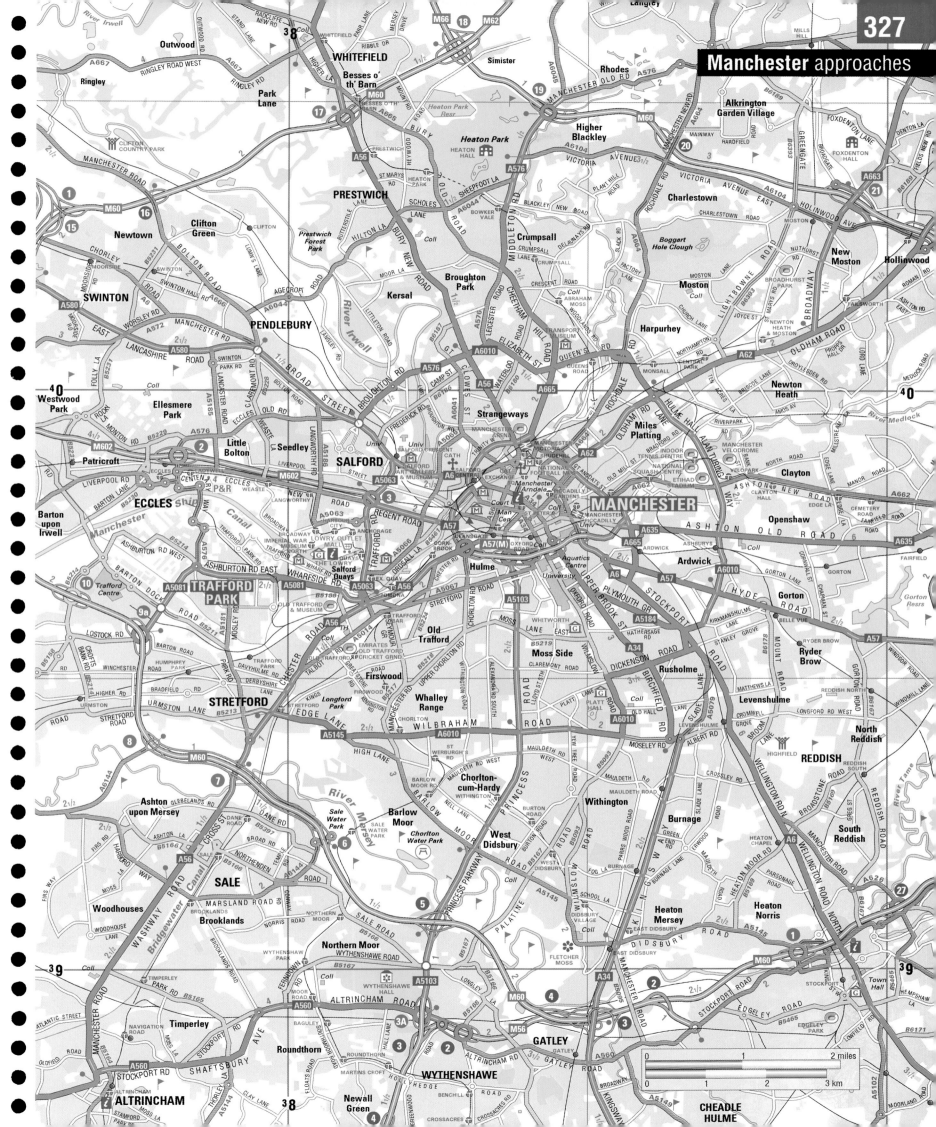

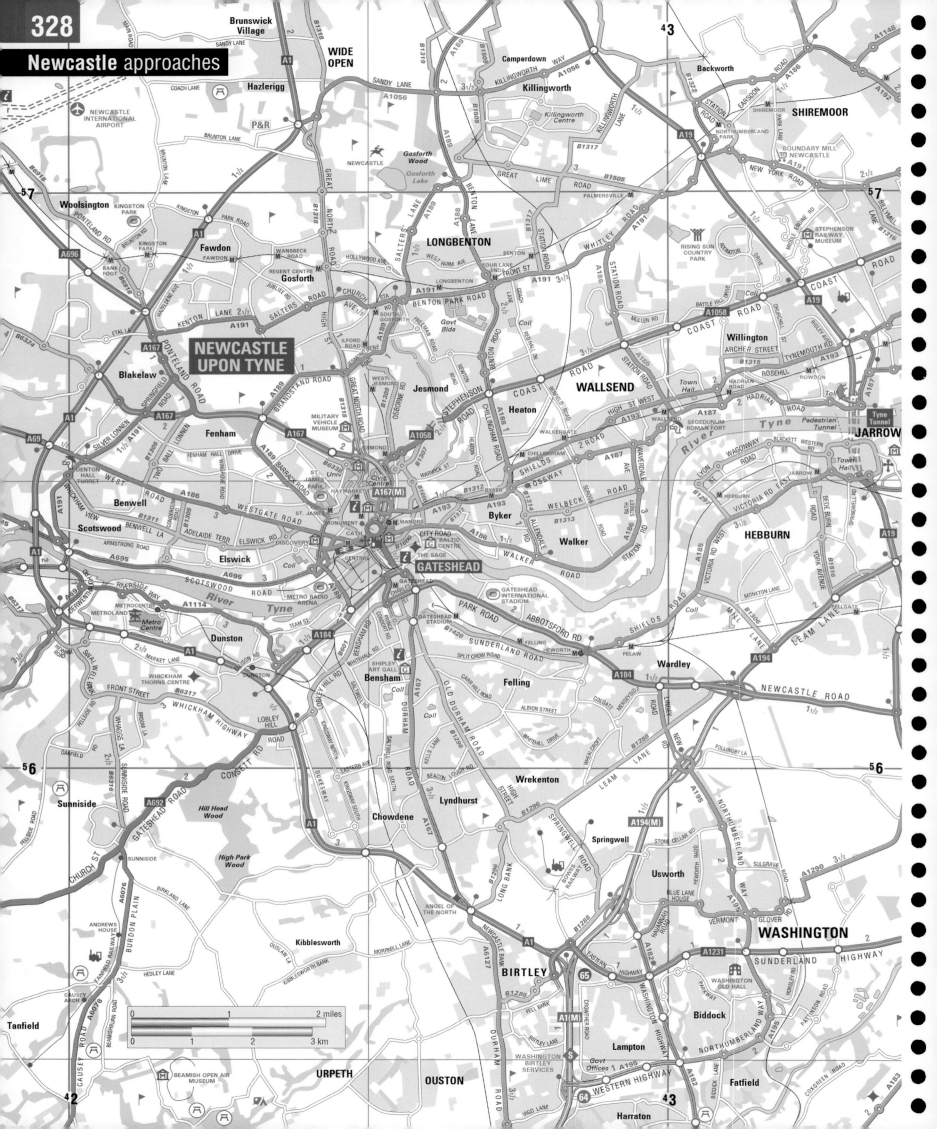

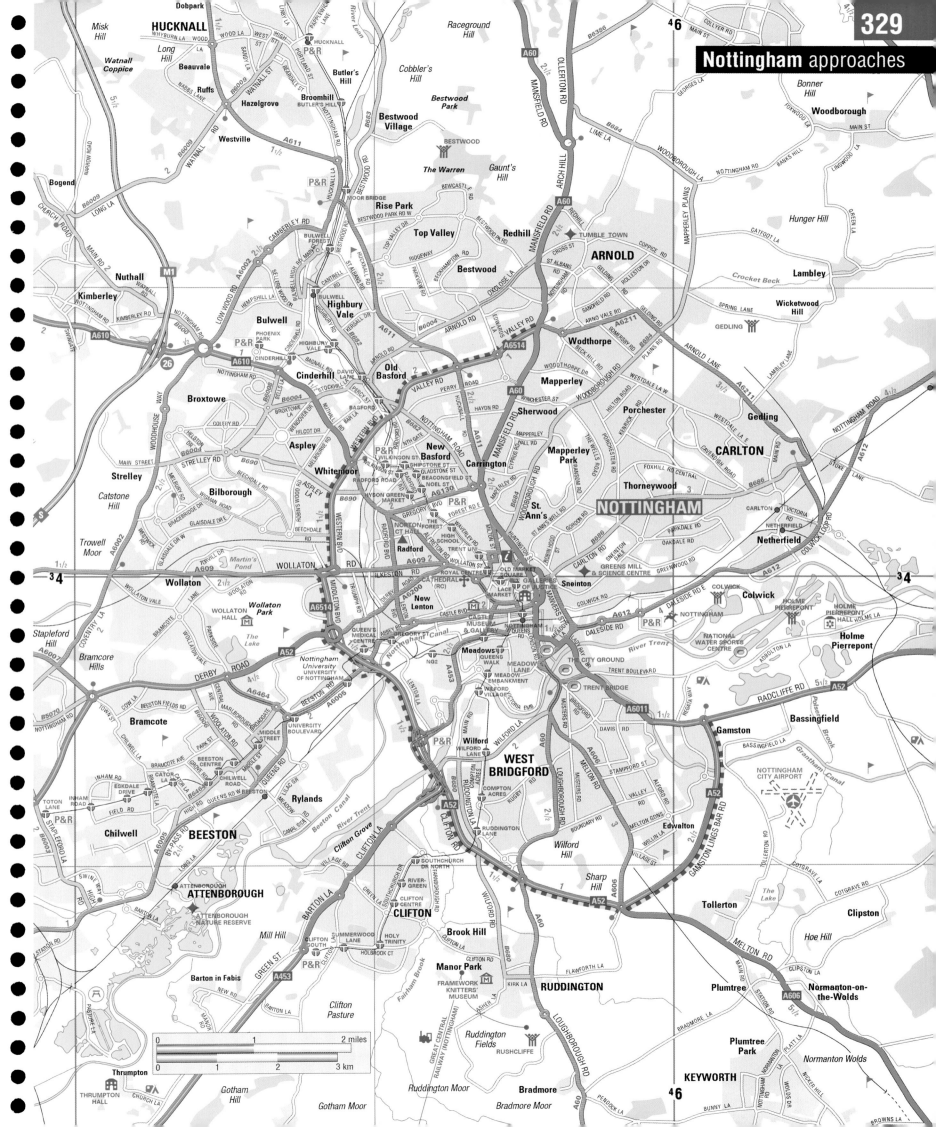

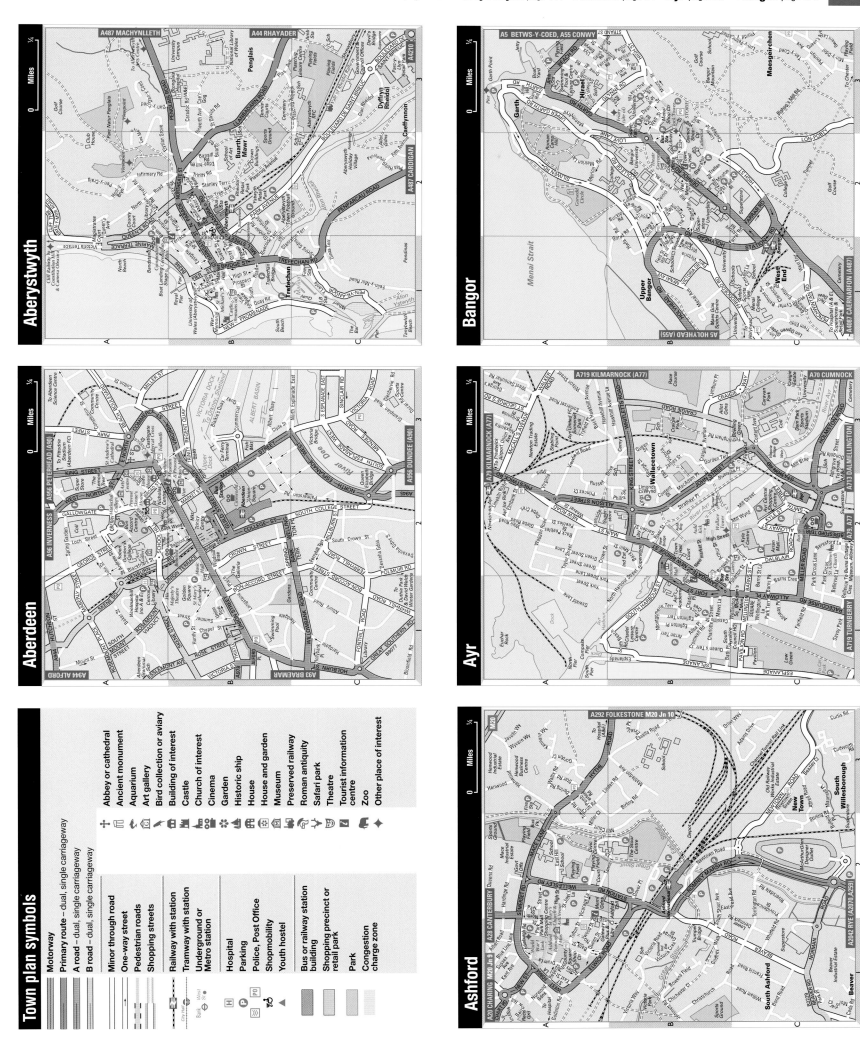

Aberystwyth

Bangor

Aberdeen

Ayr

Town plan symbols

Motorway
Primary route – dual, single carriageway
A road – dual, single carriageway
B road – dual, single carriageway

Minor through road
One-way street
Pedestrian roads
Shopping streets

Railway with station
Tramway with station
Underground or
Metro station

Hospital
Parking
Police, Post Office
Shopmobility
Youth hostel

Bus or railway station
building
Shopping precinct or
retail park
Park
Congestion
charge zone

Abbey or cathedral
Ancient monument
Aquarium
Art gallery
Bird collection or aviary
Building of interest
Castle
Church of interest
Cinema
Garden
Historic ship
House
House and garden
Museum
Preserved railway
Roman antiquity
Safari park
Theatre
Tourist information
centre
Zoo
Other place of interest

Ashford

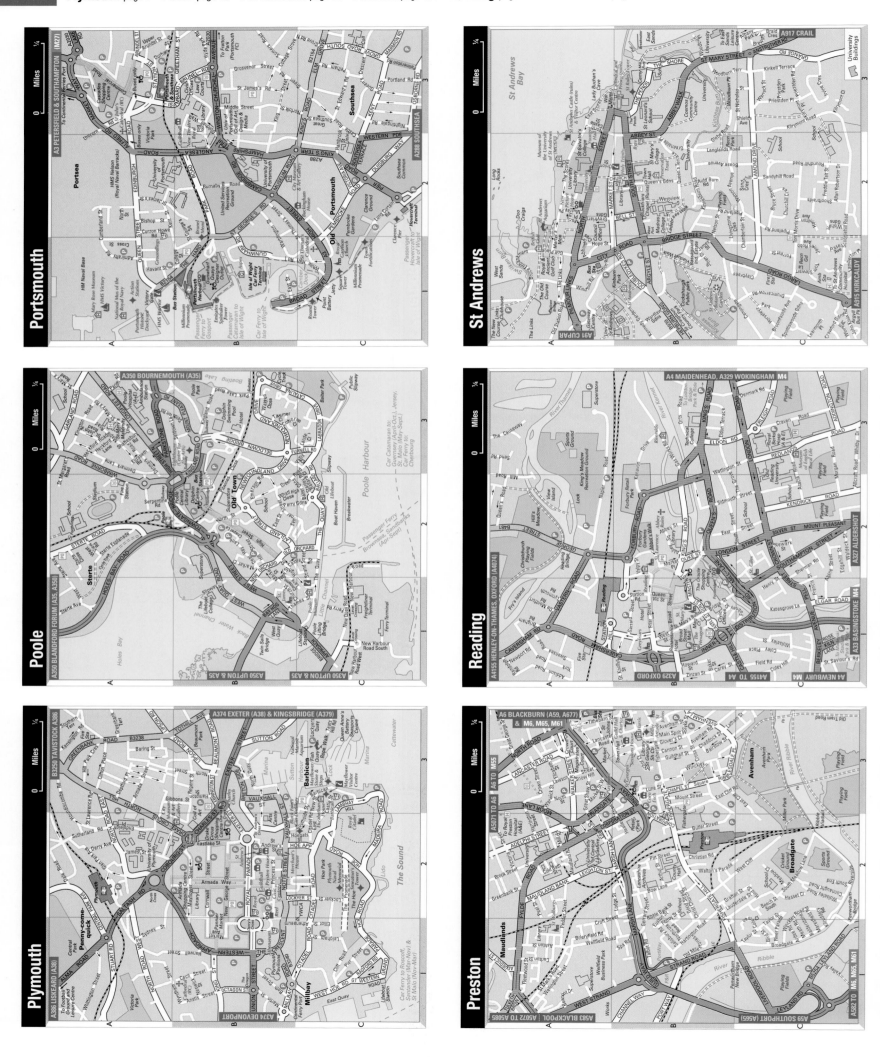

Portsmouth

St Andrews

Poole

Reading

Plymouth

Preston

Shrewsbury

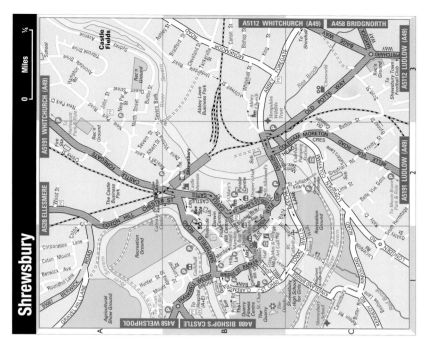

Southampton

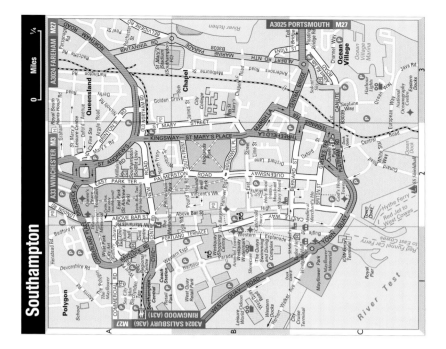

Scarborough

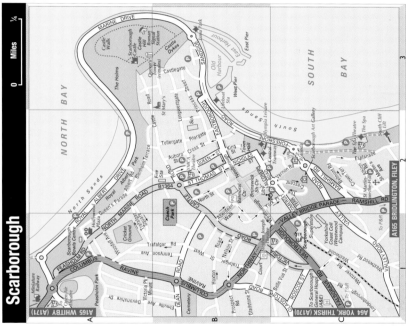

Sheffield

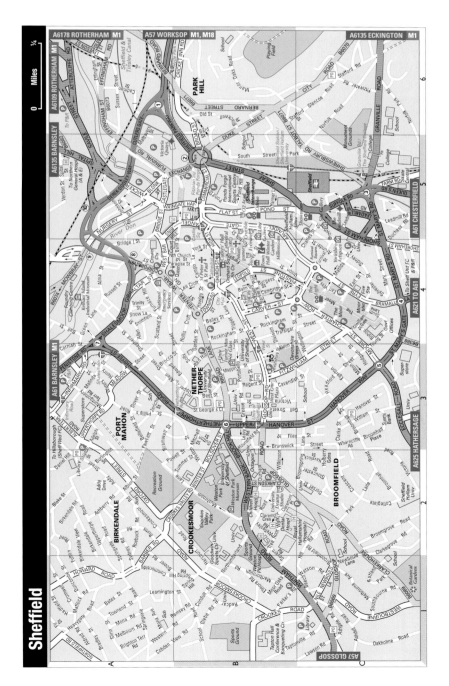

Salisbury

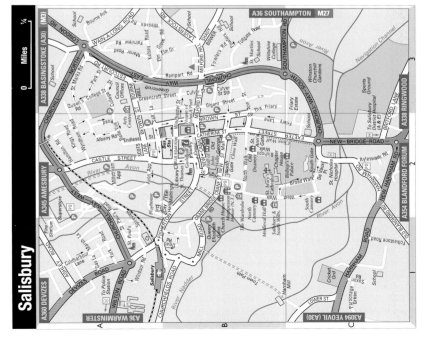

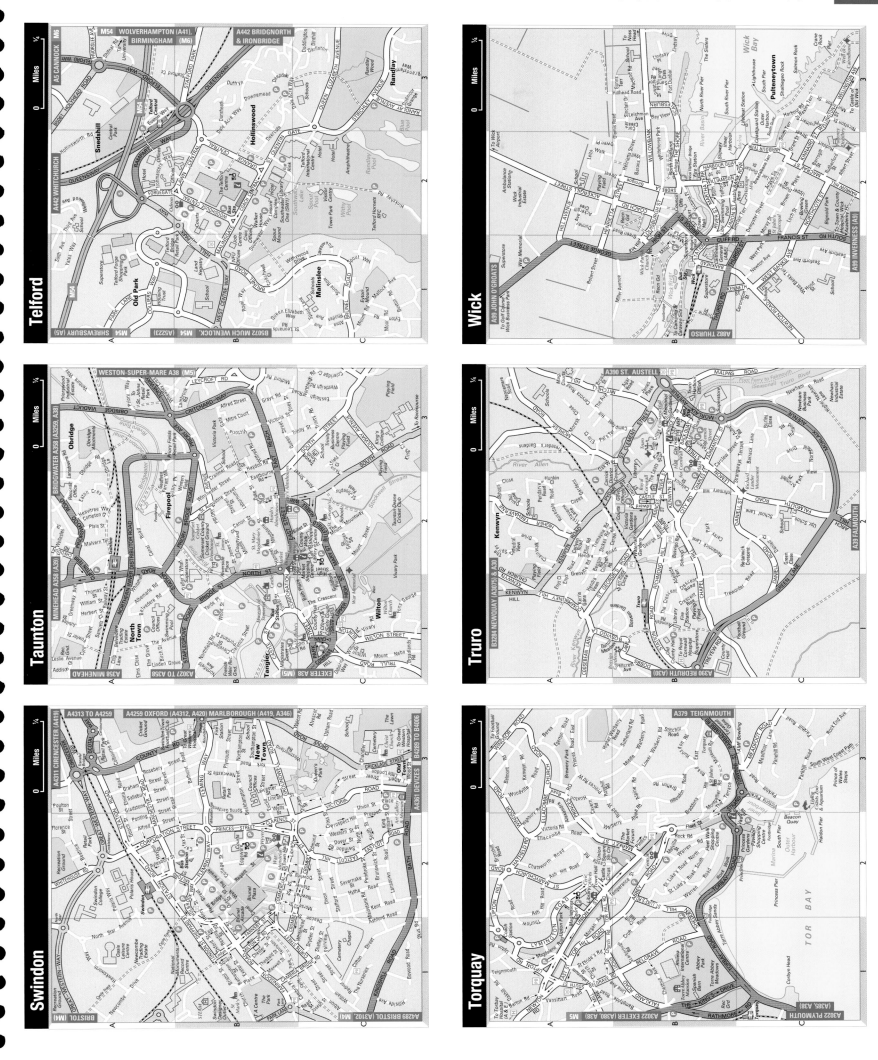

Town plan indexes

352 Blackpool • Bournemouth • Bradford • Brighton • Bristol

All Saint's St A2
All Saints Rd A2
Allcock St C5
Allesley St A4
Allison St C4
Alma Cr B6
Alston Rd C1
Arcadian Centre C4
Arena Birmingham C2
Arthur St C6
Assay Office B3
Aston Expressway A5
Aston St B4
Aston University B4/B5
Avenue Rd A5
Bacchus Rd A1
Bagot St B4
Banbury St B5
Barford Rd B1
Barford St C4
Barn St C5
Barnwell Rd C6
Barr St A3
Barrack St B5
Barwick St B4
Bath Row C3
Beaufort Rd C1
Belmont Row B5
Benson Rd A1
Berkley St C3
Bexhill Gr C3
Birchall St C5
Birmingham City FC C6
Birmingham City Hospital (A&E) A1
Birmingham City Univ B3
Birmingham Wheels Pk B6
Bishopsgate St C3
Blews St A4
Bloomsbury St A6
Blucher St C3
Bordesley St C4
Bowyer St C5
Bradburne Way A5
Bradford St C5
Branston St A3
Brearley St A4
Brewery St A4
Bridge St A3
Bridge St C3
Bridge St West A4
Brindley Dr B3
Broad St C3
Broad St Cineworld C2
Broadway Plaza C2
Bromley St C5
Bromsgrove St C4
Brookfield Rd A2
Browning St C2
Bryant St A1
BT Tower B3
Buckingham St A3
Bull St B4
Bull St B4
Bullring C4
Cambridge St C3
Camden Dr B3
Camden St B2
Cannon St C4
Cardigan St B5
Carlisle St A1
Carlyle Rd C1
Caroline St B3
Carver St B2
Cato St A6
Cattell Rd C6
Cattells Gr A6
Cawdor Cr C1
Cecil St B4
Cemetery A2/B2
Cemetery La A2
Ctr Link Industrial Est A6
Charlotte St B3
Cheapside C4
Chester St A5
Children's Hospital (A&E) B4
Church St B4
Claremont Rd A2
Clarendon Rd C1
Clark St C1
Clement St B3
Clissold St B2
Cliveland St B4
Coach Station C5
College St B2
Colmore Circus B4
Colmore Row B4
Commercial St C3
Constitution Hill B3
Convention Ctr, The C3
Cope St B2
Coplow St B1
Corporation St C4
Council House B3
County Court B4
Coveley Gr A2
Coventry Rd C6
Coventry St C5
Cox St B3
Crabtree Rd A2
Cregoe St C3
Crescent Ave A2
Crescent Theatre C3
Crescent, The A2
Cromwell St A6
Cromwell St B3
Cube, The C3
Curzon St B5
Custard Factory C5
Cuthbert Rd B1
Dale End B4
Dart St C6
Dartmouth Circus A4
Dartmouth Middleway A5
Dental Hospital B4
Deritend C5
Devon St A6
Devonshire St A1
Digbeth High St C4
Dolman St B6
Dover St A1
Duchess Rd C2
Duddeston B6
Duddeston Manor Rd B5
Duddeston Mill Rd B6
Duddeston Mill Trading Estate B6
Dudley Rd B1
Edmund St B3
Edward St B3
Elkington St A4
Ellen St B2
Ellis St C3
Erskine St B6
Essex St C4
Eyre St B2
Farm Croft A3
Farm St A3
Fazeley St B4/C5
Felstead Way B5
Finstall Cl B5
Five Ways C2
Fiveway Shopping Ctr C2
Fleet St B3
Floodgate St C5
Ford St A2
Fore St C4
Forster St B5
Francis Rd C2
Francis St B5
Frankfort St A4
Frederick St B3
Freeth St C1
Freightliner Terminal B6
Garrison La C6
Garrison St B6
Gas St C3
Geach St A4
George St B3
George St West B2
Gibb St C5
Gilby Rd C2
Gillott Rd B1
Glover St C5
Goode Ave A2
Goodrick Way A6
Gordon St B6
Graham St B3
Grand Central C4
Granville St C3
Gray St C6
Great Barr St C5
Great Charles St Queensway B3
Great Francis St B6
Great Hampton Row A3
Great Hampton St A3
Great King St A3
Great Lister St A5
Great Tindal St C2
Green La C6
Green St C5
Greenway St C6
Grosvenor St West C2
Guest Gr A3
Guild Cl C2
Guildford Dr A4
Guthrie Cl A3
Hagley Rd C1
Hall St B3
Hampton St A3
Handsworth New Rd A1
Hanley St B4
Harford St A3
Harmer Rd A2
Harold Rd C1
Hatchett St A4
Heath Mill La C5
Heath St B1
Heath St South B1
Heaton St A2
Heneage St B5
Henrietta St B4
Herbert Rd C6
High St C4
High St C5
Hilden Rd B5
Hill St C3/C4
Hindlow Cl B6
Hingeston St B2
Hippodrome Theatre C4
HM Prison A1
Hockley Circus A2
Hockley Hill A3
Hockley St A3
Holliday St C3
Holloway Circus C4
Holloway Head C3
Holt St B5
Hooper St B1
Horse Fair C4
Hospital St A4
Howard St B3
Howe St B5
Hubert St A5
Hunters Rd A2
Hunters Vale A3
Huntly Rd C2
Hurst St C4
Icknield Port Rd B1
Icknield Sq B2
Icknield St A2/B2
IKON C3
Information Ctr C4
Inge St C4
Irving St C3
James Watt Queensway B4
Jennens Rd B5
Jewellery Quarter A3
Jewellery Quarter Museum B3
John Bright St C4
Keeley St C6
Kellett Rd B5
Kent St C4
Kenyon St B3
Key Hill A3
Kilby Ave C2
King Edwards Rd B2
King Edwards Rd C3
Kingston Rd C6
Kirby Rd A1
Ladywood Arts & Leisure Ctr B1
Ladywood Middleway C2/C3
Ladywood Rd C1
Lancaster St B4
Landor St B6
Law Courts B4
Lawford Cl B5
Lawley Middleway B5
Ledbury Cl C2
Ledsam St B2
Lees St A1
Legge La B3
Lennox St A3
Library A6/C3
Lighthorne Ave B2
Link Rd B1
Lionel St B3
Lister St B5
Little Ann St C5
Little Hall Rd A6
Liverpool St C5
Livery St B3/B4
Lodge Rd A1
Lord St A5
Love La A5
Loveday St B4
Lower Dartmouth St C6
Lower Loveday St B4
Lower Tower St A4
Lower Trinity St C5
Ludgate Hill B3
Mailbox Centre & BBC C3
Margaret St B3
Markby Rd A1
Marroway St B1
Maxstoke St C6
Melvina Rd A6
Meriden St C4
Metropolitan (RC) B4
Midland St B6
Milk St C5
Mill St A5
Millennium Point B5
Miller St A4
Milton St A4
Moat La C4
Montague Rd C1
Montague St C5
Monument Rd C1
Moor St Queensway C4
Moor Street C4
Moorsom St A4
Morville St C2
Mosborough Cr A3
Moseley St C4
Mott St B3
Mus & Art Gallery B3
Musgrave Rd A1
National Sea Life Centre C3
Navigation St C3
Nechell's Park Rd A6
Nechells Parkway B5
Nechells Pl A6
New Alexandra C3
New Bartholomew St C4
New Canal St C5
New John St West A3
New Spring St B2
New St C4
New Street C4
New Summer St A4
New Town Row A4
Newhall Hill B3
Newhall St B3
Newton St B4
Newtown A4
Noel Rd C1
Norman St A1
Northbrook St B1
Northwood St B3
Norton St A2
Odeon C2
Old Crown House C5
Old Rep Theatre, The C4
Old Snow Hill B4
Oliver Rd C1
Oliver St A5
Osler St C1
Oxford St C5
Palmer St C5
Paradise Circus Queensway C3
Paradise St C3
Park Rd A2
Park St C4
Pavilions C4
Paxton Rd A2
Peel St A1
Pershore St C4
Phillips St A4
Pickford St C5
Pinfold St C4
Pitsford St A2
Plough & Harrow Rd C1
Police Station A4/B4/C2/C4
Pope St B2
Portland Rd C1
Post Office A5/B1/B3/B4/B5/C2/C3/C5
Preston Rd A1
Price St B4
Princip St B4
Printing House St B4
Priory Queensway B4
Pritchett St A4
Proctor St A5
Radnor St A2
Rea St C4
Regent Pl B3
Register Office C3
Repertory Theatre C3
Reservoir Rd C1
Richard St A5
River St C5
Rocky La A5/A6
Rodney Cl C2
Roseberry St B2
Rotton Park St B1
Rupert St A5
Ruston St C2
Ryland St C2
St Andrew's Ind Est C6
St Andrew's Rd C6
St Andrew's St C6
St Bolton St C6
St Chads B4
St Chads Queensway B4
St Clements Rd A6
St George's St A3
St James Pl B5
St Marks Cr B2
St Martin's C4
St Paul's B3
St Paul's B3
St Paul's Sq B3
St Philip's B4
St Stephen's St A4
St Thomas' Peace Garden C3
St Vincent St C2
Saltley Rd A6
Sand Pits Pde B3
Severn St C3
Shadwell St B4
Sheepcote St C2
Shefford Rd A4
Sherborne St C2
Shylton's Croft C2
Skipton Rd C2
Smallbrook Queensway C4
Smith St A3
Snow Hill B4
Snow Hill Queensway B4
Soho, Benson Rd A1
South Rd A2
Spencer St B3
Spring Hill B2
Staniforth St B4
Station St C4
Steelhouse La B4
Stephenson St C4
Steward St B2
Stirling Rd C1
Stour St B2
Suffolk St Queensway C3
Summer Hill Rd B2
Summer Hill St B2
Summer Hill Terr B2
Summer La A4
Summer Row B3
Summerfield Cr B1
Summerfield Park B1
Superstore B2
Sutton St C3
Swallow St C3
Sydney Rd C6
Symphony Hall C3
Talbot St A1
Temple Row C4
Temple St C4
Templefield St C6
Tenby St B3
Tenby St North B2
Tennant St C2/C3
Thimble Mill La A6
Thinktank (Science & Discovery) B5
Thomas St A4
Thorpe St C4
Tilton Rd C6
Tower St A4
Town Hall C3
Trent St C5
Turner's Buildings A1
Unett St A3
Union Terr B5
Upper Trinity St C5
Uxbridge St A3
Vauxhall Gr B5
Vauxhall Rd B5
Vernon Rd C1
Vesey St B4
Viaduct St B5
Victoria Sq C3
Villa St A3
Vittoria St B3
Vyse St B3
Walter St A6
Wardlow Rd A5
Warstone La B2
Washington St C3
Water St B3
Waterworks Rd C1
Watery La C5
Well St A3
Western Rd B1
Wharf St A2
Wheeler St A3
Whitehouse St A5
Whitmore St A2
Whittall St B4
Wholesale Market C4
Wiggin St B1
Willes Rd A1
Windsor Industrial Est A5
Windsor St A5
Windsor St B5
Winson Green Rd A1
Witton St C6
Wolseley St C6
Woodcock St B5

Blackpool 332

Abingdon St A1
Addison Cr A3
Adelaide St B1
Albert Rd B2
Alfred St B2
Ascot Rd A3
Ashton Rd C3
Auburn Gr C3
Bank Hey St B1
Banks St A1
Beech Ave A3
Bela Gr C2
Belmont Ave B2
Birley St A1
Blackpool & Fleetwood Tram B1
Blackpool & the Fylde College B2
Blackpool FC C2
Blackpool North A2
Blackpool Tower B1
Blundell St C1
Bonny St B1
Breck Rd B3
Bryan Rd A3
Buchanan St A2
Bus Station A2
Cambridge Rd A3
Caunce St A2/A3
Central Dr B1/C2
Central Pier C1
Central Pier C1
Central Pier Theatre C1
Chapel St C1
Charles St A2
Charnley Rd B2
Church St A1/A2
Clinton Ave B2
Coach Station A2/C1
Cocker St A1
Coleridge Rd A3
Collingwood Ave A3
Comedy Carpet B1
Condor Gr C3
Cookson St A2
Coronation St B1
Corporation St A1
Courts B1
Cumberland Ave B3
Cunliffe Rd C3
Dale St C1
Devonshire Rd A3
Devonshire Sq A3
Dickson Rd A1
Elizabeth St A2
Ferguson Rd C3
Forest Gate B3
Foxhall Rd C1
Freckleton St C2
George St A2
Gloucester Ave B3
Golden Mile, The C1
Gorse Rd B3
Gorton St A2
Grand Theatre, The B1
Granville Rd A2
Grasmere Rd C2
Grosvenor St A2
Grundy Art Gallery A1
Harvey Rd B3
Hornby Rd B2
Houndshill Shopping Centre B1
Hull Rd B1
Ibbison Ct C2
Information Ctr A1
Kent Rd C2
Keswick Rd C2
King St A2
Knox Gr C3
Laycock Gate A3
Layton Rd A3
Leamington Rd B2
Leeds Rd B3
Leicester Rd B2
Levens Gr C2
Library A1
Lifeboat Station B1
Lincoln Rd B2
Liverpool Rd B3
Livingstone Rd B2
London Rd A3
Lune Gr C2
Lytham Rd C1
Madame Tussaud's Blackpool B1
Manchester Sq C1
Manor Rd B3
Maple Ave B3
Market St A1
Marlboro Rd B3
Mere Rd B3
Milbourne St A2
Newcastle Ave B3
Newton Dr A3
North Pier A1
North Pier A1
North Pier Theatre A1
Odeon C2
Olive Gr B3
Palatine Rd B2
Park Rd B2/C3
Peter St A2
Police Station B1
Post Office A1/A3/B1/B2
Princess Parade A1
Princess St C1/C2
Promenade A1/C1
Queen St A1
Queen Victoria Rd C2
Raikes Pde B2
Reads Ave B2
Regent Rd B2
Register Office B2
Ribble Rd B2
Rigby Rd C1/C2
Ripon Rd B3
St Albans Rd B3
St Ives Ave C3
St John's Square A1
St Vincent Ave C3
Salisbury Rd B3
Salthouse Ave C2
Salvation Army Ctr A2
Sands Way C2
Sea Life Centre B1
Seasiders Way C1
Selbourne Rd A2
Sharrow Gr C3
Somerset Ave C3
South King St B2
Springfield Rd A1
Sutton Pl B2
Talbot Rd A1/A2
Thornber Gr C2
Topping St A1
Tower B1
Town Hall A1
Tram Depot C1
Tyldesley Rd C1
Vance Rd B1
Victoria St B1
Victory Rd A2
Wayman Rd A3
Westmorland Ave C2/C3
Whitegate Dr B3
Winter Gardens Theatre B1
Woodland Gr B3
Woolman Rd B2

Bournemouth 333

Ascham Rd A3
Avenue Rd B1
Ave Shopping Centre B1
Bath Rd C2
Beacon Rd C1
Beechey Rd A3
Bodorgan Rd B1
Bourne Ave B1
Bournemouth A3
Bournemouth & Poole College B3
Bournemouth Int Ctr C1
Bournemouth Pier C2
Bournemouth Sta B3
Braidley Rd A1
Cavendish Place A2
Cavendish Rd A2
Central Drive A1
Central Gdns B1
Christchurch Rd B3
Cliff Lift C1/C3
Coach House Pl A3
Coach Station A3
Commercial Rd B1
Cotlands Rd B3
Cranborne Rd C1
Cricket Ground A2
Cumnor Rd B2
Dean Park A2
Dean Park Cr B2
Dean Park Rd A2
Durrant Rd B1
East Overcliff Dr C3
Exeter Cr C1
Exeter La C2
Exeter Rd C1
Gervis Place B1
Gervis Rd B3
Glen Fern Rd B2
Golf Club B1
Grove Rd B3
Hinton Rd C2
Holdenhurst Rd B3
Horseshoe Common B2
Information Ctr C2
Lansdowne B3
Lansdowne Rd A2
Lorne Park Rd B2
Lower Gdns B1/C2
Madeira Rd B2
Methuen Rd A3
Meyrick Park A1
Meyrick Rd B3
Milton Rd A2
Nuffield Health Bournemouth Hospital (private) A2
Oceanarium C2
Odeon Cinema C2
Old Christchurch Rd B2
Ophir Rd A3
Oxford Rd B3
Park Rd A3
Parsonage Rd B2
Pavilion C2
Pier Approach C2
Pier Theatre C2
Police Station A3/B3
Portchester Rd A3
Post Office B1/B3
Priory Rd C1
Quadrant, The B2
Recreation Ground A1
Richmond Gardens Shopping Centre B2
Richmond Hill Rd B1
Russell-Cotes Art Gallery & Museum C2
Russell Cotes Rd C2
St Anthony's Rd A1
St Michael's Rd C1
St Paul's A3
St Paul's La B3
St Paul's Rd A3
St Peter's B2
St Peter's B2
St Peter's Rd B2
St Stephen's Rd B1/B2
St Swithun's B3
St Swithun's Rd B3
St Swithun's Rd South B3
St Valerie Rd A2
St Winifred's Rd A2
Square, The B1
Stafford Rd B3
Terrace Rd B1
Town Hall B1
Tregonwell Rd C1
Triangle, The B1
Trinity Rd B2
Undercliff Drive C3
Upper Hinton Rd B2
Upper Terr Rd C1
Wellington Rd A2/A3
Wessex Way A3/B1/B2
West Cliff Promenade C1
West Hill Rd C1
West Undercliff Prom C1
Westover Rd B2
Wimborne Rd A2
Wootton Mount B2
Wychwood Dr A1
Yelverton Rd B2
York Rd B3
Zig-Zag Walks C1/C3

Bradford 333

Alhambra B2
Back Ashgrove B1
Barkerend Rd A3
Barnard Rd C3
Barry St B2
Bolling Rd C3
Bolton Rd A3
Bowland St A1
Bradford Big Screen B2
Bradford College B1
Bradford Forster Sq A2
Bradford Interchange B3
Bradford Playhouse B3
Bridge St B2
Britannia St B2
Broadway Bradford, The B2
Burnett St B3
Bus Station B2
Butler St West A3
Caledonia St C2
Canal Rd A2
Carlton St B1
Cathedral A3
Centenary Sq B2
Chapel St B3
Cheapside A2
Church Bank B3
Cineworld B3
City Hall B2
City Rd A1
Claremont B1
Colour Experience B1
Croft St B2
Crown Court B3
Darfield St A1
Darley St A2
Drewton Rd A1
Drummond Trading Estate A1
Dryden St B3
Dyson St A1
Easby Rd C1
East Parade B3
Eldon Pl A1
Filey St B3
Forster Sq Retail Pk A2
Gallery II B1
Garnett St B3
Godwin St B2
Gracechurch St A1
Grattan Rd B1
Great Horton Rd B1/B2
Grove Terr B1
Hall Ings B2
Hall La C3
Hallfield Rd A1
Hammstrasse A2
Harris St B3
Holdsworth St A2
Ice Arena B2
Impressions B2
Information Ctr B2
Inland Revenue A2
Ivegate B2
Jacob's Well Municipal Offices B2
James St A2
John St A2
Kirkgate B2
Kirkgate Centre B2
Laisteridge La C1
Leeds Rd B3
L Exchange, The B3
Library B1/B2
Listerhills Rd B1
Little Horton Gn C1
Little Horton La C1
Longside La B1
Lower Kirkgate B2
Lumb La A1
Magistrates Court B2
Manchester Rd C2
Manningham La A1
Manor Row A2
Market C3
Market St B2
Melbourne Place C1
Midland Rd A2
Mill La C2
Morley St B1
National Media B2
Nelson St B2/C2
Nesfield St A2
New Otley Rd A3
Norcroft St B1
North Parade A2
North St A3
North Wing A3
Oastler Shopping Ctr A2
Otley Rd A3
Park Ave C1
Park La C1
Park Rd C2
Parma St C2
Peace Museum B2
Peckover St B3
Piccadilly A2
Police Station C2
Post Office A2/B1/B2/C3
Princes Way B2
Prospect St C3
Radwell Drive C2
Rawson Rd A1
Rebecca St A1
Richmond Rd B1
Russell St C1
St George's Hall B2
St Lukes Hospital C1
Shipley Airedale Rd A3/B3
Shopmobility A2
Simes St A1
Smith St B1
Spring Mill St C2
Stott Hill A3
Sunbridge Rd A1/B1/B2
Theatre in the Mill B1
Thornton Rd A1/B1
Trafalgar St A2
Trinity Rd C1
Tumbling Hill St B1
Tyrrel St B2
Univ of Bradford B1/C1
Usher St C3
Valley Rd A2
Vicar La B3
Wakefield Rd C3
Wapping Rd A3
Well St B3
Westgate A1
White Abbey Rd A1
Wigan Rd A1
Wilton St B1
Wood St A1
Wool Exchange B2
Worthington St A1

Brighton 333

Addison Rd A1
Albert Rd B2
Albion Hill B3
Albion St B3
Ann St A3
Baker St A3
Black Lion St C2
Brighton A2
Brighton Centre C2
Brighton Fishing Museum C2
Brighton Pier (Palace Pier) C3
Brighton Wheel C3
British Airways i360 Tower C1
Broad St C3
Buckingham Pl A2
Buckingham Rd B2
Cannon Pl C1
Carlton Hill B3
Chatham Pl A1
Cheapside A3
Church St B2
Churchill Square Shopping Centre B2
Clifton Hill B1
Clifton Pl B1
Clifton Rd B1
Clifton St A2
Clifton Terr B1
Clyde Rd A3
Coach Station C3
Compton Ave A2
Davigdor Rd A1
Denmark Terr B1
Ditchling Rd A3
Dome B2
Duke St B2
Duke's La C2
Dyke Rd A1/B2
East St C2
Edward St B3
Elmore Rd B3
Fleet St A2
Frederick St B2
Gardner St B2
Gloucester Pl B3
Gloucester Rd B2
Goldsmid Rd A1
Grand Junction Rd C2
Grand Pde B3
Grove Hill B3
Guildford St A2
Hampton Pl B1
Hanover Terr A3
High St C3
Highdown Rd A1
Information Ctr C2
John St B3
Jubilee Clock Tower B2
Kemp St B2
Kensington Pl B2
Kings Rd C1
Lanes, The C2
Law Courts B3
Lewes Rd A3
Library B2
London Rd A3
Madeira Dr C3
Marine Pde C3
Middle St C2
Montpelier Pl B1
Montpelier Rd B1
Montpelier St B1
Mus & Art Gallery B3
New England Rd A2
New England St A2
New Rd B2
Nizells Ave A1
Norfolk Rd B1
Norfolk Terr B1
North Rd B2
North St B2
Odeon C2
Old Shoreham Rd A1
Old Steine C3
Osmond Rd A1
Over St B2
Oxford St A3
Park Crescent Terr A3
Phoenix Brighton B3
Phoenix Rise A3
Police Station B3
Post Office A1/A3/C3
Preston Rd A2
Preston St B1
Prestonville Rd A1
Queen's Rd B2
Queen Sq B2
Regency Sq C1
Regent St B2
Richmond Pl B3
Richmond St B3
Richmond Terr A3
Rose Hill Terr A3
Royal Pavilion B2
St Bartholomew's A3
St James's St C3
St Nicholas Rd B2
St Nicholas' B2
St Peter's A3
Sea Life Brighton C3
Shaftesbury Rd A3
Ship St C2
Sillwood Rd B1
Sillwood St B1
Southover St A3
Spring Gdns B2
Stanford Rd A1
Stanley Rd A3
Surrey St B2
Sussex St B3
Swimming Pool B3
Sydney St B3
Temple Gdns B1
Terminus Rd A2
Theatre Royal B2
Tidy St B2
Town Hall C2
Toy & Model Mus A2
Trafalgar St B2
Union Rd A3
University of Brighton B3
Upper Lewes Rd A3
Upper North St B1
Viaduct Rd A3
Victoria Gdns B3
Victoria Rd B1
Volk's Electric Railway C3
West Pier (derelict) C1
West St C2
Western Rd B1
Whitecross St B2
York Ave B1
York Pl B3
York Rd B1

Bristol 333

Acramans Rd C4
Albert Rd C6
Alfred Hill A4
All Saint's St A4
All Saints' B4
Allington Rd C3
Alpha Rd C4
Ambra Vale B1
Ambra Vale East B2
Ambrose Rd B2
Amphitheatre & Waterfront Square C4
Anchor Rd B3
Anvil St B6
Arcade, The A5
Architecture Centre, The B4
Argyle Pl B2
Arlington Villas A2
Arnolfini Arts Centre, The B4
Art Gallery A3
Ashton Gate Rd C2
Ashton Rd C1
Avon Bridge C1
Avon Cr C1
Avon St B6
Baldwin St B4
Baltic Wharf C2
Baltic Wharf Leisure Ctr & Caravan Pk C2
Baltic Wharf Marina C2
Barossa Pl C4
Barton Manor B6
Barton Rd B6
Barton Vale B6
Bath Rd C6
Bathurst Basin C4
Bathurst Parade C4
Beauley Rd C3
Bedminster Bridge C5
Bedminster Parade C4
Bellevue B2
Bellevue Cr B2
Bellevue Rd C6
Berkeley Pl A2
Berkeley Sq A3
Birch Rd C2
Blackfriars A4
Bond St A5
Braggs La A6
Brandon Hill B3
Brandon Steep B3
Bristol Aquarium B4
Bristol Bridge B5
Bristol Cath (CE) B3
Bristol Eye Hosp (A&E) A4
Bristol Grammar School A3
Bristol Harbour Railway C3
Bristol Royal Children's Hospital A4
Bristol Royal Infirmary (A&E) A4
Bristol Temple Meads Station B6

Broad Plain B6
Broad Quay B4
Broad St A4
Broad Weir A5
Broadcasting House A3
Broadmead A5
Brunel Institute ✦ B3
Brunel Way C1
Brunswick Sq A5
Burton Cl C5
Bus Station A4
Butts Rd B3
Cabot Circus A5
Cabot Tower ✦ B3
Caledonia Pl B1
Callowhill Ct A5
Cambridge St C6
Camden Rd C3
Camp Rd A1
Canada Way C2
Cannon St A4
Canon's Way B3
Cantock's Cl A3
Canynge Rd A1
Canynge Sq A1
Castle Park A5
Castle St A5
Cathedral Walk B3
Catherine Meade St C4
Cattle Market Rd C6
Central Library B3
Charles Pl B1
Charlotte St B3
Charlotte St South B3
Chatterton House B5
Chatterton Sq C5
Chatterton St C5
Cheese La B5
Christchurch A4
Christchurch Rd A1
Christmas Steps ✦ A4
Church La B2/B5
Church St B5
City Museum A3
City of Bristol College B3
Civil and Family
Justice Centre B5
Clare St B4
Clarence Rd C5
Cliff Rd C1
Clift House Rd C1
Clifton Cath (RC) ✝ A2
Clifton Down A1
Clifton Down Rd A1
Clifton Hill B2
Clifton Park A1/A2
Clifton Park Rd A1
Clifton Rd A2
Clifton Vale B1
Cliftonwood Cr B2
Cliftonwood Rd B2
Cliftonwood Terr B2
Cobblestone Mews A1
College Green B3
College Rd A1
College St B3
Colston Almshouses
A4
Colston Ave B4
Colston Hall B4
Colston Parade C5
Colston St A4
Commercial Rd C4
Constitution Hill B2
Cooperage La C2
Corn St B4
Cornwallis Ave B1
Cornwallis Cr B1
Coronation Rd C2/C4
Council House B3
Counterslip B5
Create Centre, The ✦ C1
Crosby Row B2
Crown Court A4
Culver St B3
Cumberland Basin C1
Cumberland Cl C2
Cumberland Rd C2/C3
Dean La C4
Deanery Rd B3
Denmark St B4
Dowry Sq B1
Eaton Cr A2
Elmdale Rd A3
Elton Rd A3
Eugene St A4/A6
Exchange and St
Nicholas' Mkts, The
B4
Fairfax St A4
Fire Station B5
Floating Harbour C3
Fosseway, The A2
Foster Almshouses A4
Frayne Rd C1
Frederick Pl A2
Freeland Pl B1
Friary B5
Frogmore St B3
Fry's Hill B2
Gas La B6
Gasferry Rd C3
Georgian House B3
Glendale B1
Glentworth Rd B2
Gloucester St A1
Goldney Hall B2
Goldney Rd B1
Gordon Rd A2
Granby Hill B1
Grange Rd A1
Great Ann St A6
Great George Rd B3
Great George St A6/B3
Green St North B1
Green St South B1
Greenay Bush La C2
Greenbank Rd C2
Greville Smyth Park C1
Grove, The B4
Guildhall A4
Guinea St C4
Hamilton Rd C3
Hanbury Rd A2
Hanover Pl C2
Harley Pl A1
Haymarket A5
Hensman's Hill B1
High St B4
Highbury Villas A3
Hill St B3
Hill St C6
Hippodrome B4
Hopechapel Hill B1
Horfield Rd A4
Horsefair, The A5
Horton St B6
Host St A4
Hotwell Rd B1/B2
Houlton St A6
Howard Rd C3
IMAX Cinema B4
Information Ctr B4
Islington Rd C3
Jacob St A5/A6
Jacob's Wells Rd B2
John Carr's Terr B2
John Wesley's
Chapel A5
Joy Hill B1
Jubilee St B6
Kensington Pl A2
Kilkenny St B6
King St B4
Kingsland Rd B6
Kingston Rd C3
Lamb St A6
Lansdown Rd A2
Lawford St A6
Lawfords Gate A6
Leighton Rd C3
Lewins Mead A4
Lime Rd C2
Litfield Rd A1
Little Ann St A6
Little Caroline Pl B1
Little George St A6
Little King St B4
Llandoger Trow B4
Lloyds' Building, The C3
Lodge St A4
Lord Mayor's Chapel,
The B4
Lower Castle St A5
Lower Church La A4
Lower Clifton Hill B2
Lower Guinea St C4
Lower Lamb St B3
Lower Maudlin St A4
Lower Park Rd A4
Lower Sidney St C2
Lucky La C4
Lydstep Terr C3
M Shed C4
Magistrates' Court A4
Mall (Galleries Shopping
Centre), The A5
Mall, The A1
Manilla Rd A1
Mardyke Ferry Rd C2
Maritime Heritage
Centre B3
Marlborough Hill A4
Marlborough St A4
Marsh St B4
Mead St C5
Merchant Dock B2
Merchant Seamen's
Almshouses B4
Merchant St A5
Merchants Rd A1
Merchants Rd C1
Meridian Pl A2
Meridian Vale A2
Merrywood Rd C3
Midland Rd A6
Milford St C3
Millennium Prom B3
Millennium Sq B3
Mitchell La B5
Mortimer Rd A1
Murray Rd C4
Myrtle Rd A3
Narrow Plain B5
Narrow Quay B4
Nelson St A4
New Charlotte St C4
New Kingsley Rd B6
New Queen St C5
New St A6
Newgate A5
Newton St A6
Norland Rd A1
North St C2
O2 Academy B3
Oakfield Gr A2
Oakfield Pl A2
Oakfield Rd A2
Old Bread St B6
Old Market St A6
Old Park Hill A4
Oldfield Rd B1
Orchard Ave B4
Orchard La B4
Orchard St B4
Osbourne Rd C3
Oxford St B6
Park Pl A2
Park Rd C3
Park Row A3
Park St A3
Passage St B5
Pembroke Gr A2
Pembroke Rd A2
Pembroke Rd C3
Pembroke St A5
Penn St A5
Pennywell Rd A6
Percival Rd A1
Pero's Bridge B4
Perry Rd A4
Phipps St C2
Pip 'n' Jay B5
Plimsoll Bridge B1
Police Sta A6
Polygon Rd B1
Portland St A1
Portwall La B5
Post Office A1/A3/A5/
B1/B4/C4/C5
Prewett St C5
Prince St B4
Prince St Bridge C4
Princess St C5
Princess Victoria St B1
Priory Rd A3
Pump La C5
QEH Theatre A2
Quakers Friars A5
Quay St A4
Queen Charlotte St B4
Queen Elizabeth
Hospital School B2
Queen Sq B4
Queen St A5
Queen's Ave A3
Queen's Parade B3
Queen's Rd A2/A3
Raleigh Rd C2
Randall Rd B2
Red Lodge A4
Redcliffe Backs B5
Redcliffe Bridge B4
Redcliffe Hill C5
Redcliffe Parade C4
Redcliffe St B5
Redcliffe Way B5
Redcross St A6
Redgrave Theatre A1
Regent St B1
Richmond Hill A2
Richmond Hill Ave A2
Richmond La A2
Richmond Park Rd A2
Richmond St C6
Richmond Terr A2
River St A6
Rownham Mead B2
Royal Fort Rd A3
Royal Park A2
Royal West of England
Academy A3
Royal York Cr B1
Royal York Villas B1
Rupert St A4
Russ St B6
St Andrew's Walk B2
St George's B3
St George's Rd B3
St James A4
St John's A4
St John's Rd C4
St Luke's Rd C5
St Mary Redcliffe C5
St Matthias Park A6
St Michael's Hill A3
St Michael's Hosp A4
St Michael's Park A3
St Nicholas St B4
St Paul St A5
St Paul's Rd A2
St Peter's (ruin) A5
St Philip's Bridge B5
St Philips Rd A6
St Stephen's B4
St Stephen's St B4
St Thomas St B5
St Thomas the
Martyr B5
Sandford Rd B1
Sargent St C5
Saville Pl B1
Ship La C5
Shopmobility A5
Showcase Cinema
de Lux A5
Silver St A4
Sion Hill A1
Small St A4
Smeaton Rd C1
Somerset Sq C5
Somerset St C5
Southernhay Ave B2
Southville Rd C4
Spike Island
Artspace C2
Spring St C5
Superstore C4
SS Great Britain and
the Matthew B2
Stackpool Rd C3
Staight St B6
Stillhouse La C4
Sydney Row C2
Tankard's Cl A3
Temple Back B5
Temple Back East B5
Temple Bridge B5
Temple Church B5
Temple Circus B5
Temple Gate C5
Temple St B5
Temple Way B5
Terrell St A4
Theatre Royal
(Bristol Old Vic) B4
Thekla B4
Thomas La B5
Three Kings of
Cologne A4
Three Queens La B5
Tobacco Factory,
The C2
Tower Hill B5
Tower La A4
Trenchard St A4
Triangle South A3
Triangle West A3
Trinity Rd A6
Trinity St A6
Tyndall Ave A3
Union St A5
Union St B6
Unity St A6
Unity St B3
University of Bristol A3
University Rd A3
Upper Byron Pl A3
Upper Maudlin St A4
Upper Perry Hill C3
Upton Rd C2
Valentine Bridge B6
Victoria Gr C5
Victoria Rd C6
Victoria Rooms A2
Victoria Sq A2
Victoria St B5
Vyvyan Rd A1
Vyvyan Terr A1
Wade St A6
Walter St C2
Wapping Rd C4
Water La B5
Waterloo Rd A6
Waterloo St A1
Waterloo St A6
Watershed Media
Centre ✦ B4
We the Curious ✦ B3
Welling Terr B1
Welsh Back B4
West Mall A1
West St A6
Westfield Pl A1
Wetherell Pl A2
Whitehouse Pl C5
Whitehouse St C5
Whiteladies Rd A2
Whitson St A4
William St C5
Willway St C5
Windsor Pl B1
Wine St A4
Woodland Rd A3
Woodland Rise A3
Worcester Rd A1
Worcester Terr A1
YHA B4
York Gdns B1
York Pl A2
York Rd C5

Bury St Edmunds 333

Abbey Gardens B3
Abbey Gate B3
Abbeygate St B2
Albert Cr B1
Albert St B1
Ambulance Sta C1
Angel Hill B2
Angel La B2
Anglian Lane A1
Arc Shopping Centre B2
Athenaeum C2
Baker's La C3
Barwell Rd B3
Beetons Way A1
Bishops Rd B2
Bloomfield St B2
Bridewell La C2
Bullen Cl C1
Bury St Edmunds ≋ A2
Bury St Edmunds County
Upper School A1
Bury St Edmunds
Leisure Ctr B1
Bury Town FC B3
Bus Station B2
Business Park B3
Butter Mkt B2
Cannon St B2
Castle Rd C1
Cemetery C1
Chalk Rd (N) B1
Chalk Rd (S) B1
Church Row B2
Churchgate St C2
Cineworld B1
Citizens Advice B2
College St C2
Compiegne Way A3
Corn Exchange, The B2
Cornfield Rd B1
Cotton Lane B3
Courts B2
Covent Garden C2
Crown St C3
Cullum Rd C2
Eastern Way A3
Eastgate St B3
Enterprise Bsns Park A2
Etna Rd A2
Eyre Cl C2
Fire Station B1
Friar's Lane C2
Gage Cl A1
Garland St B2
Greene King
Brewery C3
Grove Park B1
Grove Rd B1
Guildhall C2
Guildhall St C2
Hatter St C2
High Baxter St B2
Honey Hill C3
Hospital Rd C1/C2
Ickworth Dr C1
Industrial Estate A3
Information Ctr B2
Ipswich St A2
Junction 43 A3
King Edward VI Sch A1
King's Rd C1/B2
Library B2
Long Brackland A2
Looms La B2
Lwr Baxter St B2
Malthouse La A2
Maynewater La C3
Mill Rd C1
Mill Rd (South) C1
Minden Close B3
Moyses Hall B2
Mustow St B3
Norman Tower C3
Northgate Ave A2
Northgate St B2
Nutshell, The B2
Osier Rd A2
Out Northgate A2
Out Risbygate B1
Out Westgate C2
Parkway B1/C2
Peckham St B2
Petticoat La C1
Phoenix Day Hosp C1
Pinners Way C1
Police Station C3
Post Office B2/B3
Pump La B2
Queen's Rd B1
Raingate St C3
Raynham Rd A1
Retail Park C2
Risbygate St B1/B2
Robert Boby Way C2
St Andrew's St North B2
St Andrew's St South B2
St Botolph's La C3
St Edmund's C2
St Edmund's Abbey
(Remains) ✦ B3
St Edmunds Hospital
(private) C3
St Edmundsbury ✝ C3
St John's St B2
St Marys C3
School Hall La B2
Shillitoe Cl C1
Shire Halls &
Magistrates Ct C3
South Cl C1
Southgate St C3
Sparhawk St C3
Spring Lane B1
Springfield Rd B1
Station Hill A2
Swan La C3
Tayfen Rd B2
Theatre Royal C3
Thingoe Hill A2
Victoria St B1
Vinefields, The B3
War Memorial ✦ C1
Well St B2
West Suffolk College B1
Westgarth Gdns C1
Westgate St C2
Whiting St C2
York Rd B1
York Terr B1

Cambridge 334

Abbey Rd A3
ADC A2
Anglia Ruskin Univ B3
Archaeology &
Anthropology B2
Arts Picture House B2
Arts Theatre B1
Auckland Rd A3
Backs, The B1
Bateman St C2
Benet St B1
Bradmore St B3
Bridge St A1
Broad St B3
Brookside C2
Brunswick Terr A3
Burleigh St B3
Bus Station B2
Butt Green A2
Cambridge
Contemporary Art
Gallery B1
Castle Mound A1
Castle St A1
Cemetery B3
Chesterton La A1
Christ's (Coll) B2
Christ's Lane B2
Christ's Pieces B2
City Rd B3
Clare (Coll) B1
Clarendon St C2
Coe Fen C2
Coronation St C2
Corpus Christi (Coll) B1
Court A3
Cross St C3
Crusoe Bridge C1
Darwin (Coll) C1
Devonshire Rd C3
Downing (Coll) C2
Downing St B2
Earl St B2
East Rd B3
Eden St B3
Elizabeth Way A3
Elm St B2
Emery St B3
Emmanuel (Coll) B2
Emmanuel Rd B2
Emmanuel St B2
Fair St A3
Fen Causeway, The C1
Fenner's Cricket Gd C3
Fire Station B3
Fitzroy St A3
Fitzwilliam Mus C2
Fitzwilliam St C2
Garrett Hostel Bridge B1
Glisson Rd C3
Gonville & Caius (Coll) B1
Gonville Place C2
Grafton Centre, The A3
Grand Arcade B2
Green St B1
Gresham Rd C3
Guest Rd B3
Guildhall B2
Harvey Rd C3
Hills Rd C3
Hobson St B2
Hughes Hall (Coll) B3
Information Ctr B2
James St A3
Jesus (Coll) A2
Jesus Green A2
Jesus La A2
Jesus Terr B3
John St B3
Kelsey Kerridge
Sports Centre B3
Kettle's Yard A1
King's Bridge B1
King St A2
King's (Coll) B1
King's Coll Chapel B1
King's Parade B1
Lammas Land Rec Gd C1
Lensfield Rd C2
Library B2
Lion Yard B2
Little St Mary's La B1
Lyndewod Rd C3
Magdalene (Coll) A1
Magdalene St A1
Maid's Causeway A3
Malcolm St A2
Market Hill B1
Market St B1
Mathematical Bridge B1
Mawson Rd C3
Midsummer Common A3
Mill La B1
Mill Rd B3
Mill St C3
Mumford B3
Mus of Cambridge A1
Museum of Classical
Archeology C1
Napier St A3
New Square A3
Newmarket Rd A3
Newnham Rd C1
Norfolk St B3
Northampton St A1
Norwich St C2
Orchard St B2
Panton St C2
Paradise Nature
Reserve C1
Paradise St B3
Park Parade A1
Park St A2
Park Terr B2
Parker St B2
Parker's Piece B2
Parkside B3
Parkside Pools B3
Parsonage St A3
Pemberton Terr C2
Pembroke (Coll) B2
Pembroke St B1
Perowne St B3
Peterhouse (Coll) C1
Petty Cury B2
Polar Museum, The C2
Police Station B3
Post Office A1/A3/
B2/B3/C1/C2/C3
Queen's La B1
Queen's Rd B1
Queens' (Coll) B1
Regent St B2
Regent Terr B2
Ridley Hall (Coll) C1
Riverside A3
Round Church, The A1
Russell St C2
St Andrew's St B2
St Benet's B1
St Catharine's (Coll) B1
St Eligius St C2
St John's (Coll) A1
St Mary's B1
St Paul's Rd C3
Saxon St C2
Sedgwick Museum B2
Sheep's Green C1
Shire Hall A1
Sidgwick Ave C1
Sidney St A2
Sidney Sussex (Coll) A2
Silver St B1
Station Rd C3
Tenison Ave C3
Tenison Rd C3
Tennis Court Rd B2
Thompson's La A1
Trinity (Coll) A1
Trinity Hall (Coll) B1
Trinity St B1
Trumpington Rd C2
Trumpington St B1
Union Rd C2
University Botanic
Gardens C2
Victoria Ave A2
Victoria St B2
Warkworth St B3
Warkworth Terr B3
Wesley House (Coll) A2
West Rd B1
Westcott House (Coll) A2
Westminster (Coll) A1
Whipple B2
Willis Rd B3
Willow Walk A2
YMCA C3

Canterbury 334

Artillery St B2
Barton Mill Rd A3
Beaconsfield Rd A1
Beaney, The B2
Beverley Rd A1
Bingley's Island B1
Black Griffin La B1
Broad Oak Rd A2
Broad St B2
Brymore Rd A3
Burgate B2
Bus Station C2
Canterbury College C3
Canterbury East ≋ C1
Canterbury Tales,
The ✦ B2
Canterbury West ≋ A1
Castle C1
Castle Row C1
Castle St C1
Cathedral ✝ B2
Causeway, The A2
Chaucer Rd A3
Christ Church Univ B3
Christchurch Gate ✦ B2
City Council Offices A3
City Wall B2
Coach Park A2
College Rd B3
Cossington Rd C2
Court B2
Craddock Rd A3
Crown & County
Courts B3
Dane John Gdns C2
Dane John Mound ✦ C1
Deanery B2
Dover St C2
Duck La B2
Eastbridge
Hospital B1
Edgar Rd B3
Ersham Rd C3
Ethelbert Rd C3
Fire Station C2
Forty Acres Rd A1
Friars, The B2
Gordon Rd C1
Greyfriars ✦ B1
Guildford Rd C1
Havelock St B2
Heaton Rd C1
High St B2
Information Ctr A2/B2
Ivy La B2
Ivy Pl C1
King St B2
King's School B2/B3
King's School Recreation
Centre, The A2
Kingsmead Leisure Ctr A2
Kingsmead Rd A2
Kirby's La B1
Lansdown Rd C2
Lime Kiln Rd C1
Longport B3
Lower Chantry La C3
Mandeville Rd A1
Market Way A2
Marlowe Arcade B2
Marlowe Ave C2
Marlowe Theatre B2
Martyrs Field Rd C1
Mead Way B1
Military Rd B2
Monastery St B2
Mus of Canterbury
(Rupert Bear Mus) B1
New Dover Rd C3
Norman Rd C2
North Holmes Rd B3
North La B1
Northgate A2
Nunnery Fields C2
Nunnery Rd C2
Oaten Hill C2
Odeon Cinema C2
Old Dover Rd C2
Old Palace B2
Old Ruttington La B2
Old Weavers B2
Orchard St B1
Oxford Rd C1
Palace St B2
Pilgrims Way C3
Pin Hill C1
Pine Tree Ave A1
Police Station C2
Post Office B2
Pound La B1
Puckle La C2
Raymond Ave C2
Recreation Ground A2
Registry Office A2
Rheims Way B1
Rhodaus Cl C2
Rhodaus Town C2
Roman Museum B2
Roper Gateway A1
Roper Rd A1
Rose La B2
Shopmobility B2
St Augustine's Abbey
(remains) ✝ B3
St Augustine's Rd C3
St Dunstan's A1
St Dunstan's St A1
St George's Pl C2
St George's St B2
St George's Tower ✦ B2
St Gregory's Rd B3
St John's Hospital A2
St Margaret's St B2
St Martin's B3
St Martin's Ave B3
St Martin's Rd B3
St Michael's Rd A1
St Mildred's C1
St Peter's Gr B1
St Peter's La B2
St Peter's Pl B1
St Peter's St B1
St Radigunds St B2
St Stephen's Ct A1
St Stephen's Path A1
St Stephen's Rd A2
Salisbury Rd A1
Simmonds Rd C1
Spring La C3
Station Rd West B1
Stour St B1
Sturry Rd A3
Tourtel Rd A3
Tudor Rd C1
Union St B2
University for the
Creative Arts C3
Vernon Pl C2
Victoria Rd C1
Watling St B2
Westgate Gdns B1
Westgate Towers B1
Whitefriars B2
Whitehall Gdns B1
Whitehall Rd B1
Wincheap C1
York Rd C1
Zealand Rd C2

Cardiff Caerdydd 334

Adam St B3
Alexandra Gdns A2
Allerton St C1
Arran St A3
ATRiuM (Univ of
Glamorgan) C3
Beauchamp St C1
Bedford St A3
Blackfriars Priory
(rems) ✝ B1
Boulevard De Nantes B2
Brains Brewery C2
Brook St B1
BT Sports Cardiff Arms
Park (Cardiff Blues) B1
Bus Station C2
Bute Park A1
Bute St C2
Bute Terr C3
Callaghan Sq C2/C3
Capitol Shopping
Centre, The B3
Cardiff Bridge B1
Cardiff Castle B2
Cardiff Central Sta ≋ C2
Cardiff Story, The B2
Cardiff Univ A1/A2/B3
Cardiff University
Student's Union A2
Caroline St C2
Castle Green B2
Castle Mews A1
Castle St (Heol y
Castell) B1
Cathays Station ≋ A2
Celerity Drive C3
Central Library C2
Central Sq C2
Charles St (Heol Siarl) B3
Churchill Way B3
City Hall A2
City Rd A3
Clare Rd C1
Clare St C1
Coburn St A3
Coldstream Terr B1
College Rd A1
Colum Rd A1
Court C2
Court Rd C1
Craiglee Drive C3
Cranbrook St A3
Customhouse St C2
Cyfartha St A3
Despenser Place C1
Despenser St C1
Dinas St C1
Duke St (Heol y Dug) B2
Dumfries Place B3
East Grove A3
Ellen St C3
Fire Station B3
Fitzalan Place B3
Fitzhamon Emb C1
Fitzhamon La C1
Friary, The B2
g39 B2
Gloucester St C1
Glynrhondda St A2
Gordon Rd A3
Gorsedd Gdns B2
Green St B1
Greyfriars Rd B2
Hafod St C1
Hayes, The B2
Herbert St C3
High St B2
HM Prison B3
Industrial Estate C3
John St C3
Jubilee St C1
King Edward VII Ave A1
Kingsway (Ffordd y
Brenin) B2
Knox Rd B3
Law Courts B2
Llanbleddian Gdns A2
Llantwit St A2
Lloyd George Ave C3
Lower Cathedral Rd B1
Lowther Rd A3
Magistrates Court B3
Mansion House A3
Mardy St C1
Mark St B1
Market B2
Mary Ann St C3
Merches Gdns C1
Mill La C2
Millennium Bridge B1
Miskin St A2
Monmouth St C1
Motorpoint Arena
Cardiff ✦ C3
Museum Ave A2
Museum Place A2
National Museum
Cardiff A2
National War Meml ✦ A2
Neville Place C1
New Theatre B2
Newport Rd B3
Northcote La A3
Northcote St A3
Parade, The A3
Park Grove A4
Park Place A2
Park St C2
Penarth Rd C2
Pendyris St C1
Plantaganet St C1
Post Office B2
Principality Plaza
Leisure Complex C1
Principality Stadium C1
Principality Stadium
Tours (Gate 3) ✦ B2
Quay St B2
Queen's Arcade B2
Queen Anne Sq A1
Queen St (Heol y
Frenhines) B2
Queen St Station ≋ B3
Regimental
Museums B2
Rhymney St A3
Richmond Rd A3
Royal Welsh College of
Music and Drama A1
Russell St A3
Ruthin Gdns A2
St Andrews Place A2
St David's ✝ B2
St David's B2/C2
St David's Hall ✦ B2
St John the Baptist B2
St Mary St (Heol
Eglwys Fair) B2
St Peter's St A3
Salisbury Rd A3
Sandon St B3
Schooner Way C3
Scott Rd C2
Scott St C2
Senghennydd Rd A2
Sherman Theatre A2
Sophia Gardens A1
South Wales Baptist
College A3
Sport Wales
National Ctr ✦ A1
Stafford Rd C1
Station Terr B3
Stuttgarter Strasse B2
Sussex St C1
Taffs Mead Emb C1
Talworth St A3
Temple of Peace &
Health ✦ A1
Treharris St A3
Trinity St B2
Tudor La C1
Tudor St C1
Walk, The A3
Welsh Government A1
West Grove A3
Westgate St (Heol y
Porth) B2
Windsor Place B3
Womanby St B2
Wood St C2
Working St B2
Wyeverne Rd A2

Carlisle 334

Abbey St A1
Aglionby St B3
Albion St C3
Alexander St C3
AMF Bowl ✦ C2
Annetwell St A1
Bank St B2
Bitts Park A1
Blackfriars St B2
Blencome St C1
Blunt St C1
Botchergate B2
Boustead's Grassing C2
Bowman St B3
Bridge St A1
Broad St B3
Brook St C3
Brunswick St B2
Bus Station B2
Caldew Bridge A1
Caldew St C1
Carlisle (Citadel)
Station B2
Carlisle College A2
Castle A1
Castle St A1
Castle Way A1
Cathedral ✝ A1
Cecil St B2
Chapel St A2
Charles St B3
Charlotte St B1
Chatsworth Square A2
Chiswick St B2
Citadel, The ✦ B2
City Walls A1
Civic Centre A2
Clifton St C1
Close St B3
Collingwood St C1
Colville St C1
Colville Terr C1
Court B2
Court St B2
Crosby St B2
Crown St C2

354 Chelmsford • Cheltenham • Chester • Chichester • Colchester • Coventry • Derby

Currock Rd C2
Dacre Rd A1
Dale St C1
Denton St C1
Devonshire Walk A1
Duke's Rd A2
East Dale St C1
East Norfolk St C1
Eden Bridge A2
Edward St B3
Elm St B1
English St B2
Fire Station A2
Fisher St A1
Flower St B3
Freer St C1
Fusehill St B3
Georgian Way A2
Gloucester Rd C3
Golf Course A2
Graham St C1
Grey St B3
Guildhall Museum A2
Halfey's La B3
Hardwicke Circus A2
Hart St B3
Hewson St C2
Howard Pl A3
Howe St B3
Information Ctr A2
James St B2
Junction St B1
King St B2
Lancaster St B2
Lanes Shopping Centre, The B2
Laser Quest B2
Library A2/B1
Lime St B1
Lindisfarne St C3
Linton St B3
Lismore Pl A3
Lismore St B3
London Rd C3
Lonsdale Rd B2
Lord St C3
Lorne Cres B1
Lorne St B1
Lowther St B2
Madford Retail Park B1
Magistrates' Ct A2
Market Hall A2
Mary St B2
Memorial Bridge A3
Metcalfe St C1
Milbourne St B1
Myddleton St B3
Nelson St C1
Norfolk St C1
Old Fire Sta, The A2
Old Town Hall A2
Oswald St C3
Peter St A2
Petteril St B3
Pools B2
Portland Pl B2
Portland Sq B2
Post Office A2/B2/B3/C1/C3
Princess St C2
Pugin St B1
Red Bank Terr C2
Regent St C3
Richardson St C1
Rickerby Park A3
Rickergate A2
River St B3
Rome St C2
Rydal St B3
Shopmobility A2
St Cuthbert's A2
St Cuthbert's La B2
St James' Park C1
St James' Rd C1
St Nicholas Gate Retail Park C3
St Nicholas St C3
Sands Centre, The A2
Scotch St A2
Shaddongate B1
Sheffield St B1
South Henry St B3
South John St C2
South St B3
Spencer St B2
Strand Rd A2
Superstore B1
Sybil St B3
Tait St B2
Thomas St B1
Thomson St C3
Trafalgar St C1
Trinity Leisure Ctr A2
Tullie Ho Museum A1
Tyne St C3
University of Cumbria B3
Viaduct Estate Rd B1
Victoria Pl A2
Victoria Viaduct B2
Vue B2
Warwick Rd B2
Warwick Sq B3
Water St B2
West Walls B1
Westmorland St C1

Chelmsford 334

Anchor St C1
Anglia Ruskin Univ A2
Arbour La A3
Baddow Rd B2/C3
Baker St C1
Barrack Sq B2
Bellmead B2
Bishop Hall La A2
Bishop Rd A2
Bond St B2
Boswells Dr B3
Bouverie Rd C2
Bradford St C1
Braemar Ave C1
Brook St A2
Broomfield Rd A1
Burns Cres C2
Bus Station B1
Can Bridge Way B2
Cedar Ave A1
Cedar Ave West A1
Cemetery A1
Cemetery A2
Cemetery C1
Central Park B1
Chelmsford † B2
Chelmsford ≥ A1
Chichester Dr A3
Chinery Cl A3
Civic Centre A1
Civic Theatre B1
College C1
Cottage Pl A2
County Cricket Gd B2
County Hall B2
Coval Ave B1
Coval La B1
Coval Wells B1
Crown Court B2
Duke St B2
Elm Rd C1
Elms Dr A1
Essex Record Office, The B3
Fairfield Rd B1
Falcons Mead B1
George St C2
Glebe Rd A1
Godfrey's Mews C2
Goldlay Ave C3
Goldlay Rd C2
Grove Rd C2
Hall St C2
Hamlet Rd C2
Hart St C1
Henry Rd A2
High Bridge Rd B2
High Chelmer Shopping Centre B2
High St B2
Hill Cres B3
Hill Rd B3
Hill Rd Sth B3
Hillview Rd A3
HM Prison A3
Hoffmans Way A2
Hospital B2
Lady La C2
Langdale Gdns C3
Legg St B2
Library B2
Lionfield Terr A3
Lower Anchor St C1
Lynmouth Ave C2
Lynmouth Gdns C3
Magistrates Court B2
Maltese Rd A1
Manor Rd C2
Marconi Rd A2
Market B2
Market Rd B2
Marlborough Rd C1
Meadows Shopping Centre, The B2
Meadowside A3
Mews Ct C2
Mildmay Rd C2
Moulsham Dr C2
Moulsham Mill C3
Moulsham St C1/C2
Navigation Rd B3
New London Rd B2/C1
New St A2/B2
New Writtle St C1
Nursery Rd C2
Orchard St C2
Odeon B2
Park Rd B1
Parker Rd C2
Parklands Dr A3
Parkway A1/B1/B2
Police Station A2
Post Office B2/C2
Primrose Hill A1
Prykes Dr B1
Queen St C1
Queen's Rd B3
Railway St A1
Rainsford Rd A1
Ransomes Way A2
Rectory La A2
Regina Rd A2
Riverside Ice & L Ctr B2
Riverside Retail Park A3
Rosebery Rd C2
Rothesay Ave C1
St John's Rd C2
Sandringham Pl B3
Seymour St B1
Shrublands Cl B3
Southborough Rd C1
Springfield Basin B3
Springfield Rd A3/B2/B3
Stapleford Cl C1
Superstore B2
Swiss Ave A1
Telford Pl A3
Tindal St B2
Townfield St A1
Trinity Rd B3
University B1
Upper Bridge Rd C1
Upper Roman Rd C2
Van Dieman's Rd C3
Viaduct Rd B1
Vicarage Rd C1
Victoria Rd A2
Victoria Rd South B2
Vincents Rd C2
Waterloo La B2
Weight Rd B3
Westfield Ave A1
Wharf Rd B3
Writtle Rd C1
YMCA A2
York Rd C1

Cheltenham 334

Albert Rd A3
Albion St B3
All Saints Rd B3
Ambrose St B2
Andover Rd C1
Art Gallery & Mus B2
Back Montpellier Terr C2
Bandstand C2
Bath Pde B2
Bath Rd C2
Bays Hill Rd C1
Bennington St B2
Berkeley St B3
Brewery, The A2
Brunswick St South A2
Bus Station B2
Carlton St B3
Central Cross Road A3
Cheltenham College C2
Cheltenham FC A3
Cheltenham General (A&E) C3
Cheltenham Ladies College B2
Christchurch Rd B1
Cineworld A2
Clarence Rd A2
Clarence Sq A2
Clarence St B2
Cleveland St A1
College Baths Road C3
College Rd C2
Colletts Dr A1
Corpus St C3
Council Office B1
Court B1
Devonshire St A2
Douro Rd B1
Duke St B3
Dunalley Pde A2
Dunalley St A2
Everyman B2
Evesham Rd A3
Fairview Rd B3
Fairview St A3
Fire Station C3
Folly La A2
Gloucester Rd A1
Grosvenor St B3
Grove St A1
Hanover St A2
Hatherley St C1
Henrietta St A2
Hewlett Rd B3
High St B2/B3
Holst Birthplace Museum A3
Hudson St A2
Imperial Gdns C2
Imperial La B2
Imperial Sq C2
Information Ctr B2
Keynsham Rd C3
King St A2
Knapp Rd B2
Ladies College B2
Lansdown Cr C1
Lansdown Rd C1
Leighton Rd B3
Library B2
London Rd C3
Lypiatt Rd C1
Malvern Rd B1
Manser St A2
Market St A1
Marle Hill Pde A2
Marle Hill Rd A2
Millbrook St A1
Milsom St A2
Montpellier Gdns C2
Montpellier Gr C2
Montpellier Pde C2
Montpellier Spa Rd C2
Montpellier St C1
Montpellier Terr C2
Montpellier Walk C2
New St B2
North Pl B2
Old Bath Rd C3
Oriel Rd B2
Overton Park Rd B1
Overton Rd B1
Oxford St C3
Parabola Rd B1
Park Place C1
Park St A1
Pittville Circus A3
Pittville Cres A3
Pittville Lawn A3
Pittville Park A2
Playhouse B2
Police Station C1
Portland St B3
Prestbury Rd A3
Prince's Rd C1
Priory St B3
Promenade B2
Queen St A1
Recreation Ground A2
Regent Arcade B2
Regent St B2
Rodney Rd B2
Royal Cr B2
Royal Wells Rd B2
St George's Pl B2
St Georges Rd B1
St Gregory's B2
St James St B3
St John's Ave B3
St Luke's Rd C2
St Margarets Rd A2
St Mary's B2
St Matthew's B2
St Paul's La A2
St Paul's Rd A2
St Paul's St A2
St Stephen's Rd C1
Sandford Parks Lido C3
Sandford Mill Road C3
Sandford Park C3
Sandford Rd C2
Selkirk St A3
Sherborne Pl B3
Sherborne St B3
Shopmobility B2
Suffolk Parade C2
Suffolk Rd C1
Suffolk Sq C1
Sun St A1
Swindon Rd B2
Sydenham Villas Rd C3
Tewkesbury Rd A1
The Courtyard B1
Thirlstaine Rd C2
Tivoli Rd C1
Tivoli St C1
Town Hall & Theatre B2
Townsend St A1
Trafalgar St C2
Union St B3
Univ of Gloucestershire (Francis Cl Hall) A2
Univ of Gloucestershire (Hardwick) A1
Victoria Pl B3
Victoria St A2
Vittoria Walk C2
Wel Pl B2
Wellesley Rd A2
Wellington Rd A3
Wellington Sq A3
Wellington St B2
West Drive A3
Western Rd B1
Winchcombe St B3
Winston Churchill Memorial Gardens A1

Chester 335

Abbey Gateway A2
Appleyards La C3
Bars, The B3
Bedward Row B1
Beeston View C3
Bishop Lloyd's Pal B2
Black Diamond St A2
Bottoms La C3
Boughton B3
Bouverie St A1
Bus Interchange A2
Bridge St B2
Bridgegate C2
Brook St A3
Brown's La C2
Cambrian Rd A1
Canal St A2
Carrick Rd C1
Castle C2
Castle Dr C2
Cathedral † B2
Catherine St A1
Chester ≥ A3
Cheyney Rd A1
Chichester St A1
City Rd A3
City Walls B1/B2
City Walls Rd B1
Cornwall St A2
Cross Hey C3
Cross, The B2
Crown Ct C2
Cuppin St B2
Curzon Park North C1
Curzon Park South C1
Dee Basin A1
Dee La B3
Delamere St A2
Dewa Roman Experience B2
Duke St B2
Eastgate B2
Eastgate St B2
Eaton Rd C2
Edinburgh Way C3
Elizabeth Cr B3
Fire Station A2
Foregate St B2
Forum, The B2
Frodsham St B2
Gamul House B2
Garden La A1
George St A2
Gladstone Ave A1
God's Providence House B2
Gorse Stacks A2
Greenway St C2
Grosvenor Bridge C1
Grosvenor Mus B2
Grosvenor Park B3
Grosvenor Park Terr C1
Grosvenor Shopping Centre B2
Grosvenor St B2
Groves Rd B3
Groves, The B3
Guildhall Museum B1
Handbridge C2
Hartington St C3
Hoole Way A2
Hunter St B2
Information Ctr B2
King Charles' Tower A2
King St A2
Leisure Centre A2
Library B2
Lightfoot St A3
Little Roodee C2
Liverpool Rd A2
Love St B3
Lower Bridge St B2
Lower Park Rd B3
Lyon St A2
Magistrates Court B2
Meadows La C3
Meadows, The B3
Military Museum C2
Milton St A3
New Crane St B1
Nicholas St B2
Northgate A2
Northgate St A2
Nun's Rd B1
Old Dee Bridge C2
Overleigh Rd C2
Park St B2
Police Station B2
Post Office A2/A3/B2
Princess St B2
Queen St B2
Queen's Park Rd C3
Queen's Rd A3
Race Course B1
Raymond St A1
River La C2
Roman Amphitheatre & Gardens B2
Roodee (Chester Racecourse), The B1
Russell St A3
St Anne St A2
St George's Cr C3
St Martin's Gate A1
St Martin's Way B1
St Mary's Priory B2
St Oswalds Way A2
Saughall Rd A1
Sealand Rd A1
South View Rd A1
Stanley Palace B1
Station Rd A3
Steven St A3
Storyhouse B2
Superstore B2
Tower Rd B1
Town Hall B2
Union St B3
University of Chester C2
Vicar's La B2
Victoria Cr C3
Victoria Rd A2
Walpole St A1
Water Tower St A1
Water Tower, The B1
Watergate B1
Watergate St B2
Whipcord La A1
White Friars B2
York St B3

Chichester 335

Adelaide Rd A3
Alexandra Rd A3
Arts Centre B2
Ave de Chartres B1/B2
Barlow Rd A1
Basin Rd C2
Beech Ave B1
Bishops Palace Gdns B2
Bishopsgate Walk A3
Bramber Rd C3
Broyle Rd A2
Bus Station B2
Caledonian Rd B3
Cambrai Ave B3
Canal Pl C1
Canal Wharf C2
Canon Lane B2
Cathedral † B2
Cavendish St A1
Cawley Rd B2
Cedar Dr A1
Chapel St A2
Cherry Orchard Rd C3
Chichester ≥ B2
Chichester By-Pass C2/C3
Chichester Coll B1
Chichester Cinema B3
Chichester Festival A2
Chichester Gate Leisure Park C1
Churchside A2
Cineworld C1
City Walls B2
Cleveland Rd B3
College La A2
Cory Cl C2
Council Offices B2
County Hall B2
District B2
Duncan Rd A1
Durnford Cl A1
East Pallant B2
East Row B2
East St B2
East Walls B3
Eastland Rd C3
Ettrick Cl B1
Ettrick Rd B1
Exton Rd C3
Fire Station A2
Football Ground A2
Franklin Pl A2
Friary (Rems of) A2
Garland Cl C3
Green La A3
Grove Rd C3
Guilden Rd B3
Guildhall A2
Hawthorn Cl A1
Hay Rd C3
Henty Gdns B1
Herald Dr C3
Hornet, The B3
Information Ctr B2
John's St B2
Joys Croft A3
Jubilee Pk A3
Jubilee Rd A3
Juxon Cl B2
Kent Rd A3
King George Gdns A2
King's Ave C2
Kingsham Ave C3
Kingsham Rd C2
Laburnum Gr B2
Leigh Rd C1
Lennox Rd A3
Lewis Rd A3
Library B2
Lion St B2
Litten Terr A3
Litten, The A3
Little London B2
Lyndhurst Rd B3
Market B3
Market Ave B2
Market Cross B2
Market Rd B3
Melbourne Rd A3
Minerva A2
Mount La B1
New Park Rd A3
Newlands La A1
North Pallant B2
North St A2
North Walls A2
Northgate A2
Novium, The B2
Oak Ave A1
Oak Close A1
Oaklands Park A2
Oaklands Way A2
Orchard Ave A1
Orchard St A1
Ormonde Ave B3
Pallant House B2
Parchment St A1
Parklands Rd A1/B1
Peter Weston Pl B3
Police Station C2
Post Office A1/B2/C3
Priory La A2
Priory Park A2
Priory Rd A2
Queen's Ave C1
Riverside A3
Roman Amphitheatre B3
St Cyriacs A2
St Martins' St B2
St Pancras A3
St Paul's Rd A2
St Richard's Hospital (A&E) A3
Shamrock Close A3
Sherbourne Rd A1
Somerstown A2
South Bank C2
South Downs Planetarium C2
South Pallant B2
South St B2
Southgate B2
Spitalfield La A3
Stirling Rd B3
Stockbridge Rd C1/C2
Swanfield Dr A3
Terminus Ind Est C1
Tower St A2
Tozer Way A3
Turnbull Rd A3
Upton Rd C1
Velyn Ave B3
Via Ravenna B1
Walnut Ave A1
West St B2
Westgate B1
Westgate Fields B1
Westgate Leisure Ctr B1
Weston Ave C1
Whyke Cl C3
Whyke La B3
Whyke Rd C3
Winden Ave B3

Colchester 335

Abbey Gateway † C2
Albert St A1
Albion Grove C2
Alexandra Rd C1
Artillery St C3
Arts Centre B1
Balkerne Hill B1
Barrack St C3
Beaconsfield Rd C1
Beche Rd C3
Bergholt Rd A1
Bourne Rd C3
Brick Kiln Rd A1
Brigade Gr C2
Bristol Rd B2
Broadlands Way A3
Brook St B3
Bury Cl B2
Bus Sta B2
Butt Rd C1
Campion Rd C2
Cannon St C3
Canterbury Rd C2
Captain Gardens C2
Castle B2
Castle Park B2
Castle Rd B2
Catchpool Rd A1
Causton Rd B1
Chandlers Row C3
Circular Rd East C2
Circular Rd North C1
Circular Rd West C1
Clarendon Way A1
Claudius Rd C2
Colchester ≥ A1
Colchester Camp Abbey Field C1
Colchester Retail Park B1
Colchester Town ≥ C2
Colne Bank Ave A1
Colne View Retail Pk A2
Compton Rd A3
Cowdray Ave A1/A2
Cowdray Centre, The A2
Crouch St B1
Crowhurst Rd B1
Culver Square Shopping Centre B1
Culver St East B2
Culver St West B1
Dilbridge Rd A3
East Hill B2
East St B3
East Stockwell St B1
Eld La B1
Essex Hall Rd A1
Exeter Dr B2
Fairfax Rd C2
Fire Station A2
Firstsite B2
Flagstaff Rd C1
Garrison Parade C2
George St B2
Gladstone Rd C2
Golden Noble Hill C2
Goring Rd A3
Granville Rd C3
Greenstead Rd B3
Guildford Rd B2
Harsnett Rd C3
Harwich Rd B3
Head St B1
High St B1/B2
High Woods Ctry Park A2
Hollytrees B2
Hyderabad Cl C2
Hythe Hill C3
Information Ctr B2
Jarmin Rd A2
Kendall Rd C2
Kimberley Rd C3
King Stephen Rd C3
Leisure World A2
Library B1
Lincoln Way B2
Lion Wlk Shopping Ctr B1
Lisle Rd C2
Lucas Rd C2
Magdalen Green C3
Magdalen St C2
Maidenburgh St B2
Maldon Rd C1
Manor Rd B1
Margaret Rd A1
Mason Rd A2
Mercers Way A1
Mercury B1
Mersea Rd C2
Meyrick Cr C2
Mile End Rd A1
Military Rd C2
Mill St C2
Minories B2
Moorside B3
Morant Rd C3
Napier Rd C2
Natural History B2
New Town Rd C2
Norfolk Cr A3
North Hill B1
North Station Rd A1
Northgate St B1
Nunns Rd B1
Odeon B1
Old Coach Rd B3
Old Heath Rd C3
Osborne St B2
Petrolea Cl A1
Police Station C1
Popes La B1
Port La C3
Post Office B2/C1
Priory St B2
Queen St B2
Rawstorn Rd B1
Rebon St C3
Recreation Rd C3
Ripple Way A3
Roberts Rd C2
Roman Rd B2
Roman Wall B2
Romford Cl A3
Rosebery Ave B2
St Andrews Ave B3
St Andrews Gdns B3
St Botolph St B2
St Botolphs B2
St John's Abbey (site of) † C2
St John's St B1
St Johns Walk Shopping Centre B1
St Leonards Rd C3
St Marys Fields B1
St Peter's St B1
St Peters B1
Salisbury Ave C1
Saw Mill Rd C3
Sergeant St C2
Serpentine Walk A1
Sheepen Pl B1
Sheepen Rd B1
Sir Isaac's Walk B1
Smythies Ave B2
South St C1
South Way C1
Sports Way A2
Suffolk Cl A3
Superstore A1
Town Hall B1
Valentine Dr A3
Victor Rd C3
Wakefield Cl B2
Wellesley Rd C1
Wells Rd B2/B3
West St C1
West Stockwell St B1
Weston Rd C3
Westway A1
Wickham Rd C1
Wimpole Rd C3
Winchester Rd C2
Winnock Rd C2
Worcester Rd B2

Coventry 335

Abbots La A1
Albany B1
Albany Rd B1
Alma St B3
Ambulance Sta A2
Art Faculty B3
Asthill Grove C2
Bablake School A1
Barras La A1/B1
Barr's Hill School A1
Belgrade B2
Bishop St A2
Bond's Hospital B1
Broad Gate B2
Broadway C1
Burges, The B2
Bus Station A3
Butts Radial B1
Byron St A3
Canal Basin A2
Canterbury St A3
Cathedral † B3
Central Six Retail Pk C1
Chester St A1
Cheylesmore Manor House B2
Christ Church Spire B2
City Coll A3
City Walls & Gates A2
Corporation St B2
Council House B2
Coundon Rd A1
Coventry Station ≥ C2
Coventry Transport Museum A2
Coventry University Technology Park C3
Cox St A3
Croft Rd B1
Dalton Rd C1
Deasy Rd C3
Earl St B2
Eaton Rd C2
Fairfax St B2
Foleshill Rd A2
Ford's Hospital B2
Fowler Rd A1
Friars Rd C2
Gordon St C1
Gosford St B3
Greyfriars Green B2
Greyfriars Rd B2
Gulson Rd B3
Hales St A2
Harnall Lane East A3
Harnall Lane West A2
Herbert Art Gallery & Museum B3
Hertford St B2
Hewitt Ave A1
High St B2
Hill St B1
Holy Trinity B2
Holyhead Rd A1
Howard St A3
Huntingdon Rd C1
Information Ctr B2
Jordan Well B3
King Henry VIII Sch C1
Lady Godiva Statue B2
Lamb St A2
Leicester Row A2
Library B2
Lincoln St A2
Little Park St B2
London Rd C3
Lower Ford St B3
Lower Precinct Shopping Centre B2
Magistrates & Crown Courts B2
Manor House Drive B2
Manor Rd C2
Market B2
Martyrs Memorial C2
Meadow St B1
Meriden St A1
Michaelmas Rd C2
Middleborough Rd A1
Mile La C3
Millennium Place A2
Much Park St B3
Naul's Mill Park A1
New Union B2
Odeon B1
Park Rd C2
Parkside C3
Planet Ice Arena B1
Post Office B2
Primrose Hill St A3
Priory Gardens & Visitor Centre B2
Priory St B3
Puma Way C3
Quarryfield La C3
Queen's Rd B1
Quinton Rd C2
Radford Rd A2
Raglan St B3
Ringway (Hill Cross) A1
Ringway (Queens) B1
Ringway (Rudge) B1
Ringway (St Johns) B3
Ringway (St Nicholas) A2
Ringway (St Patricks) C2
Ringway (Swanswell) A2
Ringway (Whitefriars) B3
St John St B2
St John the Baptist B2
St Nicholas St A2
Sidney Stringer Acad A3
Skydome B1
Spencer Ave C1
Spencer Rec Gnd C1
Spencer Rd C1
Spon St B1
Sports Centre B3
Stoney Rd C2
Stoney Stanton Rd A3
Superstore B2
Swanswell Pool A3
Technocentre C3
Thomas Landsdail St C2
Tomson Ave A1
Top Green C1
Trinity St B2
University B3
University Sports Ctr B3
Upper Hill St A1
Upper Well St A2
Victoria St A3
Vine St A3
Warwick Rd C2
Waveley Rd B1
West Orchards Shopping Centre B2
Westminster Rd C1
White St A3
Windsor St B1

Derby 335

Abbey St C1
Agard St B1
Albert St B2
Albion St B2
Ambulance Station B1
Arthur St A1
Ashlyn Rd B3
Assembly Rooms B2
Babington La C2
Becket St B1
Belper Rd A1
Bold La B1
Bradshaw Way C2
Bradshaw Way Retail Park C2
Bridge St B1
Brook St B1
Burton Rd C1
Bus Station B2
Business Park A3
Caesar St A2
Canal St C3
Carrington St C3
Cathedral † B2
Cathedral Rd B1
Charnwood St C2
Chester Green Rd A2
City Rd A2
Clarke St A3
Cock Pitt B3
Council House B2
Courts B1
Cranmer Rd B3
Crompton St C1
Crown & County Courts B2
Curzon St B1
Darley Grove A1
Derby ≥ C3
Derby C2
Derbyshire 3aaa County Cricket Ground B3
Derwent Business Ctr A2
Derwent St B2
Drewry La C1
Duffield Rd A1
Duke St A2
Dunton Cl B3
Eagle Market C2
East St B2
Eastgate B3
Exeter St B2
Farm St C1
Ford St B1
Forester St C1
Fox St A2
Friar Gate B1
Friary St B1
Full St B2
Gerard St C1
Gower St C2
Green La C2
Grey St C1
Guildhall B2
Harcourt St C1
Highfield Rd A1
Hill La C2
Information Ctr B2
intu Derby C2
Iron Gate B2
John St C3
Joseph Wright Centre B1
Kedleston Rd A1
Key St B2
King Alfred St C1
King St A1
Kingston St A1
Lara Croft Way C2
Leopold St C2
Library B1
Liversage St C3
Lodge La B1
London Rd C2
London Rd Community Hospital C2
Macklin St C1
Mansfield Rd A2
Market B2
Market Pl B2
May St C1
Meadow La B3
Melbourne St C2
Mercian Way C1
Midland Rd C3
Monk St C1
Morledge B2
Mount St C1
Mus & Art Gallery B1
Noble St C3
North Parade A1
North St A1
Nottingham Rd B3
Osmaston Rd C2

Otter St A1
Park St C3
Parker St A1
Pickfords House B1
Police HQ A2
Police Station B2
Post Office A1/A2/B1/C2/C3
Pride Parkway C3
Prime Enterprise Park A2
Prime Parkway A2
QUAD B2
Queens Leisure Ctr B1
Racecourse Park A3
Railway Terr C3
Register Office B2
Sadler Gate B1
St Alkmund's Way B1/B2
St Helens House A1
St Mary's A1
St Mary's Bridge A2
St Mary's Bridge Chapel A2
St Mary's Gate B1
St Paul's Rd A2
St Peter's C2
St Peter's St C2
Showcase De Lux C2
Siddals Rd C3
Sir Frank Whittle Rd A3
Spa La C1
Spring St C1
Stafford St B1
Station Approach C3
Stockbrook St C1
Stores Rd A3
Traffic St C2
Wardwick B1
Werburgh St C1
West Ave A1
West Meadows Ind Est B3
Wharf Rd A2
Wilmot St C2
Wilson St C1
Wood's La C1

Dorchester 335

Ackerman Rd B3
Acland Rd A2
Albert Rd A1
Alexandra Rd B1
Alfred Place B3
Alfred Rd B2
Alington Ave B3
Alington Rd B3
Ambulance Station B3
Ashley Rd B1
Balmoral Cres C3
Barnes Way B2/C2
Borough Gdns A1
Brewery Sq B1
Bridport Rd A1
Buckingham Way C3
Caters Place A1
Cemetery A3/C1
Charles St A2
Coburg Rd B1
Colliton St A1
Cornwall Rd A1
Cromwell Rd B1
Culliford Rd B2
Culliford Rd North B2
Dagmar Rd B1
Damer's Rd B1
Diggory Cres C2
Dinosaur Museum A2
Dorchester Bypass C2
Dorchester South Station B1
Dorchester West Station B1
Dorset County (A&E) B1
Dorset County Council Offices A1
Dorset County Mus A1
Duchy Close C3
Duke's Ave B2
Durngate St A2
Durnover Court A3
Eddison Ave B3
Edward Rd B1
Egdon Rd C2
Elizabeth Frink Statue B2
Farfrae Cres B2
Forum Centre, The B1
Friary Hill A2
Friary Lane A2
Frome Terr A2
Garland Cres C3
Glyde Path Rd A1
Government Offices B3
Grosvenor Cres C1
Grosvenor Rd C1
Grove, The A1
Gt Western Rd B1
Herringston Rd C1
High St East A2
High St Fordington A2
High Street West A1
Holloway Rd A2
Icen Way A2
Keep Military Museum, The A1
Kings Rd A3/B3
Kingsbere Cres C2
Lancaster Rd B2
Library A1
Lime Cl C1
Linden Ave B2
London Cl A3
London Rd A2/A3
Lubbecke Way A3
Lucetta La B2
Maiden Castle Rd C1
Manor Rd C2
Market B1
Marshwood Pl B2
Maumbury Rd B1
Maumbury Rings B1
Mellstock Ave C2
Mill St A3
Miller's Cl A1
Mistover Cl C1
Monmouth Rd B1/B2
Moynton Rd C2
Nature Reserve A2
North Sq A2
Northernhay A1
Odeon B1
Old Crown Court & Cells A1
Olga Rd B1
Orchard St A2
Police Station B1
Post Office A1
Pound Lane A2
Poundbury Rd A1
Prince of Wales Rd B2
Prince's St A1
Queen's Ave B1
Roman Town House A1
Roman Wall A1
Rothesay Rd C2
St George's Rd B3
Salisbury Field A2
Sandringham Sports Centre B3
Shaston Cres C2
Smokey Hole La B3
South Court Ave C1
South St B1
South Walks Rd B2
Superstore C3
Teddy Bear House A1
Temple Cl C1
Terracotta Warriors & Teddy Bear Mus A2
Town Hall A2
Town Pump A2
Trinity St A1
Tutankhamun Ex A1
Victoria Rd B1
Weatherbury Way C2
Wellbridge Cl C1
West Mills Rd A1
West Walks Rd A1
Weymouth Ave C1
Williams Ave B1
Winterbourne (BMI) C1
Wollaston Rd A2
York Rd B2

Dumfries 336

Academy St A2
Aldermanhill Rd B3
Ambulance Station C3
Annan Rd A3
Ardwall Rd A3
Ashfield Dr A1
Atkinson Rd C1
Averill Cres C1
Balliol Ave C1
Bank St B2
Bankend Rd C3
Barn Slaps B3
Barrie Ave B3
Beech Ave A1
Bowling Green A3
Brewery St B2
Bridgend Theatre B1
Brodie Ave C2
Brooke St B2
Broomlands Dr C1
Brooms Rd B3
Buccleuch St A2
Burns House B2
Burns Mausoleum B3
Burns St B2
Burns Statue A2
Bus Station B1
Cardoness St A3
Castle St A2
Catherine St A2
Cattle Market A3
Cemetery B3
Cemetery C2
Church Cres A2
Church St B2
College Rd A1
College St A1
Convent, The B1
Corbelly Hill B1
Corberry Park B1
Cornwall Mt A3
Council Offices A2
Court A2
Craigs Rd C3
Cresswell Ave B3
Cresswell Hill B3
Cumberland St B3
David Keswick Athletic Centre A3
David St B1
Dock Park C3
Dockhead B2
Dumfries A3
Dumfries Academy A2
Dumfries Museum & Camera Obscura B2
Dumfries Royal Infirmary (A&E) C3
East Riverside Dr C3
Edinburgh Rd A2
English St B2
Fire Station B3
Friar's Vennel A2
Galloway St B1
George Douglas Dr C1
George St A2
Gladstone Rd C2
Glasgow St A1
Glebe St B3
Glencaple Rd C3
Goldie Ave A1
Goldie Cres A1
Golf Course C3
Greyfriars A2
Grierson Ave B3
Hamilton Ave C1
Hamilton Starke Park C2
Hazelrigg Ave C1
Henry St B3
Hermitage Dr C1
High Cemetery C3
High St A2
Hill Ave C2
Hill St B1
HM Prison B1
Holm Ave C2
Hoods Loaning A3
Howgate St B1
Huntingdon Rd A3
Information Ctr B2
Irish St B2
Irving St A2
King St A1
Kingholm Rd C3
Kirkpatrick Ct C2
Laurieknowe B1
Leafield Rd B3
Library A2
Lochfield Rd A1
Loreburn Pk A3
Loreburn St A2
Loreburne Shopping Centre B2
Lover's Walk A2
Martin Ave B3
Maryholm Dr A1
Mausoleum B3
Maxwell St B1
McKie Ave B3
Mews La A2
Mid Steeple B2
Mill Green B2
Mill Rd B1
Moat Rd C2
Moffat Rd A3
Mountainhall Pk C3
Nelson St B1
New Abbey Rd B1/C1
New Bridge B1
Newall Terr A2
Nith Ave A2
Nith Bank C3
Nithbank Hospital C3
Nithside Ave A1
Odeon B2
Old Bridge B1
Old Bridge House B1
Palmerston Park (Queen of the South FC) A1
Park Rd C1
Pleasance Ave C1
Police HQ A3
Police Station A2
Portland Dr A1
Post Office B1/B2/B3
Priestlands Dr C1
Primrose St B1
Queen St B3
Queensberry St A2
Rae St A2
Richmond Ave C2
Robert Burns Ctr B2
Roberts Cres C1
Robertson Ave C3
Robinson Dr C1
Rosefield Rd C2
Rosemount St B1
Rotchell Park C1
Rotchell Rd B1
Rugby Football Gd C1
Ryedale Rd C2
St Andrews B2
St John the Evangelist A2
St Josephs College B3
St Mary's Ind Est A3
St Mary's St A3
St Michael St B2
St Michael's B2
St Michael's Bridge B2
St Michael's Bridge Rd B2
St Michael's Cemetery B3
Shakespeare St B2
Solway Dr C2
Stakeford St A1
Stark Cres C2
Station Rd A3
Steel Ave A1
Sunderries Ave A1
Sunderries Rd A1
Superstore B3
Suspension Brae B2
Swimming Pool A1
Terregles St B1
Theatre Royal B2
Troqueer Rd C2
Union St A1
Wallace St B3
Welldale B2
West Riverside Dr C2
White Sands B2

Dundee 336

Abertay University B2
Adelaide Pl A1
Airlie Pl C1
Albany Terr A1
Albert St A3
Alexander St A2
Ann St A2
Arthurstone Terr A3
Bank St B2
Barrack Rd A1
Barrack St B2
Bell St B2
Blinshall St B1
Broughty Ferry Rd A3
Brown St B1
Bus Station B3
Caird Hall B2
Camperdown St B3
Candle La B3
Carmichael St A1
City Churches B2
City Quay B3
City Square B2
Commercial St B2
Constable St A3
Constitution Cres A1
Constitution Ct A1
Constitution St A1/B2
Cotton Rd A3
Courthouse Sq B1
Cowgate A3
Crescent St A3
Crichton St B2
Dens Brae A3
Dens Rd A3
Discovery Point C2
Douglas St B1
Drummond St A1
Dudhope Castle A1
Dudhope St A2
Dudhope Terr A1
Dundee C2
Dundee Contemporary Arts C2
Dundee High School B2
Dundee Law A1
Dundee Repertory C2
Dunhope Park A1
Dura St A3
East Dock St B3
East Marketgait B3
East Whale La B3
Erskine St A3
Euclid Cr B2
Forebank Rd A2
Foundry La A3
Gallagher Retail Park B3
Gellatly St B3
Government Offices C2
Guthrie St B1
Hawkhill B1
Hilltown A2
HMS Unicorn B3
Howff Cemetery, The B2
Information Ctr B2
Keiller Shopping Ctr B2
Keiller Ctr, The B2
King St A3
Kinghorne Rd A1
Ladywell Ave A3
Laurel Bank A2
Law Rd A1
Law St A1
Library A2/A3
Library and Steps Theatre A2
Little Theatre, The A2
Lochee Rd B1
Lower Princes St A3
Lyon St A3
McManus Art Gallery & Museum, The B2
Meadow Side B2
Meadowside St Pauls B2
Mercat Cross B2
Murraygate B2
Nelson St A2
Nethergate B2/C1
North Lindsay St B2
North Marketgait B2
Old Hawkhill B1
Olympia Leisure Ctr B3
Overgate Shopping Ctr B2
Park Pl B1
Perth Rd C1
Police Station B1
Post Office B2
Princes St A3
Prospect Pl A2
Reform St B2
Riverside Dr C2
Riverside Esplanade C2
Roseangle C1
Rosebank St A2
RRS Discovery C2
St Andrew's C2
St Pauls Episcopal B3
Science Centre C2
Seagate B2
Sheriffs Court B1
Shopmobility B2
South George St A2
South Marketgait B3
South Tay St B2
South Victoria Dock Road B3
South Ward Rd B2
Tay Road Bridge C3
Thomson Ave B2
Trades La B3
Union St B2
Union Terr A1
University Library B2
University of Dundee B1
Upper Constitution St A1
Verdant Works B1
V&A Dundee C2
Victoria Dock B3
Victoria Rd A2
Victoria St A3
Ward Rd B1
Wellgate B2
West Bell St B1
West Marketgait B1/B2
Westfield Pl C1
William St A3
Wishart Arch A3

Durham 336

Alexander Cr B2
Allergate B2
Archery Rise C1
Avenue, The B1
Back Western Hill A1
Bakehouse La A3
Baths B3
Baths Bridge B3
Boat House B3
Bowling A2
Boyd St C3
Bus Station B2
Castle B2
Castle Chare B2
Cathedral B2
Church St C3
Clay La C1
Claypath B3
College of St Hild & St Bede B3
County Hall A1
County Hospital B1
Crescent, The A1
Crook Hall & Gardens A3
Crossgate B2
Crossgate Peth C1
Crown Court B3
Darlington Rd C1
Durham A2
Durham School C2
Durham University Science Site C3
Ellam Ave C1
Elvet Bridge B3
Elvet Court B3
Farnley Hey B1
Ferens Cl A3
Fieldhouse La A1
Flass St B1
Framwelgate Bridge B2
Framwelgate A2
Framwelgate Peth A2
Framwelgate Waterside A2
Frankland La A3
Freeman's Pl A3
Freeman's Quay L Ctr A3
Gala Theatre & Cinema B3
Geoffrey Ave C1
Gilesgate B3
Grey College C3
Grove, The A1
Hallgarth St C3
Hatfield College B3
Hawthorn Terr B1
Heritage Centre B3
HM Prison B3
Information Ctr B3
John St B1
Kingsgate Bridge B3
Laburnum Terr B1
Lawson Terr B1
Leazes Rd B2/B3
Library B2
Library C3
Margery La B2
Market B2
Mavin St C3
Millburngate B2
Millburngate Bridge B2
Millennium Bridge (foot/cycle) A2
Mountjoy Research Centre C3
Mus of Archaeology B2
Nevilledale Terr B1
New Elvet B3
New Elvet Bridge B3
North Bailey B3
North End A1
North Rd A1/B2
Observatory C1
Old Elvet B3
Open Treasure B3
Oriental Museum C2
Oswald Court C3
Parkside B2
Passport Office A2
Percy Terr B1
Pimlico C2
Police Station B3
Post Office A1/B2
Potters Bank C1/C2
Prebends Bridge C2
Prebends Walk C2
Prince Bishops Shopping Centre B3
Princes St A1
Providence Row A3
Quarryheads La C2
Redhills La B1
Redhills Terr B1
Riverwalk, The B2
Saddler St B3
St Chad's College C3
St Cuthbert's Society C2
St John's College C2
St Margaret's B2
St Mary the Less C2
St Mary's College C2
St Monica Grove B1
St Nicholas' B3
St Oswald's C3
Sands, The A3
Shopmobility B3
Sidegate A2
Silver St B2
Sixth Form College A3
South Bailey C2
South Rd C3
South St B2
Springwell Ave A1
Stockton Rd C3
Student Union B3
Sutton St B2
Town Hall B2
University Arts Block B3
University College B2
Walkergate Centre A3
Wearside Dr A3
Western Hill A1
Wharton Park A2
Whinney Hill C3
Whitehouse Ave C1
YHA C3

Edinburgh 336

Abbey Strand B6
Abbeyhill B6
Abbeyhill Cr B6
Abbeymount A6
Abercromby Pl A3
Adam St C5
Albany La A4
Albany St A4
Albert Memorial B2
Albyn Pl A2
Alva Pl A6
Alva St B1
Ann St A1
Appleton Tower C4
Archibald Place C3
Assembly Rooms & Musical Hall A3
Atholl Cr B1
Atholl Crescent La C1
Bank St B4
Barony St A4
Beaumont Pl C5
Belford Rd B1
Belgrave Cr A1
Belgrave Crescent La A1
Bell's Brae B1
Blackfriars St B4
Blair St B4
Bread St C2
Bristo Pl C4
Bristo St C4
Brougham St C2
Broughton St A4
Brown St C5
Brunton Terr A6
Buckingham Terr A1
Burial Ground A6
Bus Station A4
Caledonian Cr C1
Caledonian Rd C1
Calton Hill A4
Calton Hill A5
Calton Rd B4
Camera Obscura & Outlook Tower B3
Candlemaker Row C4
Canning St B2
Canongate B5
Canongate B5
Carlton St A1
Carlton Terr A6
Carlton Terrace La A6
Castle St B2
Castle Terr B2
Castlehill B3
Central Library B4
Chalmers Hospital C3
Chalmers St C3
Chambers St C4
Chapel St C4
Charles St C4
Charlotte Sq B2
Chester St B1
Circus La A2
Circus Pl A2
City Art Centre B4
City Chambers B4
City Observatory A5
Clarendon Cr A1
Clerk St C5
Coates Cr B1
Cockburn St B4
College of Art C3
Comely Bank Ave A1
Comely Bank Row A1
Cornwall St C2
Cowans Cl C5
Cowgate B4
Cranston St B5
Crichton St C4
Croft-An-Righ A6
Cumberland St A2
Dalry Pl C1
Dalry Rd C1
Danube St A1
Darnawy St A2
David Hume Tower C4
Davie St C5
Dean Bridge A1
Dean Gdns A1
Dean Park Cr A1
Dean Park Mews A1
Dean Park St A1
Dean Path B1
Dean St A1
Dean Terr A1
Dewar Pl C1
Dewar Place La C1
Doune Terr A2
Drummond Pl A3
Drummond St C5
Drumsheugh Gdns B1
Dublin Mews A3
Dublin St A4
Dublin Street La South A4
Dumbiedykes Rd B5
Dundas St A3
Earl Grey St C2
East Crosscauseway C5
East Market St B4
East Norton Pl A6
East Princes St Gdns B3
Easter Rd A6
Edinburgh (Waverley) B4
Edinburgh Castle B3
Edinburgh Dungeon B4
Edinburgh International Conference Ctr C2
Elder St A4
Esplanade B3
Eton Terr A1
Eye Pavilion C3
Festival Office B3
Festival Theatre Edinburgh C4
Filmhouse C2
Fire Station C2
Floral Clock B3
Forres St A2
Forth St A4
Fountainbridge C2
Frederick St A3
Freemasons' Hall B3
Fruit Market B4
Gardner's Cr C2
George Heriot's School C3
George IV Bridge B4
George Sq C4
George Sq La C4
George St B3
Georgian House B2
Gladstone's Land B4
Glen St C3
Gloucester La A2
Gloucester Pl A2
Gloucester St A2
Graham St C3
Grassmarket C3
Great King St A3
Great Stuart B1
Greenside La A5
Greenside Row A5
Greyfriars Kirk C4
Grindlay St C2
Grosvenor St C1
Grove St C1
Gullan's Cl B5
Guthrie St B4
Hanover St A3
Hart St A4
Haymarket C1
Haymarket Station C1
Heriot Pl C3
Heriot Row A2
High School Yard B5
High St B4
Hill Pl C5
Hill St A2
Hillside Cr A5
Holyrood Park C6
Holyrood Rd B5
Home St C2
Hope St B2
Horse Wynd B6
Howden St C5
Howe St A2
India Pl A2
India St A2
Infirmary St B4
Information Ctr B4
Jeffrey St B4
John Knox House B4
Johnston Terr C3
Keir St C3
Kerr St A2
King's Stables Rd B2
Lady Lawson St C3
Lauriston Gdns C3
Lauriston Park C3
Lauriston Pl C3
Lauriston St C3
Lawnmarket B3
Learmonth Gdns A1
Learmonth Terr A1
Leith St A4
Lennox St A1
Lennox St La A1
Leslie Pl A2
London Rd A5
Lothian Rd B2
Lothian St C4
Lower Menz Pl A6
Lynedoch Pl B1
Mall, The B6
Manor Pl B1
Market St B4
Marshall St C4
Maryfield A6
Maryfield Pl A6
McEwan Hall C4
Medical School C4
Melville St B1
Meuse La B4
Middle Meadow Walk C4
Milton St A6
Montrose Terr A6
Moray House (college) B5
Moray Place A2
Morrison Link C1
Morrison St C1
Mound Pl B3
Mound, The B3
Multrees Walk A4
Mus Collections Ctr A4
Mus of Childhood B5
Mus of Edinburgh B5
Museum of Fire C3
Mus on the Mound B4
National Archives of Scotland A4
National Museum of Scotland C4
National Gallery B3
National Library of Scotland B4
National Monument A5
National Portrait Gallery B4
Nelson Monument A5
Nelson St A3
New St B5
Nicolson Sq C4
Nicolson St C4
Niddry St B4
North Bank St B3
North Bridge B4
North Castle St A2
North Charlotte St A2
North Meadow Walk C3
North St Andrew St A4
North St David St A3
North West Circus Pl A2
Northumberland St A3
Odeon C2
Old Royal High School A5
Old Tolbooth Wynd B5
OMNi Centre A4
Our Dynamic Earth B6
Oxford Terr A1
Palace of Holyroodhouse B6
Palmerston Pl B1
Panmure Pl C3
Parliament House B4
Parliament Sq B4
People's Story, The B5
Playhouse Theatre A4
Pleasance C5
Police Station A4
Ponton St C2
Post Office A3/B4/B5/C1/C2/C4
Potterrow C4
Princes Mall B4
Princes St B3
Princes St B3
Prisoners of War B3
Queen St A2
Queen Street Gdns A3
Queen's Dr B6/C6
Queensferry Rd A1
Queensferry St B1
Queensferry Street La B2
Radical Rd C6
Randolph Cr B1
Regent Gdns A5
Regent Rd B5
Regent Rd Park A6
Regent Terr A5
Holyrood Abbey, remains of (AD 1128) A6
Richmond La C5
Richmond Pl C5
Rose St B2
Ross Open Air Theatre B3
Rothesay Pl B1
Rothesay Terr B1
Roxburgh Pl C5
Roxburgh St C5
Royal Bank of Scotland A4
Royal Circus A2
Royal Lyceum C2
Royal Mile, The B5
Royal Scottish Acad B3
Royal Terr A5
Royal Terrace Gdns A5
Rutland Sq B2
Rutland St B2
St Andrew Sq A4
St Andrew Sq A4
St Andrew's House A4
St Bernard's Cr A1
St Cecilia's Hall B4
St Colme St A2
St Cuthbert's B2
St Giles' B4
St John St B5
St John's B2
St John's Hill B5
St Leonard's Hill C5
St Leonard's La C5
St Leonard's St C5
St Mary's A4
St Mary's Scottish Episcopal B1
St Mary's St B5
St Stephen St A2
Salisbury Crags C6
Saunders St A2
Scotch Whisky Experience B3
Scott Monument B4
Scottish Parliament B6
Scottish Storytelling Centre B5
Semple St C2
Shandwick Pl B2
South Bridge B4
South Charlotte St B2
South College St C4
South Learmonth Gdns A1
South St Andrew St A4
South St David St A3
Spittal St C2
Stafford St B1
Student Centre C4
Surgeons' Hall C5
Tattoo Office B4
Teviot Pl C4
Thistle St A3
Torphichen Pl C1
Torphichen St C1
Traverse Theatre B2
Tron Sq B4
Tron, The B4
Union St A4
University C4
University Library C4
Upper Grove Pl C1
Usher Hall C2
Vennel C3
Victoria St B3
Viewcraig Gdns B5
Viewcraig St B5
Vue A4
Walker St B1
Waterloo Pl A4
Waverley Bridge B4
Wemyss Pl A2
West Approach Rd C1
West Crosscauseway C5
West End Princess St B1
West Maitland St C1
West of Nicholson St C4
West Port C3
West Princes St Gdns B3
West Richmond St C5
West Tollcross C2
White Horse Cl B5
William St B1
Windsor St A5
Writer's Mus, The B4
York La A4
York Pl A4
York Pl A4
Young St B2

Exeter 336

Alphington St C1
Athelstan Rd B3
Bampfylde St B2
Barnardo Rd C3
Barnfield Hill B3
Barnfield Rd B2/B3
Barnfield Theatre B2
Bartholomew St East B1
Bartholomew St West B1
Bear St B2
Beaufort Rd C1
Bedford St B2
Belgrave Rd A3
Belmont Rd A3
Blackall Rd A2
Blackboy Rd A3
Bonhay Rd B1
Bull Meadow Rd C2
Bus & Coach Sta B3
Castle St B2
Cecil Rd C1
Cheeke St A3
Church Rd C1
Chute St A3
City Wall B1/B2
Civic Centre B2
Clifton Rd B3
Clifton St B3
Clock Tower A1
College Rd B3
Colleton Cr C2
Commercial Rd C1
Coombe St B2
Cowick St C1
Crown Courts B2
Custom House C2
Cygnet New Theatre C2
Danes' Rd A2
Denmark Rd B3
Devon County Hall C3
Devonshire Pl A3
Dinham Cres B1
East Grove Rd C3
Edmund St C1
Elmgrove Rd A1
Exe St B1
Exeter Cathedral B2
Exeter Central Sta A1
Exeter City Football Ground A3
Exeter College A1
Exeter Picture Ho B1
Fire Station A1
Fore St B1
Friars Walk C2
Guildhall B2
Guildhall Shopping Ctr B2
Harlequins Shopping Centre B1
Haven Rd C2
Heavitree Rd B3
Hele Rd A1
High St B2
HM Prison A2
Holloway St C2
Hoopern St A2
Horseguards A2
Howell Rd A1
Information Ctr B3
Iron Bridge B1
Isca Rd C1
Jesmond Rd A3
King St B1
King William St A2
Larkbeare Rd C2
Leisure Centre C1
Library B2
Longbrook St A2
Longbrook Terr A2
Lower North St B1
Lucky La C2
Lyndhurst Rd C3
Magdalen Rd B3
Magdalen St B2
Market B2
Market St B2
Marlborough Rd C3
Mary Arches St B1
Matford Ave C3
Matford La C3
Matford Rd C3
May St A3
Mol's Coffee House B2
New Bridge St B1
New North Rd A1/A2
North St B1
Northernhay St B1
Norwood Ave C3
Odeon A3
Okehampton St C1
Old Mill Cl C2
Old Tiverton Rd A3
Oxford Rd A3
Paris St B2
Parr St A3
Paul St B1
Pennsylvania Rd A2
Police HQ B3
Portland Street A3
Post Office A3/B2/B3/C1
Powderham Cr A3
Preston St B1
Princesshay Shopping Centre B2
Pyramids Leisure Ctr B3
Quay, The C2
Queen St A1
Queen's Terr A1
Queens Rd C1
Radford Rd C2
Richmond Rd A1
Roberts Rd C2

356 Fort William • Glasgow • Gloucester • Grimsby • Hanley (Stoke-on-Trent) • Harrogate

Rougemont Castle .A2
Rougemont House ✦ .B2
Royal Albert Memorial Museum .B2
St David's Hill .A1
St James' Pk Sta .A3
St James' Rd .A3
St Leonard's Rd .C3
St Mary Steps .C1
St Nicholas Priory .B1
St Thomas Station .C1
Sandford Walk .B3
School for the Deaf .C2
School Rd .C1
Sidwell St .A2
Smythen St .B1
South St .B2
Southernhay East .B2
Southernhay West .B2
Spacex Gallery .B1
Spicer Rd .B3
Sports Centre .A3
Summerland St .A3
Sydney Rd .C1
Tan La .C2
Thornton Hill .A2
Topsham Rd .C3
Tucker's Hall .B1
Tudor St .B1
Underground Passages ✦ .B2
University of Exeter (St Luke's Campus) .B3
Velwell Rd .A1
Verney St .A3
Water La .C1/C2
Weirfield Rd .C2
Well St .A3
West Ave .A2
West Grove Rd .C3
Western Way .A3/B1/B2
Willeys Ave .C1
Wonford Rd .B3/C3
York Rd .A2

Fort William 337

Abrach Rd .A3
Achintore Rd .C1
Alma Rd .B2
Am Breun Chamas .A2
Ambulance Station .A3
An Aird .A2
Argyll Rd .C1
Argyll Terr .C1
Bank St .B2
Belford Hospital .B2
Ben Nevis Highland Ctr .B3
Black Parks .A3
Braemore Pl .C2
Bruce Pl .C2
Bus Station .B2
Camanachd Cr .A3/B2
Cameron Rd .C1
Cameron Sq .B1
Carmichael Way .A2
Claggan Rd .B3
Connochie Rd .C1
Cow Hill .C3
Creag Dhubh .A2
Croft Rd .B3
Douglas Pl .B2
Dudley Rd .B2
Dumbarton Rd .C1
Earl of Inverness Rd .A3
Fassifern Rd .B1
Fire Station .A2
Fort William Sta .B2
Fort William (Remains) ✦ .B2
Glasdrum Rd .C1
Glen Nevis Pl .B3
Gordon Sq .B1
Grange Rd .C1
Heathercroft Dr .C1
Heather Croft Rd .C1
Henderson Row .C2
High St .B1
Hill Rd .B2
Hosp Belhaven Annexe .B3
Information Ctr .A3
Inverlochy Ct .A3
Kennedy Rd .B2/C2
Library .B2
Lime Tree Gallery ✦ .C1
Linnhe Rd .B1
Lochaber Leisure Ctr .B3
Lochiel Rd .A3
Lochy Rd .A3
Lundavra Cres .C1
Lundavra Rd .C1
Lundy Rd .A3
Mamore Cr .B2
Mary St .B2
Middle St .B1
Montrose Ave .A3
Moray Pl .C1
Morven Pl .C2
Moss Rd .B2
Nairn Cres .C1
Nevis Bridge .B3
Nevis Centre, The .A2
Nevis Rd .A3
Nevis Terr .B2
North Rd .B3
Obelisk .B2
Parade Rd .B2
Police Station .C1
Post Office .A3/B2
Ross Pl .C1
St Andrews .B2
Shaw Pl .B2
Station Brae .B1
Superstore .B3
Treig Rd .A3
Underwater Ctr, The .A2
Union Rd .C1
Victoria Rd .B2
Wades Rd .A3
West Highland .B1
West Highland College UHI .A2
Young Pl .B2

Glasgow 337

Admiral St .C2
Albert Bridge .C5
Albion St .B5
Anderston .B3
Anderston Quay .B3
Argyle Arcade .B5
Argyle St .A1/A2/B3/B4/B5
Argyle Street .B5
Arlington St .A3
Arts Centre .B3
Ashley St .A3
Bain St .C6
Baird St .A6
Baliol St .A3
Ballater St .C5
Barras (Market), The .C6
Bath St .A3
BBC Scotland .B1
Bell St .C6
Bell's Bridge .B1
Bentinck St .A2
Berkeley St .A3
Bishop La .B3
Black St .A6
Blackburn St .C2
Blackfriars St .B6
Blantyre St .A1
Blythswood Sq .A4
Blythswood St .B4
Bothwell St .B4
Brand St .C1
Breadalbane St .A2
Bridge St .C4
Bridge St .C4
Bridgegate .C5
Briggait .C5
Broomielaw .B4
Broomielaw Quay Gdns .B3
Brown St .B4
Brunswick St .B5
Buccleuch St .A3
Buchanan Bus Station .A5
Buchanan Galleries .A5
Buchanan St .B5
Buchanan St .B5
Cadogan St .B4
Caledonian University .A5
Calgary St .A5
Cambridge St .A4
Canal St .A5
Candleriggs .B5
Carlton Pl .C4
Carnarvon St .A3
Carrick St .B4
Castle St .B6
Cathedral Sq .B6
Cathedral St .B5
Centre for Contemporary Arts .A4
Centre St .C4
Cessnock .C1
Cessnock St .C1
Charing Cross .A3
Charlotte St .C6
Cheapside St .B3
Cineworld .A5
Citizens' Theatre .C5
City Chambers Complex .B5
City Halls .B5
City of Glasgow Coll (City Campus) .B5
City of Glasgow Coll (Riverside Campus) .C5
Clairmont Gdns .A2
Claremont St .A2
Claremont Terr .A2
Claythorne St .C6
Cleveland St .A3
Clifford La .C1
Clifford St .C1
Clifton Pl .A2
Clifton St .A2
Clutha St .C1
Clyde Arc .B2
Clyde Auditorium .B2
Clyde Pl .C4
Clyde Place Quay .C4
Clyde St .C5
Clyde Walkway .C3
Clydeside Expressway .B2
Coburg St .C4
Cochrane St .B5
College St .B6
Collins St .B6
Commerce St .C4
Cook St .C4
Cornwall St .C2
Couper St .A5
Cowcaddens .A4
Cowcaddens Rd .A4
Crimea St .B3
Custom House Quay Gardens .C4
Dalhousie St .A4
Dental Hospital .A4
Derby St .A2
Dobbie's Loan .A4/A5
Dobbie's Loan Pl .A5
Dorset St .A3
Douglas St .B4
Doulton Fountain ✦ .C6
Dover St .A2
Drury St .B4
Drygate .B6
Duke St .B6
Dunaskin St .A1
Dunblane St .A4
Dundas St .B5
Dunlop St .C5
East Campbell St .C6
Eastvale Place .A1
Eglinton St .C4
Elderslie St .A3
Elliot St .B2
Elmbank St .A3
Esmond St .A1
Exhibition Centre .B2
Eye Infirmary .A2
Festival Park .C1
Film Theatre .A4
Finnieston Quay .B2
Finnieston St .B2
Fire Station .C6
Florence St .C5
Fox St .C5
Gallowgate .C6
Garnet St .A3
Garnethill St .A4
Garscube Rd .A4
George Sq .B5
George St .B5
George V Bridge .C4
Gilbert St .A1
Glasgow Bridge .C4
Glasgow Cathedral ✝ .B6
Glasgow Central .B4
Glasgow Green .C6
Glasgow Necropolis ✦ .B6
Glasgow Royal Concert Hall .A5
Glasgow Science Centre .B1
Glasgow Tower ✦ .B1
Glassford St .B5
Glebe St .A6
Gorbals Cross .C5
Gorbals St .C5
Gordon St .B4
Govan Rd .B1/C1/C2
Grace St .B3
Grafton Pl .A5
Grand Ole Opry ✦ .C2
Grant St .A3
Granville St .A3
Gray St .A2
Greendyke St .C6
Grey Eagle St .B7
Harley St .C1
Harvie St .C1
Haugh Rd .A1
Havanah St .B6
Heliport .B1
Henry Wood Hall .A2
High Court .C5
High St .B6
High Street .B6
Hill St .A3
Holland St .A3
Holm St .B4
Hope St .A5
Houldsworth St .B2
Houston Pl .C3
Houston St .C3
Howard St .C5
Hunter St .C6
Hutcheson St .B5
Hydepark St .B3
Imax Cinema .B1
India St .A3
Information Ctr .B5
Ingram St .B5
Jamaica St .B4
James Watt St .B4
John Knox St .B6
John St .B5
Kelvin Hall ✦ .A1
Kelvin Statue ✦ .A2
Kelvin Way .A2
Kelvingrove Art Gallery & Museum .A1
Kelvingrove Park .A2
Kelvingrove St .A2
Kelvinhaugh St .A1
Kennedy St .A6
Kent Rd .A2
Killermont St .A5
King St .B5
King's, The .A3
Kingston Bridge .C3
Kingston St .C4
Kinning Park .C2
Kyle St .A5
Lancefield Quay .B2
Lancefield St .B3
Langshot St .C1
Lendel Pl .C1
Lighthouse, The ✦ .B4
Lister St .A6
Little St .B3
London Rd .C6
Lorne St .C1
Lower Harbour .B1
Lumsden St .A1
Lymburn St .A1
Lyndoch Cr .A3
Lynedoch Pl .A3
Lynedoch St .A3
Maclellan St .C1
Mair St .C2
Maitland St .A4
Mansell St .C7
Mavisbank Gdns .C2
Mcalpine St .B3
Mcaslin St .A6
McLean Sq .C2
McLellan Gallery .A4
McPhater St .A4
Merchants' House .B5
Middlesex St .C2
Middleton St .C1
Midland St .B4
Miller St .B5
Millennium Bridge .B1
Millroad St .C6
Milnpark St .C2
Milton St .A4
Minerva St .B2
Mitchell Library, The .A3
Mitchell St West .B4
Mitchell Theatre, The .A3
Modern Art Gallery .B5
Moir St .C6
Molendinar St .C6
Moncur St .C6
Montieth Row .C6
Montrose St .B5
Morrison St .C3
Mosque .C5
Nairn St .A1
National Piping Centre, The ✦ .A5
Nelson Mandela Sq .B5
Nelson St .C4
Nelson's Monument .C6
New City Rd .A4
Newton Pl .A3
Newton St .A3
Nicholson St .C4
Nile St .B5
Norfolk Court .C4
Norfolk St .C4
North Frederick St .B5
North Hanover St .B5
North Portland St .B6
North St .A3
North Wallace St .A5
O2 ABC .A4
O2 Academy ✦ .C4
Odeon .C3
Old Dumbarton Rd .A1
Osborne St .B5/C5
Oswald St .B4
Overnewton St .A1
Oxford St .C4
Pacific Dr .B1
Paisley Rd .C3
Paisley Rd West .C1
Park Circus .A2
Park Gdns .A2
Park St South .A2
Park Terr .A2
Parkgrove Terr .A2
Parnie St .C5
Parson St .A6
Partick Bridge .A1
Passport Office .A5
Pavilion Theatre .A4
Pembroke St .A3
People's Palace .C6
Pinkston Rd .A6
Pitt St .A4/B4
Plantation Park .C1
Plantation Quay .B1
Police Station .A4/A6
Port Dundas Rd .A5
Port St .B2
Portman St .C2
Prince's Dock .B1
Princes Sq .B5
Provand's Lordship .B6
Queen St .B5
Queen Street .B5
Ramshorn .B5
Renfrew St .A3/A4
Renton St .A5
Richmond St .B5
Robertson St .B4
Rose St .A4
Rottenrow .B5
Royal Concert Hall .A5
Royal Conservatoire of Scotland .A4
Royal Cr .A2
Royal Exchange Sq .B5
Royal Highland Fusiliers Museum .A3
Royal Hospital For Sick Children .A1
Royal Infirmary .B6
Royal Terr .A2
Rutland Cr .C2
St Andrew's .C6
St Andrew's (RC) ✝ .C5
St Andrew's St .C5
St Enoch .B5
St Enoch Shopping Ctr .B5
St Enoch Sq .B4
St George's Rd .A3
St James Rd .B6
St Kent St .C6
St Mungo Ave .A5/A6
St Mungo Museum of Religious Life .B6
St Mungo Pl .A6
St Vincent Cr .A2
St Vincent Pl .B5
St Vincent St .B3/B4
St Vincent Street Church .B4
St Vincent Terr .B3
Saltmarket .C5
Sandyford Pl .A3
Sauchiehall St .A2/A4
School of Art .A4
Sclater St .B7
Scotland St .C2
Scott St .A4
Scottish Exhibition & Conference Centre .B1
Seaward St .C2
Shaftesbury St .B3
Sheriff Court .C5
Shields Rd .C3
Shopmobility .A5
Shuttle St .B6
Sighthill Park .A6
Somerset Pl .A2
South Portland St .C4
Springburn Rd .A6
Springfield Quay .C3
SSE Hydro The .B2
Stanley St .C2
Stevenson St .C6
Stewart St .A4
Stirling Rd .B6
Stirling's Library .B5
Stobcross Quay .B1
Stobcross Rd .B1
Stock Exchange .B5
Stockwell Pl .C5
Stockwell St .B5
Stow College .A4
Sussex St .C2
Synagogues .A3/C4
Taylor Pl .A6
Tenement House .A3
Teviot St .A1
Theatre Royal .A4
Tolbooth Steeple & Mercat Cross ✦ .C6
Tower St .C2
Trades House .B5
Tradeston St .C4
Transport Museum .A1
Tron .C5
Trongate .B5
Tunnel St .B2
Turnbull St .C5
Union St .B4
Univ of Strathclyde .B6
Victoria Bridge .C5
Virginia St .B5
Wallace St .C3
Walls St .B6
Walmer Cr .C1
Warrock St .B3
Washington St .B3
Waterloo St .B4
Watson St .B6
Watt St .C3
Wellington St .B4
West Campbell St .B4
West George St .B4
West Graham St .A4
West Greenhill Pl .B2
West Regent St .A4
West Regent St .B4
West St .C4
West St .C4
Whitehall St .B3
Wilkes St .C7
Wilson St .B5
Woodlands Gate .A3
Woodlands Rd .A3
Woodlands Terr .A2
Woodside Pl .A3
Woodside Terr .A3
York St .B4
Yorkhill Pde .A1
Yorkhill St .A1

Gloucester 337

Albion St .C1
Alexandra Rd .B3
Alfred St .C3
All Saints Rd .C2
Alvin St .B2
Arthur St .C2
Barrack Square .B1
Barton St .C2
Blackfriars ✝ .B1
Blenheim Rd .C2
Bristol Rd .C1
Brunswick Rd .C2
Bruton Way .B2
Bus Station .B2
Cineworld .C1
City Council Offices .B1
City Museum, Art Gallery & Library .B2
Clarence St .B2
Commercial Rd .B1
Council Offices .B1
Courts .B1
Cromwell St .C2
Deans Way .A2
Denmark Rd .A3
Derby Rd .C3
Docks ✦ .C1
Eastgate St .B2
Eastgate, The .B1
Edwy Pde .A2
Estcourt Cl .A3
Estcourt Rd .A3
Falkner St .C2
GL1 Leisure Centre .C2
Gloucester Cath ✝ .B1
Gloucester Life .B1
Gloucester Quays Outlet .C1
Gloucester Station .B2
Gloucester Waterways .C1
Gloucestershire Archive .B2
Gloucestershire Royal Hospital (A&E) .B3
Goodyere St .C2
Gouda Way .A1
Great Western Rd .B3
Guildhall .B2
Heathville Rd .A3
Henry Rd .B3
Henry St .B2
Hinton Rd .A2
India Rd .C3
Information Ctr .B1
Jersey Rd .C3
King's .C2
King's Walk Shopping Centre .B2
Kingsholm (Gloucester Rugby) .A2
Kingsholm Rd .A2
Lansdown Rd .A3
Library .C2
Llanthony Rd .C1
London Rd .B3
Longhorn Ave .A1
Longsmith St .B1
Malvern Rd .A3
Market .B2
Market Parade .B2
Mercia Rd .A1
Metz Way .C3
Midland Rd .C2
Millbrook St .C3
Montpellier .C1
Napier St .C3
Nettleton Rd .C2
New Inn .B2
New Olympus .C3
North Rd .A3
Northgate St .B2
Oxford Rd .A2
Oxford St .B2
Park & Ride Gloucester .A1
Park Rd .C2
Park St .B2
Park, The .C2
Parliament St .C1
Peel Centre, The .C1
Pitt St .B1
Police Station .C3
Post Office .B2
Quay St .B1
Quay, The .B1
Recreation Gd .A1/A2
Regent St .C2
Robert Raikes Ho .B1
Royal Oak Rd .B1
Russell St .B2
Ryecroft St .C2
St Aldate St .B2
St Ann Way .C1
St Catherine St .A2
St Mark St .A2
St Mary de Crypt .B1
St Mary de Lode .B1
St Nicholas's .B1
St Oswald's Rd .A1
St Oswald's Retail Pk .A1
St Peter's .B2
Seabroke Rd .A3
Sebert St .A2
Severn Rd .C1
Sherborne St .B2
Shire Hall .B1
Sidney St .C3
Soldiers of Gloucestershire .B1
Southgate St .B1/C1
Spa Field .C1
Spa Rd .C1
Sports Ground .A2/B2
Station Rd .B2
Stratton Rd .C3
Stroud Rd .C1
Superstore .A1
Swan Rd .A2
Trier Way .C1/C2
Union St .A2
Vauxhall Rd .C3
Victoria St .C2
Walham Lane .A1
Wellington St .C2
Westgate Retail Park .B1
Westgate St .B1
Widden St .C2
Worcester St .B2

Grimsby 337

Abbey Drive East .C2
Abbey Drive West .C2
Abbey Park Rd .C2
Abbey Rd .C2
Abbey Walk .C2
Abbeygate Shopping Centre .C2
Abbotsway .C2
Adam Smith St .A1/A2
Ainslie St .C2
Albert St .A3
Alexandra Dock .A2/B2
Alexandra Rd .A2/B2
Alexandra Retail Park .A2
Annesley St .A2
Armstrong St .A1
Arthur St .B1
Augusta St .C1
Bargate .C1
Beeson St .A1
Bethlehem St .C2
Bodiam Way .B3
Bradley St .B3
Brighowgate .C1/C2
Bus Station .C2
Canterbury Dr .C1
Cartergate .B1/C1
Catherine St .C3
Caxton .A3
Chantry La .B1
Charlton St .A1
Church La .C2
Church St .A3
Cleethorpe Rd .A3
Close, The .C1
College St .C1
Compton Dr .C1
Corporation Bridge .A2
Corporation Rd .A1
Court .B3
Crescent St .B1
Deansgate .C1
Doughty Rd .C2
Dover St .B1
Duchess St .C2
Dudley St .C1
Duke of York Gardens .B1
Duncombe St .B3
Earl La .B1
East Marsh St .B3
East St .B2
Eastgate .B3
Eastside Rd .A3
Eaton Ct .C1
Eleanor St .B3
Ellis Way .B3
Fisherman's Chapel .A3
Fisherman's Wharf .B2
Fishing Heritage Centre .B2
Flour Sq .A3
Frederick St .B1
Frederick Ward Way .B2
Freeman St .A3/B3
Freshney Dr .B1
Freshney Pl .B2
Garden St .C2
Garibaldi St .A3
Garth La .B2
Grime St .B3
Grimsby Docks Sta .A3
Grimsby Town Sta .C2
Hainton Ave .C3
Har Way .B3
Hare St .C3
Harrison St .B1
Haven Ave .B1
Hay Croft Ave .B1
Hay Croft St .B1
Heneage Rd .B3/C3
Henry St .B1
Holme St .B3
Hume St .C1
James St .B1
Joseph St .B1
Kent St .A3
King Edward St .A3
Lambert Rd .C2
Library .B2
Lime St .B1
Lister St .B1
Littlefield La .C1
Lockhill .A3
Lord St .B1
Lower Spring St .A3
Ludford St .C3
Macaulay St .B1
Mallard Mews .C3
Manor Ave .C2
Market .A3
Market Hall .B2
Market St .B3
Moss Rd .C2
Nelson St .A3
New St .B2
Osbourne St .B2
Pasture St .B3
Peaks Parkway .C3
Pelham Rd .C1
Police Station .B3
Post Office .B1/B2
Pyewipe Rd .A1
Railway Pl .A3
Railway St .A3
Recreation Ground .C2
Rendel St .A2
Retail Park .A2/B3
Richard St .B1
Ripon St .B1
Robinson St East .B3
Royal St .A3
St Hilda's Ave .C1
St James .C2
Sheepfold St .B3/C3
Shopmobility .B2
Sixhills St .C3
South Park .B2
Superstore .B3/B2
Tasburgh St .C3
Tennyson St .B2
Thesiger St .A3
Time Trap .C2
Town Hall .B2
Veal St .B1
Victoria Retail Park .A3
Victoria St North .A2
Victoria St South .B2
Victoria St West .B2
Watkin St .A1
Welholme Ave .C2
Welholme Rd .C3
Wellington St .B3
Wellowgate .C2
Werneth Rd .B3
West Coates Rd .A1
Westgate .A2
Westminster Dr .C1
Willingham St .C3
Wintringham Rd .C2
Wood St .B3
Yarborough Dr .B1
Yarborough Hotel .C2

Hanley 337

Acton St .A3
Albion St .B2
Argyle St .C1
Ashbourne Gr .A2
Avoca St .A3
Baskerville Rd .B3
Bedford Rd .C1
Bedford St .C1
Bethesda St .B2
Bexley St .A2
Birches Head Rd .A3
Botteslow St .C3
Boundary St .A2
Broad St .C2
Broom St .A3
Bryan St .A2
Bucknall New Rd .B3
Bucknall Old Rd .B3
Bus Station .B3
Cannon St .C2
Castlefield St .C1
Cavendish St .B1
Central Forest Pk .A2
Charles St .B3
Cheapside .B2
Chell St .A3
Clarke St .C1
Cleveland Rd .C2
Clifford St .C3
Clough St .B2
Clyde St .C1
College Rd .C2
Cooper St .C2
Corbridge Rd .A1
Cutts St .C2
Davis St .C1
Denbigh St .A1
Derby St .C3
Dilke St .A3
Dundas St .A3
Dundee Rd .C1
Dyke St .B3
Eastwood Rd .C3
Eaton St .A3
Etruria Park .B1
Etruria Rd .B1
Etruria Vale Rd .C1
Festing St .A3
Festival Retail Park .A1
Fire Station .C2
Foundry St .B2
Franklyn St .C3
Garnet St .B1
Garth St .B3
George St .A3
Gilman St .B3
Glass St .B3
Goodson St .B3
Greyhound Way .A1
Grove Pl .C1
Hampton St .C3
Hanley Park .C2
Hanley Park .C2
Harding Rd .C2
Hassall St .B3
Havelock Place .C1
Hazlehurst St .C3
Hinde St .C2
Hope St .B2
Houghton St .C2
Hulton St .A3
Information Ctr .B3
Jasper St .C2
Jervis St .A3
John Bright St .A3
John St .B2
Keelings Rd .A3
Kimberley Rd .C1
Ladysmith Rd .C1
Lawrence St .C2
Leek Rd .C3
Library .C2
Lichfield St .C3
Linfield Rd .B3
Loftus St .A2
Lower Bedford St .C1
Lower Bryan St .A2
Lower Mayer St .A3
Lowther St .A1
Magistrates Court .C2
Malham St .A2
Marsh St .B2
Matlock St .C3
Mayer St .A3
Milton St .C1
Mitchell Memorial Theatre .B2
Morley St .B2
Moston St .A3
Mount Pleasant .C1
Mulgrave St .A1
Mynors St .B3
Nelson Pl .B3
New Century St .B1
Octagon Retail Park .B1
Ogden Rd .C3
Old Hall St .B3
Old Town Rd .A3
Pall Mall .B2
Palmerston St .C3
Park and Ride .C2
Parker St .B2
Parkway, The .C2
Pavilion Dr .A1
Pelham St .C3
Percy St .B2
Piccadilly .B2
Picton St .B3
Plough St .A3
Police Station .C2
Portland St .A1
Post Office .A3/B3/C3
Potteries Museum & Art Gallery .B2
Potteries Shopping Centre .B2
Potteries Way .C2
Powell St .A1
Pretoria Rd .C1
Quadrant Rd .B2
Ranelagh St .C2
Raymond St .C2
Rectory Rd .C1
Regent Rd .C2
Regent Theatre .B2
Richmond Terr .C2
Ridgehouse Dr .A1
Robson St .C2
St Ann St .B3
St Luke St .B3
Sampson St .B2
Shaw St .A1
Sheaf St .C2
Shearer St .C1
Shelton New Rd .C1
Shirley Rd .C2
Slippery La .B2
Snow Hill .C2
Spur St .C3
Stafford St .B2
Statham St .B2
Stubbs La .C3
Sun St .C1
Supermarket .A1/B2
Talbot St .C3
Town Hall .B2
Town Rd .A3
Trinity St .B2
Union St .A2
Upper Hillchurch St .A3
Upper Huntbach St .B3
Victoria Hall Theatre .B3
Warner St .C2
Warwick St .C1
Waterloo Rd .A1
Waterloo St .B3
Well St .B3
Wellesley St .C2
Wellington Rd .B3
Wellington St .B3
Whitehaven Dr .A2
Whitmore St .C1
Windermere St .A1
Woodall St .A1
Yates St .C2
York St .A2

Harrogate 338

Albert St .C2
Alexandra Rd .B2
Arthington Ave .B2
Ashfield Rd .A2
Back Cheltenham Mount .B2
Beech Grove .C1
Belmont Rd .C1
Bilton Dr .A2
BMI The Duchy Hospital .C1
Bower Rd .B2
Bower St .B2
Bus Station .B2
Cambridge Rd .B2
Cambridge St .B2
Cemetery .A2
Chatsworth Grove .A2
Chatsworth Pl .A2
Chatsworth Rd .A2
Chelmsford Rd .B3
Cheltenham Cr .B2
Cheltenham Mt .B2
Cheltenham Pde .B2
Christ Church .B3
Christ Church Oval .B3
Chudleigh Rd .B3
Clarence Dr .B1
Claro Rd .A3
Claro Way .A3
Coach Park .B2
Coach Rd .B3
Cold Bath Rd .C1
Commercial St .B2
Coppice Ave .A1
Coppice Dr .A1
Coppice Gate .A1
Cornwall Rd .B1
Council Offices .B1
Crescent Gdns .B1
Crescent Rd .B1
Dawson Terr .A2
Devonshire Pl .B3
Dixon Rd .A2
Dixon Terrace .A2
Dragon Ave .B3
Dragon Parade .B2
Dragon Rd .B2
Duchy Rd .B1
East Parade .B2
East Park Rd .C3
Esplanade .B1
Everyman .B2
Fire Station .A2
Franklin Mount .A2
Franklin Rd .B2
Franklin Square .A2
Glebe Rd .C1
Grove Park Ct .A3
Grove Park Terr .A3
Grove Rd .A2
Hampsthwaite Rd .A1
Harcourt Dr .B3
Harcourt Rd .B3
Harrogate .B2
Harrogate Convention Centre .B1
Harrogate Justice Centre (Magistrates' and County Courts) .C2
Harrogate Ladies Coll .B1
Harrogate Theatre .B2
Heywood Rd .C1
Hollins Cr .A1
Hollins Mews .A1
Hollins Rd .A1
Hydro Leisure Ctr, The .A1
Information Ctr .B1
James St .B2
Jenny Field Dr .A1
John St .B2
Kent Dr .A1
Kent Rd .A1
Kings Rd .A2
Kingsway .B3
Kingsway Dr .B3
Lancaster Rd .C1
Leeds Rd .C2
Lime Grove .B3
Lime St .A3
Mayfield Grove .B2
Mercer .B1
Montpellier Hill .B1
Mornington Cr .A3
Mornington Terr .B3
Mowbray Sq .B3
North Park Rd .B3
Oakdale Ave .A1
Oatlands Dr .C3
Odeon .B2
Osborne Rd .A2
Otley Rd .C2
Oxford St .B2
Parade, The .B2
Park Chase .B3
Park Parade .B3
Park View .B2
Parliament St .B1
Police Station .C3
Post Office .B2/C1
Providence Terr .A2
Queen Parade .C3
Queen's Rd .C1
Raglan St .C2
Regent Ave .A3
Regent Grove .A3
Regent Parade .A3
Regent St .A3
Regent Terr .A3
Ripon Rd .A1

Luton 343

Macclesfield 343

Maidstone 343

Manchester 343

Marble St A4
Market St A2
Market St A4
Market St ᴛ............A4
Marsden St A4
Marshall St A5
Mayan Ave A2
Medlock St C3
Middlewood St B1
Miller St B4
Minshull St B4
Mosley St A4
Mount St B3
Mulberry St B3
Murray St A5
Museum of Science &
Industry (MOSI) B2
Nathan Dr A2
National Football
Museum 🏛 A4
Naval St A5
New Bailey St A3
New Elm Rd B2
New Islington A6
New Islington Sta ᴛ......B6
New Quay St A3
New Union St A6
Newgate St A5
Newton St A5
Nicholas St B4
North Western St B5
Oak St A4
Odeon 🎬 A4/B3
Old Mill St A6
Oldfield Rd A1/C1
Oldham Rd A5
Oldham St B4
Opera House 🎭 B3
Ordsall La C4
Oxford Rd C4
Oxford Rd ᴢ............C4
Oxford St B4
Paddock St C6
Palace Theatre 🎭 B4
Pall Mall A3
Palmerston St B6
Parker St B4
Peak St B5
Penfield Cl C5
Peoples' History
Museum 🏛 A3
Peru St A1
Peter St B3
Piccadilly A4
Piccadilly ᴢ............B5
Piccadilly Gardens ᴛ......B4
Piercy St A5
Poland St A6
Police Station 🛇 B3/B5
Pollard St B6
Port St B4
Portland St B4
Portugal St East B5
Post Office
🖃 ...A1/A2/A4/A5/B3/B4
Potato Wharf B2
Princess St B3/C4
Pritchard St C4
Quay St A2
Quay St B2
Queen St B3
Radium St A5
Redhill St A5
Regent Rd B1
Retail Park B5
Rice St B2
Richmond St B4
River St C3
Roby St B5
Rodney St A6
Roman Fort 🏛 A2
Rosamond St A2
Royal Exchange 🎭 A3
Sackville St B6
St Andrew's St B6
St Ann St A3
St Ann's 🕆 A3
St George's Ave B4
St James St B4
St John St A3
St John's Cath (RC) † ...A2
St Mary's 🕆 B3
St Mary's Gate A3
St Mary's Parsonage ...A3
St Peter's Sq ᴛ............A3
St Stephen St A2
Salford Approach ...A3
Salford Central ᴢ............A3
Sheffield St B5
Sherratt St A5
Shopmobility A4
Shudehill A4
Shudehill ᴛ............A4
Sidney St C4
Silk St A5
Silver St B4
Skerry Cl C5
Snell St B6
South King St A3
Sparkle St B5
Spear St A4
Spring Gdns A4
Stanley St A2/B2
Store St B5
Superstore B1
Swan St A4
Tariff St B5
Tatton St C1
Temperance St B6/C6
Thirsk St C5
Thomas St A4
Thompson St A5
Tib La B4
Tib St A4
Town Hall
(Manchester) B3
Town Hall (Salford) ...A2
Trafford St C3
Travis St B5
Trinity Way A2

Turner St A4
Union St C6
University of Manchester
(Sackville Street
Campus) C5
University of Salford ...A1
Upper Brook St C5
Upper Cleminson St......A1
Upper Wharf St A1
Urban Exchange A5
Vesta St B6
Victoria ᴛ............A4
Victoria Station ᴢ............A4
Wadesdon St A5
Water St B2
Watson St B3
West Fleet St B1
West King St A2
West Mosley St B4
Weybridge Rd A6
Whitworth St B4
Whitworth St West......C3
William St A2
William St C6
Wilmott St C3
Windmill St B3
Windsor Cr A1
Withy Gr A4
Woden St C1
Wood St A3
Woodward St A6
Worrall St C1
Worsley St B2
York St B4
York St C3

Merthyr Tydfil
Merthyr Tudful 343

Aberdare Rd B3
Abermorlais Terr A3
Alexandra Rd A3
Alma St C3
Arfryn Pl C3
Argyle St C3
Avenue De Clichy C2
Beacons Place
Shopping Centre C2
Bethesda St B2
Bishops Gr A3
Brecon Rd A1/B2
Briarmead A3
Bryn St C2
Bryntirion Rd B3/C3
Bus Station B2
Cae Mari Dwn B3
Caedraw Rd B3
Castle Sq A1
Castle St A1
Chapel A2
Chapel Bank B1
Church St B3
Civic Centre B2
Clos Penderyn B1
Coedcae'r Ct C3
County and
Crown Courts B2
Court St C3
Cromwell St B3
Cyfarthfa Castle School
and Museum 🏛 A1
Cyfarthfa Ind Est A1
Cyfarthfa Park A1
Cyfarthfa Rd A1
Dane St A2
Dane Terr A2
Danyparc B3
Darren View A1
Dixon St C3
Dyke St C3
Dynevor St B2
Elwyn Dr C3
Fire Station B2
Fothergill St B3
Galonuchaf Rd A2
Garth St B2
Georgetown B2
Grawen Terr A2
Grove Pk A2
Grove, The A2
Gurnos Rd A2
Gwaelodygarth Rd ...A2/A3
Gwaunfarren Gr A3
Gwaunfarren Rd A3
Gwendoline St A3
Hampton St C3
Hanover St B2
Heol S O Davies B1
Heol-Gerrig A1
High St A3/B2/B3/C2
Highland View B1
Howell Cl B1
Information Ctr 🛈 B2
Jackson's Bridge B2
James St C2
John St C3
Joseph Parry's Cott 🏛 B2
Lancaster St A2
Library A2
Llewellyn St B2
Llwyfen St B2
Llwyn Berry A1
Llwyn Dic Penderyn ...B1
Llwyn-y-Gelynen A1
Lower Thomas St B3
Market C2
Mary St C2
Masonic St C2
Merthyr College B2
Merthyr RFC B2
Merthyr Town FC A3
Merthyr Tydfil L Ctr ...C2
Merthyr Tydfil Sta ᴢ......C3
Meyrick Villas A2
Miniature Railway 🚂 ...A1
Mount St A2
Nantygwenith St B1
Norman Terr A2
Oak Rd A2

Old Cemetery B3
Pandy Cl A1
Pantycelynen B1
Parade, The A1
Park Terr B2
Penlan View A2
Penry St B2
Pentwyn Villas A1
Penyard Rd B3
Penydarren Park B3
Penydarren Rd B3
Plymouth St B3
Police Station 🛇 C2
Pont Marlais West B2
Post Office 🖃 B2
Quarry Row B3
Queen's Rd B3
Rees St C2
Rhydycar Link C2
Riverside Park A1
St David's 🕆 B1
St Tydfil's ᴥ............C2
St Tydfil's Ave C3
St Tydfil's Hospital
(No A&E) 🏥 C3
St Tydfil's Square
Shopping Centre C2
Saxon St A2
School of Nursing A2
Seward St A3
Shiloh La B3
Stone Circles 🗿 B3
Stuart St A3
Summerhill Pl B3
Superstore B3
Swan St C2
Swansea Rd B2
Taff Glen View C3
Taff Vale Ct C2
Theatre Soar 🎭 B2
Thomastown Park C3
Tramroad La A3
Tramroad Side A3
Tramroad Side North...B3
Tramroad Side South...C3
Trevithick Gdns C3
Trevithick St A3
Tudor Terr A1
Twynyrodyn Rd C3
Union St B3
Upper Colliers Row ...B1
Upper Thomas St B3
Victoria St B2
Vue 🎬 B2
Vulcan Rd B2
Walk, The B2
Warlow St C2
Well St A2
Welsh Assembly
Government Offices .C2
Wern La C1
West Gr C1
William St B2
Yew St C2
Ynysfach Engine Ho 🔶 C2
Ynysfach Rd C2

Middlesbrough 343

Abingdon Rd C3
Acklam Rd C1
Albert Park C2
Albert Rd B2
Albert Terr C2
Ambulance Station ...C1
Aubrey St C2
Avenue, The C2
Ayresome Gdns C2
Ayresome Green La ...C1
Ayresome St C2
Barton Rd A1
Bilsdale Rd C3
Bishopton Rd C3
Borough Rd B2/B3
Bowes Rd A2
Breckon Hill Rd B3
Bridge St East B3
Bridge St West B2
Brighouse Rd A1
Burlam Rd C1
Bus Station B2
Cannon Park B1
Cannon Park Way B1
Cannon St B1
Captain Cook Sq B2
Carlow St C1
Castle Way C2
Chipchase Rd C2
Cineworld 🎬 B2
Cleveland Centre B2
Clive Rd C2
Commercial St A2
Corporation Rd B2
Costa St C2
Council Offices B3
Crescent Rd C2
Crescent, The C2
Cumberland Rd C2
Depot Rd A2
Derwent St B2
Devonshire Rd C2
Diamond Rd B2
Dorman Museum 🏛 ...C2
Douglas St B3
Eastbourne Rd C2
Eden Rd C2
Fire Sta A3
Forty Foot Rd A2
Gilkes St B2
Gosford St B1
Grange Rd B2
Gresham Rd B2
Harehills Rd C1
Harford St C2
Hartington Rd B2
Haverton Hill Rd A1
Hey Wood St B1
Highfield Rd C3
Hillstreet Centre B2
Holwick Rd B1

Hutton Rd C3
Ironmasters Way B1
Lambton Rd C2
Lancaster Rd C2
Lansdowne Rd C3
Latham Rd C1
Law Courts B2/B3
Lees Rd C1
Leeway B3
Library B2
Linthorpe Cemetery ...C1
Linthorpe Rd B2
Lloyd St B2
Longford St B2
Longlands Rd C3
Lower East St A3
Lower Lake C2
Macmillan Academy ..C1
Maldon Rd C1
Manor St B2
Marsh St B2
Marton Rd B3
Middlehaven A2
Middlesbrough
By-Pass B2/C2
Middlesbrough Coll...B3
Middlesbrough L Park.B3
Middlesbrough ᴢ 🚌...B2
Middletown Park C2
MIMA 🏛 B3
Mulgrave Rd C2
Newport Bridge A1
Newport Bridge
Approach Rd B1
Newport Rd B2
North Ormesby Rd ...B3
North Rd B2
Northern Rd C1
Outram St B2
Oxford Rd C2
Park La C2
Park Rd North C2
Park Rd South C2
Park Vale Rd C2
Parliament Rd C1
Police Station 🛇 A2
Port Clarence Rd A3
Portman St B2
Princes Rd B2
Python ᴥ............A2
Riverside Park Rd............A1
Riverside Stadium
(Middlesbrough FC).B3
Rockliffe Rd C2
Romaldkirk Rd C1
Roman Rd C2
Roseberry Rd C3
St Barnabas' Rd C2
St Paul's Rd B2
Saltwells Rd B3
Scott's Rd A3
Seaton Carew Rd A3
Shepherdson Way B3
Shopmobility B2
Snowdon Rd A2
South West
Ironmasters Park....B1
Southfield Rd B2
Southwell Rd C2
Springfield Rd C3
Startforth Rd B1
Stockton Rd C1
Stockton St A2
Superstore B2
Surrey St C2
Sycamore Rd C2
Tax Offices B2
Tees Viaduct A2
Teessaurus Park A2
Teesside Tertiary Coll .C3
Temenos 🔶 B3
Thornfield Rd C2
Town Hall B2
Transporter Bridge
(Toll) A3
Union St B2
University of Teesside .B2
Upper Lake C2
Valley Rd C2
Ventnor Rd C2
Victoria Rd B2
Vulcan St A2
Warwick St C2
Wellesley Rd B3
West La C1
West Lane Hospital 🏥 .C1
Westminster Rd C2
Wilson St B2
Windward Way B3
Woodlands Rd C2
York Rd C3

Milton Keynes 344

Abbey Way A1
Arbrook Ave B1
Armourer Dr C2
Arncliffe Dr A1
Avebury ᴥ............C2
Avebury Blvd C2
Bankfield ᴥ............C2
Bayard Ave A2
Belvedere ᴥ............C2
Bishopstone A1
Blundells Rd A2
Boundary, The C1
Boycott Ave C2
Bradwell Comm Blvd..B1
Bradwell Rd C1
Bramble Ave B1
Brearley Ave C2
Breckland ᴥ............A2
Brill Place B1
Burnham Dr B2
Campbell Park ᴥ............B3
Cantle Ave A3
Central Retail Park....C1
Century Ave C2
Chaffron Way C3

Childs Way A1
Christ the
Cornerstone 🕆 B2
Cineworld 🎬 B2
Civic Offices B2
Cleavers Ave B1
Colesbourne Dr A3
Conniburrow Blvd ...B2
Currier Dr C2
Dansteed Way ...A2/A3/B1
Deltic Ave B1
Downs Barn ᴥ............A2
Downs Barn Blvd A2
Eaglestone ᴥ............C3
Eelbrook Ave B1
Elder Gate B2
Evans Gate C2
Fairford Cr A3
Falcon Ave B3
Fennel Dr B2
Fishermead Blvd C3
Food Centre B2
Fulwoods Dr C3
Glazier Dr A1
Glovers La A1
Grafton Gate C1
Grafton St A1/C2
Gurnards Ave B3
Harrier Dr C3
The Hub Leisure
Quarter B2/C2
Ibstone Ave B1
intu Milton Keynes....B2
Langcliffe Dr A1
Leisure Centre C3
Leisure Plaza C1
Leys Rd C3
Library B2
Linceslade Grove C1
Linford Wood A2
Magistrates Court ...B2
Marlborough Gate ...B3
Marlborough St ...A2/B3
Mercers Dr A1
Midsummer ᴥ............C2
Midsummer Blvd B2
Milton Keynes
Central ᴢ............C1
Milton Keynes
Hospital (A&E) 🏥 ...C3
Monks Way A1
Mullen Ave A3
Mullion Pl C2
Neath Hill ᴥ............A3
North Elder ᴥ............C2
North Grafton ᴥ............B1
North Overgate ᴥ............A3
North Row B2
North Saxon ᴥ............B2
North Secklow ᴥ............B2
North Skeldon ᴥ............C2
North Witan ᴥ............B1
Oakley Gdns A3
Odeon 🎬 B2
Oldbrook Blvd C2
Open-Air Theatre 🎭 ...B3
Overgate A3
Overstreet A3
Patriot Dr B1
Pencarrow Pl B3
Penryn Ave C2
Perran Ave C2
Pitcher La C1
Place Retail Park, The.C1
Police Station 🛇 B2
Portway ᴥ............B2
Post Office 🖃 ...A2/B2/B3
Precedent Dr B1
Quinton Dr B1
Ramsons Ave A2
Retail Park C2
Rockingham Dr A2
Rooksley ᴥ............B1
Saxon Gate B2
Saxon St A1/C3
Secklow Gate B2
Shackleton Pl C2
Shopmobility B2
Silbury Blvd B2
Skeldon ᴥ............A3
South Enmore B3
South Grafton ᴥ............C2
South Row C2
South Saxon ᴥ............C2
South Secklow ᴥ............B3
South Witan ᴥ............C2
Springfield ᴥ............B3
Stainton Dr A1/B1
Stanton Wood ᴥ............A2
Stantonbury ᴥ............A1
Stantonbury L Ctr 🔶 ..A1
Strudwick Dr C2
Sunrise Parkway A2
Superstore C1/C2
Theatre &
Art Gallery 🎭 B3
theCentre:mk B2
Tolcarne Ave C2
Towan Ave C2
Trueman Pl C2
Vauxhall B1
Winterhill Retail Park.C2
Witan Gate B2
Xscape B3

Newcastle upon Tyne 344

Albert St B3
Argyle St B3
Back New Bridge St...A3
BALTIC Centre for
Contemporary Art 🏛.C3
Barker St A3
Barrack Rd A1
Bath La B1
Bessie Surtees Ho 🔶 .C2
Bigg Market C2
Biscuit Factory 🏛 A3
Black Gate 🏰 C2

Blackett St B1
Blandford Square......C1
Boating Lake A1
Boyd St B3
Brandling Park A2
Bus Station B2
Buxton St B3
Byron St A3
Camden St A2
Castle Keep 🏰 C2
Central ᴥ............C1
Central Library B2
Central Motorway ...B2
Chester St A3
City Hall B2
City Rd B3/C3
City Walls 🔶 C2
Civic Centre A2
Claremont Rd A1
Clarence St B3
Clarence Walk B3
Clayton St C1/B1
Clayton St West C1
Close, The C2
Coach Station C1
College St B2
Collingwood St C2
Copland Terr B3
Coppice Way B3
Corporation St B1
Courts C3
Crawhall Rd B3
Dean St C2
Dental Hospital A1
Dinsdale Pl A3
Dinsdale Rd A3
Discovery 🏛 C1
Doncaster Rd A3
Durant Rd B2
Eldon Sq B1
Ellison Pl B2
Empire 🎭 B1
Eskdale Terr A2
Eslington Terr A2
Exhibition Park A1
Falconar St B3
Fenkle St C1
Forth Banks C1
Forth St C1
Gallowgate B1
Gate, The 🔶 B1
Gateshead Millennium
Bridge C3
Gibson St B3
Goldspink La A3
Grainger Market B2
Grainger St C2
Grantham Rd A3
Granville Rd A3
Great North
Children's Hospital ..A1
Great North
Mus:Hancock 🏛 A2
Grey St B2
Groat Market C2
Guildhall 🏛 C2
Hancock St A2
Hanover St C2
Hatton Gallery 🏛 A1
Hawks Rd C3
Haymarket ᴥ............B1
Heber St B1
Helmsley Rd A3
High Bridge B2
High Level Bridge......C2
Hillgate C2
Howard St B3
Hutton Terr A3
Information Ctr 🛈 C1
intu Eldon Square
Shopping Centre B1
Jesmond ᴥ............A2
Jesmond Rd A2/A3
John Dobson St B2
John George Joicey
Museum 🏛 C2
Jubilee Rd B3
Kelvin Gr A3
Kensington Terr A2
Laing Gallery 🏛 B2
Lambton Rd A2
Leazes Cr B1
Leazes La B1
Leazes Park B1
Leazes Park Rd B1
Leazes Terr B1
Library A2
Live 🎭 C2
Low Friar St C1
Manor Chare C2
Manors ᴥ............B2
Manors Station ᴢ............B2
Market St B2
Melbourne St B2
Mill Rd C3
Monument Ⓜ B2
Monument Mall
Shopping Centre B2
Morpeth St A1
Mosley St C2
Napier St A3
New Bridge St B2/B3
Newcastle Central
Station ᴢ............C1
Newcastle University .A1
Newgate Shopping Ctr C1
Newgate St C1
Newington Rd A3
Northern Design Ctr ..C3
Northern Stage
Theatre 🎭 A2
Northumberland Rd...B2
Northumberland St...B2
Northumbria Univ ...A2
Northwest Radial Rd ..C1
O2 Academy 🎭 C1
Oakwellgate C3
Open Univ C3
Orchard St C2
Osborne Rd A2

Osborne Terr A3
Pandon C3
Pandon Bank C3
Park Terr A1
Percy St B1
Pilgrim St B2
Pipewellgate C2
Pitt St B1
Plummer Tower 🏛 B2
Police Station 🛇 B2
Portland Rd A3/B3
Portland Terr A3
Post Office 🖃 B1/B2
Pottery La C1
Prudhoe Pl B1
Prudhoe St B1
Quayside C2
Queen Elizabeth II
Bridge C2
Queen Victoria Rd ...A1
Richardson Rd A1
Ridley Pl B2
Rock Terr B3
Rosedale Terrace A3
Royal Victoria
Infirmary 🏥 A1
Sage Gateshead 🔶 ...C3
St Andrew's St B1
St James Ⓜ B1
St James' Blvd C1
St James' Park
(Newcastle Utd FC) .B1
St Mary's Heritage
Centre 🔶 C3
St Mary's (RC) † C1
St Mary's Place B2
St Nicholas † C2
St Nicholas St C2
St Thomas' St B1
Sandyford Rd A2/A3
Science Park A3
Shield St B3
Shieldfield B3
Shopmobility B1
Side, The C2
Simpson Terr B3
South Shore Rd C3
South St C1
Starbeck Ave A3
Stepney Rd B3
Stoddart St B3
Stowell St B1
Strawberry Pl B1
Swing Bridge C2
Temple St C1
Terrace Pl B1
Theatre Royal 🎭 B2
Times Sq C1
Tower St B3
Trinity House C2
Tyne Bridge C2
Tyne Bridges 🔶 C2
Tyne Theatre & Opera
House 🎭 C1
Tyneside 🎬 B2
Victoria Sq A2
Warwick St A3
Waterloo St C1
Wellington St B1
Westgate Rd C1/C2
Windsor Terr A2
Worswick St B2
Wretham Pl B3

Newport Casnewydd 344

Albert Terr B1
Allt-yr-Yn Ave A1
Alma St C2
Ambulance Station ...C3
Bailey St B2
Barrack Hill A2
Bath St A3
Bedford Rd B3
Belle Vue La C1
Belle Vue Park C1
Bishop St A3
Blewitt St B1
Bolt Cl C3
Bolt St C3
Bond St A2
Bosworth Dr A1
Bridge St B1
Bristol St A3
Bryngwyn Rd B1
Brynhyfryd Ave C1
Brynhyfryd Rd C1
Bus Station B2
Caerau Cres C1
Caerau Rd B1
Caerleon Rd A3
Capel Cres C2
Cardiff Rd C2
Caroline St B3
Castle (Remains) A2
Cedar Rd B3
Charles St B2
Charlotte Dr C2
Chepstow Rd A3
Church Rd A3
Cineworld 🎬 B1
Civic Centre B1
Clarence Pl A2
Clifton Pl B1
Clifton Rd C1
Clyffard Cres B1
Clytha Park Rd B1
Clytha Sq C2
Coldra Rd C3
Collier St A3
Colne St A3
Comfrey Cl A1
Commercial Rd C3
Commercial St B2
Corelli St A3
Corn St B2
Corporation Rd C3
Coulson Cl C2
County Court A1
Courts A1

Courts A3
Crawford St A3
Cyril St B3
Dean St A3
Devon Pl B1
Dewsland Park Rd ...C2
Dolman 🎭 B2
Dolphin St C2
East Dock Rd C3
East St B1
East Usk Rd A3
Ebbw Vale Wharf ...B3
Emlyn St B2
Enterprise Way C2
Eton Rd B3
Evans St A2
Factory Rd A2
Fields Rd B1
Francis Dr C2
Frederick St C1
Friars Rd C1
Friars Walk B1
Gaer La C1
George St C2
George Street Bridge .C3
Godfrey Rd B1
Gold Tops B1
Gore St A3
Gorsedd Circle C1
Grafton Rd A3
Graham St B1
Granville St C2
Harlequin Dr A1
Harrow Rd A3
Herbert Rd A3
Herbert Walk C1
Hereford St A3
High St B2
Hill St B2
Hoskins St A2
Information Ctr 🛈 B2
Ivor St B2
Jones St A3
Junction Rd A3
Keynshaw Ave C2
King St C2
Kingsway B2
Kingsway Centre B2
Ledbury Dr C2
Library A3
Library, Museum &
Art Gallery 🏛 B2
Liverpool Wharf B3
Llanthewy Rd B1
Llanvair Rd A3
Locke St A2
Lower Dock St C3
Lucas St A2
Manchester St B3
Market B2
Marlborough Rd A3
Mellon St C3
Mill St A2
Morgan St A3
Mountjoy Rd C2
Newport Bridge A2
Newport Ctr B2
Newport RFC B3
Newport Station ᴢ............B2
North St B2
Oakfield Rd C1
Park Sq C2
Police Station 🛇 ...A3/C2
Post Office 🖃 B2/C3
Power St A1
Prince St A3
Pugsley St A2
Queen St B3
Queen's Cl C1
Queen's Hill B1
Queen's Hill Cres B1
Queensway B2
Railway St B2
Riverfront Theatre &
Arts Centre, The 🎭 ..B2
Riverside A2
Rodney Rd B2
Royal Gwent (A&E) 🏥 .C2
Rudry St A3
Rugby Rd B3
Ruperra La C3
Ruperra St C3
St Edmund St B1
St Mark's Cres A1
St Mary St B1
St Vincent Rd A3
St Woolos † C2
St Woolos General
(no A&E) 🏥 C1
St Woolos Rd B1
School La B2
Serpentine Rd A3
Shaftesbury Park A2
Sheaf Lane A3
Skinner St B2
Sorrel Dr A1
South Market St C3
Spencer Rd A1
Stow Hill B2/C1/C2
Stow Park Ave C1
Stow Park Dr C1
TA Centre A1
Talbot St B2
Tennis Club A1
Tregare St A3
Trostrey St A3
Tunnel Terr B1
Turner St A3
Univ of Wales Newport
City Campus B3
Upper Dock St B2
Usk St A3
Usk Way B3/C3
Victoria Cr C1
War Memorial B2
Waterloo Rd C1
West St B1
Wharves B2
Wheeler St A3
Whitby Pl A3

Windsor Terr B1
York Pl C1

Newquay 344

Agar Rd B1
Alma Pl B1
Ambulance Station ...B2
Anthony Rd C1
Atlantic Hotel A1
Bank St A1
Barrowfields A3
Bay View Terr B2
Beach Rd A2
Beachfield Ave B1
Beacon Rd A1
Belmont Pl A1
Berry Rd B2
Blue Reef
Aquarium 🔶 A1
Boating Lake B2
Bus Station B1
Chapel Hill B2
Chester Rd A3
Cheviot Rd C1/C2
Chichester Cres C1
Chynance Dr C1
Chyverton Cl C1
Cliff Rd B2
Coach Park B2
Colvreath Rd A3
Cornwall College
Newquay B3
Council Offices B1
Crantock St B1
Crescent, The B1
Criggar Rocks A3
Dale Cl C3
Dale Rd C3
Dane Rd A1
East St B2
Edgcumbe Ave B3
Edgcumbe Gdns B3
Eliot Gdns B3
Elm Cl C2
Ennor's Rd B2
Fernhill Rd B1
Fire Station C2
Fore St B1
Gannel Rd C2
Golf Driving Range...B3
Gover La B1
Great Western Beach .A2
Grosvenor Ave B3
Harbour A2
Hawkins Rd C2
Headleigh Rd B2
Hilgrove Rd A3/B3
Holywell Rd B3
Hope Terr B2
Huer's Hut, The 🔶 ...A1
Information Ctr 🛈 B1
Island Cres B2
Jubilee St B1
Kew Cl C3
Killacourt Cove A2
King Edward Cres A1
Lanhenvor Ave B2
Library B1
Lifeboat Station A1
Lighthouse 💡 B1
Linden Ave C2
Listry Rd C1
Lusty Glaze Beach ...A3
Lusty Glaze Rd A3
Manor Rd B2
Marcus Hill B2
Mayfield Rd C2
Meadowside C3
Mellanvrane La C2
Michell Ave C2
Miniature Golf Course.C3
Miniature Railway 🔶 .B3
Mount Wise B1
Mowhay Cl C3
Narrowcliff A3
Newquay ᴢ............B2
Newquay Hospital 🏥 .B2
Newquay Town
Football Ground......B3
Newquay Zoo B3
North Pier A1
North Quay Hill A1
Oakleigh Terr B2
Pargolla Rd B2
Pendragon Cres C3
Pengannel Cl C1
Penina Ave C1
Pirate's Quest 🏛 B1
Police Sta & Courts ...B2
Post Office 🖃 B1/B2
Quarry Park Rd B3
Rawley La C2
Reeds Way B1
Robartes Rd B2
St Anne's Rd A3
St Aubyn Cres C2
St George's Rd B1
St John's Rd B1
St Mary's Rd B1
St Michael's 🕆 B1
St Michael's Rd A1
St Thomas' Rd B2
Seymour Ave B2
South Pier A1
South Quay Hill A1
Superstore B2
Sweet Briar Cres C3
Sydney Rd A1
Tolcarne Beach A3
Tolcarne Point A2
Tolcarne Rd A2
Tor Rd C2
Towan Beach A1
Towan Blystra Rd ...B3
Tower Rd A1
Trebarwith Cres B2
Tredour Rd C2
Treforda Rd C3
Tregoss Rd B3

Tregunnel Hill B1/C1
Tregunnel Saltings C1
Trelawney Rd B2
Treloggan La C3
Treloggan Rd C3
Trembath Cres C1
Trenance Ave B2
Trenance Gardens B2
Trenance La C2
Trenance Leisure Pk B3
Trenance Rd B2
Trenarth Rd B2
Treninnick Hill C3
Tretherras Rd B3
Trethewey Way C1
Trevemper Rd C2
Ulalia Rd B3
Vivian Cl B2
Waterworld B3
Whitegate Rd B3
Wych Hazel Way C3

Newtown
Y Drenewydd 344

Ash Cl A3
Back La B2
Baptist Chapel B2
Barn La A2
Bear Lanes Shopping Centre B2
Beech Close A2
Beechwood Dr A2
Brimmon Cl C2
Brimmon Rd C2
Broad St B2
Bryn Bank A1
Bryn Cl A1
Bryn Gdns A1
Bryn House A1
Bryn La A1/A2
Bryn Meadows A2
Bryn St A1
Bryn, The A1
Brynglais Ave A2
Brynglais Close A2
Bus Station B2
Byrnwood Dr A1
Cambrian Bridge B3
Cambrian Gdns B2
Cambrian Way B2
Canal Rd A3
Castle Mound B2
Cedewain C1
Cefnaire C2
Cefnaire Coppice C2
Ceiriog A1
Cemetery A3
Church (Remains of) B2
Churchill Dr A3
Cledan B3
Colwyn B3
Commercial St A2
Council Offices B1
Crescent St A1
Cwm Llanfair B1
Dinas B2
Dolafon Rd B3
Dolerw Park B1
Dolfor Rd C1
Eirianell A3
Fairfield Dr A2
Ffordd Croesawdy B2
Fire Station C1
Frankwell St A2
Frolic St B2
Fron La A1
Garden La A2
Gas St B2
Glyndwr C1
Golwgydre La B2
Gorsedd Circle B1
Great Brimmon Farm C3
Hafren C1
Halfpenny Bridge B2
High St B2
Hillside Ave A3
Hoel Treowen C2
Information Ctr B2
Kerry Rd B3
Ladywell Shopping Ctr B2
Library B1
Llanfair Rd A2
Llanidloes Rd C1
Llys Ifor A2
Lon Cerddyn B1
Lon Helyg C1
Lonesome La A3
Long Bridge A2
Lower Canal Rd B3
Maldwyn Leisure Ctr C1
Market B2
Market St B2
Milford Rd B1
Mill Cl B2
Miniature Railway B1
Montgomery County Infirmary A2
Mwyn Fynydd A3
New Church St B2
New Rd B2
Newtown Football Gd B1
Newtown Station B2
Oak Tree Ave A3
Old Kerry Rd B2
Oldbarn La A2
Oriel Davies Gallery B2
Park Cl B1
Park La B1
Park St B2
Park, The B1
Parklands B1
Pavillion Ct C1
Plantation La C1
Police Station B1
Pont Brynfedw A2
Pool Rd B3
Poplar Rd A3
Post Office B2
Powys C1
Powys Theatre A2
Pryce Jones Stores & Museum B2
Quaker Meeting Ho B1
Regent B2
Robert Owen House B1
Robert Owen Mus B2
Rugby Club A3
St David's B2
School La B2
Sheaf St B3
Short Bridge St B2
Stone St B2
Superstore B3/C1
Sycamore Dr A2
Textile Museum A2
Town Hall B2
Union St A2
Upper Brimmon C3
Vastre Industrial Est B3
War Memorial B2
WHSmith Museum B2
Wynfields C1
Y Ffrydd A3

Northampton 344

78 Derngate B3
Abington Sq B3
Abington St B3
Alcombe St A3
All Saints' B2
Ambush St B1
Angel St B2
AR Centre A3
Arundel St A2
Ash St A2
Auctioneers Way C2
Bailiff St A2
Barrack Rd A2
Beaconsfield Terr A3
Becket's Park C3
Bedford Rd B3
Billing Rd B3
Brecon St A1
Brewery C2
Bridge St C2
Broad St B2
Burns St A3
Bus Station B2
Campbell St A2
Castle (Site of) B2
Castle St B2
Cattle Market Rd C2
Central Museum & Art Gallery B2
Charles St A3
Cheyne Walk B3
Church La A2
Clare St A3
Cloutsham St A3
College St B2
Colwyn Rd A3
Cotton End C2
Countess Rd A1
County Hall B2
Court A2
Craven St A3
Crown & County Courts B3
Denmark Rd B3
Derngate B3
Derngate & Royal Theatres B3
Doddridge Church B2
Drapery, The B2
Duke St A3
Dunster St A3
Earl St A3
Euston Rd C2
Fire Station A3
Foot Meadow B2
Gladstone Rd A1
Gold St B2
Grafton St A2
Gray St A3
Green St B1
Greenwood Rd B1
Greyfriars B2
Grosvenor Centre B2
Grove Rd A3
Guildhall B2
Hampton St A2
Harding Terr A2
Hazelwood Rd B3
Herbert St B2
Hervey St A3
Hester St A2
Holy Sepulchre A2
Hood St A3
Horse Market B2
Hunter St A3
Information Ctr B1
Kettering Rd A3
Kingswell St B2
Lady's La B2
Leicester St A2
Leslie Rd A2
Library B3
Lorne Rd A2
Lorry Park A1
Louise Rd A2
Lower Harding St A2
Lower Hester St A2
Lower Mounts B3
Lower Priory St A2
Main Rd C1
Marefair B2
Market Sq B2
Marlboro Rd B1
Marriott St A2
Military Rd A3
Mounts Baths L Ctr A3
Nene Valley Retail Pk C1
New South Bridge Rd C2
Northampton General Hospital (A&E) B3
Northampton Marina C3
Northampton Sta B1
Northcote St A2
Nunn Mills Rd C3
Old Towcester Rd C2
Overstone Rd A3
Peacock Pl B2
Pembroke Rd A1
Penn Court C2
Police Station B3
Post Office A1/B3
Quorn Way A2
Ransome Rd C3
Regent Sq A2
Ridings, The B3
Robert St A2
St Andrew's Rd B1
St Andrew's St A2
St Edmund's Rd B3
St George's St A2
St Giles B3
St Giles St B3
St Giles' Terr B3
St James Park Rd B1
St James Rd B1
St James Retail Park C1
St James' Mill Rd B1
St James' Mill Rd East C1
St Leonard's Rd C2
St Mary's St B2
St Michael's Rd A3
St Peter's B2
St Peter's Way Shopping Precinct B2
St Peter's Way B2
Salisbury St A2
Scarletwell St B2
Semilong Rd A2
Sheep St B2
Sol Central (Leisure Ctr) B2
Somerset St A3
South Bridge C2
Southfield Ave C2
Spencer Bridge Rd A1
Spencer Rd A3
Spring Gdns B3
Spring La B2
Superstore C2
Swan St B3
Tintern Ave A1
Towcester Rd C2
Upper Bath St B2
Upper Mounts A2
Victoria Park A1
Victoria Promenade B2
Victoria Rd B3
Victoria St A2
Wellingborough Rd B3
West Bridge B1
York Rd B3

Norwich 345

Albion Way C3
All Saints Green C2
Anchor St A3
Anglia Sq A2
Argyle St C3
Arts Centre B1
Ashby St C2
Assembly House B1
Bank Plain B2
Barker St A1
Barn Rd A1
Barrack St A3
Ber St C2
Bethel St B1
Bishop Bridge A3
Bishopbridge Rd A3
Bishopgate A3
Blackfriars St A2
Botolph St A2
Bracondale C3
Brazen Gate C2
Bridewell B2
Brunswick Rd C1
Bull Close Rd A2
Bus Station C2
Calvert St A2
Cannell Green A3
Carrow Rd C3
Castle & Museum B2
Castle Mall B2
Castle Meadow B2
Cathedral B2
Cathedral Retail Park A1
Cattlemarket St B2
Chantry Rd C1
Chapel Loke C2
Chapelfield East B1
Chapelfield Gdns B1
Chapelfield North B1
Chapelfield Rd B1
Cinema City B2
City Hall B1
City Rd C2
City Wall C1/C3
Close, The B2/B3
Colegate A2
Coslany St B1
Cow Hill B1
Cow Tower A3
Cowgate A2
Crown & Magistrates' Courts A2
Dragon Hall Heritage Centre C3
Duke St A1
Edward St A2
Elm Hill B2
Erpingham Gate B2
Fishergate A2
Forum, The B1
Foundry Bridge B3
Fye Bridge A2
Garden St C2
Gas Hill B3
Gentlemans Walk B2
Grapes Hill B1
Great Hosp Halls, The A3
Grove Ave C1
Grove Rd C1
Guildhall B1
Gurney Rd A3
Hall Rd C2
Heathgate A3
Heigham St A1
Hollywood A2
Horn's La C2
Hungate Medieval Art B2
Information Ctr B1
intu Chapelfield C1
Ipswich Rd C1
ITV Anglia C3
James Stuart Gdns B3
King St B2
King St C3
Koblenz Ave C3
Leisure Centre A3
Library B1
London St B2
Lower Clarence Rd B3
Maddermarket B1
Magdalen St A2
Mariners La C2
Market B2
Market Ave B2
Mountergate B3
Mousehold St A3
Newmarket Rd C1
Norfolk St C1
Norwich City FC C3
Norwich Gallery B2
Norwich School B2
Norwich Station B3
Oak St A1
Odeon C3
Palace St A2
Pitt St A1
Playhouse B2
Police Station B1
Post Office A2/B2/B3/C1
Pottergate B1
Prince of Wales Rd B2
Princes St B2
Pull's Ferry B3
Puppet Theatre A2
Queen St B2
Queens Rd C2
RC Cathedral B1
Recorder Rd B3
Riverside Entertainment Centre C3
Riverside Leisure Ctr C3
Riverside Rd B3
Riverside Retail Park C3
Rosary Rd B3
Rose La B3
Rouen Rd C2
St Andrews St B2
St Augustines St A1
St Benedicts St B1
St Ethelbert's Gate B2
St Faiths La B3
St Georges St A2
St Giles St B1
St James Cl A3
St Julians C2
St Leonards Rd B3
St Martin's La A1
St Peter Mancroft B2
St Peters St B1
St Stephens Rd C1
St Stephens St C1
Shopmobility C1
Silver Rd A2
Silver St A2
Southwell Rd C2
St. Andrew's & Blackfriars' Hall B2
Strangers' Hall B1
Superstore C2
Surrey St C2
Sussex St A1
Theatre Royal B1
Theatre St B1
Thorn La C2
Thorpe Rd B3
Tombland B2
Union St C1
Vauxhall St B1
Victoria St C1
Vue B2
Walpole St B1
Waterfront, The C3
Wensum St A2
Wessex St C1
Westwick St A1
Wherry Rd C3
Whitefriars A2
Willow La B1

Nottingham 345

Abbotsford Dr A3
Addison St A1
Albert Hall B1
Alfred St Central A3
Alfreton Rd B1
All Saints St A1
Annesley Gr A2
Arboretum A1
Arboretum St A1
Arthur St A1
Arts Theatre B3
Ashforth St A3
Balmoral Rd A1
Barker Gate B3
Bath St B3
BBC Nottingham C3
Beacon Hill Rise B3
Belgrave Rooms B1
Bellar Gate B3
Belward St B3
Brewhouse Yard C2
Broad Marsh Bus Sta C2
Broad St B3
Brook St B3
Burns St A1
Burton St B2
Bus Station A2
Canal St C2
Carlton St B3
Carrington St C2
Castle C2
Castle Blvd C1
Castle Gate C2
Castle Meadow Rd C1
Castle Meadow Retail Park C1
Castle Rd C2
Castle Wharf C2
Cavendish Rd East C1
Cemetery A1/B1
Chaucer St B1
Cheapside B2
Church Rd A3
City Link C3
City of Caves C2
Clarendon St B1
Cliff Rd C3
Clumber Rd East C1
Clumber St B2
College St B1
Collin St C2
Contemporary C3
Conway Cl A2
Cornerhouse, The B2
Council House B2
Cranbrook St B3
Cranmer St A2
Cromwell St B1
Curzon St B3
Derby Rd B1
Dryden St A2
Exchange Ctr, The B2
Fishpond Dr C1
Fletcher Gate B3
Forest Rd East A1
Forest Rd West A1
Friar La C2
Gedling Gr A1
Gedling St B3
George St B3
Gill St A2
Glasshouse St B2
Goldsmith St B2
Goose Gate B3
Great Freeman St A2
Guildhall B2
Hamilton Dr C1
Hampden St A1
Heathcote St B3
High Pavement C3
High School A1
HM Revenue & Customs C2
Holles Cr C1
Hope Dr C1
Hungerhill Rd A3
Huntingdon Dr C1
Huntingdon St A2
Information Ctr B2
Instow Rise A3
International Community Centre A2
intu Broadmarsh C2
intu Victoria Centre B2
Kent St B3
King St B2
Lace Market B3
Lace Mkt Theatre C3
Lamartine St B3
Leisure Ctr C3
Lenton Rd C1
Lewis Cl A3
Lincoln St B2
London Rd C3
Long Row B2
Low Pavement C2
Lower Parliament St B3
Magistrates' Court C2
Maid Marian Way B2
Mansfield Rd A2/B2
Middle Hill C2
Milton St B2
Mount St B2
National Ice Centre & Motorpoint Arena C3
National Justice Museum C3
Newcastle Dr B1
Newstead Gr A2
North Sherwood St A2
Nottingham Arena C3
Nottingham Cath B1
Nottingham College C3
Nottingham Station C3
Nottingham Station C3
Nottingham Trent University A2/B2
Old Market Square B2
Oliver St A1
Park Dr C1
Park Row C1
Park Terr B1
Park Valley C1
Park, The C1
Peas Hill Rd A3
Peel St A1
Pelham St B2
Peveril Dr C1
Plantagenet St A3
Playhouse Theatre B1
Plumptre St C3
Police Station B1/B2
Poplar St C3
Portland Rd B1
Post Office B2
Queen's Rd C3
Raleigh St A1
Regent St B1
Rick St B3
Robin Hood St B3
Robin Hood Statue C2
Ropewalk, The B1
Royal Centre B2
Royal Children Inn C2
Royal Concert Hall B2
St Ann's Hill Rd A2
St Ann's Way A2
St Ann's Well Rd A3
St James' St B2
St Mark's St B3
St Mary's Rest Garden B3
St Mary's Gate B3
St Nicholas C2
St Peter's C2
St Peter's Gate B2
Salutation Inn C2
Shakespeare St B2
Shelton St A2
Shopmobility A2
South Pde B2
South Rd C1
South Sherwood St B2
Station Street C3
Stoney St B3
Talbot St B1
Tattershall Dr C1
Tennis Dr B1
Tennyson St A1
Theatre Royal B2
Trent St C3
Trent University B2
Union Rd B3
Upper Parliament St B2
Victoria Leisure Ctr B3
Victoria Park B3
Victoria St B2
Walter St A1
Warser Gate B3
Watkin St A2
Waverley St A1
Wheeler Gate B2
Wilford Rd C2
Wilford St C2
Wollaton St B1
Woodborough Rd A2
Woolpack La B3
Ye Old Trip to Jerusalem C2
York St A2

Oban 345

Aird's Cres B2
Albany St B2
Albert La A2
Albert Rd A2
Alma Cres B1
Ambulance Station C2
Angus Terr C3
Ardconnel Rd A2
Ardconnel Terr B2
Argyll Sq B2
Argyll St B2
Atlantis Leisure Ctr A2
Bayview Rd A1
Benvoulin Rd A2
Bowling Green A2
Breadalbane St A2
Bus Station B2
Campbell St B2
College B2
Colonsay Terr C3
Columba Building B2
Combie St B2
Corran Brae A1
Corran Esplanade A1/A2
Corran Halls, The A2
Court B2
Crannaig-a-Mhinisteir B1
Crannog La C2
Croft Ave A2
Dalintart Dr C3
Dalriach Rd A2
Distillery B2
Drummore Rd C2
Duncraggan Rd A2
Dunollie Rd A2
Dunuaran Rd B1
Feochan Gr C3
Ferry Terminal B1
Gallanach Rd B1
George St A2
Glencruitten Dr C3
Glencruitten Rd B3
Glenmore Rd C1
Glenshellach Rd C1
Glenshellach Terr B2
Hazeldean Cres A3
High St B2
Highland Theatre Cinema, The A2
Hill St B2
Industrial Estate C2
Information Ctr B2
Islay Rd C3
Jacob's Ladder B2
Jura Rd C3
Knipoch Pl C3
Laurel Cres A2
Laurel Rd A2/A3
Library B1
Lifeboat Station B1
Lighthouse Pier B1
Lismore Cres A2
Lochavullin Dr B2
Lochavullin Rd C2
Lochside St B2
Longsdale Cres A3
Longsdale Rd A2/A3
Longsdale Terr A3
Lunga Rd C3
Lynn Rd C2
Market St B2
McCaig Rd C3
McCaig's Tower A2
Mill La C2
Miller Rd C2
Millpark Ave C2
Millpark Rd C2
Mossfield Ave B3
Mossfield Dr B3
Mossfield Stadium B3
Nant Dr C3
Nelson Rd C2
North Pier B2
Nursery La A2
Oban B2
Police Station B2
Polvinister Rd C3
Post Office A2/B2
Pulpit Dr C1
Pulpit Hill C1
Pulpit Hill Viewpoint B1
Quarry Rd C2
Queen's Park Pl B2
Railway Quay B1
Rockfield Rd B2
St Columba's A1
St John's A2
Scalpay Terr C3
Shore St B1
Shuna Terr C3
Sinclair Dr C2
Soroba Rd B2/C2
South Pier B2
Stevenson St B2
Tweedale St B2
Ulva Rd C2
Villa Rd B1
War & Peace A2

Oxford 345

Adelaide St A1
Albert St A1
All Souls (Coll) B2
Ashmolean Mus B2
Balliol (Coll) B2
Banbury Rd A2
Bate Collection of Musical Instruments C2
Beaumont St B1
Becket St B1
Blackhall Rd A2
Blue Boar St B2
Bodleian Library B2
Botanic Garden B3
Brasenose (Coll) B2
Brewer St C2
Broad St B2
Burton-Taylor Theatre B2
Bus Station B1
Canal St A1
Cardigan St A1
Carfax Tower B2
Castle B1
Castle St B1
Catte St B2
Cemetery C1
Christ Church (Coll) B2
Christ Church Cath C2
Christ Church Meadow C2
Clarendon Centre B2
Coach & Lorry Park C1
College B3
Coll of Further Ed C1
Cornmarket St B2
Corpus Christi (Coll) B2
County Hall B1
Covered Market B2
Cowley Pl C3
Cranham St A1
Cranham Terr A1
Cricket Ground B1
Crown & County Courts C2
Deer Park B3
Exeter (Coll) B2
Folly Bridge C2
George St B1
Great Clarendon St A1
Hart St A1
Hertford (Coll) B2
High St B3
Hollybush Row B1
Holywell St B2
Hythe Bridge St B1
Ice Rink C1
Information Ctr B2
Jericho St A1
Jesus (Coll) B2
Jowett Walk B3
Juxon St A1
Keble (Coll) A2
Keble Rd A2
Library B2
Linacre (Coll) A3
Lincoln (Coll) B2
Little Clarendon St A1
Longwall St B3
Magdalen (Coll) B3
Magdalen Bridge B2
Magdalen St B2
Magistrate's Court C2
Manchester (Coll) B2
Manor Rd B3
Mansfield (Coll) A2
Mansfield Rd A3
Market B1
Marlborough Rd C2
Martyrs' Memorial B2
Merton (Coll) B3
Merton Field B3
Merton St B2
Mus of Modern Art B2
Museum of Oxford B2
Museum Rd A2
New College (Coll) B3
New Inn Hall St B2
New Rd B1
New Theatre B2
Norfolk St C1
Nuffield (Coll) B1
Observatory A1
Observatory St A1
Odeon B1/B2
Old Fire Station B1
Old Greyfriars St C2
Oriel (Coll) B2
Oxford Station B1
Oxford University Research Centres A1
Oxpens Rd C1
Paradise Sq C1
Paradise St B1
Park End St B1
Parks Rd A2/B2
Pembroke (Coll) C2
Phoenix A1
Picture Gallery C2
Plantation Rd A1
Playhouse B2
Police Station C2
Post Office A1/B2
Pusey St B1
Queen's (Coll) B3
Queen's La B3
Radcliffe Camera B2
Rewley Rd B1
Richmond Rd A1
Rose La B3
Ruskin (Coll) B1
Said Business School B1
St Aldates C2
St Anne's (Coll) A1
St Antony's (Coll) A1
St Bernard's Rd A1
St Catherine's (Coll) B3
St Cross Building A3
St Cross Rd A3
St Edmund Hall (Coll) B3
St Giles St A2
St Hilda's (Coll) C3
St John St B2
St John's (Coll) B2
St Mary the Virgin B2
St Michael at the Northgate B2
St Peter's (Coll) B1
St Thomas St B1
Science Area A2
Science Museum B2
Sheldonian Theatre B2
Somerville (Coll) A1
South Parks Rd A2
Speedwell St C2
Sports Ground C3
Thames St C2
Town Hall B2
Trinity (Coll) B2
Turl St B2
University Coll (Coll) B3
Univ Museum & Pitt Rivers Museum A2
University Parks A2
Wadham (Coll) B2
Walton Cr A1
Walton St A1
Western Rd C2
Westgate C2
Woodstock Rd A1
Worcester (Coll) B1

Perth 345

AK Bell Library B2
Abbot Cres C1
Abbot St C1
Albany Terr A1
Albert Monument A3
Alexandra St B2
Atholl St A2
Balhousie Ave A2
Balhousie Castle Black Watch Museum A2
Balhousie St A2
Ballantine Pl A1
Barossa Pl A2
Barossa St A2
Barrack St A2
Bell's Sports Centre A2
Bellwood B3
Blair St B1
Burn Park C1
Bus Station B2
Caledonian Rd B2
Canal Cres B2
Canal St B3
Cavendish Ave C1
Charles St B2
Charlotte Pl A2
Charlotte St A3
Church St A1
City Hall B3
Club House C3
Clyde Pl C1
Commercial St A3
Concert Hall B3
Council Chambers B3
County Pl B2
Court B3
Craigie Pl C2
Crieff Rd A1
Croft Park C2
Cross St B2
Darnhall Cres C1
Darnhall Dr C1
Dewars Centre B1
Dundee Rd B3
Dunkeld Rd A1
Earl's Dykes B1
Edinburgh Rd C3
Elibank St B1
Fair Maid's House A3
Fergusson B3
Feus Rd A1
Fire Station A1
Fitness Centre B3
Foundary La A2
Friar St C1
George St B3
Glamis Pl C1
Glasgow Rd B1
Glenearn Rd C2
Glover St B1/C1
Golf Course A2
Gowrie St A3
Gray St B1
Graybank Rd B1
Greyfriars Burial Grnd B3
Hay St A2
High St B2/B3
Hotel B2
Inchaffray St A1
Industrial/Retail Park B1
Information Ctr B2
Isla Rd A3
James St B2
Keir St A3
King Edward St B3
King James VI Golf Course C3
King St B2
Kings Pl C2
Kinnoull Aisle 'Tower' B3
Kinnoull Causeway B2
Kinnoull St B2
Knowelea Pl C1
Knowelea Terr C1
Ladeside Bsns Centre A1
Leisure Pool B1
Leonard St B2
Lickley St B2
Lochie Brae A3
Long Causeway A1
Low St A2
Main St A3
Marshall Pl C3
Melville St A2
Mill St B3
Milne St B2
Murray Cres C1
Murray St B2
Needless Rd C1
New Rd B2
North Inch A3
North Methven St A2
Park Pl C1
Perth B2
Perth Bridge A3
Perth Business Park B1
Perth Museum & Art Gallery B3
Perth Station C2
Pickletulllum Rd B1
Pitheavlis Cres C1
Playhouse B2
Police Station A2
Pomarium St B2
Post Office B2/C2
Princes St B3
Priory Pl C2
Queen St C1
Queen's Bridge B3
Riggs Rd B1
Riverside B3
Riverside Park B3
Rodney Park B3
Rose Terr A2
St Catherine's Rd A1/A2
St Catherines Retail Park A1
St John St B3
St John's Kirk B3
St John's Shopping Ctr B2
St Leonards Bridge C2
St Ninians Cathedral A2
Scott Monument C2
Scott St B2
Sheriff Court B3
Shore Rd C3
Skate Park C3
South Inch C2
South Inch Bsns Ctr C3
South Inch Park C2
South Inch View C2
South Methven St B2
South St B3
South William St B2
Stables, The A1
Stanners, The B3
Stormont St A2
Strathmore St A3
Stuart Ave C1
Superstore B1/B2
Tay St B3
Union La B2
Victoria St B2
Watergate B3
Wellshill Cemetery A1
West Bridge St A3
West Mill St B2
Whitefriers Cres B1
Whitefriers St B1
Wilson St C1
Windsor Terr C1
Woodside Cres C1
York Pl B2
Young St C1

Peterborough 345

ABAX Stadium (Peterborough United) C2
Athletics Arena B3
Bishop's Palace B2
Bishop's Rd B2/B3
Boongate A3
Bourges Boulevard A1
Bourges Retail Pk B1/B2
Bridge House (Council Offices) C2
Bridge St B2
Bright St A1
Broadway A2
Broadway A2
Brook St A2
Burghley Rd A2
Bus Station B2
Cavendish St A3
Charles St A3
Church St B2
Church Walk A2
Cobden Ave A1
Cobden St A1
Cowgate B2
Craig St A2
Crawthorne Rd A2
Cromwell Rd A1
Dickens St A3
Eastfield Rd A3

Sunderland • Swansea • Swindon • Taunton • Telford • Torquay • Truro 365

Butterfly Farm ✦ C3
Cemetery C1
Chapel La B2
Cherry Orchard C1
Chestnut Walk B2
Children's Playground C3
Church St C2
Civic Hall B2
Clarence Rd B1
Clopton Bridge ✦ B3
Clopton Rd A2
College B1
College La C2
College St C2
Com Sports Centre B1
Council Offices (District) B2
Courtyard, The C2
Cox's Yard ✦ B3
Cricket Ground C3
Ely Gdns B2
Ely St B2
Evesham Rd C1
Fire Station B1
Foot Ferry C3
Fordham Ave A2
Garrick Way C1
Gower Memorial ✦ B3
Great William St B2
Greenhill St B2
Greenway, The C2
Grove Rd B2
Guild St B2
Guildhall & School B2
Hall's Croft C2
Harvard House B2
Henley St B2
Hertford Rd C1
High St B2
Holton St C2
Holy Trinity C2
Information Ctr B3
Jolyffe Park Rd A2
Kipling Rd C3
Library B2
Lodge Rd B1
Maidenhead Rd A3
Mansell St B2
Masons Court B2
Masons Rd A1
Maybird Shopping Park A2
Maybrook Retail Park A2
Maybrook Rd A1
Mayfield Ave A2
Meer St B2
Mill La C2
Moat House Hotel B3
Narrow La C2
Nash's House & New Place B2
New St C2
Old Town C2
Orchard Way C1
Other Place, The C2
Paddock La C1
Park Rd A1
Payton St B2
Percy St A2
Police Station B2
Post Office B2
Recreation Ground C2
Regal Road A2
Rother St B2
Rowley Cr A3
Royal Shakespeare Theatre B3
Ryland St C2
Saffron Meadow C2
St Andrew's Cr B1
St Gregory's A3
St Gregory's Rd A3
St Mary's Rd A2
Sanctus Dr C2
Sanctus St C1
Sandfield Rd C2
Scholars La B2
Seven Meadows Rd C2
Shakespeare Institute C2
Shakespeare St B2
Shakespeare's Birthplace ✦ B2
Sheep St B2
Shelley Rd C3
Shipston Rd C3
Shottery Rd C1
Slingates Rd A2
Southern La C2
Station Rd B1
Stratford Healthcare B2
Stratford Hospital B2
Stratford Leisure Centre B3
Stratford Sports Club B1
Stratford-upon-Avon Station B1
Swan Theatre B3
Swan's Nest La B3
Talbot Rd A2
Tiddington Rd B3
Timothy's Bridge Industrial Estate A1
Timothy's Bridge Rd A1
Town Hall & Council Offices B2
Town Sq B2
Trinity Cl C2
Tyler St B2
War Memorial Gdns B3
Warwick Rd B3
Waterside B3
Welcombe Rd A3
West St C2
Western Rd A2
Wharf Rd A2
Willows North, The B1
Willows, The B1
Wood St B2

Sunderland 348
Albion Pl C2
Alliance Pl B1
Argyle St C2
Ashwood St C1
Athenaeum St B2
Azalea Terr C2
Beach St A1
Bedford St B2
Beechwood Terr C1
Belvedere Rd C2
Blandford St B2
Borough Rd B3
Bridge Cr B2
Bridge St B2
Bridges, The B2
Brooke St A2
Brougham St B2
Burdon Rd C2
Burn Park C1
Burn Park Rd C1
Burn Park Tech Park C1
Carol St B1
Charles St A3
Chester Rd C1
Chester Terr B1
Church St A3
Civic Centre C2
Cork St B3
Coronation St B3
Cowan Terr C2
Dame Dorothy St A2
Deptford Rd B1
Deptford Terr A1
Derby St C2
Derwent St C2
Dock St A3
Dundas St A2
Durham Rd C1
Easington St A2
Egerton St C3
Empire B3
Empire Theatre B2
Farringdon Row B1
Fawcett St B2
Fire Station B1
Fox St C1
Foyle St B3
Frederick St B3
Hanover Pl A1
Havelock Terr C1
Hay St A2
Headworth Sq B3
Hendon Rd B3
High St East B3
High St West B2/B3
Holmeside B2
Hylton Rd B1
Information Ctr B2
John St B3
Kier Hardie Way A2
Lambton St B3
Laura St C3
Lawrence St B3
Library & Arts Centre B3
Lily St B1
Lime St B1
Livingstone Rd B2
Low Row B2
Matamba Terr B1
Millburn St B1
Millennium Way A2
Minster B2
Monkwearmouth Station Museum A2
Mowbray Park C3
Mowbray Rd C3
Murton St C3
National Glass Ctr ✦ A3
New Durham Rd C1
Newcastle Rd A2
Nile St B3
Norfolk St B3
North Bridge St A2
Northern Gallery for Contemporary Art B3
Otto Terr C1
Park La C2
Park Lane C2
Park Rd C2
Paul's Rd B3
Peel St C3
Point, The ✦ B2
Police Station B2
Priestly Cr A1
Queen St B2
Railway Row B1
Retail Park B1
Richmond St A2
Roker Ave A2
Royalty Theatre C1
Royalty, The C1
Ryhope Rd C2
St Mary's Way B2
St Michael's Way B2
St Peter's A3
St Peter's A2
St Peter's Way A3
St Vincent St C3
Salem Rd C3
Salem St C3
Salisbury St C3
Sans St B3
Shopmobility B2
Silkworth Row B1
Southwick Rd A2
Stadium of Light (Sunderland AFC) A2
Stadium Way A2
Stobart St A2
Stockton Rd C2
Suffolk St C3
Sunderland B2
Sunderland Aquatic Centre A2
Sunderland Mus B3
Sunderland St B3
Sunderland Station B2
Tatham St C3
Tavistock Pl B3
Thelma St C1
Thomas St North A2
Thornholme Rd C1
Toward Rd C3
Transport Interchange C2
Trimdon St Way B1
Tunstall Rd C2
University C1
University Library C1
University of Sunderland (City Campus) B1
University of Sunderland (Sir Tom Cowle at St Peter's Campus) A3
Vaux Brewery Way A2
Villiers St B3
Villiers St South B3
Vine Pl C2
Violet St B1
Walton La B3
Waterworks Rd B1
Wearmouth Bridge B2
West Sunniside B3
West Wear St B3
Westbourne Rd B1
Western Hill C1
Wharncliffe B1
Whickham St A3
White House Rd C3
Wilson St North A2
Winter Gdns C3
Wreath Quay A1

Swansea
Abertawe 348
Adelaide St C3
Albert Row C3
Alexandra Rd B3
Argyle St C1
Baptist Well Pl A2
Beach St C1
Belle Vue Way B3
Berw Rd A1
Berwick Terr A2
Bond St C1
Brangwyn Concert Hall C1
Bridge St A3
Brooklands Terrace B1
Brunswick St C1
Bryn-Syfi Terr A2
Bryn-y-Mor Rd C1
Bullins La B1
Burrows Rd C1
Bus Station C2
Bus/Rail link A3
Cadfan Rd A1
Cadrawd Rd A1
Caer St B3
Carig Cr A1
Carlton Terr B2
Carmarthen Rd A3
Castle Square B3
Castle St B3
Catherine St C1
Cinema C3
Civic Centre & Library C2
Clarence St C2
Colbourne Terr A2
Constitution Hill B1
Court B3
Creidiol Rd A2
Cromwell St B2
Crown Courts C1
Duke St B1
Dunvant Pl C2
Dyfatty Park A3
Dyfatty St A3
Dyfed Ave A1
Dylan Thomas Ctr ✦ B3
Dylan Thomas Theatre C3
Eaton Cr C1
Eigen Cr A1
Elfed Rd A1
Emlyn Rd A1
Evans Terr A3
Fairfield Terr B1
Ffynone Dr B1
Ffynone Rd B1
Fire Station B3
Firm St A2
Fleet St C1
Francis St C1
Fullers Row B2
George St B2
Glamorgan St C2
Glynn Vivian Art Gallery B3
Gower Coll Swansea C1
Graig Terr A3
Grand Theatre C3
Granogwen Rd A2
Guildhall C1
Guildhall Rd South C1
Gwent Rd A1
Gwynedd Ave A1
Hafod St A3
Hanover St B1
Harcourt St B2
Harries St A2
Heathfield B2
Henrietta St B1
Hewson St B2
High St A3/B3
High View A2
Hill St A2
Historic Ships Berth C3
HM Prison C2
Information Ctr C2
Islwyn Rd A1
King Edward's Rd C1
Kingsway, The B2
LC, The C3
Long Ridge A2
Madoc St C2
Mansel St B2
Maritime Quarter C3
Market B3
Mayhill Gdns B1
Mayhill Rd A1
Milton Terr A2
Mission Gallery C3
Montpelier Terr B1
Morfa Rd A3
Mount Pleasant B2
National Waterfront Museum C3
New Cut Rd A3
New St A3
Nicander Pde A2
Nicander Pl A2
Nicholl St B2
Norfolk St B2
North Hill Rd A2
Northampton La B2
Observatory ✦ C3
Orchard St B3
Oxford St B2
Oystermouth Rd C1
Page St B2
Pant-y-Celyn Rd B1
Parc Tawe North B3
Parc Tawe Shopping & Leisure Centre B3
Patti Pavilion C1
Paxton St C2
Pen-y-Graig Rd A1
Penmaen Terr B1
Phillips Pde C1
Picton Terr B2
Plantasia B3
Plantasia B3
Police Station B2
Post Office A1/A2/C1/C2
Powys Ave A1
Primrose St B2
Princess Way B3
Promenade B2
Pryder Gdns A1
Quadrant Shop Ctr C2
Quay Park B3
Rhianfa La B1
Rhondda St B2
Richardson St C2
Rodney St C1
Rose Hill B1
Rosehill Terr B1
Russell St B1
St David's Shop Ctr C3
St Helen's Ave C1
St Helen's Cr C1
St Helen's Rd C1
St James Gdns B1
St James's Cr B1
St Mary's B3
Sea View Terr A3
Singleton St C2
South Dock C3
Stanley Pl B2
Strand B3
Swansea Castle B3
Swansea Metropolitan University B2
Swansea Museum C3
Swansea Station A3
Taliesyn Rd B1
Tan y Marian Rd A1
Tegid Rd A2
Teilo Cr A1
Tenpin Bowling ✦ B3
Terrace Rd B1/B2
Tontine St A3
Townhill Rd A1
Tramshed, The C3
Trawler Rd C3
Union St B2
Upper Strand A3
Vernon St A3
Victoria Quay C3
Victoria Rd B3
Vincent St C1
Walter Rd B1
Watkin St A2
Waun-Wen Rd A2
Wellington St C2
Westbury St C1
Western St C1
Westway C2
William St C2
Wind St B3
Woodlands Terr B1
YMCA B2
York St C3

Swindon 349
Albert St C3
Albion St C1
Alfred St A2
Alvescot Rd C3
Art Gallery & Mus C3
Ashford Rd C1
Aylesbury St A2
Bath Rd C2
Bathampton St B1
Bathurst Rd B3
Beatrice St A2
Beckhampton St B3
Bowood Rd C1
Bristol St B1
Broad St A3
Brunel Arcade B2
Brunel Plaza B2
Brunswick St C2
Bus Station B2
Cambria Bridge Rd B1
Cambria Place B1
Canal Walk B2
Carfax St B2
Carr St B1
Cemetery C1/C3
Chandler Cl C3
Chapel C1
Chester St B1
Christ Church C3
Church Place B1
Cirencester Way A3
Clarence St B2
Clifton St C1
Cockleberry A2
Colbourne A3
Colbourne St A3
College St B2
Commercial Rd B2
Corporation St A2
Council Offices B3
County Rd A3
Courts B2
Cricket Ground A3
Cricklade Street C3
Crombey St B1/C2
Cross St C2
Curtis St B1
Deacon St C1
Designer Outlet (Great Western) B1
Dixon St C2
Dover St C2
Dowling St C2
Drove Rd C3
Dryden St C1
Durham St C3
East St B1
Eastcott Hill C2
Eastcott Rd C2
Edgeware Rd B2
Edmund St C2
Elmina Rd A3
Emlyn Square B1
Euclid St B3
Exeter St B1
Fairview C1
Faringdon Rd B1
Farnsby St B1
Fire Station B3
Fleet St B2
Fleming Way B2/B3
Florence St A2
Gladstone St A3
Gooch St A2
Graham St A3
Great Western Way A1/A2
Groundwell Rd B3
Hawksworth Way A1
Haydon St A2
Henry St B2
Hillside Ave C1
Holbrook Way B2
Hunt St C3
Hydro B1
Hythe Rd C2
Information Ctr B2
Joseph St C1
Kent Rd C2
King William St C2
Kingshill Rd C1
Lansdown Rd C2
Lawn, The C3
Leicester St B3
Library B2
Lincoln St B3
Little London C3
London St B1
Magic B3
Maidstone Rd C2
Manchester Rd A3
Maxwell St B1
Milford St B2
Milton Rd B1
Morse St C2
National Monuments Record Centre B1
Newcastle St B3
Newcombe Drive A1
Newcombe Trading Estate A1
Newhall St C2
North St C2
North Star A1
North Star Ave A1
Northampton St B3
Nurseries, The C1
Oasis Leisure Centre A1
Ocotal Way A3
Okus Rd C1
Old Town C3
Oxford St B1
Parade, The B2
Park Lane B1
Park Lane B1
Park, The B1
Pembroke St C2
Plymouth St B3
Polaris House A2
Polaris Way A2
Police Station B2
Ponting St A2
Post Office B1/B2/C1/C3
Poulton St A3
Princes St B2
Prospect Hill C2
Prospect Place C2
Queen St B2
Queen's Park C3
Radnor St C1
Read St C1
Reading St B1
Regent St B2
Retail Park A2/A3/B3
Rosebery St A3
St Mark's B1
Salisbury St A3
Savernake St C2
Shelley St C1
Sheppard St B1
South St C2
Southampton St B3
Spring Gardens B3
Stafford Street C2
Stanier St C2
Station Road A2
STEAM B1
Swindon College A2
Swindon Rd C2
Swindon Station A2
Swindon Town Football Club A3
T A Centre B1
Tennyson St B1
Theobald St B1
Town Hall B2
Transfer Bridges A3
Union St C2
Upham Rd C3
Victoria Rd C3
Walcot Rd B3
War Memorial ✦ B2
Wells St B3
Western St C2
Westmorland Rd B3
Whalebridge B2
Whitehead St C1
Whitehouse Rd A2
William St C1
Wood St C3
Wyvern Theatre & Arts Centre B2
York Rd B3

Taunton 349
Addison Gr A1
Albemarle Rd A1
Alfred St B3
Alma St C2
Avenue, The A1
Bath Pl C1
Belvedere Rd A1
Billet St B2
Billetfield C2
Birch Gr A1
Brewhouse Theatre B2
Bridge St B1
Bridgwater & Taunton Canal A2
Broadlands Rd C1
Burton Pl C1
Bus Station B1
Canal Rd A2
Cann St C1
Canon St B2
Castle B1
Castle St B1
Cheddon Rd A2
Chip Lane A1
Clarence St B1
Cleveland St B1
Clifton Terr A2
Coleridge Cres C3
Compass Hill C1
Compton Cl A2
Corporation St B1
Council Offices A1
County Walk Shopping Centre C2
Courtyard B2
Cranmer Rd B2
Crescent, The C1
Critchard Way B3
Cyril St A1
Deller's Wharf B1
Duke St B2
East Reach B3
East St B3
Eastbourne Rd B2
Eastleigh Rd C3
Eaton Cres A2
Elm Gr A1
Elms Cl A1
Fons George C1
Fore St B2
Fowler St A1
French Weir Rec Grd B1
Geoffrey Farrant Wk A2
Gray's Almshouses B2
Grays Rd B3
Greenway Ave A1
Guildford Pl C1
Hammet St B2
Haydon Rd B3
Heavitree Way A2
Herbert St A1
High St C2
Holway Ave C3
Hugo St B3
Huish's Almshouses B2
Hurdle Way C2
Information Ctr C2
Jubilee St A1
King's College C3
Kings Cl C3
Laburnum St B2
Lambrook Rd B3
Lansdowne Rd A3
Leslie Ave A1
Leycroft Rd B3
Library C2
Linden Gr A1
Magdalene St B2
Magistrates Court B1
Malvern Terr A2
Market House B2
Mary St C2
Middle St B2
Midford Rd B3
Mitre Court B3
Mount Nebo C1
Mount St C2
Mount, The C2
Mountway C2
Museum of Somerset B1
North St B2
Northern Inner Distributor Rd A1
Northfield Ave B1
Northfield Rd B1
Northleigh Rd C3
Obridge Allotments A3
Obridge Lane A3
Obridge Rd A3
Obridge Viaduct A3
Old Mkt Shopping Ctr C2
Osborne Way C1
Park St C1
Paul St C2
Plais St A2
Playing Field C3
Police Station C1
Portland St B1
Post Office B1/B2/C1
Priorswood Ind Est A3
Priorswood Rd A2
Priory Ave B2
Priory Bridge Rd B2
Priory Fields Retail Pk A3
Priory Park A2
Priory Way A3
Queen St B3
Railway St A1
Records Office A2
Recreation Grd A1
Riverside Place B2
St Augustine St B2
St George's C2
St Georges Sq C2
St James B2
St James St B2
St John's C1
St John's Rd B1
St Josephs Field C2
St Mary Magdalene's B2
Samuels Ct A1
Shire Hall & Law Courts C1
Somerset County Cricket Ground B2
Somerset County Hall C1
Somerset Cricket B2
South Rd C3
South St C3
Staplegrove Rd B1
Station Rd A1
Stephen St B2
Swimming Pool A1
Tancred St B2
Tauntfield Cl C3
Taunton Dean Cricket Club C2
Taunton Station A2
Thomas St A1
Toneway A3
Tower St B1
Trevor Smith Pl C3
Trinity Bsns Centre C3
Trinity Rd C3
Trinity St B3
Trull Rd C1
Tudor House B2
Upper High St C1
Venture Way A3
Victoria Gate B3
Victoria Park B3
Victoria St B3
Viney St B3
Vivary Park C2
Vivary Rd C1
War Memorial ✦ C1
Wellesley St A2
Wheatley Cres A3
Whitehall A1
Wilfred Rd B3
William St A1
Wilton Church C1
Wilton Cl C1
Wilton Gr C1
Wilton St C1
Winchester St B2
Winters Field B2
Wood St B1
Yarde Pl B1

Telford 349
Alma Ave C1
Amphitheatre C2
Bowling Alley B2
Brandsfarm Way C3
Brunel Rd B1
Bus Station B2
Buxton Rd C1
Central Park A2
Civic Offices B2
Coach Central B2
Coachwell Cl B1
Colliers Way A1
Courts B2
Dale Acre Way B3
Darliston C3
Deepdale B3
Deercote B2
Dinthill C3
Doddington C3
Dodmoor Grange C3
Downemead B3
Duffryn B3
Dunsheath B3
Euston Way A3
Eyton Mound C1
Eyton Rd C1
Forgegate A2
Grange Central B2
Hall Park Way B1
Hinkshay Rd C2
Hollinsworth Rd A2
Holyhead Rd A3
Housing Trust A1
Ice Rink B2
Information Ctr B2
Ironmasters Way A2
Job Centre B1
Land Registry B1
Lawn Central B2
Lawnswood C1
Library B2
Malinsgate B1
Matlock Ave C1
Moor Rd C1
Mount Rd C1
NFU Offices B1
Odeon B2
Park Lane A1
Police Station B1
Priorslee Ave A3
Queen Elizabeth Ave C3
Queen Elizabeth Way B1
Queensway A2/B3
Rampart Way A2
Randlay Ave C3
Randlay Wood C3
Rhodes Ave C1
Royal Way B1
St Leonards Rd A1
St Quentin Gate B2
Shifnal Rd A3
Sixth Ave A1
Southwater One (SW1) B2
Southwater Way B1
Spout Lane C1
Spout Mound B1
Spout Way C1
Stafford Court B3
Stafford Park B3
Stirchley Ave C3
Stone Row C1
Telford Bridge Retail Park A1
Telford Central Sta A3
Telford Centre, The B2
Telford Forge Shopping Park A1
Telford Hornets RFC C2
Telford Int Ctr C2
Telford Way A3
Third Ave A2
Town Park C2
Town Park Visitor Ctr B2
Walker House B2
Wellswood Ave A2
West Centre Way B1
Withywood Drive C1
Woodhouse Central B2
Yates Way A1

Torquay 349
Abbey Rd B2
Alexandra Rd A2
Alpine Rd B3
AMF Bowling C3
Ash Hill Rd A2
Babbacombe Rd B3
Bampfylde Rd B1
Barton Rd A1
Beacon Quay C2
Belgrave Rd A1/B1
Belmont Rd A3
Berea Rd A3
Braddons Hill Rd East B3
Brewery Park A3
Bronshill Rd A2
Castle Circus A2
Castle Rd A2
Cavern Rd A3
Central B2
Chatsworth Rd A2
Chestnut Ave B1
Church St A1
Civic Offices A2
Coach Station A1
Corbyn Head C1
Croft Hill B1
Croft Rd B1
East St A1
Egerton Rd A3
Ellacombe Church Rd A3
Ellacombe Rd A2
Falkland Rd B1
Fleet St B2
Fleet Walk Shopping Centre B2
Grafton Rd B3
Haldon Pier C2
Hatfield Rd A2
Highbury Rd A2
Higher Warberry Rd A3
Hillesdon Rd B3
Hoxton Rd A3
Hunsdon Rd B3
Information Ctr B2
Inner Harbour C3
Kenwyn Rd A3
King's Drive, The B1
Laburnum St A1
Law Courts A2
Library A2
Lime Ave B1
Living Coasts C3
Lower Warberry Rd B3
Lucius St B1
Lymington Rd A1
Magdalene Rd A1
Marina C2
Market Forum, The B2
Market St B2
Meadfoot Lane C3
Meadfoot Rd C3
Melville St B2
Middle Warberry Rd B3
Mill Lane A1
Montpellier Rd B3
Morgan Ave A1
Museum Rd B3
Newton Rd A1
Oakhill Rd A1
Outer Harbour C2
Parkhill Rd C3
Pavilion Shopping Ctr C2
Pimlico B2
Police Station A1
Post Office A1/B2
Prince of Wales Steps C3
Princes Rd A3
Princes Rd East A3
Princes Rd West A3
Princess Gdns C2
Princess Pier C2
Princess Theatre C2
Rathmore Rd B1
Recreation Grd B1
Riviera Int Ctr B1
Rock End Ave C3
Rock Rd B2
Rock Walk B2
Rosehill Rd A3
South West Coast Path C3
St Efride's Rd A1
St John's B3
St Luke's Rd B2
St Luke's Rd North B2
St Luke's Rd South B2
St Marychurch Rd A2
Scarborough Rd B1
Shedden Hill B2
South Pier C2
South St A1
Spanish Barn B1
Stitchill Rd B3
Strand B3
Sutherland Rd B3
Teignmouth Rd A1
Temperance St B2
Terrace, The B3
Thurlow Rd A1
Tor Bay B1
Tor Church Rd A1
Tor Hill Rd A1
Torbay Rd B2
Torquay Museum B3
Torquay Station C1
Torre Abbey Mansion B1
Torre Abbey Meadows B1
Torre Abbey Sands B1
Torwood Gdns B3
Torwood St C3
Town Hall A2
Union Sq Shopping Ctr A2
Union St A1
Upton Hill A2
Upton Park A1
Upton Rd A1
Vanehill Rd C3
Vansittart Rd A1
Vaughan Parade C2
Victoria Parade C3
Victoria Rd A2
Warberry Rd West B2
Warren Rd B2
Windsor Rd A2/A3
Woodville Rd A3

Truro 349
Adelaide Ter B1
Agar Rd B3
Arch Hill C2
Arundell Pl C2
Avenue, The A3
Avondale Rd B1
Back Quay B3
Barrack La C3
Barton Meadow A1
Benson Rd A2
Bishops Cl A2
Bosvean Gdns B1
Bosvigo Gardens B1
Bosvigo La A1
Bosvigo Rd B2
Broad St A3
Burley Cl C3
Bus Station B3
Calenick St B2
Campfield Hill B3
Carclew St B3
Carew Rd A2
Carey Park B2
Carlyon Rd A2
Carvoza Rd A3
Castle St B2
Cathedral View A2
Chainwalk Dr A2
Chapel Hill B1
Charles St B2
City Hall B3
City Rd B2
Coinage Hall B3
Comprigney Hill A1
Coosebean La A1
Copes Gdns A2
County Hall B1
Courtney Rd A2
Crescent Rd B1
Crescent Rise B1
Crescent, The B1
Daniell Court C2
Daniell Rd C2
Daniell St C2
Daubuz Cl A2
Dobbs La B1
Edward St B2
Eliot Rd A2
Elm Court A3
Enys Cl A1
Enys Rd A1
Fairmantle St B3
Falmouth Rd C2
Ferris Town B2
Fire Station B1
Frances St B2
George St B2
Green Cl C2
Green La C1
Grenville Rd A2
Hall For Cornwall B3
Hendra Rd A2
Hendra Vean A1
High Cross B3
Higher Newham La C3
Higher Trehaverne A2
Hillcrest Ave B1
Hospital B2
Hunkin Cl A2
Hurland Rd C3
Infirmary Hill B2
James Pl B3
Kenwyn Church Rd A1
Kenwyn Hill A1
Kenwyn Rd A2
Kenwyn St B2
Kerris Gdns A1
King St B3
Leats, The B2

Lemon Quay B3
Lemon St Gallery B3
Library B1/B3
Malpas Rd B3
Market
Memorial Gdns B3
Merrifield Close B1
Mitchell Hill A3
Moresk Cl A3
Moresk Rd A3
Morlaix Ave C3
Nancemere Rd A3
Newham Bsns Park C3
Newham Industrial Est C3
Newham Rd C3
Northfield Dr C3
Oak Way A3
Pal's Terr A3
Park View C2
Pendarves Rd A2
Plaza Cinema B3
Police Station B3
Post Office B2/B3
Prince's St B3
Pydar St A2
Quay St B3
Redannick Cres C2
Redannick La B2
Richard Lander Monument C2
Richmond Hill B1
River St B2
Rosedale Rd A2
Royal Cornwall Mus B2
St Aubyn Rd C3
St Clement St B3
St George's Rd A1
School La C2
Spires, The A2
Station Rd B1
Stokes Rd A2
Strangways Terr C3
Tabernacle St B3
Trehaverne La A2
Tremayne Rd A2
Treseder's Gdns A3
Treworder Rd B1
Treyew Rd B1
Truro Cathedral B3
Truro Harbour Office B3
Truro Station B3
Union St B2
Upper School La C2
Victoria Gdns B2
Waterfall Gdns B2

Wick 349

Ackergill Cres A2
Ackergill St A2
Albert St C2
Ambulance Station A2
Argyle Sq C2
Assembly Rooms C2
Bank Row C2
Bankhead B1
Barons Well B2
Barrogill St C2
Bay View B3
Bexley Terr C3
Bignold Park C2
Bowling Green C2
Breadalbane Terr C2
Bridge of Wick B1
Bridge St B2
Brown Pl C2
Burn St B2
Bus Station B1
Caithness General Hospital (A&E) B1
Cliff Rd B1
Coach Rd B2
Coastguard Station C3
Corner Cres B3
Coronation St C1
Council Offices B2
Court B2
Crane Rock C3
Dempster St C2
Dunnet Ave A2
Fire Station B2
Francis St C1
George St A1
Girnigoe St B2
Glamis Rd B2
Gowrie Pl B1
Grant St C2
Green Rd B2
Gunns Terr B3
Harbour Quay B2
Harbour Rd C3
Harbour Terr C2
Harrow Hill C2
Henrietta St A2/B2
Heritage Museum C2
High St B2
Hill Ave A2
Hillhead Rd B3
Hood St C1
Huddart St C2
Kenneth St C1
Kinnaird St C2
Kirk Hill B1
Langwell Cres B3
Leishman Ave B3
Leith Walk A2
Library B2
Lifeboat Station C3
Lighthouse C3
Lindsay Dr B3
Lindsay Pl B3
Loch St C2
Louisburgh St B2
Lower Dunbar St C2
Macleay La B1
Macleod Rd B3
MacRae St C2
Martha Terr B2
Miller Ave B1
Miller La B1
Moray St C2
Mowat Pl B3
Murchison St C3
Newton Ave C1
Newton Rd C1
Nicolson St C3
North Highland Coll B2
North River Pier B3
Northcote St C2
Owen Pl A2
Police Station B1
Port Dunbar B3
Post Office B2/C2
Pulteney Distillery C2
River St B2
Robert St A1
Rutherford St C2
St John's Episcopal C2
Sandigoe Rd B3
Scalesburn B3
Seaforth Ave C1
Shore La B2
Shore, The B2
Sinclair Dr B3
Sinclair Terr C2
Smith Terr C3
South Pier C3
South Quay C3
South Rd C1
South River Pier B3
Station Rd B1
Superstore A1/B1
Swimming Pool B2
Telford St B2
Thurso Rd B1
Thurso St B1
Town Hall B2
Union St B2
Upper Dunbar St C2
Vansittart St C3
Victoria Pl B2
War Memorial A1
Well of Cairndhuna C3
Wellington Ave C3
Wellington St C3
West Banks Ave C1
West Banks Terr C1
West Park C1
Whitehorse Park B2
Wick Harbour Bridge B2
Wick Industrial Estate A2
Wick Parish Church B1
Wick Station B1
Williamson St B2
Willowbank B2

Winchester 350

Andover Rd A2
Andover Rd Retail Pk A2
Archery La C2
Arthur Rd A2
Bar End Rd C3
Beaufort Rd C2
Beggar's La B3
Bereweeke Ave A1
Bereweeke Rd A1
Boscobel Rd A2
Brassey Rd A2
Broadway B3
Brooks Shopping Centre, The B3
Bus Station B3
Butter Cross B2
Canon St C2
Castle Wall C2/C3
Castle, King Arthur's Round Table B2
Cathedral C2
Cheriton Rd A1
Chesil St C3
Chesil Theatre C3
Christchurch Rd C1
City Mill B3
City Museum B2
City Rd B2
Clifton Rd B1
Clifton Terr B2
Close Wall C2/C3
Coach Park A2
Colebrook St C3
College St C2
College Walk C3
Compton Rd C2
Council Offices C3
County Council Offices B2
Cranworth Rd A2
Cromwell Rd C1
Culver Rd C2
Domum Rd C3
Durngate Pl B3
Eastgate St B3
Edgar Rd C2
Egbert Rd A2
Elm Rd B2
Everyman C2
Fairfield Rd A1
Fire Station B3
Fordington Ave B1
Fordington Rd A1
Friarsgate B3
Gordon Rd B3
Greenhill Rd B1
Guildhall B3
Hatherley Rd A1
High St B2
Hillier Way A3
HM Prison B1
Hyde Abbey (Remains) A2
Hyde Abbey Rd B2
Hyde Cl A2
Hyde St A2
Information Ctr B3
Jane Austen's Ho C2
Jewry St B2
King Alfred Pl A2
Kingsgate Arch C2
Kingsgate Park C2
Kingsgate Rd C2
Kingsgate St C2
Lankhills Rd A2
Law Courts B2
Library B2
Lower Brook St B3
Magdalen Hill B3
Market La B2
Mews La B1
Middle Brook St B3
Middle Rd B1
Military Museums B2
Milland Rd C3
Milverton Rd B1
Monks Rd A3
North Hill Cl A2
North Walls B2
North Walls Rec Gnd A3
Nuns Rd A3
Oram's Arbour B1
Owens Rd A2
Parchment St B2
Park & Ride C3
Park Ave B3
Playing Field A1
Police HQ B2
Portal Rd C3
Post Office B2/C1
Quarry Rd C3
Ranelagh Rd C1
Regiment Museum B2
River Park Leisure Ctr B3
Romans' Rd C2
Romsey Rd B1
Royal Hampshire County Hospital (A&E) B1
St Cross Rd C2
St George's St B2
St Giles Hill C3
St James Villas C2
St James' La B1
St James' Terr B1
St John's B3
St John's St B3
St Michael's Rd C2
St Paul's Hill B1
St Peter St B2
St Swithun St C2
St Thomas St C2
Saxon Rd A2
School of Art B3
Sleepers Hill Rd C1
Southgate St B2
Sparkford Rd C1
Square, The B2
Staple Gdns B2
Station Rd B2
Step Terr B1
Stockbridge Rd A1
Stuart Cres C1
Sussex St B2
Swan Lane B2
Tanner St B3
Theatre Royal B2
Tower St B2
Union St B3
Univ of Southampton (Winchester School of Art) B3
University of Winchester (King Alfred Campus) C1
Upper Brook St B2
Wales St B3
Water Lane B3
Weirs, The C3
West End Terr B1
Western Rd B1
Westgate B2
Wharf Hill C3
Winchester College C2
Winchester Station A2
Winnall Moors Wildlife Reserve A3
Wolvesey Castle C3
Worthy Lane A2
Worthy Rd A2

Windsor 350

Adelaide Sq C3
Albany Rd C2
Albert St B1
Alexandra Gdns B2
Alexandra Rd C2
Alma Rd B2
Ambulance Station B1
Arthur Rd B2
Bachelors Acre B3
Barry Ave B2
Beaumont Rd C2
Bexley St B1
Boat House B2
Brocas St B2
Brocas, The A2
Brook St C3
Bulkeley Ave C1
Castle Hill B3
Charles St B2
Claremont Rd C2
Clarence Cr B2
Clarence Rd B1
Clewer Court Rd B1
Coach Park B2
College Cr C1
Courts C2
Cricket Club A3
Cricket Ground C3
Dagmar Rd C2
Datchet Rd B3
Devereux Rd C2
Dorset Rd C2
Duke St B1
Elm Rd C1
Eton College A3
Eton Ct A2
Eton Sq A2
Eton Wick Rd A2
Farm Yard B3
Fire Station C2
Frances Rd C2
Frogmore Dr B3
Gloucester Pl C3
Goslar Way C1
Goswell Hill B2
Goswell Rd B2
Green La C1
Grove Rd C2
Guildhall B3
Helena Rd C2
Helston La B1
High St A2/B3
Holy Trinity C2
Home Park, The A3/C3
Hospital (Private) C2
Household Cavalry C2
Imperial Rd C1
Information Ctr B2/B3
Keats La A2
King Edward Ct B2
King Edward VII Ave A3
King Edward VII Hospital C2
King George V Meml B3
King Stable St A2
King's Rd C3
Library C2
Long Walk, The C3
Maidenhead Rd B1
Meadow La A2
Municipal Offices C3
Nell Gwynne's Ho B3
Osborne Rd C2
Oxford Rd B1
Park St B3
Peascod St B2
Police Station C2
Post Office A2
Princess Margaret Hospital C2
Queen Victoria's Walk B3
Queen's Rd C2
River St B2
Romney Island A3
Romney Lock A3
Romney Lock Rd A3
Russell St C2
St John's B3
St John's Chapel A2
St Leonards Rd C2
St Mark's Rd C2
Sheet St C3
South Meadow A2
South Meadow La A2
Springfield Rd C1
Stovell Rd B1
Sunbury Rd A3
Tangier La A2
Tangier St A3
Temple Rd C2
Thames St B3
Theatre Royal B3
Trinity Pl C2
Vansittart Rd B1/C1
Vansittart Rd Gdns C1
Victoria Barracks C2
Victoria St C2
Ward Royal B2
Westmead C1
White Lilies Island A1
William St B2
Windsor & Eton Central B2
Windsor & Eton Riverside A3
Windsor Arts Ctr C2
Windsor Bridge B3
Windsor Castle B3
Windsor Great Park C3
Windsor Leisure Ctr B1
Windsor Relief Rd A1
Windsor Royal Shopping B2
York Ave C1
York Rd C1

Wolverhampton 350

Albion St B3
Alexandra St C1
Arena B2
Arts Gallery B2
Ashland St C1
Austin St A1
Badger Dr A3
Bailey St B3
Bath Ave B1
Bath Rd B1
Bell St C2
Berry St B3
Bilston Rd C3
Bilston St C3
Birmingham Canal A3
Bone Mill La A2
Brewery Rd B1
Bright St A1
Burton Cres B3
Bus Station B3
Cambridge St A3
Camp St B2
Cannock Rd A3
Castle St C2
Chapel Ash C1
Cherry St C1
Chester St A1
Church La C2
Church St C2
Civic Centre B2
Civic Hall B2
Clarence Rd B2
Cleveland St C2
Clifton St C1
Coach Station B2
Compton Rd B1
Corn Hill B3
Coven St A3
Craddock St A1
Cross St North A2
Crown & County Courts C3
Crown St A2
Culwell St B3
Dale St C1
Darlington St C1
Devon Rd A1
Drummond St B2
Dudley Rd C2
Dudley St B2
Duke St C3
Dunkley St B1
Dunstall Ave A2
Dunstall Hill A2
Dunstall Rd A1/A2
Evans St A1
Fawdry St A1
Field St B3
Fire Station C1
Fiveways A2
Fowler Playing Fields A3
Fox's La A2
Francis St A2
Fryer St B3
Gloucester St A1
Gordon St C3
Graiseley St C1
Grand B3
Granville St C3
Great Brickkiln St C1
Great Hampton St A1
Great Western St A2
Grimstone St B3
Harrow St A1
Hilton St A3
Horseley Fields C3
Humber Rd C1
Jack Hayward Way A2
Jameson St A1
Jenner St C3
Kennedy Rd B3
Kimberley St C1
King St B2
Laburnum St C1
Lansdowne Rd B1
Leicester St A1
Lever St C3
Library C3
Lichfield St B2
Light House B3
Little's La B3
Lock St A3
Lord St C1
Lowe St A1
Maltings, The B2
Mander Centre C2
Mander St C3
Market C2
Market St B2
Maxwell Rd C3
Merridale St C1
Middlecross C3
Molineux St B2
Mostyn St A1
New Hampton Rd East A1
Nine Elms La A3
North Rd A2
Oaks Cres C1
Oxley St A2
Paget St A1
Park Ave B1
Park Road East A1
Park Road West B1
Paul St C2
Pelham St C1
Penn Rd C2
Piper's Row B3
Pitt St C2
Police Station C3
Pool St C2
Poole St A3
Post Office A1/B2/B2/C2
Powlett St C3
Queen St B2
Raby St C3
Railway Dr B3
Red Hill St A2
Red Lion St B2
Retreat St C1
Ring Rd B2
Royal, The C3
Rugby St A1
Russell St C1
St Andrew's B1
St David's B3
St George's C3
St George's Pde C2
St James St C3
St John's C2
St John's C2
St John's Retail Park C2
St John's Square C2
St Mark's C1
St Marks Rd C1
St Marks St C1
St Patrick's B2
St Peter's B2
St Peter's B2
Salisbury St C1
Salop St C2
School St C2
Sherwood St A2
Smestow St A3
Snow Hill C2
Springfield Rd A3
Stafford St A2/B2
Staveley Rd A1
Steelhouse La C3
Stephenson St C1
Stewart St C2
Sun St B3
Tempest St C2
Temple St C2
Tettenhall Rd B1
Thomas St C2
Thornley St B2
Tower St C2
University B2
Upper Zoar St C1
Vicarage Rd C3
Victoria St C2
Walpole St A1
Walsall St C3
Ward St C3
Warwick St C3
Water St A3
Waterloo Rd B2
Wednesfield Rd B3
West Park (not A&E) B1
West Park Swimming Pool B1
Wharf St C3
Whitmore Hill B2
Wolverhampton B3
Wolverhampton St George's C2
Wolverhampton Wanderers Football Gnd (Molineux) B2
Worcester St C2
Wulfrun Centre C2
Yarwell Cl A3
York St C3
Zoar St C1

Worcester 350

Albany Terr A1
Angel Pl B2
Angel St B2
Ashcroft Rd A2
Athelstan Rd C3
Avenue, The C1
Back Lane North A1
Back Lane South A1
Barbourne Rd A2
Bath Rd C2
Battenhall Rd C3
Bridge St B2
Britannia Sq A1
Broad St B2
Bromwich La C1
Bromwich Rd C1
Bromyard Rd C1
Bus Station B2
Butts, The B2
Carden St B3
Castle St A2
Cathedral C2
Cathedral Plaza B2
Charles St B3
Chequers La B1
Chestnut St A2
Chestnut Walk A2
Citizens' Advice Bureau B2
City Walls Rd B2
Cole Hill C3
College of Technology B2
College St C2
Commandery, The C3
Cripplegate Park B1
Croft Rd B1
Cromwell St B3
Cross, The B2
CrownGate Ctr B2
Deansway B2
Diglis Pde C2
Diglis Rd C2
Edgar Tower C2
Farrier St A2
Foregate St B2
Foregate Street B2
Fort Royal Hill C3
Fort Royal Park C3
Foundry St B3
Friar St C2
George St B3
Grand Stand Rd B1
Greenhill C3
Greyfriars B2
Guildhall B2
Henwick Rd B1
High St B2
Hill St B3
Hive, The B2
Huntingdon Hall B2
Hylton Rd B1
Information Ctr B2
King Charles Place Shopping Centre C1
King's School C2
King's School Playing Field C2
Kleve Walk C2
Lansdowne Cr A3
Lansdowne Rd A3
Lansdowne Walk A3
Laslett St A3
Leisure Centre A3
Little Chestnut St A2
Little London A2
London Rd C3
Lowell St A3
Lowesmoor B2
Lowesmoor Terr A3
Lowesmoor Wharf A3
Magistrates Court A2
Midland Rd B3
Mill St C2
Moors Severn Terrace, The A1
Mus & Art Gallery A2
Museum of Royal Worcester C2
New Rd C1
New St B2
Northfield St A2
Odeon B2
Padmore St B3
Park St C3
Pheasant St B3
Pitchcroft Racecourse A1
Police Station A2
Portland St C2
Post Office B2
Quay St B2
Queen St B2
Rainbow Hill A3
Recreation Ground A2
Reindeer Court B2
Rogers Hill A3
Sabrina Terr A1
St Dunstan's Cr C3
St John's C1
St Martin's Gate B3
St Martin's Quarter B3
St Oswald's Rd A2
St Paul's St B3
St Swithin's Church B2
St Wulstans Cr C3
Sansome Walk A2
Severn St C2
Shambles, The B2
Shaw St B2
Shire Hall Crown Ct A2
Shrub Hill B3
Shrub Hill Rd B3
Shrub Hill Retail Park B3
Slingpool Walk C1
South Parade B2
Southfield St A2
Sports Ground A2/C1
Stanley Rd B3
Swan, The A1
Swimming Pool A2
Tallow Hill B3
Tennis Walk A2
Tolladine Rd B3
Tudor House B2
Tybridge St B1
Tything, The A2
Univ of Worcester B2
Vincent Rd B3
Vue C2
Washington St A3
Woolhope Rd C3
Worcester Bridge B2
Worcester County Cricket Ground C1
Worcester Royal Grammar School A2
Wylds La C3

Wrexham Wrecsam 350

Abbot St B2
Acton Rd A3
Albert St C3
Alexandra Rd C1
Aran Rd A3
Barnfield C3
Bath Rd C2
Beeches, The A3
Beechley Rd C3
Belgrave Rd C2
Belle Vue Park C2
Belle Vue Rd C2
Belvedere Dr A1
Bennion's Rd C3
Berse Rd A1
Bersham Rd C1
Birch St C3
Bodhyfryd B3
Border Retail Park B3
Bradley Rd C2
Bright St B1
Bron-y-Nant B1
Brook St C2
Bryn-y-Cabanau Rd C3
Bury St C3
Bus Station B2
Butchers Market B3
Caia Rd C3
Cambrian Ind Est C3
Caxton Pl B2
Cemetery C1
Centenary Rd C1
Chapel St C2
Charles St B3
Chester Rd A3
Chester St B3
Cilcen Gr A3
Citizens Advice Bureau B2
Cobden Rd B1
Council Offices B3
County B2
Crescent Rd B3
Crispin La A2
Croesnewyth Rd B1
Cross St A2
Cunliffe St A2
Derby Rd C3
Dolydd Rd B1
Duke St B2
Eagles Meadow C3
Earle St C2
East Ave A2
Edward St C2
Egerton St B2
Empress Rd C1
Erddig Rd C2
Fairy Rd C2
Fire Station B2
Foster Rd A3
Foxwood Dr C1
Garden Rd A2
General Market B3
Gerald St B2
Gibson St C1
Glyndŵr University Plas Coch Campus A1
Greenbank St C3
Greenfield A2
Grosvenor Rd B2
Grove Park B2
Grove Park Rd B3
Grove Rd A3
Guildhall B2
Haig Rd C2
Hampden Rd C2
Hazel Gr A3
Henblas St B3
High St B3
Hightown Rd C3
Hill St B2
Holt Rd B3
Holt St B3
Hope St B2
Huntroyde Ave C3
Information Ctr B3
Island Gn Shopping Ctr B2
Job Centre B2
Jubilee Rd B2
King St B2
Kingsmills Rd C3
Lambpit St B3
Law Courts B3
Lawson Cl A3
Lawson Rd A3
Lea Rd C2
Library & Arts Centre B2
Lilac Way B1
Llys David Lord B1
Lorne St A2
Maesgwyn Rd B1
Maesydre Rd A3
Manley Rd B3
Market St B3
Mawddy Ave A2
Mayville Ave A2
Memorial Gallery B2
Memorial Hall B3
Mold Rd A1
Mount St C3
Neville Cres A3
New Rd A2
North Wales Regional Tennis Centre A1
North Wales School of Art & Design B2
Oak Dr A3
Park Ave A3
Park St A2
Peel St C1
Pen y Bryn C2
Pentre Felin C2
Penymaes Ave A3
Peoples Market B3
Percy St C2
Pines, The A3
Plas Coch Rd A1
Plas Coch Retail Park A1
Police Station B3
Poplar Rd C2
Post Office A2/B2/C2/C3
Powell Rd B3
Poyser St C2
Price's La A2
Primose Way B1
Princess St C1
Queen St B3
Queens Sq B2
Regent St B2
Rhosddu Rd A2/B2
Rhosnesni La A3
Rivulet Rd C3
Ruabon Rd C2
Ruthin Rd C1/C2
St Giles C3
St Giles Way C3
St James Ct A2
St Mary's B2
Salisbury Rd C3
Salop Rd C3
Sontley Rd C2
Spring Rd A2
Stanley St C3
Stansty Rd A2
Station Approach B2
Studio B2
Talbot Rd C2
Techniquest Glyndŵr A2
Town Hill C2
Trevor St C2
Trinity St B2
Tuttle St C3
Vale Park A1
Vernon St B2
Vicarage Hill B2
Victoria Rd C2
Walnut St A2
War Memorial B3
Waterworld L Ctr B3
Watery Rd B1/B2
Wellington Rd C2
Westminster Dr A3
William Aston Hall A1
Windsor Rd A1
Wrecsam
Wrexham AFC A1
Wrexham Central B2
Wrexham General B2
Wrexham Maelor Hospital (A&E) B1
Wrexham Technology Park B1
Wynn Ave A2
Yale College B3
Yale Gr A3
Yorke St C3

York 350

Aldwark B2
Barbican Rd C3
Bar Convent Living Heritage Ctr C1
Barley Hall B2
Bishopgate St C2
Bishopthorpe Rd C2
Blossom St C1
Bootham A1
Bootham Cr A1
Bootham Terr A1
Bridge St B2
Brook St A2
Brownlow St A2
Burton Stone La A1
Castle Museum C2
Castlegate B2
Cemetery Rd C3
Cherry St C2
City Screen B2
City Wall A2/B1/C3
Clarence St A2
Clementhorpe C2
Clifford St B2
Clifford's Tower B2
Clifton A1
Coach park A2
Coney St B2
Coppergate Ctr B2
Cromwell Rd C2
Crown Court C2
Davygate B2
Deanery Gdns A2
DIG B2
Ebor Industrial Estate B3
Fairfax House B2
Fishergate C3
Foss Islands Rd B3
Foss Islands Retail Pk B3
Fossbank A3
Garden St A2
George St C3
Gillygate A2
Goodramgate B2
Grand Opera House B2
Grosvenor Terr A1
Guildhall B2
Hallfield Rd A3
Heslington Rd C3
Heworth Green A3
Holy Trinity B2
Hope St C3
Huntington Rd A3
Information Ctr B2
James St B3
Jorvik Viking Ctr B2
Kent St C3
Lawrence St C3
Layerthorpe A3
Leeman Rd B1
Lendal B2
Lendal Bridge B1
Library A2/B1
Longfield Terr A1
Lord Mayor's Walk A2
Lower Eldon St A2
Lowther St A2
Mansion House B2
Margaret St C3
Marygate A1
Melbourne St C3
Merchant Adventurers' Hall B2
Merchant Taylors' Hall B2
Micklegate B1
Micklegate Bar C1
Monkgate A2
Moss St C1
Museum Gdns B1
Museum St B1
National Railway Museum B1
Navigation Rd B3
Newton Terr C2
North Pde A1
North St B2
Nunnery La C1
Nunthorpe Rd C1
Ouse Bridge B2
Paragon St C3
Park Gr A3
Park St C1
Parliament St B2
Peasholme Green B3
Penley's Grove St A2
Piccadilly B2
Police Station B2
Post Office B1/B2/C3
Priory St B1
Purey Cust Nuffield Hospital, The A2
Queen Anne's Rd A1
Reel C1
Regimental Mus B2
Richard III Experience at Monk Bar A2
Roman Bath B2
Rowntree Park C2
St Andrewgate B2
St Benedict Rd C1
St John St A2
St Olave's Rd A1
St Peter's Gr A1
St Saviourgate B2
Scarcroft Hill C1
Scarcroft Rd C1
Shambles, The B2
Shopmobility B2
Skeldergate C2
Skeldergate Bridge C2
Station Rd B1
Stonebow, The B2
Stonegate B2
Superstore A3
Sycamore Terr A1
Terry Ave C2
Theatre Royal B2
Thorpe St C1
Toft Green B1
Tower St C2
Townend St A2
Treasurer's House A2
Trinity La B1
Undercroft Mus A2
Union Terr A2
Victor St C2
Vine St C2
Walmgate B3
War Memorial B1
Wellington St C3
York Art Gallery A1
York Barbican C3
York Brewery B1
York Dungeon, The B2
York Minster A2
York St John Uni A2
York Station B1

Abbreviations used in the index

Aberdeen Aberdeen City
Aberds Aberdeenshire
Ald Alderney
Anglesey Isle of Anglesey
Angus Angus
Argyll Argyll and Bute
Bath Bath and North East Somerset
Bedford Bedford
Bl Gwent Blaenau Gwent
Blackburn Blackburn with Darwen
Blackpool Blackpool
Bmouth Bournemouth
Borders Scottish Borders
Brack Bracknell
Bridgend Bridgend
Brighton City of Brighton and Hove
Bristol City and County of Bristol
Bucks Buckinghamshire
C Beds Central Bedfordshire
Caerph Caerphilly
Cambs Cambridgeshire
Cardiff Cardiff
Carms Carmarthenshire
Ceredig Ceredigion
Ches E Cheshire East
Ches W Cheshire West and Chester
Clack Clackmannanshire
Conwy Conwy
Corn Cornwall
Cumb Cumbria
Darl Darlington
Denb Denbighshire
Derby City of Derby
Derbys Derbyshire
Devon Devon
Dorset Dorset
Dumfries Dumfries and Galloway
Dundee Dundee City
Durham Durham
E Ayrs East Ayrshire
E Dunb East Dunbartonshire
E Loth East Lothian
E Renf East Renfrewshire
E Sus East Sussex
E Yorks East Riding of Yorkshire
Edin City of Edinburgh
Essex Essex
Falk Falkirk
Fife Fife
Flint Flintshire
Glasgow City of Glasgow
Glos Gloucestershire
Gtr Man Greater Manchester
Gwyn Gwynedd
Halton Halton
Hants Hampshire
Hereford Herefordshire
Herts Hertfordshire
Highld Highland
Hrtlpl Hartlepool
Hull Hull
IoM Isle of Man
IoW Isle of Wight
Invclyd Inverclyde
Kent Kent
Lancs Lancashire
Leicester City of Leicester
Leics Leicestershire
Lincs Lincolnshire
London Greater London
Luton Luton
M Keynes Milton Keynes
M Tydf Merthyr Tydfil

Index to road maps of Britain

How to use the index

Example **Blatherwycke** Northants **137** D9

- grid square
- page number
- county or unitary authority

Mbro Middlesbrough
Medway Medway
Mers Merseyside
Midloth Midlothian
Mon Monmouthshire
Moray Moray
N Ayrs North Ayrshire
N Lincs North Lincolnshire
N Lanark North Lanarkshire
N Som North Somerset
N Yorks North Yorkshire
NE Lincs North East Lincolnshire
Neath Neath Port Talbot
Newport City and County of Newport
Norf Norfolk
Northants Northamptonshire
Northumb Northumberland
Nottingham City of Nottingham
Notts Nottinghamshire
Orkney Orkney
Oxon Oxfordshire
Pboro Peterborough
Pembs Pembrokeshire
Perth Perth and Kinross
Plym Plymouth
Poole Poole
Powys Powys
Ptsmth Portsmouth
Reading Reading
Redcar Redcar and Cleveland
Renfs Renfrewshire
Rhondda Rhondda Cynon Taff
Rutland Rutland
S Ayrs South Ayrshire
S Glos South Gloucestershire
S Lanark South Lanarkshire
S Yorks South Yorkshire
Scilly Scilly
Shetland Shetland
Shrops Shropshire
Slough Slough
Som Somerset
Soton Southampton
Staffs Staffordshire
Southend Southend-on-Sea
Stirling Stirling
Stockton Stockton-on-Tees
Stoke Stoke-on-Trent
Suff Suffolk
Sur Surrey
Swansea Swansea
Swindon Swindon
T&W Tyne and Wear
Telford Telford & Wrekin
Thurrock Thurrock
Torbay Torbay
Torf Torfaen
V Glam The Vale of Glamorgan
W Berks West Berkshire
W Dunb West Dunbartonshire
W Isles Western Isles
W Loth West Lothian
W Mid West Midlands
W Sus West Sussex
W Yorks West Yorkshire
Warks Warwickshire
Warr Warrington
Wilts Wiltshire
Windsor Windsor and Maidenhead
Wokingham Wokingham
Worcs Worcestershire
Wrex Wrexham
York City of York

A

Aaron's Hill Sur 50 E3
Aaron's Town Cumb 240 E2
Abbas Combe Som 30 C2
Abberley Worcs 116 D5
Abberton Essex 89 B8
Worcs 117 G9
Abberwick
Northumb 264 G4
Abbess End Essex 87 C9
Abbess Roding Essex 87 C9
Abbey Devon 27 E10
Abbeycwmhir
Powys 113 C11
Abbey-cwm-hir
Powys 113 C11
Abbeydale Glos 80 B5
S Yorks 186 E4
Abbeydale Park
S Yorks 186 E4
Abbey Dore Hereford 97 E7
Abbey Field Essex 107 G9
Abbey Gate Kent 53 B9
Abbey Green
Shrops 149 C10
Staffs 169 D7
Abbey Hey Gtr Man 184 B5
Abbeyhill Edin 280 G5
Abbey Hulton Stoke 168 F6
Abbey Mead Sur 66 F4
Abbey St Bathans
Borders 272 C5
Abbeystead Lancs 203 C7
Abbey Town Cumb 238 G5
Abbey Village Lancs 194 C6
Abbey Wood London 68 D3
Abbots Bickington
Devon 24 E5
Abbots Bromley
Staffs 151 E11
Abbotsbury Dorset 17 D7
Abbotsford W Sus 36 C4
Abbotsham Devon 24 B6
Abbotskerswell Devon 9 B7
Abbots Langley Herts 85 E9
Abbotsleigh Devon 8 F6
Abbots Leigh N Som 60 E4
Abbotsley Cambs 122 F4
Abbot's Meads
Ches W 166 B5
Abbots Morton
Worcs 117 F10
Abbots Ripton
Cambs 122 B4
Abbots Salford
Warks 117 G11
Abbotstone Hants 48 G5
Abbotswood Hants 32 C5
Sur 50 C4
Abbots Worthy Hants 48 G3
Abbotts Ann Hants 47 E10
Abcott Shrops 115 B7
Abdon Shrops 131 F11
Abdy S Yorks 186 B6
Aber Ceredig 93 B9
Aberaeron Ceredig 111 E9
Aberaman Rhondda 77 E8
Aberangell Gwyn 146 G6
Aber-Arad Carms 92 D6
Aberarder Highld 290 E6
Aberarder House
Highld 300 G6
Aberarder Lodge
Highld 291 E7
Aberargie Perth 286 F5
Aberarth Ceredig 111 E9
Aberavon Neath 57 C8
Aber-banc Ceredig 93 C7
Aberbargoed Caerph 77 E11
Aberbechan Powys 130 E2
Aberbeeg Bl Gwent 78 E2
Aberbran Powys 95 F9
Abercanaid M Tydf 77 E9
Abercarn Caerph 78 G2
Abercastle Pembs 91 E7
Abercegir Powys 128 C6
Aberchalder Highld 290 C5
Aberchirder Aberds 302 D6
Abercorn W Loth 279 F11
Aber Cowarch Gwyn 147 F7
Abercraf Powys 76 C4
Abercregan Neath 57 B11
Abercrombie Fife 287 G9
Abercwmboi Rhondda 77 F8
Abercych Pembs 92 C4
Abercynafon Powys 77 B9
Abercynffig /
Aberkenfig
Bridgend 57 E11
Abercynon Rhondda 77 F9
Aberdalgie Perth 286 E4
Aberdâr / Aberdare
Rhondda 77 E7
Aberdare / Aberdâr
Rhondda 77 E7
Aberdaron Gwyn 144 D3
Aberdeen
Aberdeen 293 C11
Aberdesach Gwyn 162 E6
Aberdour Fife 280 D3
Aberdovey / Aberdyfi
Gwyn 128 D2
Aberdulais Neath 76 E3
Aberdyfi / Aberdovey
Gwyn 128 D2
Aberedw Powys 95 B11
Abereiddy Pembs 90 E5
Abererch Gwyn 145 B7
Aberfan M Tydf 77 E9
Aberfeldy Perth 286 C2
Aberffraw Anglesey 162 B5
Aberffrwd
Ceredig 112 B3
Mon 78 D5
Aberford W Yorks 206 F4
Aberfoyle Stirling 285 G9
Abergarw Bridgend 58 C2
Abergarwed Neath 76 E4
Abergavenny Mon 78 C3
Abergele Conwy 180 F6
Aber-Giâr Carms 93 C10
Abergorlech Carms 93 E11
Abergwaun / Fishguard
Pembs 91 D9
Abergwesyn Powys 113 G7
Abergwili Carms 93 G8
Abergwynant Gwyn 146 F3
Abergwynfi Neath 57 B11
Aber-gwynfi Neath 57 B11
Abergwyngregyn
Gwyn 179 G11
Abergynolwyn Gwyn 128 B3
Aber-Hirnant Gwyn 147 C9
Aberhosan Powys 128 D6
Aberkenfig /
Abercynffig
Bridgend 57 E11
Aberlady E Loth 281 E9
Aberlemno Angus 287 B9
Aberlerry Ceredig 128 E2
Aberllefenni Gwyn 128 B5
Aberllydan / Broad
Haven Pembs 72 C5
Aberllynfi / Three Cocks
Powys 96 D3
Abermagwr Ceredig 112 C3
Abermaw / Barmouth
Gwyn 146 F2
Abermeurig
Ceredig 111 F11
Aber miwl / Abermule
Powys 130 E3
Abermorddu Flint 166 D4
Abermule / Aber-miwl
Powys 130 E3
Abernaint Powys 148 E2
Abernant Carms 92 G6
Powys 130 D3
Aber-nant Rhondda 77 E8
Abernethy Perth 286 F5
Abernyte Perth 286 D6
Aber-oer Wrex 166 F3
Aberogwr / Ogmore by
Sea V Glam 57 F11
Aberpennar / Mountain
Ash Rhondda 77 F8
Aberporth Ceredig 110 G5
Aber-Rhiwlech
Gwyn 147 E8
Aberriw / Berriew
Powys 130 C3
Abersoch Gwyn 144 D6
Abersychan Torf 78 E3
Abertawe / Swansea
Swansea 56 C6
Aberteifi / Cardigan
Ceredig 92 B3
Aberthin V Glam 58 D4
Abertillery Bl Gwent 78 E2
Abertridwr
Caerph 58 B6
Powys 147 F10
Abertrinant Gwyn 128 B2
Abertysswg Caerph 77 D10
Aberuchill Castle
Perth 285 E11
Aberuthven Perth 286 F3
Aber-Village Powys 96 G2
Aberyscir Powys 95 F9
Aberystwyth
Ceredig 111 A11
Abhainn Suidhe
W Isles 305 H2
Abingdon-on-Thames
Oxon 83 F7
Abinger Common
Sur 50 D6
Abinger Hammer Sur 50 D5
Abington Northants 120 E5
S Lanark 259 E10
Abington Pigotts
Cambs 104 C6
Abington Vale
Northants 120 E5
Abingworth W Sus 35 D10
Ab Kettleby Leics 154 E4
Ab Lench Worcs 117 G10
Ablington Glos 81 D10
Wilts 47 D7
Abney Derbys 185 F11
Aboyne Aberds 293 D7
Abraham Heights
Lancs 211 G9
Abram Gtr Man 194 G6
Abriachan Highld 300 F5
Abridge Essex 87 F7
Abronhill N Lanark 278 F5
Abshot Hants 33 F8
Abson S Glos 61 E8
Abthorpe Northants 102 B2
Abune-the-Hill
Orkney 314 D2
Aby Lincs 190 F6
Acaster Malbis York 207 D7
Acaster Selby
N Yorks 207 E7
Accrington Lancs 195 B9
Acha Argyll 275 B8
Argyll 288 D3
Achabraid Argyll 275 E9
Achachork Highld 298 E4
Achadh an Eas
Highld 308 F6
Achad nan Darach
Highld 284 B4
Achadunan Argyll 284 F5
Achafolla Argyll 275 B8
Achagary Highld 308 D7
Achaglass Argyll 255 C8
Achahoish Argyll 275 F8
Achalader Perth 286 C5
Achallader Argyll 285 C7
Achalone Highld 310 D5
Acha Mor W Isles 304 F5
Achanalt Highld 300 C2
Achanamara Argyll 275 E8
Achandunie Highld 300 B6
Achanelid Argyll 275 E11
Ach'an Todhair
Highld 290 F2
Achany Highld 309 J5
Achaphubuil Highld 290 F2
Acharacle Highld 289 C8
Acharn Highld 289 D9
Perth 285 C11
Acharole Highld 310 D6
Acharossan Argyll 275 F10
Acharry Muir Highld 309 K6
Achath Aberds 293 B9
Achavanich Highld 310 E5
Achavelgin Highld 301 D9
Achavraat Highld 301 E9
Achddu Carms 74 E6
Achdregnie Moray 302 G2
Achduart Highld 307 J5
Achentoul Highld 310 F2
Achfary Highld 306 F7
Achfrish Highld 309 H5
Achgarve Highld 307 K3
Achiemore Highld 308 C3
Highld 310 D2
A'Chill Highld 294 E4
Achiltibuie Highld 307 J5
Achina Highld 308 C7
Achinahuagh Highld 308 C5
Achindaul Highld 290 E3
Achindown Highld 301 E8
Achinduich Highld 309 J5
Achinduin Argyll 289 F10
Achingills Highld 310 C5
Achininver Highld 308 C5
Achintee Highld 290 F3
Highld 299 E9
Achintraid Highld 295 B10
Achlaven Argyll 289 F11
Achlean Highld 291 D10
Achleck Argyll 288 E6
Achlorachan Highld 300 D3
Achluachrach
Highld 290 E4
Achlyness Highld 306 D7
Achmelvich Highld 307 G5
Achmore Highld 295 B10
Stirling 285 D9
Achnaba Argyll 275 E10
Argyll 289 F11
Achnabat Highld 300 F5
Achnabreck Argyll 275 D9
Achnacarnin Highld 306 F5
Achnacarry Highld 290 E3
Achnacloich Argyll 289 F11
Highld 295 E7
Achnaconeran
Highld 290 B6
Achnacraig Argyll 288 E6
Achnacree Argyll 289 F11
Achnacree Bay
Argyll 289 F11
Achnacroish Argyll 289 E10
Achnadrish Argyll 288 D6
Achnafalnich Argyll 284 E6
Achnagarron Highld 300 C6
Achnaha Highld 288 C6
Achnahanat Highld 309 K5
Achnahannet Highld 301 G9
Achnahard Argyll 288 G5
Achnairn Highld 309 H5
Achnaluachrach
Highld 309 J6
Achnandarach
Highld 295 B10
Achnanellan Highld 290 E2
Achnasaul Highld 290 E3
Achnasheen Highld 299 D11
Achnashelloch
Argyll 275 D9
Achnavast Highld 310 C4
Achneigie Highld 299 B10
Achormlarie Highld 309 K6
Achorn Highld 310 F5
Achosnich Highld 288 C6
Achranich Highld 289 E9
Achreamie Highld 310 C4
Achriabhach Highld 290 G3
Achriesgill Highld 306 D7
Achrimsdale Highld 311 J3
Achtoty Highld 308 C6
Achurch Northants 137 G10
Achuvoldrach
Highld 308 D5
Achvaich Highld 309 K7
Achvarasdal Highld 310 C3
Ackenthwaite
Cumb 211 C10
Ackergill Highld 310 D7
Acklam Mbro 225 B9
N Yorks 216 G5
Ackleton Shrops 132 D5
Acklington
Northumb 252 C6
Ackton W Yorks 198 C2
Ackworth Moor Top
W Yorks 198 D2
Acle Norf 161 G8
Acock's Green
W Mid 134 G2
Acol Kent 71 F10
Acomb Northumb 241 D10
York 207 C7
Acre Gtr Man 196 F2
Lancs 195 C9
Acrefair Wrex 166 G3
Acres Nook Staffs 168 E4
Acre Street W Sus 21 B11
Acton Ches E 167 E10
Dorset 18 F5
London 67 C8
Shrops 130 G6
Staffs 168 G4
Suff 107 C7
Worcs 116 D6
Wrex 166 E4
Acton Beauchamp
Hereford 116 G3
Acton Bridge
Ches W 183 F9
Acton Burnell
Shrops 131 C10
Acton Green
Hereford 116 G3
London 67 D8
Acton Pigott
Shrops 131 C10
Acton Place Suff 107 B7
Acton Reynald
Shrops 149 E10
Acton Round
Shrops 132 D2
Acton Scott Shrops 131 F9
Acton Trussell
Staffs 151 F8
Acton Turville
S Glos 61 C10
Adabroc W Isles 304 B7
Adambrae W Loth 269 A10
Adam's Green Dorset 29 F8
Adbaston Staffs 150 D5
Adber Dorset 29 C9
Adbolton Notts 154 B2
Adderbury Oxon 101 D9
Adderley Shrops 150 B3
Adderley Green
Stoke 168 G6
Adderstone
Northumb 264 C4
Addiewell W Loth 269 C9
Addingham
W Yorks 205 D7
Addingham Moorside
W Yorks 205 D7
Addington Bucks 102 F4
Corn 6 B5
Kent 53 B7
London 67 G11
Addinston Borders 271 E10
Addiscombe London 67 F10
Addlestone Sur 66 G5
Addlestonemoor Sur 66 F4
Addlethorpe Lincs 175 B8
Adel W Yorks 205 F11
Adeney Telford 150 F4
Adeyfield Herts 85 D9
Adfa Powys 129 C11
Adforton Hereford 115 C8
Adgestone IoW 21 D7
Adisham Kent 55 C8
Adlestrop Glos 100 F4
Adlingfleet
E Yorks 199 C10
Adlington Ches E 184 E6
Lancs 194 E6
Adlington Park
Lancs 194 E5
Admaston Staffs 151 E10
Telford 150 G2
Admington Warks 100 B4
Adpar Ceredig 92 C6
Adsborough Som 28 B3
Adscombe Som 43 F7
Adstock Bucks 102 E4
Adstone Northants 119 G11
Adswood Gtr Man 184 D5
Adversane W Sus 35 C9
Advie Highld 301 F11
Adwalton W Yorks 197 B8
Adwell Oxon 83 F11
Adwick le Street
S Yorks 198 F4
Adwick upon Dearne
S Yorks 198 G3
Adziel Aberds 303 D9
Ae Dumfries 247 F11
Ae Village Dumfries 247 F11
Affetside Gtr Man 195 E9
Affleck Aberds 303 G8
Affpuddle Dorset 18 C2
Affric Lodge
Highld 299 G11
Afon Eitha Wrex 166 F3
Afon-wen Flint 181 G10
Afon Wen Gwyn 145 B8
Afton IoW 20 D2
Agar Nook Leics 153 G9
Agbrigg W Yorks 197 D10
Aggborough Worcs 116 B6
Agglethorpe
N Yorks 213 B11
Aglionby Cumb 239 F10
Agneash IoM 192 D5
Aifft Denb 165 B10
Aigburth Mers 182 D5
Aiginis W Isles 304 E6
Aike E Yorks 209 D7
Aikenway Moray 302 E2
Aikerness Orkney 314 A4
Aikers Orkney 314 G4
Aiketgate Cumb 230 B5
Aikton Cumb 239 G7
Ailby Lincs 190 F6
Ailey Hereford 96 B6
Ailstone Warks 118 G4
Ailsworth Pboro 138 D2
Aimes Green Essex 86 E5
Ainderby Quernhow
N Yorks 215 C7
Ainderby Steeple
N Yorks 224 G6
Aingers Green
Essex 108 G2
Ainley Top W Yorks 196 D6
Ainsdale Mers 193 E10
Ainsdale-on-Sea
Mers 193 E9
Ainstable Cumb 230 B6
Ainsworth Gtr Man 195 E9
Ainthorpe N Yorks 226 D4
Aintree Mers 182 B5
Aird Argyll 275 C8
Dumfries 236 C2
Highld 299 B7
W Isles 296 F3
W Isles 304 E7
Airdachuilinn Highld 306 E7
Aird a Mhachair
W Isles 297 G3
Aird a' Mhulaidh
W Isles 305 G3
Aird Asaig W Isles 305 H3
Aird Dhail W Isles 304 B6
Airdens Highld 309 K6
Airdeny Argyll 289 G11
Aird Mhidhinis
W Isles 297 L3
Aird Mhighe
W Isles 296 C6
W Isles 305 J3
Aird Mhòr W Isles 297 G4
Aird Mhor W Isles 297 L3
Aird of Sleat Highld 295 E7
Airdrie N Lanark 268 B5
Airds of Kells
Dumfries 237 B8
Aird Thunga
W Isles 304 E6
Airdtorrisdale
Highld 308 C6
Aird Uig W Isles 304 E2
Airedale W Yorks 198 B3
Aire View N Yorks 204 D5
Airidh a Bhruaich
W Isles 305 G4
Airieland Dumfries 237 D9
Airinis W Isles 304 E6
Airlie Angus 287 B7
Airlies Dumfries 236 D5
Airmyn E Yorks 199 B8
Airntully Perth 286 D4
Airor Highld 295 E9
Airth Falk 279 D7
Airthrey Castle
Stirling 278 B6
Airton N Yorks 204 B4
Airyhassen Dumfries 236 E5
Airy Hill N Yorks 227 D7
Airyligg Dumfries 236 C4
Aisby Lincs 155 B10
Lincs 188 C5
Aisgernis W Isles 297 J3
Aish Devon 8 C3
Devon 8 D6
Aisholt Som 43 F7
Aiskew N Yorks 214 B5
Aislaby N Yorks 216 B5
N Yorks 227 D7
Stockton 225 C8
Aisthorpe Lincs 188 E6
Aith Orkney 314 E2
Shetland 312 D8
Shetland 313 H5
Aithnen Powys 148 E4
Aithsetter Shetland 313 K6
Aitkenhead S Ayrs 245 B8
Aitnoch Highld 301 F9
Akeld Northumb 263 D11
Akeley Bucks 102 D4
Akenham Suff 108 B2
Albany T&W 243 F7
Albaston Corn 12 G4
Alberbury Shrops 149 G7
Albert Town Pembs 72 B6
Albert Village Leics 152 F6
Albourne W Sus 36 D3
Albourne Green
W Sus 36 D3
Albrighton Shrops 132 C6
Shrops 149 F9
Albro Castle Ceredig 92 B3
Alburgh Norf 142 F5
Albury Herts 105 G8
Sur 50 D5
Albury End Herts 105 G8
Albury Heath Sur 50 D5
Albyfield Cumb 240 G2
Alby Hill Norf 160 C3
Alcaig Highld 300 D5
Alcaston Shrops 131 F9
Alcester Dorset 30 C5
Warks 117 F11
Alcester Lane's End
W Mid 133 G11
Alciston E Sus 23 D8
Alcombe Som 42 D3
Wilts 61 F10
Alconbury Cambs 122 B3
Alconbury Weston
Cambs 122 B3
Aldbar Castle Angus 287 B9
Aldborough N Yorks 215 F8
Norf 160 C3
Aldborough Hatch
London 68 B3
Aldbourne Wilts 63 D9
Aldbrough E Yorks 209 F10
Aldbrough St John
N Yorks 224 C4
Aldbury Herts 85 C7
Aldcliffe Lancs 211 G9
Aldclune Perth 291 G11
Aldeburgh Suff 127 F9
Aldeby Norf 143 E8
Aldenham Herts 85 F10
Alderbrook E Sus 37 B8
Alderbury Wilts 31 B11
Aldercar Derbys 170 F6
Alderford Norf 160 F2
Alder Forest
Gtr Man 184 B3
Alderholt Dorset 31 E10
Alderley Glos 80 G3
Alderley Edge
Ches E 184 F4
Alderman's Green
W Mid 135 G7
Aldermaston
W Berks 64 F5
Aldermaston Soke
W Berks 64 G6
Aldermaston Wharf
W Berks 64 F6
Alderminster Warks 100 B4
Aldermoor Soton 32 D5
Alder Moor Staffs 152 D4
Alderney Poole 18 C6

B

370 Bar–Ber

Barbieston S Ayrs 257 F10
Barbon Cumb 212 C2
Barbourne Worcs 116 F6
Barbreck Ho Argyll 275 C9
Barbridge Ches E 167 D10
Barbrook Devon 41 D8
Barby Northants 119 C10
Barby Nortoft
Northants 119 C11
Barcaldine Argyll 289 E11
Barcelona Corn 6 E4
Barcheston Warks 100 D5
Barclose Cumb 239 E10
Barcombe E Sus 36 E6
Barcombe Cross
E Sus 36 D6
Barcroft W Yorks 204 F6
Barden N Yorks 224 G2
Bardennoch
Dumfries 246 E3
Barden Park Kent 52 D5
Barden Scale
N Yorks 205 B7
Bardfield End Green
Essex 106 E2
Bardfield Saling
Essex 106 F3
Bardister Shetland 312 F5
Bardnabeinne
Highld 309 K7
Bardney Lincs 173 B10
Bardon Leics 153 G8
Bardon Mill
Northumb 241 E7
Bardowie E Dunb 277 G11
Bardown E Sus 37 B11
Bardrainney Invclyd 276 G6
Bardrishaig Argyll 275 B8
Bardsea Cumb 210 E6
Bardsey W Yorks 206 E3
Bardsley Gtr Man 196 G2
Bardwell Suff 125 C8
Bare Lancs 211 G9
Bare Ash Som 43 F9
Bareless Northumb 263 B9
Bar End Hants 33 B7
Barepot Cumb 228 F6
Bareppa Corn 3 D7
Barfad Argyll 275 G9
Dumfries 236 C5
Barford Norf 142 B2
Sur 49 F11
Warks 118 E5
Barford St John
Oxon 101 E8
Barford St Martin
Wilts 46 G5
Barford St Michael
Oxon 101 E8
Barfrestone Kent 55 C9
Bargaly Dumfries 236 C6
Bargarran Renfs 277 G9
Bargate Derbys 170 F5
Bargeddie N Lanark 268 C4
Bargoed Caerph 77 F10
Bargrennan
Dumfries 236 B5
Barham Cambs 122 B2
Kent 55 C8
Suff 126 G2
Barharrow Dumfries 237 D8
Barhill Dumfries 237 C10
Bar Hill Cambs 123 E7
Staffs 168 G3
Barholm Dumfries 237 D7
Lincs 155 G11
Barkby Leics 136 B2
Barkby Thorpe
Leics 136 B2
Barkers Green
Shrops 149 D10
Barkers Hill Wilts 30 B6
Barkestone-le-Vale
Leics 154 C5
Barkham Wokingham 65 F9
Barking London 68 C2
Suff 125 G11
Barkingside London 68 B2
Barking Tye Suff 125 G11
Barkisland W Yorks 196 D5
Barkla Shop Corn 4 E4
Barkston Lincs 172 G6
N Yorks 206 F5
Barkston Ash
N Yorks 206 F5
Barkway Herts 105 D7
Barlake Som 45 D7
Barlanark Glasgow 268 C3
Barland Powys 114 E5
Barland Common
Swansea 56 D5
Barlaston Staffs 151 B7
Barlavington W Sus 35 D7
Barlborough Derbys 187 F7
Barlby N Yorks 207 G8
Barlestone Leics 135 B8
Barley Herts 105 D7
Lancs 204 E2
Barleycroft End
Herts 105 F8
Barley End Bucks 85 C7
Barley Green Lancs 204 E2
Barley Mow T&W 243 G7
Barleythorpe
Rutland 136 B6
Barling Essex 70 B2
Barlings Lincs 189 G9
Barlow Derbys 186 G4
N Yorks 198 B6
T&W 242 E5
Barlow Moor
Gtr Man 184 C4
Barmby Moor
E Yorks 207 D11
Barmby on the Marsh
E Yorks 199 B7
Barmer Norf 158 C6
Barming Heath Kent 53 B8
Barmolloch Argyll 275 D9
Bar Moor T&W 242 E4
Barmoor Castle
Northumb 263 B11
Barmoor Lane End
Northumb 264 B2
Barmouth / Abermaw
Gwyn 146 F2
Barmpton Darl 224 B6
Barmston E Yorks 209 B9
T&W 243 F8
Barmulloch Glasgow 268 B2
Barnaby Green Suff 127 B9
Barnacabber Argyll 276 D3
Barnack Pboro 137 B11
Barnacle Warks 135 G7
Barnaline Argyll 275 B10
Barnard Castle
Durham 223 B11
Barnard Gate Oxon 82 C6
Barnardiston Suff 106 B4
Barnard's Green
Worcs 98 B5
Barnardtown
Newport 59 B10
Barnbarroch
Dumfries 237 D10
Barnbow Carr
W Yorks 206 F3
Barnburgh S Yorks 198 G3
Barnby Suff 143 F9
Barnby Dun S Yorks 198 F6
Barnby in the Willows
Notts 172 E5
Barnby Moor Notts 187 E11
Barncluith S Lanark 268 E4
Barndennoch
Dumfries 247 F9
Barne Barton Plym 7 D8
Barnehurst London 68 D4
Barnes Cray London 68 D4
Barnes Hall S Yorks 186 B4
Barnes Street Kent 52 D6
Barnet London 86 F2
Barnetby le Wold
N Lincs 200 F5
Barnet Gate London 86 F2
Barnettbrook Worcs 117 B7
Barnett Brook
Ches E 167 G10
Barney Norf 159 C9
Barnfield Kent 54 D2
Barnfields Hereford 97 C9
Staffs 169 D7
Barnham Suff 125 B7
W Sus 35 G7
Barnham Broom
Norf 141 B11
Barnhead Angus 287 B10
Barnhill Ches W 167 E7
Dundee 287 D8
Moray 301 D11
Barnhills Dumfries 236 B1
Barningham
Durham 223 C11
Suff 125 B9
Barningham Green
Norf 160 C2
Barnmoor Green
Warks 118 E3
Barnoldby le Beck
NE Lincs 201 G8
Barnoldswick Lancs 204 D3
N Yorks 212 E3
Barns Borders 260 B6
Barnsbury London 67 C10
Barnsdale Rutland 137 B8
Barns Green W Sus 35 B10
Barnside W Yorks 197 F7
Barnsley Glos 81 D9
S Yorks 197 F10
Shrops 132 E5
Barnsole Kent 55 B9
Barnstaple Devon 40 G5
Barnston Essex 87 B10
Mers 182 E3
Barnstone Notts 154 B4
Barnt Green Worcs 117 C10
Barnton Ches W 183 F10
Edin 280 F3
Barnwell Northants 137 G10
Barnwell All Saints
Northants 137 G10
Barnwell St Andrew
Northants 137 F10
Barnwood Glos 80 B5
Barochreal Argyll 289 G10
Barons Cross
Hereford 115 F9
Barr Highld 289 D8
S Ayrs 245 E7
Som 27 C11
Barra Castle Aberds 303 G7
Barrachan Dumfries 236 E5
Barrachnie Glasgow 268 C3
Barrack Aberds 303 E8
Barrack Hill
Newport 59 B10
Barraer Dumfries 236 C5
Barraglom W Isles 304 E3
Barrahormid Argyll 275 E8
Barran Argyll 289 G10
Barranrioch Argyll 289 G10
Barrapol Argyll 288 E1
Barras Aberds 293 E10
Cumb 222 C6
Barrasford
Northumb 241 C10
Barravullin Argyll 275 C9
Barr Common
W Mid 133 D11
Barregarrow IoM 192 D4
Barrets Green
Ches E 167 D9
Barrhead E Renf 267 D9
Barrhill S Ayrs 244 G6
Barrington Cambs 105 B7
Som 28 D5
Barripper Corn 2 B4
Barrmill N Ayrs 267 E7
Barrock Highld 310 B6
Barrock Ho Highld 310 C6
Barrow Glos 99 G7
Lancs 203 F10
Rutland 155 F7
S Yorks 186 B5
Shrops 132 C3
Som 44 E5
Suff 124 E5
Barroway Drove
Norf 139 C11
Barrow Bridge
Gtr Man 195 E7
Barrowburn
Northumb 263 G9
Barrow Burn
Northumb 263 G9
Barrowby Lincs 155 B7
Barrowcliff
N Yorks 217 B10
Barrow Common
N Som 60 F4
Barrowden Rutland 137 C8
Barrowford Lancs 204 F3
Barrow Green Kent 70 G3
Barrow Gurney
N Som 60 F4
Barrow Hann
N Lincs 200 C5
Barrow Haven
N Lincs 200 C5
Barrowhill Kent 54 F6
Barrow Hill Derbys 186 F6
Dorset 18 B5
Barrow-in-Furness
Cumb 210 F4
Barrow Island Cumb 210 F3
Barrowmore Estate
Ches W 167 B7
Barrow Nook Lancs 194 G2
Barrows Green
Ches E 167 D11
Cumb 211 B10
Notts 171 E7
Barrow's Green
Mers 183 D8
Barrow Street Wilts 45 G10
Barrow upon Humber
N Lincs 200 C5
Barrow upon Soar
Leics 153 F11
Barrow upon Trent
Derbys 153 D7
Barrow Vale Bath 60 G6
Barrow Wake Glos 80 B6
Barry Angus 287 D9
V Glam 58 F6
Barry Dock V Glam 58 F6
Barry Island V Glam 58 F6
Barsby Leics 154 G3
Barsham Suff 143 F7
Barshare E Ayrs 258 F3
Barstable Essex 69 B8
Barston W Mid 118 B4
Bartestree Hereford 97 C11
Barthol Chapel
Aberds 303 F8
Bartholomew Green
Essex 106 G4
Barthomley Ches E 168 E3
Bartington Ches W 183 F10
Bartley Hants 32 E4
Bartley Green
W Mid 133 G10
Bartlow Cambs 105 B11
Barton Cambs 123 F8
Ches W 166 E6
Glos 80 B4
Glos 99 F11
IoW 20 D6
Lancs 193 F11
Lancs 202 F6
N Som 43 B11
N Yorks 224 D4
Oxon 83 D9
Torbay 9 B8
Warks 118 G2
Barton Abbey Oxon 101 G9
Barton Bendish
Norf 140 B4
Barton Court
Hereford 98 C4
Barton End Glos 80 F4
Barton Gate Devon 41 E7
Staffs 152 F3
Barton Green Staffs 152 F3
Barton Hartshorn
Bucks 102 E2
Barton Hill Bristol 60 E6
N Yorks 216 G4
Barton in Fabis
Notts 153 C10
Barton in the Beans
Leics 135 B7
Barton-le-Clay
C Beds 103 E11
Barton-le-Street
N Yorks 216 E4
Barton-le-Willows
N Yorks 216 G4
Barton Mills Suff 124 C4
Barton on Sea
Hants 19 C10
Barton on the Heath
Warks 100 E5
Barton St David Som 44 G4
Barton Seagrave
Northants 121 B7
Bartonsham
Hereford 97 D10
Barton Stacey Hants 48 E2
Barton Town Devon 41 E7
Barton Turf Norf 161 E7
Barton Turn Staffs 152 F4
Barton-under-Needwood Staffs 152 F3
Barton-upon-Humber
N Lincs 200 C4
Barton Upon Irwell
Gtr Man 184 B3
Barton Waterside
N Lincs 200 C4
Barugh S Yorks 197 F10
Barugh Green
S Yorks 197 F10
Barway Cambs 123 B10
Barwell Leics 135 D8
London 67 G7
Barwick Devon 25 F9
Herts 86 B5
Som 29 E9
Barwick in Elmet
W Yorks 206 F3
Baschurch Shrops 149 E8
Bascote Warks 119 E8
Bascote Heath
Warks 119 E7
Base Green Suff 125 E10
Basford Shrops 131 F7
Staffs 168 F5
Basford Green
Staffs 169 E7
Bashall Eaves Lancs 203 E9
Bashley Hants 19 B10
Bashley Park Hants 19 B10
Basildon Essex 69 B8
Basingstoke Hants 48 C6
Baslow Derbys 186 G3
Bason Bridge Som 43 D10
Bassaleg Newport 59 B9
Bassenthwaite
Cumb 229 E10
Bassett S Yorks 186 E3
Soton 32 D6
Bassett Green Soton 32 D6
Bassingbourn
Cambs 104 C6
Bassingfield Notts 154 B2
Bassingham Lincs 172 C6
Bassingthorpe Lincs 155 D9
Bassus Green Herts 104 F6
Basta Shetland 312 D7
Basted Kent 52 B6
Baston Lincs 156 G2
Bastonford Worcs 116 G6
Bastwick Norf 161 F8
Baswich Staffs 151 E8
Baswick Steer
E Yorks 209 D7
Batavaime Stirling 285 D8
Batch Som 43 B10
Batchcott Shrops 115 C9
Batchfields Hereford 98 B3
Batchley Worcs 117 D10
Batchworth Herts 85 G9
Batchworth Heath
Herts 85 G9
Batcombe Dorset 29 G10
Som 45 F7
Bate Heath Ches E 183 F11
Bateman's Green
Worcs 117 B11
Bateman's Hill Pembs 73 E8
Batemoor S Yorks 186 E5
Batford Herts 85 B10
Bath Bath 61 F8
Bathampton Bath 61 F9
Bathealton Som 27 C9
Batheaston Bath 61 F9
Bathford Bath 61 F9
Bathgate W Loth 269 B9
Bathley Notts 172 D3
Bathpool Corn 11 G11
Som 28 B3
Bath Side Essex 108 E5
Bath Vale Ches E 168 C5
Bathville W Loth 269 B8
Bathway Som 44 C5
Bathwick Bath 61 F9
Batlers Green Herts 85 F11
Batley W Yorks 197 C8
Batley Carr W Yorks 197 C8
Batsford Glos 100 E3
Batson Devon 9 G9
Batsworthy Devon 26 D4
Batten's Green Som 28 D3
Battenton Green
Worcs 116 D6
Battersby N Yorks 225 D11
Battersea London 67 D9
Battisborough Cross
Devon 7 F11
Battisford Suff 125 G11
Battisford Tye Suff 125 G10
Battle E Sus 38 D2
Powys 95 E10
Battledown Glos 99 G9
Battledown Cross
Devon 25 F7
Battlefield Shrops 149 F10
Battle Hill T&W 243 D8
Battlesbridge Essex 88 G3
Battlescombe Glos 80 D6
Battlesden C Beds 103 F9
Battlesea Green
Suff 126 B4
Battleton Som 26 B6
Battlies Green Suff 125 E7
Battram Leics 135 B8
Battramsley Hants 20 B2
Battramsley Cross
Hants 20 B2
Batt's Corner Hants 49 E10
Battyeford W Yorks 197 C7
Batworthy Devon 13 D10
Bauds of Cullen
Moray 302 C4
Baugh Argyll 288 E2
Baughton Worcs 99 C7
Baughurst Hants 48 B5
Baulking Oxon 82 G4
Baumber Lincs 190 G2
Baunton Glos 81 E8
Baverstock Wilts 46 G4
Bawburgh Norf 142 B3
Bawdeswell Norf 159 E10
Bawdrip Som 43 F10
Bawdsey Suff 108 C6
Bawsey Norf 158 F3
Bawtry S Yorks 187 C11
Baxenden Lancs 195 B9
Baxterley Warks 134 D5
Baxter's Green Suff 124 F5
Bay Dorset 30 B4
Highld 298 D2
Baybridge Hants 33 C8
Northumb 241 G11
Baycliff Cumb 210 E5
Baydon Wilts 63 D9
Bayford Herts 86 D4
Som 30 B2
Bay Gate Lancs 203 D11
Bay Horse Lancs 202 C5
Bayles Cumb 231 C10
Bayley's Hill Kent 52 C4
Baylham Suff 126 G2
Baylis Green
Worcs 117 C11
Baynard's Green
Oxon 101 F10
Baynhall Worcs 99 B7
Baysham Hereford 97 F11
Bayston Hill Shrops 131 B9
Bayswater London 67 C9
Baythorne End
Essex 106 C4
Baythorpe Lincs 174 G2
Bayton Worcs 116 C3
Bayton Common
Worcs 116 C4
Bay View Kent 70 E4
Bayworth Oxon 83 E8
Beach Highld 289 D9
S Glos 61 E8
Beachampton Bucks 102 D5
Beachamwell Norf 140 B5
Beachans Moray 301 E10
Beacharr Argyll 255 C7
Beachborough Kent 55 F7
Beach Hay Worcs 116 C4
Beachlands E Sus 23 E11
Beachley Glos 79 G9
Beacon Corn 2 B5
Devon 27 F11
Devon 28 F2
Beacon Down E Sus 37 C9
Beacon End Essex 107 G9
Beaconhill Northumb 243 B7
Beacon Hill Bath 61 F9
Bucks 84 G6
Cumb 210 E4
Dorset 18 C5
Essex 88 C5
Kent 53 G10
Notts 172 E4
Suff 108 B4
Sur 49 F11
Beacon Lough T&W 243 F7
Beacon's Bottom
Bucks 84 F3
Beaconsfield Bucks 66 B2
Beaconside Staffs 151 E8
Beacrabhaic
W Isles 305 J3
Beadlam N Yorks 216 C3
Beadlow C Beds 104 D2
Beadnell Northumb 264 D6
Beaford Devon 25 E9
Beal N Yorks 198 B4
Northumb 273 G11
Bealach Highld 289 D11
Bealach Maim
Argyll 275 E10
Bealbury Corn 7 B7
Beal's Green Kent 53 G9
Bealsmill Corn 12 F3
Beambridge
Shrops 131 F10
Beam Bridge Som 27 D10
Beam Hill Staffs 152 D4
Beamhurst Staffs 151 B11
Beamhurst Lane
Staffs 151 B11
Beaminster Dorset 29 G7
Beamish Durham 242 G6
Beamond End Bucks 84 F6
Beamsley N Yorks 205 C7
Bean Kent 68 E5
Beanacre Wilts 62 F2
Beancross Falk 279 F8
Beanhill M Keynes 103 D7
Beanley Northumb 264 F3
Beansburn E Ayrs 257 B10
Beanthwaite Cumb 210 C4
Beaquoy Orkney 314 D3
Bear Cross Bmouth 19 B7
Beard Hill Som 44 E6
Beardly Batch Som 44 E6
Beardwood
Blackburn 195 B7
Beare Devon 27 G7
Beare Green Sur 51 E7
Bearley Warks 118 E3
Bearley Cross
Warks 118 E3
Bearnus Argyll 288 E5
Bearpark Durham 233 C10
Bearsbridge
Northumb 241 F7
Bearsden E Dunb 277 G10
Bearsted Kent 53 B9
Bearstone Shrops 150 B4
Bearwood Hereford 115 F7
Poole 18 B6
W Mid 133 F10
Beasley Staffs 168 F4
Beattock Dumfries 248 C3
Beauchamp Roding
Essex 87 C9
Beauchief S Yorks 186 E4
Beauclerc Northumb 242 E2
Beaudesert Warks 118 D3
Beaufort Bl Gwent 77 C11
Beaufort Castle
Highld 300 E5
Beaulieu Hants 32 G5
Beaulieu Park Essex 88 C2
Beaulieu Wood
Dorset 30 F2
Beauly Highld 300 E5
Beaumaris
Anglesey 179 F10
Beaumont Cumb 239 F8
Essex 108 G3
Windsor 66 E3
Beaumont Hill Darl 224 B5
Beaumont Leys
Leicester 135 B11
Beausale Warks 118 C4
Beauvale Notts 171 F8
Beauworth Hants 33 B9
Beavan's Hill
Hereford 98 G3
Beaworthy Devon 12 B5
Beazley End Essex 106 F4
Bebington Mers 182 E4
Bebside Northumb 253 G7
Beccles Suff 143 E8
Becconsall Lancs 194 C2
Beck Bottom Cumb 210 C5
W Yorks 197 C10
Beckbury Shrops 132 C5
Beckces Cumb 230 F4
Beckenham London 67 F11
Beckermet Cumb 219 D10
Beckermonds
N Yorks 213 C7
Beckery Som 44 F3
Beckett End Norf 140 D5
Beckfoot Cumb 220 E3
Cumb 229 B7
Beck Foot Cumb 222 F2
W Yorks 205 F8
Beckford Worcs 99 D9
Beckhampton Wilts 62 F5
Beck Head Cumb 211 C8
Beck Hole N Yorks 226 E6
Beck Houses Cumb 221 F11
Beckingham Lincs 172 E5
Notts 188 D3
Beckington Som 45 C10
Beckjay Shrops 115 B7
Beckley E Sus 38 C5
Hants 19 B10
Oxon 83 C9
Beckley Furnace
E Sus 38 C4
Beck Row Suff 124 B3
Beckside Cumb 212 B2
Beck Side Cumb 210 C4
Cumb 211 C7
Beckton London 68 C2
Beckwith N Yorks 205 C11
Beckwithshaw
N Yorks 205 C11
Becontree London 68 B3
Bedale N Yorks 214 B5
Bedburn Durham 233 E8
Bedchester Dorset 30 D5
Beddau Rhondda 58 B5
Beddgelert Gwyn 163 F9
Beddingham E Sus 36 F6
Beddington London 67 G10
Beddington Corner
London 67 F9
Bedfield Suff 126 D4
Bedford Beds 121 G11
Gtr Man 183 B11
Bedford Park London 67 D8
Bedgebury Cross
Kent 53 G8
Bedgrove Bucks 84 C4
Bedham W Sus 35 C8
Bedhampton Hants 22 B2
Bedingfield Suff 126 D3
Bedingham Green
Norf 142 E5
Bedlam N Yorks 214 G5
Som 45 D9
Bedlam Street
W Sus 36 D3
Bedlar's Green
Essex 105 G10
Bedlington
Northumb 253 G7
Bedlington Station
Northumb 253 G7
Bedlinog M Tydf 77 E9
Bedminster Bristol 60 E5
Bedminster Down
Bristol 60 F5
Bedmond Herts 85 E9
Bednall Staffs 151 F9
Bednall Head Staffs 151 F9
Bedrule Borders 262 F4
Bedstone Shrops 115 B7
Bedwas Caerph 59 B7
Bedwell Herts 104 G4
Wrex 166 F5
Bedwellty Caerph 77 E11
Bedwellty Pits
Bl Gwent 77 D11
Bedwlwyn Wrex 148 B4
Bedworth Warks 135 F7
Bedworth Heath
Warks 134 F6
Bedworth Woodlands
Warks 134 F6
Bed-y-coedwr
Gwyn 146 D4
Beeby Leics 136 B3
Beech Hants 49 F7
Staffs 151 B7
Beechcliff Staffs 151 B7
Beechcliffe
W Yorks 205 E7
Beechen Cliff Bath 61 G9
Beech Hill Gtr Man 194 F5
W Berks 65 G7
Beechingstoke Wilts 46 B5
Beech Lanes
W Mid 133 F10
Beechwood Halton 183 E8
Newport 59 B10
W Mid 118 B5
W Yorks 206 F2
Beecroft C Beds 103 G10
Beedon W Berks 64 D3
Beedon Hill W Berks 64 D3
Beeford E Yorks 209 C8
Beeley Derbys 170 B3
Beelsby NE Lincs 201 G8
Beenham W Berks 64 F5
Beenham's Heath
Windsor 65 D10
Beenham Stocks
W Berks 64 F5
Beeny Corn 11 C8
Beer Devon 15 D10
Som 44 G2
Beercrocombe Som 28 C4
Beer Hackett Dorset 29 E9
Beesands Devon 8 G6
Beesby Lincs 191 E7
Beeslack Midloth 270 C4
Beeson Devon 8 G6
Beeston C Beds 104 B3
Ches W 167 D8
Norf 159 F8
Notts 153 B10
W Yorks 205 G11
Beeston Hill
W Yorks 205 G11
Beeston Park Side
W Yorks 197 B9
Beeston Regis
Norf 177 E11
Beeston Royds
W Yorks 205 G11
Beeston St Lawrence
Norf 160 E6
Beeswing Dumfries 237 C10
Beetham Cumb 211 D9
Som 28 E3
Beetley Norf 159 F9
Beffcote Staffs 150 F6
Began Cardiff 59 C8
Begbroke Oxon 83 C7
Begdale Cambs 139 B9
Begelly Pembs 73 D10
Beggar Hill Essex 87 E10
Beggarington Hill
W Yorks 197 C9
Beggars Ash
Hereford 98 D4
Beggars Bush
W Sus 35 F11
Beggar's Bush
Powys 114 E5
Beggars Pound
V Glam 58 F4
Beggearn Huish Som 42 F4
Beguildy Powys 114 B3
Beighton Norf 143 B7
S Yorks 186 E6
Beighton Hill
Derbys 170 E3
Beili-glas Mon 78 C4
Beitearsaig W Isles 305 G1
Beith N Ayrs 266 E6
Bekesbourne Kent 55 B7
Bekesbourne Hill
Kent 55 B7
Belah Cumb 239 F9
Belan Powys 130 C4
Belaugh Norf 160 F5
Belbins Hants 32 C5
Belbroughton
Worcs 117 B8
Belchalwell Dorset 30 F3
Belchalwell Street
Dorset 30 F3
Belchamp Otten
Essex 106 C6
Belchamp St Paul
Essex 106 C5
Belchamp Walter
Essex 106 C6
Belcher's Bar Leics 135 B8
Belchford Lincs 190 F3
Beleybridge Fife 287 F9
Belfield Gtr Man 196 E2
Belford Northumb 264 C4
Belgrano Conwy 181 F7
Belgrave Ches W 166 C5
Leicester 135 B11
Staffs 134 C4
Belgravia London 67 D9
Belhaven E Loth 282 F3
Belhelvie Aberds 293 B11
Belhinnie Aberds 302 G4
Bellabeg Aberds 292 B5
Bellamore S Ayrs 244 F6
Bellanoch Argyll 275 D8
Bellanrigg Borders 260 B6
Bellasize E Yorks 199 B10
Bellaty Angus 286 B6
Bell Bar Herts 86 D3
Bell Busk N Yorks 204 B4
Bell Common Essex 86 E6
Belleau Lincs 190 F6
Belle Eau Park
Notts 171 D11
Belle Green
S Yorks 197 F11
Bellehiglash Moray 301 F11
Belle Isle W Yorks 197 B10
Bell End Worcs 117 B8
Bellerby N Yorks 224 G2
Belle Vale Mers 182 D6
W Mid 133 G9
Bellever Devon 13 F9
Bellevue Worcs 117 C9
Belle Vue Cumb 229 E8
Cumb 239 F9
Gtr Man 184 B5
S Yorks 198 G5
Shrops 149 G9
W Yorks 197 D10
Bellfield E Ayrs 257 B10
Bellfields Sur 50 C3
Bell Green London 67 E11
W Mid 135 G7
Bell Heath Worcs 117 B9
Bell Hill Hants 34 C2
Belliehill Angus 293 G7
Bellingdon Bucks 84 D6
Bellingham London 67 E11
Northumb 251 G8
Bellmount Norf 157 E10
Belloch Argyll 255 D7
Bellochantuy Argyll 255 D7
Bell o' th' Hill
Ches W 167 F8
Bellsbank E Ayrs 245 C11
Bell's Close T&W 242 E5
Bell's Corner Suff 107 D9
Bellshill N Lanark 268 C4
Northumb 264 C4
Bellside N Lanark 268 D6
Bellsmyre W Dunb 277 F8
Bellspool Borders 260 B5
Bellsquarry
W Loth 269 C10
Bells Yew Green
E Sus 52 F6
Belluton Bath 60 G6
Bellyeoman Fife 280 D2
Belmaduthy Highld 300 D6
Belmesthorpe
Rutland 155 G10
Belmont Blackburn 195 D7
Durham 234 C2
E Sus 38 E4
London 67 G9
London 85 G11
Oxon 63 B11
S Ayrs 257 E8
Shetland 312 C7
Belnacraig Aberds 292 B5
Belnagarrow Moray 302 E3
Belnie Lincs 156 C5
Belowda Corn 5 C9
Belper Derbys 170 F4
Belper Lane End
Derbys 170 F4
Belph Derbys 187 F8
Belsay Northumb 242 B4
Belses Borders 262 D3
Belsford Devon 8 D5
Belsize Herts 85 E8
Belstead Suff 108 C2
Belston S Ayrs 257 E9
Belstone Devon 13 C8
Belstone Corner
Devon 13 B8
Belthorn Blackburn 195 C8
Beltinge Kent 71 F7
Beltingham
Northumb 241 E7
Beltoft N Lincs 199 F10
Belton Leics 153 E8
Lincs 155 B8
N Lincs 199 F9
Norf 143 C9
Belton in Rutland
Rutland 136 C6
Beltring Kent 53 D7
Belts of Collonach
Aberds 293 D8
Belvedere London 68 D3
W Loth 269 B9
Belvoir Leics 154 C6
Bembridge IoW 21 D8
Bemersyde Borders 262 C3
Bemerton Wilts 46 G6
Bemerton Heath
Wilts 46 G6
Bempton E Yorks 218 E3
Benacre Suff 143 G10
Ben Alder Lodge
Highld 291 F7
Ben Armine Lodge
Highld 309 H7
Benbuie Dumfries 246 D6
Ben Casgro W Isles 304 F6
Benchill Gtr Man 184 D4
Bencombe Glos 80 F3
Benderloch Argyll 289 F11
Bendish Herts 104 G3
Bendronaig Lodge
Highld 299 F10
Benenden Kent 53 G10
Benfield Dumfries 236 C5
Benfieldside
Durham 242 G3
Bengal Pembs 91 E9
Bengate Norf 160 D6
Bengeo Herts 86 C4
Bengeworth Worcs 99 C10
Bengrove Glos 99 E9
Benhall Glos 99 G8
Benhall Green Suff 127 E7
Benhall Street Suff 127 E7
Benhilton London 67 F9
Benholm Aberds 293 G10
Beningbrough
N Yorks 206 B6
Benington Herts 104 G5
Lincs 174 F5
Benington Sea End
Lincs 174 F6
Benllech Anglesey 179 E8
Benmore Argyll 276 E2
Stirling 285 E8
Benmore Lodge
Argyll 289 F7
Highld 309 H3
Bennacott Corn 11 C11
Bennah Devon 14 E2
Bennan N Ayrs 255 E10
Bennane Lea S Ayrs 244 F3
Bennetland
E Yorks 199 B10
Bennetsfield Highld 300 D6
Bennett End Bucks 84 F3
Bennetts End Herts 85 D9
Benniworth Lincs 190 E2
Benover Kent 53 D8
Ben Rhydding
W Yorks 205 D8
Bensham T&W 242 E6
Benslie N Ayrs 266 G6
Benson Oxon 83 G10
Benston Shetland 313 H6
Bent Aberds 293 F8
Benter Som 44 D6
Bentfield Bury
Essex 105 F9
Bentfield Green
Essex 105 F10
Bentgate Gtr Man 196 E2
Bent Gate Lancs 195 C9
Benthall Northumb 264 D6
Shrops 132 C3
Bentham Glos 80 B6
Benthoul Aberdeen 293 C10
Bentilee Stoke 168 F6
Bentlass Pembs 73 E7
Bentlawnt Shrops 130 C6
Bentley E Yorks 208 F6
Essex 87 F9
Hants 49 E9
S Yorks 198 F5
Suff 108 D2
W Mid 133 D9
Warks 134 D5
Worcs 117 D9
Bentley Common
Warks 134 D5
Bentley Heath Herts 86 F2
W Mid 118 B3
Bentley Rise
S Yorks 198 G5
Benton Devon 41 F7
Benton Green
W Mid 118 B5
Bentpath Dumfries 249 E8
Bents W Loth 269 C9
Bents Head
W Yorks 205 F7
Bentwichen Devon 41 G8
Bentworth Hants 49 E7
Benvie Dundee 287 D7
Benville Dorset 29 G8
Benwell T&W 242 E6
Benwick Cambs 138 E6
Beobridge Shrops 132 E5
Beoley Worcs 117 D11
Beoraidbeg Highld 295 F8
Bepton W Sus 34 D5
Berden Essex 105 F9
Bere Alston Devon 7 B8
Berechurch Essex 107 G9
Bere Ferrers Devon 7 C9
Berefold Aberds 303 F9
Berepper Corn 2 E5
Bere Regis Dorset 18 C2
Bergh Apton Norf 142 C6
Berghers Hill Bucks 66 B2
Berhill Som 44 F2
Berinsfield Oxon 83 F9
Berkeley Glos 79 F11
Berkeley Heath Glos 79 F11
Berkeley Road Glos 80 E2

Berkeley Towers
Ches E 167 E11
Berkhamsted Herts 85 D7
Berkley Som 45 D10
Berkley Down Som 45 D9
Berkley Marsh Som 45 D10
Berkswell W Mid 118 B4
Bermondsey London 67 D10
Bermuda Warks 135 F7
Bernards Heath
Herts 85 D11
Bernera Highld 295 C10
Berner's Cross
Devon 25 F10
Berner's Hill E Sus 53 G8
Berners Roding
Essex 87 D10
Bernice Argyll 276 C2
Bernisdale Highld 298 D4
Berrick Salome
Oxon 83 G10
Berriedale Highld 311 G5
Berrier Cumb 230 F3
Berriew / Aberriw
Powys 130 C3
Berrington
Northumb 273 G10
Shrops 131 B10
Worcs 115 D11
Berrington Green
Worcs 115 D11
Berriowbridge Corn 11 F11
Berrow Som 43 C10
Worcs 98 E5
Berrow Green
Worcs 116 F4
Berry Swansea 56 D3
Berry Brow W Yorks 196 E6
Berry Cross Devon 25 E7
Berry Down Cross
Devon 40 E5
Berryfield Oxon 84 B3
Wilts 61 G11
Berrygate Hill
E Yorks 201 C8
Berry Hill Glos 79 C9
Pembs 91 C11
Stoke 168 F6
Worcs 117 E7
Berryhillock Moray 302 C5
Berrylands London 67 F7
Berry Moor S Yorks 197 G9
Berrynarbor Devon 40 D5
Berry Pomeroy Devon 8 C6
Berrysbridge Devon 26 G6
Berry's Green London 52 B2
Bersham Wrex 166 F4
Berstane Orkney 314 E4
Berth-ddu Flint 166 B2
Berthengam Flint 181 F10
Berwick E Sus 23 D8
Kent 54 F6
S Glos 60 C5
Berwick Bassett
Wilts 62 E5
Berwick Hill
Northumb 242 B5
Berwick Hills Mbro 225 B10
Berwick St James
Wilts 46 F5
Berwick St John
Wilts 30 C6
Berwick St Leonard
Wilts 46 G2
Berwick-upon-Tweed
Northumb 273 E9
Berwick Wharf
Shrops 149 G10
Berwyn Denb 165 G11
Bescaby Leics 154 D6
Bescar Lancs 193 E11
Bescot W Mid 133 D10
Besford Shrops 149 E11
Worcs 99 C8
Bessacarr S Yorks 198 G6
Bessels Green Kent 52 B4
Bessels Leigh Oxon 83 E7
Besses o' th' Barn
Gtr Man 195 F10
Bessingby E Yorks 218 F3
Bessingham Norf 160 B3
Best Beech Hill
E Sus 52 G6
Besthorpe Norf 141 D11
Notts 172 C4
Bestwood
Nottingham 171 G9
Bestwood Village
Notts 171 F9
Beswick E Yorks 208 D6
Gtr Man 184 B5
Betchcott Shrops 131 D8
Betchton Heath
Ches E 168 C3
Betchworth Sur 51 D8
Bethania Ceredig 111 E11
Gwyn 163 E10
Gwyn 164 F2
Bethany Corn 6 D6
Bethel Anglesey 178 G5
Corn 5 E10
Gwyn 147 B9
Gwyn 163 B8
Bethelnie Aberds 303 F7
Bethersden Kent 54 E2
Bethesda Gwyn 163 B10
Pembs 73 B9
Bethlehem Carms 94 F3
Bethnal Green
London 67 C10
Betley Staffs 168 F3
Betley Common
Staffs 168 F2
Betsham Kent 68 E6
Betteshanger Kent 55 C10
Bettiscombe Dorset 16 B3
Bettisfield Wrex 149 B9
Betton Shrops 130 C6
Shrops 150 B3
Betton Strange
Shrops 131 B10
Bettws
Bridgend 58 B2
Mon 78 B3
Newport 78 G3
Bettws Cedewain
Powys 130 D2
Bettws Gwerfil Goch
Denb 165 F8
Bettws Ifan Ceredig 92 B6
Bettws Newydd Mon 78 D5
Bettws-y-crwyn
Shrops 130 G4
Bettyhill Highld 308 C7
Betws Bridgend 57 D11
Carms 75 C10
Betws Bledrws
Ceredig 111 G11
Betws-Garmon
Gwyn 163 D8
Betws Ifan Ceredig 92 B6
Betws-y-Coed
Conwy 164 D4
Betws-yn-Rhos
Conwy 180 G6
Beulah Ceredig 92 B5
Powys 113 G8
Bevendean Brighton 36 F4
Bevercotes Notts 187 G11
Bevere Worcs 116 F6
Beverley E Yorks 208 F6
Beverston Glos 80 G5
Bevington Glos 79 F11
Bewaldeth Cumb 229 E10
Bewbush W Sus 51 F8
Bewcastle Cumb 240 C3
Bewdley Worcs 116 B5
Bewerley N Yorks 214 G3
Bewholme E Yorks 209 C9
Bewley Common
Wilts 62 F2
Bewlie Borders 262 D3
Bewlie Mains
Borders 262 D3
Bewsey Warr 183 D9
Bexfield Norf 159 D10
Bexhill E Sus 38 F2
Bexley London 68 E3
Bexleyheath London 68 D3
Bexleyhill W Sus 34 B6
Bexon Kent 53 B11
Bexwell Norf 140 C2
Beyton Suff 125 E8
Beyton Green Suff 125 E8
Bhalasaigh W Isles 304 E3
Bhaltos W Isles 304 E2
Bhatarsaigh
W Isles 297 M2
Bhlàraidh Highld 290 B5
Bibstone S Glos 79 G11
Bibury Glos 81 D10
Bicester Oxon 101 G11
Bickenhall Som 28 D3
Bickenhill W Mid 134 G3
Bicker Lincs 156 B4
Bicker Bar Lincs 156 B4
Bicker Gauntlet
Lincs 156 B4
Bickershaw
Gtr Man 194 G6
Bickerstaffe Lancs 194 G2
Bickerton Ches E 167 E8
Devon 9 G11
N Yorks 206 C5
Bickford Staffs 151 G7
Bickham Som 42 E3
Bickingcott Devon 26 B3
Bickington Devon 13 G11
Devon 40 G4
Bickleigh Devon 7 C10
Devon 26 F6
Bickleton Devon 40 G4
Bickley Ches W 167 F8
London 68 F2
Worcs 116 C2
Bickley Moss
Ches W 167 F8
Bickley Town
Ches W 167 F8
Bickleywood
Ches W 167 F8
Bickmarsh Warks 100 B2
Bicknacre Essex 88 E3
Bicknoller Som 42 F6
Bicknor Kent 53 B11
Bickton Hants 31 E11
Bicton Hereford 115 E9
Pembs 72 D4
Shrops 130 G5
Shrops 149 F8
Bicton Heath
Shrops 149 G9
Bidborough Kent 52 E5
Bidden Hants 49 D8
Biddenden Kent 53 F11
Biddenden Green
Kent 53 E11
Biddenham Beds 103 B10
Biddestone Wilts 61 E11
Biddick T&W 243 F8
Biddick Hall T&W 243 E9
Biddisham Som 43 C11
Biddlesden Bucks 102 C2
Biddlestone
Northumb 251 B11
Biddulph Staffs 168 D5
Biddulph Moor
Staffs 168 D6
Bideford Devon 25 B7
Bidford-on-Avon
Warks 118 G2
Bidlake Devon 12 D5
Bidston Mers 182 C3
Bidston Hill Mers 182 D3
Bidwell C Beds 103 G10
Bielby E Yorks 207 E11
Bieldside Aberdeen 293 C10
Bierley IoW 20 F6
W Yorks 205 G9
Bierton Bucks 84 B4
Bigbury Devon 8 F3
Bigbury-on-Sea
Devon 8 G3
Bigby Lincs 200 F5
Bigfrith Windsor 65 C11
Biggar Cumb 210 F3
S Lanark 260 B2
Biggar Road
N Lanark 268 C5
Biggin Derbys 169 D11
Derbys 170 F3
N Yorks 206 F6
Thurrock 69 D7
Biggings Shetland 313 G3
Biggin Hill London 52 B2
Biggleswade
C Beds 104 C3
Bighouse Highld 310 C2
Bighton Hants 48 G6
Biglands Cumb 239 G7
Big Mancot Flint 166 B4
Bignall End Staffs 168 E4
Bignor W Sus 35 E7
Bigods Essex 106 G2
Bigram Stirling 285 G10
Bigrigg Cumb 219 C10
Big Sand Highld 299 B7
Bigswell Orkney 314 E3
Bigton Shetland 313 L5
Bilberry Corn 5 C10
Bilborough
Nottingham 171 G8
Bilbrook Som 42 E4
Staffs 133 C7
Bilbrough N Yorks 206 D6
Bilbster Highld 310 D6
Bilby Notts 187 E10
Bildershaw
Durham 233 G10
Bildeston Suff 107 B9
Billacombe Plym 7 E10
Billacott Corn 11 C11
Billericay Essex 87 G11
Billesdon Leics 136 C4
Billesley W Mid 133 G11
Warks 118 F2
Billesley Common
W Mid 133 G11
Billingborough
Lincs 156 C2
Billinge Mers 194 G4
Billingford Norf 126 B3
Norf 159 E10
Billingham Stockton 234 G5
Billinghay Lincs 173 E11
Billingley S Yorks 198 G2
Billingshurst W Sus 35 B9
Billingsley Shrops 132 F4
Billington C Beds 103 G8
Lancs 203 F10
Staffs 151 E7
Billockby Norf 161 G8
Billy Mill T&W 243 D8
Billy Row Durham 233 D9
Bilmarsh Shrops 149 D9
Bilsborrow Lancs 202 F6
Bilsby Lincs 191 F7
Bilsby Field Lincs 191 F7
Bilsdon Devon 14 C2
Bilsham W Sus 35 G7
Bilsington Kent 54 G4
Bilson Green Glos 79 C11
Bilsthorpe Notts 171 C10
Bilsthorpe Moor
Notts 171 D11
Bilston Midloth 270 C5
W Mid 133 D9
Bilstone Leics 135 B7
Bilting Kent 54 D5
Bilton E Yorks 209 G9
N Yorks 206 B2
Northumb 264 G6
Warks 119 C9
Bilton Haggs
N Yorks 206 D5
Bilton in Ainsty
N Yorks 206 D5
Bimbister Orkney 314 E3
Binbrook Lincs 190 C2
Binchester Blocks
Durham 233 E10
Bincombe Dorset 17 E9
Bindal Highld 311 L3
Bindon Som 27 C10
Binegar Som 44 D6
Bines Green W Sus 35 D11
Binfield Brack 65 E10
Binfield Heath Oxon 65 D8
Bingfield Northumb 241 C11
Bingham Notts 154 B4
Bingley W Yorks 205 F8
Bings Heath
Shrops 149 F10
Binham Norf 159 B9
Binley Hants 48 C2
W Mid 119 B7
Binley Woods
Warks 119 B7
Binnegar Dorset 18 D3
Binniehill Falk 279 G7
Binscombe Sur 50 D3
Binsey Oxon 83 D7
Binsoe N Yorks 214 D4
Binstead Hants 49 E9
IoW 21 C7
Binsted Hants 49 E9
W Sus 35 F7
Binton Warks 118 G2
Bintree Norf 159 E10
Binweston Shrops 130 C6
Birch Essex 88 B6
Gtr Man 195 F11
Birch Acre Worcs 117 C11
Birchall Hereford 98 D3
Staffs 169 E7
Bircham Newton
Norf 158 C5
Bircham Tofts Norf 158 C5
Birchan Coppice
Worcs 116 C6
Birchanger Essex 105 G10
Birch Berrow Worcs 116 E4
Birchburn N Ayrs 255 E10
Birch Cross Staffs 152 C2
Birchden E Sus 52 F4
Birchencliffe
W Yorks 196 D6
Birchend Hereford 98 C3
Birchendale Staffs 151 B11
Bircher Hereford 115 D9
Birches Green
W Mid 134 E2
Birches Head Stoke 168 F5
Birchett's Green
E Sus 53 G7
Birchfield Highld 301 G9
W Mid 133 E11
Birch Green Essex 88 B6
Birch Green *continued*
Herts 86 C3
Lancs 194 F3
Worcs 99 B7
Birchgrove Cardiff 59 D7
E Sus 36 B6
Swansea 57 B8
Birchhall Corner
Essex 107 E10
Birch Heath
Ches W 167 C8
Birch Hill Brack 65 F11
Ches W 183 G8
Birchill Devon 28 G4
Birchills W Mid 133 D10
Birchington Kent 71 F9
Birchley Heath
Warks 134 E5
Birchmoor Warks 134 C5
Birchmoor Green
C Beds 103 E8
Bircholt Forstal Kent 54 E5
Birchover Derbys 170 C2
Birch Vale Derbys 185 D8
Birchwood Herts 86 D2
Lincs 172 B6
Som 28 E2
Warr 183 C10
Birchy Hill Hants 19 B11
Bircotes Notts 187 C10
Birdbrook Essex 106 C4
Birdbush Wilts 30 C6
Birdfield Argyll 275 D10
Birdforth N Yorks 215 D9
Birdham W Sus 22 D4
Birdholme Derbys 170 B5
Birdingbury Warks 119 D8
Birdlip Glos 80 C6
Birdsall N Yorks 216 F6
Birds Edge W Yorks 197 F8
Birds End Suff 124 E5
Birdsgreen Shrops 132 F5
Birds Green Essex 87 D9
Birdsmoorgate
Dorset 28 G5
Birdston E Dunb 278 F3
Bird Street Suff 125 G10
Birdwell S Yorks 197 G10
Birdwood Glos 80 B2
Birgham Borders 263 B7
Birichen Highld 309 K7
Birkacre Lancs 194 D5
Birkby Cumb 229 D7
N Yorks 224 E6
W Yorks 196 D6
Birkdale Mers 193 D10
Birkenbog Aberds 302 C5
Birkenhead Mers 182 D4
Birkenhills Aberds 303 E7
Birkenshaw
N Lanark 268 C3
S Lanark 268 F5
W Yorks 197 B8
Birkenshaw Bottoms
W Yorks 197 B8
Birkenside Borders 271 G11
Birkett Mire Cumb 230 G2
Birkhall Aberds 292 D5
Birkhill Angus 287 D7
Borders 260 F6
Borders 271 G11
Birkholme Lincs 155 E9
Birkhouse W Yorks 197 C7
Birkin N Yorks 198 B4
Birks Cumb 222 G3
W Yorks 197 B9
Birkshaw Northumb 241 D7
Birley Hereford 115 G9
Birley Carr S Yorks 186 C4
Birley Edge S Yorks 186 C4
Birleyhay Derbys 186 E5
Birling Kent 69 G7
Northumb 252 B6
Birling Gap E Sus 23 F9
Birlingham Worcs 99 C8
Birmingham
W Mid 133 F11
Birnam Perth 286 C4
Birniehill S Lanark 268 E2
Birse Aberds 293 D7
Birsemore Aberds 293 D7
Birstall Leics 135 B11
W Yorks 197 B8
Birstall Smithies
W Yorks 197 B8
Birstwith N Yorks 205 B10
Birthorpe Lincs 156 C2
Birtle Gtr Man 195 E10
Birtley
Hereford 115 D7
Northumb 241 B9
Shrops 131 E9
T&W 243 F7
Birtley Green Sur 50 E4
Birtsmorton Worcs 98 D6
Birts Street Worcs 98 D5
Bisbrooke Rutland 137 D7
Biscathorpe Lincs 190 D2
Biscombe Som 27 E11
Biscot Luton 103 G11
Biscovey Corn 5 E11
Bisham Windsor 65 C10
Bishampton Worcs 117 G9
Bish Mill Devon 26 B2
Bishon Common
Hereford 97 C8
Bishop Auckland
Durham 233 F10
Bishopbridge Lincs 189 C8
Bishopbriggs
E Dunb 278 G2
Bishop Burton
E Yorks 208 F5
Bishopdown Wilts 47 G7
Bishop Kinkell
Highld 300 D5
Bishop Middleham
Durham 234 E2
Bishopmill Moray 302 C2
Bishop Monkton
N Yorks 214 F6
Bishop Norton Lincs 189 C7
Bishopsbourne Kent 55 C7
Bishops Cannings
Wilts 62 G4
Bishop's Castle
Shrops 130 F6
Bishop's Caundle
Dorset 29 E11
Bishop's Cleeve Glos 99 F9
Bishop's Down
Dorset 29 E11
Bishops Frome
Hereford 98 B3
Bishopsgarth
Stockton 234 G4
Bishopsgate Sur 66 E3
Bishops Green Essex 87 B5
Bishop's Green
W Berks 64 G4
Bishop's Hull Som 28 C2
Bishop's Itchington
Warks 119 F7
Bishops Lydeard
Som 27 B11
Bishop's Norton Glos 98 G6
Bishops Nympton
Devon 26 C3
Bishop's Offley
Staffs 150 D5
Bishop's Quay Corn 2 D6
Bishop's Stortford
Herts 105 G9
Bishop's Sutton
Hants 48 G6
Bishop's Tachbrook
Warks 118 E6
Bishops Tawton
Devon 40 G5
Bishopsteignton
Devon 14 G4
Bishopstoke Hants 33 D7
Bishopston Bristol 60 D5
Swansea 56 D5
Bishopstone Bucks 84 C4
E Sus 23 E7
Hereford 97 C8
Kent 71 F8
Swindon 63 C8
Wilts 31 B9
Bishopstrow Wilts 45 E11
Bishop Sutton Bath 44 B5
Bishop's Waltham
Hants 33 D9
Bishopswood Som 28 E3
Bishop's Wood
Staffs 132 B6
Bishopsworth Bristol 60 F5
Bishop Thornton
N Yorks 214 G5
Bishopthorpe York 207 D7
Bishopton Darl 234 G3
Dumfries 236 E6
N Yorks 214 E6
Renfs 277 G8
Warks 118 F3
Bishopwearmouth
T&W 243 F9
Bishop Wilton
E Yorks 207 B11
Bishpool Newport 59 B10
Bishton Newport 59 B11
Staffs 151 E10
Bisley Glos 80 D6
Sur 50 B3
Bisley Camp Sur 50 B2
Bispham Blackpool 202 E2
Bispham Green
Lancs 194 E3
Bissoe Corn 4 G5
Bissom Corn 3 C7
Bisterne Hants 31 G10
Bisterne Close Hants 32 G2
Bitchet Green Kent 52 C5
Bitchfield Lincs 155 D9
Bittadon Devon 40 E4
Bittaford Devon 8 D3
Bittering Norf 159 F8
Bitterley Shrops 115 B11
Bitterne Soton 33 E7
Bitterne Park Soton 32 E6
Bitterscote Staffs 134 C4
Bitteswell Leics 135 F10
Bittles Green Dorset 30 C5
Bitton S Glos 61 F7
Bix Oxon 65 B8
Bixter Shetland 313 H5
Blaby Leics 135 D11
Blackacre Dumfries 248 E2
Blackadder West
Borders 272 E6
Blackawton Devon 8 E6
Black Bank Cambs 139 F10
Warks 135 F7
Black Banks Darl 224 C5
Black Barn Lincs 157 D8
Blackbeck Cumb 219 D10
Blackbird Leys Oxon 83 E9
Blackborough Devon 27 F9
Norf 158 G3
Blackborough End
Norf 158 G3
Black Bourton Oxon 82 E3
Blackboys E Sus 37 C8
Blackbraes Aberds 293 B10
Blackbrook Derbys 170 F4
Derbys 185 E9
Mers 183 B8
Staffs 150 B5
Sur 51 D7
Blackburn Aberds 293 B10
Aberds 302 F5
Blackburn 195 B7
S Yorks 186 C5
W Loth 269 B9
Black Callerton
T&W 242 D5
Black Carr Norf 141 D11
Blackcastle Midloth 271 D8
Blackchambers
Aberds 293 B9
Black Clauchrie
S Ayrs 245 G7
Black Corner W Sus 51 F9
Black Corries Lodge
Highld 284 B6
Blackcraig Dumfries 246 G6
Blackcraigs Angus 293 E7
Black Crofts Argyll 289 F11
Black Cross Corn 5 C8
Black Dam Hants 48 C6
Blackden Heath
Ches E 184 G3
Blackditch Oxon 82 D6
Blackdog Aberds 293 B11
Black Dog Devon 26 F4
Blackdown Dorset 28 G5
Hants 33 C8
Warks 118 D6
Blackdyke Cumb 238 G4
Blackdykes E Loth 281 E11
Blacker Hill
S Yorks 197 G11
Blacketts Kent 70 F2
Blackfell T&W 243 F7
Blackfen London 68 E3
Blackfield Hants 32 G6
Blackford Cumb 239 E9
Dumfries 248 G4
Perth 286 G2
Shrops 131 G11
Som 29 B11
Som 42 D2
Som 44 D2
Blackford Bridge
Gtr Man 195 F10
Blackfordby Leics 152 F6
Blackfords Staffs 151 G9
Blackgang IoW 20 F5
Blackgate Angus 287 B8
Blackhall Aberds 293 D8
Edin 280 G4
Renfs 267 C9
Blackhall Colliery
Durham 234 D5
Blackhall Mill T&W 242 F4
Blackhall Rocks
Durham 234 D5
Blackham E Sus 52 F3
Blackhaugh
Borders 261 B10
Blackheath Essex 107 G10
London 67 D11
Suff 127 C8
Sur 50 D4
W Mid 133 F9
Blackheath Park
London 68 D2
Black Heddon
Northumb 242 B3
Blackhill Aberds 303 D10
Aberds 303 E10
Aberds 303 F10
Durham 242 G3
Hants 32 D4
Highld 298 D3
Black Hill W Yorks 204 E6
Blackhillock Moray 302 E4
Blackhills Highld 301 D9
Moray 302 D2
Swansea 56 C5
Blackhorse Devon 14 C5
S Glos 61 D7
Black Horse Drove
Cambs 139 E11
Blackjack Lincs 156 B5
Black Lake W Mid 133 E9
Blackland Wilts 62 F4
Blacklands E Sus 38 E4
Hereford 98 C2
Black Lane Gtr Man 195 F9
Blacklaw Aberds 302 D6
Blackleach Lancs 202 G5
Blackley Gtr Man 195 G11
W Yorks 196 D6
Blacklunans Perth 292 G3
Black Marsh Shrops 130 D6
Blackmarstone
Hereford 97 D10
Blackmill Bridgend 58 B2
Blackminster Worcs 99 C11
Blackmoor Bath 60 G5
Gtr Man 195 G7
Hants 49 G9
N Som 60 G3
Som 27 D11
Black Moor Lancs 194 E3
W Yorks 205 F11
Blackmoorfoot
W Yorks 196 E5
Blackmoor Gate
Devon 41 E7
Blackmore Essex 87 E10
Shrops 130 B6
Blackmore End
Essex 106 E4
Herts 85 B11
Worcs 98 C6
Black Mount Argyll 284 C6
Blackness Aberds 293 D8
E Sus 52 G4
Falk 279 F11
Blacknest Hants 49 E9
Windsor 66 F3
Blacknoll Dorset 18 D2
Black Notley Essex 106 G5
Blacko Lancs 204 E3
Blackoe Shrops 149 B10
Blackpark Dumfries 236 C5
Black Park Wrex 166 G4
Black Pill Swansea 56 C6
Blackpole Worcs 117 F7
Black Pole Lancs 202 F5
Blackpool Blackpool 202 F2
Devon 7 E11
Devon 9 F7
Devon 14 G2
Pembs 73 C9
Blackpool Gate
Cumb 240 B2
Blackridge W Loth 269 B7
Blackrock Argyll 274 G4
Bath 60 F6
Mon 78 C2
Black Rock Brighton 36 G4
Corn 2 C5
Blackrod Gtr Man 194 E6
Blackshaw Dumfries 238 D2
Blackshaw Head
W Yorks 196 B3
Blackshaw Moor
Staffs 169 D8
Blacksmith's Corner
Suff 108 C2
Blacksmith's Green
Suff 126 D2
Blacksnape
Blackburn 195 C8
Blackstone W Sus 36 D2
Worcs 116 C5
Black Street Suff 143 F10
Black Tar Pembs 73 D7
Blackthorn Oxon 83 B10
Blackthorpe Suff 125 E8
Blacktoft E Yorks 199 C10
Blacktop Aberdeen 293 C10
Black Torrington
Devon 25 F7
Blacktown Newport 59 C9
Black Vein Caerph 78 G2
Blackwall Derbys 170 F3
London 67 C11
Blackwall Tunnel
London 67 C11
Blackwater Corn 4 F4
Dorset 19 B8
Hants 49 B10
IoW 20 D6
Norf 159 E11
Som 28 D3
Blackwaterfoot
N Ayrs 255 E9
Blackwater Lodge
Moray 302 G3
Blackweir Cardiff 59 D7
Blackwell Cumb 239 G10
Darl 224 C5
Derbys 170 D6
Derbys 185 G10
Devon 27 B8
W Sus 51 F11
Warks 100 C4
Worcs 117 C9
Blackwood Caerph 77 F11
S Lanark 268 G5
Warr 183 C10
Blackwood Hill
Staffs 168 D6
Blacon Ches W 166 B5
Bladbean Kent 55 D7
Blades N Yorks 223 F9
Bladnoch Dumfries 236 D6
Bladon Oxon 82 C6
Blaenannerch
Ceredig 92 B4
Blaenau Carms 75 C10
Flint 166 D2
Blaenau Dolwyddelan
Conwy 164 E2
Blaenau Ffestiniog
Gwyn 164 F2
Blaenau-Gwent
Bl Gwent 78 E2
Blaenavon Torf 78 D3
Blaenbedw Fawr
Ceredig 111 G7
Blaencaerau
Bridgend 57 C11
Blaencelyn Ceredig 111 G7
Blaen-Cil-Llech
Ceredig 92 C6
Blaen Clydach
Rhondda 77 G7
Blaencwm Rhondda 76 F6
Blaendulais / Seven
Sisters Neath 76 D4
Blaendyryn Powys 95 D8
Blaenffos Pembs 92 D3
Blaengarw Bridgend 76 G6
Blaengwrach Neath 76 D5
Blaengwynfi Neath 57 B11
Blaen-gwynfi Neath 57 B11
Blaenllechau Rhondda 77 F8
Blaen-pant Ceredig 92 C5
Blaenpennal Ceredig 112 E2
Blaenplwyf Ceredig 111 B11
Blaenporth Ceredig 92 B5
Blaenrhondda
Rhondda 76 E6
Blaenwaun Carms 92 F4
Blaen-waun Carms 92 F4
Blaen-y-coed Carms 92 F6
Blaenycwm Ceredig 112 B6
Blaen-y-cwm
Bl Gwent 77 C10
Denb 147 C10
Gwyn 146 E4
Powys 147 E11
Blagdon N Som 44 B4
Torbay 9 C7
Blagdon Hill Som 28 D2
Blagill Cumb 231 B10
Blaguegate Lancs 194 F3
Blaich Highld 290 F2
Blain Highld 289 C8
Blaina Bl Gwent 78 D2
Blainacraig Ho
Aberds 293 D7
Blair Fife 280 C6
Blair Atholl Perth 291 G10
Blairbeg N Ayrs 256 C2
Blairburn Fife 279 D9
Blairdaff Aberds 293 B8
Blair Drummond
Stirling 278 B4
Blairdryne Aberds 293 D9
Blairglas Argyll 276 D6
Blairgorm Highld 301 G10
Blairgowrie Perth 286 C5
Blairhall Fife 279 D10
Blairhill N Lanark 268 B4
Blairingone Perth 279 B9
Blairland N Ayrs 266 F6
Blairlinn N Lanark 278 G5
Blairlogie Stirling 278 B6
Blairlomond Argyll 276 B3
Blairmore Argyll 276 E3
Highld 306 D6
Blairnamarrow
Moray 292 B4
Blairquhosh
Stirling 277 E10
Blair's Ferry Argyll 275 G10
Blairskaith E Dunb 277 F11
Blaisdon Glos 80 B2
Blake Hamlet Bristol 60 D5
Blakebrook Worcs 116 B6
Blakedown Worcs 117 B7
Blake End Essex 106 G4
Blakelands
M Keynes 103 C7
Blakelaw Borders 263 C7
T&W 242 D6
Blakeley Staffs 133 E7
Blakeley Lane Staffs 169 F7
Blakelow Ches E 167 E11
Blakemere Hereford 97 C7
Blakenall Heath
W Mid 133 C10
Blakeney Glos 79 D11
Norf 177 E8
Blakenhall Ches E 168 F2
W Mid 133 D8
Blakeshall Worcs 132 G6
Blakesley Northants 120 G2
Blanchland
Northumb 241 G11
Blandford Camp
Dorset 30 F6
Blandford Forum
Dorset 30 F5
Blandford St Mary
Dorset 30 F5
Bland Hill N Yorks 205 C10
Blandy Highld 308 D6
Blanefield Stirling 277 F11
Blanerne Borders 272 D6
Blank Bank Staffs 168 F4
Blankney Lincs 173 C9
Blantyre S Lanark 268 D3
Blar a'Chaorainn
Highld 290 G3
Blaran Argyll 275 B9
Blarghour Argyll 275 B10
Blarmachfoldach
Highld 290 G2
Blarnalearoch
Highld 307 K6
Blasford Hill Essex 88 C2
Blashford Hants 31 F11
Blaston Leics 136 D6
Blatchbridge Som 45 D9
Blatherwycke
Northants 137 D9
Blawith Cumb 210 B5
Blaxhall Suff 127 F7
Blaxton S Yorks 199 G7
Blaydon T&W 242 E5
Blaydon Burn T&W 242 E5
Blaydon Haughs
T&W 242 E5
Bleach Green Cumb 219 B9
Suff 126 B4
Bleadney Som 44 D3
Bleadon N Som 43 B10
Bleak Acre Hereford 98 B2
Bleak Hall
M Keynes 103 D7
Bleak Hey Nook
Gtr Man 196 F4
Bleak Hill Hants 31 E10
Blean Kent 70 G6
Bleasby Lincs 189 E10
Notts 172 F2
Bleasby Moor
Lincs 189 E10
Bleasdale Lancs 203 D7
Bleatarn Cumb 222 C4
Blebocraigs Fife 287 F8
Bleddfa Powys 114 D4
Bledington Glos 100 G4
Bledlow Bucks 84 E3
Bledlow Ridge Bucks 84 F3
Bleet Wilts 45 B11
Blegbie E Loth 271 C9
Blegbury Devon 24 B2
Blencarn Cumb 231 E8
Blencogo Cumb 229 B9
Blendworth Hants 34 E2
Blenheim Oxon 83 D9
Oxon 83 E9
Blenheim Park Norf 158 C6
Blenkinsopp Hall
Northumb 240 E5
Blennerhasset
Cumb 229 C9
Blervie Castle
Moray 301 D10
Bletchingdon Oxon 83 B8
Bletchingley Sur 51 C10
Bletchley M Keynes 103 E7
Shrops 150 C2
Bletherston Pembs 91 G11
Bletsoe Beds 121 F10
Blewbury Oxon 64 B4
Blickling Norf 160 D3
Blidworth Notts 171 D9
Blidworth Bottoms
Notts 171 E9
Blidworth Dale
Notts 171 E9
Blindburn Northumb 263 G8
Blindcrake Cumb 229 E8
Blindley Heath Sur 51 D11
Blindmoor Som 28 E3
Blingery Highld 310 E7
Blisland Corn 11 G8
Blissford Hants 31 E11
Bliss Gate Worcs 116 C4
Blisworth Northants 120 G4
Blithbury Staffs 151 E11
Blitterlees Cumb 238 G4
Blockley Glos 100 D3
Blofield Norf 142 B6
Blofield Heath Norf 160 G6
Blo' Norton Norf 125 B10
Bloodman's Corner
Suff 143 D10
Bloomfield Bath 45 B7
Bath 61 G8
Borders 262 E3
W Mid 133 E9
Bloomsbury London 67 C10
Blore Staffs 150 C4
Staffs 169 F10
Bloreheath Staffs 150 B4
Blossomfield
W Mid 118 B2
Blount's Green
Staffs 151 C11
Blowick Mers 193 D11
Blowinghouse Corn 4 E4
Bloxham Oxon 101 D8
Bloxholm Lincs 173 E9
Bloxwich W Mid 133 C9
Bloxworth Dorset 18 C3
Blubberhouses
N Yorks 205 B9
Blue Anchor Corn 5 D8
Som 42 E4

Brandon Bank
Cambs 140 F2
Brandon Creek Norf 140 E2
Brandon Parva
Norf 141 B11
Brandsby N Yorks 215 E11
Brands Hill Windsor 66 D4
Brandwood Shrops 149 D9
Brandwood End
W Mid 117 B11
Brandy Carr
W Yorks 197 C10
Brandy Hole Essex 88 F4
Brandyquoy Orkney 314 G4
Brandy Wharf Lincs 189 B8
Brane Corn 1 D4
Bran End Essex 106 F3
Branksome Darl 224 B5
Poole 18 C6
Branksome Park
Poole 19 C7
Bransbury Hants 48 E2
Bransby Lincs 188 F5
Branscombe Devon 15 D9
Bransford Worcs 116 G5
Bransgore Hants 19 B9
Branshill Clack 279 C7
Bransholme Hull 209 G8
Branson's Cross
Worcs 117 C11
Branston Leics 154 D6
Lincs 173 B8
Staffs 152 E4
Branston Booths
Lincs 173 B9
Branstone IoW 21 E7
Bransty Cumb 219 B9
Brant Broughton
Lincs 172 E6
Brantham Suff 108 E2
Branthwaite Cumb 229 D11
Cumb 229 G7
Branthwaite Edge
Cumb 229 G7
Brantingham
E Yorks 200 B2
Branton Northumb 264 F2
S Yorks 198 G6
Branton Green
N Yorks 215 G8
Branxholme
Borders 261 G11
Branxholm Park
Borders 261 G11
Branxton Northumb 263 B9
Brascote Leics 135 C8
Brassey Green
Ches W 167 C8
Brassington Derbys 170 E2
Brasted Kent 52 C3
Brasted Chart Kent 52 C3
Brathens Aberds 293 D8
Bratoft Lincs 175 B7
Brattle Kent 54 G2
Brattleby Lincs 188 E6
Bratton Som 42 D2
Telford 150 G2
Wilts 46 C2
Bratton Clovelly
Devon 12 C5
Bratton Fleming
Devon 40 F6
Bratton Seymour
Som 29 B11
Braughing Herts 105 F7
Braughing Friars
Herts 105 G8
Braulen Lodge
Highld 300 F2
Braunston
Northants 119 D10
Braunstone Leics 135 C11
Braunstone Town
Leicester 135 C11
Braunston-in-Rutland
Rutland 136 B6
Braunton Devon 40 F3
Brawby N Yorks 216 D4
Brawith N Yorks 225 D10
Brawl Highld 310 C2
Brawlbin Highld 310 D4
Bray Windsor 66 D2
Braybrooke
Northants 136 G5
Braydon Side Wilts 62 B4
Brayford Devon 41 G7
Brayfordhill Devon 41 G7
Brays Grove Essex 87 D7
Bray Shop Corn 12 G2
Braystones Cumb 219 D10
Brayswick Worcs 98 B6
Braythorn N Yorks 205 D10
Brayton N Yorks 207 G8
Braytown Dorset 18 D2
Bray Wick Windsor 65 D11
Braywoodside
Windsor 65 D11
Brazacott Corn 11 C11
Brazenhill Staffs 151 E7
Brea Corn 4 G3
Breach Bath 60 G6
Kent 69 F10
W Sus 22 B3
Breachacha Castle
Argyll 288 D3
Breachwood Green
Herts 104 G2
Breacleit W Isles 304 E3
Breaden Heath
Shrops 149 B8
Breadsall Derbys 153 B7
Breadsall Hilltop
Derby 153 B7
Breadstone Glos 80 E2
Bread Street Glos 80 D4
Breage Corn 2 D4
Breakachy Highld 300 E4
Brealeys Devon 25 D8
Bream Glos 79 D10
Breamore Hants 31 D11
Bream's Meend Glos 79 D9
Brean Som 43 B9
Breanais W Isles 304 F1
Brearley W Yorks 196 B4
Brearton N Yorks 214 G6
Breascleit W Isles 304 E4
Breaston Derbys 153 C9
Brechfa Carms 93 E10
Brechin Angus 293 G7
Breckan Orkney 314 F2
Breckles Norf 141 E9
Breck of Cruan
Orkney 314 E3
Breckrey Highld 298 C5
Brecks S Yorks 187 C7
Brecon Powys 95 F10
Bredbury Gtr Man 184 C6
Bredbury Green
Gtr Man 184 C6
Brede E Sus 38 D4
Bredenbury
Hereford 116 F2
Bredfield Suff 126 G5
Bredgar Kent 69 G11
Bredhurst Kent 69 G9
Bredicot Worcs 117 G8
Bredon Worcs 99 D8
Bredon's Hardwick
Worcs 99 D8
Bredon's Norton
Worcs 99 D8
Bredwardine
Hereford 96 C6
Breedon on the Hill
Leics 153 E8
Breeds Essex 87 C11
Breedy Butts Lancs 202 E2
Breibhig W Isles 297 M2
W Isles 304 E6
Breich W Loth 269 C9
Breightmet Gtr Man 195 F8
Breighton E Yorks 207 G10
Breinton Hereford 97 D9
Breinton Common
Hereford 97 C9
Breiwick Shetland 313 J6
Brelston Green
Hereford 97 G11
Bremhill Wilts 62 E3
Bremhill Wick Wilts 62 E3
Bremirehoull
Shetland 313 L6
Brenachoile Lodge
Stirling 285 G8
Brenchley Kent 53 E7
Brenchoillie Argyll 284 G4
Brendon Devon 24 E5
Devon 24 F5
Devon 41 D9
Brenkley T&W 242 B6
Brent Corn 6 E4
Brent Cross London 67 B8
Brent Eleigh Suff 107 B8
Brentford London 67 D7
Brentford End
London 67 D7
Brentingby Leics 154 F5
Brent Knoll Som 43 C10
Brent Mill Devon 8 D3
Brent Pelham Herts 105 E8
Brentry Bristol 60 D5
Brentwood Essex 87 G9
Brenzett Kent 39 B8
Brenzett Green Kent 39 B8
Brereton Staffs 151 F11
Brereton Cross
Staffs 151 F11
Brereton Green
Ches E 168 C3
Brereton Heath
Ches E 168 C4
Breretonhill Staffs 151 F11
Bressingham Norf 141 G11
Bressingham Common
Norf 141 G11
Bretby Derbys 152 E5
Bretford Warks 119 B8
Bretforton Worcs 99 C11
Bretherdale Head
Cumb 221 E11
Bretherton Lancs 194 C3
Brettabister
Shetland 313 H6
Brettenham Norf 141 G8
Suff 125 G9
Bretton Derbys 186 F2
Flint 166 C5
Pboro 138 C3
Brewer's End
Essex 105 G11
Brewers Green Norf 142 G2
Brewer Street Sur 51 C10
Brewlands Bridge
Angus 292 G3
Brewood Staffs 133 B7
Briach Moray 301 D10
Briants Puddle
Dorset 18 C2
Briar Hill Northants 120 F4
Brick End Essex 105 F11
Brickendon Herts 86 D4
Bricket Wood Herts 85 E10
Brickfields Worcs 117 F7
Brickhill Beds 121 G11
Brick Hill Sur 66 G3
Brick House End
Essex 105 F9
Brickhouses Ches E 168 C3
Brick Houses
S Yorks 186 E4
Brick-kiln End
Notts 171 D9
Brickkiln Green
Essex 106 E4
Bricklehampton
Worcs 99 C9
Bride IoM 192 B5
Bridekirk Cumb 229 E8
Bridell Pembs 92 C3
Bridestowe Devon 12 D6
Brideswell Aberds 302 F5
Bridford Devon 14 D2
Bridfordmills Devon 14 D2
Bridge Corn 2 D6
Corn 4 G3
Kent 55 C7
Som 28 F5
Bridge Ball Devon 41 D8
Bridge End Beds 121 G10
Cumb 230 B3
Devon 8 F3
Durham 232 D6
Essex 106 E3
Flint 166 D4
Bridge End *continued*
Hereford 98 B2
Lincs 156 B2
Northumb 241 D10
Northumb 241 E10
Oxon 83 G9
Bridge-End Shetland 313 K5
Bridge End Sur 50 B5
Warks 118 E5
Worcs 98 E6
Bridgefoot Aberds 292 C6
Angus 287 D7
Cumb 229 F7
Bridge Green Essex 105 D9
Norf 142 G2
Bridgehampton Som 29 C9
Bridge Hewick
N Yorks 214 E6
Bridgehill Durham 242 G3
Bridge Ho Argyll 254 B4
Bridgeholm Green
Derbys 185 E8
Bridgehouse Gate
N Yorks 214 F3
Bridgelands
Borders 261 C11
Bridgemary Hants 33 G9
Bridgemere Ches E 168 F2
Bridgemont Derbys 185 E8
Bridgend Aberds 293 B7
Aberds 302 F5
Angus 293 G7
Argyll 255 D8
Argyll 274 G4
Argyll 275 D9
Corn 6 D2
Cumb 221 C7
Devon 7 F11
Fife 287 F7
Glos 80 E4
Highld 300 D3
Invclyd 276 F5
Moray 302 F3
N Lanark 278 G3
Pembs 92 B3
W Loth 279 F10
Bridgend of Lintrathen
Angus 286 B6
Bridgend / Pen-y-Bont
ar-ogwr Bridgend 58 C2
Bridgeness Falk 279 E10
Bridge of Alford
Aberds 293 B7
Bridge of Allan
Stirling 278 B5
Bridge of Avon
Moray 301 F11
Moray 301 G11
Bridge of Awe
Argyll 284 E4
Bridge of Balgie
Perth 285 C9
Bridge of Cally
Perth 286 B5
Bridge of Canny
Aberds 293 D8
Bridge of Craigisla
Angus 286 B6
Bridge of Dee
Dumfries 237 D9
Bridge of Don
Aberdeen 293 B11
Bridge of Dun
Angus 287 B10
Bridge of Dye
Aberds 293 E8
Bridge of Earn
Perth 286 F5
Bridge of Ericht
Perth 285 B9
Bridge of Feugh
Aberds 293 D9
Bridge of Forss
Highld 310 C4
Bridge of Gairn
Aberds 292 D5
Bridge of Gaur
Perth 285 B9
Bridge of Lyon
Perth 285 C11
Bridge of Muchalls
Aberds 293 D10
Bridge of Muick
Aberds 292 D5
Bridge of Oich
Highld 290 C5
Bridge of Orchy
Argyll 284 D6
Bridge of Waith
Orkney 314 E2
Bridge of Walls
Shetland 313 H4
Bridge of Weir
Renfs 267 B7
Bridge Reeve Devon 25 E11
Bridgerule Devon 24 G3
Bridges Corn 5 D10
Shrops 131 D7
Bridge Sollers
Hereford 97 C8
Bridge Street Suff 107 B7
Bridgeton Glasgow 268 C2
Bridgetown Corn 12 D2
Devon 8 C6
Som 42 G2
Staffs 133 B9
Bridge Town Warks 118 G4
Bridge Trafford
Ches W 183 G7
Bridge Yate S Glos 61 E7
Bridgham Norf 141 F9
Bridgnorth Shrops 132 E4
Bridgtown Staffs 133 B9
Bridgwater Som 43 F10
Bridlington E Yorks 218 F3
Bridport Dorset 16 C5
Bridstow Hereford 97 G11
Brierfield Lancs 204 F2
Brierholme Carr
S Yorks 199 E7
Brierley Glos 79 B10
Hereford 115 F9
S Yorks 198 E2
Brierley Hill W Mid 133 F8
Brierton Hrtlpl 234 E5
Briery Cumb 229 G11
Briery Hill Bl Gwent 77 D11
Briestfield W Yorks 197 D8
Brigflatts Cumb 222 G3
Brigg N Lincs 200 F3
N Lincs 200 F4
Briggate Norf 160 D6
Briggswath N Yorks 227 D7
Brigham Cumb 229 E7
Cumb 229 G11
E Yorks 209 C7
Brighouse W Yorks 196 C6
Brighstone IoW 20 E4
Brightgate Derbys 170 D3
Brighthampton Oxon 82 E5
Brightholmlee
S Yorks 186 B3
Brightley Devon 13 B7
Brightling E Sus 37 C11
Brightlingsea Essex 89 B9
Brighton Brighton 36 G4
Corn 5 E8
Brighton Hill Hants 48 D6
Brighton le Sands
Mers 182 B4
Brightons Falk 279 F8
Brightside S Yorks 186 D5
Brightwalton
W Berks 64 D2
Brightwalton Green
W Berks 64 D2
Brightwalton Holt
W Berks 64 D2
Brightwell Suff 108 C4
Brightwell Baldwin
Oxon 83 F11
Brightwell cum Sotwell
Oxon 83 G9
Brigmerston Wilts 47 D7
Brignall Durham 223 C11
Brig o'Turk Stirling 285 G9
Brigsley NE Lincs 201 G9
Brigsteer Cumb 211 B9
Brigstock Northants 137 F8
Brill Bucks 83 C11
Corn 2 D6
Brilley Hereford 96 B5
Brilley Mountain
Powys 114 G5
Brimaston Pembs 91 G8
Brimfield Hereford 115 D10
Brimington Derbys 186 G6
Brimington Common
Derbys 186 G6
Brimley Devon 13 F11
Devon 28 G4
Brimpsfield Glos 80 C6
Brimps Hill Glos 79 B11
Brimpton W Berks 64 G5
Brimpton Common
W Berks 64 G5
Brims Orkney 314 H2
Brims Castle Highld 310 B4
Brimscombe Glos 80 E5
Brimsdown London 86 F5
Brimstage Mers 182 E4
Brinacory Highld 295 F9
Brincliffe S Yorks 186 D4
Brind E Yorks 207 G10
Brindham Som 44 E4
Brindister Shetland 313 H4
Shetland 313 K6
Brindle Lancs 194 C6
Brindle Heath
Gtr Man 195 G10
Brindley Ches E 167 E9
Brindley Ford Stoke 168 E5
Brindwoodgate
Derbys 186 F4
Brineton Staffs 150 G6
Bringewood Forge
Hereford 115 C9
Bringhurst Leics 136 E6
Bringsty Common
Hereford 116 F4
Brington Cambs 121 B11
Brinian Orkney 314 D4
Briningham Norf 159 C10
Brinkhill Lincs 190 G5
Brinkley Cambs 124 G2
Notts 172 E2
Brinkley Hill
Hereford 97 E11
Brinklow M Keynes 103 D8
Warks 119 B8
Brinkworth Wilts 62 C4
Brinmore Highld 300 G6
Brinnington
Gtr Man 184 C6
Brinscall Lancs 194 C6
Brinsea N Som 60 G2
Brinsford Staffs 133 B8
Brinsley Notts 171 F7
Brinsop Hereford 97 C8
Brinsop Common
Hereford 97 C8
Brinsworth S Yorks 186 D6
Brinsworthy Devon 41 G9
Brinton Norf 159 B10
Brisco Cumb 239 G10
Briscoe Cumb 219 C10
Briscoerigg
N Yorks 205 C11
Brisley Norf 159 E8
Brislington Bristol 60 E6
Brissenden Green
Kent 54 F2
Bristnall Fields
W Mid 133 F9
Bristol Bristol 60 E5
Briston Norf 159 C11
Britain Bottom
S Glos 61 B9
Britannia Lancs 195 C11
Britford Wilts 31 B11
Brithdir Caerph 77 E11
Ceredig 92 B6
Gwyn 146 F5
Brithem Bottom
Devon 27 E8
British Torf 78 E3
Briton Ferry / Llansawel
Neath 57 C8
Britten's Bath 45 B7
Britwell Slough 66 C3
Britwell Salome
Oxon 83 G11
Brixham Torbay 9 D8
Brixton Devon 7 E11
Brixton *continued*
London 67 D10
Brixton Deverill
Wilts 45 F11
Brixworth Northants 120 C4
Brize Norton Oxon 82 D4
Broad Alley Worcs 117 D7
Broad Blunsdon
Swindon 81 G11
Broadbottom
Gtr Man 185 C7
Broadbridge W Sus 22 B4
Broadbridge Heath
W Sus 50 G6
Broadbury Devon 12 B5
Broadbush Swindon 81 G11
Broad Campden
Glos 100 D3
Broad Carr W Yorks 196 D5
Broad Chalke Wilts 31 B8
Broad Clough
Lancs 195 C11
Broadclyst Devon 14 B5
Broad Colney Herts 85 E11
Broad Common
Worcs 117 D7
Broadfield
Gtr Man 195 E10
Invclyd 276 G6
Lancs 194 C4
Lancs 195 B8
Pembs 73 E10
W Sus 51 G9
Broadford Highld 295 C8
Sur 50 D3
Broad Ford Kent 53 F8
Broadford Bridge
W Sus 35 C9
Broadgate Hants 32 C6
Broadgrass Green
Suff 125 E9
Broad Green
C Beds 103 C9
Cambs 124 F3
Essex 105 D8
Essex 107 G7
London 67 F10
Mers 182 C6
Suff 124 F5
Suff 125 F11
Worcs 116 F5
Worcs 117 C9
Broadgreen Wood
Herts 86 D4
Broadhalgh
Gtr Man 195 E11
Broadham Green
Sur 51 C11
Broadhaugh
Borders 249 B10
Broadhaven Highld 310 D7
Broad Haven /
Aberllydan Pembs 72 C5
Broadheath
Gtr Man 184 D3
Broad Heath Powys 114 E6
Staffs 151 D7
Worcs 116 D3
Broadhembury
Devon 27 G10
Broadhempston Devon 8 B6
Broad Hill Cambs 123 B11
Broad Hinton Wilts 62 D6
Broadholm Derbys 170 F4
Broadholme Derbys 170 F5
Lincs 188 G5
Broad Ings E Yorks 208 C2
Broadland Row
E Sus 38 D4
Broadlands Devon 14 G3
Broadlane Corn 2 C4
Broad Lane Corn 4 G3
Broad Lanes Shrops 132 F5
Broadlay Carms 74 D5
Broad Laying Hants 64 G2
Broad Layings Hants 64 G2
Broadley Lancs 195 D11
Moray 302 C3
Broadley Common
Essex 86 D6
Broadleys Aberds 303 C8
Broad Marston
Worcs 100 B2
Broadmayne Dorset 17 D10
Broad Meadow
Staffs 168 F4
Broadmeadows
Borders 261 C10
Broadmere Hants 48 D6
Broadmoor Pembs 73 D9
Sur 50 D6
Broadmoor Common
Hereford 98 D2
Broadmore Green
Worcs 116 G6
Broadoak Dorset 16 B4
Glos 80 C2
Hants 33 E8
Shrops 149 F9
Wrex 166 D5
Broad Oak Carms 93 G11
Cumb 220 G2
Dorset 30 E3
E Sus 37 C10
E Sus 38 D4
Hants 49 C9
Hereford 97 G9
Kent 54 F4
Kent 71 G7
Mers 183 B8
Shrops 132 F5
Broadoak End Herts 86 C4
Broadoak Park
Gtr Man 195 G9
Broad Parkham
Devon 24 C5
Broadplat Oxon 65 C8
Broadrashes Moray 302 D4
Broadrock Glos 79 F8
Broadsands Torbay 9 D7
Broadsea Aberds 303 C9
Broad's Green
Essex 87 C11
Wilts 62 F3
Broadshard Som 28 E6
Broadstairs Kent 71 F11
Broadstone Kent 53 D11
Broadstone *continued*
Mon 79 E8
Poole 18 B6
Shrops 131 F10
Broad Street E Sus 38 D5
Kent 53 B10
Kent 54 E6
Kent 55 E7
Medway 69 E9
Suff 107 C9
Wilts 46 B6
Broadstreet Common
Newport 59 C11
Broad Street Green
Essex 88 D5
Broad Tenterden
Kent 53 G11
Broad Town Wilts 62 D5
Broadwas Worcs 116 F5
Broadwater Herts 104 G4
W Sus 35 G11
Broadwater Down
Kent 52 F5
Broadwaters Worcs 116 B6
Broadwath Cumb 239 F11
Broadway Carms 74 D3
Carms 74 D5
Pembs 72 C5
Som 28 D4
Suff 127 B7
Worcs 99 D11
Broadway Lands
Hereford 97 E11
Broadwell Glos 79 C9
Glos 100 F4
Oxon 82 E3
Warks 119 D9
Broadwey Dorset 17 E9
Broadwindsor Dorset 28 G6
Broadwood Kelly
Devon 25 F10
Broadwoodwidger
Devon 12 D4
Brobury Hereford 96 C6
Brochel Highld 298 E5
Brochroy Argyll 284 D4
Brock Lancs 202 E6
Brockamin Worcs 116 G5
Brockbridge Hants 33 D10
Brockdish Norf 126 B4
Brockencote Worcs 117 C7
Brockenhurst Hants 32 G4
Brocketsbrae
S Lanark 259 B8
Brockfield Devon 28 F4
Brockford Green
Suff 126 D2
Brockford Street
Suff 126 D2
Brockhall Northants 120 E2
Brockhall Village
Lancs 203 F10
Brockham Sur 51 D7
Brockham End Bath 61 F8
Brockham Park Sur 51 D8
Brockhampton Glos 99 F8
Glos 99 G10
Hants 22 B2
Hereford 97 E11
Brockhampton Green
Dorset 30 F2
Brockhill Borders 261 E9
Brock Hill Essex 88 F2
Brockholes W Yorks 197 E7
Brockhollands Glos 79 D10
Brockhurst Derbys 170 C4
Hants 33 G10
Warks 135 G9
Brocklebank Cumb 230 C2
Brocklehirst
Dumfries 238 C3
Brocklesby Lincs 200 E6
Brockley London 67 E11
N Som 60 F3
Brockley Corner
Suff 124 C6
Brockley Green Suff 106 B4
Suff 124 G6
Brockleymoor
Cumb 230 D5
Brockloch Dumfries 246 D2
Brockmanton
Hereford 115 F10
Brockmoor W Mid 133 F8
Brockscombe Devon 12 C5
Brock's Green Hants 64 G4
Brock's Watering
Norf 142 E2
Brockton Shrops 130 C6
Shrops 130 F6
Shrops 131 E11
Shrops 132 C4
Staffs 150 C6
Telford 150 F4
Brockweir Glos 79 E8
Brockwell Som 42 E2
Brockwood Hants 33 B10
Brockworth Glos 80 B5
Brocton Corn 5 B10
Staffs 151 F9
Brodick N Ayrs 256 B2
Brodie Moray 301 D9
Brodiesord Aberds 302 C5
Brodsworth S Yorks 198 F4
Brogaig Highld 298 C4
Brogborough
C Beds 103 D9
Broke Hall Suff 108 C3
Brokenborough Wilts 62 B2
Broken Cross
Ches E 184 G5
Ches W 183 G11
Broken Green Herts 105 G8
Brokerswood Wilts 45 C10
Brokes N Yorks 224 F3
Brombil Neath 57 D9
Bromborough Mers 182 E4
Bromborough Pool
Mers 182 E4
Bromdon Shrops 132 G2
Brome Suff 126 B2
Bromesberrow Glos 98 E4
Bromesberrow Heath
Glos 98 E4
Brome Street Suff 126 B3
Bromeswell Suff 126 G6
Bromfield Cumb 229 B9
Bromfield *continued*
Shrops 115 B9
Bromford W Mid 134 E2
Bromham Beds 121 G10
Wilts 62 F3
Bromley Herts 105 G8
London 67 C11
London 68 F2
S Yorks 186 B4
Shrops 132 D4
Shrops 149 D8
W Mid 133 F8
Bromley Common
London 68 F2
Bromley Cross
Essex 107 F11
Gtr Man 195 E8
Bromley Green Kent 54 F3
Bromley Hall Staffs 150 C5
Bromley Heath
S Glos 61 D7
Bromley Park
London 67 F11
Bromley Wood
Staffs 152 E2
Bromlow Shrops 130 C6
Brompton London 67 D9
Medway 69 F9
N Yorks 217 C8
N Yorks 225 F7
Shrops 131 B10
Brompton-by-Sawdon
N Yorks 217 C8
Brompton-on-Swale
N Yorks 224 F4
Brompton Ralph Som 42 G5
Brompton Regis Som 42 G3
Bromsash Hereford 98 G2
Bromsberrow Heath
Glos 98 E4
Bromsgrove Worcs 117 C9
Bromstead Common
Staffs 150 F6
Bromstead Heath
Staffs 150 F6
Bromstone Kent 71 F11
Bromyard Hereford 116 G3
Bromyard Downs
Hereford 116 F3
Bronaber Gwyn 146 C4
Broncroft Shrops 131 F10
Brondesbury London 67 C8
Brondesbury Park
London 67 C8
Broneirion Powys 129 F10
Brongest Ceredig 92 B6
Brongwyn Ceredig 92 C5
Bronington Wrex 149 B9
Bronllys Powys 96 D2
Bronnant Ceredig 112 D2
Bronwydd Ceredig 93 C7
Bronwydd Arms
Carms 93 G8
Bronydd Powys 96 B4
Bronygarth Shrops 148 B5
Brook Carms 74 D3
Devon 12 G5
Devon 14 C2
Hants 32 B4
Hants 32 E3
IoW 20 E3
Kent 54 E5
Sur 50 D5
Sur 50 F2
Brook Bottom
Gtr Man 185 D7
Gtr Man 196 G3
Lancs 202 E6
Brooke Norf 142 D5
Rutland 136 B6
Brookenby Lincs 190 B2
Brookend Glos 79 E11
Glos 79 F9
Oxon 100 G6
Brook End Beds 121 E11
C Beds 104 B3
Cambs 121 C11
Herts 104 F6
M Keynes 103 C8
Wilts 61 C10
Worcs 99 B7
Brookfield Derbys 185 B8
Lancs 203 G7
Mbro 225 B9
Renfs 267 C8
Brookfoot W Yorks 196 C6
Brookgreen IoW 20 E3
Brook Green London 67 D8
Suff 125 F7
Brookhampton
Oxon 83 F10
Shrops 131 E11
Som 29 B10
Brook Hill Hants 32 E3
Notts 153 C11
Brookhouse
Blackburn 195 B7
Ches E 184 F6
Denb 165 B9
Lancs 211 G10
S Yorks 187 D8
W Yorks 196 B5
Brookhouse Green
Ches E 168 C4
Brookhouses
Derbys 185 D8
Staffs 169 G7
Brookhurst Mers 182 E4
Brookland Kent 39 B7
Brooklands
Dumfries 237 B10
Gtr Man 184 C3
Shrops 167 G8
Sur 66 G5
W Yorks 206 F2
Brookleigh Devon 14 B5
Brookmans Park
Herts 86 E2
Brookpits W Sus 35 G8
Brook Place Sur 66 G3
Brookrow Shrops 116 C2
Brooks Corn 6 C3
Powys 130 D2
Brooksbottoms
Gtr Man 195 D9
Brooksby Leics 154 F3
Brooks End Kent 71 F9
Brooks Green
W Sus 35 C10
Brookside Brack 66 E2
Derbys 186 G5
Telford 132 B3
Brook Street Essex 87 G9
Kent 52 D5
Kent 54 G2
Suff 106 B6
W Sus 36 B4
Brookthorpe Glos 80 C4
Brookvale Halton 183 E8
Brookville Norf 140 D4
Brook Waters Wilts 30 C6
Brookwood Sur 50 B2
Broom C Beds 104 C3
Cumb 231 G9
Devon 28 G4
E Renf 267 D10
Pembs 73 D10
S Yorks 186 C5
Warks 117 G11
Broombank Worcs 116 C3
Broome Norf 143 E7
Shrops 131 D10
Shrops 131 G8
Worcs 117 B8
Broomedge Warr 184 D2
Broome Park
Northumb 264 G4
Broomer's Corner
W Sus 35 C10
Broomershill W Sus 35 D9
Broomfield Aberds 303 F9
Cumb 230 B2
Essex 88 D2
Kent 53 C10
Kent 71 F7
Som 43 G8
Wilts 61 D11
Broomfields Shrops 149 F8
Broomfleet
E Yorks 199 B11
Broom Green Norf 159 E9
Broomhall Ches E 167 F10
Windsor 66 F3
Broomhall Green
Ches E 167 F10
Broomham E Sus 23 C8
Broomhaugh
Northumb 242 E2
Broomhill Borders 261 D11
Bristol 60 D6
Ches W 167 B7
Highld 301 G9
Kent 55 B8
Norf 140 C2
Northumb 252 C6
Notts 171 F8
S Yorks 198 G2
Broom Hill Bristol 60 E6
Dorset 31 G8
Durham 242 G4
London 68 F3
Suff 108 B5
Worcs 117 B8
Broomhill Bank Kent 52 E5
Broomholm Norf 160 C6
Broomhouse
Glasgow 268 C3
Broomlands N Ayrs 257 B8
Broomley Northumb 242 E2
Broompark
Durham 233 C10
Broomridge Stirling 278 C6
Broom's Barn Suff 124 D5
Broom's Green Glos 98 E4
Broomsgrove E Sus 38 E4
Broomsthorpe Norf 158 D6
Broom Street Kent 70 G4
Broomton Highld 301 B8
Broomy Hill Hereford 97 D9
Broomy Lodge Hants 32 E2
Broomyshaw Staffs 169 F9
Brora Highld 311 J3
Broseley Shrops 132 C3
Brotherhouse Bar
Lincs 156 G5
Brotheridge Green
Worcs 98 C6
Brotherlee Durham 232 D4
Brotherstone
Borders 262 B4
Brothertoft Lincs 174 F3
Brotherton N Yorks 198 B3
Brothybeck Cumb 230 C2
Brotton Redcar 226 B3
Broubster Highld 310 C4
Brough Cumb 222 C5
Derbys 185 E11
E Yorks 200 B2
Highld 310 B6
Notts 172 D4
Orkney 314 E3
Orkney 314 H4
Shetland 312 C7
Shetland 312 F6
Shetland 312 F7
Shetland 313 G7
Shetland 313 H6
Shetland 313 J7
Broughall Shrops 167 G9
Brough Lodge
Shetland 312 D7
Brough Sowerby
Cumb 222 C5
Broughton
Borders 260 B4
Bucks 84 C4
Cambs 122 B5
Edin 280 F5
Flint 166 C4
Hants 47 G10
Lancs 202 F6
M Keynes 103 C7
N Lincs 200 F3
N Yorks 204 C4
N Yorks 216 E5
Northants 120 B6
Orkney 314 B4
Oxon 101 D8
Shrops 132 E6
Staffs 150 C5
V Glam 58 E2

Broughton Astley Leics 135 E10
Broughton Beck Cumb 210 C5
Broughton Common N Lincs 200 E3; Wilts 61 G11
Broughton Cross Cumb 229 E7
Broughton Gifford Wilts 61 G11
Broughton Green Worcs 117 E9
Broughton Hackett Worcs 117 G8
Broughton in Furness Cumb 210 B4
Broughton Lodges Leics 154 E4
Broughton Mills Cumb 220 G4
Broughton Moor Cumb 228 E6
Broughton Park Gtr Man 195 G10
Broughton Poggs Oxon 82 E2
Broughtown Orkney 314 B6
Broughty Ferry Dundee 287 D8
Brow Edge Cumb 211 C7
Browhouses Dumfries 239 D7
Browland Shetland 313 H4
Brown Bank N Yorks 205 C10
Brownber Cumb 222 D4
Brownbread Street E Sus 23 B11
Brown Candover Hants 48 F5
Brownedge Ches E 168 C3
Brown Edge Lancs 193 E11; Mers 183 C8; Staffs 168 E6
Brownheath Devon 27 D10; Shrops 149 D9
Brown Heath Ches W 167 B7; Hants 33 D8
Brownheath Common Worcs 117 E7
Brownhill Aberds 302 E6; Aberds 303 E8; Blackburn 203 G9; Shrops 149 E8
Brownhills Fife 287 F9; Shrops 150 B3; W Mid 133 B10
Brownieside Northumb 264 E5
Browninghill Green Hants 48 B5
Brown Knowl Ches W 167 E7
Brown Lees Staffs 168 D5
Brownlow Ches E 168 C4; Mers 194 G4
Brownlow Fold Gtr Man 195 E8
Brownlow Heath Ches E 168 C4
Brown Moor W Yorks 206 G3
Brownmuir Aberds 293 F9
Brown's Bank Ches E 167 G10
Brown's End Glos 98 E4
Brown's Green W Mid 133 E10
Brownshill Glos 80 E5
Brownshill Green W Mid 134 G6
Brownside Lancs 204 G3
Brownsover Warks 119 B10
Brownston Devon 8 E3
Brown Street Suff 125 E11
Browns Wood M Keynes 103 D8
Browsburn N Lanark 268 C5
Browston Green Norf 143 C9
Browtop Cumb 229 G7
Broxa N Yorks 227 G8
Broxbourne Herts 86 D5
Broxburn E Loth 282 F3; W Loth 279 G11
Broxfield Northumb 264 F6
Broxholme Lincs 188 F6
Broxted Essex 105 F11
Broxton Ches W 167 E7
Broxtowe Nottingham 171 G8
Broxwood Hereford 115 G7
Broyle Side E Sus 23 C7
Brù W Isles 304 D5
Bruairnis W Isles 297 L3
Bruan Highld 310 F7
Bruar Lodge Perth 291 F10
Brucefield Fife 280 D2
Brucehill W Dunb 277 F7
Bruche Warr 183 D10
Brucklebog Aberds 293 D9
Bruera Ches W 166 C6
Bruern Abbey Oxon 100 G5
Bruichladdich Argyll 274 G3
Bruisyard Suff 126 D6
Brumby N Lincs 199 F11
Brunant Powys 130 B5
Brund Staffs 169 C10
Brundall Norf 142 B6
Brundish Norf 143 D7; Suff 126 D5
Brundish Street Suff 126 C5
Brundon Suff 107 C7
Brunery Highld 289 B9
Brunnion Corn 2 B2
Brunshaw Lancs 204 G3
Brunstane Edin 280 G6
Brunstock Cumb 239 F10
Brunswick Gtr Man 184 B4
Brunswick Park London 86 G3
Brunswick Village T&W 242 C6
Bruntcliffe W Yorks 197 B9
Brunt Hamersland Shetland 313 H6
Brunthwaite W Yorks 205 D7
Bruntingthorpe Leics 136 F2
Brunton Fife 287 E7; Northumb 264 E6; Wilts 47 B8
Brushes Gtr Man 185 B7
Brushfield Derbys 185 G11
Brushford Devon 25 F11; Som 26 B6
Bruton Som 45 G7
Bryans Midloth 270 C6
Bryan's Green Worcs 117 D7
Bryanston Dorset 30 F5
Bryant's Bottom Bucks 84 F5
Brydekirk Dumfries 238 C5
Bryher Scilly 1 G3
Brymbo Conwy 180 G4; Wrex 166 E3
Brympton Som 29 D8
Brympton D'Evercy Som 29 D8
Bryn Caerph 77 F11; Carms 75 E8; Ches W 183 G10; Gtr Man 194 G5; Gwyn 179 G9; Neath 57 C10; Powys 130 C3; Rhondda 76 D6; Shrops 130 F5; Swansea 56 C4
Brynafan Ceredig 112 C4
Brynamman Carms 76 C2
Brynawel Caerph 77 G11
Brynberian Pembs 92 D2
Brynbryddan Neath 57 C9; Neath 57 C9
Bryn Bwbach Gwyn 146 B2
Bryncae Rhondda 58 C3; Rhondda 58 C3
Bryn Celyn Anglesey 179 F10; Flint 181 F11
Bryncethin Bridgend 58 C2; Bridgend 58 C2
Bryncir Gwyn 163 G7
Bryncoch Bridgend 58 C2
Bryn-coch Neath 57 B8
Bryn Common Flint 166 D3
Bryncroes Gwyn 144 C4
Bryncrug Gwyn 128 C2
Brynderwen Powys 130 D3
Bryndu Carms 75 D8
Bryn Du Anglesey 178 G4
Bryn Dulas Conwy 180 F6
Bryneglwys Denb 165 F10
Bryn Eglwys Gwyn 163 B10
Brynford Flint 181 G11
Bryn Gates Gtr Man 194 G5
Brynglas Newport 59 B10
Bryn-glas Conwy 164 B4
Brynglas Sta Gwyn 128 C2
Bryn Golau Rhondda 58 B3
Bryngwran Anglesey 178 F4
Bryngwyn Ceredig 92 B5; Mon 78 D5; Powys 96 B3
Brynhenllan Pembs 91 D10
Bryn-henllan Pembs 91 D10
Brynheulog Bridgend 57 C11
Brynhoffnant Ceredig 110 G6
Bryniau Denb 181 E9
Bryning Lancs 194 B2
Brynithel Bl Gwent 78 E2
Bryn-Iwan Carms 92 E6
Brynllywarch Powys 130 F3
Brynmawr Bl Gwent 77 C11
Bryn-mawr Gwyn 144 C4
Bryn Mawr Powys 148 F5
Brynmenyn Bridgend 58 B2
Brynmill Swansea 56 C6
Brynmorfudd Conwy 164 C4
Bryn Myrddin Carms 93 G8
Brynna Rhondda 58 C3
Bryn-nantllech Conwy 164 B6
Brynnau Gwynion Rhondda 58 C3
Bryn-newydd Denb 165 G11
Bryn Offa Wrex 166 F4
Brynore Shrops 149 B7
Bryn-penarth Powys 130 C2
Bryn Pen-y-lan Wrex 166 G4
Bryn Pydew Conwy 180 F4
Brynrefail Anglesey 179 D7; Gwyn 163 C9
Bryn Rhyd-yr-Arian Conwy 165 B7
Bryn-rhys Conwy 180 F4
Brynsadler Rhondda 58 C4
Bryn Saith Marchog Denb 165 E9
Brynsiencyn Anglesey 163 B7
Bryn Sion Gwyn 147 F7
Brynsworthy Devon 40 G4
Bryn Tanat Powys 148 E4
Brynteg Anglesey 179 E7; Ceredig 93 C9; Wrex 166 E4
Bryntirion Bridgend 57 E11
Bryn-y-cochin Shrops 149 B7
Bryn-y-gwenin Mon 78 B4
Bryn-y-maen Conwy 180 F4
Bryn-yr-Eos Wrex 166 G3
Bryn-yr-eryr Gwyn 162 F5
Bryn-yr-ogof Denb 165 D11
Buaile nam Bodach W Isles 297 L3
Bualintur Highld 294 C6
Bualnaluib Highld 307 K3
Buarthmeini Gwyn 146 C6
Bubbenhall Warks 119 C7
Bubblewell Glos 80 E5
Bubnell Derbys 186 G2
Bubwith E Yorks 207 F10
Buccleuch Borders 261 G8
Buchanan Smithy Stirling 277 D9
Buchanhaven Aberds 303 E11
Buchan Hill W Sus 51 G9
Buchanty Perth 286 E3
Buchley E Dunb 277 G11
Buchlyvie Stirling 277 C11
Buckabank Cumb 230 B3
Buckbury Worcs 98 E6
Buckden Cambs 122 D3; N Yorks 213 D8
Buckenham Norf 143 B7
Buckerell Devon 27 G10
Bucket Corner Hants 32 C6
Buckfast Devon 8 B4
Buckfastleigh Devon 8 B4
Buckham Dorset 29 G7
Buckhaven Fife 281 B7
Buck Hill Wilts 62 E3
Buckholm Borders 261 B11
Buckholt Mon 79 B8
Buckhorn Devon 12 B3
Buckhorn Weston Dorset 30 C3
Buckhurst Kent 53 E10
Buckhurst Hill Essex 86 G6
Buckie Moray 302 C4
Buckies Highld 310 C5
Buckingham Bucks 102 E3
Buckland Bucks 84 C5; Devon 8 G3; Devon 14 G3; Glos 99 D11; Hants 20 B2; Herts 105 E7; Kent 55 E10; Oxon 82 F4; Sur 51 C8
Buckland Brewer Devon 24 C6
Buckland Common Bucks 84 D6
Buckland Dinham Som 45 C9
Buckland Down Som 45 C8
Buckland End W Mid 134 F2
Buckland Filleigh Devon 25 F7
Buckland in the Moor Devon 13 G10
Buckland Marsh Oxon 82 F4
Buckland Monachorum Devon 7 B9
Buckland Newton Dorset 29 F11
Buckland Ripers Dorset 17 E8
Bucklands Borders 262 F2
Buckland St Mary Som 28 E3
Buckland Valley Kent 55 E10
Bucklandwharf Bucks 84 C5
Bucklebury W Berks 64 E5
Bucklebury Alley W Berks 64 E4
Bucklegate Lincs 156 B6
Buckleigh Devon 24 B6
Bucklerheads Angus 287 D8
Bucklers Hard Hants 20 B4
Bucklesham Suff 108 C4
Buckley / Bwcle Flint 166 C3
Buckley Green Warks 118 D3
Buckley Hill Mers 182 B4
Bucklow Hill Ches E 184 E2
Buckminster Leics 155 E7
Buckmoorend Bucks 84 E4
Bucknall Lincs 173 B11; Stoke 168 F6
Bucknell Oxon 101 F11; Shrops 115 C7
Buckoak Ches W 183 G8
Buckover S Glos 79 G11
Buckpool Moray 302 C4; W Mid 133 F7
Buckridge Worcs 116 C4
Bucksburn Aberdeen 293 C10
Buck's Cross Devon 24 C4
Bucks Green W Sus 50 G5
Buckshaw Village Lancs 194 C5
Bucks Hill Herts 85 E9
Bucks Horn Oak Hants 49 E10
Buckskin Hants 48 C6
Buck's Mills Devon 24 C5
Buckton E Yorks 218 E3; Hereford 115 C7; Northumb 264 B3
Buckton Vale Gtr Man 196 G3
Buckworth Cambs 122 B2
Budbrooke Warks 118 D5
Budby Notts 171 B10
Buddgbrake Shetland 312 B8
Buddileigh Staffs 168 F3
Budd's Titson Corn 24 G2
Bude Corn 24 F2
Budge's Shop Corn 6 D6
Budlake Devon 14 B5
Budle Northumb 264 B5
Budleigh Som 27 D11
Budleigh Salterton Devon 15 E7
Budlett's Common E Sus 37 C7
Budock Water Corn 3 C7
Budworth Heath Ches W 183 F11
Buersil Head Gtr Man 196 E2
Buerton Ches E 167 G11
Buffler's Holt Bucks 102 D3
Bufton Leics 135 B8
Bugbrooke Northants 120 F3
Bugford Devon 40 E6
Bughtlin Edin 280 G3
Buglawton Ches E 168 C5
Bugle Corn 5 D10
Bugle Gate Worcs 116 D6
Bugley Dorset 30 C3; Wilts 45 E11
Bugthorpe E Yorks 207 B11
Building End Essex 105 D8
Buildwas Shrops 132 C2
Builth Road Powys 113 G10
Builth Wells Powys 113 G10
Buirgh W Isles 305 J2
Bulbourne Herts 84 C6
Bulbridge Wilts 46 G5
Bulby Lincs 155 D11
Bulcote Notts 171 G11
Buldoo Highld 310 C3
Bulford Wilts 47 E7
Bulford Camp Wilts 47 E7
Bulkeley Ches E 167 E8
Bulkeley Hall Shrops 168 G2
Bulkington Warks 135 F7; Wilts 46 B2
Bulkworthy Devon 24 E5
Bullamoor N Yorks 225 G7
Bull Bay / Porthllechog Anglesey 178 C6
Bullbridge Derbys 170 E5
Bullbrook Brack 65 F11
Bulleign Kent 53 G11
Bullenhill Wilts 45 B11
Bullen's Green Herts 86 D2
Bulley Glos 80 B3
Bullgill Cumb 229 D7
Bull Hill Hants 20 B2
Bullhurst Hill Derbys 170 G3
Bullinghope Hereford 97 D10
Bullington Hants 48 E3; Lincs 189 F9
Bullo Glos 79 D11
Bullock's Horn Wilts 81 G7
Bullockstone Kent 71 F7
Bulls Cross London 86 F4
Bulls Green Som 45 D8
Bull's Green Herts 86 B3; Norf 143 E8
Bull's Hill Hereford 97 G11
Bullwood Argyll 276 G3
Bullyhole Bottom Mon 79 F7
Bulmer Essex 106 C6; N Yorks 216 F3
Bulmer Tye Essex 106 D6
Bulphan Thurrock 68 B6
Bulstrode Herts 85 E8
Bulthy Shrops 148 G6
Bulverhythe E Sus 38 F3
Bulwark Aberds 303 E9; Mon 79 G8
Bulwell Nottingham 171 F8
Bulwell Forest Nottingham 171 F8
Bulwick Leics 136 E3; Northants 137 E9
Bumble's Green Essex 86 D6
Bumwell Hill Norf 142 E2
Bun Abhainn Eadarra W Isles 305 H3
Bunacaimb Highld 295 G8
Bun a'Mhuillin W Isles 297 K3
Bunarkaig Highld 290 E3
Bunbury Ches E 167 D9
Bunbury Heath Ches E 167 D9
Bunce Common Sur 51 D8
Bunchrew Highld 300 E6
Bundalloch Highld 295 C10
Buness Shetland 312 C8
Bunessan Argyll 288 G5
Bungay Suff 142 F6
Bunkers Hill Gtr Man 184 D6; Oxon 83 B7
Bunker's Hill Cambs 139 B8; Lincs 174 E3; Lincs 189 G7; Norf 142 B3; Suff 143 C10
Bunloit Highld 300 G5
Bun Loyne Highld 290 C4
Bunnahabhain Argyll 274 F5
Bunny Notts 153 D11
Bunny Hill Notts 153 D11
Bunree Highld 290 G2
Bunroy Highld 290 E4
Bunsley Bank Ches E 167 G11
Bunstead Hants 32 C6
Buntait Highld 300 F3
Buntingford Herts 105 F7
Bunting's Green Essex 106 E6
Bunwell Norf 142 E2
Bunwell Bottom Norf 142 D2
Buoltach Highld 310 F5
Burbage Derbys 185 G8; Leics 135 E8; Wilts 63 G8
Burcher Hereford 114 E6
Burchett's Green Windsor 65 C10
Burcombe Wilts 46 G5
Burcot Oxon 83 F9; Worcs 117 C9
Burcote Shrops 132 D4
Burcott Bucks 84 B4; Bucks 103 G7; Som 44 D4
Burdiehouse Edin 270 B5
Burdon T&W 243 G9
Burdonshill V Glam 58 E6
Burdrop Oxon 101 D7
Bures Suff 107 E8
Bures Green Suff 107 D8
Burford Ches E 167 E10; Devon 24 C4; Oxon 82 C3; Shrops 115 D11; Som 44 E5
Burg Argyll 288 E5; Argyll 288 G6
Burgar Orkney 314 D3
Burgate Hants 31 D11; Suff 125 B11
Burgates Hants 34 B3
Burgedin Powys 148 G4
Burge End Herts 104 E2
Burgess Hill W Sus 36 D4
Burgh Suff 126 G4
Burgh by Sands Cumb 239 F8
Burgh Castle Norf 143 B9
Burghclere Hants 64 G3
Burghclere Common Hants 64 G3
Burgh Common Norf 141 E11
Burghead Moray 301 C11
Burghfield W Berks 65 F7
Burghfield Common W Berks 64 F6
Burghfield Hill W Berks 65 F7
Burgh Heath Sur 51 B8
Burgh Hill E Sus 23 C8; E Sus 38 B2
Burghill Hereford 97 C9
Burgh le Marsh Lincs 175 B8
Burgh Muir Aberds 293 B9; Aberds 303 G7
Burgh next Aylsham Norf 160 D4
Burgh on Bain Lincs 190 D2
Burgh St Margaret / Fleggburgh Norf 161 G8
Burgh St Peter Norf 143 E9
Burgh Stubbs Norf 159 C10
Burghwallis S Yorks 198 E4
Burgois Corn 10 G4
Burham Kent 69 G8
Burham Court Kent 69 G8
Buriton Hants 34 C2
Burland Ches E 167 E10
Burlawn Corn 10 G5
Burleigh Brack 65 F11; Glos 80 E5
Burlescombe Devon 27 D9
Burleston Dorset 17 C11
Burlestone Devon 8 F6
Burley Hants 32 G2; Rutland 155 G7; Shrops 131 G9; W Yorks 205 G11
Burley Beacon Hants 32 G2
Burleydam Ches E 167 G10
Burley Gate Hereford 97 B11
Burley in Wharfedale W Yorks 205 D9
Burley Lawn Hants 32 G2
Burley Lodge Hants 32 F2
Burley Street Hants 32 G2
Burley Woodhead W Yorks 205 E9
Burlinch Som 28 B3
Burlingham Green Norf 161 G7
Burlingjobb Powys 114 F5
Burlish Park Worcs 116 C6
Burlorne Tregoose Corn 5 B10
Burlow E Sus 23 B9
Burlton Shrops 149 D9
Burmantofts W Yorks 206 G2
Burmarsh Hereford 97 B10; Kent 54 G5
Burmington Warks 100 D5
Burn N Yorks 198 B5
Burnage Gtr Man 184 C5
Burnard's Ho Devon 24 G4
Burnaston Derbys 152 C5
Burnbank S Lanark 268 D4
Burn Bridge N Yorks 206 C2
Burnby E Yorks 208 D2
Burncross S Yorks 186 B4
Burndell W Sus 35 G7
Burnden Gtr Man 195 F8
Burnedge Gtr Man 196 E2
Burnend Aberds 303 E8
Burneside Cumb 221 F10
Burness Orkney 314 B6
Burneston N Yorks 214 B6
Burnett Bath 61 F7
Burnfoot Borders 261 G10; Borders 262 F2; Dumfries 239 C7; Dumfries 247 E11; E Ayrs 245 B10; N Lanark 268 B5; Perth 286 G3
Burngreave S Yorks 186 D5
Burnham Bucks 66 C2; N Lincs 200 D5
Burnham Deepdale Norf 176 E4
Burnham Green Herts 86 B3
Burnham Market Norf 176 E4
Burnham Norton Norf 176 E4
Burnham-on-Crouch Essex 88 F6
Burnham-on-Sea Som 43 D10
Burnham Overy Staithe Norf 176 E4
Burnham Overy Town Norf 176 E4
Burnham Thorpe Norf 176 E5
Burnhead Aberds 293 D10; Borders 262 F2; Dumfries 247 D9; Dumfries 247 G10; S Ayrs 244 C6
Burnhervie Aberds 293 B9
Burnhill Green Staffs 132 C5
Burnhope Durham 233 B9
Burnhouse N Ayrs 267 E7
Burnhouse Mains Borders 271 F8
Burniere Corn 10 G5
Burniestrype Moray 302 C3
Burniston N Yorks 227 G10
Burnlee W Yorks 196 F6
Burnley Lancs 204 G2
Burnley Lane Lancs 204 G2
Burnley Wood Lancs 204 G2
Burnmouth Borders 273 C9
Burn Naze Lancs 202 E2
Burn of Cambus Stirling 285 G11
Burnopfield Durham 242 F5
Burnrigg Cumb 239 F11
Burnsall N Yorks 213 G10
Burn's Green Herts 104 G6
Burnside Aberds 303 E8; Angus 287 B9; E Ayrs 258 G3; Fife 286 G5; Perth 286 E4; S Lanark 268 C2; Shetland 312 F4; T&W 243 G8; W Loth 279 G11
Burnside of Duntrune Angus 287 D8
Burnstone Devon 24 C4
Burnswark Dumfries 238 B5
Burnt Ash Glos 80 E5
Burntcommon Sur 50 C4
Burntheath Derbys 152 C4
Burnt Heath Derbys 186 F2; Essex 107 F11
Burnt Hill W Berks 64 E5
Burnthouse Corn 3 B7
Burnt Houses Durham 233 G8
Burntisland Fife 280 D4
Burnt Mills Essex 88 G2
Burnt Oak E Sus 37 B8; London 86 G2
Burnton E Ayrs 245 B11
Burnt Tree W Mid 133 E9
Burnturk Fife 287 G7
Burntwood Staffs 133 B11
Burntwood Green Staffs 133 B11
Burntwood Pentre Flint 166 C3
Burnt Yates N Yorks 214 G5
Burnworthy Som 27 D11
Burnwynd Edin 270 B2
Burpham Sur 50 C4; W Sus 35 F8
Burradon Northumb 251 B11; T&W 243 C7
Burrafirth Shetland 312 B8
Burraland Shetland 312 F5; Shetland 313 J4
Burras Corn 2 C5
Burrastow Shetland 313 J4
Burraton Corn 7 D8
Burraton Coombe Corn 7 D8
Burravoe Shetland 312 F7; Shetland 312 G5
Burray Village Orkney 314 G4
Burreldales Aberds 303 F7
Burrells Cumb 222 B3
Burrelton Perth 286 D6
Burridge Devon 28 F4; Devon 40 F5; Hants 33 E8
Burrigill Highld 310 F6
Burrill N Yorks 214 B4
Burringham N Lincs 199 F10
Burrington Devon 25 D10; Hereford 115 C8; N Som 44 B3
Burrough End Cambs 124 F2
Burrough Green Cambs 124 F2
Burrough on the Hill Leics 154 G5
Burroughs Grove Bucks 65 B11
Burroughston Orkney 314 D5
Burrow Devon 14 B5; Som 28 C6; Som 42 E2
Burrowbridge Som 43 G11
Burrow-bridge Som 28 B5
Burrowhill Sur 66 G3
Burrows Cross Sur 50 D5
Burrowsmoor Holt Notts 172 G2
Burrsville Park Essex 89 B11
Burrswood Kent 52 F4
Burry Swansea 56 C3
Burry Green Swansea 56 C3
Burry Port / Porth Tywyn Carms 74 E6
Burscott Devon 24 C4
Burscough Lancs 194 E2
Burscough Bridge Lancs 194 E2
Bursdon Devon 24 D3
Bursea E Yorks 208 G2
Burshill E Yorks 209 D7
Bursledon Hants 33 F7
Burslem Stoke 168 F5
Burstall Suff 107 C11
Burstallhill Suff 107 B11
Burstock Dorset 28 G6
Burston Devon 26 G2; Norf 142 G2; Staffs 151 C8
Burstow Sur 51 E10
Burstwick E Yorks 201 B8
Burtersett N Yorks 213 B7
Burtholme Cumb 240 E2
Burthorpe Suff 124 E5
Burthwaite Cumb 230 B4
Burtle Som 43 E11
Burtle Hill Som 43 E11
Burtoft Lincs 156 B5
Burton Ches W 167 C8; Ches W 182 G4; Dorset 17 C9; Dorset 19 C9; Lincs 189 G7; Northumb 264 C5; Pembs 73 D7; Som 29 E8; Som 43 E7; V Glam 58 F4; Wilts 45 G10; Wilts 61 D10; Wrex 166 D5
Burton Agnes E Yorks 218 G2
Burton Bradstock Dorset 16 D5
Burton Corner Lincs 174 F4
Burton Dassett Warks 119 G7
Burton End Cambs 106 B2; Essex 105 G10
Burton Ferry Pembs 73 D7
Burton Fleming E Yorks 217 E11
Burton Green Essex 106 F6; W Mid 118 B5; Wrex 166 D4
Burton Hastings Warks 135 E8
Burton-in-Kendal Cumb 211 D10
Burton in Lonsdale N Yorks 212 E3
Burton Joyce Notts 171 G10
Burton Latimer Northants 121 C8
Burton Lazars Leics 154 F5
Burton-le-Coggles Lincs 155 D9
Burton Leonard N Yorks 214 G6
Burton Manor Staffs 151 E8
Burton on the Wolds Leics 153 E11
Burton Overy Leics 136 D3
Burton Pedwardine Lincs 173 G10
Burton Pidsea E Yorks 209 G10
Burton Salmon N Yorks 198 B3
Burton Stather N Lincs 199 D11
Burton upon Stather N Lincs 199 D11
Burton upon Trent Staffs 152 E5
Burton Westwood Shrops 132 D2
Burtonwood Warr 183 C9
Burwardsley Ches W 167 D8
Burwarton Shrops 132 F2
Burwash E Sus 37 C11
Burwash Common E Sus 37 C10
Burwash Weald E Sus 37 C10
Burwell Cambs 123 D11; Lincs 190 F5
Burwen Anglesey 178 C6
Burwick Orkney 314 H4; Shetland 313 J5
Burwood Shrops 131 F9
Burwood Park Sur 66 G6
Bury Cambs 138 G5; Gtr Man 195 E10; Som 26 B6; W Sus 35 E8
Buryas Br Corn 1 D4
Burybank Staffs 151 B7
Bury End Beds 121 G9; C Beds 104 E2; Worcs 99 D11
Bury Green Herts 86 E4; Herts 105 G8
Bury Hollow W Sus 35 E8
Bury Park Luton 103 G11
Bury St Edmunds Suff 125 E7
Bury's Bank W Berks 64 F3
Burythorpe N Yorks 216 G5
Busbiehill N Ayrs 257 B9
Busbridge Sur 50 E3
Busby E Renf 267 D11
Buscot Oxon 82 F2
Buscott Som 44 F2
Bush Aberds 293 G9; Corn 24 F2
Bush Bank Hereford 115 G9
Bushbury Sur 51 D7; W Mid 133 C8
Bushby Leics 136 C3
Bush Crathie Aberds 292 D4
Bush End Essex 87 B9
Bush Estate Norf 161 D8
Bushey Dorset 18 E5; Herts 85 G10
Bushey Ground Oxon 82 D4
Bushey Heath Herts 85 G11
Bushey Mead London 67 F8
Bushfield Cumb 249 G11
Bush Green Norf 141 D10; Norf 142 F4; Suff 125 F8
Bush Hill Park London 86 F4
Bushley Worcs 99 E7
Bushley Green Worcs 99 E7
Bushmead Beds 122 E2
Bushmoor Shrops 131 F8
Bushton Wilts 62 D5
Bushy Common Norf 159 G9
Bushy Hill Sur 50 C4
Busk Cumb 231 C8; Gtr Man 196 F2
Buslingthorpe Lincs 189 D9
Bussage Glos 80 E5
Bussex Som 43 F11
Busta Shetland 312 G5
Bustard Green Essex 106 F2
Bustard's Green Norf 142 E3
Bustatoun Orkney 314 A7
Busveal Corn 4 G4
Butcher's Common Norf 160 E6
Butcher's Cross E Sus 37 B9
Butcombe N Som 60 G4
Butetown Cardiff 59 D7
Bute Town Caerph 77 D10
Butlane Head Shrops 149 G8
Butleigh Som 44 G4
Butleigh Wootton Som 44 G4
Butlersbank Shrops 149 E11
Butlers Cross Bucks 85 G7
Butler's Cross Bucks 84 D4
Butler's End Warks 134 G4
Butler's Hill Notts 171 F8
Butlers Marston Warks 118 G6
Butley Suff 127 G7
Butley High Corner Suff 109 B7
Butley Low Corner Suff 109 B7
Butley Town Ches E 184 F6
Butlocks Heath Hants 33 F7
Butter Bank Staffs 151 E7
Butterburn Cumb 240 C5
Buttercrambe N Yorks 207 B10
Butteriss Gate Corn 2 C6
Butterknowle Durham 233 F8
Butterleigh Devon 27 F7
Butterley Derbys 170 C4; Derbys 170 E6
Buttermere Cumb 220 B3; Wilts 63 G10
Butterrow Glos 80 E5
Butters Green Staffs 168 E4
Buttershaw W Yorks 196 B6
Butterstone Perth 286 C4
Butterton Staffs 168 G4; Staffs 169 D9
Butterwick Cumb 221 B10; Durham 234 F3; Lincs 174 G5; N Yorks 216 D4; N Yorks 217 E9
Butteryhaugh Northumb 250 E4
Butt Green Ches E 167 E11
Buttington Powys 130 B5
Butt Lane Staffs 168 E4
Buttonbridge Shrops 116 B4
Button Haugh Green Suff 125 D9
Buttonoak Worcs 116 B5
Button's Green Suff 125 G8
Butts Devon 14 D2
Buttsash Hants 32 F6
Buttsbear Cross Corn 24 G3
Buttsbury Essex 87 F11
Butts Green Essex 105 E9
Butt's Green Essex 88 E3; Hants 32 B3
Buttsole Kent 55 C10
Butt Yeats Lancs 211 F11
Buxhall Suff 125 F10
Buxhall Fen Street Suff 125 F10
Buxley Borders 272 E6
Buxted E Sus 37 C7
Buxton Derbys 185 G9; Norf 160 E4
Buxworth Derbys 185 E8
Bwcle / Buckley Flint 166 C3
Bwlch Flint 181 G11; Powys 96 G2
Bwlch-derwin Gwyn 163 F7
Bwlchgwyn Wrex 166 E3
Bwlch-Llan Ceredig 111 F11
Bwlchnewydd Carms 93 G7
Bwlch-newydd Carms 93 G7
Bwlchtocyn Gwyn 144 D6
Bwlch-y-cibau Powys 148 F3
Bwlch-y-cwm Cardiff 58 C6
Bwlchyddar Powys 148 E3
Bwlch-y-fadfa Ceredig 93 B8
Bwlch-y-ffridd Powys 129 D11
Bwlchygroes Pembs 92 D4
Bwlchyllyn Gwyn 163 D8
Bwlch-y-Plain Powys 114 B4
Bwlch-y-sarnau Powys 113 C10
Bybrook Kent 54 E4
Bycross Hereford 97 C7
Byeastwood Bridgend 58 C2
Byebush Aberds 303 F7
Bye Green Bucks 84 C5
Byerhope Northumb 232 B3
Byermoor T&W 242 F5
Byers Green Durham 233 E10
Byfield Northants 119 G10
Byfleet Sur 66 G5
Byford Hereford 97 C7
Byford Common Hereford 97 C7
Bygrave Herts 104 D5
Byker T&W 243 E7
Byland Abbey N Yorks 215 D10
Bylchau Conwy 165 C7
Byley Ches W 168 B2
Bynea Carms 56 B4
Byram N Yorks 198 B3
Byrness Northumb 251 C7
Bythorn Cambs 121 B11
Byton Hereford 115 E7

Catton N Yorks 215 D7
Northumb 241 F8
Catwick E Yorks 209 D8
Catworth Cambs 121 C11
Caudle Green Glos 80 C6
Caudlesprings Norf 141 C8
Caulcott C Beds 103 C9
Oxon 101 G10
Cauld Borders 261 G11
Cauldcoats Holdings
Falk 279 F10
Cauldcots Angus 287 C10
Cauldhame Stirling 278 C2
Cauldmill Borders 262 G2
Cauldon Staffs 169 F9
Cauldon Lowe
Staffs 169 F9
Cauldwells Aberds 303 D7
Caulkerbush
Dumfries 237 D11
Caulside Dumfries 249 G10
Caundle Marsh
Dorset 29 E11
Caunsall Worcs 132 G6
Caunton Notts 172 D2
Causeway Hants 33 E11
Hants 34 C2
Mon 60 B2
Causewayend
S Lanark 260 B2
Causeway End
Cumb 210 C6
Cumb 211 B9
Dumfries 236 C6
Essex 87 B11
Wilts 62 C4
Causeway Foot
W Yorks 197 E7
W Yorks 205 G7
Causeway Green
W Mid 133 F9
Causewayhead
Cumb 238 G4
Stirling 278 B6
Causewaywood
Shrops 131 D10
Causey Durham 242 F6
Causeyend Aberds 293 B11
Causey Park Bridge
Northumb 252 E5
Causeyton Aberds 293 B8
Caute Devon 24 E6
Cautley Cumb 222 G3
Cavendish Suff 106 B6
Cavendish Bridge
Leics 153 D8
Cavenham Suff 124 D5
Cavers Carre
Borders 262 D3
Caversfield Oxon 101 F11
Caversham Reading 65 E8
Caversham Heights
Reading 65 D8
Caverswall Staffs 169 G7
Cavil E Yorks 207 G11
Cawdor Highld 301 D8
Cawkeld E Yorks 208 C5
Cawkwell Lincs 190 F3
Cawood N Yorks 207 F7
Cawsand Corn 7 E8
Cawston Norf 160 E2
Warks 119 C9
Cawthorne N Yorks 216 B5
S Yorks 197 F9
Cawthorpe Lincs 155 E11
Cawton N Yorks 216 D2
Caxton Cambs 122 F6
Caynham Shrops 115 C11
Caythorpe Lincs 172 F6
Notts 171 F11
Cayton N Yorks 217 C11
Ceallan W Isles 296 F4
Ceann a Bhaigh
W Isles 296 E3
Ceann a Bhàigh
W Isles 305 J4
Ceannacroc Lodge
Highld 290 B4
Ceann a Deas Loch
Baghasdail
W Isles 297 K3
Ceann Shiphoirt
W Isles 305 G4
Ceann Tarabhaigh
W Isles 305 G4
Cearsiadair W Isles 304 F5
Ceathramh Meadhanach
W Isles 296 D4
Cefn Newport 59 B9
Powys 148 G5
Cefn Berain Conwy 165 B7
Cefn-brith Conwy 164 E6
Cefn-bryn-brain
Carms 76 C2
Cefn-bychan
Swansea 56 B4
Wrex 166 G3
Cefncaeau Carms 56 B4
Cefn Canol Powys 148 C4
Cefn-coch Conwy 164 B5
Cefn Coch Powys 129 C10
Powys 148 D2
Cefn-coed-y-cymmer
M Tydf 77 D9
Cefn Cribbwr
Bridgend 57 E11
Cefn Cross Bridgend 57 E11
Cefn-ddwysarn
Gwyn 147 B9
Cefn Einion Shrops 130 F5
Cefneithin Carms 75 C9
Cefn-eurgain Flint 166 B2
Cefn Fforest Caerph 77 F11
Cefn Glas Bridgend 57 E11
Cefn Golau
Bl Gwent 77 D10
Cefn-gorwydd Powys 95 B8
Cefn Hengoed
Caerph 77 F10
Cefn-hengoed
Swansea 57 B7
Cefn Llwyd Ceredig 128 G2
Cefn-mawr Wrex 166 G3
Cefnpennar Rhondda 77 E8
Cefn Rhigos Rhondda 76 D6
Cefn-y-bedd Flint 166 D4
Cefn-y-Crib Torf 78 F2
Cefn-y-Garth
Swansea 76 E2
Cefn-y-pant Carms 92 F3
Cegidfa / Guilsfield
Powys 148 G4
Cei-bach Ceredig 111 F8
Ceinewydd / New Quay
Ceredig 111 F7
Ceint Anglesey 179 F7
Ceinws Powys 128 B5
Cellan Ceredig 94 B2
Cellarhead Staffs 169 F7
Cellarhill Kent 70 G3
Celyn-Mali Flint 165 B11
Cemaes Anglesey 178 C5
Cemmaes Powys 128 B6
Cemmaes Road / Glantwymyn
Powys 128 C6
Cenarth Carms 92 C5
Cenin Gwyn 163 F7
Central Invclyd 276 F5
Central Milton Keynes
M Keynes 102 D6
Ceos W Isles 304 F5
Ceres Fife 287 F8
Ceri / Kerry Powys 130 F2
Cerne Abbas Dorset 29 G11
Cerney Wick Glos 81 F9
Cerrigceinwen
Anglesey 178 G6
Cerrig Llwydion
Neath 57 C9
Cerrig-mân
Anglesey 179 C7
Cerrigydrudion
Conwy 165 F7
Cess Norf 161 F8
Cessford Borders 262 E6
Ceunant Gwyn 163 C8
Chaceley Glos 99 E7
Chaceley Hole Glos 98 E6
Chaceley Stock Glos 99 F7
Chacewater Corn 4 G4
Chackmore Bucks 102 D3
Chacombe
Northants 101 C9
Chadbury Worcs 99 B10
Chadderton
Gtr Man 196 F2
Chadderton Fold
Gtr Man 195 F11
Chaddesden Derby 153 B7
Chaddesley Corbett
Worcs 117 C7
Chaddlehanger
Devon 12 F5
Chaddlewood Plym 7 D11
Chaddleworth
W Berks 64 D2
Chadkirk Gtr Man 184 D6
Chadlington Oxon 100 G6
Chadshunt Warks 118 G6
Chadsmoor Staffs 151 G9
Chadstone Northants 121 F7
Chad Valley W Mid 133 F10
Chadwell Leics 154 E5
Shrops 150 G5
Chadwell End
Beds 121 D11
Chadwell Heath
London 68 B3
Chadwell St Mary
Thurrock 68 D6
Chadwick Worcs 116 D6
Chadwick End
W Mid 118 C4
Chadwick Green
Mers 183 B8
Chaffcombe Som 28 E5
Chafford Hundred
Thurrock 68 D5
Chagford Devon 13 D10
Chailey E Sus 36 D5
Chainbridge Cambs 139 C8
Chain Bridge Lincs 174 G4
Chainhurst Kent 53 D8
Chalbury Dorset 31 F8
Chalbury Common
Dorset 31 F8
Chaldon Sur 51 B10
Chaldon Herring or East
Chaldon Dorset 17 E11
Chale IoW 20 F5
Chale Green IoW 20 F5
Chalfont Common
Bucks 85 G8
Chalfont Grove Bucks 85 G7
Chalfont St Giles
Bucks 85 G7
Chalfont St Peter
Bucks 85 G8
Chalford Glos 80 E5
Oxon 84 E2
Wilts 45 C11
Chalford Hill Glos 80 E5
Chalgrave C Beds 103 F10
Chalgrove Oxon 83 F10
Chalk Kent 69 E7
Chalk End Essex 87 C10
Chalkfoot Cumb 230 B2
Chalkhill Norf 141 C7
Chalkhouse Green
Oxon 65 D8
Chalkshire Bucks 84 D4
Chalksole Kent 55 E9
Chalkway Som 28 F5
Chalkwell Kent 69 G11
Southend 69 B11
Challaborough Devon 8 G3
Challacombe Devon 41 E7
Challister Shetland 312 G7
Challoch Dumfries 236 C5
Challock Kent 54 C4
Chalmington Dorset 29 G9
Chalton C Beds 103 F10
Hants 34 D2
Chalvedon Essex 69 B8
Chalvey Slough 66 D3
Chalvington E Sus 23 D8
Chambercombe
Devon 40 D4
Chamber's Green
Kent 54 E2
Champson Devon 26 B4
Chance Inn Fife 287 F7
Chancery / Rhydgaled
Ceredig 111 B11
Chance's Pitch
Hereford 98 C4
Chandler's Cross
Herts 85 F9
Worcs 98 D5
Chandler's Ford
Hants 32 C6
Chandlers Green
Hants 49 B8
Channel's End Beds 122 F2
Channel Tunnel Kent 55 F7
Channerwick
Shetland 313 L6
Chantry Devon 25 C9
Som 45 D8
Suff 108 C2
Chapel Corn 4 C6
Cumb 229 E10
Fife 280 C5
Chapel Allerton Som 44 C2
W Yorks 206 F2
Chapel Amble Corn 10 F5
Chapel Brampton
Northants 120 D4
Chapel Chorlton
Staffs 150 B6
Chapel Cleeve Som 42 E4
Chapel Cross E Sus 37 C10
Chapel End Beds 103 B11
Beds 122 F2
C Beds 103 C11
Cambs 138 G2
Ches E 167 G11
Essex 105 G11
Northants 138 F2
Warks 134 E6
Chapel-en-le-Frith
Derbys 185 E9
Chapel Field
Gtr Man 195 F9
Norf 161 E7
Chapel Fields
W Mid 118 B6
York 207 C7
Chapelgate Lincs 157 E8
Chapel Green Herts 104 D6
Warks 119 E9
Warks 134 F5
Chapel Haddlesey
N Yorks 198 B5
Chapelhall N Lanark 268 C5
Chapel Head Cambs 138 G6
Chapelhill Dumfries 248 E3
Highld 301 B8
N Ayrs 266 G4
Perth 286 D4
Perth 286 E3
Perth 286 E6
Chapel Hill Aberds 303 F10
Glos 79 E10
Lincs 174 E2
Mon 79 F8
N Yorks 206 D2
Chapel House Lancs 194 F3
Chapel Knapp Wilts 61 F11
Chapelknowe
Dumfries 239 C8
Chapel Lawn Shrops 114 B6
Chapel-le-Dale
N Yorks 212 D4
Chapel Leigh Som 27 B10
Chapel Mains
Borders 271 G11
Chapel Milton
Derbys 185 E9
Chapel of Garioch
Aberds 303 G7
Chapel of Stoneywood
Aberdeen 293 B10
Chapel on Leader
Borders 271 G11
Chapel Outon
Dumfries 236 E6
Chapel Plaister
Wilts 61 F10
Chapel Row E Sus 23 C10
Essex 88 E3
W Berks 64 F5
Chapels Blackburn 195 C7
Cumb 210 C4
Chapel St Leonards
Lincs 191 G9
Chapel Stile Cumb 220 D6
Chapelthorpe
W Yorks 197 D10
Chapelton
Angus 287 C10
Devon 25 B9
Highld 291 B11
S Lanark 268 F3
Chapelton Row
Dumfries 237 E8
Chapeltown
Blackburn 195 D8
Moray 302 G2
S Yorks 186 B5
W Yorks 206 F2
Chapel Town Corn 5 D7
Chapman's Hill
Worcs 117 B9
Chapmanslade
Wilts 45 D10
Chapman's Town
E Sus 23 B10
Chapmans Well
Devon 12 C3
Chapmore End Herts 86 B4
Chappel Essex 107 F7
Charaton Cross Corn 6 B6
Charcott Kent 52 D4
Chard Som 28 F4
Chard Junction
Dorset 28 G4
Chardleigh Green
Som 28 E4
Chardstock Devon 28 G4
Charfield S Glos 80 G2
Charfield Green
S Glos 80 G2
Charfield Hill S Glos 80 G2
Charford Worcs 117 D9
Chargrove Glos 80 B6
Charing Kent 54 D3
Charing Cross
Dorset 31 E10
Charing Heath Kent 54 D2
Charing Hill Kent 54 C3
Charingworth Glos 100 D4
Charlbury Oxon 82 B5
Charlcombe Bath 61 F8
Charlcutt Wilts 62 D3
Charlecote Warks 118 F5
Charlemont W Mid 133 E10
Charles Devon 41 G7
Charles Bottom
Devon 41 G7
Charlesfield
Borders 262 D3
Dumfries 238 D5
Charleshill Sur 49 E11
Charleston Angus 287 C7
Renfs 267 C9
Charlestown
Aberdeen 293 C11
Corn 5 E10
Derbys 185 C8
Dorset 17 F9
Fife 279 E11
Gtr Man 195 G10
Gtr Man 195 G11
Highld 299 B8
Highld 300 E6
W Yorks 196 B3
W Yorks 205 F9
Charlestown of Aberlour
Moray 302 E2
Charles Tye Suff 125 G10
Charlesworth
Derbys 185 C8
Charleton Devon 8 G5
Charlinch Som 43 F8
Charlottetown Fife 286 F6
Charlton Hants 47 D11
Herts 104 F3
London 68 D2
Northants 101 D10
Northumb 251 F8
Oxon 64 B2
Redcar 226 B2
Som 28 B3
Som 44 E6
Som 45 C7
Sur 66 F5
Telford 149 G11
W Sus 34 E5
Wilts 30 C6
Wilts 46 B6
Wilts 62 B3
Worcs 99 B10
Worcs 116 C6
Charlton Abbots
Glos 99 G10
Charlton Adam Som 29 B8
Charlton-All-Saints
Wilts 31 C11
Charltonbrook
S Yorks 186 B4
Charlton Down
Dorset 17 C9
Charlton Horethorne
Som 29 C11
Charlton Kings Glos 99 G9
Charlton Mackrell
Som 29 B8
Charlton Marshall
Dorset 30 G5
Charlton Musgrove
Som 30 B2
Charlton on Otmoor
Oxon 83 B9
Charlton on the Hill
Dorset 30 G5
Charlton Park Glos 99 G9
Charlton St Peter
Wilts 46 B6
Charlwood E Sus 51 G11
Hants 49 G7
Sur 51 E8
Charlynch Som 43 F8
Charminster Bmouth 19 C8
Dorset 17 C9
Charmouth Dorset 16 C3
Charnage Wilts 45 G10
Charndon Bucks 102 G3
Charnes Staffs 150 C5
Charney Bassett
Oxon 82 G5
Charnock Green
Lancs 194 D5
Charnock Hall
S Yorks 186 E5
Charnock Richard
Lancs 194 D5
Charsfield Suff 126 F5
Chart Corner Kent 53 C9
Charter Alley Hants 48 B5
Charterhouse Som 44 B3
Chartershall Stirling 278 C6
Charterville Allotments
Oxon 82 C4
Chartham Kent 54 C6
Chartham Hatch Kent 54 B6
Chart Hill Kent 53 D9
Chartridge Bucks 84 E6
Chart Sutton Kent 53 D10
Charvil Wokingham 65 D9
Charwelton
Northants 119 F10
Chase Cross London 87 G8
Chase End Street
Worcs 98 D5
Chase Hill S Glos 61 B8
Chase Terrace
Staffs 133 B10
Chasetown Staffs 133 B10
Chastleton Oxon 100 F4
Chasty Devon 24 G4
Chatburn Lancs 203 E11
Chatcull Staffs 150 C5
Chatford Shrops 131 B9
Chatham Caerph 59 B8
Medway 69 F9
Chatham Green
Essex 88 B2
Chathill Northumb 264 D5
Chat Hill W Yorks 205 G8
Chatley Worcs 117 E7
Chattenden Medway 69 E9
Chatter End Essex 105 F9
Chatteris Cambs 139 F7
Chatterley Staffs 168 E4
Chattern Hill Sur 66 E5
Chatterton Lancs 195 D9
Chattisham Suff 107 C11
Chattle Hill Warks 134 E3
Chatto Borders 263 F7
Chatton Northumb 264 D3
Chaulden Herts 85 D8
Chaul End C Beds 103 G11
Chavel Shrops 149 G8
Chavenage Green
Glos 80 F5
Chavey Down Brack 65 F11
Chawleigh Devon 26 E2
Chawley Oxon 83 E7
Chawson Worcs 117 E7
Chawston Beds 122 F3
Chawton Hants 49 F8
Chaxhill Glos 80 C2
Chazey Heath Oxon 65 D7
Cheadle Gtr Man 184 D5
Staffs 169 G8
Cheadle Heath
Gtr Man 184 D5
Cheadle Hulme
Gtr Man 184 D5
Cheadle Park Staffs 169 G8
Cheam London 67 G8
Cheapside Herts 105 E8
Sur 50 B4
Windsor 66 F2
Chearsley Bucks 84 C2
Chebsey Staffs 151 D7
Checkendon Oxon 65 C7
Checkley Ches E 168 F2
Hereford 97 D11
Staffs 151 B10
Checkley Green
Ches E 168 F2
Chedburgh Suff 124 F5
Cheddar Som 44 C3
Cheddington Bucks 84 B6
Cheddleton Staffs 169 E7
Cheddleton Heath
Staffs 169 E7
Cheddon Fitzpaine
Som 28 B2
Chedglow Wilts 80 G6
Chedgrave Norf 143 D7
Chedington Dorset 29 F7
Chediston Suff 127 B7
Chediston Green
Suff 127 B7
Chedworth Glos 81 C9
Chedworth Laines
Glos 81 C8
Chedzoy Som 43 F10
Cheeklaw Borders 272 E5
Cheeseman's Green
Kent 54 F4
Cheetam Hill
Gtr Man 195 G10
Cheglinch Devon 40 E4
Chegworth Kent 53 C10
Cheldon Devon 26 E2
Chelfham Devon 40 F6
Chelford Ches E 184 G4
Chellaston Derby 153 C7
Chell Heath Stoke 168 E5
Chellington Beds 121 F9
Chells Herts 104 F5
Chelmarsh Shrops 132 F4
Chelmer Village
Essex 88 D2
Chelmick Shrops 131 E9
Chelmondiston Suff 108 D4
Chelmorton Derbys 169 B10
Chelmsford Essex 88 D2
Chelmsine Som 27 D11
Chelmsley Wood
W Mid 134 F3
Chelsea London 67 D9
Chelsfield London 68 G3
Chelsham Sur 51 B11
Chelston Som 27 C11
Torbay 9 C7
Chelston Heathfield
Som 27 C11
Chelsworth Suff 107 B9
Chelsworth Common
Suff 107 B9
Cheltenham Glos 99 G8
Chelveston
Northants 121 D9
Chelvey N Som 60 F3
Chelvey Batch N Som 60 F3
Chelwood Bath 60 G6
Chelwood Common
E Sus 36 B6
Chelwood Gate
E Sus 36 B6
Chelworth Wilts 81 G7
Chelworth Lower Green
Wilts 81 G9
Chelworth Upper Green
Wilts 81 G9
Chelynch Som 45 E7
Chemistry Shrops 167 G8
Cheney Longville
Shrops 131 G8
Chenhalls Corn 2 B3
Chenies Bucks 85 F8
Cheny Longville
Shrops 131 G8
Chepstow Mon 79 G8
Chequerbent
Gtr Man 195 F7
Chequerfield
W Yorks 198 C3
Chequers Corner
Norf 139 B9
Chequertree Kent 54 F4
Cherhill Wilts 62 E4
Cherington Glos 80 F6
Warks 100 D5
Cheristow Devon 24 B3
Cheriton
Devon 41 D8
Hants 33 B9
Kent 55 F7
Swansea 56 C3
Cheriton Bishop
Devon 13 C11
Cheriton Cross
Devon 13 C11
Cheriton Fitzpaine
Devon 26 F5
Cheriton or Stackpole
Elidor Pembs 73 F7
Cherrington Telford 150 E3
Cherrybank Perth 286 E5
Cherry Burton
E Yorks 208 E5
Cherry Green
Essex 105 F11
Herts 105 F7
Cherry Hinton
Cambs 123 F9
Cherry Orchard
Shrops 149 G9
Worcs 117 G7
Cherry Tree
Blackburn 195 B7
Gtr Man 185 C7
Cherrytree Hill
Derby 153 B7
Cherry Willingham
Lincs 189 G8
Chertsey Sur 66 F4
Chertsey Meads Sur 66 F5
Cheselbourne
Dorset 17 B11
Chesham Bucks 85 E7
Gtr Man 195 E10
Chesham Bois Bucks 85 F7
Cheshunt Herts 86 E5
Chesley Kent 69 G11
Cheslyn Hay Staffs 133 B9
Chessetts Wood
Warks 118 C3
Chessington London 67 G7
Chessmount Bucks 85 E7
Chestall Staffs 151 G11
Chester Ches W 166 B6
Chesterblade Som 45 E7
Chesterfield Derbys 186 G5
Staffs 134 B2
Chesterhill Midloth 271 B7
Chesterhope
Northumb 251 F9
Chesterknowes
Borders 262 D2
Chester-le-Street
Durham 243 G7
Chester Moor
Durham 233 B11
Chesters Borders 262 E4
Borders 262 G4
Chesterton Cambs 123 E9
Cambs 138 D2
Glos 81 E8
Oxon 101 G11
Shrops 132 D5
Staffs 168 F4
Warks 118 F6
Chesterton Green
Warks 118 F6
Chesterwood
Northumb 241 D8
Chestfield Kent 70 F6
Chestnut Hill
Cumb 229 G11
Chestnut Street
Kent 69 G11
Cheston Devon 8 D3
Cheswardine
Shrops 150 D4
Cheswell Telford 150 F4
Cheswick Northumb 273 F10
Cheswick Buildings
Northumb 273 F10
Cheswick Green
W Mid 118 B2
Chetnole Dorset 29 F10
Chettiscombe Devon 27 E7
Chettisham Cambs 139 G10
Chettle Dorset 31 E7
Chetton Shrops 132 E3
Chetwode Bucks 102 F2
Chetwynd Aston
Telford 150 F5
Cheveley Cambs 124 E3
Chevening Kent 52 B3
Cheverell's Green
Herts 85 B9
Chevin End W Yorks 205 E9
Chevington Suff 124 F5
Chevithorne Devon 27 D7
Chew Magna Bath 60 G5
Chew Moor Gtr Man 195 F7
Chew Stoke Bath 60 G5
Chewton Keynsham
Bath 61 F7
Chewton Mendip
Som 44 C5
Cheylesmore
W Mid 118 B6
Chichacott Devon 13 B8
Chicheley M Keynes 103 B8
Chichester W Sus 22 C5
Chickenley W Yorks 197 C9
Chickerell Dorset 17 E8
Chicklade Wilts 46 G2
Chickney Essex 105 F11
Chicksands C Beds 104 D2
Chicksgrove Wilts 46 G3
Chickward Hereford 114 G5
Chidden Hants 33 D11
Chiddingfold Sur 50 F3
Chiddingly E Sus 23 C8
Chiddingstone Kent 52 D3
Chiddingstone
Causeway Kent 52 D4
Chiddingstone Hoath
Kent 52 E3
Chideock Dorset 16 C4
Chidgley Som 42 F4
Chidham W Sus 22 C3
Chidswell W Yorks 197 C9
Chieveley W Berks 64 E3
Chignall St James
Essex 87 D11
Chignall Smealy
Essex 87 C11
Chigwell Essex 86 G6
Chigwell Row Essex 87 G7
Chilbolton Hants 47 F11
Chilbolton Down
Hants 48 F2
Chilbridge Dorset 31 G7
Chilcomb Hants 33 B8
Chilcombe Dorset 16 C6
Som 42 F6
Chilcompton Som 44 C6
Chilcote Leics 152 G5
Childerditch Essex 68 B6
Childerley Gate
Cambs 123 F7
Childer Thornton
Ches W 182 F5
Child Okeford Dorset 30 E4
Childrey Oxon 63 B11
Childsbridge Kent 52 B5
Child's Ercall Shrops 150 E3
Child's Hill London 67 B8
Childswickham
Worcs 99 D11
Childwall Mers 182 D6
Childwick Bury
Herts 85 C10
Childwick Green
Herts 85 C10
Chilfrome Dorset 17 B7
Chilgrove W Sus 34 E4
Chilham Kent 54 C5
Chilhampton Wilts 46 G5
Chilla Devon 24 G6
Chillaton Devon 12 E4
Chillenden Kent 55 C9
Chillerton IoW 20 E5
Chillesford Suff 127 G7
Chillingham
Northumb 264 D3
Chillington Devon 8 G5
Som 28 E5
Chillmill Kent 53 E7
Chilmark Wilts 46 G3
Chilmington Green
Kent 54 E3
Chilsham E Sus 23 C10
Chilson Oxon 82 B4
Som 28 G4
Chilson Common
Som 28 G4
Chilsworthy Corn 12 G4
Devon 24 F4
Chiltern Green Beds 85 B10
Chilthorne Domer
Som 29 D8
Chiltington E Sus 36 D5
Chilton Bucks 83 C11
Durham 233 F11
Kent 71 G11
Oxon 64 B3
Suff 107 C7
Chilton Candover
Hants 48 E5
Chilton Cantelo Som 29 C9
Chilton Foliat Wilts 63 E10
Chilton Lane
Durham 234 E2
Chilton Moor T&W 234 B2
Chilton Polden Som 43 F11
Chilton Street Suff 106 B5
Chilton Trinity Som 43 F9
Chilvers Coton
Warks 135 E7
Chilwell Notts 153 B10
Chilworth Hants 32 D6
Sur 50 D4
Chilworth Old Village
Hants 32 D6
Chimney Oxon 82 E5
Chimney-end Oxon 82 B4
Chimney Street Suff 106 B4
Chineham Hants 49 C7
Chingford London 86 G5
Chingford Green
London 86 G5
Chingford Hatch
London 86 G5
Chinley Derbys 185 E8
Chinley Head
Derbys 185 E9
Chinnor Oxon 84 E3
Chipley Som 27 C10
Chipmans Platt Glos 80 D3
Chipnall Shrops 150 C4
Chippenhall Green
Suff 126 B5
Chippenham Cambs 124 D3
Wilts 62 E2
Chipperfield Herts 85 E8
Chipping Herts 105 E7
Lancs 203 E8
Chipping Barnet
London 86 F2
Chipping Campden
Glos 100 D3
Chipping Hill Essex 88 B4
Chipping Norton
Oxon 100 F6
Chipping Ongar
Essex 87 E8
Chipping Sodbury
S Glos 61 C8
Chipping Warden
Northants 101 B9
Chipstable Som 27 B8
Chipstead Kent 52 B3
Sur 51 B9
Chirbury Shrops 130 D5
Chirk Bank Shrops 148 B5
Chirk Green Wrex 148 B5
Chirk / Y Waun
Wrex 148 B5
Chirmorrie S Ayrs 236 B4
Chirnside Borders 273 D7
Chirnsidebridge
Borders 273 D7
Chirton T&W 243 D8
Wilts 46 B5
Chisbridge Cross
Bucks 65 B10
Chisbury Wilts 63 F9
Chiselborough Som 29 E7
Chiseldon Swindon 63 D7
Chiserley W Yorks 196 B4
Chislehampton Oxon 83 F9
Chislehurst London 68 E2
Chislehurst West
London 68 E2
Chislet Kent 71 G8
Chislet Forstal Kent 71 G8
Chiswell Dorset 17 G9
Chiswell Green
Herts 85 E10
Chiswick London 67 D8
Chiswick End
Cambs 105 B7
Chisworth Derbys 185 C7
Chitcombe E Sus 38 C4
Chithurst W Sus 34 C4
Chittering Cambs 123 C9
Chitterley Devon 26 G6
Chitterne Wilts 46 E3
Chittlehamholt
Devon 25 C11
Chittlehampton
Devon 25 B10
Chittoe Wilts 62 F3
Chitts Hills Essex 107 F9
Chitty Kent 71 G8
Chivelstone Devon 9 G10
Chivenor Devon 40 G4
Chivery Bucks 84 D6
Chobham Sur 66 G3
Choicelee Borders 272 E4
Cholderton Wilts 47 E8
Cholesbury Bucks 84 D6
Chollerford
Northumb 241 C10
Chollerton
Northumb 241 C10
Cholmondeston
Ches E 167 C10
Cholsey Oxon 64 B5
Cholstrey Hereford 115 F9
Cholwell Bath 44 B6
Chop Gate N Yorks 225 F11
Choppington
Northumb 253 G7
Chopwell T&W 242 F4
Chorley Ches E 167 E9
Lancs 194 D5
Shrops 132 G3
Staffs 151 G11
Chorley Common
W Sus 34 B4
Chorleywood Herts 85 F8
Chorleywood Bottom
Herts 85 F8
Chorleywood West
Herts 85 F8
Chorlton Ches E 168 E2
Chorlton-cum-Hardy
Gtr Man 184 C4
Chorlton Lane
Ches W 167 F7
Choulton Shrops 131 F7
Chowdene T&W 243 F7
Chowley Ches W 167 D7
Chownes Mead
W Sus 36 C4
Chreagain Highld 289 C10
Chrishall Essex 105 D8
Christchurch Cambs 139 D9
Dorset 19 C9
Glos 79 C9
Newport 59 B10
Christian Malford
Wilts 62 D3
Christleton Ches W 166 B6
Christmas Common
Oxon 84 G2
Christon N Som 43 B11
Christon Bank
Northumb 264 E6
Christow Devon 14 D2
Chryston N Lanark 278 G3
Chub Tor Devon 7 B10
Chuck Hatch E Sus 52 G3
Chudleigh Devon 14 F3
Chudleigh Knighton
Devon 14 F2
Chulmleigh Devon 25 E11
Chunal Derbys 185 C8
Church Lancs 195 B8
Churcham Glos 80 B3
Church Aston
Telford 150 F4
Churchbank Shrops 114 B6
Church Brampton
Northants 120 D4
Churchbridge Corn 6 D4
Staffs 133 B9
Church Brough
Cumb 222 C5
Church Broughton
Derbys 152 C4
Church Charwelton
Northants 119 F10
Church Clough
Lancs 204 F3
Church Common
Hants 34 B2
Church Coombe Corn 4 G3
Church Cove Corn 2 G6
Church Crookham
Hants 49 C10
Churchdown Glos 80 B5
Church Eaton Staffs 150 F6
Churchend Essex 89 G8
Essex 106 G2
Glos 80 D3
Reading 65 E7
S Glos 80 G2
Church End Beds 121 G12
Beds 122 F2
Bucks 84 D6
Bucks 84 D2
C Beds 85 B8
C Beds 103 E9
C Beds 103 G9
C Beds 104 D3
C Beds 122 G3
Cambs 121 C11
Cambs 123 C7
Cambs 123 D7
Cambs 138 G4
Cambs 139 B7
E Yorks 209 C7
Essex 88 B2
Essex 105 C11
Essex 105 F11
Essex 106 F4
Glos 80 D2
Glos 99 D7
Hants 49 B7
Herts 85 C10
Herts 85 F8
Herts 104 E5
Herts 105 G8
Lincs 156 C4
Lincs 190 B6
London 67 C8
London 86 G2
Norf 157 F10

Colestocks Devon 27 G9
Colethrop Glos 80 C4
Coley Bath 44 B5
Reading 65 E8
W Yorks 196 B6
Colfin Dumfries 236 D2
Colgate W Sus 51 G8
Colgrain Argyll 276 E6
Colham Green
London 66 C5
Colindale London 67 B8
Colinsburgh Fife 287 G8
Colinton Edin 270 B4
Colintraive Argyll 275 F11
Colkirk Norf 159 D8
Collace Perth 286 D6
Collafield Glos 79 C11
Collafirth Shetland 312 G6
Collam W Isles 305 J3
Collamoor Head
Corn 11 C9
Collaton Devon 9 G9
Collaton St Mary
Torbay 9 D7
College Milton
S Lanark 268 D2
College of Roseisle
Moray 301 C11
College Park London 67 C8
College Town Brack 65 G11
Collennan S Ayrs 257 C8
Collessie Fife 286 F6
Colleton Mills
Devon 25 D11
Collett's Br Norf 139 B9
Collett's Green
Worcs 116 G6
Collier Row London 87 G8
Collier's End Herts 105 G7
Collier's Green E Sus 38 C3
Kent 53 F9
Colliers Hatch Essex 87 E8
Collier Street Kent 53 D8
Collier's Wood
London 67 E9
Colliery Row T&W 234 B2
Collieston Aberds 303 G10
Collin Dumfries 238 B2
Collingbourne Ducis
Wilts 47 C8
Collingbourne Kingston
Wilts 47 B8
Collingham Notts 172 C4
W Yorks 206 D3
Collington Hereford 116 E2
Collingtree
Northants 120 F5
Collingwood
Northumb 243 B7
Collins End Oxon 65 D7
Collins Green Warr 183 C9
Worcs 116 F4
Collipriest Devon 27 E7
Colliston Angus 287 C10
Colliton Devon 27 G9
Collycroft Warks 135 F7
Collyhurst Gtr Man 195 G11
Collynie Aberds 303 F8
Collyweston
Northants 137 C9
Colmonell S Ayrs 244 F4
Colmslie Borders 262 B2
Colmsliehill
Borders 271 G10
Colmworth Beds 122 F2
Colnabaichin
Aberds 292 C4
Colnbrook Slough 66 D4
Colne Cambs 123 B7
Lancs 204 E3
Colne Bridge
W Yorks 197 C7
Colne Edge Lancs 204 E3
Colne Engaine
Essex 107 E7
Colnefields Cambs 123 B7
Colney Norf 142 B3
Colney Hatch London 86 G3
Colney Heath Herts 86 D2
Colney Street Herts 85 E11
Coln Rogers Glos 81 D9
Coln St Aldwyns
Glos 81 D10
Coln St Dennis Glos 81 C9
Cologin Argyll 289 G10
Colpitts Grange
Northumb 241 F11
Colpy Aberds 302 F6
Colquhar Borders 270 G6
Colscott Devon 24 E5
Colshaw Staffs 169 B8
Colsterdale N Yorks 214 C2
Colsterworth Lincs 155 E8
Colston E Dunb 268 B2
Pembs 91 F9
Colston Bassett
Notts 154 C3
Colstrope Bucks 65 B9
Coltfield Moray 301 C11
Colt Hill Hants 49 C8
Colthouse Cumb 221 F7
Colthrop W Berks 64 F4
Coltishall Norf 160 F5
Coltness N Lanark 268 D6
Colton
Cumb 210 B6
N Yorks 206 E6
Norf 142 B2
Staffs 151 E11
Suff 125 D7
W Yorks 206 G3
Colton Hills Staffs 133 D8
Colt Park Cumb 210 E5
Colt's Green S Glos 61 C8
Colt's Hill Kent 52 E6
Col Uarach W Isles 304 E6
Columbia T&W 243 F8
Columbjohn Devon 14 B5
Colva Powys 114 G4
Colvend Dumfries 237 D10
Colvister Shetland 312 D7
Colwall Hereford 98 C4
Colwall Green
Hereford 98 C4
Colwall Stone
Hereford 98 C5
Colwell IoW 20 D2
Northumb 241 B11
Colwich Staffs 151 E10
Colwick Notts 171 G10
Colwinston / Tregolwyn
V Glam 58 D2
Colworth W Sus 22 C6
Colwyn Bay / Bae
Colwyn Conwy 180 F4
Colychurch Bridgend 58 D2
Colyford Devon 15 C10
Colyton Devon 15 C10
Colzie Fife 286 F6
Combe Devon 7 E10
Devon 8 B4
Devon 9 G9
E Sus 37 B10
Hereford 114 E6
Oxon 82 B6
Som 28 B6
W Berks 63 G11
Combe Almer Dorset 18 B5
Combebow Devon 12 D5
Combe Common Sur 50 F3
Combe Down Bath 61 G9
Combe Fishacre
Devon 8 C6
Combe Florey Som 43 G7
Combe Hay Bath 45 B8
Combeinteignhead
Devon 14 G4
Combe Martin Devon 40 D5
Combe Moor
Hereford 115 E7
Combe Pafford Torbay 9 B8
Combe Raleigh
Devon 27 G11
Comberbach
Ches W 183 F10
Comberford Staffs 134 B3
Comberton Cambs 123 F7
Hereford 115 D9
Combe St Nicholas
Som 28 E4
Combe Throop Som 30 C2
Combpyne Devon 15 C11
Combrew Devon 40 G4
Combridge Staffs 151 B11
Combrook Warks 118 G6
Combs Derbys 185 F8
Suff 125 F10
W Yorks 197 D8
Combs Ford Suff 125 F11
Combwich Som 43 E9
Comers Aberds 293 C8
Come-to-Good Corn 4 G6
Comeytrowe Som 28 C2
Comford Corn 2 B6
Comfort Corn 2 D6
Comhampton
Worcs 116 D6
Comins Coch
Ceredig 128 G2
Comiston Edin 270 B4
Comley Shrops 131 D9
Commercial End
Cambs 123 E11
Commins Denb 165 C10
Commins Capel Betws
Ceredig 112 F2
Commins Coch
Powys 128 C6
Common Cefn-llwyn
Mon 78 G4
Commondale
N Yorks 226 C3
Common Edge
Blackpool 202 G2
Common End Cumb 228 G6
Derbys 170 C6
Common Hill
Hereford 97 E11
Commonmoor Corn 6 B4
Common Moor Corn 6 B4
Common Platt Wilts 62 B6
Commonside
Ches W 183 G8
Derbys 170 G2
Notts 171 D7
Common Side
Ches W 167 B9
Derbys 170 F6
Derbys 186 F4
Commonwood Herts 85 E8
Shrops 149 D9
Wrex 166 E5
Common-y-coed
Mon 60 B2
Comp Kent 52 B6
Compass Som 43 G9
Compstall Gtr Man 185 C7
Compton Derbys 169 F11
Devon 9 C7
Hants 32 B4
Hants 33 B7
Plym 7 D9
Staffs 132 G6
Sur 49 D11
Sur 50 D3
W Berks 64 D4
W Mid 133 D7
W Sus 34 E3
W Yorks 206 E3
Wilts 46 C6
Compton Abbas
Dorset 30 D5
Compton Abdale
Glos 81 B9
Compton Bassett
Wilts 62 E4
Compton Beauchamp
Oxon 63 B9
Compton Bishop
Som 43 B11
Compton Chamberlayne
Wilts 31 B8
Compton Common
Bath 60 G6
Compton Dando
Bath 60 G6
Compton Dundon
Som 44 G3
Compton Durville
Som 28 D6
Compton End Hants 33 B7
Compton Green Glos 98 F4
Compton Greenfield
S Glos 60 C5
Compton Martin
Bath 44 B4
Compton Pauncefoot
Som 29 B10
Compton Valence
Dorset 17 C7
Comrie Fife 279 D10
Highld 300 D4
Perth 285 C11
Perth 285 E11
Comrue Dumfries 248 F3
Conaglen House
Highld 290 G2
Conanby S Yorks 187 B7
Conchra Argyll 275 E11
Highld 295 C10
Concord T&W 243 F8
Concraig Perth 286 F2
Concraigie Perth 286 C5
Conder Green Lancs 202 B5
Conderton Worcs 99 D9
Condicote Glos 100 F3
Condorrat N Lanark 278 G4
Condover Shrops 131 B9
Coney Hall London 67 G11
Coney Hill Glos 80 B5
Coneyhurst W Sus 35 C10
Coneysthorpe
N Yorks 216 E4
Coneythorpe
N Yorks 206 B3
Coney Weston Suff 125 B9
Conford Hants 49 G10
Congash Highld 301 G10
Congdon's Shop
Corn 11 F11
Congeith Dumfries 237 C10
Congelow Kent 53 D7
Congerstone Leics 135 B7
Congham Norf 158 E4
Congleton Ches E 168 C5
Congleton Edge
Ches E 168 C5
Congl-y-wal Gwyn 164 G2
Congresbury N Som 60 G2
Congreve Staffs 151 G8
Conham Bristol 60 E6
Conicavel Moray 301 D9
Coningsby Lincs 174 D2
Conington Cambs 122 D6
Cambs 138 F3
Conisbrough
S Yorks 187 B8
Conisby Argyll 274 G3
Conisholme Lincs 190 B6
Coniston Cumb 220 F6
E Yorks 209 F9
Coniston Cold
N Yorks 204 B4
Conistone N Yorks 213 F9
Conkwell Wilts 61 G9
Connage Moray 302 C4
Connah's Quay Flint 166 B3
Connel Argyll 289 F11
Connel Park E Ayrs 258 G4
Conniburrow
M Keynes 103 D7
Connista Highld 298 B4
Connon Corn 6 C3
Connor Downs Corn 2 B3
Conock Wilts 46 B5
Conon Bridge
Highld 300 D5
Conon House Highld 300 D5
Cononish Stirling 285 E7
Cononley N Yorks 204 D5
Cononley Woodside
N Yorks 204 D5
Cononsyth Angus 287 C9
Conordan Highld 295 B7
Conquermoor Heath
Telford 150 F3
Conshall Staffs 169 F7
Consett Durham 242 G4
Constable Burton
N Yorks 224 G3
Constable Lee
Lancs 195 C10
Constantine Corn 2 D6
Constantine Bay
Corn 10 G3
Contin Highld 300 D4
Contlaw Aberdeen 293 C10
Conwy Conwy 180 F3
Conyer Kent 70 G3
Conyers Green Suff 125 D7
Cooden E Sus 38 F2
Cooil IoM 192 E4
Cookbury Devon 24 F6
Cookbury Wick
Devon 24 F5
Cookham Windsor 65 B11
Cookham Dean
Windsor 65 C11
Cookham Rise
Windsor 65 C11
Cookhill Worcs 117 F11
Cookley Suff 126 B6
Worcs 132 G6
Cookley Green
Oxon 83 G11
Cookney Aberds 293 D10
Cookridge
W Yorks 205 E11
Cooksbridge E Sus 36 E6
Cooksey Corner
Worcs 117 D8
Cooksey Green
Worcs 117 D8
Cook's Green Essex 89 B11
Suff 125 G9
Cookshill Staffs 168 G6
Cooksland Corn 5 B11
Cooksmill Green
Essex 87 D10
Cooksongreen
Ches W 183 G9
Coolham W Sus 35 C10
Cooling Medway 69 D9
Coolinge Kent 55 F8
Cooling Street
Medway 69 E8
Coombe Bucks 84 D4
Corn 4 G2
Coombe *continued*
Corn 4 G5
Corn 4 G6
Corn 5 E9
Corn 6 C4
Corn 24 E2
Devon 14 G4
Devon 27 D8
Glos 80 G3
Hants 33 C11
Kent 55 B9
London 67 E8
Som 28 B3
Som 28 F6
Wilts 30 C5
Wilts 47 C7
Coombe Bissett
Wilts 31 B10
Coombe Dingle
Bristol 60 D5
Coombe Hill Glos 99 F7
Coombe Keynes
Dorset 18 E2
Coombes W Sus 35 F11
Coombesdale Staffs 150 B6
Coombeswood
W Mid 133 F9
Coomb Hill Kent 69 G7
Coombs End S Glos 61 C9
Coombses Som 28 F4
Coopersale Common
Essex 87 E7
Coopersale Street
Essex 87 E7
Cooper's Corner
Kent 52 D3
Cooper's Green
E Sus 37 C7
Herts 85 D11
Cooper's Hill
C Beds 103 D10
Sur 66 E3
Cooper Street Kent 55 B10
Cooper Turning
Gtr Man 194 F6
Cootham W Sus 35 E9
Copcut Worcs 117 E7
Copdock Suff 108 C2
Coped Hall Wilts 62 C5
Copenhagen Denb 165 B8
Copford Essex 107 G8
Copford Green
Essex 107 G8
Copgrove N Yorks 214 G6
Copister Shetland 312 F6
Cople Beds 104 B2
Copley Durham 233 F7
Gtr Man 185 B7
W Yorks 196 C5
Copley Hill W Yorks 197 B8
Coplow Dale
Derbys 185 F11
Copmanthorpe York 207 D7
Copmere End Staffs 150 D6
Copnor Ptsmth 33 G11
Copp Lancs 202 F4
Coppathorne Corn 24 G2
Coppenhall Ches E 168 D2
Staffs 151 F8
Coppenhall Moss
Ches E 168 D2
Copperhouse Corn 2 B3
Coppice Gtr Man 196 G2
Coppicegate Shrops 132 G4
Coppingford Cambs 138 G3
Coppins Corner Kent 54 D2
Coppleham Som 42 G2
Copplestone Devon 26 G3
Coppull Lancs 194 E5
Coppull Moor Lancs 194 E5
Copsale W Sus 35 C11
Copse Hill London 67 E8
Copster Green
Lancs 203 G9
Copster Hill
Gtr Man 196 G2
Copston Magna
Warks 135 F9
Cop Street Kent 55 B9
Copt Green Warks 118 D3
Copthall Green Essex 86 E6
Copt Heath W Mid 118 B3
Copt Hewick
N Yorks 214 E6
Copthill Durham 232 C3
Copthorne Ches E 167 G11
Corn 11 C11
Shrops 149 G9
Sur 51 F10
Coptiviney Shrops 149 B8
Copt Oak Leics 153 G9
Copton Kent 54 B4
Copy's Green Norf 159 B8
Copythorne Hants 32 E4
Corbets Tey London 68 B5
Corbridge
Northumb 241 E11
Corbriggs Derbys 170 B6
Corby Northants 137 F7
Corby Glen Lincs 155 E9
Corby Hill Cumb 239 F11
Cordon N Ayrs 256 C2
Cordwell Norf 142 E2
Coreley Shrops 116 C2
Cores End Bucks 66 B2
Corfe Som 28 D2
Corfe Castle Dorset 18 E5
Corfe Mullen Dorset 18 B5
Corfton Shrops 131 F9
Corfton Bache
Shrops 131 F9
Corgarff Aberds 292 C4
Corgee Corn 5 C10
Corhampton Hants 33 C10
Corlae Dumfries 246 D5
Corlannau Neath 57 C9
Corley Warks 134 F6
Corley Ash Warks 134 F5
Corley Moor Warks 134 F5
Cornaa IoM 192 D5
Cornabus Argyll 254 C4
Cornaigbeg Argyll 288 E1
Cornaigmore Argyll 288 C4
Argyll 288 E1
Cornard Tye Suff 107 C8
Cornbank Midloth 270 C4
Cornbrook Shrops 116 B2
Corncatterach
Aberds 302 F5
Cornel Conwy 164 C2
Corner Row Lancs 202 F4
Cornett Hereford 97 B11
Corney Cumb 220 G2
Cornforth Durham 234 E2
Cornharrow
Dumfries 246 E5
Cornhill Aberds 302 D5
Powys 96 C2
Stoke 168 E5
Cornhill-on-Tweed
Northumb 263 B9
Cornholme W Yorks 196 B2
Cornish Hall End
Essex 106 D3
Cornquoy Orkney 314 G5
Cornriggs Durham 232 C2
Cornsay Durham 233 C8
Cornsay Colliery
Durham 233 C9
Cornton Stirling 278 B5
Corntown Highld 300 D5
V Glam 58 D2
Cornwell Oxon 100 F5
Cornwood Devon 8 D2
Cornworthy Devon 8 D6
Corpach Highld 290 F2
Corpusty Norf 160 C2
Corran Highld 290 G2
Highld 295 E10
Corran a Chan
Uachdaraich
Highld 295 C7
Corranbuie Argyll 275 G9
Corrany IoM 192 D5
Corrichoich Highld 311 G4
Corrie N Ayrs 255 C11
Corrie Common
Dumfries 248 F6
Corriecravie
N Ayrs 255 E10
Corriecravie Moor
N Ayrs 255 E10
Corriedoo Dumfries 246 G5
Corriegarth Lodge
Highld 291 B7
Corriemoillie Highld 300 C3
Corriemulzie Lodge
Highld 309 K3
Corrievarkie Lodge
Perth 291 F7
Corrievorrie Highld 301 G7
Corrigall Orkney 314 E3
Corrimony Highld 300 F3
Corringham Lincs 188 C5
Thurrock 69 C8
Corris Gwyn 128 B5
Corris Uchaf Gwyn 128 B4
Corrour Highld 290 G5
Corrour Shooting Lodge
Highld 290 G6
Corrow Argyll 284 G5
Corry Highld 295 C8
Corrybrough Highld 301 G8
Corrydon Perth 292 G3
Corryghoil Argyll 284 E5
Corrykinloch Highld 309 G3
Corrylach Argyll 255 D8
Corrymuckloch
Perth 286 D2
Corrynachenchy
Argyll 289 E8
Corry of Ardnagrask
Highld 300 E5
Corsback Highld 310 B6
Corscombe Dorset 29 F8
Corse Aberds 302 E6
Glos 98 F5
Corse Lawn Worcs 98 E6
Corse of Kinnoir
Aberds 302 E5
Corsewall Dumfries 236 C2
Corsham Wilts 61 E11
Corsindae Aberds 293 C8
Corsley Wilts 45 D10
Corsley Heath Wilts 45 D10
Corsock Dumfries 237 B9
Corston Bath 61 F7
Orkney 314 E3
Wilts 62 C2
Corstorphine Edin 280 G3
Cors-y-Gedol
Gwyn 145 E11
Cortachy Angus 287 B7
Corton Suff 143 D10
Wilts 46 E2
Corton Denham
Som 29 C10
Cortworth S Yorks 186 B6
Coruanan Lodge
Highld 290 G2
Corunna W Isles 296 E4
Corvast Highld 309 K5
Corwen Denb 165 G9
Cory Devon 24 D5
Coryates Dorset 17 D8
Coryton Cardiff 58 C6
Devon 12 E5
Thurrock 69 C8
Còsag Highld 295 D10
Cosby Leics 135 E10
Coscote Oxon 64 B4
Coseley W Mid 133 E8
Cosford Warks 119 B9
Cosgrove Northants 102 C5
Cosham Ptsmth 33 F11
Cosheston Pembs 73 E8
Cosmeston V Glam 59 F7
Cosmore Dorset 29 F11
Cossall Notts 171 G7
Cossall Marsh Notts 171 G7
Cosses S Ayrs 244 G4
Cossington Leics 154 G2
Som 43 E11
Costa Orkney 314 D3
Costessey Norf 160 G3
Costessey Park
Norf 160 G3
Costhorpe Notts 187 D9
Costislost Corn 10 G6
Costock Notts 153 D11
Coston Leics 154 E6
Norf 141 B11
Coswinsawsin Corn 2 B4
Cote Oxon 82 E4
Cote *continued*
Som 43 E10
W Sus 35 F10
Cotebrook Ches W 167 B9
Cotehill Cumb 239 G11
Cotes Cumb 211 B9
Leics 153 E11
Staffs 150 C6
Cotesbach Leics 135 G10
Cotes Heath Staffs 150 C6
Cotes Park Derbys 170 E6
Cotford St Lukes
Som 27 B11
Cotgrave Notts 154 B2
Cothall Aberds 293 B10
Cotham Bristol 60 E5
Notts 172 F3
Cothelstone Som 43 G7
Cotheridge Worcs 116 G5
Cotherstone
Durham 223 B10
Cothill Oxon 83 F7
Cotland Mon 79 E8
Cotleigh Devon 28 G2
Cotmanhay Derbys 171 G7
Cotmarsh Wilts 62 D5
Cotmaton Devon 15 D8
Coton Cambs 123 F8
Northants 120 C3
Shrops 149 C10
Staffs 134 B3
Staffs 150 E6
Staffs 151 C9
Coton Clanford
Staffs 151 E7
Coton Hayes Staffs 151 C9
Coton Hill Shrops 149 G9
Staffs 151 C9
Coton in the Clay
Staffs 152 D3
Coton in the Elms
Derbys 152 F4
Coton Park Derbys 152 F5
Cotonwood Shrops 149 B10
Staffs 150 E6
Cotswold Community
Wilts 81 F8
Cott Devon 8 C5
Cottam E Yorks 217 F9
Lancs 202 G6
Notts 188 F4
Cottartown Highld 301 F10
Cottenham Cambs 123 D8
Cottenham Park
London 67 F8
Cotterdale N Yorks 222 G6
Cottered Herts 104 F6
Cotterhill Woods
S Yorks 187 E9
Cotteridge W Mid 117 B10
Cotterstock
Northants 137 E10
Cottesbrooke
Northants 120 C4
Cottesmore Rutland 155 G8
Cotteylands Devon 26 E6
Cottingham E Yorks 208 G6
Northants 136 E6
Cottingley W Yorks 205 F8
Cottisford Oxon 101 E11
Cotton Staffs 169 F9
Suff 125 D11
Cotton End Beds 103 B11
Northants 120 F5
Cotton Stones
W Yorks 196 C4
Cotton Tree Lancs 204 F4
Cottonworth Hants 47 F11
Cottown Aberds 293 B9
Aberds 302 G5
Aberds 303 E8
Cotts Devon 7 B8
Cottwood Devon 25 E10
Cotwall Telford 150 F2
Cotwalton Staffs 151 B8
Couch Green Hants 48 G4
Couch's Mill Corn 6 D2
Coughton Hereford 97 G11
Warks 117 E11
Coughton Fields
Warks 117 F11
Cougie Highld 300 G2
Coulaghailtro Argyll 275 G8
Coulags Highld 299 E9
Coulby Newham
Mbro 225 B10
Coulderton Cumb 219 D9
Couldoran Highld 299 E8
Couligartan Stirling 285 G8
Coulin Highld 299 D10
Coulin Lodge
Highld 299 D10
Coull Aberds 293 C7
Argyll 274 G3
Coulmony Ho Highld 301 E9
Coulport Argyll 276 D4
Coulsdon London 51 B9
Coulshill Perth 286 G3
Coulston Wilts 46 C3
Coulter S Lanark 260 C2
Coultings Som 43 E8
Coulton N Yorks 216 E2
Coultra Fife 287 E7
Cound Shrops 131 C11
Coundlane Shrops 131 B11
Coundmoor Shrops 131 C11
Coundon Durham 233 F10
W Mid 134 G6
Coundongate
Durham 233 F10
Coundon Grange
Durham 233 F10
Counters End Herts 85 D8
Countersett N Yorks 213 B8
Countess Wilts 47 E7
Countess Cross
Essex 107 E7
Countess Wear
Devon 14 D4
Countesthorpe
Leics 135 D11
Countisbury Devon 41 D8
County Oak W Sus 51 F9
Coupar Angus Perth 286 C6
Coup Green Lancs 194 B5
Coupland Cumb 222 B4
Coupland *continued*
Northumb 263 C10
Cour Argyll 255 C9
Courance Dumfries 248 E3
Coursley Som 42 G6
Court-at-Street Kent 54 F5
Court Barton Devon 14 D2
Court Colman
Bridgend 57 E11
Court Corner Hants 48 B6
Courteenhall
Northants 120 G5
Court Henry Carms 93 G11
Courthill Perth 286 C5
Court House Green
W Mid 135 G7
Courtsend Essex 89 G8
Courtway Som 43 G8
Cousland Midloth 271 B7
Cousley Wood E Sus 53 G7
Couston Argyll 275 F11
Cova Shetland 313 J5
Cove Argyll 276 E4
Borders 282 G5
Devon 27 D7
Hants 49 B11
Highld 307 K3
Cove Bay Aberdeen 293 C11
Cove Bottom Suff 127 B9
Covehithe Suff 143 G10
Coven Staffs 133 B8
Covender Hereford 98 C2
Coveney Cambs 139 G9
Covenham St
Bartholomew
Lincs 190 C4
Covenham St Mary
Lincs 190 C4
Coven Heath Staffs 133 C8
Coven Lawn Staffs 133 B8
Coventry W Mid 118 B6
Coverack Corn 3 F7
Coverack Bridges
Corn 2 C5
Coverham N Yorks 214 B2
Covesea Moray 301 B11
Covingham Swindon 63 B7
Covington Cambs 121 C11
S Lanark 259 B11
Cowan Bridge
Lancs 212 D2
Cow Ark Lancs 203 D9
Cowbar Redcar 226 B5
Cowbeech E Sus 23 C10
Cowbeech Hill
E Sus 23 C10
Cowbit Lincs 156 F5
Cowbog Aberds 303 D8
Cowbridge Lincs 174 F4
Som 42 E3
Cowbridge / Y Bont-
Faen V Glam 58 E3
Cowcliffe W Yorks 196 D6
Cowdale Derbys 185 G9
Cowden Kent 52 E3
Cowdenbeath Fife 280 C3
Cowdenburn
Borders 270 E4
Cowen Head Cumb 221 F9
Cowers Lane Derbys 170 F4
Cowes IoW 20 B5
Cowesby N Yorks 215 B9
Cowesfield Green
Wilts 32 C3
Cowfold W Sus 36 C2
Cowgill Cumb 212 B5
Cow Green Suff 125 D11
Cowgrove Dorset 18 B5
Cowhill Derbys 170 F5
S Glos 79 G10
Cow Hill Lancs 203 G7
Cowhorn Hill S Glos 61 E7
Cowie Aberds 293 E10
Stirling 278 D6
Cowlands Corn 4 G6
Cowleaze Corner
Oxon 82 E4
Cowley Derbys 186 F4
Devon 14 B4
Glos 81 C7
London 66 C5
Oxon 83 E8
Cowleymoor Devon 27 E7
Cowley Peachy
London 66 C5
Cowling Lancs 194 D5
N Yorks 204 E5
N Yorks 214 B4
Cowlinge Suff 124 G4
Cowlow Derbys 185 G9
Cowmes W Yorks 197 D7
Cowpe Lancs 195 C10
Cowpen Northumb 253 G7
Cowpen Bewley
Stockton 234 G5
Cowplain Hants 33 E11
Cow Roast Herts 85 C7
Cowshill Durham 232 C3
Cowslip Green
N Som 60 G3
Cowstrandburn
Fife 279 C10
Cowthorpe N Yorks 206 C4
Coxall Hereford 115 C7
Coxbank Ches E 167 G11
Coxbench Derbys 170 G5
Coxbridge Som 44 F4
Cox Common Suff 143 G8
Coxford Corn 11 B9
Norf 158 D6
Soton 32 D5
Coxgreen Staffs 132 F6
Cox Green Gtr Man 195 E8
Sur 50 G5
Windsor 65 D11
Coxheath Kent 53 C8
Coxhill Kent 55 D8
Cox Hill Corn 4 G4
Coxhoe Durham 234 D2
Coxley Som 44 E4
W Yorks 197 D9
Coxley Wick Som 44 E4
Coxlodge T&W 242 D6
Cox Moor Notts 171 D8
Coxpark Corn 12 G4
Coxtie Green Essex 87 F9
Coxwold N Yorks 215 D10
Coychurch Bridgend 58 D2
Coylton S Ayrs 257 E10
Coylumbridge
Highld 291 B11
Coynach Aberds 292 C6
Coynachie Aberds 302 F4
Coytrahen Bridgend 57 D11
CoytrahÛn Bridgend 57 D11
Crabadon Devon 8 E5
Crabbet Park W Sus 51 F10
Crabble Kent 55 E9
Crabbs Cross
Worcs 117 E10
Crabbs Green Herts 105 F9
Crabgate Norf 159 D11
Crab Orchard Dorset 31 F9
Crabtree Plym 7 D10
W Sus 36 B2
Crabtree Green
Wrex 166 G4
Crackaig Argyll 274 G6
Crackenedge
W Yorks 197 C8
Crackenthorpe
Cumb 231 G9
Crackington Haven
Corn 11 B8
Crackley Staffs 168 E4
Warks 118 C5
Crackleybank
Shrops 150 G5
Crackpot N Yorks 223 F9
Crackthorn Corner
Suff 125 B10
Cracoe N Yorks 213 G9
Cracow Moss
Ches E 168 F2
Staffs 168 F3
Craddock Devon 27 E9
Cradhlastadh
W Isles 304 E2
Cradle Edge
W Yorks 205 F7
Cradle End Herts 105 G9
Cradley Hereford 98 B4
W Mid 133 G8
Cradley Heath
W Mid 133 F8
Cradoc Powys 95 E10
Crafthole Corn 7 E7
Crafton Bucks 84 B5
Crag Bank Lancs 211 E9
Crag Foot Lancs 211 E9
Craggan Highld 301 G10
Moray 301 F11
Stirling 285 E9
Cragganvallie
Highld 300 F5
Craggenmore
Moray 301 F11
Cragg Hill W Yorks 205 F10
Craggie Highld 301 F7
Highld 311 H2
Craggiemore Highld 309 J7
Cragg Vale W Yorks 196 C4
Craghead Durham 242 G6
Crahan Corn 2 C5
Crai Powys 95 G7
Craibstone Moray 302 D4
Craichie Angus 287 C9
Craig Dumfries 237 B8
Dumfries 237 C8
Highld 299 E10
Craiganor Lodge
Perth 285 B10
Craig Berthlwyd
M Tydf 77 F9
Craig Castle Aberds 302 G4
Craig-cefn-parc
Swansea 75 E11
Craigdallie Perth 286 E6
Craigdam Aberds 303 F8
Craigdarroch
Dumfries 246 E6
Highld 300 D4
Craigdhu Highld 300 E4
Craig Douglas
Borders 261 E7
Craigearn Aberds 293 B9
Craigellachie Moray 302 E2
Craigencallie Ho
Dumfries 237 B7
Craigencross
Dumfries 236 C2
Craigend Borders 271 F9
Glasgow 268 B3
Perth 286 E3
Perth 286 E5
Stirling 278 D5
Craigendive Argyll 275 E11
Craigendoran Argyll 276 E6
Craigendowie
Angus 293 G7
Craigends Renfs 267 B8
Craigens Argyll 274 G3
E Ayrs 258 F3
Craigentinny Edin 280 G5
Craigerne Borders 261 B7
Craighall Perth 286 C5
Craighat Stirling 277 E9
Craighead Fife 287 G10
Highld 301 C7
Craighill Aberds 303 E7
Craighlaw Mains
Dumfries 236 C5
Craighouse Argyll 274 G6
Craigie Aberds 293 B11
Dundee 287 D8
Perth 286 C5
Perth 286 E5
S Ayrs 257 C10
S Ayrs 257 E8
Craigiefield Orkney 314 E4
Craigiehall Edin 280 F3
Craigielaw E Loth 281 F9
Craigierig Borders 260 E6
Craigleith Edin 280 G4
Craig Llangiwg
Neath 76 D2
Craig-llwyn Shrops 148 D4
Craiglockhart Edin 280 G4
Craig Lodge Argyll 275 G10
Craigmalloch
E Ayrs 245 E11
Craigmaud Aberds 303 D8
Craigmill Stirling 278 B6
Craigmillar Edin 280 G5

Cwm-y-glo continued
Gwyn 163 C8
Cwmynyscoy Torf 78 F3
Cwmyoy Mon 96 G5
Cwmystwyth
Ceredig 112 C5
Cwrt Gwyn 128 C3
Cwrt-newydd Ceredig 93 B9
Cwrt-y-cadno Carms 94 C3
Cwrt-y-gollen Powys 78 B2
Cydweli / Kidwelly
Carms 74 D6
Cyffordd Llandudno / Llandudno Junction
Conwy 180 F3
Cyffylliog Denb 165 D9
Cyfronydd Powys 130 B2
Cymau Flint 166 D3
Cymdda Bridgend 58 C2
Cymer Neath 57 B11
Cymmer Rhondda 77 G8
Cyncoed Cardiff 59 C7
Cynghordy Carms 94 C6
Cynheidre Carms 75 D7
Cynonville Neath 57 B10
Cyntwell Cardiff 58 D6
Cynwyd Denb 165 G9
Cynwyl Elfed Carms 93 F7
Cywarch Gwyn 147 F7

D

Daccombe Devon 9 B8
Dacre Cumb 230 F5
N Yorks 214 G3
Dacre Banks
N Yorks 214 G3
Daddry Shield
Durham 232 D3
Dadford Bucks 102 D3
Dadlington Leics 135 D8
Dafarn Faig Gwyn 163 F7
Dafen Carms 75 E8
Daffy Green Norf 141 B9
Dagdale Staffs 151 C11
Dagenham London 68 C3
Daggons Dorset 31 E10
Daglingworth Glos 81 D7
Dagnall Bucks 85 B7
Dagtail End Worcs 117 E10
Dagworth Suff 125 E10
Dail Beag W Isles 304 D4
Dail bho Dheas
W Isles 304 B6
Dail bho Thuath
W Isles 304 B6
Daill Argyll 274 G4
Dailly S Ayrs 245 C7
Dail Mor W Isles 304 D4
Dainton Devon 9 B7
Dairsie or Osnaburgh
Fife 287 F8
Daisy Green Suff 125 D10
Suff 125 D11
Daisy Hill Gtr Man 195 G7
W Yorks 197 B9
W Yorks 205 G8
Daisy Nook Gtr Man 196 G2
Dalabrog W Isles 297 J3
Dalavich Argyll 275 B10
Dalbeattie
Dumfries 237 C10
Dalbeg Highld 291 B8
Dalblair E Ayrs 258 F4
Dalbog Angus 293 F7
Dalbrack Stirling 285 G11
Dalbury Derbys 152 C5
Dalby IoM 192 E3
Lincs 190 G6
N Yorks 216 E2
Dalchalloch Perth 291 G9
Dalchalm Highld 311 J3
Dalchenna Argyll 284 G4
Dalchirach Moray 301 F11
Dalchonzie Perth 285 E11
Dalchork Highld 309 H5
Dalchreichart
Highld 290 B4
Dalchruin Perth 285 F11
Dalderby Lincs 174 B2
Dale Cumb 230 C6
Gtr Man 196 F3
Pembs 72 D4
Shetland 312 G6
Dale Abbey Derbys 153 B8
Dalebank Derbys 170 C5
Dale Bottom Cumb 229 G11
Dale Brow Ches E 184 F6
Dale End Derbys 170 C2
N Yorks 204 D5
Dale Head Cumb 221 B8
Dale Hill E Sus 53 G7
E Sus 53 G8
Dalelia Highld 289 C9
Dale Moor Derbys 153 B8
Dale of Walls
Shetland 313 H3
Dales Brow
Gtr Man 195 G9
Dales Green Staffs 168 D5
Daless Highld 301 F8
Dalestie Moray 292 B3
Dalestorth Notts 171 C8
Dalfaber Highld 291 B11
Dalfoil Stirling 277 D11
Dalganachan Highld 310 E4
Dalgarven N Ayrs 266 F5
Dalgety Bay Fife 280 E3
Dalginross Perth 285 E11
Dalguise Perth 286 C3
Dalhalvaig Highld 310 D2
Dalham Suff 124 E4
Dalhastnie Angus 293 F7
Dalhenzean Perth 292 G3
Dalinlongart Argyll 276 E2
Dalkeith Midloth 270 B6
Dallam Warr 183 C9
Dallas Moray 301 D11
Dallas Lodge
Moray 301 D11
Dallcharn Highld 308 D6
Dalleagles E Ayrs 258 G3
Dallicott Shrops 132 E5
Dallimores IoW 20 C6
Dallinghoo Suff 126 G5
Dallington E Sus 23 B11
Northants 120 E4
Dallow N Yorks 214 E3
Dalmadilly Aberds 293 B9
Dalmally Argyll 284 E5
Dalmarnock
Glasgow 268 C2
Perth 286 C3
Dalmary Stirling 277 B10
Dalmellington
E Ayrs 245 B11
Dalmeny Edin 280 F2
Dalmigavie Highld 291 B9
Dalmigavie Lodge
Highld 301 G7
Dalmilling S Ayrs 257 E9
Dalmore Highld 300 C6
Dalmuir W Dunb 277 G9
Dalnabreck Highld 289 C8
Dalnacardoch Lodge
Perth 291 F9
Dalnacroich Highld 300 D3
Dalnaglar Castle
Perth 292 G3
Dalnahaitnach
Highld 301 G8
Dalnamein Lodge
Perth 291 G9
Dalnarrow Argyll 289 F9
Dalnaspidal Lodge
Perth 291 F8
Dalnavaid Perth 292 G2
Dalnavie Highld 300 B6
Dalnaw Dumfries 236 B5
Dalnawillan Lodge
Highld 310 E4
Dalness Highld 284 B5
Dalnessie Highld 309 H6
Dalphaid Highld 309 H3
Dalqueich Perth 286 G4
Dalrannoch Argyll 289 E11
Dalreavoch Highld 309 J7
Dalriach Highld 301 F10
Dalrigh Stirling 285 E7
Dalry Edin 280 G4
N Ayrs 266 F5
Dalrymple E Ayrs 257 G9
Dalscote Northants 120 G3
Dalserf S Lanark 268 E6
Dalshannon
N Lanark 278 G4
Dalston Cumb 239 G9
London 67 C10
Dalswinton
Dumfries 247 F10
Dalton
Cumb 211 D10
Dumfries 238 C4
Lancs 194 F3
N Yorks 215 D8
N Yorks 224 D2
Northumb 241 F10
Northumb 242 C4
S Lanark 268 D3
S Yorks 187 C7
W Yorks 197 D7
Dalton-in-Furness
Cumb 210 E4
Dalton-le-Dale
Durham 234 B4
Dalton Magna
S Yorks 187 C7
Dalton-on-Tees
N Yorks 224 D5
Dalton Parva
S Yorks 187 C7
Dalton Piercy Hrtlpl 234 E5
Dalveallan Highld 300 F6
Dalveich Stirling 285 E10
Dalvina Lo Highld 308 E6
Dalwey Telford 132 B3
Dalwhinnie Highld 291 E8
Dalwood Devon 28 G3
Dalwyne S Ayrs 245 D8
Damask Green
Herts 104 F5
Damems W Yorks 204 F6
Damerham Hants 31 D10
Damery Glos 80 G2
Damgate Norf 143 B8
Norf 161 F9
Dam Green Norf 141 F11
Damhead Moray 301 D10
Dam Head W Yorks 196 B6
Damhead Holdings
Midloth 270 B5
Dam Mill Staffs 133 C7
Damnaglaur
Dumfries 236 F3
Dam of Quoiggs
Perth 286 G2
Damside Borders 270 F3
Dam Side Lancs 202 D4
Danaway Kent 69 G11
Danbury Essex 88 E3
Danbury Common
Essex 88 E3
Danby N Yorks 226 D4
Danby Wiske
N Yorks 224 F6
Dan Caerlan Rhondda 58 C5
Dancers Hill Herts 86 F2
Dancing Green
Hereford 98 G2
Dandaleith Moray 302 E2
Danderhall Midloth 270 B6
Dandy Corner Suff 125 D11
Danebank Ches E 185 E7
Dane Bank Gtr Man 184 B6
Danebridge Ches E 169 B7
Dane End Herts 104 G6
Danegate E Sus 52 G5
Danehill E Sus 36 B6
Dane in Shaw
Ches E 168 C5
Danemoor Green
Norf 141 B11
Danesbury Herts 86 B2
Danesfield Bucks 65 C10
Danesford Shrops 132 E4
Daneshill Hants 49 C7
Danesmoor Derbys 170 C6
Danes Moss Ches E 184 G6
Dane Street Kent 54 C5
Daneway Glos 80 E6
Dangerous Corner
Gtr Man 195 G7
Lancs 194 E4
Daniel's Water Kent 54 E3
Danna na Cloiche
Argyll 275 F7
Dannonchapel Corn 10 E6
Danskine E Loth 271 B11
Danthorpe E Yorks 209 G10
Danygraig Caerph 78 G2
Danzey Green
Warks 118 D2
Dapple Heath
Staffs 151 D10
Darby End W Mid 133 F9
Darby Green Hants 65 G10
Darbys Green Worcs 116 F4
Darby's Hill W Mid 133 F9
Darcy Lever
Gtr Man 195 F8
Dardy Powys 78 B2
Darenth Kent 68 E5
Daresbury Halton 183 E9
Daresbury Delph
Halton 183 E9
Darfield S Yorks 198 G2
Darfoulds Notts 187 F9
Dargate Kent 70 G5
Dargate Common
Kent 70 G5
Dargavel Village
Renfs 277 G8
Darite Corn 6 B5
Darkland Moray 302 C2
Darland Wrex 166 D5
Darlaston W Mid 133 D9
Darlaston Green
W Mid 133 D9
Darley N Yorks 205 B10
Shrops 132 D3
Darley Abbey Derby 153 B7
Darley Bridge
Derbys 170 C3
Darley Dale Derbys 170 C3
Darleyford Corn 11 G11
Darley Green Warks 118 C3
Darleyhall Herts 104 G2
Darley Head
N Yorks 205 B9
Darley Hillside
Derbys 170 C3
Darlingscott Warks 100 C4
Darlington Darl 224 C5
Darliston Shrops 149 C11
Darlton Notts 188 G3
Darmsden Suff 125 G11
Darnall S Yorks 186 D5
Darnaway Castle
Moray 301 D9
Darnford Staffs 134 B2
Darnhall Ches W 167 C10
Darnhall Mains
Borders 270 F4
Darn Hill Gtr Man 195 E10
Darnick Borders 262 C2
Darowen Powys 128 C6
Darra Aberds 303 E7
Darracott Devon 24 D2
Devon 40 F3
Darras Hall
Northumb 242 C5
Darrington W Yorks 198 D3
Darrow Green Norf 142 F5
Darsham Suff 127 D8
Darshill Som 44 E6
Dartford Kent 68 E4
Dartford Crossing
Kent 68 D5
Dartington Devon 8 C5
Dartmeet Devon 13 G9
Dartmouth Devon 9 E7
Dartmouth Park
London 67 B9
Darton S Yorks 197 F10
Darvel E Ayrs 258 B3
Darvillshill Bucks 84 F4
Darwell Hole E Sus 23 B11
Darwen Blackburn 195 C7
Dassels Herts 105 F7
Datchet Windsor 66 D3
Datchet Common
Windsor 66 D3
Datchworth Herts 86 B3
Datchworth Green
Herts 86 B3
Daubhill Gtr Man 195 F8
Daugh of Kinermony
Moray 302 E2
Dauntsey Wilts 62 C3
Dauntsey Lock Wilts 62 C3
Dava Moray 301 F10
Davenham Ches W 183 G11
Davenport Ches E 168 B4
Gtr Man 184 D5
Davenport Green
Ches E 184 F4
Gtr Man 184 D4
Daventry Northants 119 E11
Davidson's Mains
Edin 280 F4
Davidston Highld 301 C7
Davidstow Corn 11 D9
David Street Kent 68 G6
David's Well Powys 113 B11
Davington Dumfries 248 C6
Kent 70 G4
Daviot Aberds 303 G7
Highld 301 F7
Davis's Town E Sus 23 B8
Davoch of Grange
Moray 302 D4
Davo Mains Aberds 293 F9
Davyhulme Gtr Man 184 B3
Daw Cross
N Yorks 205 C11
Dawdon Durham 234 B4
Daw End W Mid 133 C10
Dawesgreen Sur 51 D8
Dawker Hill N Yorks 207 F7
Dawley Telford 132 B3
Dawley Bank Telford 132 B3
Dawlish Devon 14 F5
Dawlish Warren
Devon 14 F5
Dawn Conwy 180 G5
Daw's Cross Essex 107 E7
Daw's Green Som 27 C11
Daws Heath Essex 69 B10
Dawshill Worcs 116 G6
Daw's House Corn 12 E2
Dawsmere Lincs 157 C8
Daybrook Notts 171 F9
Day Green Ches E 168 D3
Dayhills Staffs 151 C9
Dayhouse Bank
Worcs 117 B9
Daylesford Glos 100 F4
Daywall Shrops 148 C5
Ddol Flint 181 G10
Ddôl Cownwy
Powys 147 F10
Ddrydwy Anglesey 178 G5
Deacons Hill Herts 85 F11
Deadman's Cross
C Beds 104 C2
Deadman's Green
Staffs 151 B10
Deadwater Hants 49 F10
Northumb 250 D4
Deaf Hill Durham 234 D3
Deal Hall Essex 89 F8
Kent 55 C11
Dean Cumb 229 F7
Devon 8 C4
Devon 40 D6
Devon 40 E4
Devon 41 D8
Dorset 31 D7
Edin 280 G4
Hants 33 D9
Hants 48 G2
Lancs 195 B11
Oxon 100 G6
Som 45 E7
Dean Bank Durham 233 E11
Deanburnhaugh
Borders 261 G9
Dean Court Oxon 83 D7
Dean Cross Devon 40 E4
Deane Gtr Man 195 F7
Hants 48 C4
Deanend Dorset 31 D7
Dean Head S Yorks 197 G9
Deanich Lodge
Highld 309 L3
Deanland Dorset 31 D7
Deanlane End W Sus 34 E2
Dean Lane Head
W Yorks 205 G7
Dean Park Renfs 267 B10
Dean Prior Devon 8 C4
Dean Row Ches E 184 E5
Deans W Loth 269 B10
Deans Bottom Kent 69 G11
Deanscales Cumb 229 F7
Deansgreen
Ches E 183 D11
Dean's Green Warks 118 D2
Deanshanger
Northants 102 D5
Deans Hill Kent 69 G11
Deanston Stirling 285 G11
Dean Street Kent 53 C8
Dearham Cumb 229 D7
Dearnley Gtr Man 196 D2
Debach Suff 126 G4
Debdale Gtr Man 184 B5
Debden Essex 86 F6
Essex 105 E11
Debden Cross
Essex 105 E11
Debden Green Essex 86 F6
Essex 105 E11
De Beauvoir Town
London 67 C10
Debenham Suff 126 E3
Deblin's Green Worcs 98 B6
Dechmont W Loth 279 G10
Deckham T&W 243 E7
Deddington Oxon 101 E9
Dedham Essex 107 E11
Dedham Heath
Essex 107 E11
Dedridge W Loth 269 B11
Dedworth Windsor 66 D2
Deebank Aberds 293 D8
Deecastle Aberds 292 D6
Deene Northants 137 E8
Deenethorpe
Northants 137 E9
Deepcar S Yorks 186 B3
Deepclough Derbys 185 B8
Deepcut Sur 50 B2
Deepdale C Beds 104 B4
Cumb 212 C4
N Yorks 213 D7
Deepdene Sur 51 D7
Deepfields W Mid 133 E8
Deeping Gate Lincs 138 B2
Deeping St James
Lincs 138 B3
Deeping St Nicholas
Lincs 156 F4
Deepthwaite Cumb 211 C10
Deepweir Mon 60 B3
Deerhill Moray 302 D4
Deerhurst Glos 99 F7
Deerhurst Walton
Glos 99 F7
Deerland Pembs 73 C7
Deerness Orkney 314 F5
Deer's Green Essex 105 E9
Deerstones N Yorks 205 C7
Deerton Street Kent 70 G3
Defford Worcs 99 C8
Defynnog Powys 95 F8
Deganwy Conwy 180 F3
Degar V Glam 58 D4
Degibna Corn 2 D5
Deighton N Yorks 225 E7
W Yorks 197 D7
York 207 E8
Deiniolen Gwyn 163 C9
Deishar Highld 291 B11
Delabole Corn 11 E7
Delamere Ches W 167 B9
Delfour Highld 291 C10
Delfrigs Aberds 303 G9
Delliefure Highld 301 F10
Dell Lodge Highld 292 B2
Dell Quay W Sus 22 C4
Delly End Oxon 82 C5
Delnabo Moray 292 B3
Delnadamph Aberds 292 C4
Delnamer Angus 292 G3
Delph Gtr Man 196 F3
Delves Durham 233 B8
Delvine Perth 286 C5
Delvin End Essex 106 D5
Dembleby Lincs 155 B10
Demelza Corn 5 C9
Denaby Main
S Yorks 187 B7
Denbeath Fife 281 B7
Denbigh Denb 165 B9
Denbury Devon 8 B6
Denby Derbys 170 F5
Denby Bottles
Derbys 170 F5
Denby Common
Derbys 170 F6
Denby Dale
W Yorks 197 F8
Denchworth Oxon 82 G5
Dendron Cumb 210 E4
Denel End C Beds 103 D10
Denend Aberds 302 F6
Dene Park Kent 52 C5
Deneside Durham 234 B4
Denford Northants 121 B9
Staffs 169 E7
Dengie Essex 89 E7
Denham Bucks 66 B4
Bucks 102 G5
Suff 124 E5
Suff 126 C3
Denham Corner
Suff 126 C3
Denham End Suff 124 E5
Denham Green Bucks 66 B4
Denham Street Suff 126 C3
Denhead Aberds 303 D9
Fife 287 F8
Denhead of Arbilot
Angus 287 C9
Denhead of Gray
Dundee 287 D7
Denholm Borders 262 F3
Denholme W Yorks 205 G7
Denholme Clough
W Yorks 205 G7
Denholme Edge
W Yorks 205 G7
Denholme Gate
W Yorks 205 G7
Denholmhill Borders 262 F3
Denio Gwyn 145 B7
Denmead Hants 33 E11
Denmore Aberdeen 293 B11
Denmoss Aberds 302 E6
Dennington Suff 126 D5
Dennington Corner
Suff 126 D5
Dennington Hall
Suff 126 D5
Denny Falk 278 E6
Denny Bottom Kent 52 F5
Denny End Cambs 123 D9
Dennyloanhead
Falk 278 E6
Denny Lodge Hants 32 F4
Dennystown
W Dunb 277 F7
Denshaw Gtr Man 196 E3
Denside Aberds 293 D10
Densole Kent 55 E8
Denston Suff 124 G5
Denstone Staffs 169 G9
Denstroude Kent 70 G6
Dent Cumb 212 B4
Dent Bank Durham 232 F4
Denton Cambs 138 F2
Darl 224 B4
E Sus 23 E7
Gtr Man 184 B6
Kent 55 D8
Kent 69 E7
Lincs 155 C7
N Yorks 205 D8
Norf 142 F5
Northants 120 F6
Oxon 83 E9
Denton Burn T&W 242 D5
Denton Holme
Cumb 239 G10
Denton's Green
Mers 183 B7
Denver Norf 140 C2
Denvilles Hants 22 B2
Denwick Northumb 264 G6
Deopham Norf 141 C11
Deopham Green
Norf 141 D10
Deopham Stalland
Norf 141 D10
Depden Suff 124 F5
Depden Green Suff 124 F5
Deppers Bridge
Warks 119 F7
Deptford London 67 D11
T&W 243 F9
Wilts 46 F4
Derby Derbys 153 B7
Devon 40 G5
Derbyhaven IoM 192 F3
Derbyshire Hill
Mers 183 C8
Dereham Norf 159 G9
Dergoals Dumfries 236 D4
Deri Caerph 77 E10
Derriford Plym 7 D9
Derril Devon 24 G4
Derringstone Kent 55 D8
Derrington Shrops 132 E2
Staffs 151 E7
Derriton Devon 24 G4
Derry Stirling 285 E10
Derrydaroch Stirling 285 E7
Derry Downs London 68 F3
Derry Fields Wilts 81 G8
Derryguaig Argyll 288 F6
Derry Hill Wilts 62 E3
Derry Lodge Aberds 292 D2
Derrythorpe
N Lincs 199 F10
Dersingham Norf 158 C3
Dertfords Wilts 45 D10
Dervaig Argyll 288 D6
Derwen Bridgend 58 C2
Denb 165 E9
Derwenlas Powys 128 D4
Derwydd Carms 75 B10
Desborough
Northants 136 G6
Desford Leics 135 C9
Deskryshiel Aberds 292 B6
Detchant Northumb 264 B3
Detling Kent 53 B9
Deuchar Angus 292 G6
Deuddwr Powys 148 F4
Deuxhill Shrops 132 F3
Devauden Mon 79 F7
Deveral Corn 2 B3
Devil's Bridge / Pontarfynach
Ceredig 112 B4
Devitts Green
Warks 134 E5
Devizes Wilts 62 G4
Devol Invclyd 276 G6
Devonport Plym 7 E9
Devonside Clack 279 B8
Devon Village Clack 279 B8
Devoran Corn 3 B7
Dewar Borders 270 F6
Dewartown Midloth 271 C7
Dewes Green Essex 105 E9
Dewlands Common
Dorset 31 F9
Dewlish Dorset 17 B11
Dewsbury W Yorks 197 C8
Dewsbury Moor
W Yorks 197 C8
Dewshall Court
Hereford 97 E9
Dhoon IoM 192 D5
Dhoor IoM 192 C5
Dhowin IoM 192 B5
Dhustone Shrops 115 B11
Dial Green W Sus 34 B6
Dial Post W Sus 35 D11
Dibberford Dorset 29 G7
Dibden Hants 32 F6
Dibden Purlieu Hants 32 F6
Dickens Heath
W Mid 118 B2
Dickleburgh Norf 142 G3
Dickleburgh Moor
Norf 142 G3
Dickon Hills Lincs 174 D6
Didbrook Glos 99 E11
Didcot Oxon 64 B4
Diddington Cambs 122 D3
Diddlebury Shrops 131 F10
Diddywell Devon 25 B7
Didley Hereford 97 E9
Didling W Sus 34 D4
Didlington Norf 140 D5
Didmarton Glos 61 B10
Didsbury Gtr Man 184 C4
Didworthy Devon 8 C3
Diebidale Highld 309 L4
Digbeth W Mid 133 F11
Digby Lincs 173 E9
Digg Highld 298 C4
Diggle Gtr Man 196 F4
Diglis Worcs 116 G6
Digmoor Lancs 194 F3
Digswell Herts 86 B3
Digswell Park Herts 86 C2
Digswell Water Herts 86 C3
Dihewyd Ceredig 111 F9
Dilham Norf 160 D6
Dilhorne Staffs 169 G7
Dillarburn S Lanark 268 G6
Dill Hall Lancs 195 B8
Dillington Cambs 122 D2
Som 28 D5
Dilston Northumb 241 E11
Dilton Marsh Wilts 45 D11
Dilwyn Hereford 115 G8
Dimlands V Glam 58 F3
Dimmer Som 44 G6
Dimple Derbys 170 C3
Gtr Man 195 D8
Dimsdale Staffs 168 F4
Dimson Corn 12 G4
Dinas Carms 92 E5
Corn 10 G4
Gwyn 144 B5
Gwyn 163 D7
Dinas Cross Pembs 91 D10
Dinas Dinlle Gwyn 162 D6
Dinas-Mawddwy
Gwyn 147 G7
Dinas Mawr Conwy 164 E4
Dinas Powys V Glam 59 E7
Dinbych y Pysgod / Tenby Pembs 73 E10
Dinckley Lancs 203 F9
Dinder Som 44 E5
Dinedor Hereford 97 D10
Dinedor Cross
Hereford 97 D10
Dines Green Worcs 116 F6
Dingestow Mon 79 C7
Dinghurst N Som 44 B2
Dingle Mers 182 D5
Dingleden Kent 53 G10
Dingleton Borders 262 C2
Dingley Northants 136 F5
Dingwall Highld 300 D5
Dinlabyre Borders 250 E2
Dinmael Conwy 165 G8
Dinnet Aberds 292 D6
Dinnington S Yorks 187 D8
Som 28 E6
T&W 242 C6
Dinorwic Gwyn 163 C9
Dinton Bucks 84 C3
Wilts 46 G4
Dinwoodie Mains
Dumfries 248 E4
Dinworthy Devon 24 D4
Dipford Som 28 C2
Dipley Hants 49 B8
Dippenhall Sur 49 D10
Dippertown Devon 12 E4
Dippin N Ayrs 256 E2
Dipple Devon 24 D4
Moray 302 D3
S Ayrs 244 C6
Diptford Devon 8 D4
Dipton Durham 242 G5
Diptonmill
Northumb 241 E10
Dirdhu Highld 301 G10
Direcleit W Isles 305 J3
Dirleton E Loth 281 E10
Dirt Pot Northumb 232 B3
Discoed Powys 114 E5
Discove Som 45 G7
Diseworth Leics 153 E9
Dishes Orkney 314 D6
Dishforth N Yorks 215 E7
Dishley Leics 153 E10
Disley Ches E 185 E7
Diss Norf 126 B2
Disserth Powys 113 F10
Distington Cumb 228 G6
Ditchampton Wilts 46 G5
Ditcheat Som 44 F6
Ditchfield Bucks 84 G4
Ditchford Hill
Worcs 100 D4
Ditchingham Norf 142 E6
Ditchling E Sus 36 D4
Ditherington
Shrops 149 G10
Ditteridge Wilts 61 F10
Dittisham Devon 9 E7
Ditton Halton 183 D7
Kent 53 B8
Ditton Green Cambs 124 F3
Ditton Priors Shrops 132 F2
Dittons E Sus 23 E10
Divach Highld 300 G4
Divlyn Carms 94 D5
Dixton Glos 99 E9
Mon 79 C8
Dizzard Corn 11 B9
Dobcross Gtr Man 196 F3
Dobs Hill Flint 166 C4
Dobson's Bridge
Shrops 149 C9
Dobwalls Corn 6 C4
Doccombe Devon 13 D11
Dochfour Ho Highld 300 F6
Dochgarroch Highld 300 E6
Dockeney Norf 143 E7
Dockenfield Sur 49 E10
Docker Lancs 211 E11
Docking Norf 158 B5
Docklow Hereford 115 F11
Dockray Cumb 230 G3
Dockroyd W Yorks 204 F6
Doc Penfro / Pembroke Dock Pembs 73 E7
Docton Devon 24 C2
Dodbrooke Devon 8 G4
Dodburn Borders 249 B11
Doddenham Worcs 116 F5
Doddinghurst Essex 87 F9
Doddington Cambs 139 E7
Kent 54 B2
Lincs 188 G6
Northumb 263 C11
Shrops 116 B2
Doddiscombsleigh
Devon 14 D3
Doddshill Norf 158 C3
Doddycross Corn 6 C6
Dodford Northants 120 E2
Worcs 117 C8
Dodington S Glos 61 C9
Som 43 E7
Dodleston Ches W 166 C5
Dodmarsh Hereford 97 C11
Dodscott Devon 25 D8
Dods Leigh Staffs 151 C10
Dodworth S Yorks 197 F10
Dodworth Bottom
S Yorks 197 G10
Dodworth Green
S Yorks 197 G10
Doe Bank W Mid 134 D2
Doe Green Warr 183 D9
Doehole Derbys 170 D5
Doe Lea Derbys 171 B7
Doffcocker Gtr Man 195 E7
Dogdyke Lincs 174 D2
Dog & Gun Mers 182 B5
Dog Hill Gtr Man 196 F3
Dogingtree Estate
Staffs 151 G9
Dogley Lane
W Yorks 197 E7
Dogmersfield Hants 49 C9
Dogridge Wilts 62 B5
Dogsthorpe Pboro 138 C3
Dog Village Devon 14 B5
Doirlinn Highld 289 D8
Dolanog Powys 147 G11
Dolau Powys 114 D2
Rhondda 58 C3
Dolbenmaen Gwyn 163 G8
Dole Ceredig 128 F2
Dolemeads Bath 61 G9
Doley Staffs 150 D4
Dolfach Powys 129 C8
Dol-ffanog Gwyn 146 G4
Dolfor Powys 130 F2
Dol-fôr Powys 128 B6
Dolgarrog Conwy 164 B3
Dolgellau Gwyn 146 F4
Dolgerdd Ceredig 111 G8
Dolgoch Gwyn 128 C3
Dolgran Carms 93 E8
Dolhelfa Powys 113 C8
Dolhendre Gwyn 147 C7
Doll Highld 311 J2
Dollar Clack 279 B9
Dolley Green Powys 114 D5
Dollis Hill London 67 B8
Dollwen Ceredig 128 G3
Dolphin Flint 181 G11
Dolphingstone
E Loth 281 G7
Dolphinholme
Lancs 202 C6
Dolphinston Borders 262 F5
Dolphinton S Lanark 270 F2
Dolton Devon 25 E9
Dolwen Conwy 180 G5
Powys 129 B9
Dolwyd Conwy 180 F4
Dolwyddelan Conwy 164 E2
Dôl-y-Bont Ceredig 128 F2
Dol-y-cannau Powys 96 B3
Dolydd Gwyn 163 D7
Dolyhir Powys 114 F4
Dolymelinau
Powys 129 D11
Dolywern Wrex 148 B4
Domewood Sur 51 E10
Domgay Powys 148 F5
Dommett Som 28 E3
Doncaster S Yorks 198 G5
Doncaster Common
S Yorks 198 G6
Dones Green
Ches W 183 F10
Donhead St Andrew
Wilts 30 C6
Donhead St Mary
Wilts 30 C6
Donibristle Fife 280 D3
Doniford Som 42 E5
Donington Lincs 156 B4
Shrops 132 C6
Donington Eaudike
Lincs 156 B4
Donington le Heath
Leics 153 G8
Donington on Bain
Lincs 190 E2
Donington South Ing
Lincs 156 C4
Donisthorpe Leics 152 G6
Don Johns Essex 106 F6
Donkey Street Kent 54 G6
Donkey Town Sur 66 G2
Donna Nook Lincs 190 B6
Donnington Glos 100 F3
Hereford 98 E4
Shrops 131 B11
Telford 150 G4
W Berks 64 F3
W Sus 22 C5
Donnington Wood
Telford 150 G4
Donwell T&W 243 F7
Donyatt Som 28 E4
Doomsday Green
W Sus 35 B11
Doonfoot S Ayrs 257 F8
Dora's Green Hants 49 D10
Dorback Lodge
Highld 292 B2
Dorcan Swindon 63 C7
Dorchester Dorset 17 C9
Oxon 83 G9
Dordale Worcs 117 C8
Dordon Warks 134 C5
Dore S Yorks 186 E4
Dores Highld 300 F5
Dorking Sur 51 D7
Dorking Tye Suff 107 D8
Dorley's Corner
Suff 127 D7
Dormansland Sur 52 E2
Dormans Park Sur 51 E11
Dormanstown
Redcar 235 G7
Dormer's Wells
London 66 C6
Dormington
Hereford 97 C11
Dormston Worcs 117 F9
Dorn Glos 100 E4
Dornal S Ayrs 236 B4
Dorney Bucks 66 D2
Dorney Reach Bucks 66 D2
Dorn Hill Worcs 100 E3
Dornie Highld 295 C10
Dornoch Highld 309 L7
Dornock Dumfries 238 D6
Dorrery Highld 310 D4
Dorridge W Mid 118 B3
Dorrington Lincs 173 E9
Shrops 131 C9
Dorsington Warks 100 B2
Dorstone Hereford 96 C6
Dorton Bucks 83 C11
Dorusduain Highld 295 C11
Doseley Telford 132 B3
Dosmuckeran
Highld 300 C2
Dosthill Staffs 134 C4
Staffs 134 D4
Dothan Anglesey 178 G5
Dothill Telford 150 G2
Dottery Dorset 16 B5
Doublebois Corn 6 C3
Double Hill Bath 45 B8
Dougarie N Ayrs 255 D9
Doughton Glos 80 G5
Norf 159 D7
Douglas IoM 192 E4
S Lanark 259 C8
Douglas & Angus
Dundee 287 D8
Douglastown Angus 287 C8
Douglas Water
S Lanark 259 B9
Douglas West
S Lanark 259 C8
Doulting Som 44 E6
Dounby Orkney 314 D2
Doune Highld 291 C10
Highld 309 J4
Stirling 285 G11
Doune Park Aberds 303 C7
Douneside Aberds 292 C6
Dounie Argyll 275 D8
Highld 309 K5
Highld 309 L6
Dounreay Highld 310 C3
Doura N Ayrs 266 G6
Dousland Devon 7 B10
Dovaston Shrops 149 E7
Dovecot Mers 182 C6
Dovecothall
Glasgow 267 D10
Dove Green Notts 171 E7
Dove Holes Derbys 185 F9
Dovenby Cumb 229 E7
Dovendale Lincs 190 E4
Dove Point Mers 182 C2
Dover Gtr Man 194 G6
Kent 55 E10
Dovercourt Essex 108 E5
Doverdale Worcs 117 D7
Doverhay Som 41 D11
Doveridge Derbys 152 C2
Doversgreen Sur 51 D9
Dowally Perth 286 C4
Dowanhill Glasgow 267 B11
Dowbridge Lancs 202 G4
Dowdeswell Glos 81 B7
Dowe Hill Norf 161 F10
Dowlais M Tydf 77 D10

Dowlais Top M Tydf 77 D9
Dowland Devon 25 E9
Dowles Worcs 116 B5
Dowlesgreen
Wokingham 65 F10
Dowlish Ford Som 28 E5
Dowlish Wake Som 28 E5
Downall Green
Gtr Man 194 G5
Down Ampney Glos 81 F10
Downan Moray 301 F11
S Ayrs 244 G3
Downcraig Ferry
N Ayrs 266 D3
Downderry Corn 6 E6
Downe London 68 G2
Downend Glos 80 F4
IoW 20 D6
S Glos 60 D6
W Berks 64 D3
Down End Som 43 E10
Downfield Dundee 287 D7
Down Field Cambs 124 C2
Downgate Corn 11 G11
Corn 12 G3
Down Hall Cumb 239 G7
Downham Essex 88 F2
Lancs 203 E11
London 67 E11
Northumb 263 C9
Downham Market
Norf 140 C2
Down Hatherley Glos 99 G7
Downhead Som 29 B9
Som 45 D7
Downhead Park
M Keynes 103 C7
Downhill Corn 5 B7
Perth 286 D4
T&W 243 F9
Downholland Cross
Lancs 193 F11
Downholme
N Yorks 224 F2
Downicary Devon 12 C3
Downies Aberds 293 D11
Downinney Corn 11 C10
Downley Bucks 84 G4
Down Park W Sus 51 F10
Downs V Glam 58 E6
Down St Mary Devon 26 G2
Downside C Beds 103 G10
E Sus 23 E9
N Som 60 F3
Som 44 D6
Sur 50 B6
Sur 51 B7
Down Street E Sus 36 C6
Down Thomas Devon 7 E10
Downton Hants 19 C11
Powys 114 E4
Shrops 149 G10
Wilts 31 C11
Downton on the Rock
Hereford 115 C8
Dowsby Lincs 156 D2
Dowsdale Lincs 156 G5
Dowslands Som 28 C2
Dowthwaitehead
Cumb 230 G3
Doxey Staffs 151 E8
Doxford Park T&W 243 G9
Doynton S Glos 61 E8
Drabblegate Norf 160 D4
Draethen Newport 59 B8
Draffan S Lanark 268 F5
Dragley Beck Cumb 210 D5
Dragonby N Lincs 200 E2
Dragons Green
W Sus 35 C10
Drakehouse S Yorks 186 E6
Drakeland Corner
Devon 7 D11
Drakelow Worcs 132 G6
Drakemyre Aberds 303 F9
N Ayrs 266 E5
Drake's Broughton
Worcs 99 B8
Drakes Cross
Worcs 117 B11
Drakestone Green
Suff 107 B9
Drakewalls Corn 12 G4
Draughton N Yorks 204 C6
Northants 120 B5
Drawbridge Corn 6 B3
Drax N Yorks 199 B7
Draycot Oxon 83 D10
Draycot Cerne Wilts 62 D2
Draycote Warks 119 C8
Draycot Fitz Payne
Wilts 62 G6
Draycot Foliat
Swindon 63 D7
Draycott Derbys 153 C8
Glos 80 E2
Glos 100 D3
Shrops 132 E6
Som 29 C8
Som 44 C3
Worcs 99 B7
Draycott in the Clay
Staffs 152 D3
Draycott in the Moors
Staffs 169 G7
Drayford Devon 26 E3
Drayton Leics 136 E6
Lincs 156 B4
Norf 160 G3
Northants 119 E11
Oxon 83 G7
Oxon 101 C8
Ptsmth 33 F11
Som 28 C6
Som 29 D7
Warks 118 F3
Worcs 117 B8
Drayton Bassett
Staffs 134 C3
Drayton Beauchamp
Bucks 84 C6
Drayton Parslow
Bucks 102 F6
Drayton St Leonard
Oxon 83 F10
Drebley N Yorks 205 B7
Dreemskerry IoM 192 C5
Dreenhill Pembs 72 C6
Drefach Carms 75 C8
Carms 92 G5
Carms 93 D7
Dre-fach Carms 75 B11
Ceredig 93 B10
Drefelin Carms 93 D7
Dreggie Highld 301 G10
Dreghorn Edin 270 B4
N Ayrs 257 B9
Dre-gôch Denb 165 B10
Drellingore Kent 55 E8
Drem E Loth 281 F10
Dresden Stoke 168 G6
Dreumasdal
W Isles 297 H3
Drewsteignton
Devon 13 C10
Driby Lincs 190 G5
Driffield E Yorks 208 B6
Glos 81 F9
Drift Corn 1 D4
Drigg Cumb 219 F11
Drighlington
W Yorks 197 B8
Drimnin Highld 289 D7
Drimnin Ho Highld 289 D7
Drimpton Dorset 28 F6
Drimsynie Argyll 284 G5
Dringhoe E Yorks 209 C9
Dringhouses York 207 D7
Drinisiadar W Isles 305 J3
Drinkstone Suff 125 E9
Drinkstone Green
Suff 125 E9
Drishaig Argyll 284 F5
Drissaig Argyll 275 B10
Drive End Dorset 29 F9
Driver's End Herts 86 B2
Drochedlie Aberds 302 C5
Drochil Borders 270 G3
Drointon Staffs 151 D10
Droitwich Spa
Worcs 117 E7
Droman Highld 306 D6
Dromore Dumfries 237 C7
Dron Perth 286 F5
Dronfield Derbys 186 F5
Dronfield Woodhouse
Derbys 186 F4
Drongan E Ayrs 257 F10
Dronley Angus 287 D7
Droop Dorset 30 F3
Drope Cardiff 58 D6
Dropping Well
S Yorks 186 C5
Droughduil
Dumfries 236 D3
Droxford Hants 33 D10
Droylsden Gtr Man 184 B6
Drub W Yorks 197 B7
Druggers End Worcs 98 D5
Druid Denb 165 G8
Druidston Pembs 72 B5
Druim Highld 301 D9
Druimarbin Highld 290 F2
Druimavuic Argyll 284 C4
Druimdrishaig
Argyll 275 F8
Druimindarroch
Highld 295 G8
Druimkinnerras
Highld 300 F4
Druimnacroish
Argyll 288 E6
Druimsornaig Argyll 289 F9
Druimyeon More
Argyll 255 B7
Drum Argyll 275 F10
Edin 270 B6
Perth 286 G4
Drumardoch
Stirling 285 F10
Drumbeg Highld 306 F6
Drumblade Aberds 302 E5
Drumblair Aberds 302 E6
Drumbuie Dumfries 246 G3
Highld 295 B9
Drumburgh Cumb 239 F7
Drumburn
Dumfries 237 C11
Drumchapel
Glasgow 277 G10
Drumchardine
Highld 300 E5
Drumchork Highld 307 L3
Drumclog S Lanark 258 B4
Drumdelgie Aberds 302 E4
Drumderfit Highld 300 D6
Drumdollo Aberds 302 F6
Drumeldrie Fife 287 G8
Drumelzier Borders 260 C4
Drumfearn Highld 295 D8
Drumgask Highld 291 D8
Drumgelloch
N Lanark 268 B5
Drumgley Angus 287 B8
Drumgreen Angus 292 F6
Drumguish Highld 291 D9
Drumhead Aberds 293 B11
Drumin Moray 301 F11
Drumindorsair
Highld 300 E4
Drumlasie Aberds 293 C8
Drumlean Stirling 285 G8
Drumlemble Argyll 255 F7
Drumliah Highld 309 K6
Drumligair Aberds 293 B11
Drumlithie Aberds 293 E9
Drumloist Stirling 285 G10
Drummersdale
Lancs 193 E11
Drummick Perth 286 E3
Drummoddie
Dumfries 236 E5
Drummond Highld 300 C6
Drummore Dumfries 236 F3
Drummuir Moray 302 E3
Drummuir Castle
Moray 302 E3
Drumnadrochit
Highld 300 G5
Drumnagorrach
Moray 302 D5
Drumness Perth 286 F2
Drumoak Aberds 293 D9
Drumore Argyll 255 E8
Drumpark Dumfries 247 G9
Drumpellier
N Lanark 268 B4
Drumphail Dumfries 236 C4
Drumrash Dumfries 237 B8
Drumrunie Highld 307 J6
Drumry W Dunb 277 G10
Drums Aberds 303 G9
Drumsallie Highld 289 B11
Drumsmittal Highld 300 E6
Drumstinchall
Dumfries 237 D10
Drumsturdy Angus 287 D8
Drumtochty Castle
Aberds 293 F8
Drumtroddan
Dumfries 236 E5
Drumuie Highld 298 E4
Drumuillie Highld 301 G9
Drumvaich Stirling 285 G10
Drumwalt Dumfries 236 D5
Drumwhindle
Aberds 303 F9
Drunkendub Angus 287 C10
Drury Flint 166 C3
Drurylane Norf 141 C8
Drury Lane Wrex 167 G7
Drury Square Norf 159 F8
Drybeck Cumb 222 B3
Drybridge Moray 302 C4
N Ayrs 257 B9
Drybrook Glos 79 B10
Dryburgh Borders 262 C3
Dryden Borders 261 E11
Dry Doddington
Lincs 172 F4
Dry Drayton Cambs 123 E7
Dryhill Kent 52 B3
Dry Hill Hants 49 F7
Dryhope Borders 261 E7
Drylaw Edin 280 F4
Drym Corn 2 C4
Drymen Stirling 277 D9
Drymere Norf 140 B5
Drymuir Aberds 303 E9
Drynachan Lodge
Highld 301 F8
Drynain Argyll 276 D3
Drynham Wilts 45 B11
Drynie Park Highld 300 D5
Drynoch Highld 294 B6
Dry Sandford Oxon 83 E7
Dryslwyn Carms 93 G11
Dry Street Essex 69 B7
Dryton Shrops 131 B11
Drywells Aberds 302 D6
Duag Bridge Highld 309 K3
Duartbeg Highld 306 F6
Duartmore Bridge
Highld 306 F6
Dubbs Cross Devon 12 C3
Dubford Aberds 303 C8
Dubhchladach
Argyll 275 G9
Dublin Suff 126 D3
Dubton Angus 287 B9
Dubwath Cumb 229 E9
Duchally Highld 309 H3
Duchlage Argyll 276 D6
Duchrae Dumfries 246 G5
Duck Corner Suff 109 C7
Duck End Beds 103 C11
Beds 121 G9
Bucks 102 F5
Cambs 122 E4
Essex 105 G10
Essex 106 E3
Essex 106 F3
Duckend Green
Essex 106 G4
Duckhole S Glos 79 G10
Duckington Ches W 167 E7
Ducklington Oxon 82 D5
Duckmanton Derbys 186 G6
Duck's Cross Beds 122 F2
Ducks Island London 86 F2
Duckswich Worcs 98 D6
Dudbridge Glos 80 E4
Dudden Hill London 67 B8
Duddenhoe End
Essex 105 D9
Duddingston Edin 280 G5
Duddington
Northants 137 C9
Duddlestone Som 28 C2
Duddleswell E Sus 37 B7
Duddlewick Shrops 132 G3
Duddo Northumb 273 G8
Duddon Ches W 167 C8
Duddon Bridge
Cumb 210 B3
Duddon Common
Ches W 167 B8
Dudleston Shrops 148 B6
Dudleston Grove
Shrops 149 B7
Dudleston Heath
(Criftins) Shrops 149 B7
Dudley T&W 243 C7
W Mid 133 E8
Dudley Hill W Yorks 205 G9
Dudley Port W Mid 133 E9
Dudley's Fields
W Mid 133 C9
Dudley Wood
W Mid 133 F8
Dudlows Green
Warr 183 E10
Dudsbury Dorset 19 B7
Dudswell Herts 85 D7
Dudwells Pembs 91 G8
Duerdon Devon 24 D4
Duffield Derbys 170 G4
Duffieldbank
Derbys 170 G5
Duffryn Neath 57 B10
Newport 59 B9
Shrops 130 G4
Dufftown Moray 302 F3
Duffus Moray 301 C11
Dufton Cumb 231 F9
Duggleby N Yorks 217 F7
Duich Argyll 254 B4
Duiletter Argyll 284 D5
Duinish Perth 291 G8
Duirinish Highld 295 B9
Duisdalebeg Highld 295 D8
Duisdalemore
Highld 295 D9
Duisky Highld 290 F2
Duke End Warks 134 F4
Dukesfield
Northumb 241 F10
Dukestown
Bl Gwent 77 C10
Dukinfield Gtr Man 184 B6
Dulas Anglesey 179 D7
Dulcote Som 44 E5
Dulford Devon 27 F9
Dull Perth 286 C2
Dullatur N Lanark 278 F4
Dullingham Cambs 124 F2
Dullingham Ley
Cambs 124 F2
Dulnain Bridge
Highld 301 G9
Duloch Fife 280 D2
Duloe Beds 122 E3
Corn 6 D4
Dulsie Highld 301 E9
Dulverton Som 26 B6
Dulwich London 67 E10
Dulwich Village
London 67 E10
Dumbarton W Dunb 277 F7
Dumbleton Glos 99 D10
Dumcrieff Dumfries 248 C4
Dumfries Dumfries 237 B11
Dumgoyne Stirling 277 E10
Dummer Hants 48 D5
Dumpford W Sus 34 C4
Dumpinghill Devon 24 F6
Dumpling Green
Norf 159 G10
Dumplington
Gtr Man 184 B3
Dumpton Kent 71 F11
Dun Angus 287 B10
Dunach Argyll 289 G10
Dunadd Argyll 275 D9
Dunain Ho Highld 300 E6
Dunalastair Perth 285 B11
Dunan Highld 295 C7
Dunans Argyll 275 D9
Argyll 275 D11
Dunball Som 43 E10
Dunbar E Loth 282 F3
Dunbeath Highld 311 G5
Dunbeg Argyll 289 F10
Dunblane Stirling 285 G11
Dunbog Fife 286 F6
Dunbridge Hants 32 B4
Duncansclett
Shetland 313 K5
Duncanston Highld 300 D5
Duncanstone
Aberds 302 G5
Dun Charlabhaigh
W Isles 304 D3
Dunchideock Devon 14 D3
Dunchurch Warks 119 C9
Duncombe Lancs 202 F6
Duncote Northants 120 G3
Duncow Dumfries 247 G11
Duncraggan Stirling 285 G9
Duncrievie Perth 286 G5
Duncroisk Stirling 285 D9
Duncton W Sus 35 D7
Dundas Ho Orkney 314 H4
Dundee Dundee 287 D8
Dundeugh Dumfries 246 F3
Dundon Som 44 G3
Dundonald Fife 280 C4
S Ayrs 257 C9
Dundon Hayes Som 44 G3
Dundonnell Highld 307 L5
Dundonnell Hotel
Highld 307 L5
Dundonnell House
Highld 307 L6
Dundraw Cumb 229 B10
Dundreggan Highld 290 B5
Dundreggan Lodge
Highld 290 B5
Dundrennan
Dumfries 237 E9
Dundridge Hants 33 D9
Dundry N Som 60 F5
Dundurn Perth 285 E11
Dundyvan N Lanark 268 C4
Dunecht Aberds 293 C9
Dunfermline Fife 279 D11
Dunfield Glos 81 F10
Dunford Bridge
S Yorks 197 G7
Dungate Kent 54 B2
Dunge Wilts 45 C11
Dungeness Kent 39 D9
Dungworth S Yorks 186 D3
Dunham Notts 188 G4
Dunham-on-the-Hill
Ches W 183 G7
Dunham on Trent
Notts 188 G4
Dunhampstead
Worcs 117 E8
Dunhampton Worcs 116 D6
Dunham Town
Gtr Man 184 D2
Dunham Woodhouses
Gtr Man 184 D2
Dunholme Lincs 189 F8
Dunino Fife 287 F9
Dunipace Falk 278 E6
Dunira Perth 285 E11
Dunkeld Perth 286 C4
Dunkerton Bath 45 B8
Dunkeswell Devon 27 F10
Dunkeswick
N Yorks 206 D2
Dunkirk Cambs 139 F10
Ches W 182 G5
Kent 54 B5
Norf 160 D4
Nottingham 153 B11
S Glos 61 B9
Staffs 168 E4
Wilts 62 G3
Dunk's Green Kent 52 C6
Dunlappie Angus 293 G7
Dunley Hants 48 C3
Worcs 116 D5
Dunlichity Lodge
Highld 300 F6
Dunlop E Ayrs 267 F8
Dunmaglass Lodge
Highld 300 G5
Dunmere Corn 5 B10
Dunmore Argyll 275 G8
Falk 279 D7
Highld 300 E5
Dunnerholme Cumb 210 D4
Dunnet Highld 310 B6
Dunnichen Angus 287 C9
Dunnikier Fife 280 C5
Dunninald Angus 287 B11
Dunning Perth 286 F4
Dunnington E Yorks 209 C9
Warks 117 G11
York 207 C9
Dunningwell Cumb 210 C3
Dunnockshaw
Lancs 195 B10
Dunnose IoW 21 F7
Dunnsheath Shrops 149 F9
Dunn Street Kent 54 D3
Kent 69 G9
Dunollie Argyll 289 F10
Dunoon Argyll 276 F3
Dunragit Dumfries 236 D3
Dunrobin Mains
Highld 311 J2
Dunrostan Argyll 275 E8
Duns Borders 272 E5
Dunsa Derbys 186 G2
Dunsby Lincs 156 D2
Dunscar Gtr Man 195 E8
Dunscore Dumfries 247 G9
Dunscroft S Yorks 199 F7
Dunsdale Redcar 226 B2
Dunsden Green Oxon 65 D8
Dunsfold Sur 50 F4
Dunsfold Common
Sur 50 F4
Dunsfold Green Sur 50 F4
Dunsford Devon 14 D2
Sur 50 F4
Dunshalt Fife 286 F6
Dunshillock Aberds 303 E9
Dunsill Notts 171 C7
Dunsinnan Perth 286 D5
Dunskey Ho
Dumfries 236 D2
Dunslea Corn 11 G11
Dunsley N Yorks 227 C7
Staffs 133 G7
Dunsmore Bucks 84 D5
Warks 119 B10
Dunsop Bridge
Lancs 203 C9
Dunstable C Beds 103 G10
Dunstal Staffs 151 D11
Dunstall Staffs 152 E3
Dunstall Common
Worcs 99 C7
Dunstall Green Suff 124 E4
Dunstall Hill W Mid 133 C8
Dunstan Northumb 265 F7
Dunstan Steads
Northumb 264 E6
Dunster Som 42 E3
Duns Tew Oxon 101 F9
Dunston Derbys 186 G5
Lincs 173 C9
Norf 142 C4
Staffs 151 F8
T&W 242 E6
Dunstone Devon 7 E11
Devon 8 G5
Dunston Heath
Staffs 151 F8
Dunston Hill T&W 242 E6
Dunsville S Yorks 198 F6
Dunswell E Yorks 209 F7
Dunsyre S Lanark 269 F11
Dunterton Devon 12 F3
Dunthrop Oxon 101 F7
Duntisbourne Abbots
Glos 81 D7
Duntisbourne Leer
Glos 81 D7
Duntisbourne Rouse
Glos 81 D7
Duntish Dorset 29 F11
Duntocher W Dunb 277 G9
Dunton Bucks 102 G6
C Beds 104 C4
Norf 159 C7
Dunton Bassett
Leics 135 E10
Dunton Green Kent 52 B4
Dunton Patch Norf 159 C7
Dunton Wayletts
Essex 87 G11
Duntrune Castle
Argyll 275 D8
Duntulm Highld 298 B4
Dunure S Ayrs 257 F7
Dunvant / Dynfant
Swansea 56 C5
Dunvegan Highld 298 E2
Dunveth Corn 10 G5
Dunwear Som 43 F10
Dunwich Suff 127 C9
Dunwood Staffs 168 D6
Dupplin Castle
Perth 286 F4
Durdar Cumb 239 G10
Durgan Corn 3 D7
Durgates E Sus 52 G6
Durham Durham 233 C11
Durisdeer Dumfries 247 C9
Durisdeermill
Dumfries 247 C9
Durkar W Yorks 197 D10
Durleigh Som 43 F9
Durleighmarsh
W Sus 34 C3
Durley Hants 33 D8
Wilts 63 G8
Durley Street Hants 33 D8
Durlock Kent 55 B9
Durlow Common
Hereford 98 D2
Durn Gtr Man 196 D2
Durnamuck Highld 307 K5
Durness Highld 308 C4
Durnfield Som 29 C7
Durno Aberds 303 G7
Durns Town Hants 19 B11
Duror Highld 289 D11
Durran Argyll 275 C10
Highld 310 C5
Durrant Green Kent 53 F11
Durrants Hants 22 B2
Durrington W Sus 35 F10
Wilts 47 E7
Durrisdale Orkney 314 D3
Dursley Glos 80 F3
Wilts 45 C11
Dursley Cross Glos 98 G3
Durston Som 28 B3
Durweston Dorset 30 F5
Dury Shetland 313 G6
Duryard Devon 14 C4
Duston Northants 120 E4
Dutch Village Essex 69 C9
Duthil Highld 301 G9
Dutlas Powys 114 B4
Duton Hill Essex 106 F2
Dutson Corn 12 D2
Dutton Ches W 183 F9
Duxford Cambs 105 B9
Oxon 82 F5
Duxmoor Shrops 115 B8
Dwygyfylchi Conwy 180 F2
Dwyran Anglesey 162 B6
Dwyrhiw Powys 129 C11
Dyce Aberdeen 293 B10
Dyche Som 43 E7
Dye House
Northumb 241 F10
Dyer's Common
S Glos 60 C5
Dyer's Green Cambs 105 B7
Dyffryn Bridgend 57 C11
Carms 92 G6
Ceredig 110 G5
Pembs 91 D8
Dyffryn Ardudwy
Gwyn 145 E11
Dyffryn-bern
Ceredig 110 G5
Dyffryn Castell
Ceredig 128 G5
Dyffryn Ceidrych
Carms 94 F4
Dyffryn Cellwen
Neath 76 D5
Dyke Lincs 156 E2
Moray 301 D9
Dykehead Angus 292 G5
N Lanark 269 D7
Stirling 277 B11
Dykelands Aberds 293 G9
Dykends Angus 286 B6
Dykeside Aberds 303 E7
Dykesmains N Ayrs 266 G5
Dylife Powys 129 E7
Dymchurch Kent 39 B9
Dymock Glos 98 E4
Dynfant / Dunvant
Swansea 56 C5
Dyrham S Glos 61 D8
Dysart Fife 280 C6
Dyserth Denb 181 F9

E

Eabost Highld 294 B5
Eabost West Highld 298 E3
Each End Kent 55 B10
Eachway Worcs 117 B9
Eachwick Northumb 242 C4
Eadar Dha Fhadhail
W Isles 304 E2
Eagland Hill Lancs 202 D4
Eagle Lincs 172 B5
Eagle Barnsdale
Lincs 172 B5
Eagle Moor Lincs 172 B5
Eaglesfield Cumb 229 F7
Dumfries 238 C6
Eaglesham E Renf 267 E11
Eaglestone
M Keynes 103 D7
Eaglethorpe
Northants 137 E11
Eagle Tor Derbys 170 C2
Eagley Gtr Man 195 E8
Eairy IoM 192 E3
Eakley Lanes
M Keynes 120 G6
Eakring Notts 171 C11
Ealand N Lincs 199 E9
Ealing London 67 C7
Eals Northumb 240 F5
Eamont Bridge
Cumb 230 F6
Earby Lancs 204 D3
Earcroft Blackburn 195 C7
Eardington Shrops 132 E4
Eardisland Hereford 115 F8
Eardisley Hereford 96 B6
Eardiston Shrops 149 D7
Worcs 116 D3
Earith Cambs 123 C7
Earle Northumb 263 D11
Earlestown Mers 183 B9
Earley Wokingham 65 E9
Earlham Norf 142 B4
Earlish Highld 298 C3
Earls Barton
Northants 121 E7
Earls Colne Essex 107 F7
Earl's Common
Worcs 117 F9
Earl's Court London 67 D9
Earl's Croome Worcs 99 C7
Earlsdon W Mid 118 B6
Earl's Down E Sus 23 B10
Earlsferry Fife 281 B9
Earlsfield Lincs 155 B8
London 67 E9
Earlsford Aberds 303 F8
Earl's Green Suff 125 D10
Earlsheaton
W Yorks 197 C9
Earl Shilton Leics 135 D9
Earlsmill Moray 301 D9
Earl Soham Suff 126 E4
Earl Sterndale
Derbys 169 B9
Earlston Borders 262 B3
E Ayrs 257 B10
Earlstone Common
Hants 64 G3
Earl Stoneham Suff 126 F2
Earl Stonham Suff 126 F2
Earlstoun Dumfries 246 G4
Earlswood Mon 79 F7
Sur 51 D9
Warks 118 C2
Earnley W Sus 22 D4
Earnock S Lanark 268 E3
Earnshaw Bridge
Lancs 194 C4
Earsairidh W Isles 297 M3
Earsdon T&W 243 C8
Earsham Norf 142 F6
Earsham Street Suff 126 B4
Earswick York 207 B8
Eartham W Sus 22 B6
Earthcott Green
S Glos 61 B7
Easby N Yorks 224 E3
N Yorks 225 D11
Easdale Argyll 275 B8
Easebourne W Sus 34 C5
Easenhall Warks 119 B9
Eashing Sur 50 E2
Easington Bucks 83 C11
Durham 234 C4
E Yorks 201 D11
Lancs 203 C10
Northumb 264 C4
Oxon 83 F11
Oxon 101 D9
Redcar 226 B4
Easington Colliery
Durham 234 C4
Easington Lane
T&W 234 B3
Easingwold
N Yorks 215 F10
Easole Street Kent 55 C9
Eason's Green E Sus 23 B8
Eassie Angus 287 C7
East Aberthaw
V Glam 58 F4
Eastacombe Devon 25 B8
Devon 25 C9
Eastacott Devon 25 C10
East Acton London 67 C8
East Adderbury
Oxon 101 D9
East Allington Devon 8 F5
East Amat Highld 309 K4
East Anstey Devon 26 B5
East Anton Hants 47 D11
East Appleton
N Yorks 224 F4
East Ardsley
W Yorks 197 B10
East Ashling W Sus 22 B4
East Aston Hants 48 D2
East Auchronie
Aberds 293 C10
East Ayton N Yorks 217 B9
East Bank Bl Gwent 78 D2
East Barkwith
Lincs 189 E11
East Barming Kent 53 C8
East Barnby
N Yorks 226 C6
East Barnet London 86 F3
East Barns E Loth 282 F4
East Barsham Norf 159 C8
East Barton Suff 125 D8
East Beach W Sus 22 E5
East Beckham Norf 177 E11
East Bedfont London 66 E5
East Bergholt Suff 107 D11
East Bierley
W Yorks 197 B7
East Bilney Norf 159 F9
East Blackdene
Durham 232 D3
East Blatchington
E Sus 23 E7
East Bloxworth
Dorset 18 C3
East Boldon T&W 243 E9
East Boldre Hants 32 G5
East Bonhard Perth 286 E5
Eastbourne Darl 224 C6
E Sus 23 F10
East Bower Som 43 F10
East Brent Som 43 C11
Eastbridge Suff 127 D9
East Bridgford
Notts 171 G11
East Briscoe
Durham 223 B9
Eastbrook Som 28 C2
V Glam 59 E7
East Buckland Devon 41 G7
East Budleigh Devon 15 E7
Eastburn E Yorks 208 B5
W Yorks 204 E6
Eastburn Br
W Yorks 204 E6
East Burnham Bucks 66 C3
East Burrafirth
Shetland 313 H5
East Burton Dorset 18 D2
Eastbury London 85 G9
W Berks 63 D10
East Butsfield
Durham 233 B8
East Butterleigh
Devon 27 F7
East Butterwick
N Lincs 199 F10
Eastby N Yorks 204 C6
East Cairnbeg
Aberds 293 F9
East Calder
W Loth 269 B11
East Carleton Norf 142 C3
East Carlton
Northants 136 F6
W Yorks 205 E10
East Chaldon or Chaldon
Herring Dorset 17 E11
East Challow Oxon 63 B11
East Charleton Devon 8 G5
East Chelborough
Dorset 29 F9
East Chiltington
E Sus 36 D5
East Chinnock Som 29 E7
East Chisenbury
Wilts 46 C6
East Cholderton
Hants 47 D9
Eastchurch Kent 70 E3
East Clandon Sur 50 C5
East Claydon Bucks 102 F4
East Clevedon N Som 60 E2
East Clyne Highld 311 J3
East Clyth Highld 310 F7
East Coker Som 29 E8
Eastcombe Glos 80 E5
East Combe Som 43 G7
East Common
N Yorks 207 G8
East Compton Dorset 30 D5
Som 44 E6
East Cornworthy
Devon 8 D6
Eastcote London 66 B6
Northants 120 G3
W Mid 118 B3
Eastcote Village
London 66 B6
Eastcott Corn 24 D3
Wilts 46 B4
East Cottingwith
E Yorks 207 E10
Eastcotts Beds 103 B11
Eastcourt Wilts 63 G8
Wilts 81 G7
East Cowes IoW 20 B6
East Cowick
E Yorks 199 C7
East Cowton
N Yorks 224 E6
East Cramlington
Northumb 243 B7
East Cranmore Som 45 E7
East Creech Dorset 18 E4
East Croachy Highld 300 G6
East Croftmore
Highld 291 B11
East Curthwaite
Cumb 230 B2
East Dean E Sus 23 F9
Glos 98 G3
Hants 32 B3
W Sus 34 E6
East Dene S Yorks 186 C6
East Denton T&W 242 D6
East Didsbury
Gtr Man 184 C5
Eastdon Devon 14 F5
Eastdown Devon 8 F6
East Down Devon 40 E6
East Drayton Notts 188 F3
East Dulwich London 67 E10
East Dundry N Som 60 F5
East Ella Hull 200 B5
Eastend Essex 86 C6
Oxon 100 G6
East End Beds 122 F2
Bucks 84 B4
C Beds 103 C9
Dorset 18 B5
E Yorks 201 B9
E Yorks 209 B9
E Yorks 209 G9
Essex 89 D8
Glos 81 E11
Hants 20 B3
Hants 33 C11
Hants 64 G2
Herts 105 F9
Kent 53 E11
Kent 53 F10
Kent 70 E3
M Keynes 103 C8
N Som 60 E3
Oxon 82 C5
Oxon 101 D9
Oxon 101 E7
S Glos 61 E9
Som 29 B10
Som 44 C5
Som 45 D7
Suff 108 E2
Suff 126 F3
East End Green Herts 86 C3
Easter Aberchalder
Highld 291 B7
Easter Ardross
Highld 300 B6
Easter Balgedie
Perth 286 G5
Easter Balmoral
Aberds 292 D4
Easter Boleskine
Highld 300 G5
Easter Brackland
Stirling 285 G10
Easter Brae Highld 300 C6
Easter Cardno
Aberds 303 C9
Easter Compton
S Glos 60 C5
Easter Cringate
Stirling 278 D4
Easter Culfosie
Aberds 293 C9
Easter Davoch
Aberds 292 C6
Easter Earshaig
Dumfries 248 C2
Easter Ellister Argyll 254 B3
Easter Fearn Highld 309 L6
Easter Galcantray
Highld 301 E8
Eastergate W Sus 22 B6
Easterhouse
Glasgow 268 B3
Easter Housebyres
Borders 262 B2
Easter Howgate
Midloth 270 C4
Easter Howlaws
Borders 272 G4
Easter Kinkell
Highld 300 D5
Easter Knox Angus 287 D9
Easter Langlee
Borders 262 B2
Easter Lednathie
Angus 292 G5
Easter Milton Highld 301 D9

Easter Moniack Highld 300 E5
Eastern Green W Mid 134 G5
Easter Ord Aberdeen 293 C10
Easter Quarff Shetland 313 K6
Easter Rhynd Perth 286 F5
Easter Row Stirling 278 B5
Easterside Mbro 225 B10
Easter Silverford Aberds 303 C7
Easter Skeld Shetland 313 J5
Easter Softlaw Borders 263 C7
Easterton Wilts 46 C4
Easterton of Lenabo Aberds 303 E10
Easterton Sands Wilts 46 B4
Eastertown Som 43 C10
Eastertown of Auchleuchries Aberds 303 F10
Easter Tulloch Highld 291 B11
Easter Whyntie Aberds 302 C6
East Everleigh Wilts 47 C8
East Ewell Sur 67 G8
East Farleigh Kent 53 C8
East Farndon Northants 136 F4
East Fen Common Cambs 124 C2
East Ferry Lincs 188 B4
Eastfield Borders 262 D2
Bristol 60 D5
N Lanark 269 C7
N Lanark 278 G4
N Yorks 217 C10
Northumb 243 B7
Pboro 138 D4
S Lanark 268 C2
S Yorks 197 G9
Eastfield Hall Northumb 252 B6
East Fields W Berks 64 F3
East Finchley London 67 B9
East Finglassie Fife 280 B5
East Firsby Lincs 189 D8
East Fleet Dorset 17 E8
East Fortune E Loth 281 F10
East Garforth W Yorks 206 G4
East Garston W Berks 63 D11
Eastgate Durham 232 D5
Norf 160 E2
Pboro 138 D4
East Gateshead T&W 243 E7
East Ginge Oxon 64 B2
East Gores Essex 107 G7
East Goscote Leics 154 G2
East Grafton Wilts 63 G9
East Grange Moray 301 C10
East Green Hants 49 E9
Suff 124 G3
Suff 127 D8
East Grimstead Wilts 32 B2
East Grinstead W Sus 51 F11
East Guldeford E Sus 38 C6
East Haddon Northants 120 D3
East Hagbourne Oxon 64 B4
Easthall Herts 104 G3
East Halton N Lincs 200 D6
Eastham Mers 182 E5
Worcs 116 D3
East Ham London 68 C2
Eastham Ferry Mers 182 E5
East Hampnett W Sus 22 B6
Easthampstead Brack 65 F11
Easthampton Hereford 115 E8
East Hanney Oxon 82 G6
East Hanningfield Essex 88 E3
East Hardwick W Yorks 198 D3
East Harling Norf 141 F9
East Harlsey N Yorks 225 F8
East Harnham Wilts 31 B10
East Harptree Bath 44 B5
East Hartford Northumb 243 B7
East Harting W Sus 34 D3
East Hatch Wilts 30 B6
East Hatley Cambs 122 G5
Easthaugh Norf 159 F11
East Hauxwell N Yorks 224 G3
East Haven Angus 287 D9
Eastheath Wokingham 65 F10
East Heckington Lincs 173 G11
East Hedleyhope Durham 233 C9
East Helmsdale Highld 311 H4
East Hendred Oxon 64 B3
East Herringthorpe S Yorks 187 C7
East Herrington T&W 243 G9
East Heslerton N Yorks 217 D8
East Hewish N Som 59 G11
East Hill Kent 68 G5
East Hoathly E Sus 23 B8
East Hogaland Shetland 313 K5
East Holme Dorset 18 D3
East Holton Dorset 18 C5
East Holywell Northumb 243 C8
Easthope Shrops 131 D11
Easthopewood Shrops 131 D11
East Horndon Essex 68 B6
Easthorpe Essex 107 G8
Leics 154 B6
Notts 172 E2
East Horrington Som 44 D5
East Horsley Sur 50 C5
East Horton Northumb 264 C2
Easthouse Shetland 313 J5
Easthouses Midloth 270 B6
East Howdon T&W 243 D8
East Howe Bmouth 19 B7
East Huntspill Som 43 E10
East Hyde C Beds 85 B10
East Ilkerton Devon 41 D8
East Ilsley W Berks 64 C3
Easting Orkney 314 A7
Eastington Devon 26 F2
Glos 80 D3
Glos 81 C10
East Keal Lincs 174 C5
East Kennett Wilts 62 F6
East Keswick W Yorks 206 E3
East Kilbride S Lanark 268 E2
East Kimber Devon 12 B5
East Kingston W Sus 35 G9
East Kirkby Lincs 174 C4
East Knapton N Yorks 217 D7
East Knighton Dorset 18 D2
East Knowstone Devon 26 C4
East Knoyle Wilts 45 G11
East Kyloe Northumb 264 B3
East Kyo Durham 242 G5
East Lambrook Som 28 D6
East Lamington Highld 301 B7
Eastland Gate Hants 33 E11
East Langdon Kent 55 D10
East Langton Leics 136 E4
East Langwell Highld 309 J7
East Lavant W Sus 22 B5
East Lavington W Sus 34 D6
East Law Northumb 242 G3
East Layton N Yorks 224 D3
Eastleach Martin Glos 82 D2
Eastleach Turville Glos 81 D11
East Leake Notts 153 D11
East Learmouth Northumb 263 B9
Eastleigh Devon 25 B7
Hants 32 D6
East Leigh Devon 8 E3
Devon 25 F11
East Lexham Norf 159 F7
East Lilburn Northumb 264 E2
Eastling Kent 54 B3
East Linton E Loth 281 F11
East Liss Hants 34 B3
East Lockinge Oxon 64 B2
East Loftus Redcar 226 B4
East Looe Corn 6 E5
East Lound N Lincs 188 B3
East Lulworth Dorset 18 E3
East Lutton N Yorks 217 F8
East Lydeard Som 27 B11
East Lydford Som 44 G5
East Lyng Som 28 B4
East Mains Aberds 293 D8
Borders 271 F11
S Lanark 268 E2
East Malling Kent 53 B8
East Malling Heath Kent 53 B7
East March Angus 287 D8
East Marden W Sus 34 E4
East Markham Notts 188 G2
East Marsh NE Lincs 201 E9
East Martin Hants 31 D9
East Marton N Yorks 204 C4
East Melbury Dorset 30 C5
East Meon Hants 33 C11
East Mere Devon 27 D7
East Mersea Essex 89 C9
East Mey Highld 310 B7
East Molesey Sur 67 F7
Eastmoor Derbys 186 G4
Norf 140 C4
East Moor W Yorks 197 C10
East Moors Cardiff 59 D8
East Morden Dorset 18 B4
East Morton W Yorks 205 E7
East Moulsecoomb Brighton 36 F4
East Ness N Yorks 216 D3
East Newton E Yorks 209 F11
N Yorks 216 D2
Eastney Ptsmth 21 B9
Eastnor Hereford 98 D4
East Norton Leics 136 C5
East Nynehead Som 27 C11
East Oakley Hants 48 C5
Eastoft N Lincs 199 D10
East Ogwell Devon 14 G2
Eastoke Hants 21 B10
Easton Bristol 60 E6
Cambs 122 C2
Cumb 239 C10
Cumb 239 F7
Devon 8 F3
Devon 13 D10
Dorset 17 G9
Hants 48 G4
IoW 20 D2
Lincs 155 D8
Norf 160 G2
Som 44 D4
Suff 126 F5
W Berks 64 E2
Easton *continued*
Wilts 61 E11
Easton Grey Wilts 61 B11
Easton in Gordano N Som 60 D4
Easton Maudit Northants 121 F7
Easton on the Hill Northants 137 C10
Easton Royal Wilts 63 G8
Easton Town Som 44 G5
Wilts 61 B11
East Orchard Dorset 30 D4
East Ord Northumb 273 E9
Eastover Som 43 F10
East Panson Devon 12 C3
Eastpark Dumfries 238 D2
East Parley Dorset 19 B8
East Peckham Kent 53 D7
East Pennard Som 44 F5
East Perry Cambs 122 D3
East Portholland Corn 5 G9
East Portlemouth Devon 9 G9
East Prawle Devon 9 G10
East Preston W Sus 35 G9
East Pulham Dorset 30 F2
East Putford Devon 24 D5
East Quantoxhead Som 42 E6
East Rainton T&W 234 B2
East Ravendale NE Lincs 190 B2
East Raynham Norf 159 D7
Eastrea Cambs 138 D5
East Rhidorroch Lodge Highld 307 K7
Eastriggs Dumfries 238 D6
East Rigton W Yorks 206 E3
Eastrington E Yorks 199 B9
Eastrip Wilts 61 E10
East Rolstone N Som 59 G11
Eastrop Hants 48 C6
East Rounton N Yorks 225 E8
East Row N Yorks 227 C7
East Rudham Norf 158 D6
East Runton Norf 177 E11
East Ruston Norf 160 D6
Eastry Kent 55 C10
East Saltoun E Loth 271 B9
East Sheen London 67 D8
East Skelston Dumfries 247 F8
East Sleekburn Northumb 253 G7
East Somerton Norf 161 F9
East Stanley Durham 242 G6
East Stockwith Lincs 188 C3
East Stoke Dorset 18 D3
Notts 172 F3
Som 29 D7
East Stour Dorset 30 C4
East Stour Common Dorset 30 C4
East Stourmouth Kent 71 G9
East Stowford Devon 25 B10
East Stratton Hants 48 F4
East Street Kent 55 B10
Som 44 F4
East Studdal Kent 55 D10
East Suisnish Highld 295 B7
East Taphouse Corn 6 C3
East-the-Water Devon 25 B7
East Third Borders 262 B4
East Thirston Northumb 252 D5
East Tilbury Thurrock 69 D7
East Tisted Hants 49 G8
East Torrington Lincs 189 E10
East Town Som 42 G6
Som 44 E6
Wilts 45 B11
East Trewent Pembs 73 F8
East Tuddenham Norf 159 G11
East Tuelmenna Corn 6 B4
East Tytherley Hants 32 B3
East Tytherton Wilts 62 E3
East Village Devon 26 F4
V Glam 58 E3
Eastville Bristol 60 E6
Lincs 174 D6
East Wall Shrops 131 E10
East Walton Norf 158 F4
East Water Som 44 C4
East Week Devon 13 C9
Eastwell Leics 154 D5
East Wellow Hants 32 C4
Eastwell Park Kent 54 D4
East Wemyss Fife 280 B6
East Whitburn W Loth 269 B9
Eastwick Herts 86 C6
Shetland 312 F5
East Wickham London 68 D3
East Williamston Pembs 73 E9
East Winch Norf 158 F3
East Winterslow Wilts 47 G8
East Wittering W Sus 21 B11
East Witton N Yorks 214 B2
Eastwood Hereford 98 C2
Notts 171 F7
S Yorks 186 C6
Southend 69 B10
W Yorks 196 B3
East Woodburn Northumb 251 F10
Eastwood End Cambs 139 E8
Eastwood Hall Notts 171 F7
East Woodhay Hants 64 G2
East Woodlands Som 45 E9
East Worldham Hants 49 F8
East Worlington Devon 26 E3
East Worthing W Sus 35 G11
East Wretham Norf 141 E8
East Youlstone Devon 24 D3
Eathorpe Warks 119 D7
Eaton Ches E 168 B5
Ches W 167 C9
Hereford 115 F10
Leics 154 D5
Norf 142 B4
Notts 188 F2
Oxon 82 E6
Shrops 131 F7
Shrops 131 F10
Eaton Bishop Hereford 97 D8
Eaton Bray C Beds 103 G9
Eaton Constantine Shrops 131 B11
Eaton Ford Cambs 122 E3
Eaton Green C Beds 103 G9
Eaton Hastings Oxon 82 F3
Eaton Mascott Shrops 131 B10
Eaton on Tern Shrops 150 E3
Eaton Socon Cambs 122 F3
Eaton upon Tern Shrops 150 E3
Eau Brink Norf 157 F11
Eau Withington Hereford 97 C10
Eaves Green W Mid 134 G5
Eavestone N Yorks 214 F4
Ebberly Hill Devon 25 D9
Ebberston N Yorks 217 C7
Ebbesbourne Wake Wilts 31 C7
Ebblake Hants 31 F10
Ebbw Vale Bl Gwent 77 D11
Ebchester Durham 242 F4
Ebdon N Som 59 G11
Ebernoe W Sus 35 B7
Ebford Devon 14 D5
Ebley Glos 80 D4
Ebnal Ches W 167 F7
Ebnall Hereford 115 F9
Ebreywood Shrops 149 F10
Ebrington Glos 100 C3
Ecchinswell Hants 48 B4
Ecclaw Borders 272 B5
Ecclefechan Dumfries 238 C5
Eccle Riggs Cumb 210 B4
Eccles Borders 272 G5
Gtr Man 184 B3
Kent 69 G8
Ecclesall S Yorks 186 E4
Ecclesfield S Yorks 186 C5
Ecclesgreig Aberds 293 G9
Eccleshall Staffs 150 D6
Eccleshill W Yorks 205 F9
Ecclesmachan W Loth 279 G11
Eccles on Sea Norf 161 D8
Eccles Road Norf 141 E10
Eccleston Ches W 166 C6
Lancs 194 D4
Mers 183 B7
Eccleston Park Mers 183 C7
Eccliffe Dorset 30 B3
Eccup W Yorks 205 E11
Echt Aberds 293 C9
Eckford Borders 262 D6
Eckfordmoss Borders 262 D6
Eckington Derbys 186 F6
Worcs 99 C8
Eckington Corner E Sus 23 D8
Ecklands S Yorks 197 G8
Eckworthy Devon 24 D6
Ecton Northants 120 E6
Staffs 169 D9
Ecton Brook Northants 120 E6
Edale Derbys 185 D10
Edale End Derbys 185 D11
Edbrook Som 43 E8
Edburton W Sus 36 E2
Edderside Cumb 229 B7
Edderton Highld 309 L7
Eddington Kent 71 F7
W Berks 63 F10
Eddistone Devon 24 C3
Eddleston Borders 270 F4
Eddlewood S Lanark 268 E4
Edenbridge Kent 52 D2
Edenfield Lancs 195 D9
Edenhall Cumb 231 E7
Edenham Lincs 155 E11
Eden Mount Cumb 211 D8
Eden Park London 67 F11
Edensor Derbys 170 B2
Edentaggart Argyll 276 C6
Edenthorpe S Yorks 198 F6
Edentown Cumb 239 F9
Eden Vale Durham 234 D4
Wilts 45 C11
Ederline Argyll 275 C9
Edern Gwyn 144 B5
Edford Som 45 D7
Edgarley Som 44 F4
Edgbaston W Mid 133 G11
Edgcote Northants 101 B10
Edgcott Bucks 102 G3
Som 41 F10
Edgcumbe Corn 2 C6
Edge Glos 80 D4
Shrops 131 B7
Edgebolton Shrops 149 E11
Edge End Glos 79 C9
Lancs 203 G10
Edgefield Norf 159 C11
Edgefield Street Norf 159 C11
Edge Fold Blackburn 195 D8
Gtr Man 195 F8
Edge Green Ches W 167 E7
Gtr Man 183 B9
Norf 141 F10
Edgehill Warks 101 B7
Edge Hill Mers 182 C5
Warks 134 D4
Edgeley Gtr Man 184 D5
Edge Mount S Yorks 186 C3
Edgerley Shrops 148 F6
Edgerston Borders 262 G5
Edgerton W Yorks 196 D6
Edgeside Lancs 195 C10
Edgeworth Glos 80 D6
Edginswell Devon 9 B7
Edgiock Worcs 117 E10
Edgmond Telford 150 F4
Edgmond Marsh Telford 150 E4
Edgton Shrops 131 F7
Edgware London 85 G11
Edgwick W Mid 134 G6
Edgworth Blackburn 195 D8
Edham Borders 262 B6
Edial Staffs 133 B11
Edinample Stirling 285 E9
Edinbane Highld 298 D3
Edinburgh Edin 280 G5
Edinchip Stirling 285 E9
Edingale Staffs 152 G4
Edingight Ho Moray 302 D5
Edinglassie Ho Aberds 292 B5
Edingley Notts 171 D11
Edingthorpe Norf 160 C6
Edingthorpe Green Norf 160 C6
Edington Som 43 F11
Wilts 46 C2
Edingworth Som 43 C11
Edintore Moray 302 E4
Edistone Devon 24 C2
Edithmead Som 43 D10
Edith Weston Rutland 137 B8
Edlaston Derbys 169 G11
Edlesborough Bucks 85 B7
Edlingham Northumb 252 B4
Edlington Lincs 190 G2
Edmondsham Dorset 31 E9
Edmondsley Durham 233 B10
Edmondstown Rhondda 77 G8
Edmondthorpe Leics 155 F7
Edmonston S Lanark 269 G11
Edmonstone Orkney 314 D5
Edmonton Corn 10 G5
London 86 G4
Edmundbyers Durham 242 G2
Ednam Borders 262 B6
Ednaston Derbys 170 G2
Edney Common Essex 87 E11
Edradynate Perth 286 B2
Edrom Borders 272 D6
Edstaston Shrops 149 C10
Edstone Warks 118 E3
Edvin Loach Hereford 116 F3
Edwalton Notts 153 B11
Edwardstone Suff 107 C8
Edwardsville M Tydf 77 F9
Edwinsford Carms 94 E2
Edwinstowe Notts 171 B10
Edworth C Beds 104 C4
Edwyn Ralph Hereford 116 F2
Edzell Angus 293 G7
Efail-fôch Neath 57 B9
Efail Isaf Rhondda 58 C5
Efailnewydd Gwyn 145 B7
Efailwen Carms 92 F2
Efenechtyd Denb 165 D10
Effingham Sur 50 C6
Effirth Shetland 313 H5
Effledge Borders 262 F3
Efflinch Staffs 152 F3
Efford Devon 26 G5
Plym 7 D10
Egbury Hants 48 C2
Egdon Worcs 117 G8
Egerton Gtr Man 195 E8
Kent 54 D2
Egerton Forstal Kent 53 D11
Egerton Green Ches E 167 E8
Egford Som 45 D9
Eggbeare Corn 12 D2
Eggborough N Yorks 198 C5
Eggbuckland Plym 7 D10
Eggesford Station Devon 25 E11
Eggington C Beds 103 F9
Egginton Derbys 152 D5
Egginton Common Derbys 152 D5
Egglesburn Durham 232 G5
Egglescliffe Stockton 225 C8
Eggleston Durham 232 G5
Egham Sur 66 E4
Egham Hythe Sur 66 E4
Egham Wick Sur 66 E3
Egleton Rutland 137 B7
Eglingham Northumb 264 F4
Egloshayle Corn 10 G5
Egloskerry Corn 11 D11
Eglwysbach Conwy 180 G4
Eglwys-Brewis V Glam 58 F4
Eglwys Cross Wrex 167 G7
Eglwys Fach Ceredig 128 D3
Eglwyswen Pembs 92 D3
Eglwyswrw Pembs 92 D2
Egmanton Notts 172 B2
Egmere Norf 159 B8
Egremont Cumb 219 C10
Mers 182 C4
Egton N Yorks 226 D6
Egton Bridge N Yorks 226 D6
Egypt Bucks 66 B3
Egypt *continued*
Hants 48 E3
W Berks 64 D2
W Yorks 205 G7
Eiden Highld 309 J7
Eight Ash Green Essex 107 F8
Eighton Banks T&W 243 F7
Eignaig Highld 289 E9
Eign Hill Hereford 97 D10
Eil Highld 291 B10
Eilanreach Highld 295 D10
Eildon Borders 262 C3
Eileanach Lodge Highld 300 C5
Eilean Anabaich W Isles 305 H4
Eilean Darach Highld 307 L6
Eilean Shona Ho Highld 289 B8
Einacleite W Isles 304 F3
Einsiob / Evenjobb Powys 114 E5
Eisgean W Isles 305 G5
Eisingrug Gwyn 146 C2
Eland Green Northumb 242 C5
Elan Village Powys 113 D8
Elberton S Glos 60 B6
Elborough N Som 43 B11
Elbridge Shrops 149 E7
W Sus 22 C6
Elburton Plym 7 E10
Elcho Perth 286 E5
Elcock's Brook Worcs 117 E10
Elcombe Glos 80 F3
Swindon 62 C6
Elcot W Berks 63 F11
Eldene Swindon 63 C7
Eldernell Cambs 138 D6
Eldersfield Worcs 98 E6
Elderslie Renfs 267 C8
Elder Street Essex 105 E11
Eldon Durham 233 F10
Eldon Lane Durham 233 F10
Eldrick S Ayrs 245 G7
Eldroth N Yorks 212 F5
Eldwick W Yorks 205 E8
Elemore Vale T&W 234 B3
Elerch / Bont-goch Ceredig 128 F3
Elfhowe Cumb 221 F9
Elford Northumb 264 C5
Staffs 152 G3
Elford Closes Cambs 123 C10
Elgin Moray 302 C2
Elgol Highld 295 D7
Elham Kent 55 E7
Eliburn W Loth 269 B10
Elie Fife 287 G8
Elim Anglesey 178 D5
Eling Hants 32 E5
W Berks 64 D4
Elishader Highld 298 C5
Elishaw Northumb 251 D9
Elizafield Dumfries 238 C2
Elkesley Notts 187 F11
Elkington Northants 120 B2
Elkins Green Essex 87 E10
Elkstone Glos 81 C7
Ellacombe Torbay 9 C8
Ellan Highld 301 G8
Elland W Yorks 196 C6
Elland Lower Edge W Yorks 196 C6
Elland Upper Edge W Yorks 196 C6
Ellary Argyll 275 F8
Ellastone Staffs 169 G10
Ellel Lancs 202 B5
Ellemford Borders 272 C4
Ellenborough Cumb 228 D6
Ellenbrook Herts 86 D2
IoM 192 E4
Ellenglaze Corn 4 D5
Ellenhall Staffs 150 D6
Ellen's Green Sur 50 F5
Ellerbeck N Yorks 225 F8
Ellerburn N Yorks 216 C6
Ellerby N Yorks 226 C5
Ellerdine Telford 150 E2
Ellerdine Heath Telford 150 E2
Ellerhayes Devon 27 G7
Elleric Argyll 284 C4
Ellerker E Yorks 200 B2
Ellerton E Yorks 207 F10
N Yorks 224 F5
Shrops 150 D4
Ellesborough Bucks 84 D4
Ellesmere Shrops 149 C8
Ellesmere Park Gtr Man 184 B3
Ellesmere Port Ches W 182 F6
Ellicombe Som 42 E3
Ellingham Hants 31 F10
Norf 143 E7
Northumb 264 D5
Ellingstring N Yorks 214 C3
Ellington Cambs 122 C3
Northumb 253 E7
Ellington Thorpe Cambs 122 C3
Elliot Angus 287 D10
Elliots Green Som 45 D9
Elliot's Town Caerph 77 E10
Ellisfield Hants 48 D6
Elliston Borders 262 D3
Ellistown Leics 153 G8
Ellon Aberds 303 F9
Ellonby Cumb 230 D4
Ellough Suff 143 F8
Elloughton E Yorks 200 B2
Ellwood Glos 79 D9
Elm Cambs 139 B9
Elmbridge Glos 80 B5
Worcs 117 D8
Elm Corner Sur 50 B5
Elm Cross Wilts 62 D6
Elmdon Essex 105 D9
W Mid 134 G3
Elmdon Heath W Mid 134 G3
Elmer W Sus 35 G7
Elmers End London 67 F11
Elmers Green Lancs 194 F3
Elmers Marsh W Sus 34 B5
Elmesthorpe Leics 135 D9
Elmfield IoW 21 C8
Elm Hill Dorset 30 B4
Elmhurst Bucks 84 B4
Staffs 152 G2
Elmley Castle Worcs 99 C9
Elmley Lovett Worcs 117 D7
Elmore Glos 80 B3
Elmore Back Glos 80 B3
Elm Park London 68 B4
Elmscott Devon 24 C2
Elmsett Suff 107 B11
Elms Green Hereford 115 F10
Worcs 116 D4
Elmslack Lancs 211 D9
Elmstead Essex 107 F11
London 68 E2
Elmstead Heath Essex 107 G11
Elmstead Market Essex 107 G11
Elmsted Kent 54 E6
Elmsthorpe Leics 135 D9
Elmstone Kent 71 G9
Elmstone Hardwicke Glos 99 F8
Elmswell E Yorks 208 B5
Suff 125 E9
Elmton Derbys 187 G8
Elness Orkney 314 C6
Elphin Highld 307 H7
Elphinstone E Loth 281 G7
Elrick Aberds 293 C10
Elrig Dumfries 236 E5
Elrigbeag Argyll 284 F5
Elrington Northumb 241 E9
Elscar S Yorks 197 G11
Elsdon Hereford 114 G6
Northumb 251 E10
Elsecar S Yorks 186 B5
S Yorks 197 G11
Elsenham Essex 105 F10
Elsenham Sta Essex 105 F10
Elsfield Oxon 83 C8
Elsham N Lincs 200 E4
Elsing Norf 159 F11
Elslack N Yorks 204 D4
Elson Hants 33 G10
Shrops 149 B7
Elsrickle S Lanark 269 G11
Elstead Sur 50 E2
Elsted W Sus 34 D4
Elsthorpe Lincs 155 E11
Elstob Durham 234 G2
Elston Devon 26 G3
Notts 172 F3
Wilts 46 E5
Elstone Devon 25 D11
Elstow Beds 103 B11
Elstree Herts 85 F11
Elstronwick E Yorks 209 G10
Elswick Lancs 202 F4
T&W 242 E6
Elswick Leys Lancs 202 F4
Elsworth Cambs 122 E6
Elterwater Cumb 220 E6
Eltham London 68 E2
Eltisley Cambs 122 F5
Elton Cambs 137 E11
Ches W 183 F7
Derbys 170 C2
Glos 80 C2
Gtr Man 195 E9
Hereford 115 C9
Notts 154 B5
Stockton 225 B8
Elton Green Ches W 183 G7
Elton's Marsh Hereford 97 C9
Eltringham Northumb 242 E3
Elvanfoot S Lanark 259 F11
Elvaston Derbys 153 C8
Elveden Suff 124 B6
Elvet Hill Durham 233 C11
Elvingston E Loth 281 G9
Elvington Kent 55 C9
York 207 D9
Elwell Devon 41 G7
Dorset 17 E9
Elwick Hrtlpl 234 E5
Northumb 264 B4
Elworth Ches E 168 C2
Elworthy Som 42 G5
Ely Cambs 139 G10
Cardiff 58 D6
Emberton M Keynes 103 B7
Embleton Cumb 229 E9
Durham 234 F4
Northumb 264 E6
Embo Highld 311 K2
Emborough Som 44 C6
Embo Street Highld 311 K2
Embsay N Yorks 204 C6
Emerson Park London 68 B4
Emerson's Green S Glos 61 D7
Emerson Valley M Keynes 102 E6
Emery Down Hants 32 F3
Emley W Yorks 197 E8
Emmbrook Wokingham 65 F9
Emmer Green Reading 65 D8
Emmett Carr Derbys 187 F7
Emmington Oxon 84 E2
Emneth Norf 139 B9
Emneth Hungate Norf 139 B10
Emorsgate Norf 157 E10
Empingham Rutland 137 B8
Empshott Hants 49 G9
Empshott Green Hants 49 G8
Emscote Warks 118 D5
Emstrey Shrops 149 G10
Emsworth Hants 22 B2
Enborne W Berks 64 F2
Enborne Row W Berks 64 G2
Enchmarsh Shrops 131 D10
Enderby Leics 135 D10
Endmoor Cumb 211 C10
Endon Staffs 168 E6
Endon Bank Staffs 168 E6
Energlyn Caerph 58 B6
Enfield London 86 F4
Worcs 117 D10
Enfield Highway London 86 F5
Enfield Lock London 86 F5
Enfield Town London 86 F4
Enfield Wash London 86 F5
Enford Wilts 46 C6
Engamoor Shetland 313 H4
Engedi Anglesey 178 F5
Engine Common S Glos 61 C7
Englefield W Berks 64 E6
Englefield Green Sur 66 E3
Englesea-brook Ches E 168 E3
English Bicknor Glos 79 B9
Englishcombe Bath 61 G8
English Frankton Shrops 149 D9
Engollan Corn 10 G3
Enham Alamein Hants 47 D11
Enis Devon 25 B9
Enisfirth Shetland 312 F5
Enmore Som 43 G8
Enmore Field Hereford 115 E9
Enmore Green Dorset 30 C5
Ennerdale Bridge Cumb 219 B11
Enniscaven Corn 5 D9
Enoch Dumfries 247 C9
Enochdhu Perth 292 G2
Ensay Argyll 288 E5
Ensbury Bmouth 19 B7
Ensbury Park Bmouth 19 C7
Ensdon Shrops 149 F8
Ensis Devon 25 B9
Enslow Oxon 83 B7
Enstone Oxon 101 G7
Enterkinfoot Dumfries 247 C9
Enterpen N Yorks 225 D9
Enton Green Sur 50 E3
Enville Staffs 132 F6
Eolaigearraidh W Isles 297 L3
Eorabus Argyll 288 G5
Eòropaidh W Isles 304 B7
Epney Glos 80 C3
Epperstone Notts 171 F11
Epping Essex 87 E7
Epping Green Essex 86 D6
Herts 86 D3
Epping Upland Essex 86 E6
Eppleby N Yorks 224 C3
Eppleworth E Yorks 208 G6
Epsom Sur 67 G8
Epwell Oxon 101 C7
Epworth N Lincs 199 G9
Epworth Turbary N Lincs 199 G9
Erbistock Wrex 166 G5
Erbusaig Highld 295 C9
Erchless Castle Highld 300 E4
Erdington W Mid 134 E2
Eredine Argyll 275 C10
Eriboll Highld 308 D4
Ericstane Dumfries 260 G3
Eridge Green E Sus 52 F5
Erines Argyll 275 F9
Eriswell Suff 124 B4
Erith London 68 D4
Erlestoke Wilts 46 C3
Ermine Lincs 189 G7
Ermington Devon 8 E2
Ernesettle Plym 7 D8
Erpingham Norf 160 C3
Erriottwood Kent 54 B2
Errogie Highld 300 G5
Errol Perth 286 E6
Errol Station Perth 286 E6
Erskine Renfs 277 G9
Erskine Bridge Renfs 277 G9
Ervie Dumfries 236 C2
Erwarton Suff 108 E4
Erwood Powys 95 C11
Eryholme N Yorks 224 D6
Eryrys Denb 166 D2
Escomb Durham 233 E9
Escott Som 42 F5
Escrick N Yorks 207 E8
Esgairdawe Carms 94 C2
Esgairgeiliog Powys 128 B5
Esgyryn Conwy 180 F4
Esh Durham 233 C9
Esher Sur 66 G6
Eshiels Borders 261 B7
Esholt W Yorks 205 E9
Eshott Northumb 252 D6
Eshton N Yorks 204 B4
Esh Winning Durham 233 C9
Eskadale Highld 300 F4
Eskbank Midloth 270 B6
Eskdale Green Cumb 220 E2
Eskdalemuir Dumfries 249 D7
Eske E Yorks 209 E7
Eskham Lincs 190 B5
Eskholme S Yorks 198 D6
Esknish Argyll 274 G4
Esk Valley N Yorks 226 E6
Eslington Park Northumb 264 G2
Esperley Lane Ends Durham 233 G8
Esprick Lancs 202 F4
Essendine Rutland 155 G10
Essendon Herts 86 D3
Essich Highld 300 F6
Essington Staffs 133 C9
Esslemont Aberds 303 G9

Gearraidh Bhaird W Isles 304 F5
Gearraidh Dubh W Isles 296 F4
Gearraidh na h-Aibhne W Isles 304 E4
Gearraidh na Monadh W Isles 297 K3
Geàrraidh Sheilidh W Isles 297 J3
Geary Highld 298 C2
Geat Wolford Warks 100 E4
Geddes House Highld 301 D8
Gedding Suff 125 F9
Geddington Northants 137 G7
Gedgrave Hall Suff 109 B8
Gedintailor Highld 295 B7
Gedling Notts 171 G10
Gedney Lincs 157 E8
Gedney Broadgate Lincs 157 E8
Gedney Drove End Lincs 157 D9
Gedney Dyke Lincs 157 D8
Gedney Hill Lincs 156 G6
Gee Cross Gtr Man 185 C7
Geeston Rutland 137 C9
Gegin Wrex 166 E3
Geilston Argyll 276 F6
Geinas Denb 165 B9
Geirinis W Isles 297 G3
Geise Highld 310 C5
Geisiadar W Isles 304 E3
Geldeston Norf 143 E7
Gell Conwy 164 B5
Gelli Pembs 73 B9
Rhondda 77 G7
Gellideg M Tydf 77 D8
Gellifor Denb 165 C10
Gelligaer Caerph 77 F10
Gelli-gaer Neath 57 C9
Gelligroes Caerph 77 G11
Gelli-hôf Caerph 77 F11
Gellilydan Gwyn 146 B3
Gellinud Neath 76 E2
Gellinudd Neath 76 E2
Gellyburn Perth 286 D4
Gellygron Neath 76 E2
Gellywen Carms 92 G5
Gelsmoor Leics 153 F8
Gelston Dumfries 237 D9
Lincs 172 G6
Gembling E Yorks 209 B8
Gemini Warr 183 C9
Gendros Swansea 56 B6
Genesis Green Suff 124 F4
Gentleshaw Staffs 151 G11
Geocrab W Isles 305 J3
Georgefield Dumfries 249 E7
George Green Bucks 66 C4
Georgeham Devon 40 F3
George Nympton Devon 26 C2
Georgetown Bl Gwent 77 D10
Georgia Corn 1 B5
Gergask Highld 291 D8
Gerlan Gwyn 163 B10
Germansweek Devon 12 C4
Germiston Glasgow 268 B2
Germoe Corn 2 D3
Gerrans Corn 3 B9
Gerrard's Bromley Staffs 150 C5
Gerrards Cross Bucks 66 B4
Gerrick Redcar 226 C4
Geseilfa Powys 129 E8
Gestingthorpe Essex 106 D6
Gesto Ho Highld 294 B5
Geufforدd Powys 148 G4
Geufron Denb 166 G2
Gibbet Hill W Mid 118 C6
Warks 135 G10
Gibb Hill Ches W 183 F10
Gibbshill Dumfries 237 B9
Gib Heath W Mid 133 F11
Gibraltar Beds 103 B10
Bucks 84 C3
Kent 55 F8
Gibralter Oxon 83 B7
Gibshill Invclyd 276 G6
Gibsmere Notts 172 F2
Giddeahall Wilts 61 E11
Giddy Green Dorset 18 D2
Gidea Park London 68 B4
Gidleigh Devon 13 D9
Giffard Park M Keynes 103 C7
Giffnock E Renf 267 D11
Gifford E Loth 271 B10
Giffordland N Ayrs 266 F5
Giffordtown Fife 286 F6
Gigg Gtr Man 195 F10
Giggetty Staffs 133 E7
Giggleswick N Yorks 212 G6
Giggshill Sur 67 F7
Gignog Pembs 91 G7
Gilberdyke E Yorks 199 B10
Gilbert's Coombe Corn 4 G3
Gilbert's End Worcs 98 C6
Gilbert's Green Warks 118 C2
Gilbertstone W Mid 134 G2
Gilbert Street Hants 49 G7
Gilchriston E Loth 271 B9
Gilcrux Cumb 229 D8
Gildersome W Yorks 197 B8
Gildersome Street W Yorks 197 B8
Gildingwells S Yorks 187 D9
Gilesgate Durham 233 C11
Gilesgate Moor Durham 233 C11
Gileston V Glam 58 F4
Gilfach Caerph 77 F11
Hereford 96 E6
Gilfach Goch Rhondda 58 B3
Gilfachrheda Ceredig 111 F8
Gilgarran Cumb 228 G6
Gill N Yorks 204 E5
Gillamoor N Yorks 216 B3
Gillan Corn 3 E7
Gillar's Green Mers 183 B7
Gillbank Cumb 221 F7
Gillbent Gtr Man 184 E5
Gillen Highld 298 D2
Gillesbie Dumfries 248 E5
Gilling East N Yorks 216 D2
Gillingham Dorset 30 B4
Medway 69 F9
Norf 143 E8
Gilling West N Yorks 224 D3
Gillmoss Mers 182 B6
Gillock Highld 310 D6
Gillow Heath Staffs 168 D5
Gills Highld 310 B7
Gill's Green Kent 53 G9
Gillway Staffs 134 C4
Gilmanscleuch Borders 261 E8
Gilmerton Edin 270 B5
Perth 286 E2
Gilmonby Durham 223 C9
Gilmorton Leics 135 F11
Gilmourton S Lanark 268 G3
Gilnow Gtr Man 195 F8
Gilroyd S Yorks 197 G10
Gilsland Northumb 240 D4
Gilsland Spa Cumb 240 D4
Gilson Warks 134 E3
Gilstead W Yorks 205 F8
Gilston Borders 271 D8
Herts 86 C6
Gilston Park Herts 86 C6
Giltbrook Notts 171 F7
Gilver's Lane Worcs 98 C6
Gilwell Park Essex 86 F5
Gilwern Mon 78 C2
Gimingham Norf 160 B5
Ginclough Ches E 185 F7
Ginger's Green E Sus 23 C10
Giosla W Isles 304 F3
Gipping Suff 125 E11
Gipsey Bridge Lincs 174 F3
Gipsy Row Suff 107 D11
Gipsyville Hull 200 B5
Gipton W Yorks 206 F2
Gipton Wood W Yorks 206 F2
Girdle Toll N Ayrs 266 G6
Girlington W Yorks 205 G8
Girlsta Shetland 313 H6
Girsby Lincs 190 D2
N Yorks 225 D7
Girt Som 29 C10
Girtford C Beds 104 B3
C Beds 122 G3
Girthon Dumfries 237 D8
Girton Cambs 123 E8
Notts 172 B4
Girvan S Ayrs 244 D5
Gisburn Lancs 204 D2
Gisleham Suff 143 F10
Gislingham Suff 125 C11
Gissing Norf 142 F2
Gittisham Devon 15 B8
Givons Grove Sur 51 C7
Glachavoil Argyll 275 F11
Glackmore Highld 300 D6
Glack of Midthird Moray 302 E3
Gladestry Powys 114 F4
Gladsmuir E Loth 281 G9
Glaichbea Highld 300 F5
Glais Swansea 76 E2
Glaisdale N Yorks 226 D5
Glame Highld 298 E5
Glamis Angus 287 C7
Glan Adda Gwyn 179 G9
Glanafon Pembs 73 B7
Glanaman Carms 75 C11
Glan-Conwy Conwy 164 E4
Glandford Norf 177 E8
Glan-Duar Carms 93 C10
Glandwr Caerph 78 E2
Pembs 92 F3
Glan-Dwyfach Gwyn 163 G7
Glandy Cross Carms 92 F2
Glandyfi Ceredig 128 D3
Glan Gors Anglesey 179 F7
Glangrwyney Powys 78 B2
Glanhanog Powys 129 D8
Glanmule Powys 130 E3
Glanrafon Ceredig 128 G2
Glanrhyd Gwyn 144 B5
Pembs 92 C2
Glan-rhyd Gwyn 163 D7
Powys 76 D3
Glantlees Northumb 252 B4
Glanton Northumb 264 G3
Glanton Pike Northumb 264 G3
Glan-traeth Anglesey 178 F3
Glantwymyn / Cemmaes Road Powys 128 C6
Glanvilles Wootton Dorset 29 F11
Glanwern Ceredig 128 F2
Glanwydden Conwy 180 E4
Glan-y-don Flint 181 F11
Glan y Ffer / Ferryside Carms 74 C5
Glan-y-llyn Rhondda 58 C6
Glan-y-môr Carms 74 C4
Glan-y-nant Caerph 77 F10
Powys 129 G8
Glan-yr-afon Anglesey 179 E10
Flint 181 E10
Gwyn 164 G6
Gwyn 165 G8
Shrops 148 E4
Glan-y-wern Gwyn 146 C2
Glapthorn Northants 137 E10
Glapwell Derbys 171 B7
Glas-allt Shiel Aberds 292 E4
Glasbury Powys 96 D3
Glaschoil Highld 301 F10
Glascoed Denb 181 G7
Mon 78 E4
Powys 129 F11
Powys 148 G2
Wrex 166 E3
Glascorrie Aberds 292 D5
Perth 286 E2
Glascote Staffs 134 C4
Glascwm Powys 114 G3
Glasdir Flint 181 E10
Glasdrum Argyll 284 C4
Glasfryn Conwy 164 E6
Glasgoed Ceredig 92 B6
Glasgoforest Aberds 293 B10
Glasgow Glasgow 267 B11
Glashvin Highld 298 C4
Glasinfryn Gwyn 163 B9
Glasllwch Newport 59 B9
Glasnacardoch Highld 295 F8
Glasnakille Highld 295 D7
Glasphein Highld 297 G7
Glaspwll Powys 128 D4
Glassburn Highld 300 F3
Glassenbury Kent 53 F8
Glasserton Dumfries 236 F6
Glassford S Lanark 268 F4
Glassgreen Moray 302 C2
Glass Houghton W Yorks 198 C2
Glasshouse Glos 98 G4
Glasshouse Hill Glos 98 G4
Glasshouses N Yorks 214 G3
Glasslie Fife 286 G6
Glasson Cumb 228 D6
Cumb 239 E7
Lancs 202 B4
Glassonby Cumb 231 D7
Glasterlaw Angus 287 B9
Glaston Rutland 137 C7
Glastonbury Som 44 F4
Glatton Cambs 138 F3
Glazebrook Warr 183 C11
Glazebury Warr 183 B11
Glazeley Shrops 132 F4
Gleadless S Yorks 186 E5
Gleadless Valley S Yorks 186 E5
Gleadmoss Ches E 168 B4
Gleadsmoss Ches E 168 B4
Gleanhead Perth 292 F2
Dumfries 245 G10
Gleann Tholàstaidh W Isles 304 D7
Gleaston Cumb 210 E5
Glebe Hants 33 D9
Shetland 313 J6
T&W 243 F8
Glecknabae Argyll 275 G11
Gledhow W Yorks 206 F2
Gledrid Shrops 148 B5
Gleiniant Powys 129 E9
Glemsford Suff 106 B6
Glen Dumfries 237 B10
Dumfries 237 D7
Glenallachie Moray 302 E2
Glenalmond College Perth 286 E3
Glenalmond Ho Perth 286 E3
Glenamachrie Argyll 289 G11
Glenample Stirling 285 E9
Glenancross Highld 295 F8
Glenapp Castle S Ayrs 244 G3
Glenaros Ho Argyll 289 E7
Glen Auldyn IoM 192 C5
Glenbarr Argyll 255 D7
Glenbeg Highld 289 C7
Highld 301 G10
Glen Bernisdale Highld 298 E4
Glenbervie Aberds 293 E9
Glenboig N Lanark 268 B4
Glenborrodale Highld 289 C8
Glenbranter Argyll 276 B2
Glenbreck Borders 260 E3
Glenbrein Lodge Highld 290 B6
Glenbrittle House Highld 294 C6
Glenbrook Edin 270 B2
Glenbuchat Castle Aberds 292 B5
Glenbuchat Lodge Aberds 292 B5
Glenbuck E Ayrs 259 D7
Glenburn Renfs 267 C9
Glenbyre Argyll 289 G7
Glencalvie Lodge Highld 309 L4
Glencanisp Lodge Highld 307 G6
Glencaple Dumfries 237 C11
Glencarron Lodge Highld 299 D10
Glencarse Perth 286 E5
Glencassley Castle Highld 309 J4
Glencat Aberds 293 D7
Glenceitlein Highld 284 C5
Glencoe Highld 284 B4
Glencraig Fife 280 B3
Glencripesdale Highld 289 D8
Glencrosh Dumfries 247 F7
Glendavan Ho Aberds 292 C6
Glendearg Borders 262 B2
Glendevon Perth 286 G3
Glendoebeg Highld 290 C6
Glendoe Lodge Highld 290 C6
Glendoick Perth 286 E6
Glendoll Lodge Angus 292 F4
Glendoune S Ayrs 244 D5
Glenduckie Fife 286 F6
Glendye Lodge Aberds 293 E8
Gleneagles Hotel Perth 286 F3
Gleneagles House Perth 286 G3
Glenearn Perth 286 F5
Glenegedale Argyll 254 B4
Glenelg Highld 295 D10
Glenernie Moray 301 E10
Glenfarg Perth 286 F5
Glenfarquhar Lodge Aberds 293 E9
Glenferness House Highld 301 E9
Glenfeshie Lodge Highld 291 D10
Glenfiddich Lodge Moray 302 F3
Glenfield Leics 135 B10
Glenfinnan Highld 295 G10
Glenfinnan Lodge Highld 295 G11
Glenfintaig Ho Highld 290 E4
Glenfoot Perth 286 F5
Glenfyne Lodge Argyll 284 F6
Glengap Dumfries 237 D8
Glengarnock N Ayrs 266 E6
Glengolly Highld 310 C5
Glengorm Castle Argyll 288 D6
Glengoulandie Perth 285 B11
Glengrasco Highld 298 E4
Glenhead Farm Angus 292 G4
Glen Ho Borders 261 C7
Glenholt Plym 7 C10
Glenhoul Dumfries 246 F4
Glenhurich Highld 289 C10
Glenkerry Borders 261 G7
Glenkiln Dumfries 237 B10
Glenkindie Aberds 292 B6
Glenlair Dumfries 237 B9
Glenlatterach Moray 301 D11
Glenlee Dumfries 246 G4
Glenleigh Park E Sus 38 F2
Glenleraig Highld 306 F6
Glenlichorn Perth 285 F11
Glenlicht Ho Highld 290 B2
Glenlivet Moray 301 G11
Glenlochar Dumfries 237 C9
Glenlochsie Perth 292 F2
Glenlocksie Lodge Perth 292 F2
Glenloig N Ayrs 255 D10
Glenlomond Perth 286 G5
Glenluce Dumfries 236 D4
Glenlussa Ho Argyll 255 E8
Glenmallan Argyll 276 B5
Glenmark Angus 292 E6
Glenmarkie Lodge Angus 292 G4
Glenmarksie Highld 300 D3
Glenmavis N Lanark 268 B4
W Loth 269 B9
Glenmaye IoM 192 E3
Glenmayne Borders 261 C11
Glenmeanie Highld 300 D2
Glenmidge Dumfries 247 F9
Glenmoidart Ho Highld 289 B9
Glen Mona IoM 192 D5
Glen Mor Highld 295 B10
Glenmore Argyll 275 B9
Argyll 275 G11
Highld 298 E4
Glenmore Lodge Highld 291 C11
Glenmoy Angus 292 G6
Glen Nevis House Highld 290 F3
Glennoe Argyll 284 D4
Glen of Newmill Moray 302 D4
Glenogil Angus 292 G6
Glenowen Pembs 73 D7
Glen Parva Leics 135 D11
Glenprosen Lodge Angus 292 G4
Glenprosen Village Angus 292 G5
Glenquaich Lodge Perth 286 D2
Glenquiech Angus 292 G6
Glenquithle Aberds 303 C8
Glenrath Borders 260 C6
Glenrazie Dumfries 236 C5
Glenreasdell Mains Argyll 255 B9
Glenree N Ayrs 255 E10
Glenridding Cumb 221 B7
Glenrosa N Ayrs 256 B2
Glenrossal Highld 309 J4
Glenrothes Fife 286 G6
Glensanda Highld 289 E10
Glensaugh Aberds 293 F8
Glensburgh Falk 279 E8
Glenshero Lodge Highld 291 D7
Glenshoe Lodge Perth 292 G3
Glen Sluain Argyll 275 D11
Glenstockadale Dumfries 236 C2
Glenstriven Argyll 275 F11
Glentaggart S Lanark 259 D8
Glen Tanar House Aberds 292 D6
Glentarkie Perth 286 F5
Glenternie Borders 260 B6
Glentham Lincs 189 C8
Glentirranmuir Stirling 278 C3
Glenton Aberds 302 G6
Glentress Borders 261 B7
Glentromie Lodge Highld 291 D9
Glen Trool Lodge Dumfries 245 G10
Glentrool Village Dumfries 236 B5
Glentruan IoM 192 B5
Glentruim House Highld 291 D8
Glentworth Lincs 188 D6
Glenuaig Lodge Highld 299 E11
Glenuig Highld 289 B8
Glenure Argyll 284 C4
Glenurquhart Highld 301 C7
Glen Vic Askil Highld 298 E3
Glenview Argyll 284 E5
Glen Village Falk 279 F7
Glen Vine IoM 192 E4
Glespin S Lanark 259 D8
Gletness Shetland 313 H6
Glewstone Hereford 97 G11
Glinton Pboro 138 B3
Globe Town London 67 C11
Glodwick Gtr Man 196 G2
Glogue Pembs 92 E4
Glooston Leics 136 D4
Glororum Northumb 264 C5
Glossop Derbys 185 C8
Gloster Hill Northumb 253 C7
Gloucester Glos 80 B4
Gloup Shetland 312 C7
Glowleth Corn 4 G5
Glusburn N Yorks 204 E6
Glutt Lodge Highld 310 F3
Glutton Bridge Staffs 169 B9
Gluvian Corn 5 C8
Glympton Oxon 101 G8
Glyn Mon 79 F7
Powys 129 F8
Glynarthen Ceredig 92 B6
Glynbrochan Powys 129 G8
Glyn Castle Neath 76 E4
Glyn-Ceiriog Wrex 148 B4
Glyncoch Rhondda 77 G9
Glyncoed Bl Gwent 77 C11
Glyncorrwg Neath 57 B11
Glyn-cywarch Gwyn 146 C2
Glynde E Sus 23 D7
Glyndebourne E Sus 23 C7
Glyndyfrdwy Denb 165 G10
Glynedd / Glyn neath Neath 76 D5
Glyne Gap E Sus 38 F3
Glyn Etwy Bl Gwent 77 D11
Glynhafren Powys 129 G7
Glynllan Bridgend 58 B2
Glynmorlas Shrops 148 B6
Glyn-neath / Glynedd Neath 76 D5
Glynogwr Bridgend 58 B3
Glyntaff Rhondda 58 B5
Glyntawe Powys 76 B4
Gnosall Staffs 150 E6
Gnosall Heath Staffs 150 E6
Goadby Leics 136 D4
Goadby Marwood Leics 154 D5
Goatacre Wilts 62 D4
Goatham Green E Sus 38 C4
Goathill Dorset 29 D11
Goathland N Yorks 226 E6
Goathurst Som 43 G9
Goathurst Common Kent 52 C3
Goat Lees Kent 54 D4
Gobernuisgach Lodge Highld 308 E4
Gobernuisgeach Highld 310 F3
Gobhaig W Isles 305 H2
Gobley Hole Hants 48 D6
Gobowen Shrops 148 C6
Godalming Sur 50 E3
Goddards Bucks 84 G3
Goddard's Corner Suff 126 D5
Goddard's Green Kent 53 G10
W Berks 65 F7
Goddards' Green W Sus 36 C3
Godden Green Kent 52 B5
Goddington London 68 F3
Godley Gtr Man 185 B7
Godleybrook Staffs 169 G7
Godley Hill Gtr Man 185 C7
Godleys Green E Sus 36 D5
Godmanchester Cambs 122 C4
Godmanstone Dorset 17 B9
Godmersham Kent 54 C5
Godney Som 44 E3
Godolphin Cross Corn 2 C4
Godre'r-graig Neath 76 D3
God's Blessing Green Dorset 31 G8
Godshill Hants 31 E11
IoW 20 E6
Godstone Sur 51 C10
Godswinscroft Hants 19 B9
Godwell Devon 8 D2
Godwick Norf 159 E8
Godwinscroft Hants 19 B9
Goetre Mon 78 D4
Goferydd Anglesey 178 E2
Goff's Oak Herts 86 E4
Gogar Edin 280 G3
Goginan Ceredig 128 G3
Goirtean a'Chladaich Highld 290 F2
Golan Gwyn 163 G8
Golant Corn 6 E2
Golberdon Corn 12 G2
Golborne Gtr Man 183 B10
Golcar W Yorks 196 D6
Golch Flint 181 F11
Goldcliff Newport 59 C11
Golden Balls Oxon 83 F9
Golden Cross E Sus 23 C8
E Sus 23 C10
Golden Green Kent 52 D6
Golden Grove Carms 75 B9
Goldenhill Stoke 168 E5
Golden Hill Bristol 60 D5
Hants 19 B11
Pembs 73 E7
Pembs 91 G9
Golden Park Devon 24 C2
Golden Pot Hants 49 E8
Golden Valley Derbys 170 E6
Glos 99 G8
Golden Valley *continued*
Hereford 98 B3
Golder Field Hereford 115 E11
Golders Green London 67 B9
Goldfinch Bottom W Berks 64 G4
Goldhanger Essex 88 D6
Gold Hill Dorset 30 E4
Norf 139 E10
Golding Shrops 131 C10
Goldington Beds 121 G11
Goldsborough N Yorks 206 B3
N Yorks 226 C6
Gold's Cross Bath 60 G5
Golds Green W Mid 133 E9
Goldsithney Corn 2 C2
Goldstone Shrops 150 D4
Goldthorn Park W Mid 133 D8
Goldthorpe S Yorks 198 G3
Goldworthy Devon 24 C5
Golford Kent 53 F9
Golftyn Flint 182 G3
Golgotha Kent 55 D9
Gollanfield Highld 301 D8
Gollawater Corn 4 E5
Gollinglith Foot N Yorks 214 C3
Golly Wrex 166 D4
Golsoncott Som 42 F4
Golspie Highld 311 J2
Golval Highld 310 C2
Golynos Torf 78 E3
Gomeldon Wilts 47 F7
Gomersal W Yorks 197 B8
Gometra Ho Argyll 288 E5
Gomshall Sur 50 D5
Gonalston Notts 171 F11
Gonamena Corn 11 G11
Gonerby Hill Foot Lincs 155 B8
Gonfirth Shetland 313 G5
Good Easter Essex 87 C10
Gooderstone Norf 140 C5
Goodleigh Devon 40 G6
Goodley Stock Kent 52 C2
Goodmanham E Yorks 208 E3
Goodmayes London 68 B3
Goodnestone Kent 55 C9
Kent 70 G4
Goodrich Hereford 79 B9
Goodrington Torbay 9 D7
Good's Green Worcs 132 G5
Goodshaw Lancs 195 B10
Goodshaw Chapel Lancs 195 B10
Goodshaw Fold Lancs 195 B10
Goodstone Devon 13 G11
Goodwick / Wdig Pembs 91 D8
Goodworth Clatford Hants 47 E11
Goodyers End Warks 134 F6
Goodyhills Cumb 229 B8
Goole E Yorks 199 C8
Goom's Hill Worcs 117 G10
Goonabarn Corn 5 E9
Goonbell Corn 4 F4
Goon Gumpas Corn 4 G4
Goonhavern Corn 4 E5
Goonhusband Corn 2 D5
Goonlaze Corn 2 B6
Goonown Corn 4 E4
Goonpiper Corn 3 B8
Goonvrea Corn 4 F4
Gooseberry Green Essex 87 F11
Goose Eye W Yorks 204 E6
Gooseford Devon 13 C9
Goose Green Cumb 211 C10
Essex 108 F2
Gtr Man 194 G5
Hants 32 F4
Herts 86 D5
Kent 52 C6
Kent 53 F10
Lancs 194 C3
Norf 142 F2
S Glos 61 C8
W Sus 34 C3
W Sus 35 D10
Gooseham Mill Devon 24 D2
Goosehill W Yorks 197 C11
Goose Hill Hants 64 G4
Goosehill Green Worcs 117 E8
Goosemoor Staffs 150 F6
Goosemoor Green Staffs 151 G11
Goosenford Som 28 B2
Goose Pool Hereford 97 D9
Goosewell Devon 40 D5
Goosey Oxon 82 G5
Goosnargh Lancs 203 F7
Goostrey Ches E 184 G3
Gorbals Glasgow 267 C11
Gorcott Hill Warks 117 D11
Gord Shetland 313 L6
Gordinog Conwy 179 G11
Gordon Borders 272 G2
Gordonbush Highld 311 J2
Gordonsburgh Moray 302 C4
Gordonstoun Moray 301 C11
Gordonstown Aberds 302 D5
Aberds 303 F7
Gore Dorset 29 D9
Kent 55 B10
Gorebridge Midloth 270 C6
Gore Cross Wilts 46 C4
Gore End Hants 64 G2
Gorefield Cambs 157 G8
Gorehill W Sus 35 C7
Gore Pit Essex 88 B5
Gore Street Kent 71 F9
Gorgie Edin 280 G4
Gorhambury Herts 85 D10
Goring Oxon 64 C6
Goring-by-Sea W Sus 35 G10
Goring Heath Oxon 65 D7
Gorleston-on-Sea Norf 143 C10
Gornalwood W Mid 133 E8
Gorrachie Aberds 303 D7
Gorran Churchtown Corn 5 G9
Gorran Haven Corn 5 G10
Gorran High Lanes Corn 5 G9
Gorrenberry Borders 249 D11
Gorrig Ceredig 93 C8
Gorse Covert Warr 183 C11
Gorsedd Flint 181 F11
Gorse Hill Gtr Man 184 B4
Swindon 63 B7
Gorseinon Swansea 56 B5
Gorseness Orkney 314 E4
Gorsethorpe Notts 171 B9
Gorseybank Derbys 170 E3
Gorsgoch Ceredig 111 G9
Gorslas Carms 75 C9
Gorsley Glos 98 F3
Gorsley Common Hereford 98 F3
Gorsley Ley Staffs 133 B11
Gorstage Ches W 183 G10
Gorstan Highld 300 C3
Gorstanvorran Highld 289 B10
Gorstella Ches W 166 C5
Gorsteyhill Ches E 168 E2
Gorst Hill Worcs 116 C4
Gorstyhill Staffs 168 E2
Gorsty Hill Staffs 151 D11
Gortan Argyll 274 G3
Gortantaoid Argyll 274 F4
Gortenacullish Highld 295 G8
Gorteneorn Highld 289 C8
Gortenfern Highld 289 C8
Gortinanane Argyll 255 C8
Gorton Gtr Man 184 B5
Gortonallister N Ayrs 256 D2
Gosbeck Suff 126 F3
Gosberton Lincs 156 C4
Gosberton Cheal Lincs 156 D4
Gosberton Clough Lincs 156 D3
Goscote W Mid 133 C10
Goseley Dale Derbys 152 E6
Gosfield Essex 106 F5
Gosford Hereford 115 D10
Oxon 83 C7
Gosford Green W Mid 118 B6
Gosforth Cumb 219 E11
T&W 242 D6
Gosforth Valley Derbys 186 F4
Gosland Green Suff 124 G5
Gosling Green Suff 107 C9
Gosmere Kent 54 B4
Gosmore Herts 104 F3
Gospel Ash Staffs 132 E6
Gospel End Village Staffs 133 E7
Gospel Green W Sus 50 G2
Gospel Oak London 67 B9
Gosport Hants 21 B8
Hants 32 C5
Gossabrough Shetland 312 E7
Gossard's Green C Beds 103 C9
Gossington Glos 80 E2
Gossops Green W Sus 51 F9
Goswick Northumb 273 F11
Gotham Dorset 31 E9
E Sus 38 F2
Notts 153 C10
Gothelney Green Som 43 F9
Gotherington Glos 99 F9
Gothers Corn 5 D9
Gott Argyll 288 E2
Shetland 313 J6
Gotton Som 28 B2
Goudhurst Kent 53 F8
Goukstone Moray 302 D4
Goulceby Lincs 190 F3
Goulton N Yorks 225 E9
Gourdas Aberds 303 E7
Gourdon Aberds 293 F10
Gourock Invclyd 276 F4
Govan Glasgow 267 B11
Govanhill Glasgow 267 C11
Gover Hill Kent 52 C6
Goverton Notts 172 E2
Goveton Devon 8 F5
Govilon Mon 78 C3
Gowanhill Aberds 303 C10
Gowanwell Aberds 303 E8
Gowdall E Yorks 198 C6
Gowerton / Tre-Gwyr Swansea 56 B5
Gowhole Derbys 185 E8
Gowkhall Fife 279 D11
Gowkthrapple N Lanark 268 E5
Gowthorpe E Yorks 207 C11
Goxhill E Yorks 209 E9
N Lincs 200 C6
Goxhill Haven N Lincs 200 B6
Goybre Neath 57 D9
Goytre Neath 57 D9
Gozzard's Ford Oxon 83 F7
Grabhair W Isles 305 G5
Graby Lincs 155 D11
Gracca Corn 5 D10
Gracemount Edin 270 B5
Grade Corn 2 G6
Graffham W Sus 34 D6
Grafham Cambs 122 D3
Sur 50 E4
Grafton Hereford 97 D9
N Yorks 215 G8
Grafton *continued*
Oxon 82 E3
Shrops 149 F8
Worcs 99 D9
Worcs 115 E11
Grafton Flyford Worcs 117 F9
Grafton Regis Northants 102 B5
Grafton Underwood Northants 137 G8
Grafty Green Kent 53 D11
Grahamston Falk 279 E7
Graianrhyd Denb 166 D2
Graig Carms 74 E6
Conwy 180 G4
Denb 181 G9
Rhondda 58 B5
Wrex 148 B4
Graig-Fawr Swansea 75 E10
Graig-fechan Denb 165 E10
Graig Felen Swansea 75 E11
Graig Penllyn V Glam 58 D3
Graig Trewyddfa Swansea 57 B7
Grain Medway 69 D11
Grains Bar Gtr Man 196 F3
Grainsby Lincs 190 B3
Grainthorpe Lincs 190 B5
Grainthorpe Fen Lincs 190 B5
Graiselound N Lincs 188 B3
Grampound Corn 5 F8
Grampound Road Corn 5 E8
Gramsdal W Isles 296 F4
Granborough Bucks 102 F5
Granby Notts 154 B5
Grandborough Warks 119 D9
Grandpont Oxon 83 D8
Grandtully Perth 286 B3
Grange Cumb 220 B5
Dorset 31 G8
E Ayrs 257 B10
Fife 287 G8
Halton 183 E8
Lancs 203 G7
Medway 69 F9
Mers 182 D2
N Yorks 223 G8
NE Lincs 201 F9
Perth 286 E6
Warr 183 C10
Grange Crossroads Moray 302 D4
Grange Estate Dorset 31 G10
Grange Hall Moray 301 C10
Grange Hill Durham 233 F10
Essex 86 G6
Grangemill Derbys 170 D2
Grange Moor W Yorks 197 D8
Grangemouth Falk 279 E8
Grangemuir Fife 287 G9
Grange of Cree Dumfries 236 D6
Grange of Lindores Fife 286 F6
Grange-over-Sands Cumb 211 D8
Grangepans Falk 279 E10
Grange Park London 86 F4
Mers 183 C7
Northants 120 F5
Swindon 62 C6
Grangetown Cardiff 59 E7
Redcar 235 G7
T&W 243 G10
Grange Villa Durham 242 G6
Grange Village Glos 79 C11
Granish Highld 291 B11
Gransmoor E Yorks 209 B8
Gransmore Green Essex 106 G3
Granston / Treopert Pembs 91 E7
Grantchester Cambs 123 F8
Grantham Lincs 155 B8
Grantley N Yorks 214 F4
Grantley Hall N Yorks 214 F4
Grantlodge Aberds 293 B9
Granton Dumfries 248 B3
Edin 280 F4
Grantown Aberds 302 D5
Grantown-on-Spey Highld 301 G10
Grantsfield Hereford 115 E10
Grantshouse Borders 272 B6
Grant Thorold NE Lincs 201 F9
Graplin Dumfries 237 E8
Grappenhall Warr 183 D10
Grasby Lincs 200 G5
Grasmere Cumb 220 D6
Grasscroft Gtr Man 196 G3
Grassendale Mers 182 D5
Grassgarth Cumb 221 F8
Cumb 230 C2
Grass Green Essex 106 D4
Grassholme Durham 232 G4
Grassington N Yorks 213 G10
Grassmoor Derbys 170 B6
Grassthorpe Notts 172 B3
Grasswell T&W 243 G8
Grateley Hants 47 E9
Gratton Devon 24 E5
Gratwich Staffs 151 C11
Gravel Ches W 167 B11
Gravel Castle Kent 55 D8
Graveley Cambs 122 E4
Herts 104 F4
Gravelhill Shrops 149 G9
Gravel Hill Bucks 85 G8
Gravel Hole Gtr Man 196 F2

Haughton *continued*
Shrops 132 D3
Shrops 149 D7
Shrops 149 F11
Staffs 151 E7
Haughton Castle
Northumb 241 C10
Haughton Green
Gtr Man 184 C6
Haughton Le Skerne
Darl 224 B6
Haughurst Hill
W Berks 64 G5
Haulkerton Aberds 293 F9
Haultwick Herts 104 G6
Haunn Argyll 288 E5
W Isles 297 K3
Haunton Staffs 152 G4
Hauxton Cambs 123 G8
Havannah Ches E 168 C5
Havant Hants 22 B2
Haven Hereford 97 B11
Hereford 115 G8
Haven Bank Lincs 174 E2
Haven Side E Yorks 201 B7
Havenstreet IoW 21 C7
Havercroft
W Yorks 197 E11
Haverfordwest / Hwlffordd Pembs 73 B7
Haverhill Suff 106 B3
Haverigg Cumb 210 D3
Havering-atte-Bower
London 87 G8
Haveringland Norf 160 E3
Haversham
M Keynes 102 C6
Haverthwaite Cumb 210 C6
Haverton Hill
Stockton 234 G5
Haviker Street Kent 53 D8
Havyatt Som 44 F4
Havyatt Green
N Som 60 G3
Hawarden / Penarlâg
Flint 166 B4
Hawbridge Worcs 99 B8
Hawbush Green
Essex 106 G5
Hawcoat Cumb 210 E4
Hawcross Glos 98 E5
Hawddamor Gwyn 146 F3
Hawen Ceredig 92 B6
Hawes N Yorks 213 B7
Hawes' Green Norf 142 D4
Hawes Side
Blackpool 202 G2
Hawford Worcs 116 E6
Hawgreen Shrops 150 D2
Hawick Borders 262 F2
Hawkchurch Devon 28 G4
Hawkcombe Som 41 D11
Hawkedon Suff 124 G5
Hawkenbury Kent 52 F5
Kent 53 E10
Hawkeridge Wilts 45 C11
Hawkerland Devon 15 D7
Hawkersland Cross
Hereford 97 B10
Hawkesbury S Glos 61 B9
Warks 135 G7
Hawkesbury Upton
S Glos 61 B9
Hawkes End W Mid 134 G6
Hawkesley W Mid 117 B10
Hawk Green
Gtr Man 185 D7
Hawkhill Northumb 264 G6
Hawk Hill Cumb 228 F6
Hawkhope Northumb 250 F6
Hawkhurst Kent 53 G9
Hawkhurst Common
E Sus 23 B8
Hawkinge Kent 55 F8
Hawkin's Hill Essex 106 E3
Hawkley Gtr Man 194 G5
Hants 34 B2
Hawkridge Som 41 G11
Hawksdale Cumb 230 B3
Hawks Green Staffs 151 G9
Hawkshaw
Blackburn 195 D9
Hawkshead Cumb 221 F7
Hawkshead Hill
Cumb 220 F6
Hawks Hill Bucks 66 B2
Hawk's Hill Sur 51 B7
Hawksland S Lanark 259 B8
Hawkspur Green
Essex 106 E3
Hawks Stones
W Yorks 196 B2
Hawkswick N Yorks 213 E9
Hawksworth Notts 172 G3
W Yorks 205 E9
W Yorks 205 F11
Hawkwell Essex 88 G4
Hawley Hants 49 B11
Kent 68 E4
Hawley Bottom
Devon 28 G2
Hawley Lane Hants 49 B11
Hawling Glos 99 G11
Hawn Orkney 314 D4
Hawnby N Yorks 215 B10
Hawne W Mid 133 G9
Haworth W Yorks 204 F6
Haws Bank Cumb 220 F6
Hawstead Suff 125 F7
Hawstead Green
Suff 125 F7
Hawthorn Durham 234 B4
Hants 49 G7
Rhondda 58 B6
Wilts 61 F11
Hawthorn Corner
Kent 71 F8
Hawthorn Hill Brack 65 E11
Lincs 174 D2
Hawthorns Staffs 168 F4
Hawthorpe Lincs 155 D10
Hawton Notts 172 E3
Haxby York 207 B8
Haxey N Lincs 188 B3
Haxey *continued*
N Lincs 199 G9
Haxey Carr N Lincs 199 G9
Haxted Sur 52 D2
Haxton Wilts 46 D6
Hay Corn 10 G5
Haybridge Shrops 116 C2
Som 44 D4
Telford 150 G3
Hayden Glos 99 G8
Haydock Mers 183 B9
Haydon Bath 45 C7
Dorset 29 D11
Som 28 C3
Som 44 D5
Swindon 62 B6
Haydon Bridge
Northumb 241 E8
Haydon Wick Swindon 62 B6
Haye Corn 7 B7
Haye Fm Corn 6 B6
Hayes London 66 C6
London 68 F2
Staffs 169 C9
Hayes End London 66 C5
Hayes Knoll Wilts 81 G10
Hayes Town London 66 C6
Hayfield Derbys 185 D8
Fife 280 C5
Hay Field S Yorks 187 B10
Hayfield Green
S Yorks 187 B11
Haygate Telford 150 G2
Haygrass Som 28 C2
Hay Green Essex 87 E10
Herts 104 D6
Norf 157 F10
Hayhill E Ayrs 257 F11
Hayhillock Angus 287 C9
Haylands IoW 21 C7
Hayle Corn 2 B3
Hayley Green
W Mid 133 G8
Hay Mills W Mid 134 G2
Haymoor End Som 28 B4
Haymoor Green
Ches E 167 E11
Hayne Devon 26 F5
Haynes C Beds 103 C11
Haynes Church End
C Beds 103 C11
Haynes West End
C Beds 103 C11
Hay-on-Wye Powys 96 C4
Hayscastle Pembs 91 F7
Hayscastle Cross
Pembs 91 G8
Haysford Pembs 91 G8
Hayshead Angus 287 C10
Hayston E Dunb 278 G2
Haystoun Borders 261 B7
Hay Street Herts 105 F7
Haythorne Dorset 31 F8
Hayton Aberdeen 293 C11
Cumb 229 C8
Cumb 240 F2
E Yorks 208 D2
Notts 188 E2
Hayton's Bent
Shrops 131 G10
Haytor Vale Devon 13 F11
Haytown Devon 24 E5
Haywards Heath
W Sus 36 C4
Haywood S Lanark 269 E9
S Yorks 198 E5
Haywood Oaks
Notts 171 D10
Hazard's Green
E Sus 23 C11
Hazelbank S Lanark 268 F6
Hazelbeach Pembs 72 E6
Hazelbury Bryan
Dorset 30 F2
Hazeleigh Essex 88 E4
Hazel End Essex 105 G9
Hazeley Hants 49 B8
Hazeley Bottom
Hants 49 B9
Hazeley Heath Hants 49 B9
Hazeley Lea Hants 49 B8
Hazelgrove Notts 171 F8
Hazel Grove
Gtr Man 184 D6
Hazelhurst Gtr Man 195 D9
Gtr Man 195 G9
Gtr Man 196 G3
Hazelslack Cumb 211 D9
Hazelslade Staffs 151 G10
Hazel Street Kent 53 B11
Kent 53 F7
Hazel Stub Suff 106 C3
Hazelton Glos 81 B9
Hazelton Walls Fife 287 E7
Hazelwood Derbys 170 F4
Devon 8 E4
London 68 G2
Hazlehead S Yorks 197 G7
Hazlemere Bucks 84 F5
Hazler Shrops 131 E9
Hazlerigg T&W 242 C6
Hazles Staffs 169 F8
Hazlescross Staffs 169 F8
Hazleton Glos 81 B9
Hazlewood N Yorks 205 C7
Hazon Northumb 252 C5
Heacham Norf 158 B3
Headbourne Worthy
Hants 48 G3
Headbrook Hereford 114 F6
Headcorn Kent 53 E10
Headingley
W Yorks 205 F11
Headington Oxon 83 D8
Headington Hill Oxon 83 D8
Headlam Durham 224 B3
Headless Cross
Cumb 211 D7
Worcs 117 D10
Headley Hants 49 F10
Hants 64 G4
Sur 51 C8
Headley Down
Hants 49 F10
Headley Heath
Worcs 117 B11
Headley Park Bristol 60 F5
Head of Muir Falk 278 E6
Headon Devon 24 G5
Notts 188 F2
Heads S Lanark 268 F4
Headshaw Borders 261 E11
Heads Nook Cumb 239 F11
Headstone London 66 B6
Headwell Fife 279 D11
Heady Hill Gtr Man 195 E10
Heage Derbys 170 E5
Healaugh N Yorks 206 D5
N Yorks 223 F10
Heald Green
Gtr Man 184 D4
Healds Green
Gtr Man 195 F11
Heale Devon 40 D6
Som 28 B5
Som 28 D2
Som 45 E7
Healey Gtr Man 195 D11
N Yorks 214 C3
Northumb 242 F2
W Yorks 197 C8
W Yorks 197 D9
Healey Cote
Northumb 252 C4
Healeyfield Durham 233 B7
Healey Hall
Northumb 242 F2
Healing NE Lincs 201 E8
Heamoor Corn 1 C5
Heaning Cumb 221 F8
Heanish Argyll 288 E2
Heanor Derbys 170 F6
Heanor Gate Derbys 170 F6
Heanton Punchardon
Devon 40 F4
Heap Bridge
Gtr Man 195 E10
Heapham Lincs 188 D5
Hearn Hants 49 F10
Hearnden Green
Kent 53 D10
Hearthstane
Borders 260 D4
Hearthstone Derbys 170 D4
Hearts Delight Kent 69 G11
Heasley Mill Devon 41 G8
Heast Highld 295 D8
Heath Cardiff 59 D7
Derbys 170 B6
Halton 183 E8
Heath and Reach
C Beds 103 F8
Heath Charnock
Lancs 194 E5
Heath Common
W Sus 35 E10
W Yorks 197 D11
Heathcot Aberds 293 C10
Heathcote Derbys 169 C10
Shrops 150 D3
Warks 118 E6
Heath Cross Devon 13 B10
Devon 14 C2
Heath End Bucks 84 F5
Bucks 85 D7
Derbys 153 E7
Hants 64 G2
Hants 64 G5
S Glos 61 B7
Sur 49 D10
W Mid 133 C10
W Sus 35 D7
Warks 118 E4
Heather Leics 153 G7
Heathercombe
Devon 13 E10
Heatherfield Highld 298 E4
Heather Row Hants 49 C8
Heatherside Sur 50 B2
Heatherwood Park
Highld 311 K2
Heatherybanks
Aberds 303 E7
Heathfield Cambs 105 B9
Devon 14 F2
E Sus 37 C9
Glos 80 F2
Hants 33 F9
Lincs 189 C10
N Yorks 214 F2
S Ayrs 257 E9
Som 27 B11
Som 43 G7
Heathfield Village
Oxon 83 B8
Heath Green Hants 48 F6
Worcs 117 C11
Heathhall Dumfries 237 B11
Heath Hayes Staffs 151 G10
Heath Hill Shrops 150 G5
Heath House Som 44 D2
Heathlands
Wokingham 65 F10
Heath Lanes Telford 150 E2
Heath Park London 68 B4
Heathrow Airport
London 66 D5
Heath Side Kent 68 E4
Heathstock Devon 28 G2
Heathton Shrops 132 E6
Heathtop Derbys 152 C4
Heath Town W Mid 133 D8
Heathwaite Cumb 221 F8
N Yorks 225 E9
Heatley Staffs 151 D11
Warr 184 D2
Heaton Gtr Man 195 F7
Lancs 211 G8
Staffs 169 C7
T&W 243 D7
W Yorks 205 G8
Heaton Chapel
Gtr Man 184 C5
Heaton Mersey
Gtr Man 184 C5
Heaton Moor
Gtr Man 184 C5
Heaton Norris
Gtr Man 184 C5
Heaton Royds
W Yorks 205 F8
Heaton's Bridge
Lancs 194 E2
Heaton Shay
W Yorks 205 F8
Heaven's Door Som 29 C10
Heaverham Kent 52 B5
Heaviley Gtr Man 184 D6
Heavitree Devon 14 C4
Hebburn T&W 243 E8
Hebburn Colliery
T&W 243 D8
Hebburn New Town
T&W 243 E8
Hebden N Yorks 213 G10
Hebden Bridge
W Yorks 196 B3
Hebden Green
Ches W 167 B10
Hebing End Herts 104 G6
Hebron Anglesey 179 E7
Carms 92 F3
Northumb 252 F5
Heck Dumfries 248 G3
Heckdyke N Lincs 188 B3
Heckfield Hants 65 G8
Heckfield Green
Suff 126 B3
Heckfordbridge
Essex 107 G8
Heckingham Norf 143 D7
Heckington Lincs 173 G10
Heckmondwike
W Yorks 197 C8
Heddington Wilts 62 F3
Heddington Wick
Wilts 62 F3
Heddle Orkney 314 E3
Heddon Devon 25 B11
Heddon-on-the-Wall
Northumb 242 D4
Hedenham Norf 142 E6
Hedge End Dorset 30 F4
Hants 33 E7
Hedgehog Bridge
Lincs 174 F3
Hedgerley Bucks 66 B3
Hedgerley Green
Bucks 66 B3
Hedgerley Hill Bucks 66 B3
Hedging Som 28 B4
Hedley Hill Durham 233 C9
Hedley on the Hill
Northumb 242 F3
Hednesford Staffs 151 G9
Hedon E Yorks 201 B7
Hedsor Bucks 66 B2
Hedworth T&W 243 E8
Heelands M Keynes 102 D6
Heeley S Yorks 186 E5
Hegdon Hill
Hereford 115 G11
Heggerscales Cumb 222 C6
Heggle Lane Cumb 230 D3
Heglibister Shetland 313 H5
Heighington Darl 233 G11
Lincs 173 B8
Heighley Staffs 168 F3
Height End Lancs 195 C9
Heightington Worcs 116 C5
Heights Gtr Man 196 F3
Heights of Brae
Highld 300 C5
Heights of Kinlochewe
Highld 299 C10
Heilam Highld 308 C4
Heiton Borders 262 C6
Helbeck Cumb 222 B5
Hele Devon 12 C2
Devon 13 G10
Devon 27 G7
Devon 40 D4
Som 27 C11
Torbay 9 B8
Helebridge Corn 24 G2
Helensburgh Argyll 276 E5
Helford Corn 3 D7
Helford Passage Corn 3 D7
Helham Green Herts 86 B5
Helhoughton Norf 159 D7
Helions Bumpstead
Essex 106 C3
Hellaby S Yorks 187 C8
Helland Corn 11 G7
Som 28 C4
Hellandbridge Corn 11 G7
Hell Corner
W Berks 63 G11
Hellesdon Norf 160 G4
Hellesveor Corn 2 A2
Hellidon Northants 119 F10
Hellifield N Yorks 204 B3
Hellifield Green
N Yorks 204 B3
Hellingly E Sus 23 C9
Hellington Norf 142 C6
Hellister Shetland 313 J5
Hellman's Cross
Essex 87 B9
Helm N Yorks 223 G8
Northumb 252 D5
Helmburn Borders 261 E9
Helmdon Northants 101 C11
Helme W Yorks 196 E5
Helmingham Suff 126 F3
Helmington Row
Durham 233 D9
Helmsdale Highld 311 H4
Helmshore Lancs 195 C9
Helmside Cumb 212 B3
Helmsley N Yorks 216 C2
Helperby N Yorks 215 F8
Helperthorpe
N Yorks 217 E9
Helpringham Lincs 173 G10
Helpston Pboro 138 B2
Helsby Ches W 183 F7
Helscott Corn 24 G2
Helsey Lincs 191 G8
Helston Corn 2 D5
Helstone Corn 11 E7
Helston Water Corn 4 G5
Helton Cumb 230 G6
Helwith Bridge
N Yorks 212 F6
Helygain / Halkyn
Flint 182 G2
Hemblington Norf 160 G6
Hemblington Corner
Norf 160 G6
Hembridge Som 44 F5
Hemel Hempstead
Herts 85 D9
Hemerdon Devon 7 D11
Hemford Shrops 130 C6
Hem Heath Stoke 168 G5
Hemingbrough
N Yorks 207 G9
Hemingby Lincs 190 G2
Hemingfield
S Yorks 197 G11
Hemingford Abbots
Cambs 122 C5
Hemingford Grey
Cambs 122 C5
Hemingstone Suff 126 G3
Hemington Leics 153 D9
Northants 137 F11
Som 45 C8
Hemley Suff 108 C5
Hemlington Mbro 225 C10
Hemp Green Suff 127 D7
Hempholme
E Yorks 209 C7
Hempnall Norf 142 E4
Hempnall Green
Norf 142 E4
Hempriggs House
Highld 310 E7
Hemp's Green Essex 107 F8
Hempshill Vale
Notts 171 G8
Hempstead Essex 106 D2
Medway 69 G9
Norf 160 B2
Norf 161 D8
Hempsted Glos 80 B4
Hempton Norf 159 D8
Oxon 101 E8
Hempton Wainhill
Oxon 84 E3
Hemsby Norf 161 F9
Hemsted Kent 54 E6
Hemswell Lincs 188 C6
Hemswell Cliff
Lincs 188 D6
Hemsworth Dorset 31 F7
S Yorks 186 E5
W Yorks 198 E2
Hemyock Devon 27 E10
Henaford Devon 24 D2
Hen Bentref Llandegfan
Anglesey 179 G9
Henbrook Worcs 117 D8
Henbury Bristol 60 D5
Ches E 184 G5
Dorset 18 B5
Hendomen Powys 130 D4
Hendon London 67 B8
T&W 243 F10
Hendra Corn 2 B6
Corn 2 C5
Corn 2 D3
Corn 2 F6
Corn 5 C9
Corn 5 D9
Corn 11 E7
Hendrabridge Corn 6 B5
Hendraburnick Corn 11 D8
Hendra Croft Corn 4 D5
Hendre Flint 165 B11
Gwyn 110 B2
Powys 129 D9
Hendre-ddu Conwy 164 B5
Hendredenny Park
Caerph 58 B6
Hendreforgan
Rhondda 58 B3
Hendrerwydd
Denb 165 C10
Hendrewen
Swansea 75 D10
Hendy Carms 75 E9
Hendy-Gwyn Carms 74 B2
Hendy Gwyn / Whitland
Carms 73 B11
Hên-efail Denb 165 C9
Heneglwys Anglesey 178 F6
Hen-feddau fawr
Pembs 92 E4
Henfield S Glos 61 D7
W Sus 36 D2
Henford Devon 12 C3
Henfords Marsh
Wilts 45 E11
Henghurst Kent 54 F3
Hengoed Caerph 77 F10
Denb 165 D9
Powys 114 G4
Shrops 148 C5
Hengrave Norf 160 F2
Suff 124 D6
Hengrove Bristol 60 F6
Hengrove Park
Bristol 60 F5
Henham Essex 105 F10
Heniarth Powys 130 B2
Henlade Som 28 C3
Henleaze Bristol 60 D5
Henley Dorset 29 G11
Glos 80 B6
Shrops 115 B10
Shrops 131 F9
Som 44 G2
Suff 126 G3
W Sus 34 B5
Wilts 47 B10
Wilts 61 F10
Henley Common
W Sus 34 B5
Henley Green
W Mid 135 G7
Henley-in-Arden
Warks 118 D3
Henley-on-Thames
Oxon 65 C9
Henley's Down E Sus 38 E2
Henley Street Kent 69 F7
Henllan Ceredig 93 C7
Denb 165 B8
Henllan Amgoed
Carms 92 G3
Henlle Shrops 148 C6
Henllys Torf 78 G3
Henllys Vale Torf 78 G3
Henlow C Beds 104 D3
Hennock Devon 14 E2
Henny Street Essex 107 D7
Henryd Conwy 180 G3
Henry's Moat Pembs 91 F10
Hensall N Yorks 198 C5
Henshaw Northumb 241 E7
W Yorks 205 E10
Hensingham Cumb 219 B9
Hensington Oxon 83 B7
Henstead Suff 143 F9
Hensting Hants 33 C7
Henstridge Devon 40 E5
Som 30 D2
Henstridge Ash Som 30 C2
Henstridge Bowden
Som 29 C11
Henstridge Marsh
Som 30 C2
Henton Oxon 84 E3
Som 44 D3
Henwood Corn 11 G11
Oxon 83 E7
Henwood Green Kent 52 E6
Heogan Shetland 313 J6
Heol-ddu Carms 75 E7
Swansea 56 B6
Heolgerrig M Tydf 77 D8
Heol-laethog
Bridgend 58 C2
Heol-las Bridgend 58 C2
Swansea 57 B7
Heol Senni Powys 95 G8
Heol-y-gaer Powys 96 D3
Heol-y-mynydd
V Glam 57 G11
Hepburn Northumb 264 E3
Hepple Northumb 251 C11
Hepscott Northumb 252 G6
Hepthorne Lane
Derbys 170 C6
Heptonstall
W Yorks 196 B3
Hepworth Suff 125 C9
W Yorks 197 F7
Herbrandston Pembs 72 D5
Hereford Hereford 97 C10
Heribusta Highld 298 B4
Heriot Borders 271 E7
Hermiston Edin 280 G3
Hermitage Borders 250 D2
Dorset 29 F10
W Berks 64 E4
W Sus 22 B3
Hermitage Green
Mers 183 C10
Hermit Hill
S Yorks 197 G10
Hermit Hole
W Yorks 205 F7
Hermon Anglesey 162 B5
Carms 93 E7
Carms 94 F3
Pembs 92 E4
Herne Kent 71 F7
Herne Bay Kent 71 F7
Herne Common Kent 71 F7
Herne Hill London 67 E10
Herne Pound Kent 53 C7
Herner Devon 25 B9
Hernhill Kent 70 G5
Herniss Corn 2 C6
Herodsfoot Corn 6 C4
Heron Cross Stoke 168 G5
Heronden Kent 55 C9
Herongate Essex 87 G10
Heronsford S Ayrs 244 G4
Heronsgate Herts 85 G8
Heron's Ghyll E Sus 37 B7
Herons Green Bath 44 B5
Heronston Bridgend 58 D2
Herra Shetland 312 D8
Herriard Hants 49 D7
Herringfleet Suff 143 D9
Herring's Green
Beds 103 C11
Herringswell Suff 124 C4
Herringthorpe
S Yorks 186 C6
Hersden Kent 71 G8
Hersham Corn 24 F3
Sur 66 G6
Herstmonceux
E Sus 23 C10
Herston Dorset 18 F6
Orkney 314 G4
Hertford Herts 86 C4
Hertford Heath Herts 86 C4
Hertingfordbury
Herts 86 C4
Hesketh Bank Lancs 194 C2
Hesketh Lane Lancs 203 E8
Hesketh Moss Lancs 194 C2
Hesket Newmarket
Cumb 230 D2
Heskin Green Lancs 194 D4
Hesleden Durham 234 D4
Hesleyside
Northumb 251 G8
Heslington York 207 C8
Hessay York 206 C6
Hessenford Corn 6 D6
Hessett Suff 125 E8
Hessle E Yorks 200 B4
W Yorks 198 D2
Hest Bank Lancs 211 F9
Hester's Way Glos 99 G8
Hestinsetter
Shetland 313 J4
Heston London 66 D6
Hestwall Orkney 314 E2
Heswall Mers 182 E3
Hethe Oxon 101 F11
Hethel Norf 142 C3
Hethelpit Cross Glos 98 F5
Hethersett Norf 142 C3
Hethersgill Cumb 239 D11
Hetherside Cumb 239 D10
Hetherson Green
Ches W 167 F8
Hethpool Northumb 263 D9
Hett Durham 233 D11
Hetton N Yorks 204 B5
Hetton Downs T&W 234 B3
Hetton-le-Hill T&W 234 B3
Hetton-le-Hole
T&W 234 B3
Hetton Steads
Northumb 264 B2
Heugh Northumb 242 C3
Heugh-head Aberds 292 B5
Heveningham Suff 126 C6
Hever Kent 52 E3
Heversham Cumb 211 C9
Hevingham Norf 160 E3
Hewas Water Corn 5 F9
Hewelsfield Glos 79 E9
Hewelsfield Common
Glos 79 E8
Hewer Hill Cumb 230 D3
Hew Green
N Yorks 205 B10
Hewish N Som 60 G2
Som 28 F6
Hewood Dorset 28 G5
Heworth T&W 243 E7
York 207 C8
Hexham Northumb 241 E10
Hextable Kent 68 E4
Hexthorpe S Yorks 198 G5
Hexton Herts 104 E2
Hexworthy Devon 13 G9
Hey Lancs 204 E3
Heybridge Essex 87 F10
Essex 88 D5
Heybridge Basin
Essex 88 D5
Heybrook Bay Devon 7 F10
Heydon Cambs 105 C8
Norf 160 D2
Heydour Lincs 155 B10
Hey Green W Yorks 196 E4
Heyheads Gtr Man 196 G3
Hey Houses Lancs 193 B10
Heylipol Argyll 288 E1
Heylor Shetland 312 E4
Heyope Powys 114 C4
Heyrod Gtr Man 185 B7
Heysham Lancs 211 G8
Heyshaw N Yorks 214 G3
Heyshott W Sus 34 D5
Heyshott Green
W Sus 34 D5
Heyside Gtr Man 196 F2
Heytesbury Wilts 46 E2
Heythrop Oxon 101 F7
Heywood Gtr Man 195 E11
Wilts 45 C11
Hibaldstow N Lincs 200 G3
Hibb's Green Suff 125 G7
Hickford Hill Essex 106 C5
Hickleton S Yorks 198 F3
Hickling Norf 161 E8
Notts 154 D3
Hickling Green Norf 161 E8
Hickling Heath Norf 161 E8
Hickling Pastures
Notts 154 D3
Hickmans Green
Kent 54 B5
Hicks Forstal Kent 71 G7
Hicks Gate Bath 60 F6
Hick's Mill Corn 4 G5
Hickstead W Sus 36 C3
Hidcote Bartrim
Glos 100 C3
Hidcote Boyce Glos 100 C3
Hifnal Shrops 132 D4
Higginshaw
Gtr Man 196 F2
High Ackworth
W Yorks 198 D2
Higham Derbys 170 D5
Fife 286 F6
Kent 69 E8
Lancs 204 F2
S Yorks 197 F10
Suff 107 D10
Suff 124 E4
Higham Common
S Yorks 197 F10
Higham Dykes
Northumb 242 B4
Higham Ferrers
Northants 121 D9
Higham Gobion
C Beds 104 E2
Higham Hill London 86 G5
Higham on the Hill
Leics 135 D7
Highampton Devon 25 G7
Highams Park
London 86 G5
Higham Wood Kent 52 D5
High Angerton
Northumb 252 F3
High Bankhill Cumb 231 C7
High Banton
N Lanark 278 E4
High Barn Lincs 174 C5
High Barnes T&W 243 F9
High Barnet London 86 F2
High Beach Essex 86 F6
High Bentham
N Yorks 212 F3
High Bickington
Devon 25 C10
High Biggins Cumb 212 D2
High Birkwith
N Yorks 212 D5
High Birstwith
N Yorks 205 B10
High Blantyre
S Lanark 268 D3
High Bonnybridge
Falk 278 F6
High Bradfield
S Yorks 186 C3
High Bradley
N Yorks 204 D6
High Bray Devon 41 G7
Highbridge Cumb 230 C3
Hants 33 C7
Highld 290 E3
Som 43 D10
W Mid 133 C10
Highbrook W Sus 51 G11
High Brooms Kent 52 E5
High Brotheridge
Glos 80 C5
High Bullen Devon 25 C8
Highburton
W Yorks 197 E7
Highbury London 67 B10
Ptsmth 33 G11
Som 45 D7
Highbury Vale
Nottingham 171 G8
High Buston
Northumb 252 B6
High Callerton
Northumb 242 C5
High Cark Cumb 211 C7
High Casterton
Cumb 212 D2
High Catton
E Yorks 207 C10
High Church
Northumb 252 F5
Highclere Hants 64 G2
Highcliffe Derbys 186 F2
Dorset 19 C10
High Cogges Oxon 82 D5
High Common Norf 141 B9
High Coniscliffe
Darl 224 B4
High Crompton
Gtr Man 196 F2
High Cross Cambs 123 F8
Corn 2 D6
E Sus 37 B9
Hants 34 B2
Herts 85 F10
Herts 86 B5
Newport 59 B9
W Sus 36 D2
Warks 118 D3
High Crosshill
S Lanark 268 C2
High Cunsey Cumb 221 G7
High Dubmire T&W 234 B2
High Dyke Durham 232 F5
High Easter Essex 87 C10
High Eggborough
N Yorks 198 C5
High Eldrig
Dumfries 236 C4
High Ellington
N Yorks 214 C3
Higher Alham Som 45 E7
Higher Ansty Dorset 30 G3
Higher Ashton Devon 14 E3
Higher Audley
Blackburn 195 B7
Higher Bal Corn 4 E4
Higher Ballam
Lancs 202 G3
Higher Bartle Lancs 202 G6
Higher Bebington
Mers 182 D4
Higher Berry End
C Beds 103 E9
Higher Blackley
Gtr Man 195 G10
Higher Boarshaw
Gtr Man 195 F11
Higher Bockhampton
Dorset 17 C10
Higher Bojewyan Corn 1 C3
Higher Boscaswell
Corn 1 C3
Higher Brixham
Torbay 9 D8
Higher Broughton
Gtr Man 195 G10
Higher Burrow Som 28 C6
Higher Burwardsley
Ches W 167 D8
High Ercall Telford 149 F11
Higher Chalmington
Dorset 29 G9
Higher Cheriton
Devon 27 G10
Higher Chillington
Som 28 E5
Higher Chisworth
Derbys 185 C7
Highercliff Corn 6 D4
Higher Clovelly
Devon 24 C4
Higher Condurrow
Corn 2 B5
Higher Crackington
Corn 11 B9
Higher Cransworth
Corn 5 B9
Higher Croft
Blackburn 195 B7
Higher Denham
Bucks 66 B4
Higher Dinting
Derbys 185 C8
Higher Disley
Ches E 185 E7
Higher Downs Corn 2 C3
Higher Durston Som 28 B3
Higher End Gtr Man 194 G4
Higher Folds
Gtr Man 195 G7
Higherford Lancs 204 E3
Higher Gabwell Torbay 9 B8
Higher Green
Gtr Man 195 G8
Higher Halstock Leigh
Dorset 29 F8
Higher Heysham
Lancs 211 G8
Higher Hogshead
Lancs 195 C11
Higher Holton Som 29 B11
Higher Hurdsfield
Ches E 184 G6
Higher Kingcombe
Dorset 16 B6
Higher Kinnerton
Flint 166 C4
Higher Land Corn 12 G3
Higher Marsh Som 30 C2
Higher Melcombe
Dorset 30 G2
Higher Menadew
Corn 5 D10
Higher Molland
Devon 41 G8
Higher Muddiford
Devon 40 F5
Higher Nyland Dorset 30 C2
Higher Penwortham
Lancs 194 B4
Higher Pertwood
Wilts 45 F11
Higher Porthpean
Corn 5 E10

Hig–Hoo 389

Higher Poynton
Ches E 184 E6
Higher Prestacott
Devon 12 B3
Higher Rads End
C Beds 103 E9
Higher Ridge
Shrops 149 C7
Higher Rocombe Barton
Devon 9 B8
Higher Row Dorset 31 G8
Higher Runcorn
Halton 183 E8
Higher Sandford
Dorset 29 C10
Higher Shotton
Flint 166 B4
Higher Shurlach
Ches W 183 G11
Higher Slade Devon 40 D4
Higher Street Som 42 E6
Higher Tale Devon 27 G9
Higher Tolcarne Corn 5 B7
Higher Totnell
Dorset 29 F10
Highertown Corn 4 G6
Corn 11 E8
Higher Town Corn 5 C10
Scilly 1 F4
Som 42 D3
Higher Tremarcoombe
Corn 6 B5
Higher Vexford Som 42 F6
Higher Walreddon
Devon 12 G5
Higher Walton
Lancs 194 B5
Warr 183 D9
Higher Wambrook
Som 28 F3
Higher Warcombe
Devon 40 D3
Higher Weaver
Devon 27 G9
Higher Whatcombe
Dorset 30 G4
Higher Wheelton
Lancs 194 C6
Higher Whitley
Ches W 183 E10
Higher Wincham
Ches W 183 F11
Higher Woodsford
Dorset 17 D11
Higher Wraxall
Dorset 29 G9
Higher Wych
Ches W 167 G7
High Etherley
Durham 233 F9
High Ferry Lincs 174 F5
Highfield E Yorks 207 F10
Glos 79 E10
Gtr Man 194 G5
Gtr Man 195 F8
Herts 85 D9
N Ayrs 266 E6
Oxon 101 G11
S Yorks 186 D5
Soton 32 E6
T&W 242 F4
High Field Lancs 203 C10
Highfields Cambs 123 F7
Derbys 170 B6
Essex 88 B5
Glos 80 F3
Leicester 136 C2
Northumb 273 E9
S Yorks 198 F4
Staffs 151 E8
High Flatts W Yorks 197 F8
High Forge Durham 242 G6
High Friarside
Durham 242 F5
High Gallowhill
E Dunb 278 G2
High Garrett Essex 106 F5
Highgate E Sus 52 G2
Kent 53 G9
London 67 B9
Powys 130 D2
S Yorks 198 G3
W Mid 133 F11
High Grange
Durham 233 E9
High Grantley
N Yorks 214 F4
High Green
Cumb 221 E8
Norf 141 B8
Norf 142 B2
Norf 159 G8
S Yorks 186 B4
Shrops 132 G4
Suff 125 E7
W Yorks 197 E7
Worcs 99 B7
High Halden Kent 53 F11
High Halstow
Medway 69 D9
High Ham Som 44 G2
High Handenhold
Durham 242 G6
High Harrington
Cumb 228 F6
High Harrogate
N Yorks 206 B2
High Haswell
Durham 234 C3
High Hatton Shrops 150 E2
High Hauxley
Northumb 253 C7
High Hawsker
N Yorks 227 D8
High Heath Shrops 150 D3
W Mid 133 C10
High Hesket Cumb 230 C5
High Hesleden
Durham 234 D5
High Hill Cumb 229 G11
High Houses Essex 87 C11
High Hoyland
S Yorks 197 E9
High Hunsley
E Yorks 208 F4
High Hurstwood
E Sus 37 B7
High Hutton
N Yorks 216 F5
High Ireby Cumb 229 D10
High Kelling Norf 177 E10
High Kilburn
N Yorks 215 D10
High Lands Durham 233 F8
Highlane Ches E 168 B5
Derbys 186 E6
High Lane Gtr Man 185 D7
Worcs 116 E3
Highlanes Corn 10 G4
Staffs 150 C5
High Lanes Corn 2 B3
High Laver Essex 87 D8
Highlaws Cumb 229 B8
Highleadon Glos 98 G5
High Legh Ches E 184 E2
Highleigh W Sus 22 D4
High Leven Stockton 225 C8
Highley Shrops 132 G4
High Littleton Bath 44 B6
High Longthwaite
Cumb 229 B11
High Lorton Cumb 229 F9
High Marishes
N Yorks 216 D6
High Marnham
Notts 188 G4
High Melton
S Yorks 198 G4
High Mickley
Northumb 242 E3
High Mindork
Dumfries 236 D5
Highmoor Cumb 229 B11
Oxon 65 B8
High Moor Derbys 187 E7
Lancs 194 E4
Highmoor Cross
Oxon 65 C8
Highmoor Hill Mon 60 B3
High Moorsley T&W 234 B2
Highnam Glos 80 B3
Highnam Green Glos 98 G5
High Nash Glos 79 C9
High Newton Cumb 211 C8
High Newton-by-the-Sea Northumb 264 D6
High Nibthwaite
Cumb 210 B5
Highoak Norf 141 C11
High Oaks Cumb 222 G2
High Offley Staffs 150 D5
High Ongar Essex 87 E9
High Onn Staffs 150 F6
High Onn Wharf
Staffs 150 F6
High Park Cumb 221 G10
Mers 193 D11
Highridge Bristol 60 F5
High Risby N Lincs 200 E2
Highroad Well Moor
W Yorks 196 B5
High Roding Essex 87 B10
High Rougham Suff 125 E8
High Row Cumb 230 D3
Cumb 230 G3
High Salvington
W Sus 35 F10
High Scales Cumb 229 B9
High Sellafield
Cumb 219 E10
High Shaw N Yorks 223 G7
High Shields T&W 243 D9
High Shincliffe
Durham 233 C11
High Side Cumb 229 E10
High Southwick
T&W 243 F9
High Spen T&W 242 F4
High Stakesby
N Yorks 227 C7
Highstead Kent 71 F8
Highsted Kent 70 G2
High Stoop Durham 233 C8
Highstreet Kent 70 G5
High Street Corn 5 E9
Kent 53 G8
Pembs 73 B11
Suff 107 B7
Suff 127 C8
Suff 127 F8
Suff 143 G7
Highstreet Green
Essex 106 E5
Sur 50 F3
High Street Green
Suff 125 F10
High Sunderland
Borders 261 C11
Hightae Dumfries 238 B3
Highter's Heath
W Mid 117 B11
High Throston
Hrtlpl 234 E5
High Tirfergus
Argyll 255 F7
Hightown Ches E 168 C5
Hants 31 G11
Mers 193 G10
Soton 33 E7
W Yorks 197 C7
Wrex 166 F4
High Town Luton 103 G11
Shrops 132 E4
Staffs 151 G9
Hightown Green
Suff 125 F9
Hightown Heights
W Yorks 197 C7
High Toynton Lincs 174 B3
High Trewhitt
Northumb 252 B2
High Urpeth
Durham 242 G6
High Valleyfield
Fife 279 D10
High Walton Cumb 219 C9
High Warden
Northumb 241 D10
High Water Head
Cumb 220 F6
Highway Corn 4 G4
Hereford 97 B9
Som 29 C7
Wilts 62 E4
Highway *continued*
Windsor 65 C11
Highweek Devon 14 G2
High Westwood
Durham 242 F4
High Whinnow
Cumb 239 G8
Highwood Devon 27 F10
Dorset 18 D3
Essex 87 E10
Hants 31 F11
Worcs 116 D3
Highwood Hill
London 86 G2
High Woolaston Glos 79 F9
High Worsall
N Yorks 225 D7
Highworth Swindon 82 G2
Highworthy Devon 24 F6
High Wray Cumb 221 F7
High Wych Herts 87 C7
High Wycombe
Bucks 84 G5
Hilborough Norf 140 C6
Hilborough Ho Norf 140 C6
Hilcot Glos 81 B7
Hilcote Derbys 171 D7
Hilcot End Glos 81 E9
Hilcott Wilts 46 B6
Hildenborough Kent 52 D5
Hilden Park Kent 52 D5
Hildersham Cambs 105 B10
Hildersley Hereford 98 G2
Hilderstone Staffs 151 C8
Hilderthorpe
E Yorks 218 F3
Hilfield Dorset 29 F10
Hilgay Norf 140 D2
Hill S Glos 79 G10
W Mid 134 D2
Warks 119 D9
Hillam N Yorks 198 B4
Hillbeck Cumb 222 B5
Hillblock Pembs 73 B8
Hillborough Kent 71 F8
Hill Bottom Oxon 64 D6
Hillbourne Poole 18 C6
Hillbrae Aberds 302 E6
Aberds 303 G7
Hill Brow W Sus 34 B3
Hillbutts Dorset 31 G7
Hill Chorlton Staffs 150 B5
Hillclifflane Derbys 170 F3
Hillcommon Som 27 B11
Hill Common Norf 161 E8
Hill Corner Som 45 D10
Hill Croome Worcs 99 C7
Hillcross Derbys 152 C6
Hill Dale Lancs 194 E3
Hill Deverill Wilts 45 E11
Hilldyke Lincs 174 F4
Hill Dyke Lincs 174 F4
Hillend Fife 280 E2
N Lanark 268 B6
N Som 43 B11
Shrops 132 E6
Swansea 56 C2
Hill End Durham 232 D6
Fife 279 B10
Glos 99 D8
London 85 G8
N Yorks 205 C7
Som 29 E8
Worcs 117 E8
Hillend Green Glos 98 F4
Hillersland Glos 79 C9
Hillerton Devon 13 B10
Hillesden Bucks 102 F3
Hillesden Hamlet
Bucks 102 E3
Hillesley Glos 61 B9
Hillfarance Som 27 C11
Hillfarrance Som 27 C11
Hillfield Devon 8 E6
W Mid 118 B2
Hillfields S Glos 60 D6
W Mid 118 B6
Hillfoot Aberds 303 D9
W Yorks 205 G10
Hillfoot End C Beds 104 E2
Hill Furze Worcs 99 B9
Hill Gate Hereford 97 F9
Hillgreen W Berks 64 D3
Hill Green Essex 105 E9
Kent 69 G10
Hillgrove W Sus 34 B6
Hillhampton
Hereford 97 B11
Hillhead
Aberds 302 F5
Aberds 303 G8
Corn 5 C11
Devon 9 E8
E Ayrs 257 B10
S Ayrs 257 F10
Hill Head Hants 33 G8
Northumb 241 D10
Hillhead of Auchentumb
Aberds 303 D9
Hillhead of Blairy
Aberds 302 D6
Hillhead of Cocklaw
Aberds 303 E10
Hill Hoath Kent 52 E3
Hill Hook W Mid 134 C2
Hillhouse Borders 271 D10
Hill Houses Shrops 116 B2
Hilliard's Cross
Staffs 152 G3
Hilliclay Highld 310 C5
Hillingdon London 66 C5
Hillingdon Heath
London 66 C5
Hillington Glasgow 267 C10
Norf 158 D4
Hillis Corner IoW 20 C5
Hillmoor Devon 27 E10
Hillmorton Warks 119 C10
Hill Mountain Pembs 73 D7
Hillockhead Aberds 292 B6
Aberds 292 C5
Hillock Vale Lancs 195 B9
Hill of Beath Fife 280 C3
Hill of Drip Stirling 278 B5
Hill of Fearn Highld 301 B8
Hill of Keillor Angus 286 C6
Hill of Mountblairy
Aberds 302 D6
Hill of Overbrae
Aberds 303 C8
Hill Park Hants 33 F9
Kent 52 B2
Hillpool Worcs 117 B7
Hillpound Hants 33 D9
Hill Ridware Staffs 151 F11
Hillsborough
S Yorks 186 C4
Hillside Aberds 293 D11
Angus 293 G9
Devon 8 C4
Devon 27 F11
Hants 49 C9
Mers 193 E10
Orkney 314 D3
Orkney 314 G4
Shetland 313 G6
Shrops 131 F11
Wilts 81 G9
Hill Side Hants 34 B3
S Yorks 197 G8
W Yorks 197 D7
Worcs 116 E5
Hill Somersal
Derbys 152 C2
Hills Town Derbys 171 B7
Hillstreet Hants 32 D4
Hill Street Kent 54 D6
Hillswick Shetland 312 F4
Hilltop Bl Gwent 77 D11
Bucks 85 E7
Derbys 170 C4
Hill Top Derbys 186 F5
Durham 232 G5
Durham 233 C10
Durham 242 G5
Gtr Man 195 G8
Hants 32 G6
N Yorks 214 G3
N Yorks 214 G5
Notts 171 F7
S Yorks 186 C5
S Yorks 186 D3
S Yorks 187 B7
S Yorks 197 F9
Staffs 133 B7
W Mid 133 E9
W Sus 34 C5
W Yorks 196 E5
W Yorks 197 D10
W Yorks 205 G7
W Yorks 205 G11
Warks 134 E5
Warks 135 E7
Hillview T&W 243 G9
Hill View Dorset 18 B5
Hillway IoW 21 D8
Hillwell Shetland 313 M5
Hill Wood W Mid 134 C2
Hill Wootton Warks 118 D6
Hillyfields Hants 32 D5
Hilmarton Wilts 62 D4
Hilperton Wilts 45 B11
Hilperton Marsh
Wilts 45 B11
Hilsea Ptsmth 33 G11
Hilston E Yorks 209 G11
Hiltingbury Hants 32 C6
Hilton Aberds 303 F9
Borders 273 E7
Cambs 122 D5
Cumb 231 G10
Derbys 152 C4
Dorset 30 G3
Durham 233 G9
Highld 309 L7
Highld 311 L3
Shrops 132 D5
Staffs 133 B11
Stockton 225 C9
Hilton House
Gtr Man 194 F6
Hilton Lodge Highld 300 G2
Hilton of Cadboll
Highld 301 B8
Hilton Park
Gtr Man 195 G10
Himbleton Worcs 117 F8
Himley Staffs 133 E7
Hincaster Cumb 211 C10
Hinchley Wood Sur 67 F7
Hinchliffe Mill
W Yorks 196 F6
Hinchwick Glos 100 E2
Hinckley Leics 135 E8
Hinderclay Suff 125 B10
Hinderton Ches W 182 F4
Hinderwell N Yorks 226 B5
Hindford Shrops 148 C6
Hindhead Sur 49 F11
Hindle Fold Lancs 203 G10
Hindley Gtr Man 194 G6
Northumb 242 F2
Hindley Green
Gtr Man 194 G6
Hindlip Worcs 117 F7
Hindolveston Norf 159 D10
Hindon Wilts 46 G2
Hindpool Cumb 210 F3
Hindringham Norf 159 B9
Hindsford Gtr Man 195 G7
Hingham Norf 141 C10
Hinstock Shrops 150 D3
Hintlesham Suff 107 C11
Hinton
Glos 79 E11
Hants 19 B10
Hereford 96 D6
Northants 119 G10
S Glos 61 D8
Shrops 131 B8
Som 29 C10
Hinton Ampner Hants 33 B9
Hinton Blewett Bath 44 B5
Hinton Charterhouse
Bath 45 B9
Hinton Cross Worcs 99 C10
Hinton-in-the-Hedges
Northants 101 D11
Hinton Martell Dorset 31 F8
Hinton on the Green
Worcs 99 C10
Hinton Parva Dorset 31 G7
Swindon 63 C8
Hinton St George
Som 28 E6
Hinton St Mary
Dorset 30 D3
Hinton Waldrist Oxon 82 F5
Hints Shrops 116 C2
Staffs 134 C3
Hinwick Beds 121 E8
Hinwood Shrops 131 B7
Hinxhill Kent 54 E5
Hinxton Cambs 105 B9
Hinxworth Herts 104 C4
Hipperholme
W Yorks 196 B6
Hipplecote Worcs 116 F4
Hipsburn Northumb 264 G6
Hipswell N Yorks 224 F3
Hirael Gwyn 179 G9
Hiraeth Carms 92 G3
Hirn Aberds 293 C9
Hirnant Powys 147 E11
Hirst N Lanark 269 C7
Northumb 253 F7
Hirst Courtney
N Yorks 198 C6
Hirwaen Denb 165 C10
Hirwaun Rhondda 77 D7
Hirwaun Common
Bridgend 58 C2
Hiscott Devon 25 B8
Hislop Borders 249 C9
Hisomley Wilts 45 D11
Histon Cambs 123 E8
Hitcham Suff 125 G9
Hitchill Dumfries 238 D4
Hitchin Herts 104 F3
Hitchin Hill Herts 104 F3
Hitcombe Bottom
Wilts 45 E10
Hither Green London 67 E11
Hittisleigh Devon 13 C10
Hittisleigh Barton
Devon 13 B10
Hive E Yorks 208 G2
Hixon Staffs 151 D10
Hoaden Kent 55 B9
Hoar Cross Staffs 152 E2
Hoarwithy Hereford 97 F10
Hoath Kent 71 G8
Hoath Corner Kent 52 E3
Hobarris Shrops 114 B6
Hobbister Orkney 314 F3
Hobble End Staffs 133 B10
Hobbles Green Suff 124 G4
Hobbs Cross Essex 87 C7
Essex 87 F7
Hobbs Wall Bath 61 G7
Hob Hill Ches W 167 E7
Hobkirk Borders 262 G3
Hobroyd Derbys 185 C8
Hobson Durham 242 F5
Hoby Leics 154 F3
Hoccombe Som 27 B10
Hockenden London 68 F3
Hockerill Herts 105 G9
Hockering Norf 159 G11
Hockering Heath
Norf 159 G11
Hockerton Notts 172 D2
Hockholler Som 27 C11
Hockholler Green
Som 27 C11
Hockley Ches E 184 E6
Essex 88 G4
Kent 54 B3
Staffs 134 C4
W Mid 118 B5
Hockley Heath
W Mid 118 C3
Hockliffe C Beds 103 F9
Hockwold cum Wilton
Norf 140 F4
Hockworthy Devon 27 D8
Hocombe Hants 32 C6
Hoddesdon Herts 86 D5
Hoddlesden
Blackburn 195 C8
Hoddomcross
Dumfries 238 C5
Hoddom Mains
Dumfries 238 C5
Hoden Worcs 99 B11
Hodgefield Staffs 168 E6
Hodgehill Ches E 168 B4
W Mid 134 F2
Hodgeston Pembs 73 F8
Hodley Powys 130 E3
Hodnet Shrops 150 D2
Hodnetheath
Shrops 150 D2
Hodsock Notts 187 D10
Hodsoll Street Kent 68 G6
Hodson Swindon 63 C7
Hodthorpe Derbys 187 F8
Hoe
Hants 33 D9
Norf 159 F9
Sur 50 D5
Hoe Benham
W Berks 64 F2
Hoe Gate Hants 33 E10
Hoff Cumb 222 B3
Hoffleet Stow Lincs 156 B4
Hogaland Shetland 312 F5
Hogben's Hill Kent 54 B4
Hogganfield
Glasgow 268 B2
Hoggard's Green
Suff 125 F7
Hoggeston Bucks 102 G6
Hoggington Wilts 45 B10
Hoggrill's End
Warks 134 E4
Hogha Gearraidh
W Isles 296 D3
Hog Hatch Sur 49 D10
Hoghton Lancs 194 B6
Hoghton Bottoms
Lancs 194 B6
Hogley Green
W Yorks 196 F6
Hognaston Derbys 170 E2
Hogpits Bottom
Herts 85 E8
Hogsthorpe Lincs 191 G8
Hogstock Dorset 31 F7
Holbeach Lincs 157 E7
Holbeach Bank
Lincs 157 D7
Holbeach Clough
Lincs 156 D6
Holbeach Drove
Lincs 156 G6
Holbeache Worcs 116 B5
Holbeach Hurn
Lincs 157 D7
Holbeach St Johns
Lincs 156 F6
Holbeach St Marks
Lincs 157 C7
Holbeach St Matthew
Lincs 157 C8
Holbeck Notts 187 G8
W Yorks 205 G11
Holbeck Woodhouse
Notts 187 G8
Holberrow Green
Worcs 117 F10
Holbeton Devon 8 E2
Holborn London 67 C10
Holborough Kent 69 G8
Holbrook Derbys 170 G5
S Yorks 186 E6
Suff 108 D3
Holbrook Common
S Glos 61 E7
Holbrook Moor
Derbys 170 F5
Holbrooks W Mid 134 G6
Holburn Northumb 264 B2
Holbury Hants 32 G6
Holcombe Devon 14 G5
Gtr Man 195 D9
Som 45 D7
Holcombe Brook
Gtr Man 195 E9
Holcombe Rogus
Devon 27 D9
Holcot Northants 120 D5
Holdbrook London 86 F5
Holden Lancs 203 D11
Holdenby Northants 120 D3
Holden Fold
Gtr Man 196 F2
Holdenhurst Bmouth 19 B8
Holder's Green
Essex 106 F2
Holders Hill London 86 G2
Holdfast Worcs 99 D7
Holdgate Shrops 131 F11
Holdingham Lincs 173 F9
Holditch Dorset 28 G4
Holdsworth
W Yorks 196 B5
Holdworth S Yorks 186 C3
Hole Devon 24 D4
W Yorks 204 F6
Hole Bottom
W Yorks 196 C2
Holefield Borders 263 C8
Holehills N Lanark 268 B5
Holehouse Derbys 185 C8
Holehouses Ches E 184 F2
Hole-in-the-Wall
Hereford 98 F2
Holemill Aberdeen 293 C10
Holemoor Devon 24 F6
Hole's Hole Devon 7 B8
Holestane Dumfries 247 D9
Holestone Derbys 170 C4
Hole Street W Sus 35 E10
Holewater Devon 41 F8
Holford Som 43 E7
Holgate York 207 C7
Holker Cumb 211 D7
Holkham Norf 176 E5
Hollacombe Devon 24 G5
Devon 26 G4
Hollacombe Hill
Devon 7 E10
Holland Orkney 314 A4
Orkney 314 D6
Sur 52 C2
Holland Fen Lincs 174 F2
Holland Lees Lancs 194 F4
Holland-on-Sea
Essex 89 B12
Hollands Som 29 D9
Hollandstoun
Orkney 314 A7
Hollee Dumfries 239 D7
Hollesley Suff 109 C7
Hollicombe Torbay 9 C7
Hollies Common
Staffs 150 E6
Hollinfare Warr 183 C11
Hollingbourne Kent 53 B10
Hollingbury Brighton 36 F4
Hollingdean Brighton 36 F4
Hollingdon Bucks 103 F7
Hollingrove E Sus 37 C11
Hollingthorpe
W Yorks 197 D10
Hollington Derbys 152 B4
E Sus 38 E3
Hants 48 B2
Staffs 151 B11
Hollington Cross
Hants 48 B2
Hollington Grove
Derbys 152 B4
Hollingwood Derbys 186 G6
Hollingworth
Gtr Man 185 B8
Hollin Hall Lancs 204 F4
Hollin Park W Yorks 206 F2
Hollins
Cumb 222 G3
Derbys 186 G4
Gtr Man 195 F8
Gtr Man 195 F10
Gtr Man 195 F11
Staffs 168 D6
Staffs 168 E4
Staffs 169 F7
Hollinsclough Staffs 169 B9
Hollins End S Yorks 186 E5
Hollinsgreen
Ches E 168 C2
Hollins Green
Warr 183 C11
Hollins Lane Lancs 202 C5
Shrops 149 B10
Hollinswood Telford 132 B4
Hollinthorpe
W Yorks 206 G3
Hollinwood
Gtr Man 196 G2
Shrops 149 B10
Hollis Green Devon 27 F9
Hollis Head Devon 27 G7
Hollocombe Devon 25 E10
Hollocombe Town
Devon 25 E10
Holloway Derbys 170 D4
Wilts 45 G11
Windsor 65 C10
Holloway Hill Sur 50 E3
Hollow Brook Bath 60 G5
Hollowell Northants 120 C3
Hollow Meadows
S Yorks 186 D2
Hollowmoor Heath
Ches W 167 B7
Hollow Oak Dorset 18 C2
Hollows Dumfries 239 B9
Hollow Street Kent 71 G8
Holly Bank W Mid 133 C11
Hollyberry End
W Mid 134 G5
Holly Brook Som 44 D4
Hollybush Caerph 77 E11
E Ayrs 257 G9
Stoke 168 G5
Torf 78 G3
Worcs 98 D5
Holly Bush Wrex 166 G6
Hollybush Corner
Bucks 66 B3
Suff 125 F8
Hollybushes Kent 54 B2
Hollybush Hill Bucks 66 C3
Essex 89 B10
Hollycroft Leics 135 E8
Holly Cross Windsor 65 C10
Holly End Norf 139 B9
Holly Green Bucks 84 E3
Worcs 99 C7
Holly Hill N Yorks 224 E3
Hollyhurst Shrops 131 D9
Warks 135 F7
Hollym E Yorks 201 B10
Hollywaste Shrops 116 B2
Hollywater Hants 49 G10
Hollywood Worcs 117 B11
Holmacott Devon 25 B8
Holman Clavel Som 28 D2
Holmbridge
W Yorks 196 F6
Holmbury St Mary
Sur 50 E6
Holmbush Corn 5 E10
Dorset 28 G5
Holmcroft Staffs 151 D8
Holme C Beds 104 C3
Cambs 138 F3
Cumb 211 D10
N Lincs 200 F2
N Yorks 215 C7
Notts 172 D4
W Yorks 196 F6
W Yorks 205 G9
Holmebridge Dorset 18 D3
Holme Chapel
Lancs 195 B11
Holme Green
C Beds 104 C3
N Yorks 207 E7
Wokingham 65 F10
Holme Hale Norf 141 B7
Holme Hill NE Lincs 201 F9
Holme Lacy
Hereford 97 D11
Holme Lane Notts 154 B2
Holme Marsh
Hereford 114 G6
Holme Mills Cumb 211 D10
Holme next the Sea
Norf 176 E2
Holme-on-Spalding-Moor E Yorks 208 F2
Holme on the Wolds
E Yorks 208 D5
Holme Pierrepont
Notts 154 B2
Holmer Hereford 97 C10
Holmer Green Bucks 84 F6
Holmes Lancs 194 D2
Holme St Cuthbert
Cumb 229 B8
Holmes Chapel
Ches E 168 B3
Holmesdale Derbys 186 F5
Holmesfield Derbys 186 F4
Holme Slack Lancs 203 G7
Holmes's Hill E Sus 23 C8
Holmeswood Lancs 194 D2
Holmethorpe Sur 51 C9
Holmewood Derbys 170 B6
Holme Wood
W Yorks 205 G9
Holmfield W Yorks 196 B5
Holmfirth W Yorks 196 F6
Holmhead Angus 293 F7
Dumfries 246 F6
E Ayrs 258 E3
Holmhill Dumfries 247 D9
Holmisdale Highld 297 G7
Holmley Common
Derbys 186 F5
Holmpton E Yorks 201 C11
Holmrook Cumb 219 F11
Holmsgarth Shetland 313 J6
Holmside Durham 233 B10
Holmsleigh Green
Devon 28 G2
Holmston S Ayrs 257 E9
Holmwood Corner
Sur 51 E7
Holmwrangle Cumb 230 B6
Holne Devon 8 B4
Holnest Dorset 29 E11
Holnicote Som 42 D2
Holsworthy Devon 24 G4
Holsworthy Beacon
Devon 24 F5
Holt Dorset 31 G8
Hants 49 C8
Mers 183 C7
Norf 159 B11
Wilts 61 G11
Holt *continued*
Worcs 116 E6
Wrex 166 E6
Holtby York 207 C9
Holt End Hants 49 F7
Worcs 117 D11
Holt Fleet Worcs 116 E6
Holt Green Lancs 193 G11
Holt Head W Yorks 196 E5
Holt Heath Dorset 31 G9
Worcs 116 E6
Holt Hill Kent 53 B8
Staffs 152 D2
Holton Oxon 83 D10
Som 29 B11
Suff 127 B7
Holton cum Beckering
Lincs 189 E10
Holton Heath Dorset 18 C4
Holton le Clay Lincs 201 G9
Holton le Moor
Lincs 189 B9
Holton St Mary
Suff 107 D11
Holt Park W Yorks 205 E11
Holt Pound Hants 49 E10
Holts Gtr Man 196 G3
Holtspur Bucks 84 G6
Holt Wood Dorset 31 F8
Holtye E Sus 52 F3
Holway Dorset 28 G5
Dorset 29 C10
Flint 181 F11
Som 28 C2
Holwell Dorset 30 E2
Herts 104 E3
Leics 154 E4
Oxon 82 D2
Som 45 D8
Holwellbury C Beds 104 E3
Holwick Durham 232 F4
Holworth Dorset 17 E11
Holybourne Hants 49 E8
Holy City Devon 28 G3
Holy Cross T&W 243 D8
Worcs 117 B8
Holyfield Essex 86 E5
Holyhead / Caergybi
Anglesey 178 E2
Holy Island
Northumb 273 B11
Holylee Borders 261 B9
Holymoorside
Derbys 170 B4
Holyport Windsor 65 D11
Holystone
Northumb 251 C11
Holytown N Lanark 268 C5
Holy Vale Scilly 1 G4
Holywell C Beds 85 B8
Cambs 122 C6
Corn 4 D5
Dorset 29 G9
E Sus 23 F9
Glos 80 G3
Hereford 97 C7
Herts 85 F9
Northumb 243 C8
Som 29 E8
Warks 118 D3
Holywell Green
W Yorks 196 D5
Holywell Lake Som 27 C10
Holywell Row Suff 124 B4
Holywell / Treffynnon
Flint 181 F11
Holywood Dumfries 247 G10
Homedowns Glos 99 E8
Homer Shrops 132 C2
Homer Green
Mers 193 G10
Homersfield Suff 142 F5
Homerton London 67 B11
Hom Green
Hereford 97 G11
Homington Wilts 31 B10
Honeybourne
Worcs 100 C2
Honeychurch Devon 25 G10
Honeydon Beds 122 F2
Honey Hall N Som 60 G2
Honeyhill
Wokingham 65 F10
Honey Hill Kent 70 G6
Honeystreet Wilts 62 G6
Honey Street Wilts 62 G6
Honey Tye Suff 107 D9
Honeywick C Beds 103 G9
Honicknowle Plym 7 D9
Honiley Warks 118 C4
Honing Norf 160 D6
Honingham Norf 160 G2
Honington Lincs 172 G6
Suff 125 C8
Warks 100 C5
Honiton Devon 27 G11
Honkley Wrex 166 D4
Honley W Yorks 196 E6
Honley Moor
W Yorks 196 E6
Honnington Telford 150 F4
Honor Oak London 67 E11
Honor Oak Park
London 67 E11
Honresfeld Gtr Man 196 D2
Hoo Kent 71 G9
Hoober S Yorks 186 B6
Hoobrook Worcs 116 C6
Hood Green
S Yorks 197 G10
Hood Hill S Yorks 186 B5
Hood Manor Warr 183 D9
Hooe E Sus 23 D11
Plym 7 E10
Hooe Common
E Sus 23 C11
Hoo End Herts 85 B11
Hoofield Ches W 167 C8
Hoo Green Ches E 184 E2
Hoohill Blackpool 202 F2
Hoo Hole W Yorks 196 B4
Hook Cambs 139 E8
Devon 28 F4
E Yorks 199 B9

J

K

Little Bromley Essex 107 F11
Little Bromwich W Mid 134 F2
Little Broughton Cumb 229 E7
Little Budworth Ches W 167 B9
Little Burstead Essex 87 G11
Littlebury Essex 105 D10
Littlebury Green Essex 105 D9
Little Bytham Lincs 155 F10
Little Cambridge Essex 106 F2
Little Canfield Essex 105 G11
Little Canford Poole 18 B6
Little Carleton Lancs 202 F2
Little Carlton Lincs 190 D5
Notts 172 D3
Little Casterton Rutland 137 B10
Little Catwick E Yorks 209 E8
Little Catworth Cambs 122 C2
Little Cawthorpe Lincs 190 E5
Little Chalfield Wilts 61 G11
Little Chalfont Bucks 85 F7
Little Chart Kent 54 D2
Little Chart Forstal Kent 54 D3
Little Chell Stoke 168 E5
Little Chester Derby 153 B7
Little Chesterford Essex 105 C10
Little Chesterton Oxon 101 G11
Little Cheverell Wilts 46 C3
Little Chishill Cambs 105 D8
Little Clacton Essex 89 B11
Little Clanfield Oxon 82 E3
Little Clegg Gtr Man 196 E2
Little Clifton Cumb 229 F7
Little Coates NE Lincs 201 F8
Little Colp Aberds 303 E7
Little Comberton Worcs 99 C9
Little Comfort Corn 12 E2
Little Common E Sus 38 F2
Lincs 156 D6
Shrops 115 B7
W Sus 34 C6
Little Compton Warks 100 E5
Little Corby Cumb 239 F11
Little Cornard Suff 107 D7
Littlecote Bucks 102 G6
Littlecott Wilts 46 C6
Little Cowarne Hereford 116 G2
Little Coxwell Oxon 82 G3
Little Crakehall N Yorks 224 G4
Little Cransley Northants 120 B6
Little Crawley M Keynes 103 B8
Little Creaton Northants 120 C4
Little Creich Highld 309 L6
Little Cressingham Norf 141 D7
Little Crosby Mers 193 G10
Little Cubley Derbys 152 B3
Little Dalby Leics 154 G5
Little Dawley Telford 132 B3
Littledean Glos 79 C11
Littledean Hill Glos 79 C11
Little Dens Aberds 303 E10
Little Dewchurch Hereford 97 E10
Little Ditton Cambs 124 F3
Little Doward Hereford 79 B8
Littledown Bmouth 19 C8
Hants 47 B10
Little Downham Cambs 139 G10
Little Drayton Shrops 150 C3
Little Driffield E Yorks 208 B6
Little Drybrook Glos 79 D9
Little Dunham Norf 159 G7
Little Dunkeld Perth 286 C4
Little Dunmow Essex 106 G3
Little Durnford Wilts 46 G6
Little Eastbury Worcs 116 F6
Little Easton Essex 106 G2
Little Eaton Derbys 170 G5
Little Eccleston Lancs 202 E4
Little Ellingham Norf 141 D10
Little End Cambs 122 F3
E Yorks 208 F2
Essex 87 E8
Little Everdon Northants 119 F11
Little Eversden Cambs 123 G7
Little Faringdon Oxon 82 E2
Little Fencote N Yorks 224 G5
Little Fenton N Yorks 206 F6
Littleferry Highld 311 K2
Littlefield NE Lincs 201 F9
Littlefield Common Sur 50 C3
Littlefield Green Windsor 65 D11
Little Finborough Suff 125 G10
Little Fransham Norf 159 G8
Little Frith Kent 54 B2
Little Gaddesden Herts 85 C7
Littlegain Shrops 132 D5
Little Gidding Cambs 138 G2
Little Gight Aberds 303 F8
Little Glemham Suff 126 F6
Little Glenshee Perth 286 D3
Little Gorsley Glos 98 F3
Little Gransden Cambs 122 F5
Little Green Cambs 104 B5
Notts 172 G2
Som 45 D8
Suff 125 C11
Wrex 167 G7
Little Grimsby Lincs 190 C4
Little Gringley Notts 188 E2
Little Gruinard Highld 307 L4
Little Habton N Yorks 216 D4
Little Hadham Herts 105 G8
Little Hale Lincs 173 G10
Norf 141 B8
Little Hallam Derbys 171 G7
Little Hallingbury Essex 87 B7
Littleham Devon 14 E6
Devon 24 C6
Little Hampden Bucks 84 E5
Littlehampton W Sus 35 G8
Little Haresfield Glos 80 D4
Little Harrowden Northants 121 C7
Little Harwood Blackburn 195 B7
Little Haseley Oxon 83 E10
Little Hatfield E Yorks 209 E9
Little Hautbois Norf 160 E5
Little Haven Pembs 72 C5
W Sus 51 G7
Little Hay Staffs 134 C2
Little Hayfield Derbys 185 D8
Little Haywood Staffs 151 E10
Little Heath Ches E 167 G11
Ches W 166 B6
Herts 85 D8
Herts 86 E3
London 68 B3
Staffs 151 F8
Sur 66 G6
W Berks 65 E7
W Mid 134 G6
Little Heck N Yorks 198 C5
Littlehempston Devon 8 C6
Little Henham Essex 105 E10
Little Henny Essex 107 D7
Little Herbert's Glos 81 B7
Little Hereford Hereford 115 D11
Little Hill Hereford 97 F9
Som 28 E3
Little Holbury Hants 32 G6
Little Honeyborough Pembs 73 D7
Little Hoole Moss Houses Lancs 194 C3
Little Horkesley Essex 107 E9
Little Hormead Herts 105 F8
Little Horsted E Sus 23 B7
Little Horton W Yorks 205 G9
Wilts 62 G4
Little Horwood Bucks 102 E5
Littlehoughton Northumb 264 F6
Little Houghton Northants 120 F6
S Yorks 198 G2
Little Hucklow Derbys 185 F11
Little Hulton Gtr Man 195 G8
Little Humber E Yorks 201 C8
Little Hungerford W Berks 64 E4
Little Ilford London 68 B2
Little Ingestre Staffs 151 E9
Little Inkberrow Worcs 117 F10
Little Irchester Northants 121 D8
Little Keyford Som 45 D9
Little Kimble Bucks 84 D4
Little Kineton Warks 118 G6
Little Kingshill Bucks 84 F5
Little Knowles Green Suff 124 F5
Little Langdale Cumb 220 E6
Little Langford Wilts 46 F4
Little Laver Essex 87 D8
Little Lawford Warks 119 B9
Little Layton Blackpool 202 F2
Little Leigh Ches W 183 F10
Little Leighs Essex 88 B2
Little Lepton W Yorks 197 E8
Little Leven E Yorks 209 D8
Little Lever Gtr Man 195 F9
Little Limber Lincs 200 E6
Little Linford M Keynes 102 C6
Little Load Som 29 C7
Little London Bucks 83 C10
Bucks 84 D5
Cambs 139 D8
E Sus 23 B9
Essex 105 F9
Essex 106 D3
Glos 80 B2
Hants 47 D11
Hants 48 B6
Lincs 156 E4
Lincs 157 E8
Lincs 189 D10
Lincs 190 F4
Norf 140 D5
Norf 160 C2
Norf 160 C5
Norf 160 E3
Oxon 83 E8
Powys 129 F10
Shrops 131 F10
Som 44 D6
Suff 125 F10
W Yorks 205 F10
Worcs 116 C2
Little Longstone Derbys 185 G11
Little Lynturk Aberds 293 B7
Little Lyth Shrops 131 B9
Little Madeley Staffs 168 F3
Little Malvern Worcs 98 C5
Little Mancot Flint 166 B4
Little Maplestead Essex 106 E6
Little Marcle Hereford 98 D3
Little Marlow Bucks 65 B11
Little Marsden Lancs 204 F3
Little Marsh Bucks 102 G3
Norf 159 B10
Wilts 45 B11
Little Marton Blackpool 202 G2
Little Mascalls Essex 88 E2
Little Massingham Norf 158 E5
Little Melton Norf 142 B3
Little Merthyr Hereford 96 B5
Little Milford Pembs 73 C7
Littlemill Aberds 292 D5
E Ayrs 257 F11
Highld 301 D9
Northumb 264 F6
Little Mill Kent 53 D7
Mon 78 E4
Little Milton Newport 59 B11
Oxon 83 E10
Little Minster Oxon 82 C4
Little Missenden Bucks 84 F6
Little Mongeham Kent 55 C10
Littlemoor Derbys 170 C5
Dorset 17 E9
Little Moor Gtr Man 184 D6
Lancs 203 E10
Little Moor End Lancs 195 B8
Littlemore Oxon 83 E8
Little Morrell Warks 118 F6
Littlemoss Gtr Man 184 B6
Little Mountain Flint 166 C3
Little Musgrave Cumb 222 C5
Little Ness Shrops 149 F8
Little Neston Ches W 182 F3
Little Newcastle Pembs 91 F9
Little Newsham Durham 224 B2
Little Norlington E Sus 23 C7
Little Norton Som 29 D7
Little Oakley Essex 108 F4
Northants 137 F7
Little Odell Beds 121 F9
Little Offley Herts 104 F2
Little Onn Staffs 150 F6
Little Ormside Cumb 222 B4
Little Orton Cumb 239 F9
Leics 134 B6
Little Ouse Norf 140 F2
Little Ouseburn N Yorks 215 G8
Littleover Derby 152 C6
Little Overton Wrex 166 G5
Little Oxney Green Essex 87 D11
Little Packington Warks 134 G4
Little Parndon Essex 86 C6
Little Paxton Cambs 122 E3
Little Petherick Corn 10 G4
Little Pitlurg Moray 302 E4
Little Plumpton Lancs 202 G3
Little Plumstead Norf 160 G6
Little Ponton Lincs 155 C8
Littleport Cambs 139 F11
Little Posbrook Hants 33 G8
Little Poulton Lancs 202 F3
Little Preston Kent 53 B8
W Yorks 206 G3
Littler Ches W 167 B10
Little Raveley Cambs 122 B5
Little Reedness E Yorks 199 C10
Little Reynoldston Swansea 56 D3
Little Ribston N Yorks 206 C3
Little Rissington Glos 81 B11
Little Rogart Highld 309 J7
Little Rollright Oxon 100 E5
Little Ryburgh Norf 159 D9
Little Ryle Northumb 264 G2
Little Ryton Shrops 131 C9
Little Salisbury Wilts 63 G7
Little Salkeld Cumb 231 D7
Little Sampford Essex 106 E3
Little Sandhurst Brack 65 G10
Little Saredon Staffs 133 B8
Little Saxham Suff 124 E5
Little Scatwell Highld 300 D3
Little Scotland Gtr Man 194 E6
Little Sessay N Yorks 215 E9
Little Shelford Cambs 123 G9
Little Shoddesden Hants 47 D9
Little Shrewley Warks 118 D4
Little Shurdington Glos 80 B6
Little Silver Devon 26 F6
Devon 40 E4
Little Singleton Lancs 202 F3
Little Skillymarno Aberds 303 D9
Little Skipwith N Yorks 207 F9
Little Smeaton N Yorks 198 D4
N Yorks 224 E6
Little Snoring Norf 159 C9
Little Sodbury S Glos 61 C9
Little Sodbury End S Glos 61 C8
Little Somborne Hants 47 G11
Little Somerford Wilts 62 C3
Little Soudley Shrops 150 D4
Little Stainforth N Yorks 212 F6
Little Stainton Darl 234 G2
Little Stanmore London 85 G11
Little Stanney Ches W 182 G6
Little Staughton Beds 122 E2
Littlestead Green Oxon 65 D8
Little Steeping Lincs 174 C6
Little Stoke S Glos 60 C6
Staffs 151 C8
Littlestone-on-Sea Kent 39 C9
Little Stonham Suff 126 E2
Little Stretton Leics 136 C3
Shrops 131 E8
Little Strickland Cumb 221 B11
Little Studley N Yorks 214 E6
Little Stukeley Cambs 122 B4
Little Sugnall Staffs 150 C6
Little Sutton Ches W 182 F5
Lincs 157 E9
Shrops 131 G10
Little Swinburne Northumb 241 B10
Little Tarrington Hereford 98 C2
Little Tew Oxon 101 F7
Little Tey Essex 107 G7
Little Thetford Cambs 123 B10
Little Thirkleby N Yorks 215 D9
Little Thornage Norf 159 B11
Little Thornton Lancs 202 E3
Littlethorpe Leics 135 D10
N Yorks 214 F6
Little Thorpe Durham 234 C4
W Yorks 197 C7
Little Thurlow Suff 124 G3
Little Thurlow Green Suff 124 G3
Little Thurrock Thurrock 68 D6
Littleton Bath 60 G5
Ches W 166 B6
Dorset 30 G5
Hants 48 G3
Perth 286 D6
Som 44 G3
Sur 50 D3
Sur 66 F5
Wilts 62 G2
Littleton Common Sur 66 E5
Littleton Drew Wilts 61 C10
Littleton-on-Severn S Glos 60 B5
Littleton Panell Wilts 46 C4
Littleton-upon-Severn S Glos 79 G9
Little Torboll Highld 309 K7
Little Torrington Devon 25 D7
Little Totham Essex 88 C5
Little Toux Aberds 302 D5
Littletown Durham 234 C2
IoW 20 C6
W Yorks 197 C8
Little Town Cumb 220 B4
Lancs 203 F9
Warr 183 C10
Little Tring Herts 84 C6
Little Twycross Leics 134 B6
Little Urswick Cumb 210 E5
Little Vantage W Loth 270 C2
Little Wakering Essex 70 B2
Little Walden Essex 105 C10
Little Waldingfield Suff 107 B8
Little Walsingham Norf 159 B8
Little Waltham Essex 88 C2
Little Walton Warks 135 G9
Little Warley Essex 87 G10
Little Warton Warks 134 C5
Little Washbourne Glos 99 E9
Little Weighton E Yorks 208 G5
Little Weldon Northants 137 F8
Little Welland Worcs 98 D6
Little Welnetham Suff 125 E7
Little Welton Lincs 190 D4
Little Wenham Suff 107 D11
Little Wenlock Telford 132 B2
Little Weston Som 29 B10
Little Whitehouse IoW 20 C5
Little Whittingham Green Suff 126 B5
Littlewick Green Windsor 65 D10
Little Wigborough Essex 89 B7
Little Wilbraham Cambs 123 F10
Littlewindsor Dorset 28 G6
Little Wisbeach Lincs 156 C2
Little Wishford Wilts 46 F5
Little Witcombe Glos 80 B6
Little Witley Worcs 116 E5
Little Wittenham Oxon 83 G9
Little Wolford Warks 100 D5
Littlewood Staffs 133 B9
Little Wood Corner Bucks 84 E6
Little Woodcote London 67 G9
Littlewood Green Warks 117 E11
Little Woolgarston Dorset 18 E5
Littleworth Beds 103 C11
Glos 80 E4
Glos 100 D2
Oxon 82 F4
Oxon 83 D9
Oxon 83 G10
S Yorks 187 B10
Staffs 151 E8
Staffs 151 G10
W Sus 35 C11
Warks 118 E4
Wilts 63 G7
Worcs 117 E9
Worcs 117 G7
Littleworth Common Bucks 66 B2
Little Worthen Shrops 130 B6
Littleworth End Warks 134 D3
Little Wratting Suff 106 B3
Little Wymington Beds 121 D9
Little Wymondley Herts 104 F4
Little Wyrley Staffs 133 B10
Little Wytheford Shrops 149 F11
Little Yeldham Essex 106 D5
Littley Green Essex 87 B11
Litton Derbys 185 F11
N Yorks 213 E8
Som 44 C5
Litton Cheney Dorset 17 C7
Litton Mill Derbys 185 G11
Liurbost W Isles 304 F5
Livermead Torbay 9 C8
Liverpool Mers 182 C4
Liverpool Airport Mers 182 E6
Liversedge W Yorks 197 C8
Liverton Devon 14 F2
Redcar 226 B4
Liverton Mines Redcar 226 B4
Liverton Street Kent 53 C11
Livesey Street Kent 53 C8
Livingshayes Devon 27 G7
Livingston W Loth 269 B11
Livingston Village W Loth 269 B10
Lix Toll Stirling 285 D9
Lixwm Flint 181 G11
Lizard Corn 2 G6
Llaingoch Anglesey 178 E2
Llaithddu Powys 129 G11
Llampha V Glam 58 D2
Llan Powys 129 C7
Llanaber Gwyn 146 F2
Llanaelhaearn Gwyn 162 G5
Llanafan Ceredig 112 C3
Llanafan-fawr Powys 113 F9
Llanallgo Anglesey 179 D7
Llananno Powys 113 C11
Llanarmon Gwyn 145 B8
Llanarmon Dyffryn Ceiriog Wrex 148 C3
Llanarmon Mynydd-mawr Powys 148 D2
Llanarmon-yn-Ial Denb 165 D11
Llanarth Ceredig 111 F8
Mon 78 C5
Llanarthne Carms 93 G10
Llanasa Flint 181 E10
Llanbabo Anglesey 178 D5
Llanbad Rhondda 58 C3
Llanbadarn Fawr Ceredig 128 G2
Llanbadarn Fynydd Powys 114 B2
Llanbadarn-y-Garreg Powys 96 B2
Llanbadoc Mon 78 E5
Llanbadrig Anglesey 178 C5
Llanbeder Newport 78 G5
Llanbedr Gwyn 145 D11
Powys 96 B2
Powys 96 G4
Llanbedr-Dyffryn-Clwyd Denb 165 D10
Llanbedrgoch Anglesey 179 E8
Llanbedrog Gwyn 144 C6
Llanbedr Pont Steffan / Lampeter Ceredig 93 B11
Llanbedr-y-cennin Conwy 164 B3
Llanberis Gwyn 163 C9
Llanbethery V Glam 58 F4
Llanbister Powys 114 C2
Llanblethian / Llanfleiddan V Glam 58 E3
Llanboidy Carms 92 G4
Llanbradach Caerph 77 G10
Llanbrynmair Powys 129 C7
Llancadle / Llancatal V Glam 58 F4
Llancaiach Caerph 77 F10
Llancarfan V Glam 58 E5
Llancatal / Llancadle V Glam 58 F4
Llancayo Mon 78 E5
Llancloudy Hereford 97 G9
Llancowrid Powys 130 E3
Llancynfelyn Ceredig 128 E2
Llan-dafal Bl Gwent 77 E11
Llandaff Cardiff 59 D7
Llandaff North Cardiff 59 D7
Llandanwg Gwyn 145 D11
Llandarcy Neath 57 B8
Llandawke Carms 74 C3
Llanddaniel Fab Anglesey 179 G7
Llanddarog Carms 75 B8
Llanddeiniol Ceredig 111 C11
Llanddeiniolen Gwyn 163 B8
Llandderfel Gwyn 147 B9
Llanddeusant Anglesey 178 D4
Carms 94 G5
Llanddew Powys 95 E11
Llanddewi Swansea 56 D3
Llanddewi-Brefi Ceredig 112 F3
Llanddewi Fach Mon 78 F4
Llanddewi'r Cwm Powys 95 B10
Llanddewi Rhydderch Mon 78 C5
Llanddewi Skirrid Mon 78 B4
Llanddewi Velfrey Pembs 73 B10
Llanddewi Ystradenni Powys 114 D2
Llanddoged Conwy 164 C4
Llanddona Anglesey 179 F9
Llanddowror Carms 74 C3
Llanddulas Conwy 180 F6
Llanddwywe Gwyn 145 E11
Llanddyfynan Anglesey 179 F8
Llandecwyn Gwyn 146 B2
Llandefaelog Powys 95 E10
Llandefaelog Fach Powys 95 E10
Llandefaelog-tre'r-graig Powys 96 F2
Llandefalle Powys 96 D2
Llandegai Gwyn 179 G9
Llandegfan Anglesey 179 G9
Llandegla Denb 165 E11
Llandegley Powys 114 E2
Llandegveth Mon 78 F4
Llandegwning Gwyn 144 C5
Llandeilo Carms 94 G2
Llandeilo Graban Powys 95 C11
Llandeilo'r Fan Powys 95 E7
Llandeloy Pembs 91 F7
Llandenny Mon 78 E6
Llandenny Walks Mon 78 E5
Llandevaud Newport 78 G6
Llandevenny Mon 60 B2
Llandewi Ystradenny Powys 114 D2
Llandilo Pembs 92 F2
Llandilo-yr-ynys Carms 93 G9
Llandinabo Hereford 97 F10
Llandinam Powys 129 F10
Llandissilio Pembs 92 G2
Llandogo Mon 79 E8
Llandough V Glam 58 E3
V Glam 59 E7
Llandovery / Llanymddyfri Carms 94 E5
Llandow / Llandw V Glam 58 E2
Llandre Carms 94 C3
Ceredig 128 F2
Llandrillo Denb 147 B10
Llandrillo-yn-Rhôs Conwy 180 E4
Llandrindod Wells Powys 113 E11
Llandrinio Powys 148 F5
Llandruidion Pembs 90 G5
Llandudno Conwy 180 E3
Llandudno Junction / Cyffordd Llandudno Conwy 180 F3
Llandudoch / St Dogmaels Pembs 92 B3
Llandw / Llandow V Glam 58 E2
Llandwrog Gwyn 163 D7
Llandybie Carms 75 B10
Llandyfaelog Carms 74 C6
Llandyfan Carms 75 B10
Llandyfriog Ceredig 92 C6
Llandyfrydog Anglesey 178 D6
Llandygwydd Ceredig 92 C4
Llandynan Denb 165 F11
Llandyrnog Denb 165 B10
Llandysilio Powys 148 F5
Llandyssil Powys 130 D3
Llandysul Ceredig 93 C8
Llanedeyrn Cardiff 59 C8
Llanedi Carms 75 D9
Llanedwen Anglesey 163 B8
Llaneglwys Powys 95 D11
Llanegryn Gwyn 110 B2
Llanegwad Carms 93 G10
Llaneilian Anglesey 179 C7
Llanelian yn-Rhôs Conwy 180 F5
Llanelidan Denb 165 E10
Llanelieu Powys 96 E3
Llanellen Mon 78 C4
Llanelli Carms 56 B4
Llanelltyd Gwyn 146 F4
Llanelly Mon 78 C2
Llanelly Hill Mon 78 C2
Llanelwedd Powys 113 G10
Llanelwy / St Asaph Denb 181 G8
Llanenddwyn Gwyn 145 E11
Llanengan Gwyn 144 D5
Llanerch Powys 130 E6
Llanerch Emrys Powys 148 E4
Llanerchymedd Anglesey 178 E6
Llanerfyl Powys 129 B10
Llaneuddog Anglesey 179 D7
Llan eurgain / Northop Flint 166 B2
Llanfabon Caerph 77 G10
Llanfachraeth Anglesey 178 E4
Llanfachreth Gwyn 146 E5
Llanfaelog Anglesey 178 G4
Llanfaelrhys Gwyn 144 D4
Llanfaenor Mon 78 B6
Llanfaes Anglesey 179 F10
Powys 95 F10
Llanfaethlu Anglesey 178 D4
Llanfaglan Gwyn 163 C7
Llanfair Gwyn 145 D11
Llanfair Caereinion Powys 130 B2
Llanfair Clydogau Ceredig 112 G2
Llanfair-Dyffryn-Clwyd Denb 165 D10
Llanfairfechan Conwy 179 F11
Llanfair Kilgeddin Mon 78 D4
Llanfair Kilgheddin Mon 78 D4
Llanfair-Nant-Gwyn Pembs 92 D3
Llanfairpwll-gwyngyll Anglesey 179 G8
Llanfair Talhaiarn Conwy 180 G6
Llanfair Waterdine Shrops 114 B4
Llanfairyneubwll Anglesey 178 F3
Llanfairynghornwy Anglesey 178 C4
Llanfallteg Carms 73 B11
Llanfallteg West Carms 73 B10
Llanfaredd Powys 113 G11
Llanfarian Ceredig 111 B11
Llanfechain Powys 148 E3
Llanfechan Powys 113 G9
Llanfechell Anglesey 178 C5
Llanferres Denb 165 C11
Llan Ffestiniog Gwyn 164 G2
Llanfflewyn Anglesey 178 D5
Llanfigael Anglesey 178 E4
Llanfihangel-ar-arth Carms 93 D9
Llanfihangel-Crucorney Mon 96 G6
Llanfihangel Glyn Myfyr Conwy 165 F7
Llanfihangel-helygen Powys 113 E10
Llanfihangel Nant Bran Powys 95 E8
Llanfihangel-nant-Melan Powys 114 F3
Llanfihangel Rhydithon Powys 114 D3
Llanfihangel Rogiet Mon 60 B2
Llanfihangel Tal-y-llyn Powys 96 F2
Llanfihangel Tor y Mynydd Mon 79 E7
Llanfihangel-uwch-Gwili Carms 93 G9
Llanfihangel-y-Creuddyn Ceredig 112 B3
Llanfihangel-yng-Ngwynfa Powys 147 F11
Llanfihangel yn Nhowyn Anglesey 178 F4
Llanfihangel-y-pennant Gwyn 128 B3
Gwyn 163 F8
Llanfilo Powys 96 E2
Llanfleiddan / Llanblethian V Glam 58 E3
Llanfoist Mon 78 C3
Llanfor Gwyn 147 B8
Llanfrechfa Torf 78 G4
Llanfrothen Gwyn 163 G10
Llanfrynach Powys 95 F11
Llanfwrog Anglesey 178 E4
Denb 165 D10
Llanfyllin Powys 148 F2
Llanfynydd Carms 93 F11
Flint 166 D3
Llanfyrnach Pembs 92 E4
Llangadfan Powys 147 G10
Llangadog Carms 74 D6
Carms 94 F4
Llangadwaladr Anglesey 162 B5
Powys 148 C3
Llangaffo Anglesey 162 B6
Llangain Carms 74 B5
Llangammarch Wells Powys 95 B8
Llangan V Glam 58 D3
Llangarron Hereford 97 G10
Llangasty Talyllyn Powys 96 F2
Llangathen Carms 93 G11
Llangattock Powys 78 B2
Llangattock Lingoed Mon 97 G7
Llangattock nigh Usk Mon 78 D4
Llangattock-Vibon-Avel Mon 79 B7
Llangedwyn Powys 148 E3
Llangefni Anglesey 179 F7
Llangeinor Bridgend 58 B2
Llangeitho Ceredig 112 F2
Llangeler Carms 93 D7
Llangendeirne Carms 75 C7
Llangennech Carms 75 E9
Llangennith Swansea 56 C2
Llangenny Powys 78 B2
Llangernyw Conwy 164 B5
Llangeview Mon 78 E5
Llangewydd Court Bridgend 57 E11
Llangian Gwyn 144 D5
Llanglofan Pembs 91 E8
Llanglydwen Carms 92 F3
Llangoed Anglesey 179 F10
Llangoedmor Ceredig 92 B3
Llangollen Denb 166 G2
Llangolman Pembs 92 F2
Llangors Powys 96 F2
Llangorwen Ceredig 128 G2
Llangovan Mon 79 D7
Llangower Gwyn 147 C8
Llangrannog Ceredig 110 G6
Llangristiolus Anglesey 178 G6
Llangrove Hereford 79 B8
Llangua Mon 97 F7
Llangunllo Powys 114 C4
Llangunnor Carms 74 B6
Llangurig Powys 113 B8
Llangwm Conwy 165 G7
Mon 78 E6
Pembs 73 D7
Llangwnnadl Gwyn 144 C4
Llangwyfan Denb 165 B10
Llangwyfan-isaf Anglesey 162 B4
Llangwyllog Anglesey 178 F6
Llangwyryfon Ceredig 111 C11
Llangybi Ceredig 112 G2
Gwyn 162 G6
Mon 78 F5
Llangyfelach Swansea 56 B6
Llangyndeyrn Carms 75 C7
Llangynhafal Denb 165 C10
Llangynidr Powys 77 B11
Llangyniew Powys 130 B2
Llangynin Carms 74 B2
Llangynog Carms 74 B4
Powys 147 D11
Llangynwyd Bridgend 57 D11
Llanhamlach Powys 95 F11
Llanharan Rhondda 58 C4
Llanharry Rhondda 58 C4
Llanhennock Mon 78 G5
Llanhilleth Bl Gwent 78 E2
Llanhowel Pembs 90 F6
Llanidloes Powys 129 G9
Llaniestyn Gwyn 144 C5
Llanifyny Powys 129 G7
Llanigon Powys 96 D4
Llanilar Ceredig 112 C2
Llanilid Rhondda 58 C3
Llanilltud Fawr / Llantwit Major V Glam 58 F3
Llanio Ceredig 112 F2
Llanion Pembs 73 E7
Llanishen Cardiff 59 C7
Mon 79 E7
Llanllawddog Carms 93 F9
Llanllechid Gwyn 163 B10
Llanllowell Mon 78 F5
Llanllugan Powys 129 C11
Llanllwch Carms 74 B5
Llanllwchaiarn Powys 130 E2
Llanllwni Carms 93 D9
Llanllwyd Shrops 130 G3
Llanllyfni Gwyn 163 E7
Llanmadoc Swansea 56 C2
Llanmaes Cardiff 58 D6
V Glam 58 F3
Llanmartin Newport 59 B11
Llanmerwig Powys 130 E3
Llanmihangel V Glam 58 E3
Llan-mill Pembs 73 C10
Llanmiloe Carms 74 D3
Llanmorlais Swansea 56 C4
Llannefydd Conwy 181 G7
Llannerch-y-môr Flint 181 F11
Llannon Carms 75 D8
Llan-non / Llanon Ceredig 111 D10
Llannor Gwyn 145 B7
Llanon Pembs 90 E6
Llanon / Llan-non Ceredig 111 D10
Llanover Mon 78 D4
Llanpumsaint Carms 93 F8
Llanreath Pembs 73 E7
Llanreithan Pembs 91 F7
Llanrhaeadr Denb 165 C9
Llanrhaeadr-ym-Mochnant Powys 148 D2
Llanrhian Pembs 90 E6
Llanrhidian Swansea 56 C3
Llanrhos Conwy 180 E3

396 Low–Map

Lower Largo Fife 287 G8
Lower Layham Suff 107 C10
Lower Ledwyche Shrops 115 C10
Lower Leigh Staffs 151 B10
Lower Lemington Glos 100 E4
Lower Lenie Highld 300 G5
Lower Lode Glos 99 E7
Lower Lovacott Devon 25 B8
Lower Loxhore Devon 40 F6
Lower Lydbrook Glos 79 B9
Lower Lye Hereford 115 D8
Lower Machen Newport 59 B8
Lower Maes-coed Hereford 96 E6
Lower Mains Clack 279 B9
Lower Mannington Dorset 31 F9
Lower Marsh Som 30 C2
Lower Marston Som 45 E9
Lower Meend Glos 79 E9
Lower Menadue Corn 5 D10
Lower Merridge Som 43 G8
Lower Mickletown W Yorks 198 B2
Lower Middleton Cheney Northants 101 C10
Lower Midway Derbys 152 E6
Lower Mill Corn 3 B10
Lower Milovaig Highld 296 F7
Lower Milton Som 44 D4
Lower Moor Wilts 81 G8
Worcs 99 B9
Lower Morton S Glos 79 G10
Lower Mountain Flint 166 D4
Lower Nazeing Essex 86 D5
Lower Netchwood Shrops 132 E2
Lower Netherton Devon 14 G3
Lower New Inn Torf 78 F4
Lower Ninnes Corn 1 C5
Lower Nobut Staffs 151 C10
Lower North Dean Bucks 84 F5
Lower Norton Warks 118 E4
Lower Nyland Dorset 30 C2
Lower Ochrwyth Caerph 59 B8
Lower Odcombe Som 29 D8
Lower Oddington Glos 100 F4
Lower Ollach Highld 295 B7
Lower Padworth W Berks 64 F6
Lower Penarth V Glam 59 F7
Lower Penn Staffs 133 D7
Lower Pennington Hants 20 C2
Lower Penwortham Lancs 194 B4
Lower Peover Ches W 184 G2
Lower Pexhill Ches E 184 G5
Lower Pilsley Derbys 170 C6
Lower Pitkerrie Highld 311 L2
Lower Place Gtr Man 196 E2
London 67 C8
Lower Pollicot Bucks 84 C2
Lower Porthkerry V Glam 58 F5
Lower Porthpean Corn 5 E10
Lower Quinton Warks 100 B3
Lower Rabber Hereford 114 G5
Lower Race Torf 78 E3
Lower Radley Oxon 83 F8
Lower Rainham Medway 69 F10
Lower Ratley Hants 32 C4
Lower Raydon Suff 107 D10
Lower Rea Glos 80 B4
Lower Ridge Devon 28 G2
Shrops 148 C6
Lower Roadwater Som 42 F4
Lower Rochford Worcs 116 D2
Lower Rose Corn 4 E5
Lower Row Dorset 31 G8
Lower Sapey Worcs 116 E3
Lower Seagry Wilts 62 C3
Lower Sheering Essex 87 C7
Lower Shelton C Beds 103 C9
Lower Shiplake Oxon 65 D9
Lower Shuckburgh Warks 119 E9
Lower Skelty Swansea 56 C6
Lower Slackstead Hants 32 B5
Lower Slade Devon 40 D4
Lower Slaughter Glos 100 G3
Lower Solva Pembs 87 G11
Lower Soothill W Yorks 197 C9
Lower Soudley Glos 79 D11
Lower Southfield Hereford 98 C3
Lower Stanton St Quintin Wilts 62 C2
Lower Stoke Medway 69 D10
W Mid 119 B7
Lower Stondon C Beds 104 D3
Lower Stone Glos 79 G11
Lower Stonnall Staffs 133 C11
Lower Stow Bedon Norf 141 E9
Lower Stratton Som 28 D6
Swindon 63 B7
Lower Street E Sus 38 E2
Norf 160 B5
Norf 160 C3
Norf 160 F6
Suff 108 E3
Suff 124 G5
Lower Strensham Worcs 99 C8
Lower Stretton Warr 183 E10
Lower Studley Wilts 45 B11
Lower Sundon C Beds 103 F10
Lower Swainswick Bath 61 F9
Lower Swanwick Hants 33 F7
Lower Swell Glos 100 F3
Lower Sydenham London 67 E11
Lower Tadmarton Oxon 101 D8
Lower Tale Devon 27 G9
Lower Tasburgh Norf 142 D3
Lower Tean Staffs 151 B10
Lower Thorpe Northants 101 B10
Lower Threapwood Wrex 166 G6
Lower Thurlton Norf 143 D8
Lower Thurnham Lancs 202 C5
Lower Thurvaston Derbys 152 B4
Lower Todding Hereford 115 B8
Lower Tote Highld 298 C5
Lowertown Corn 2 D5
Corn 5 C11
Devon 12 E5
Lower Town Devon 27 E8
Hereford 98 C2
Pembs 91 D9
W Yorks 204 G6
Worcs 117 F7
Lower Trebullett Corn 12 F2
Lower Tregunnon Corn 11 E10
Lower Treworrick Corn 6 B4
Lower Tuffley Glos 80 C4
Lower Turmer Hants 31 F10
Lower Twitchen Devon 24 D5
Lower Twydall Medway 69 F10
Lower Tysoe Warks 100 B6
Lower Upham Hants 33 D8
Lower Upnor Medway 69 E9
Lower Vexford Som 42 F6
Lower Wainhill Oxon 84 E3
Lower Walton Warr 183 D10
Lower Wanborough Swindon 63 C8
Lower Weacombe Som 42 E6
Lower Weald M Keynes 102 D5
Lower Wear Devon 14 D4
Lower Weare Som 44 C2
Lower Weedon Northants 120 F2
Lower Welson Hereford 114 G5
Lower Westholme Som 44 E5
Lower Westhouse N Yorks 212 E3
Lower Westmancote Worcs 99 D8
Lower Weston Bath 61 F8
Lower Whatcombe Dorset 30 G4
Lower Whatley Som 45 D8
Lower Whitley Ches W 183 F10
Lower Wick Glos 80 F2
Worcs 116 G6
Lower Wield Hants 48 E6
Lower Willingdon E Sus 23 E9
Lower Winchendon or Nether Winchendon Bucks 84 C2
Lower Withington Ches E 168 B4
Lower Wolverton Worcs 117 G8
Lower Woodend Aberds 293 B8
Bucks 65 B10
Lower Woodford Wilts 46 G6
Lower Woodley Corn 5 B10
Lower Woodside Herts 86 D2
Lower Woolston Som 29 B11
Lower Woon Corn 5 C10
Lower Wraxall Dorset 29 G9
Som 44 F6
Wilts 61 G10
Lower Wych Ches W 167 G7
Lower Wyche Worcs 98 C5
Lower Wyke W Yorks 197 B7
Lower Yelland Devon 40 G3
Lower Zeals Wilts 45 G9
Lowes Barn Durham 233 C11
Lowesby Leics 136 B4
Lowestoft Suff 143 E10
Loweswater Cumb 229 G8
Low Etherley Durham 233 F9
Low Fell T&W 243 F7
Lowfield S Yorks 186 D5
Lowfield Heath W Sus 51 E9
Low Fold W Yorks 205 F10
Lowford Hants 33 E7
Low Fulney Lincs 156 E5
Low Garth N Yorks 226 D4
Low Gate N Yorks 214 F5
Northumb 241 E10
Low Geltbridge Cumb 240 F2
Lowgill Cumb 222 F2
Lancs 212 G3
Low Grantley N Yorks 214 E4
Low Green N Yorks 205 B10
Suff 125 E7
W Yorks 205 F10
Low Greenside T&W 242 E4
Low Habberley Worcs 116 B6
Low Ham Som 28 B6
Low Hauxley Northumb 253 C7
Low Hawsker N Yorks 227 D8
Low Hesket Cumb 230 B5
Low Hesleyhurst Northumb 252 D3
Low Hill W Mid 133 C8
Low Hutton N Yorks 216 F5
Lowick Cumb 210 B5
Northants 137 G9
Northumb 264 B2
Lowick Bridge Cumb 210 B5
Lowick Green Cumb 210 B5
Low Knipe Cumb 230 G6
Low Laithe N Yorks 214 G3
Low Laithes S Yorks 197 G11
Lowlands Torf 78 F3
Low Leighton Derbys 185 D8
Low Lorton Cumb 229 F9
Low Marishes N Yorks 216 D6
Low Marnham Notts 172 B4
Low Mill N Yorks 226 F3
Low Moor Lancs 203 E10
W Yorks 197 B7
Lowmoor Row Cumb 231 F8
Low Moorsley T&W 234 B2
Low Moresby Cumb 228 G5
Lowna N Yorks 226 G3
Low Newton Cumb 211 C8
Low Newton-by-the-Sea Northumb 264 E6
Lownie Moor Angus 287 C8
Lowood Borders 262 B2
Low Prudhoe Northumb 242 E4
Low Risby N Lincs 200 E2
Low Row Cumb 229 C9
Cumb 240 E3
N Yorks 223 F9
Low Salchrie Dumfries 236 C2
Low Smerby Argyll 255 E8
Low Snaygill N Yorks 204 D5
Lowsonford Warks 118 D3
Low Street Norf 141 B10
Thurrock 69 D7
Low Tharston Norf 142 D3
Lowther Cumb 230 G6
Lowthertown Dumfries 238 D6
Lowtherville IoW 21 F7
Low Thornley T&W 242 E5
Lowthorpe E Yorks 217 G11
Lowton Gtr Man 183 B10
Som 27 D11
Lowton Common Gtr Man 183 B10
Lowton Heath Gtr Man 183 B10
Lowton St Mary's Gtr Man 183 B10
Low Torry Fife 279 D10
Low Town Shrops 132 E4
Low Toynton Lincs 190 G3
Low Valley S Yorks 198 G2
Low Valleyfield Fife 279 D10
Low Walton Cumb 219 C9
Low Waters S Lanark 268 E4
Low Westwood Durham 242 F4
Low Whinnow Cumb 239 G8
Low Whita N Yorks 223 F10
Low Wood Cumb 210 C6
Low Worsall N Yorks 225 C7
Low Wray Cumb 221 E7
Loxbeare Devon 26 D6
Loxford London 68 B2
Loxhill Sur 50 F4
Loxhore Devon 40 F6
Loxhore Cott Devon 40 F6
Loxley S Yorks 186 D4
Warks 118 G5
Loxley Green Staffs 151 C11
Loxter Hereford 98 C4
Loxton N Som 43 B11
Loxwood W Sus 50 G4
Loyter's Green Essex 87 C8
Loyterton Kent 70 G3
Lozells W Mid 133 F11
Lubachlaggan Highld 300 B3
Lubachoinnich Highld 309 K4
Lubberland Shrops 116 B2
Lubcroy Highld 309 J3
Lubenham Leics 136 F4
Lubinvullin Highld 308 C5
Lucas End Herts 86 E4
Lucas Green Lancs 194 C5
Sur 50 B2
Luccombe Som 42 E2
Luccombe Village IoW 21 F7
Lucker Northumb 264 C5
Luckett Corn 12 G3
Lucking Street Essex 106 E6
Luckington Wilts 61 C10
Lucklawhill Fife 287 E8
Luckwell Bridge Som 42 F2
Lucton Hereford 115 E8
Ludag W Isles 297 K3
Ludborough Lincs 190 B3
Ludbrook Devon 8 E3
Ludchurch Pembs 73 C10
Luddenden W Yorks 196 B4
Luddenden Foot W Yorks 196 C4
Ludderburn Cumb 221 G8
Luddesdown Kent 69 F7
Luddington N Lincs 199 D10
Warks 118 G3
Luddington in the Brook Northants 138 G2
Lude House Perth 291 G10
Ludford Lincs 190 D2
Shrops 115 C10
Ludgershall Bucks 83 B11
Wilts 47 C9
Ludgvan Corn 2 C2
Ludham Norf 161 F7
Ludlow Shrops 115 C10
Ludney Lincs 190 B5
Som 28 E5
Ludstock Hereford 98 D3
Ludstone Shrops 132 E6
Ludwell Wilts 30 C6
Ludworth Durham 234 C3
Luffenhall Herts 104 F5
Luffincott Devon 12 C2
Lufton Som 29 D8
Lugar E Ayrs 258 E3
Lugate Borders 271 G8
Luggate Burn E Loth 282 G2
Lugg Green Hereford 115 E9
Luggiebank N Lanark 278 G5
Lugsdale Halton 183 D8
Lugton E Ayrs 267 E8
Lugwardine Hereford 97 C11
Luib Highld 295 C7
Luibeilt Highld 290 G4
Lulham Hereford 97 C8
Lullenden Sur 52 E2
Lullington Derbys 152 G5
Som 45 C9
Lulsgate Bottom N Som 60 F4
Lulsley Worcs 116 F4
Lulworth Camp Dorset 18 E2
Lumb Lancs 195 C10
Lancs 195 D9
W Yorks 196 C4
W Yorks 197 E7
Lumb Foot W Yorks 204 F6
Lumburn Devon 12 G5
Lumbutts W Yorks 196 C3
Lumby N Yorks 206 G5
Lumley W Sus 22 B3
Lumley Thicks Durham 243 G8
Lumloch E Dunb 268 B2
Lumphanan Aberds 293 C7
Lumphinnans Fife 280 C3
Lumsdaine Borders 273 B7
Lumsden Aberds 302 G4
Lunan Angus 287 B10
Lunanhead Angus 287 B8
Luncarty Perth 286 E4
Lund E Yorks 208 D5
N Yorks 207 G9
Shetland 312 C7
Lundal W Isles 304 E3
Lundavra Highld 290 G2
Lunderton Aberds 303 E11
Lundie Angus 286 D6
Highld 290 B3
Lundin Links Fife 287 G8
Lundwood S Yorks 197 F11
Lundy Green Norf 142 E4
Lunga Argyll 275 C8
Lunna Shetland 312 G6
Lunning Shetland 312 G7
Lunnister Shetland 312 F5
Lunnon Swansea 56 D4
Lunsford Kent 53 B7
Lunsford's Cross E Sus 38 E2
Lunt Mers 193 G10
Luntley Hereford 115 F7
Lunts Heath Halton 183 D8
Lupin Staffs 152 F2
Luppitt Devon 27 F11
Lupridge Devon 8 E4
Lupset W Yorks 197 D10
Lupton Cumb 211 C11
Lurg Aberds 293 C8
Lurgashall W Sus 34 B6
Lurignich Argyll 289 D11
Lurley Devon 26 E6
Lusby Lincs 174 B4
Luscott Shrops 131 D11
Luson Devon 8 F2
Luss Argyll 277 C7
Lussagiven Argyll 275 E7
Lusta Highld 298 D2
Lustleigh Devon 13 E11
Lustleigh Cleave Devon 13 E11
Luston Hereford 115 E9
Lusty Som 45 G7
Luthermuir Aberds 293 G8
Luthrie Fife 287 F7
Lutley W Mid 133 G8
Luton Devon 14 F4
Devon 27 G9
Luton 103 G11
Medway 69 F9
Lutsford Devon 24 D3
Lutterworth Leics 135 G10
Lutton Devon 7 D11
Devon 8 C3
Lincs 157 D8
Northants 138 F2
Lutton Gowts Lincs 157 E8
Lutworthy Devon 26 D3
Luxborough Som 42 F3
Luxley Glos 98 G3
Luxted London 68 G2
Luxton Devon 28 E2
Luxulyan Corn 5 D11
Luzley Gtr Man 196 G3
Luzley Brook Gtr Man 196 F2
Lyatts Som 29 E8
Lybster Highld 310 F6
Lydbury North Shrops 131 F7
Lydcott Devon 41 F7
Lydd Kent 39 C8
Lydden Kent 55 D9
Kent 71 F11
Lyddington Rutland 137 D7
Lydd on Sea Kent 39 C9
Lyde Orkney 314 E3
Shrops 130 C6
Lydeard St Lawrence Som 42 G6
Lyde Cross Hereford 97 C10
Lyde Green Hants 49 B8
S Glos 61 D7
Lydford Devon 12 E6
Lydford Fair Place Som 44 G5
Lydford-on-Fosse Som 44 G5
Lydgate Derbys 186 F4
Gtr Man 196 G3
W Yorks 196 B2
Lydham Shrops 130 E6
Lydiard Green Wilts 62 B5
Lydiard Millicent Wilts 62 B5
Lydiard Plain Wilts 62 B5
Lydiard Tregoze Swindon 62 C6
Lydiate Mers 193 G11
Lydiate Ash Worcs 117 B9
Lydlinch Dorset 30 E2
Lydmarsh Som 28 F5
Lydney Glos 79 E10
Lydstep Pembs 73 F9
Lye W Mid 133 G8
Lye Cross N Som 60 G3
Lye Green Bucks 85 E7
E Sus 52 G4
Warks 118 D3
Wilts 45 B10
Lye Head Worcs 116 C5
Lye Hole N Som 60 G4
Lyewood Common E Sus 52 F4
Lyford Oxon 82 G5
Lymbridge Green Kent 54 E6
Lyme Green Ches E 184 G6
Lyme Regis Dorset 16 C2
Lymiecleuch Borders 249 C9
Lyminge Kent 55 E7
Lymington Hants 20 B2
Lyminster W Sus 35 G8
Lymm Warr 183 D11
Lymore Hants 19 C11
Lympne Kent 54 F6
Lympsham Som 43 C10
Lympstone Devon 14 E5
Lynbridge Devon 41 D8
Lynch Hants 48 D4
Som 42 D2
Lynchat Highld 291 C9
Lynchgate Shrops 131 F7
Lynch Hill Hants 48 D3
Slough 66 C2
Lyndale Ho Highld 298 D3
Lyndhurst Hants 32 F4
Lyndon Rutland 137 C8
Lyndon Green W Mid 134 F2
Lyne Borders 270 G4
Sur 66 F4
Lyneal Shrops 149 C8
Lyneal Mill Shrops 149 C9
Lyneal Wood Shrops 149 C9
Lyne Down Hereford 98 E2
Lyneham Oxon 100 G5
Wilts 62 D4
Lynemore Highld 301 G10
Lynemouth Northumb 253 E7
Lyne of Gorthleck Highld 300 G5
Lyne of Skene Aberds 293 B9
Lyness Orkney 314 G3
Lyne Station Borders 260 B6
Lynford Norf 140 E6
Lyng Norf 159 F11
Som 28 B4
Lyngate Norf 160 C5
Lyngford Som 28 B2
Lynmore Highld 301 F10
Lynmouth Devon 41 D8
Lynn Staffs 133 C11
Telford 150 F5
Lynnwood Borders 261 G11
Lynsore Bottom Kent 55 D7
Lynsted Kent 70 G2
Lynstone Corn 24 F2
Lynton Devon 41 D8
Lynwilg Highld 291 B10
Lynworth Glos 99 G9
Lyons T&W 234 B3
Lyon's Gate Dorset 29 F11
Lyon's Green Norf 159 G8
Lyonshall Hereford 114 F6
Lyons Hall Essex 88 B2
Lypiatt Glos 80 D6
Lyrabus Argyll 274 G3
Lytchett Matravers Dorset 18 B4
Lytchett Minster Dorset 18 C5
Lyth Highld 310 C6
Lytham Lancs 193 B11
Lytham St Anne's Lancs 193 B10
Lythbank Shrops 131 B9
Lythe N Yorks 226 C6
Lythes Orkney 314 H4
Lythmore Highld 310 C4

M

Maam Argyll 284 F5
Mabe Burnthouse Corn 3 C7
Mabie Dumfries 237 B11
Mableton Kent 52 E5
Mablethorpe Lincs 191 D8
Macclesfield Ches E 184 G6
Macclesfield Forest Ches E 185 G7
Macduff Aberds 303 C7
Mace Green Suff 108 C2
Machan S Lanark 268 E5
Macharioch Argyll 255 G8
Machen Caerph 59 B8
Machrie N Ayrs 255 D9
Machrie Hotel Argyll 254 C4
Machrihanish Argyll 255 E7
Machroes Gwyn 144 D6
Machynlleth Powys 128 C4
Machynys Carms 56 B4
Mackerel's Common W Sus 35 B8
Mackerye End Herts 85 B11
Mackham Devon 27 F11
Mackney Oxon 64 B5
Mackside Borders 262 G4
Mackworth Derbys 152 B6
Macmerry E Loth 281 G8
Madderty Perth 286 E3
Maddington Wilts 46 E5
Maddiston Falk 279 F8
Maddox Moor Pembs 73 C7
Madehurst W Sus 35 E7
Madeley Staffs 168 G3
Telford 132 C3
Madeley Heath Staffs 168 F3
Worcs 117 B9
Madeley Park Staffs 168 G3
Madeleywood Telford 132 C3
Maders Corn 12 G2
Madford Devon 27 E10
Madingley Cambs 123 E7
Madjeston Dorset 30 B4
Madley Hereford 97 D8
Madresfield Worcs 98 B6
Madron Corn 1 C5
Maenaddwyn Anglesey 179 E7
Maenclochog Pembs 91 F11
Maendy V Glam 58 D4
Maenporth Corn 3 D7
Maentwrog Gwyn 163 G11
Maen-y-groes Ceredig 111 F7
Maer Corn 24 F2
Staffs 150 B5
Maerdy Carms 94 G2
Conwy 165 G8
Rhondda 77 F7
Maes-bangor Ceredig 128 G3
Maesbrook Shrops 148 E5
Maesbury Shrops 148 D6
Maesbury Marsh Shrops 148 D6
Maesgeirchen Gwyn 179 G9
Maes-glas Newport 59 B9
Maes Glas / Greenfield Flint 181 F11
Maesgwyn-Isaf Powys 148 G3
Maeshafn Denb 166 C2
Maesllyn Ceredig 93 C7
Maes llyn Ceredig 93 C7
Maesmynis Powys 95 B10
Maes Pennant Flint 181 F11
Maesteg Bridgend 57 C10
Maes-Treylow Powys 114 D5
Maesybont Carms 75 B9
Maesycoed Rhondda 58 B5
Maesycrugiau Carms 93 C9
Maesycwmmer Caerph 77 G11
Maes-y-dre Flint 166 C2
Maesygwartha Mon 78 C2
Maesymeillion Ceredig 93 B8
Maesypandy Powys 129 D9
Maesyrhandir Powys 129 E11
Magdalen Laver Essex 87 D8
Maggieknockater Moray 302 E3
Maggots End Essex 105 F9
Magham Down E Sus 23 C10
Maghull Mers 193 G11
Magor Mon 60 B2
Magpie Green Suff 125 B11
Mahaar Dumfries 236 B2
Maida Vale London 67 C9
Maidenbower W Sus 51 F9
Maiden Bradley Wilts 45 F10
Maidencombe Torbay 9 B8
Maidenhall Suff 108 C3
Maidenhead Windsor 65 C11
Maiden Head N Som 60 F5
Maidenhead Court Windsor 66 C2
Maiden Law Durham 233 B9
Maiden Newton Dorset 17 B7
Maidenpark Falk 279 E9
Maidens S Ayrs 244 B6
Maidensgrave Suff 108 B5
Maiden's Green Brack 65 E11
Maidensgrove Oxon 65 B8
Maiden's Hall Northumb 252 D6
Maidenwell Corn 11 G8
Lincs 190 F4
Maiden Wells Pembs 73 F7
Maidford Northants 120 G2
Maids Moreton Bucks 102 D4
Maidstone Kent 53 B9
Maidwell Northants 120 B4
Mail Shetland 313 L6
Mailand Shetland 312 C8
Mailingsland Borders 270 G4
Main Powys 148 F3
Maindee Newport 59 B10
Maindy Cardiff 59 D7
Mainholm S Ayrs 257 E9
Mains Cumb 229 G7
Mainsforth Durham 234 E2
Mains of Airies Dumfries 236 C1
Mains of Allardice Aberds 293 F10
Mains of Annochie Aberds 303 E9
Mains of Ardestie Angus 287 D9
Mains of Arnage Aberds 303 F9
Mains of Auchoynanie Moray 302 E4
Mains of Baldoon Dumfries 236 D6
Mains of Balhall Angus 293 G7
Mains of Ballindarg Angus 287 B8
Mains of Balnakettle Aberds 293 F8
Mains of Birness Aberds 303 F9
Mains of Blackhall Aberds 303 G7
Mains of Burgie Moray 301 D10
Mains of Cairnbrogie Aberds 303 G8
Mains of Cairnty Moray 302 D3
Mains of Clunas Highld 301 E8
Mains of Crichie Aberds 303 E9
Mains of Daltulich Highld 301 E7
Mains of Dalvey Highld 301 F11
Mains of Dellavaird Aberds 293 E9
Mains of Drum Aberds 293 D10
Mains of Edingight Moray 302 D5
Mains of Fedderate Aberds 303 E8
Mains of Flichity Highld 300 G6
Mains of Hatton Aberds 303 D9
Aberds 303 E7
Mains of Inkhorn Aberds 303 F9
Mains of Innerpeffray Perth 286 F3
Mains of Kirktonhill Aberds 293 G8
Mains of Laithers Aberds 302 E6
Mains of Mayen Moray 302 E5
Mains of Melgund Angus 287 B9
Mains of Taymouth Perth 285 C11
Mains of Thornton Aberds 293 F8
Mains of Towie Aberds 303 E7
Mains of Ulbster Highld 310 E7
Mains of Watten Highld 310 D6
Mainsriddle Dumfries 237 D11
Mainstone Shrops 130 F5
Maisemore Glos 98 G6
Maitland Park London 67 C9
Major's Green W Mid 118 B2
Makeney Derbys 170 G5
Malacleit W Isles 296 D3
Malborough Devon 9 G9
Malcoff Derbys 185 E9
Malden Rushett London 67 G7
Maldon Essex 88 D4
Malehurst Shrops 131 B7
Malham N Yorks 213 G8
Maligar Highld 298 C4
Malinbridge S Yorks 186 D4
Malinslee Telford 132 B3
Malkin's Bank Ches E 168 D3
Mallaig Highld 295 F8
Mallaig Bheag Highld 295 F8
Malleny Mills Edin 270 B3
Malling Stirling 285 G9
Mallows Green Essex 105 F9
Malltraeth Anglesey 162 B6
Mallwyd Gwyn 147 G7
Malmesbury Wilts 62 B2
Malmsmead Devon 41 D9
Malpas Ches W 167 F7
Corn 4 G6
Newport 78 G4
W Berks 64 E6
Malswick Glos 98 F4
Maltby Lincs 190 E4
S Yorks 187 C8
Stockton 225 C9
Maltby le Marsh Lincs 191 E7
Malting End Suff 124 G4
Malting Green Essex 107 G9
Maltings Angus 293 G9
Maltman's Hill Kent 54 E2
Malton N Yorks 216 E5
Malvern Common Worcs 98 C5
Malvern Link Worcs 98 B5
Malvern Wells Worcs 98 C5
Mambeg Argyll 276 D4
Mamble Worcs 116 C3
Mamhilad Mon 78 E4
Manaccan Corn 3 E7
Manadon Plym 7 D9
Manafon Powys 130 C2
Manais W Isles 296 C7
Manar Ho Aberds 303 G7
Manaton Devon 13 E11
Manby Lincs 190 D5
Mancetter Warks 134 D6
Manchester Gtr Man 184 B4
Manchester Airport Gtr Man 184 D4
Mancot Flint 166 B4
Mancot Royal Flint 166 B4
Mandally Highld 290 C4
Manea Cambs 139 F9
Maney W Mid 134 D2
Manfield N Yorks 224 C4
Mangaster Shetland 312 F5
Mangotsfield S Glos 61 D7
Mangrove Green Herts 104 G2
Mangurstadh W Isles 304 E2
Manhay Corn 2 C5
Manian-fawr Pembs 92 B3
Mankinholes W Yorks 196 C3
Manley Ches W 183 G8
Devon 27 E7
Manley Common Ches W 183 G8
Manmoel Caerph 77 E11
Man-moel Caerph 77 E11
Mannal Argyll 288 E1
Mannamead Plym 7 D9
Mannerston W Loth 279 F10
Manningford Abbots Wilts 46 B6
Manningford Bohune Wilts 46 B6
Manningford Bruce Wilts 46 B6
Manningham W Yorks 205 G9
Mannings Heath W Sus 36 B2
Mannington Dorset 31 F9
Manningtree Essex 107 E11
Mannofield Aberdeen 293 C11
Manor London 68 B2
Manorbier Pembs 73 F9
Manorbier Newton Pembs 73 F8
Manor Bourne Devon 7 F9
Manordeilo Carms 94 F3
Manor Estate S Yorks 186 D5
Manorhill Borders 262 C5
Manor Hill Corner Lincs 157 F8
Manor House W Mid 135 G7
Manorowen Pembs 91 D8
Manor Park Bucks 84 C4
Ches W 167 B11
E Sus 37 C7
London 68 B2
Notts 153 C11
S Yorks 186 D5
Slough 66 C3
W Yorks 205 D9
Manor Parsley Corn 4 F4
Manor Royal W Sus 51 F9
Man's Cross Essex 106 D5
Mansegate Dumfries 247 G9
Manselfield Swansea 56 D5
Mansel Lacy Hereford 97 B8
Mansell Gamage Hereford 97 C7
Manselton Swansea 57 B7
Mansergh Cumb 212 C2
Mansewood Glasgow 267 C11
Mansfield E Ayrs 258 G4
Notts 171 C8
Mansfield Woodhouse Notts 171 C8
Manson Green Norf 141 C10
Mansriggs Cumb 210 C5
Manston Dorset 30 D4
Kent 71 F10
W Yorks 206 F3
Manswood Dorset 31 F7
Manthorpe Lincs 155 B8
Lincs 155 F11
Mantles Green Bucks 85 F7
Manton N Lincs 200 G2
Notts 187 F9
Rutland 137 C7
Wilts 63 F7
Manton Warren N Lincs 200 F2
Manuden Essex 105 F9
Manwood Green Essex 87 C8
Manywells Height W Yorks 205 F7
Maperton Som 29 B11
Maplebeck Notts 172 C2
Maple Cross Herts 85 G8
Mapledurham Oxon 65 D7
Mapledurwell Hants 49 C7
Maple End Essex 105 D11
Maplehurst W Sus 35 C11
Maplescombe Kent 68 G5
Mapleton Derbys 169 F11
Mapperley Derbys 170 G6
Nottingham 171 G9
Mapperley Park Nottingham 171 G9

398 Mid–Mou

Middletown *continued*
N Som 60 E3
Powys 148 G6
Warks 117 E11
Middle Town Scilly 1 F4
Middle Tysoe Warks 100 C6
Middle Wallop Hants 47 F9
Middle Weald
M Keynes 102 D5
Middlewich
Ches E 167 B11
Middlewick Wilts 61 E11
Middle Wick Glos 80 F2
Middle Winterslow
Wilts 47 G8
Middlewood Ches E 184 E6
Corn 11 F11
S Yorks 186 C4
Middle Woodford
Wilts 46 F6
Middlewood Green
Suff 125 E11
Middleyard Glos 80 E4
Middlezoy Som 43 G11
Middridge Durham 233 F11
Midelney Som 28 C6
Midfield Highld 308 C5
Midford Bath 61 G9
Midgard Borders 262 F3
Mid Garrary
Dumfries 237 B7
Midge Hall Lancs 194 C4
Midgehole W Yorks 196 B3
Midgeholme Cumb 240 F4
Midgham W Berks 64 F5
Midgham Green
W Berks 64 F5
Midgley W Yorks 196 B4
W Yorks 197 E9
Mid Holmwood Sur 51 D7
Midhopestones
S Yorks 186 B2
Midhurst W Sus 34 C5
Mid Lambrook Som 28 D6
Midland Orkney 314 F3
Mid Lavant W Sus 22 B5
Midlem Borders 262 D2
Mid Letter Argyll 284 G4
Midlock S Lanark 259 E11
Mid Main Highld 300 F4
Midmar Aberds 293 C8
Midmuir Argyll 289 G11
Mid Murthat
Dumfries 248 D3
Midpark Argyll 255 B11
Midplaugh Aberds 302 E5
Midsomer Norton
Bath 45 C7
Midton Invclyd 276 F4
Midtown Highld 307 L3
Highld 308 C5
Midtown of Buchromb
Moray 302 E3
Midtown of Glass
Aberds 302 E4
Mid Urchany Highld 301 E8
Midville Lincs 174 D5
Mid Walls Shetland 313 H4
Midway Ches E 184 E6
Som 45 D7
Mid Yell Shetland 312 D7
Miekle Toux Aberds 302 D5
Migdale Highld 309 K6
Migvie Aberds 292 C6
Milarrochy Stirling 277 C8
Milber Devon 14 G3
Milborne Port Som 29 D11
Milborne St Andrew
Dorset 18 B2
Milborne Wick Som 29 C11
Milbourne Northumb 242 B4
Wilts 62 B2
Milburn Aberds 302 E5
Aberds 302 F6
Cumb 231 F9
Milbury Heath
S Glos 79 G11
Milby N Yorks 215 F8
Milch Hill Essex 106 G4
Milcombe Corn 6 D4
Oxon 101 E8
Milden Suff 107 B9
Mildenhall Suff 124 C4
Wilts 63 F8
Milebrook Powys 114 C6
Milebush Kent 53 D9
Mile Cross Norf 160 G4
Mile Elm Wilts 62 F3
Mile End Cambs 140 G2
Devon 14 G2
Essex 107 F9
Glos 79 C9
London 67 C11
Suff 124 G6
Mileham Norf 159 F8
Mile Oak Brighton 36 F2
Kent 53 E7
Shrops 148 D6
Staffs 134 C3
Miles Green Staffs 168 F4
Sur 50 B3
Miles Hill W Yorks 205 F11
Milesmark Fife 279 D11
Miles Platting
Gtr Man 184 B5
Miles's Green
W Berks 64 F4
Mile Town Kent 70 E2
Milfield Northumb 263 C10
Milford Derbys 170 F5
Devon 24 C2
Powys 129 E11
Shrops 149 E8
Staffs 151 E9
Sur 50 E2
Wilts 31 B11
Milford Haven Pembs 72 D6
Milford on Sea
Hants 19 C11
Milkhouse Water
Wilts 63 G7
Milkieston Borders 270 F4
Milkwall Glos 79 D9
Milkwell Wilts 30 C6
Milland W Sus 34 B4
Millarston Renfs 267 C9
Millbank Aberds 303 E11
Highld 310 C5
Kent 71 F8
Mill Bank W Yorks 196 C4
Millbeck Cumb 229 F11
Millbounds Orkney 314 C5
Millbreck Aberds 303 E10
Millbridge Sur 49 E10
Millbrook C Beds 103 D10
Corn 7 E8
Devon 41 G9
Gtr Man 185 B7
Soton 32 E5
Mill Brow Gtr Man 185 D7
Millburn S Ayrs 257 D10
Millcombe Devon 8 F6
Mill Common Norf 142 C6
Suff 143 G8
Mill Corner E Sus 38 C4
Milldale Staffs 169 E10
Mill Dam N Yorks 212 F3
Millden Lodge
Angus 293 F7
Milldens Angus 287 B9
Millend Glos 80 D3
Glos 80 F3
Mill End Bucks 65 C9
Cambs 124 F3
Glos 81 C10
Herts 85 G8
Herts 104 E6
Mill End Green
Essex 106 F2
Millendreath Corn 6 E5
Millerhill Midloth 270 B6
Miller's Dale
Derbys 185 G10
Miller's Green
Derbys 170 E3
Essex 87 D9
Millersneuk E Dunb 278 G3
Millerston Glasgow 268 B2
Mill Farm Aberds 303 C8
Millfield Pboro 138 C3
T&W 243 F9
Millgate Lancs 195 D11
Norf 160 D3
Millgillhead Cumb 229 G7
Mill Green Cambs 106 B2
Essex 87 E10
Hants 64 G4
Herts 86 D2
Norf 142 G2
Shrops 150 D3
Suff 107 C9
Suff 125 F9
Suff 126 E2
W Mid 133 C11
Millhalf Hereford 96 B5
Millhall Kent 53 B8
Mill Hall Dumfries 237 E8
Millhayes Devon 27 E10
Devon 28 G2
Millhead Lancs 211 E9
Millheugh S Lanark 268 E5
Millhill Devon 12 G5
Mill Hill Blackburn 195 B7
E Sus 23 D10
Essex 88 G4
Glos 79 D10
Gtr Man 195 F8
Kent 55 C11
Lincs 175 B8
London 86 G2
Suff 125 G7
Mill Hills Suff 108 B5
Mill Hirst N Yorks 214 G3
Millholme Cumb 221 G11
Millhouse Argyll 275 F10
Cumb 230 D3
Millhousebridge
Dumfries 248 F4
Millhouse Green
S Yorks 197 G8
Millhouses S Yorks 186 E4
S Yorks 198 G2
Millikenpark Renfs 267 C8
Millin Cross Pembs 73 C7
Millington E Yorks 208 C2
Millington Green
Derbys 170 F3
Mill Lane Hants 49 C9
Mill Meads London 67 C11
Millmeece Staffs 150 C6
Millmoor Devon 27 E10
Millness Cumb 211 C10
Mill of Brydock
Aberds 302 D6
Mill of Chon Stirling 285 G8
Mill of Haldane
W Dunb 277 E8
Mill of Kingoodie
Aberds 303 G8
Mill of Lynebain
Aberds 302 F4
Mill of Muiresk
Aberds 302 E6
Mill of Rango
Orkney 314 E2
Mill of Sterin
Aberds 292 D5
Mill of Uras Aberds 293 E10
Millom Cumb 210 C3
Millook Corn 11 B9
Millow C Beds 104 C4
Mill Park Argyll 255 G8
Mill Place N Lincs 200 F3
Millpool Corn 2 C3
Corn 11 G8
Millport N Ayrs 266 E3
Millquarter
Dumfries 246 G4
Mill Shaw W Yorks 205 G11
Mill Side Cumb 211 C8
Mill Street Kent 53 B7
Norf 159 F11
Suff 107 D9
Milltack Aberds 303 D7
Millthorpe Derbys 186 F4
Lincs 156 C2
Mill Throop Bmouth 19 B8
Millthrop Cumb 222 G3
Milltimber
Aberdeen 293 C10
Milltown Aberds 292 C4
Milltown *continued*
Corn 6 B2
Corn 6 D2
Derbys 170 C5
Devon 40 F5
Highld 301 E9
Milltown of Aberdalgie
Perth 286 E4
Milltown of Auchindoun
Moray 302 E3
Milltown of Craigston
Aberds 303 D7
Milltown of Edinvillie
Moray 302 E2
Milltown of Kildrummy
Aberds 292 B6
Milltown of Rothiemay
Moray 302 E5
Milltown of Towie
Aberds 292 B6
Millwall London 67 D11
Milnathort Perth 286 G5
Milner's Heath
Ches W 167 C7
Milngavie E Dunb 277 G11
Milnquarter Falk 278 F6
Milnrow Gtr Man 196 E2
Milnsbridge
W Yorks 196 D6
Milnshaw Lancs 195 B9
Milnthorpe Cumb 211 C9
W Yorks 197 D10
Milnwood N Lanark 268 D4
Milo Carms 75 B9
Milson Shrops 116 C2
Milstead Kent 54 B2
Milston Wilts 47 D7
Milthorpe
Northants 101 B11
Milton
Angus 287 C7
Angus 292 E6
Cambs 123 E9
Cumb 211 C10
Cumb 240 E3
Derbys 152 D6
Dumfries 236 D4
Dumfries 237 B10
Dumfries 247 G8
Fife 287 E8
Glasgow 267 B11
Highld 299 E7
Highld 300 D3
Highld 300 E5
Highld 300 F4
Highld 301 B7
Highld 301 E7
Highld 310 D7
Kent 69 E7
Moray 292 B3
Moray 302 C5
N Som 59 G10
Notts 188 G2
Oxon 83 G7
Oxon 101 E9
Pembs 73 E8
Perth 286 F3
Powys 114 G4
Ptsmth 21 B9
S Yorks 197 G11
Som 29 C7
Stirling 285 G9
Stoke 168 E6
W Dunb 277 G8
Wilts 45 G11
Milton Abbas Dorset 30 G4
Milton Bridge
Midloth 270 C4
Milton Bryan
C Beds 103 E9
Milton Clevedon Som 45 F7
Milton Coldwells
Aberds 303 F9
Milton Combe Devon 7 B9
Milton Common
Oxon 83 E11
Milton Coombe Devon 7 B9
Milton Damerel
Devon 24 E5
Miltonduff Moray 301 C11
Milton End Glos 80 C2
Glos 81 E10
Milton Ernest Beds 121 F10
Milton Green
Ches W 167 D7
Devon 12 F4
Milton Heights Oxon 83 G7
Miltonhill Moray 301 C10
Milton Hill Devon 14 F4
Oxon 83 G7
Miltonise Dumfries 236 B3
Milton Keynes
M Keynes 103 D7
Milton Keynes Village
M Keynes 103 D7
Milton Lilbourne
Wilts 63 G7
Milton Malsor
Northants 120 F4
Milton Morenish
Perth 285 D10
Milton of Auchinhove
Aberds 293 C7
Milton of Balgonie
Fife 287 G7
Milton of Buchanan
Stirling 277 C8
Milton of Campfield
Aberds 293 C8
Milton of Campsie
E Dunb 278 F3
Milton of Corsindae
Aberds 293 C8
Milton of Cullerlie
Aberds 293 C9
Milton of Cultoquhey
Perth 286 E2
Milton of Cushnie
Aberds 293 B7
Milton of Dalcapon
Perth 286 B3
Milton of Drimmie
Perth 286 B5
Milton of Edradour
Perth 286 B3
Milton of Gollanfield
Highld 301 D7
Milton of Lesmore
Aberds 302 G4
Milton of Logie
Aberds 292 C6
Milton of Machany
Perth 286 F3
Milton of Mathers
Aberds 293 G9
Milton of Murtle
Aberdeen 293 C10
Milton of Noth
Aberds 302 G5
Milton of Tullich
Aberds 292 D5
Milton on Stour
Dorset 30 B3
Milton Regis Kent 70 F2
Milton Street E Sus 23 E8
Milton under Wychwood
Oxon 82 B3
Milverton Som 27 B10
Warks 118 D6
Milwich Staffs 151 C9
Milwr Flint 181 G11
Mimbridge Sur 66 G3
Minard Argyll 275 D10
Minard Castle
Argyll 275 D10
Minchington Dorset 31 E7
Minchinhampton
Glos 80 E5
Mindrum Northumb 263 C8
Minehead Som 42 D3
Minera Wrex 166 E3
Mineshope Corn 11 B9
Minety Wilts 81 G8
Minffordd Gwyn 145 B11
Gwyn 146 G4
Gwyn 179 G9
Mingarrypark
Highld 289 C8
Mingoose Corn 4 F4
Miningsby Lincs 174 C4
Minions Corn 11 G11
Minishant S Ayrs 257 G8
Minllyn Gwyn 147 G7
Minnes Aberds 303 G9
Minngearraidh
W Isles 297 J3
Minnigaff Dumfries 236 C6
Minnonie Aberds 303 C7
Minnow End Essex 88 C2
Minnygap Dumfries 248 D2
Minshull Vernon
Ches E 167 C11
Minskip N Yorks 215 G7
Minstead Hants 32 E3
Minsted W Sus 34 C5
Minster Kent 70 E3
Kent 71 G10
Minsterley Shrops 131 C7
Minster Lovell Oxon 82 C4
Minsterworth Glos 80 B3
Minterne Magna
Dorset 29 G11
Minterne Parva
Dorset 29 G11
Minting Lincs 189 G11
Mintlaw Aberds 303 E10
Minto Borders 262 E3
Minto Kames
Borders 262 E3
Minton Shrops 131 E8
Mintsfeet Cumb 221 G10
Minwear Pembs 73 C8
Minworth W Mid 134 E3
Mirbister Orkney 314 E2
Mirehouse Cumb 219 B9
Mireland Highld 310 C7
Mirfield W Yorks 197 D8
Miserden Glos 80 D6
Misery Corner Norf 142 F5
Miskin Rhondda 58 C4
Rhondda 77 F8
Misselfore Wilts 31 C8
Misson Notts 187 C11
Misterton Leics 135 G11
Notts 188 C3
Som 29 F7
Misterton Soss
Notts 188 B3
Mistley Essex 108 E2
Mistley Heath Essex 108 E2
Mitcham London 67 F9
Mitcheldean Glos 79 B11
Mitchell Corn 5 E7
Mitchell Hill
Borders 260 C3
Mitchellslacks
Dumfries 247 D11
Mitchelston Borders 271 F9
Mitchel Troy Mon 79 C7
Mitcheltroy Common
Mon 79 D7
Mite Houses Cumb 219 F11
Mitford Northumb 252 F5
Mithian Corn 4 E4
Mithian Downs Corn 4 F4
Mitton Staffs 151 F7
Worcs 99 E8
Mixbury Oxon 102 E2
Mixenden W Yorks 196 B5
Mixtow Corn 6 E2
Moat Cumb 239 C10
Moats Tye Suff 125 F10
Mobberley Ches E 184 F3
Staffs 169 G8
Moblake Ches E 167 G11
Mobwell Bucks 84 E5
Moccas Hereford 97 C7
Mochdre Conwy 180 F4
Powys 129 F11
Mochrum Dumfries 236 E5
Mockbeggar Hants 31 F11
Kent 54 E6
Medway 69 E8
Mockerkin Cumb 229 G7
Moclett Orkney 314 B4
Modbury Devon 8 E3
Moddershall Staffs 151 B8
Model Village
Derbys 187 G8
Warks 119 E8
Modest Corner Kent 52 E5
Moelfre Anglesey 179 D8
Conwy 181 G7
Powys 148 D3
Moel Tryfan Gwyn 163 D8
Moel-y-crio Flint 165 B11
Moffat Dumfries 248 B3
Moffat Mills
N Lanark 268 C5
Mogador Sur 51 C8
Moggerhanger
C Beds 104 B2
Mogworthy Devon 26 D5
Moira Leics 152 F6
Moity Powys 96 C3
Molash Kent 54 C4
Mol-chlach Highld 294 D6
Mold Flint 166 C2
Moldgreen W Yorks 197 D7
Molehill Green
Essex 105 G11
Essex 106 G4
Molescroft E Yorks 208 E6
Molesden Northumb 252 G4
Molesworth Cambs 121 B11
Molinnis Corn 5 D10
Moll Highld 295 B7
Molland Devon 26 B4
Mollington Ches W 182 G5
Oxon 101 B8
Mollinsburn
N Lanark 278 G4
Monachty Ceredig 111 E10
Monachylemore
Stirling 285 F8
Monar Lodge Highld 300 E2
Monaughty Powys 114 D4
Monboddo House
Aberds 293 F9
Mondaytown Shrops 130 B6
Mondynes Aberds 293 F9
Monemore Stirling 285 D9
Monevechadan
Argyll 284 G5
Monewden Suff 126 F4
Moneyacres E Ayrs 267 E8
Moneydie Perth 286 E4
Moneyhill Herts 85 G8
Money Hill Leics 153 F7
Moneyrow Green
Windsor 65 D11
Moneystone Staffs 169 F9
Mongleath Corn 3 C7
Moniaive Dumfries 247 E7
Monifieth Angus 287 D8
Monikie Angus 287 D8
Monimail Fife 286 F6
Monington Pembs 92 C2
Monk Bretton
S Yorks 197 F11
Monk End N Yorks 224 D5
Monken Hadley
London 86 F3
Monkerton Devon 14 C5
Monk Fryston
N Yorks 198 B4
Monk Hesleden
Durham 234 D5
Monkhide Hereford 98 C2
Monkhill Cumb 239 F8
W Yorks 198 C3
Monkhopton Shrops 132 E2
Monkland Hereford 115 F9
Monkleigh Devon 25 C7
Monkmoor Shrops 149 G10
Monknash V Glam 58 E2
Monkokehampton
Devon 25 F9
Monkscross Corn 12 G3
Monkseaton T&W 243 C8
Monks Eleigh Suff 107 B9
Monk's Gate W Sus 36 B2
Monks Heath
Ches E 184 G4
Monk Sherborne
Hants 48 B6
Monkshill Aberds 303 E7
Monks Hill Kent 53 E11
Monksilver Som 42 F5
Monks Kirby Warks 135 G9
Monk Soham Suff 126 D4
Monks Orchard
London 67 F11
Monk's Park Wilts 61 F11
Monkspath W Mid 118 B2
Monks Risborough
Bucks 84 E4
Monksthorpe Lincs 174 B6
Monkston Park
M Keynes 103 D7
Monk Street Essex 106 F2
Monkswood Midloth 270 C6
Mon 78 E4
W Yorks 206 F2
Monkton Devon 27 G11
Kent 71 G9
Pembs 73 E7
S Ayrs 257 D9
T&W 243 E8
V Glam 58 E2
Monkton Combe
Bath 61 G9
Monkton Deverill
Wilts 45 F11
Monkton Farleigh
Wilts 61 F10
Monktonhall E Loth 280 G6
Monkton Heathfield
Som 28 B3
Monkton Up Wimborne
Dorset 31 E8
Monkwearmouth
T&W 243 F9
Monkwood Hants 49 G7
Monkwood Green
Worcs 116 E6
Monmarsh Hereford 97 B10
Monmore Green
W Mid 133 D8
Monmouth Cap Mon 97 F7
Monmouth / Trefynwy
Mon 79 C8
Monnington on Wye
Hereford 97 C7
Monreith Dumfries 236 E5
Monreith Mains
Dumfries 236 E5
Montacute Som 29 D7
Montcliffe Gtr Man 195 E7
Montcoffer Ho
Aberds 302 C6
Montford Argyll 266 C2
Shrops 149 G8
Montford Bridge
Shrops 149 F8
Montgarrie Aberds 293 B7
Montgomery Powys 130 D4
Montgomery Lines
Hants 49 C11
Monton Gtr Man 184 B3
Montpelier Bristol 60 E5
Montrave Fife 287 G7
Montrose Angus 287 B11
Montsale Essex 89 F8
Monwode Lea
Warks 134 E5
Monxton Hants 47 E10
Monyash Derbys 169 B11
Monymusk Aberds 293 B8
Monzie Perth 286 E2
Monzie Castle Perth 286 E2
Moodiesburn
N Lanark 278 G3
Moolham Som 28 E5
Moon's Green Kent 38 B5
Moon's Moat
Worcs 117 D11
Moonzie Fife 287 F7
Moor Som 28 D6
Mooradale Shetland 312 F6
Moor Allerton
W Yorks 205 F11
Mooray Wilts 46 G3
Moorby Lincs 174 C3
Moorclose Cumb 228 F5
Gtr Man 195 F11
Moor Common Bucks 84 G4
Moorcot Hereford 115 F7
Moor Crichel Dorset 31 F7
Moor Cross Devon 8 D2
Moordown Bmouth 19 C7
Moore Halton 183 E9
Moor Edge W Yorks 205 F7
Moorend Cumb 239 G8
Derbys 170 F2
Dumfries 239 C7
Glos 80 C5
Glos 80 E2
Gtr Man 185 D7
S Glos 61 D7
Moor End Bucks 84 G4
C Beds 103 G9
Cambs 105 B7
Durham 234 C2
E Yorks 208 F2
Glos 99 G9
Lancs 202 E3
N Yorks 207 F7
N Yorks 215 G7
S Yorks 197 G9
W Yorks 196 B5
W Yorks 206 D4
Worcs 117 F8
York 207 B9
Moorend Cross
Hereford 98 B4
Moor End Field
N Yorks 215 F8
Moorends S Yorks 199 D7
Moorfield Derbys 185 C8
Moorgate Norf 160 C3
S Yorks 186 C6
Moorgreen Hants 33 D7
Notts 171 F7
Moor Green Herts 104 F6
Staffs 169 G7
W Mid 133 G11
Wilts 61 F11
Moorhaigh Notts 171 C8
Moorhall Derbys 186 G4
Moor Hall W Mid 134 D2
Moorhampton
Hereford 97 B7
Moorhaven Village
Devon 8 D3
Moorhayne Devon 28 F2
Moorhead W Yorks 205 F8
Moor Head W Yorks 197 B8
W Yorks 197 E8
Moorhey Gtr Man 196 G2
Moorhole S Yorks 186 E6
Moorhouse Cumb 239 F8
Cumb 239 G7
Notts 172 B3
S Yorks 198 E3
Moorhouse Bank Sur 52 C2
Moorhouses Lincs 174 D3
Moorland or Northmoor
Green Som 43 G10
Moorledge Bath 60 G5
Moorlinch Som 43 F11
Moor Monkton
N Yorks 206 B6
Moor Monkton Moor
N Yorks 206 B6
Moor of Balvack
Aberds 293 B8
Moor of Granary
Moray 301 D10
Moor of Ravenstone
Dumfries 236 E5
Moor Park Cumb 229 D7
Hereford 97 C9
Herts 85 G9
Sur 49 D11
Moor Row Cumb 219 C10
Cumb 229 B10
Moorsholm Redcar 226 C3
Moorside Ches W 182 F3
Dorset 30 D3
Durham 233 B7
Gtr Man 195 G9
Gtr Man 196 F3
W Yorks 197 B8
W Yorks 205 F10
Moor Side Lancs 202 F5
Lancs 202 G4
Lincs 174 D2
W Yorks 197 B7
W Yorks 204 F6
Moorstock Kent 54 F6
Moor Street Kent 69 F10
Moorswater Corn 6 C4
Moorthorpe
W Yorks 198 E3
Moor Top W Yorks 197 C7
Moortown Devon 12 B2
Devon 12 G6
Moortown *continued*
Devon 25 C8
Hants 31 G11
IoW 20 E4
Lincs 189 B9
Telford 150 F2
W Yorks 206 F2
Morangie Highld 309 L7
Morar Highld 295 F8
Moravian Settlement
Derbys 153 B8
Môrawelon
Anglesey 178 E3
Morayhill Highld 301 E7
Morborne Cambs 138 E2
Morchard Bishop
Devon 26 F3
Morchard Road
Devon 26 G3
Morcombelake
Dorset 16 C4
Morcott Rutland 137 C8
Morda Shrops 148 D5
Morden Dorset 18 B4
London 67 F9
Morden Green
Cambs 104 C5
Morden Park London 67 F8
Mordiford Hereford 97 D11
Mordington Holdings
Borders 273 D8
Mordon Durham 234 F2
More Shrops 130 E6
Morebath Devon 27 C7
Morebattle Borders 263 E7
Morecambe Lancs 211 G8
More Crichel Dorset 31 F7
Moredon Swindon 62 B6
Moredun Edin 270 B5
Morefield Highld 307 K6
Morehall Kent 55 F8
Morelaggan Argyll 284 G6
Moreleigh Devon 8 E5
Morenish Perth 285 D9
Moresby Cumb 228 G5
Moresby Parks
Cumb 219 B9
Morestead Hants 33 B8
Moreton Dorset 18 D2
Essex 87 D8
Hereford 115 E10
Mers 182 C3
Oxon 82 E6
Oxon 83 E11
Staffs 150 F5
Staffs 152 D2
Moreton Corbet
Shrops 149 E11
Moretonhampstead
Devon 13 D11
Moreton-in-Marsh
Glos 100 E4
Moreton Jeffries
Hereford 98 B2
Moreton Morrell
Warks 118 F6
Moreton on Lugg
Hereford 97 B10
Moreton Paddox
Warks 118 G6
Moreton Pinkney
Northants 101 B11
Moreton Say Shrops 150 C2
Moreton Valence
Glos 80 D3
Moretonwood
Shrops 150 C2
Morfa Carms 56 B4
Carms 75 C9
Ceredig 110 G6
Gwyn 144 C3
Morfa Bach Carms 74 C5
Morfa Bychan
Gwyn 145 B10
Morfa Dinlle Gwyn 162 D6
Morfa Glas Neath 76 D5
Morfa Nefyn Gwyn 162 G3
Morfydd Denb 165 F10
Morganstown Cardiff 58 C6
Morgan's Vale Wilts 31 C11
Moriah Ceredig 112 B2
Mork Glos 79 D9
Morland Cumb 231 G7
Morley Ches E 184 E4
Derbys 170 G5
Durham 233 F8
W Yorks 197 B9
Morley Green
Ches E 184 E4
Morleymoor Derbys 170 G5
Morley Park Derbys 170 F5
Morley St Botolph
Norf 141 D11
Morley Smithy
Derbys 170 G5
Mornick Corn 12 G2
Morningside Edin 280 G3
N Lanark 268 D6
Morningthorpe Norf 142 E4
Morpeth Northumb 252 F6
Morphie Aberds 293 G9
Morrey Staffs 152 F2
Morridge Side
Staffs 169 E8
Morrilow Heath
Staffs 151 B9
Morris Green Essex 106 E4
Morriston / Treforys
Swansea 57 B7
Morristown V Glam 59 E7
Morston Norf 177 E8
Mortehoe Devon 40 D3
Morthen S Yorks 187 D7
Mortimer W Berks 65 G7
Mortimer's Cross
Hereford 115 E8
Mortimer West End
Hants 64 G6
Mortlake London 67 D8
Mortomley S Yorks 186 B4
Morton Cumb 230 D4
Cumb 239 G9
Derbys 170 C6
IoW 21 D8
Lincs 155 E11
Lincs 172 C5
Lincs 188 C4
Morton *continued*
Norf 160 F2
Notts 172 E2
S Glos 79 G10
Shrops 148 E5
Morton Bagot
Warks 118 E2
Morton Common
Shrops 148 E5
Morton Mains
Dumfries 247 D9
Morton Mill Shrops 149 E11
Morton-on-Swale
N Yorks 224 G6
Morton Spirt
Warks 117 G10
Morton Tinmouth
Durham 233 G9
Morton Underhill
Worcs 117 F10
Morvah Corn 1 B4
Morval Corn 6 D5
Morven Lodge
Aberds 292 C5
Morvich Highld 295 C11
Highld 309 J7
Morville Shrops 132 E3
Morville Heath
Shrops 132 E3
Morwellham Quay
Devon 7 B8
Morwenstow Corn 24 E2
Mosborough
S Yorks 186 E6
Moscow E Ayrs 267 G9
Mose Shrops 132 E5
Mosedale Cumb 230 E3
Moseley W Mid 133 D8
W Mid 133 G11
Worcs 116 F6
Moses Gate
Gtr Man 195 F8
Mosley Common
Gtr Man 195 G8
Moss Argyll 288 E1
Highld 289 C8
S Yorks 198 E5
Wrex 166 E4
Mossat Aberds 292 B6
Mossbank Shetland 312 F6
Moss Bank Halton 183 D8
Mers 183 B8
Mossbay Cumb 228 F5
Mossblown S Ayrs 257 E10
Mossbrow Gtr Man 184 D2
Mossburnford
Borders 262 F5
Mossdale Dumfries 237 B8
Mossedge Cumb 239 D11
Moss Edge Lancs 202 D4
Lancs 202 E4
Mossend N Lanark 268 C4
Moss End Brack 65 E11
Ches E 183 F11
Mosser Mains Cumb 229 F8
Mossfield Highld 300 B6
Mossgate Staffs 151 B8
Mossgiel E Ayrs 257 D11
Mosshouses Borders 262 B2
Moss Houses
Ches E 184 G5
Mosside Angus 287 B8
Moss Lane Ches E 184 G6
Mossley Ches E 168 C5
Gtr Man 196 G3
Mossley Brow
Gtr Man 196 G3
Mossley Hill Mers 182 D5
Moss Nook Gtr Man 184 D4
Mers 183 C8
Moss of Barmuckity
Moray 302 C2
Moss of Meft Moray 302 C2
Mosspark Glasgow 267 C10
Moss Pit Staffs 151 E8
Moss Side Cumb 238 G5
Gtr Man 184 B4
Moss-side Highld 301 D8
Moss Side Lancs 193 G11
Lancs 194 C4
Lancs 202 G3
Mers 182 B6
Moss-side Moray 302 D5
Mosstodloch Moray 302 D3
Mosston Angus 287 C9
Mosstown Aberds 303 C10
Mossy Lea Lancs 194 E4
Mosterton Dorset 29 F7
Moston Ches E 168 C2
Ches W 182 G6
Gtr Man 195 G11
Shrops 149 D11
Moston Green
Ches E 168 C2
Mostyn Flint 181 E11
Mostyn Quay Flint 181 E11
Motcombe Dorset 30 B5
Mothecombe Devon 8 F2
Motherby Cumb 230 F4
Motherwell
N Lanark 268 D5
Motspur Park London 67 F8
Mottingham London 68 E2
Mottisfont Hants 32 B4
Mottistone IoW 20 E4
Mottram in Longdendale
Gtr Man 185 B7
Mottram Rise
Gtr Man 185 B7
Mottram St Andrew
Ches E 184 F5
Mott's Green Essex 87 B8
Mott's Mill E Sus 52 F4
Mouldsworth
Ches W 183 G8
Moulin Perth 286 B3
Moulsecoomb
Brighton 36 F4
Moulsford Oxon 64 C5
Moulsham Essex 88 D2
Moulsoe M Keynes 103 C8
Moultavie Highld 300 B6
Moulton Ches W 167 B11
Lincs 156 E6
N Yorks 224 E4
Northants 120 D5
Suff 124 E3

Moulton *continued*
V Glam 58 E5
Moulton Chapel
Lincs 156 F5
Moulton Eaugate
Lincs 156 F6
Moulton Park
Northants 120 E5
Moulton St Mary
Norf 143 B7
Moulton Seas End
Lincs 156 D6
Moulzie Angus 292 F4
Mounie Castle
Aberds 303 G7
Mount Corn 4 D5
Corn 6 B2
Highld 301 E9
W Yorks 196 D5
Mountain Anglesey 178 E2
W Yorks 205 G7
Mountain Air
Bl Gwent 77 D11
Mountain Ash / Aberpennar
Rhondda 77 F8
Mountain Bower
Wilts 61 D10
Mountain Cross
Borders 270 F2
Mountain Street
Kent 54 C5
Mountain Water
Pembs 91 G8
Mount Ambrose Corn 4 G4
Mount Ballan Mon 60 B3
Mount Batten Plym 7 E9
Mountbenger
Borders 261 D8
Mountbengerburn
Borders 261 D8
Mountblow W Dunb 277 G9
Mount Bovers Essex 88 G4
Mount Bures Essex 107 E8
Mount Canisp
Highld 301 B7
Mount Charles Corn 5 B10
Corn 5 E10
Mount Cowdown
Wilts 47 C9
Mount End Essex 87 E7
Mount Ephraim
E Sus 23 B7
Mounters Dorset 30 D3
Mountfield E Sus 38 C2
Mountgerald Highld 300 C5
Mount Gould Plym 7 D9
Mount Hawke Corn 4 F4
Mount Hermon Corn 2 F6
Sur 50 B4
Mount Hill S Glos 61 E7
Mountjoy Corn 5 C7
Mount Lane Devon 12 B3
Mountnessing Essex 87 F10
Mounton Mon 79 G8
Mount Pleasant
Bucks 102 E3
Ches E 168 D4
Corn 5 C10
Derbys 152 D6
Derbys 152 F5
Derbys 170 F4
Devon 27 G11
Durham 233 E11
E Sus 23 E7
E Sus 36 D6
Flint 182 G2
Hants 19 B11
Kent 71 F10
London 85 G8
M Tydf 77 F9
Neath 57 B9
Norf 141 E9
Pembs 73 D8
Shrops 149 G9
Stockton 234 G4
Stoke 168 G5
Suff 106 B4
T&W 243 E7
W Yorks 197 C8
Warks 135 F7
Worcs 99 D10
Worcs 117 E10
Mount Sion Wrex 166 E3
Mount Skippett
Oxon 82 B5
Mountsolie Aberds 303 D9
Mountsorrel Leics 153 F11
Mount Sorrel Wilts 31 C8
Mount Tabor
W Yorks 196 B5
Mount Vernon
Glasgow 268 C3
Mount Wise Corn 7 E9
Mousehill Sur 50 E2
Mousehole Corn 1 D5
Mousen Northumb 264 C4
Mousley End Warks 118 D4
Mouswald Dumfries 238 C3
Mouth Mill Devon 24 B3
Mowbreck Lancs 202 G4
Mow Cop Ches E 168 D5
Mowden Darl 224 B5
Essex 88 C3
Mowhaugh Borders 263 E8
Mowmacre Hill
Leicester 135 B11
Mowshurst Kent 52 D3
Mowsley Leics 136 F2
Moxby N Yorks 215 F11
Moxley W Mid 133 D9
Moy Argyll 255 E8
Highld 290 E6
Highld 301 F7
Moy Hall Highld 301 F7
Moy Ho Moray 301 C10
Moyles Court Hants 31 F11
Moylgrove / Trewyddel
Pembs 92 C2
Moy Lodge Highld 290 E6
Muasdale Argyll 255 C7
Muchalls Aberds 293 D11
Much Birch Hereford 97 E10
Much Cowardne
Hereford 98 B2
Much Cowarne
Hereford 98 B2
Much Dewchurch
Hereford 97 E9
Muchelney Som 28 C6
Muchelney Ham Som 28 C6
Much Hadham Herts 86 B5
Much Hoole Lancs 194 C3
Much Hoole Moss Houses Lancs 194 C3
Much Hoole Town
Lancs 194 C3
Muchlarnick Corn 6 D4
Much Marcle
Hereford 98 E3
Muchrachd Highld 300 F2
Much Wenlock
Shrops 132 C2
Muckairn Argyll 289 F11
Muckernich Highld 300 D5
Mucking Thurrock 69 C7
Muckle Breck
Shetland 312 G7
Muckleford Dorset 17 C8
Mucklestone Staffs 150 B4
Muckleton Norf 158 B6
Shrops 149 E11
Muckletown Aberds 302 G5
Muckley Shrops 132 D2
Muckley Corner
Staffs 133 B11
Muckley Cross
Shrops 132 D2
Muckton Lincs 190 E5
Muckton Bottom
Lincs 190 E5
Mudale Highld 308 F5
Mudd Gtr Man 185 C7
Muddiford Devon 40 F5
Muddlebridge Devon 40 G4
Muddles Green
E Sus 23 C8
Mudeford Dorset 19 C9
Mudford Som 29 D9
Mudford Sock Som 29 D9
Mudgley Som 44 D2
Mugdock Stirling 277 F11
Mugeary Highld 294 B6
Mugginton Derbys 170 G3
Muggintonlane End
Derbys 170 G3
Muggleswick
Durham 232 B6
Mugswell Sur 51 C9
Muie Highld 309 J6
Muir Aberds 292 E2
Muircleugh
Borders 271 F10
Muirden Aberds 303 D7
Muirdrum Angus 287 D9
Muiredge Fife 281 B7
Muirend Glasgow 267 C11
Muirhead Angus 287 D7
Fife 286 G6
Fife 287 F8
N Lanark 268 B3
S Ayrs 257 C8
Muirhouse Edin 280 F4
N Lanark 268 D5
Muirhouselaw
Borders 262 D4
Muirhouses Falk 279 E10
Muirkirk E Ayrs 258 D5
Muirmill Stirling 278 E4
Muir of Alford
Aberds 293 B7
Muir of Fairburn
Highld 300 D4
Muir of Fowlis
Aberds 293 B7
Muir of Kinellar
Aberds 293 B10
Muir of Miltonduff
Moray 301 D11
Muir of Ord Highld 300 D5
Muir of Pert Angus 287 D8
Muirshearlich
Highld 290 E3
Muirskie Aberds 293 D10
Muirtack Aberds 303 F9
Muirton Aberds 303 D7
Highld 301 C7
Perth 286 E5
Perth 286 F3
Muirton Mains
Highld 300 D4
Muirton of Ardblair
Perth 286 C5
Muirton of Ballochy
Angus 293 G8
Muiryfold Aberds 303 D7
Muker N Yorks 223 F8
Mulbarton Norf 142 C3
Mulben Moray 302 D3
Mulberry Corn 5 B10
Mulfra Corn 1 C5
Mulindry Argyll 254 B4
Mulla Shetland 313 G6
Mullardoch House
Highld 300 F2
Mullenspond Hants 47 D9
Mullion Corn 2 F5
Mullion Cove Corn 2 F5
Mumbles Hill
Swansea 56 D6
Mumby Lincs 191 G8
Mumps Gtr Man 196 F2
Mundale Moray 301 D10
Munderfield Row
Hereford 116 G2
Munderfield Stocks
Hereford 116 G2
Mundesley Norf 160 B6
Mundford Norf 140 E6
Mundham Norf 142 D6
Mundon Essex 88 E5
Mundurno
Aberdeen 293 B11
Mundy Bois Kent 54 D2
Munerigie Highld 290 C4
Muness Shetland 312 C8
Mungasdale Highld 307 K4
Mungrisdale Cumb 230 E3
Munlochy Highld 300 D6
Munsary Cottage
Highld 310 E6
Munsley Hereford 98 C3
Munslow Shrops 131 F10
Munstone Hereford 97 C10
Murch V Glam 59 E7
Murchington Devon 13 D9
Murcot Worcs 99 C11
Murcott Oxon 83 B9
Wilts 81 G7
Murdieston Stirling 278 B3
Murdishaw Halton 183 E9
Murieston W Loth 269 C11
Murkle Highld 310 C5
Murlaggan Highld 290 D2
Highld 290 E5
Murra Orkney 314 F2
Murrayfield Edin 280 G4
Murrayshall Perth 286 E5
Murraythwaite
Dumfries 238 C4
Murrell Green Hants 49 B8
Murrell's End Glos 98 E4
Glos 98 G5
Murrion Shetland 312 F4
Murrow Cambs 139 B7
Mursley Bucks 102 F6
Murston Kent 70 G2
Murthill Angus 287 B8
Murthly Perth 286 D4
Murton
Cumb 231 G10
Durham 234 B3
Northumb 273 F9
Swansea 56 D5
T&W 243 C8
York 207 C8
Murton Grange
N Yorks 215 B10
Murtwell Devon 8 D5
Musbury Devon 15 C11
Muscliff Bmouth 19 B7
Muscoates N Yorks 216 C3
Muscott Northants 120 E2
Musdale Argyll 289 G11
Mushroom Green
W Mid 133 F8
Musselburgh
E Loth 280 G6
Musselwick Pembs 72 D4
Mustard Hyrn Norf 161 F8
Muston Leics 154 B6
N Yorks 217 D11
Mustow Green
Worcs 117 C7
Muswell Hill London 86 G3
Mutehill Dumfries 237 E8
Mutford Suff 143 F9
Muthill Perth 286 F2
Mutley Plym 7 D9
Mutterton Devon 27 G8
Mutton Hall E Sus 37 C9
Muxton Telford 150 G4
Mwdwl-eithin Flint 181 F11
Mwynbwll Flint 165 B11
Mybster Highld 310 D5
Myddfai Carms 94 F5
Myddle Shrops 149 E9
Myddlewood Shrops 149 E9
Myddyn-fych Carms 75 C10
Mydroilyn Ceredig 111 F9
Myerscough Lancs 202 F5
Myerscough Smithy
Lancs 203 G8
Mylor Bridge Corn 3 B8
Mylor Churchtown
Corn 3 B8
Mynachdy Cardiff 59 D7
Rhondda 77 F8
Mynachlog-ddu
Pembs 92 E2
Mynd Shrops 115 C7
Myndd Llandegai
Gwyn 163 B10
Myndtown Shrops 131 F7
Mynydd Bach
Ceredig 112 B4
Mynydd-bach Mon 79 G7
Swansea 57 B7
Mynydd-bach-y-glo
Swansea 56 B6
Mynydd Bodafon
Anglesey 179 D7
Mynydd Fflint / Flint Mountain Flint 182 G2
Mynydd Gilan Gwyn 144 E5
Mynydd-isa Flint 166 C3
Mynyddislwyn
Caerph 77 G11
Mynydd-llan Flint 181 G11
Mynydd Marian
Conwy 180 F5
Mynydd Mechell
Anglesey 178 D5
Mynyddygarreg
Carms 74 D6
Mynytho Gwyn 144 C6
Myrebird Aberds 293 D9
Myrelandhorn
Highld 310 D6
Myreside Perth 286 E6
Myrtle Hill Carms 94 E5
Mytchett Sur 49 B11
Mytchett Place Sur 49 C11
Mytholm W Yorks 196 B3
Mytholmes W Yorks 204 F6
Mytholmroyd
W Yorks 196 B4
Mythop Lancs 202 G3
Mytice Aberds 302 F4
Myton Warks 118 E6
Myton Hall N Yorks 215 F8
Myton-on-Swale
N Yorks 215 F8
Mytton Shrops 149 F8

N

Naast Highld 307 L3
Nab Hill W Yorks 197 D7
Nab's Head Lancs 194 B6
Naburn York 207 D7
Nab Wood W Yorks 205 F8
Naccolt Kent 54 E4
Nackington Kent 55 C7
Nacton Suff 108 C4
Nadderwater Devon 14 C3
Nafferton E Yorks 209 B7
Na Gearrannan
W Isles 304 D3
Nag's Head Glos 80 F5
Naid-y-march
Flint 181 F11
Nailbridge Glos 79 B10
Nailsbourne Som 28 B2
Nailsea N Som 60 D3
Nailstone Leics 135 B8
Nailsworth Glos 80 F5
Nailwell Bath 61 G8
Nairn Highld 301 D8
Nalderswood Sur 51 D8
Nance Corn 4 G3
Nanceddan Corn 2 C2
Nancegollan Corn 2 C4
Nancemellin Corn 4 G2
Nancenoy Corn 2 D6
Nancledra Corn 1 B5
Nangreaves Lancs 195 D10
Nanhoron Gwyn 144 C5
Nanhyfer / Nevern
Pembs 91 D11
Nannau Gwyn 146 E4
Nannerch Flint 165 B11
Nanpantan Leics 153 F10
Nanpean Corn 5 D9
Nanquidno Corn 1 D3
Nanstallon Corn 5 B10
Nant Carms 74 B6
Denb 165 D11
Nant Alyn Flint 165 B11
Nant-ddu Powys 77 B8
Nanternis Ceredig 111 F7
Nantgaredig Carms 93 G9
Nantgarw Rhondda 58 B6
Nant-glas Powys 113 E9
Nantglyn Denb 165 C8
Nantgwyn Powys 113 B9
Nantithet Corn 2 E5
Nantlle Gwyn 163 E8
Nantmawr Shrops 148 E5
Nant Mawr Flint 166 C3
Nantmel Powys 113 D10
Nantmor Gwyn 163 F10
Nant Peris / Old Llanberis Gwyn 163 D10
Nantserth Powys 113 C9
Nant Uchaf Denb 165 D8
Nantwich Ches E 167 E11
Nant-y-Bai Carms 94 C5
Nant-y-Bwch
Bl Gwent 77 C10
Nant-y-cafn Neath 76 D4
Nantycaws Carms 75 B7
Nant y Caws Shrops 148 D5
Nant-y-ceisiad
Caerph 59 B8
Nant-y-derry Mon 78 D4
Nant-y-felin
Conwy 179 G11
Nant-y-ffin Carms 93 E11
Nantyffyllon
Bridgend 57 C11
Nantyglo Bl Gwent 77 C11
Nant-y-gollen
Shrops 148 D4
Nant-y-moel
Bridgend 76 G6
Nant-y-pandy
Conwy 179 G11
Nant-y-Rhiw Conwy 164 D4
Nantyronen Station
Ceredig 112 B3
Napchester Kent 55 D10
Naphill Bucks 84 F4
Napleton Worcs 99 B7
Napley Staffs 150 B4
Napley Heath Staffs 150 B4
Nappa N Yorks 204 C3
Nappa Scar N Yorks 223 G9
Napton on the Hill
Warks 119 E9
Narberth / Arberth
Pembs 73 C10
Narberth Bridge
Pembs 73 C10
Narborough Leics 135 D10
Norf 158 G4
Narfords Som 28 F3
Narkurs Corn 6 D6
Narracott Devon 24 D5
Narrowgate Corner
Norf 161 F8
Nasareth Gwyn 163 E7
Naseby Northants 120 B3
Nash Bucks 102 E5
Hereford 114 E6
Kent 55 B9
London 68 G2
Newport 59 C10
Shrops 116 C2
Som 29 E8
Nashend Glos 80 D5
Nash End Worcs 132 G5
Nashes Green Hants 49 D7
Nash Lee Bucks 84 D4
Nash Mills Herts 85 E9
Nash Street E Sus 23 C8
Kent 68 F6
Nassington
Northants 137 D11
Nastend Glos 80 D3
Nast Hyde Herts 86 D2
Nasty Herts 105 G7
Natcott Devon 24 C3
Nateby Cumb 222 D5
Lancs 202 E5
Nately Scures Hants 49 C8
Natland Cumb 211 B10
Natton Glos 99 E8
Naughton Suff 107 B10
Naunton Glos 100 G2
Worcs 99 D7
Naunton Beauchamp
Worcs 117 G9
Navant Hill W Sus 34 B6
Navenby Lincs 173 D7
Navestock Heath
Essex 87 F8
Navestock Side Essex 87 F9
Navidale Highld 311 H4
Navity Highld 301 C7
Nawton N Yorks 216 C3
Nayland Suff 107 E9
Nazeing Essex 86 D6
Nazeing Gate Essex 86 D6
Nazeing Long Green
Essex 86 E6
Nazeing Mead Essex 86 D5
Neacroft Hants 19 B9
Nealhouse Cumb 239 G8
Neal's Green Warks 134 G6
Neames Forstal Kent 54 B5
Neap Shetland 313 H7
Near Hardcastle
N Yorks 214 F2
Near Sawrey Cumb 221 F7
Neasden London 67 B8
Neasham Darl 224 C6
Neat Enstone Oxon 101 G7
Neath Abbey Neath 57 B8
Neatham Hants 49 E8
Neath / Castell-nedd
Neath 57 B8
Neath Hill M Keynes 103 C7
Neatishead Norf 160 E6
Neat Marsh E Yorks 209 G9
Neaton Norf 141 C8
Nebo Anglesey 179 C7
Ceredig 111 D10
Conwy 164 D4
Gwyn 163 E7
Nebsworth Warks 100 C3
Nechells W Mid 133 F11
Necton Norf 141 B7
Nedd Highld 306 F6
Nedderton
Northumb 252 G6
Nedge Hill Som 44 C5
Telford 132 B4
Nedging Suff 107 B9
Nedging Tye Suff 107 B10
Needham Norf 142 G4
Needham Green
Essex 87 B9
Needham Market
Suff 125 G11
Needham Street
Suff 124 D4
Needingworth
Cambs 122 C6
Needwood Staffs 152 E3
Neen Savage Shrops 116 B3
Neen Sollars Shrops 116 C3
Neenton Shrops 132 F2
Nefod Shrops 148 B6
Nefyn Gwyn 162 G4
Neighbourne Som 44 D6
Neight Hill Worcs 117 F8
Neilston E Renf 267 D9
Neinthirion Powys 129 B9
Neithrop Oxon 101 C8
Nelly Andrews Green
Powys 130 B5
Nelson Caerph 77 F10
Lancs 204 F3
Nelson Village
Northumb 243 B7
Nemphlar S Lanark 269 G7
Nempnett Thrubwell
N Som 60 G4
Nene Terrace Lincs 138 B5
Nenthall Cumb 231 B11
Nenthead Cumb 231 C11
Nenthorn Borders 262 B5
Neopardy Devon 13 B11
Nepcote W Sus 35 F10
Nepgill Cumb 229 F7
Nep Town W Sus 36 D2
Nerabus Argyll 254 B3
Nercwys Flint 166 C2
Nerston S Lanark 268 D2
Nesbit Northumb 263 C11
Ness Ches W 182 F4
Orkney 314 C4
Nesscliffe Shrops 149 F7
Nessholt Ches W 182 F4
Nesstoun Orkney 314 A7
Neston Ches W 182 F3
Wilts 61 F11
Netchells Green
W Mid 133 F11
Netham Bristol 60 E6
Nethanfoot
S Lanark 268 F6
Nether Alderley
Ches E 184 F4
Netheravon Wilts 46 D6
Nether Blainslie
Borders 271 G10
Nether Booth
Derbys 185 D10
Netherbrae Aberds 303 D7
Netherbrough
Orkney 314 E3
Nether Broughton
Leics 154 D3
Netherburn
S Lanark 268 F6
Nether Burrow
Lancs 212 D2
Nether Burrows
Derbys 152 B5
Netherbury Dorset 16 B5
Netherby Cumb 239 C9
N Yorks 206 D2
Nether Cassock
Dumfries 248 C6
Nether Cerne Dorset 17 B9
Nether Chanderhill
Derbys 186 G4
Netherclay Som 28 C3
Nether Compton
Dorset 29 D9
Nethercote Oxon 101 C9
Warks 119 E10
Nethercott Devon 12 B3
Devon 40 F3
Oxon 101 G9
Som 42 G6
Nether Crimond
Aberds 303 G8
Netherdale Shetland 313 H3
Nether Dalgliesh
Borders 249 B7
Nether Dallachy
Moray 302 C3
Nether Edge
S Yorks 186 E4
Netherend Glos 79 E9
Nether End Derbys 186 G3
Leics 154 G4
W Yorks 197 F8
Nether Exe Devon 26 G6
Netherfield E Sus 38 D2
Netherfield *continued*
M Keynes 103 D7
Notts 171 G10
Nethergate Norf 159 D11
Nether Glasslaw
Aberds 303 D8
Nether Hall
Leicester 136 B2
Netherhampton
Wilts 31 B10
Nether Handley
Derbys 186 F6
Nether Handwick
Angus 287 C7
Nether Haugh
S Yorks 186 B6
Nether Headon
Notts 188 F2
Nether Heage
Derbys 170 E5
Nether Heyford
Northants 120 F3
Nether Hindhope
Borders 263 G7
Nether Horsburgh
Borders 261 B8
Nether Howecleuch
S Lanark 260 G2
Nether Kellet
Lancs 211 F10
Nether Kidston
Borders 270 G4
Nether Kinmundy
Aberds 303 E10
Nether Kirton
E Renf 267 D9
Netherland Green
Staffs 152 C2
Nether Langwith
Notts 187 G8
Netherlaw Dumfries 237 E9
Netherlay Dorset 28 F6
Nether Leask
Aberds 303 F10
Netherlee E Renf 267 D11
Nether Lenshie
Aberds 302 E6
Netherley Aberds 293 D10
Mers 182 D6
W Yorks 196 E4
Nether Loads
Derbys 170 B4
Nethermill Dumfries 248 F2
Nethermills Moray 302 D5
Nether Monynut
Borders 272 C4
Nether Moor Derbys 170 B5
Nethermuir Aberds 303 E9
Netherne on-the-Hill
Sur 51 B9
Netheroyd Hill
W Yorks 196 D6
Nether Padley
Derbys 186 F3
Nether Park
Aberds 303 D10
Netherplace
E Renf 267 D10
Nether Poppleton
York 207 B7
Netherraw Borders 262 E3
Nether Row Cumb 230 D2
Nether Savock
Aberds 303 E10
Netherseal Derbys 152 G5
Nether Shiels
Borders 271 F8
Nether Silton
N Yorks 225 G9
Nether Skyborry
Shrops 114 C5
Nether St Suff 125 E8
Netherstoke Dorset 29 F8
Nether Stowe Staffs 152 G2
Nether Stowey Som 43 F7
Nether Street Essex 87 C9
Herts 86 B6
Netherthird E Ayrs 258 F3
Netherthong
W Yorks 196 F6
Netherthorpe
Derbys 186 G6
S Yorks 187 E8
Netherton
Aberds 303 E8
Angus 287 B9
Ches W 183 F8
Corn 11 G11
Cumb 228 D6
Devon 14 G3
Glos 81 E11
Hants 47 B11
Hereford 97 F10
Mers 193 G11
N Lanark 268 E5
Northumb 251 B11
Oxon 82 F6
Perth 286 B5
Shrops 132 G4
Stirling 277 F11
W Mid 133 F8
W Yorks 196 E6
W Yorks 197 D9
Worcs 99 C9
Netherton of Lonmay
Aberds 303 C10
Nethertown Cumb 219 D9
Highld 310 B7
Lancs 203 F10
Staffs 152 F2
Nether Urquhart
Fife 286 G5
Nether Wallop
Hants 47 F10
Nether Warden
Northumb 241 D10
Nether Wasdale
Cumb 220 E2
Nether Welton
Cumb 230 B3
Nether Westcote
Glos 100 G4
Nether Whitacre
Warks 134 E4
Nether Winchendon or Lower Winchendon
Bucks 84 C2
Netherwitton
Northumb 252 E4
Netherwood E Ayrs 258 D5
Nether Worton
Oxon 101 E8
Nether Yeadon
W Yorks 205 E10
Nethy Bridge
Highld 301 G10
Netley Hants 33 F7
Netley Hill Soton 33 E7
Netley Marsh Hants 32 E4
Nettacott Devon 14 B4
Netteswell Essex 87 C7
Nettlebed Oxon 65 B8
Nettlebridge Som 44 D6
Nettlecombe Dorset 16 B6
IoW 20 F6
Nettleden Herts 85 C8
Nettleham Lincs 189 F8
Nettlestead Kent 53 C7
Suff 107 B11
Nettlestead Green
Kent 53 C7
Nettlestone IoW 21 C8
Nettlesworth
Durham 233 B11
Nettleton Glos 80 C6
Lincs 200 G6
Wilts 61 D10
Nettleton Green
Wilts 61 D10
Nettleton Hill
W Yorks 196 D5
Nettleton Shrub
Wilts 61 D10
Nettleton Top
Lincs 189 B10
Netton Wilts 46 F6
Neuadd Carms 94 G3
Nevendon Essex 88 G2
Nevern / Nanhyfer
Pembs 91 D11
Nevilles Cross
Durham 233 C11
New Abbey
Dumfries 237 C11
New Aberdour
Aberds 303 C8
New Addington
London 67 G11
Newall W Yorks 205 D10
Newall Green
Gtr Man 184 D4
New Alresford Hants 48 G5
New Alyth Perth 286 C6
Newark Orkney 314 B7
Pboro 138 C4
Newark-on-Trent
Notts 172 E3
New Arley Warks 134 F5
New Arram E Yorks 208 E6
Newarthill N Lanark 268 D5
New Ash Green Kent 68 F6
New Balderton
Notts 172 E4
Newball Lincs 189 F9
Newbarn Kent 55 F7
New Barn Kent 68 F6
New Barnet London 86 F3
New Barnetby
N Lincs 200 E5
Newbarns Cumb 210 E4
New Barton
Northants 121 E7
New Basford
Nottingham 171 G9
Newbattle Midloth 270 B6
New Beaupre V Glam 58 E4
New Beckenham
London 67 E11
New Bewick
Northumb 264 E3
Newbie Dumfries 238 D5
Newbiggin Cumb 210 F5
Cumb 211 D11
Cumb 219 G11
Cumb 230 F5
Cumb 231 B7
Cumb 231 F8
Durham 232 B5
Durham 232 F4
Durham 233 B8
N Yorks 213 B9
N Yorks 223 G9
Newbiggin-by-the-Sea
Northumb 253 F8
Newbigging Aberds 303 G7
Angus 287 D8
Borders 262 F6
Edin 280 F2
S Lanark 269 F10
New-bigging Angus 286 C6
Newbiggings Orkney 314 B6
Newbiggin Hall Estate
T&W 242 D6
Newbiggin-on-Lune
Cumb 222 D4
New Bilton Warks 119 B9
Newbold Derbys 186 G5
Gtr Man 196 E2
Leics 136 B5
Leics 153 F8
Newbold Heath
Leics 135 B8
Newbold on Avon
Warks 119 B9
Newbold on Stour
Warks 100 B4
Newbold Pacey
Warks 118 F5
Newbolds W Mid 133 C8
Newbold Verdon
Leics 135 C8
New Bolingbroke
Lincs 174 D4
New Bolsover
Derbys 187 G7
Newborough Pboro 138 B4
Staffs 152 D2
New Boston Mers 183 B9
New Botley Oxon 83 D7
Newbottle
Northants 101 D10
T&W 243 G8
New Boultham
Lincs 189 G7
Newbourne Suff 108 C5
New Bradwell
M Keynes 102 C6
New Brancepeth
Durham 233 C10
Newbridge Bath 61 F8
Caerph 78 F2
Ceredig 111 F10
Corn 1 C4
Corn 4 G5
Corn 7 B7
Dumfries 237 B11
E Sus 52 G3
Edin 280 G2
Hants 32 D3
IoW 20 D4
Lancs 204 F3
N Yorks 216 B6
Oxon 82 E6
Pembs 91 E8
Shrops 148 D6
W Mid 133 D7
Wrex 166 G3
New Bridge Wrex 166 G3
Newbridge Green
Worcs 98 D6
Newbridge-on-Usk
Mon 78 G5
Newbridge-on-Wye
Powys 113 F10
New Brighton Flint 166 B3
Mers 182 C4
W Sus 22 B3
W Yorks 197 B9
W Yorks 205 F8
Wrex 166 E3
New Brimington
Derbys 186 G6
New Brinsley Notts 171 E7
New Brotton Redcar 235 G9
Newbrough
Northumb 241 D9
New Broughton
Wrex 166 E4
New Buckenham
Norf 141 E11
Newbuildings Devon 26 G3
New Buildings Bath 45 B7
Dorset 18 E5
Newburgh Aberds 303 D9
Aberds 303 G9
Borders 261 F8
Fife 286 F6
Lancs 194 E3
Newburn T&W 242 D5
Newbury Kent 54 B2
W Berks 64 F3
Wilts 45 E10
New Bury Gtr Man 195 F8
Newbury Park London 68 B2
Newby Cumb 231 G7
Lancs 204 D2
N Yorks 205 D11
N Yorks 212 E4
N Yorks 215 F7
N Yorks 225 C10
N Yorks 227 G10
Newby Bridge Cumb 211 B7
Newby Cote
N Yorks 212 E4
Newby East Cumb 239 F11
Newby Head Cumb 231 G7
New Byth Aberds 303 D8
Newby West Cumb 239 G9
Newby Wiske
N Yorks 215 B7
Newcastle Bridgend 58 D2
Mon 78 B6
Shrops 130 G4
Newcastle Emlyn / Castell Newydd Emlyn
Carms 92 C6
Newcastleton or Copshaw Holm
Borders 249 F11
Newcastle-under-Lyme
Staffs 168 F4
Newcastle upon Tyne
T&W 242 E6
New Catton Norf 160 G4
Newchapel Powys 129 G9
Staffs 168 E5
Sur 51 E11
Newchapel / Capel Newydd Pembs 92 D4
New Charlton London 68 D2
New Cheltenham
S Glos 61 E7
New Cheriton Hants 33 B9
Newchurch
Bl Gwent 77 C11
Carms 93 G7
Hereford 115 G7
IoW 21 D7
Kent 54 G5
Lancs 195 C10
Mon 79 F7
Powys 114 G4
Staffs 152 E2
Newchurch in Pendle
Lancs 204 F2
New Clipstone
Notts 171 C9
New Costessey Norf 160 G3
Newcott Devon 28 F2
New Coundon
Durham 233 E10
New Cowper Cumb 229 B8
Newcraighall Edin 280 G6
New Crofton
W Yorks 197 D11
New Cross Ceredig 112 B2
London 67 D11
Oxon 65 D9
Som 28 D6
New Cross Gate
London 67 D11
New Cumnock
E Ayrs 258 G4
New Deer Aberds 303 E8
New Delaval
Northumb 243 B7
New Delph Gtr Man 196 F3
New Denham Bucks 66 C4

Pen–Pon 403

Penny's Green Norf 142 D3
Pennytinney Corn 10 F6
Pennywell T&W 243 F9
Pen-onn V Glam 58 F5
Penparc Ceredig 92 B4
Pembs 91 E7
Penparcau Ceredig 111 B11
Penpedairheol
Caerph 77 F10
Mon 78 E4
Penpergym Mon 78 C4
Penperlleni Mon 78 E4
Penpethy Corn 11 D7
Penpillick Corn 5 D11
Penplas Carms 74 B5
Penpol Corn 3 B8
Penpoll Corn 6 E2
Penponds Corn 2 B4
Penpont Corn 11 G7
Dumfries 247 E8
Powys 95 F9
Penprysg Bridgend 58 C3
Penquit Devon 8 E2
Penrallt Gwyn 145 B7
Powys 129 F9
Penrherber Carms 92 D5
Penrhiw Caerph 78 G2
Penrhiwceiber
Rhondda 77 F8
Pen-Rhiw-fawr
Neath 76 C2
Penrhiwgarreg
Bl Gwent 78 E2
Penrhiw-llan Ceredig 93 C7
Penrhiw-pal Ceredig 92 B6
Penrhiwtyn Neath 57 B8
Penrhos Anglesey 178 E3
Gwyn 144 C6
Hereford 114 F6
Mon 78 C6
Penrhôs Mon 78 C6
Penrhos Powys 76 C3
Pen-rhos Wrex 166 E3
Penrhosfeilw
Anglesey 178 E2
Penrhos-garnedd
Gwyn 179 G9
Penrhyd Lastra
Anglesey 178 C6
Penrhyn Bay / Bae-
Penrhyn Conwy 180 E4
Penrhyn Castle
Pembs 92 B2
Penrhyn-coch
Ceredig 128 G2
Penrhyndeudraeth
Gwyn 146 B2
Penrhynside Conwy 180 E4
Penrhyn side Conwy 180 E4
Penrhys Rhondda 77 F8
Penrice Swansea 56 D3
Penrith Cumb 230 E6
Penrose Corn 10 G3
Corn 11 F7
Penrose Hill Corn 2 D4
Penruddock Cumb 230 F4
Penryn Corn 3 C7
Pensarn Carms 74 B6
Conwy 181 F7
Pen-sarn Gwyn 145 D11
Gwyn 162 G6
Pensax Worcs 116 D4
Pensby Mers 182 E3
Penselwood Som 45 G9
Pensford Bath 60 G6
Pensham Worcs 99 C8
Penshaw T&W 243 G8
Penshurst Kent 52 E4
Pensilva Corn 6 B5
Pensnett W Mid 133 F8
Penston E Loth 281 G8
Penstone Devon 26 G3
Penstraze Corn 4 F5
Pentewan Corn 5 F10
Pentiken Shrops 130 G4
Pentir Gwyn 163 B9
Pentire Corn 4 C5
Pentirvin Shrops 130 C6
Pentlepoir Pembs 73 D10
Pentlow Essex 106 B6
Pentlow Street
Essex 106 B6
Pentney Norf 158 G4
Penton Corner
Hants 47 D10
Penton Grafton
Hants 47 D10
Penton Mewsey
Hants 47 D10
Pentonville London 67 C10
Pentowin Carms 74 B3
Pentraeth Anglesey 179 F8
Pentrapeod Caerph 77 E11
Pentre Carms 75 C8
Denb 165 D10
Flint 165 C11
Flint 166 B4
Flint 166 C2
Flint 166 D2
Powys 129 F11
Powys 130 B4
Powys 130 E5
Powys 147 D11
Powys 148 G3
Rhondda 77 F7
Shrops 148 D4
Shrops 149 F7
Wrex 148 B2
Wrex 166 G3
Pentrebach Carms 94 E6
M Tydf 77 E9
Rhondda 58 B5
Swansea 75 D10
Pentre-bâch
Ceredig 93 B11
Pentre-bach Powys 95 E8
Pentrebane Cardiff 58 D6
Pentrebeirdd Powys 148 G3
Pentre Berw
Anglesey 179 G7
Pentre-bont Conwy 164 E2
Pentre Broughton
Wrex 166 E4
Pentre Bychan
Wrex 166 F4
Pentrecagal Carms 92 C6
Pentre-cefn Shrops 148 D4
Pentre-celyn Denb 165 E11
Powys 129 B7
Pentre-chwyth
Swansea 57 B7
Pentre Cilgwyn
Wrex 148 B4
Pentre-clawdd
Shrops 148 C5
Pentre-coed Shrops 149 B7
Pentre-cwrt Carms 93 D7
Pentre Dolau-Honddu
Powys 95 C9
Pentredwr Denb 165 F11
Pentre-dwr Swansea 57 B7
Pentrefelin
Anglesey 178 C6
Carms 93 G11
Ceredig 94 B2
Conwy 180 G4
Denb 166 G2
Gwyn 145 B10
Pentre-Ffwrndan
Flint 182 G3
Pentrefoelas Conwy 164 E5
Pentref-y-groes
Caerph 77 F11
Pentre-galar Pembs 92 E3
Pentregat Ceredig 111 G7
Pentre-Gwenlais
Carms 75 B10
Pentre Gwynfryn
Gwyn 145 D11
Pentre Halkyn Flint 182 G2
Pentreheyling
Shrops 130 E4
Pentre Hodre
Shrops 114 B6
Pentre Isaf Conwy 164 B5
Pentre Llanrhaeadr
Denb 165 C9
Pentre Llifior
Powys 130 D2
Pentrellwyn Ceredig 93 C8
Pentre-llwyn-llwyd
Powys 113 G9
Pentre-llyn Ceredig 112 C2
Pentre-llyn cymmer
Conwy 165 E7
Pentre Maelor Wrex 166 F5
Pentre Meyrick
V Glam 58 D3
Pentre-newydd
Shrops 148 B5
Pentre-Piod Torf 78 E3
Pentre-Poeth Carms 75 E8
Newport 59 B9
Pentre'r beirdd
Powys 148 G3
Pentre'r Felin
Conwy 164 B4
Pentre'r-felin
Denb 165 B10
Powys 95 E8
Pentre-rhew
Ceredig 112 G3
Pentre-tafarn-y-fedw
Conwy 164 C4
Pentre-ty-gwyn
Carms 94 D6
Pentreuchaf Gwyn 145 B7
Pentre-uchaf Conwy 180 F5
Pentrich Derbys 170 E5
Pentridge Dorset 31 D8
Pentrisil Pembs 91 E11
Pentwyn Caerph 77 E10
Cardiff 59 C8
Pen-twyn Caerph 78 E2
Carms 75 C9
Mon 79 D8
Torf 78 E3
Pentwyn Berthlwyd
Caerph 77 F10
Pentwyn-mawr
Caerph 77 F11
Pentwyn / Pendine
Carms 74 D2
Pentyrch Cardiff 58 C6
Penuchadre V Glam 57 G11
Pen-Uchar Plwyf
Flint 181 G11
Penuwch Ceredig 111 E11
Penwartha Corn 4 E5
Penwartha Coombe
Corn 4 E5
Penweathers Corn 4 G6
Penwithick Corn 5 D10
Penwood Hants 64 G2
Penwortham Lane
Lancs 194 B4
Penwyllt Powys 76 B5
Pen-y-Ball Top
Flint 181 F11
Penybanc Carms 75 C10
Pen-y-banc Carms 93 G8
Carms 94 G2
Pen-y-bank Caerph 77 E10
Penybedd Carms 74 E6
Penybont Ceredig 128 F2
Powys 114 E2
Pen-y-Bont
Bl Gwent 78 D2
Carms 92 G6
Gwyn 128 C4
Gwyn 146 D2
Powys 148 E4
Pen y Bont ar ogwr /
Bridgend Bridgend 58 C2
Penybontfawr
Powys 147 E11
Penybryn Caerph 77 F10
Pen-y-Bryn
Gwyn 145 B9
Gwyn 146 F3
Pembs 92 C3
Powys 130 C3
Shrops 148 B6
Wrex 166 G3
Penycae Wrex 166 F3
Pen-y-cae Bridgend 58 C2
Neath 57 D9
Powys 76 C4
Pen-y-cae-mawr
Mon 78 F6
Penycaerau Gwyn 144 D3
Pen-y-cefn Flint 181 F10
Pen-y-clawdd Mon 79 D7
Pen-y-coed Shrops 148 E5
Pen-y-coedcae
Rhondda 58 B5
Penycwm Pembs 90 G6
Pen-y-Darren
M Tydf 77 D9
Penydre Swansea 75 E11
Pen-y-fai Bridgend 57 E11
Carms 75 E7
Pen-y-fan Carms 56 B4
Mon 79 D8
Penyfeidr Pembs 91 F7
Pen-y-felin Flint 165 B11
Penyffordd Flint 166 C4
Pen-y-ffordd Denb 181 F8
Flint 181 E10
Penyffridd Gwyn 163 D8
Pen y Foel Shrops 148 E5
Penygarn Torf 78 E3
Pen-y-garn Carms 93 E11
Ceredig 128 F2
Penygarnedd Powys 148 E2
Pen-y-garnedd
Anglesey 179 F8
Penygelli Powys 130 E2
Pen-y-gop Conwy 164 G6
Penygraig Rhondda 77 G7
Pen-y-graig Gwyn 144 C3
Penygraigwen
Anglesey 178 D6
Penygroes Gwyn 163 E7
Pembs 92 D3
Pen-y-groes Carms 75 C9
Pen-y-groeslon
Gwyn 144 C4
Pen-y-Gwryd Hotel
Gwyn 163 D11
Pen-y-lan Cardiff 59 D7
Newport 59 B9
V Glam 58 D3
Pen-y-maes Flint 181 F11
Pen-y-Myndd Carms 75 E7
Penymynydd Flint 166 C4
Pen-y-Park Hereford 96 C5
Penyraber Pembs 91 D9
Pen-yr-englyn
Rhondda 76 F6
Penyrheol Caerph 58 B6
Swansea 56 B5
Torf 78 F3
Pen-yr-heol Bridgend 58 C2
Mon 78 C6
Pen-yr-Heolgerrig
M Tydf 77 D8
Pen-y-rhiw Rhondda 58 B5
Penysarn Anglesey 179 C7
Pen-y-stryt Denb 165 E11
Penywaun Rhondda 77 E7
Pen-y-wern Shrops 114 B6
Penzance Corn 1 C5
Peopleton Worcs 117 G8
Peover Heath
Ches E 184 G3
Peper Harow Sur 50 E2
Peppercombe Devon 24 C5
Pepper Hill Som 43 F7
W Yorks 196 B6
Peppermoor
Northumb 264 F6
Pepper's Green
Essex 87 C10
Pepperstock C Beds 85 B9
Perceton N Ayrs 267 G7
Percie Aberds 293 D7
Percuil Corn 3 C9
Percyhorner Aberds 303 C9
Percy Main T&W 243 D8
Per-ffordd-llan
Flint 181 F10
Perham Down Wilts 47 D9
Periton Som 42 D3
Perivale London 67 C7
Perkhill Aberds 293 C7
Perkinsville Durham 243 G7
Perlethorpe Notts 187 G11
Perranarworthal Corn 3 B7
Perrancoombe Corn 4 E5
Perran Downs Corn 2 C3
Perranporth Corn 4 E5
Perranuthnoe Corn 2 D2
Perranwell Corn 3 B7
Corn 4 E5
Perranwell Station
Corn 3 B7
Perran Wharf Corn 3 B7
Perranzabuloe Corn 4 E5
Perrott's Brook Glos 81 D8
Perry Devon 26 F5
Kent 55 B9
W Mid 133 E11
Perry Barr W Mid 133 E11
Perry Beeches
W Mid 133 E11
Perry Common
W Mid 133 E11
Perry Crofts Staffs 134 C4
Perryfields Worcs 117 C8
Perryfoot Derbys 185 E10
Perry Green Essex 106 G6
Herts 86 B6
Som 43 F9
Wilts 62 B3
Perrymead Bath 61 G9
Perrystone Hill
Hereford 98 F2
Perry Street Kent 68 E6
Som 28 F4
Perrywood Kent 54 B4
Pershall Staffs 150 C6
Pershore Worcs 99 B8
Pert Angus 293 G8
Pertenhall Beds 121 D11
Perth Perth 286 E5
Perthcelyn Rhondda 77 F9
Perthy Shrops 149 C7
Perton Hereford 97 C11
Staffs 133 D7
Pertwood Wilts 45 F11
Pested Kent 54 C4
Peterborough
Pboro 138 D3
Peterburn Highld 307 L2
Peterchurch Hereford 96 D6
Peterculter
Aberdeen 293 C10
Peterhead Aberds 303 E11
Peterlee Durham 234 C4
Petersburn
N Lanark 268 C5
Petersfield Hants 34 C2
Peter's Finger Devon 12 D3
Peter's Green Herts 85 B10
Petersham London 67 E7
Peters Marland
Devon 25 E7
Peterstone Wentlooge
Newport 59 C9
Peterston-super-Ely
V Glam 58 D5
Peterstow Hereford 97 G11
Peter Tavy Devon 12 F6
Petertown Orkney 314 F3
Peterville Corn 4 E4
Petham Kent 54 C6
Petherwin Gate
Corn 11 D11
Petrockstow Devon 25 F8
Petsoe End
M Keynes 103 B7
Pett E Sus 38 E5
Pettaugh Suff 126 F3
Pett Bottom Kent 54 E6
Kent 55 C7
Petteridge Kent 53 E7
Pettinain S Lanark 269 G9
Pettings Kent 68 G6
Pettistree Suff 126 G5
Pett Level E Sus 38 E5
Petton Devon 27 C8
Shrops 149 D8
Petts Wood London 68 F2
Petty Aberds 303 F7
Pettycur Fife 280 D5
Petty France S Glos 61 B9
Pettymuick Aberds 303 G9
Pettywell Norf 159 E11
Petworth W Sus 35 C7
Pevensey E Sus 23 E10
Pevensey Bay E Sus 23 E11
Peverell Plym 7 D9
Pewsey Wilts 63 G7
Pewsey Wharf Wilts 63 G7
Pewterspear Warr 183 E10
Phantassie E Loth 281 F11
Pharisee Green
Essex 106 G2
Pheasants Bucks 65 B9
Pheasant's Hill Bucks 65 B9
Pheasey W Mid 133 D11
Pheonix Green Hants 49 B9
Phepson Worcs 117 F8
Philadelphia T&W 243 G8
Philham Devon 24 C3
Philiphaugh
Borders 261 D10
Phillack Corn 2 B3
Philleigh Corn 3 B9
Phillip's Town
Caerph 77 E10
Philpot End Essex 87 B10
Philpstoun W Loth 279 F10
Phocle Green
Hereford 98 F2
Phoenix Green Hants 49 B9
Phoenix Row
Durham 233 F9
Phorp Moray 301 D10
Pibsbury Som 28 B6
Pibwrlwyd Carms 74 B6
Pica Cumb 228 G6
Piccadilly S Yorks 187 B7
Warks 134 D4
Piccadilly Corner
Norf 142 F5
Piccotts End Herts 85 D9
Pickburn S Yorks 198 F4
Picken End Worcs 98 C6
Pickering N Yorks 216 C5
Pickering Nook
Durham 242 F5
Picket Hill Hants 31 F11
Picket Piece Hants 47 D11
Picket Post Hants 31 F11
Pickford W Mid 134 G5
Pickford Green
W Mid 134 G5
Pickhill N Yorks 214 C6
Picklenash Glos 98 F4
Picklescott Shrops 131 D8
Pickles Hill W Yorks 204 F6
Pickletillem Fife 287 E8
Pickley Green
Gtr Man 195 G7
Pickmere Ches E 183 F11
Pickney Som 27 B11
Pickstock Telford 150 E4
Pickup Bank
Blackburn 195 C8
Pickwell Devon 40 E3
Leics 154 G5
Pickwick Wilts 61 E11
Pickwood Scar
W Yorks 196 C5
Pickworth Lincs 155 C10
Rutland 155 G9
Picton Ches W 182 G6
Flint 181 E10
N Yorks 225 D8
Pict's Hill Som 28 B6
Piddinghoe E Sus 36 G6
Piddington Bucks 84 G4
Northants 120 G6
Oxon 83 B10
Piddlehinton Dorset 17 B10
Piddletrenthide
Dorset 17 B10
Pidley Cambs 122 B6
Pidney Dorset 30 F2
Piece Corn 2 B5
Piercebridge Darl 224 B4
Piercing Hill Essex 86 F6
Pierowall Orkney 314 B4
Piff's Elm Glos 99 F8
Pigdon Northumb 252 F5
Pightley Som 43 F8
Pig Oak Dorset 31 G8
Pigstye Green Essex 87 D10
Pike End W Yorks 196 D4
Pikehall Derbys 169 D11
Pike Hill Lancs 204 G3
Pike Law W Yorks 196 D4
Pikeshill Hants 32 F3
Pikestye Hereford 97 B10
Pilford Dorset 31 G8
Pilgrims Hatch Essex 87 F9
Pilham Lincs 188 C5
Pilhough Derbys 170 C3
Pill N Som 60 D4
Pembs 72 D6
Pillaton Corn 7 C7
Staffs 151 G8
Pillerton Hersey
Warks 100 B6
Pillerton Priors
Warks 100 B5
Pilleth Powys 114 D5
Pilley Glos 81 B7
Hants 20 B2
S Yorks 197 G10
Pilley Bailey Hants 20 B2
Pillgwenlly Newport 59 B10
Pilling Lancs 202 D4
Pilling Lane Lancs 202 D3
Pillmouth Devon 25 C7
Pillowell Glos 79 D10
Pillows Green Glos 98 F5
Pillwell Dorset 30 D3
Pilmuir Borders 261 G11
Pilning S Glos 60 B5
Pilrig Edin 280 F5
Pilsbury Derbys 169 C10
Pilsdon Dorset 16 B4
Pilsgate Pboro 137 B11
Pilsley Derbys 170 C6
Derbys 186 G2
Pilsley Green
Derbys 170 C6
Pilson Green Norf 161 G7
Piltdown E Sus 36 C6
Pilton Devon 40 G5
Edin 280 F4
Northants 137 G10
Rutland 137 C8
Som 44 E5
Pilton Green
Swansea 56 D2
Piltown Som 44 F5
Pimhole Gtr Man 195 E10
Pimlico Herts 85 D9
Lancs 203 E10
London 67 D9
Northants 102 C2
Pimperne Dorset 29 F9
Dorset 30 F6
Pinchbeck Lincs 156 D4
Pinchbeck Bars
Lincs 156 D3
Pinchbeck West
Lincs 156 E4
Pincheon Green
S Yorks 199 D7
Pinckney Green
Wilts 61 G10
Pincock Lancs 194 D5
Pineham Kent 55 D10
M Keynes 103 C7
Pinehurst Swindon 63 B7
Pinfarthings Glos 80 E5
Pinfold Lancs 193 E11
Pinfold Hill S Yorks 197 G9
Pinfoldpond C Beds 103 E8
Pinford End Suff 124 F6
Pinged Carms 74 E6
Pingewood W Berks 65 F7
Pin Green Herts 104 F4
Pinhoe Devon 14 C5
Pinkett's Booth
W Mid 134 G5
Pink Green Worcs 117 D11
Pinkie Braes E Loth 281 G7
Pinkney Wilts 61 B11
Pinkneys Green
Windsor 65 C11
Pinksmoor Som 27 D10
Pinley W Mid 119 B7
Pinley Green Warks 118 D4
Pin Mill Suff 108 D4
Pinminnoch
Dumfries 236 D2
S Ayrs 244 E5
Pinmore S Ayrs 244 E6
Pinmore Mains
S Ayrs 244 E6
Pinnacles Essex 86 D6
Pinner London 66 B6
Pinner Green
London 85 G10
Pinnerwood Park
London 85 G10
Pin's Green Worcs 98 B6
Pinsley Green
Ches E 167 F9
Pinstones Shrops 131 F9
Pinvin Worcs 99 B9
Pinwall Leics 134 C6
Pinwherry S Ayrs 244 F5
Pinxton Derbys 171 E7
Pipe and Lyde
Hereford 97 C10
Pipe Aston Hereford 115 C9
Pipe Gate Shrops 168 G2
Pipehill Staffs 133 B11
Pipehouse Bath 45 B9
Piperhall Argyll 266 D2
Piperhill Highld 301 D8
Pipe Ridware
Staffs 151 F11
Piper's Ash Ches W 166 B6
Piper's End Worcs 98 E6
Piper's Hill Worcs 117 D9
Piper's Pool Corn 11 E11
Pipewell Northants 136 F6
Pippacott Devon 40 F4
Pippin Street Lancs 194 C5
Pipps Hill Essex 69 B7
Pipsden Kent 53 G9
Pipton Powys 96 D3
Pirbright Sur 50 B2
Pirbright Camp Sur 50 B2
Pirnmill N Ayrs 255 C9
Pirton Herts 104 E2
Worcs 99 B7
Pisgah Ceredig 112 B3
Stirling 285 G11
Pishill Oxon 65 B8
Pishill Bank Oxon 84 G2
Pismire Hill S Yorks 186 C5
Pistyll Gwyn 162 G4
Pit Mon 78 D5
Pitagowan Perth 291 G10
Pitblae Aberds 303 C9
Pitcairngreen Perth 286 E4
Pitcalnie Highld 301 B8
Pitcaple Aberds 303 G7
Pitchcombe Glos 80 D5
Pitchcott Bucks 102 G5
Pitcher's Green Suff 125 F8
Pitchford Shrops 131 C10
Pitch Green Bucks 84 E3
Pitch Place Sur 49 F11
Sur 50 C3
Pitcombe Som 45 G7
Pitcorthie Fife 280 D2
Fife 287 G9
Pitcot Som 45 D7
V Glam 57 G11
Pitcox E Loth 282 F2
Pitcur Perth 286 D6
Pitfancy Aberds 302 E5
Pitfichie Aberds 293 B8
Pitforthie Aberds 293 F10
Pitgair Aberds 303 D7
Pitgrudy Highld 309 K7
Pithmaduthy Highld 301 B7
Pitkennedy Angus 287 B9
Pitkevy Fife 286 G6
Pitkierie Fife 287 G9
Pitlessie Fife 287 G7
Pitlochry Perth 286 B3
Pitmachie Aberds 302 G6
Pitmain Highld 291 C9
Pitmedden Aberds 303 G8
Pitminster Som 28 D2
Pitmuies Angus 287 C9
Pitmunie Aberds 293 B8
Pitney Som 29 B7
Pitrocknie Perth 286 C6
Pitscottie Fife 287 F8
Pitsea Essex 69 B8
Pitses Gtr Man 196 G2
Pitsford Northants 120 D5
Pitsford Hill Som 42 G6
Pitsmoor S Yorks 186 D5
Pitstone Bucks 84 B6
Pitstone Green Bucks 84 B6
Pitstone Hill Bucks 85 C7
Pitt Hants 33 B7
Pittachar Perth 286 E2
Pitt Court Glos 80 F3
Pittendreich
Moray 301 C11
Pittentrail Highld 309 J7
Pittenweem Fife 287 G9
Pitteuchar Fife 280 B5
Pittington Durham 234 C2
Pittodrie Aberds 302 G6
Pitton Swansea 56 D2
Wilts 47 G8
Pitts Hill Stoke 168 E5
Pittswood Kent 52 D6
Pittulie Aberds 303 C9
Pittville Glos 99 G9
Pityme Corn 10 F5
Pity Me Durham 233 B11
Pityoulish Highld 291 B11
Pixey Green Suff 126 B4
Pixham Sur 51 C7
Worcs 98 B6
Pixley Hereford 98 D3
Shrops 150 D3
Pizien Well Kent 53 C7
Place Newton
N Yorks 217 E7
Plaidy Aberds 303 D7
Corn 6 E5
Plain-an-Gwarry Corn 4 G3
Plain Dealings Pembs 73 B9
Plains N Lanark 268 B5
Plainsfield Som 43 F7
Plain Spot Notts 171 E7
Plain Street Corn 10 F5
Plaish Shrops 131 D10
Plaistow
London 68 C2
London 68 E2
W Sus 50 G4
Plaistow Green
Essex 106 F6
Plaitford Wilts 32 D3
Plaitford Green
Hants 32 C3
Plank Lane Gtr Man 194 G6
Plans Dumfries 238 D3
Plantation Bridge
Cumb 221 F9
Plantationfoot
Dumfries 248 E4
Plardiwick Staffs 150 E6
Plasau Shrops 149 E7
Plâs Berwyn Denb 165 G11
Plas-canol Gwyn 145 F11
Plas Coch Wrex 166 E4
Plas Dinam Powys 129 F10
Plas Gogerddan
Ceredig 128 G2
Plashet London 68 C2
Plashett Carms 74 D3
Plasiolyn Powys 129 C11
Plas Llwyngwern
Powys 128 C5
Plas Meredydd
Powys 130 D3
Plas Nantyr Wrex 148 B3
Plasnewydd Powys 129 D9
Plaster's Green Bath 60 G4
Plastow Green Hants 64 G4
Plas-yn-Cefn Denb 181 G8
Platt Kent 52 B6
Platt Bridge
Gtr Man 194 G6
Platt Lane Shrops 149 B10
Platts Common
S Yorks 197 G11
Platt's Heath Kent 53 C11
Plawsworth
Durham 233 B11
Plaxtol Kent 52 C6
Playden E Sus 38 C6
Playford Suff 108 B4
Play Hatch Oxon 65 D8
Playing Place Corn 4 G6
Playley Green Glos 98 E5
Plealey Shrops 131 B8
Pleamore Cross
Som 27 D10
Plean Stirling 278 D6
Pleasant Valley
Pembs 73 D10
Pleasington
Blackburn 194 B6
Pleasley Derbys 171 C8
Pleasleyhill Notts 171 C8
Pleck Dorset 30 D3
Dorset 30 E2
W Mid 133 D9
Pleckgate Blackburn 203 G9
Pleck or Little Ansty
Dorset 30 G3
Pledgdon Green
Essex 105 F11
Pledwick W Yorks 197 D10
Plemstall Ches W 183 G7
Plenmeller
Northumb 240 E6
Pleshey Essex 87 C11
Plockton Highld 295 B10
Plocrapol W Isles 305 J3
Plot Gate Som 44 G4
Plot Street Som 44 F5
Ploughfield Hereford 97 C7
Plough Hill Warks 134 E6
Plowden Shrops 131 F7
Ploxgreen Shrops 131 C7
Pluckley Kent 54 D2
Pluckley Thorne Kent 54 E2
Plucks Gutter Kent 71 G9
Plumbland Cumb 229 D9
Plumbley S Yorks 186 E6
Plumford Kent 54 B4
Plumley Ches E 184 F2
Plump Hill Glos 79 B11
Plumpton Cumb 230 D5
E Sus 36 E5
Northants 101 B11
Plumpton End
Northants 102 B4
Plumpton Foot
Cumb 230 D5
Plumpton Green
E Sus 36 D5
Plumpton Head
Cumb 230 E6
Plumstead London 68 D3
Norf 160 C2
Plumstead Common
London 68 D3
Plumstead Green
Norf 160 C2
Plumtree Notts 154 C2
Plumtree Green
Kent 53 D10
Plumtree Park
Notts 154 C2
Plungar Leics 154 C5
Plush Dorset 30 G2
Plusha Corn 11 E11
Plushabridge Corn 12 G2
Plusterwine Glos 79 F9
Plwmp Ceredig 111 G7
Plymouth Plym 7 E9
Plympton Plym 7 D10
Plymstock Plym 7 E10
Plymtree Devon 27 G9
Pobgreen Gtr Man 196 F4
Pochin Houses
Caerph 77 E11
Pocket Nook
Gtr Man 183 B10
Pockley N Yorks 216 B2
Pocklington
E Yorks 208 D2
Pockthorpe Norf 141 D8
Norf 158 D6
Norf 159 E10
Norf 159 F11
Pode Hole Lincs 156 E4
Podimore Som 29 C8
Podington Beds 121 E8
Podmoor Worcs 117 C7
Podmore Norf 159 G9
Staffs 150 B5
Podsmead Glos 80 B4
Poffley End Oxon 82 C5
Pogmoor S Yorks 197 F10
Point Corn 3 B8
Point Clear Essex 89 C9
Pointon Lincs 156 C2
Pokesdown Bmouth 19 C8
Pol a Charra
W Isles 297 K3
Polbae Dumfries 236 B4
Polbain Highld 307 H4
Polbathic Corn 7 D7
Polbeth W Loth 269 C10
Polborder Corn 7 C7
Polbrock Corn 5 B10
Polchar Highld 291 C10
Polebrook
Northants 137 F11
Pole Elm Worcs 98 B6
Polegate E Sus 23 D9
Pole Moor W Yorks 196 D5
Poles Highld 309 K7
Polesden Lacey Sur 50 C6
Poleshill Som 27 C9
Pole's Hole Wilts 45 C10
Polesworth Warks 134 C5
Polgear Corn 2 B5
Polgigga Corn 1 E3
Polglass Highld 307 J5
Polgooth Corn 5 E9
Poling W Sus 35 G8
Poling Corner W Sus 35 F8
Polkerris Corn 5 E11
Polla Highld 308 D3
Polladras Corn 2 C4
Pollard Street Norf 160 C6
Pollhill Kent 53 C11
Poll Hill Mers 182 E3
Pollie Highld 309 H7
Pollington E Yorks 198 D6
Polliwilline Argyll 255 G8
Polloch Highld 289 C9
Pollok Glasgow 267 C10
Pollokshields
Glasgow 267 C11
Polmadie Glasgow 267 C11
Polmarth Corn 2 B6
Polmassick Corn 5 F9
Polmear Corn 5 E11
Polmont Falk 279 F8
Polmorla Corn 10 G5
Polnessan E Ayrs 257 G10
Polnish Highld 295 G9
Polopit Northants 121 B10
Polpenwith Corn 2 D6
Polpeor Corn 2 B2
Polperro Corn 6 E4
Polruan Corn 6 E2
Polsham Som 44 E4
Polsloe Devon 14 C4
Polstead Suff 107 D9
Polstead Heath Suff 107 C9
Poltalloch Argyll 275 D9
Poltesco Corn 2 F6
Poltimore Devon 14 B5
Polton Midloth 270 C5
Polwarth Borders 272 E4
Polwheveral Corn 2 D6
Polyphant Corn 11 E11
Polzeath Corn 10 F4
Pomeroy Derbys 169 B10
Pomphlett Plym 7 E10
Ponciau Wrex 166 F3
Pond Close Som 27 B10
Ponde Powys 96 D2
Pondersbridge
Cambs 138 E5
Ponders End London 86 F5
Pond Park Bucks 85 E7
Pond Street Essex 105 D9
Pondtail Hants 49 C10
Pondwell IoW 21 C8
Poniou Corn 1 B4
Ponjeravah Corn 2 D6
Ponsanooth Corn 3 B7
Ponsford Devon 27 F8
Ponsonby Cumb 219 D11
Ponsongath Corn 3 F7
Ponsworthy Devon 13 G10
Pont Corn 6 E2
Pont Aber Carms 94 G4
Pont Aber-Geirw
Gwyn 146 D5
Pontamman Carms 75 C10
Pontantwn Carms 74 C6
Pontardawe Neath 76 E2
Pontarddulais
Swansea 75 E9
Pontarfynach / Devils
Bridge Ceredig 112 B4
Pont-ar-gothi
Carms 93 G10
Pont ar Hydfer Powys 95 F7
Pont-ar-llechau
Carms 94 G4
Pontarsais Carms 93 F8
Pontblyddyn Flint 166 C3
Pontbren Araeth
Carms 94 G3
Pontbren Llwyd
Rhondda 76 D6
Pontcanna Cardiff 59 D7
Pont Cyfyng Conwy 164 D2
Pont Cysyllte Wrex 166 G3
Pontdolgoch
Powys 129 E10
Pont Dolydd Prysor
Gwyn 146 B4
Pontefract W Yorks 198 C3
Ponteland Northumb 242 C5
Ponterwyd Ceredig 128 G4
Pontesbury Shrops 131 B7
Pontesbury Hill
Shrops 131 B7
Pontesford Shrops 131 B8
Pontfadog Wrex 148 B4
Pontfaen Pembs 91 E10
Pont-faen Powys 95 E9
Shrops 148 B5
Pont Fronwydd
Gwyn 146 E6
Pont-gareg Pembs 92 C2
Pontgarreg Ceredig 110 G6
Ponthen Shrops 148 F6
Pont-Henri Carms 75 D7
Ponthir Torf 78 G4
Ponthirwaun
Ceredig 92 B5
Pont Hwfa Anglesey 178 E2
Pontiago Pembs 91 D8
Pont iets / Pontyates
Carms 75 D7
Pontithel Powys 96 D3
Pontllanfraith
Caerph 77 F11
Pontlliw Swansea 75 E10
Pont-Llogel Powys 147 F10
Pontllyfni Gwyn 162 E6
Pontlottyn Caerph 77 D10
Pontneddfechan
Powys 76 D6
Pontnewydd Torf 78 F3
Pont-newydd Carms 74 D6
Flint 165 B11
Pontnewynydd Torf 78 E3
Pont Pen-y-benglog
Gwyn 163 C10
Pontrhydfendigaid
Ceredig 112 D4
Pont Rhydgaled
Powys 128 G6
Pont Rhyd-goch
Conwy 163 C11
Pont-Rhyd-sarn
Gwyn 147 D7
Pont Rhyd-y-berry
Powys 95 D9
Pont Rhyd-y-cyff
Bridgend 57 D11
Pontrhydyfen Neath 57 C9
Pont-rhyd-y-groes
Ceredig 112 C4
Pontrhydyrun Torf 78 F3
Pont-Rhythallt
Gwyn 163 C8
Pontrilas Hereford 97 F7
Pontrobert Powys 148 G2
Pont-rug Gwyn 163 C8
Pont Senni /
Sennybridge Powys 95 F8
Ponts Green E Sus 23 B11
Pontshill Hereford 98 G2
Pont-siôn Ceredig 93 B8
Pont Siôn Norton
Rhondda 77 G9
Pontsticill M Tydf 77 C9
Pont-Walby Neath 76 D5
Pontwgan Conwy 180 G3

406 Ros–San

Rosemount Perth 286 C5
Rosenannon Corn 5 B9
Rosenithon Corn 3 E8
Roser's Cross E Sus 37 C9
Rose Valley Pembs 73 E8
Rosevean Corn 5 D10
Rosevear Corn 2 E5
Roseville W Mid 133 E8
Rosevine Corn 3 B9
Rosewarne Corn 2 B4
Corn 4 G2
Rosewell Midloth 270 C5
Roseworth Stockton 234 G4
Roseworthy Corn 2 B4
Corn 4 F5
Roseworthy Barton
Corn 2 B4
Rosgill Cumb 221 B10
Rosherville Kent 68 E6
Roshven Highld 289 B9
Roskear Croft Corn 4 G3
Roskhill Highld 298 E2
Roskill House
Highld 300 D6
Roskorwell Corn 3 E7
Rosley Cumb 230 B2
Roslin Midloth 270 C5
Rosliston Derbys 152 F4
Rosneath Argyll 276 E5
Ross Borders 273 C9
Dumfries 237 E8
Northumb 264 B4
Perth 285 E11
Rossett Wrex 166 D5
Rossett Green
N Yorks 206 C2
Ross Green Worcs 116 E5
Rossie Ochill Perth 286 F4
Rossie Priory Perth 286 D6
Rossington
S Yorks 187 B10
Rosskeen Highld 300 C6
Rossland Renfs 277 G8
Rossmore Poole 19 C7
Ross-on-Wye
Hereford 98 G2
Roster Highld 310 F6
Rostherne Ches E 184 E2
Rostholme S Yorks 198 F5
Rosthwaite Cumb 220 C5
Cumb 220 G4
Roston Derbys 169 G10
Rosudgeon Corn 2 D3
Rosyth Fife 280 E2
Rotchfords Essex 107 E8
Rotcombe Bath 44 B6
Rothbury Northumb 252 C3
Rotherbridge W Sus 35 C7
Rotherby Leics 154 F3
Rotherfield E Sus 37 B9
Rotherfield Greys
Oxon 65 C8
Rotherfield Peppard
Oxon 65 C8
Rotherham S Yorks 186 C6
Rotherhithe London 67 D11
Rothersthorpe
Northants 120 F4
Rotherwas Hereford 97 D10
Rotherwick Hants 49 B8
Rothes Moray 302 E2
Rothesay Argyll 275 G11
Rothiebrisbane
Aberds 303 F7
Rothiemay Crossroads
Moray 302 E5
Rothiemurchus Lodge
Highld 291 C11
Rothienorman
Aberds 303 F7
Rothiesholm Orkney 314 D6
Rothley Leics 153 G11
Northumb 252 F2
Rothley Plain Leics 153 G11
Rothley Shield East
Northumb 252 E2
Rothmaise Aberds 302 F6
Rothwell Lincs 189 B11
Northants 136 G6
W Yorks 197 B10
Rothwell Haigh
W Yorks 197 B10
Rotsea E Yorks 209 C7
Rottal Angus 292 G5
Rotten End Essex 106 F4
Suff 127 D7
Rotten Green Hants 49 B9
Rotten Row W Berks 64 E5
W Mid 118 B3
Rottingdean Brighton 36 G5
Rottington Cumb 219 C9
Rotton Park
W Mid 133 F10
Roud IoW 20 E6
Rougham Norf 158 E6
Suff 125 E8
Rougham Green
Suff 125 E8
Rough Bank
Gtr Man 196 E2
Roughbirchworth
S Yorks 197 G9
Roughburn Highld 290 E5
Rough Close Staffs 151 B8
Rough Common Kent 54 B6
Roughcote Staffs 168 G6
Rough Haugh Highld 308 E7
Rough Hay Staffs 152 E4
Roughlee Lancs 204 E2
Roughley W Mid 134 D2
Roughmoor Som 28 B2
Swindon 62 B6
Roughrigg N Lanark 278 G6
Roughsike Cumb 240 B2
Roughton Lincs 174 C2
Norf 160 B4
Shrops 132 E5
Roughton Moor
Lincs 174 C2
Roughway Kent 52 C6
Roundbush Essex 88 E5
Round Bush Herts 85 F10
Roundbush Green
Essex 87 C9
Round Green
Luton 103 G11
Roundham Som 28 F6
Roundhay W Yorks 206 F2
Round Maple Suff 107 C9
Round Oak Shrops 131 G7
W Mid 133 F8
Round's Green
W Mid 133 F9
Roundshaw London 67 G10
Round Spinney
Northants 120 D5
Roundstonefoot
Dumfries 248 B4
Round Street Kent 69 F7
Roundstreet Common
W Sus 35 B9
Roundswell Devon 40 G4
Roundthorn
Gtr Man 184 D4
Roundthwaite Cumb 222 E2
Roundway Wilts 62 G4
Roundyhill Angus 287 B7
Rousdon Devon 15 C11
Rousham Oxon 101 G9
Rous Lench Worcs 117 G10
Routenburn N Ayrs 266 C3
Routh E Yorks 209 E7
Rout's Green Bucks 84 F3
Row Corn 11 F7
Cumb 211 B8
Cumb 231 E8
Rowanburn
Dumfries 239 B10
Rowanfield Glos 99 G8
Rowardennan
Stirling 277 B7
Rowarth Derbys 185 D8
Row Ash Hants 33 E8
Rowbarton Som 28 B2
Rowberrow Som 44 B3
Row Brow Cumb 229 D7
Rowde Wilts 62 G3
Rowden Devon 13 B8
N Yorks 205 B11
Rowe Head Cumb 210 D5
Rowen Conwy 180 G3
Rowfoot Northumb 240 E5
Rowford Som 28 B2
Row Green Essex 106 G4
Row Heath Essex 89 B10
Rowhedge Essex 107 G10
Rowhill Sur 66 G4
Rowhook W Sus 50 G6
Rowington Warks 118 D4
Rowington Green
Warks 118 D4
Rowland Derbys 186 G2
Rowlands Castle
Hants 34 E2
Rowlands Gill T&W 242 F5
Rowland's Green
Hereford 98 D3
Rowledge Sur 49 E10
Rowlestone Hereford 97 F7
Rowley E Yorks 208 G5
Shrops 130 B6
Rowley Green London 86 F2
Rowley Hill W Yorks 197 E7
Rowley Park Staffs 151 E8
Rowley Regis
W Mid 133 F9
Rowley's Green
W Mid 134 G6
Rowling Kent 55 C9
Rowly Sur 50 E4
Rownall Staffs 169 F7
Rowner Hants 33 G9
Rowney Green
Worcs 117 C10
Rownhams Hants 32 D5
Row-of-trees
Ches E 184 F4
Rowrah Cumb 219 B11
Rowsham Bucks 84 B4
Rowsley Derbys 170 B3
Rowstock Oxon 64 B3
Rowston Lincs 173 D9
Rowthorne Derbys 171 C7
Rowton Ches W 166 C6
Shrops 149 G7
Telford 150 F2
Rowton Moor
Ches W 166 C6
Row Town Sur 66 G4
Roxburgh Borders 262 C5
Roxburgh Mains
Borders 262 D5
Roxby N Lincs 200 D2
N Yorks 226 B5
Roxeth London 66 B6
Roxton Beds 122 G3
Roxwell Essex 87 D10
Royal British Legion
Village Kent 53 B8
Royal Leamington Spa
Warks 118 D6
Royal Oak Darl 233 G10
Lancs 194 G2
N Yorks 218 D2
Royal's Green
Ches E 167 G10
Royal Tunbridge Wells /
Tunbridge Wells
Kent 52 F5
Royal Wootton Bassett
Wilts 62 C5
Roybridge Highld 290 E4
Royd S Yorks 197 G8
Roydhouse W Yorks 197 E8
Royd Moor S Yorks 197 G8
W Yorks 198 E2
Roydon Essex 86 D6
Norf 141 G11
Norf 158 E4
Roydon Hamlet
Essex 86 D6
Royds Green
W Yorks 197 B11
Royston Glasgow 268 B2
Herts 105 C7
S Yorks 197 E11
Royston Water Som 28 E2
Royton Gtr Man 196 F2
Ruabon / Rhiwabon
Wrex 166 G4
Ruaig Argyll 288 E2
Ruan High Lanes
Corn 3 B10
Ruan Lanihorne Corn 5 G7
Ruan Major Corn 2 F6
Ruan Minor Corn 2 F6
Ruarach Highld 295 C11
Ruardean Glos 79 B10
Ruardean Hill Glos 79 B10
Ruardean Woodside
Glos 79 B10
Rubery Worcs 117 B9
Rubha Ghaisinis
W Isles 297 G4
Rubha Stoer Highld 306 F5
Ruchazie Glasgow 268 B3
Ruchill Glasgow 267 B11
Ruckcroft Cumb 230 C6
Ruckhall Hereford 97 D9
Ruckinge Kent 54 G4
Ruckland Lincs 190 F4
Rucklers Lane Herts 85 E9
Ruckley Shrops 131 C10
Rudbaxton Pembs 91 G9
Rudby N Yorks 225 D9
Ruddington Notts 153 C11
Ruddle Glos 79 C11
Rudford Glos 98 G5
Rudge Shrops 132 D6
Som 45 C10
Rudge Heath
Shrops 132 D5
Rudgeway S Glos 60 B6
Rudgwick W Sus 50 G5
Rudhall Hereford 98 F2
Rudheath Ches W 183 G11
Rudheath Woods
Ches W 184 G2
Rudhja Garbh
Argyll 289 E11
Rudley Green Essex 88 E4
Rudloe Wilts 61 E10
Rudry Caerph 59 B7
Rudston E Yorks 217 F11
Rudyard Staffs 169 D7
Ruewood Shrops 149 D9
Rufford Lancs 194 D3
Rufforth York 206 C6
Ruffs Notts 171 F8
Rugby Warks 119 B10
Rugeley Staffs 151 F10
Ruggin Som 27 D11
Ruglen S Ayrs 245 C7
Rugley Northumb 264 G5
Ruilick Highld 300 E5
Ruishton Som 28 C3
Ruisigearraidh
W Isles 296 C5
Ruislip London 66 B5
Ruislip Common
London 66 B5
Ruislip Gardens
London 66 B5
Ruislip Manor London 66 B6
Ruiton W Mid 133 E8
Ruloe Ches W 183 G9
Rumach Highld 295 G8
Rumbling Bridge
Perth 279 B10
Rumbow Cottages
Worcs 117 B8
Rumburgh Suff 142 G6
Rumbush W Mid 118 B2
Rumer Hill Staffs 133 B9
Rumford Corn 10 G3
Falk 279 F8
Rumney Cardiff 59 D8
Rumsam Devon 40 G5
Rumwell Som 27 C11
Runcorn Halton 183 E8
Runcton W Sus 22 C5
Runcton Holme
Norf 140 B2
Rundlestone Devon 13 G7
Runfold Sur 49 D11
Runhall Norf 141 B11
Runham Norf 143 B10
Norf 161 G9
Runham Vauxhall
Norf 143 B10
Running Hill Head
Gtr Man 196 F4
Runnington Som 27 C10
Running Waters
Durham 234 C2
Runsell Green Essex 88 D3
Runshaw Moor
Lancs 194 D4
Runswick Bay
N Yorks 226 B6
Runwell Essex 88 G2
Ruscombe Glos 80 D4
Wokingham 65 D9
Ruscote Oxon 101 C8
Rushall Hereford 98 E3
Norf 142 G3
W Mid 133 C10
Wilts 46 B6
Rushbrooke Suff 125 E7
Rushbury Shrops 131 E10
Rushcombe Bottom
Poole 18 B5
Rushden Herts 104 E6
Northants 121 D9
Rushenden Kent 70 E2
Rusher's Cross
E Sus 37 B10
Rushey Mead
Leicester 136 B2
Rushford Devon 12 F4
Norf 141 G8
Rushgreen Warr 183 D11
Rush Green Essex 89 B11
Herts 86 C5
Herts 104 G4
London 68 B4
Norf 141 B11
Rush-head Aberds 303 E8
Rush Hill Bath 61 G8
Rushington Hants 32 E5
Rushlake Green
E Sus 23 B10
Rushland Cross
Cumb 210 B6
Rushley Green
Essex 106 D5
Rushmere C Beds 103 F8
Suff 143 F9
Rushmere St Andrew
Suff 108 B4
Rushmere Street
Suff 108 B4
Rushmoor Sur 49 E11
Telford 150 G2
Rushmore Hants 33 E11
Rushmore Hill
London 68 G3
Rushock Hereford 114 F6
Worcs 117 C7
Rusholme Gtr Man 184 B5
Rushton Ches W 167 C9
Dorset 18 D3
N Yorks 217 C9
Northants 136 G6
Shrops 132 B2
Rushton Spencer
Staffs 168 C6
Rushwick Worcs 116 G6
Rushyford Durham 233 F11
Rushy Green E Sus 23 C7
Ruskie Stirling 285 G10
Ruskington Lincs 173 E9
Rusland Cumb 210 B6
Rusling End Herts 104 G4
Rusper W Sus 51 F8
Ruspidge Glos 79 C11
Russel Highld 299 E8
Russell Hill London 67 G10
Russell's Green
E Sus 38 E2
Russell's Hall
W Mid 133 F8
Russell's Water Oxon 65 B8
Russel's Green Suff 126 C5
Russ Hill Sur 51 E8
Rusthall Kent 52 F5
Rustington W Sus 35 G9
Ruston N Yorks 217 C9
Ruston Parva
E Yorks 217 G11
Ruswarp N Yorks 227 D7
Ruthall Shrops 131 F11
Rutherford Borders 262 C4
Rutherglen
S Lanark 268 C2
Ruthernbridge Corn 5 B10
Ruthin Denb 165 D10
V Glam 58 D3
Ruthrieston
Aberdeen 293 C11
Ruthven Aberds 302 E5
Angus 286 C6
Highld 291 D9
Highld 301 F8
Ruthven House
Angus 287 C7
Ruthvoes Corn 5 C8
Ruthwaite Cumb 229 D10
Ruthwell Dumfries 238 D3
Ruxley London 68 E3
Ruxton Hereford 97 F11
Ruxton Green
Hereford 79 B8
Ruyton-XI-Towns
Shrops 149 E7
Ryal Northumb 242 C2
Ryal Fold Blackburn 195 C7
Ryall Dorset 16 C4
Worcs 99 C7
Ryarsh Kent 53 B7
Rychraggan Highld 300 F4
Rydal Cumb 221 D7
Ryde IoW 21 C7
Rydens Sur 66 F6
Rydeshill Sur 50 C3
Rydon Devon 14 G3
Rye E Sus 38 C6
Ryebank Shrops 149 C10
Rye Common Hants 49 C9
Ryecroft S Yorks 186 B6
W Yorks 205 F7
Ryecroft Gate Staffs 168 C6
Ryeford Glos 80 E4
Rye Foreign E Sus 38 C5
Rye Harbour E Sus 38 D6
Ryehill E Yorks 201 B8
Ryeish Green
Wokingham 65 F8
Ryelands Hereford 115 F9
Rye Park Herts 86 C5
Rye Street Worcs 98 D5
Ryeworth Glos 99 G9
Ryhall Rutland 155 G10
Ryhill W Yorks 197 E11
Ryhope T&W 243 G10
Rylah Derbys 171 B7
Rylands Notts 153 B10
Rylstone N Yorks 204 B5
Ryme Intrinseca
Dorset 29 E9
Ryther N Yorks 207 F7
Ryton Glos 98 E4
N Yorks 216 D5
Shrops 132 C5
T&W 242 E5
Warks 135 F7
Ryton-on-Dunsmore
Warks 119 C7
Ryton Woodside
T&W 242 E4

S

Sabden Lancs 203 F11
Sabine's Green Essex 87 F8
Sackers Green Suff 107 D8
Sacombe Herts 86 B4
Sacombe Green
Herts 86 B4
Sacriston Durham 233 B10
Sadberge Darl 224 B6
Saddell Argyll 255 D8
Saddell Ho Argyll 255 D8
Saddington Leics 136 E3
Saddle Bow Norf 158 F2
Saddlescombe
W Sus 36 E3
Saddle Street Dorset 28 G5
Sadgill Cumb 221 D9
Saffron's Cross
Hereford 115 G10
Saffron Walden
Essex 105 D10
Sageston Pembs 73 E9
Saham Hills Norf 141 C8
Saham Toney Norf 141 C8
Saighdinis W Isles 296 E4
Saighton Ches W 166 C6
Sain Dunwyd / St
Donats V Glam 58 F2
St Abbs Borders 273 B8
St Abb's Haven
Borders 273 B8
St Agnes Corn 4 E4
Scilly 1 H3
St Albans Herts 85 D10
St Allen Corn 4 E6
St Andrews Fife 287 F9
St Andrew's Major
V Glam 58 E6
St Andrew's Wood
Devon 27 F9
St Annes Lancs 193 B10
St Anne's Park Bristol 60 E6
St Ann's Dumfries 248 E3
Nottingham 171 G9
St Ann's Chapel Corn 12 G4
Devon 8 F3
St Anthony Corn 3 C9
St Anthony-in-Meneage
Corn 3 D7
St Anthony's T&W 243 E7
St Anthony's Hill
E Sus 23 E10
St Arvans Mon 79 F8
St Asaph / Llanelwy
Denb 181 G8
St Athan / Sain Tathon
V Glam 58 F4
Sain Tathon / St Athan
V Glam 58 F4
St Augustine's Kent 54 C6
St Austell Corn 5 E10
St Austins Hants 20 B2
St Bees Cumb 219 C9
St Blazey Corn 5 E11
St Blazey Gate Corn 5 E11
St Boswells Borders 262 C3
St Breock Corn 10 G5
St Breward Corn 11 F7
St Briavels Glos 79 E9
St Briavels Common
Glos 79 E8
St Bride's Pembs 72 C4
St Brides Major / Saint-
y-Brid V Glam 57 G11
St Bride's Netherwent
Mon 60 B2
St Brides-super-Ely
V Glam 58 D5
St Brides Wentlooge
Newport 59 C9
Saintbridge Glos 80 B5
St Budeaux Plym 7 D8
Saintbury Glos 100 D2
St Buryan Corn 1 D4
St Catherine Bath 61 E9
St Catherine's Argyll 284 G5
St Catherine's Hill
Dorset 19 B8
St Chloe Glos 80 E4
St Clears / Sanclêr
Carms 74 B3
St Cleer Corn 6 B5
St Clement Corn 4 G6
St Clether Corn 11 E10
St Colmac Argyll 275 G11
St Columb Major Corn 5 C8
St Columb Minor Corn 4 C6
St Columb Road Corn 5 D8
St Combs Aberds 303 C10
St Cross Hants 33 B7
St Cross South Elmham
Suff 142 G5
St Cyrus Aberds 293 G9
St David's Perth 286 E3
St David's / Tyddewi
Pembs 90 F5
St Day Corn 4 G4
St Decumans Som 42 E5
St Dennis Corn 5 D9
St Denys Soton 32 E6
St Devereux Hereford 97 E8
St Dials Torf 78 G3
St Dogmaels /
Llandudoch Pembs 92 B3
St Dominick Corn 7 B8
St Donat's / Sain
Dunwyd V Glam 58 F2
St Edith's Wilts 62 G3
St Endellion Corn 10 F5
St Enoder Corn 5 D7
St Erme Corn 4 E6
St Erney Corn 7 D7
St Erth Corn 2 B3
St Erth Praze Corn 2 B3
St Ervan Corn 10 G3
St Eval Corn 5 B7
St Ewe Corn 5 F9
St Fagans Cardiff 58 D6
St Fergus Aberds 303 D10
St Fillans Perth 285 E10
St Florence Pembs 73 E9
St Gennys Corn 11 B8
St George Bristol 60 E6
Conwy 181 F7
St George in the East
London 67 C10
St Georges N Som 59 G11
St George's Gtr Man 184 B4
Telford 150 G4
V Glam 58 D5
St George's Hill Sur 66 G5
St George's Well
Devon 27 F8
St Germans Corn 7 D7
St Giles Lincs 189 G7
London 67 C10
St Giles in the Wood
Devon 25 D8
St Giles on the Heath
Devon 12 C3
St Giles's Hill Hants 33 B7
St Gluvias Corn 3 C7
St Godwalds Worcs 117 D9
St Harmon Powys 113 C9
St Helena Warks 134 C5
St Helen Auckland
Durham 233 F9
St Helens Cumb 228 E6
IoW 21 D8
St Helens *continued*
Mers 183 B8
St Helen's E Sus 38 E4
S Yorks 197 F11
St Helen's Wood
E Sus 38 E4
St Helier London 67 F9
St Hilary Corn 2 C3
V Glam 58 E4
Saint Hill Devon 27 F9
W Sus 51 F11
St Ibbs Herts 104 F3
St Illtyd Bl Gwent 78 E2
St Ippollytts Herts 104 F3
St Ishmael's Pembs 72 D4
St Issey Corn 10 G4
St Ive Corn 6 B6
St Ive Cross Corn 6 B6
St Ives Cambs 122 C6
Corn 2 A2
Dorset 31 G10
St James Dorset 30 C5
London 67 C9
Norf 160 E5
St James's End
Northants 120 E4
St James South Elmham
Suff 142 G6
St Jidgey Corn 5 B8
St John Corn 7 E8
St Johns London 67 D11
Warks 118 C5
St John's
E Sus 52 G4
IoM 192 D3
Kent 52 B4
Kent 52 E5
Sur 50 B3
W Yorks 206 F4
Worcs 116 G6
St John's Chapel
Devon 25 B8
Durham 232 D3
St John's Fen End
Norf 157 G10
St John's Highway
Norf 157 G10
St John's Park IoW 21 C8
St John's Town of Dalry
Dumfries 246 G4
St John's Wells
Aberds 303 F7
St John's Wood
London 67 C9
St Judes IoM 192 C4
St Julians Herts 85 D10
Newport 59 B10
St Just Corn 1 C3
St Justinian Pembs 90 F4
St Just in Roseland
Corn 3 B9
St Katharines Wilts 63 G9
St Katherine's
Aberds 303 F7
St Keverne Corn 3 E7
St Kew Corn 10 F6
St Kew Highway Corn 10 F6
St Keyne Corn 6 C4
St Lawrence Corn 5 B10
Essex 89 E7
IoW 20 F6
Kent 71 F11
St Leonards Dorset 31 G10
E Sus 38 F3
S Lanark 268 E2
St Leonard's Bucks 84 D6
St Leonard's Street
Kent 53 B7
St Levan Corn 1 E3
St Luke's Derby 152 B6
London 67 C10
St Lythans V Glam 58 E6
St Mabyn Corn 10 G6
St Madoes Perth 286 E5
St Margarets Herts 86 C5
London 67 E7
St Margaret's
Hereford 97 E7
St Margaret's at Cliffe
Kent 55 E11
St Margaret's Hope
Orkney 314 G4
St Margaret South
Elmham Suff 142 G6
St Mark's Glos 99 G8
IoM 192 E3
St Martin Corn 2 E6
Corn 6 E5
St Martins Perth 286 D5
St Martin's Shrops 148 B6
St Martin's Moor
Shrops 148 B6
St Mary Bourne
Hants 48 C2
St Marychurch Torbay 9 B8
St Mary Church
V Glam 58 E4
St Mary Cray London 68 F3
St Mary Hill V Glam 58 D3
St Mary Hoo
Medway 69 D10
St Mary in the Marsh
Kent 39 B9
St Mary's Orkney 314 F4
St Mary's Bay Kent 39 B9
St Maughans Mon 79 B7
St Maughans Green
Mon 79 B7
St Mawes Corn 3 C8
St Mawgan Corn 5 B7
St Mellion Corn 7 B7
St Mellons Cardiff 59 C8
St Merryn Corn 10 G3
St Mewan Corn 5 E9
St Michael Caerhays
Corn 5 G9
St Michael Church
Som 43 G10
St Michael Penkevil
Corn 5 G7
St Michaels Kent 53 F11
Torbay 9 C7
Worcs 115 D11
St Michael's Hamlet
Mers 182 D5
St Michael's on Wyre
Lancs 202 E5
St Michael South
Elmham Suff 142 G6
St Minver Corn 10 F5
St Monans Fife 287 G9
St Neot Corn 6 B3
St Neots Cambs 122 E3
St Newlyn East Corn 4 D6
St Nicholas Herts 104 F5
Pembs 91 D7
V Glam 58 E5
St Nicholas at Wade
Kent 71 F9
St Nicholas South
Elmham Suff 142 G6
St Nicolas Park
Warks 135 E7
St Ninians Stirling 278 C5
St Olaves Norf 143 D9
St Osyth Essex 89 B10
St Osyth Heath
Essex 89 B10
St Owens Cross
Hereford 97 G10
St Pancras London 67 C10
St Paul's Glos 80 B4
St Paul's Cray London 68 F3
St Paul's Walden
Herts 104 G3
St Peters Kent 71 F11
St Peter's Glos 99 G8
T&W 243 E7
St Peter South Elmham
Suff 142 G6
St Peter The Great
Worcs 117 G7
St Petrox Pembs 73 F7
St Pinnock Corn 6 C4
St Quivox S Ayrs 257 E9
St Ruan Corn 2 F6
Saint's Hill Kent 52 E4
St Stephen Corn 5 E8
St Stephens Corn 7 D8
Herts 85 D10
St Stephen's Corn 12 D2
St Teath Corn 11 E7
St Thomas Devon 14 C4
Swansea 57 C7
St Tudy Corn 11 F7
St Twynnells Pembs 73 F7
St Veep Corn 6 E2
St Vigeans Angus 287 C10
St Vincent's Hamlet
Essex 87 G9
St Wenn Corn 5 C9
St Weonards
Hereford 97 G9
St Winnow Corn 6 D2
Saint y Brid / St Brides
Major V Glam 57 G11
St y-Nyll V Glam 58 D5
Saith ffynnon Flint 181 F11
Salcombe Devon 9 G9
Salcombe Regis
Devon 15 D9
Salcott-cum-Virley
Essex 88 C6
Salden Bucks 102 F6
Sale Gtr Man 184 C3
Saleby Lincs 191 F7
Sale Green Worcs 117 F8
Salehurst E Sus 38 C2
Salem Carms 94 F2
Ceredig 128 G3
Corn 4 G4
Salen Argyll 289 E7
Highld 289 C8
Salendine Nook
W Yorks 196 D6
Salenside Borders 261 E11
Salesbury Lancs 203 G9
Saleway Worcs 117 F8
Salford C Beds 103 D8
Gtr Man 184 B4
Oxon 100 F5
Salford Ford
C Beds 103 D8
Salford Priors
Warks 117 G11
Salfords Sur 51 D9
Salhouse Norf 160 G6
Saligo Argyll 274 G3
Salisbury Wilts 31 B10
Salkeld Dykes Cumb 230 D6
Sallachan Highld 289 C11
Sallachy Highld 295 B11
Highld 309 J5
Salle Norf 160 E2
Salmans Kent 52 E4
Salmonby Lincs 190 G4
Salmond's Muir
Angus 287 D9
Salmonhutch Devon 14 B2
Salperton Glos 99 G11
Salperton Park Glos 81 B9
Salph End Beds 121 G11
Salsburgh N Lanark 268 C6
Salt Staffs 151 D9
Salta Cumb 229 B7
Saltaire W Yorks 205 F8
Saltash Corn 7 D8
Saltburn Highld 301 C7
Saltburn-by-the-Sea
Redcar 235 G9
Saltby Leics 155 D7
Salt Coates Cumb 238 G5
Saltcoats
Cumb 219 F11
E Loth 281 E9
N Ayrs 266 G4
Saltcotes Lancs 193 B11
Saltdean Brighton 36 G5
Salt End E Yorks 201 B7
Salter Lancs 212 G2
Salterbeck Cumb 228 F5
Salterforth Lancs 204 D3
Salters Heath Hants 48 B6
Saltershill Shrops 150 D2
Salters Lode Norf 139 C11
Salter Street W Mid 118 C2
Salterswall
Ches W 167 B10
Salterton Wilts 46 F6
Saltfleet Lincs 191 C7
Saltfleetby All Saints
Lincs 191 C7
Saltfleetby St Clement
Lincs 191 C7
Saltfleetby St Peter
Lincs 190 D6
Saltford Bath 61 F7
Salt Hill Slough 66 C3
Salthouse Cumb 210 F4
Norf 177 E9
Saltley W Mid 133 F11
Saltmarsh Newport 59 C11
Saltmarshe E Yorks 199 C9
Saltness Orkney 314 G2
Shetland 313 J4
Saltney Flint 166 B5
Salton N Yorks 216 D4
Saltrens Devon 25 C7
Saltwell T&W 243 E7
Saltwick Northumb 242 B5
Saltwood Kent 55 F7
Salum Argyll 288 E2
Salvington W Sus 35 F10
Salwarpe Worcs 117 E7
Salwayash Dorset 16 B5
Sambourne Warks 117 E11
Wilts 45 E11
Sambrook Telford 150 E4
Samhla W Isles 296 E3
Samlesbury Lancs 203 G7
Samlesbury Bottoms
Lancs 194 B6
Sampford Arundel
Som 27 D10
Sampford Brett Som 42 E5
Sampford Chapple
Devon 25 G10
Sampford Courtenay
Devon 25 G10
Sampford Moor
Som 27 D10
Sampford Peverell
Devon 27 E8
Sampford Spiney
Devon 12 G6
Sampool Bridge
Cumb 211 B9
Samuel's Corner
Essex 70 B3
Samuelston E Loth 281 G9
Sanachan Highld 299 E8
Sanaigmore Argyll 274 F3
Sanclêr / St Clears
Carms 74 B3
Sancreed Corn 1 D4
Sancton E Yorks 208 F4
Sand Highld 307 K4
Shetland 313 J5
Som 44 D2
Sandaig Highld 295 E9
Sandal W Yorks 197 D10
Sandale Cumb 229 C10
Sandal Magna
W Yorks 197 D10
Sandavore Highld 294 G6
Sandbach Ches E 168 C3
Sandbach Heath
Ches E 168 C3
Sandbank Argyll 276 E3
Sandbanks Kent 70 G4
Poole 18 D6
Sandborough Staffs 152 F2
Sandbraes Lincs 200 G6
Sandend Aberds 302 C5
Sanderstead London 67 G10
Sandfields Glos 99 G8
Neath 57 C8
Staffs 134 B2
Sandford Cumb 222 B4
Devon 26 G4
Dorset 18 D4
Hants 31 G11
IoW 20 E6
N Som 44 B2
S Lanark 268 G4
Shrops 148 E6
Shrops 149 C11
W Yorks 205 F11
Worcs 99 B7
Sandford Batch
N Som 44 B2
Sandfordhill
Aberds 303 E11
Sandford Hill Stoke 168 G6
Sandford on Thames
Oxon 83 E8
Sandford Orcas
Dorset 29 C10
Sandford St Martin
Oxon 101 F8
Sandgate Kent 55 G7
Sand Gate Cumb 211 D7
Sandgreen Dumfries 237 D7
Sandhaven Aberds 303 C9
Argyll 276 E3
Sandhead Dumfries 236 E2
Sandhill Bucks 102 F4
Cambs 139 F11
S Yorks 198 F2
Sandhills Dorset 29 E11
Dorset 29 G9
Mers 182 C4
Oxon 83 D9
Sur 50 F2
W Yorks 206 F3
Sandhoe Northumb 241 D11
Sandhole Argyll 275 D11
Sand Hole E Yorks 208 F2
Sandholme E Yorks 208 G2
Lincs 156 B6
Sandhurst Brack 65 G10
Glos 98 G6
Kent 38 B3
Sandhurst Cross
Kent 38 B3
Sandhutton N Yorks 215 C7
Sand Hutton
N Yorks 207 B9
Sandiacre Derbys 153 B9
Sandilands Lincs 191 E8
S Lanark 259 B9
Sandiway Ches W 183 G10
Sandleheath Hants 31 E10
Sandling Kent 53 B9
Sandlow Green
Ches E 168 B3
Sandness Shetland 313 H3
Sandon Essex 88 E2
Herts 104 E6
Staffs 151 C8
Sandonbank Staffs 151 D8

Shiptonthorpe
E Yorks 208 E3
Shipton-under-Wychwood Oxon 82 B3
Shirburn Oxon 83 F11
Shirdley Hill Lancs 193 E11
Shirebrook Derbys 171 B8
Shirecliffe S Yorks 186 C4
Shiregreen S Yorks 186 C5
Shirehampton Bristol 60 D4
Shiremoor T&W 243 C8
Shirenewton Mon 79 G7
Shire Oak W Mid 133 C11
Shireoaks Derbys 185 E9
Notts 187 E9
Shires Mill Fife 279 D10
Shirkoak Kent 54 F2
Shirland Derbys 170 D6
Shirlett Shrops 132 D3
Shirley Derbys 170 G2
Hants 19 B9
London 67 F11
Soton 32 E6
W Mid 118 B2
Shirley Heath
W Mid 118 B2
Shirley holms Hants 19 B11
Shirley Warren Soton 32 E5
Shirl Heath Hereford 115 F8
Shirrell Heath Hants 33 E9
Shirwell Devon 40 F5
Shirwell Cross Devon 40 F5
Shiskine N Ayrs 255 E10
Shitterton Dorset 18 C2
Shobdon Hereford 115 E8
Shobley Hants 31 F11
Shobnall Staffs 152 E4
Shobrooke Devon 26 G5
Shoby Leics 154 F3
Shocklach Ches W 166 F6
Shocklach Green
Ches W 166 F6
Shoeburyness
Southend 70 C2
Sholden Kent 55 C11
Sholing Soton 32 E6
Sholing Common
Soton 33 E7
Sholver Gtr Man 196 F3
Shootash Hants 32 C4
Shooters Hill London 68 D2
Shootersway Herts 85 D7
Shoot Hill Shrops 149 G8
Shop Corn 10 G3
Corn 24 E2
Devon 24 E5
Shop Corner Suff 108 E4
Shopford Cumb 240 C3
Shopnoller Som 43 G7
Shopp Hill W Sus 34 B6
Shopwyke W Sus 22 B5
Shore Gtr Man 196 D2
W Yorks 196 B2
Shore Bottom Devon 28 G2
Shoreditch London 67 C10
Som 28 C2
Shoregill Cumb 222 E5
Shoreham Kent 68 G4
Shoreham Beach
W Sus 36 G2
Shoreham-by-Sea
W Sus 36 F2
Shore Mill Highld 301 C7
Shoresdean
Northumb 273 F9
Shores Green Oxon 82 D5
Shoreside Shetland 313 J4
Shoreswood
Northumb 273 F8
Shoreton Highld 300 C6
Shorley Hants 33 B9
Shorncliffe Camp
Kent 55 F7
Shorncote Glos 81 F8
Shorne Kent 69 E7
Shorne Ridgeway
Kent 69 E7
Shorne West Kent 69 E7
Shortacombe Devon 12 D6
Shortacross Corn 6 D5
Shortbridge E Sus 37 C7
Short Cross W Mid 133 G9
Shortfield Common
Sur 49 E10
Shortgate E Sus 23 B7
Short Green Norf 141 F11
Shorthampton Oxon 100 G6
Shortheath Hants 49 F9
Sur 49 E10
Short Heath Derbys 152 G6
W Mid 133 C9
W Mid 133 E11
Shorthill Shrops 131 B8
Shortlands London 67 F11
Shortlanesend Corn 4 F6
Shortlees E Ayrs 257 B10
Shortmoor Devon 28 G2
Dorset 29 G7
Shorton Torbay 9 C7
Shortroods Renfs 267 B9
Shortstanding Glos 79 C9
Shortstown Beds 103 B11
Short Street Wilts 45 D10
Shortwood Glos 80 F4
S Glos 61 D7
Shorwell IoW 20 E5
Shoscombe Bath 45 B8
Shoscombe Vale
Bath 45 B8
Shotatton Shrops 149 E7
Shotesham Norf 142 D5
Shotgate Essex 88 G3
Shotley Northants 137 D8
Suff 108 D4
Shotley Bridge
Durham 242 G3
Shotleyfield
Northumb 242 G3
Shotley Gate Suff 108 E4
Shottenden Kent 54 C4
Shottermill Sur 49 G11
Shottery Warks 118 G3
Shotteswell Warks 101 B8
Shottisham Suff 108 C6
Shottle Derbys 170 F4
Shottlegate Derbys 170 F4
Shotton Durham 234 D4
Durham 234 F3
Flint 166 B4
Northumb 242 B6
Northumb 263 C8
Shotton Colliery
Durham 234 C3
Shotts N Lanark 269 C7
Shotwick Ches W 182 G4
Shouldham Norf 140 B3
Shouldham Thorpe
Norf 140 B3
Shoulton Worcs 116 F6
Shover's Green
E Sus 53 G7
Shraleybrook Staffs 168 F3
Shrawardine Shrops 149 F8
Shrawley Worcs 116 E6
Shreding Green
Bucks 66 C4
Shrewley Warks 118 D4
Shrewley Common
Warks 118 D4
Shrewsbury Shrops 149 G9
Shrewton Wilts 46 E5
Shripney W Sus 22 C6
Shrivenham Oxon 63 B8
Shropham Norf 141 E9
Shroton or Iwerne
Courtney Dorset 30 E5
Shrub End Essex 107 G9
Shrubs Hill Sur 66 F3
Shrutherhill
S Lanark 268 F5
Shucknall Hereford 97 C11
Shudy Camps
Cambs 106 C2
Shulishadermor
Highld 298 E4
Shulista Highld 298 B4
Shuna Ho Argyll 275 C8
Shurdington Glos 80 B6
Shurlock Row
Windsor 65 E10
Shurnock Worcs 117 E10
Shurrery Highld 310 D4
Shurrery Lodge
Highld 310 D4
Shurton Som 43 E8
Shustoke Warks 134 E4
Shute Devon 15 B11
Devon 26 G5
Shute End Wilts 31 B11
Shutford Oxon 101 C7
Shut Heath Staffs 151 E7
Shuthonger Glos 99 D7
Shutlanger
Northants 120 G4
Shutta Corn 6 E5
Shutt Green Staffs 133 B7
Shuttington Warks 134 B5
Shuttlesfield Kent 55 E7
Shuttlewood Derbys 187 G7
Shuttleworth
Gtr Man 195 D10
Shutton Hereford 98 F3
Shwt Bridgend 57 D11
Siabost bho Dheas
W Isles 304 D4
Siabost bho Thuath
W Isles 304 D4
Siadar W Isles 304 C5
Siadar Iarach
W Isles 304 C5
Siadar Uarach
W Isles 304 C5
Sibbaldbie Dumfries 248 F4
Sibbertoft Northants 136 G3
Sibdon Carwood
Shrops 131 G8
Sibford Ferris Oxon 101 D7
Sibford Gower
Oxon 101 D7
Sible Hedingham
Essex 106 E5
Sibley's Green Essex 106 F2
Sibsey Lincs 174 E5
Sibsey Fen Side
Lincs 174 E4
Sibson Cambs 137 D11
Leics 135 C7
Sibster Highld 310 D7
Sibthorpe Notts 172 F3
Notts 188 G2
Sibton Suff 127 D7
Sibton Green Suff 127 C7
Sicklesmere Suff 125 E7
Sicklinghall
N Yorks 206 D3
Sid Devon 15 D8
Sidbrook Som 28 B3
Sidbury Devon 15 C8
Shrops 132 F3
Sidcot N Som 44 B2
Sidcup London 68 E3
Siddal W Yorks 196 C6
Siddick Cumb 228 E6
Siddington Ches E 184 G4
Glos 81 F8
Siddington Heath
Ches E 184 G4
Sidemoor Worcs 117 C9
Side of the Moor
Gtr Man 195 E8
Sidestrand Norf 160 B5
Sideway Stoke 168 G5
Sidford Devon 15 C8
Sidlesham W Sus 22 D5
Sidlesham Common
W Sus 22 C5
Sidley E Sus 38 F2
Sidlow Sur 51 D9
Sidmouth Devon 15 D8
Sidway Staffs 150 B5
Sigford Devon 13 G11
Sigglesthorne
E Yorks 209 D9
Sighthill Edin 280 G3
Glasgow 268 B2
Sigingstone / Tresigin
V Glam 58 E3
Signet Oxon 82 C2
Sigwells Som 29 C10
Silchester Hants 64 G6
Sildinis W Isles 305 G4
Sileby Leics 153 F11
Silecroft Cumb 210 C2
Silfield Norf 142 D2
Silford Devon 24 B6
Silian Ceredig 111 G11
Silkstead Hants 32 C6
Silkstone S Yorks 197 F9
Silkstone Common
S Yorks 197 G9
Silk Willoughby
Lincs 173 G9
Silloth Cumb 238 G4
Sills Northumb 251 C8
Sillyearn Moray 302 D5
Siloh Carms 94 D4
Silpho N Yorks 227 G9
Silsden W Yorks 204 D6
Silsoe C Beds 103 D11
Silton Dorset 30 B3
Silverburn Midloth 270 C4
Silverdale Lancs 211 E9
Staffs 168 F4
Silverdale Green
Lancs 211 E9
Silver End Essex 88 B4
W Mid 133 F8
Silvergate Norf 160 D3
Silver Green Norf 142 E5
Silverhill E Sus 38 E3
Silver Hill E Sus 38 B2
Silverhill Park E Sus 38 E4
Silver Knap Som 29 C11
Silverknowes Edin 280 F4
Silverley's Green
Suff 126 B5
Silvermuir S Lanark 269 F8
Silverstone
Northants 102 C3
Silver Street Glos 80 E3
Kent 69 G11
Som 27 C11
Som 44 G4
Worcs 117 B11
Silverton Devon 27 G7
W Dunb 277 F8
Silvertonhill
S Lanark 268 E4
Silvertown London 68 D2
Silverwell Corn 4 F4
Silvington Shrops 116 B2
Silwick Shetland 313 J4
Sim Hill S Yorks 197 G9
Simister Gtr Man 195 F10
Simmondley Derbys 185 C8
Simm's Cross
Halton 183 D8
Simm's Lane End
Mers 194 G4
Simonburn
Northumb 241 C9
Simonsbath Som 41 F9
Simonsburrow
Devon 27 D10
Simonside T&W 243 E8
Simonstone Lancs 203 G11
N Yorks 223 G7
Simprim Borders 272 F6
Simpson M Keynes 103 D7
Pembs 72 B5
Simpson Cross
Pembs 72 B5
Simpson Green
W Yorks 205 F9
Sinclair's Hill
Borders 272 E6
Sinclairston
E Ayrs 257 F11
Sinclairtown Fife 280 C5
Sinderby N Yorks 214 C6
Sinderhope
Northumb 241 G8
Sinderland Green
Gtr Man 184 C2
Sindlesham
Wokingham 65 F9
Sinfin Derby 152 C6
Sinfin Moor Derby 153 C7
Singdean Borders 250 C3
Singleborough
Bucks 102 E5
Single Hill Bath 45 B8
Singleton Lancs 202 F3
W Sus 34 E5
Singlewell Kent 69 E7
Singret Wrex 166 D4
Sinkhurst Green
Kent 53 E10
Sinnahard Aberds 292 B6
Sinnington N Yorks 216 B4
Sinton Worcs 116 E6
Sinton Green Worcs 116 E6
Sion Hill Bath 61 F8
Sipson London 66 D5
Sirhowy Bl Gwent 77 C11
Sisland Norf 142 D6
Sissinghurst Kent 53 F9
Sisterpath Borders 272 F5
Siston S Glos 61 D7
Sithney Corn 2 D4
Sithney Common Corn 2 D4
Sithney Green Corn 2 D4
Sittingbourne Kent 70 G2
Six Ashes Staffs 132 F5
Six Bells Bl Gwent 78 E2
Sixhills Lincs 189 D11
Six Hills Leics 154 E2
Sixmile Kent 54 E6
Six Mile Bottom
Cambs 123 F11
Sixpenny Handley
Dorset 31 D7
Sizewell Suff 127 E9
Skaigh Devon 13 C8
Skail Highld 308 E7
Skaill Orkney 314 C4
Orkney 314 E2
Orkney 314 F5
Skares E Ayrs 258 F2
Skateraw E Loth 282 F4
Skaw Shetland 312 B8
Shetland 312 G7
Skeabost Highld 298 E4
Skeabrae Orkney 314 D2
Skeeby N Yorks 224 E4
Skeete Kent 54 E6
Skeffington Leics 136 C4
Skeffling E Yorks 201 D11
Skegby Notts 171 C7
Notts 188 G3
Skegness Lincs 175 C9
Skelberry Shetland 313 G6
Shetland 313 M5
Skelbo Highld 309 K7
Skelbo Street Highld 309 K7
Skelbrooke S Yorks 198 E4
Skeldyke Lincs 156 B6
Skelfhill Borders 249 C11
Skellingthorpe
Lincs 188 G6
Skellister Shetland 313 H6
Skellorn Green
Ches E 184 E6
Skellow S Yorks 198 E4
Skelmanthorpe
W Yorks 197 E8
Skelmersdale Lancs 194 F3
Skelmonae Aberds 303 F8
Skelmorlie N Ayrs 266 B3
Skelmuir Aberds 303 E9
Skelpick Highld 308 D7
Skelton Cumb 230 D4
E Yorks 199 B9
N Yorks 223 E11
Redcar 226 B3
York 207 B7
Skelton-on-Ure
N Yorks 215 F7
Skelwick Orkney 314 B4
Skelwith Bridge
Cumb 220 E6
Skendleby Lincs 174 B6
Skendleby Psalter
Lincs 190 G6
Skene Ho Aberds 293 C9
Skenfrith Mon 97 G9
Skerne E Yorks 208 B6
Skerne Park Darl 224 C5
Skeroblingarry
Argyll 255 E8
Skerray Highld 308 C6
Skerricha Highld 306 D7
Skerryford Pembs 72 C6
Skerton Lancs 211 G9
Sketchley Leics 135 E8
Sketty Swansea 56 C6
Skewen / Sgiwen
Neath 57 B8
Skewes Corn 5 B9
Skewsby N Yorks 216 E2
Skeyton Norf 160 D4
Skeyton Corner
Norf 160 D5
Skiag Bridge Highld 307 G7
Skibo Castle Highld 309 L7
Skidbrooke Lincs 190 C6
Skidbrooke North End
Lincs 190 B6
Skidby E Yorks 208 G6
Skilgate Som 27 B7
Skillington Lincs 155 D7
Skinburness Cumb 238 F4
Skinflats Falk 279 E8
Skinidin Highld 298 E2
Skinner's Bottom Corn 4 F4
Skinners Green
W Berks 64 F2
Skinnet Highld 308 C5
Skinningrove
Redcar 226 B4
Skipness Argyll 255 B9
Skippool Lancs 202 E3
Skiprigg Cumb 230 B3
Skipsea E Yorks 209 B9
Skipsea Brough
E Yorks 209 C9
Skipton N Yorks 204 C5
Skipton-on-Swale
N Yorks 215 D7
Skipwith N Yorks 207 F9
Skirbeck Lincs 174 G4
Skirbeck Quarter
Lincs 174 G4
Skirethorns
N Yorks 213 G9
Skirlaugh E Yorks 209 F8
Skirling Borders 260 B3
Skirmett Bucks 65 B9
Skirpenbeck
E Yorks 207 B10
Skirwith Cumb 231 E8
Skirza Highld 310 C7
Skitby Cumb 239 D10
Skitham Lancs 202 E4
Skittle Green Bucks 84 E3
Skulamus Highld 295 C8
Skullomie Highld 308 C6
Skyborry Green
Shrops 114 C5
Skye Green Essex 107 G7
Skye of Curr Highld 301 G9
Skyfog Pembs 90 F6
Skyreholme
N Yorks 213 G11
Slack Derbys 170 C4
W Yorks 196 B3
W Yorks 196 D5
Slackcote Gtr Man 196 F3
Slackhall Derbys 185 E9
Slackhead Moray 302 C4
Slack Head Cumb 211 D9
Slackholme End
Lincs 191 G8
Slacks of Cairnbanno
Aberds 303 E8
Slad Glos 80 D5
Sladbrook Glos 98 F5
Slade Devon 27 F10
Devon 40 D4
Kent 54 C2
Pembs 72 B6
Slade End Oxon 83 G9
Slade Green London 68 D4
Slade Heath Staffs 133 B8
Slade Hooton
S Yorks 187 D8
Sladen Green Hants 48 C2
Sladesbridge Corn 10 G6
Slades Green Worcs 99 E7
Slaggyford
Northumb 240 G5
Slaidburn Lancs 203 C10
Slaithwaite W Yorks 196 E5
Slaley Derbys 170 D3
Northumb 241 F11
Slamannan Falk 279 G7
Slape Cross Som 43 F10
Slapewath Redcar 226 B2
Slapton Bucks 103 G8
Devon 8 G6
Northants 102 B2
Slateford Edin 280 G4
Slate Haugh Moray 302 C4
Slatepit Dale Derbys 170 B4
Slattocks Gtr Man 195 F11
Slaugham W Sus 36 B3
Slaughterbridge
Corn 11 D8
Slaughterford Wilts 61 E10
Slaughter Hill
Ches E 168 D2
Slawston Leics 136 E5
Slay Pits S Yorks 199 F7
Sleaford Hants 49 F10
Lincs 173 F9
Sleagill Cumb 221 B11
Sleap Shrops 149 D9
Sleapford Telford 150 F2
Sleapshyde Herts 86 D2
Sleastary Highld 309 K6
Slebech Pembs 73 B8
Sledge Green Worcs 98 E6
Sledmere E Yorks 217 G8
Sleeches Cross
E Sus 52 G5
Sleepers Hill Hants 33 B7
Sleetbeck Cumb 240 B2
Sleet Moor Derbys 170 E6
Sleight Dorset 18 B5
Sleights N Yorks 227 D7
Slepe Dorset 18 C4
Sliabhna h-Airde
W Isles 296 F3
Slickly Highld 310 C6
Sliddery N Ayrs 255 E10
Slideslow Worcs 117 C9
Sligachan Hotel
Highld 294 C6
Sligneach Argyll 288 G4
Sligrachan Argyll 276 C3
Slimbridge Glos 80 E2
Slindon Staffs 150 C6
W Sus 35 F7
Slinfold W Sus 50 G6
Sling Glos 79 D9
Gwyn 163 B10
Slingsby N Yorks 216 E3
Slioch Aberds 302 F5
Slip End C Beds 85 B9
Herts 104 D5
Slippery Ford
W Yorks 204 E6
Slipton Northants 121 B9
Slitting Mill Staffs 151 F10
Slochd Highld 301 G8
Slockavullin Argyll 275 D9
Slogan Moray 302 E3
Sloley Norf 160 E5
Sloncombe Devon 13 D10
Sloothby Lincs 191 G7
Slough Slough 66 D3
Slough Green Som 28 C3
W Sus 36 B3
Slough Hill Suff 125 G7
Sluggan Highld 301 G8
Sluggans Highld 298 E4
Slumbay Highld 295 B10
Sly Corner Kent 54 G3
Slyfield Sur 50 C3
Slyne Lancs 211 F9
Smailholm Borders 262 B4
Smallbridge
Gtr Man 196 D2
Smallbrook Devon 14 B3
Glos 79 E9
Smallburgh Norf 160 E6
Smallburn Aberds 303 E10
E Ayrs 258 D5
Smalldale Derbys 185 E11
Derbys 185 F9
Small Dole W Sus 36 E2
Small End Lincs 174 D6
Smalley Derbys 170 G6
Smalley Common
Derbys 170 G6
Smalley Green
Derbys 170 G6
Smallfield Sur 51 E10
Smallford Herts 85 D11
Small Heath W Mid 134 F2
Smallholm Dumfries 238 B4
Small Hythe Kent 53 G11
Smallmarsh Devon 25 C10
Smallrice Staffs 151 C9
Smallridge Devon 28 G4
Smallshaw Gtr Man 196 G2
Smallthorne Stoke 168 E5
Small Way Som 44 G6
Smallwood Ches E 168 C4
Worcs 117 D10
Smallwood Green
Suff 125 F8
Smallwood Hey
Lancs 202 D3
Smallworth Norf 141 G10
Smannell Hants 47 D11
Smardale Cumb 222 D4
Smarden Kent 53 E11
Smarden Bell Kent 53 E11
Smart's Hill Kent 52 E4
Smaull Argyll 274 G3
Smeatharpe Devon 27 E11
Smeaton Fife 280 C5
Smeeth Kent 54 F5
Smeeton Westerby
Leics 136 E3
Smelthouses
N Yorks 214 G3
Smercleit W Isles 297 K3
Smerral Highld 310 F5
Smestow Staffs 133 E7
Smethcott Shrops 131 D9
Smethwick W Mid 133 F10
Smethwick Green
Ches E 168 C4
Smirisary Highld 289 B8
Smisby Derbys 152 F6
Smite Hill Worcs 117 F7
Smithaleigh Devon 7 D11
Smithbrook W Sus 34 C6
Smith End Green
Worcs 116 G5
Smithfield Cumb 239 D10
Smith Green Lancs 202 C5
Smithies S Yorks 197 F11
Smithincott Devon 27 E9
Smithley S Yorks 197 G11
Smith's End Herts 105 D8
Smiths Green
Ches E 184 G4
Smith's Green
Ches E 168 E3
Essex 105 G11
Essex 106 C3
Smithston Aberds 302 G5
Smithstown Highld 299 B7
Smithton Highld 301 E7
Smithwood Green
Suff 125 G8
Smithy Bridge
Gtr Man 196 D2
Smithy Gate Flint 181 F11
Smithy Green
Ches E 184 G2
Gtr Man 184 D5
Smithy Houses
Derbys 170 F5
Smithy Lane Ends
Lancs 194 E2
Smock Alley W Sus 35 D9
Smockington Leics 135 F9
Smoky Row Bucks 84 D4
Smoogro Orkney 314 F3
Smug Oak Herts 85 E10
Smyrton S Ayrs 244 G4
Smythe's Green
Essex 88 B6
Snagshall E Sus 38 C3
Snaigow House
Perth 286 C4
Snailbeach Shrops 131 C7
Snails Hill Som 29 E7
Snailswell Herts 104 E3
Snailwell Cambs 124 D2
Snainton N Yorks 217 C8
Snaisgill Durham 232 F5
Snaith E Yorks 198 C6
Snape N Yorks 214 C5
Suff 127 F7
Snape Green Lancs 193 E11
Snape Hill Derbys 186 F5
S Yorks 198 G2
Snapper Devon 40 G5
Snaresbrook London 67 B11
Snarestone Leics 134 B6
Snarford Lincs 189 E9
Snargate Kent 39 B7
Snarraness Shetland 313 H4
Snatchwood Torf 78 E3
Snave Kent 39 B8
Sneachill Worcs 117 G8
Snead Powys 130 E6
Snead Common
Worcs 116 D4
Sneads Green
Worcs 117 D7
Sneath Common
Norf 142 F3
Sneaton N Yorks 227 D7
Sneatonthorpe
N Yorks 227 D8
Snedshill Telford 132 B4
Sneinton
Nottingham 153 B11
Snelland Lincs 189 E9
Snelston Derbys 169 G11
Snetterton Norf 141 E9
Snettisham Norf 158 C3
Sneyd Green Stoke 168 F5
Sneyd Park Bristol 60 D5
Snibston Leics 153 G8
Snig's End Glos 98 F5
Snipeshill Kent 70 G2
Sniseabhal W Isles 297 H3
Snitter Northumb 252 C2
Snitterby Lincs 189 C7
Snitterfield Warks 118 F4
Snitterton Derbys 170 C3
Snitton Shrops 115 B11
Snittongate Shrops 115 B11
Snodhill Hereford 96 C6
Snodland Kent 69 G7
Snods Edge
Northumb 242 G3
Snowden Hill
S Yorks 197 G9
Snowdown Kent 55 C8
Snow End Herts 105 E8
Snow Hill Ches E 167 E10
W Yorks 197 C10
Snow Lea W Yorks 196 D5
Snowshill Glos 99 E11
Snow Street Norf 141 G11
Snydale W Yorks 198 D2
Soake Hants 33 E11
Soar
Anglesey 178 G5
Carms 94 F2
Devon 9 G9
Gwyn 146 B2
Powys 95 E9
Soar-y-Mynydd
Ceredig 112 G5
Soberton Hants 33 D10
Soberton Heath
Hants 33 E10
Sockbridge Cumb 230 F6
Sockburn Darl 224 D6
Sockety Dorset 29 F7
Sodom Denb 181 G9
Shetland 313 G7
Wilts 62 C4
Sodylt Bank Shrops 148 B6
Soham Cambs 123 C11
Soham Cotes
Cambs 123 B11
Soho London 67 C9
Som 45 D7
W Mid 133 F10
Solas W Isles 296 D4
Soldon Cross Devon 24 E4
Soldridge Hants 49 G7
Sole Street Kent 54 D5
Kent 69 F7
Solfach / Solva
Pembs 90 G5
Solihull W Mid 118 B2
Solihull Lodge
W Mid 117 B11
Sollers Dilwyn
Hereford 115 F8
Sollers Hope
Hereford 98 E2
Sollom Lancs 194 D3
Solva / Solfach
Pembs 90 G5
Somerby Leics 154 G5
Lincs 200 F5
Somercotes Derbys 170 E6
Somerdale Bath 61 F7
Somerford Ches E 168 B4
Dorset 19 C9
Staffs 133 B7
Somerford Keynes
Glos 81 G8
Somerley W Sus 22 D4
Somerleyton Suff 143 D9
Somersal Herbert
Derbys 152 B2
Somersby Lincs 190 G4
Somersham Cambs 123 B7
Suff 107 B11
Somers Town London 67 C9
Ptsmth 21 B8
Somerton Newport 59 B10
Oxon 101 F9
Som 29 B7
Suff 124 G6
Somerton Hill Som 29 B7
Somerwood
Shrops 149 G11
Sompting W Sus 35 G11
Sompting Abbotts
W Sus 35 F11
Sonning Wokingham 65 D9
Sonning Common
Oxon 65 C8
Sonning Eye Oxon 65 D9
Sontley Wrex 166 F4
Sookholme Notts 171 B8
Sopley Hants 19 B9
Sopwell Herts 85 D11
Sopworth Wilts 61 B10
Sorbie Dumfries 236 E6
Sordale Highld 310 C5
Sorisdale Argyll 288 C4
Sorley Devon 8 F4
Sorn E Ayrs 258 D3
Sornhill E Ayrs 258 C2
Sortat Highld 310 C6
Sotby Lincs 190 F2
Sothall S Yorks 186 E6
Sots Hole Lincs 173 C10
Sotterley Suff 143 G9
Soudley Shrops 131 E9
Shrops 150 D4
Soughley S Yorks 197 G7
Soughton / Sychdyn
Flint 166 B2
Soulbury Bucks 103 F7
Soulby Cumb 222 C4
Cumb 230 F5
Souldern Oxon 101 E10
Souldrop Beds 121 E9
Sound Ches E 167 F10
Shetland 313 H5
Shetland 313 J6
Sound Heath
Ches E 167 F10
Soundwell S Glos 60 D6
Sourhope Borders 263 E8
Sourin Orkney 314 C4
Sourlie N Ayrs 266 G6
Sour Nook Cumb 230 C3
Sourton Devon 12 C6
Soutergate Cumb 210 C4
South Acre Norf 158 G6
South Acton London 67 D7
South Alkham Kent 55 E8
Southall London 66 C6
South Allington
Devon 9 G10
South Alloa Falk 279 C7
Southam Cumb 219 C9
Glos 99 F9
Warks 119 E8
South Ambersham
W Sus 34 C6
Southampton Soton 32 E6
South Anston
S Yorks 187 E8
South Ascot Windsor 66 F2
South Ashford Kent 54 E4
South Auchmachar
Aberds 303 E9
Southay Som 28 D6
South Baddesley
Hants 20 B3
South Ballachulish
Highld 284 B4
South Balloch
S Ayrs 245 D8
South Bank Redcar 234 G6
York 207 C7
South Barrow Som 29 B10
South Beach
Northumb 243 B8
South Beach / Marian-y-de Gwyn 145 C7
South Beddington
London 67 G9
South Benfleet Essex 69 B9
South Bents T&W 243 E10
South Bersted
W Sus 22 C6
South Blainslie
Borders 271 G10
South Bockhampton
Dorset 19 B9
Southborough Kent 52 E5
London 67 F7
London 68 F2
Southbourne Bmouth 19 C8
W Sus 22 B3
South Bramwith
S Yorks 198 E6
South Brent Devon 8 D3
South Brewham Som 45 F8
South Bromley
London 67 C11
Southbrook Wilts 45 G10
South Broomage
Falk 279 E7
South Broomhill
Northumb 252 D6
Southburgh Norf 141 C9
South Burlingham
Norf 143 B7
Southburn E Yorks 208 C5
South Cadbury Som 29 B10
South Cairn
Dumfries 236 C1
South Carlton Lincs 189 F7
Notts 187 E9
South Carne Corn 11 E10
South Cave E Yorks 208 G4
South Cerney Glos 81 F8
South Chailey E Sus 36 D5
South Chard Som 28 F4
South Charlton
Northumb 264 E5
South Cheriton Som 29 C11
Southchurch
Southend 70 B2
South Church
Durham 233 F10
South Cliffe E Yorks 208 F3
South Clifton Notts 188 G4
South Clunes Highld 300 E5
South Cockerington
Lincs 190 D5
South Common
Devon 28 G4
Southcoombe Oxon 100 F6
South Cornelly
Bridgend 57 E10
South Corriegills
N Ayrs 256 C2
South Corrielaw
Dumfries 248 G5
Southcote Reading 65 E7
Southcott Corn 11 B9
Devon 24 D6
Wilts 47 B7
Southcourt Bucks 84 C4
South Cove Suff 143 G9
South Creagan
Argyll 289 E11
South Creake Norf 159 B7
Southcrest Worcs 117 D10
South Crosland
W Yorks 196 E6
South Croxton Leics 154 G3
South Croydon
London 67 G10
South Cuil Highld 298 C3
South Dalton
E Yorks 208 D5
South Darenth Kent 68 F5
Southdean Borders 250 B4
Southdene Mers 182 B6
South Denes Norf 143 C10
Southdown Bath 61 G8
Corn 7 E8
South Down Hants 33 C7
Som 28 E2
South Duffield
N Yorks 207 G9
South Dunn Highld 310 D5
South Earlswood Sur 51 D9
Southease E Sus 36 F6
South Elkington
Lincs 190 D3
South Elmsall
W Yorks 198 E3
South Elphinstone
E Loth 281 G7
Southend Argyll 255 G7
Bucks 65 B9
Glos 80 F2
London 67 E11
Oxon 83 E9
W Berks 64 D2
W Berks 64 E5
Wilts 63 E7
South End Beds 103 B10
Bucks 103 F7
Cumb 210 G4
E Yorks 209 E9
Hants 31 D10
South-end Herts 86 B6
South End N Lincs 200 C6
Norf 141 E9
Southend-on-Sea
Southend 69 B11
Southerhouse
Shetland 313 K5
Southerly Devon 12 D6
Southernby Cumb 230 D3
Southern Cross
Brighton 36 F3
Southernden Kent 53 D11
Southerndown
V Glam 57 G11
Southerness
Dumfries 237 D11
Southern Green
Herts 104 E6
South Erradale
Highld 299 B7
Southery Norf 140 E2
Southey Green
Essex 106 E5
South Fambridge
Essex 88 F5
South Farnborough
Hants 49 C11
South Fawley
W Berks 63 C11
South Ferriby
N Lincs 200 C3
Southfield Northumb 243 B7
South Field E Yorks 200 B4
Windsor 66 D3
Southfields London 67 E9
Thurrock 69 C7
Southfleet Kent 68 E6
South Flobbets
Aberds 303 F7
Southford IoW 20 F6
South Garth
Shetland 312 D7
South Garvan
Highld 289 B11
Southgate
Ceredig 111 A11
London 86 G3
Norf 159 C7
Norf 160 E2
Swansea 56 D5
W Sus 51 F9
South Glendale
W Isles 297 K3

South Gluss Shetland 312 F5
South Godstone Sur 51 D11
South Gorley Hants 31 E11
South Gosforth T&W 242 D6
South Green Essex 87 G11
Essex 89 B8
Kent 69 G11
Norf 157 F10
Norf 159 G11
Suff 126 B3
South Gyle Edin 280 G3
South-haa Shetland 312 E5
South Hackney London 67 C11
South Ham Hants 48 C6
South Hampstead London 67 C9
South Hanningfield Essex 88 F2
South Harefield London 66 B5
South Harrow London 66 B6
South Harting W Sus 34 D3
South Hatfield Herts 86 D2
South Hayling Hants 21 B10
South Hazelrigg Northumb 264 C3
South Heath Bucks 84 E6
Essex 89 B10
South Heighton E Sus 23 E7
South-heog Shetland 312 E5
South Hetton Durham 234 B3
South Hiendley W Yorks 197 E11
South Hill Corn 12 G2
N Som 43 B10
Pembs 72 C4
South Hinksey Oxon 83 E8
South Hole Devon 24 C2
South Holme N Yorks 216 D3
South Holmwood Sur 51 D7
South Hornchurch London 68 C4
South Huish Devon 8 G3
South Hykeham Lincs 172 C6
South Hylton T&W 243 F9
Southill C Beds 104 C3
Dorset 17 E9
Southington Hants 48 D4
South Kelsey Lincs 189 B8
South Kensington London 67 D9
South Kessock Highld 300 E6
South Killingholme N Lincs 201 D7
South Kilvington N Yorks 215 C8
South Kilworth Leics 136 G2
South Kirkby W Yorks 198 E2
South Kirkton Aberds 293 C9
South Kiscadale N Ayrs 256 D2
South Knighton Devon 14 G2
Leicester 136 C2
South Kyme Lincs 173 F11
South Lambeth London 67 D10
South Lancing W Sus 35 G11
Southlands Dorset 17 F9
South Lane S Yorks 197 F9
Southleigh Devon 15 C10
South Leigh Oxon 82 D5
South Leverton Notts 188 E3
South Littleton Worcs 99 B11
South Lopham Norf 141 G10
South Luffenham Rutland 137 C8
South Malling E Sus 36 E6
Southmarsh Som 45 G8
South Marston Swindon 63 B7
Southmead Bristol 60 D5
South Merstham Sur 51 C9
South Middleton Northumb 263 E11
South Milford N Yorks 206 G5
South Millbrex Aberds 303 E8
South Milton Devon 8 G4
South Mimms Herts 86 E2
Southminster Essex 89 F7
South Molton Devon 26 B2
Southmoor Oxon 82 F5
South Moor Durham 242 G5
South Moreton Oxon 64 B5
South Mundham W Sus 22 C5
South Muskham Notts 172 D3
South Newbald E Yorks 208 F4
South Newbarns Cumb 210 F4
South Newington Oxon 101 E8
South Newsham Northumb 243 B8
South Newton Wilts 46 G5
South Normanton Derbys 170 D6
South Norwood London 67 F10
South Nutfield Sur 51 D10
South Ockendon Thurrock 68 C5
Southoe Cambs 122 E3
Southolt Suff 126 D3
South Ormsby Lincs 190 F5
Southorpe Pboro 137 C11
South Ossett W Yorks 197 D9
South Otterington N Yorks 215 B7
Southover Dorset 17 C8
E Sus 36 F6
E Sus 37 B11
South Owersby Lincs 189 C9
Southowram W Yorks 196 C6
South Oxhey Herts 85 G10
South Park Sur 51 D8
South Pelaw Durham 243 G7
South Perrott Dorset 29 F7
South Petherton Som 28 D6
South Petherwin Corn 12 E2
South Pickenham Norf 141 C7
South Pill Corn 7 D8
South Pool Devon 8 G5
South Poorton Dorset 16 B6
Southport Mers 193 D10
South Port Argyll 284 E4
Southpunds Shetland 313 L6
South Quilquox Aberds 303 F8
South Radworthy Devon 41 G9
South Rauceby Lincs 173 F8
South Raynham Norf 159 E7
South Reddish Gtr Man 184 C5
Southrepps Norf 160 B5
South Reston Lincs 190 E6
Southrey Lincs 173 B10
Southrop Glos 81 E11
Oxon 101 E7
Southrope Hants 49 E7
South Ruislip London 66 B6
South Runcton Norf 140 B2
South Scarle Notts 172 C4
Southsea Ptsmth 21 B8
Wrex 166 E4
South Shian Argyll 289 E11
South Shields T&W 243 D9
South Shore Blackpool 202 G2
South Side Durham 233 F8
Orkney 314 D5
South Somercotes Lincs 190 C6
South Stainley N Yorks 214 G6
South Stainmore Cumb 222 C6
South Stanley Durham 242 G5
South Stifford Thurrock 68 D6
Southstoke Bath 61 G8
South Stoke Oxon 64 C6
W Sus 35 F8
South Stour Kent 54 F4
South Street E Sus 36 D5
Kent 54 B5
Kent 68 G6
Kent 69 G10
Kent 70 F6
London 52 B2
South Tawton Devon 13 C9
South Tehidy Corn 4 G3
South Thoresby Lincs 190 F6
South Tidworth Wilts 47 D8
South Tottenham London 67 B10
Southtown Norf 143 B10
Orkney 314 G4
Som 28 D4
Som 44 F5
South Town Devon 14 E5
Hants 49 F7
South Twerton Bath 61 G8
South Ulverston Cumb 210 D6
South View Hants 48 C6
Southville Devon 8 G4
Torf 78 F3
South Voxter Shetland 313 G5
Southwaite Cumb 230 C4
South Walsham Norf 161 G7
Southwark London 67 D10
South Warnborough Hants 49 D8
Southwater W Sus 35 B11
Southwater Street W Sus 35 B11
Southway Plym 7 C9
Som 44 E4
South Weald Essex 87 G9
South Weirs Hants 32 G3
Southwell Dorset 17 G9
Notts 172 E2
South Weston Oxon 84 F2
South Wheatley Corn 11 C10
Notts 188 D3
South Whiteness Shetland 313 J5
Southwick Hants 33 F10
Northants 137 E10
Som 43 D11
T&W 243 F9
W Sus 36 F2
Wilts 45 B10
South Widcombe Bath 44 B5
South Wigston Leics 135 D11
South Willesborough Kent 54 E4
South Willingham Lincs 189 E11
South Wimbledon London 67 E9
South Wingate Durham 234 E4
South Wingfield Derbys 170 D5
South Witham Lincs 155 F8
Southwold Suff 127 B10
South Wonford Devon 24 F5
South Wonston Hants 48 F3
Southwood Derbys 153 E7
Hants 49 B10
Norf 143 B7
Som 44 G5
Worcs 116 E4
South Woodford London 86 G6
South Woodham Ferrers Essex 88 F4
South Wootton Norf 158 E2
South Wraxall Wilts 61 G10
South Yardley W Mid 134 G2
South Yarrows Highld 310 E7
South Yeo Devon 25 G8
South Zeal Devon 13 C9
Soval Lodge W Isles 304 F5
Sowber Gate N Yorks 215 B7
Sowerby N Yorks 215 C8
W Yorks 196 C4
Sowerby Bridge W Yorks 196 C5
Sowerby Row Cumb 230 D3
Sower Carr Lancs 202 E3
Sowley Green Suff 124 G4
Sowood W Yorks 196 D5
Sowood Green W Yorks 196 D5
Sowton Devon 14 C5
Sowton Barton Devon 14 D2
Soyal Highld 309 K5
Soyland Town W Yorks 196 C4
Spacey Houses N Yorks 206 C2
Spa Common Norf 160 C5
Spalding Lincs 156 E4
Spaldington E Yorks 207 G11
Spaldwick Cambs 122 C2
Spalford Notts 172 B4
Spanby Lincs 155 B11
Spango Invclyd 276 G4
Spanish Green Hants 49 B7
Sparham Norf 159 F11
Sparhamhill Norf 159 F11
Spark Bridge Cumb 210 C6
Sparkbrook W Mid 133 G11
Sparkford Som 29 B10
Sparkhill W Mid 133 G11
Sparkwell Devon 7 D11
Sparl Shetland 312 G5
Sparnon Corn 1 E3
Sparnon Gate Corn 4 G3
Sparrow Green Norf 159 G9
Sparrow Hill Som 44 C2
Sparrowpit Derbys 185 E9
Sparrow's Green E Sus 52 G6
Sparsholt Hants 48 G2
Oxon 63 B10
Spartylea Northumb 232 B3
Spath Staffs 151 B11
Spaunton N Yorks 226 G4
Spaxton Som 43 F8
Spean Bridge Highld 290 E4
Spear Hill W Sus 35 D10
Spearywell Hants 32 B4
Speckington Som 29 C9
Speed Gate Kent 68 F5
Speedwell Bristol 60 E6
Speen Bucks 84 F4
W Berks 64 F3
Speeton N Yorks 218 E2
Speke Mers 182 E6
Speldhurst Kent 52 E5
Spellbrook Herts 87 B7
Spelsbury Oxon 101 G7
Spelter Bridgend 57 C11
Spen W Yorks 197 B7
Spencers Wood Wokingham 65 F8
Spen Green Ches E 168 C4
Spennells Worcs 116 C6
Spennithorne N Yorks 214 B2
Spennymoor Durham 233 E11
Spernall Warks 117 E11
Spetchley Worcs 117 G7
Spetisbury Dorset 30 G6
Spexhall Suff 143 G7
Speybank Highld 291 C10
Spey Bay Moray 302 C3
Speybridge Highld 301 G10
Speyview Moray 302 E2
Spillardsford Aberds 303 D10
Spilsby Lincs 174 B6
Spindlestone Northumb 264 C5
Spinkhill Derbys 187 F7
Spinney Hill Northants 120 E5
Spinney Hills Leicester 136 C2
Spinningdale Highld 309 L6
Spion Kop Notts 171 B9
Spirthill Wilts 62 D3
Spital Mers 182 E4
Windsor 66 D3
Spitalbrook Herts 86 D5
Spitalfields London 67 C10
Spitalhill Derbys 169 F11
Spital Hill S Yorks 187 C10
Spital in the Street Lincs 189 D7
Spital Tongues T&W 242 D6
Spithurst E Sus 36 D6
Spittal Dumfries 236 D5
E Loth 281 F9
Spittal *continued*
E Yorks 207 C11
Highld 310 D5
Northumb 273 E10
Pembs 91 G9
Stirling 277 D10
Spittalfield Perth 286 C5
Spittal Houses S Yorks 186 B5
Spittal of Glenmuick Aberds 292 E5
Spittal of Glenshee Perth 292 F3
Spittlegate Lincs 155 C8
Spixworth Norf 160 F4
Splatt Corn 10 F4
Corn 11 D10
Devon 25 F10
Som 43 F8
Splayne's Green E Sus 36 C6
Splott Cardiff 59 D7
Spofforth N Yorks 206 C3
Spondon Derby 153 B8
Spon End W Mid 118 B6
Spon Green Flint 166 C3
Spooner Row Norf 141 D11
Spoonleygate Shrops 132 D6
Sporle Norf 158 G6
Spotland Bridge Gtr Man 195 E11
Spott E Loth 282 F3
Spratton Northants 120 C4
Spreakley Sur 49 E10
Spreyton Devon 13 B9
Spriddlestone Devon 7 E10
Spridlington Lincs 189 E8
Sprig's Alley Oxon 84 F3
Springbank Glos 99 G8
Spring Bank Cumb 229 G10
Springboig Glasgow 268 C3
Springbourne Bmouth 19 C8
Springburn Glasgow 268 B2
Spring Cottage Leics 152 F6
Spring End N Yorks 223 F9
Springfield Argyll 275 F11
Caerph 77 F11
Dumfries 239 D8
Essex 88 D2
Fife 287 F7
Gtr Man 194 F5
Highld 300 C6
M Keynes 103 D7
Moray 301 D10
W Mid 133 D8
W Mid 133 F9
W Mid 133 G11
Springfields Stoke 168 G5
Spring Gardens Som 45 D9
Spring Green Lancs 204 E4
Spring Grove London 67 D7
Springhead Gtr Man 196 G3
Springhill E Renf 267 D10
IoW 20 B6
N Lanark 269 D7
Staffs 133 B11
Staffs 133 C9
Spring Hill Gtr Man 196 F2
Lancs 195 B8
W Mid 133 D7
Springholm Dumfries 237 C10
Springkell Dumfries 239 B7
Spring Park London 67 F11
Springside N Ayrs 257 B9
Springthorpe Lincs 188 D5
Spring Vale S Yorks 197 G9
Spring Valley IoM 192 E4
Springwell Essex 105 C10
T&W 243 F7
T&W 243 F9
Springwells Dumfries 248 E3
Sproatley E Yorks 209 G9
Sproston Green Ches W 168 B2
Sprotbrough S Yorks 198 G4
Sproughton Suff 108 C2
Sprouston Borders 263 B7
Sprowston Norf 160 G4
Sproxton Leics 155 E7
N Yorks 216 C2
Sprunston Cumb 230 B3
Spunhill Shrops 149 C8
Spurlands End Bucks 84 F5
Spurstow Ches E 167 D9
Spurtree Shrops 116 D2
Spynie Moray 302 C2
Spyway Dorset 16 C6
Square and Compass Pembs 91 E7
Squires Gate Blackpool 202 G2
Sraid Ruadh Argyll 288 E1
Srannda W Isles 296 C6
Sronphadruig Lodge Perth 291 F9
Stableford Shrops 132 D5
Staffs 150 B6
Stacey Bank S Yorks 186 C3
Stackhouse N Yorks 212 F6
Stackpole Pembs 73 F7
Stackpole Quay Pembs 73 F7
Stacksford Norf 141 E11
Stacksteads Lancs 195 C10
Stackyard Green Suff 107 B9
Staddiscombe Plym 7 E10
Staddlethorpe E Yorks 199 B10
Staddon Devon 24 C3
Devon 24 G5
Staden Derbys 185 G9
Stadhampton Oxon 83 F10
Stadhlaigearraidh W Isles 297 H3
Stadmorslow Staffs 168 D5
Staffield Cumb 230 C6
Staffin Highld 298 C4
Stafford Staffs 151 E8
Stafford Park Telford 132 B4
Stafford's Corner Essex 89 B7
Stafford's Green Dorset 29 C10
Stagbatch Hereford 115 F9
Stagden Cross Essex 87 C10
Stagehall Borders 271 G9
Stagsden Beds 103 B9
Stagsden West End Beds 103 B9
Stag's Head Devon 25 B11
Stain Highld 310 C7
Stainburn Cumb 228 F6
N Yorks 205 D10
Stainby Lincs 155 E8
Staincliffe W Yorks 197 C8
Staincross S Yorks 197 E10
Staindrop Durham 233 G8
Staines Green Herts 86 C3
Staines-upon-Thames Sur 66 E4
Stainfield Lincs 155 D11
Lincs 189 G10
Stainforth N Yorks 212 F6
S Yorks 198 E6
Staining Lancs 202 F3
Stainland W Yorks 196 D5
Stainsacre N Yorks 227 D8
Stainsby Derbys 170 B6
Lincs 190 G4
Stainton Cumb 211 B10
Cumb 230 F5
Cumb 239 F9
Durham 223 B11
Mbro 225 C9
N Yorks 224 F2
S Yorks 187 C9
Stainton by Langworth Lincs 189 F9
Staintondale N Yorks 227 F9
Stainton le Vale Lincs 189 C11
Stainton with Adgarley Cumb 210 E5
Stair Cumb 229 G10
E Ayrs 257 E10
Stairfoot S Yorks 197 F11
Stairhaven Dumfries 236 D4
Staithes N Yorks 226 B5
Stakeford Northumb 253 F7
Stake Hill Gtr Man 195 F11
Stakenbridge Worcs 117 B7
Stake Pool Lancs 202 D4
Stalbridge Dorset 30 D2
Stalbridge Weston Dorset 30 D2
Stalham Norf 161 D7
Stalham Green Norf 161 E7
Stalisfield Green Kent 54 C3
Stallen Dorset 29 D10
Stallingborough NE Lincs 201 E7
Stalling Busk N Yorks 213 B8
Stallington Staffs 151 B8
Stalmine Lancs 202 D3
Stalmine Moss Side Lancs 202 D3
Stalybridge Gtr Man 185 B7
Stambermill W Mid 133 G8
Stamborough Som 42 F4
Stambourne Essex 106 D4
Stambourne Green Essex 106 D4
Stamford Lincs 137 B10
Stamford Bridge Ches W 167 B7
E Yorks 207 B10
Stamfordham Northumb 242 C3
Stamford Hill London 67 B10
Stamperland E Renf 267 D11
Stamshaw Ptsmth 33 G10
Stanah Cumb 220 B6
Lancs 202 E3
Stanborough Herts 86 C2
Stanbridge C Beds 103 G9
Dorset 31 G8
Stanbridgeford C Beds 103 G9
Stanbrook Essex 106 F2
Worcs 98 B6
Stanbury W Yorks 204 F6
Stand Gtr Man 195 F9
N Lanark 268 B5
Standburn Falk 279 G8
Standeford Staffs 133 B8
Standen Kent 53 E11
Standen Hall Lancs 203 E10
Standen Street Kent 53 G10
Standerwick Som 45 C10
Standford Hants 49 G10
Standford Bridge Telford 150 E4
Standingstone Cumb 229 B11
Cumb 229 E7
Standish Glos 80 D4
Gtr Man 194 E5
Standish Lower Ground Gtr Man 194 F5
Standlake Oxon 82 E5
Standon Hants 32 B6
Herts 105 G7
Staffs 150 B6
Standon Green End Herts 86 B5
Stane N Lanark 269 D7
Stanecastle N Ayrs 257 B8
Stanfield Norf 159 E8
Stoke 168 E5
Stanford C Beds 104 C3
Kent 54 F6
Norf 141 E7
Shrops 148 G6
Stanford Bishop Hereford 116 G3
Stanford Bridge Worcs 116 D4
Stanford Dingley W Berks 64 E5
Stanford End Wokingham 65 G8
Stanford Hills Notts 153 E10
Stanford in the Vale Oxon 82 G4
Stanford-le-Hope Thurrock 69 C7
Stanford on Avon Northants 119 B11
Stanford on Soar Notts 153 E10
Stanford on Teme Worcs 116 D4
Stanford Rivers Essex 87 E8
Stanfree Derbys 187 G7
Stanground Pboro 138 D4
Stanhill Lancs 195 B8
Stanhoe Norf 158 B6
Stanhope Borders 260 D4
Durham 232 D5
Kent 54 E3
Stanion Northants 137 F8
Stank Cumb 210 E4
Stanklyn Worcs 117 C7
Stanks W Yorks 206 F3
Stanley Derbys 170 G6
Durham 242 G5
Lancs 194 F3
Notts 171 C7
Perth 286 D5
Shrops 132 G3
Shrops 132 G5
Staffs 168 E6
W Yorks 197 C10
Wilts 62 E3
Stanley Common Derbys 170 G6
Stanley Crook Durham 233 D9
Stanley Downton Glos 80 E4
Stanley Ferry W Yorks 197 C11
Stanley Gate Lancs 194 G2
Stanley Green Ches E 184 E5
Poole 18 C6
Shrops 149 B10
Stanley Hill Hereford 98 C3
Stanley Moor Staffs 168 E6
Stanley Pontlarge Glos 99 E9
Stanleytown Rhondda 77 G8
Stanlow Ches W 182 F6
Staffs 132 D5
Stanmer Brighton 36 F4
Stanmore Hants 33 B7
London 85 G11
Shrops 132 E4
W Berks 64 D3
Stanner Powys 114 F5
Stannergate Dundee 287 D8
Stannersburn Northumb 250 F6
Stanners Hill Sur 66 G3
Stanningfield Suff 125 F7
Stanningley W Yorks 205 G10
Stannington Northumb 242 B6
S Yorks 186 D4
Stanpit Dorset 19 C9
Stansbatch Hereford 114 E6
Stansfield Suff 124 G5
Stanshope Staffs 169 E10
Stanstead Suff 106 B6
Stanstead Abbotts Herts 86 C5
Stansted Kent 68 G6
Stansted Airport Essex 105 G11
Stansted Mountfitchet Essex 105 G10
Stanthorne Ches W 167 B11
Stanton Glos 99 E11
Mon 96 G6
Northumb 252 F4
Staffs 169 F10
Suff 125 C9
Stantonbury M Keynes 102 C6
Stanton by Bridge Derbys 153 D7
Stanton-by-Dale Derbys 153 B9
Stanton Chare Suff 125 C9
Stanton Drew Bath 60 G5
Stanton Fitzwarren Swindon 81 G11
Stanton Gate Notts 153 B9
Stanton Harcourt Oxon 82 D6
Stanton Hill Notts 171 C7
Stanton in Peak Derbys 170 C2
Stanton Lacy Shrops 115 B9
Stanton Lees Derbys 170 C3
Stanton Long Shrops 131 E11
Stanton-on-the-Wolds Notts 154 C2
Stanton Prior Bath 61 G7
Stanton St Bernard Wilts 62 G5
Stanton St John Oxon 83 D9
Stanton St Quintin Wilts 62 D2
Stanton Street Suff 125 D9
Stanton under Bardon Leics 153 G9
Stanton upon Hine Heath Shrops 149 E11
Stanton Wick Bath 60 G6
Stantway Glos 80 C2
Stanwardine in the Fields Shrops 149 E8
Stanwardine in the Wood Shrops 149 D8
Stanway Essex 107 G8
Glos 99 E11
Stanway Green Essex 107 G9
Suff 126 C4
Stanwell Sur 66 E5
Stanwell Moor Sur 66 E4
Stanwick Northants 121 C9
Stanwick-St-John N Yorks 224 C3
Stanwix Cumb 239 F10
Stanycliffe Gtr Man 195 F11
Stanydale Shetland 313 H4
Staoinebrig W Isles 297 H3
Stape N Yorks 226 G5
Stapehill Dorset 31 G9
Stapeley Ches E 167 F11
Stapenhill Staffs 152 E5
Staple Kent 55 B9
Som 42 E6
Staplecross E Sus 38 C3
Staple Cross Devon 27 C8
Staplefield W Sus 36 B3
Staple Fitzpaine Som 28 D3
Stapleford Cambs 123 G9
Herts 86 B4
Leics 154 F6
Lincs 172 D5
Notts 153 B9
Wilts 46 F5
Stapleford Abbotts Essex 87 G8
Stapleford Tawney Essex 87 F8
Staplegrove Som 28 B2
Staplehay Som 28 C2
Staple Hill S Glos 61 D7
Worcs 117 C9
Staplehurst Kent 53 E9
Staple Lawns Som 28 D3
Staplers IoW 20 D6
Staples Hill W Sus 35 B8
Staplestreet Kent 70 G5
Stapleton Bristol 60 D6
Cumb 240 C2
Hereford 114 D6
Leics 135 D8
N Yorks 198 D4
N Yorks 224 C5
Shrops 131 C9
Som 29 C7
Stapley Som 27 E11
Staploe Beds 122 E2
Staplow Hereford 98 C3
Stapness Shetland 313 J4
Star Anglesey 179 G8
Fife 287 G7
Pembs 92 E4
Som 44 B2
Stara Orkney 314 D2
Starbeck N Yorks 206 B2
Starbotton N Yorks 213 E9
Starcross Devon 14 E5
Stareton Warks 118 C6
Stargate T&W 242 E5
Star Hill Mon 79 E7
Starkholmes Derbys 170 D4
Starling Gtr Man 195 E9
Starlings Green Essex 105 E9
Starr's Green E Sus 38 D3
Starston Norf 142 G4
Start Devon 8 G6
Startforth Durham 223 B10
Start Hill Essex 105 G10
Startley Wilts 62 C2
Startop's End Bucks 84 C6
Starveall S Glos 61 B9
Starvecrow Kent 52 D5
Statenborough Kent 55 B10
Statford St Andrew Suff 127 E7
Statham Warr 183 D11
Stathe Som 28 B5
Stathern Leics 154 C5
Station Hill Cumb 229 B11
Station Town Durham 234 D4
Statland Common Norf 141 D10
Staughton Green Cambs 122 D2
Staughton Highway Cambs 122 E2
Staughton Moor Beds 122 E2
Staunton Glos 79 C8
Glos 98 F5
Staunton in the Vale Notts 172 G4
Staunton on Arrow Hereford 115 E7
Staunton on Wye Hereford 97 B7
Staupes N Yorks 205 B10
Staveley Cumb 211 B7
Cumb 221 F9
Derbys 186 G6
N Yorks 215 G7
Staveley-in-Cartmel Cumb 211 B7
Staverton Devon 8 C5
Glos 99 G7
Northants 119 E10
Wilts 61 G11
Staverton Bridge Glos 99 G7
Stawell Som 43 F11
Stawley Som 27 C9
Staxigoe Highld 310 D7
Staxton N Yorks 217 D10
Staylittle Ceredig 128 F2
Staylittle / Penffordd-Lâs Powys 129 E7
Staynall Lancs 202 E3
Staythorpe Notts 172 E3
Stead W Yorks 205 D8
Steam Mills Glos 79 B10
Stean N Yorks 213 E11
Steanbow Som 44 F5
Stearsby N Yorks 216 E2
Steart Som 29 B9
Som 43 D9
Stebbing Essex 106 G3
Stebbing Green Essex 106 G3
Stechford W Mid 134 F2
Stede Quarter Kent 53 F11
Stedham W Sus 34 C5
Steel Northumb 241 F10
Northumb 251 G9
Steel Bank S Yorks 186 D4
Steel Cross E Sus 52 G4
Steelend Fife 279 C10
Steele Road Borders 250 E2
Steeleroad-end Borders 250 E2
Steel Green Cumb 210 D3
Steel Heath Shrops 149 B10
Steen's Bridge Hereford 115 F10
Steep Hants 34 B2
Steephill IoW 21 F7
Steep Lane W Yorks 196 C4
Steeple Dorset 18 E4
Essex 88 E6
Steeple Ashton Wilts 46 B2
Steeple Aston Oxon 101 F9
Steeple Barton Oxon 101 G8
Steeple Bumpstead Essex 106 C3
Steeple Claydon Bucks 102 F3
Steeple Gidding Cambs 138 G2
Steeple Langford Wilts 46 F4
Steeple Morden Cambs 104 C5
Steep Marsh Hants 34 B3
Steeraway Telford 132 B3
Steeton W Yorks 204 E6
Stein Highld 298 D2
Steinmanhill Aberds 303 E7
Stella T&W 242 E5
Stelling Minnis Kent 54 D6
Stelvio Newport 59 B9
Stembridge Som 28 C6
Swansea 56 C3
Stemster Highld 310 C5
Stemster Ho Highld 310 C5
Stenalees Corn 5 D10
Stenaquoy Orkney 314 C5
Stencoose Corn 4 F4
Stenhill Devon 27 E9
Stenhouse Dumfries 247 E8
Edin 280 G4
Stenhousemuir Falk 279 E7
Stenigot Lincs 190 E3
Stennack Corn 2 B5
Stenness Shetland 312 F4
Stenscholl Highld 298 C4
Stenso Orkney 314 D3
Stenson Derbys 152 D6
Stenton E Loth 282 G2
Fife 280 B5
Stentwood Devon 27 F10
Stenwith Lincs 154 B6
Stepaside Corn 5 F9
Pembs 73 D10
Powys 129 F11
Stepping Hill Gtr Man 184 D6
Steppingley C Beds 103 D10
Stepps N Lanark 268 B3
Sterndale Moor Derbys 169 B10
Sternfield Suff 127 E7
Sterridge Devon 40 D5
Stert Wilts 46 B4
Sterte Poole 18 C6
Stetchworth Cambs 124 F2
Stevenage Herts 104 G4
Steven's Crouch E Sus 38 D2
Stevenston N Ayrs 266 G5
Stevenstone Devon 25 D8
Steventon Hants 48 D4
Oxon 83 G7
Shrops 115 C10
Steventon End Essex 105 C11
Stevington Beds 121 G9
Stewards Essex 87 D7
Steward's Green Essex 87 E7
Stewartby Beds 103 C10
Stewarton Argyll 255 F7
E Ayrs 267 F8
Stewkley Bucks 103 F7
Stewkley Dean Bucks 102 F6
Stewley Som 28 D4
Stewton Lincs 190 D5
Steyne Cross IoW 21 D8
Steyning W Sus 35 E11
Steynton Pembs 72 D6
Stibb Corn 24 E2
Stibbard Norf 159 D9
Stibb Cross Devon 24 E6
Stibb Green Wilts 63 G8
Stibbington Cambs 137 D11
Stichill Borders 262 B6
Sticker Corn 5 E9
Stickford Lincs 174 D5
Stick Hill Kent 52 E3
Sticklepath Devon 13 C8
Devon 40 G5
Som 28 E4
Som 42 F4
Sticklinch Som 44 F5
Stickling Green Essex 105 E9
Stickney Lincs 174 D4
Stiffkey Norf 177 E7
Stifford's Bridge Hereford 98 B4
Stiff Street Kent 69 G11
Stileway Som 44 E3
Stillingfleet N Yorks 207 E7
Stillington N Yorks 215 F11
Stockton 234 G3
Stilton Cambs 138 F3
Stinchcombe Glos 80 F2
Stinsford Dorset 17 C10
Stiperstones Shrops 131 C7
Stirchley Telford 132 B4
W Mid 133 G11
Stirkoke Ho Highld 310 D7

Swa–Tho 411

Swallows Cross Essex 87 F10
Swalwell T&W 242 E6
Swampton Hants 48 C2
Swanage Dorset 18 F6
Swanbach Ches E 167 G11
Swanbister Orkney 314 F3
Swanborough Swindon 81 G11
Swan Bottom Bucks 84 D6
Swanbourne Bucks 102 F6
Swanbridge V Glam 59 F7
Swan Green
Ches W 184 G2
Suff 126 C5
Swanland E Yorks 200 B3
Swanley Glos 80 F2
Kent 68 F4
Swanley Bar Herts 86 E3
Swanley Village Kent 68 F4
Swanmore Hants 33 D9
IoW 21 C7
Swannay Orkney 314 D2
Swannington Leics 153 F8
Norf 160 F2
Swanpool Lincs 189 G7
Swanscombe Kent 68 E6
Swansea / Abertawe
Swansea 56 C6
Swanside Mers 182 C6
Swanston Edin 270 B4
Swan Street Essex 107 F7
Swanton Abbott
Norf 160 D5
Swanton Hill Norf 160 D5
Swanton Morley
Norf 159 F10
Swanton Novers
Norf 159 C10
Swanton Street
Kent 53 B11
Swan Village
W Mid 133 E9
Swanwick Derbys 170 E6
Hants 33 F8
Swanwick Green
Ches E 167 F9
Swarby Lincs 173 G8
Swarcliffe W Yorks 206 F3
Swardeston Norf 142 C4
Swarister Shetland 312 E7
Swarkestone
Derbys 153 D7
Swarland Northumb 252 C5
Swarraton Hants 48 F5
Swartha W Yorks 205 D7
Swarthmoor Cumb 210 D5
Swartland Orkney 314 D2
Swathwick Derbys 170 B5
Swaton Lincs 156 B2
Swavesey Cambs 123 D7
Sway Hants 19 B11
Swayfield Lincs 155 E9
Swaythling Soton 32 D6
Sweet Green Worcs 116 E2
Sweetham Devon 14 B3
Sweethaws E Sus 37 B8
Sweethay Som 28 C2
Sweetholme Cumb 221 B11
Sweethouse Corn 5 C11
Sweets Corn 11 B9
Sweetshouse Corn 5 C11
Sweffling Suff 126 E6
Swell Som 28 C5
Swelling Hill Hants 49 G7
Swepstone Leics 153 G7
Swerford Oxon 101 E7
Swettenham Ches E 168 B4
Swetton N Yorks 214 E3
Swffryd Caerph 78 F2
Swiftsden E Sus 38 B2
Swift's Green Kent 53 E11
Swilland Suff 126 G3
Swillbrook Lancs 202 G5
Swillington
W Yorks 206 G3
Swillington Common
W Yorks 206 G3
Swimbridge Devon 25 B10
Swimbridge Newland
Devon 40 G6
Swinbrook Oxon 82 C3
Swincliffe N Yorks 205 B10
W Yorks 197 B8
Swincombe Devon 41 E7
Swinden N Yorks 204 C3
Swinderby Lincs 172 C5
Swindon Glos 99 G8
Staffs 133 E7
Swindon 63 C7
Swine E Yorks 209 F8
Swinefleet E Yorks 199 C9
Swineford S Glos 61 F7
Swineshead Beds 121 D11
Lincs 174 G2
Swineshead Bridge
Lincs 174 G2
Swinethorpe Lincs 172 B5
Swiney Highld 310 F6
Swinford Leics 119 B11
Oxon 82 D6
Swingate Notts 171 G8
Swingbrow Cambs 139 F7
Swingfield Minnis
Kent 55 E8
Swingfield Street
Kent 55 E8
Swingleton Green
Suff 107 B9
Swinhoe Northumb 264 D6
Swinhope Lincs 190 B2
Swining Shetland 312 G6
Swinister Shetland 312 E5
Shetland 313 L6
Swinithwaite
N Yorks 213 B10
Swinmore Common
Hereford 98 C3
Swinnie Borders 262 F4
Swinnow Moor
W Yorks 205 G10
Swinscoe Staffs 169 F10
Swinside Cumb 229 G10
Swinside Townfoot
Borders 262 F6
Swinstead Lincs 155 E10
Swinton Borders 272 F6
Swinton *continued*
Glasgow 268 C3
Gtr Man 195 G9
N Yorks 214 D4
N Yorks 216 E5
S Yorks 186 B6
Swinton Bridge
S Yorks 187 B7
Swinton Hill Borders 272 F6
Swintonmill Borders 272 F6
Swinton Park
Gtr Man 195 G9
Swiss Valley Carms 75 E8
Swithland Leics 153 G10
Swordale Highld 300 C5
Highld 309 K6
Swordland Highld 295 F9
Swordly Highld 308 C7
Sworton Heath
Ches E 183 E11
Swyddffynnon
Ceredig 112 D3
Swynnerton Staffs 151 B7
Swyre Dorset 16 D6
Sycamore Devon 28 F3
Sychdyn / Soughton
Flint 166 B2
Sychtyn Powys 129 B9
Sydallt Wrex 166 D4
Syde Glos 81 C7
Sydenham London 67 E11
Oxon 84 E2
Som 43 F10
Sydenham Damerel
Devon 12 F4
Syderstone Norf 158 C6
Sydling St Nicholas
Dorset 17 B8
Sydmonton Hants 48 B3
Sydney Ches E 168 D2
Syerston Notts 172 F2
Syke Gtr Man 195 D11
Sykehouse S Yorks 198 D6
Sykes Lancs 203 C8
Syleham Suff 126 B4
Sylen Carms 75 D8
Symbister Shetland 313 G7
Symington Borders 271 F8
S Ayrs 257 C9
S Lanark 259 B11
Symondsbury Dorset 16 C4
Symonds Green
Herts 104 F4
Symonds Yat
Hereford 79 B9
Synderford Dorset 28 G5
Synod Inn / Post Mawr
Ceredig 111 G8
Synton Borders 261 E11
Synton Mains
Borders 261 E11
Synwell Glos 80 G3
Syre Highld 308 E6
Syreford Glos 99 G10
Syresham Northants 102 C2
Syster Highld 310 C6
Syston Leics 154 G2
Lincs 172 G6
Sytchampton Worcs 116 D6
Sytch Ho Green
Shrops 132 E5
Sytch Lane Telford 150 E2
Sywell Northants 120 D6

T

Taagan Highld 299 C10
Tabley Hill Ches E 184 F2
Tabor Gwyn 146 F5
Tàbost W Isles 304 B7
Tabost W Isles 305 G5
Tachbrook Mallory
Warks 118 E6
Tacker Street Som 42 F4
Tackley Oxon 101 G9
Tacleit W Isles 304 E3
Tacolneston Norf 142 D2
Tadcaster N Yorks 206 E5
Tadden Dorset 31 G7
Taddington Derbys 185 G10
Glos 99 E11
Taddiport Devon 25 D7
Tadhill Som 45 D7
Tadley Hants 64 G6
Oxon 64 B4
Tadlow Beds 104 B5
C Beds 104 B5
Tadmarton Oxon 101 D7
Tadnoll Dorset 17 D11
Tadwick Bath 61 E8
Tadworth Sur 51 B8
Tafarnau-bach
Bl Gwent 77 C10
Tafarn-y-bwlch
Pembs 91 E11
Tafarn-y-gelyn
Denb 165 C11
Taff Merthyr Garden
Village M Tydf 77 F10
Taff's Well Rhondda 58 C6
Tafolwern Powys 129 C7
Tai Conwy 164 C3
Taibach Neath 57 D9
Tai-bach Powys 148 D3
Taigh a Ghearraidh
W Isles 296 D3
Taigh Bhalaigh
W Isles 296 D3
Tai-mawr Conwy 165 G7
Tai-morfa Gwyn 144 D5
Tain Highld 309 L7
Highld 310 C6
Tai-nant Wrex 166 F3
Tainlon Gwyn 162 E6
Tairbeart W Isles 305 H3
Tai'r-Bull Powys 95 F9
Tairgwaith Neath 76 C2
Tai'r-heol Caerph 77 G10
Tai'r-ysgol Swansea 57 B7
Tai-Ucha Denb 165 D8
Takeley Essex 105 G11
Takeley Street
Essex 105 G10
Talacharn / Laugharne
Carms 74 C4
Talachddu Powys 95 E11
Talacre Flint 181 E10
Talardd Gwyn 147 D7
Talaton Devon 15 B7
Talbenny Pembs 72 C4
Talbot Green
Rhondda 58 C4
Talbot Heath Poole 19 C7
Talbot's End S Glos 80 G2
Talbot Village Poole 19 C7
Talbot Woods
Bmouth 19 C7
Tale Devon 27 G9
Talerddig Powys 129 C8
Talgarreg Ceredig 111 G8
Talgarth Powys 96 E3
Talgarth's Well
Swansea 56 D2
Talisker Highld 294 B5
Talke Staffs 168 E4
Talke Pits Staffs 168 E4
Talkin Cumb 240 F3
Talladale Highld 299 B9
Talla Linnfoots
Borders 260 E4
Tallaminnoch
S Ayrs 245 D10
Talland Corn 6 E4
Tallarn Green Wrex 166 G6
Tallentire Cumb 229 D8
Talley Carms 94 E2
Tallington Lincs 137 B11
Talmine Highld 308 C5
Talog Carms 92 F6
Talsarn Carms 94 F5
Tal-sarn Ceredig 111 F10
Talsarnau Gwyn 146 B2
Talskiddy Corn 5 B8
Talwrn Anglesey 179 F7
Wrex 166 F3
Tal-y-bont Ceredig 128 F3
Conwy 164 B3
Gwyn 145 E11
Gwyn 179 G10
Talybont-on-Usk
Powys 96 G2
Tal-y-cafn Conwy 180 G3
Tal-y-coed Mon 78 B6
Talygarn Rhondda 58 C4
Talyllyn Powys 96 F2
Tal-y-llyn Gwyn 128 B4
Talysarn Gwyn 163 E7
Tal-y-waenydd
Gwyn 163 F11
Talywain Torf 78 E3
Tal-y-wern Powys 128 C6
Tamanabhagh
W Isles 304 F2
Tame Bridge
N Yorks 225 D10
Tamer Lane End
Gtr Man 194 G6
Tamerton Foliot Plym 7 C9
Tame Water
Gtr Man 196 F3
Tamfourhill Falk 279 F7
Tamworth Staffs 134 C4
Tamworth Green
Lincs 174 G5
Tancred N Yorks 206 B5
Tandem W Yorks 197 D7
Tanden Kent 54 F2
Tandlehill Renfs 267 C8
Tandridge Sur 51 C11
Tanerdy Carms 93 G8
Tanfield Durham 242 F5
Tanfield Lea
Durham 242 G5
Tang N Yorks 205 B10
Tangasdal W Isles 297 M2
Tang Hall York 207 C8
Tangiers Pembs 73 B7
Tangley Hants 47 C10
Tanglwst Carms 92 E6
Tangmere W Sus 22 B6
Tangwick Shetland 312 F4
Tangy Argyll 255 E7
Tan Hills Durham 233 B11
Tan Hinon Powys 129 F7
Tanhouse Lancs 194 F3
Tanis Wilts 62 G3
Tankersley
S Yorks 197 G10
Tankerton Kent 70 F6
Tanlan Flint 181 E10
Tan-lan Conwy 164 C3
Gwyn 163 G10
Tanlan Banks Flint 181 E10
Tannach Highld 310 E7
Tannachie Aberds 293 E9
Tannadice Angus 287 B8
Tanner's Green
Worcs 117 C11
Tannington Suff 126 D4
Tannington Place
Suff 126 D4
Tannochside
N Lanark 268 C4
Tan Office Suff 126 E2
Tan Office Green
Suff 124 F5
Tansley Derbys 170 D4
Tansley Hill W Mid 133 F9
Tansley Knoll
Derbys 170 C4
Tansor Northants 137 E11
Tanterton Lancs 202 G6
Tantobie Durham 242 G5
Tanton N Yorks 225 C10
Tanwood Worcs 117 C8
Tanworth-in-Arden
Warks 118 C2
Tan-y-bwlch
Gwyn 163 G11
Tanyfron Wrex 166 E3
Tan-y-fron Conwy 165 C7
Tan-y-graig
Anglesey 179 F8
Gwyn 144 B6
Tanygrisiau Gwyn 163 F11
Tan-y-groes
Ceredig 92 B5
Tan-y-mynydd
Gwyn 144 C6
Tan-y-pistyll
Powys 147 D11
Tan-yr-allt Denb 181 E9
Gwyn 163 E7
Tanyrhydiau
Ceredig 112 D4
Tanysgafell Gwyn 163 B10
Taobh a Chaolais
W Isles 297 K3
Taobh a' Ghlinne
W Isles 305 G5
Taobh a Thuath Loch
Aineort W Isles 297 J3
Taobh a Tuath Loch
Baghasdail
W Isles 297 J3
Taobh Siar W Isles 305 H3
Taobh Tuath
W Isles 296 C5
Taplow Bucks 66 C2
Tapnage Hants 33 E9
Tapton Derbys 186 G5
Tapton Hill S Yorks 186 D4
Tarbat Ho Highld 301 B7
Tarbert Argyll 255 B7
Argyll 275 E7
Argyll 275 G9
Tarbet Argyll 285 G7
Highld 295 F9
Highld 306 E6
Tarbock Green
Mers 183 D7
Tarbolton S Ayrs 257 D10
Tarbrax S Lanark 269 D10
Tardebigge Worcs 117 D10
Tardy Gate Lancs 194 B4
Tarfside Angus 292 F6
Tarland Aberds 292 C6
Tarleton Lancs 194 C3
Tarleton Moss
Lancs 194 C2
Tarlogie Highld 309 L7
Tarlscough Lancs 194 E2
Tarlton Glos 81 F7
Tarn W Yorks 205 F9
Tarnbrook Lancs 203 B7
Tarnock Som 43 C11
Tarns Cumb 229 B8
Tarnside Cumb 221 G8
Tarporley Ches W 167 C9
Tarpots Essex 69 B9
Tarr Som 42 G6
Tarraby Cumb 239 F10
Tarrant Crawford
Dorset 30 G6
Tarrant Gunville
Dorset 30 E6
Tarrant Hinton
Dorset 30 E6
Tarrant Keyneston
Dorset 30 G6
Tarrant Launceston
Dorset 30 F6
Tarrant Monkton
Dorset 30 F6
Tarrant Rawston
Dorset 30 F6
Tarrant Rushton
Dorset 30 F6
Tarrel Highld 311 L2
Tarring Neville
E Sus 36 G6
Tarrington Hereford 98 C2
Tarrington Common
Hereford 98 D2
Tarryblake Ho
Moray 302 E5
Tarsappie Perth 286 E5
Tarskavaig Highld 295 E7
Tarts Hill Shrops 149 B8
Tarves Aberds 303 F8
Tarvie Highld 300 D4
Perth 292 G2
Tarvin Ches W 167 B7
Tarvin Sands
Ches W 167 B7
Tasburgh Norf 142 D4
Tasley Shrops 132 E3
Taston Oxon 101 G7
Tat Bank W Mid 133 F9
Tatenhill Staffs 152 E4
Tatenhill Common
Staffs 152 E3
Tathall End
M Keynes 102 B6
Tatham Lancs 212 F2
Tathwell Lincs 190 E4
Tatling End Bucks 66 B4
Tatsfield Sur 52 B2
Tattenhall Ches W 167 D7
Tattenhoe M Keynes 102 E6
Tatterford Norf 159 D7
Tattersett Norf 158 C6
Tattershall Lincs 174 D2
Tattershall Bridge
Lincs 173 D11
Tattershall Thorpe
Lincs 174 D2
Tattingstone Suff 108 D2
Tattingstone White
Horse Suff 108 D2
Tattle Bank Warks 118 E3
Tatton Dale Ches E 184 E2
Tatworth Som 28 F4
Taunton Gtr Man 196 G2
Som 28 C2
Taverham Norf 160 G3
Taverners Green
Essex 87 B9
Tavernspite Pembs 73 C11
Tavistock Devon 12 G5
Taw Green Devon 13 B9
Tawstock Devon 25 B9
Taxal Derbys 185 F8
Tay Bridge Dundee 287 E8
Tayinloan Argyll 255 C7
Taymouth Castle
Perth 285 C11
Taynish Argyll 275 E8
Taynton Glos 98 G4
Oxon 82 C2
Taynuilt Argyll 284 D4
Tayport Fife 287 E8
Tayvallich Argyll 275 E8
Tea Green Herts 104 G2
Tealby Lincs 189 C11
Tealing Angus 287 D8
Teams T&W 242 E6
Team Valley T&W 242 E6
Teanford Staffs 169 G8
Teangue Highld 295 E8
Teanna Mhachair
W Isles 296 E3
Teasley Mead E Sus 52 F4
Tebay Cumb 222 E2
Tebworth C Beds 103 F9
Tedburn St Mary
Devon 14 C2
Teddington Glos 99 E9
London 67 E7
Teddington Hands
Worcs 99 E9
Tedsmore Shrops 149 D7
Tedstone Delamere
Hereford 116 F3
Tedstone Wafer
Hereford 116 F3
Teesville Redcar 225 B10
Teeton Northants 120 C3
Teffont Evias Wilts 46 G3
Teffont Magna Wilts 46 G3
Tegryn Pembs 92 E4
Teigh Rutland 155 F7
Teigncombe Devon 13 D9
Teigngrace Devon 14 G2
Teignmouth Devon 14 G4
Teign Village Devon 14 E2
Telford Telford 132 B3
Telham E Sus 38 E3
Tellisford Som 45 B10
Telscombe E Sus 36 G6
Telscombe Cliffs
E Sus 36 G5
Templand Dumfries 248 F3
Temple Corn 11 G8
Glasgow 267 B10
Midloth 270 D6
Wilts 45 E10
Windsor 65 C10
Temple Balsall
W Mid 118 B4
Temple Bar Carms 75 B9
Ceredig 111 G10
W Sus 22 B5
Templeborough
S Yorks 186 C6
Temple Cloud Bath 44 B6
Templecombe Som 30 C2
Temple Cowley Oxon 83 E8
Temple End Essex 106 C6
Suff 124 G3
Temple Ewell Kent 55 E9
Temple Fields Essex 87 C7
Temple Grafton
Warks 118 G2
Temple Guiting Glos 99 F11
Templehall Fife 280 C5
Temple Herdewyke
Warks 119 G7
Temple Hill Kent 68 D5
Temple Hirst
N Yorks 198 C6
Templeman's Ash
Dorset 28 G6
Temple Normanton
Derbys 170 B6
Temple Sowerby
Cumb 231 F8
Templeton Devon 26 E5
Pembs 73 C10
W Berks 63 F11
Templeton Bridge
Devon 26 E5
Templetown
Durham 242 G4
Tempsford C Beds 122 G3
Ten Acres W Mid 133 G11
Tenandry Perth 291 G11
Tenbury Wells
Worcs 115 D11
Tenby / Dinbych-y-
Pysgod Pembs 73 E10
Tencreek Corn 6 E4
Tendring Essex 108 G2
Tendring Green
Essex 108 F2
Tendring Heath
Essex 108 F2
Ten Mile Bank Norf 140 D2
Tenston Orkney 314 E2
Tenterden Kent 53 G11
Terfyn Conwy 180 F6
Gwyn 163 C9
Terhill Som 43 G7
Terling Essex 88 B3
Ternhill Shrops 150 C2
Terpersie Castle
Aberds 302 G5
Terras Corn 5 E8
Terregles Banks
Dumfries 237 B11
Terrible Down E Sus 23 B7
Terrick Bucks 84 D4
Terriers Bucks 84 G5
Terrington N Yorks 216 E3
Terrington St Clement
Norf 157 E10
Terrington St John
Norf 157 G10
Terryhorn Aberds 302 F4
Terry's Green Warks 118 C2
Terwick Common
W Sus 34 C4
Teston Kent 53 C8
Testwood Hants 32 E5
Tetbury Glos 80 G5
Tetbury Upton Glos 80 F5
Tetchill Shrops 149 C7
Tetchwick Bucks 83 B11
Tetcott Devon 12 B2
Tetford Lincs 190 G4
Tetley N Lincs 199 E9
Tetney Lincs 201 G10
Tetney Lock Lincs 201 G10
Tetsworth Oxon 83 E11
Tettenhall W Mid 133 D7
Tettenhall Wood
W Mid 133 D7
Tetworth Cambs 122 G4
Teuchan Aberds 303 F10
Teversal Notts 171 C7
Teversham Cambs 123 F9
Teviothead Borders 249 B10
Tewel Aberds 293 E10
Tewin Herts 86 C3
Tewin Wood Herts 86 B3
Tewitfield Lancs 211 E10
Tewkesbury Glos 99 E7
Teynham Kent 70 G3
Teynham Street Kent 70 G3
Thackley W Yorks 205 F9
Thackley End
W Yorks 205 F9
Thackthwaite Cumb 229 G8
Thainston Aberds 293 F8
Thakeham W Sus 35 D10
Thame Oxon 84 D2
Thames Ditton Sur 67 F7
Thames Haven
Thurrock 69 C8
Thames Head Glos 81 F7
Thamesmead London 68 C3
Thanington Kent 54 B6
Thankerton
S Lanark 259 B11
Tharston Norf 142 E3
Thatcham W Berks 64 F4
Thatto Heath Mers 183 C8
Thaxted Essex 106 E2
The Aird Highld 298 D4
Theakston N Yorks 214 B6
Thealby N Lincs 199 D11
The Alders Staffs 134 C3
Theale Som 44 D3
W Berks 64 E6
The Arms Norf 141 D7
Thearne E Yorks 209 F7
The Bage Hereford 96 C5
The Balloch Perth 286 F2
The Bank Ches E 168 D4
The Banks Gtr Man 185 D7
Wilts 62 D4
The Barony Ches E 167 E11
Orkney 314 D2
The Barton Wilts 62 D5
The Batch S Glos 61 E7
The Beeches Glos 81 E8
The Bell Gtr Man 194 F4
The Bents Staffs 151 C10
Theberton Suff 127 D8
The Blythe Staffs 151 D10
The Bog Shrops 131 D7
The Borough Dorset 30 E2
London 67 D10
The Bourne Sur 49 E10
Worcs 117 F9
The Bows Stirling 285 G11
The Braes Highld 295 B7
The Brampton
Staffs 168 F4
The Brand Leics 153 G10
The Bratch Staffs 133 E7
The Breck Orkney 314 F3
The Brents Kent 70 G4
The Bridge Dorset 30 E3
The Broad Hereford 115 E9
The Brook Suff 125 B11
The Brushes Derbys 186 F5
The Bryn Mon 78 D4
The Burf Worcs 116 D6
The Butts Hants 49 F8
Som 45 D9
The Camp Glos 80 D6
Herts 85 D11
The Cape Warks 118 D5
The Chart Kent 52 C3
The Chequer Wrex 167 G7
The Chuckery
W Mid 133 D10
The City Bucks 84 F3
The Cleaver
Hereford 97 F10
The Close W Sus 22 C5
The Colony Oxon 100 D6
The Common Bath 60 G6
Bucks 102 E5
Dorset 30 E3
Shrops 150 D3
Suff 108 B2
Swansea 56 C4
W Sus 51 G7
Wilts 47 G8
Wilts 61 G11
Wilts 62 C4
The Corner Kent 53 E8
Shrops 131 F8
The Cot Mon 79 F8
The Craigs Highld 309 K4
The Crofts E Yorks 218 E4
The Cronk IoM 192 C4
The Cross Hands
Leics 134 C6
The Cwm Mon 79 G7
Theddingworth
Leics 136 F3
Theddlethorpe All Saints
Lincs 191 D7
Theddlethorpe St Helen
Lincs 191 D7
The Dell Suff 143 D9
The Delves W Mid 133 D10
The Den N Ayrs 266 E6
The Dene Durham 242 G4
Hants 47 C11
The Down Kent 53 F7
Shrops 132 E3
The Downs Sur 50 F3
The Dunks Wrex 166 E4
The Eals Northumb 251 F7
The Eaves Glos 79 D10
The Fall W Yorks 197 B10
The Fence Glos 79 D8
The Flat Glos 80 B3
The Flatt Cumb 240 B3
The Flourish Derbys 153 B8
The Folly Herts 85 C11
S Glos 61 E8
The Fording Hereford 98 F3
The Forge Hereford 114 F6
The Forstal Kent 54 F4
The Forties Derbys 152 F6
The Four Alls
Shrops 150 C3
The Fox Wilts 62 B6
The Foxholes
Shrops 132 G2
The Frenches Hants 32 C4
The Frythe Herts 86 C2
The Garths Shetland 312 B8
The Gibb Wilts 61 D10
The Glack Borders 260 B6
The Gore Shrops 131 G11
The Grange
N Yorks 225 F11
Norf 160 E2
The Green C Beds 85 B8
Cambs 122 D5
Cumb 210 C3
Cumb 211 D7
Essex 88 B3
Hants 32 B3
M Keynes 103 C7
Norf 141 C11
Norf 159 B11
Northants 102 C5
Oxon 101 F9
S Yorks 197 G8
Shrops 130 G6
Warks 118 F4
Wilts 45 G11
The Grove
Dumfries 237 B11
Durham 242 G3
Herts 85 F9
Shrops 131 B7
Shrops 131 G8
Worcs 99 C7
The Gutter Derbys 170 F5
Worcs 117 B9
The Hacket S Glos 61 B7
The Hague Derbys 185 C8
The Hall Shetland 312 D8
The Hallands
N Lincs 200 C5
The Ham Wilts 45 C11
The Handfords
Staffs 151 E7
The Harbour Kent 53 D10
The Haven W Sus 50 G5
The Headland Hrtlpl 234 E6
The Heath Norf 159 D8
Norf 160 E3
Norf 160 E4
Staffs 151 C11
Suff 108 D2
The Hem Shrops 132 B4
The Hendre Mon 79 C7
The Herberts V Glam 58 E3
The Hermitage
Cambs 123 C7
The High Essex 86 C6
The Highlands E Sus 38 F2
The Hill Cumb 210 C3
The Hobbins Shrops 132 E4
The Hollands Staffs 168 D6
The Hollies Notts 172 E4
The Holmes Derbys 153 B7
The Holt Wokingham 65 D10
The Hook Worcs 98 C6
The Hope Shrops 115 B10
The Howe Cumb 211 B9
IoM 192 F2
The Humbers
Telford 150 G3
The Hundred
Hereford 115 E10
The Hyde London 67 B8
Worcs 98 C6
The Hythe Essex 107 G10
The Inch Edin 280 G5
The Knab Swansea 56 D6
The Knap V Glam 58 F5
The Knapp Hereford 116 G3
S Glos 79 G11
The Knowle W Mid 133 F9
The Laches Staffs 133 B8
The Lake Dumfries 237 E8
The Lakes Worcs 116 B5
The Lawe T&W 243 D9
The Lawns E Yorks 208 G6
Thelbridge Barton
Devon 26 E3
The Leacon Kent 54 G3
The Leath Shrops 131 F11
The Lee Bucks 84 E6
The Lees Kent 54 C4
The Leigh Glos 99 F7
The Leys Staffs 134 C4
The Lhen IoM 192 B4
The Ling Norf 142 D6
The Lings Norf 141 B10
S Yorks 199 F7
The Linleys Wilts 61 F11
Thelnetham Suff 125 B10
The Lunt W Mid 133 D9
Thelveton Norf 142 G3
Thelwall Warr 183 D10
The Manor W Sus 22 C4
The Marsh Ches E 168 C4
Hereford 115 F9
Powys 130 D6
Shrops 150 D3
Staffs 150 D6
Suff 125 B11
Suff 126 B2
Wilts 62 C5
Themelthorpe
Norf 159 E11
The Middles
Durham 242 G6
The Mint Hants 34 B3
The Moor Flint 166 B4
Kent 38 B3
The Moors Hereford 97 E10
The Mount Hants 64 G2
Reading 65 E8
The Mumbles / Y
Mwmbwls Swansea 56 D6
The Murray
S Lanark 268 E2
The Mythe Glos 99 E7
The Nant Wrex 166 E3
The Narth Mon 79 D8
The Neuk Aberds 293 D9
Thenford Northants 101 C10
The Node Herts 104 G4
The Nook Shrops 149 C11
Shrops 150 E3
The North Mon 79 D8
Theobald's Green
Wilts 62 F4
The Oval Bath 61 G8
The Park Glos 99 G8
The Parks S Yorks 198 F6
The Pitts Wilts 31 B9
The Platt Oxon 83 E9
The Pludds Glos 79 B10
The Point Devon 14 E5
The Pole of Itlaw
Aberds 302 D6
The Port of Felixstowe
Suff 108 E5
The Potteries Stoke 168 F5
The Pound Glos 98 E4
The Quarry Glos 80 F2
Shrops 149 G9
The Quarter Kent 53 E11
Kent 53 G11
The Rampings Worcs 99 E7
The Rectory Lincs 156 G2
The Reddings Glos 99 G8
Therfield Herts 104 D6
The Rhos Pembs 73 C8
The Rhydd Hereford 97 E9
The Riddle Hereford 115 E9
The Ridge Wilts 61 F11
The Ridges
Wokingham 65 G10
The Ridgeway Herts 86 E3
The Riding
Northumb 241 D10
The Riggs Borders 261 C8
The Rink Borders 261 C11
The Rise Windsor 66 F2
The Rock Telford 132 B3
The Rocks Kent 53 B8
S Glos 61 C8
The Roe Denb 181 G8
The Rookery Herts 85 G10
Staffs 168 D5
The Row Lancs 211 D9
The Rowe Staffs 150 B6
The Ryde Herts 86 D2
The Sands Sur 49 D11
The Scarr Glos 98 F4
The Shoe Wilts 61 E10
The Shruggs Staffs 151 C8
The Slack Durham 233 F8
The Slade W Berks 64 F4
The Smeeth Norf 157 G10
The Smithies
Shrops 132 D3
The Spa Wilts 62 G2
The Spring Warks 118 C5
The Square Torf 78 F3
The Stocks Kent 38 B6
Wilts 62 G2
The Straits Hants 49 F9
W Mid 133 E8
The Strand Wilts 46 B2
The Swillett Herts 85 F8
The Sydnall Shrops 150 C3
Thetford Lincs 156 F2
Norf 141 G7
The Thrift Cambs 104 D6
The Throat
Wokingham 65 F10
The Toft Staffs 151 F8
The Towans Corn 2 B3
The Town Scilly 1 F3
The Twittocks Glos 99 D7
The Tynings Glos 80 B6
The Vale W Mid 133 G11
The Valley Ches E 167 D11
Kent 54 C3
Leics 154 F4
Pembs 73 D10
The Vauld Hereford 97 B10
The Village Newport 78 G4
W Mid 133 F7
Windsor 66 E3
The Walshes Worcs 116 C6
The Warren Kent 54 E3
Wilts 63 F8
The Waterwheel
Shrops 131 C7
The Weaven
Hereford 97 E10
The Wells Sur 67 G7
The Wern Wrex 166 E3
The Willows
NE Lincs 201 F8
The Wood Shrops 148 E6
Shrops 149 D9
The Woodlands
Leics 136 D3
Suff 107 C11
Suff 108 D3
The Woods W Mid 133 D10
The Wrangle Bath 44 B4
The Wrythe London 67 F9
The Wyke Shrops 132 B4
The Wymm Hereford 97 B10
Theydon Bois Essex 86 F6
Theydon Garnon
Essex 87 F7
Theydon Mount
Essex 87 F7
The Yeld Shrops 131 G11
Thicket Mead Bath 45 B7
Thick Hollins
W Yorks 196 E6
Thickthorn Hall
Norf 142 B3
Thickwood Wilts 61 E10
Thimbleby Lincs 190 G2
N Yorks 225 F9
Thimble End W Mid 134 E2
Thinford Durham 233 E11
Thingley Wilts 61 E11
Thingwall Mers 182 E3
Thirdpart N Ayrs 266 F3
Thirlby N Yorks 215 C9
Thirlestane
Borders 271 F11
Thirn N Yorks 214 B4
Thirsk N Yorks 215 C8
Thirtleby E Yorks 209 G9
Thistleton Lancs 202 F4
Rutland 155 F8
Thistley Green Essex 88 B2
Suff 124 B3
Thixendale N Yorks 216 G6
Thockrington
Northumb 241 B11
Tholomas Drove
Cambs 139 B7
Tholthorpe N Yorks 215 F9
Thomas Chapel
Pembs 73 D10
Thomas Close Cumb 230 C4
Thomastown Aberds 302 F5
Rhondda 58 B4
Thompson Norf 141 D8
Thomshill Moray 302 D2
Thong Kent 69 E7

Underling Green
Kent 53 D9
Underriver Kent 52 C5
Underriver Ho Kent 52 C5
Under the Wood Kent 71 F8
Under Tofts S Yorks 186 D4
Underton Shrops 132 E3
Underwood Newport 59 B11
Notts 171 E7
Pembs 73 C7
Plym 7 D10
Undley Suff 140 G3
Undy Mon 60 B2
Ungisiadar W Isles 304 F3
Unifirth Shetland 313 H4
Union Cottage
Aberds 293 D10
Union Mills IoM 192 E4
Union Street E Sus 53 G8
United Downs Corn 4 G4
Unstone Derbys 186 F5
Unstone Green
Derbys 186 F5
Unsworth Gtr Man 195 F10
Unthank Cumb 230 B3
Cumb 230 D5
Cumb 231 C8
Derbys 186 F4
Unthank End Cumb 230 D5
Upavon Wilts 46 C6
Up Cerne Dorset 29 G11
Upchurch Kent 69 F10
Upcott Devon 24 D2
Devon 25 F9
Devon 25 F11
Devon 40 F3
Hereford 114 G6
Som 27 C11
Upend Cambs 124 F3
Up End M Keynes 103 B8
Up Exe Devon 26 G6
Upgate Norf 160 F2
Upgate Street Norf 141 E11
Norf 142 E5
Up Green Hants 65 G9
Uphall Dorset 29 G9
W Loth 279 G11
Uphall Station
W Loth 279 G11
Upham Devon 26 F5
Hants 33 C8
Uphampton
Hereford 115 E7
Worcs 116 E6
Up Hatherley Glos 99 G8
Uphempston Devon 8 C6
Uphill N Som 43 B10
Uphill Manor
N Som 43 B10
Up Holland Lancs 194 F4
Uplands Glos 80 D5
Swansea 56 C6
Uplawmoor E Renf 267 D8
Upleadon Glos 98 F5
Upleadon Court Glos 98 F5
Upleatham Redcar 226 B2
Uplees Kent 70 G3
Uploders Dorset 16 C6
Uplowman Devon 27 D8
Uplyme Devon 16 C2
Up Marden W Sus 34 E3
Upminster London 68 B5
Up Mudford Som 29 D9
Up Nately Hants 49 C7
Upnor Medway 69 E9
Upottery Devon 28 F2
Uppacott Devon 25 B9
Uppat Highld 311 J2
Uppend Essex 105 F9
Upper Affcot Shrops 131 F8
Upper Ardchronie
Highld 309 L6
Upper Ardgrain
Aberds 303 F9
Upper Ardroscadale
Argyll 275 G11
Upper Arley Worcs 132 G5
Upper Armley
W Yorks 205 G11
Upper Arncott Oxon 83 B10
Upper Astley
Shrops 149 F10
Upper Aston Shrops 132 E6
Upper Astrop
Northants 101 D10
Upper Badcall
Highld 306 E6
Upper Bangor Gwyn 179 G9
Upper Basildon
W Berks 64 D5
Upper Batley
W Yorks 197 B8
Upper Battlefield
Shrops 149 F10
Upper Beeding
W Sus 35 E11
Upper Benefield
Northants 137 F9
Upper Bentley
Worcs 117 D9
Upper Bighouse
Highld 310 D2
Upper Birchwood
Derbys 170 E6
Upper Blainslie
Borders 271 G10
Upper Boat Rhondda 58 B6
Upper Boddam
Aberds 302 F6
Upper Boddington
Northants 119 G9
Upper Bogrow
Highld 309 L7
Upper Bogside
Moray 302 D2
Upper Bonchurch
IoW 21 F7
Upper Booth
Derbys 185 D10
Upper Borth Ceredig 128 F2
Upper Boyndlie
Aberds 303 C9
Upper Brailes
Warks 100 D6
Upper Brandon Parva
Norf 141 B10
Upper Breakish
Highld 295 C8
Upper Breinton
Hereford 97 C9
Upper Broadheath
Worcs 116 F6
Upper Brockholes
W Yorks 196 B5
Upper Broughton
Notts 154 D3
Upper Broxwood
Hereford 115 G7
Upper Bruntingthorpe
Leics 136 F2
Upper Brynamman
Carms 76 C2
Upper Buckenhill
Hereford 97 E11
Upper Bucklebury
W Berks 64 F4
Upper Bullington
Hants 48 E3
Upper Burgate
Hants 31 D11
Upper Burnhaugh
Aberds 293 D10
Upper Bush Medway 69 F7
Upperby Cumb 239 G10
Upper Caldecote
C Beds 104 B3
Upper Cam Glos 80 F3
Upper Canada
N Som 43 B11
Upper Canterton
Hants 32 E3
Upper Catesby
Northants 119 F10
Upper Catshill
Worcs 117 C9
Upper Chapel
Powys 95 C10
Upper Cheddon Som 28 B2
Upper Chicksgrove
Wilts 31 B7
Upper Church Village
Rhondda 58 B5
Upper Chute Wilts 47 C9
Upper Clapton
London 67 B10
Upper Clatford
Hants 47 E11
Upper Coberley Glos 81 B7
Upper College
Shrops 149 C11
Upper Colwall
Hereford 98 C5
Upper Common
Hants 48 D6
Upper Cotburn
Aberds 303 D7
Upper Cotton Staffs 169 F9
Upper Coullie
Aberds 293 B9
Upper Cound
Shrops 131 C11
Upper Coxley Som 44 E4
Upper Cudworth
S Yorks 197 F11
Upper Culphin
Aberds 302 D6
Upper Cumberworth
W Yorks 197 F8
Upper Cwmbran Torf 78 F3
Upper Cwm-twrch
Powys 76 C3
Upperdale Derbys 185 G11
Upper Dallachy
Moray 302 C3
Upper Deal Kent 55 C11
Upper Dean Beds 121 D10
Devon 8 C4
Upper Denby
W Yorks 197 D8
W Yorks 197 F8
Upper Denton Cumb 240 D4
Upper Derraid
Highld 301 F10
Upper Diabaig
Highld 299 C8
Upper Dicker E Sus 23 D9
Upper Dinchope
Shrops 131 G9
Upper Dormington
Hereford 97 D11
Upper Dounreay
Highld 310 C4
Upper Dovercourt
Essex 108 E4
Upper Dowdeswell
Glos 81 B8
Upper Druimfin
Argyll 289 D7
Upper Dunsforth
N Yorks 215 G8
Upper Dunsley Herts 84 C6
Upper Eashing Sur 50 E3
Upper Eastern Green
W Mid 134 G5
Upper Eathie Highld 301 C7
Upper Edmonton
London 86 G4
Upper Egleton
Hereford 98 C2
Upper Elkstone
Staffs 169 D9
Upper Ellastone
Staffs 169 G10
Upper Elmers End
London 67 F11
Upper End Derbys 185 F9
Glos 81 C10
Glos 81 D8
Leics 154 G4
Upper Enham Hants 47 D11
Upper Farmcote
Shrops 132 E5
Upper Farringdon
Hants 49 F8
Upper Feorlig
Highld 298 E2
Upper Fivehead Som 28 C4
Upper Forge Shrops 132 F4
Upper Framilode
Glos 80 C3
Upper Froyle Hants 49 E9
Upper Gambolds
Worcs 117 D9
Upper Gills Highld 310 B7
Upper Glenfintaig
Highld 290 E4
Upper Godney Som 44 E3
Upper Goldstone
Kent 71 G9
Upper Gornal
W Mid 133 E8
Upper Gravenhurst
C Beds 104 D2
Upper Green
Essex 105 E8
Mon 78 B5
Suff 124 E4
W Berks 63 G11
W Yorks 197 B9
Upper Grove Common
Hereford 97 F11
Upper Guist Norf 159 D10
Upper Hackney
Derbys 170 C3
Upper Hale Sur 49 D10
Upper Halistra
Highld 298 D2
Upper Halliford Sur 66 F5
Upper Halling
Medway 69 G7
Upper Ham Worcs 99 D7
Upper Hambleton
Rutland 137 B8
Upper Hamnish
Hereford 115 F10
Upper Harbledown
Kent 54 B6
Upper Hardres Court
Kent 55 C7
Upper Hardwick
Hereford 115 F8
Upper Hartfield
E Sus 52 G3
Upper Hartshay
Derbys 170 E5
Upper Haselor
Worcs 99 C10
Upper Hatton Staffs 150 B6
Upper Haugh
S Yorks 186 B6
Upper Hawkhillock
Aberds 303 F10
Upper Hayesden
Kent 52 E5
Upper Hayton
Shrops 131 G10
Upper Heath
Shrops 131 F11
Upper Heaton
W Yorks 197 D7
Upper Hellesdon
Norf 160 G4
Upper Helmsley
N Yorks 207 B9
Upper Hengoed
Shrops 148 C5
Upper Hergest
Hereford 114 G5
Upper Heyford
Northants 120 F3
Oxon 101 F9
Upper Hill Glos 79 F11
Hereford 115 G9
Upper Hindhope
Borders 251 B7
Upper Holloway
London 67 B9
Upper Holton Suff 127 B8
Upper Hopton
W Yorks 197 D7
Upper Horsebridge
E Sus 23 C9
Upper Howsell Worcs 98 B5
Upper Hoyland
S Yorks 197 G11
Upper Hulme Staffs 169 C8
Upper Hyde IoW 21 E7
Upper Ifold Sur 50 G4
Upper Inglesham
Swindon 82 F2
Upper Inverbrough
Highld 301 F8
Upper Kergord
Shetland 313 H6
Upper Kidston
Borders 270 G4
Upper Kilcott Glos 61 B9
Upper Killay Swansea 56 C5
Upper Killeyan
Argyll 254 C3
Upper Kinsham
Hereford 115 D7
Upper Knockando
Moray 301 E11
Upper Lambourn
W Berks 63 C10
Upper Landywood
Staffs 133 B9
Upper Langford
N Som 44 B3
Upper Langwith
Derbys 171 B8
Upper Layham
Suff 107 C10
Upper Leigh Staffs 151 B10
Upper Lenie Highld 300 G5
Upper Littleton
N Som 60 G5
Upper Loads Derbys 170 B4
Upper Lochton
Aberds 293 D8
Upper Lode Worcs 99 E7
Upper Longdon
Staffs 151 G11
Upper Longwood
Shrops 132 B2
Upper Ludstone
Shrops 132 D6
Upper Lybster
Highld 310 F6
Upper Lydbrook
Glos 79 B10
Upper Lyde Hereford 97 C9
Upper Lye Hereford 115 D7
Upper Maes-coed
Hereford 96 D6
Upper Marsh
W Yorks 204 F6
Upper Midhope
S Yorks 186 B2
Upper Midway
Derbys 152 E5
Uppermill Gtr Man 196 F3
Upper Milovaig
Highld 297 G7
Upper Milton Oxon 82 B3
Som 44 D4
Upper Minety Wilts 81 G8
Upper Mitton Worcs 116 C6
Upper Moor Worcs 99 B9
Upper Moor Side
W Yorks 205 G10
Upper Morton
S Glos 79 G11
Upper Nash Pembs 73 E8
Upper Netchwood
Shrops 132 E2
Upper Newbold
Derbys 186 G5
Upper Nobut Staffs 151 B10
Upper North Dean
Bucks 84 F4
Upper Norwood
London 67 F10
W Sus 34 D6
Upper Obney Perth 286 D4
Upper Ochrwyth
Caerph 59 B8
Upper Oddington
Glos 100 F4
Upper Ollach Highld 295 B7
Upper Padley
Derbys 186 F2
Upper Pickwick
Wilts 61 E11
Upper Pollicott
Bucks 84 C2
Upper Poppleton
York 207 C7
Upper Port Highld 301 G10
Upper Postern Kent 52 D6
Upper Quinton
Warks 100 B3
Upper Race Torf 78 F3
Upper Ratley Hants 32 C4
Upper Ridinghill
Aberds 303 D10
Upper Rissington
Glos 82 B2
Upper Rochford
Worcs 116 D2
Upper Rodmersham
Kent 70 G2
Upper Sandaig
Highld 295 D9
Upper Sanday
Orkney 314 F5
Upper Sapey
Hereford 116 E3
Upper Saxondale
Notts 154 B3
Upper Seagry Wilts 62 C2
Upper Shelton
C Beds 103 C9
Upper Sheringham
Norf 177 E10
Upper Shirley
London 67 G11
Soton 32 E6
Upper Siddington
Glos 81 F8
Upper Skelmorlie
N Ayrs 266 B4
Upper Slackstead
Hants 32 B5
Upper Slaughter
Glos 100 G3
Upper Solva Pembs 90 G5
Upper Soudley Glos 79 C11
Uppersound
Shetland 313 J6
Upper Stanton Drew
Bath 60 G6
Upper Staploe Beds 122 F2
Upper Stoke Norf 142 C5
W Mid 135 G7
Upper Stondon
C Beds 104 D2
Upper Stowe
Northants 120 F2
Upper Stratton
Swindon 63 B7
Upper Street Hants 31 D11
Norf 142 G3
Norf 160 B5
Norf 160 E6
Norf 160 F6
Norf 161 F7
Suff 108 E2
Suff 124 G5
Suff 126 G2
Upper Strensham
Worcs 99 D8
Upper Studley Wilts 45 B10
Upper Sundon
C Beds 103 F10
Upper Swainswick
Bath 61 F9
Upper Swanmore
Hants 33 D9
Upper Swell Glos 100 F3
Upper Sydenham
London 67 E10
Upper Tankersley
S Yorks 186 B4
Upper Tean Staffs 151 B10
Upperthong
W Yorks 196 F6
Upperthorpe Derbys 187 E7
N Lincs 199 G9
Upper Threapwood
Ches W 166 F6
Upper Thurnham
Lancs 202 C5
Upper Tillyrie Perth 286 G5
Upperton E Sus 23 E10
Oxon 83 G11
W Sus 35 C7
Upper Tooting
London 67 E9
Upper Tote Highld 298 D5
Uppertown Derbys 170 C4
Highld 300 F4
Highld 310 B7
Northumb 241 C9
Uppertown *continued*
Orkney 314 G4
Upper Town Derbys 170 D3
Derbys 170 E2
Durham 233 D7
Hereford 97 B11
N Som 60 F4
Suff 125 D8
W Yorks 204 G6
Wilts 62 D3
Upper Treverward
Shrops 114 B5
Upper Tysoe Warks 100 C6
Upper Up Glos 81 F8
Upper Upham Wilts 63 D8
Upper Upnor Medway 69 E9
Upper Vobster Som 45 D8
Upper Walthamstow
London 67 B11
Upper Wardington
Oxon 101 B9
Upper Wardley
W Sus 34 B4
Upper Weald
M Keynes 102 D5
Upper Weedon
Northants 120 F2
Upper Welland
Worcs 98 C5
Upper Wellingham
E Sus 36 E6
Upper Welson
Hereford 114 G5
Upper Westholme
Som 44 E5
Upper Weston Bath 61 F8
Upper Weybread
Suff 126 B4
Upper Whiston
S Yorks 187 D7
Upper Wick Glos 80 F2
Worcs 116 G6
Upper Wield Hants 48 F6
Upper Wigginton
Shrops 148 B6
Upper Winchendon
Bucks 84 C2
Upper Witton
W Mid 133 E11
Upper Wolvercote
Oxon 83 D7
Upper Wolverton
Worcs 117 G8
Upperwood Derbys 170 D3
Upper Woodend
Aberds 293 B8
Upper Woodford
Wilts 46 F6
Upper Woolhampton
W Berks 64 F5
Upper Wootton
Hants 48 C5
Upper Wraxall Wilts 61 E10
Upper Wyche
Hereford 98 C5
Uppincott Devon 26 G5
Uppingham Rutland 137 D7
Uppington Dorset 31 F8
Shrops 132 B2
Upsall N Yorks 215 B9
Upsher Green Suff 107 C8
Upshire Essex 86 E6
Up Somborne Hants 47 G11
Upstreet Kent 71 G8
Up Sydling Dorset 29 G10
Upthorpe Glos 80 E3
Suff 125 C9
Upton Bucks 84 C3
Cambs 122 B3
Ches W 166 B6
Corn 11 G11
Corn 24 G2
Cumb 230 D2
Devon 8 G4
Devon 27 G9
Dorset 17 E10
Dorset 18 C5
E Yorks 209 C8
Hants 32 D5
Hants 47 B11
IoW 21 C7
Kent 71 F11
Leics 135 D7
Lincs 188 D5
London 68 C2
Mers 182 D3
Mers 183 D7
Norf 161 G7
Northants 120 E4
Notts 172 E2
Notts 188 F2
Oxon 64 B4
Oxon 82 C2
Pboro 138 C2
Slough 66 D3
Som 27 B7
Som 29 B7
W Yorks 198 E3
Warks 118 F2
Wilts 45 G11
Upton Bishop
Hereford 98 F2
Upton Cheyney
S Glos 61 F7
Upton Cressett
Shrops 132 E3
Upton Crews
Hereford 98 F2
Upton Cross Corn 11 G11
Upton End C Beds 104 E2
Upton Field Notts 172 E2
Upton Green Norf 161 G7
Upton Grey Hants 49 D7
Upton Heath
Ches W 166 B6
Upton Hellions
Devon 26 G4
Upton Lea Bucks 66 C3
Upton Lovell Wilts 46 E2
Upton Magna
Shrops 149 G11
Upton Noble Som 45 F8
Upton Park London 68 C2
Upton Pyne Devon 14 B4
Upton Rocks Halton 183 D8
Upton St Leonards
Glos 80 C5
Upton Scudamore
Wilts 45 D11
Upton Snodsbury
Worcs 117 G8
Upton upon Severn
Worcs 99 C7
Upton Warren
Worcs 117 D8
Upwaltham W Sus 34 E6
Upware Cambs 123 C10
Upwell Norf 139 C9
Upwey Dorset 17 E9
Upwick Green Herts 105 G9
Upwood Cambs 138 G5
Uradale Shetland 313 K6
Urafirth Shetland 312 F5
Uragaig Argyll 274 D4
Urchfont Wilts 46 B4
Urdimarsh Hereford 97 B10
Ure Shetland 312 F4
Ure Bank N Yorks 214 E6
Urgashay Som 29 C9
Urgha W Isles 305 J3
Urgha Beag
W Isles 305 H3
Urishay Common
Hereford 96 D6
Urlar Perth 286 C2
Urlay Nook Stockton 225 C7
Urmston Gtr Man 184 C3
Urpeth Durham 242 G6
Urquhart Highld 300 D5
Moray 302 C2
Urra N Yorks 225 E11
Urray Highld 300 D5
Ushaw Moor
Durham 233 C10
Usk Mon 78 E5
Usselby Lincs 189 C9
Usworth T&W 243 F8
Utkinton Ches W 167 B8
Utley W Yorks 204 E6
Uton Devon 14 B2
Utterby Lincs 190 C4
Uttoxeter Staffs 151 C11
Uwchmynydd Gwyn 144 D3
Uxbridge London 66 C5
Uxbridge Moor
London 66 C5
Uyea Shetland 312 D5
Uyeasound Shetland 312 C7
Uzmaston Pembs 73 C7

V

Vachelich Pembs 90 F5
Vadlure Shetland 313 J4
Vagg Som 29 D8
Vaila Hall Shetland 313 J4
Vaivoe Shetland 312 G7
Vale W Yorks 196 B2
Vale Down Devon 12 D6
Vale of Health
London 67 B9
Valeswood Shrops 149 E7
Valleyfield Dumfries 237 D8
Valley Park Hants 32 C6
Valley Truckle Corn 11 E7
Valley / Y Fali
Anglesey 178 F3
Valsgarth Shetland 312 B8
Valtos Highld 298 C5
Van Caerph 59 B7
Powys 129 F9
Vange Essex 69 B8
Vanlop Shetland 313 M5
Varchoel Powys 148 G4
Varfell Corn 2 C2
Varteg Torf 78 D3
Vassa Shetland 313 H6
Vastern Wilts 62 C5
Vatsetter Shetland 312 E7
Shetland 313 L5
Vatten Highld 298 E2
Vaul Argyll 288 E2
Vauxhall London 67 D10
Mers 182 C4
W Mid 133 F11
Vaynol Hall Gwyn 163 B8
Vaynor M Tydf 77 C8
Veensgarth Shetland 313 J6
Velator Devon 40 F3
Veldo Hereford 97 C11
Velindre Powys 96 D3
Vellanoweth Corn 2 C2
Vellow Som 42 F5
Velly Devon 24 C3
Veness Orkney 314 D5
Venn Devon 8 F4
Venngreen Devon 24 E5
Venn Green Devon 24 E5
Vennington Shrops 130 B6
Venn Ottery Devon 15 C7
Venn's Green
Hereford 97 B10
Venny Tedburn
Devon 14 B2
Venterdon Corn 12 G3
Vention Devon 40 E3
Ventnor IoW 21 F7
Venton Devon 7 D11
Ventongimps Corn 4 E5
Ventonleague Corn 2 B3
Venus Hill Herts 85 E8
Veraby Devon 26 B3
Vermentry Shetland 313 H5
Vernham Bank
Hants 47 B10
Vernham Dean
Hants 47 B10
Vernham Row Hants 47 B10
Vernham Street
Hants 47 B11
Vernolds Common
Shrops 131 G9
Verwood Dorset 31 F9
Veryan Corn 3 B10
Veryan Green Corn 5 G8
Vicarage Devon 15 D10
Vicarscross Ches W 166 B6
Vickerstown Cumb 210 F3
Victoria Corn 5 C9
S Yorks 197 F7
Victoria Dock Village
Hull 200 B6
Victoria Park Bucks 84 C4
Victory Gardens
Renfs 267 B10
Vidlin Shetland 312 G6
Viewpark N Lanark 268 C4
Vigo W Mid 133 C10
Vigo Village Kent 68 G6
Vinegar Hill Mon 60 B2
Vinehall Street
E Sus 38 C3
Vines Cross E Sus 23 B9
Viney Hill Glos 79 D11
Vinney Green S Glos 61 D7
Virginia Water Sur 66 F3
Virginstow Devon 12 C3
Viscar Corn 2 C6
Vobster Som 45 D8
Voe Shetland 312 E5
Shetland 313 G6
Vogue Corn 4 G4
Vole Som 43 D11
Vowchurch Hereford 97 D7
Vowchurch Common
Hereford 97 D7
Voxmoor Som 27 D10
Voxter Shetland 312 F5
Voy Orkney 314 E2
Vron Gate Shrops 130 B6
Vulcan Village Mers 183 C9

W

Waberthwaite Cumb 220 G2
Wackerfield Durham 233 G9
Wacton Hereford 116 F2
Norf 142 E3
Wacton Common
Norf 142 F3
Wadbister Shetland 313 J6
Wadborough Worcs 99 B8
Wadbrook Devon 28 G4
Waddesdon Bucks 84 B2
Waddeton Devon 9 D7
Waddicar Mers 182 B5
Waddicombe Devon 26 B5
Waddingham Lincs 189 B7
Waddington Lancs 203 E10
Lincs 173 C7
Waddingworth
Lincs 189 G11
Waddon Devon 14 F3
London 67 G10
Wadebridge Corn 10 G5
Wadeford Som 28 E4
Wade Hall Lancs 194 C4
Wadenhoe
Northants 137 G10
Wades Green
Ches E 167 C11
Wadesmill Herts 86 B5
Wadhurst E Sus 52 G6
Wadshelf Derbys 186 G4
Wadsley S Yorks 186 C4
Wadsley Bridge
S Yorks 186 C4
Wadswick Wilts 61 F10
Wadwick Hants 48 C2
Wadworth S Yorks 187 B9
Waen Denb 165 B10
Denb 165 C7
Flint 181 G11
Powys 129 E9
Waen Aberwheeler
Denb 165 B9
Waen-fâch Powys 148 F4
Waen Goleugoed
Denb 181 G9
Waen-pentir Gwyn 163 B9
Waen-wen Gwyn 163 B9
Wag Highld 311 G4
Wagbeach Shrops 131 C7
Wagg Som 28 B6
Waggersley Staffs 151 B7
Waggs Plot Devon 28 G4
Wainfelin Torf 78 E3
Wainfleet All Saints
Lincs 175 D7
Wainfleet Bank
Lincs 175 D7
Wainfleet St Mary
Lincs 175 D8
Wainfleet Tofts
Lincs 175 D7
Wainford Norf 142 E6
Waingroves Derbys 170 F6
Wainhouse Corner
Corn 11 B9
Wain Lee Staffs 168 D5
Wainscott Medway 69 E8
Wainstalls W Yorks 196 B4
Waitby Cumb 222 D5
Waithe Lincs 201 G9
Wakefield
W Yorks 197 C10
Wake Green
W Mid 133 G11
Wake Hill N Yorks 214 E3
Wake Lady Green
N Yorks 226 F3
Wakeley Herts 104 F6
Wakerley Northants 137 D9
Wakes Colne Essex 107 F7
Wakes Colne Green
Essex 107 E7
Walberswick Suff 127 C9
Walberton W Sus 35 F7
Walbottle T&W 242 D5
Walby Cumb 239 E10
Walcombe Som 44 D5
Walcot Bath 61 F9
Lincs 155 B11
N Lincs 199 C11
Oxon 82 B4
Shrops 130 F6
Swindon 63 C7
Telford 149 G11
Worcs 99 B8
Walcote Leics 135 G11
Warks 118 F2
Walcot Green Norf 142 G2
Walcott Lincs 173 D10
Norf 161 C7
Walden N Yorks 213 C10
Walden Head
N Yorks 213 C9
Walden Stubbs
N Yorks 198 D5
Waldersey Cambs 139 C8
Waldershaigh
S Yorks 186 B3
Walderslade Medway 69 G9
Walderton W Sus 34 E3
Walditch Dorset 16 C5
Waldley Derbys 152 B2
Waldridge Durham 243 G7
Waldringfield Suff 108 C5
Waldringfield Heath
Suff 108 B5
Waldron E Sus 23 B8
Waldron Down E Sus 37 C8
Wales S Yorks 187 E7
Som 29 C9
Wales Bar S Yorks 187 E7
Walesby Lincs 189 C10
Notts 187 G11
Walesby Grange
Lincs 189 C10
Wales End Suff 106 B5
Waleswood S Yorks 187 E7
Walford Hereford 97 G11
Hereford 115 C7
Shrops 149 E8
Som 28 B3
Staffs 150 C6
Walford Heath
Shrops 149 F8
Walgherton
Ches E 167 F11
Walgrave Northants 120 C6
Walham Glos 98 G6
Walham Green
London 67 D9
Walhampton Hants 20 B2
Walkden Gtr Man 195 G8
Walker T&W 243 E7
Walker Barn Ches E 185 G7
Walkerburn Borders 261 B9
Walker Fold Lancs 203 E9
Walkeringham
Notts 188 C3
Walkerith Lincs 188 C3
Walkern Herts 104 F5
Walker's Green
Hereford 97 B10
Walker's Heath
W Mid 117 B11
Walkerville N Yorks 224 F4
Walkford Dorset 19 C10
Walkhampton Devon 7 B10
Walkington E Yorks 208 F5
Walkley S Yorks 186 D4
Walkmill Shrops 131 E7
Walk Mill Lancs 204 G3
Walkmills Shrops 131 D9
Wall Corn 2 B4
Northumb 241 D10
Staffs 134 B2
Wallacestone Falk 279 F8
Wallaceton Dumfries 247 F8
Wallacetown
S Ayrs 245 C7
S Ayrs 257 E8
Shetland 313 H5
Wallands Park E Sus 36 E6
Wallasey Mers 182 C4
Wallbank Lancs 195 D11
Wall Bank Shrops 131 E10
Wallbrook W Mid 133 E8
Wallcrouch E Sus 53 G7
Wallend London 68 C2
Wall End Cumb 210 C4
Kent 71 G8
Waller's Green
Hereford 98 D3
Walley's Green
Ches E 167 C11
Wall Heath W Mid 133 F7
Wall Hill Gtr Man 196 F3
Wallingford Oxon 64 B6
Wallington
Hants 33 F9
Herts 104 E5
London 67 G9
Wallington Heath
W Mid 133 C9
Wallingwells Notts 187 E9
Wallis Pembs 91 F10
Wallisdown Poole 19 C7
Walliswood Sur 50 F6
Wall Mead Bath 45 B7
Wall Nook Durham 233 B10
Wallow Green Glos 80 F4
Wallridge Northumb 242 B3
Walls Shetland 313 J4
Wallsend T&W 243 D7
Wallston V Glam 58 E6
Wallsuches Gtr Man 195 E7
Wallsworth Glos 98 G6
Wall under Heywood
Shrops 131 E10
Wallyford E Loth 281 G7
Walmer Kent 55 C11
Walmer Bridge
Lancs 194 C3
Walmersley
Gtr Man 195 E10
Walmgate Stray
York 207 C8
Walmley W Mid 134 E2
Walmsgate Lincs 190 F5
Walnut Grove Perth 286 E5
Walnut Tree
M Keynes 103 D7
Walnuttree Green
Herts 105 G9
Walpole Som 43 E10
Suff 127 C7
Walpole Cross Keys
Norf 157 F10
Walpole Highway
Norf 157 G10
Walpole Marsh Norf 157 F9
Walpole St Andrew
Norf 157 F10
Walpole St Peter
Norf 157 F9
Walrow Som 43 D10
Walsal End W Mid 118 B4
Walsall W Mid 133 D10
Walsall Wood
W Mid 133 C10
Walsden W Yorks 196 C2
Walsgrave on Sowe
W Mid 135 G7

Walsham le Willows
Suff 125 C9
Walshaw Gtr Man . . 195 E9
Walshford N Yorks . 206 C4
Walsoken Cambs. . . 157 G9
Walson Mon 97 G8
Walston S Lanark . . 269 F11
Walsworth Herts. . . . 104 E4
Walters Ash Bucks . . 84 F4
Walter's Green Kent . 52 E4
Walterston V Glam . . 58 E5
Walterstone Hereford . 96 F6
Waltham Kent 54 D6
NE Lincs. 201 G9
Waltham Abbey
Essex. 86 E5
Waltham Chase
Hants. 33 D9
Waltham Cross Herts . 86 E5
Waltham on the Wolds
Leics 154 E6
Waltham St Lawrence
Windsor. 65 D10
Waltham's Cross
Essex. 106 E3
Walthamstow
London. 67 B11
Walton Bucks. 84 C4
Cumb 240 E2
Derbys. 170 B5
Leics 135 F11
M Keynes. 103 D7
Mers 182 C5
Pboro. 138 C3
Powys 114 F5
Shrops. 115 B9
Som. 44 F3
Staffs. 151 C7
Staffs. 151 D7
Suff 108 D5
Telford. 149 F11
W Yorks 197 D11
W Yorks 206 D4
Warks 118 G5
Walton Cardiff Glos. . 99 E8
Walton Court Bucks. . 84 C4
Walton East Pembs . . 91 G10
Walton Elm Dorset . . 30 D3
Walton Grounds
Northants 101 E10
Walton Heath Hants. 33 F10
Walton Highway
Norf 157 G9
Walton in Gordano
N Som 60 E2
Walton-le-Dale
Lancs. 194 B5
Walton Manor Oxon. . 83 D8
Walton-on-Thames
Sur. 66 F6
Walton on the Hill
Staffs. 151 E7
Sur. 51 B8
Walton-on-the-Naze
Essex. 108 G5
Walton on the Wolds
Leics 153 F11
Walton-on-Trent
Derbys. 152 F4
Walton Pool Worcs. . 117 B8
Walton St Mary
N Som 60 E2
Walton Summit
Lancs. 194 B5
Walton Warren Norf . 158 F4
Walton West Pembs. . 72 C5
Walwen Flint 181 F10
Flint 181 G11
Flint 182 F2
Walwick Northumb . 241 C10
Walworth Darl. 224 B4
London. 67 D10
Walworth Gate
Darl 233 G10
Walwyn's Castle
Pembs 72 C5
Wambrook Som 28 F3
Wampool Cumb. . . . 238 G6
Wanborough Sur . . . 50 D2
Swindon. 63 C8
Wandel Dyke
S Lanark 259 D11
Wandle Park London. 67 F10
Wandon End Herts. . 104 G2
Wandsworth London. . 67 E9
Wangford Suff. 127 B9
Wanlip Leics 154 G2
Wanlockhead
Dumfries 259 G9
Wannock E Sus 23 E9
Wansford E Yorks . . 209 B7
Pboro. 137 D11
Wanshurst Green
Kent. 53 D9
Wanson Corn 24 G1
Wanstead London . . 68 B2
Wanstrow Som 45 E8
Wanswell Glos. 79 E11
Wantage Oxon 63 B11
Wants Green Worcs. 116 F5
Wapley S Glos 61 D8
Wappenbury Warks. 119 D7
Wappenham
Northants 102 B2
Wapping London . . . 67 C10
Warbleton E Sus . . . 23 B10
Warblington Hants. . 22 B2
Warborough Oxon . . 83 G9
Warboys Cambs. . . . 138 G6
Warbreck Blackpool . 202 F2
Warbstow Corn 11 C10
Warbstow Cross
Corn. 11 C10
Warburton Gtr Man. 184 D2
Warburton Green
Gtr Man 184 E3
Warcop Cumb 222 B4
Warden Kent 70 E4
Northumb 241 D10
Powys 114 E6
Ward End W Mid . . . 134 F2
Warden Hill Glos . . . 99 G8
Warden Point IoW . . 20 D2
Warden Street
C Beds 104 C2
Ward Green
S Yorks 197 G10

Ward Green continued
Suff 125 E10
Ward Green Cross
Lancs. 203 F8
Wardhedges
C Beds 103 D11
Wardhill Orkney . . . 314 D6
Wardington Oxon. . . 101 B9
Wardlaw Borders . . 261 F7
Wardle Ches E 167 D10
Gtr Man 196 D2
Wardle Bank
Ches E 167 D10
Wardley Gtr Man . . 195 G9
Rutland 136 C6
T&W 243 E7
W Sus 34 B4
Wardlow Derbys . . . 185 G11
Wardour Wilts. 30 B6
Wardpark N Lanark . 278 F5
Wardrobes Bucks . . . 84 E4
Wardsend Ches E . . 184 E6
Wardy Hill Cambs . . 139 G9
Ware Herts. 86 C5
Kent. 71 G9
Wareham Dorset. . . . 18 D4
Warehorne Kent . . . 54 G3
Warenford
Northumb 264 D4
Waren Mill
Northumb 264 C4
Warenton Northumb . 264 C4
Wareside Herts. 86 B5
Waresley Cambs. . . . 122 G4
Worcs 116 C6
Ware Street Kent . . . 53 B9
Warfield Brack. 65 E11
Warfleet Devon 9 E7
Wargate Lincs 156 C4
Wargrave Mers 183 C9
Wokingham 65 D9
Warham Hereford . . . 97 D9
Norf 176 E6
Warhill Gtr Man . . . 185 B7
Waring's Green
W Mid 118 C2
Wark Northumb . . . 241 B9
Northumb 263 B8
Wark Common
Northumb 263 B8
Warkleigh Devon . . . 25 C10
Warkton Northants . 121 B7
Warkworth
Northants 101 C9
Northumb 252 B6
Warlaby N Yorks . . . 224 G6
Warland W Yorks. . . 196 C2
Warleggan Corn 6 B3
Warleigh Bath 61 G9
Warley Essex 87 G9
Warley Town
W Yorks 196 B5
Warley Woods
W Mid 133 F10
Warlingham Sur . . . 51 B11
Warmbrook Derbys . 170 E3
Warmfield
W Yorks 197 C11
Warmingham
Ches E 168 C2
Warminghurst
W Sus 35 D10
Warmington
Northants 137 E11
Warks 101 B8
Warminster Wilts. . . 45 D11
Warminster Common
Wilts 45 E11
Warmlake Kent 53 C10
Warmley S Glos 61 E7
Warmley Hill S Glos . 61 E7
Warmley Tower
S Glos 61 E7
Warmonds Hill
Northants 121 D9
Warmsworth
S Yorks 198 G4
Warmwell Dorset . . . 17 D11
Warnborough Green
Hants. 49 C8
Warndon Worcs . . . 117 F7
Warners End Herts. . 85 D8
Warnford Hants 33 C10
Warnham W Sus 51 G7
Warningcamp W Sus . 35 F8
Warninglid W Sus . . 36 B2
Warpsgrove Oxon . . 83 F10
Warren Ches E 184 G5
Dorset 18 C3
Pembs 72 F6
S Yorks 186 B5
Dumfries 248 E5
Warrenby Redcar . . 235 F7
Warren Corner Hants . 34 B2
Hants. 49 D10
Warren Heath Suff . . 108 C4
Warren Row
Windsor. 65 C10
Warren's Green
Herts. 104 F5
Warren Street Kent . 54 C2
Warrington
M Keynes. 121 G7
Warr 183 D10
Warriston Edin 280 F5
Warsash Hants 33 F7
Warsill N Yorks. . . . 214 F4
Warslow Staffs 169 D9
Warsop Vale Notts . . 171 B8
Warstock W Mid . . . 117 B11
Warstone Staffs . . . 133 B9
Warter E Yorks 208 C3
Warthermarske
N Yorks 214 D4
Warthill N Yorks. . . 207 B9
Wartle Aberds 293 C7
Wartling E Sus 23 D11
Wartnaby Leics 154 E4
Warton Lancs 194 B2
Lancs 211 E9
Northumb 252 C3
Warks 134 C5
Warton Bank Lancs . 194 B2
Warwick Warks 118 E5
Warwick Bridge
Cumb 239 F11
Warwick on Eden
Cumb 239 F11

Warwicksland
Cumb 239 B10
Warwick Wold Sur. . 51 C10
Wasbister Orkney . . 314 C3
Wasdale Head
Cumb 220 D3
Wash Derbys 185 E9
Washall Green
Herts. 105 E8
Washaway Corn 5 B10
Washbourne Devon . . 8 E5
Washbrook Som. . . . 44 C2
Suff 108 C2
Washbrook Street
Suff 108 C2
Wash Common
W Berks 64 G3
Wash Dyke Norf . . . 157 F10
Washerwall Staffs . . 168 F6
Washfield Devon . . . 26 D6
Washfold N Yorks . . 223 E11
Washford Som 42 E5
Worcs 117 D11
Washford Pyne
Devon 26 E4
Washingborough
Lincs 189 G8
Washingley Cambs. . 138 F2
Washington T&W . . 243 F8
W Sus 35 E10
Washington Village
T&W 243 F8
Washmere Green
Suff 107 B8
Washpit W Yorks. . . 196 F6
Wash Water W Berks . 64 G3
Washwood Heath
W Mid 134 F2
Wasing W Berks. . . . 64 G5
Waskerley Durham . 233 B7
Wasperton Warks. . 118 F5
Wasp Green Sur . . . 51 D10
Wasps Nest Lincs . . 173 C9
Wass N Yorks 215 D11
Waste Green Warks . 118 D4
Wastor Devon. 8 F2
Watchet Som 42 E5
Watchfield Oxon. . . . 63 B8
Som 43 D10
Watchgate Cumb. . . 221 F10
Watchhill Cumb . . . 229 C9
Watch House Green
Essex 106 G3
Watchill Dumfries . . 238 D6
Dumfries 248 G3
Watcombe Torbay . . . 9 B8
Watendlath Cumb. . 220 B5
Watergate Corn 5 B8
Water Devon 13 E11
Waterbeach Cambs . 123 D9
W Sus 22 B5
Waterbeck Dumfries. 238 B6
Waterden Norf 159 B7
Waterditch Hants . . 19 B9
Water Eaton
M Keynes. 103 E7
Oxon 83 C8
Watereud Bucks . . . 84 F3
Cumb 229 G8
Glos 80 C3
Herts. 86 C2
Water End Beds . . . 104 B2
C Beds 103 C11
C Beds 104 B5
E Yorks 207 F11
Essex 105 C11
Hants. 49 C7
Herts. 85 C8
Herts. 86 E2
Waterfall Staffs . . . 169 E9
Waterfoot Argyll. . . 255 D9
Cumb 230 G5
E Renf 267 D11
Lancs 195 C10
Waterford Hants . . . 20 B2
Herts. 86 C4
Water Fryston
W Yorks 198 B3
Water Garth Nook
Cumb 210 F3
Watergate Corn 6 E4
Corn. 11 E8
Watergore Som. . . . 28 D6
Waterhales Essex . . 87 F8
Waterham Kent . . . 70 G5
Waterhay Wilts . . . 81 G9
Waterhead Angus . . 292 F6
Cumb 221 E7
Devon 8 F3
Dumfries 248 E5
Waterhead on Minnoch
S Ayrs 245 G9
Waterheads Borders 270 E4
Waterheath Norf . . 143 E8
Waterhouses
Durham 233 C9
Staffs. 169 E9
Water Houses
N Yorks 213 F7
Wateringbury Kent . . 53 C7
Waterlane Glos 80 E6
Waterlip Som. 45 E7
Waterloo Blackburn . 195 B7
Corn. 11 G8
Derbys. 170 C6
Gtr Man 196 G2
Highld 295 C8
Mers 182 B4
N Lanark 268 E6
Norf 126 B2
Norf 143 E8
Norf 160 F4
Pembs 73 E7
Perth 286 D4
Poole 18 C6
Shrops. 132 E2
Waterloo Park Mers 182 B4
Waterloo Port Gwyn .163 C7
Waterlooville Hants. 33 F11
Waterman Quarter
Kent. 53 E10
Watermead Glos. . . 80 B5
Watermeetings
S Lanark 259 G11
Watermill E Sus. . . . 38 E2
Watermillock Cumb. 230 G4

Watermoor Glos. . . . 81 E8
Water Newton
Cambs 138 D2
Water Orton Warks. 134 E3
Waterperry Oxon . . . 83 D10
Waterrow Som. 27 B9
Watersfield W Sus . . 35 D8
Watersheddings
Gtr Man 196 F2
Waterside Aberds . . 292 B5
Aberds. 303 D10
Blackburn 195 C8
Bucks. 85 E7
Cumb 229 B10
Derbys. 185 E8
E Ayrs. 245 B10
E Ayrs. 267 G9
E Dunb 278 G3
E Renf 267 D10
S Yorks 199 E7
Waterslack Lancs . . 211 D9
Water's Nook
Gtr Man 195 F7
Waterstein Highld . . 297 G2
Waterstock Oxon . . . 83 D10
Waterston Pembs . . 72 D6
Water Stratford
Bucks. 102 E3
Waters Upton
Telford. 150 F2
Waterthorpe
S Yorks 186 E6
Waterton Aberds. . . 303 F9
Bridgend 58 D2
Water Yeat Cumb . . 210 B5
Watford Herts. 85 F10
Northants 120 D2
Watford Gap Staffs. 134 C2
Watford Heath
Herts. 85 G10
Watford St Mary Corn . 11 B10
Watford Park Caerph. 58 B6
Wath Cumb 222 D3
N Yorks 214 D6
N Yorks 214 F2
N Yorks 216 D3
Wath Brow Cumb . . 219 C10
Watherston Borders. 271 F8
Wath upon Dearne
S Yorks 198 G2
Watledge Glos. 80 E4
Watley's End S Glos. . 61 C7
Watlington Norf . . . 158 G2
Oxon 83 G11
Watnall Notts. 171 E8
Watsness Shetland . 313 H3
Watten Highld 310 D6
Wattisfield Suff . . . 125 C10
Wattisham Suff . . . 125 G10
Wattisham Stone
Suff 125 G10
Wattlefield Norf . . . 142 D2
Wattlesborough Heath
Shrops. 149 G7
Watton E Yorks. . . . 208 C6
Norf 141 C8
Watton at Stone
Herts. 86 B4
Watton Green Norf . 141 C8
Watton's Green Essex. 87 F8
Wattston N Lanark. . 268 B5
Wattstown Rhondda . 77 G8
Wattsville Caerph . . 78 G2
Wauchan Highld . . 295 G11
Waulkmill Lodge
Orkney. 314 F3
Waun Gwyn 163 C9
Powys 148 F4
Waunarlwydd
Swansea 56 B6
Waun Beddau Pembs. 90 F5
Waunclunda Carms . 94 E3
Waunfawr Gwyn . . . 163 D8
Waun Fawr Ceredig . 128 G2
Waun Gilwen Carms .92 D6
Waungron Swansea . 75 E9
Waunlwyd BI Gwent . 77 D11
Waun-Lwyd
BI Gwent 207 G11
Waun-y-clyn Carms . 75 E7
Waun y Gilfach
Bridgend 57 D10
Wavendon
M Keynes. 103 D8
Wavendon Gate
M Keynes. 103 D8
Waverbridge Cumb .229 B10
Waverton Ches W . . 167 C7
Cumb 229 B10
Wavertree Mers . . . 182 D5
Wawcott W Berks . . 63 F11
Wawne E Yorks. . . . 209 F7
Waxham Norf 161 D8
Waxholme E Yorks . 201 B10
Way Kent 71 F10
Waye Devon 13 G11
Wayend Street
Hereford 98 D4
Wayfield Medway . . 69 F9
Wayford Som. 28 F6
Waymills Shrops . . . 167 G9
Wayne Green Mon . . 78 B6
Way's Green
Ches W 167 B10
Waytown Devon . . . 24 C5
Devon 40 G5
Way Village Devon . . 26 E5
Way Wick N Som . . . 59 G11
Wdig / Goodwick
Pembs 91 D8
Weachyburn Aberds . 302 D6
Weacombe Som . . . 42 E6
Weald Oxon 82 E4
Wealdstone London. . 67 B7
Wearde Corn 7 D8
Weardley W Yorks . . 205 E11
Weare Som. 44 C2
Weare Giffard Devon. 25 C7
Wearhead Durham . 232 D3
Wearne Som 28 B6
Weasdale Cumb . . . 222 E4
Weasenham All Saints
Norf 158 E6
Weasenham St Peter
Norf 159 E7
Weaste Gtr Man . . .184 B4

Weatherhill Sur 51 E10
Weatheroak Hill
Worcs 117 C11
Weaverham
Ches W 183 G10
Weavering Street
Kent. 53 B9
Weaverslake Staffs . 152 F2
Weaverthorpe
N Yorks 217 E7
Webbington Som . . . 43 B11
Webheath Worcs . . 117 D10
Webscott Shrops. . . 149 E9
Wecock Hants 33 E11
Wedderlairs Aberds . 303 F8
Wedderlie Borders . 272 E2
Weddington Kent . . . 55 B9
Warks 135 E7
Wedhampton Wilts . 46 B5
Wedmore Som 44 D2
Wednesbury W Mid . 133 D9
Wednesbury Oak
W Mid 133 E9
Wednesfield W Mid .133 C8
Weecar Notts. 172 B4
Weedon Bucks. 84 B4
Weedon Bec
Northants 120 F2
Weedon Lois
Northants 102 B2
Weeford Staffs 134 C2
Week Devon 8 C5
Devon 12 E5
Devon 25 B9
Devon 26 D2
Hants. 48 G3
Week Green Corn . . 11 B10
Weekley Northants . 137 G7
Weekmoor Som . . . 27 B10
Weeks IoW 21 C7
Weel E Yorks 209 F7
Weeley Essex 108 G2
Weeley Heath Essex 108 G3
Weelsby NE Lincs . . 201 F9
Weem Perth 286 C2
Weeping Cross
Staffs. 151 E8
Weethley Warks . . . 117 F11
Weethley Bank
Warks 117 G11
Weethley Gate
Warks 117 G11
Weeting Norf 140 F5
Weeton E Yorks . . . 201 C11
Lancs 202 G3
N Yorks. 205 D11
Weetwood
W Yorks 205 F11
Weetwood Common
Ches W 167 B8
Weetwood Hall
Northumb 264 D2
Weir Essex 69 B10
Lancs 195 B11
Weirbrook Shrops . . 148 E6
Weir Quay Devon . . 7 C8
Welborne Norf 159 G11
Welborne Common
Norf 141 B11
Welbourn Lincs . . . 173 E7
Welburn N Yorks . . 216 C3
N Yorks. 216 F4
Welbury N Yorks . . . 225 E7
Welby Lincs 155 B9
Welches Dam
Cambs 139 F9
Welcombe Devon . . 24 D2
Weld Bank Lancs. . . 194 D5
Weldon Northants . 137 F8
Northumb 252 D4
Welford Northants . 136 G2
W Berks 64 E2
Welford-on-Avon
Warks 118 G3
Welham Leics 136 E5
Notts 188 E2
Som 45 G7
Welhambridge
E Yorks. 207 G11
Welham Green Herts..86 D2
Well Hants 49 D9
Lincs 190 G6
N Yorks. 214 C5
Welland Worcs 98 C5
Welland Stone
Worcs 98 D6
Wellbank Angus . . . 287 D8
Well Bottom Dorset . 30 D6
Wellbrook E Sus . . . 37 B9
Welldale Dumfries. . 238 D5
Well End Bucks 65 B11
Herts. 86 F2
Weller's Town Kent . 52 E4
Wellesbourne
Warks 118 F5
Well Heads
W Yorks 205 G7
Well Hill Kent. 68 G3
Wellhouse W Berks . 64 E4
W Yorks 196 E5
Welling London 68 D3
Wellingborough
Northants 121 D7
Wellingham Norf . . 159 E7
Wellingore Lincs. . . 173 D7
Wellington Cumb . . 219 E11
Hereford 97 B9
Som. 27 C10
Telford. 150 G3
Wellington Heath
Hereford 98 C4
Wellington Hill
W Yorks 206 F2
Wellisford Som . . . 27 C9
Wellow Bath 45 B8
IoW 20 D3
Notts 171 B11
Wellow Wood Hants . 32 C3
Well Place Oxon . . . 65 B7
Wellpond Green
Herts. 105 G8
Wellroyd W Yorks ..205 F10

Wells 44 D5
Wellsborough Leics . 135 C7
Wells Green
Ches E 167 E11
Wells-next-the-Sea
Norf 176 E6
Wellsprings Som . . . 28 B2
Well Street Kent . . . 53 B7
Wellstye Green
Essex. 87 B10
Wellswood Torbay . . 9 C8
Welltown Corn 6 B2
Well Town Devon . . 26 F6
Wellwood Fife. 279 D11
Welney Norf 139 E10
Welsh Bicknor
Hereford 79 B9
Welsh End Shrops. . 149 B10
Welsh Frankton
Shrops. 149 C7
Welsh Harp London . 67 B8
Welsh Hook Pembs . 91 F8
Welsh Newton
Hereford 79 B7
Welsh Newton Common
Hereford 79 B8
Welshpool Powys . . 130 B4
Welsh St Donats
V Glam 58 D4
Welshwood Park
Essex 107 F10
Welstor Devon 13 G10
Welton Bath 45 C7
Cumb 230 C3
E Yorks 208 G5
E Yorks 200 B3
Lincs 189 F8
Northants 119 D11
Welton Hill Lincs. . . 189 E8
Welton le Marsh
Lincs 175 B7
Welton le Wold
Lincs 190 D3
Welwick E Yorks . . . 201 C10
Welwyn Herts 86 B2
Welwyn Garden City
Herts. 86 C2
Wem Shrops 149 D10
Wembdon Som. . . . 43 F9
Wembley London . . . 67 B7
Wembley Park
London. 67 B7
Wembury Devon . . . 7 F10
Wembworthy Devon . 25 F11
Wemyss Bay Invclyd .266 B3
Wenallt Ceredig. . . . 112 C3
Gwyn 146 F4
Gwyn 165 G2
Wendens Ambo
Essex 105 E10
Wendlebury Oxon. . .83 B9
Wendling Norf. . . . 159 G8
Wendover Bucks. . . 84 D5
Wendover Dean
Bucks. 84 E5
Wendron Corn 2 C5
Wendy Cambs 104 B6
Wenfordbridge Corn. 11 F7
Wenhaston Suff . . . 127 B8
Wenhaston Black Heath
Suff 127 C8
Wennington Cambs .122 B4
Lancs 212 E2
London. 68 C4
Wensley Derbys . . . 170 C3
N Yorks. 213 B11
Wentbridge
W Yorks 198 D3
Wentnor Shrops . . . 131 E7
Wentworth Cambs . 123 B9
S Yorks 186 B5
Wenvoe V Glam . . . 58 E6
Weobley Hereford . . 115 G8
Weobley Marsh
Hereford 115 G8
Weoley Castle
W Mid 133 G10
Wepham W Sus 35 F8
Wepre Flint 166 B3
Wereham Norf. . . . 140 C3
Wereham Row Norf. 140 C3
Wereton Staffs 168 E3
Wergs W Mid 133 C7
Wern Gwyn 145 B10
Powys 77 B10
Powys 147 G9
Powys 148 E5
Powys 148 G5
Shrops. 148 C5
Swansea 56 C4
Wern ddu Shrops. . 148 D4
Werneth Gtr Man . . 196 G2
Werneth Low
Gtr Man 185 C7
Wernffrwd Swansea . 56 C4
Wern-Gifford Mon . . 96 G6
Wernlas Shrops . . . 148 E6
Wern-heolydd Mon . 78 C5
Wern Tarw Bridgend. 58 C3
Wern-y-cwrt Mon . . 78 C5
Wern-y-gaer Flint . . 166 B2
Wernyrheolydd Mon . 78 C5
Werrington Corn . . 12 D2
Pboro. 138 C3
Staffs. 168 F6
Wervin Ches W . . . 182 G6
Wescoe Hill
N Yorks 205 D11
Wesham Lancs. . . . 202 G4
Wessington Derbys . 170 D5
West Aberthaw
V Glam 58 F4
Westacott Devon. . . 40 G5
West Acre Norf . . . 158 F5
West Acton London . 67 C8
West Adderbury
Oxon 101 D9
West Allerdean
Northumb 273 F9
West Allotment
T&W 243 C8
West Alvington Devon. .8 G4
West Amesbury Wilts. 46 E6

West Anstey Devon. . 26 C3
N Yorks 224 G4
West Appleton
N Yorks 224 G4
West Ardsley
W Yorks 197 B9
West Ardwell
Dumfries 236 E2
West Arthurlie
E Renf 267 D9
West Ashby Lincs . . 190 G3
West Ashford Devon . 40 F4
West Ashling W Sus . 22 B4
West Ashton Wilts . . 45 B11
West Auckland
Durham 233 F9
West Ayton N Yorks . 217 C9
West Bagborough
Som. 43 G7
West Bank BI Gwent . 78 D2
Halton 183 E8
West Barkwith
Lincs 189 E11
West Barnby
N Yorks 226 C6
West Barnes
London. 67 F8
West Barns E Loth . . 282 F3
West Barsham Norf . 159 C8
West Bay Dorset . . . 16 C5
West Beckham Norf . 160 B2
West Bedfont Sur. . . 66 E5
West Benhar
N Lanark 269 C7
Westbere Kent 71 G7
West Bergholt
Essex 107 F9
West Bexington
Dorset 16 D6
West Bilney Norf. . . 158 F4
West Blackdene
Durham 232 D3
West Blackdown
Devon 12 E5
West Blatchington
Brighton 36 F3
West Bold Borders . 261 B9
West Boldon T&W . . 243 E9
Westborough Lincs . 172 G5
Westbourne Bmouth . 19 C7
Suff 108 B2
W Sus 22 B3
Westbourne Green
London. 67 C9
West Bourton Dorset. 30 B3
West Bowling
W Yorks 205 G9
West Bradford
Lancs 203 E10
West Bradley Som . . 44 F5
West Bretton
W Yorks 197 E9
West Bridgford
Notts 153 B11
West Brompton
London. 67 E10
West Bromwich
W Mid 133 E10
Westbrook Hereford . 96 C5
Kent. 71 E10
Sur. 50 E3
W Berks 64 E2
Wilts 62 F3
Westbrook Green
Norf 142 G2
Westbrook Hay Herts. 85 D8
West Broughton
Derbys. 152 C2
West Buckland
Devon 41 G7
Som 27 C11
Westburn S Lanark . 268 C3
West Burnside
Aberds. 293 F8
West Burrafirth
Shetland 313 H4
West Burton
N Yorks. 213 B10
W Sus 35 E7
Westbury Bucks . . . 102 D2
Shrops. 131 B7
Wilts 45 C11
Westbury Leigh
Wilts 45 C11
Westbury-on-Severn
Glos 80 C2
Westbury on Trym
Bristol 60 D5
Westbury Park
Bristol 60 D5
Westbury-sub-Mendip
Som. 44 D4
West Butsfield
Durham 233 C8
West Butterwick
N Lincs. 199 F10
West Byfleet Sur. . . 66 G5
West Caister Norf. . 161 G10
West Calder
W Loth 269 C10
West Camel Som . . 29 C9
West Carlton
W Yorks 205 E10
West Carr Hull 209 G7
N Lincs. 199 F8
West Chadsmoor
Staffs. 151 G9
West Challow Oxon ..63 B11
West Charleton Devon. .8 G5
West Chelborough
Dorset 29 F8
West Chevington
Northumb 252 D6
West Chilcompton

Westcliff-on-Sea
Southend. 69 B11
West Clyne Highld . . 311 J2
West Clyth Highld . . 310 F6
West Coker Som . . . 29 E8
Westcombe Som . . . 29 B7
Som. 45 F7
West Common Hants. 32 G6
West Compton
Dorset 17 C7
Som. 44 E5
West Cornforth
Durham 234 E2
Westcot Oxon 63 B10
Westcote Glos. 100 G4
Westcotes
Leicester 135 C11
Westcott Bucks 84 B2
Devon 27 G8
Shrops. 131 C8
Sur. 50 D6
Westcott Barton
Oxon 101 F8
West Cowick
E Yorks. 199 C7
West Cranmore Som . 45 E7
Westcroft M Keynes . 102 E6
W Mid 133 C8
West Cross Kent . . . 53 G10
Swansea 56 D6
West Crudwell Wilts .80 G6
West Cullery Aberds .293 C9
West Curry Corn . . . 11 C11
West Curthwaite
Cumb 230 B2
West Darlochan
Argyll 255 E7
Westdean E Sus . . . 23 F8
West Dean W Sus . . . 34 E5
Wilts 32 B3
West Deeping Lincs . 138 B2
West Denant Pembs. 72 C6
Westdene Brighton . 36 F3
West Denton T&W . . 242 D5
West Derby Mers . . 182 C5
West Dereham Norf . 140 C3
West Didsbury
Gtr Man 184 C4
West Down Devon . . 40 E4
Hants. 47 F11
Westdown Camp
Wilts 46 D4
Westdowns Corn . . 11 E7
West Downs Corn . . 5 C10
West Drayton London .66 D5
Notts 188 G2
West Dulwich
London. 67 E10
West Ealing London . 67 C7
West Edge Derbys. . 170 C4
West Ella E Yorks . . 200 B4
West End Oxon . . . 100 G6
Beds 121 E11
Beds 121 G9
Brack. 65 E11
Brack. 66 G2
Caerph. 78 F2
Cumb 239 F8
Dorset 30 G6
E Yorks 201 B9
E Yorks 208 G4
E Yorks 209 B9
E Yorks 209 G9
E Yorks 217 G11
Glos. 80 F5
Hants. 33 F7
Hants. 33 F9
Hants. 48 F6
Herts. 86 D3
Kent. 54 B2
Lancs 195 B8
Leics 153 F8
Lincs 174 F5
Lincs 190 B5
Mon 78 F6
N Som 60 F3
N Yorks. 205 B8
N Yorks. 206 E6
N Yorks. 207 F7
Norf 141 B8
Norf 161 G10
Oxon 64 B5
Oxon 82 E6
S Glos. 61 B8
S Lanark 269 F9
S Yorks 199 F7
Som. 44 G5
Som. 45 G7
Suff 143 G9
Sur. 49 E10
Sur. 66 G6
W Sus 36 D2
W Sus 197 B7
W Yorks 205 F10
Wilts 30 C6
Wilts 31 C7
Wilts 62 D3
Windsor. 65 D10
Worcs 99 D11
West End Green
Hants. 65 G7
West End / Marian-y-
mor Gwyn. 145 C7
Westend Town
Northumb 241 D7
West-end Town
V Glam 58 F3
Wester Aberchalder
Highld 300 G5
Wester Arboll
Highld 311 L2
Wester Auchinloch
N Lanark 278 G3
Wester Auchnagallin
Highld 301 F10
Wester Balgedie
Perth 286 G5

Wester Brae Highld 300 C6
Wester Broomhouse
E Loth 282 F3
Wester Craiglands
Highld 301 D7
Wester Culbeuchly
Aberds 302 C6
Westerdale Highld 310 D5
N Yorks 226 D3
Wester Dalvoult
Highld 291 B11
Wester Dechmont
W Loth 269 B10
Wester Deloraine
Borders 261 E8
Wester Denoon
Angus 287 C7
Wester Ellister
Argyll 254 B2
Wester Essendy
Perth 286 C5
Wester Essenside
Borders 261 E10
Wester Feddal
Perth 286 G2
Westerfield
Shetland 313 H5
Suff 108 B3
Wester Fintray
Aberds 293 B10
Westerfolds Moray 301 C11
Wester Galgantray
Highld 301 E8
Westergate W Sus 22 C6
Wester Gospetry
Fife 286 G5
Wester Gruinards
Highld 309 K5
Wester Hailes Edin 270 B4
Westerham Kent 52 C2
Westerhope T&W 242 D5
Wester Housebyres
Borders 262 B2
Wester Kershope
Borders 261 D9
Wester Lealty
Highld 300 B6
Westerleigh S Glos 61 D8
Westerleigh Hill
S Glos 61 D8
Wester Lix Stirling 285 E9
Wester Milton
Highld 301 D9
Wester Mosshead
Aberds 302 F5
Western Bank
Cumb 229 B10
Western Downs
Staffs 151 E8
Wester Newburn
Fife 287 G8
Western Heights
Kent 55 E10
Western Hill
Durham 233 C11
Western Park
Leicester 135 C11
Wester Ord Aberds 293 C10
Wester Parkgate
Dumfries 248 F2
Wester Quarff
Shetland 313 K6
Wester Skeld
Shetland 313 J4
Wester Strath
Highld 300 D6
Westerton Aberds 293 B9
Aberds 302 E5
Angus 287 B10
Durham 233 E10
Moray 302 D3
W Sus 22 B5
Westertown Aberds 303 F7
Wester Watten
Highld 310 D6
Westerwick Shetland 313 J4
West Ewell Sur 67 G8
West Farleigh Kent 53 C8
West Farndon
Northants 119 G10
West Felton Shrops 148 D6
West Fenton E Loth 281 E9
West Ferry Dundee 287 D8
Westfield Bath 45 C7
Cumb 228 F5
E Sus 38 D4
Hants 21 B10
Hereford 98 B4
Highld 310 C4
N Lanark 278 G4
Norf 141 B9
Redcar 235 G7
S Yorks 186 E6
Sur 50 B4
W Loth 279 G8
W Yorks 197 C8
W Yorks 205 E9
West Field N Lincs 200 D6
York 207 C7
Westfields Dorset 30 F2
Hereford 97 C9
West Fields W Berks 64 F3
Westfields of Rattray
Perth 286 C5
Westfield Sole Kent 69 G9
West Firle E Sus 23 D7
West Fleetham
Northumb 264 D5
West Flodden
Northumb 263 C10
Westford Som 27 C10
West Garforth
W Yorks 206 G3
Westgate Durham 232 D4
N Lincs 199 F9
Norf 176 E4
Norf 177 E7
Westgate Hill
W Yorks 197 B8
Westgate on Sea
Kent 71 E10
Westgate Street
Norf 160 E3
West Ginge Oxon 64 B2
West Gorton
Gtr Man 184 B5
West Grafton Wilts 63 G8
West Green Hants 49 B8
London 67 B10
S Yorks 197 F11
W Sus 51 F9
West Greenskares
Aberds 303 C7
West Grimstead
Wilts 32 B2
West Grinstead
W Sus 35 C11
West Haddlesey
N Yorks 198 B5
West Haddon
Northants 120 C2
West Hagbourne
Oxon 64 B4
West Hagley Worcs 133 G8
Westhall Aberds 302 G6
Suff 143 G8
West Hall Cumb 240 D3
West Hallam Derbys 170 G6
Westhall Hill Oxon 82 C3
West Halton
N Lincs 200 C2
Westham Dorset 17 F9
E Sus 23 E10
Som 44 D2
West Ham Hants 48 C6
London 68 C2
Westhampnett
W Sus 22 B5
West Hampstead
London 67 B9
West Handley
Derbys 186 F5
West Hanney Oxon 82 G6
West Hanningfield
Essex 88 F2
West Hardwick
W Yorks 198 D2
West Harling Norf 141 G9
West Harlsey
N Yorks 225 F8
West Harnham
Wilts 31 B10
West Harptree Bath 44 B5
West Harrow London 66 B6
West Harting W Sus 34 C3
West Harton T&W 243 E9
West Hatch Som 28 C3
Wilts 30 B6
Westhay Som 44 E2
Westhead Lancs 194 F2
West Head Norf 139 B11
West Heath Ches E 168 C4
Hants 48 B5
Hants 49 B11
London 68 D3
W Mid 117 B10
West Helmsdale
Highld 311 H4
West Hendon London 67 B8
West Hendred Oxon 64 B2
West Herrington
T&W 243 G8
West Heslerton
N Yorks 217 D8
West Hewish
N Som 59 G11
Westhide Hereford 97 C11
Westhill Aberds 293 C10
E Yorks 209 F10
Highld 301 E7
West Hill
Devon 15 C7
E Sus 38 E4
E Yorks 218 F3
London 67 E8
N Som 60 D3
Som 30 B2
Staffs 151 G9
W Sus 51 G10
Wilts 61 F11
West Hoathly
W Sus 51 G11
West Holme Dorset 18 D3
West Holywell T&W 243 C8
Westhope Hereford 115 G9
Shrops 131 F9
West Horndon Essex 68 B6
Westhorp
Northants 119 G10
Westhorpe Lincs 156 C4
Notts 171 E11
Suff 125 D10
West Horrington
Som 44 D5
West Horsley Sur 50 C5
West Horton
Northumb 264 C2
West Hougham Kent 55 E9
Westhoughton
Gtr Man 195 F7
West Houlland
Shetland 313 H4
Westhouse N Yorks 212 E3
Westhouses Derbys 170 D6
West Houses Lincs 174 E4
West Howe Bmouth 19 B7
West Howetown Som 42 G2
Westhumble Sur 51 C7
West Huntington
York 207 B8
West Huntspill Som 43 E10
West Hurn Dorset 19 B8
West Hyde Herts 85 G8
West Hynish Argyll 288 F1
West Hythe Kent 54 G6
West Ilkerton Devon 41 D8
West Ilsley W Berks 64 C3
Westing Shetland 312 C7
Westington Glos 100 D2
West Itchenor W Sus 22 C3
West Jesmond
T&W 243 D7
West Keal Lincs 174 C5
West Kennett Wilts 62 F6
West Kensington
London 67 D8
West Kilbride
N Ayrs 266 F4
West Kilburn London 67 C8
West Kingsdown
Kent 68 G5
West Kingston
W Sus 35 G9
West Kington Wilts 61 D10
West Kington Wick
Wilts 61 D10
West Kinharrachie
Aberds 303 F9
West Kirby Mers 182 D2
West Kirkby Mers 182 D2
West Knapton
N Yorks 217 D7
West Knighton
Dorset 17 D10
West Knoyle Wilts 45 G11
West Kyloe
Northumb 273 G11
West Kyo Durham 242 G5
Westlake Devon 8 E2
West Lambrook Som 28 D6
Westland Argyll 275 G11
Westland Green
Herts 105 G8
Westlands Staffs 168 G4
Worcs 117 E7
West Langdon Kent 55 D10
West Langwell
Highld 309 J6
West Lavington
W Sus 34 C5
Wilts 46 C4
West Layton
N Yorks 224 D2
Westlea Northumb 252 G6
Swindon 62 C6
West Lea Durham 234 B4
West Leake Notts 153 D10
West Learmouth
Northumb 263 B9
Westleigh Devon 25 B7
Devon 27 D9
Gtr Man 194 G6
West Leigh Devon 25 F11
Hants 22 B2
Som 42 G6
Westleton Suff 127 D8
West Lexham Norf 158 F6
Westley Shrops 131 B7
Suff 124 E6
Westley Heights
Essex 69 B7
Westley Waterless
Cambs 124 F2
West Lilling N Yorks 216 F2
Westlington Bucks 84 C3
Westlinton Cumb 239 E9
West Linton Borders 270 E2
West Liss Hants 34 B3
West Littleton S Glos 61 D9
West Lockinge Oxon 64 B2
West Looe Corn 6 E5
West Luccombe
Som 41 D11
West Lulworth Dorset 18 E2
West Lutton
N Yorks 217 F8
West Lydford Som 44 G5
West Lydiatt
Hereford 97 C11
West Lyn Devon 41 D8
West Lyng Som 28 B4
West Lynn Norf 158 E2
West Mains
Borders 271 F11
S Lanark 268 E2
West Malling Kent 53 B7
West Malvern Worcs 98 B5
Westmancote Worcs 99 D8
West Marden W Sus 34 E3
West Marina E Sus 38 F3
West Markham
Notts 188 G2
Westmarsh Kent 71 G9
West Marsh
NE Lincs 201 E9
West Marton
N Yorks 204 C3
West Mathers
Aberds 293 G9
West Melbury Dorset 30 C5
West Melton
S Yorks 198 G2
West Meon Hants 33 C10
West Meon Woodlands
Hants 33 B10
West Merkland
Highld 308 F3
West Mersea Essex 89 C8
Westmeston E Sus 36 E4
Westmill Herts 104 E3
Herts 105 F7
West Milton Dorset 16 B6
Westminster London 67 D10
West Minster Kent 70 E2
West Molesey Sur 66 F6
West Monkseaton
T&W 243 C8
West Monkton Som 28 B3
West Moor T&W 243 C7
Westmoor End
Cumb 229 D8
West Moors Dorset 31 G9
West Morden Dorset 18 B4
West Morriston
Borders 272 G2
West Morton
W Yorks 205 E7
West Mudford Som 29 C9
Westmuir Angus 287 B7
West Muir Angus 293 G7
West Myreriggs
Perth 286 C6
Westness Orkney 314 D3
West Ness N Yorks 216 D3
West Newham
Northumb 242 B3
Westnewton Cumb 229 C8
Northumb 263 C10
West Newton
E Yorks 209 F9
Norf 158 D3
Som 28 B3
West Norwood
London 67 E10
Westoe T&W 243 D9
West Ogwell Devon 14 G2
Weston Bath 61 F8
Ches E 168 E2
Weston *continued*
Ches E 184 G5
Devon 15 D9
Devon 27 G10
Dorset 17 G9
Dorset 29 F8
Halton 183 E8
Hants 34 C2
Hereford 115 F7
Herts 104 E5
Lincs 156 D5
N Yorks 205 D9
Northants 101 B11
Notts 172 B3
Pembs 73 C8
S Lanark 269 F10
Shrops 114 C6
Shrops 131 E11
Shrops 148 D5
Shrops 149 D11
Soton 32 E6
Staffs 151 D9
Suff 143 F8
W Berks 63 E11
Weston Bampfylde
Som 29 C10
Weston Beggard
Hereford 97 C11
Westonbirt Glos 61 B11
Weston by Welland
Northants 136 E5
Weston Colley Hants 48 F4
Weston Colville
Cambs 124 G2
Westoncommon
Shrops 149 D8
Weston Common
Soton 33 E7
Weston Corbett
Hants 49 D7
Weston Coyney
Stoke 168 G6
Weston Ditch Suff 124 B3
Weston Favell
Northants 120 E5
Weston Green
Cambs 124 G2
Norf 160 G2
Sur 67 F7
Weston Heath
Shrops 150 G5
Weston Hills Lincs 156 E5
Weston in Arden
Warks 135 F7
Westoning C Beds 103 E10
Weston-in-Gordano
N Som 60 E2
Weston Jones
Staffs 150 E5
Weston Longville
Norf 160 F2
Weston Lullingfields
Shrops 149 E8
Weston Manor IoW 20 D2
Weston Mill Plym 7 D9
Weston-on-Avon
Warks 118 G3
Weston-on-the-Green
Oxon 83 B8
Weston-on-Trent
Derbys 153 D8
Weston Park Bath 61 F8
Weston Patrick
Hants 49 D7
Weston Point
Halton 183 E7
Weston Rhyn
Shrops 148 B5
Weston-sub-Edge
Glos 100 C2
Weston-super-Mare
N Som 59 G10
Weston Town Som 45 E8
Weston Turville
Bucks 84 C5
Weston under Lizard
Staffs 150 G6
Weston under Penyard
Hereford 98 G2
Weston under Wetherley
Warks 119 D7
Weston Underwood
Derbys 170 G3
M Keynes 121 G7
Westonwharf
Shrops 149 D8
Westonzoyland Som 43 G11
West Orchard Dorset 30 D4
West Overton Wilts 62 F6
Westow N Yorks 216 F5
Westowe Som 42 G6
Westown Devon 27 E10
Perth 286 E6
West Panson Devon 12 C2
West Park Hrtlpl 234 E5
Hull 200 B5
Mers 183 B7
T&W 243 D9
W Yorks 205 F11
West Parley Dorset 19 B7
West Pasture
Durham 232 G4
West Peckham Kent 52 C6
West Pelton
Durham 242 G6
West Pennard Som 44 F4
West Pentire Corn 4 C5
West Perry Cambs 122 D2
West Pontnewydd
Torf 78 F3
West Poringland
Norf 142 C5
West Porlock Som 41 D11
Westport Argyll 255 E7
Som 28 D5
West Portholland
Corn 5 G9
West Porton Renfs 277 G8
West Pulham Dorset 30 F2
West Putford Devon 24 D5
West Quantoxhead
Som 42 E6
Westquarter Falk 279 F8
Westra V Glam 58 E6
West Rainton
Durham 234 B2
West Rasen Lincs 189 D9
West Ravendale
NE Lincs 190 B2
West Raynham Norf 159 D7
West Retford Notts 187 E11
Westridge Green
W Berks 64 D5
Westrigg W Loth 269 B8
Westrip Glos 80 D4
Westrop Wilts 61 E11
Westrop Green
W Berks 64 E4
West Rounton
N Yorks 225 E8
West Row Suff 124 B3
West Royd W Yorks 205 F9
West Rudham Norf 158 D6
West Ruislip London 66 B5
Westrum N Lincs 200 F4
West Runton Norf 177 E11
Westruther Borders 272 F2
Westry Cambs 139 D7
West Saltoun
E Loth 271 B9
West Sandford
Devon 26 G4
West Sandwick
Shetland 312 E6
West Scholes
W Yorks 205 G7
West Scrafton
N Yorks 213 C11
West Shepton Som 44 E6
West Side Bl Gwent 77 D11
Orkney 314 C5
West Skelston
Dumfries 247 F8
West Sleekburn
Northumb 253 G7
West Somerton
Norf 161 F9
West Southbourne
Bmouth 19 C8
West Stafford
Dorset 17 D10
West Stockwith
Notts 188 C3
West Stoke Devon 13 G9
Som 29 D7
W Sus 22 B4
West Stonesdale
N Yorks 223 E7
West Stoughton Som 44 D2
West Stour Dorset 30 C3
West Stourmouth
Kent 71 G9
West Stow Suff 124 C6
West Stowell Wilts 62 G6
West Strathan
Highld 308 C5
West Stratton Hants 48 E4
West Street Kent 54 C2
Kent 55 C10
Medway 69 D8
Suff 125 C9
West Tanfield
N Yorks 214 D5
West Taphouse Corn 6 C3
West Tarbert Argyll 275 G9
West Tarring
W Sus 35 G10
West Third Borders 262 B4
West Thirston
Northumb 252 D5
West Thorney W Sus 22 C3
Westthorpe Derbys 187 F7
West Thurrock
Thurrock 68 D5
West Tilbury
Thurrock 69 D7
West Tisted Hants 33 B11
West Tofts Norf 140 E6
Perth 286 D5
West Tolgus Corn 4 G3
West Torrington
Lincs 189 E10
West Town Bath 60 G4
Devon 14 B3
Devon 24 C4
Hants 21 B10
Hereford 115 E8
N Som 60 F3
Som 44 F4
W Sus 36 D3
West Tytherley Hants 32 B3
West Tytherton Wilts 62 E2
Westvale Mers 182 B6
West Vale W Yorks 196 C5
West View Hrtlpl 234 D5
West Village V Glam 58 E3
Westville Devon 8 G4
Notts 171 F8
West Walton Norf 157 G9
West Walton Highway
Norf 157 G9
Westward Cumb 229 C11
Westward Ho! Devon 24 B6
West Watergate Corn 6 E4
West Watford Herts 85 F10
Westweekmoor
Devon 12 C4
Westwell Kent 54 D3
Oxon 82 D2
Westwell Leacon
Kent 54 D3
West Wellow Hants 32 D3
Westwells Wilts 61 F11
West Wemyss Fife 280 C6
Westwick Cambs 123 D8
Durham 223 B11
Norf 160 D5
West Wick N Som 59 G11
West Wickham
Cambs 106 B2
London 67 F11
Westwick Row Herts 85 D9
West Williamston
Pembs 73 D8
West Willoughby
Lincs 173 G7
West Winch Norf 158 F2
West Winterslow
Wilts 47 G8
West Wittering
W Sus 21 B11
West Witton
N Yorks 213 B11
Westwood Devon 14 B6
Westwood *continued*
Devon 14 E5
Kent 55 D7
Kent 71 F11
Notts 171 E7
Pboro 138 D3
S Lanark 268 E2
Wilts 45 B10
Wilts 46 G6
West Woodburn
Northumb 251 F9
West Woodhay
W Berks 63 G11
Westwood Heath
W Mid 118 B5
West Woodlands
Som 45 E9
Westwood Park
Essex 107 E9
Gtr Man 184 B3
Westwoodside
N Lincs 188 B3
West Worldham
Hants 49 F8
West Worlington
Devon 26 E3
West Worthing
W Sus 35 G10
West Wratting
Cambs 124 G2
West Wycombe
Bucks 84 G4
West Wylam
Northumb 242 E4
Westy Warr 183 D10
West Yatton Wilts 61 E11
West Yell Shetland 312 E6
West Yeo Som 43 G10
West Yoke Kent 68 F5
West Youlstone Corn 24 D3
Wetham Green Kent 69 F10
Wetheral Cumb 239 G11
Wetheral Plain
Cumb 239 F11
Wetherby W Yorks 206 D4
Wetherden Suff 125 E10
Wetherden Upper Town
Suff 125 D10
Wetheringsett Suff 126 D2
Wethersfield Essex 106 E4
Wethersta Shetland 312 G5
Wetherup Street
Suff 126 E2
Wetley Rocks Staffs 169 F7
Wetmore Staffs 152 E5
Wettenhall Ches E 167 C10
Wettenhall Green
Ches E 167 C10
Wettles Shrops 131 F8
Wetton Staffs 169 D10
Wetwang E Yorks 208 B4
Wetwood Staffs 150 C5
Wexcombe Wilts 47 B9
Wexham Street
Bucks 66 C3
Weybourne Norf 177 E10
Sur 49 D11
Weybread Suff 142 G4
Weybridge Sur 66 G5
Weycroft Devon 16 B2
Weydale Highld 310 C5
Weyhill Hants 47 D10
Weymouth Dorset 17 F9
Weythel Powys 114 F4
Whaddon Bucks 102 E6
Cambs 104 B6
Glos 80 C4
Glos 99 G9
Wilts 31 B11
Wilts 61 G11
Whaddon Gap
Cambs 104 B6
Whale Cumb 230 G6
Whaley Derbys 187 G8
Whaley Bridge
Derbys 185 E8
Whaley Thorns
Derbys 187 G8
Whaligoe Highld 310 E7
Whalley Lancs 203 F10
Whalley Banks
Lancs 203 F10
Whalley Range
Gtr Man 184 C4
Whalleys Lancs 194 F3
Whalton Northumb 252 G4
Wham N Yorks 212 G5
Whaplode Lincs 156 E6
Whaplode Drove
Lincs 156 G6
Whaplode St Catherine
Lincs 156 E6
Wharf Warks 119 G8
Wharfe N Yorks 212 F5
Wharles Lancs 202 F4
Wharley End
C Beds 103 C8
Wharmley Northumb 241 D9
Wharncliffe Side
S Yorks 186 C3
Wharram le Street
N Yorks 217 F7
Wharram Percy
N Yorks 217 G7
Wharton Ches W 167 B11
Hereford 115 F10
Lincs 188 C4
Wharton Green
Ches W 167 B11
Whashton N Yorks 224 D3
Whasset Cumb 211 C10
Whatcombe Dorset 30 G4
Whatcote Warks 100 C6
Whatcroft Ches W 167 B11
Whateley Staffs 134 D4
Whatfield Suff 107 B10
Whatley Som 28 F5
Som 45 D8
Whatlington E Sus 38 D3
Whatmore Shrops 116 C2
Whatsole Street Kent 54 E6
Whatstandwell
Derbys 170 E4
Whatton Notts 154 B4
Whauphill Dumfries 236 E6
Whaw N Yorks 223 E9
Wheal Alfred Corn 2 B3
Wheal Baddon Corn 4 G5
Wheal Busy Corn 4 G4
Wheal Frances Corn 4 E5
Wheal Kitty Corn 4 E4
Wheal Rose Corn 4 G4
Wheatacre Norf 143 E9
Wheatcroft Derbys 170 D5
Wheatenhurst Glos 80 D3
Wheathall Shrops 131 C9
Wheathampstead
Herts 85 C11
Wheathill Shrops 132 G2
Som 44 G5
Wheat Hold Hants 64 G5
Wheatley Devon 14 C4
Hants 49 E9
Oxon 83 D9
S Yorks 198 G5
W Yorks 196 B5
Wheatley Hill
Durham 234 D3
Wheatley Hills
S Yorks 198 G6
Wheatley Lane
Lancs 204 F2
Wheatley Park
S Yorks 198 F5
Wheaton Aston
Staffs 151 G7
Wheddon Cross Som 42 F2
Wheedlemont
Aberds 302 G4
Wheelbarrow Town
Kent 55 D7
Wheeler End Bucks 84 G4
Wheelerstreet Sur 50 E2
Wheelock Ches E 168 D3
Wheelock Heath
Ches E 168 D2
Wheelton Lancs 194 C5
Lancs 194 C6
Lancs 194 D5
Lancs 194 D6
Wheen Angus 292 F5
Wheldale W Yorks 198 B3
Wheldrake York 207 D9
Whelford Glos 81 F11
Whelley Gtr Man 194 F5
Whelpley Hill Herts 85 E7
Whelpo Cumb 230 D2
Whelp Street Suff 107 B8
Whelston Flint 182 F2
Whempstead Herts 104 G6
Whenby N Yorks 216 F2
Whepstead Suff 124 F6
Wherry Town Corn 1 D5
Wherstead Suff 108 C3
Wherwell Hants 47 E11
Wheston Derbys 185 F10
Whetley Cross Dorset 29 G7
Whetsted Kent 53 D7
Whetstone Leics 135 D11
London 86 G3
Whettleton Shrops 131 G8
Whicham Cumb 210 C2
Whichford Warks 100 E6
Whickham T&W 242 E6
Whickham Fell T&W 242 F6
Whiddon Devon 40 F5
Whiddon Down
Devon 13 C9
Whifflet N Lanark 268 C4
Whigstreet Angus 287 C8
Whilton Northants 120 E2
Whilton Locks
Northants 120 E2
Whimble Devon 24 G5
Whim Farm Borders 270 E4
Whimple Devon 14 B6
Whimpwell Green
Norf 161 D7
Whinburgh Norf 141 B10
Whinfield Darl 224 B6
Whinhall N Lanark 268 B5
Whin Lane End
Lancs 202 E3
Whinmoor W Yorks 206 F3
Whinney Hill
S Yorks 187 C7
Stockton 225 B7
Whinnieliggate
Dumfries 237 D9
Whinnyfold Aberds 303 F10
Whinny Heights
Blackburn 195 B7
Whins of Milton
Stirling 278 C5
Whins Wood
W Yorks 205 F7
Whipcott Devon 27 D9
Whippendell Botton
Herts 85 E9
Whippingham IoW 20 C6
Whipsiderry Corn 4 C6
Whipsnade C Beds 85 B8
Whipton Devon 14 C5
Whirley Grove
Ches E 184 F5
Whirlow S Yorks 186 E4
Whisby Lincs 172 B6
Whissendine
Rutland 154 G6
Whissonsett Norf 159 E8
Whisterfield Ches E 184 G4
Whistlefield Argyll 276 C2
Argyll 276 C4
Whistley Green
Wokingham 65 E9
Whistlow Oxon 101 F9
Whiston Mers 183 C7
Northants 120 E6
S Yorks 186 D6
Staffs 151 G7
Staffs 169 F8
Whiston Cross
Mers 183 C7
Shrops 132 C5
Whitacre Heath
Warks 134 E4
Whitbarrow Village
Cumb 230 F4
Whitbeck Cumb 210 C2
Whitbourne
Hereford 116 F4
Whitbourne Moor
Wilts 45 D10
Whitburn T&W 243 E10
Whitburn *continued*
W Loth 269 C8
Whitburn Colliery
T&W 243 E10
Whitby Ches W 182 F5
N Yorks 227 C7
Whitbyheath
Ches W 182 F5
Whitchurch Bath 60 F6
Bucks 102 G5
Cardiff 59 C7
Devon 12 G5
Hants 48 D3
Hereford 79 B9
Pembs 90 F5
Shrops 167 G8
Som 30 C2
Whitchurch
Canonicorum
Dorset 16 B3
Whitchurch Hill Oxon 64 D6
Whitchurch-on-Thames
Oxon 64 D6
Whitcombe Dorset 17 D10
Som 29 C10
Whitcot Shrops 131 E7
Whitcott Keysett
Shrops 130 G5
Whiteacen Moray 302 E2
Whiteacre Kent 54 D6
Whiteacre Heath
Warks 134 E4
Whiteash Green
Essex 106 E5
White Ball Som 27 D9
Whitebirk Blackburn 195 B8
Whitebog Highld 301 C7
Whitebridge Highld 290 B6
Whitebrook Mon 79 D8
Whiteburn Borders 271 F11
Whitebushes Sur 51 D9
Whitecairn Dumfries 236 D4
Whitecairns
Aberds 293 B11
Whitecastle
S Lanark 269 G10
Whitechapel Lancs 203 E7
London 67 C10
Whitechurch Maund
Hereford 97 B11
Whitecleat Orkney 314 F5
Whitecliff Glos 79 C9
Whiteclosegate
Cumb 239 F10
White Colne Essex 107 F7
White Coppice
Lancs 194 D6
Whitecote W Yorks 205 F10
Whitecraig E Loth 281 G7
Whitecraigs
E Renf 267 D11
Whitecroft Glos 79 D10
Whitecrook
W Dunb 267 B10
Whitecross Corn 2 C2
Corn 6 E2
Corn 10 G5
Falk 279 F9
Som 28 C6
Staffs 151 E7
White Cross Bath 44 B5
Bath 44 B6
Corn 2 E5
Corn 5 D7
Hereford 97 C9
Som 43 D10
Wilts 45 G9
White Cross Hill
Cambs 123 B9
White End Worcs 98 E5
Whiteface Highld 309 L7
Whitefarland
N Ayrs 255 C9
Whitefaulds S Ayrs 245 B7
Whitefield Aberds 303 G7
Dorset 18 C4
Gtr Man 195 F10
Perth 286 D5
Som 27 B9
Whitefield Lane End
Mers 183 D7
Whiteflat E Ayrs 258 D2
Whiteford Aberds 303 G7
Whitegate Ches W 167 B10
White Gate
Gtr Man 195 G11
Som 28 F4
White Grit Shrops 130 D6
Whitehall
Blackburn 195 C7
Bristol 60 E6
Devon 27 E10
Devon 40 F4
Hants 49 C8
Herts 104 E6
W Sus 35 C10
White Hall Herts 104 G5
Whitehall Village
Orkney 314 D6
Whitehaven Cumb 219 B9
Shrops 148 E5
Whitehawk Brighton 36 G4
Whiteheath Gate
W Mid 133 F9
Whitehill E Sus 37 B8
Hants 49 G9
Kent 54 B4
Midloth 271 B7
Moray 302 D5
S Lanark 268 D4
Staffs 168 E3
White Hill Bath 45 B8
W Yorks 204 E6
Wilts 45 G10
Whitehills Aberds 302 C6
S Lanark 268 E2
T&W 243 E7
White Hills
Northants 120 E4
Whiteholme
Blackpool 202 E2
Whitehough Derbys 185 E8
Whitehouse Aberds 293 B8
Argyll 275 G9
White House Suff 108 B2
Whitehouse Common
W Mid 134 D2